THE PENGUIN
SPELLING DICTIONARY

THE PENGUIN

Spelling
Dictionary

MARKET HOUSE BOOKS

PENGUIN BOOKS

PENGUIN BOOKS

Published by the Penguin Group
27 Wrights Lane, London W8 5TZ, England
Viking Penguin Inc., 40 West 23rd Street, New York, New York 10010, USA
Penguin Books Australia Ltd, Ringwood, Victoria, Australia
Penguin Books Canada Ltd, 2801 John Street, Markham, Ontario, Canada L3R 1B4
Penguin Books (NZ) Ltd, 182–190 Wairau Road, Auckland 10, New Zealand

Penguin Books Ltd, Registered Offices: Harmondsworth, Middlesex, England

First published 1990
1 3 5 7 9 10 8 6 4 2

Made and printed in Great Britain by
Richard Clay Ltd, Bungay, Suffolk
Set in Times by Market House Books Ltd in conjunction
with Alexander Typesetting, Indianapolis, USA

TABLE OF CONTENTS

PREFACE

English is a difficult language to spell correctly – and not only for the foreigner. Native speakers, too, find it hard. The problem is that modern English is such a rich and resourceful language, derived from so many sources, that its spelling does not obey simple rules. Although much of the language *is* regular, in the sense that it does obey rules, there are very large numbers of exceptions to the common patterns. While the only safe way to be sure of a spelling is to look it up in this dictionary, the basic rules are given on the following pages.

The Penguin Spelling Dictionary is divided into three sections: the main spelling list; a list of first names; and a list of biographical names.

SPELLING LIST

This, the largest section, contains normal vocabulary words, place names, some trademarks, and biblical and mythological names not included in the names lists (see below). Unhyphenated two-word compounds (e.g. phrasal verbs and nouns) are usually not listed, as each element will have its own entry. Exceptions include compounds with irregular inflections (see below) and some eponymous terms (terms derived from the name of a person), in which both elements are included as an aid to the sense.

Centred dots within a word indicate the points at which it can be hyphenated. These divisions are phonetic, rather than etymological, and correspond to syllabification breaks; note, however, that when syllabification breaks are not acceptable hyphenation points are not shown. Monosyllabic words should never be hyphenated, nor – if possible – should people's names.

Inflections (changes in the form of a word to indicate changes in grammatical function) are included if they are irregular. In general, regular inflections are not included. For rules on the formation of regular and irregular inflections, see under **The Rules of Spelling** on the following pages.

US spellings and British variant spellings are included after the preferred spelling of the word; they also have their own entries, with an appropriate gloss, if they are widely separated alphabetically from the preferred spelling.

Short glosses are provided for unfamiliar words and to avoid confusion between similarly spelt or pronounced words. Most of the proper names in this section are also glossed.

A few common misspellings are included in the list. These words are bracketed and the correct spelling indicated.

FIRST NAMES

This section comprises a comprehensive list of English first names, together with their spelling variants. It does not include the more obscure biblical and mythological names (many of which are listed in the main section of the dictionary) or the names of monarchs and other rulers that are unfamiliar or foreign (many of these are listed under the biographical names).

BIOGRAPHICAL NAMES

This section includes the names of people from all countries, past and present, who have achieved fame in some sphere of human activity. Monarchs are generally not included if their names appear in the first names list. Biographical names are listed in alphabetical order of the surname, followed by first names and any titles; the less familiar names of a subject are bracketed. Variant spellings and pseudonyms are also listed, and similar names are glossed to avoid confusion.

THE RULES OF SPELLING

Nouns

Regular plurals are formed by adding -*s*; for nouns ending in -*s*, -*x*, -*z*, -*ch*, or -*sh*, add -*es*.

1

Nouns of Latin origin ending in -*a*, especially in scientific or technical usage, usually have the plural ending -*ae* (e.g. **alga/algae; nebula/nebulae**).

Such nouns ending in -*ma* usually have the plural ending -*mata* (e.g. **stoma/stomata**).

2

Nouns ending in -*f* either form regular plurals (e.g. **chief/chiefs**) or have the plural ending -*ves* (e.g. **calf/calves**).

Most nouns ending in -*fe* from regular plurals (e.g. **safe/safes**) but a few have the plural ending -*ves* (e.g. **wife/wives**).

3

Nouns ending in -*i* usually form regular plurals but a few have the plural ending -*ies* (e.g. **chilli/chillies**).

4

Nouns ending in -*is* either form regular plurals (e.g. **iris/irises**) or having the plural ending -*es* (e.g. **basis/bases**). Some scientific and technical nouns have the plural ending -*ides* (e.g. **apsis/apsides**).

5

Most nouns ending in -*o* either form regular plurals (e.g. **albino/abinos**) or have the plural ending (-*oes* (e.g. **tomato/tomatoes**). Nouns of Italian origin have the plural form -*i*, either as the only plural or as an alternative (e.g. **graffito/graffiti; virtuoso/virtuosos** *or* **virtuosi**).

6

Some nouns of Greek origin ending in -*on* have the plural ending -*a* (e.g. **criterion/criteria**).

7

Nouns of Latin origin ending in -*um*, especially in scientific or technical usage, have the plural ending -*a* (e.g. **bacterium/bacteria; stratum/strata**).

Many nouns of Latin origin ending in *-us*, especially in scientific or technical usage, have the preferred or alternative plural ending *-i* (e.g. **fungus/fungi**; **stylus/styli** *or* **styluses**). A few such nouns have the plural ending *-era* or *-ora* (e.g. **genus/genera**; **corpus/corpora**).

9

Most nouns ending in *-x* form regular plurals (e.g. **tax/taxes**) but a few, usually in scientific or technical usage, have the plural ending *-ces* (e.g. **appendix/appendices**).

Such nouns ending in *-ex* have the plural ending *-ices* (e.g. **index/indices**).

Such nouns ending in *-nx* have the plural ending *-nges* (e.g. **meninx/meninges**).

10

Nouns ending in *-y* preceded by a vowel form regular plurals (e.g. **donkey/donkeys**). Nouns ending in *-y* preceded by a consonant or *-qu-* have the plural ending *-ies* (e.g. **family/families**; **colloquy/colloquies**). Note that proper names ending in *-y* form regular plurals, irrespective of the preceding letter (e.g. **Sally/Sallys**).

11

In phrasal nouns and most other hyphenated nouns, the final element is pluralized (e.g. **lay-by/lay-bys**), but in some hyphenated and multiword nouns the noun element may be pluralized irrespective of its position (e.g. **looker-on/lookers-on**; **court martial/court martials** *or* **courts martial**).

Note, however, that this does not apply to nouns ending in *-ful* (e.g. **spoonful/spoonfuls**; *not* **spoonsful**).

12

Some nouns, especially animals, have the same singular and plural forms (e.g. **sheep/sheep**; **fish/fish** *or* **fishes**).

13

Abbreviations and numberals usually have the plural ending *-s* (e.g. **MPs**; **1920s**).

SUFFIXES

Many nouns are formed by adding suffixes to the corresponding verb or adjective. A few general rules apply.

1   *-ation*

For words ending in *-l* preceded by a single vowel, the *-l* is doubled (e.g. **cancel/cancellation**).

2   -er and -or

Either of these suffixes may be added to form nouns meaning the 'doer' of the corresponding verb, but the -er forms greatly outnumber the -or forms. For some verbs, both forms exist; in these cases the following rules may apply:

(a) the -or form is used for objects and the -er form for people (e.g. **resister**, person who resists; **resistor**, electrical component).

(b) the or form is preferred in legal or scientific contexts (e.g. **bailer**, one who bails; **bailor**, transferer of goods by bailment).

3   -ment

(a) For words ending in -dge, the preferred form is to drop the -e (e.g. **judge/judgment**).

(b) For words ending in -ll, the terminal -l is dropped (e.g. **install/instalment**).

(c) For words of more than one syllable ending in -y preceded by a consonant, the -y is changed to -i (e.g. **merry/merriment**).

4   -ness

For words of more than one syllable preceded by a consonant, the -y is changed to -i (e.g. **happy/happiness**).

Adjectives

REGULAR INFLECTIONS

Regular comparatives and superlatives, for adjectives of one or two syllables, are formed by adding -er and -est, respectively.

For adjectives ending in -e, the -e is dropped before adding -er or -est (e.g. **nice/nicer, nicest; free/freer, freest**).

Adjectives of three or more syllables are preceded by *more* and *most* to form the comparative and superlative respectively.

IRREGULAR INFLECTIONS

1

For adjectives ending in -y preceded by a consonant, the comparative and superlative are formed by dropping the -y and adding -ier and -iest respectively (e.g. **tidy/tidier, tidiest**).

2

For monosyllabic adjectives ending in a consonant preceded by a single vowel, the comparative and superlative are formed by doubling the terminal consonant before adding -er and -est respectively (e.g. **hot/hotter, hottest**).

-able and -ible

The great majority of these adjectives have the ending -*able*; they are derived from native English verbs and nouns. Certain verbs and nouns of Latin origin, however, take the suffix -*ible*; some common examples are **accessible, comprehensible, convertible, divisible, eligible, perceptible, permissible, tangible**. Some can end in either -*able* or -*ible* (e.g. **collectable/collectible, discussible/discussable**).

For adjectives ending in -*able*, the following rules generally apply, although there are exceptions:

(a) For verbs and nouns ending in -*e*, the -*e* is dropped before adding -*able* unless it is preceded by -*c*- or -*g*- (e.g. **noticeable, changeable**) or when its retention aids pronunciation (e.g. **blameable, saleable**).

(b) For words ending in -*y* preceded by a consonant, the -*y* is changed to -*i* before adding -*able* (e.g. **justifiable**).

(c) For verbs ending in -*l* preceded by a single vowel, the -*l* is doubled before adding -*able* (e.g. **distil/distillable**).

Verbs

REGULAR INFLECTIONS

1

The third person singular is formed by adding -*s* or, for verbs ending in -*s*, -*x*, -*z*, -*ch*, or -*sh*, by adding -*es*.

2

The present participle is formed by adding -*ing*.

3

The past tense and past participle are formed by adding -*ed*.

4

For verbs ending in -*e* preceded by a consonant, the -*e* is dropped before adding -*ing* or -*ed* (compare **Irregular inflections** 3 and 4).

IRREGULAR INFLECTIONS

1

For verbs ending in -*y* preceded by a consonant, the past tense and past participle are formed by dropping the -*y* and adding -*ied* (e.g. **marry/married**).

2

In monosyllabic verbs ending in a consonant preceded by a single vowel, the terminal consonant is doubled when inflecting (e.g. **pat/patting, patted**).

With some exceptions, this rule also applies to verbs of more than one syllable, notably when:

(a) the terminal consonant is *-l* (e.g. **marvel/marvelling, marvelled**); note that in American English the *-l* is not doubled.

(b) the stress is on the last syllable (e.g. **refer/referring, referred**).

3

For verbs ending in *-e* preceded by a vowel, the *-e* is dropped before adding *-ed* but retained before *-ing* (e.g. **hoe/hoeing, hoed**).

4 For a few verbs ending in *-e* preceded by a consonant, the *-e* is dropped before adding *-ed* but retained before *-ing*, usually to avoid confusion with very similar words (e.g. **singe/singeing, singed**).

5

For verbs ending in *-ac-* or *-ic*, the present participle is formed by adding *-king* and the past tense and participle by adding *-ked* (e.g. **traffic/trafficking, trafficked**).

SUFFIXES

1 *-ize* and *-ise*

Most of these verbs have the preferred ending *-ize*, with *-ise* as an acceptable variant in British English (but not in American English); the same applies to the derived nouns (e.g. **specialize/specialization**). Exceptions include **advertise, compromise, improvise, supervise**; for these verbs *-ise* is the only acceptable ending in British and American English.

2 *-yse* and *-yze*

-yse is the only acceptable form in British English; *-yze* is the US spelling (e.g. **catalyse**/*US* **catalyze**; **paralyse**/*US* **paralyze**).

Adverbs

Many adverbs are formed by adding *-ly* to the corresponding adjectives or noun. Note:

1

For adjectives or nouns ending in *-e*, the *-e* is usually, but not always, retained (e.g. **pale/palely; rude/rudely**). Exceptions include **true/truly, whole/wholly**.

2

For adjectives or nouns ending in *-l*, the *-l* is retained (e.g. **eventual/eventually**).

3

For adjectives ending in *-ll*, the penultimate *-l* is dropped before adding *-ly* (e.g. **full/fully**).

4

For adjectives or nouns ending in *-y*, the adverb is formed by dropping the *-y* and adding *-ily* (e.g. **merry/merrily**).

Common spelling problems

1   *-cede* or *-ceed*

There is no general rule here: the usual ending is *-cede* (e.g. **concede**, **precede**); the only verbs ending in *-ceed* are **exceed**, **proceed**, and **succeed**. Note particularly the spelling of **supersede**.

2   *-ei-* or *-ie-*

The rule 'i before e except after c' works fairly well when the sound is pronounced 'ee' (e.g. **niece**, **siege**; but **receipt**, **receive**). Exceptions include **seize**, **weir**, **weird**.

When the sound is pronounced 'ai' (as in paid), the spelling is *-ei-* (e.g. **deign**, **neighbour**, **weigh**).

3   *Difficult words*

A few words cause many people problems because they follow no rules:

accommodate	exaggerate	phenomenon
anomalous	forty	pursue
business	gauge	surprise
commemorate	harass	threshold
desiccate	inoculate	withhold
ecstasy	necessary	
embarrass	parallel	

A

aa rock
Aachen West German city
Aal·borg (or Ål·) Danish port
aalii shrub
aard·vark
aard·wolf (plural ·wolves)
Aar·gau Swiss canton
Aar·hus (or År·) Danish port
aba·ca fibre
aback
ab·ac·ti·nal zoology term
aba·cus (plural ·ci or ·cuses)
Aba·dan Iranian port
Abad·don the devil
abaft nautical term
aba·lo·ne mollusc
ab·am·pere electrical unit
aban·don
aban·doned
aban·doned·ly
aban·donee legal term
aban·don·ment
abase
abase·ment
abash
abash·ed·ly
abat·able
abate
abate·ment
aba·tis (or ab·at·tis) fortifications term
aba·tor legal term
ab·at·toir
ab·ax·ial away from the axis; compare adaxial
ab·ba·cy (plural ·cies)
Abbasid dynasty of caliphs
ab·ba·tial
abbé French abbott
ab·bess
Abbe·vill·ian archaeological period
ab·bey
ab·bot
ab·bre·vi·ate
ab·bre·via·tion

ab·bre·via·tor
(abcess) incorrect spelling of abscess
ab·cou·lomb electrical unit
ab·di·cable
ab·di·cate
ab·di·ca·tion
ab·dica·tive
ab·di·ca·tor
ab·do·men
ab·domi·nal
ab·domi·nal·ly
ab·du·cens nerve
ab·du·cent anatomy term
ab·duct
ab·duc·tion
abeam nautical term
abece·dar·ian learner
abed
abele poplar
Abelian maths term
abel·mosk plant
Ab·eo·ku·ta Nigerian town
Ab·er·dare Welsh town
Ab·er·deen
Ab·er·do·nian
ab·er·nethy biscuit
ab·er·rance (or ·ran·cy)
ab·er·rant
ab·er·ra·tion
Ab·er·yst·wyth
abet (abet·ting, abet·ted)
abet·ment
abet·ter (or esp. in legal contexts ·tor)
abey·ance
abey·ant
ab·far·ad electrical unit
ab·hen·ry (plural ·ries) electrical unit
ab·hor (·hor·ring, ·horred)
ab·hor·rence
ab·hor·rent
ab·hor·rer
abid·ance
abide (abid·ing, abode or abid·ed)
abid·er

abid·ing
abid·ing·ly
Abid·jan Ivory Coast port
abi·et·ic acid
abi·gail maid
Abi·lene Texan city
abil·ity (plural ·ities)
Ab·ing·don
ab ini·tio Latin from the start
abio·gen·esis biological theory
abio·genet·ic
abiog·enist
abio·sis absence of life
abiot·ic
ab·ir·ri·tant relieving irritation
ab·ir·ri·tate
ab·ject
ab·jec·tion
ab·ju·ra·tion
ab·jure renounce; compare adjure
ab·jur·er
Ab·khaz (plural ·khaz) Soviet people
Ab·kha·zia Soviet republic
ab·late
ab·la·tion
ab·la·tive grammar term
ab·la·tor heat shield
ab·laut linguistics term
ablaze
able
able-bodied
abloom
ab·lu·tion
ab·lu·tion·ary
ably
ab·ne·gate
ab·ne·ga·tion
ab·ne·ga·tor
ab·nor·mal
ab·nor·mal·ity (plural ·ities)
ab·nor·mal·ly
aboard
abode

ab·ohm electrical unit
aboi·deau (*plural* ·deaus *or* ·deaux) Canadian dyke
abol·ish
abol·ish·er
abol·ish·ment
abo·li·tion
abo·li·tion·ary
abo·li·tion·ism
abo·li·tion·ist
abo·ma·sum ruminant's stomach
abomi·nable
abomi·nably
abomi·nate
abomi·na·tion
abomi·na·tor
ab·oral zoology term
Abo·rigi·nal
abo·rigi·nal
Abo·rigi·ne native Australian
abo·rigi·ne an original inhabitant
abort
abor·ti·cide
abor·ti·fa·cient inducing abortion
abor·tion
abor·tion·al
abor·tion·ist
abor·tive
Abou·kir battle site
abou·lia *variant spelling of* abulia
abound
about
about-turn (*or esp. US* about-face)
above
ab·ra·ca·dab·ra
abra·dant
abrade
abrad·er
abran·chi·ate (*or* ·chial) zoology term
abra·sion
abra·sive
abrax·as magic charm
ab·re·act psychology term
ab·re·ac·tion
ab·re·ac·tive
abreast
abridg·able (*or* abridge·)

abridge
abridg·er
abridg·ment (*or* abridge·)
abroad
ab·ro·gate
ab·ro·ga·tion
ab·ro·ga·tor
ab·rupt
ab·rup·tion breaking off
ab·rupt·ness
Abruz·zi Italian region
ab·scess
ab·scise to separate
ab·scis·sa (*plural* ·sas *or* ·sae) maths term
ab·scis·sion shedding of plant parts
ab·scond
ab·scond·er
ab·seil mountaineering term
ab·sence
ab·sent
ab·sen·tee
ab·sen·tee·ism
ab·sent·er
ab·sen·te reo *Latin* the defendant being absent
absent-minded
absent-minded·ness
ab·sinthe (*or* ·sinth)
ab·sit omen *Latin* may the foreboding not be realized
ab·so·lute
ab·so·lute·ly
ab·so·lu·tion
ab·so·lut·ism
ab·solu·tory
ab·solv·able
ab·solve
ab·solv·er
ab·sorb take into or permeate; *compare* adsorb
ab·sorb·abil·ity
ab·sorb·able
ab·sorb·ance physics term
ab·sorb·ed·ly
ab·sor·be·fa·cient inducing absorption
ab·sorb·en·cy
ab·sorb·ent
ab·sorb·er
ab·sorb·ing
ab·sorb·ing·ly
ab·sorp·tance physics term
ab·sorp·tion

ab·sorp·tive
ab·sorp·tiv·ity physics term
ab·squatu·late decamp
ab·stain
ab·stain·er
ab·ste·mi·ous
ab·sten·tion
ab·sten·tious
ab·ster·gent cleansing
ab·sti·nence
ab·sti·nent
ab·stract
ab·stract·ed·ly
ab·stract·ed·ness
ab·strac·tion
ab·strac·tion·ism theory of abstract art
ab·strac·tive
ab·stric·tion biology term
ab·struse
ab·struse·ness
ab·surd
ab·surd·ity (*or* ·ness; *plural* ·ities *or* ·nesses)
Abu Dha·bi sheikdom
abu·lia (*or* abou·) loss of willpower
abu·lic
abun·dance
abun·dant
abuse
abus·er
Abu Sim·bel Egyptian temple
abu·sive
abu·sive·ness
abut (abut·ting, abut·ted)
abu·ti·lon shrub
abut·ment (*or* abut·tal)
abut·tals legal term
abut·ter owner of adjoining property
abuzz
ab·volt electrical unit
ab·watt electrical unit
Aby·dos ancient Egyptian town
abysm *Archaic* abyss
abys·mal immeasurable; very bad
abys·mal·ly
abyss
abys·sal of ocean depths
Ab·ys·sinia *former name of* Ethiopia

Ab·ys·sin·ian
aca·cia
aca·deme
aca·demia
aca·dem·ic
aca·dem·ical·ly
aca·dem·icals academic
dress
acad·emi·cian
aca·demi·cism (*or*
acad·emism)
conventionalism
acad·emy (*plural* ·emies)
Aca·dia Canadian region;
compare Arcadia
Aca·dian of Acadia;
compare Accadian
aca·jou mahogany
ac·an·tha·ceous botany
term
acan·thine
acan·tho·cepha·lan
wormlike animal
acan·thoid spiny
ac·an·thop·ter·yg·ian fish
acan·thous thornlike
acan·thus (*plural* ·thuses
or ·thi) plant;
architectural ornament
a cap·pel·la musical term
Aca·pul·co Mexican port
aca·ria·sis tick or mite
infestation
aca·rid (*or* acari·dan) tick
or mite
aca·roid
aca·rol·ogy
acar·pel·lous lacking
carpels
acar·pous producing no
fruit
aca·rus mite
acata·lec·tic verse form
acau·dal (*or* ·date) having
no tail
acau·les·cent having no
stem
Ac·cad *variant spelling of*
Akkad
Ac·cad·ian *variant spelling*
of Akkadian; *compare*
Acadian
ac·cede
ac·ced·ence
ac·ced·er
ac·cel·era·able

ac·cel·er·an·do (*plural*
·dos) musical term
ac·cel·er·ant
ac·cel·er·ate
ac·cel·era·tion
ac·cel·era·tive (*or* ·tory)
ac·cel·era·tor
ac·cel·er·om·eter
ac·cent
ac·cen·tor bird
ac·cen·tual rhythmical
ac·cen·tu·ate
ac·cen·tua·tion
ac·cept
ac·cept·abil·ity (*or*
·able·ness)
ac·cept·able
ac·cept·ably
ac·cept·ance
ac·cept·ant
ac·cep·ta·tion
ac·cept·ed·ly
ac·cep·ter (*or esp. in legal*
contexts, chemistry,
and electronics ·tor)
ac·cess
ac·ces·sa·ry (*plural* ·ries)
variant spelling of
accessory
ac·ces·sibil·ity
ac·ces·sible
ac·ces·sibly
ac·ces·sion
ac·ces·sion·al
ac·ces·so·rial
ac·ces·so·ri·ly
ac·ces·so·ri·ness
ac·ces·so·ry (*or in legal*
contexts ·sa·ry; *plural*
·ries)
ac·ciac·ca·tu·ra (*plural*
·ras *or* ·re) musical term
ac·ci·dence linguistics term
ac·ci·dent
ac·ci·den·tal
ac·ci·den·tal·ly
ac·ci·die apathy
ac·cipi·ter hawk
ac·cipi·tral (*or* ·trine)
ac·claim
ac·cla·ma·tion
ac·clama·tory
ac·cli·ma·tiz·able (*or*
·ma·tis·able, ·mat·able)

ac·cli·ma·ti·za·tion (*or*
·ma·ti·sa·tion, ·ma·tion)
ac·cli·ma·tize (*or* ·ma·tise,
·mate)
ac·cli·ma·tiz·er (*or* ·tis·er)
ac·clivi·tous (*or* ·cli·vous)
ac·cliv·ity (*plural* ·ities)
upward slope
ac·co·lade
ac·com·mo·date
ac·com·mo·dat·ing
ac·com·mo·dat·ing·ly
ac·com·mo·da·tion
ac·com·mo·da·tive
(accomodate) *incorrect*
spelling of accommodate
ac·com·pa·ni·er
ac·com·pa·ni·ment
ac·com·pa·nist (*or esp.*
US ·pa·ny·ist)
ac·com·pa·ny (·nies,
·ny·ing, ·nied)
ac·com·plice
ac·com·plish
ac·com·plish·able
ac·com·plish·er
ac·com·plish·ment
ac·cord
ac·cord·able
ac·cord·ance
ac·cord·ant
ac·cord·er
ac·cord·ing
ac·cord·ing·ly
ac·cor·di·on
ac·cor·di·on·ist
ac·cost
ac·cost·able
ac·count
ac·count·abil·ity
ac·count·able
ac·count·ably
ac·count·an·cy
ac·count·ant
ac·count·ing
ac·cou·ple·ment supporting
beam
ac·cou·tre (*US* ·ter)
ac·cou·tre·ment (*US*
·ter·)
Ac·cra Ghanaian capital
ac·cred·it
ac·credi·ta·tion
ac·cres·cent botany term
ac·crete

ac·cre·tion

ac·cre·tive (*or* ac·cre·tion·ary)

Ac·cring·ton

ac·cru·al (*or* ·ment)

ac·crue (·cru·ing, ·crued)

ac·cul·tur·ate

ac·cul·tura·tion

ac·cum·ben·cy

ac·cum·bent botany term

ac·cu·mu·lable

ac·cu·mu·late

ac·cu·mu·la·tion

ac·cu·mu·la·tive

ac·cu·mu·la·tor

ac·cu·ra·cy (*plural* ·cies)

ac·cu·rate

ac·cu·rate·ly

ac·curs·ed

ac·cus·al

ac·cu·sa·tion

ac·cu·sa·ti·val

ac·cu·sa·tive grammar term

ac·cu·sa·to·rial (*or* ·tory)

ac·cuse

ac·cused

ac·cus·er

ac·cus·ing·ly

ac·cus·tom

ac·cus·tomed

Ac·cu·tron (*Trademark*) watch

ace

acedia apathy

acel·lu·lar

acen·tric

acepha·lous headless

ac·er·ate *variant of* acerose

ac·er·bate embitter

acer·bic

acer·bity (*plural* ·bities)

ac·er·ose (*or* ·ous, ·ate) needle-shaped

acer·vate growing in clusters

aces·cence (*or* ·cen·cy)

aces·cent turning sour

ac·etabu·lum (*plural* ·la) cavity in hipbone

ac·etal chemical compound

ac·et·al·de·hyde

ac·et·am·ide (*or* ·id)

ac·et·ani·lide (*or* ·lid)

ac·etate

acetic acid

aceti·fi·ca·tion

aceti·fi·er

aceti·fy (·fies, ·fy·ing, ·fied) convert into vinegar

ac·etom·eter

ac·etone

ac·etous (*or* ·etose) resembling vinegar

acetum vinegar

ac·etyl

acety·late

acety·la·tion

acetyl·cho·line biochemical compound

acety·lene

acety·len·ic

acety·lide

ac·etyl·sali·cyl·ic acid *chemical name for* aspirin

acey-deucy backgammon

Achaea (*or* Achaia) region of Greece

Achae·an (*or* Achaian)

Achaemenid member of Persian dynasty

Acha·tes loyal friend

ache

ach·ing·ly

achene (*or* akene) botany term

achenial (*or* akenial)

Acher·nar star

Ach·er·on mythological river

Acheu·lian (*or* ·lean) archaeological period

achiev·able

achieve

achieve·ment

achiev·er

Ach·il·lean

Achilles

ach·la·myd·eous lacking petals and sepals

achlor·hy·dria lacking stomach acid

achon·drite meteorite

achon·drit·ic

achon·dro·pla·sia skeletal disorder

achon·dro·plas·tic

ach·ro·mat type of lens

ach·ro·mat·ic

ach·ro·mati·cal·ly

achro·ma·tin part of cell nucleus

achro·ma·tism (*or* ·tic·ity)

achro·ma·ti·za·tion (*or* ·sa·tion)

achro·ma·tize (*or* ·tise) remove colour from

achro·ma·tous

a·chro·mic (*or* achro·mous) colourless

ach-y-fi Welsh expression of disgust

acicu·la (*plural* ·lae) needle-shaped structure

acicu·lar

acicu·late (*or* ·lat·ed)

acicu·lum (*plural* ·lums *or* ·la) zoology term

acid

acid-fast

acid-forming

acid·ic

acidi·fi·able

acidi·fi·ca·tion

acidi·fi·er

acidi·fy (·fies, ·fy·ing, ·fied)

aci·dim·eter

acidi·met·ric (*or* ·ri·cal)

aci·di·met·ri·cal·ly

aci·dim·etry

acid·ity (*plural* ·ities)

acid·ness

aci·dom·eter hydrometer for acids

aci·do·phil (*or* ·phile) biology term

aci·do·phil·ic (*or* ·dophi·lous)

aci·dophi·lus bacterium

aci·do·sis medical condition

aci·dot·ic

acidu·late make acid

acidu·la·tion

acidu·lous (*or* ·lent)

aci·er·ate change into steel

aci·era·tion

aci·naci·form botany term

acin·ic (*or* aci·nous, aci·nose)

acini·form

aci·nus (*plural* ·ni) biology term

Acis mythological character

ack-ack anti-aircraft fire

ackee (*or* akee) fruit

ac·knowl·edge

acumen

ac·knowl·edge·able
ac·knowl·edg·er
ac·knowl·edg·ment (*or* ·edge·)
aclin·ic line magnetic equator
acme peak
acne skin disease
ac·no·dal
ac·node maths term
Acol bridge term
aco·lyte
aco·nite (*or* ·ni·tum)
aco·nit·ic
acorn
acoty·ledon botany term
acoty·ledon·ous
acou·chi (*or* ·chy) rodent
acous·tic (*or* ·ti·cal)
acous·ti·cal·ly
acous·ti·cian
acous·tics
ac·quaint
ac·quaint·ance
ac·quaint·ance·ship
ac·quaint·ed
ac·qui·esce
ac·qui·es·cence
ac·qui·es·cent
ac·quir·able
ac·quire
ac·quire·ment
ac·quir·er
ac·qui·si·tion
ac·quisi·tive
ac·quisi·tive·ness
ac·quit (·quit·ting, ·quit·ted)
ac·quit·tal
ac·quit·tance
ac·quit·ter
acre
acre·age
acred having acres of land
acre-foot (*plural* -feet)
acre-inch
ac·rid
ac·ri·dine chemical compound
acrid·ity (*or* ·ness)
ac·ri·fla·vine antiseptic
Ac·ri·lan (*Trademark*)
ac·ri·mo·ni·ous
ac·ri·mo·ny (*plural* ·nies)
ac·ro·bat

ac·ro·bat·ic
ac·ro·bati·cal·ly
ac·ro·bat·ics
ac·ro·car·pous botany term
ac·ro·dont zoology term
ac·ro·drome botany term
ac·ro·gen botany term
ac·ro·gen·ic (*or* acrog·enous)
acro·lein chemical compound
ac·ro·lith type of sculpture
ac·ro·me·gal·ic
ac·ro·mega·ly hormonal disease
acro·mi·on (*plural* ·mia) part of shoulder blade
acrony·chal (*or* ·cal) occurring at sunset
ac·ro·nym
ac·ro·nym·ic (*or* acrony·mous)
acrop·etal botany term
ac·ro·pho·bia fear of heights
ac·ro·pho·bic
Acropo·lis
ac·ro·spire botany term
across
acros·tic
acros·ti·cal·ly
acro·ter architectural term
acryl·ic
ac·ry·lo·ni·trile
ac·ry·lyl
act
act·abil·ity
act·able
ac·tin protein
ac·ti·nal zoology term
act·ing
ac·tinia (*plural* ·tiniae *or* ·tinias) sea anemone
ac·tin·ic type of radiation
ac·tini·cal·ly
ac·ti·nide (*or* ·non)
ac·tini·form (*or* ac·ti·noid) star-shaped
ac·tin·ism
ac·tin·ium radioactive element
ac·ti·noid *variant of* actiniform
ac·tino·lite mineral
ac·ti·no·mere biology term

ac·ti·nom·eter radiation measurer
ac·ti·no·met·ric (*or* ·ri·cal)
ac·ti·nom·etry
ac·ti·no·mor·phic (*or* ·phous) botany term
ac·ti·no·my·cete bacterium
ac·ti·no·my·cin antibiotic
ac·ti·no·my·co·sis bacterial infection
ac·ti·no·my·cot·ic
ac·ti·non *variant of* actinide
ac·tino·pod protozoan
ac·ti·no·thera·py radiotherapy
ac·ti·no·ura·nium isotope of uranium
ac·ti·no·zo·an marine organism
ac·tion
ac·tion·able
ac·tion·ably
action-packed
Ac·ti·um ancient Greek town
ac·ti·vate
ac·ti·va·tion
ac·ti·va·tor
ac·tive
ac·tive·ly
ac·tive·ness
ac·tiv·ism
ac·tiv·ist
ac·tiv·ity (*plural* ·ities)
ac·to·myo·sin protein
Ac·ton London district
ac·tor
ac·tress
ac·tual
ac·tu·al·ity (*plural* ·ities)
ac·tu·ali·za·tion (*or* ·sa·tion)
ac·tu·al·ize (*or* ·ise)
ac·tu·al·ly
ac·tu·ari·al
ac·tu·ary (*plural* ·aries)
ac·tu·ate
ac·tua·tion
ac·tua·tor
acu·ity
acu·leate (*or* ·leat·ed) pointed
acu·leus (*plural* ·lei) prickle
acu·men

acu·mi·nate pointed
acu·mi·na·tion
acu·mi·nous
acu·punc·ture
acut·ance photography term
acute
acute·ly
acute·ness
acy·clic chemistry term
acyl
ad Slang advertisement
adac·ty·lous without fingers
or toes
ad·age
ada·gio (plural ·gios)
musical term
ada·mant
ada·man·tine very hard
Ada·ma·wa language group
Ad·am·ite nudist
Ad·ams US mountain
ad·ams·ite tear gas
Ada·na Turkish city
adapt
adapt·abil·ity (or
·able·ness)
adapt·able
adapt·ably
ad·ap·ta·tion
adapt·er one who adapts;
compare adaptor
adap·tive
adapt·or electrical device;
compare adapter
ad·ax·ial towards the axis;
compare abaxial
add
ad·dax antelope
ad·dend number added to
ad·den·dum (plural ·da)
ad·der snake
add·er calculator
ad·dict
ad·dic·tion
ad·dic·tive
Ad·dis Aba·ba Ethiopian
capital
ad·di·tion
ad·di·tion·al
ad·di·tion·al·ly
ad·di·tive
ad·dle
ad·dress
ad·dressee
ad·dress·er (or ·dres·sor)

Ad·dres·so·graph
(Trademark)
ad·duce
ad·duce·able (or
·duc·ible)
ad·du·cent
ad·duct pull towards
ad·duc·tion
ad·duc·tor muscle
Ad·elaide Australian city
ademp·tion legal term
Aden capital of South
Yemen
ad·enec·to·my (plural
·mies) removal of gland
ad·enine biochemical
compound
ad·eni·tis inflammation of a
gland
ad·eno·car·ci·no·ma
(plural ·mas or ·ma·ta)
tumour
ad·eno·hy·phophy·sis part
of pituitary gland
ad·enoid resembling a gland
ad·enoi·dal affected by
enlarged adenoids
ad·enoid·ec·to·my (plural
·mies)
ad·enoids tonsil tissue
ad·eno·ma (plural ·mas or
·ma·ta) glandular tumour
adeno·sine biochemical
compound
ad·eno·vi·rus
adept
ad·equa·cy
ad·equate
à deux French of or for two
persons
ad·here
ad·her·ence
ad·her·ent (noun, adj)
ad·he·sion
ad·he·sive
ad·he·sive·ness
ad hoc Latin for a particular
purpose
ad ho·mi·nem Latin to the
man
adia·bat·ic physics term
adi·aph·or·ism theological
term
adi·apho·rist
adi·apho·ris·tic
adi·apho·rous medical term

adieu (plural adieus or
adieux) goodbye
ad in·fi·ni·tum Latin
without end
ad in·ter·im Latin for the
meantime
adi·os Spanish goodbye
adi·po·cere waxy substance
adi·poc·er·ous
adi·pose fatty
adi·pos·ity
Adi·ron·dacks US
mountains
adit mine shaft
Adi·va·si Indian people
ad·ja·cen·cy
ad·ja·cent
ad·jec·ti·val
ad·jec·tive
ad·join
ad·join·ing
ad·joint maths term
ad·journ
ad·journ·ment
ad·judge
ad·ju·di·cate
ad·ju·di·ca·tion
ad·ju·di·ca·tive
ad·ju·di·ca·tor
ad·junct
ad·junc·tive
ad·ju·ra·tion
ad·jura·tory
ad·jure appeal to solemnly;
compare abjure
ad·jur·er (or ·ju·ror)
ad·just
ad·just·able
ad·just·ment
ad·ju·tan·cy
ad·ju·tant
ad·ju·vant helping; auxiliary
ad lib spontaneously; freely
ad-lib (-libbing, -libbed)
improvise
ad·libber
ad·man (plural ·men)
ad·mass people susceptible
to advertising
ad·meas·ure
ad·meas·ure·ment
Admetus mythological king
ad·min short for
administration
ad·mini·cle legal term

ad·min·is·ter
ad·min·is·trable
ad·min·is·trate
ad·min·is·tra·tion
ad·min·is·tra·tive
ad·min·is·tra·tor (*fem*
·trix *in legal contexts*)
ad·mi·rable
ad·mi·rably
ad·mi·ral
ad·mi·ral·ty (*plural* ·ties)
ad·mi·ra·tion
ad·mire
ad·mirer
ad·mir·ing·ly
ad·mis·sibil·ity (*or*
·sible·ness)
ad·mis·sible
ad·mis·sion
ad·mis·sive
ad·mit (·mit·ting,
·mit·ted)
ad·mit·tance
ad·mit·ted·ly
ad·mix
ad·mix·ture
ad·mon·ish
ad·mon·ish·er (*or*
·moni·tor)
ad·mo·ni·tion
ad·moni·tory
ad·nate botany term
ad nau·seam *Latin* to a
disgusting extent
ad·nomi·nal word
modifying a noun
ad·noun adjective used as
noun
ado
ado·be building term
ado·les·cence
ado·les·cent
Adon·ic type of verse line
Adonis mythological
character
adopt
adopt·able
adopt·ed
adop·tee
adopt·er
adop·tion
adop·tion·ism (*or* ·tian·)
adop·tion·ist (*or* ·tian·)
adop·tive
ador·able

ador·ably
ado·ra·tion
adore
ador·er
adorn
adorn·ment
ad rem *Latin* to the point
ad·re·nal gland
adrena·line hormone
ad·ren·er·gic biology term
adre·no·cor·ti·co·troph·ic
(*US* ·trop·ic) stimulating
adrenal cortex
Adri·at·ic
adrift
adroit
adroit·ness
ad·sci·ti·tious additional
ad·sorb accumulate on a
surface; *compare* absorb
ad·sorb·abil·ity
ad·sorb·able
ad·sorb·ate
ad·sor·bent
ad·sorp·tion
adu·laria mineral
adu·late
adu·la·tion
adu·la·tor
adu·la·tory
adult
adul·ter·ant
adul·ter·ate
adul·tera·tion
adul·ter·ator
adul·ter·er (*fem* ·ess)
adul·ter·ine fake
adul·ter·ous
adul·tery (*plural* ·teries)
adult·hood
ad·um·bral shadowy
ad·um·brate
ad·um·bra·tion
ad·um·bra·tive
Adu·wa Ethiopian town
ad va·lo·rem *Latin*
according to value
ad·vance
ad·vanced
ad·vance·ment
ad·vanc·er
ad·vanc·ing·ly
ad·van·tage
ad·van·ta·geous
ad·van·ta·geous·ness

ad·vec·tion
Ad·vent coming of Christ
ad·vent arrival
Ad·ven·tist
ad·ven·ti·tia anatomy term
ad·ven·ti·tious happening
by chance; growing in
abnormal position
ad·ven·tive
ad·ven·ture
ad·ven·tur·er (*fem* ·ess)
ad·ven·tur·ism
ad·ven·tur·ist
ad·ven·tur·ous
ad·verb
ad·ver·bial
ad·ver·sary (*plural*
·saries)
ad·ver·sa·tive linguistics
term
ad·verse
ad·ver·sity (*plural* ·sities)
ad·vert refer to; *Slang*
advertisement
ad·vert·ence (*or* ·en·cy)
ad·vert·ent·ly
ad·ver·tise
ad·ver·tise·ment
ad·ver·tis·er
ad·ver·tis·ing
(advertize) *incorrect spelling
of* advertise
ad·vice
ad·vis·abil·ity
ad·vis·able
ad·vise
ad·vised
ad·vis·ed·ly
ad·vise·ment *US* careful
consideration
ad·vis·er (*or* ·vi·sor)
ad·vi·so·ry
ad·vo·caat
ad·vo·ca·cy (*plural* ·cies)
ad·vo·cate
ad·vo·ca·tion
ad·vo·ca·tory
Ady·gei (*plural* ·gei *or*
·geis) Soviet people
ady·na·mia weakness
ady·nam·ic
adze (*US* adz) tool
Adzhar
Adzha·ria Soviet republic
ad·zuki (*or* ·su·ki) bean

aecio·spore

aecium (*or* aecid·ium; *plural* aecia *or* ·ia) fungal structure

aedes mosquito

aedile (*US also* edile) Roman magistrate

Aeëtes mythological king

Aegean

Aegi·na Greek island

Aegir Norse god

aegis (*US also* egis)

aegro·tat university degree

Aegyptus mythological king

Aeneas mythological prince

Aene·id epic poem

Aeo·lian

aeo·lian harp

Aeol·ic ancient Greek dialect

aeoli·pile model steam turbine

Aeo·lis Greek god

aeon (*US* eon)

aeo·nian (*or* eo·) everlasting

aepy·or·nis extinct bird

aer·ate

aera·tion

aera·tor

aer·en·chy·ma plant tissue

aer·ial relating to air; radio or TV device; *compare* ariel

aeri·al·ist trapeze artist

aerie *variant spelling of* eyrie

aeri·fi·ca·tion

aeri·form gaseous

aeri·fy (·fies, ·fy·ing, ·fied)

aero·bal·lis·tics

aero·bat·ics

aer·obe (*or* aero·bium; *plural* ·obes *or* ·bia)

aero·bic requiring oxygen

aero·bics exercises

aero·bio·sis

aero·bio·tic

aero·bium *variant of* aerobe

aero·do·net·ics study of gliding flight

aero·drome

aero·dy·nam·ic

aero·dy·nami·cal·ly

aero·dy·nam·ics

aero·dyne heavier-than-air machine

aero·em·bo·lism nitrogen in the blood

aero·engine

aero·foil

aero·gel solid foam

aero·gram (*or* ·gramme)

aer·og·ra·phy

aero·lite meteorite

aero·lo·gic (*or* ·logi·cal)

aer·olo·gist

aer·ol·ogy study of the atmosphere

aero·mechan·ic

aero·mechani·cal

aero·mechan·ics

aer·om·eter

aero·met·ric

aer·om·etry branch of physics

aero·naut

aero·nau·ti·cal (*or* aero·nau·tic)

aero·naut·ics

aero·neu·ro·sis

aero·pause region of upper atmosphere

aero·pha·gia swallowing of air

aero·pho·bia

aero·pho·bic afraid of draughts

aero·plane

aero·sol

aero·space

aero·sphere earth's atmosphere

aero·stat lighter-than-air craft

aero·stat·ic (*or* ·stati·cal)

aero·stat·ics

aero·sta·tion

aero·ther·mo·dy·nam·ic

aero·ther·mo·dy·nam·ics

aeru·go verdigris

aeru·gin·ous

aery *variant spelling of* eyrie; *poetic* airy; insubstantial

Aes·cu·la·pian

Aesculapius Roman god

Aesir Norse gods

aes·the·sia (*US* es·) normal sensitivity

aes·thete (*US also* es·)

aes·thet·ic (*or* ·theti·cal; *US also* es·)

aes·theti·cal·ly (*US also* es·)

aes·the·ti·cian (*US also* es·)

aes·theti·cism (*US also* es·)

aes·thet·ics (*US also* es·)

aes·ti·val (*US* es·) occurring in the summer

aes·ti·vate (*US* es·)

aes·ti·va·tion (*US* es·) biology term

aes·ti·va·tor (*US* es·)

aether *former spelling of* ether (anaesthetic); *variant spelling of* ether (hypothetical medium)

aethe·real *rare spelling of* ethereal

aethe·real·ity *rare spelling of* ethereality

aetio·logi·cal (*US* etio·)

aeti·olo·gist (*US* eti·)

aeti·ol·ogy (*US* eti·) study of causes

Aeto·lia Greek region

afar

afebrile without fever

af·fabil·ity

af·fable

af·fably

af·fair

af·faire *French* love affair

af·fect have an effect on; *compare* effect (*verb*)

af·fec·ta·tion

af·fect·ed

af·fect·ed·ly

af·fect·ed·ness

af·fect·ing

af·fect·ing·ly

af·fec·tion

af·fec·tion·al

af·fec·tion·ate

af·fec·tive arousing emotions

af·fec·tiv·ity (*or* ·tive·ness)

af·fen·pin·scher dog

af·fer·ent conducting inwards; *compare* efferent

af·fet·tuo·so musical term

af·fi·ance betroth

af·fi·ant *US* person who makes an affidavit
af·fi·da·vit
af·fili·ate
af·filia·tion
af·fine maths term
af·fined closely related
af·fini·tive
af·fin·ity (*plural* ·ities)
af·firm
af·firm·able
af·fir·ma·tion
af·firma·tive
af·firm·er (*or* ·ant)
af·fix
af·fix·ture
af·fla·tus creative power
af·flict
af·flic·tion
af·flic·tive
af·flu·ence
af·flu·ent
af·flux flowing towards
af·ford
af·for·est
af·for·esta·tion
af·fran·chise release from obligation
af·fran·chise·ment
af·fray
af·freight·ment
af·fri·cate
af·frica·tive phonetics term
af·fright
af·front
af·fu·sion baptism
Af·ghan hound
Af·ghan (*or* ·ghani) people
af·ghan shawl
af·ghani Afghan currency
Af·ghani·stan
afi·cio·na·do (*plural* ·dos) supporter
afield
afire
aflame
af·la·tox·in
afloat
aflut·ter
afoot
afore
afore·men·tioned
afore·said
afore·thought

a for·tio·ri *Latin* for a stronger reason
afoul
afraid
af·reet Arabian demon
afresh
Af·ri·ca
Af·ri·can
Af·ri·can·ism
Af·ri·kaans language of Afrikaners
Af·ri·kan·der (*or* ·can·) cattle
Af·ri·ka·ner White South African
Af·ri·ka·ner·dom
Afro (*plural* **Afros**) hairstyle
Afro-American
Afro-Asian
Afro-Asiatic
af·ror·mo·sia wood
aft
af·ter
after·birth
after·body (*plural* ·bodies) discarded part of rocket
after·brain
after·burner
after·burning
after·care
after·damp gas in mines
after·deck
after·effect
after·glow
after·heat
after·image
after·life
after·math
after·noon
after·pains
after·piece brief additional comic play
af·ters *Slang* dessert
after·sensation
after·shaft type of feather
after·shave
after·shock
after·taste
after·thought
after·wards (*or esp. US* ·ward)
after·word postscript
after·world

aga (*or* **agha**) Turkish title
Aga·dir Moroccan port
again
against
agal·loch tree
aga·ma lizard
Agamemnon mythological king
agam·ete biology term
agam·ic biology term
agami·cal·ly
aga·mo·gen·esis biology term
aga·mo·genet·ic
aga·mo·geneti·cal·ly
aga·pan·thus lily
Agape Christian love
agape gaping
agar seaweed product
aga·ric mushroom
agari·ca·ceous
Agar·ta·la Indian city
ag·ate
agate·ware
aga·ve plant
age (**age·ing** *or esp. US* **ag·ing**, **aged**)
aged (*adj, noun*)
agee *Scot* awry
age·ing (*or esp. US* **ag·ing**)
age·less
agen·cy (*plural* ·cies)
agen·da (*or* ·dum; *plural* ·das *or* ·dums)
agen·esis imperfect development
agenet·ic
agent
agen·tial
agen·tive (*or* ·tial) linguistics term
agent pro·vo·ca·teur (*plural* **agents pro·vo·ca·teurs**)
ag·era·tum plant
ag·ger Roman earthwork
ag·gior·na·men·to (*plural* ·ti) updating Catholic church
ag·glom·er·ate
ag·glom·era·tion
ag·glom·era·tive
ag·glu·ti·nabil·ity
ag·glu·ti·nable

ag·glu·ti·nant
ag·glu·ti·nate
ag·glu·ti·na·tion
ag·glu·ti·na·tive
ag·glu·ti·nin antibody
à·glu·tino·gen
ag·grada·tion
ag·grade geology term
ag·gran·dize (or ·dise)
ag·gran·dize·ment (or ·dise·ment)
ag·gran·diz·er (or ·dis·er)
ag·gra·vate
ag·gra·va·tion
ag·gre·gate
ag·gre·ga·tion
ag·gress
ag·gres·sion
ag·gres·sive
ag·gres·sor
ag·grieve
ag·griev·ed·ly
ag·gro Slang aggression
aghast
ag·ile
agil·ity
Ag·in·court
ag·ing variant spelling (esp. US) of ageing
agio·tage business of currency exchange
agist legal term
agi·tate
agi·ta·tion
agi·ta·to musical term
agi·ta·tor
agit·prop communist propaganda
Aglaia Greek goddess
agleam
ag·let (or aiglet) shoelace tag
agley Scot awry
aglit·ter
aglow
agma phonetic symbol
ag·mi·nate gathered together
ag·nate having common male ancestor
ag·no·men (plural ·nomi·na) ancient Roman's fourth name
ag·nomi·nal
ag·nos·tic

ag·nos·ti·cism
Ag·nus Dei liturgical chant
ago
agog
à gogo French as much as one likes
agon (plural ago·nes) ancient Greek festival
agon·ic forming no angle
ago·nist
ago·nis·tic
ago·nize (or ·nise)
ago·niz·ing·ly (or ·nis·)
ago·ny (plural ·nies)
ago·ra (plural ·rae or ·ras) Greek marketplace
ago·ra (plural ·rot) Israeli coin
ago·ra·pho·bia
ago·ra·pho·bic
agou·ti (plural ·tis or ·ties) rodent
Agra Indian city
agraffe fastening
agran·ulo·cy·tosis blood disorder
ag·ra·pha sayings of Christ
agraphia inability to write
agrar·ian
agrari·an·ism
agree (agree·ing, agreed)
agree·able
agree·able·ness
agree·ably
agreed
agree·ment
agres·tal growing as a weed
agres·tic rural
ag·ri·busi·ness
ag·ri·cul·tur·al
ag·ri·cul·ture
ag·ri·cul·tur·ist (or ·tur·al·ist)
ag·ri·mo·ny (plural ·nies) plant
ag·ro·bio·logi·cal
ag·ro·bi·olo·gist
ag·ro·bi·ol·ogy
ag·ro·logi·cal
agrol·ogy study of soils
ag·ro·nom·ic (or ·nomi·cal)
ag·ro·nom·ics land economics
agrono·mist

agrono·my science of cultivation
ag·ros·tol·ogy study of grasses
aground
ag·ryp·not·ic of insomnia
Aguas·ca·lien·tes Mexican state
ague malaria
ague·weed
Agul·has South African headland
ah
aha
ahead
ahem
Ah·meda·bad (or ·mada·) Indian city
Ah·med·na·gar (or ·mad·) Indian city
ahoy
Ah·waz (or ·vaz) Iranian town
ai (plural ais) animal
aid help
aide assistant
aide-de-camp (plural aides-)
aide-mémoire (plural aides-)
aid·er
aigrette (or aigret) feather on hat
aiguille mountain peak
aiguil·lette military ornament
aikido self-defence
ail
ailan·thus (plural ·thuses) tree
ailer·on
ail·ing
ail·ment
ailu·ro·phile cat lover
ailu·ro·philia
ailu·ro·phobe fearer of cats
ailu·ro·phobia
aim
aim·less
aim·less·ness
ain Scot own
ain't Nonstandard am not
Ainu (plural Ainus or Ainu) Japanese people
aïoli garlic mayonnaise
Aïr Saharan region

air
air·borne
air·brick
air·brush
air·burst
air·bus
air-conditioned
air-conditioner
air-conditioning
air-cool
air·craft (plural ·craft)
air·craft·man (or ·crafts·; plural ·men)
air·craft·woman (or ·crafts·; plural ·women)
air·crew
Air·drie Scottish town
air·drop (·drop·ping, ·dropped) delivery by parachute
air-dry (-dries, -dry·ing, -dried)
Aire·dale Yorkshire district; terrier
air·field
air·flow
air·foil
air·frame part of aircraft
air·glow
air·head military term
airi·ly
airi·ness
air·ing
air·intake
air·less
air·less·ness
air·lift
air·line
air·lin·er
air·lock
air·man (plural ·men)
air·plane US aeroplane
air·port
air·screw propeller
air·ship
air·sick
air·sick·ness
air·space
air·speed
air·stream
air·strip
air·tight
air·waves
air·way

air·woman (plural ·women)
air·worthi·ness
air·worthy
airy (airi·er, airi·est)
airy-fairy
aisle
Aisne French river
ait Dialect islet
aitch letter H
aitch·bone cut of beef
Aix-en-Provence French city
Ajac·cio Corsican port
ajar
Ajax mythological character
Aj·mer Indian city
Ake·la cub-scout leader
akha·ra Indian gymnasium
akim·bo
akin
Ak·kad (or Ac·cad) Babylonian city
Ak·ka·dian (or Ac·ca·)
Ak·tyu·binsk Soviet city
à la French in the style of
ala (plural alae) winglike structure
Ala·bama
Ala·bam·ian
ala·bas·ter
à la carte
alack
alacka·day
alac·ri·tous
alac·rity
Aladdin
Ala·go·as Brazilian state
Alai Soviet mountain range
ala·meda US tree-lined promenade
Ala·mo
à la mode fashionable
ala·mode silk
ala·nine amino acid
alan·nah Irish term of endearment
alap Indian music
alar of wings
alarm
alarmed
alarm·ing
alarm·ing·ly
alarm·ism
alarm·ist

alar·um Archaic alarm
alary of wings
alas
Alas·ka
Alas·kan
alate winged
al·ba·core fish
Alba Lon·ga ancient city
Al·ba·nia
Al·ba·nian
Al·ba·ny US city; Canadian river; Australian port
al·ba·ta alloy
al·ba·tross
al·be·do (plural ·dos) physics term
al·be·it
Al·bert former name of Mobutu
Al·ber·ta Canadian province
al·bert·ite variety of bitumen
al·bes·cence
al·bes·cent becoming white
Al·bi·gen·ses medieval heretics
Al·bi·gen·sian
al·bin·ic (or ·bin·is·tic)
al·bi·nism
al·bi·no (plural ·nos)
Al·bi·on Archaic Britain
al·bite mineral
al·bit·ic
Ål·borg variant spelling of Aalborg
al·bum
al·bu·men white of egg; compare albumin
al·bu·menize (or ·menise)
al·bu·min a protein; compare albumen
al·bu·mi·nate
al·bu·mi·noid
al·bu·mi·nous
al·bu·mi·nu·ria urine containing albumin
Al·bu·quer·que US city
al·bur·num sapwood
Al·bu·ry Australian city
Al·ca·ic verse form
al·caide Spanish commander
al·cal·de Spanish mayor
Al·ca·traz US island
al·ca·zar Moorish palace
Alcestis mythological queen

al·chem·ic (*or* ·chemi·cal,
·chem·is·tic)
al·che·mist
al·che·mize (*or* ·mise)
al·che·my (*plural* ·mies)
al·che·rin·ga Aboriginal
golden age
al·ci·dine ornithology term
al·co·hol
al·co·hol·ic
al·co·hol·ic·ity
al·co·hol·ism
al·co·holi·za·tion (*or*
·sa·tion)
al·co·hol·ize (*or* ·ise)
al·co·hol·om·eter
Al·co·ran Koran
al·cove
Alcyone (*or* Halcyone)
mythological character
Al·dab·ra Indian Ocean
islands
Al·deba·ran star
al·de·hyde
al den·te *Italian* cooked
until still firm
al·der
al·der·man (*plural* ·men)
al·der·man·ic
Al·der·mas·ton
Al·der·ney Channel Island
Al·der·shot
al·dol chemical compound
al·dose sugar
al·dos·terone hormone
ald·ox·ime chemical
compound
al·drin insecticide
ale
alea·to·ry dependent on
chance
ale·cost plant
alee nautical term
al·egar malt vinegar
ale·house
Ale·man·ni Germanic
people
Al·eman·nic
alem·bic
alem·bi·cat·ed excessively
refined
aleph Hebrew letter
aleph-null (*or* -zero)
maths term
Alep·po Syrian city

alert
alert·ness
Ales·san·dria Italian town
alethic logic term
aleu·rone (*or* ·ron) plant
protein
al·evin young fish
ale·wife fish
al·ex·an·ders plant
Al·ex·an·dria Egyptian port
Al·ex·an·drian
Al·ex·an·drine type of
verse
al·ex·an·drite gemstone
alexia word blindness
alex·in immunology term
al·fal·fa
al·fila·ria (*or* ·fil·eria)
plant
al·fres·co
al·gae (*sing.* alga)
al·gal
al·gar·ro·ba (*or* ·ga·ro·ba)
tree
al·ge·bra
al·ge·bra·ic (*or* ·brai·cal)
al·ge·brai·cal·ly
al·ge·bra·ist
Al·ge·ci·ras Spanish port
Al·ge·ria
Al·ge·rian (*or* ·rine)
al·gerine fabric
al·gi·cide
al·gid chilly
Al·giers Algerian capital
al·gin biochemical
compound
al·gi·nate
al·gin·ic acid
al·goid resembling algae
Al·gol star; computer
language
al·go·lag·nia sexual
perversion
al·go·lag·nic
al·go·lag·nist
al·golo·gist
al·gol·ogy study of algae
al·gom·eter
al·gom·etry
Al·gon·quian (*or* ·kian)
Al·gon·quin (*or* ·kin;
plural ·quins, ·quin *or*
·kins, ·kin) American
Indian

al·go·pho·bia fear of pain
al·gor chill
al·go·rism counting system
al·go·ris·mic
al·go·rithm maths term
al·go·rith·mic
al·go·rith·mi·cal·ly
Al·ham·bra Spanish citadel
Al·ham·bresque
Al Hasa Saudi Arabian
province
Al Hu·fuf (*or* Ho·fuf)
Saudi Arabian town
ali·as (*plural* ·ases)
Ali Baba
ali·bi (*plural* ·bis)
Ali·can·te Spanish town
ali·cy·clic chemistry term
ali·dade (*or* ·dad)
surveying instrument
al·ien
al·ien·abil·ity
al·ien·able
al·ien·age
al·ien·ate
al·iena·tion
al·iena·tor
al·ienee legal term
al·ien·ism
al·ien·ist *US* psychiatrist
al·ien·or legal term
ali·form wing-shaped
Ali·garh Indian city
alight (alight·ing,
alight·ed *or* alit)
align
align·ment
alike
ali·ment
ali·men·ta·ry
ali·men·ta·tion
ali·men·ta·tive
ali·mo·ny
aline *rare spelling of* align
ali·ped having winglike
limbs
ali·phat·ic chemistry term
ali·quant maths term
ali·quot maths term
aliun·de from another
source
alive
aliza·rin dye
al·ka·hest (*or* ·ca·)
alchemical solvent

al·ka·li (*plural* ·lis *or* ·lies)
al·kal·ic
al·ka·li·fy (·fies, ·fy·ing, ·fied)
al·ka·lim·eter
al·ka·li·met·ric
al·ka·lim·etry
al·ka·line
al·ka·lin·ity
al·ka·liz·able (*or* ·lis·able)
al·ka·lize (*or* ·lise)
al·ka·loid plant compound
al·ka·lo·sis medical condition
al·kanfe chemistry term
al·ka·net plant
al·kene chemistry term
al·kyd
al·kyl
al·kyla·tion chemistry term
al·kyne chemistry term
all
Allah
Al·laha·bad Indian city
al·lan·ite mineral
al·lan·to·ic
al·lan·toid
al·lan·toi·dal
al·lan·to·is (*plural* ·ides) embryology term
al·lar·gan·do musical term
al·lay
(alledge) *incorrect spelling of* allege
al·le·ga·tion
al·lege
al·leged
al·leg·ed·ly
al·le·giance
al·le·gori·cal (*or* ·gor·ic)
al·le·gori·cal·ly
al·le·go·rist
al·le·gori·za·tion (*or* ·sa·tion)
al·le·go·rize (*or* ·rise)
al·le·go·ry (*plural* ·ries)
al·le·gret·to (*plural* ·tos) musical term
al·le·gro (*plural* ·gros)
al·lele (*or* al·le·lo·morph) genetics term
al·lel·ic
al·lel·ism

al·le·luia (*or* hal·le·lu·jah; *note Handel's* **Hallelujah Chorus**)
alle·mande musical term
Al·len Irish bog
Al·len·town US city
Al·lep·pey Indian port
al·ler·gen allergy-causing substance
al·ler·gen·ic
al·ler·gic
al·ler·gist allergy specialist
al·ler·gy (*plural* ·gies)
al·le·thrin insecticide
al·le·vi·ate
al·le·via·tion
al·le·via·tive
al·le·via·tor
al·ley narrow lane; *compare* ally
alley·way
All·hal·lows
All·hal·low·tide
all·heal plant
al·lia·ceous of allium
al·li·ance
al·lied
Al·lier French river
Al·lies in World War II
al·lies *plural of* ally
al·li·ga·tor
all-important
all-inclusive
al·lit·er·ate
al·lit·era·tion
al·lit·era·tive
al·lium onion genus
Al·loa Scottish town
al·lo·cate
al·lo·ca·tion
al·loch·tho·nous geology term
al·lo·cu·tion formal speech
al·lo·dial
al·lo·dium (*or* al·lod; *plural* ·dia *or* ·lods) legal term
al·loga·mous
al·loga·my biology term
al·lo·graph signature written for another
al·lo·graph·ic
al·lom·er·ism chemistry term
al·lom·er·ous

al·lo·met·ric
al·lom·etry biology term
al·lo·morph
al·lo·mor·phic
al·lo·mor·phism chemistry term
al·lo·nym assumed name
al·lo·path (*or* ·lopa·thist) medical practitioner
al·lo·path·ic
al·lo·pathi·cal·ly
al·lopa·thy
al·lo·pat·ric biology term
al·lo·pat·ri·cal·ly
al·lo·phane mineral
al·lo·phone linguistics term
al·lo·phon·ic
al·lo·plasm biology term
al·lo·plas·mic
al·lo·pu·ri·nol anti-gout drug
al·lot (·lot·ting, ·lot·ted)
al·lot·ment
al·lo·trope chemistry term
al·lo·trop·ic
al·lo·tropi·cal·ly
al·lot·ro·py (*or* ·pism)
al·lot·tee
al·low
al·low·able
al·low·ance
Al·lo·way Scottish village
al·low·ed·ly
al·loy
all-round
all·rounder
all·seed plant
all·spice
all-star (*adj*)
all-time (*adj*)
al·lude refer; *compare* elude; illude
al·lure
al·lure·ment
al·lur·er
al·lur·ing
al·lu·sion reference; *compare* illusion
al·lu·sive
al·lu·sive·ness
al·lu·vial
al·lu·vion overflow
al·lu·vium (*plural* ·viums *or* ·via) soil; *compare* eluvium

ally (*verb* **allies**, **ally·ing**, **allied**; *noun, plural* **allies**) friend; *compare* alley

al·lyl

Alma-Ata Soviet city

Al·ma·da Portuguese city

Al·ma·gest astronomy treatise

alma ma·ter *Latin* one's school or university

al·ma·nac

al·ma·nack almanac; *Archaic except in proper names, as* **Whitaker's Almanack**

al·man·dine gemstone

Al Marj Libyan town

al·me·mar platform in synagogue

Al·mería Spanish port

al·mighti·ly

al·mighti·ness

Al·mighty God

al·mighty

Al·mo·hades Muslim group

al·mond

al·mon·er

al·mon·ry

Al·mo·ra·vides Muslim group

al·most

alms

alms·house

al·mu·can·tar astronomy term

al·muce monk's cape

Al·ni·co (*Trademark*)

aloe (*plural* **aloes**) plant

aloes purgative drug

alo·etic

aloft

alo·ha Hawaiian greeting

alo·in chemical compound

alone

along

along·shore

along·side

aloof

aloof·ness

alo·pecia

aloud

alow nautical term

alp

al·paca

alpen·glow

alpen·horn *variant of* alphorn

alpen·stock

Alpes-de-Haute-Pro·vence French department

Alpes Ma·ri·times French department

al·pes·trine

al·pha

al·pha·bet

al·pha·beti·cal (*or* ·**bet·ic**)

al·pha·beti·cal·ly

al·pha·beti·za·tion (*or* ·**sa·tion**)

al·pha·bet·ize (*or* ·**ise**)

al·pha·bet·iz·er (*or* ·**is·er**)

Al·pha Cen·tau·ri constellation

al·pha·nu·mer·ic (*or* al·pha·mer·ic)

al·pha·nu·meri·cal·ly (*or* al·pha·meri·cal·ly)

alp·horn (*or* alpen·horn)

al·pho·sis absence of skin pigmentation

Al·pine of the Alps

al·pine of mountains

al·pin·ism

al·pin·ist

Alps

al·ready

al·right *variant spelling of* all right, *regarded by some as nonstandard*

Al·sace French region

Alsace-Lor·raine French region

Al·sa·tia *ancient name of* Alsace

Al·sa·tian

al·sike plant

also

also-ran

alt high in pitch

Al·tai Asian mountains

Al·ta·ic language group

Al·tair star

al·tar table in church; *compare* alter

altar·piece

alt·azi·muth astronomical instrument

al·ter to change; *compare* altar

al·ter·abil·ity

al·ter·able

al·tera·tion

al·tera·tive therapeutic drug

al·ter·cate

al·ter·ca·tion

al·ter ego

al·ter·nant

al·ter·nate

al·ter·nate·ly

al·ter·na·tion

al·ter·na·tive

al·ter·na·tive·ly

al·ter·na·tor

al·thaea (*US* ·**thea**) plant

Al·thing Icelandic parliament

alt·horn brass instrument

al·though

al·time·ter

al·ti·met·ri·cal

al·tim·etry

Al·ti·pla·no Andean plateau

al·tis·si·mo musical term

al·ti·tude

al·ti·tu·di·nal

alto (*plural* **altos**)

alto·cu·mu·lus (*plural* ·**li**) cloud

al·to·geth·er entirely; *note* all together all at the same time

Al·to·na German port

al·to re·lie·vo (*or* ri·; *plural* ·**vos**) sculpture term

al·to·stra·tus (*plural* ·**ti**) cloud

al·tri·cial ornithology term

Al·trin·cham English town

al·tru·ism

al·tru·ist

al·tru·is·tic

al·tru·is·ti·cal·ly

alu·del chemical vessel

alu·la (*plural* ·**lae**) tuft of feathers

alum

alu·mi·na aluminium oxide

alu·mi·nate

alu·mi·nif·er·ous

alu·min·ium (*US* ·**min·um**)

alu·mi·nize (*or* ·**nise**)

alu·mi·nos·ity

An·dor·ra

An·dor·ra La Vel·la
capital of Andorra

An·dor·ran

And·over

an·dra·dite gemstone

Androcles legendary
character

an·dro·clin·ium botany
term

an·droe·cial

an·droe·cium (plural ·cia)
stamens of flower

an·dro·gen hormone

an·dro·gen·ic

an·drog·enous producing
only male offspring;
compare androgynous

an·dro·gyne

an·drogy·nous having male
and female characteristics;
compare androgenous

an·droid

Andromache mythological
character

An·drom·eda constellation

An·dros Greek island

an·dro·sphinx (plural
·sphinxes or ·sphinges)

an·dros·ter·one hormone

Andvari mythological
character

ane Scot one

an·ec·dot·age

an·ec·do·tal

an·ec·dote

an·ec·dot·ic

an·ec·dot·ist

an·echo·ic

anemia US spelling of
anaemia

anemic US spelling of
anaemic

anemo·chore botany term

anemo·graph

anemo·graph·ic

anemo·graphi·cal·ly

an·emog·ra·phy recording
wind measurements

an·emol·ogy

an·emom·eter

an·emo·met·ric

an·emo·met·ri·cal

an·emom·etry

anemo·ne

an·emophi·lous wind-
pollinated

an·emophi·ly

anemo·scope

anent Scot concerning

aner·gic lacking energy

an·er·gy

an·er·oid

an·es·the·sia US spelling of
anaesthesia

an·es·thesi·olo·gist US
anaesthetist

an·es·thesi·ology US
anaesthetics

an·es·the·tist US person
qualified to administer
anaesthetics, not
necessarily a doctor;
compare anaesthetist

an·es·trus US spelling of
anoestrus

an·ethole organic
compound

an·eu·ploid biology term

aneu·rin vitamin

aneu·rysm (or ·rism)
blood-vessel defect

aneu·rys·mal (or ·ris·mal,
·rys·mat·ic, ·ris·mat·ic)

anew

an·frac·tu·os·ity (plural
·ities)

an·frac·tu·ous convoluted

An·garsk Soviet city

an·ga·ry legal term

an·gel

An·ge·leno (plural ·nos)
inhabitant of Los Angeles

angel·fish (plural ·fish or
·fishes)

an·gel·ic

an·gel·ica

an·geli·cal

an·gel·ol·ogy

An·ge·lus Roman Catholic
prayers

an·ger

An·gers French town

An·ge·vin inhabitant of
Anjou

an·gi·na

an·gi·nal

an·gi·na pec·to·ris

an·gi·nose (or ·nous)

an·gi·ol·ogy branch of
medicine

an·gio·ma (plural ·mas or
·ma·ta) tumour

an·gi·oma·tous

an·gio·sperm botany term

an·gio·sper·mous

Ang·kor Cambodian region

An·gle ancient German
invader

an·gle

an·gler

An·gle·sey

an·gle·site mineral

angle·worm

An·glian of Angles or East
Anglia

An·gli·can of Church of
England

An·gli·can·ism

An·gli·cism English idiom

An·gli·cist

an·gli·ci·za·tion (or
·sa·tion)

an·gli·cize (or ·cise)

an·gli·fy (·fies, ·fy·ing,
·fied)

an·gling

Anglo-American

Anglo-Catholic

Anglo-Catholicism

Anglo-Irish

An·glo·ma·nia

An·glo·phile (or ·phil)

An·glo·philia

An·glo·phili·ac (or
·phil·ic)

An·glo·phobe

An·glo·pho·bia

An·glo·phone native
English speaker

Anglo-Saxon

An·go·la

An·go·lan

an·go·ra

an·gos·tu·ra bitter-tasting
bark

An·gos·tu·ra Bit·ters
(Trademark)

an·gri·ly

an·gry (·gri·er, ·gri·est)

angst anxiety

ang·strom unit of length

An·guil·la West Indian
island

an·guil·li·form eel-shaped

an·guine snakelike

an·guish
an·gu·lar
an·gu·lar·ity (*plural* ·ities)
an·gu·late
an·gu·la·tion
An·gus former Scottish
   county
ang·wan·ti·bo (*plural*
   ·bos) animal
An·halt German region
an·he·dral
an·hin·ga bird
An·hwei Chinese province
an·hy·dride
an·hy·drite
an·hy·drous
ani (*plural* anis) bird
Ani·ak·chak Alaskan
   volcano
an·icon·ic
anil shrub
an·ile like an old woman
ani·line organic compound
anil·ity
ani·ma
ani·mad·ver·sion
ani·mad·vert
ani·mal
ani·mal·cu·lar
ani·mal·cule (*or* ·cu·lum;
   plural ·cules *or* ·cu·la)
   microscopic animal
ani·mal·ism
ani·mal·ist
ani·mal·ity
ani·mali·za·tion (*or*
   ·sa·tion)
ani·mal·ize (*or* ·ise)
ani·mate
ani·ma·tion
ani·ma·tism
ani·ma·to music term
ani·ma·tor (*or* ·mat·er)
ani·mé resin
ani·mism
ani·mist
ani·mis·tic
ani·mos·ity (*plural* ·ities)
ani·mus
an·ion chemistry term
ani·on·ic
an·ise plant
ani·seed
an·isei·ko·nia visual defect
an·isei·kon·ic

ani·sette liqueur
ani·so·dac·tyl zoology term
ani·so·dac·ty·lous
ani·soga·mous
ani·soga·my type of sexual
   reproduction
ani·sole chemical compound
an·isom·er·ous botany term
an·iso·met·ric
an·iso·metro·pia visual
   disorder
an·iso·trop·ic
an·isot·ro·py
An·jou French province
An·ka·ra Turkish city
an·ker·ite mineral; *compare*
   anchorite
ankh Egyptian cross
An·king Chinese city
an·kle
ankle·bone
an·klet
an·ky·lo·saur dinosaur
an·ky·lose (*or* ·chy·)
an·ky·lo·sis (*or* ·chy·)
   immobility of joint
an·ky·lot·ic (*or* ·chy·)
an·lace medieval dagger
an·la·ge (*plural* ·gen *or*
   ·ges) biology term
An·na·ba Algerian port
an·na·berg·ite mineral
an·nal
an·nal·ist compiler of
   annals; *compare* analyst
an·nal·is·tic
an·nals
An·nam (*or* Anam) part of
   Vietnam
An·napo·lis US city
An·na·pur·na (*or* Ana·)
   Nepalese mountains
an·nates pope's revenue
an·nat·to (*or* anat·; *plural*
   ·tos) tree
an·neal
an·neal·er
Anne·cy French lake
an·nelid worm
an·neli·dan
an·nex take over or add on;
   compare annexe
an·nexa·tion
an·nexa·tion·al
an·nexa·tion·ism

an·nexa·tion·ist
an·nexe addition to
   building; *compare* annex
an·ni·hil·able
an·ni·hi·late
an·ni·hi·la·tion
an·ni·hi·la·tive
an·ni·hi·la·tor
an·ni·ver·sa·ry (*plural*
   ·saries)
anno Domi·ni *Latin* year of
   our Lord
an·no·tate
an·no·ta·tion
an·no·ta·tive
an·no·ta·tor
an·nounce
an·nounce·ment
an·nounc·er
an·noy
an·noy·ance
an·nual
an·nual·ly
an·nui·tant
an·nu·ity (*plural* ·ities)
an·nul (·nul·ling, ·nulled)
an·nu·lar
an·nu·late ringed
an·nu·la·tion
an·nu·let architectural
   moulding
an·nul·lable
an·nul·ment
an·nu·lose segmented
an·nu·lus (*plural* ·li *or*
   ·luses)
an·nun·ci·ate announce;
   compare enunciate
An·nun·cia·tion Christian
   feast
an·nun·cia·tion
   announcement
an·nun·cia·tive (*or* ·tory)
an·nun·cia·tor
anoa cattle
an·ode
an·od·ic
ano·dize (*or* ·dise)
ano·dyne painkiller
an·oes·trus (*US* ·es·)
anoint
anoint·er
anoint·ment
anole lizard
anoma·lis·tic

anoma·lis·ti·cal·ly
anoma·lous
anoma·ly (*plural* ·lies)
anom·ic
an·omie (*or* ·omy) lack of
social standards
anon *Archaic* soon
ano·nym pseudonym
ano·nym·ity
anony·mous
anophe·les (*plural* ·les)
mosquito
ano·rak
ano·rexia ner·vo·sa
ano·rex·ic
an·or·thite mineral
an·or·thit·ic
an·or·tho·site rock
an·os·mat·ic (*or*
an·os·mic)
an·os·mia inability to smell
an·oth·er
an·ox·aemia (*US* ·emia)
oxygen deficiency in blood
an·ox·aemic (*US* ·emic)
an·oxia lack of oxygen
an·ox·ic
an·sate having a handle
An·schluss union of Austria
with Germany
an·ser·ine (*or* ·ous) of
geese
An·shan Chinese city
an·swer
an·swer·abil·ity (*or*
·able·ness)
an·swer·able
ant
anta architectural term
An·ta·buse (*Trademark*)
ant·acid
an·tago·nism
an·tago·nist
an·tago·nis·tic
an·tago·nis·ti·cal·ly
an·tago·niz·able (*or*
·nis·able)
an·tago·ni·za·tion (*or*
·sa·tion)
an·tago·nize (*or* ·nise)
ant·al·ka·li (*plural* ·lis *or*
·lies)
ant·al·ka·line
An·ta·na·na·ri·vo
Madagascan capital

Ant·arc·tic
Ant·arc·ti·ca
An·tar·es star
ante stake in poker; advance
payment; *compare* anti
ant·eater
ante·bel·lum
ante·cede
ante·ced·ence
ante·ced·ent
an·te·ced·ents
ante·choir part of church
ante·date
ante·di·lu·vian
ante·fix (*plural* ·fixes *or*
·fixa) roof ornament
ante·fix·al
ante·lope
ante·me·rid·ian (*adj*)
ante me·ridi·em *Latin*
before noon
ante-mortem (*adj*) before
death
ante·na·tal
an·ten·na (*plural* ·nae)
insect feelers
an·ten·na (*plural* ·nas)
aerial
an·ten·nule
ante·pen·dium (*plural*
·dia) altar covering
ante·penult
ante·penul·ti·mate
ante·ri·or
ante·room
ante·type earlier form
ante·ver·sion
ante·vert tilt forwards
ant·he·li·on (*plural* ·lia)
meteorology term
ant·he·lix (*or* anti·; *plural*
·heli·ces *or* ·he·lixes)
ear cartilage
an·thel·min·tic (*or* ·thic)
vermifuge
an·them
an·themi·on (*plural* ·mia)
Greek design
an·ther
an·ther·idial
an·ther·id·ium (*plural* ·ia)
botany term
an·thero·zo·id botany term
an·thesis flowering
an·tho·cya·nin (*or* ·cy·an)
pigment

an·tho·dium (*plural* ·dia)
botany term
an·tho·logi·cal
an·tholo·gist
an·tholo·gize (*or* ·gise)
an·thol·ogy (*plural* ·ogies)
an·tho·phore botany term
an·tho·taxy botany term
an·tho·zo·an marine
organism
an·thra·cene chemical
compound
an·thra·cite coal
an·thra·cit·ic
an·thrac·nose fungal
disease
an·thra·coid
an·thra·qui·none chemical
compound
an·thrax (*plural* ·thra·ces)
an·thro·po·cen·tric
an·thro·po·cen·trism
an·thro·po·gen·esis (*or*
·geny) study of man's
origin
an·thro·po·genet·ic (*or*
·gen·ic)
an·thro·poid
an·thro·poi·dal
an·thro·po·logi·cal
an·thro·polo·gist
an·thro·pol·ogy
an·thro·po·met·ric (*or*
·ri·cal)
an·thro·po·met·ri·cal·ly
an·thro·pome·trist
an·thro·pom·etry
an·thro·po·mor·phic
an·thro·po·mor·phism
an·thro·po·mor·phist
an·thro·po·mor·phize (*or*
·phise)
an·thro·po·mor·pho·sis
an·thro·po·mor·phous
an·thro·po·path·ic
an·thro·popa·thy (*or*
·thism) attribution of
human passions to a deity
an·thro·popha·gi (*sing.*
·gus) cannibals
an·thro·po·phag·ic
an·thro·popha·gite
an·thro·popha·gy
cannibalism
an·thro·po·soph·ic
an·thro·poso·phy

an·thu·rium plant

anti Slang opposed to; compare ante

anti·aircraft

an·ti·ar tree

anti·bary·on physics term

An·tibes French port

anti·bio·sis

anti·bi·ot·ic

anti·body (plural ·bodies)

an·tic

anti·cata·lyst

anti·cath·ode

anti·chlor

anti·chlo·ris·tic

anti·cho·lin·er·gic physiology term

anti·cho·lin·es·ter·ase enzyme

Anti·christ

an·tici·pant

an·tici·pate

an·tici·pa·tion

an·tici·pa·tive

an·tici·pa·tor

an·tici·pa·to·ri·ly

an·tici·pa·tory

anti·clas·tic maths term

anti·cleri·cal

anti·cli·mac·tic

anti·cli·mac·ti·cal·ly

anti·cli·max

anti·cli·nal

anti·cline geology term

anti·cli·no·rium (plural ·ria) geology term

anti·clock·wise

anti·co·agu·lant

anti·con·vul·sant

An·ti·cos·ti Canadian island

anti·cy·clone

anti·cy·clon·ic

anti·de·pres·sant

anti·dote

anti·drom·ic biology term

An·tie·tam US battle site

anti·febrile

anti·fer·ro·mag·ne·tism

anti·foul·ing protective paint

anti·freeze

anti·gen

anti·gen·ic

anti·geni·cal·ly

Antigone mythological character

An·ti·gua West Indian island

anti·ha·la·tion photography term

anti·he·ro (plural ·roes)

anti·his·ta·mine

anti·icer

anti·imperi·al·ism

anti·imperi·al·ist

anti·knock petrol additive

anti·lep·ton physics term

An·til·les West Indian islands

anti·log

anti·loga·rithm

anti·loga·rith·mic

an·tilo·gism philosophy term

an·til·ogy (plural ·ogies) contradiction in terms

anti·ma·cas·sar

anti·mag·net·ic

anti·ma·lar·ial

anti·masque grotesque dance

anti·mat·ter

anti·mere biology term

anti·mer·ic

an·tim·er·ism

anti·mis·sile

anti·mo·nar·chic

anti·mo·nar·chist

anti·mo·nial

anti·mo·nic

anti·mo·nous

anti·mo·ny chemical element; compare antinomy

anti·mo·nyl

anti·na·tion·al·ist

anti·na·tion·al·is·tic

anti·neu·tri·no (plural ·nos)

anti·neu·tron

anti·nod·al

anti·node physics term

anti·nom·ic

anti·nomi·cal·ly

an·tino·my (plural ·mies) paradox; compare antimony

anti·nu·cleon

An·ti·och Turkish city

anti·oxi·dant

anti·par·al·lel

anti·par·ticle

anti·pas·to (plural ·ti) Italian hors d'oeuvres

anti·pa·thet·ic (or ·ical)

anti·pa·theti·cal·ly

an·tipa·thy (plural ·thies)

anti·peri·od·ic

anti·peri·stal·sis physiology term

anti·per·son·nel

anti·per·spi·rant

anti·phlo·gis·tic

anti·phon

an·tipho·nal

an·tipho·nal·ly

an·tipho·nary (plural ·naries) collection of biblical passages

an·tipho·ny (plural ·nies) type of choral singing

an·tiph·ra·sis rhetorical device

an·tipo·dal

anti·pode

an·tipo·dean

An·tipo·des Australia and New Zealand

an·tipo·des points diametrically opposite on Earth

anti·pope

anti·prag·mat·ic

anti·prag·ma·tism

anti·pro·ton

anti·psy·chia·try

anti·py·resis

anti·py·ret·ic

anti·py·rine

anti·quar·ian

anti·quary (plural ·quaries)

anti·quate

anti·quat·ed

anti·qua·ted·ness

an·tique

an·tiq·uity (plural ·uities)

anti·ra·chit·ic preventing rickets

anti·racism

anti·racist

anti·repub·li·can

anti·revo·lu·tion·ary

an·tir·rhi·num

anti·scor·bu·tic preventing scurvy
anti-Semite
anti-Semitic
anti-Semitism
anti·sep·sis
anti·sep·tic
anti·sep·ti·cal·ly
anti·serum (*plural* ·serums *or* ·sera)
anti·slav·ery
anti·so·cial
anti·spas·mod·ic
anti·stat·ic
an·tis·tro·phe
anti·stroph·ic
anti·sub·ma·rine
anti·tank
an·tith·esis (*plural* ·ses)
anti·theti·cal (*or* ·thet·ic)
anti·theti·cal·ly
anti·tox·ic
anti·tox·in
anti·trades winds
an·tit·ra·gus (*plural* ·gi) part of ear
anti·tus·sive alleviating coughing
anti·type
anti·ven·in
anti·vivi·sec·tion
anti·vivi·sec·tion·ist
anti·world world composed of antimatter
ant·ler
ant·lered
Ant·lia constellation
ant·like
ant·li·on insect
An·to·fa·gas·ta Chilean port
an·to·no·ma·sia figure of speech
an·to·no·mas·tic
an·to·no·mas·ti·cal·ly
an·to·nym
an·tony·mous
an·tre cavern
An·trim
an·trorse directed upwards
an·trum (*plural* ·tra) anatomy term
An·tung Chinese port
Ant·werp
Anubis Egyptian god

anu·ran tailless amphibian
anu·resis inability to urinate
anu·ria inability to form urine
anu·rous tailless
anus
an·vil
anxi·ety (*plural* ·eties)
anx·ious
anx·ious·ness
any
An·yang Chinese town
any·body
any·how
any·one
any·thing
any·way
any·where
any·wise
An·zac Australian and New Zealand Army Corps
An·zio Italian port
aorist linguistics term
aoris·tic
aoris·ti·cal·ly
aor·ta (*plural* ·tas *or* ·tae)
aor·tic (*or* ·tal)
aou·dad sheep
apace
Apache (*plural* **Apaches** *or* **Apache**) American Indian
apache gangster
apa·go·ge logic term
apa·gog·ic (*or* ·gogi·cal)
apa·gogi·cal·ly
ap·an·age *variant spelling of* áppanage
Apar·ri Philippine port
apart
apart·heid
apart·ment
apa·tet·ic of animal coloration
apa·thet·ic
apa·theti·cal·ly
apa·thy
apa·tite mineral
ape
apeak
Apel·doorn Dutch town
ape·like
ape·man (*plural* ·men)
Ap·en·nines

aper·çu *French* outline or insight
aperi·ent
aperi·od·ic at irregular intervals
aperi·odi·cal·ly
aperio·dic·ity
apé·ri·tif drink before meal; *compare* **aperitive**
ape·ri·tive laxative; *compare* apéritif
ap·er·ture
ap·ery (*plural* ·eries) imitative behaviour
apet·al·ous petal-less
apet·aly
apex (*plural* **apexes** *or* **api·ces**)
aphaer·esis (*or* apher·; *plural* ·ses) linguistics term
apha·gia inability to swallow
apha·nite rock
apha·sia language disorder
apha·sic
ap·he·lian
ap·he·li·on (*plural* ·lia) point in planet's orbit
ap·he·lio·trop·ic botany term
apher·esis *variant spelling of* **aphaeresis**
aph·esis linguistics term
aphet·ic
apheti·cal·ly
aphid
aphidi·ous
aphis (*plural* **aphi·des**)
apho·nia (*or* ·ny) loss of voice
aphon·ic
apho·rism
apho·rist
apho·ris·tic
apho·rize (*or* ·rise)
apho·tic without light
aph·ro·di·sia
aph·ro·disi·ac
Aphrodite Greek goddess
aph·tha (*plural* ·thae) ulcer
aphyl·lous leafless
aphyl·ly
apian of bees
api·ar·ian of beekeeping

apia·rist
api·ary (*plural* ·aries)
  beehive; *compare* aviary
api·cal
api·cal·ly
api·ces *plural of* apex
apicu·late
api·cul·tur·al
api·cul·ture
api·cul·tur·ist
apiece
à pied *French* on foot
Api·ezon (*Trademark*)
Apis sacred bull
ap·ish
ap·ish·ness
apiv·or·ous bee-eating
apla·cen·tal
ap·la·nat·ic physics term
ap·la·nati·cal·ly
aplano·sphere
aplano·spore
apla·sia congenital absence
  of organ
aplas·tic
aplen·ty
ap·lite (*or* hap·) rock
ap·lit·ic (*or* hap·)
aplomb
ap·noea (*US* ·nea)
  inability to breath
Apo Philippine mountain
apoca·lypse
apoca·lyp·tic
apoca·lyp·ti·cal·ly
apo·carp
apo·car·pous botany term
apo·chro·mat
apo·chro·mat·ic physics
  term
apo·chro·ma·tism
apoco·pate
apoco·pa·tion
apoco·pe linguistics term
apo·crine physiology term
Apoc·ry·pha Old Testament
  appendix
apoc·ry·phal of doubtful
  authenticity
apoc·ry·phal·ly
apocy·na·ceous botany
  term
apo·cyn·thi·on astronomy
  term
apo·dal without feet

apo·dic·tic (*or* ·deic·)
  unquestionably true
apo·dic·ti·cal·ly (*or* ·deic·)
apodo·sis (*plural* ·ses)
  grammar term
apo·en·zyme
apo·gam·ic
apoga·mous
apoga·my type of plant
  reproduction
apo·gee
apo·geo·trop·ic botany
  term
apo·geot·ro·pism
apo·liti·cal
apo·liti·cal·ly
Apol·li·naris mineral water
Apollo Greek god
Apol·lo spacecraft
Ap·ol·lo·nian
Apollyon the Devil
apolo·get·ic
apolo·geti·cal·ly
apolo·get·ics branch of
  theology
apo·lo·gia
apolo·gist
apolo·gize (*or* ·gise)
apolo·giz·er (*or* ·gis·er)
apo·logue moral fable
apol·ogy (*plural* ·ogies)
apo·lune astronomy term
apo·mict
apo·mic·tic
apo·mixis (*plural* ·mixes)
  asexual reproduction
apo·mor·phine alkaloid
apo·neu·ro·sis (*plural*
  ·ses) anatomy term
apo·neu·rot·ic
apopha·sis rhetorical device
apo·phthegm (*or*
  apo·thegm) cryptic
  remark; *compare* apothem
apophy·ge architectural
  term
apophyl·lite mineral
apophy·sate
apophy·sial
apophy·sis (*plural* ·ses)
  outgrowth
apo·plec·tic
apo·plexy
aport nautical term
apo·semat·ic zoology term

apo·sio·pe·sis (*plural* ·ses)
  rhetorical device
apo·sio·pet·ic
apo·spory botany term
apos·ta·sy (*plural* ·sies)
apos·tate
apos·ta·tize (*or* ·tise)
a pos·terio·ri *Latin* from
  effect to cause; *compare* a
  priori
apos·til marginal note
apos·tie
apos·to·late
ap·os·tol·ic
apos·tro·phe
apo·stroph·ic
apos·tro·phize (*or* ·phise)
apoth·ecary (*plural*
  ·ecaries)
apo·the·cial
apo·the·cium (*plural* ·cia)
apo·thegm *variant spelling*
  of apophthegm
apo·them geometry term;
  compare apophthegm
apoth·eo·sis (*plural* ·ses)
apoth·eo·size (*or* ·sise)
  glorify
apo·tro·pa·ic preventing
  evil
ap·pal (*US* ·pall;
  ·pal·ling, ·palled)
Ap·pa·la·chia US region
Appa·la·chian
ap·pal·ling
ap·pal·ling·ly
Ap·pa·loo·sa horse
ap·pa·nage (*or* apa·nage)
  perquisite
ap·pa·rat·us (*plural*
  rat·us *or* ·rat·uses)
ap·par·el (·el·ling, ·elled;
  US ·el·ing, ·eled)
ap·par·ent
ap·par·ent·ness
ap·pa·ri·tion
ap·pari·tor ecclesiastical
  court officer
ap·pas·sio·na·to musical
  term
ap·peal
ap·peal·able
ap·peal·er
ap·peal·ing·ly
ap·pear
ap·pear·ance

ap·peas·able
ap·pease
ap·peas·er
ap·pease·ment
ap·pel fencing term
ap·pel·lant
ap·pel·late
ap·pel·la·tion
ap·pel·la·tive
ap·pel·lee
ap·pend
ap·pend·age
ap·pen·dant
ap·pen·di·cec·to·my (or esp. US
ap·pen·dec·to·my; plural ·mies)
ap·pen·di·ci·tis
ap·pen·di·cle small appendage
ap·pen·dicu·lar
ap·pen·dix (plural ·dixes or ·di·ces)
Ap·pen·zell Swiss canton
ap·per·ce.ve
ap·per·cep·tion psychology term
ap·per·cep·tive
ap·per·tain
ap·pes·tat hunger control centre in brain
ap·pe·tence (or ·ten·cy; plural ·tences or ·ten·cies)
ap·pe·tite
ap·pe·tiz·er (or ·tis·er)
ap·pe·tiz·ing (or ·tis·ing)
ap·plaud
ap·plaud·er
ap·plaud·ing·ly
ap·plause
ap·ple
apple·cart
apple·jack
apple·snits Canadian apple dish
ap·pli·ance
ap·plic·abil·ity
ap·pli·cable
ap·pli·cably
ap·pli·cant
ap·pli·ca·tion
ap·plica·tive
ap·pli·ca·tor
ap·pli·ca·tory

ap·plied
ap·pli·er
ap·pli·qué (·qué·ing, ·quéd)
ap·ply (·plies, ·ply·ing, ·plied)
ap·pog·gia·tu·ra (plural ·ras or ·re) musical term
ap·point
ap·poin·tee
ap·point·er
ap·point·ment
ap·poin·tor legal term
Ap·po·mat·tox US battle site
ap·por·tion
ap·por·tion·able
ap·por·tion·er
ap·por·tion·ment
ap·pose
ap·po·site apt; compare opposite
ap·po·si·tion
ap·posi·tive linguistics term
ap·prais·able
ap·prais·al (or ·praise·ment)
ap·praise assess; compare apprise
ap·prais·er
ap·prais·ing·ly
ap·prais·ive
ap·pre·ci·able
ap·pre·ci·ate
ap·pre·cia·tion
ap·pre·cia·tive (or ·tory)
ap·pre·cia·tive·ness
ap·pre·hend
ap·pre·hen·sibil·ity
ap·pre·hen·sible
ap·pre·hen·sion
ap·pre·hen·sive
ap·pre·hen·sive·ness
ap·pren·tice
ap·pren·tice·ship
ap·pressed pressed closely against
ap·prise (or ·prize) inform; compare appraise
ap·proach
ap·proach·abil·ity (or ·able·ness)
ap·proach·able
ap·pro·bate Scottish legal term; US approve

ap·pro·ba·tion
ap·pro·ba·tive (or ·tory)
ap·pro·pri·able
ap·pro·pri·ate
ap·pro·pri·ate·ness
ap·pro·pria·tion
ap·pro·pria·tor
ap·prov·al
ap·prove
ap·proved
ap·proxi·mal situated side by side
ap·proxi·mate
ap·proxi·mate·ly
ap·proxi·ma·tion
ap·proxi·ma·tive
ap·pulse astronomy term
ap·pul·sive
ap·pur·te·nance
ap·pur·te·nant
apraxia disorder of nervous system
aprax·ic (or aprac·tic)
après-ski
apri·cot
April
a prio·ri Latin from cause to effect; compare a posteriori
apri·or·ism
apri·or·ity
apron
ap·ro·pos
apse recess in church
ap·si·dal
ap·sis (plural ·si·des) point in planet's orbit
apt
ap·ter·al architectural term
ap·ter·ous wingless
ap·ter·yg·ial lacking fins or wings
ap·ter·yx kiwi
ap·ti·tude
apt·ness
Apu·lia Italian region
Apu·ri·mac Peruvian river
apy·re·tic
Aqa·ba (or Aka·ba) Jordanian port
aqua (plural aquae or aquas)
aqua·cul·ture cultivation of marine organisms; compare aquiculture
aqua·lung

aqua·marine
aqua·naut
aqua·pho·bia
aqua·plane
aqua re·gia strong acid
aqua·relle
aqua·rel·list water-colour
  painter
aqua·rist aquarium curator
aquar·ium (*plural*
  aquar·iums *or* aquaria)
Aquar·ius
aquat·ic
aquat·ics
aqua·tint
aqua·vit aromatic spirit
aqua vi·tae *Archaic* brandy
aque·duct
aque·ous
aqui·cul·tur·al
aqui·cul·ture hydroponics;
  compare aquaculture
aqui·cul·tur·ist
aqui·fer water-containing
  rock
Aqui·la constellation
aqui·legia
aqui·line
Aqui·taine French region
Ara constellation
Arab
ara·besque
Ara·bia
Ara·bian
Ara·bic language
arabi·nose sugar
Ar·ab·ist
ar·able
Ara·by *Archaic* Arabia
Ara·ca·jú Brazilian port
Arachne mythological
  character
arach·nid spider
arach·ni·dan
arach·noid membrane
  covering brain
Arad Romanian city
Ara·gon Spanish region
Ara·go·nese
arago·nite mineral
Ara·guaia Brazilian river
Arak Iranian town
arak *variant spelling of*
  arrack
Aral·dite (*Trademark*)

ara·lia·ceous botany term
Ara·ma·ic language
Aran Irish islands; type of
  sweater; *compare* Arran
ara·neid spider
Arapa·ho (*plural* ·hos *or*
  ·ho) American Indian
ara·pai·ma fish
Ara·rat Turkish mountain
ara·ro·ba tree; medicinal
  substance
Aras Asian river
Arau·ca·nia Chilean region
Arau·ca·nian
arau·ca·ria tree
Ara·wak·an American
  Indian language
ar·ba·lest crossbow
ar·bi·ter
ar·bi·trable
ar·bi·trage financial term
ar·bi·tral
ar·bit·ra·ment
ar·bi·trari·ly
ar·bi·trari·ness
ar·bi·trary
ar·bi·trate
ar·bi·tra·tion
ar·bi·tra·tor
ar·bi·tress
ar·bor rotating shaft; *US
  spelling of* arbour
ar·bora·ceous
ar·bor·eal
ar·bo·reous
ar·bo·res·cence
ar·bo·res·cent
ar·bo·retum (*plural* ·ta *or*
  ·tums)
ar·bori·cul·ture
ar·bor·ist
ar·bori·za·tion (*or*
  ·sa·tion)
ar·bor vi·tae tree
ar·bour (*US* ·bor) tree-
  lined shelter; *compare*
  arbor
Ar·broath Scottish port
ar·bu·tus (*plural* ·tuses)
  shrub
arc part of curve; *compare*
  ark
ar·cade
Ar·ca·dia department of
  Greece; *compare* Acadia

Ar·ca·dian
Ar·ca·dy (*or* ·dia) rustic
  paradise
ar·ca·na tarot cards
ar·cane
ar·ca·num (*plural* ·na)
ar·ca·ture small arcade
arch
Ar·chaean (*or esp. US*
  ·chean) geology term
ar·chaeo·logi·cal (*US also*
  ·cheo·)
ar·chaeo·logi·cal·ly (*US
  also* ·cheo·)
ar·chae·olo·gist (*US also*
  ·che·)
ar·chae·ol·ogy (*US also*
  ·che·)
ar·chaeo·mag·net·ism
  (*US also* ·cheo·)
ar·chae·op·ter·yx
ar·chae·or·nis extinct bird
Ar·chaeo·zo·ic (*US also*
  ·cheo·)
ar·cha·ic
ar·chai·cal·ly
ar·cha·ism
ar·cha·ist
ar·cha·is·tic
ar·cha·is·ti·cal·ly
ar·cha·ize (*or* ·ise)
ar·cha·iz·er (*or* ·is·er)
Arch·an·gel Soviet port
arch·angel
arch·angelic
arch·bishop
arch·bishop·ric
arch·deacon
arch·deacon·ry (*plural*
  ·ries)
arch·dioc·esan
arch·dio·cese
arch·ducal
arch·duchess
arch·duchy (*plural*
  ·duchies)
arch·duke
arched
ar·che·go·nium (*plural*
  ·nia) botany term
arch·en·emy (*plural*
  ·emies)
ar·chen·ter·ic
ar·chen·ter·on embryology
  term

ar·che·ol·ogy *US variant spelling of* **archaeology**
arch·er
archer·fish (*plural* ·fish *or* ·fishes)
ar·chery
ar·che·spore (*or* ·spo·rium; *plural* ·spores *or* ·spo·ria) spore-making cell
ar·che·spo·rial
ar·che·typ·al (*or* ·typi·cal)
ar·che·typ·al·ly (*or* ·typi·cal·ly)
ar·che·type
arch·fiend
archi·carp fungal structure
archi·di·aco·nal
archi·di·aco·nate
archi·epis·co·pal
archi·epis·co·pate (*or* ·co·pa·cy)
ar·chil *variant spelling of* orchil
archi·mage great magician
archi·man·drite head of Orthodox monastery
Archi·medean
archi·pelag·ic (*or* ·pe·lagian)
archi·pela·go (*plural* ·gos *or* ·goes)
archi·tect
archi·tec·ton·ic
archi·tec·toni·cal·ly
archi·tec·ton·ics
archi·tec·tur·al
archi·tec·tur·al·ly
archi·tec·ture
archi·trave moulding
ar·chiv·al
ar·chive
archi·vist
archi·volt moulding around arch
arch·ness
ar·cho·plasm (*or* archi·) type of protoplasm
ar·cho·plas·mic
arch·priest
arch·way
arco·graph geometric instrument
Arc·tic North Pole region
arc·tic very cold

Arc·to·gaea (*US* ·gea) zoogeographical area
Arc·to·gaean (*US* ·gean)
Arc·tu·rian
Arc·tu·rus star
ar·cu·ate arc-shaped
ar·cua·tion
ar·deb unit of measure
Ar·dèche French department
Arden (Forest of)
ar·den·cy
Ar·dennes W European hills
ar·dent
ar·dour (*US* ·dor)
ar·du·ous
ar·du·ous·ness
are
area
areal
area·way passageway
ar·eca palm tree
arena
ar·ena·ceous geology term
ar·enico·lous living in sandy places
ar·enite sandstone
ar·enit·ic
aren't are not
ar·eog·ra·phy description of Mars
areo·la (*plural* ·lae *or* ·las)
areo·lar (*or* ·late)
areo·la·tion
Arequi·pa Peruvian city
Ares Greek god
arête mountain ridge
ar·ethu·sa plant
Arez·zo Italian city
ar·ga·li (*or* ar·gal; *plural* ·ga·li *or* ·gals) wild sheep
ar·gent silver
Ar·gen·teuil Parisian suburb
ar·gen·tic
ar·gen·tif·er·ous
Ar·gen·ti·na
Ar·gen·tine of Argentina
ar·gen·tine of silver
Ar·gen·tin·ean
ar·gen·tite mineral
ar·gen·tous

ar·gil potter's clay
ar·gil·la·ceous
ar·gil·lif·er·ous
ar·gil·lite rock
ar·gil·lit·ic
ar·gi·nine amino acid
Argo Jason's ship; constellation
ar·gol deposit in wine vats
Ar·go·lis region of ancient Greece
ar·gon chemical element
Ar·go·naut
Ar·gonne French region
ar·go·non gas
Ar·gos ancient Greek city
ar·go·sy (*plural* ·sies) large merchant ship
ar·got
ar·got·ic
ar·gu·able
ar·gu·ably
ar·gue (·gu·ing, ·gued)
ar·gu·er
ar·gu·fy (·fies, ·fy·ing, ·fied)
ar·gu·ment
ar·gu·men·ta·tion
ar·gu·men·ta·tive
ar·gu·men·ta·tive·ness
ar·gu·men·tum (*plural* ·ta) *Latin* argument
Argus mythological giant
argy-bargy (*plural* -bargies)
ar·gyle fabric
Ar·gyll (*or* ·gyll·shire) former Scottish county
År·hus *variant spelling of* Aarhus
aria
Arian follower of Arianism; *compare* Aryan
Ari·an·ism heretical doctrine
arid
arid·ity (*or* ar·id·ness)
Ariège French department
Ari·el satellite of Uranus
ari·el gazelle; *compare* aerial
Aries constellation; sign of the zodiac
ari·et·ta (*plural* ·et·tas, ·et·te *or* ·ettes) short aria
aright

aril botany term

ar·il·late

ar·il·lode

Ar·i·ma·thea Palestinian town

ar·io·so musical term

arise (aris·ing, arose, aris·en)

aris·ta (plural ·tae) bristle

Ar·is·tar·chus moon crater

aris·tate

ar·is·toc·ra·cy (plural ·cies)

aris·to·crat

aris·to·crat·ic

aris·to·crati·cal·ly

Ar·is·to·telian

arith·me·tic (noun)

arith·met·ic (or ·meti·cal; adj)

arith·meti·cal·ly

arith·meti·cian

Ari·zo·na

ark Noah's boat; compare arc

Ar·kan·sas

ar·kose sandstone

Ar·ling·ton US county

arm

ar·ma·da

ar·ma·dil·lo (plural ·los)

Ar·ma·ged·don

Ar·magh

Ar·ma·gnac French brandy

ar·ma·ment

ar·ma·men·tar·ium (plural ·tar·iums or ·taria) doctor's equipment

ar·ma·ture moving electrical part

arm·band

arm·chair

Arm·co (Trademark) safety barrier

armed

Ar·me·nia

Ar·me·nian

Ar·men·tières French town

ar·met medieval helmet

arm·ful

arm·hole

ar·mi·ger heraldic term

ar·mil·lary of bracelets

arm·ing

Ar·mini·an

Ar·mini·an·ism Protestant doctrine

ar·mipo·tence

ar·mipo·tent strong in battle

ar·mi·stice

arm·less

arm·let

ar·moire cabinet

ar·mo·ri·al

ar·mour (US ·mor)

ar·moured (US ·mored)

ar·mour·er (US ·mor·)

ar·moury (US ·mory; plural ·mouries, US ·mories)

arm·pit

arm·rest

arms

ar·mure fabric

army (plural armies)

Arn·hem Dutch city

ar·ni·ca plant

Arno Italian river

ar·oid botany term

aro·ma

aro·mat·ic

aro·mati·cal·ly

aro·ma·tic·ity

aro·ma·ti·za·tion (or ·sa·tion)

aro·ma·tize (or ·tise)

arose

around

arous·al

arouse

arous·er

ar·peg·gio (plural ·gios)

ar·que·bus (or har·) early musket

ar·rack (or arak) alcoholic spirit

ar·raign

ar·raign·er

ar·raign·ment legal term

Ar·ran Scottish island; compare Aran

ar·range

ar·range·able

ar·range·ment

ar·rang·er

ar·rant

Ar·ras French town

ar·ras hanging tapestry; compare arris

ar·ray

ar·ray·al

ar·rears

ar·rest

ar·rest·able

ar·rest·er

ar·rest·ing

ar·rest·ing·ly

ar·rhyth·mia abnormal heartbeat

arrière-pensée (plural arrière-pensées) French mental reservation

Ar Ri·mal Arabian desert

ar·ris (plural ·ris or ·rises) sharp edge; compare arras

ar·ri·val

ar·rive

ar·riv·er

ar·ri·viste ambitious person

ar·ro·ba unit of weight

ar·ro·gance

ar·ro·gant

ar·ro·gate claim without justification

ar·ro·ga·tion

ar·roga·tive

ar·ro·ga·tor

ar·ron·disse·ment French district

ar·row

arrow·head

arrow·root

arrow·wood

arrow·worm

arro·yo US gully

ars antiqua 13th-century music style; compare ars nova

arse

ar·senal

ar·senate

ar·senic

ar·seni·cal

ar·senide

ar·seni·ous (or ·sen·ous)

ar·senite

ar·seno·py·rite mineral

ar·sine chemical compound

ar·sis (plural ·ses) prosody term

ars nova 14th-century music style; compare ars antiqua

ar·son

ars·phena·mine drug
arsy-versy *Slang* backwards
art
Art Deco 1920–40 art
style; *compare* Art
Nouveau
ar·te·fact (*or* ·ti·)
ar·tel Soviet cooperative
union
Artemis Greek goddess
ar·te·mi·sia plant
ar·te·rial
ar·te·ri·ali·za·tion (*or*
·sa·tion)
ar·te·ri·al·ize (*or* ·ise)
ar·te·ri·ole subdivision of
artery
ar·te·rio·sclero·sis
ar·te·rio·sclerot·ic
ar·te·rio·venous
ar·te·ri·tis
ar·tery (*plural* ·teries)
ar·te·sian
art·ful
art·ful·ly
art·ful·ness
ar·thral·gia joint pain
ar·thral·gic
ar·thrit·ic
ar·thri·tis
arthro·mere zoology term
arthro·mer·ic
arthro·pod
ar·thropo·dous (*or* ·dal)
arthro·spore
ar·thro·spor·ic (*or* ·ous)
Ar·thu·rian
ar·ti·choke
ar·ti·cle
ar·ticu·lar
ar·ticu·late
ar·ticu·late·ness (*or*
·la·cy)
ar·ticu·la·tion
ar·ticu·la·tor
ar·ticu·la·tory
ar·ti·fact *variant spelling of*
artefact
ar·ti·fice
ar·tifi·cer
ar·ti·fi·cial
ar·ti·fi·ci·al·ity
ar·til·lery
ar·tillery·man (*plural*
·men)

arti·ness
ar·tio·dac·tyl zoology term
ar·tio·dac·ty·lous
ar·ti·san
art·ist person skilled in art,
etc.
ar·tiste entertainer
ar·tis·tic
ar·tis·ti·cal·ly
art·ist·ry
art·less
art·less·ness
Art Nouveau 1890–1910
art style; *compare* Art
Deco
Ar·tois former French
province
art·work
arty (arti·er, arti·est)
Aru·ba West Indian island
arum
Aru·na·chal Pra·desh
Indian state
Ar·un·del
arun·di·na·ceous
resembling a reed
Aru·wi·mi Zaïrian river
Aryan (*or* Arian) non-
Jewish Caucasian; *compare*
Arian
Ary·an·ize (*or* ·ise)
aryl chemistry term
ary·te·noid (*or* ·tae·)
anatomy term
ary·te·noid·al
as
asa·foeti·da (*or esp. US*
·feti·) resin
Asan·te·he·ne Ghanaian
ruler
asa·ra·bac·ca plant
asa·rum dried ginger root
as·bes·tos (*US also* ·tus)
as·bes·to·sis
as·ca·ria·sis
as·ca·rid parasitic worm
as·cend
as·cend·ancy (*or* ·ency,
·ance, ·ence)
as·cend·ant (*or* ·ent)
as·cend·er
As·cen·sion Christian feast;
S Atlantic island
as·cen·sion
as·cen·sion·al
As·cen·sion·tide

as·cent upward movement;
compare assent
as·cer·tain
as·cer·tain·able
as·cer·tain·ment
as·cesis (*plural* ·ceses)
self-discipline
as·cet·ic
as·ceti·cal·ly
as·ceti·cism
asci *plural of* ascus
Ascii computer language
as·cid·ian marine animal
as·cid·ium (*plural* ·cidia)
botany term
as·ci·tes medical term
as·cit·ic
as·cle·pia·da·ceous botany
term
Asclepius Greek god
as·co·carp part of a fungus
as·co·go·nium (*plural*
·nia) fungal reproductive
body
as·co·my·cete fungus
as·co·my·cetous
ascor·bic acid
as·co·spore
As·cot Berkshire town;
racecourse
as·cot cravat
as·crib·able
as·cribe
as·crip·tion (*or* ad·scrip·)
as·cus (*plural* asci) fungal
part
as·dic echo sounder
ase·ity philosophy term
asep·al·ous
asep·sis
asep·tic
asexu·al
asexu·al·ity
asexu·al·ly
As·gard home of Norse gods
ash
ashamed
asham·ed·ly
Ashan·ti Ghanaian region
ash·en
Ashes cricket trophy
ashet *Dialect* dish
Ash·ke·na·zi (*plural* ·zim)
Jew of E European
descent

ash·key
Ash·kha·bad Soviet city
ash·lar (or ·ler)
ash·lar·ing building
  material
ashore
(ashphalt) incorrect spelling
  of asphalt
ash·plant
ash·ram Hindu religious
  retreat
Ashtoreth biblical character
ash·tray
ashy (ashi·er, ashi·est)
Asia
Asian
Asi·at·ic
aside
asi·nine
asi·nin·ity
Asir Saudi Arabian region
ask
askance (or askant)
ask·er
askew
aslant
asleep
As·ma·ra Ethiopian city
Asmodeus Jewish demon
As·nières Parisian suburb
aso·cial
aso·cial·ly
asp
as·para·gine amino acid
as·para·gus
as·par·tic acid
as·pect
as·pec·tual linguistics term
as·pen
as·per Turkish coin
as·per·gil·lo·sis (plural
  ·ses)
as·per·gil·lus (plural ·li)
  fungus
as·per·ity (plural ·ities)
as·perse
as·pers·er
as·per·sion
as·per·sive
as·per·so·rium (plural
  ·ria) basin for holy water
as·phalt
as·phal·tic
as·phal·tite
as·phal·tum

as·pho·del plant
as·phyxia
as·phyx·ial
as·phyxi·ant
as·phyxi·ate
as·phyxia·tion
as·phyxia·tor
as·pic
as·pi·dis·tra
as·pir·ant
as·pi·rate
as·pi·ra·tion
as·pi·ra·tor
as·pira·tory
as·pire
as·pir·er
as·pi·rin (plural ·rin or
  ·rins)
as·pir·ing
(asprin) incorrect spelling of
  aspirin
asquint
ass
as·sai musical term; palm
  tree
as·sail
assail·able
as·sail·ant
as·sail·er
assail·ment
As·sam Indian state
As·sa·mese (plural ·mese)
as·sas·sin
as·sas·si·nate
as·sas·si·na·tion
as·sault
as·sault·er
as·say test; compare essay
as·say·able
as·say·er
as·se·gai (or ·sa·; plural
  ·gais) spear
as·sem·blage
as·sem·ble
as·sem·bler
as·sem·bly (plural ·blies)
as·sembly·man (plural
  ·men)
as·sent consent; compare
  ascent
as·sen·ta·tion servile
  agreement
as·sen·tient approving
as·sen·tor
as·sert

as·sert·er (or ·ser·tor)
as·sert·ible
as·ser·tion
as·ser·tive
as·ser·tive·ness
as·sess
as·sess·able
as·sess·ment
as·ses·sor
as·ses·so·rial
as·set
asset-stripper
asset-stripping
as·sev·er·ate declare
  emphatically
as·sev·era·tion
as·sibi·late phonetics term
as·sibi·la·tion
as·si·du·ity (plural ·ities)
as·sidu·ous
as·sidu·ous·ness
as·sign
as·sign·abil·ity
as·sign·able
as·sig·nat former French
  currency
as·sig·na·tion
as·signee legal term
as·sign·er
as·sign·ment
as·sign·or legal term
as·simi·lable
as·simi·late
as·simi·la·tion
as·simi·la·tive (or ·tory)
As·sini·boine Canadian
  river
as·sist
as·sis·tance
as·sis·tant
as·sist·er
as·size
as·sizes
as·so·ci·able
as·so·ci·ate
as·so·cia·tion
as·so·cia·tion·ism
  psychology term
as·so·cia·tive
as·so·nance grammar term
as·so·nant
as·so·nan·tal
as·sort
as·sorta·tive (or ·sort·ive)
as·sort·ed

as·sort·er
as·sort·ment
as·suage
as·suage·ment
as·suag·er
as·sua·sive
as·sum·able
as·sume
as·sumed
as·sum·er
as·sum·ing
As·sump·tion Christian
  feast
as·sump·tion
as·sump·tive
Assur Assyrian god
as·sur·able
as·sur·ance *note* life
  assurance; *compare*
  insurance
as·sure
as·sured
as·sur·ed·ly
as·sur·ed·ness
as·sur·er
as·sur·gent curving
  upwards
(assymetric) *incorrect
  spelling of* **asymmetric**
(assymptote) *incorrect
  spelling of* **asymptote**
As·syria
As·syr·ian
As·syri·olo·gist
As·syri·ol·ogy
Astarte Phoenician goddess
astat·ic unstable
astati·cal·ly
astati·cism
as·ta·tine chemical element
as·ter
as·te·ri·at·ed
  crystallography term
as·ter·isk
as·ter·ism
astern
aster·nal anatomy term
as·ter·oid
as·teroi·dal
as·the·nia (*or* ·ny)
as·then·ic weak
as·the·no·pia eyestrain
as·the·nop·ic
as·theno·sphere layer of
  atmosphere

asth·ma
asth·mat·ic
asthmati·cal·ly
Asti Italian town
as·tig·mat·ic
as·tig·mati·cal·ly
astig·ma·tism (*or*
  astig·mia)
astil·be plant
astir
Asti Spumante wine
As·to·lat Arthurian town
astoma·tous biology term
aston·ish
aston·ish·ing
aston·ish·ing·ly
aston·ish·ment
As·to·ria US port
astound
astound·ed
astound·ing
astound·ing·ly
astrad·dle
as·tra·gal architectural
  moulding
astraga·lus anklebone
As·tra·khan Soviet city
as·tra·khan fur
as·tral
as·tra·pho·bia (*or* ·tro·)
  fear of thunderstorms
as·tra·pho·bic (*or* ·tro·)
astray
astride
as·trin·gen·cy (*or* ·gence)
as·trin·gent
as·tro·bi·ol·ogy
as·tro·bota·ny
as·tro·com·pass
as·tro·cyte cytology term
as·tro·dome
as·tro·dy·nam·ics
as·tro·geol·ogy
as·troid maths term
as·tro·labe astronomers'
  instrument
as·trolo·ger (*or* ·gist)
as·tro·logi·cal
as·tro·logi·cal·ly
as·trol·ogy
as·tro·met·ric (*or* ·ri·cal)
as·trom·etry branch of
  astronomy
as·tro·naut
as·tro·nau·tic (*or* ·ti·cal)

as·tro·nau·ti·cal·ly
as·tro·nau·tics
as·tro·navi·ga·tion
as·tro·navi·ga·tor
as·trono·mer
as·tro·nomi·cal (*or*
  ·nom·ic)
as·tro·nomi·cal·ly
as·trono·my
as·tro·photo·graph·ic
as·tro·pho·tog·ra·phy
as·tro·physi·cal
as·tro·physi·cist
as·tro·phys·ics
as·tro·sphere cytology term
As·tu·ri·as former Spanish
  kingdom
as·tute
as·tute·ness
Astyanax mythological
  character
asty·lar architectural term
Asun·ción Paraguayan
  capital
asun·der
As·wan Egyptian city
aswarm
asyl·lab·ic
asy·lum
asym·met·ric (*or* ·ri·cal)
asym·met·ri·cal·ly
asym·me·try
asymp·to·mat·ic
asymp·to·mati·cal·ly
as·ymp·tote geometry term
as·ymp·tot·ic (*or* ·toti·cal)
as·ymp·toti·cal·ly
asyn·chro·nism
asyn·chro·nous
as·yn·det·ic
as·yn·deti·cal·ly
asyn·de·ton (*plural* ·deta)
  grammar term
Asyut (*or* **As·siut**)
  Egyptian city
at
atac·tic chemistry term
Atalanta mythological
  character; *compare* **Atlanta**
ata·man (*plural* ·mans)
  Cossack leader
ata·rac·tic (*or* ·rax·ic)
ata·raxia (*or* ·raxy) peace
  of mind
ata·vism

ata·vist
ata·vis·tic (*or* ·vic)
ata·vis·ti·cal·ly
ataxia (*or* ataxy) lack of muscular coordination
atax·ic (*or* atac·tic)
At·ba·ra Sudanese town
Ate Greek goddess
ate
at·elec·ta·sis lung collapse
at·el·ier *French* workshop
Atha·bas·ka Canadian lake
athe·ism
athe·ist
athe·is·tic (*or* ·ti·cal)
athe·is·ti·cal·ly
ath·el·ing Anglo-Saxon prince
ath·emat·ic musical term
Athena Greek goddess
Ath·enaeum
ath·enaeum (*US also* ath·eneum) institution of learning
Athe·nian
Ath·ens
ather·man·cy
ather·ma·nous opaque to radiant heat
ath·ero·ma (*plural* ·mas *or* ·ma·ta)
ath·er·oma·tous
ath·ero·scle·ro·sis (*plural* ·ses)
ath·ero·scle·rot·ic
athirst
ath·lete
ath·let·ic
ath·leti·cal·ly
ath·leti·cism
ath·let·ics
atho·dyd ramjet
at·home social gathering
athwart
athwart·ships
atilt
At·lan·ta US city; *compare* Atalanta
At·lan·tean
at·lan·tes architectural term
At·lan·tic
At·lan·tis legendary continent
At·las mountain range
at·las

Atli legendary king
at·man Hindu self
at·moly·sis (*plural* ·ses)
at·mom·eter
at·mom·etry
at·mos·phere
at·mos·pher·ic (*or* ·pheri·cal)
at·mos·pheri·cal·ly
at·mos·pher·ics
at·oll
atom
atom·ic
atomi·cal·ly
ato·mic·ity
at·om·ism
at·om·ist
at·om·is·tic (*or* ·ti·cal)
at·om·is·ti·cal·ly
at·omi·za·tion (*or* ·sa·tion)
at·om·ize (*or* ·ise)
at·om·iz·er (*or* ·is·er)
aton·able (*or* atone·)
aton·al musical term
aton·al·ism
ato·nal·ity
ato·nal·ly
atone
atone·able *variant spelling* of atonable
atone·ment
aton·er
aton·ic
ato·nic·ity
ato·ny
atop
atrial
atrio·ven·tricu·lar
atrip nautical term
atrium (*plural* atria)
atro·cious
atro·cious·ness
atroc·ity (*plural* ·ities)
atroph·ic
at·ro·phy (*noun, plural* ·phies; *verb* ·phies, ·phy·ing, ·phied)
at·ro·pine (*or* ·pin) alkaloid
atta·boy
at·tach
at·tach·able
at·ta·ché diplomat
at·tach·er

at·tach·ment
at·tack
at·tack·er
at·tain
at·tain·abil·ity (*or* ·able·ness)
at·tain·able
at·tain·der legal term
at·tain·ment
at·taint
at·tar (*or* ot·) essential oil
(attachment) *incorrect spelling of* attachment
at·tempt
at·tempt·able
at·tempt·er
at·tend
at·tend·ance
at·tend·ant
at·tend·er
at·ten·tion
at·ten·tive
at·ten·tive·ness
at·tenu·ant
at·tenu·ate
at·tenua·tion
at·tenua·tor physics term
at·test
at·test·able
at·test·ant (*or* ·test·er)
at·tes·ta·tion
at·test·or (*or* ·test·ta·tor) legal term
At·tic of Attica
at·tic
At·ti·ca Greek region
at·ti·cism clear expression
at·tire
at·ti·tude
at·ti·tu·di·nal
at·ti·tu·di·nize (*or* ·nise)
at·ti·tu·di·niz·er (*or* ·nis·er)
at·torn
at·tor·ney
at·torn·ment
at·tract
at·tract·able
at·tract·ant
at·trac·tion
at·trac·tive
at·trac·tive·ness
at·trac·tor (*or* ·tract·er)
at·trib·ut·able
at·trib·ute

at·trib·ut·er (*or* ·tribu·tor)
at·tribu·tion
at·tribu·tive
at·tri·tion
at·tri·tion·al
at·tri·tive
Attu island off Alaska
at·tune
atypi·cal
atypi·cal·ly
aubade ode
Aube French river
auberge *French* inn
auber·gine
Auber·vil·liers Parisian
  suburb
aubrie·tia (*or* aubre·)
  plant
au·burn
Aubus·son French town
Auck·land New Zealand
  city; S Pacific islands
au cou·rant *French* up-to-
  date
auc·tion
auc·tion·eer
auc·to·rial of an author
auda·cious
auda·cious·ness
audac·ity (*plural* ·ities)
Aude French department
audibil·ity (*or*
  audible·ness)
audible
audi·ence
audile psychology term
audio
audio·gen·ic
audio·logi·cal
audi·olo·gist
audi·ol·ogy
audi·om·eter
audio·met·ric
audio·met·ri·cal·ly
audi·om·etrist
audi·om·etry
audio·phile hi-fi enthusiast
audio·typ·ing
audio·typist
audio·visual
audi·phone hearing aid
audit
audi·tion
audi·tor

audi·to·rium (*plural*
  ·riums *or* ·ria)
audi·tory
au fait *French* well-informed
au fond *French*
  fundamentally
auf Wie·der·seh·en
  German goodbye
Augean mythological
  stables; very dirty
augend number added
auger boring tool; *compare*
  augur
aught (*or* ought) *Archaic*
  anything; zero; *compare*
  ought
augite mineral
au·git·ic
aug·ment
aug·ment·able
aug·men·ta·tion
aug·menta·tive
aug·men·tor (*or* ·ment·er)
Augs·burg West German
  city
augur predict; *compare*
  auger
augur·al
augu·ry (*plural* ·ries)
August month
august imposing
Au·gus·ta Sicilian port
Augus·tan of Emperor
  Augustus; literary period
Augus·tin·ian of St
  Augustine
auk
auk·let
au lait *French* with milk
auld lang syne *Scot* old
  times; *compare* langsyne
aulic of a royal court
Aulis ancient Greek town
aum·bry *variant spelling of*
  ambry
au na·tu·rel *French* nude or
  raw
aunt
auntie (*or* aunty; *plural*
  aunties)
au pair
aura (*plural* auras *or*
  aurae)
aural of the ear; *compare*
  oral
aural·ly

aure·ate gilded
aure·ole (*or* aureo·la) halo
Aureo·my·cin
  (*Trademark*) antibiotic
aure·us (*plural* aurei)
  Roman coin
au re·voir
auric chemistry term
auri·cle anatomical part
auricu·la (*plural* ·lae *or*
  ·las) primrose
auricu·lar
auricu·late (*or* ·lat·ed)
  having ears
aurif·er·ous
Auri·ga constellation
Aurig·na·cian Palaeolithic
  culture
aurist ear specialist
aurochs extinct cattle
Aurora Roman goddess
auro·ra (*plural* ·ras *or*
  ·rae)
auro·ra aus·tra·lis
auro·ra bo·real·is
auro·ral
aur·ous
aurum gold
Ausch·witz
aus·cul·tate
aus·cul·ta·tion
aus·cul·ta·tor
aus·form·ing steel heat
  treatment
aus·pex (*plural* ·pices)
  Roman soothsayer
aus·pice (*plural* ·pices)
  omen; guidance
aus·pi·cious
aus·pi·cious·ness
aus·ten·ite metallurgy term
aus·ten·it·ic
aus·tere
aus·tere·ness
aus·ter·ity (*plural* ·ities)
Aus·ter·litz battle site
aus·tral of the south
Aus·tral·asia
Aus·tral·asian
Aus·tralia
Aus·tral·ian
Aus·tral·ia·na
Aus·trali·an·ism
Aus·trali·an·ize (*or* ·ise)
Aus·tra·loid

aus·tra·lo·pithe·cine fossil man

Aus·tra·lo·pithe·cus genus of fossil men

Aus·tral·orp domestic fowl

Aus·tria

Aus·trian

Austro-Asiatic

Aus·tro·nesia S Pacific islands

Aus·tro·nesian

auta·coid body secretion

autar·chic (or ·chi·cal)

autar·chy (plural ·chies) unrestricted rule; compare autarky

autar·kic (or ·ki·cal, ·chic, ·chi·cal)

autar·ky (or ·chy; plural ·kies or ·chies) economic self-sufficiency; compare autarchy

aut·eco·logi·cal

aut·ecol·ogy

auteur film director

authen·tic

authen·ti·cal·ly

authen·ti·cate

authen·ti·ca·tion

au·then·ti·ca·tor

au·then·tic·ity

author

author·ess

autho·rial

authori·tar·ian

authori·tari·an·ism

authori·ta·tive

authori·ta·tive·ness

author·ity (plural ·ities)

authori·za·tion (or ·sa·tion)

author·ize (or ·ise)

author·iz·er (or ·is·er)

author·ship

autism

autis·tic

auto (plural autos) Slang motor car

auto·anti·body (plural ·bodies)

auto·bahn

auto·bi·og·ra·pher

auto·bio·graphi·cal

auto·bi·og·ra·phy (plural ·phies)

auto·cade US motorcade

auto·ca·taly·sis (plural ·ses) chemistry term

auto·chang·er record-changing device

autoch·thon (plural ·thons or ·tho·nes) earliest known inhabitant

autoch·thon·ism (or ·tho·ny)

autoch·tho·nous (or ·tho·nal)

auto·clave

auto·cor·re·la·tion

autoc·ra·cy (plural ·cies)

auto·crat

auto·crat·ic

auto·crati·cal·ly

auto·cross

auto·cue

auto-da·fé (plural autos-da·fé) ceremony of Spanish Inquisition

auto·di·dact self-taught person

autoe·cious botany term

autoe·cism

autoga·mous (or auto·gam·ic)

autoga·my biology term

auto·gen·esis (or autog·eny)

auto·genet·ic

autog·enous

auto·gi·ro (or ·gy·; plural ·ros)

auto·graft

auto·graph

auto·graph·ic

auto·graphi·cal·ly

autog·ra·phy

auto·hyp·no·sis

auto·hyp·not·ic

auto·hyp·noti·cal·ly

autoi·cous botany term

auto·im·mune

auto·im·mun·ity

auto·ioni·za·tion (or ·sa·tion)

auto·ki·net·ic

Autoly·cus moon crater

Autolycus mythological character

auto·lyse (US ·lyze)

autoly·sin

autoly·sis self-destruction of cells

auto·lyt·ic

auto·mat

automa·ta plural of automaton

auto·mate

auto·mat·ic

auto·mati·cal·ly

auto·ma·tion

automa·tism

automa·tist

automa·tize (or ·tise)

automa·ton (plural ·tons or ·ta)

automa·tous

auto·mo·bile

auto·mo·bil·ist

auto·mo·tive

auto·nom·ic

auto·nomi·cal·ly

autono·mist

autono·mous

autono·my (plural ·mies)

auto·phyte botany term

auto·phyt·ic

auto·phyti·cal·ly

auto·pi·lot

auto·pis·ta Spanish motorway

auto·plas·tic

auto·plas·ty transplantation from own body

autop·sy (plural ·sies)

auto·put Yugoslav motorway

auto·radio·graph

auto·radio·graph·ic

auto·ra·di·og·ra·phy

auto·ro·ta·tion

auto·so·mal

auto·some type of chromosome

auto·sta·bil·ity

auto·stra·da Italian motorway

auto·sug·ges·tion

auto·sug·ges·tive

auto·tim·er

auto·tom·ic

autoto·mize (or ·mise)

autoto·my (plural ·mies) shedding of body part

auto·tox·ic

auto·tox·in

auto·trans·form·er

auto·troph·ic biology term

auto·type
auto·typ·ic
auto·typy
autoxi·da·tion chemistry term
autumn
autum·nal
autun·ite mineral
Auvergne French region
auxa·nom·eter
aux·esis biology term
aux·ilia·ry (plural ·ries)
aux·in hormone
auxo·chrome chemistry term
ava·da·vat (or ama·) bird
avail
avail·abil·ity
avail·able
avail·ably
ava·lanche
Ava·lon Arthurian paradise
avant-garde
Avar former European people
ava·rice
ava·ri·cious
avast nautical interjection
ava·tar manifestation of Hindu deity
ave Latin welcome; farewell
Ave·bury Wiltshire village; Neolithic stone circle
Ave·lla·ne·da Argentine city
avenge
aveng·er
av·ens (plural ·ens) plant
Av·en·tine Roman hill
aven·tu·rine (or aven·tu·rin, avan·tu·rine) dark glass
av·enue
aver (aver·ring, averred)
av·er·age
aver·ment
averse
aver·sion
aver·sive
avert
avert·ible (or ·able)
Aves·ta Zoroastrian scriptures
Aves·tan

Avey·ron French department
avian of birds
aviary (plural aviaries) place for keeping birds; compare apiary
avi·ate
avia·tion
avia·tor
avia·trix (or ·tress)
avi·cul·ture bird-rearing
avi·cul·tur·ist
avid
avi·din a protein
avid·ity
avid·ness
Avie·more Scottish resort
avi·fau·na
avi·fau·nal
Avi·gnon French city
avi·on·ic
avi·on·ics
aviru·lent
avita·mino·sis (plural ·ses)
avi·zan·dum Scottish legal term
avo·ca·do (plural ·dos)
avo·cet (or ·set) bird
avoid
avoid·able
avoid·ance
avoid·er
av·oir·du·pois system of weights
Avon English county and river
avow
avow·able
avow·al
avowed
avow·er
avul·sion
avun·cu·lar
avun·cu·late
await
awake (awak·ing, awoke or awaked, awok·en or awaked)
awak·en
award
award·able
awardee
award·er
aware

aware·ness
awash
away
awe
aweath·er nautical term
aweigh
awe-inspiring
awe·some
awe·some·ness
awe-stricken (or awe-struck)
aw·ful
aw·ful·ly
aw·ful·ness
awhile
awk·ward
awk·ward·ness
awl
awl·wort plant
awn plant bristle
awn·ing
awoke
awry
axe (US ax)
axel ice-skating jump; compare axil; axle
axen·ic uncontaminated
ax·ial
axil angle between leaf and stem; compare axel; axle
ax·ile attached to an axis
ax·il·la (plural ·lae) armpit
ax·il·lary (plural ·laries) of armpit; feather
axio·logi·cal
axi·olo·gist
axi·ol·ogy study of values
axi·om
axio·mat·ic (or ·mati·cal)
axio·mati·cal·ly
Axis Nazi alliance
axis (plural axes)
axle mechanical part; compare axel; axil
axle·tree carriage axle
Ax·min·ster Devon town; carpet
axo·lotl salamander
axon part of nerve cell
ax·seed plant
ay (or aye) Archaic always; compare aye
ayah maid
aya·huas·ca plant
ayatollah

Ay·cliffe English town
aye (*or* **ay**) *Archaic or dialect* yes; *compare* **ay**
aye-aye animal
Ayles·bury
Ay·ma·ra (*plural* **·ras** *or* **·ra**) South American Indian
Ayr Scottish port
Ayr·shire cattle
Ayur·veda Hindu medical treatise
Ayut·tha·ya Thai city
azalea
azan Islamic call to prayer

aza·thio·prine drug
Az·bine Saharan region
azeda·rach medicinal bark
azeo·trope chemistry term
azeo·trop·ic
Azer·bai·jan region of Iran; Soviet republic
Azer·bai·ja·ni (*plural* **·ni** *or* **·nis**)
az·ide
azi·muth astronomy term
azi·muth·al
az·ine
azo·ben·zene
azo·ic without life

az·ole chemical compound
Azores Atlantic islands
az·ote *Obsolete* nitrogen
azo·tae·mia (*US* **·te·**) uraemia
azo·tae·mic (*US* **·te·**)
az·oth mercury
azot·ic of nitrogen
azo·to·bac·ter bacterium
Az·tec
az·ure
az·ur·ite mineral
azy·gous

B

Ba soul in Egyptian mythology
baa (**baa·ing, baaed**)
Baal Semitic god
Baal·bek Lebanese town
baba cake
ba·bas·su palm tree
bab·bitt line with alloy
Bab·bitt met·al
bab·ble
bab·bler
babe
Ba·bel biblical tower
ba·biche rawhide thongs
babi·ru·sa wild pig
ba·boon
(babtize) *incorrect spelling of* **baptize**
ba·bul acacia tree
baby (*noun, plural* **babies**; *verb* **babies, ba·by·ing, ba·bied**)
ba·by·hood
ba·by·ish
Baby·lon city
Baby·lo·nia kingdom
Baby·lo·nian
baby's-breath (*or* **babies'-**) plant
baby-sit (**-sitting, -sat**)
baby-sitter
baby-snatch·er
bac·ca·lau·re·ate
bac·ca·rat

bac·cate berry-like
Bac·chae priestesses of Bacchus
bac·cha·nal
bac·cha·na·lia
bac·cha·na·lian
bac·chant (*fem* **·chan·te**; *plural* **·chants** *or* **·chan·tes**, *fem* **·chan·tes**) drunken reveller
Bac·chic
bac·chius (*plural* **·chii**) metrical foot
Bacchus god of wine
bac·cif·er·ous
bac·ci·form
bac·civ·or·ous
bac·cy *Slang* tobacco
bach·elor
bachelor's-buttons plant
ba·cil·lary (*or* **·lar**)
ba·cil·li·form
ba·cil·lus (*plural* **·li**) rod-shaped bacterium
baci·tra·cin antibiotic
back
back·ache
back·bencher
back·bend
back·bite (**·bit·ing, bit, bit·ten** *or* **bit**)
back·board
back·bone

back·breaker
back·breaking
back·chat
back·cloth (*or* **·drop**)
back·comb
back·cross genetics term
back·date
back·door
back·er
back·fill archaeology term
back·fire
back·gam·mon
back·ground
back·hand
back·hand·ed
back·handed·ly
back·handed·ness
back·hand·er
back·ing
back·lash
back·less
back·list
back·log
back·most
back-pedal (**-pedalling, -pedalled**; *US* **-pedaling, -pedaled**)
back·saw
Backs Cambridge college grounds
back·scratch·er
back·side
back·sight
back-slapping

balancer

back·slide (·slid·ing, ·slid,
·slid *or* ·slid·den)
back·slid·er
back·space
back·spin
back·stage
back·stairs
back·stay nautical term
back·stitch
back·stop
back·street
back·stroke
back·swept
back·track
back·up (*noun*)
back·veld South African
rural area
back·ward (*adj*)
back·warda·tion stock
exchange term
back·ward·ness
back·wards (*US* ·ward;
adv)
back·wash
back·water
back·woods·man (*plural*
·men)
Ba·co·lod Philippine town
ba·con
ba·con·er pig
bac·te·rae·mia (*US* ·re·)
bacteria in the blood
bac·te·ria *plural of*
bacterium
bac·te·rial
bac·te·ri·cid·al
bac·te·ri·cide
bac·te·rin vaccine
bac·te·rio·logi·cal
bac·te·ri·olo·gist
bac·te·ri·ol·ogy
bac·te·ri·oly·sis
disintegration of bacteria
bac·te·rio·lyt·ic
bac·te·rio·phage virus that
destroys bacteria
bac·te·rio·phag·ic
bac·te·ri·opha·gous
bac·te·rio·sta·sis
bac·te·rio·stat·ic
bac·te·rio·stati·cal·ly
bac·te·rium (*plural* ·ria)
bac·ter·oid
Bac·tria ancient Asian
country

Bac·trian
ba·cu·li·form rod-shaped
bacu·lum (*plural* ·la *or*
·lums)
bad (worse, worst)
Ba·da·joz Spanish city
Ba·da·lo·na Spanish port
bad·der·locks seaweed
bad·dy (*or* ·die; *plural*
·dies)
bade
Ba·den former German
state; Swiss spa
Baden-Baden West
German spa
Baden-Wurttem·berg
West German state
badge
badg·er
badi·nage
bad·lands
bad·ly
bad·man (*plural* ·men)
bad·min·ton
bad·mouth
bad·ness
Bae·de·ker travel
guidebook
bael tree
Baf·fin Canadian island and
bay
baf·fle
baf·fle·ment
baf·fler
bag (bag·ging, bagged)
Ba·gan·da (*plural* ·da *or*
·das) African people
ba·gasse sugar-cane pulp
baga·telle
ba·gel (*or* bei·) bread roll
bag·gage
bag·gi·ly
bag·gi·ness
bag·ging
bag·gy (·gier, ·gi·est)
bagh Indian garden
Bagh·dad (*or* Bag·dad)
bag·man (*plural* ·men)
bag·pipe
ba·guette (*or* ·guet)
bag·wig 18th-century wig
bag·worm
Ba·hai
Ba·ha·ism religion
Ba·ha·ist

Ba·ha·mas
Ba·ha·mian
Ba·hia Brazilian town
Ba·hía Blan·ca Argentine
port
Bah·rain (*or* ·rein)
Bah·rai·ni (*or* ·rei·)
baht Thai currency
ba·hu·vri·hi linguistics term
Bai·kal Soviet lake
bail (*noun*) security for
prisoner; part of wicket;
compare bale
bail (*or* bale; *verb*) remove
water from boat
bail·able
bailee legal term
bail·er (*or* bal·) one who
bails water
bai·ley castle wall
Bailey bridge
bailie *Scot* magistrate
bail·iff
baili·wick legal term
bail·ment legal term
bail·or legal term
bails·man (*plural* ·men)
one who stands bail
bain·ite component of steel
bain-marie (*plural* bains-
marie) cooking utensil
Bai·ram Muslim festival
bairn
bait enticement; to torment;
compare bate
baize
bake
bake·house
Ba·ke·lite (*Trademark*)
bak·er
bak·ery (*plural* ·eries)
Bake·well English town;
tart
bak·la·va cake
bak·sheesh
Baku Soviet port
Bala Welsh lake
Balaam biblical character
Bala·cla·va helmet
Bala·kla·va (*or* ·cla·)
Soviet port
bala·lai·ka
bal·ance
bal·ance·able
bal·anc·er

bal·as gemstone

bala·ta tree

Ba·la·ton Hungarian lake

Bal·boa Panamanian port

bal·boa Panamanian currency

bal·brig·gan fabric

bal·co·nied

bal·co·ny (*plural* ·nies)

bald

bal·da·chin brocade

Balder Norse god

bal·der·dash

bald·headed

bald·ing

bald·money plant

bald·ness

bald·pate

bal·dric sash for sword

bale (*noun*) block of hay; *compare* bail

bale (*verb*) make bales; jump from aircraft; *variant spelling of* bail

Bal·ear·ic Is·lands

ba·leen whalebone

bale·ful

bale·ful·ly

bale·ful·ness

bal·er agricultural machine; *variant spelling of* bailer

Bali Indonesian island

bali·bun·tal straw hat

Ba·lik·pa·pan Indonesian city

Ba·li·nese (*plural* ·nese)

balk (*or* baulk) stop short; avoid; timber beam; *compare* baulk

Bal·kan

Bal·kani·za·tion (*or* ·sa·tion)

balk·er (*or* baulk·)

balky (*or* baulky; balki·er *or* baulki·er, balki·est *or* baulki·est)

ball

bal·lad

bal·lade verse form

bal·lad·eer

bal·lad·ry

Bal·la·rat Australian town

bal·last

bal·le·ri·na

bal·let

bal·let·ic

bal·leto·mane

bal·leto·ma·nia

ball·flower architectural ornament

bal·lis·ta (*plural* ·tae) ancient catapult

bal·lis·tic

bal·lis·ti·cal·ly

bal·lis·tics

bal·locks *variant spelling of* bollocks

bal·lo·net gas compartment in balloon

bal·loon

bal·loon·ist

bal·lot (·lot·ing, ·lot·ed)

bal·lotte·ment medical term

ball·park

ball·point

ball·room

bal·ly slang term

bal·ly·hoo

balm

bal·ma·caan overcoat

balmi·ly

balmi·ness

Bal·mor·al Scottish castle; flat cap

balmy (balmi·er, balmi·est) soft and soothing; *variant spelling* (*esp. US*) *of* barmy

bal·ne·al

bal·neo·logi·cal

bal·ne·olo·gist

bal·ne·ol·ogy study of therapeutic baths

ba·lo·ney (*or* bo·)

bal·sa wood

bal·sam

bal·sam·ic

bal·sam·if·er·ous

bal·sa·mi·na·ceous

Balt person from Baltic States

Bal·tic

Bal·ti·more

Ba·lu·chi (*or* ·lo·; *plural* ·chis *or* ·chi) Muslim people

Ba·lu·chi·stan region of Asia

bal·us·ter

bal·us·trade

Ba·ma·ko capital of Mali

Bam·ba·ra (*plural* ·ra *or* ·ras) African people

Bam·berg West German town

bam·bi·no (*plural* ·nos *or* ·ni)

bam·boo (*plural* ·boos)

bam·boo·zle

bam·boo·zle·ment

bam·boo·zler

ban (ban·ning, banned)

ba·nal

ba·nal·ity

ba·na·na

Ban·at plain in E Europe

ba·nau·sic utilitarian

Ban·bury

banc legal term

band

band·age

ban·dan·na (*or* ban·dana)

band·box

ban·deau (*plural* ·deaux) headband

ban·de·ril·la bullfighter's dart

ban·de·ril·lero (*plural* ·leros) bullfighter's assistant

ban·de·role (*or* ·de·rol, ·ne·rol) flag

ban·di·coot

ban·dit (*plural* ·dits *or* ·dit·ti)

ban·dit·ry

Band·jar·ma·sin (*or* Ban·jer·ma·sin) Indonesian port

band·master

ban·do·leer (*or* ·lier) shoulder belt

ban·do·line hairdressing substance

ban·dora (*or* pan·) musical instrument

bands·man (*plural* ·men)

band·spreading radio tuning control

band·stand

Ban·dung Indonesian city

band·wagon

band·width

ban·dy (*adj* ·di·er, ·di·est; *verb* ·dies, ·dy·ing, ·died)

bandy-bandy (*plural*
  -bandies) snake
bane
bane·berry (*plural*
  ·berries)
bane·ful
Banff former Scottish
  county; Canadian town
bang
Ban·ga·lore Indian city
bang·er
Bang·ka Indonesian island
Bang·kok
Bang·la·desh
Bang·la·deshi
ban·gle
Bangor Welsh or Northern
  Irish town
Ban·gui capital of Central
  African Republic
ban·ish
ban·ish·ment
ban·is·ter
ban·jo (*plural* ·jos *or*
  ·joes)
ban·jo·ist
Ban·jul Gambian capital
bank
bank·able
bank·book
bank·er
bank·et gold-bearing rock
bank·ing
bank·roll
bank·rupt
bank·rupt·cy (*plural* ·cies)
bank·sia shrub
banned
ban·ner
ban·ner·ette
ban·ning
(**bannister**) *incorect spelling
  of* **banister**
ban·nock Scottish cake
Ban·nock·burn Scottish
  battle site
banns (*or* bans) of
  marriage
ban·quet feast
ban·quette seat
ban·shee
bant *Dialect* string
ban·tam
bantam·weight
ban·ter

ban·ter·er
Ban·toid language
Ban·tu (*plural* ·tu *or* ·tus)
Ban·tu·stan South African
  homeland
ban·yan (*or* ·ian) tree
ban·zai Japanese salutation
bao·bab tree
bap
bap·tism
bap·tis·mal
Bap·tist member of
  Christian sect
bap·tist·ry (*or* ·tis·tery;
  plural ·ries *or* ·teries)
bap·tize (*or* ·tise)
bar (bar·ring, barred)
Barabbas biblical character
bara·thea fabric
barb
Bar·ba·dian
Bar·ba·dos
bar·bar·ian
bar·bar·ian·ism
bar·bar·ic
bar·bari·cal·ly
bar·bar·ism
bar·bar·ity (*plural* ·ities)
bar·ba·rize (*or* ·rise)
bar·ba·rous
bar·ba·rous·ness
Bar·ba·ry N African region
bar·bate
bar·becue (·becu·ing,
  ·becued)
bar·bel fish; bristle
bar·bell weight
bar·bel·late covered with
  bristles
bar·ber
bar·ber·ry (*plural* ·ries)
barber·shop
bar·bet bird
bar·bette gun platform
Bar·bi·can area of London
bar·bi·can fortified place
bar·bi·cel
bar·bi·tone (*US* ·tal)
bar·bi·tu·rate
Bar·bu·da West Indian
  island
bar·bule
bar·ca·role (*or* ·rolle)
Bar·ce·lo·na

bar·chan (*or* ·khan,
  ·chane, ·kan) sand dune
bard
bard·ic
bar·dola·try
bare uncovered; naked;
  expose; *compare* bear
bare·back (*or* ·backed)
bare·faced
bare·fac·ed·ness
bare·foot (*or* ·footed)
bare·handed
bare·headed
Ba·reil·ly Indian city
bare·ly
bare·ness
Bar·ents Arctic sea
bar·gain
barge
bar·gee
barge·pole
Bari Italian port
bar·ic of atmospheric
  pressure
ba·ril·la plant extract
bari·tone
bar·ium
bark dog's cry; outer layer
  of tree; *compare* barque
bark·er
Bark·ing London borough
bar·ley
barley·corn
barm *Dialect* yeast
bar·maid
bar·man (*plural* ·men)
Bar·mecide (*or* ·mecid·al)
  illusory
bar mitz·vah
bar·my (*or esp. US*
  balmy; ·mi·er, ·mi·est)
  Slang crazy; *compare*
  balmy
barn
bar·na·cle
Bar·na·ul Soviet city
barn-brack *Dialect* fruit
  muffin
Bar·net London borough
bar·ney *Slang* argument
barn·storm
barn·yard
Ba·ro·da Indian state
baro·gram
baro·graph

baro·graphic
ba·rom·eter
baro·met·ric
baro·met·ri·cal·ly
bar·on
bar·on·age
bar·on·ess
bar·on·et
bar·on·et·age
bar·on·et·cy (*plural* ·cies)
ba·rong Philippine knife
ba·ro·nial
baro·ny (*plural* ·nies)
ba·roque
baro·recep·tor
baro·scope
baro·stat
Ba·rot·se (*plural* ·se *or* ·ses) African people
Ba·rot·se·land Zambian region
ba·rouche horse-drawn carriage
barque (*US also* bark) boat; *compare* bark
bar·quen·tine (*or* ·quan·)
Bar·qui·si·me·to Venezuelan city
bar·rack (*verb*)
bar·racks
bar·ra·cou·ta fish
bar·ra·cu·da (*plural* ·da *or* ·das) fish
bar·rage
bar·ra·mun·da (*or* ·di; *plural* ·das, ·da; *or* ·dis, ·dies, di) fish
bar·ran·ca *US* ravine
Bar·ran·quil·la Colombian port
bar·ra·tor
bar·ra·trous (*or* bar·retrous)
bar·ra·try (*or* bar·retry) legal term
bar·ré music term
barred
bar·rel (·rel·ling, ·relled; *US* ·rel·ing, ·reled)
bar·ren
bar·ren·ness
bar·rens *US* barren land
barren·wort plant
bar·ret cap
bar·rette hair clasp

bar·ri·cade
bar·ri·cad·er
bar·ri·er
bar·ring
bar·ris·ter
bar·room
bar·row
Bar·ry Welsh port
Bar·sac wine
bar·tender
bar·ter
bar·ter·er
bar·ti·zan small turret
Bart·lett pear
bary·cen·tre centre of mass
bar·ye unit
bary·on physics term
bary·sphere
ba·ry·tes mineral
bary·ton bass viol
ba·sal
bas·alt
basalt·ware
bas·cule bridge
base
base·ball
base·board
base·born
Ba·sel (*or* Basle) Swiss city
base·less
base·line
base·man (*plural* ·men) baseball fielder
base·ment
base·ness
Ba·sen·ji dog
ba·ses *plural of* base *or* basis
bash
Ba·shan biblical region
bash·ful
bash·ful·ly
bash·ful·ness
bashi·ba·zouk Turkish soldier
Bash·kir (*plural* ·kir *or* ·kirs) Mongoloid people
ba·sic
ba·si·cal·ly
ba·sic·ity chemistry term
ba·sid·ial
ba·sidio·my·cete fungus
ba·sidio·my·cet·ous
ba·sidio·spore
ba·sidio·spor·ous

ba·sid·ium (*plural* ·ia) fungal structure
basi·fixed botany term
basi·fy (·fies, ·fy·ing, ·fied) make basic
bas·il herb
basi·lar anatomy term
basi·lary
Ba·sil·don Essex town
Ba·sil·ian Eastern monk
ba·sil·ic vein
ba·sili·ca Roman building
ba·sil·i·can (*or* ·sil·ic)
Ba·si·li·ca·ta Italian region
basi·lisk lizard
ba·sin
basi·net medieval helmet; *compare* bassinet
ba·sin·ful
Ba·sing·stoke Hampshire town
ba·sion anatomy term
ba·sip·etal botany term
ba·sis (*plural* ·ses)
bask
Baskerville style of type
bas·ket
basket·ball
bas·ket·ry
basket·star starfish
basket·work
Basle *variant spelling of* Basel
ba·so·phil (*or* ·phile, ·phil·ic) stained by basic dyes
Ba·so·tho (*plural* ·tho *or* ·thos) African people
Basque Pyrenean people and language
Bas·ra (*or* Bas·rah, Bus·ra, Bus·rah) Iraqi port
bas-relief (*or* bas·relief)
Bas-Rhin French department
bass voice; singer
bass (*plural* bass *or* basses) fish
Bas·sein Burmese city
Bas·sen·thwaite
bas·set
Basse-Terre West Indian island
bas·si·net cradle; *compare* basinet

bass·ist double bass player
bas·so (*plural* **·sos** *or* **·si**) bass singer
bas·soon
bas·soon·ist
bass·wood
bast plant tissue
bas·tard
bas·tardi·za·tion (*or* **·sa·tion**)
bas·tard·ize (*or* **·ise**)
bas·tard·ry *Austral* malicious behaviour
bas·tardy illegitimacy
baste
Bas·tille fortress
bas·ti·na·do (*noun, plural* **·does;** *verb* **·does,** **·do·ing, ·doed**) torture
bast·ing
bas·ti·on
bast·naes·ite (*or* **·nas·ite**) mineral
Ba·su·to·land *former name of* **Lesotho**
bat (**bat·ting, bat·ted**)
Ba·tan·gas Philippine port
batch
(**batchelor**) *incorrect spelling of* **bachelor**
bate restrain; *Slang* rage; *compare* **bait**
ba·teau boat
bat·ed
bat·fish (*plural* **·fish** *or* **·fishes**)
Bath English city; order of knighthood
bath container; wash in bath
bathe swim; wash wound, etc.
bath·er
ba·thet·ic
bath·house
bath·ing
batho·lith (*or* **·lite**) granite mass
batho·lith·ic (*or* **·lit·ic**)
ba·thom·eter
batho·met·ric
batho·met·ri·cal·ly
ba·thom·etry
ba·thos
bath·robe
bath·room
bath·tub

Bath·urst Australian city; *former name of* **Banjul**
bathy·al of ocean depths
bathy·met·ric
bathy·met·ri·cal·ly
ba·thym·etry
bathy·scaph (*or* **·scaphe,** **·scape**)
bathy·sphere
ba·tik (*or* **bat·tik**) fabric-printing process
ba·tiste fabric
Bat·ley Yorkshire town
bat·man (*plural* **·men**)
ba·ton
Bat·on Rouge US city
ba·tra·chi·an amphibian
bats·man (*plural* **·men**)
bats·man·ship
batt quilt wadding
bat·tal·ion
bat·ted
bat·ten
Bat·ten·burg cake
bat·ter
bat·ter·er
bat·tery (*plural* **·teries**)
bat·ting
bat·tle
battle-axe
bat·tle·dore racket game
battle·field
bat·tle·ment
battle·piece
bat·tler
battle-scarred
battle·ship
bat·tue hunting term
bat·ty (**·ti·er, ·ti·est**)
Ba·tum (*or* **Ba·tu·mi**) Soviet city
bat·wing
bat·woman (*plural* **·women**)
bau·ble
Bau·chi Nigerian state
baud unit of speed; *compare* **bawd**
Bau·haus school of arts
bau·hinia plant
baulk billiards term (*US* **balk**); *variant spelling of* **balk**
Bau·tzen East German city
baux·ite

Ba·varia
Ba·var·ian
baw·bee former Scottish coin
bawd brothel keeper; *compare* **baud**
bawdi·ly
bawdi·ness
bawd·ry
bawdy (**bawdi·er,** **bawdi·est**)
bawdy·house
bawl
bawl·er
bay
ba·ya·dere Hindu dancing girl
Ba·ya·mon Puerto Rican city
bay·berry (*plural* **·berries**)
Ba·yeux French town
bayo·net (**·net·ing, ·net·ed** *or* **·net·ting, ·net·ted**)
bayou marshy stream
bay·wood
ba·zaar (*or* **·zar**)
ba·zoo *US* mouth
ba·zoo·ka
bdel·lium tree
be
beach shore; *compare* **beech**
beach·comber
beach·head
Beach-la-Mar Pacific language
bea·con
Bea·cons·field English town
bead
beadi·ly
beadi·ness
bead·ing
bea·dle
beady (**beadi·er,** **beadi·est**)
bea·gle
beak
beaked
beak·er
beaky
beam
beam-ends
beamy
bean

bean·bag
bean·ery (*plural* ·eries)
　US cheap restaurant
bean·feast
beanie US close-fitting hat
beano (*plural* beanos)
　Slang party
bean·pole
beanstalk
bear (bear·ing, bore,
　borne) support; convey;
　endure; compare bare
bear (bear·ing, bore,
　born) give birth to
bear (*plural* bears *or*
　bear) animal
bear·able
bear·ably
bear·berry (*plural*
　·berries)
beard
beard·ed
beard·less
bear·er
bear·ish
Bé·ar·naise sauce
bear's-breech (*or*
　-breeches) plant
bear's-foot plant
bear·skin
beast
beast·ings US spelling of
　beestings
beast·li·ness
beast·ly (·lier, ·liest)
beat (beat·ing, beat,
　beat·en *or* beat)
beat·able
beat·er
bea·tif·ic
bea·tifi·cal·ly
be·ati·fi·ca·tion
be·ati·fy (·fies, ·fy·ing,
　·fied)
be·ati·tude
beat·nik
beau (*plural* beaus *or*
　beaux)
Beau·fort meteorological
　scale
beau·jo·lais (*or* Beau·)
　wine
beau monde fashionable
　society
Beau·mont Texan city
Beaune French city; wine

beaut Slang good
beau·te·ous
beau·ti·cian
beau·ti·fi·ca·tion
beau·ti·ful
beau·ti·ful·ly
beau·ti·fy (·fies, ·fy·ing,
　·fied)
beau·ty (*plural* ·ties)
Beau·vais French town
beaux-arts fine art
bea·ver
Beaver·board
　(*Trademark*)
be·bee·rine alkaloid
Beb·ing·ton English town
be·bop jazz
be·calmed
be·came
be·cause
bec·ca·fi·co (*plural* ·cos)
　bird
bé·cha·mel sauce
bêche-de-mer marine
　organism
Bechua·na·land *former
　name of* Botswana
beck
beck·et nautical term
beck·on
beck·on·er
be·cloud
be·come (·com·ing,
　·came, ·come)
be·com·ing·ly
bed (bed·ding, bed·ded)
be·daub
be·daz·zle
be·daz·zle·ment
bed·bug
bed·dable
bed·ded
bed·der
bed·ding
be·deck
be·dev·il (·il·ling, ·illed;
　US ·il·ing, ·iled)
be·dev·il·ment
be·dew
bed·fellow
Bed·ford
Bed·ford·shire
be·dim (·dim·ming,
　·dimmed)
bed·lam

Bed·ling·ton terrier
Bedou·in (*or* Bedu·in;
　plural ·ins *or* ·in)
bed·pan
bed·plate
bed·post
be·drag·gle
bed·rail
bed·rid·den
bed·rock
bed·roll
bed·room
bed·side
bed·sitter (*or* ·sit)
bed·sore
bed·spread
bed·stead
bed·straw plant
bed·time
bed·warmer
bee
bee·bread
beech tree; compare beach
beech·nut
bee-eater
beef (*plural* beeves) cattle
beef (*plural* beefs) cut of
　meat; complaint
beef·bur·ger
beef·cake
beef·eater
beefi·ness
beef·steak
beef·wood
beefy (beefi·er, beefi·est)
bee·hive
bee·keeper
bee·line
Beelzebub the Devil
been
beep
beep·er
beer
beeri·ness
Beer·she·ba Israeli town
beery (beeri·er, beeri·est)
beest·ings (*or* biest·ings;
　US *also* beast·ings)
　cow's first milk
bees·wax
bees·wing crust in port
beet
beet·fly (*plural* ·flies)
bee·tle
beet·root

bee·zer *Slang* fellow
be·fall (·fal·ling, ·fell,
  ·fall·en)
be·fit (·fit·ting, ·fit·ted)
be·fit·ting·ly
be·fog (·fog·ging, ·fogged)
be·fool
be·fore
before·hand
be·foul
be·foul·er
be·foul·ment
be·friend
be·fud·dle
beg (beg·ging, begged)
be·gan
be·get (·get·ting, ·got *or*
  ·gat, ·got·ten *or* ·got)
be·get·ter
beg·gar
beg·gar·li·ness
beg·gar·ly
beggar·weed
beg·gary
begged
beg·ging
be·gin (gin·ning, ·gan,
  ·gun)
be·gin·ner
be·gird surround
be·gone
be·gonia
be·gor·ra Irish exclamation
be·got
be·got·ten
be·grime
be·grudge
be·grudg·ing·ly
be·guile (·guil·ing,
  ·guiled)
be·guile·ment
be·guil·er
be·guil·ing·ly
be·guine dance
be·gum (*or* ·gam) Muslim
  woman ruler
be·gun
be·half
be·have
be·hav·iour (*US* ·ior)
be·hav·iour·al (*US* ·ior·)
be·hav·iour·ism (*US* ·ior·)
be·hav·iour·ist (*US* ·ior·)
be·hav·iour·is·tic (*US*
  ·ior·)

be·head
be·held
be·he·moth biblical monster
be·hest
be·hind
behind·hand
be·hold (·hold·ing, ·held)
be·hold·en
be·hold·er
be·hove (*US* ·hoove)
beige
bei·gel *variant spelling of*
  bagel
Bei·jin *Chinese name for*
  Peking
be·ing
Bei·ra Mozambique port
Bei·rut (*or* Bey·routh)
  Lebanese capital
be·jew·el (·el·ling, ·elled;
  US ·el·ing, ·eled)
bel unit of power
be·la·bour (*US* ·bor)
be·lah tree
be·lat·ed
be·lat·ed·ness
be·lay (·lay·ing, ·layed)
  make secure
belch
belch·er
be·lea·guer
Be·lém Brazilian port
be·lem·nite fossil
Bel·fast
Bel·fort French department
bel·fry (*plural* ·fries)
Bel·gae Celtic people
Bel·gian
Bel·gium
Bel·grade Yugoslav capital
Bel·gra·via London district
Belial demon
be·lie (·ly·ing, ·lied)
be·lief
be·li·er
be·liev·able
be·lieve
be·liev·er
Belisha traffic beacon
be·lit·tle
be·lit·tle·ment
be·lit·tler
be·lit·tling·ly
Be·lize Central American
  state

bell
bel·la·don·na
bel·lar·mine jar
Bel·la·trix star
bell·bird
bell·boy
belle beautiful woman
belle époque *French* period
  before World War I
Bel·leek porcelain
Bellerophon mythological
  hero
belles-lettres *French*
  literary works
bel·let·rist
bel·let·ris·tic
bell·hop
bel·li·cose
bel·li·cos·ity
bel·lig·er·ence
bel·lig·er·en·cy
bel·lig·er·ent
Bellona Roman goddess
bel·low
bel·low·er
bel·lows
bell·pull
bell·push
bell·ringer
bell·ringing
bell·wether flock leader
bell·wort plant
bel·ly (*noun, plural* ·lies;
  verb ·lies, ·ly·ing, ·lied)
belly·band part of harness
belly·button
belly-flop (·flopping,
  -flopped)
bel·ly·ful
Bel·mo·pan Belize capital
Belo Ho·ri·zon·te
  Brazilian city
be·long
be·long·ings
Be·lo·rus·sia (*or* Bye·)
  Soviet republic
Be·lo·rus·sian (*or* Bye·)
be·lov·ed
Be·lo·vo (*or* Bye·) Soviet
  city
be·low
Bel Pa·ese cheese
Bel·sen concentration camp
Belshazzar biblical
  character

belt

belt
Bel·tane Celtic festival
belt·way *US* ring road
be·lu·ga sturgeon
bel·vedere building with
　view
bema Athenian speaker's
　platform
Bem·ba (*plural* ·**ba** *or*
　·**bas**) African people
be·mire
be·moan
be·muse
be·mused
ben *Scot* mountain peak
Bena·dryl (*Trademark*)
Be·na·res Indian city
bench
bench·er a judge
bend (**bend·ing, bent**)
Ben·del Nigerian state
bend·er
Ben·di·go Australian city
bends decompression
　sickness
bendy (**bendi·er,**
　bendi·est)
be·neath
Ben·edi·ci·te canticle
ben·edi·ci·te blessing
Ben·edic·tine order of
　monks; liqueur
ben·edic·tion
ben·edic·tory
Ben·edic·tus canticle
ben·efac·tion
ben·efac·tor
ben·efac·tress
be·nef·ic *rare variant of*
　beneficient
ben·efice
be·nefi·cence
be·nefi·cent
ben·efi·cial
ben·efi·cial·ly
bene·fi·ciary (*plural*
　·**ciaries**)
ben·efit
Bene·lux
Be·ne·ven·to Italian city
be·nevo·lence
be·nevo·lent
Ben·gal
Ben·ga·lese
Ben·ga·li

ben·ga·line fabric
Ben·gha·zi (*or* ·**ga·si**)
　Libyan port
be·night·ed
be·nign
be·nig·nan·cy
be·nig·nant
be·nig·nity (*plural* ·**nities**)
Be·nin African republic
beni·son
ben·ne plant
Ben Ne·vis
ben·ny *Slang* amphetamine
　tablet
Be·no·ni South African city
bent
ben·thic
ben·thos (*or* ·**thon**)
　biology term
ben·ton·ite clay
bent·wood
Be·nue Nigerian state
be·numb
ben·zal·de·hyde
Ben·ze·drine
　(*Trademark*)
ben·zene chemical
　compound; *compare*
　benzine
ben·zi·dine
ben·zine (*or* ·**zin**) petrol;
　compare benzene
ben·zo·ate
ben·zo·caine anaesthetic
Ben·zo·drine
　(*Trademark*)
ben·zo·fu·ran
ben·zo·ic
ben·zo·in gum resin
ben·zol (*or* ·**zole**)
ben·zo·phe·none
ben·zo·qui·none
ben·zo·yl
ben·zyl
Beo·wulf epic poem
be·queath
be·queath·er
be·quest
Be·rar Indian region
be·rate
Ber·ber Caucasoid Muslim
Ber·bera Somalian port
ber·beri·da·ceous botany
　term
ber·ber·ine alkaloid

ber·ber·is shrub
ber·ceuse lullaby
Berch·tes·ga·den West
　German town
be·reave
be·reave·ment
be·reft
be·ret
Be·rez·ni·ki Soviet city
berg iceberg; mountain;
　compare burg; burgh
Ber·ga·mo Italian city
ber·ga·mot tree; oil
Ber·gen Norwegian port
berg·schrund crevasse in
　glacier
beri·beri disease
Bering Arctic sea and strait
berk *variant spelling of* burk
Berkeley Californian city
ber·kelium radioactive
　element
Berk·shire
Ber·lin
berm narrow ledge
Ber·mu·da
Bern (*or* **Berne**) Swiss
　capital
Ber·nese
ber·ry (*noun, plural* ·**ries;**
　verb ·**ries,** ·**ry·ing,**
　·**ried**)
ber·sa·gliere Italian soldier
ber·seem plant
ber·serk
berth
Ber·wick former Scottish
　county
Berwick-upon-Tweed
　English town
ber·yl mineral
ber·yl·ine
be·ryl·lium chemical
　element
Bes Egyptian god
Be·san·çon French city
be·seech (·**seech·ing,**
　·**sought**)
be·set (·**set·ting,** ·**set**)
be·side
be·sides
be·siege
be·sieg·er
be·smear
be·smirch

be·som
be·sot·ted
be·span·gle
be·spat·ter
be·speak (·speak·ing,
·spoke, spo·ken or
·spoke)
be·spec·ta·cled
be·spoke
be·spread
be·sprent sprinkled over
be·sprin·kle
Bes·sa·ra·bia Soviet region
best
bes·tial
bes·ti·al·ity (plural ·ities)
bes·ti·al·ize (or ·ise)
bes·tial·ly
bes·ti·ary (plural ·aries)
be·stir (·stir·ring, ·stirred)
be·stow
be·stow·al (or ·ment)
be·stow·er
be·strew (·strew·ing,
·strewed, ·strewn or
·strewed)
be·stride (·strid·ing,
·strode or ·strid,
·strid·den or ·strid)
bet (bet·ting, bet or
bet·ted)
beta
be·ta·ine alkaloid
be·take (·tak·ing, ·took,
·tak·en)
be·ta·tron particle
accelerator
be·tel plant
Be·tel·geuse (or ·geux)
star
bête noire (plural bêtes
noires) pet hate
beth Hebrew letter
Betha·ny biblical village
Beth·el biblical town
Beth·le·hem
be·tide
bê·tise folly
be·to·ken
beto·ny (plural ·nies)
plant
be·took
be·tray
be·tray·al
be·tray·er

be·troth
be·troth·al
be·trothed
bet·ta fish
bet·ter improved
bett·er one who bets
bet·ter·ment
betu·la·ceous botany term
be·tween
be·tween·times
be·twixt
Beu·lah biblical place
beva·tron synchrotron
bev·el (·el·ling, ·elled; US
·el·ing, ·eled)
bev·er·age
Bev·er·ly Hills Californian
city
bev·vy (plural ·vies)
Dialect alcoholic drink
bevy (plural bevies) flock
be·wail
be·wail·er
be·ware
be·wil·der
be·wil·der·ing·ly
be·wil·der·ment
be·witch
be·witch·ing·ly
bey Turkish title
Bey·og·lu district of
Istanbul
be·yond
bez·ant gold coin
bez·el face of tool or gem
be·zique card game
be·zoar hairball
Bha·gal·pur Indian city
Bha·ga·vad-Gita Hindu
text
bhang narcotic
Bha·rat Hindi India
Bha·ra·ti·ya Indian
Bhat·pa·ra Indian city
bha·van house
Bhav·na·gar Indian port
bhin·di vegetable
Bho·pal Indian port
Bhu·ba·nes·war Indian city
Bhu·tan Asian kingdom
Bhu·tan·ese
Bi·afra Nigerian region
Bia·ly·stok Polish city
bi·an·nual twice a year;
compare biennial

bi·an·nual·ly
bi·an·nu·late zoology term
Biar·ritz French town
bias (·as·ing, ·ased or
·as·sing, ·assed)
bi·ath·lon sport
bi·auricu·late (or ·lar)
bi·ax·ial
bib (bib·bing, bibbed)
bib·ber
bib·cock tap with nozzle
bi·belot trinket
Bi·ble
bib·li·cal
Bib·li·cist
bib·lio·graph·er (or
·graph)
bib·lio·graph·ic (or
·graphi·cal)
bib·li·og·ra·phy (plural
·phies)
bib·li·ola·try
bib·lio·man·cy
bib·lio·ma·nia
bib·lio·ma·ni·ac
bib·lio·phile (or ·phil)
bib·li·ophi·lis·tic
bib·li·oph·ism
bib·lio·pole (or
·li·opo·list) dealer in rare
books
bib·lio·the·ca (plural ·cas
or ·cae) library
bibu·lous
bi·cam·er·al
bi·cap·su·lar
bicarb
bi·car·bo·nate
bice blue colour
bi·cen·tenary (plural
·tenaries)
bi·cepha·lous two-headed
bi·ceps (plural ·ceps or
·cepses)
bi·chlo·ride
bi·cip·i·tal of the biceps
bick·er
bick·er·er
bi·col·lat·er·al
bi·col·our (or ·oured; US
·or or ·ored)
bi·con·cave
bi·con·cav·ity
bi·con·vex

bi·corn (*or* ·cor·nate,
·cor·nu·ate)
bi·cus·pid
bi·cus·pi·date
bi·cy·cle
bi·cy·clic (*or* ·cli·cal)
bi·cy·clist (*or* ·cler)
bid (bid·ding; bad, bade,
or bid; bid·den *or* bid)
bi·dar·ka (*or* ·kee) Eskimo
canoe
bid·dable
bid·der
bid·dy (*plural* ·dies)
bide (bid·ing, bid·ed *or*
bode, bid·ed)
bi·den·tate
bi·det
Bie·der·mei·er furniture
and art style
(biege) *incorrect spelling of*
beige
Biel Swiss town
bield *Dialect* refuge
Bie·lefeld West German
city
Bielskó-Biala Polish town
bi·en·nial every two years;
compare biannual
bi·en·nial·ly
bier coffin support; *compare*
byre
bier·kel·ler
bi·fa·cial
bi·fari·ous botany term
biff
bif·fin apple
bi·fid divided into two lobes
bi·fid·ity
bi·fi·lar having two parallel
threads
bi·flag·el·late biology term
bi·fo·cal
bi·fo·cals
bi·fo·li·ate having two
leaves
bi·fo·lio·late having two
leaflets
bi·fo·rate having two
openings
bi·form
Bif·rost Norse mythological
rainbow
bi·fur·cate forked
bi·fur·ca·tion
big (big·ger, big·gest)

biga·mist
biga·mous
biga·my (*plural* ·mies)
big·ar·reau cherry
bi·gen·er hybrid organism
bi·gener·ic
big·eye fish
big·ger
big·gest
big·gin close-fitting cap
big·gish
big·head
big·headed
big·headed·ness
big·horn (*plural* ·horns *or*
·horn)
bight bay; bend in rope;
compare bite; byte
big·mouth
big·no·nia shrub
big·no·nia·ceous
big·ot
big·ot·ed
big·ot·ry (*plural* ·ries)
bi·gua·nide biochemical
compound
big·wig
Bi·har Indian state
Bi·ha·ri
Bi·ja·pur Indian city
bi·jec·tion maths term
bi·jec·tive
bi·jou (*plural* ·joux)
bi·jou·terie jewellery
bi·ju·gate (*or* ·gous)
botany term
Bi·ka·ner Indian city
bike
bi·ki·ni
bi·la·bial
bi·la·bi·ate
bil·an·der cargo ship
bi·lat·er·al
bi·lat·er·al·ly
Bil·bao Spanish port
bil·berry (*plural* ·berries)
bil·boes ankle shackles
bile
bile·stone
bilge
bil·har·zia parasite
bil·har·zia·sis
bili·ary
bi·lin·ear
bi·lin·gual

bi·lin·gual·ism
bili·ous
bil·ious·ness
bili·ru·bin bile pigment
bili·ver·din bile pigment
bilk thwart
bilk·er
bill
bil·la·bong
bill·board
bil·let
billet-doux (*plural* billets-
doux) love letter
bill·fish (*plural* ·fish *or*
·fishes)
bill·fold
bill·hook
bil·liard
bill·ing
Bil·lings·gate
bil·lion (*plural* ·lions *or*
·lion)
bil·lion·aire
bil·lionth
bil·lon alloy
bil·low
bil·lowi·ness
bil·lowy
bill·poster
bil·ly (*plural* ·lies)
bil·ly·can
bill·yo slang term
bi·lo·bate (*or* ·lobed)
bi·locu·lar (*or* ·late)
Bim native of Barbados
bima·nous two-handed
bim·bo (*plural* ·bos *or*
·boes)
bi·mes·trial lasting two
months
bi·me·tal·lic
bi·met·al·lism economic
doctrine
bi·mo·lec·u·lar
bi·month·ly (*plural* ·lies)
bi·morph electronics term
bin (bin·ning, binned)
bi·nal twofold
bi·na·ry (*plural* ·ries)
bi·nate occurring in pairs
bin·aural
bind (bind·ing, bound)
bind·er
bind·ery (*plural* ·eries)
bindi-eye plant

bind·weed
bine botany term
binge
bin·gey Austral stomach
bin·gle Austral minor crash
bin·go
bin·na·cle
binned
bin·ning
bin·ocu·lar (adj)
bin·ocu·lars
bi·no·mial
bi·nomi·nal biology term
bint Slang girl
bin·tu·rong animal
bi·nu·cle·ar
bi·nu·cle·ate
bio·assay
bio·as·tro·nau·tics
bio·cata·lyst
bio·cata·lyt·ic
bi·oc·el·late biology term
bio·cenol·ogy branch of
  ecology
bio·chemi·cal
bio·chemi·cal·ly
bio·chem·ist
bio·chem·is·try
bio·cid·al
bio·cide
bio·cli·ma·tol·ogy
bio·cy·cle ecological region
bio·degrad·able
bio·deg·ra·da·tion
bio·dy·nam·ic (or
  ·nami·cal)
bio·dy·nam·ics
bio·en·er·get·ics
bio·en·gi·neer
bio·en·gi·neer·ing
bio·feed·back
bio·fla·vo·noid vitamin
bio·gen hypothetical protein
bio·gen·esis
bio·genet·ic (or
  bio·geneti·cal,
  biog·enous)
bio·geneti·cal·ly
bio·geo·graphi·cal
bio·geog·ra·phy
bi·og·ra·pher
bio·graphi·cal
bi·og·ra·phy (plural
  ·phies)
bio·herm organic rock

bio·logi·cal (or ·log·ic)
bio·logi·cal·ly
bi·olo·gist
bi·ol·ogy
bio·lu·mi·nes·cence
bio·lu·mi·nes·cent
bi·oly·sis
bio·lyt·ic
bio·mass ecology term
bi·ome ecology term
bio·met·ric
bio·met·ri·cal·ly
bi·om·etry (or
  bio·met·rics)
bi·on·ic
bi·on·ics
bio·nom·ic
bio·nomi·cal·ly
bio·nom·ics ecology
bi·ono·mist
bio·physi·cal
bio·physi·cist
bio·phys·ics
bio·plasm
bio·plas·mic
bio·poi·esis biology term
bi·op·sy (plural ·sies)
bi·op·tic
bio·rhythm
bio·scope
bi·os·co·py (plural ·pies)
bio·sphere ecology term
bio·stat·ic
bio·stati·cal·ly
bio·stat·ics
bio·strome fossil-rich rock
bio·syn·the·sis
bio·syn·thet·ic
bio·syn·theti·cal·ly
bio·ta biology term
bio·tech·no·logi·cal
bio·tech·nolo·gist
bio·tech·nol·ogy
bi·ot·ic
bio·tin vitamin
bio·tite mineral
bio·tit·ic
bio·tope ecological area
bio·type biology term
bio·typ·ic
bi·pa·ri·etal
bip·ar·ous
bi·par·ti·san (or ·zan)
bi·par·ti·san·ship (or
  ·zan·)

bi·par·tite
bi·par·ti·tion
bi·ped
bi·ped·al
bi·pet·al·ous
bi·phen·yl
bi·pin·nate botany term
bi·plane
bi·pod
bi·po·lar
bi·pro·pel·lant
bi·quad·rate maths term
bi·quad·rat·ic
bi·quar·ter·ly
bi·ra·cial
bi·ra·dial
bi·ra·mous divided into two
  parts
birch
bird
bird·bath
bird-brained
bird-cage
bird-house
birdie
bird-like
bird·lime
bird·man (plural ·men)
bird·seed
bird's-eye (adj)
bird's-foot (or bird-;
  plural -foots) plant
bird-watcher
bird-watching
bi·refrin·gence
bi·refrin·gent
bi·reme ship
bi·ret·ta (or ber·ret·ta)
  clerical cap
bi·ria·ni Indian food
Bir·ken·head
Bir·ming·ham
Biro (Trademark; plural
  Biros)
Bi·ro·bi·dzhan Soviet city
birr make whirring sound;
  compare bur; burr
birth
birth·day
birth·mark
birth·place
birth·right
birth·root plant
birth·stone
birth·wort plant

Bis·cay (Bay of)
bis·cuit
bise wind
bi·sect
bi·sec·tion
bi·sec·tor
bi·sec·trix (*plural* ·tri·ces)
  maths term
bi·ser·rate botany term
bi·sex·ual
bi·sexu·al·ism (*or* ·ity)
bish *Slang* mistake
bish·op
bishop·bird
bish·op·ric
Bis·kra Algerian town
Bis·marck US city
bis·muth
bis·muth·al
bis·mu·thic
bis·muth·in·ite mineral
bis·muth·ous
bi·son (*plural* ·son)
bisque colour; soup; sports
  term
Bis·sau (*or* ·sao) capital of
  Guinea-Bissau
bis·sex·tile of a leap year
bis·ter US spelling of bistre
bis·tort plant
bis·tou·ry (*plural* ·ries)
  surgical knife
bis·tre (*US* ·ter) drawing
  pigment
bis·tro (*plural* ·tros)
  restaurant
bi·sul·cate cleft
bi·sul·phate (*US* ·fate)
bi·sul·phide (*US* ·fide)
bi·sul·phite (*US* ·fite)
bi·sym·met·ric (*or* ·ri·cal)
bi·sym·met·ri·cal·ly
bi·sym·met·ry
bit
bi·tar·trate
bitch
bitchi·ly
bitchy (bitchi·er,
  bitchi·est)
bite (bit·ing, bit, bit·ten)
  grip with teeth; *compare*
  bight; byte
Bi·thynia ancient Asian
  country
bit·ing·ly

bit·ing·ness
bit·ser *Austral* mongrel dog
bit·stock
bitt mooring post
bit·ten
bit·ter
Bit·ter Lakes
bit·ter·ling fish
bit·tern bird
bit·ter·ness
bitter·nut
bit·ters drink
bitter·sweet
bitter·weed
bitter·wood
bit·ty (·ti·er, ·ti·est)
bi·tu·men
bi·tu·mi·ni·za·tion (*or*
  ·sa·tion)
bi·tu·mi·nize (*or* ·nise)
bi·tu·mi·nous
bi·va·len·cy
bi·va·lent
bi·valve
bi·val·vu·lar
bivou·ac (·ack·ing,
  ·acked)
biv·vy (*plural* ·vies) *Slang*
  tent
bi·week·ly (*plural* ·lies)
bi·year·ly
Biysk (*or* Biisk, Bisk)
  Soviet town
bi·zarre
Bi·zer·te (*or* ·ta) Tunisian
  port
blab (blab·bing, blabbed)
blab·ber
blabber·mouth
black
black·ball
black·berry (*plural*
  ·berries)
black·bird
black·board
black·buck antelope
Black·burn
black·butt tree
black·cap bird
black·cock male grouse
black·cur·rant
black·damp
black·en
black·fish (*plural* ·fish *or*
  ·fishes)

black·fly (*plural* ·flies)
Black·foot (*plural* ·feet *or*
  ·foot) American Indian
black·guard
black·guard·ism
black·guard·ly
black·head
black·heart plant disease
black-hearted
black·ing
black·ish
black·jack
black·leg (·leg·ging,
  ·legged)
black·list
black·mail
black·mail·er
black-market (*verb*)
black·ness
black·out
black·poll bird
Black·pool
Black·shirt fascist
black·smith
black·snake
black·tail deer
black·thorn
black·top *US* paving
  material
Black·wood bridge term
black·wood Australian tree
blad·der
blad·der ket·mia plant
bladder·nose seal
bladder·nut
bladder·wort
bladder·wrack
blade
blah silly talk
blain blister
blam·able (*or* blame·)
blame
blame·ful
blame·ful·ness
blame·less
blame·less·ness
blame·worthi·ness
blame·worthy
blanch make white; *compare*
  blench
blanc·mange
bland
blan·dish
blan·dish·ment
bland·ness

blank
blan·ket
blank·ly
Blan·tyre-Limbe
  Malawian city
blare
blar·ney
bla·sé indifferent
blas·pheme
blas·phem·er
blas·phe·mous
blas·phe·my (*plural*
  ·mies)
blast
blasted
blas·te·ma (*plural* ·mas or
  ·ma·ta) biology term
blas·tem·ic
blast·ing
blas·to·coel (*or* ·coele)
  embryology term
blas·to·cyst
blas·to·derm (*or* ·disc)
  embryology term
blas·to·derm·ic
blast·off
blas·to·gen·esis
blas·to·gen·ic (*or*
  ·genet·ic)
blas·to·mere embryology
  term
blas·to·mer·ic
blas·to·pore embryology
  term
blas·to·por·ic (*or* ·al)
blas·to·sphere
blas·tu·la (*plural* ·las or
  ·lae) embryology term
blas·tu·lar
blat *US* bleat
bla·tan·cy
bla·tant
blath·er (*or* bleth·)
blather·skite talkative
  person
blau·bok (*plural* ·bok or
  ·boks) antelope
Blay·don English town
blaze
blaz·er
bla·zon
bla·zon·ry (*plural* ·ries)
bleach
bleach·able
bleach·er

bleak
bleak·ness
blear
bleari·ness
bleary (bleari·er,
  bleari·est)
bleat
bleat·er
bleat·ing·ly
bleb blister
bleed (bleed·ing, bled)
bleed·er
bleep
blem·ish
blem·ish·er
blench shy away; *compare*
  blanch
blench·er
blench·ing·ly
blend combine
blende type of ore
blend·er
Blen·heim West German
  village
blen·ni·oid fish
blen·ny (*plural* ·nies)
blepha·ri·tic
blepha·ri·tis inflammation
  of eyelids
bles·bok (*or* ·buck; *plural*
  ·boks, ·bok or ·bucks,
  ·buck) antelope
bless (bless·ing, blessed
  or blest)
bless·ed (*adj*)
bless·ed·ness
blest
blet fruit decay
blew
blew·its edible fungus;
  compare bluet
Bli·da Algerian city
blight
blight·er
Blighty *Slang* England
bli·mey
blimp
blimp·ish
blind
blind·age military screen
blind·er
blind·fish (*plural* ·fish or
  ·fishes)
blind·fold
blind·ing

blind·ly
blind·ness
blind·storey (*or* ·story)
blind·worm
blini (*or* blin·is) pancake
blink
blink·er
blink·ers
blink·ing
blintz (*or* blintze) filled
  pancake
blip (blip·ping, blipped)
bliss
bliss·ful
bliss·ful·ly
bliss·ful·ness
blis·ter
blis·ter·ing·ly
blithe
blithe·ness
blith·er·ing
blithe·some
blitz
blitz·krieg
bliz·zard
bloat
bloated
bloat·er
blob (blob·bing, blobbed)
bloc group of nations
block
block·ade
block·ad·er
block·age
block·board
block·bust·er
block·bust·ing
block·er
block·head
block·house
Bloem·fon·tein South
  African city
bloke
blond (*fem* blonde)
blond·ness (*fem*
  blonde·ness)
blood
blood·curdling
blood·ed
blood·fin
blood·hound
bloodi·ly
bloodi·ness
blood·less
blood·letting

blood·root
blood·shed
blood·shot
blood·stain
blood·stained
blood·stock
blood·stone
blood·sucker
blood·thirsti·ly
blood·thirsti·ness
blood·thirsty (·thirsti·er,
·thirsti·est)
blood·worm
bloody (adj bloodi·er,
bloodi·est; verb
blood·ies, bloody·ing,
blood·ied)
bloody-minded
bloom
bloom·er
bloom·ers
bloom·ery (plural ·eries)
ironworks
bloom·ing
Blooms·bury
bloop·er US blunder
blos·som
blot (blot·ting, blot·ted)
blotch
blotchi·ly
blotchi·ness
blotchy (blotchi·er,
blotchi·est)
blot·ter
blot·to Slang drunkenly
unconscious
blouse
blou·son
blow (blow·ing, blew,
blown)
blow-dry (-dries, -dry·ing,
-dried)
blow·er
blow·fish (plural ·fish or
·fishes)
blow·fly (plural ·flies)
blow·hard boastful person
blow·hole
blow·lamp
blown
blow·out (noun)
blow·pipe
blow·torch
blow-wave

blowy (blowi·er,
blowi·est)
blowzi·ly (or blowsi·)
blowzi·ness (or
blowsi·ness)
blowzy (or blowsy;
blowzi·er, blowzi·ier or
blowsi·er, blowsi·est)
blub (blub·bing, blubbed)
blub·ber
blub·bery
bludge Austral scrounge
bludg·eon
bludg·eon·er
blue (adj blu·er, blu·est;
verb blue·ing or
blu·ing, blued)
Blue·beard
blue·bell
blue·berry (plural
·berries)
blue·bill
blue·bird
blue-blooded
blue·bonnet Scottish hat
blue·book government
publication
blue·bottle
blue·fish (plural ·fish or
·fishes)
blue·gill fish
blue·grass
blue·ing (or blu·ing)
blue·jacket
blue·ness
blue·nose US puritanical
person
blue·print
blues
blue·stocking
blue·stone
bluet plant; compare blewits
blue·throat bird
blue·tit
blue·tongue lizard
blu·ey Austral blanket
bluff
bluff·er
bluff·ness
blu·ing variant spelling of
blueing
blu·ish (or blue·ish)
blun·der
blun·der·buss
blun·der·er

blun·der·ing·ly
blunge ceramics term
blung·er
blunt
blunt·ness
blur (blur·ring, blurred)
blurb
blur·red·ly
blur·red·ness
blur·ry
blurt
blush
blush·er
blush·ing·ly
blus·ter
blus·ter·er
blus·ter·ing·ly (or ·ous·ly)
blus·tery (or ·ter·ous)
Blyth English port
B'nai B'rith Jewish society
boa
boar male pig; compare
boor; bore
board
board·er
board·ing
board·room
board·walk US wooden
promenade
boar·fish (plural ·fish or
·fishes)
boar·hound
boar·ish coarse; sensual;
compare boorish
boar·ish·ness
boast
boast·er
boast·ful
boast·ful·ly
boast·ful·ness
boast·ing·ly
boat
boat·el waterside hotel
boat·er
boat·hook
boat·house
boat·ing
boat·load
boat·man (plural ·men)
boat·swain (or bo·sun)
bob (bob·bing, bobbed)
bob·bery (plural ·beries)
pack of dogs
bob·bin
bob·bi·net fabric

bob·ble
bob·by (*plural* ·bies)
bob·cat
bob·float fishing float
bob·let bobsleigh
bobo·link bird
bo·bo·tie curried dish
bob·owler *Dialect* moth
bob·sleigh (*or esp. US* ·sled)
bob·stay
bob·tail
bob·white bird
bo·cage wooded country
boc·cia bowls game
Boche *Slang* German
Bo·chum West German city
bock beer
bod *Slang* person
bode
bo·dega wine shop
bodge
bodg·er
bodgie *Austral* unruly man
Bo·dhi·satt·va Buddhist divine
bod·ice
bodi·less
bodi·ly
bod·kin
Bod·lei·an Oxford library
Bod·min
Bo·do·ni style of type
body (*noun, plural* bodies; *verb* bodies, body·ing, bod·ied)
body-centred
body-check
body-guard
body-snatcher
body-work
boehm·ite mineral
Boeo·tia region of ancient Greece
Boeo·tian
Boer Dutch South African
boeuf Bour·gui·gnon beef casserole
bof·fin
bog (bog·ging, bogged)
bo·gan *Canadian* side stream
bo·gey golf term; *compare* bogie

bo·gey (*or* bogy; *plural* ·geys *or* bogies) evil spirit; *compare* bogie
bogey·man (*plural* ·men)
bog·gart *Dialect* poltergeist
bog·gi·ness
bog·gle
bog·gy (·gi·er, ·gi·est)
bo·gie wheeled undercarriage; *compare* bogey
bo·gle *Dialect* bogey
Bog·nor Re·gis
bo·gong moth
Bo·gor Indonesian city
Bo·go·tá Colombian capital
bo·gus
bog·wood
bogy *variant spelling of* bogey
bo·hea China tea
Bo·he·mia
Bo·he·mian
Bo·hol Philippine island
boil
boil·able
boil·er
boiler·maker
boiler·plate
boiler·suit
boil·ing·ly
Bois de Bou·logne Parisian park
Boi·se US city
bois·ter·ous
bois·ter·ous·ness
bok·ma·kie·rie bird
bola weapon
Bo·land South African region
bold
bold·face (*adj*)
bold·ness
bole tree trunk; *compare* bowl
bo·lec·tion architectural term
bo·lero (*plural* ·ros)
bo·letus (*plural* ·letuses *or* ·leti) fungus
bo·lide meteor
boli·var (*plural* ·vars *or* ·vares) Venezuelan currency
Bo·livia

Bo·liv·ian
boll
bol·lard
bol·locks (*or* bal·locks)
boll·worm
bolo (*plural* bolos) knife
Bo·lo·gna Italian city
Bo·lo·gnese
bo·lom·eter
bo·lo·met·ric
bo·lo·met·ri·cal·ly
bo·lo·ney *variant spelling of* baloney
Bol·she·vik (*plural* ·viks *or* ·vi·ki)
Bol·she·vism
Bol·she·vist
Bol·shie (*or* ·shy)
bol·son US desert valley
bol·ster
bol·ster·er
bol·ster·ing·ly
bolt
bolt·er
Bol·ton
bol·to·nia plant
bolt·rope rope on a sail
bo·lus (*plural* ·luses) chewed food
Bol·za·no Italian city
bomb
bom·ba·ca·ceous botany term
bom·bard
bom·bar·dier
bom·bard·ment
bom·bar·don musical instrument
bom·bast
bom·bas·tic
bom·bas·ti·cal·ly
Bom·bay
bom·ba·zine
bom·be dessert
bom·bé furniture style
bomb·er
bom·bora submerged reef
bomb·shell
bomb·sight bomb-aiming device
bomb site bomb-destroyed area
bom·by·cid moth
bona fide genuine
bona fides good faith

Bon·aire West Indian island
bo·nan·za
Bo·na·part·ism
bona va·can·tia unclaimed
 goods
bon·bon
bonce *Slang* head
bond
bond·age
bond·ed
bond·holder
bond·maid
bond·servant
bonds·man (*plural* **·men**)
bone
bone·black
bone·fish (*plural* **·fish** *or*
 ·fishes)
bone·head
bone·less
bon·er *Slang* blunder
bone·set plant
bone·set·ter
bone·shaker
bone·yard
bon·fire
bong
bon·go (*plural* **·gos** *or*
 ·goes) drum
bon·go (*plural* **·go** *or*
 ·gos) antelope
bon·ho·mie
boni·ness
bon·ism
bo·ni·to (*plural* **·tos** *or*
 ·toes) fish
bonk·ers
bon mot (*plural* **bons**
 mots) fitting remark
Bonn West German capital
bon·net
bon·ny (**·ni·er**, **·ni·est**)
bon·sai (*plural* **·sai**)
bon·sela African gift
bon·spiel curling match
bon·te·bok (*plural* **·boks**
 or **·bok**) antelope
bo·nus
bony (**boni·er**, **boni·est**)
bonze Buddhist priest
boo (**boo·ing**, **booed**)
boob
boo·bi·al·la shrub
boo·book owl
boo·by (*plural* **·bies**)

booby-trap (*verb*;
 ·trap·ping, **·trapped**)
boo·dle
booed
boo·gie
boogie-woogie
boo·hoo (**·hoo·ing**,
 ·hooed)
boo·ing
book
book·binder
book·bindery (*plural*
 ·binderies)
book·bind·ing
book·case
bookie
book·ing
book·ish
book·ish·ness
book·keeper
book·keeping
book·learning
book·let
book·louse insect
book·maker
book·making
book·mark (*or* **·marker**)
book·plate
book·rack
book·sell·er
book·shelf (*plural*
 ·shelves)
book·shop
book·stall
book·stand
book·worm
Bool·ean type of algebra
boom
boom·er
boom·er·ang
boom·slang snake
boon
boon·docks *US* wild
 country
boon·dog·gle *US* do futile
 work
boor unpleasant person;
 compare **boar; bore**
boor·ish ill-mannered;
 insensitive; *compare*
 boarish
boor·ish·ness
boost
boost·er
boot

boot·black
boot·ed
bootee
Boö·tes constellation
booth
boot·lace
Boo·tle
boot·leg (**·leg·ging**,
 ·legged)
boot·leg·ger
boot·less
boot·lick
boot·lick·er
boot·loader
boot·strap
boo·ty (*plural* **·ties**)
booze
booz·er
boozi·ness
boozy (**boozi·er**,
 boozi·est)
bop (**bop·ping**, **bopped**)
bora north wind
Bora Bora Pacific island
bo·ra·cic
bo·ra·cite mineral
bor·age plant
bo·ra·gi·na·ceous
bo·rak *Austral* nonsense
bo·rane chemical compound
bo·rate
bo·rax (*plural* **·raxes** *or*
 ·ra·ces)
bo·ra·zon chemical
 compound
bor·bo·ryg·mus (*plural*
 ·mi) stomach rumbling
Bor·deaux French port;
 wine
Bor·delaise sauce
bor·del·lo (*plural* **·los**)
bor·der
bor·dereau (*plural*
 ·dereaux) insurance
 invoice
bor·der·er
border·land
border·line
Bor·ders Scottish region
bor·dure heraldry term
bore dull person; drill hole;
 compare **boar; boor**
bo·real of the north
Boreas Greek god
bore·dom

boree tree
bor·er
bo·ric
bo·ride chemical compound
bor·ing
born given birth to
borne carried
Bor·neo Malaysian island
bor·neol chemical compound
born·ite mineral
Bor·nu Nigerian state
Bo·ro·di·no battle site
bo·ron chemical element
bo·ro·nia shrub
bo·ro·sili·cate
bor·ough
bor·row
bor·row·er
bor·stal
bort (*or* **boart, bortz**) inferior diamond
bor·zoi (*plural* **·zois**)
bos·cage (*or* **·kage**) thicket
bosch·vark wild pig
bosh
bosk small wood
bos·ket (*or* **·quet**) thicket
Bos·kop prehistoric African race
bosky (**boski·er, boski·est**)
Bos·nia Yugoslav region
Bos·nian
bos·om
bos·omy
bos·on physics term
Bos·po·rus (*or* **Bos·pho·rus**) Turkish strait
boss
bos·sa nova dance
bossi·ly
bossi·ness
bossy (**bossi·er, bossi·est**)
Bos·ton
bo·sun *variant spelling of* boatswain
Bos·worth battle site
bot (*or* **bott**) botfly larva
bo·tani·cal (*or* **·tan·ic**)
bota·nist
bota·nize (*or* **·nise**)
bota·ny (*plural* **·nies**)

bo·tar·go (*plural* **·goes**) fish roe
botch
botch·er
botchi·ly
botchiness
botchy (**botchi·er, botchi·est**)
bot·fly (*plural* **·flies**)
both
both·er
both·era·tion
both·er·some
bothy (*plural* **bothies**) *Scot* small shelter
bot·ryoi·dal (*or* **·ry·ose**)
bots horse disease
Bot·swa·na
bot·tle
bottle·brush shrub
bottle·neck
bottle·nose dolphin
bot·tom
bot·tom·less
bottom·most
bot·tom·ry (*plural* **·ries**) legal term
Bot·trop West German city
botu·lin toxin
botu·li·nus (*plural* **·nuses**) bacterium
botu·lism
Boua·ke Ivory Coast town
bou·chée vol-au-vent
Bouches-du-Rhone French department
bou·clé knobbly yarn
bou·clée support for billiard cue
bou·doir
bouf·fant
Bou·gain·ville Pacific island
bou·gain·vil·lea (*or* **·laea**) plant
bough
bought
bought·en *Dialect* bought
bou·gie catheter
bouil·la·baisse fish soup
bouil·lon broth
boul·der
boule gem; *compare* boulle
boule·vard

boule·var·di·er fashionable man
boule·verse·ment *French* upheaval
boulle (*or* **boule, buhl**) marquetry; *compare* boule
Bou·logne
bounce
bounc·er
bounci·ly
bounci·ness
bounc·ing
bouncy (**bounci·er, bounci·est**)
bound
bounda·ry (*plural* **·ries**)
bound·en
bound·er
bound·less
bound·less·ness
bounds
boun·te·ous
boun·te·ous·ness
boun·ti·ful
boun·ti·ful·ness
boun·ty (*plural* **·ties**)
bou·quet
bou·quet gar·ni (*plural* **bou·quets gar·nis**)
bour·bon US whiskey
bour·don organ stop
bourg French market town
bour·geois (*fem* **·geoise**)
bour·geoi·sie
bourn stream
bourne (*or* **bourn**) destination; boundary
Bourne·mouth
bour·rée dance
Bourse French stock exchange
bouse (*or* **bowse**) nautical term
bou·stro·phedon alternately ordered word lines
bout
bou·tique
bou·ton·ni·ere buttonhole flower
bou·zouki
bo·vid
bo·vine
Bov·ril (*Trademark*)
bov·ver *Slang* rowdiness

bow
bowd·ler·ism
bowd·leri·za·tion (*or* ·sa·tion)
bowd·ler·ize (*or* ·ise)
bow·el
bow·er
bower·bird
Bow·ery New York street and area
bow·fin fish
bow·head whale
bow·ing
bow·knot
bowl basin; wooden ball; *compare* bole
bow-legged
bowl·er
bowl·ful
bow·line
bowl·ing
bowls
bow·man (*plural* ·men)
bow·saw
bowse *variant spelling of* bouse
bow·ser fuel tanker
bow·shot
bow·sprit
bow·string
bow-wow
bow·yer maker of archery bows
box
box·berry (*plural* ·berries)
box·board
box·car US closed railway van
box·er
box·ing
box·room
box·wood
boy
boy·ar
boy·cott
boy·friend
boy·hood
boy·ish
boy·ish·ness
boy·la Aboriginal witch doctor
Boyne Irish river
boysen·berry (*plural* ·berries)

bra
Bra·bant Belgian province
brace
brace·let
brac·er
bra·chial of the arm
bra·chi·ate
bra·chia·tion
bra·chio·pod marine invertebrate
bra·chio·saur·us
bra·chium (*plural* ·chia) armlike part
brachy·cephal·ic (*or* ·cepha·lous) broad-headed
brachy·cepha·ly (*or* ·lism)
brachy·dac·tylia (*or* ·tyl·ism)
brachy·dac·tyl·ic
bra·chylo·gous
bra·chyl·ogy (*plural* ·ogies) concise style
bra·chyp·ter·ous short-winged
brachy·ur·an crustacean
brac·ing
brac·ing·ly
brack·en
brack·et
brack·ish
brack·ish·ness
Brack·nell Berkshire town
bract
bract·eal
brac·te·ate
brac·teo·late
brac·te·ole
brad small nail
brad·awl
Brad·ford
Bradshaw railway timetable
brady·car·dia abnormally slow heartbeat
brady·car·di·ac
brady·kin·in blood protein
brae *Scot* hill
brag (brag·ging, bragged)
Bra·ga Portuguese city
brag·ga·do·cio (*plural* ·cios) boasting
brag·gart
brag·ger
brag·ging·ly
Brah·ma Hindu god

Brah·man (*or* ·min; *plural* ·mans, ·min, *or* ·mins) Hindu caste
Brah·ma·na Hindu treatise
Brah·ma·ni (*plural* ·nis) woman Brahman
Brah·man·ic (*or* ·min·ic)
Brah·man·ism (*or* ·min·ism)
Brah·ma·pu·tra Asian river
Brah·min *variant spelling of* Brahman
Bra·hui Pakistani language
braid
braid·ed
braid·er
braid·ing
brail nautical term
Braille writing for blind
brain
brain·child (*plural* ·children)
braini·ness
brain·less
brain·less·ness
brain·pan
brain·sick
brain·stem
brain·storm
brain·storm·er
brain·storm·ing
brain·wash
brain·wash·er
brain·wash·ing
brainy (braini·er, braini·est)
braise cook; *compare* braze
brake
brakes·man (*plural* ·men)
bram·ble
bram·bling bird
Bram·ley apple
bran
branch
bran·chia (*plural* ·chiae) animal's gill
bran·chial
bran·chi·ate
branch·ing
bran·chio·pod crustacean
brand
Bran·den·burg East German city
bran·dish
bran·dish·er

brand·ling earthworm
brand-new
bran·dy (*plural* ·dies)
bran·le dance
brash
brashi·ness state of being
   brashy
brash·ly
brash·ness
brashy (brashi·er,
   brashi·est) fragmented
Bra·sília Brazilian capital
Bra·şou Romanian city
brass
bras·sard (*or* ·sart)
   armband
brass·bound
bras·se·rie
bras·si·ca vegetable
bras·si·ca·ceous
brassie (*or* brassy; *plural*
   brassies) golf club
bras·siere
brassi·ly
brassi·ness
brassy (brassi·er,
   brassi·est)
brat
Bra·ti·sla·va Czech city
brat·tice mining term
brat·tish·ing architectural
   term
brat·wurst sausage
braun·ite mineral
bra·va·do (*plural* ·does *or*
   ·dos)
brave
brave·ness
brav·ery (*plural* ·eries)
bra·vo (*plural* ·voes *or*
   ·vos)
bra·vu·ra
braw *Scot* excellent
brawl
brawl·er
brawn
brawni·ly
brawni·ness
brawny (brawni·er,
   brawni·est)
braxy sheep disease
bray
bray·er
braze solder metal; *compare*
   braise

bra·zen
bra·zen·ness
braz·er one who brazes
bra·zi·er brass worker;
   charcoal-burning pot
Bra·zil
bra·zil·ein (*or* ·sil·ein) red
   dye
Bra·zil·ian
brazi·lin (*or* brasi·lin)
   yellow dye
Braz·za·ville Congolese
   capital
breach break; gap; *compare*
   breech
bread
bread·board
bread-crumb
bread·fruit (*plural* ·fruits
   or ·fruit)
bread·line
bread·nut
bread·root plant
breadth
bread·winner
break (break·ing, broke,
   brok·en)
break·able
break·age
break·away
break·down
break·er
break·fast
break·front
break-in (*noun*)
break·neck
break-out (*noun*)
break·point
break·through (*noun*)
break-up (*noun*)
break·water
bream (*plural* bream)
breast
breast·bone
breast-feed (-feed·ing,
   -fed)
breast·pin
breast·plate
breast·stroke
breast·work fortification
breath
breatha·lyse
Breatha·lyz·er (*or* ·lys·er)
   (*Trademark*)
breathe

breath·er
breathi·ly
breathi·ness
breath·ing
breath·less
breath·less·ness
breath·taking
breathy (breathi·er,
   breathi·est)
brec·cia rock
brec·ci·at·ed
Brec·on (*or* Breck·nock)
   Welsh town
Brec·on·shire (*or*
   Breck·nock·shire)
   former Welsh county
bred
Bre·da Dutch city
bree *Scot* thin soup
breech part of gun;
   buttocks (*note* breech
   birth); *compare* breach
breech·block
breech·clout loincloth
breeches
breech·ing harness strap
breech·loader
breech-loading
breed (breed·ing, bred)
breed·er
breeze
breezi·ly
breezi·ness
breezy (breezi·er,
   breezi·est)
breg·ma (*plural* ·ma·ta)
   part of skull
Bre·men West German city
Brem·er·ha·ven West
   German port
brems·strah·lung physics
   term
Bren gun
Bren·ner Pass
Brent London borough
brent (*plural* brents *or*
   brent) goose
br'er *US dialect* brother
Bre·scia Italian city
Brest French port
breth·ren
Bret·on of Brittany
breve accent; musical note
bre·vet (·vet·ting, ·vet·ted
   or ·vet·ing, ·vet·ed)
   military term

brev·et·cy
brevia·ry (*plural* ·ries)
bre·vier size of type
brevi·ros·trate ornithology
   term
brev·ity (*plural* ·ities)
brew
brew·age
brew·er
brew·ery (*plural* ·eries)
brew·ing
brew·is *Dialect* gravy-soaked
   bread
bri·ar (*or* ·er) tobacco pipe;
   variant spelling of brier
Briareus Greek giant
briar·root (*or* brier·)
brib·able (*or* bribe·able)
bribe
brib·er
brib·ery (*plural* ·eries)
bric-a-brac
brick
brick·bat
brickie *Slang* bricklayer
brick·layer
brick·laying
brick·le *Dialect* brittle
brick·work
brick·yard
bri·cole billiards term
brid·al
bride
bride·groom
brides·maid
bride·well jail
bridge
bridge·able
bridge·board
bridge·head
Bridge·port US port
bridge·work
bridg·ing
Bridg·wa·ter Somerset town
bri·die *Scot* meat pie
bri·dle
bri·dler
bri·doon horse's bit
Brie cheese
brief
brief·case
brief·ing
brief·ly
bri·er (*or* ·ar) thorny shrub;
   compare briar

bri·ery (*or* ·ary)
brig
bri·gade
briga·dier
briga·low tree
brig·and
brig·an·dine armour
brig·an·tine ship
bright
bright·en
bright·en·er
bright·ness
Bright·on
brights US headlights
bright·work metal car
   trimmings
brill (*plural* brill *or* brills)
bril·liance (*or* ·lian·cy)
bril·liant
bril·lian·tine
brim (brim·ming,
   brimmed)
brim·ful (*or* ·full)
brim·mer
brim·stone
brin·dle
brin·dled
brine
bring (bring·ing, brought)
brini·ness
brink
brink·man·ship
brin·ny (*plural* ·nies)
   Austral a stone
briny (brini·er, brini·est)
bri·oche
brio·lette jewel
bri·quette
bri·sance power of
   explosion
Bris·bane
brise-soleil window
   protection
brisk
bris·ket
bris·ling fish
bris·tle
bristle-grass
bristle·tail insect
bris·tly
Bris·tol
bris·tols *Slang* breasts
Brit *Slang* Briton
brit young herring
Brit·ain

Bri·tan·nia
Bri·tan·nic
Briti·cism
Brit·ish
Brit·ish·er
Brit·ish·ism
Brit·on
Brit·ta·ny
brit·tle
brit·tle·ness
brittle·star starfish
Brno Czech city
broach raise topic; tap
   container; *compare* brooch
broach·er
broad
broad·bill bird
broad·brim hat
broad·cast (cast·ing, ·cast
   or ·cast·ed)
broad·cast·er
broad·cloth
broad·en
broad·leaf (*plural* ·leaves)
   tobacco plant
broad-leaved denoting
   nonconiferous trees
broad·loom
broad·ly
broad-minded
broad-minded·ness
Broad·moor
Broads East Anglian lakes
broad·sheet
broad·side
broad·sword
broad·tail Persian lamb
Broad·way
Brob·ding·nag
bro·cade
broca·telle brocade
broc·co·li
broch Scottish tower
bro·ché woven with raised
   design
bro·chette skewer
bro·chure
brock badger
brock·et deer
brod·dle *Dialect* poke
bro·de·rie an·glaise
Broeder·bond South
   African society
bro·gan boot
brogue

broil
broil·er
broke
bro·ken
broken-down
broken-hearted
bro·ker
bro·ker·age
brol·ga bird
brol·ly (plural ·lies)
bro·mal sedative
bro·mate
brome grass
bro·melia·ceous
bro·meli·ad botany term
brom·eo·sin dye
bro·mic
bro·mide
bro·mid·ic dull
bro·min·ate chemistry term
bro·mina·tion
bro·mine chemical element
bro·mism (or
 bro·min·ism) bromine
 poisoning
bro·mo·form chemical
 compound
Broms·grove English town
bron·chi plural of bronchus
bron·chia bronchial tubes
bron·chial
bron·chi·ec·ta·sis bronchial
 disease
bron·chio·lar
bron·chi·ole
bron·chit·ic
bron·chi·tis
bron·cho·pneu·mo·nia
bron·cho·scope
bron·cho·scop·ic
bron·chos·co·pist
bron·chos·co·py
bron·chus (plural ·chi)
bron·co (or ·cho; plural
 ·cos or ·chos) wild pony
bronco·buster
bron·to·sau·rus (or
 ·to·saur)
Bronx New York borough
bronze
bronzy
brooch piece of jewellery;
 compare broach
brood
brood·er

broodi·ness
broody (broodi·er,
 broodi·est)
brook
brook·able
brook·ite mineral
brook·let
brook·lime trailing plant
Brook·lyn New York
 borough
brook·weed
broom
broom·corn sorghum
broom·rape plant
broom·stick
brose Scot porridge
broth
broth·el
broth·er
brother·hood
brother-in-law (plural
 brothers-)
broth·er·li·ness
broth·er·ly
brough·am carriage
brought
brou·ha·ha
brow
brow·band part of bridle
brow·beat (·beat·ing,
 ·beat, ·beat·en)
brown
browned-off
Brownie junior Guide
brownie chocolate cake
brown·ing
brown·ish
brown·out US power
 reduction
browse
brows·er
bru·cel·lo·sis
bruc·ine alkaloid
Bruges Belgian city
bru·in
bruise
bruised
bruis·er
bruis·ing
bruit Archaic report
bru·mal wintry
brume mist
Brum·ma·gem Slang
 Birmingham

Brum·mie Slang
 Birmingham native
brum·ous
brunch
Bru·nei Malaysian state
bru·nette
Brunhild (or Brünnhilde)
 legendary queen
Bruns·wick West German
 city
brunt
brush
brush·er
brush·off (noun)
brush-up (noun)
brush·wood
brush·work
brusque
brusque·ness
Brus·sels
brut denoting dry
 champagne
bru·tal
bru·tal·ity (plural ·ities)
bru·tali·za·tion (or
 ·sa·tion)
bru·tal·ize (or ·ise)
bru·tal·ly
brute
bru·ti·fy (·fies, ·fy·ing,
 ·fied) brutalize
brut·ish
brut·ish·ness
Bry·ansk Soviet city
bryo·logi·cal
bry·olo·gist
bry·ol·ogy study of mosses
bryo·ny (or brio·; plural
 ·nies)
bryo·phyte botany term
bryo·phyt·ic
bryo·zoan invertebrate
 animal
Bry·thon·ic language group
bu·bal (or bu·ba·lis)
 antelope
bu·ba·line
bub·ble
bub·bler
bub·bly (·bli·er, ·bli·est)
bubo (plural buboes)
 swelling
bu·bon·ic
bu·bono·cele medical term

Bu·ca·ra·man·ga
 Colombian city
buc·cal of the cheek
buc·ca·neer
buc·ci·na·tor muscle
bu·cen·taur Venetian barge
Bu·cha·rest Romanian
 capital
Buch·en·wald
 concentration camp
bu·chu shrub
buck
bucka·roo US cowboy
buck·bean
buck·board carriage
buck·et
buck·et·ful (*plural* **·fuls**)
buck·eye tree
buck·horn
buck·hound
Buck·ing·ham
Buck·ing·ham·shire
buck·jump·er *Austral*
 untamed horse
buck·le
buckler-fern
buck·ling bloater
bucko *Irish* young fellow
buck·ram (**ram·ing,**
 ·ramed)
buck·saw
buck·shee
buck·shot
buck·skin
buck·thorn
buck·tooth (*plural* **·teeth**)
buck·wheat
bu·col·ic
bu·coli·cal·ly
bud (**bud·ding, bud·ded**)
Bu·da·pest Hungarian
 capital
Bud·dhism
Bud·dhist
bud·ding
bud·dle trough
bud·dleia
bud·dy (*plural* **·dies**)
budge
budg·eri·gar
budg·et
budgie
Bue·na·ven·tu·ra
 Colombian port
Bue·nos Aires

buff
Buf·fa·lo port in New York
 State
buf·fa·lo (*plural* **·loes,**
 ·los, *or* **·lo**)
buff·er
buf·fet restaurant; sideboard
buf·fet (**·fet·ing, ·fet·ed**) to
 batter; a blow
buf·fet·er
buffle·head duck
buf·foon
buf·foon·ery
bug (**bug·ging, bugged**)
buga·boo source of fear
Bu·gan·da Ugandan state
bug·bane plant
bug·bear
bugged
bug·ger
bug·gery
bug·ging
bug·gy (*noun, plural*
 ·gies; *adj* **·gi·er, ·gi·est**)
bu·gle
bu·gler
bugle·weed
bu·gloss
buhl *variant spelling of* boulle
buhr·stone (*or* **bur·** *or*
 burr·)
build (**build·ing, built**)
build·er
build·ing
build-up (*noun*)
built
built-in
built-up
(buisness) *incorrect spelling*
 of business
Bu·jum·bu·ra capital of
 Burundi
Bu·kha·ra (*or* **Bo·**) Soviet
 city
Bu·ko·vi·na (*or* **·co·**) E
 European region
Bu·la·wa·yo Zimbabwean
 city
bul·ba·ceous
bulb·ar
bulb·if·er·ous
bul·bil (*or* **·bel**) small bulb
bulb·ous
bul·bul bird
Bul·garia

Bul·gar·ian
bulge
bulgi·ness
bulg·ing·ly
bulgy
bu·limia insatiable hunger
bulk
bulk·head
bulki·ly
bulki·ness
bulky (**bulki·er, bulki·est**)
bull
bul·la (*plural* **·lae**) seal on
 papal bull; blister
bul·lace damson
bul·late blistered
bull·bat bird
bull·dog
bull·doze
bull·doz·er
bul·let
bul·letin
bullet·proof
bull·fight
bull·fighter
bull·fighting
bull·finch
bull·frog
bull·head fish
bul·lion
bull·ish
bull-necked
bull·ock
bull·pen
bull·ring
bull's-eye
bull·shit
bull·whip
bul·ly (*noun, plural* **·lies;**
 verb **·lies, ·ly·ing, ·lied**)
bully·rag (**·rag·ging,**
 ·ragged)
bul·rush
bul·wark
bum (**bum·ming,**
 bummed)
bum·bailiff
bum·ble
bumble-bee
bum·bler
bum·boat
bum·ma·lo (*plural* **·lo**)
 Bombay duck
bum·mer
bump

bump·er

bumph (*or* bumf) *Slang* documents

bumpi·ly

bumpi·ness

bump·kin

bump·tious

bump·tious·ness

bumpy (bumpi·er, bumpi·est)

bun

Buna (*Trademark*) rubber

bunch

bunchi·ness

bunchy (bunchi·er, bunchi·est)

bun·combe *US variant spelling of* bunkum

Bund (*plural* Bunds *or* Bün·de) federation

bund embankment

Bun·da·berg Australian city

Bun·del·khand Indian region

Bun·des·rat West German federal council

Bun·des·tag West German legislative assembly

bundh Indian strike

bun·dle

bun·dler

bun·du *S African* wild region

bung

bun·ga·low

bung·hole

bun·gle

bun·gler

bun·gling

bun·ion

bunk

bun·ker

bun·kum (*US also* ·combe)

bun·ny (*plural* ·nies)

bun·raku Japanese puppet theatre

Bun·sen burn·er

bunt

bunt·al straw

bunt·ing

bunt·line

bunya-bunya tree

bun·yip Australian monster

buoy

buoy·age

buoy·an·cy

buoy·ant

bu·pres·tid beetle

bur (bur·ring, burred) seed vessel; *compare* birr; burr

bu·ran blizzard

Bu·ray·dah (*or* ·rai·da) Saudi Arabian town

Bur·ber·ry (*Trademark*; *plural* ·ries)

bur·ble

bur·bler

bur·bot (*plural* ·bots *or* ·bot) fish

bur·den

bur·den·some

bur·dock

bu·reau (*plural* ·reaus *or* ·reaux)

bu·reau·cra·cy (*plural* ·cies)

bu·reau·crat

bu·reau·crat·ic

bu·reau·crati·cal·ly

bu·reau·crat·ism

bu·reau·cra·tize (*or* ·tise)

bu·rette (*or esp. US* ·ret)

burg fortified town; *compare* berg; burgh

Bur·gas Bulgarian port

bur·gee ship's flag

Bur·gen·land Austrian province

bur·geon (*or* bour·geon)

burg·er hamburger

burg·ess citizen of borough

burgh Scottish town; *compare* berg; burg

burgh·al

burgh·er citizen

bur·glar

bur·glar·ize *US* burgle

bur·gla·ry (*plural* ·ries)

bur·gle

bur·go·mas·ter

bur·go·net helmet

bur·grave German governor

Bur·gun·dian

Bur·gun·dy

bur·ial

buri·er

bu·rin chisel

burk (*or* berk) *Slang* fool

bur·ka Muslim garment

burke suffocate

Bur·kina Faso African country

burl small lump

bur·lap fabric

burl·er

bur·lesque (*or* ·lesk; ·lesqu·ing, ·lesqued *or* ·lesk·ing, ·lesked)

bur·les·quer (*or* ·lesk·er)

bur·ley tobacco

bur·li·ness

Bur·ling·ton Canadian and US cities

bur·ly (·li·er, ·li·est)

Bur·ma

Bur·mese

burn (burn·ing, burnt *or* burned)

burn·er

bur·net plant

burn·ing

burn·ing·ly

bur·nish

burn·ish·able

burn·ish·er

Burn·ley Lancashire town

bur·noose (*or* bur·nous *or* bur·nouse) Arab hood

burn·sides *US* side-whiskers

burnt

bu·roo *Dialect* dole

burp

burr rough edge; small drill; dialect characteristic; *compare* birr; bur

bur·ra·wang plant

burred

bur·ring

bur·ro (*plural* ·ros) donkey

bur·row

bur·row·er

bur·ry (·ri·er, ·ri·est) prickly

Bur·sa Turkish city

bur·sa (*plural* ·sae *or* ·sas) medical term; *compare* bursar

bur·sal

bur·sar financial official; *compare* bursa

bur·sar·ial

bur·sa·ry (*plural* ·ries)

burse *Scot* student allowance

bur·ser·aceous botany term
bur·si·form
bur·si·tis
burst (burst·ing, burst)
burst·er
bur·ton hoisting tackle
Burton-upon-Trent
Bu·run·di African republic
bur·weed
Bury town in Greater
Manchester
bury (buries, bury·ing,
bur·ied)
Bur·yat Mongoloid people
Bury St Ed·munds
bus (noun, plural buses
or busses; verb bus·ing
or bus·sing, bused or
bussed)
bus·bar electrical conductor
bus·by (plural ·bies)
bu·sera Ugandan drink
bush
bush·baby (plural
·babies)
bush·buck (or bosch·bok;
plural ·bucks, ·buck or
·boks, ·bok) antelope
bush·el (·el·ing, ·elled;
US ·el·ing, ·eled) unit;
US mend garment
bush·el·ler (US ·el·er)
bush·hammer
Bu·shi·do samurai code
bushi·ness
bush·ing
Bu·shire Iranian port
Bush·man (plural ·man or
·men) S African people
bush·man (plural ·men)
bush dweller
bush·master snake
bush·pig
bush·ranger
bush·tit bird
Bush·veld
bush·whack
bush·whacker
bushy (bushi·er,
bushi·est)
busi·ly
busi·ness trade, etc.;
compare busyness
business·like
business·man (plural
·men)

business·woman (plural
·women)
bus·ing (or bus·sing)
busk
busk·er
bus·kin boot
bust
bus·tard
bust·er
bus·tle
bus·tler
busty (busti·er, busti·est)
bu·suu·ti garment
busy (adj busi·er,
busi·est; verb busies,
busy·ing bus·ied)
busy·body (plural
·bodies)
busy Liz·zie plant
busy·ness state of being
busy; compare business
but
bu·ta·di·ene
bu·tane
bu·ta·nol
bu·ta·none
butch
butch·er
butcher·bird
butcher's-broom shrub
butch·ery (plural ·eries)
bu·tene
but·ler
but·lery (plural ·leries)
butt
butte steep-sided hill
but·ter food
butt·er one that butts
but·ter·bur plant
butter·cup
butter·fat
butter·fingered
butter·fingers
butter·fish (plural ·fish or
·fishes)
butter·fly (plural ·flies)
but·ter·ine artificial butter
But·ter·mere lake
butter·milk
butter·nut
butter·scotch
butter·wort plant
but·tery (plural ·teries)
but·tock
but·ton

button·hole
button·hook
button·mould (US ·mold)
but·ton·wood
but·tress
but·ty (plural ·ties) Dialect
sandwich
bu·tyl
bu·tyra·ceous
bu·tyr·al·de·hyde
bu·tyr·ate
bu·tyr·ic acid
bu·tyr·in
bux·om
bux·om·ness
Bux·ton Derbyshire town
buy (buys, buy·ing,
bought)
buy·er
buzz
buz·zard
buzz·er
bwa·na
by
by-bidder
by-blow
Byd·goszcz Polish city
bye sports term; something
incidental
by-election (or bye-
election)
Bye·lo·rus·sia variant
spelling of **Belorussia**
Bye·lo·rus·sian variant
spelling of **Belorussian**
Bye·lo·vo variant spelling of
Belovo
by·gone
by·law (or bye-law)
by·line
by·pass (·pass·ing,
·passed or ·past)
by·path
by·product
byre cowshed; compare bier
byr·nie armour
by·road
By·ron·ic
bys·si·no·sis lung disease
bys·sus (plural ·suses or
·si) zoology term
by·stander
by·street
byte computer term;
compare bight; bite

C

cab
ca·bal (**·bal·ling**, **·balled**)
 secret group
ca·bal·le·ro (*plural* **·ros**)
ca·ba·na tent
Ca·ba·na·tuan Philippine
 city
caba·ret
cab·bage
cabbage·town city slum
cab·ba·la (*or* **ca·ba·la**,
 kab·ba·la, **ka·ba·la**)
 Jewish teaching
cab·ba·lism (*or* **caba·**,
 kab·ba·, **kaba·**)
cab·ba·list (*or* **caba·**,
 kab·ba·, **kaba·**)
cab·ba·lis·tic (*or* **caba·**,
 kab·ba·, **kaba·**)
cab·by (*or* **cab·bie**; *plural*
 ·bies)
ca·ber
cab·ezon (*or* **·ezone**) fish
Ca·bi·mas Venezuelan town
cab·in
Cabi·net government
cabi·net furniture
cabinet-maker
cabinet·work
ca·ble
ca·ble·gram
cable-laid
ca·blet small cable
cable·way
cab·man (*plural* **·men**)
cabo·chon polished gem
ca·boo·dle
ca·boose
Ca·bo·ra Bas·sa African
 dam
cabo·tage coastal
 navigation
ca·bret·ta leather
ca·bril·la fish
cab·ri·ole furniture leg
cab·rio·let horse-drawn
 carriage
ca·cao cocoa tree

cac·cia·to·re (*or* **·ra**)
 cookery term
cacha·lot whale
cache
ca·chec·tic weakened
cache·pot flowerpot
 container
ca·chet
ca·chexia (*or* **·chexy**)
 weakness
cach·in·nate laugh loudly
cach·in·na·tion
ca·chou lozenge; *variant of*
 catechu; *compare* **cashew**
ca·chu·cha dance
ca·cique American Indian
 chief
cack-handed
cack·le
cack·ler
caco·demon
caco·dyl chemical
 compound
caco·epy bad pronunciation
caco·ethes uncontrollable
 urge
caco·eth·ic
caco·gen·ics
caco·graph·ic
ca·cog·ra·phy bad
 handwriting
ca·col·ogy bad speech
caco·mis·tle (*or* **·mix·le**)
 animal
caco·phon·ic
ca·copho·nous
ca·copho·ny (*plural* **·nies**)
cac·ta·ceous
cac·tus (*plural* **·tuses** *or*
 ·ti)
ca·cu·mi·nal phonetics term
cad
ca·das·ter (*or* **·tre**)
 property register
ca·dav·er
ca·dav·er·ic
ca·dav·er·ine chemical
 compound

ca·dav·er·ous
ca·dav·er·ous·ness
cad·die (*or* **·dy**; *noun*,
 plural **·dies**; *verb* **·dies**,
 ·dy·ing, **·died**) golf term;
 compare **caddy**
cad·dis fly
cad·dis (*or* **·dice**) textile
cad·dish
Cad·do·an language group
cad·dy (*plural* **·dies**) tea
 container; *compare* **caddie**
cade tree
ca·delle beetle
ca·dence
ca·den·cy (*plural* **·cies**)
 heraldic term
ca·dent
ca·den·za
ca·det
cadge
cadg·er
cadi Muslim judge
Cadillac (*Trademark*)
Cá·diz Spanish port
cad·mium
ca·dre trained personnel
ca·du·ceus (*plural* **·cei**)
 medical emblem
ca·du·city senility
ca·du·cous biology term
cae·cal (*US* **ce·**)
cae·cil·ian amphibian
cae·cum (*US* **ce·**; *plural*
 ·ca) part of intestine
Cae·lian Roman hill
Cae·lum constellation
Caen French city
cae·no·gen·esis (*or* **cai·**,
 kai·; *US* **ce·** *or* **ke·**)
 biology term
cae·no·genet·ic (*or* **cai·**,
 kai·; *US* **ce·** *or* **ke·**)
caeo·ma botany term
Caer·leon Welsh town
Caer·nar·von
Caer·nar·von·shire
Caer·phil·ly

caes·al·pinia·ceous botany term

Caesa·rea Israeli port

Cae·sar·ean (*or* ·**ian**) of Caesar

Cae·sar·ean sec·tion (*or* **cae·**; *US* **ce·sar·ean sec·tion**)

Cae·sar·ism autocratic government

cae·sium (*US* **ce·**)

caes·pi·tose (*US* **ces·**) growing in tufts

cae·su·ra (*plural* ·**ras** *or* ·**rae**)

café

caf·eteria

caf·feine (*or* ·**fein**)

caf·tan *variant spelling of* **kaftan**

cage

cage·ling

cag·ey (*or* **cagy; cagi·er, cagi·est**)

cagi·ly

cagi·ness

Ca·glia·ri Sardinian port

cag·mag *Dialect* chat

ca·goule

ca·hier *French* notebook

ca·hoots

Caiaphas biblical character

Cai·cos West Indian islands

Cain biblical character

Cai·no·zo·ic *variant spelling of* **Cenozoic**

caïque boat

cairn

cairn·gorm quartz

Cairngorm Scottish mountains

Cai·ro

cais·son watertight structure

Caith·ness

cai·tiff cowardly person

ca·jole

ca·jol·ery (*plural* ·**eries**)

Ca·jun Acadian descendant

caju·put (*or* **caj·eput**) shrub

cake

cake·walk

Cala·bar Nigerian port

cala·bash tree

Ca·lab·ria Italian region

ca·la·dium plant

Cal·ais

cala·lu Caribbean leaves

cala·man·co fabric

cala·man·der wood

cala·mine lotion

cala·mint plant

cala·mite plant

ca·lami·tous

ca·lam·ity (*plural* ·**ities**)

cala·mon·din fruit

cala·mus (*plural* ·**mi**) plant; cane

cal·an·dria heat-exchanger vessel

ca·lash (*or* ·**leche**) carriage

cala·thus (*plural* ·**thi**) Greek symbol

ca·lav·er·ite mineral

cal·ca·neal (*or* ·**nean**)

cal·ca·neus (*or* ·**neum**; *plural* ·**nei**) heel bone

cal·car (*plural* ·**caria**) spur

cal·car·eous containing lime

cal·ca·rif·er·ous

cal·cei·form (*or* ·**ceo·late**) botany term

cal·ceo·lar·ia plant

cal·ces (*plural of* **calx**)

cal·cic containing calcium

cal·ci·cole lime-loving plant

cal·cico·lous

cal·cif·er·ol vitamin

cal·cif·er·ous

cal·cif·ic

cal·ci·fi·ca·tion

cal·ci·fu·gal

cal·ci·fuge acid-loving plant

cal·cifu·gous

cal·ci·fy (·**fies**, ·**fy·ing**, ·**fied**)

cal·ci·mine (*or* **kal·so·mine**) wash for walls

cal·ci·na·tion

cal·cine chemistry term

cal·cite mineral

cal·cit·ic

cal·ci·ton·in hormone

cal·cium

calc·sinter rock

cal·cu·la·bil·ity (*plural* ·**ities**)

cal·cu·lable

cal·cu·late

cal·cu·la·tion

cal·cu·la·tive

cal·cu·la·tor

cal·cu·lous

cal·cu·lus (*plural* ·**luses**) maths term

cal·cu·lus (*plural* ·**li**) stone in body

Cal·cut·ta

cal·dar·ium Roman bathroom

cal·de·ra volcanic crater

cal·dron *variant spelling of* **cauldron**

Cale·do·nia

Cale·do·nian

cal·efa·cient

cal·efac·tion

cal·efac·tory (*plural* ·**tories**)

cal·en·dar dates; *compare* **colander**

cal·en·der smoothing machine; *compare* **colander**

cal·ends (*or* **kal·ends**)

ca·len·du·la plant

cal·en·ture fever

calf (*plural* **calves**)

calf·skin

Cal·ga·ry Canadian city

Cali Colombian city

cali·brate

cali·bra·tion

cali·bra·tor (*or* ·**brat·er**)

cali·bre (*US* ·**ber**)

cali·bred (*US* ·**bered**)

cali·ces *plural of* **calix**

ca·li·che geology term

cali·co (*plural* ·**coes** *or* ·**cos**)

Cali·cut Indian port

Cali·for·nia

cali·for·nium radioactive element

cali·pash (*or* **cal·li·pash**) turtle meat

cali·pee turtle meat

cali·per *US spelling of* **calliper**

ca·liph (*or* **ca·lif, ka·lif, kha·lif**)

ca·li·phate (*or* **ca·li·fate, ka·li·fate**)

cali·sa·ya cinchona bark

cal·is·then·ic *variant spelling of* callisthenic

ca·lix (*plural* cali·ces) chalice; *compare* calyx

calk *variant spelling of* caulk

calk (*or* cal·kin) spike on shoe

call

cal·la plant

call·able

cal·lais ornamental stone

cal·lant (*or* ·lan) youth

Ca·llao Peruvian port

call·boy

call·er one who calls

cal·ler *Scot* fresh food

cal·lig·ra·pher (*or* ·phist)

cal·li·graph·ic

cal·li·graphi·cal·ly

cal·lig·ra·phy

call·ing

cal·lio·pe *US* steam organ

cal·li·pash *variant spelling of* calipash

cal·li·per (*US* cali·per)

cal·li·pyg·ian (*or* ·py·gous) having shapely buttocks

cal·lis·then·ic (*or* cal·is·)

cal·lis·then·ics (*or* cal·is·)

Cal·lis·to satellite of Jupiter

cal·los·ity (*plural* ·ities)

cal·lous (*adj*)

cal·lous·ness

cal·low

cal·low·ness

cal·lus (*noun*; *plural* ·luses)

calm

cal·ma·tive

calm·ness

calo·mel purgative

Cal·or (*Trademark*)

ca·lor·ic

calo·ric·ity (*plural* ·ities)

Calo·rie kilocalorie

calo·rie

calo·rif·ic

calo·rifi·cal·ly

calo·rim·eter

calo·ri·met·ric (*or* ·ri·cal)

calo·ri·met·ri·cal·ly

calo·rim·etry

ca·lotte priest's skullcap

calo·yer Greek Orthodox monk

cal·pac (*or* cal·pack, kal·pak) brimless hat

calque (calqu·ing, calqued) linguistics term

cal·trop (*or* ·trap, ·throp) plant

calu·met peace pipe

ca·lum·ni·ate

ca·lum·nia·tion

ca·lum·ni·ous (*or* ·nia·tory)

cal·um·ny (*plural* ·nies)

calu·tron physics term

Cal·va·dos French department; brandy

cal·varia top of skull

Cal·va·ry Crucifixion site

cal·va·ry (*plural* ·ries) suffering

calve (*verb*)

calves *plural of* calf

Cal·vin·ism

Cal·vin·ist

Cal·vin·is·tic

cal·vi·ti·es baldness

calx (*plural* calxes *or* cal·ces) oxide

caly·cate having a calyx

caly·cine (*or* ca·lyci·nal) of a calyx

caly·cle (*or* ca·lycu·lus; *plural* ·cles *or* ·li) biology term

Calypso mythological character

ca·lyp·so (*plural* ·sos) song

ca·lyp·tra botany term

ca·lyp·trate

ca·lyp·tro·gen

ca·lyx (*plural* ca·lyxes *or* caly·ces) sepals of plant; *compare* calix

Cam river

cam machinery

Ca·ma·güey Cuban city

ca·mail armour

ca·ma·ra·derie

cama·ril·la Spanish cabal

cam·ass (*or* ·as) plant

cam·ber

Cam·ber·well

cam·bial of cambium

cam·bist foreign-exchange dealer

cam·bist·ry (*plural* ·ries)

cam·bium (*plural* ·biums *or* ·bia) plant tissue

Cam·bo·dia

Cam·bo·dian

cam·bo·gia gum resin

cam·boose lumberjack's cabin

Cam·brai French town

Cam·bria *Latin* Wales

Cam·brian geological period

cam·bric fabric

Cam·bridge

Cam·bridge·shire

Cam·den London borough

came

cam·el

cam·el·eer

ca·mel·lia

ca·melo·pard giraffe

Ca·melo·par·dus (*or* ·da·lis) constellation

Cam·elot

Cam·em·bert cheese

cameo (*noun, plural* cameos; *verb* cameos, cameo·ing, cam·eoed)

cam·era

cam·er·al

cam·era lu·ci·da

camera·man (*plural* ·men)

cam·era ob·scu·ra

camera-ready

cam·er·len·go (*or* ·lin·go; *plural* ·gos) papal treasurer

Cam·eroon

cami·knick·ers

cami·on lorry

ca·mise smock

cami·sole

cam·let cloth

camo·mile (*or* chamo·)

ca·moo·di snake

Ca·mor·ra secret society

camou·flage

camp

Cam·pa·gna Italian plain

cam·paign

cam·paign·er

Cam·pa·nia Italian region

cam·pa·ni·le bell tower
cam·pa·nolo·gist
cam·pa·nol·ogy
cam·panu·la flower
cam·panu·la·ceous
cam·panu·late bell-shaped
Cam·peche Mexican state
camp·er
cam·pes·tral of fields
cam·phene
cam·phire henna
cam·phor
cam·pho·rate
cam·phor·ic
Cam·pi·nas Brazilian city
camp·ing
cam·pi·on
cam·po Brazilian savanna
campo·ree Scout meeting
Cam·pos Brazilian city
cam·pus (*plural* ·puses)
cam·shaft
cam·wood
can (can·ning, canned)
Cana biblical town
Ca·naan biblical region
Ca·naan·ite
Cana·da
Ca·na·dian
Ca·na·di·an·ism
ca·nai·gre plant
ca·naille *French* mob
ca·nal (·nal·ling, ·nalled;
    US ·nal·ing, ·naled)
cana·licu·lar
cana·licu·lus (*plural* ·li)
    small channel
cana·li·za·tion (*or*
    ·sa·tion)
cana·lize (*or* ·lise)
cana·pé
ca·nard rumour
ca·nary (*plural* ·naries)
Ca·nary Is·lands (*or*
    Ca·naries)
ca·nas·ta card game
can·as·ter tobacco
Ca·nav·er·al *US* cape
Can·ber·ra
can·can
can·cel (·cel·ling, ·celled;
    US ·cel·ing, ·celed)
can·cel·late (*or* ·lous,
    ·lat·ed) medical term
can·cel·la·tion

can·cel·ler (*US* ·cel·er)
Can·cer sign of zodiac
can·cer disease
can·cer·ous
can·croid
can·de·la unit
can·de·la·brum (*or* ·bra;
    plural ·bra, ·brums, *or*
    ·bras)
can·did
can·di·da·cy (*or* ·da·ture)
can·di·date
can·did·ness
can·died
Can·di·ot Cretan
can·dle
candle·berry (*plural*
    ·berries)
candle·fish (*plural* ·fish *or*
    ·fishes)
candle·light
Candle·mas
candle·nut
candle·pins bowling game
candle·power
can·dler
candle·stick
candle·wick
candle·wood
can·dour (*US* ·dor)
can·dy (*noun, plural*
    ·dies; *verb* ·dies,
    ·dy·ing, ·died)
candy·floss
candy-striped
candy·tuft
cane
cane·brake US thicket
ca·nel·la spice
can·er
ca·nes·cent hoary
can·field card game
cangue wooden collar
Ca·nicu·la the star Sirius
ca·nicu·lar of Sirius
ca·nine
can·ing
can·is·ter
can·ker
can·ker·ous
canker·worm
can·na plant
can·na·bic
can·na·bin
can·na·bis

Can·nae battle site
canned
can·nel coal
can·nel·lo·ni (*or* ·ne·lo·ni)
can·ne·lure groove
can·ner
can·nery (*plural* ·neries)
Cannes French town
can·ni·bal
can·ni·bal·ism
can·ni·bal·is·tic
can·ni·bali·za·tion (*or*
    ·sa·tion)
can·ni·bal·ize (*or* ·ise)
can·ni·kin (*or* cana·kin,
    cani·kin) small can
can·ni·ly
can·ni·ness
can·ning
Can·nock Staffordshire
    town
can·non (*plural* ·nons *or*
    ·non) artillery; *compare*
    canon
can·non·ade
cannon·ball
can·non·eer
can·non·ry (*plural* ·ries)
    artillery; *compare* canonry
can·not
can·nu·la (*or* canu·la;
    plural ·las *or* ·lae)
    surgical tube
can·nu·late (*or* canu·late)
can·ny (·ni·er, ·ni·est)
ca·noe (·noes, ·noe·ing,
    ·noed)
ca·noe·ist
can·on priest; decree;
    compare cannon
can·on·ess
ca·noni·cal
ca·noni·cate office of canon
can·on·ic·ity
can·on·ist
can·oni·za·tion (*or*
    ·sa·tion)
can·on·ize (*or* ·ise)
can·on·ry (*plural* ·ries)
    office of canon; *compare*
    cannonry
ca·noo·dle
Ca·no·pus Egyptian port
cano·py (*noun, plural*
    ·pies; *verb* ·pies,
    ·py·ing, ·pied)

Ca·nos·sa Italian castle
cans *Slang* headphones
cant platitudes; slope
can't cannot
can·ta·bi·le musical term
Can·ta·brian Spanish
  mountains
Can·ta·brig·ian of
  Cambridge
Can·tal French department;
  cheese
can·ta·la plant
can·ta·loupe (*or* ·loup)
can·tan·ker·ous
can·ta·ta
can·ta·trice singer
can·teen
can·ter
Can·ter·bury
can·thari·des (*sing.*
  ·tha·ris) medicine
can·thus (*plural* ·thi)
  corner of eye
cant·ic
can·ti·cle
can·ti·lena musical term
can·ti·lever
can·til·late
can·til·la·tion
can·ti·na Spanish bar
cant·ing
can·tle saddle part
can·to (*plural* ·tos)
Can·ton Chinese port
can·ton division of
  Switzerland
can·ton·al
Can·ton·ese (*plural* ·ese)
can·ton·ment
can·tor religious singer
can·tor·is musical term
can·trip magic spell
can·tus (*plural* ·tus)
  medieval church singing
canty *Dialect* lively
can·vas cloth
canvas·back (*plural*
  ·backs *or* ·back) duck
can·vass solicit
can·vass·er
can·yon
can·zo·na musical term
can·zo·ne (*plural* ·ni) song
can·zo·net song
caou·tchouc rubber

cap (cap·ping, capped)
ca·pa·bil·ity (*plural* ·ities)
ca·pable
ca·pably
ca·pa·cious
ca·paci·tance physics term
ca·paci·tate
ca·paci·ta·tion
ca·paci·tive
ca·paci·tor
ca·pac·ity (*plural* ·ities)
cap·a·pie from head to foot
ca·pari·son
cape
cap·elin (*or* cap·lin) fish
Ca·pel·la star
ca·per
cap·er·cail·lie (*or*
  ·cail·zie)
Ca·per·na·um Israeli town
Cape Roca Portuguese cape
cape·skin
Capet French dynasty
Ca·petian
Cape Verde island country
ca·pi·as legal term
cap·il·la·ceous hairy
cap·il·lar·ity surface tension
ca·pil·lary (*plural* ·laries)
capi·tal
capi·tal·ism
capi·tal·ist
capi·tal·is·tic
capi·tali·za·tion (*or*
  ·sa·tion)
capi·tal·ize (*or* ·ise)
capi·tal·ly
capi·tate headlike
capi·ta·tion
capi·ta·tive
Capi·tol US Congress
  building
Capi·to·line Roman hill
ca·pitu·lar
ca·pitu·lary (*plural*
  ·laries)
ca·pitu·late
ca·pitu·la·tion
ca·pitu·la·tor
ca·pitu·lum (*plural* ·la)
  biology term
capo (*plural* capos) guitar
  attachment
ca·pon
ca·pon·ize (*or* ·ise)

capo·ral tobacco; *compare*
  corporal
ca·pote cloak
Cap·pa·do·cia ancient
  Asian region
cap·pa·ri·da·ceous botany
  term
capped
cap·per
cap·pie *Scot* ice-cream cone
cap·ping
cap·puc·ci·no (*plural*
  ·nos)
cap·reo·late botany term
Ca·pri
ca·pric·cio (*plural* ·cios *or*
  ·ci) musical work
ca·pric·cio·so musical term
ca·price
ca·pri·cious
ca·pri·cious·ness
Cap·ri·corn sign of zodiac
Cap·ri·cor·nus (*plural* ·ni)
  constellation
cap·ri·fi·ca·tion
cap·ri·fig wild fig
cap·ri·fo·lia·ceous botany
  term
cap·rine of goats
cap·ri·ole
cap·sai·cin alkaloid
cap·si·cum
cap·sid plant bug
cap·size
cap·stan
cap·stone (*or* cope·)
cap·su·lar
cap·su·late (*or* ·lat·ed)
cap·su·la·tion
cap·sule
cap·sul·ize (*or* ·ise)
cap·tain
cap·tain·cy (*or* ·tain·ship;
  plural ·cies *or* ·ships)
cap·tion
cap·tious
cap·ti·vate
cap·ti·va·tion
cap·ti·va·tor
cap·tive
cap·tiv·ity (*plural* ·ities)
cap·tor
cap·ture
Capua Italian town
ca·puche friar's hood

Capu·chin friar
capu·chin monkey
ca·put (*plural* capi·ta) head; *compare* kaput
capy·ba·ra rodent
car
cara·bao water buffalo
cara·bid beetle
cara·bi·neer (*or* ·nier) *variants of* carbineer
ca·ra·bi·nie·re (*plural* ·ri) Italian policeman
cara·cal lynx
ca·ra·ca·ra bird
Ca·ra·cas Venezuelan capital
cara·cole (*or* ·col) dressage term
cara·cul fur; *variant spelling of* karakul
ca·rafe
cara·geen *variant spelling of* carrageen
ca·ram·ba (*or* ·bo·la) tree; fruit
cara·mel
cara·mel·ize (*or* ·ise)
ca·ran·gid (*or* ·goid) fish
cara·pace
car·at weight; *compare* caret
cara·van (·van·ning, ·vanned)
cara·van·se·rai (*or* ·sa·ry; *plural* ·rais *or* ·ries)
cara·vel (*or* car·vel) ship
cara·way
car·ba·mate
car·bami·dine
car·ban·ion chemistry term
car·ba·zole
car·bene chemistry term
car·bide
car·bine rifle
car·bi·neer (*or* cara·bi·neer, cara·bi·nier) soldier
car·bo·hy·drate
car·bo·lat·ed
car·bol·ic
car·bo·lize (*or* ·lise)
car·bon
car·bo·na·ceous
car·bo·nade beef stew
car·bo·na·do (*noun, plural* ·does *or* ·dos; *verb*

·do·ing, ·doed) grilled meat; industrial diamond
Car·bo·na·ri political society
car·bon·ate
car·bona·tion
car·bon·ic
car·bon·if·er·ous
car·boni·za·tion (*or* ·sa·tion)
car·bon·ize (*or* ·ise)
car·bon·ous
car·bon·yl
Car·bo·run·dum (*Trademark*)
car·box·yl
car·box·yl·ase enzyme
car·box·yl·ate
car·box·yl·ic
car·boy large bottle
car·bun·cle
car·bun·cu·lar
car·bu·ra·tion
car·bu·ret (·ret·ting, ·ret·ted; *US* ·ret·ing, ·ret·ed)
car·bu·ret·tor (*or* ·ter; *US* ·retor)
car·bu·ri·za·tion (*or* ·sa·tion)
car·bu·rize (*or* ·rise)
car·byla·mine
car·cass (*or* ·case)
Car·chem·ish ancient Syrian city
car·cino·gen
car·cino·gen·ic
car·ci·no·ma (*plural* ·mas *or* ·ma·ta)
car·ci·no·ma·toid (*or* ·tous)
car·ci·no·ma·to·sis
card
car·da·mom (*or* ·mum, ·mon) spice
card·board
card-carrying
car·di·ac
car·di·al·gia heart pain
car·di·al·gic
Car·diff
Car·di·gan Welsh bay
car·di·gan
car·di·nal
car·di·nal·ate (*or* ·ship)

car·di·nal·ly
card·ing
car·dio·gram record
car·dio·graph instrument
car·di·og·ra·pher
car·dio·graph·ic (*or* ·graphi·cal)
car·di·og·ra·phy
car·di·oid
car·dio·logi·cal
car·di·olo·gist
car·di·ol·ogy
car·dio·mega·ly heart enlargement
car·dio·vas·cu·lar
car·di·tis
car·doon plant
card·sharp (*or* ·sharper)
car·dua·ceous botany term
care
ca·reen nautical term
ca·reer
ca·reer·ist
care·free
care·ful
care·ful·ly
care·ful·ness
care·less
care·less·ness
ca·ress
ca·ress·er
ca·ress·ing·ly
car·et printing symbol; *compare* carat
care·taker
care·worn
car·fare *US* bus fare
car·fax crossroads
car·go (*plural* ·goes *or* ·gos)
car·hop
Caria ancient Asian region
Car·ib (*plural* ·ibs *or* ·ib) American Indian
Car·ib·bean
Car·ib·bees West Indian islands
cari·bou (*plural* ·bous *or* ·bou)
cari·ca·ture
cari·ca·tur·ist
cari·es (*plural* cari·es) tooth decay
ca·ril·lon (·lon·ning, ·lonned)

ca·ril·lon·neur

Ca·ri·na constellation

ca·ri·na (*plural* ·nae *or* ·nas) keel-shaped part

cari·nate (*or* ·nat·ed)

Ca·rin·thia Austrian province

cario·ca dance

cario·gen·ic producing tooth decay

cari·ole (*or* car·ri·ole) cart

cari·os·ity (*or* cari·ous·ness)

cari·ous

car·line plant

car·ling (*or* ·line) ship's beam

Car·lisle Cumbrian city

Car·low Irish county

Carl·ton English town

car·ma·gnole French costume

car·man (*plural* ·men)

Car·mar·then

Car·mar·then·shire former Welsh county

Car·mel Israeli mountain

Car·mel·ite friar or nun

car·mina·tive

car·mine

car·nage

car·nal

car·nal·ist

car·nal·ity

car·nall·ite mineral

car·nal·ly

car·nas·sial tooth

Car·nat·ic Indian region

car·na·tion

car·nau·ba wax

car·nel·ian *variant spelling of* cornelian

car·net travel document; customs licence

car·ni·fi·ca·tion

car·ni·fy (·fies, ·fy·ing, ·fied) medical term

Car·nio·la Yugoslav region

car·ni·val

car·ni·vore

car·nivo·rous

car·no·tite

car·ny (*or* ·ney; ·nies, ·ny·ing, ·nied *or* ·neys, ·ney·ing, ·neyed) coax

car·ob

ca·roche carriage

car·ol (·ol·ling, ·olled; *US* ·ol·ing, ·oled)

car·ol·er

Caro·li·na

Caro·line (*or* Caro·lean) of King Charles

Caro·lin·gian Frankish dynasty

Caro·lin·ian of Carolina

caro·lus (*plural* ·luses *or* ·li) coin

car·om billiards term

caro·tene (*or* ·tin) orange pigment

ca·rot·enoid

ca·rot·id artery

ca·rot·id·al

ca·rous·al drinking party; *compare* carousel

ca·rouse

carou·sel *US* merry-go-round; *compare* carousal

ca·rous·er

carp

car·pal of the wrist; *compare* carpel

Car·pa·thian Moun·tains

car·pel flower part; *compare* carpal

car·pel·lary

car·pel·late

Car·pen·ta·ria Australian gulf

car·pen·ter

car·pen·try

car·pet

carpet·bag

carpet·bag·ger

car·phol·ogy medical term; *compare* carpology

car·po·go·nial

car·po·go·nium (*plural* ·nia) botany term

car·po·logi·cal

car·polo·gist

car·pol·ogy branch of botany; *compare* carphology

car·po·meta·car·pus bird bone

car·popha·gous feeding on fruit

car·po·phore botany term

car·port

car·po·spore

car·pus (*plural* ·pi) wrist

car·rack galleon

car·ra·geen (*or* ·gheen, cara·geen) seaweed

Car·ra·ra Italian town

car·re·four crossroads

car·rel (*or* ·rell) library cubicle

car·riage

carriage·way

car·rick

car·ri·er

car·ri·on

car·ron·ade cannon

car·rot

car·roty

car·ry (·ries, ·ry·ing, ·ried)

carry·all

carry·cot

carse *Scot* low-lying land

car·sey *variant spelling of* carzey

car·sick

car·sick·ness

cart

cart·age

Car·ta·gena Colombian port

carte blanche (*plural* cartes blanches)

car·tel

car·tel·ize

car·teli·za·tion

Car·tesian of Descartes

cart·ful

Car·thage

Car·tha·gin·ian

cart·horse

Car·thu·sian monk

car·ti·lage

car·ti·lagi·nous

cart·load

car·to·gram map

car·tog·ra·pher

car·to·graph·ic

car·to·graphi·cal

car·tog·ra·phy

carto·man·cy fortune-telling

car·ton

car·toon

car·toon·ist

car·touche (*or* ·touch)

car·tridge
car·tu·lary (*or* char·; *plural* ·laries) legal records
cart·wheel
car·un·cle fleshy outgrowth
car·un·cu·lar (*or* ·lous)
car·un·cu·late (*or* ·lat·ed)
carve
car·vel *variant of* caravel
carvel-built
carv·er
carv·ery (*plural* ·eries)
carv·ing
cary·at·id (*plural* ·ids *or* ·ati·des)
cary·ati·dal (*or* ·dean, **cary·at·ic, cary·atid·ic**)
caryo·phyl·la·ceous botany term
cary·op·sis (*plural* ·ses *or* ·si·des) botany term
car·zey (*or* ·sey) *Slang* lavatory
ca·sa·ba (*or* cas·sa·ba) melon
Casa·blan·ca
cas·bah *variant spelling of* kasbah
cas·cade
cas·ca·ra
cas·ca·ril·la shrub
case
ca·sease enzyme
ca·seate medical term
ca·sea·tion
case·bound
ca·sefy (·sefies, ·sefy·ing, ·sefied) become cheesy
case-harden
ca·sein protein
ca·seino·gen protein
case·mate part of ship
case·ment
ca·seose biochemical compound
ca·seous cheeselike
ca·sern (*or* ·serne) soldier's billet
Ca·ser·ta Italian town
case·work
cash
cash·able
cash-and-carry
cash-book

cash·ew nut; *compare* cachou
cash·ier
cash·mere
cas·ing
ca·si·no (*plural* ·nos) gaming house; *compare* cassino
cask
cas·ket
Cas·lon style of type
Cas·pian Sea
casque helmet
casqued
cas·sa·reep cassava juice
cas·sa·ta ice cream
cas·sa·tion legal term
cas·sa·va plant
Cas·se·grain·ian telescope
cas·se·role
cas·sette
cas·sia plant
cas·si·mere (*or* casi·mere) cloth
cas·si·no (*or* ca·si·no) card game; *compare* casino
Cas·sio·peia constellation
cas·sis liqueur
cas·sit·er·ite mineral
cas·sock priest's garment; *compare* hassock
cas·socked
cas·sou·let French stew
cas·so·wary (*plural* ·waries) bird
cast (·ing, cast)
cas·ta·net
cast·away
caste Hindu class
cas·tel·lan keeper of castle
cas·tel·lat·ed
cas·tel·la·tion
cast·er one who casts; *compare* castor
cas·ter (*or* ·tor) sugar dispenser; wheel on furniture; *compare* castor
cas·ti·gate
cas·ti·ga·tion
cas·ti·ga·tor
Cas·tile (*or* Cas·til·la)
Cas·til·ian
cast·ing
cas·tle
cas·tled

cast-off (*adj*)
cast-off (*noun*)
Cas·tor star; mythological character
cas·tor plant oil; beaver secretion; *compare* caster
cas·trate
cas·tra·tion
cas·tra·to (*plural* ·ti *or* ·tos)
cas·tra·tor
cas·ual
casu·al·ly
casu·al·ty (*plural* ·ties)
casua·ri·na tree
casu·ist
casu·is·tic (*or* ·ti·cal)
casu·is·ti·cal·ly
casu·ist·ry (*plural* ·ries)
ca·sus bel·li *Latin* occasion of war
cat
ca·taba·sis (*plural* ·ses) descent
cata·bat·ic
cata·bol·ic (*or* kata·)
cata·boli·cal·ly (*or* kata·)
ca·tabo·lism (*or* ka·)
ca·tabo·lite
cata·caus·tic physics term
cata·chre·sis incorrect use of words
cata·chres·tic (*or* ·ti·cal)
cata·cla·sis (*plural* ·ses) geology term
cata·clas·tic
cata·cli·nal geology term
cata·clysm
cata·clys·mic (*or* ·mal)
cata·comb
ca·tad·ro·mous migrating down river; *compare* anadromous
cata·falque
Cata·lan language or inhabitant of Catalonia
cata·lase enzyme
cata·lec·tic prosody term
cata·lep·sy medical term
cata·lep·tic
cata·logue (*US* ·log)
cata·logu·er (*or* ·logu·ist; *US* ·log·)
Cata·lo·nia Spanish region
ca·tal·pa tree

cata·lyse (*US* ·lyze)
cata·lys·er (*US* ·lyz·)
ca·taly·sis (*plural* ·ses)
cata·lyst
cata·lyt·ic
cata·ma·ran
cata·menia menstruation
cata·menial
cata·mite homosexual boy
cata·mount (*or* ·mount·ain) animal
Ca·ta·nia Sicilian port
cata·pho·resis chemistry term
cata·phyll leaf
cata·pla·sia pathology term
cata·plasm poultice
cata·plas·tic
cata·plexy paralysis
cata·pult
cata·ract
ca·tarrh
ca·tarrh·al (*or* ·ous)
cat·arrh·ine zoology term
ca·tas·tro·phe
cata·stroph·ic
cata·strophi·cal·ly
ca·tas·tro·phism geological theory
ca·tas·tro·phist
cata·to·nia schizophrenia
cata·ton·ic
Ca·taw·ba (*plural* ·bas *or* ·ba) American Indian people
cat·bird
cat·boat
cat·call
catch (catch·ing, caught)
catch·er
catch·fly (*plural* ·flies) plant
catchi·ness
catch·ing
catch·ment
catch·penny (*plural* ·pennies)
catch·pole sheriff's officer
catch·up *US variant of* ketchup
catch·weight
catch·word
catchy (catchi·er, catchi·est)

cate·cheti·cal (*or* cat·echet·ic) teaching method
cat·echeti·cal·ly
cat·echin chemical compound
cat·echism
cat·echis·mal
cat·echist (*or* cate·chiz·er, cate·chis·er)
cat·echis·tic (*or* ·ti·cal)
cat·echi·za·tion (*or* ·sa·tion)
cat·echize (*or* ·ise)
cat·echol chemical compound
cat·echola·mine
cat·echu (*or* ca·chou, cutch) resin
cat·echu·men convert
cat·ego·rial
cat·egori·cal (*or* ·egor·ic)
cat·egori·cal·ly
cat·ego·ri·za·tion (*or* ·sa·tion)
cat·ego·rize (*or* ·rise)
cat·ego·ry (*plural* ·ries)
ca·tena (*plural* ·tenae) biblical comments
cat·enane chemistry term
cat·enar·ian
ca·tena·ry (*plural* ·ries) geometric curve
cat·enate biology term
cat·ena·tion
cat·enoid geometric surface
ca·tenu·late botany term
ca·ter
cat·er·an brigand
ca·ter·er
ca·ter·ing
cat·er·pil·lar
cat·er·waul
cat·fall nautical term
cat·fish (*plural* ·fish *or* ·fishes)
cat·gut
Cath·ar (*plural* ·ars *or* ·ari) heretical Christian
Cath·ar·ism
ca·thar·sis
ca·thar·tic purgative
ca·thar·ti·cal·ly
Ca·thay *Archaic* China
cat·head nautical term

ca·thec·tic psychology term
ca·thedra (*plural* ·thedrae) bishop's throne
ca·thedral
ca·thep·sin enzyme
Cathe·rine wheel firework
cath·eter
cath·eteri·za·tion (*or* ·sa·tion)
cath·eter·ize (*or* ·ise)
ca·thex·is (*plural* ·thexes) psychiatry term
ca·thod·al
cath·ode
ca·thod·ic (*or* ·thodi·cal)
Catholic religion
catho·lic universal
Ca·tholi·cism
catho·lic·ity
ca·tholi·ci·za·tion (*or* ·sa·tion)
ca·tholi·cize (*or* ·cise)
ca·tholi·con universal remedy
cati·on positive ion
cati·on·ic
cat·kin
cat·like
cat·ling surgical knife
cat·mint (*or esp. US* ·nip)
cat·nap (*verb* ·nap·ping, ·napped)
cat-o'-nine-tails (*plural* -tails)
ca·top·tric (*or* ·tri·cal)
ca·top·trics branch of optics
cat's-ear plant
cat's-eye
cat's-foot (*plural* -feet) plant
cat's-paw
cat·sup *US variant of* ketchup
cat·ta·lo (*or* cata·lo; *plural* ·loes *or* ·los) cattle
cat·tery (*plural* ·teries)
cat·ti·ly
cat·ti·ness
cat·tish
cat·tle
cattle·man (*plural* ·men)
catt·leya orchid
cat·ty (·ti·er, ·ti·est)
cat·walk

Cau·ca·sia
Cau·ca·sian
Cau·ca·soid
Cau·ca·sus mountain range
cau·cus (*plural* ·cuses)
cau·dad towards the tail
cau·dal of the tail
cau·dal·ly
cau·date (*or* ·dat·ed)
cau·da·tion
cau·dex (*plural* ·di·ces *or* ·dexes) stem
cau·dil·lo (*plural* ·los) Spanish leader
cau·dle spiced wine
caught
caul
caul·dron (*or* cal·dron)
cau·les·cent
cau·li·cle plant stalk
cau·li·flow·er
cau·line
caulk (*or* calk) fill cracks
caulk·er (*or* calk·er)
caus·abil·ity
caus·able
caus·al
cau·sal·gia pathology term
cau·sal·ity (*plural* ·ities)
cau·sal·ly
cau·sa·tion
causa·tive
cause cé·lè·bre (*plural* causes cé·lè·bres)
caus·er
cau·serie informal talk
cause·way
caus·tic
caus·ti·cal·ly
caus·tic·ness (*or* ·tic·ity)
cau·ter·ant caustic
cau·teri·za·tion (*or* ·sa·tion)
cau·ter·ize (*or* ·ise)
cau·tery (*plural* ·teries)
cau·tion
cau·tion·ary
cau·tious
cau·tious·ness
cav·al·cade
cava·lier
cava·lier·ism
ca·val·la (*or* ·ly; *plural* ·la, ·las, *or* ·lies) fish
cav·al·ry (*plural* ·ries)

cav·al·ry·man (*plural* ·men)
Cav·an Irish county
cava·ti·na (*plural* ·ne) musical work
cave
ca·veat warning
ca·veat emp·tor *Latin* let the buyer beware
ca·vea·tor legal term
cave·fish (*plural* ·fish *or* ·fishes)
cave·man (*plural* ·men)
cav·en·dish tobacco
cav·er
cav·ern
cav·ern·ous
cav·es·son horse's noseband
ca·vet·to (*plural* ·ti) architectural moulding
cavi·ar (*or* ·are)
cavi·corn hollow-horned
ca·vie *Scot* hen coop
cav·il (·il·ling, ·illed; *US* ·il·ing, ·iled)
cav·il·ler
cav·ing
cavi·ta·tion
Ca·vi·te Philippine port
cav·ity (*plural* ·ities)
cavo-relievo (*or* -rilievo; *plural* cavo-relievos *or* cavi-rilievi) architectural term
ca·vort
cavy (*plural* cavies) rodent
caw
Cawn·pore Indian city
Cax·ton style of type
cay low island or bank
cay·enne
cay·man (*or* cai·man; *plural* ·mans) crocodile
Cay·man Is·lands
cay·use *US* small pony
cea·no·thus shrub
Cea·ra Brazilian state
cease
cease·fire
cease·less
ce·cal *US spelling of* caecal
ce·ci·ty blindness
Cecrops mythological character

ce·cum *US spelling of* caecum
ce·dar tree; *compare* ceder
cede
ced·er one who cedes; *compare* cedar
cedi Ghanaian currency
ce·dil·la
cei·ba tree
cei·lidh Gaelic party
ceil·ing
ceil·om·eter
cela·don porcelain
cel·an·dine
Ce·la·ya Mexican city
Cel·ebes Indonesian island
cel·ebrant
cel·ebrate
cel·ebra·tion
cel·ebra·tive
cel·ebra·tor
cel·ebra·tory
ce·leb·rity (*plural* ·rities)
ce·leri·ac vegetable
ce·ler·ity speed
cel·ery
ce·les·ta (*or* ·leste) musical instrument
ce·les·tial
ce·les·tial·ly
cel·es·tite (*or* ·tine) mineral
ce·li·ac *US spelling of* coeliac
celi·ba·cy (*plural* ·cies)
celi·bate
cell
cel·la (*plural* ·lae) room in temple
cel·lar
cel·lar·age
cel·lar·er monastic official
cel·lar·et bottle stand
Cel·le West German city
cel·list
cel·lo (*plural* ·los)
cel·lo·bi·ose (*or* cel·lose) biochemical compound
cel·loi·din chemical compound
cel·lo·phane
cel·lu·lar
cel·lu·lase enzyme
cel·lule
cel·lu·li·tis

Cel·lu·loid (*Trademark*)

cel·lu·lose

cel·lu·lo·sic

ce·lom *US spelling of* **coelom**

ce·lo·mate *US spelling of* **coelomate**

Celsius temperature scale

celt axe

Celt (*or* **Kelt**) people

Celt·ic (*or* **Kelt·ic**)

Celti·cist (*or* **Celt·ist, Kelti·cist, Kelt·ist**)

cem·ba·lo (*plural* **·los**) harpsichord

ce·ment

ce·men·ta·tion

ce·ment·er

ce·ment·ite chemical compound

ce·men·tum tooth substance

cem·etery (*plural* **·eteries**)

cena·cle (*or* **coena·cle**) supper room

ce·nes·the·sia *variant spelling of* **coenesthesia**

ce·no·bite *variant spelling of* **coenobite**

ce·no·gen·esis *US spelling of* **caenogenesis**

ce·no·genet·ic *US spelling of* **caenogenetic**

ce·no·spe·cies (*plural* **·spe·cies**) biology term

ceno·taph

ceno·taph·ic

ce·no·te well

Ce·no·zo·ic (*or* **Cai·**) geological era

cense burn incense

cen·ser incense container

cen·sor suppressor; to ban; *compare* **sensor**

cen·sor·able

cen·so·rial

cen·so·ri·ous

cen·so·ri·ous·ness

cen·sor·ship

cen·sual of a census; *compare* **sensual**

cen·sur·able

cen·sure

cen·sus (*plural* **·suses**)

cent

cen·tal unit

cen·taur

Cen·tau·rus constellation

cen·tau·ry (*plural* **·ries**) plant

cen·te·nar·ian

cen·te·nary (*plural* **·naries**)

cen·ten·nial

cen·ter *US spelling of* **centre**

cen·tesi·mal hundredth

cen·tesi·mo (*plural* **·mos**) monetary unit

cen·ti·are (*or* **cen·tare**) unit

cen·ti·grade

cen·ti·gram (*or* **·gramme**)

cen·ti·li·tre (*US* **·ter**)

cen·til·lion (*plural* **·lions** *or* **·lion**) 10^{600}

cen·time

cen·ti·me·tre (*US* **·ter**)

cen·ti·pede

centi·poise unit

cent·ner

cen·to (*plural* **·tos**) type of poem

cen·tral

cen·tral·ism

cen·tral·ity (*plural* **·ities**)

cen·trali·za·tion (*or* **·sa·tion**)

cen·tral·ize (*or* **·ise**)

cen·tral·ly

cen·tre (*US* **·ter**)

centre·board (*US* **center·**) keel

centre·fire (*US* **center·**)

centre·fold (*US* **center·**)

centre·piece (*US* **center·**)

cen·tric (*or* **·tri·cal**)

cen·tric·ity

cen·trifu·gal

cen·trifu·gal·ly

cen·trifu·ga·tion

cen·tri·fuge

cen·tring (*US* **·tering**)

cen·tri·ole biology term

cen·trip·etal

cen·trip·etal·ly

cen·trist moderate

cen·tro·bar·ic

cen·tro·cli·nal geology term

cen·troid

cen·tro·mere chromosome part

cen·tro·mer·ic

cen·tro·some cell part

cen·tro·som·ic

cen·tro·sphere

cen·trum (*plural* **·trums** *or* **·tra**) part of vertebra

cen·tum linguistics term

cen·tu·pli·cate

cen·tu·rial

cen·tu·ri·on

cen·tu·ry (*plural* **·ries**)

cep fungus

cepha·lad towards the head

cepha·lal·gia headache

ce·phal·ic

cepha·lin (*or* **kepha·**) biochemical compound

cepha·li·za·tion (*or* **·sa·tion**)

cepha·lo·chor·date zoology term

cepha·lom·eter

cepha·lo·met·ric

cepha·lom·etry

Cepha·lo·nia Greek island

cepha·lo·pod mollusc

cepha·lopo·dan

cepha·lo·pod·ic (*or* **·lopo·dous**)

cepha·lo·tho·rac·ic

cepha·lo·tho·rax (*plural* **·raxes** *or* **·races**)

Ce·pheus constellation

ce·ra·ceous waxy

Ce·ram Indonesian island

ce·ram·ic

ce·ram·ics

cera·mist (*or* **ce·rami·cist**)

ce·rar·gy·rite mineral

ce·ras·tes (*plural* **·tes**) snake

ce·rate ointment

ce·rat·ed ornithology term

ce·rato·dus (*plural* **·duses**) extinct fish

Cerberus mythological dog

cer·cal zoology term

cer·caria (*plural* **·cariae**) larva

cer·car·ial (*or* **·ian**)

cer·cis plant

cer·co·pi·thecoid monkey

cer·cus (*plural* **·ci**) zoology term

cere swelling on bird's beak; *compare* **sere**
ce·real crop; *compare* **serial**
cer·ebel·lar
cer·ebel·lum (*plural* **·lums** *or* **·la**)
cer·ebral
cer·ebral·ly
cer·ebrate
cer·ebra·tion
cer·ebric
cer·ebroid
cer·ebro·side biochemical compound
cer·ebro·spi·nal
cer·ebro·vas·cu·lar
cer·ebrum (*plural* **·ebrums** *or* **·ebra**)
cere·cloth waxed cloth
cere·ment burial clothes
cer·emo·nial
cer·emo·ni·al·ism
cer·emo·ni·al·ist
cer·emo·nial·ly
cer·emo·ni·ous
cer·emo·ny (*plural* **·nies**)
Ce·res asteroid
Ceres Roman goddess
cer·esin wax
ce·reus cactus
ce·ria chemical compound
ce·ric
ce·rise
ce·rium chemical element
cer·met metal–ceramic material
cer·nu·ous drooping
cero (*plural* **cero** *or* **ceros**) fish
ce·ro·graph·ic (*or* **·graphi·cal**)
ce·rog·ra·phist
ce·rog·ra·phy engraving on wax
ce·ro·plas·tic
ce·ro·plas·tics
ce·ro·type printing process
ce·rous
cert *Slang* certainty
cer·tain
cer·tain·ly
cer·tain·ty (*plural* **·ties**)
cer·ti·fi·able
cer·ti·fi·ably
cer·tifi·cate
cer·ti·fi·ca·tion
cer·tifi·ca·tory

cer·ti·fy (**·fies**, **·fy·ing**, **·fied**)
cer·tio·ra·ri legal term
cer·ti·tude
ce·ru·lean deep blue
ce·ru·men earwax
ce·ru·mi·nous
ce·ruse white lead
ce·rus·site (*or* **·ru·site**) mineral
cer·ve·lat sausage
cer·vi·cal
cer·vi·ci·tis
cer·vid zoology term
cer·vine of deer
cer·vix (*plural* **·vixes** *or* **·vi·ces**)
ce·sar·ean sec·tion US spelling of **Caesarean section**
ce·sium US spelling of **caesium**
ces·pi·tose US spelling of **caespitose**
cess
ces·sa·tion
ces·ser legal term
ces·sion act of ceding; *compare* **session**
ces·sion·ary (*plural* **·aries**) legal term
cess·pool (*or* **·pit**)
ces·tode tapeworm
ces·toid ribbon-shaped
ce·ta·cean whale
ce·ta·ceous
ce·tane chemical compound
cete group of badgers
ce·teris pa·ri·bus *Latin* other things being equal
ce·to·logi·cal
ce·tolo·gist
ce·tol·ogy study of whales
Ce·tus constellation
Ce·vennes mountain range
Cey·lon
Cey·lon·ese
chaba·zite mineral
chab·lis wine
cha-cha (*or* **cha-cha-cha**)
chac·ma baboon
cha·conne musical term
Chad African republic; lake
Chad·ean
Chad·ic language group
chae·ta (*plural* **·tae**) bristle on worm

chae·tog·nath wormlike animal
chae·to·pod worm
chafe
chaf·er beetle
chaff
chaff·er (*noun*)
chaf·fer (*verb*) haggle
chaf·finch
chaffy
chaf·ing
Cha·gas' dis·ease
cha·grin
chain
chain·man (*plural* **·men**)
chain·plate
chain-react
chain-smoke
chain-stitch
chain-store
chair
chair·borne
chair·man (*plural* **·men**)
chair·man·ship
chair·person
chair·woman (*plural* **·women**)
chaise carriage
chaise longue (*plural* **chaise longues** *or* **chaises longues**)
cha·la·za (*plural* **·zas** *or* **·zae**) biology term
cha·la·zal
chal·can·lite mineral
chal·cedon·ic
chal·cedo·ny (*plural* **·nies**)
chal·cid insect
Chal·cidi·ce Greek peninsula
Chal·cis Greek city
chal·co·cite mineral
chal·cog·ra·pher (*or* **·phist**)
chal·co·graph·ic (*or* **·graphi·cal**)
chal·cog·ra·phy engraving
chal·co·lith·ic archaeology term
chal·co·py·rite mineral
Chal·dea (*or* **·daea**) Babylonian region
Chal·dean (*or* **·daean**)
Chal·dee language
chal·dron unit
cha·let

chal·ice goblet; *compare* challis

chali·co·there extinct mammal

chalk

chalk·board *US* blackboard

chalki·ness

chalk·pit

chalky (chalki·er, chalki·est)

chal·lah (*or* hal·lah; *plural* ·lahs *or* ·loth) Jewish bread

chal·lenge

chal·lenge·able

chal·leng·er

chal·lis (*or* ·lie) fabric; *compare* chalice

chal·one internal secretion

cha·lyb·eate containing iron

cha·made military signal

cham·ber

cham·ber·lain

chamber·maid

cham·bray cloth

cha·me·le·on

cha·meleon·ic

cham·fer

cham·fer·er

cham·ois (*plural* ·ois)

Cha·mo·nix French town

champ

cham·pac (*or* ·pak) tree

Cham·pagne French region

cham·pagne wine

cham·paign open country

cham·pers *Slang* champagne

cham·per·tous

cham·per·ty (*plural* ·ties) legal term

cham·pi·gnon mushroom

cham·pi·on

cham·pion·ship

champ·le·vé enamelling process

Champs Ély·sées

chance

chan·cel

chan·cel·lery (*or* ·lo·ry; *plural* ·leries *or* ·lo·ries)

chan·cel·lor

chan·cel·lor·ship

chan·cery (*plural* ·ceries)

chanci·ly

chan·cre pathology term

chan·croid ulcer

chan·croi·dal

chan·crous

chancy (chanci·er, chanci·est)

chan·de·lier

chan·delle aeronautics term

Chan·der·na·gore Indian port

Chan·di·garh Indian city

chan·dler

chan·dlery (*plural* ·dleries)

Chang·chia·kow (*or* ·k'ou) Chinese city

Chang·chow (*or* Ch'ang-chou) Chinese city

Chang·chun (*or* Ch'ang Ch'un) Chinese city

change

change·abil·ity (*or* ·able·ness)

change·able

change·ably

change·ful

change·less

change·less·ness

change·ling

change·over

chang·er

change-ringing

Chang·sha (*or* Ch'ang-sha) Chinese port

Chang·teh (*or* Ch'ang-te) Chinese port

chan·nel (·nel·ling, ·nelled; *US* ·nel·ing, ·neled)

chan·nel·ize (*or* ·ise)

chan·nel·ler (*US* ·nel·er)

chan·son *French* song

chant

chant·er

chan·te·relle mushroom

chan·teuse

chan·tey *US spelling of* shanty

chan·ti·cleer (*or* ·cler) cock

Chan·til·ly French town

chan·try (*plural* ·tries)

chan·ty *variant spelling of* shanty

Chao·an Chinese city

cha·os

cha·ot·ic

cha·oti·cal·ly

chap (chap·ping, chapped)

chapa·rejos cowboy's overalls

chap·ar·ral wooded area

cha·pat·ti (*or* ·pa·ti; *plural* ·ti *or* ·tis) bread

chap·book

chape scabbard mounting

cha·peau (*plural* ·peaux *or* ·peaus) hat

chap·el

chap·er·on (*or* ·one)

chap·er·on·age

chap·fallen (*or* chop·) dejected

chapi·ter architectural term

chap·lain

chap·lain·cy (*plural* ·cies)

chap·let strung beads

chap·let·ed

chap·pal sandal

chapped

chap·pie *Slang* fellow

chap·ping

chaps *short for* chaparejos

chap·stick *US* lip salve

chap·ter

chap·ter·house

char (char·ring, charred)

char (*or* charr; *plural* char, chars *or* charr, charrs) fish

chara·banc

chara·cin (*or* ·cid) fish

char·ac·ter

char·ac·ter·ful

char·ac·ter·is·tic

char·ac·ter·is·ti·cal·ly

char·ac·teri·za·tion (*or* ·sa·tion)

char·ac·ter·ize (*or* ·ise)

char·ac·ter·less

cha·rade

char·as hashish

char·coal
chard
Cha·rente *French river*
Charent-Maritime *French department*
charge
charge·abil·ity
charge·able
char·gé d'af·faires (*plural* char·gés d'af·faires)
charg·er
Cha·ri *African river*
chari·ly
chari·ness
Char·ing Cross
Chari-Nile *language group*
chari·ot
chari·ot·eer
cha·ris·ma (*or* char·ism)
char·is·mat·ic
char·is·mati·cal·ly
chari·table
chari·table·ness
chari·tably
char·ity (*plural* ·ities)
cha·ri·va·ri (*or* shiva·ree) *mock serenade*
char·kha (*or* ·ka) *spinning wheel*
char·lady (*plural* ·ladies)
char·la·tan
char·la·tan·ism (*or* ·ry)
char·la·tan·is·tic
Charles·ton *US city*
charles·ton *dance*
char·lie *Slang fool*
char·lock *plant*
Char·lotte *US city*
char·lotte *pudding*
Charlotte Ama·lie *capital of Virgin Islands*
charm
charm·er
Char·meuse (*Trademark*) *fabric*
Char·mi·nar *Indian monument*
charm·ing
char·nel *sepulchral*
Char·ol·lais *cattle*
Charon *mythological character*
char·poy (*or* ·pai) *bedstead*
char·qui *dried meat*
char·quid

chart
chart·able
char·ter
char·tered
Char·ter·house *Carthusian monastery*
Chart·ism *reform movement*
Chart·ist
chart·ist *share analyst*
Char·tres *French city*
char·treuse *liqueur*
char·woman *plural* ·women
chary (chari·er, chari·est)
Cha·ryb·dis *mythological monster*
chase
chas·er
chasm
chas·mal (*or* ·mic)
chas·sé *ballet step*
chas·seur *French huntsman*
chas·sis (*plural* ·sis)
chaste
chas·ten
chas·ten·er
chas·tis·able
chas·tise
chas·tise·ment
chas·tity
chasu·ble
chat (chat·ting, chat·ted)
cha·teau (*or* châ·; *plural* ·teaux *or* ·teaus)
chat·elain (*fem* ·elaine) *castle keeper*
Chat·ham *Kent town; Pacific islands*
cha·toy·an·cy
cha·toy·ant *changing in lustre*
Chat·ta·noo·ga *US city*
chat·tel
chat·ter
chatter·box
chat·ter·er
chat·ti·ly
chat·ty (·ti·er, ·ti·est)
Chau·cerian
chaud·froid *sauce*
chauf·fer (*or* chau·fer) *heater*
chauf·feur (*fem* ·feuse)
chaul·moo·gra *tree*
chausses *medieval garment*

chau·vin·ism
chau·vin·ist
chau·vin·is·tic
chau·vin·is·ti·cal·ly
chaw *Dialect chew tobacco*
cha·yo·te *plant*
cheap *inexpensive; compare* cheep
cheap·en
cheap·ness
cheap·skate
cheat
cheat·er
Che·bo·ksa·ry *Soviet port*
Che·chen (*plural* ·chens *or* ·chen) *Soviet people*
Checheno-Ingush *Soviet republic*
check *pause; pattern; etc.; US spelling of* cheque
check·able
check·book *US spelling of* chequebook
check·er *one who checks; US spelling of* chequer
check·ered *US spelling of* chequered
checker·berry (*plural* ·berries)
checker·bloom *plant*
checker·board *US draughtboard*
check·ers *US draughts*
check-in (*noun*)
check·mate
check·out (*noun*)
check·point
check·up (*noun*)
checky *heraldic term*
Ched·dar
chedd·ite *explosive*
cheek
cheek·bone
cheeki·ly
cheeki·ness
cheek·piece
cheeky (cheeki·er, cheeki·est)
cheep *chirp; compare* cheap
cheep·er
cheer
cheer·ful
cheer·ful·ly
cheer·ful·ness
cheeri·ly

cheeri·ness
cheerio
cheer·leader
cheer·less
cheer·less·ness
cheers
cheery (cheeri·er, cheeri·est)
cheese
cheese·board
cheese·burg·er
cheese·cake
cheese·cloth
cheese·mon·ger
cheese·paring
cheesi·ness
cheesy (cheesi·er, cheesi·est)
chee·tah (or che·tah)
chef
chef-d'oeuvre (plural chefs-d'oeuvre) French masterpiece
Che·kiang Chinese province
che·la (plural ·lae) claws
che·la (plural ·las) Hindu disciple
che·la·ship
che·late chemistry term
che·la·tion
che·lic·era (plural ·erae) spider's claw
che·lic·er·al
che·lic·er·ate
che·lif·er·ous
che·li·form
Chelms·ford
che·loid variant spelling of keloid
che·lo·nian tortoise or turtle
chelp Dialect chatter
Chel·sea
Chel·ten·ham
Chel·ya·binsk Soviet city
chemi·cal
chemi·cal·ly
chemi·lu·mi·nes·cence
chemi·lu·mi·nes·cent
che·min de fer gambling game
che·mise
chemi·sette underbodice
chemi·sorb (or chemo·)
chemi·sorp·tion
chem·ist

chem·is·try (plural ·tries)
chemo·pro·phy·lac·tic
chemo·pro·phy·lax·is
chemo·recep·tor (or chemo·cep·tor)
chem·os·mo·sis
chem·os·mot·ic
chemo·sphere layer of atmosphere
chemo·spher·ic
che·mo·stat
chemo·syn·thesis
chemo·syn·thet·ic
chemo·syn·theti·cal·ly
chemo·tac·tic
chemo·tac·ti·cal·ly
chemo·tax·is biology term
chemo·thera·pist
chemo·thera·py
chemo·trop·ic
chemo·tropi·cal·ly
che·mot·ro·pism botany term
chem·pa·duk tree
chem·ur·gic (or ·gi·cal)
chem·ur·gy branch of chemistry
Che·nab Himalayan river
Cheng·chow (or Cheng-chou) Chinese city
Cheng·teh Chinese city
Cheng·tu (or Ch'eng-tu) Chinese city
che·nille
che·no·pod plant
che·no·po·dia·ceous
cheong·sam Chinese dress
cheque (US check)
cheque·book (US check·)
cheq·uer (US check·) pattern of squares; compare checker
chequer·board (US checker·)
cheq·uered (US check·ered)
Cheq·uers premier's country house
cheq·uers US draughts game
Cher French river
Cher·bourg French port
Che·rem·kho·vo Soviet city
cher·ish
cher·ish·able

cher·ish·er
Cher·nov·tsy Soviet city
cher·no·zem (or tscher·no·sem) black soil
Chero·kee (plural ·kees or ·kee)
che·root
cher·ry (plural ·ries)
cher·so·nese peninsula
chert quartz
Chert·sey Surrey town
cherty
cher·ub (plural ·ubs or cheru·bim)
che·ru·bic
che·ru·bi·cal
cher·vil
cher·vo·nets Soviet coin
Chesa·peake US bay
Chesh·ire
chess
chess·board
ches·sel cheese mould
chess·man (plural ·men)
chest
chest·ed
Ches·ter
Ches·ter·field Derbyshire town
ches·ter·field sofa
chesti·ly
chesti·ness
chest·nut
chesty (chesti·er, chesti·est)
cheval-de-frise barrier of spikes
cheva·lier
che·vet part of church
Che·vi·ot hills; sheep
che·vi·ot fabric
chev·rette goat skin
chev·ron
chev·ro·tain animal
chew
chew·able
chew·er
chewy (chewi·er, chewi·est)
Chey·enne American Indian; US city
chez French at the home of
chi Greek letter
chi·ack Austral to tease

chi·an·ti
Chi·apas Mexican state
chia·ro·scur·ism
chia·ro·scu·rist
chia·ro·scu·ro (*plural* ·ros) art term
chi·as·ma (*or* chi·asm; *plural* ·mas, ·ma·ta, *or* ·asms) biology term
chi·as·mal
chi·as·mic
chi·as·mus (*plural* ·mi) rhetoric term
chi·as·tic
chi·as·to·lite mineral
Chi·ba Japanese city
chi·bouk (*or* ·bouque) Turkish pipe
chic
Chi·ca·go
chi·ca·lo·te poppy
chi·cane
chi·can·er
chi·can·ery (*plural* ·eries)
Chich·es·ter
chi·chi
Chi·chi·haerh (*or* Ch'i-ch'i-haerh) Chinese city
chick
chicka·bid·dy
chicka·dee bird
chicka·ree squirrel
Chicka·saw (*plural* ·saws *or* ·saw) American Indian
chick·en
chicken-hearted (*or* -livered)
chicken-pox
chick·pea
chick·weed
Chi·cla·yo Peruvian city
chic·le gum
chi·co shrub
chico·ry (*or* chic·co·ry; *plural* ·ries)
chide (chid·ing; chid·ed *or* chid; chid·ed, chid, *or* chid·den)
chid·er
chief
chief·ly
chief·tain
chiff·chaff bird
chif·fon

chif·fo·nier (*or* ·fon·nier) furniture
chig·etai wild ass
chig·ger larva
chi·gnon
chigoe flea
Chi·hua·hua Mexican state; dog
chil·blain
child (*plural* chil·dren)
child·bed
child·birth
child·hood
child·ish
child·ish·ness
child·less
child·less·ness
child·like
chil·dren *plural of* child
Chile
Chil·ean
chili·ad group of one thousand
chili·ad·al (*or* ·ad·ic)
chili·asm theology term
chili·ast
chili·as·tic
chill
chil·li (*plural* ·lies)
chil·li con car·ne
chil·li·ness
Chil·lon Swiss castle
chil·lum clay pipe
chil·ly (·li·er, ·li·est)
chi·lo·pod invertebrate
Chil·tern Hills; Hundreds
Chi·lung (*or* Chi-lung) Taiwanese port
chi·maera fish; *compare* chimera
Chim·bo·te Peruvian port
chime
chi·mera (*or* ·maera) monster; biology term; *compare* chimaera
chi·mere (*or* chim·er, chim·ar) bishop's gown
chi·meri·cal (*or* ·mer·ic) fanciful
Chim·kent Soviet city
chim·ney
chimney·piece
chimney·pot
chimp
chim·pan·zee

chin
Chi·na country
chi·na porcelain
china·berry (*plural* ·berries)
China·graph (*Trademark*)
China·man (*plural* ·men)
China·town
china·ware
chinch US bedbug
chin·che·rin·chee plant
chin·chil·la
Chin-Chou (*or* Chin·chow) Chinese city
Chin·dit
Chin·dwin Burmese river
chine
chi·né mottled
Chi·nee *Slang* Chinaman
Chi·nese (*plural* ·nese)
Ching (*or* Ch'ing) Chinese dynasty
chink
Chin·kiang (*or* Cheng-chiang) Chinese port
chin·less
chino (*plural* chinos) cloth
chi·noi·serie
Chi·nook (*plural* ·nook *or* ·nooks) American Indian
chi·nook wind
Chi·nook·an
chin·qua·pin (*or* ·ca·pin, ·ka·pin) tree
chintz
chintzy (chintzi·er, chintzi·est)
chin·wag (·wag·ging, ·wagged)
chi·ono·doxa plant
Chios Greek island
chip (chip·ping, chipped)
chip·board
chip·munk
chipo·la·ta
chip·per
chip·ping
chip·py (*noun, plural* ·pies; *adj* ·pi·er, ·pi·est)
chir·al chemistry term
chi·ral·ity
chirm chirp
chi·rog·ra·pher

chi·ro·graph·ic (*or* ·graphi·cal)
chi·rog·ra·phy calligraphy
chi·ro·man·cy palmistry
Chiron centaur
chi·ropo·dist
chi·ropo·dy
chi·ro·prac·tic
chi·ro·prac·tor
chi·rop·ter bat
chi·rop·ter·an
chirp
chirp·er
chirpi·ly
chirpi·ness
chirpy (chirpi·er, chirpi·est)
chirr (*or* chirre, churr) make shrill sound
chir·rup
chir·rup·er
chir·rupy
chis·el (·el·ling, ·elled; *US* ·el·ing, ·eled)
chis·el·ler (*US* ·el·er)
chi-square statistics term
chit
Chi·ta Soviet city
chi·tal deer
chi·tar·ro·ne (*plural* ·ni) lute
chit-chat (·chat·ting, ·chat·ted)
chi·tin biochemical compound
chi·tin·oid
chi·tin·ous
chi·ton Greek tunic
Chit·ta·gong Bangladeshi port
chit·ter *US* twitter
chit·ter·lings (*or* chit·lins, chit·lings) pig intestines
chiv *Slang* knife
chiv·al·ric
chiv·al·rous
chiv·al·ry (*plural* ·ries)
chive (*or* chives)
chivy (*or* chiv·vy; chivies, chivy·ing, chiv·ied *or* chiv·vies, ·vy·ing, ·vied)
chlamy·date zoology term
chla·myd·eous botany term
chla·mydo·spore
chlor·acne skin disease

chlo·ral chemical compound
chlo·ram·bu·cil drug
chlo·ra·mine chemical compound
chlo·ram·pheni·col antibiotic
chlo·rate
chlor·dane (*or* ·dan) insecticide
chlo·rel·la alga
chlo·ren·chy·ma plant tissue
chlo·ric
chlo·ride
chlo·rid·ic
chlo·rin·ate
chlo·rina·tion
chlo·rina·tor
chlo·rine (*or* ·rin)
chlo·rite mineral
chlo·rit·ic
chlo·ro·ben·zene
chlo·ro·form
chlo·ro·hy·drin
Chlo·ro·my·ce·tin (*Trademark*)
chlo·ro·phyll (*or* ·phyl)
chlo·ro·phyl·loid
chlo·ro·phyl·lous
chlo·ro·pic·rin (*or* chlor·pic·rin) pesticide
chlo·ro·plast
chlo·ro·plast·ic
chlo·ro·prene chemical compound
chlo·ro·quine drug
chlo·ro·sis disease
chlo·ro·thia·zide
chlo·rot·ic
chlo·rous of chlorine
chlor·proma·zine drug
chlor·pro·pa·mide drug
cho·ano·cyte zoology term
choc-ice
chock
chock-a-block
chock·er *Slang* fed up
chock-full
choco·late
choco·laty
Choc·taw (*plural* ·taws *or* ·taw) American Indian
Chog·yal Indian ruler
choice
choice·ly

choice·ness
choir choral group; *compare* quire
choir·boy
choir·master
Choi·seul Pacific island
choke
choke·able
choke·berry (*plural* ·berries)
choke·bore shotgun
choke·cherry (*plural* ·cherries)
chok·er
choky (*or* ·ey)
cho·lecal·cif·er·ol vitamin
chol·an·gi·og·raphy bile-duct examination
chol·ecys·tec·to·my (*plural* ·mies) removal of gall bladder
chol·ecys·tog·raphy gall-bladder examination
chol·er anger
chol·era
chol·er·ic
chol·eroid
cho·les·ter·ol (*or* ·ter·in)
cho·li bodice
cho·line biochemical compound
cho·lin·er·gic biology term
cho·lin·es·ter·ase enzyme
chol·la cactus
Cho·lon Vietnamese city
chomp
chon Korean coin
chon·dri·fi·ca·tion
chon·dri·fy (·fies, ·fy·ing, ·fied) change into cartilage
chon·drio·so·mal
chon·drio·some biology term
chon·drite meteorite
chon·drit·ic
chon·dro·ma (*plural* ·mas *or* ·ma·ta) tumour
chon·dro·ma·tous
chon·drule meteorology term
Chong·jin (*or* Chung·) Korean port
Chon·ju Korean city
choose (choos·ing, chose, cho·sen)

choos·er
choosi·ly
choosi·ness
choosy (choosi·er, choosi·est)
chop (chop·ping, chopped)
cho·pine shoe
chop·logic
chop·per
chop·pi·ly
chop·pi·ness
chop·py (·pi·er, ·pi·est)
chop·stick
cho·ra·gus Greek chorus leader
cho·ral (*adj*)
cho·rale (*noun*)
cho·ral·ly
chord maths and music senses; *compare* cord
chord·al
chor·date animal with notochord; *compare* cordate
chord·ing musical term
chordo·phone musical instrument
chore
cho·rea neurological disorder
cho·real (*or* cho·re·ic)
cho·reo·dra·ma
cho·reo·graph
cho·reog·ra·pher (*or* ·reg·ra·pher)
cho·reo·graph·ic (*or* ·regraph·ic)
cho·reo·graphi·cal·ly (*or* ·regraphi·)
cho·reog·ra·phy (*or* ·reg·ra·phy)
cho·ri·amb (*or* ·am·bus; *plural* ·ambs *or* ·am·bi) prosody term
cho·ri·am·bic
cho·ric of a chorus
cho·ri·on embryonic membrane
cho·ri·on·ic (*or* cho·rial)
chor·is·ter
Chor·ley Lancashire town
cho·rog·ra·pher
cho·ro·graph·ic (*or* ·graphi·cal)
cho·ro·graphi·cal·ly

cho·rog·ra·phy mapping regions
cho·roid membrane of eyeball
cho·rol·ogy geography term
chor·tle
cho·rus (*plural* ·ruses)
Chor·zow Polish city
chose
cho·sen
Cho·ta Nag·pur Indian plateau
Chou Chinese dynasty
chou (*plural* choux) cabbage; *compare* choux
chough bird
choux pastry; *plural of* chou
chow
chow-chow
chow·der soup
chow mein Chinese food
chre·ma·tis·tic of money-making
chres·ard biology term
chrism (*or* chris·om) anointing oil; *compare* chrisom
chris·mal
chris·ma·tory (*plural* ·tories) receptacle for consecrated oil
chris·om baptismal robe; *compare* chrism
Christ
Chris·ta·del·phian
Christ·church New Zealand city; Dorset town
chris·ten
Chris·ten·dom
chris·ten·er
chris·ten·ing
Chris·tian
Chris·tia·nia *former name for* Oslo
Chris·ti·an·ity
Chris·tiani·za·tion (*or* ·sa·tion)
Chris·tian·ize (*or* ·ise)
Chris·tian·iz·er (*or* ·is·er)
Chris·tian·ly
Christ·like
Christ·mas
Christ·mas·sy
Christmas·tide
Chris·to·logi·cal
Chris·tol·ogist

Chris·tol·ogy
Christ's-thorn plant
chro·ma physics term
chro·mate
chro·mat·ic
chro·mati·cal·ly
chro·mati·cism
chro·ma·tic·ity physics term
chro·mat·ic·ness physics term
chro·mat·ics (*or* chro·ma·tol·ogy) science of colour
chro·ma·tid chromosome part
chro·ma·tin substance of chromosomes
chro·ma·tin·ic
chro·ma·tist (*or* chro·ma·tolo·gist)
chro·ma·to·gram
chro·ma·tog·ra·pher
chro·ma·to·graph·ic
chro·ma·to·graphi·cal·ly
chro·ma·tog·ra·phy chemical analysis
chro·ma·tol·ogy *variant of* chromatics
chro·ma·toly·sis cytology term
chro·ma·to·phore zoology term
chro·ma·to·phor·ic
chro·ma·toph·or·ous
chrome
chro·mic
chro·mi·nance physics term
chro·mite mineral
chro·mium
chro·mo·gen
chro·mo·gen·ic colour-producing
chro·mo·litho·graph
chro·mo·li·thog·ra·pher
chro·mo·litho·graph·ic
chro·mo·li·thog·ra·phy
chro·mo·mere cytology term
chro·mo·nema (*plural* ·nema·ta) biology term
chro·mo·nemal (*or* ·nemat·ic, ·nemic)
chro·mo·phore chemistry term
chro·mo·phor·ic (*or* ·ous)

chro·mo·plast part of cell
chro·mo·pro·tein
chro·mo·so·mal
chro·mo·some
chro·mo·sphere layer of sun
chro·mo·spher·ic
chro·mous
chro·myl
chro·naxie (or ·naxy) physiology term
chron·ic
chroni·cal·ly
chro·nic·ity
chroni·cle
chroni·cler
Chroni·cles Old Testament book
chrono·bi·ol·ogy
chrono·gram
chrono·gram·mat·ic (or ·mati·cal)
chrono·graph time recorder
chro·nog·ra·pher
chrono·graph·ic
chrono·logi·cal
chrono·logi·cal·ly
chro·nolo·gist
chro·nol·ogy (plural ·ogies)
chro·nom·eter timepiece
chrono·met·ric (or ·ri·cal)
chrono·metri·cal·ly
chro·nom·etry
chro·non unit
chrono·scope
chrono·scop·ic
chrysa·lis (plural ·lises, ·lids, or chry·sali·des)
chry·san·themum
chrysa·ro·bin drug
chrys·el·ephan·tine statuary term
chryso·ber·yl
chryso·lite gemstone
chryso·lit·ic
chryso·prase gemstone
chryso·tile mineral
chtho·nian (or ·nic) of the underworld
chub (plural chub or chubs)
Chubb (Trademark) lock
chub·bi·ness
chub·by (·bi·er, ·bi·est)

chuck
chuck·le
chuck·ler
chuck·wal·la lizard
chuck-will's-widow bird
chud·dar Indian shawl
chu·fa sedge
chuff
chuffed
chuf·fy Scot chubby
chug (chug·ging, chugged)
chu·kar partridge
Chuk·chi Soviet peninsula
chuk·ker (or ·ka) polo term
chum (chum·ming, chummed)
chum·mi·ly
chum·mi·ness
chum·my (·mi·er, ·mi·est)
chump
chump·ing Dialect collecting wood
chun·der
chun·der·ous Austral nauseating
Chung·king (or Ch'ung-ch'ing) Chinese port
chunk
chunki·ly
chunki·ness
chunky (chunki·er, chunki·est)
Chun·nel Channel tunnel
chun·ter
church
church·goer
church·going
Church·ill Canadian river
church·man (plural ·men)
church·warden
church·woman (plural ·women)
church·yard
chu·ri·dars Indian trousers
chu·rin·ga Aboriginal amulet
churl
churl·ish
churn
churr variant spelling of chirr
chute
chut·ney (or ·nee)

chut·tie Austral chewing gum
Chu·vash (plural ·vash or ·vashes) Soviet people
chy·la·ceous (or chy·lous)
chyle intestinal fluid
chyme digested food
chy·mo·sin rennin
chy·mo·tryp·sin enzyme
chy·mo·tryp·sino·gen enzyme precursor
chy·mous
ciao Italian greeting
ci·bo·rium (plural ·ria) communion vessel
ci·ca·da (or ci·ca·la; plural ·das, ·dae or ·las, ·le)
cica·tri·cial
cica·tric·le biology term
ci·cat·ri·cose
cica·trix (plural ·tri·ces) scar
cica·tri·zant (or ·sant)
cica·tri·za·tion (or ·sa·tion)
cica·trize (or ·trise) heal
cica·triz·er (or ·tris·er)
cic·ely plant
cic·ero (plural ·eros) unit
cic·ero·ne (plural ·nes or ·ni) tourist guide
Cic·ero·nian eloquent
cich·lid fish
cich·loid
ci·der
ci·gar
ciga·rette
ciga·ril·lo (plural ·los) cigar
cig·gy (plural ·gies) Slang cigarette
cilia plural of cilium
cili·ary
cili·ate
cili·at·ed
cili·ation
cil·ice haircloth
cilio·late
cil·ium (plural cilia) minute hair
cim·ba·lom dulcimer
Cim·bri Germanic people
Cim·brian
Cim·bric

ci·mex (*plural* cimi·ces)
bedbug
Cim·me·rian very dark
cinch
cin·cho·na tree bark
cin·choni·dine alkaloid
cin·cho·nine alkaloid
cin·chon·ism poisoning
cin·cho·ni·za·tion (*or*
·sa·tion)
cin·cho·nize (*or* ·nise)
Cin·cin·nati
cinc·ture surround
cin·der
cin·dery
cine film
cin·easte film enthusiast
cin·ema
Cin·ema·scope
(*Trademark*)
cin·ema·theque small
cinema
cin·emat·ic
cin·emati·cal·ly
cin·emato·graph
cin·ema·tog·ra·pher
cin·emato·graph·ic
cin·ema·tog·ra·phy
cin·eol (*or* ·eole)
eucalyptol
Cin·era·ma (*Trademark*)
cin·eraria plant
cin·erar·ium (*plural*
·eraria) place for
cremation ashes
cin·erary (*adj*)
cin·era·tor cremation
furnace
ci·ner·eous (*or*
cin·eri·tious) greyish
cin·erin chemical compound
cin·gu·late (*or* ·lat·ed)
cin·gu·lum (*plural* ·la)
anatomical part
cin·na·bar mineral
cin·na·mon
cin·na·mon·ic (*or*
ci·nam·ic)
cin·quain poem
cinque five
cinque·foil plant
Cinque Ports
Cin·za·no (*Trademark*)
ci·pher (*or* cy·pher) secret
writing; *compare* sypher

cipo·lin marble
cir·ca
cir·ca·dian daily
Cir·cas·sia Soviet region
Cir·cas·sian
Circe mythological character
cir·ci·nate botany term
Cir·ci·nus constellation
cir·cle
cir·cler
cir·clet
cir·cuit
cir·cuit·al of a circuit
cir·cui·tous indirect
cir·cui·tous·ly
cir·cuit·ry circuit system
cir·cu·ity (*plural* ·ities)
cir·cu·lar
cir·cu·lar·ity (*or* ·ness)
cir·cu·lari·za·tion (*or*
·sa·tion)
cir·cu·lar·ize (*or* ·ise)
cir·cu·lar·iz·er (*or* ·is·er)
cir·cu·late
cir·cu·la·tion
cir·cu·la·tive
cir·cu·la·tor
cir·cu·la·tory
cir·cum·am·bi·ence (*or*
·en·cy)
cir·cum·am·bi·ent
cir·cum·am·bu·late
cir·cum·am·bu·la·tion
cir·cum·am·bu·la·tor
cir·cum·am·bu·la·tory
cir·cum·ben·di·bus
circumlocution
cir·cum·cise
cir·cum·ci·sion
cir·cum·fer·ence
cir·cum·fer·en·tial
cir·cum·flex
cir·cum·flex·ion
cir·cum·flu·ous surrounded
by water
cir·cum·fuse
cir·cum·fu·sion
cir·cum·lo·cu·tion
cir·cum·locu·tory
cir·cum·lu·nar
cir·cum·navi·gable
cir·cum·navi·gate
cir·cum·navi·ga·tion
cir·cum·navi·ga·tor

cir·cum·nu·tate botany
term
cir·cum·nu·ta·tion
cir·cum·po·lar
cir·cum·scis·sile botany
term
cir·cum·scribe
cir·cum·scrip·tion
cir·cum·spect
cir·cum·spec·tion
cir·cum·spec·tive
cir·cum·stance
cir·cum·stan·tial
cir·cum·stan·ti·ality
(*plural* ·alities)
cir·cum·stan·tial·ly
cir·cum·stan·ti·ate
cir·cum·stan·tia·tion
cir·cum·val·late surround
with fortification
cir·cum·val·la·tion
cir·cum·vent
cir·cum·vent·er (*or*
ven·tor)
cir·cum·ven·tion
cir·cum·vo·lu·tion
cir·cum·vo·lu·tory
cir·cus (*plural* ·cuses)
ciré waxed
Ci·ren·ces·ter
cirque mountain feature
cir·rate (*or* cir·rose,
cir·rous) biology term
cir·rhosed
cir·rho·sis
cir·rhot·ic
cir·ri·pede (*or* ·ped)
marine animal
cir·ro·cu·mu·lus (*plural*
·li)
cir·rose (*or* ·rous)
cir·ro·stra·tus (*plural* ·ti)
cir·rus (*plural* ·ri) cloud;
tentacle; *compare* schirrhus
cir·soid medical term
cis·al·pine
cis·co (*plural* ·coes *or*
·cos) fish
cis·lu·nar between earth and
moon
cis·mon·tane
cis·soid curve
cist box; *compare* cyst
cis·ta·ceous botany term
Cis·ter·cian monk

cis·tern

cis·ter·na (*plural* ·nae)
  anatomy term

cis·tron genetics term

cit·able (*or* cite·able)

cita·del

ci·ta·tion

cite

cithа·ra (*or* kitha·ra)
  musical instrument

citi·fy (*or* city·fy; ·fies,
  ·fy·ing, ·fied)

citi·zen

citi·zen·ry (*plural* ·ries)

citi·zen·ship

Ci·tlal·té·petl Mexican
  volcano

cit·ral plant oil

cit·rate

cit·re·ous greenish-yellow

cit·ric

cit·ri·cul·ture

cit·rin vitamin

cit·rine gemstone

cit·ron fruit

cit·ron·el·la grass

cit·ron·el·lal plant oil

cit·rul·line amino acid

cit·rus (*plural* ·ruses)

cit·tern musical instrument

City London's commercial
  area

city (*plural* cities)

civ·et

civ·ic

civi·cal·ly

civ·ics

civ·il

ci·vil·ian

ci·vil·ity (*plural* ·ities)

civi·li·za·tion (*or* ·sa·tion)

civi·lize (*or* ·lise)

civi·liz·er (*or* ·lis·er)

civ·il·ly

civ·vy (*plural* ·vies) *Slang*
  civilian

clack

Clack·man·nan former
  Scottish county

Clac·ton Essex town

Clac·to·nian Palaeolithic
  culture

clad (clad·ding, clad)

clade

cla·dis·tic

cla·dis·tics

cla·doc·er·an animal

clad·ode (*or* clado·phyll)
  plant stem

claim

claim·able

claim·ant

claim·er

clair·audi·ence psychology
  term

clair-obscure art term

clair·voy·ance

clair·voy·ant

clam (clam·ming,
  clammed)

cla·mant noisy

clama·to·rial ornithology
  term

clam·bake

clam·ber

clam·mi·ly

clam·mi·ness

clam·my (·mi·er, ·mi·est)

clam·or·ous

clam·our (*US* ·or)

clamp

clamp·er shoe spike

clan

clan·des·tine

clang

clang·er that which clangs;
  mistake

clang·or (*or* ·our) loud
  noise

clang·or·ous (*or* ·our·ous)

clank

clan·nish

clans·man (*plural* ·men)

clans·woman (*plural*
  ·women)

clap (clap·ping, clapped)

clap·board

Clap·ham

clap·per

clapper·board

clap·trap

claque hired applauders

clara·bel·la (*or* clari··)
  organ stop

clar·ence carriage

Clar·en·don village near
  Salisbury

clar·en·don typeface

clar·et

clari·fi·ca·tion

clari·fier

clari·fy (·fies, ·fy·ing,
  ·fied)

clari·net

clari·net·ist (*or* ·net·tist)

cla·rino musical term

clari·on

clario·net *Obsolete* clarinet

clar·ity

clarkia plant

cla·ro cigar

clarts *Dialect* lumps of mud

clary (*plural* claries) plant

clash

clash·er

clasp

clasp·er

class

class-conscious

class-conscious·ness

clas·sic

clas·si·cal

clas·si·cal·ism

clas·si·cal·ity

clas·si·cal·ly

clas·si·cism (*or*
  clas·si·cal·ism)

clas·si·cist (*or*
  clas·si·cal·ist)

clas·si·cis·tic

clas·sics

clas·si·fi·able

clas·si·fi·ca·tion

clas·si·fi·ca·tion·al

clas·si·fi·ca·tory

clas·si·fi·er

clas·si·fy (·fies, ·fy·ing,
  ·fied)

classi·ly

classi·ness

clas·sis (*plural* ·ses)
  church elders

class·less

class·less·ness

class·mate

class·room

classy (classi·er,
  classi·est)

clas·tic geology term

clath·rate netlike

clat·ter

clat·tery

clau·di·ca·tion lameness

claus·al

clause

claus·tral *variant spelling of* cloistral

claus·tro·phobe

claus·tro·pho·bia

claus·tro·pho·bic

claus·tro·pho·bi·cal·ly

cla·vate (*or* clavi·form) club-shaped

clav·er *Scot* gossip

clavi·chord

clavi·chord·ist

clavi·cle

clavi·corn beetle

cla·vicu·lar

cla·vier musical instrument

Cla·vi·us moon crater

claw

claw·er

clay

clay·bank *US* brown colour

clay·ey

clay·like

clay·more sword

clay·pan clay layer

clay·stone

clay·to·nia plant

clean

clean·able

clean-cut

clean·er

clean-limbed

clean·li·ness

clean·ly (·li·er, ·li·est)

clean·ness

cleans·able

cleanse

cleans·er

clean-shaven

clear

clear·ance

clear·cole wall whiting

clear-cut

clear-eyed

clear-headed

clear-headed·ness

clear·ing

clear·ness

clear-sighted

clear·way

clear·wing moth

cleat

cleav·able

cleav·age

cleave (cleav·ing; cleaved *or* clove; cleft, cleaved, *or* clo·ven)

cleav·er

cleav·ers goosegrass

cleck *Dialect* gossip

cleek golf club

Clee·thorpes English resort

clef

cleft

cleg horsefly

cleis·toga·mous (*or* ·to·gam·ic)

cleis·toga·my botany term

clem (clem·ming, clemmed) *Dialect* be hungry

clema·tis

clem·en·cy (*plural* ·cies)

clem·ent

clem·en·tine

clench

cleo·me plant

clep·to·ma·nia *variant spelling of* kleptomania

clere·storied (*or* clear-storied)

clere·story (*or* clear-; *plural* ·stories) church windows

cler·gy (*plural* ·gies)

clergy·man (*plural* ·men)

cler·ic

cleri·cal

cleri·cal·ism

cleri·cal·ly

cleri·hew verse

clerk

clerk·dom

clerk·ly

clerk·ship

Clermont-Ferrand French city

cle·ru·chy Athenian colony

cleve·ite mineral

Cleve·land

clev·er

clev·er·ly

clev·er·ness

clev·is coupling device

clew yarn; *compare* clue

cli·ché

cli·ché'd (*or* ·chéd)

Cli·chy Parisian suburb

click

click·er

cli·ent

cli·en·tal of a client

cli·en·tele customers

cliff

cliff·hanger

cliff·hanging

cli·mac·ter·ic critical period

cli·mac·teri·cal

cli·mac·tic (*or* ·ti·cal) of a climax

cli·mate

cli·mat·ic (*or* ·mati·cal *or* ·mat·al)

cli·ma·to·log·ic (*or* ·logi·cal)

cli·ma·tolo·gist

cli·ma·tol·ogy

cli·max

climb

climb·er

clime climate

clin·al of a cline

cli·nan·drium (*plural* ·dria) botany term

clinch

clinch·er

cline ecology term

cling (cling·ing, clung)

cling·er

cling·fish (*plural* ·fish *or* ·fishes)

clingi·ness (*or* cling·ing·ness)

cling·stone peach

clingy

clin·ic

clini·cal

cli·ni·cian

clink

clink·er

clinker-built (*or* clincher-)

clink·stone

cli·nom·eter surveying instrument

cli·no·met·ric (*or* ·ri·cal)

cli·nom·etry

cli·no·stat botany term

clin·quant tinsel

clin·to·nia plant

clip (clip·ping, clipped)

clip·board

clip-clop

clip·per

clip·pers
clip·pie *Slang* bus
 conductress
clip·ping
clique
cli·quey (*or* ·quy)
cli·quish
clish·ma·clav·er *Scot* gossip
cli·tel·lum (*plural* ·la) part
 of worm
clit·ic unstressed
clito·ral
clito·ris
cloa·ca (*plural* ·cae)
 zoology term
cloa·cal
cloak
cloak·room
clob·ber
cloche
clock
clock·maker
clock·wise
clock·work
clod
clod·dish
clod·dy
clod·hop·per
clod·hop·ping
clog (clog·ging, clogged)
clog·gi·ness
clog·gy (·gi·er, ·gi·est)
cloi·son·né enamel work
clois·ter
clois·tered
clois·tral (*or* claus·tral)
clomp
clon·al
clone (*or* clon)
clon·ic medical term
clo·nic·ity
clonk
clo·nus convulsion
clop (clop·ping, clopped)
close
close-down (*noun*)
close-fisted
close-grained
close-hauled sailing term
close-knit
close·ly
close·ness
clos·er
close-stool
clos·et

close-up (*noun*)
clos·ing
clos·trid·ial (*or* ·ian)
clos·trid·ium (*plural*
 ·iums *or* ·ia) bacterium
clo·sure
clot (clot·ting, clot·ted)
cloth
cloth·bound
clothe (cloth·ing, clothed
 or clad)
clothes
clothes·horse
clothes·line
clothes·press
clo·thi·er
cloth·ing
clo·ture *US* closure
cloud
cloud·berry (*plural*
 ·berries)
cloud·burst
cloud-cuckoo-land
cloudi·ly
cloudi·ness
cloud·less
cloud·let
cloud·scape
cloudy (cloudi·er,
 cloudi·est)
clough *Dialect* gorge
clout
clove
clo·ven
clo·ver
clover·leaf (*plural*
 ·leaves)
clown
clown·ery
clown·ish
cloy
cloy·ed·ness
cloy·ing·ly
cloy·ing·ness
club (club·bing, clubbed)
club·bable (*or* ·able)
club·by (·bi·er, ·bi·est)
club-footed
club·haul nautical term
club·house
club·land
club·man (*plural* ·men)
cluck
clucky *Austral* pregnant

clue (clu·ing, clued)
 evidence; *compare* clew
clue·less
Cluj Romanian city
clum·ber spaniel
clump
clump·ish (*or* clump·like)
clumpy
clum·si·ly
clum·si·ness
clum·sy (·si·er, ·si·est)
clung
Clu·ni·ac of Cluny
clunk
Clu·ny French town
clu·peid fish
clu·peoid
clus·ter
clus·tery
clutch
clut·ter
Clw·yd Welsh county
Clyde Scottish river
Clyde·bank Scottish town
Clydes·dale horse
clype *Scot* tell tales
clyp·eal (*or* clype·ate)
clyp·eus (*plural* clypei)
 part of insect's head
clys·ter enema
cni·dar·ian zoology term
cnido·blast zoology term
Cni·dus ancient Greek city
Cnos·sus *variant spelling of*
 Knossos
co·ac·er·vate chemistry
 term
co·ac·er·va·tion
coach
coach·er
coach·ing
coach·man (*plural* ·men)
coach·work
co·ac·tion
co·ac·tive
co·ac·tiv·ity
co·ad·ju·tant
co·ad·ju·tor bishop's
 assistant
co·adu·nate biology term
co·adu·na·tion
co·adu·na·tive
co·agu·lable
co·agu·lant (*or*
 co·agu·la·tor)

co·agu·lase enzyme
co·agu·late
co·agu·la·tion
co·agu·la·tive
co·agu·lum (*plural* ·la)
  coagulated mass
Coa·hui·la Mexican state
coal
coal·er coal transporter
coa·lesce
coa·les·cence
coa·les·cent
coal·face
coal·field
coal·fish (*plural* ·fish *or*
  ·fishes)
coa·li·tion
coa·li·tion·al
coa·li·tion·ist (*or* ·er)
coal·man (*plural* ·men)
Coal·port china
coaly
coam·ing nautical term
co·ap·ta·tion joining two
  surfaces
co·arc·tate zoology term
co·arc·ta·tion
coarse rough; *compare*
  corse; course
coarse·ly
coars·en
coarse·ness
coast
coast·al
coast·er
coast·guard
coast·line
coat
coat·ed
coatee small coat
coa·ti (*or* coati-mundi)
  animal
coat·ing
coat·less
coat·tail
co·author
coax
coax·er
co·ax·ial (*or* ·ax·al)
cob
co·balt
co·bal·tic
co·bal·tite (*or* ·tine)
  mineral
co·bal·tous

cob·ber *Austral* friend
cob·ble
cob·bler
cobble·stone
co·bel·lig·er·ent
co·bia fish
co·ble *Scot* fishing boat
Co·blenz *variant spelling of*
  Koblenz
cob·nut
Cobol computer language
co·bra
Co·burg West German city
co·burg loaf
cob·web
cob·webbed
cob·web·by
coca shrub
Coca-Cola (*Trademark*)
co·caine (*or* ·cain)
co·cain·ism
co·caini·za·tion (*or*
  ·sa·tion)
co·cain·ize (*or* ·ise)
coc·cal
coc·ci *plural of* coccus
coc·cid insect
coc·cidi·oi·do·my·co·sis
  fungal disease
coc·cidio·sis (*plural* ·ses)
  animal disease
coc·cif·er·ous
coc·coid
coc·co·lith geology term
coc·cous (*adj*)
coc·cus (*plural* ·ci)
  bacterium
coc·cyg·eal
coc·cyx (*plural* ·cy·ges)
Co·cha·bam·ba Bolivian
  city
Co·chin Indian region and
  port
cochi·neal
coch·lea (*plural* ·leae) ear
  part
coch·lear
coch·leate shell-shaped
cock
cock·ade
cock-a-doodle-doo
cock-a-hoop
Cock·aigne imaginary land
cock-a-leekie soup

cocka·lo·rum self-
  important person
cocka·tiel (*or* ·teel) parrot
cocka·too (*plural* ·toos)
  parrot
cocka·trice monster
cock·chafer beetle
cock·crow
cock·er
cock·er·el
cock·eye
cock·eyed
cock·fight
cock·horse
cocki·ly
cocki·ness
cock·le
cockle·bur weed
cockle·shell
cock·loft garret
cock·ney
cock·ney·fi·ca·tion (*or*
  ·ni·)
cock·ney·fy (*or* ·ni·; ·fies,
  ·fy·ing, ·fied)
cock·ney·ism
cock·pit
cock·roach
cocks·comb (*or*
  cox·comb)
cocks·foot (*plural* ·foots)
  grass
cock·shy throw
cock·spur grass
cock·sure
cock·swain *variant spelling*
  of coxswain
cock·tail
cock·up
cocky (cocki·er,
  cocki·est)
coco (*plural* cocos) *short*
  for coconut
co·coa
coco de mer tree
coco·nut
co·coon
co·co·pan mining wagon
co·cotte
co·co·yam vegetable
cod (*noun, plural* cod *or*
  cods; *verb* cod·ding,
  cod·ded)
coda
cod·dle

cod·dler
code
co·dec·li·na·tion
co·deine
cod·er
co·dex (*plural* co·di·ces)
cod·fish (*plural* ·fish *or*
·fishes)
codg·er
codi·cil
codi·cil·la·ry
co·di·col·ogy
codi·fi·ca·tion
codi·fi·er
codi·fy (·fies, ·fy·ing,
·fied)
cod·ling (*or* ·lin) apple
co·do·main maths term
co·don genetics term
cod·piece
co-driver
cods·wallop
co-ed
co-edit
co·edi·tion
co·edi·tor
co·edu·ca·tion
co·edu·ca·tion·al
co·edu·ca·tion·al·ly
co·ef·fi·cient
coe·la·canth primitive fish
coe·len·ter·ate animal
coe·len·ter·ic
coe·len·ter·on (*plural*
·tera) zoology term
coe·li·ac (*US* ce·) of the
abdomen
coe·lom (*US* ce·) body
cavity
coe·lo·mate (*US* ce·)
coe·lo·stat astronomical
instrument
coe·nes·the·sia (*or* ·sis,
ce·)
coe·nes·thet·ic (*or* ce·)
coe·no·bite (*or* ce·)
member of religious order
coe·no·cyte botany term
coe·no·cyt·ic
coe·no·sarc zoology term
coe·nu·rus larva
co·en·zyme
co·equal
co·equali·ty
co·equal·ly

co·erce
co·er·cible
co·er·cion
co·er·cion·ary
co·er·cion·ist
co·er·cive
co·er·cive·ness
co·er·civ·ity physics term
co·es·sen·tial
co·es·sen·tial·ity (*or*
·ness)
co·eter·nity
co·eval contemporary
co·eval·ity
co·eval·ly
co·ex·ist
co·ex·ist·ence
co·ex·ist·ent
co·ex·tend
co·ex·ten·sion
co·ex·ten·sive
coff *Scot* buy
cof·fee
coffee·pot
cof·fer
coffer·dam underwater
chamber
cof·fin
cof·fle chained slaves
cog (cog·ging, cogged)
co·gen·cy
co·gent
cogi·tate
cogi·ta·tion
cogi·ta·tive
cogi·ta·tor
Cog·nac French town;
brandy
cog·nate
cog·na·tion relatedness
cog·ni·tion perception
cog·ni·tive
cog·ni·zable (*or* ·sable)
cog·ni·zance (*or* ·sance)
cog·ni·zant (*or* ·sant)
cog·nize (*or* ·nise) perceive
cog·no·men Roman family
name
co·gno·scen·ti (*or*
cono·scen·ti; *sing.* ·te)
co·gon grass
cog·wheel
co·hab·it
co·hab·it·ant (*or* ·it·er)
co·habi·ta·tion

co·heir
co·here
co·her·ence (*or* ·en·cy)
co·her·ent
co·her·er
co·he·sion
co·he·sive
coho (*plural* coho *or*
cohos) fish
co·ho·bate redistil
co·hort
co·hosh plant
co·hune palm tree
coif cap
coif·feur (*fem* ·feuse)
hairdresser
coif·fure hair style
coign (*or* coigne) *variant
spellings of* quoin; *compare*
coin
coil
coil·er
Co·im·ba·tore Indian city
Coim·bra Portuguese city
coin currency; *compare*
quoin
coin·age
co·in·cide
co·in·ci·dence
co·in·ci·dent
co·in·ci·dent·al
co·in·ci·dent·al·ly
coin·er
coin-op
co·in·sur·ance
co·in·sure
Coin·treau (*Trademark*)
coir coconut fibre
coit *Austral* buttocks
coi·tal
coi·tus (*or* ·tion)
Coke (*Trademark*) Coca-
Cola
coke
coku·lo·ris film term
col
cola (*or* kola) tree; nut
col·an·der sieve; *compare*
calendar; calender
co·lati·tude
col·can·non cabbage dish
Col·ches·ter
col·chi·cine alkaloid
col·chi·cum plant

Col·chis ancient Asian country

col·co·thar rouge

cold

cold-blooded

cold-blooded·ness

cold-drawn metallurgy term

cold-hearted

cold·ish

cold·ness

cold-weld

cole cabbage

co·lec·to·my (*plural* ·mies)

cole·man·ite mineral

col·eop·ter·an (*plural* ·ter·ans *or* ·tera) beetle

col·eop·ter·ist

col·eop·ter·ous

col·eop·tile botany term

col·eo·rhi·za (*plural* ·zae) botany term

cole·slaw

co·leus (*plural* ·uses) plant

col·ey fish; *compare* coly

col·ic

col·icky

colic·root

colic·weed

Co·li·ma Mexican state and city

coli·seum (*or* col·os·seum)

co·li·tic

co·li·tis (*or* colo·ni·tis)

col·labo·rate

col·labo·ra·tion

col·labo·ra·tive

col·labo·ra·tor

col·lage

col·la·gen protein

col·la·gen·ic (*or* ·gen·ous)

col·lag·ist

col·lap·sar black hole

col·lapse

col·laps·ibil·ity

col·laps·ible (*or* ·able)

col·lar

collar·bone

col·lard cabbage

col·lar·ette

col·late

col·lat·er·al

col·lat·er·al·ly

col·la·tion

col·la·tive

col·la·tor

col·league

col·lect

col·lect·able (*or* ·ible)

col·lec·ta·nea miscellany

col·lec·tion

col·lec·tive

col·lec·tiv·ism

col·lec·tiv·ist

col·lec·tiv·is·tic

col·lec·tiv·ity (*plural* ·ities)

col·lec·tivi·za·tion (*or* ·sa·tion)

col·lec·ti·vize (*or* ·vise)

col·lec·tor

col·lec·to·rate

col·leen *Irish* girl

col·lege

col·le·gial

col·legian

col·legi·ate

col·legium (*plural* ·legiums *or* ·legia)

col·lem·bo·lan insect

col·len·chy·ma plant tissue

Colles' frac·ture

col·let jewellery setting

col·lide

col·lie

col·li·er

col·liery (*plural* ·lieries)

col·li·gate join

col·li·ga·tion

col·li·ga·tive

col·li·mate

col·li·ma·tion

col·li·ma·tor optical device

col·lin·ear

col·lin·ear·ity

col·lin·sia plant

col·li·sion

col·lo·cate

col·lo·ca·tion

col·lo·cu·tor

col·lo·di·on (*or* ·dium) liquid

col·logue (·lo·guing, ·logued) conspire

col·loid

col·loi·dal

col·loi·dal·ity

col·lop *Dialect* meat slice

col·lo·quial

col·lo·qui·al·ism

col·lo·qui·al·ly

col·lo·quium (*plural* ·quiums *or* ·quia)

col·lo·quy (*plural* ·quies)

(collossus) *incorrect spelling of* colossus

col·lo·type printing process

col·lo·typ·ic

col·lude

col·lu·sion

col·lu·sive

col·lu·vial

col·lu·vium (*plural* ·via *or* ·viums) rock fragments

col·ly *Dialect* soot

col·lyr·ium (*plural* ·lyria *or* ·lyr·iums) eye lotion

col·ly·wob·bles

colo·bus monkey

colo·cynth plant

co·loga·rithm

co·logne perfume

Co·logne West German city

Co·lom·bia South American republic; *compare* Columbia

Co·lom·bian

Co·lom·bo Sri Lankan capital

co·lon

Co·lón Panamanian port

colo·nel

colo·nel·cy (*or* colo·nel·ship)

co·lo·nial

co·lo·ni·al·ism

co·lo·ni·al·ist

co·lo·ni·al·ly

co·lon·ic

colo·nist

colo·ni·tis *variant of* colitis

colo·niz·able (*or* ·nis·able)

colo·ni·za·tion (*or* ·sa·tion)

colo·nize (*or* ·nise)

colo·niz·er (*or* ·nis·er)

col·on·nade

col·on·nad·ed

Col·on·say Hebridean island

colo·ny (*plural* ·nies)

colo·phon emblem

co·lopho·ny rosin

col·or *US spelling of* colour

Colo·ra·do

col·or·ant

col·ora·tion

colo·ra·tu·ra (*or* col·ora·ture) musical term

col·or·if·ic

col·or·im·eter

col·ori·met·ric (*or* ·ri·cal)

col·or·im·etry

co·los·sal

co·los·sal·ly

Col·os·seum Roman amphitheatre

col·os·seum *variant spelling of* coliseum

co·los·sus (*plural* ·si *or* ·suses)

co·los·to·my (*plural* ·mies) artificial colon opening

co·los·tral

co·los·trum first breast milk

co·loto·my (*plural* ·mies)

col·our (*US* col·or)

col·our·able (*US* ·or·)

col·our·ant (*US* ·or·)

(colouration) *incorrect spelling of* coloration

colour-blind (*US* color-)

col·oured (*US* ·ored)

colour·fast (*US* color·)

col·our·ful (*US* ·or·)

col·our·ful·ly (*US* ·or·)

col·our·ing (*US* ·or·)

col·our·ist (*US* ·or·)

col·our·is·tic (*US* ·or·)

col·our·ize (·ise; *US* col·or·ize)

col·our·less (*US* ·or·)

colour·man (*US* color·; *plural* ·men) paint dealer

col·oury (*or* ·ory)

col·pi·tis medical term

col·por·teur book pedlar

Colt (*Trademark*) revolver

colt

col·ter *US spelling of* coulter

colt·ish

colts·foot (*plural* ·foots) plant

colu·brid snake

colu·brine of snakes

co·lu·go lemur

Co·lum·ba constellation

col·um·bar·ium (*plural* ·ia) dovecote

Co·lum·bia US river and city; *compare* Colombia

Co·lum·bian

co·lum·bic

Col·um·bine pantomime character

col·um·bine plant

co·lum·bite mineral

co·lum·bium chemical element

Co·lum·bus US city

colu·mel·la (*plural* ·lae) biology term

colu·mel·lar

col·umn

co·lum·nar

col·umned (*or* ·um·nat·ed)

co·lum·nia·tion

col·umn·ist

co·lure circle on sphere

Col·wyn Bay

coly (*plural* colies) bird; *compare* coley

col·za rape plant

coma (*plural* comas) unconsciousness

coma (*plural* comae) cloud round comet

com·al

Co·man·che (*plural* ·ches *or* ·che)

Co·man·chean

co·mate hairy

co·ma·tose

co·matu·lid (*or* ·matu·la; *plural* ·lids *or* ·lae) marine animal

comb

com·bat

com·bat·able

com·bat·ant

com·bat·er

com·bat·ive

combe *variant spelling of* coomb

comb·er

com·bin·able

com·bi·na·tion

com·bi·na·tive (*or* ·to·rial, ·tory)

com·bine

com·bin·er

comb·ing

com·bo (*plural* ·bos) jazz band

com·bust

com·bus·tibil·ity (*or* ·tible·ness)

com·bus·tible

com·bus·tion

com·bus·tor engine part

come (com·ing, came)

come·back

Com·econ Communist economic association

co·median

co·medic

co·medi·enne

com·edo (*plural* ·edos *or* ·edo·nes) blackhead

come·down

com·edy (*plural* ·edies)

come·ly (·li·er, ·li·est)

come-on (*noun*)

com·er

co·mes·tible

com·et

come·up·pance

com·fit sweet

com·fort

com·fort·able

com·fort·ably

com·fort·er

com·fort·ing

com·fort·less

com·frey plant

com·fy (·fi·er, ·fi·est)

com·ic

comi·cal

comi·cal·ly

Com·in·form Communist Information Bureau

com·ing

Com·in·tern international Communist organization

co·mi·tia Roman assembly

com·ity (*plural* ·ities) courtesy

com·ma

com·mand

com·man·dant

com·man·deer

com·mand·er

com·mand·er·ship

com·mand·ing

com·mand·ment

com·man·do (*plural* ·dos
or ·does)
com·mea·sure
com·media dell'arte
Italian comic theatre
comme il faut *French* as it
should be
com·memo·rate
com·memo·ra·tion
com·memo·ra·tive (*or*
·tory)
com·memo·ra·tor
com·mence
com·mence·ment
com·mend
com·mend·able
com·mend·ably
com·men·dam Church
office
com·men·da·tion
com·menda·tory
com·men·sal biology term
com·men·sal·ism (*or*
·sal·ity)
com·men·su·rable
com·men·su·rate
com·men·su·ra·tion
com·ment
com·men·tar·ial
com·men·tary (*plural*
·taries)
com·men·tate
com·men·ta·tor
com·ment·er
com·merce
com·mer·cial
com·mer·cial·ism
com·mer·cial·ist
com·mer·cial·is·tic
com·mer·ci·al·ity
com·mer·ciali·za·tion (*or*
·sa·tion)
com·mer·cial·ize (*or* ·ise)
com·mer·cial·ly
com·mère female compere
com·mi·na·tion threatening
vengeance
com·mina·tory
com·min·gle
com·mi·nute reduce to
fragments
com·mi·nu·tion
com·mis agent
com·mis·er·ate
com·mis·era·tion

com·mis·era·tive
com·mis·era·tor
com·mis·sar
com·mis·sar·ial
com·mis·sari·at
com·mis·sary (*plural*
·saries)
com·mis·sion
com·mis·sion·aire
com·mis·sion·al (*or* ·ary)
com·mis·sion·er
com·mis·su·ral
com·mis·sure anatomy
term
com·mit (·mit·ting,
·mit·ted)
com·mit·ment
com·mit·tal
com·mit·tee
committee·man (*plural*
·men)
com·mit·ter
(committment) *incorrect
spelling of* commitment
com·mode
com·mo·di·ous
com·mod·ity (*plural*
·ities)
com·mo·dore
com·mon
com·mon·able legal term
com·mon·age legal term
com·mon·al·ity
commonness
com·mon·al·ty (*or* ·ity)
ordinary people
com·mon·er
com·mon·ly
com·mon·ness
common·place
Com·mons (House of)
common·weal *Archaic*
common goods;
commonwealth
Common·wealth of
Nations; republican
England
common·wealth
independent community
com·mo·tion
com·mo·tion·al
com·mu·nal
com·mu·nal·ism
com·mu·nal·ist
com·mu·nal·is·tic
com·mu·nal·ity

commu·nali·za·tion (*or*
·sa·tion)
com·mu·nal·ize (*or* ·ise)
Com·mu·nade supporter of
Paris Commune
com·mu·nard member of a
commune
Com·mune Paris
Revolutionary government
com·mune
com·mu·ni·cabil·ity (*or*
·cable·ness)
com·mu·ni·cable
com·mu·ni·cant
com·mu·ni·cate
com·mu·ni·ca·tion
com·mu·ni·ca·tive
com·mu·ni·ca·tor
com·mu·ni·ca·tory
Com·mun·ion Eucharist
com·mun·ion
com·mun·ion·al
com·mun·ion·ist
com·mu·ni·qué
com·mun·ism
Com·mun·ist political party
com·mun·ist supporter of
communism
com·mu·nis·tic
com·mu·ni·tar·ian
com·mu·nity (*plural*
·nities)
com·mu·ni·za·tion (*or*
·sa·tion)
com·mu·nize (*or* ·nise)
nationalize
com·mut·able exchangeable
com·mu·tate
com·mu·ta·tion
com·mu·ta·tive involving
substitution
com·mu·ta·tor electrical
device
com·mute
com·mut·er
Como Italian city and lake
Como·ros island country
co·mose hairy
comp *Slang* compositor
com·pact
com·pact·er
com·pact·ness
com·pan·der sound
transmission
com·pan·ion

com·pan·ion·able
com·pan·ion·ably
com·pan·ion·able
com·pan·ion·ate
com·pan·ion·ship
com·pan·ion·way stairway
 on ship
com·pa·ny (*plural* ·nies)
com·pa·rabil·ity
com·pa·rable
com·pa·rably
com·para·tive
com·para·tive·ly
com·para·tor
com·pare
com·par·er
com·pari·son
com·part·ment
com·part·men·tal
com·part·men·tali·za·tion
 (*or* ·sa·tion)
com·part·men·tal·ize (*or*
 ·ise)
com·part·men·ted
com·pass
com·pass·able
com·pas·sion
com·pas·sion·ate
com·pat·ibil·ity
com·pat·ible
com·pat·ibly
com·pat·ri·ot
com·pat·ri·ot·ic
com·pat·ri·ot·ism
com·peer equal status
com·pel (·pel·ling,
 ·pelled)
com·pel·ler
com·pen·di·ous
com·pen·dium (*plural*
 ·diums *or* ·dia)
com·pen·sate
com·pen·sa·tion
com·pen·sa·tive
com·pen·sa·tor
com·pen·sa·tory
com·pere
com·pete
com·pe·tence
com·pe·ten·cy (*plural*
 ·cies) legal term
com·pe·tent
com·pe·ti·tion
com·peti·tive
com·peti·tor

com·pi·la·tion
com·pile
com·pil·er
com·pla·cen·cy (*or*
 com·pla·cence; *plural*
 ·cencies *or* ·cences)
 self-satisfaction; *compare*
 complaisance
com·pla·cent
com·plain
com·plain·ant
com·plain·er
com·plaint
com·plai·sance willingness
 to comply; *compare*
 complacency
com·plai·sant
com·ple·ment complete;
 that which completes;
 compare compliment
com·ple·men·tary (*or* ·tal)
com·ple·men·tiz·er
 grammar term
com·plete
com·plete·ness
com·plet·er
com·ple·tion
com·ple·tive
com·plex
com·plex·ion
com·plex·ity (*plural*
 ·ities)
com·pli·ance (*or* ·an·cy)
com·pli·ant (*or* ·able)
com·pli·cate
com·pli·cat·ed
com·pli·ca·tion
com·plic·ity (*plural* ·ities)
com·pli·er
com·pli·ment praise;
 compare complement
com·pli·men·tary
com·pline (*or* ·plin)
 canonical hour
com·ply (·plies, ·ply·ing,
 ·plied)
com·po (*plural* ·pos)
 mixture; *Austral*
 compensation
com·po·nent
com·po·nen·tial
com·po·ny (*or* ·ne)
 heraldic term
com·port
com·port·ment
com·pose

com·pos·er
com·po·site
com·po·si·tion
com·po·si·tion·al
com·posi·tor
com·pos men·tis *Latin*
 sane
com·post
com·po·sure
com·pote
com·pound
com·pound·er
com·pra·dor foreign agent
com·pre·hend
com·pre·hen·sibil·ity (*or*
 ·sible·ness)
com·pre·hen·sible (*or*
 ·hend·ible)
com·pre·hen·sibly
com·pre·hen·sion
com·pre·hen·sive
com·press
com·press·ibil·ity (*or*
 ·ible·ness)
com·press·ible
com·pres·sion
com·pres·sion·al
com·pres·sive
com·pres·sor
com·pris·able
com·pris·al
com·prise
com·pro·mise
com·pro·mis·er
Comp·tom·eter
 (*Trademark*)
comp·trol·ler
com·pul·sion
com·pul·sive
com·pul·so·ry
com·pul·so·ri·ly
com·punc·tion
com·punc·tious
com·put·abil·ity
com·put·able
com·pu·ta·tion
com·pu·ta·tion·al
com·pute
com·put·er
com·put·eri·za·tion (*or*
 ·sa·tion)
com·put·er·ize (*or* ·ise)
com·rade
com·rade·ship

com·sat *short for* communications satellite

com·stock·ery *US* excessive censorship

Comus Roman god

con (**con·ning, conned**)

con amo·re musical term

co·na·tion psychology term

cona·tive linguistics term

co·na·tus (*plural* ·**tus**) striving

con brio musical term

con·cat·enate

con·cat·ena·tion series of events

con·cave

con·cav·ity (*plural* ·**ities**)

concavo-concave

concavo-convex

con·ceal

con·ceal·ment

con·cede

con·ced·er

con·ceit

con·ceit·ed

con·ceiv·able

con·ceiv·ably

con·ceive

con·cel·ebrate

con·cel·ebra·tion

(**concensus**) *incorrect spelling of* **consensus**

con·cen·trate

con·cen·tra·tion

con·cen·tra·tive

con·cen·tra·tor

con·cen·tre to concentrate

con·cen·tric (*or* ·**tri·cal**)

con·cen·tri·cal·ly

con·cen·tric·ity

Con·cep·ción Chilean city

con·cept

con·cep·ta·cle botany term

con·cep·tion

con·cep·tion·al

con·cep·tive

con·cep·tual

con·cep·tu·al·ism

con·cep·tu·al·ist

con·cep·tu·al·is·tic

con·cep·tu·ali·za·tion (*or* ·**sa·tion**)

con·cep·tu·al·ize (*or* ·**ise**)

con·cern

con·cerned

con·cern·ed·ly

con·cern·ing

con·cert

con·cer·tan·te musical work

con·cert·ed

con·cert·go·er

con·cer·ti·na (·**nas**, ·**na·ing**, ·**naed**)

con·cer·ti·no (*plural* ·**ni**) musical work

con·cer·tize

con·cer·to (*plural* ·**tos** *or* ·**ti**)

con·cer·to gros·so (*plural* ·**ti gros·si**)

con·ces·sible

con·ces·sion

con·ces·sion·aire (*or* ·**er**, ·**ary**; *plural* ·**aires**, ·**ers**, *or* ·**aries**)

con·ces·sion·ary

con·ces·sive

conch (*plural* **conchs** *or* **conches**) mollusc

con·cha (*plural* ·**chae**) shell-shaped part

con·chal

con·chif·er·ous

con·chio·lin protein

con·choid geometric curve

con·choi·dal geology term

con·cho·logi·cal

con·cholo·gist

con·chol·ogy study of shells

con·chy (*plural* ·**chies**) *Slang* conscientious objector

con·ci·erge

con·cili·ar of ecclesiastical councils

con·cili·ate

con·cili·ation

con·cilia·tive

con·cili·ator

con·cilia·tory (*or* ·**tive**)

con·cin·nity (*plural* ·**nities**) harmonious arrangement

con·cin·nous

con·cise

con·ci·sion

con·clave

con·clav·ist

con·clude

con·clu·sion

con·clu·sive

con·coct

con·coct·er (*or* ·**coc·tor**)

con·coc·tion

con·coc·tive

con·comi·tance

con·comi·tant

Con·cord US and Australian cities; *compare* Concorde

con·cord agreement

con·cord·ance

con·cord·ant

con·cor·dat treaty

Con·corde airliner; *compare* Concord

con·course

con·cres·cence biology term

con·crete

con·cre·tion

con·cre·tion·ary

con·cre·tive

con·creti·za·tion (*or* ·**sa·tion**)

con·cre·tize (*or* ·**tise**)

con·cu·bi·nage

con·cu·bine

con·cu·pis·cence

con·cu·pis·cent

con·cur (·**cur·ring**, ·**curred**)

con·cur·rence

con·cur·rent

con·cuss

con·cus·sion

con·cus·sive

con·demn

con·demn·able

con·dem·na·tion

con·dem·na·tory

con·demn·er

con·den·sabil·ity (*or* ·**sibil·ity**)

con·den·sable (*or* ·**sible**)

con·den·sate

con·den·sa·tion

con·dense

con·dens·er

con·de·scend

con·de·scend·ence legal term

con·de·scend·ing

con·de·scen·sion

con·dign well-deserved

con·di·ment

con·di·tion
con·di·tion·al
con·di·tion·al·ity
con·di·tion·al·ly
con·di·tioned
con·di·tion·er
con·di·tion·ing
con·do·la·tory
con·dole
con·do·lence (*or* ·dole·ment)
con·dol·er
con·dom
con·do·min·ium (*plural* ·iums)
con·do·na·tion
con·done
con·don·er
con·dor vulture
con·dot·tiere (*plural* ·tieri) mercenary
con·duce
con·duc·er
con·duc·ible
con·du·cive
con·duct
con·duct·ance physics term
con·duct·ible
con·duc·tion
con·duc·tive
con·duc·tiv·ity (*plural* ·ities)
con·duc·tor (*fem* ·tress)
con·duit
con·du·pli·cate botany term
con·du·pli·ca·tion
con·dy·lar
con·dyle bone projection
con·dy·loid
con·dy·lo·ma (*plural* ·mas *or* ·ma·ta) tumour
con·dy·loma·tous
cone
cone·flower
co·ney *variant spelling of* cony
Co·ney Is·land US resort
con·fab *Slang* chat
con·fabu·late
con·fabu·la·tion
con·fabu·la·tor
con·fabu·la·tory
con·fect combine ingredients
con·fec·tion

con·fec·tion·ary (*plural* ·aries) place where confections are made
con·fec·tion·er
con·fec·tion·ery (*plural* ·eries) sweets
Con·fed·era·cy seceding US states
con·fed·era·cy (*plural* ·cies)
Con·fed·er·ate
con·fed·er·ate
Con·fed·era·tion original US states
con·fed·era·tion
con·fed·era·tion·ism
con·fed·era·tion·ist
con·fer (·fer·ring, ·ferred)
con·feree (*or* ·fer·ree)
con·fer·ence
con·fer·en·tial
con·fer·ment (*or* ·fer·ral)
con·fer·rable
con·fer·rer
con·fer·va (*plural* ·vae *or* ·vas) alga
con·fer·val
con·fer·void
con·fess
confessant
con·fess·ed·ly
con·fes·sion
con·fes·sion·al
con·fes·sion·ary
con·fes·sor
con·fet·ti
con·fi·dant (*fem* ·dante) person in whom one confides
con·fide
con·fi·dence
con·fi·dent self-assured
con·fi·den·tial
con·fi·den·ti·al·ity (*or* ·tial·ness)
con·fi·den·tial·ly
con·fid·er
con·fid·ing
con·figu·ra·tion
con·figu·ra·tion·al (*or* ·ra·tive)
con·figu·ra·tion·ism Gestalt psychology
con·figu·ra·tion·ist
con·fin·able (*or* ·fine·able)

con·fine
con·fine·ment
con·firm
con·firm·and candidate for confirmation
con·fir·ma·tion
con·firma·tory (*or* ·tive)
con·fis·cable
con·fis·cate
con·fis·ca·tor
con·fis·ca·tory
Con·fit·eor prayer
con·fi·ture confection
con·fla·gra·tion
con·fla·gra·tive
con·flate combine
con·fla·tion
con·flict
con·flic·tion
con·flic·tive (*or* ·tory)
con·flu·ence (*or* con·flux)
con·flu·ent
con·fo·cal
con·form
con·form·abil·ity (*or* ·able·ness)
con·form·able
con·form·ably
con·for·mal maths term
con·for·ma·tion
con·form·er
con·form·ist
con·form·ity (*or* ·ance; *plural* ·ities *or* ·ances)
con·found
con·found·er
con·fra·ter·nal
con·fra·ter·nity (*plural* ·nities)
con·frère fellow member
con·front
con·fron·ta·tion (*or* con·front·ment)
con·front·er
Con·fu·cian
Con·fu·cian·ism
Con·fu·cian·ist
con fuo·co musical term
con·fus·able
con·fuse
con·fus·ed·ly
con·fus·ing
con·fus·ing·ly
con·fu·sion
con·fu·ta·tion

con·fu·ta·tive
con·fute
con·fut·er
con·ga (·ga·ing, ·gaed) dance; compare conger
con·gé dismissal
con·geal
con·geal·ment
con·ge·la·tion
con·ge·ner member of group
con·ge·ner·ic
con·gen·ial
con·ge·ni·al·ity (or con·gen·ial·ness)
con·gen·ial·ly
con·geni·tal present from birth
con·geni·tal·ly
con·ger eel; compare conga
con·ge·ries collection
con·gest
con·gest·ible
con·ges·tion
con·ges·tive
con·gi·us (plural ·gii) unit
con·glo·bate form into ball
con·glo·ba·tion
con·glom·er·ate
con·glom·er·at·ic (or ·it·ic)
con·glom·era·tion
con·glu·ti·nant
con·glu·ti·nate heal together
con·glu·ti·na·tive
Con·go African republic
con·go eel
Con·go·lese
con·gou (or ·go) China tea
con·grats
con·gratu·late
con·gratu·la·tion
con·gratu·la·tor
con·gratu·la·tory
con·gre·gant
con·gre·gate
con·gre·ga·tion
Con·gre·ga·tion·al evangelical church
con·gre·ga·tion·al
Con·gre·ga·tion·al·ism
Con·gre·ga·tion·al·ist
con·gre·ga·tive

con·gre·ga·tor (or ·gre·gant)
Con·gress US legislature
con·gress
Con·gres·sion·al
con·gres·sion·al
Con·gres·sion·al·ist
con·gres·sion·al·ist
Congress·man (plural ·men)
Congress·woman (plural ·women)
con·gru·ence (or ·en·cy; plural ·ences or ·cies)
con·gru·ent
con·gru·ity (plural ·ities)
con·gru·ous
con·ic (or coni·cal)
con·ics
co·nid·ial (or ·ian)
co·nidio·phore
co·nid·ium (plural ·nidia) fungal spore
co·ni·fer
co·nif·er·ous
co·ni·ine (or co·nin, co·nine) alkaloid
Con·is·ton lake
co·nium hemlock
con·jec·tur·al
con·jec·ture
con·jec·tur·er
con·join
con·join·ed·ly
con·join·er
con·joint
con·ju·gable
con·ju·gal
con·ju·gal·ly
con·ju·gal·ity
con·ju·gant
con·ju·gate
con·ju·ga·tion
con·ju·ga·tion·al
con·ju·ga·tive
con·ju·ga·tor
con·junct
con·junc·tion
con·junc·tion·al
con·junc·ti·va (plural ·vas or ·vae) eyeball membrane
con·junc·ti·val
con·junc·tive
con·junc·ti·vi·tis

con·junc·tur·al
con·junc·ture
con·jura·tion
con·jure
con·jur·er (or ·or)
conk
conk·er
con moto musical term
Con·nacht Northern Irish province
con·nate
con·natu·ral
Con·naught former name of Connacht
con·nect
con·nect·ible (or ·able)
Con·necti·cut
con·nec·tion (or ·nex·ion)
con·nec·tion·al (or ·nex·ion·al)
con·nec·tive
con·nect·or (or ·er)
conned
Con·ne·ma·ra
con·ning
con·nip·tion US rage
con·niv·ance (or ·ence)
con·nive
con·niv·ent
con·niv·er
con·nois·seur
con·no·ta·tion
con·no·ta·tive (or con·no·tive)
con·note
con·nu·bial
con·nu·bi·al·ity
con·nu·bi·al·ly
co·no·dont fossil tooth
co·noid geometry term
co·noi·dal
con·quer
con·quer·or
con·quest
con·quis·ta·dor (plural ·dors or ·do·res)
con·san·guin·eous (or ·guine)
con·san·guin·ity
con·science
conscience-stricken
con·sci·en·tious
con·sci·en·tious·ness
con·scion·able
con·scious

con·scious·ness
con·script
con·scrip·tion
con·scrip·tion·al
con·scrip·tion·ist
con·se·crate
con·se·cra·tion
con·se·cra·tor
con·se·cra·tory (or ·tive)
con·se·cu·tion sequence of events
con·secu·tive
con·sen·sual
con·sen·sus
con·sent
con·sent·er
con·sen·tience
con·sen·tient in agreement
con·se·quence
con·se·quent
con·se·quen·tial
con·se·quen·tial·ly
con·se·quen·ti·al·ity (or ·tial·ness)
con·se·quent·ly
con·serv·able
con·serv·an·cy (plural ·cies)
con·ser·va·tion
con·ser·va·tion·al
con·ser·va·tion·ist
con·serva·tism
Con·serva·tive political party
con·serva·tive opposed to change
con·serva·toire musical institution
con·ser·va·tor custodian
con·serva·tory (plural ·tories)
con·serve
con·serv·er
Con·sett Durham town
con·sid·er
con·sid·er·able
con·sid·er·ably
con·sid·er·ate
con·sid·era·tion
con·sid·er·er
con·sign
con·sign·able
con·signa·tion
con·signee
con·sign·ment

con·sign·or (or ·er)
con·sist
con·sist·en·cy (or ·ence; plural ·cies or ·ences)
con·sist·ent
con·sis·to·rial (or ·rian)
con·sis·tory (plural ·tories) diocesan court
con·so·ci·ate
con·so·cia·tion
con·so·cies (plural ·cies) ecology term
con·sol·able
con·so·la·tion
con·sola·tory
con·sole
con·sol·er
con·soli·date
con·soli·da·tion
con·soli·da·tor
con·sols government securities
con·so·lute chemistry term
con·som·mé
con·so·nance (or ·nan·cy; plural ·nances or ·cies) agreement
con·so·nant
con·so·nan·tal
con·sort
con·sort·er
con·sor·tial
con·sor·tium (plural ·tia)
con·spe·cif·ic
con·spec·tus overall view
con·spicu·ous
con·spicu·ous·ness
con·spira·cy (plural ·cies)
con·spira·tor
con·spira·to·rial (or con·spira·tory)
con·spira·to·rial·ly
con·spira·tress
con·spire
con·sta·ble
con·stabu·lary (plural ·laries)
Con·stance European lake
Con·stance (or Kon·stanz) West German city
con·stan·cy
con·stant
Con·stan·ţa Romanian port
con·stant·an alloy

Con·stan·tine Algerian city
Con·stan·ti·no·ple
con·sta·ta·tion establishing truth
con·stel·late form clusters
con·stel·la·tion
con·stel·la·tory
con·ster·nate
con·ster·na·tion
con·sti·pate
con·sti·pat·ed
con·sti·pa·tion
con·stitu·en·cy (plural ·cies)
con·stitu·ent
con·sti·tute
con·sti·tut·er (or ·tu·tor)
con·sti·tu·tion
con·sti·tu·tion·al
con·sti·tu·tion·al·ism
con·sti·tu·tion·al·ist
con·sti·tu·tion·al·ity
con·sti·tu·tion·al·ly
con·sti·tu·tive
con·strain
con·strain·er
con·straint
con·strict
con·stric·tion
con·stric·tive
con·stric·tor
con·struct
con·struct·ible
con·struc·tion
con·struc·tion·al
con·struc·tive
con·struc·tiv·ism art movement
con·struc·tiv·ist
con·struc·tor (or ·ter)
con·strue (·stru·ing, ·strued)
con·stru·er
con·sub·stan·tia·tion Christian doctrine
con·suetude custom
con·suetu·di·nary
con·sul
con·su·lar
con·su·late
con·sult
con·sul·tan·cy (plural ·cies)
con·sul·tant
con·sul·ta·tion

con·sul·ta·tive (*or* ta·tory, con·sul·tive)
con·sult·er (*or* ·sul·tor)
con·sum·able
con·sume
con·sum·er
con·sum·er·ism
con·sum·mate
con·sum·ma·tion
con·sum·ma·tive (*or* ·tory)
con·sum·ma·tor
con·sump·tion
con·sump·tive
con·tact
con·tac·tor
con·tac·tual
con·ta·gion
con·ta·gious
con·ta·gious·ness
con·ta·gium (*plural* ·gia) transmission of disease
con·tain
con·tain·er
con·tain·eri·za·tion (*or* ·sa·tion)
con·tain·er·ize (*or* ·ise)
con·tain·ment
con·tami·nant
con·tami·nate
con·tami·na·tion
con·tami·na·tor
con·tan·go (*noun, plural* ·gos; *verb* ·goes, ·go·ing, ·goed) stock-exchange term
conte *French* short story
con·té crayon
con·temn scorn
con·temn·er (*or* ·tem·nor)
con·tem·nible
con·tem·plate
con·tem·pla·tion
con·tem·pla·tive
con·tem·pla·tor
con·tem·po·ra·neity
con·tem·po·ra·neous
con·tem·po·rari·ly
con·tem·po·rary (*plural* ·raries)
con·tem·po·rize (*or* ·rise) synchronize
con·tempt
con·tempt·ibil·ity (*or* ·ible·ness)

con·tempt·ible
con·temp·tu·ous
con·tend
con·tend·er
con·tent
con·tent·ed
con·ten·tion
con·ten·tion·al
con·ten·tious
con·tent·ment
con·ter·mi·nous
con·test
con·test·able
con·test·ant
con·tes·ta·tion
con·test·er
con·text
con·tex·tual
con·tex·tu·al·ize (*or* ·ise)
con·tex·tual·ly
con·tex·tur·al
con·tex·ture weaving
con·ti·gu·ity
con·tigu·ous
con·ti·nence (*or* con·ti·nen·cy)
Con·ti·nent mainland Europe
con·ti·nent large landmass
Con·ti·nen·tal
con·ti·nen·tal
Con·ti·nen·tal·ism
Con·ti·nen·ta·list
con·ti·nen·tal·ity
con·tin·gence
con·tin·gen·cy (*plural* ·cies)
con·tin·gent
con·tinu·able
con·tin·ual
con·tinu·al·ity (*or* ·al·ness)
con·tin·ual·ly
con·tinu·ance
con·tinu·ant
con·tinu·ation
con·tinu·ative linguistics term
con·tinu·ator
con·tinue
con·tinu·er
con·tinu·ing·ly
con·ti·nu·ity (*plural* ·ities)
con·tinuo (*plural* ·tinuos) musical term

con·tinu·ous
con·tin·uum (*plural* ·tinua *or* ·tin·uums)
con·to (*plural* ·tos) Portuguese currency
con·tort
con·tor·tion
con·tor·tion·al
con·tor·tion·ist
con·tor·tion·is·tic
con·tour
contra·band
contra·band·ist
contra·bass musical instrument
contra·bass·ist
contra·bas·soon
contra·bas·soon·ist
contra·cep·tion
contra·cep·tive
con·tract
con·tract·able able to enter contract
con·tract·ibil·ity (*or* ·ible·ness)
con·tract·ible able to be shortened
con·trac·tile
con·trac·til·ity
con·trac·tion
con·trac·tion·al
con·trac·tive
con·trac·tor
con·trac·tual
con·trac·tual·ly
con·trac·ture muscle disorder
contra·dict
contra·dict·able
contra·dict·er (*or* ·dic·tor)
contra·dic·tion
contra·dic·tive (*or* ·tious)
contra·dic·tory
contra·dis·tinc·tion
contra·dis·tinc·tive
contra·dis·tin·guish
con·trail aircraft vapour trail
contra·in·di·cant
contra·in·di·cate
contra·in·di·ca·tion
con·tral·to (*plural* ·tos *or* ·ti)
contra·po·si·tion
con·trap·tion

contra·pun·tal
contra·pun·tal·ly
contra·pun·tist (*or* ·tal·ist)
contra·ri·ety (*plural*
　·eties)
con·tra·ri·ly
con·tra·ri·ness
con·tra·ri·wise
con·tra·ry (*plural* ·ries)
con·trast
con·tras·tive
con·trasty
contra·val·la·tion
　fortifications
contra·vene
contra·ven·er
contra·ven·tion
contra·yer·va plant root
con·tre·danse dance
con·tre·temps (*plural*
　·temps)
con·trib·ute
con·tri·bu·tion
con·tribu·tive
con·tribu·tor
con·tribu·to·rial
con·tribu·tory
con·trite
con·tri·tion
con·triv·ance
con·trive
con·trol (·trol·ling,
　·trolled)
con·trol·lable
con·trol·lably
con·trol·ler
con·tro·ver·sial
contro·ver·sial·ism
contro·ver·sial·ist
con·tro·ver·sial·ly
con·tro·ver·sy (*plural*
　·sies)
con·tro·vert deny
contro·vert·er
contro·vert·ible
con·tu·ma·cious obstinate
con·tu·ma·cy (*plural*
　·cies)
con·tu·meli·ous insolent
con·tu·mely (*plural*
　·melies)
con·tuse bruise
con·tu·sion
con·tu·sioned
con·tu·sive

co·nun·drum
con·ur·ba·tion
con·ure parrot
con·va·lesce
con·va·les·cence
con·va·les·cent
con·vec·tion
con·vec·tion·al
con·vec·tive
con·vec·tor
con·ven·able
con·ve·nance *French*
　propriety
con·vene
con·ven·er
con·veni·ence
con·veni·ent
con·vent
con·ven·ti·cle secret
　assembly
con·ven·tion
con·ven·tion·al
con·ven·tion·al·ism
con·ven·tion·al·ist
con·ven·tion·al·ity (*plural*
　·ities)
con·ven·tion·ali·za·tion
　(*or* ·sa·tion)
con·ven·tion·al·ize (*or*
　·ise)
con·ven·tion·al·ly
con·ven·tual of a convent
con·verge
con·ver·gence
con·ver·gen·cy
con·ver·gent
con·vers·able
con·ver·sance (*or* ·san·cy)
con·ver·sant
con·ver·sa·tion
con·ver·sa·tion·al
con·ver·sa·tion·al·ist (*or*
　·tion·ist)
con·ver·sa·tion·al·ly
con·ver·sa·zio·ne (*plural*
　·zio·ni *or* ·zio·nes)
　Italian artistic discussion
con·verse
con·vers·er
con·ver·sion
con·ver·sion·al (*or* ·ary)
con·vert
con·vert·er (*or* ·ver·tor)
con·vert·ibil·ity (*or*
　·ible·ness)

con·vert·ible
con·verti·plane (*or*
　·verta·, ·verto·)
con·vex
con·vex·ity (*plural* ·ities)
convexo-concave
convexo-convex
con·vey
con·vey·able
con·vey·ance
con·vey·anc·er
con·vey·anc·ing
con·vey·or (*or* ·er)
con·vict
con·vict·able (*or* ·ible)
con·vic·tion
con·vic·tive convincing
con·vince
con·vinc·er
con·vinc·ible
con·vinc·ing
con·viv·ial
con·vivi·al·ity
con·vivi·al·ly
con·vo·ca·tion legislative
　assembly
con·vo·ca·tion·al
con·voca·tive
con·vo·ca·tor
con·voke summon
con·vok·er
con·vo·lute
con·vo·lut·ed
con·vo·lu·tion
con·volve coil
con·vol·vu·la·ceous
con·vol·vu·lus (*plural*
　·luses *or* ·li) plant
con·voy
con·vul·sant
con·vulse
con·vul·sion
con·vul·sive
cony (*or* co·ney; *plural*
　conies *or* ·neys)
coo (coo·ing, cooed)
Cooch Be·har Indian city
cooee (*or* coo·ey)
cook
cook·able
cook·book
cook·er
cook·ery
cook·house
cookie

cook·ing
cook·out *US* barbecue
cool
coo·la·bah (*or* ·li·) tree
cool·ant
cool·er
coolie (*or* cooly; *plural*
  coolies)
cool·ly (*adv*)
cool·ness
coomb (*or* combe,
  coombe) valley
coon
coon·can card game
coon·skin
coon·tie plant
coop
co-op
coop·er barrel-maker
coop·er·age
co·oper·ate (*or* co-
  operate)
co·opera·tion (*or* co-
  operation)
co·opera·tive (*or* co-
  operative)
co·opera·tor (*or* co-
  operator)
coop·ery
co·opt (*or* co-opt)
co·opta·tion (*or* co-
  optation)
co·opta·tive (*or* co-
  optative)
co·option (*or* co-option)
co·or·di·nal (*or* co-
  ordinal) biology term
co·or·di·nate (*or* co-
  ordinate)
co·or·di·na·tion (*or* co-
  ordina·tion)
co·or·di·na·tor (*or* co-
  ordina·tor)
Coorg former Indian
  province
coot
cootch hiding place
cootie *US* louse
cop (cop·ping, copped)
co·pai·ba (*or* ·va) resin
co·pal resin
co·palm resin
co·par·cenary (*or* ·ceny)
  joint ownership
co·par·cener
co·part·ner

cope
Co·pen·ha·gen
co·pepod plankton
  constituent
co·per horse dealer
Co·per·ni·can
cope·stone
copi·er
co·pilot
cop·ing
co·pi·ous
co·pla·nar
co·pla·nar·ity
co·poly·mer chemistry term
co·poly·meri·za·tion (*or*
  ·sa·tion)
co·poly·mer·ize (*or* ·ise)
cop·per
cop·per·as chemical
  compound
copper·head snake
copper·plate
copper·smith
cop·pery
cop·pice *variant of* copse
cop·ra coconut kernel
cop·ro·la·lia obscene
  language
cop·ro·lite fossilized faeces
cop·ro·lit·ic
cop·ropha·gous
cop·ropha·gy
cop·ro·philia abnormal
  interest in faeces
co·prophi·lous growing on
  dung
copse (*or* cop·pice)
Copt
cop·ter *short for* helicopter
Cop·tic language; Church
copu·la (*plural* ·las *or*
  ·lae) linking verb;
  compare cupola
copu·lar
copu·late
copu·la·tion
copu·la·tive
copy (*noun, plural*
  copies; *verb* copies,
  copy·ing, copied)
copy·book
copy-edit
copy-editor
copy·hold
copy·holder

copy·ist
copy·read *US* subedit
copy·right
copy·writer
copy·writing
coq au vin chicken dish
coque·li·cot corn poppy
co·quet (·quet·ting,
  ·quet·ted) to flirt
co·quet·ry (*plural* ·ries)
co·quette
co·quet·tish
co·quille seafood
co·qui·na limestone
co·qui·to (*plural* ·tos) tree
cora·cii·form ornithology
  term
cora·cle
cora·coid zoology term
cor·al animal; jewellery;
  compare corral
cor·al·line (*or* ·loid)
cor·al·lite fossil coral
coral·root
cor an·glais (*plural* cors
  an·glais) musical
  instrument
cor·ban biblical gift
cor·beil (*or* ·beille)
  architectural ornament
cor·bel (·bel·ling, ·belled)
  bracket on building
cor·bicu·la (*plural* ·lae)
  pollen basket
cor bli·mey
cord string; anatomical
  senses; *compare* chord
cord·age
cor·date heart-shaped;
  compare chordate
cord·ed
Cor·delier Franciscan friar
Cor·deliers French political
  club
cor·dial
cor·di·al·ity (*plural* ·ities)
cor·di·al·ly
cor·di·er·ite mineral
cor·di·form heart-shaped
cor·dil·lera mountain range
Cor·dil·leras American
  mountain range
cord·ite explosive
cord·less
Cór·do·ba Argentinian and
  Spanish cities

cor·do·ba Nicaraguan
  currency
cor·don
cor·don bleu
cor·do·van leather
cords corduroy trousers
cor·du·roy
cord·wood
core
co·reli·gion·ist
co·reop·sis plant
corer
co·respon·den·cy
co·respond·ent adulterer;
  compare correspondent
corf (*plural* corves) wagon
Cor·fam (*Trademark*)
Cor·fu
cor·gi (*plural* ·gis)
co·ria·ceous of leather
co·ri·an·der
Cor·inth Greek port; region
  of ancient Greece
Co·rin·thian
Co·rin·thians New
  Testament book
co·rium (*plural* ·ria) layer
  beneath skin
Cork
cork
cork·age
cork·board
corked
cork·er
cork·ing
cork·screw
cork·wood
corky
corm
cor·mel new corm
cor·mo·phyte botany term
cor·mo·phyt·ic
cor·mo·rant
cor·mous
corn
cor·na·ceous botany term
corn·cob
corn·cockle plant
corn·crake bird
corn·crib US maize store
cor·nea (*plural* ·neas or
  ·neae) eye layer
cor·neal
corned
cor·nel plant

cor·nel·ian of cornel
cor·nel·ian (*or* car·)
  gemstone
cor·neous horny
cor·ner
corner·stone
cor·net
cor·net·ist (*or* ·net·tist)
cor·nett (*or* ·net) old
  woodwind instrument
corn·field
corn·flakes
corn·flour cooking
  ingredient
corn·flower plant
corn·husk
cor·nice architectural
  embellishment
cor·niche coastal road
cor·nicu·late horned
Cor·nish
corn·stalk Austral native
  Australian
corn·starch US cornflour
cor·nu (*plural* ·nua)
  anatomical part
cor·nual
cor·nu·co·pia
cor·nute (*or* ·nut·ed)
  hornlike
Corn·wall
corny (corni·er, corni·est)
co·rol·la flower petals
cor·ol·la·ceous
cor·ol·lary (*plural* ·laries)
co·ro·na (*plural* ·nas or
  ·nae)
Co·ro·na Aus·tra·lis
  constellation
Co·ro·na Bo·real·is
  constellation
co·ro·nach Scot dirge
co·ro·na·graph (*or* ·no·)
  optical instrument
coro·nal
coro·nary (*plural* ·naries)
  artery; thrombosis
coro·na·tion
coro·ner
coro·ner·ship
coro·net
coro·net·ed
cor·po·ra *plural of* corpus
cor·po·ral NCO; of the
  body; *compare* corporeal;
  caporal

cor·po·ra·le altar cloth
cor·po·ral·ity
cor·po·ral·ship
cor·po·rate
cor·po·ra·tion
cor·po·ra·tive
cor·po·ra·tor member of
  corporation
cor·po·real physical;
  compare corporal
cor·po·real·ly
cor·po·real·ity (*or* ·ness)
cor·po·reity bodily nature
cor·po·sant atmospheric
  phenomenon
corps (*plural* corps) group
  of people
corpse dead body
cor·pu·lence (*or* ·len·cy)
cor·pu·lent
cor·pus (*plural* ·po·ra)
Cor·pus Chris·ti Christian
  festival
cor·pus·cle
cor·pus·cu·lar
cor·pus de·lic·ti legal term
cor·pus lu·teum (*plural*
  cor·po·ra lu·tea) tissue
  in ovary
cor·pus stria·tum (*plural*
  cor·po·ra stria·ta) brain
  part
cor·pus vile (*plural*
  cor·po·ra vilia) Latin
  worthless body
cor·rade geology term
cor·ral (·ral·ling, ·ralled)
  animal enclosure; *compare*
  coral
cor·ra·sion geology term;
  compare corrosion
cor·ra·sive
cor·rect
cor·rect·able (*or* ·ible)
cor·rec·tion
cor·recti·tude
cor·rec·tive
cor·rect·ness
cor·rec·tor
Cor·regi·dor Philippine
  island
cor·re·late
cor·re·la·tion
cor·rela·tive mutually
  related

cor·rela·tive·ness (or
  ·tiv·ity)
cor·re·spond
cor·re·spond·ence
cor·re·spond·ent one who
  corresponds; compare co-
  respondent
Cor·rèze French region
cor·ri·da Spanish bullfight
cor·ri·dor
cor·rie hollow in hill
Cor·rie·dale sheep
Cor·ri·en·tes Argentine
  port
cor·ri·gen·dum (plural
  ·da)
cor·ri·gibil·ity
cor·ri·gible
cor·robo·rant
cor·robo·rate
cor·robo·ra·tion
cor·robo·ra·tive
cor·robo·ra·tor
cor·robo·ree Austral noisy
  gathering
cor·rod·ant (or ·ent)
cor·rode
cor·rod·er
cor·rod·ibil·ity
cor·rod·ible
cor·ro·sion wearing away;
  compare corrasion
cor·ro·sive
cor·ru·gate
cor·ru·gat·ed
cor·ru·ga·tion
cor·ru·ga·tor muscle
cor·rupt
cor·rupt·er (or ·rup·tor)
cor·rupt·ibil·ity (or
  ·ible·ness)
cor·rup·tible
cor·rup·tion
cor·rup·tion·ist
cor·rup·tive
cor·sac fox
cor·sage
cor·sair
corse Archaic corpse;
  compare coarse; course
corse·let (or cors·let)
cor·set
cor·setière (masc ·setier)
cor·set·ry
Cor·si·ca

Cor·si·can
cor·tege (or ·tège)
Cor·tes Spanish parliament
cor·tex (plural ·ti·ces)
cor·ti·cal
cor·ti·cate (or ·cat·ed)
  having rind or bark
cor·ti·ca·tion
cor·ti·co·ster·oid (or
  cor·ti·coid) hormone
cor·ti·co·ster·one
cor·ti·co·tro·phic (US
  ·pic)
cor·ti·co·tro·phin (US
  ·pin) hormone
cor·ti·sol hormone
cor·ti·sone
co·run·dum mineral
Co·run·na variant of La
  Coruña
co·rus·cate sparkle
co·rus·ca·tion
cor·vée feudal labour
corves plural of corf
cor·vette
cor·vine of crows
co·ryda·lis plant
cor·ymb botany term
co·rym·bose (or ·bous)
cory·phaeus (plural
  ·phaei) chorus leader
cory·phée ballet dancer
co·ry·za head cold
cos lettuce; short for cosine
co·sec short for cosecant
co·secant geometry term
co·sech geometry term
co·seis·mal (or ·mic)
Co·sen·za Italian city
cosh
cosh·er
co·sig·na·tory
co·si·ly (US ·zi·)
co·sine geometry term
co·si·ness
cos·met·ic
cos·meti·cal·ly
cos·me·ti·cian
cos·mic (or ·mi·cal)
cos·mine (or ·min) zoology
  term
cos·mo·drome zoology
  term
cos·mo·go·nal

cos·mo·gon·ic (or
  ·goni·cal)
cos·mogo·nist
cos·mogo·ny (plural
  ·nies) origin of universe
cos·mog·ra·phy mapping of
  universe
cos·moid fish scale
cos·mo·logi·cal (or
  ·log·ic)
cos·molo·gist
cos·mol·ogy study of
  universe
cos·mo·naut
cos·mopo·lis international
  city
cos·mo·poli·tan
cos·mo·poli·tan·ism
cos·mopo·lite cosmopolitan
  plant or animal
cos·mopo·lit·ism
cos·mos
Cos·mo·tron particle
  accelerator
coss Indian unit
Cos·sack
cos·set
cost (cost·ing, cost)
cos·ta (plural ·tae) rib
Cos·ta Bra·va
cos·tal of ribs
co·star (-star·ring,
  -starred)
cos·tard apple
Cos·ta Rica
Cos·ta Ri·can
cos·tate
cost-effective
cos·ter·mon·ger
cost·ing
cos·tive constipated
cost·li·ness
cost·ly (·li·er, ·li·est)
cost·mary (plural
  ·maries) plant
cos·toto·my (plural ·mies)
cost-plus
cos·tume
cos·tumi·er (or ·tum·er)
cosy (US cozy; noun,
  plural cosies; adj cosi·er,
  cosi·est, US coz·ier,
  cozi·est)
cot
co·tan·gent geometry term

cote shelter for doves
Côte d'Azur
Côte-d'Or French
    department
co·ten·an·cy
co·ten·ant
co·terie
co·ter·mi·nous
Côtes-du-Nord French
    department
co·tid·al
co·til·lion dance
co·tin·ga bird
co·to·neas·ter shrub
Coto·paxi volcano in
    Ecuador
Cots·wold sheep
Cots·wolds hills
cot·ta surplice; *compare*
    cotter
cot·tage
cot·tag·er
cot·ter securing pin; peasant
    farmer; *compare* cotta
cot·tier Irish smallholder
cot·ton
cot·ton·ade fabric
cotton·seed (*plural* ·seeds
    or ·seed)
cotton·tail US rabbit
cotton·weed
cotton·wood
cot·tony
coty·ledon seed leaf
coty·ledo·nal
coty·ledo·na·ry
coty·ledo·nous (*or* ·noid)
coty·loid (*or* ·oi·dal) cup-
    shaped
cou·cal bird
couch
cou·chant heraldic term
couch·er
cou·chette
couch·ing embroidery; eye
    surgery
cou·dé telescope
cou·gar
cough
could
couldn't
cou·lee lava
cou·lisse timber
cou·loir gully
cou·lomb unit

cou·lom·eter (*or*
    ·lomb·meter)
coul·ter (*US* col·) plough
    blade
cou·ma·ric (*or* cu·)
cou·ma·rin (*or* cu·)
cou·ma·rone
coun·cil assembly
coun·cil·lor (*US* ·ci·lor)
    council member
coun·cil·lor·ship (*US*
    ·ci·lor·)
coun·sel (·sel·ling,
    ·selled; *US* ·sel·ing,
    ·seled) advice; advise
coun·sel·lor (*US* ·sel·or)
    advisor
count
count·down
coun·te·nance
count·er
counter·act
counter·ac·tion
counter·ac·tive
counter·at·tack
counter·bal·ance
counter·blast
counter·change
counter·charge
counter·check
counter·claim
counter·claim·ant
counter·clockwise *US*
    anticlockwise
counter·culture
counter·es·pio·nage
counter·feit
counter·feit·er
counter·foil
counter·glow glow in sky
counter·in·sur·gen·cy
counter·in·tel·li·gence
counter·ir·ri·tant
counter·ir·ri·ta·tion
counter·mand
counter·march
counter·meas·ure
counter·mine
counter·move
counter·of·fen·sive
counter·pane
counter·part
counter·plot (·plot·ting,
    ·plot·ted)
counter·point

counter·poise
counter·pro·duc·tive
counter·proof printing term
counter·pro·pos·al
Counter-Reformation
    religious movement
counter·revo·lu·tion
counter·revo·lu·tion·ary
counter·scarp fortification
counter·shad·ing
counter·shaft
counter·sign
counter·sink (·sink·ing,
    ·sank, ·sunk)
counter·spy (*plural*·
    ·spies)
counter·ten·or
counter·type
counter·vail
counter·weigh
counter·weight
counter·word
counter·work
coun·tess
count·less
coun·tri·fy (*or* ·try·fy;
    ·fies, ·fy·ing, ·fied)
coun·try (*plural* ·tries)
country·man (*plural*
    ·men)
country·side
country·woman (*plural*
    ·women)
coun·ty (*plural* ·ties)
coup
coup de grâce (*plural*
    coups de grâce)
coup d'état (*plural* coups
    d'état)
coupe dish; ice-cream
cou·pé car; carriage
cou·ple
cou·pler
cou·plet
cou·pling
cou·pon
cour·age
cou·ra·geous
cou·rante musical work
cour·gette
cou·ri·er messenger;
    compare currier
cour·lan bird
Cour·land (*or* Kur·land)
    Soviet region

course direction, etc.;
  compare **coarse; corse**
cours·er
cours·ing hunting
court
Cour·telle (*Trademark*)
cour·teous
cour·tesan (*or* ·**tezan**)
cour·tesy (*plural* ·**tesies**)
court·house
court·ti·er
court·ing
court·ly (·**li·er**, ·**li·est**)
court mar·tial (*noun,
  plural* **court mar·tials**
  or **courts mar·tial**)
court-martial (*verb
  -martial·ling,
  -martialled*; *US
  -martial·ing,
  -martialed*)
court·room
court·ship
court·yard
cous·cous spicy dish;
  compare **cuscus**
cous·in relation; *compare*
  cozen
cou·teau knife
couth refined
couthie *Scot* friendly
cou·ture
cou·tu·ri·er (*fem* ·**ère**)
cou·vade primitive custom
co·va·len·cy (*US
  ·**va·lence**) chemistry term
co·va·lent
co·vari·ance
cove
cov·en
cov·enant
cov·enan·tal
cov·enan·tee
Cov·enant·er Scottish
  Presbyterian
cov·enan·tee
cov·enant·er (*or
  ·**enan·tor**)
Cov·en·try
cov·er
cov·er·age
cov·er·er
cov·er·ing
cov·er·less
cov·er·let
co·vers maths term

cov·ert
cov·er·ture legal term
cover-up
cov·et
cov·et·er
cov·et·ous
cov·et·ous·ness
cov·ey flock
cov·in conspiracy
cow
cow·age (*or* ·**hage**) plant
cow·ard
cow·ard·ice
cow·ard·li·ness
cow·ard·ly
cow·bane plant
cow·bell
cow·berry (*plural
  ·**berries**)
cow·bind plant
cow·bird
cow·boy
cow·er
Cowes
cow·fish (*plural* ·**fish** *or
  ·**fishes**)
cow·girl
cow·hand
cow·herb
cow·herd
cow·hide
cow·itch plant
cowl
cow·lick
cowl·ing
cow·man (*plural* ·**men**)
co-worker
cow·pat
cow·pea plant
cow·pox
cow·ry (*or* ·**rie**; *plural
  ·**ries**) mollusc
cow·shed
cow·slip
cox
coxa (*plural* **coxae**) hip
  joint
cox·al
cox·al·gia
cox·al·gic
cox·comb
cox·comb·ry (*plural* ·**ries**)
cox·swain (*or* **cock·**)
coy
coy·ness

coy·ote (*plural* ·**otes** *or
  ·**ote**)
co·yo·til·lo (*plural* ·**los**)
  shrub
coy·pu (*plural* ·**pus** *or
  ·**pu**)
co·zen to trick; *compare*
  cousin
coz·en·age
coz·en·er
cozy *US spelling of* **cosy**
crab (**crab·bing, crabbed**)
crab-apple
crab·ber fisherman
crab·by (·**bi·er**, ·**bi·est**)
crab·stick
crab·wise
crack
crack·brain
crack·brained
cracked
crack·er
cracker·jack
crack·et *Dialect* stool
crack·ing
crack·jaw
crack·le
crack·ling
crack·nel
crack·pot
Cra·cow Polish city
cra·dle
cradle-snatch·er
cradle-song
craft skill; *compare* **kraft**
crafti·ly
crafti·ness
crafts·man (*plural* ·**men**)
crafts·man·ship
crafty (**crafti·er,
  crafti·est**)
crag
crag·ged *US* craggy
crag·gy (·**gi·er**, ·**gi·est**)
Cra·iova Romanian city
crake bird
cram (**cram·ming,
  crammed**)
cram·bo (*plural* ·**boes**)
  word game
cram·mer
cramoi·sy crimson
cramp
cram·pon (*or* ·**poon**)
cran herring measure

cran·age
cran·berry (*plural* ·berries)
crane
cranes·bill
cra·nial
cra·ni·ate having a skull
cra·nio·logi·cal
cra·ni·olo·gist
cra·ni·ol·ogy
cra·ni·om·eter
cra·nio·met·ric (*or* ·ri·cal)
cra·ni·om·etry
cra·ni·oto·my (*plural* ·mies)
cra·nium (*plural* ·niums *or* ·nia)
crank
crank·case
cranki·ly
cranki·ness
crank·pin
crank·shaft
cranky (cranki·er, cranki·est)
cran·nied
cran·ny (*plural* ·nies)
crap (crap·ping, crapped)
crape *variant spelling of* crepe
crap·pie (*plural* ·pies) fish
crap·py *Slang* worthless
craps US dice game
crap·shooter
crapu·lence
crapu·lous (*or* ·lent) drunken
cra·que·lure cracks on paintings
crash
crash·ing
crash-land
crash-landing
cra·sis (*plural* ·ses) linguistics term
crass
crass·ness (*or* cras·si·tude)
cras·su·la·ceous botany term
cratch fodder rack
crate
cra·ter
cra·ter·ous
craunch *Dialect* crunch

cra·vat
crave
cra·ven
crav·ing
craw animal stomach
craw·fish *variant spelling of* crayfish
crawl
crawl·er
Craw·ley Sussex town
cray *Austral* crayfish
cray·fish (*or* craw·; *plural* ·fish *or* ·fishes)
cray·on
cray·on·ist
craze
crazed
cra·zi·ly
cra·zi·ness
cra·zy (·zi·er, ·zi·est)
creak noise; *compare* creek
creaki·ness
creaky (creaki·er, creaki·est)
cream
cream·cups flower
cream·er
cream·ery (*plural* ·eries)
cream-laid (*or* ·woven) type of paper
creamy (creami·er, creami·est)
crease
crease·less
cre·ate
crea·tine (*or* ·tin) biochemical compound
cre·ati·nine biochemical compound
crea·tion
crea·tion·al
crea·tion·ism theological belief
crea·tive
crea·tive·ly
crea·tiv·ity
crea·tor
crea·tur·al (*or* ·ture·ly)
crea·ture
crèche
Cré·cy battlefield
cred·al *variant spelling of* creedal
cre·dence

cre·den·dum (*plural* ·da) article of faith
cre·dent *Archaic* believing
cre·den·tial
cre·den·za sideboard
cred·ibil·ity (*or* ·ible·ness)
cred·ible
cred·ibly
cred·it
cred·it·able
cred·it·able·ness (*or* ·abil·ity)
cred·it·ably
credi·tor
cre·do (*plural* ·dos)
cre·du·lity
credu·lous
Cree American Indian
creed
creed·al (*or* cred·al)
creek inlet; *compare* creak
creel basket
creep (creep·ing, crept)
creep·er
creepie *Scot* stool
creepi·ly
creepi·ness
creeps (*noun*)
creepy (creepi·er, creepi·est)
creepy-crawly (*plural* -crawlies)
cre·mate
cre·ma·tion
cre·ma·tion·ism
cre·ma·tion·ist
cre·ma·tor
crema·to·rium (*plural* ·riums *or* ·ria)
crema·tory (*adj*)
crème *French* cream
crème cara·mel
crème de menthe liqueur
Cre·mo·na Italian city
cre·nate (*or* ·nat·ed) scalloped
cre·na·tion (*or* crena·ture)
cren·el (*or* ·nelle)
cren·el·late (US ·el·ate) supply with battlements; indent
cren·el·la·tion (US ·ela·tion)

crenu·late (*or* ·lat·ed)
notched
crenu·la·tion
creo·dont extinct mammal
Cre·ole people
cre·ole language
creo·lized (*or* ·lised)
Creon legendary king
cre·opha·gous flesh-eating
cre·opha·gy
creo·sol constituent of
creosote; *compare* cresol
creo·sote
creo·sot·ic
crepe (*or* crape) fabric
crêpe pancake
crepe de Chine fabric
crêpe su·zette (*plural*
crêpes su·zettes) orange
pancake
crepi·tant
crepi·tate crackle
crepi·ta·tion
crepi·tus medical term
crept
cre·pus·cu·lar active at
dusk
cre·scen·do (*plural* ·dos)
cres·cent
cres·cen·tic
cre·sol disinfectant; *compare*
creosol
cress
cres·set
crest
crest·ed
crest·fallen
crest·ing
cre·syl·ic
Cre·ta·ceous geological
period
cre·ta·ceous of chalk
Cre·tan
Crete
cre·tic metrical foot
cret·in
cret·in·ism
cret·in·oid
cret·in·ous
cre·tonne fabric
Creuse French region
cre·vasse glacier crack
crev·ice cleft
crew
Crewe Cheshire town

crew·el yarn; *compare* cruel
crew·el·ist
crewel·work
crew-neck (*or* -necked)
crib (crib·bing, cribbed)
crib·bage
cri·bel·lum spider's organ
crib·ri·form (*or* crib·rous)
sievelike
crib·work timber framework
crick
crick·et
crick·et·er
cri·coid anatomy term
cried
cri·er
cri·key
crim *Austral* criminal
crime
Cri·mea
Cri·mean
crime pas·sio·nel (*plural*
crimes pas·sio·nel)
crimi·nal
crimi·nal·ity (*plural* ·ities)
crimi·nal·ly
crimi·no·logi·cal (*or*
·log·ic)
crimi·nolo·gist
crimi·nol·ogy
crimp
crimp·er
crim·ple crumple
Crimp·lene (*Trademark*)
crim·son
cringe
crin·gle nautical term
cri·nite having hairs
crin·kle
crinkle·root plant
crin·kly
crinkum-crankum twisted
object
cri·noid marine organism
crino·line
cri·num plant
cri·ol·lo (*plural* ·los) cocoa
cripes slang expression
crip·ple
crip·pling
cri·sis (*plural* ·ses)
crisp
cris·pate (*or* ·pat·ed)
curled
cris·pa·tion

crisp·bread
crisp·er
crisp·ness
crispy (crispi·er,
crispi·est)
cris·sal of a crissum
criss·cross
cris·sum (*plural* ·sa)
ornithology term
cris·ta (*plural* ·tae) biology
term
cris·tate (*or* ·tat·ed)
crested
cri·teri·on (*plural* ·teria
or ·terions)
crit·ic
criti·cal
criti·cal·ly
criti·cism
criti·cize (*or* ·cise)
criti·cizer (*or* ·ciser)
cri·tique
crit·ter *US* creature
croak
croak·er
croaki·ly
croaki·ness
croaky
Cro·at
Croa·tia Yugoslav republic
Croa·tian
cro·cein dye
cro·chet (·chet·ing,
·cheted) knitting;
compare crotchet
cro·chet·er
cro·cido·lite asbestos
crock
crock·ery
crock·et architectural
ornament
Crock·ford clergy directory
croco·dile
croco·dil·ian
cro·co·ite (*or* ·coi·site)
mineral
cro·cus (*plural* ·cuses)
croft
croft·er
crois·sant
Cro-Magnon prehistoric
man
crom·bec bird
crom·lech prehistoric
structure

Crom·wel·lian
crone
cronk *Austral* unsound
Cronus Titan
cro·ny (*plural* ·nies)
crook
crook·ed
crook·ed·ness
croon
croon·er
crop (crop·ping, cropped)
crop-eared
crop·per
cro·quet (·quet·ing, ·queted) game
cro·quette savoury cake
cro·sier (*or* ·zier) bishop's crook
cross
cross·bar
cross·beam
cross·bill
cross·bones
cross·bow
cross·breed (·breed·ing, ·bred)
cross·check
cross-country
cross·current
cross·cut (·cut·ting, cut)
crosse lacrosse stick
cross-examina·tion
cross-examine
cross-examiner
cross-eye
cross-eyed
cross-fertili·za·tion (*or* ·sa·tion)
cross-fertilize (*or* -fertilise)
cross·fire
cross-garnet hinge
cross-grained
cross·hatch
cross·head
cross-index
cross·ing
cross·jack sail
cross-legged
cross·let heraldry term
cross·link
cros·sop·te·ryg·ian primitive fish
cross·over
cross·patch

cross·piece
cross-ply (*adj*)
cross-pollinate
cross-pollina·tion
cross-purposes
cross-question
cross-question·ing
cross-refer
cross-reference
cross·road (*or* ·roads)
cross-ruff bridge term
cross-section·al
cross·slide
cross·stitch
cross·talk
cross·tree nautical term
cross·walk *US* pedestrian crossing
cross·wind
cross·wise (*or* ·ways)
cross·word
cross·wort plant
crotch
crotch·et musical note; *compare* crochet
crotch·ety *Slang* irritable
cro·ton shrub
crouch
croup disease
croup (*or* croupe) horse's hindquarters
crou·pi·er
croup·ous (*or* croupy)
crouse *Dialect* saucy
croute toast
crou·ton cookery garnish
crow (crow·ing, crowed *or* crew)
crow·bar
crow·berry (*plural* ·berries)
crow·boot Eskimo boot
crowd
crowd·ed
crow·er
crow·foot (*plural* ·foots) plant
crown
crown·piece bridle part
crown·work
crow's-foot (*plural* -feet)
crow's-nest
Croy·don
croze barrel recess

cro·zier *variant spelling of* crosier
cru vineyard
cru·ces *plural of* crux
cru·cial important
cru·cial·ly
cru·cian fish
cru·ci·ate
cru·ci·ble
cru·ci·fer plant
cru·cif·er·ous
cru·ci·fier
cru·ci·fix
cru·ci·fix·ion
cru·ci·form
cru·ci·fy (·fies, ·fy·ing, ·fied)
cruck roof timber
crud *Slang* rubbish
crude
crud·ity (*or* crude·ness; *plural* ·ities *or* ·nesses)
cru·el (·el·ler, ·el·lest) unkind; *compare* crewel
cru·el·ly
cru·el·ty (*plural* ·ties)
cru·et
cruise sea trip; *compare* cruse
cruis·er
cruiser·weight
cruise·way
crul·ler cake
crumb
crum·ble
crum·bly (·bli·er, ·bli·est)
crumby (crumbi·er, crumbi·est) full of crumbs; *compare* crummy
crum·horn musical instrument
crum·my (·mi·er, ·mi·est) *Slang* inferior; *compare* crumby
crump to thud
crum·pet
crum·ple
crum·ply
crunch
crunchi·ly
crunchi·ness
crunchy (crunchi·er, crunchi·est)
cru·node maths term
crup·per saddle strap

cru·ra *plural of* crus
cru·ral
crus (*plural* cru·ra) lower
  leg
cru·sade
cru·sad·er
cruse small pot; *compare*
  cruise
crush
crush·er
crust
crus·ta·cean
crus·ta·ceous
crus·tal
crust·ed
crusti·ly
crusti·ness
crusty (crusti·er,
  crusti·est)
crutch
crux (*plural* cruxes *or*
  cru·ces)
crux an·sa·ta ankh
cru·zei·ro (*plural* ·ros)
  Brazilian currency
crwth musical instrument
cry (*noun, plural* cries;
  verb cries, cry·ing,
  cried)
cry·baby (*plural* ·babies)
cryo·bi·olo·gist
cryo·bi·ol·ogy
cryo·gen freezing mixture
cryo·gen·ics
cryo·hy·drate
cryo·lite mineral
cry·om·eter
cry·om·etry
cry·on·ics
cryo·phil·ic
cryo·phyte plant growing
  on snow
cryo·plank·ton
cryo·scope
cryo·scop·ic
cry·os·co·py
cryo·stat
cryo·sur·gery
cryo·thera·py (*or*
  cry·mo·thera·py)
cryo·tron electronic device
crypt
cryp·taes·thesia (*US*
  ·tes·) extrasensory
  perception

crypt·al of crypts; *compare*
  cryptic
crypt·analy·sis study of
  codes
crypt·ana·lyst
crypt·ana·lyt·ic
cryp·tic (*or* ·ti·cal)
  obscure; *compare* cryptal
cryp·ti·cal·ly
cryp·to·clas·tic geology
  term
cryp·to·crys·tal·line
cryp·to·gam plant
cryp·to·gam·ic (*or*
  ·toga·mous)
cryp·to·gen·ic of unknown
  origin
cryp·to·gram
cryp·to·graph
cryp·tog·ra·pher (*or*
  ·phist)
cryp·to·graph·ic (*or*
  ·graphi·cal)
cryp·tog·ra·phy (*or*
  ·tol·ogy) study of codes
cryp·tolo·gist
cryp·to·meria tree
cryp·to·zo·ic living in dark
  places
cryp·to·zo·ite malarial
  parasite
crys·tal
crys·tal·line
crys·tal·lin·ity
crys·tal·lite
crys·tal·lit·ic
crys·tal·lize (*or* ·tal·ize,
  ·tal·lise, ·tal·ise)
crys·tal·log·ra·pher
crys·tal·lo·graph·ic
crys·tal·log·ra·phy
crys·tal·loid
cte·nid·ium (*plural* ·ia)
  mollusc's gill
cte·noid comblike
cte·nopho·ran
cteno·phore invertebrate
cub (cub·bing, cubbed)
Cuba
cub·age
Cu·ban
cub·ane chemical compound
cu·ba·ture cubic contents
cubbed
cub·bing
cubby·hole

cube
cu·beb plant
cu·bic
cu·bi·cal (*adj*) of volume
cu·bi·cle (*noun*) small
  room
cu·bicu·lum burial chamber
cu·bi·form
cub·ism
cub·ist
cu·bis·tic
cu·bit unit
cu·bi·tal of the forearm
cu·boid
Cu-bop jazz music
cuck·old
cuck·old·ry
cuckoo (*plural* cuckoos)
cuckoo·pint
cu·cu·li·form ornithology
  term
cu·cul·late hood-shaped
cu·cum·ber
cu·cur·bit plant
cu·cur·bi·ta·ceous
Cú·cu·ta Colombian city
cud
cud·bear lichen
cud·dle
cud·dle·some
cud·dly (·dli·er, ·dli·est)
cud·dy (*plural* ·dies) cabin
cudg·el (·el·ling, ·elled;
  US ·el·ing, ·eled)
cudg·el·ler (*US* ·el·er)
cudg·erie tree
cud·weed
cue (cu·ing, cued) signal;
  billiard shaft; *compare*
  queue
Cuer·na·va·ca Mexican city
cues·ta ridge
cuff
Cuia·bá (*or* Cu·ya·bá)
  Brazilian port and river
cu·ing
cui·rass armour
cui·ras·sier
cuir-bouilli leather
cui·sine
cuisse armour
culch (*or* cultch) oyster
  bed
cul-de-sac (*plural* culs-
  de-sac *or* cul-de-sacs)

cu·let armour
cu·lex (*plural* ·li·ces)
  mosquito
Cu·lia·cán Mexican city
cu·lic·id mosquito
culi·nary
cull
cull·er
cul·let waste glass
cul·lis gutter
Cul·lod·en battlefield
cul·ly (*plural* ·lies) *Slang*
  pal
culm stem
cul·mif·er·ous
cul·mi·nant
cul·mi·nate
cul·mi·na·tion
cu·lottes women's trousers
cul·pa (*plural* ·pae) fault
cul·pabil·ity
cul·pable
cul·pably
cul·prit
cult
cul·tic
cul·ti·gen plant
cult·ism
cult·ist
cul·ti·vable (*or*
  cul·ti·vat·able)
cul·ti·var plant
cul·ti·vate
cul·ti·vat·ed
cul·ti·va·tion
cul·ti·va·tor
cul·trate (*or* ·trat·ed)
  knife-shaped
cul·tur·al
cul·tur·al·ly
cul·ture
cul·tured
cul·tur·ist
cul·ver *Archaic* dove
cul·ver·in cannon
cul·vert
Cu·ma·ná Venezuelan city
cum·ber
Cum·ber·land former
  English county
Cum·ber·nauld Scottish
  town
cum·ber·some
cum·brance
Cum·bria

Cum·brian
cum·in (*or* cum·min) herb
cum·mer·bund (*or* kum·)
cum·shaw tip; gift
cu·mu·late
cu·mu·la·tion
cu·mu·la·tive
cu·mul·et pigeon
cu·mu·li·form cloud-shaped
cu·mu·lo·nim·bus (*plural*
  ·bi *or* ·buses) cloud
cu·mu·lo·stra·tus (*plural*
  ·ti)
cu·mu·lous (*adj*)
cu·mu·lus (*noun*; *plural*
  ·li)
cu·neal
cu·neate
cu·nei·form writing
cun·jevoi plant
cun·ni·lin·gus
cun·ning
cunt
cup (cup·ping, cupped)
cup·bearer
cup·board
cup·cake
cu·pel (·pel·ling, ·pelled;
  US ·pel·ing, ·peled)
cu·pel·la·tion metallurgical
  process
cup·ful (*plural* ·fuls)
Cupid
cu·pid·ity
cu·po·la dome; *compare*
  copula
cu·po·lat·ed
cup·pa (*or* ·per) *Slang* cup
  of tea
cupped
cup·ping
cu·pre·ous
cu·pric
cu·prif·er·ous
cu·prite mineral
cu·pro·nick·el
cu·prous
cu·pu·late (*or* ·lar) cup-
  shaped
cu·pule
cur
cur·abil·ity
cur·able
Cu·ra·çao Carribean island;
  liqueur

cu·ra·cy (*plural* ·cies)
cu·ra·re (*or* ·ri) poison
cu·ra·rine muscle relaxant
cu·ra·ri·za·tion (*or*
  ·sa·tion)
cu·ra·rize (*or* ·rise)
cu·ras·sow bird
cu·rate
cu·ra·tive
cu·ra·tor museum keeper
cu·ra·to·rial
curb restrain; *US spelling of*
  kerb
curch woman's cap
cur·cu·lio (*plural* ·lios)
  weevil
cur·cu·ma plant
curd
curdi·ness
cur·dle
cur·dler
curdy
cur·able
cure
cure-all
cu·rette (*or* ·ret; ·ret·ting,
  ·ret·ted) surgical
  instrument
cu·ret·tage (*or*
  ·rette·ment)
cur·few
cu·ria (*plural* ·riae) papal
  court
Cu·ria Re·gis Norman
  king's court
cu·rie unit
cu·rio (*plural* ·rios)
  collector's item
cu·rio·sa curiosities
cu·ri·os·ity (*plural* ·ities)
cu·ri·ous
cu·ri·ous·ness
Cu·ri·ti·ba Brazilian city
cu·rium radioactive element
curl
curl·er
cur·lew
cur·li·cue (*or* ·ly·)
curli·ness
curl·ing
curl·paper
curly (curli·er, curli·est)
cur·mudg·eon
cur·mudg·eon·ly

cur·rant fruit; *compare* current

cur·ra·jong *variant spelling of* kurrajong

cur·ra·wong bird

cur·ren·cy (*plural* ·cies)

cur·rent flow; up-to-date; *compare* currant

cur·ri·cle carriage

cur·ricu·lar

cur·ricu·lum (*plural* ·la *or* ·lums)

cur·ricu·lum vi·tae (*plural* ·la vi·tae)

cur·ri·er leather worker; *compare* courier

cur·ri·ery (*plural* ·eries)

cur·rish rude

cur·ry (*noun, plural* ·ries; *verb* ·ries, ·ry·ing, ·ried)

curry·comb

curse

curs·ed (*or* curst)

cur·sive printing term

cur·sor VDU device

cur·so·rial adapted for running

cur·sori·ly

cur·sory hasty

curt

cur·tail

cur·tail·ment

cur·tain

curtain-raiser

cur·ta·na sword

cur·ti·lage enclosed land

curt·ness

curt·sy (*or* ·sey; *noun, plural* ·sies *or* ·seys; *verb* ·sies, ·sy·ing, ·sied *or* ·seys, ·sey·ing, ·seyed)

cur·va·ceous

cur·va·ture

curve

cur·vet (·vet·ting *or* ·vet·ing, ·vet·ted *or* ·vet·ed) dressage term

cur·vi·lin·ear (*or* ·eal)

cur·vi·lin·ear·ity

curvy (curvi·er, curvi·est)

cus·cus marsupial; *compare* couscous

cu·sec unit

Cush biblical character

cush·ion

cush·iony

Cush·it·ic language

cushy *Slang* easy

cus·pate (*or* ·pat·ed, cusped)

cus·pid

cus·pi·date (*or* ·dat·ed, ·pidal)

cus·pi·da·tion architectural term

cus·pi·dor spittoon

cuss

cuss·ed

cuss·ed·ness

cus·tard

cus·to·dial

cus·to·dian

cus·to·dy (*plural* ·dies)

cus·tom

cus·tom·ari·ly

cus·tom·ary

custom-built

cus·tom·er

cus·tom·ize (*or* ·ise)

cus·tos (*plural* cus·to·des) Franciscan

cus·tu·mal customary

cut (cut·ting, cut)

cu·ta·neous

cut·away

cut·back

Cutch *variant spelling of* Kutch

cutch *variant of* catechou

cute

cute·ness

cu·ti·cle

cu·ticu·la (*plural* ·lae) cuticle

cu·ticu·lar (*adj*)

cutie

cu·tin plant substance

cu·tin·ize (*or* ·ise)

cu·tis (*plural* ·tes *or* ·tises) skin

cut·lass

cut·ler

cut·lery

cut·let

cut-price

cut·purse pickpocket

Cut·tack Indian city

cut·ter

cut·throat

cut·ting

cut·tle

cuttle·bone

cuttle·fish (*plural* ·fish *or* ·fishes)

cut·ty *Dialect* short

cut·water

cut·work embroidery

cut·worm caterpillar

cu·vette dish

Cux·ha·ven West German port

Cuz·co (*or* Cus·co) Peruvian city

cwm valley

Cwm·bran Welsh town

cyan blue colour

cy·ana·mide (*or* ·mid)

cy·anate

cy·an·ic

cya·ni·da·tion

cya·nide

cya·nine (*or* ·nin) dye

cya·nite mineral

cya·nit·ic

cya·no·co·bala·min vitamin

cy·ano·gen poisonous gas

cya·no·hy·drin

cya·no·sis blueness of skin

cya·not·ic

cy·ano·type blueprint

Cybele Phrygian goddess

cy·ber·nate

cy·ber·na·tion

cy·ber·net·ic

cy·ber·neti·cist

cy·ber·net·ics

cy·cad plant

cyca·da·ceous

Cyc·la·des Aegean islands

cy·cla·mate

cyc·la·men

cy·cle

cy·clic (*or* ·cli·cal)

cy·cli·cal·ly

cy·clist

cy·clo·al·kane

cy·clo·hex·ane

cy·cloid

cy·cloi·dal

cy·clom·eter

cy·clom·etry

cy·clone

cy·clon·ic (*or* ·cloni·cal, ·clo·nal)
cy·clo·nite explosive
Cy·clo·pean
cy·clo·pedia (*or* ·pae·dia)
cy·clo·pedic (*or* ·pae·dic)
cy·clo·pen·tane
cy·clo·plegia medical term
cy·clo·pro·pane
Cy·clops one-eyed giant
cy·clops crustacean
cy·clo·rama
cy·clo·ram·ic
cy·clo·sis (*plural* ·ses) biological process
cy·clos·to·mate (*or* ·clo·stoma·tous)
cy·clo·stome primitive vertebrate
cy·clo·style
cy·clo·thy·mia mood swings
cy·clo·thy·mic (*or* ·mi·ac)
cy·clo·tron physics term
cyg·net young swan; *compare* signet
Cyg·nus constellation
cyl·in·der
cy·lin·dri·cal (*or* ·dric)
cy·lin·dri·cal·ly
cyl·in·droid
cyma (*plural* cymae *or* cymas) architectural moulding
cy·mar woman's jacket
cy·ma·tium architectural moulding
cym·bal musical instrument; *compare* symbol
cym·bal·er (*or* ·eer, ·bal·ist)
cym·ba·lo (*plural* ·los) dulcimer
cyme botany term
cy·mene chemical compound
cy·mif·er·ous
cy·mo·gene *US* petroleum distillate

cy·mo·graph *variant spelling of* kymograph
cy·moid like a cyma
cy·mo·phane mineral
cy·mose of a cyme
Cym·ric (*or* Kym·) Welsh language
Cym·ry (*or* Kym·) Welsh people
cyn·ic
cyni·cal
cyni·cal·ly
cyni·cism
cy·no·sure
cy·pher *variant spelling of* cipher
cy·pera·ceous botany term
cy pres legal term
cy·press tree; *compare* Cyprus
Cyp·rian
cy·pri·nid fish
cy·prino·dont fish
cy·pri·noid carplike
Cyp·ri·ot (*or* ·ote)
cyp·ri·pedium orchid
Cy·prus country; *compare* cypress
cyp·sela (*plural* ·selae) botany term
Cyr·enai·ca (*or* Cir·) Libyan region
Cy·ril·lic Slavonic alphabet
cyst lump; sac; *compare* cist
cys·tec·to·my (*plural* ·mies) removal of bladder
cys·teine amino acid
cys·tein·ic
cyst·ic
cys·ti·cer·coid larva
cys·ti·cer·cus (*plural* ·ci) larva
cys·tine amino acid
cys·ti·tis bladder inflammation
cys·to·carp botany term

cys·to·carp·ic
cys·to·cele
cys·toid
cys·to·lith bladder stone
cys·to·scope medical term
cys·to·scop·ic
cys·tos·co·py (*plural* ·pies)
cys·toto·my (*plural* ·mies)
cy·tas·ter cytology term
Cyth·era Greek island
cyti·dine biochemical compound
cy·to·chemi·cal
cy·to·chem·is·try
cy·to·chrome biochemical compound
cy·to·gen·esis (*or* ·tog·eny) origin of cells
cy·to·genet·ics
cy·to·ki·nesis
cy·to·logi·cal
cy·tolo·gist
cy·tol·ogy study of cells
cy·toly·sin
cy·toly·sis
cy·ton nerve-cell body
cy·to·plasm
cy·to·plasm·ic
cy·to·plast
cy·to·sine biochemical compound
cy·to·taxo·nom·ic
cy·to·tax·ono·mist
cy·to·tax·on·omy
Cyzi·cus ancient Greek colony
czar *variant spelling of* tsar
czar·das dance
Czech
Czecho·slo·vak
Czecho·slo·va·kia
Czecho·slo·va·kian
Czę·sto·cho·wa Polish city

D

dab (dab·bing, dabbed)
dab·ber

dab·ble
dab·bler

dab·chick
da capo musical term

Dac·ca *variant of* **Dhaka**
dace
da·cha (*or* **·tcha**) Russian country house
dachs·hund
da·coit armed robber
da·coity
Da·cron (*Trademark*)
dac·tyl metrical foot; finger
dac·tyl·ic
dac·tyli·cal·ly
dac·tylo·gram *US* fingerprint
dac·tyl·og·ra·phy
dac·ty·lol·ogy (*plural* **·ogies**) sign language
dad
Dada artistic movement
Da·da·ism
Da·da·ist
Da·da·is·tic
Da·da·is·ti·cal·ly
dad·dy (*plural* **·dies**)
dado (*plural* **da·does** *or* **da·dos**) lower part of wall
Daedalus mythological character
dae·mon (*or* **dai·**) spirit; demigod; *compare* **demon**
dae·mon·ic (*or* **dai·**)
daff *Scot* to frolic; *Slang* daffodil
daf·fo·dil
daffy (**daffi·er, daffi·est**) *Slang* daft
daft
Da·gan Babylonian god
Dag·en·ham
Da·ge·stan (*or* **Da·ghe·stan**) Soviet republic
dag·ga narcotic
dag·ger
dagger·board
dag·lock encrusted wool
da·go (*plural* **·gos** *or* **·goes**)
da·go·ba Buddhist shrine
da·guerreo·type
da·guerreo·typ·er (*or* **·ist**)
da·guerreo·typy
dah Morse code sound
dahl·ia
Dah·na Arabian desert

Da·ho·man (*or* **Da·ho·mean**)
Da·ho·mey *former name of* Benin
Dáil Ei·rann Irish parliament
dai·ly (*plural* **·lies**)
dai·mon *variant spelling of* daemon
dain·ti·ly
dain·ti·ness
dain·ty (*noun, plural* **·ties**; *adj* **·ti·er, ·ti·est**)
dai·qui·ri (*plural* **·ris**) drink
dairy (*plural* **dairies**)
dairy·ing
dairy·man (*plural* **·men**)
dais platform
dai·sy (*plural* **·sies**)
daisy·cutter cricket
Da·kar Senegalese capital
Da·ko·ta
Da·ko·tan
dal Indian food
Dalai Lama Tibetan leader
da·la·si Gambian currency
dale
Dales Yorkshire region
dales·man (*plural* **·men**)
Dal·las US city
dal·li·ance
dal·ly (**·lies, ·ly·ing, ·lied**)
Dal·ma·tia Yugoslav region
Dal·ma·tian
dal·mat·ic tunic
dal·ton unit
dal·ton·ic
dal·ton·ism colour blindness
dam (**dam·ming, dammed**) river barrier; female parent; *compare* **damn**
dam·age
dam·age·abil·ity
dam·age·able
dam·ag·er
dam·ages
Da·man Indian region
Da·man·hûr Egyptian city
Da·ma·ra (*plural* **·ras** *or* **·ra**) African people
Dama·scene of Damascus
dama·scene decorate metal

Da·mas·cus Syrian capital
dam·ask
dame
Dami·et·ta Egyptian town
dam·mar (*or* **da·mar, dam·mer**) resin
dammed obstructed; *compare* **damned**
dam·ming
damn condemn; *compare* **dam**
dam·nabil·ity
dam·nable
dam·nably
dam·na·tion
dam·na·tory
damned condemned; *compare* **dammed**
damned·est
dam·ni·fi·ca·tion
dam·ni·fy (**·fies, ·fy·ing, ·fied**) injure
Damocles mythological character
damp
damp·course
damp·en
damp·en·er
damp·er
damp·ly
damp·ness
dam·sel
damsel·fish (*plural* **·fish** *or* **·fishes**)
damsel·fly (*plural* **·flies**)
dam·son
dan buoy; judo grade
Danaë mythological character
dance
danc·er
danc·ing
dan·de·lion
dan·der
Dan·die Din·mont terrier
dan·di·fi·ca·tion
dan·di·fy (**·fies, ·fy·ing, ·fied**)
dan·di·prat coin
dan·dle fondle
dan·dler
dan·druff (*or* **·driff**)
dan·druffy (*or* **·driffy**)
dan·dy (*plural* **·dies**)
dandy·ish

dandy·ism
Dane
Dane·geld (or ·gelt)
 Anglo-Saxon tax
Dane·law (or ·lagh)
 England under Danish law
dane·wort shrub
dang damn
dan·ger
dan·ger·ous
dan·ger·ous·ness
dan·gle
dan·gler
danio (plural danios) fish
Dan·ish
dank
dank·ness
dan·seur (fem ·seuse)
 French dancer
Dan·ube
Danu·bian
Dan·zig Gdańsk; pigeon
dap (dap·ping, dapped)
daphne shrub
daph·nia flea
Daph·nis mythological
 character
dap·per
dap·ple
dapple-grey (US -gray)
dar·af unit
dar·bies Slang handcuffs
Dar·dan (or ·da·nian)
 Trojan
Dar·da·nelles
Dar·da·nus mythological
 character
Dar·dic language group
dare
dare·devil
dare·devil·ry (or ·try)
dar·er
Dar es Sa·laam Tanzanian
 capital
Dar·fur Sudanese province
darg Dialect day's work
dar·ic coin
Dari·en part of Panama
dar·ing
dari·ole cookery mould
Dar·jee·ling Indian town;
 tea
dark
dark·en
dark·en·er

dar·kle darken
dark·ly
dark·ness
dark·room
dark·some
darky (or darkie,
 dark·ey; plural darkies
 or ·eys)
Dar·ling Australian river
dar·ling
Dar·ling·ton Durham town
Darm·stadt West German
 city
darn
darned
dar·nel grass
darn·er
darn·ing
dart
dart·board
dart·er
Dart·ford Kent town
Dart·moor
Dart·mouth Devon port
darts
Dar·win Australian port
Dar·win·ian
Dar·win·ism
Dar·win·ist
dash
dash·board
da·sheen plant
dash·er
da·shi·ki garment
dash·ing
dash·pot vibration damper
Dasht-i-Lut (or -e-)
 Iranian desert
das·sie animal
das·tard
das·tard·li·ness
das·tard·ly
dasy·ure marsupial
da·ta information; plural of
 datum
dat·able (or date·)
dat·able·ness (or date·)
da·ta·ry (plural ·ries)
 Catholic official
date
dat·ed
dat·ed·ness
date·less
date·line
dat·er

dat·ing
da·ti·val
da·tive
dato Philippine chief
da·to·lite mineral
da·tum (plural ·ta) fact;
 compare data
da·tu·ra plant
daub smear
daube stew
daub·er
daub·ery (or ·ry)
dauby
Dau·gav·pils Soviet city
daugh·ter
daughter-in-law (plural
 daughters-)
daugh·ter·li·ness
daugh·ter·ly
daunt
daunt·er
daunt·ing
daunt·less
dau·phin heir to French
 throne
Dau·phi·né former French
 province
dau·phine (or ·phin·ess)
 wife of dauphin
dav·en·port desk
dav·it
daw jackdaw
daw·dle
daw·dler
dawn
Daw·son Canadian town
day
day·book
day·boy
day·break
day·dream
day·dream·er
day·dream·ing
day·dreamy
day·flower
day·light
day·long
day-neutral botany term
day·star sun
day·time
day-to-day
Day·ton US city
Day·to·na Beach US city
day-tripper
daze

daz·zle
dea·con
dea·con·ess
dea·con·ry (*plural* ·ries)
dea·con·ship
de·ac·tiv·ate
de·ac·ti·va·tion
de·ac·ti·va·tor
dead
dead·beat
dead·en
dead·en·er
dead·eye nautical term
dead·fall trap
dead·head
dead·light nautical term
dead·line
dead·li·ness
dead·lock
dead·ly (·li·er, ·li·est)
dead·ness
dead·nettle
dead·pan
dead·wood
deaf
deaf-and-dumb
deaf·en
deaf-mute
deaf-muteness (*or*
  -mutism)
deaf·ness
deal (deal·ing, dealt) take
  action, etc.; *compare* dele
dea·late (*or* ·lat·ed)
  wingless
dea·la·tion
deal·er
deal·fish (*plural* ·fish *or*
  ·fishes)
deal·ing
dealt
de·ami·nate (*or*
  ·am·in·ize, ·am·in·ise)
  biochemistry term
de·ami·na·tion (*or*
  ·ami·ni·za·tion,
  ·ami·ni·sa·tion)
dean university official, etc.;
  compare dene
dean·ery (*plural* ·eries)
dean·ship
dear
dear·ly
dear·ness
dearth

deary (*or* dearie; *plural*
  dearies)
death
death·bed
death·blow
death·less
death·li·ness
death·ly
death's-head
death·trap
death·watch
Deau·ville French resort
deb *short for* debutante
de·ba·cle
de·bag (·bag·ging,
  ·bagged)
de·bar (·bar·ring, ·barred)
de·bark disembark
de·bar·ka·tion
de·bar·ment
de·base
de·bas·ed·ness
de·base·ment
de·bas·er
de·bat·able (*or* ·bate·able)
de·bat·ably
de·bate
de·bat·er
de·bauch
debau·chee
de·bauch·er
de·bauch·ery (*or* ·ment)
de·ben·ture bond
de·bili·tate
de·bili·ta·tion
de·bili·ta·tive
de·bil·ity (*plural* ·ities)
deb·it
debo·nair (*or*
  deb·on·naire)
de·bouch move into larger
  space
de·bouch·ment (*or*
  ·bou·chure)
De·bre·cen Hungarian city
dé·bride·ment surgical term
de·brief
de·bris (*or* dé·)
debt
debt·or
de·bug (·bug·ging,
  ·bugged)
de·bunk
de·bunk·er

de·bus (·bus·ing, ·bused
  or ·bus·sing, ·bussed)
  unload; alight
de·but
debu·tante
de·ca·dal
dec·ade
deca·dence (*or* ·den·cy)
deca·dent
de·caf·fein·ate
deca·gon
de·cago·nal
deca·he·dral
deca·he·dron
de·cal transferred design
de·cal·ci·fi·ca·tion
de·cal·ci·fi·er
de·cal·ci·fy (·fies, ·fy·ing,
  ·fied)
de·cal·co·ma·nia
  transferring designs
de·ca·les·cence physics
  term
de·ca·les·cent
Deca·logue Ten
  Commandments
de·camp
de·camp·ment
de·ca·nal of a dean
dec·ane chemical compound
dec·ane·dio·ic acid
de·ca·ni musical term
deca·no·ic acid
de·cant
de·cant·er
de·capi·tate
de·capi·ta·tion
de·capi·ta·tor
deca·pod crustacean
de·capo·dal (*or* ·dan,
  ·dous)
de·car·bon·ate
de·car·boni·za·tion (*or*
  ·sa·tion)
de·car·bon·ize (*or* ·ise)
de·car·bon·iz·er (*or* ·is·er)
de·car·boxy·la·tion
dec·are unit
deca·style architectural
  term
deca·syl·lab·ic
deca·syl·lable
de·cath·lete
de·cath·lon
de·cay

Dec·can Indian plateau
de·cease
de·ceased
de·cedent deceased
de·ceit
de·ceit·ful
de·ceit·ful·ly
de·ceiv·able
de·ceiv·able·ness (or
·abil·ity)
de·ceive
de·ceiv·er
de·cel·er·ate
de·cel·era·tion
de·cel·era·tor
de·cel·erom·eter
De·cem·ber
De·cem·brist Russian
revolutionary
de·cena·ry (or
de·cen·na·ry) of tithing
de·cen·cy (plural ·cies)
de·cen·nial
de·cen·nium (or
de·cen·na·ry; plural
·niums, ·nia, or ·naries)
decade
de·cent
de·cen·tral·ist
de·cen·trali·za·tion (or
·sa·tion)
de·cen·tral·ize (or ·ise)
de·cep·tion
de·cep·tive
de·ce·rebrate remove brain
de·ce·rebra·tion
de·cern legal term
deci·are unit
deci·bel
de·cid·able
de·cide
de·cid·ed
de·cid·ed·ly
de·cid·er
de·cidua (plural ·cid·uas
or ·ciduae) anatomy
term
de·cid·ual (or ·cidu·ate)
de·cidu·ous
dec·ile statistics term
de·cil·lion 10^{60}
de·cil·lionth
deci·mal
deci·mali·za·tion (or
·sa·tion)

deci·mal·ize (or ·ise)
deci·mate
deci·ma·tion
deci·ma·tor
deci·metre (US ·meter)
de·ci·pher
de·ci·pher·abil·ity
de·ci·pher·able
de·ci·pher·er
de·ci·pher·ment
de·ci·sion
de·ci·sion·al
de·ci·sive
de·ci·sive·ness
deck
deck·house
deck·le (or ·el) frame
deckle-edged
de·claim
de·claim·er
dec·la·ma·tion
de·clama·to·ri·ly
de·clama·tory
de·clar·able
de·clar·ant
dec·la·ra·tion
de·clara·tive
de·clara·tor legal term
de·clara·to·ri·ly
de·clara·tory
de·clare
de·clar·er
de·class
dé·clas·sé (fem ·sée)
French having lost status
de·clas·si·fi·able
de·clas·si·fi·ca·tion
de·clas·si·fy (·fies, ·fy·ing,
·fied)
de·clen·sion
de·clen·sion·al
de·clen·sion·al·ly
de·clin·able
dec·li·nate drooping
dec·li·na·tion
de·cli·na·tory
de·cline
de·clin·er
dec·li·nom·eter
de·clivi·tous
de·cliv·ity (plural ·ities)
downward slope
de·clutch
de·coct
de·coc·tion

de·code
de·cod·er
de·coke
de·col·late separate
de·col·la·tion
de·col·la·tor
dé·colle·tage low neckline
dé·colle·té
de·colo·nize (or ·nise)
de·col·or·ant
de·col·ori·za·tion (or
·sa·tion,
de·col·ora·tion)
de·col·or·ize (or ·ise,
de·col·our)
de·com·pos·abil·ity
de·com·pos·able
de·com·pose
de·com·pos·er
de·com·po·si·tion
de·com·pound type of leaf
de·com·press
de·com·pres·sion
de·com·pres·sive
de·com·pres·sor
de·con·gest·ant
de·con·secrate
de·con·tami·nant
de·con·tami·nate
de·con·tami·na·tion
de·con·tami·na·tive
de·con·tami·na·tor
de·con·trol (·trol·ling,
·trolled)
dé·cor (or de·)
deco·rate
deco·ra·tion
deco·ra·tive
deco·ra·tor
deco·rous
de·cor·ti·cate remove shell
de·cor·ti·ca·tion
de·cor·ti·ca·tor
de·co·rum
de·cou·page decoration
de·cou·pling electronics
term
de·coy
de·coy·er
de·crease
de·creas·ing·ly
de·cree (·cree·ing, ·creed)
de·cree·able
de·cree nisi
de·cre·er

dec·re·ment diminution
de·crep·it
de·crepi·tate crackle on heating
de·crepi·ta·tion
de·crepi·tude
de·cres·cence
de·cres·cent decreasing
de·cre·tal papal edict
de·cre·tal·ist
de·cre·tive
dec·re·tory
de·cri·al
de·cri·er
de·cry (·cries, ·cry·ing, ·cried)
de·crypt decode
de·cum·bence (or ·ben·cy)
de·cum·bent lying flat
de·cu·ple increase tenfold
de·cu·ri·on Roman councillor
de·cur·rent botany term
de·curved bent downwards
decu·ry (plural ·ries) ten Roman soldiers
de·cus·sate intersect
de·cus·sa·tion
De·dé·ag·ach Greek port
dedi·cate
dedi·cat·ed
dedi·ca·tee
dedi·ca·tion
dedi·ca·tor
dedi·ca·tory (or ·tive)
de·dif·fer·en·tia·tion
de·duce
de·duc·ibil·ity (or ·ible·ness)
de·duc·ible
de·duct
de·duct·ibil·ity
de·duct·ible
de·duc·tion
de·duc·tive
Dee river
deed
deek Dialect look at
deem consider; compare deme
deem·ster (or demp·) Manx magistrate
deep
deep·en

deep·en·er
deep-freeze (noun)
deep-freeze (verb; -freez·ing, -froze or -freezed, -frozen or -freezed)
deep-fry (-fries, -fry·ing, -fried)
deep-laid
deep·ness
deep-rooted (or -seated)
deer (plural deer or deers)
deer·grass
deer·hound
deer·skin
deer·stalker
de-escalate
de-escala·tion
de·face
de·face·able
de·face·ment
de·fac·er
de fac·to
(defaecate) incorrect spelling of defecate
de·fal·cate legal term
de·fal·ca·tion
de·fal·ca·tor
defa·ma·tion
de·fama·to·ri·ly
de·fama·tory
de·fame
de·fam·er
de·fault
de·fault·er
de·fea·sance annulment
de·fea·sible
de·feat
de·feat·er
de·feat·ism
de·feat·ist
def·ecate
def·eca·tion
def·eca·tor
de·fect
de·fec·tion
de·fec·tive
de·fec·tor
de·fence (US ·fense)
de·fence·less (US ·fense·)
de·fence·less·ness (US ·fense·)
de·fend
de·fend·able

de·fend·ant
de·fend·er
de·fen·es·tra·tion throwing from window
de·fen·sibil·ity (or ·sible·ness)
de·fen·sible
de·fen·sibly
de·fen·sive
de·fer (·fer·ring, ·ferred)
def·er·ence
def·er·ent
def·er·en·tial
def·er·en·tial·ly
de·fer·ment (or ·fer·ral)
de·fer·rable (or ·fer·able)
de·fer·ral
de·ferred
de·fer·rer
de·fi·cient
defi·cit
de·fi·er
defi·lade military term
de·file
de·file·ment
de·fil·er
de·fin·able
de·fine
de·fin·er
de·fini·en·dum (plural ·da) thing defined
de·fini·ens (plural ·en·tia) definition
defi·nite
defi·nite·ly
defi·nite·ness
defi·ni·tion
defi·ni·tion·al
de·fini·tive
de·fini·tive·ly
de·fini·tude
def·la·grate burn
def·la·gra·tion
de·flate
de·fla·tion
de·fla·tion·ary
de·fla·tion·ist
de·fla·tor
de·flect
de·flec·tion (or ·flex·ion)
de·flec·tive
de·flec·tor
de·flexed
de·floc·cu·late disperse
de·floc·cu·la·tion

de·flo·ra·tion
de·flow·er
de·flow·er·er
de·fo·li·ant
de·fo·li·ate
de·fo·lia·tion
de·fo·lia·tor
de·force withhold
de·force·ment
de·for·ciant legal term
de·for·est
de·for·esta·tion
de·for·est·er
de·form
de·form·able
de·for·ma·tion
de·formed
de·form·ed·ness
de·form·er
de·form·ity (plural ·ities)
de·fraud
de·frau·da·tion
de·fraud·er
de·fraud·ment
de·fray
de·fray·able
de·fray·al (or ·ment)
de·fray·er
de·frock
de·frost
de·frost·er
deft
deft·ness
de·funct
de·func·tive
de·fuse
defy (·fies, ·fy·ing, ·fied)
dé·ga·gé French casual
de·gas (·gas·ses or ·gases, ·gas·sing, ·gassed)
de·gas·ser
de·gauss demagnetize
de·gen·era·cy (plural ·cies)
de·gen·er·ate
de·gen·er·ate·ness
de·gen·era·tion
de·gen·era·tive
de·glu·ti·nate extract gluten
de·glu·ti·na·tion
de·glu·ti·tion swallowing
de·gra·dable
deg·ra·da·tion
de·grade
de·grad·ed

de·grad·er
de·grad·ing
de·grease
de·gree
degree-day unit
de·gres·sion decrease
de·hisce burst open
de·his·cence
de·his·cent
de·horn
Deh·ra Dun Indian city
de·hu·mani·za·tion (or ·sa·tion)
de·hu·man·ize (or ·ise)
de·hu·midi·fi·ca·tion
de·hu·midi·fi·er
de·hu·midi·fy (·fies, ·fy·ing, ·fied)
de·hy·drate
de·hy·dra·tion
de·hy·dra·tor
de·hydro·gen·ase enzyme
de·hydro·gen·ate (or ·ize, ·ise) remove hydrogen
de·hydro·gena·tion
de·hydro·geni·za·tion (or ·sa·tion)
de·hyp·no·tize (or ·ise)
de·ice
de·icer
dei·ci·dal
dei·cide killing a god
deic·tic logic term
deic·ti·cal·ly
de·ific godlike
dei·fi·ca·tion
dei·fi·er
dei·form
dei·fy (·fies, ·fy·ing, ·fied)
deign
deil Scot devil
de·in·dus·tri·ali·za·tion (or ·sa·tion)
de·in·dus·tri·al·ize (or ·ise)
de·ism
de·ist
de·ist·ic (or ·is·ti·cal)
de·ity (plural ·ities)
deix·is linguistics term
déjà vu
de·ject
de·jec·ta body waste
de·ject·ed
de·ject·ed·ness

de·jec·tion
de jure Latin according to law
dek·ko (plural ·kos) Slang look
de·laine fabric
de·lami·nate divide into layers
de·lami·na·tion
(delapidate) incorrect spelling of dilapidate
de·late denounce
Dela·ware US state
Dela·war·ean
de·lay
de·lay·er
dele (de·leing, de·led) symbol for deletion; compare deal
de·lec·table
de·lec·table·ness (or ·tabil·ity)
de·lec·tably
de·lec·ta·tion
del·egable
del·ega·cy (plural ·cies) committee
del·egate
del·ega·tion
de·lete
del·eteri·ous
de·letion
Delft Dutch town; earthenware
Del·hi Indian capital
deli short for delicatessen
De·lian of Delos
de·lib·er·ate
de·lib·er·ate·ness
de·lib·era·tion
de·lib·era·tive
de·lib·era·tor
deli·ca·cy (plural ·cies)
deli·cate
deli·ca·tes·sen
de·li·cious
de·lict civil wrong
de·light
de·light·ed
de·light·er
de·light·ful
de·light·ful·ly
de·light·ful·ness
de·lim·it (or ·limi·tate)
de·limi·ta·tion

de·limi·ta·tive
de·lin·eable
de·lin·eate
de·lin·ea·tion
de·lin·ea·tive
de·lin·ea·tor tailor's pattern
de·lin·quen·cy (plural
·cies)
de·lin·quent
deli·quesce chemistry term
deli·ques·cence
deli·ques·cent
de·liri·ant
de·liri·ous
de·liri·ous·ness
de·lir·ium (plural ·lir·iums
or ·liria)
de·lir·ium tre·mens
deli·tes·cence medical term
deli·tes·cent
de·liv·er
de·liv·er·able
de·liv·er·ance
de·liv·er·er
de·liv·ery (plural ·eries)
dell
Del·mar·va US peninsula
de·lo·cali·za·tion (or
·sa·tion)
de·lo·cal·ize (or ·ise)
De·los Greek island
de·louse
Del·phi Greek oracle
Del·phian
Del·phic
del·phin·ium (plural
·phin·iums or ·phinia)
Del·phi·nus constellation
del·ta
del·ta·ic (or del·tic)
del·ti·olo·gist
del·ti·ol·ogy collecting
postcards
del·toid muscle
de·lude
de·lud·er
del·uge
de·lu·sion
de·lu·sion·al
de·lu·sive
de·lu·so·ry
de luxe
delve
delv·er

de·mag·neti·za·tion (or
·sa·tion)
de·mag·net·ize (or ·ise)
de·mag·net·iz·er (or
·is·er)
dema·gog·ic (or ·gogi·cal)
dema·gogi·cal·ly
dema·gogue (US also
·gog)
dema·gogu·ery (or ·ism)
dema·gogy (plural
·gogies)
de·mand
de·mand·able
de·mand·ant
de·mand·er
de·mand·ing
de·man·toid gemstone
de·mar·cate
de·mar·ca·tion (or
·ka·tion)
de·mar·ca·tor
dé·marche French
diplomatic manoeuvre
de·ma·teri·al·ize (or ·ise)
Dema·vend Iranian volcano
deme biology term; ancient
local-government unit;
compare deem
de·mean
de·mean·ing
de·mean·our (US ·or)
de·ment
de·ment·ed
de·ment·ed·ness
de·men·tia
Dem·erara Guyanese river
dem·erara sugar
de·mer·it
de·meri·to·ri·ous
de·mer·sal living in deep
water
de·mesne land
Demeter Greek goddess
demi·bas·ti·on fortification
demi·can·ton
demi·god (fem ·god·dess)
demi·john bottle
de·mili·ta·ri·za·tion (or
·sa·tion)
de·mili·ta·rize (or ·rise)
demi·lune crescent shape
demi·mon·daine
unrespectable woman
demi·monde

de·min·er·al·ize (or ·ise)
demi·relief
de·mis·able
de·mise
demi·semi·qua·ver
de·mis·sion giving up office
de·mist
de·mist·er
demi·tasse small coffee cup
demi·urge philosophy term
demi·vierge French
promiscuous virgin
demi·volt (or ·volte)
demo (plural demos)
Slang demonstration
de·mob (·mob·bing,
·mobbed)
de·mo·bi·li·za·tion (or
·sa·tion)
de·mo·bi·lize (or ·lise)
de·moc·ra·cy (plural
·cies)
Demo·crat political party
member
demo·crat
Demo·crat·ic
demo·crat·ic
demo·crati·cal·ly
de·moc·ra·ti·za·tion (or
·sa·tion)
de·moc·ra·tize (or ·tise)
dé·mo·dé French out of
fashion
de·modu·late
de·modu·la·tion electronics
term
de·modu·la·tor
De·mo·gor·gon underworld
god
de·mog·ra·pher (or ·phist)
de·mo·graph·ic (or
·graphi·cal)
de·mo·graphi·cal·ly
de·mog·ra·phy
demoi·selle damsel; bird
de·mol·ish
de·mol·ish·er
de·mol·ish·ment
demo·li·tion
demo·li·tion·ist
de·mon devil; compare
daemon
de·mon·eti·za·tion (or
·sa·tion)
de·mon·etize (or ·etise)
de·mo·ni·ac (or ·nia·cal)

de·mo·nia·cal·ly
de·mon·ic
de·moni·cal·ly
de·mon·ism
de·mon·ist
de·mon·ize (*or* ·ise)
de·mon·ola·ter demon
worshipper
de·mon·ola·try
de·mono·logi·cal
de·mon·olo·gist
de·mon·ol·ogy
de·mon·strabil·ity (*or* ·strable·ness)
de·mon·strable
de·mon·strably
dem·on·strate
dem·on·stra·tion
de·mon·stra·tion·al
de·mon·stra·tion·ist
de·mon·stra·tive
de·mon·stra·tor
de·mor·ali·za·tion (*or* ·sa·tion)
de·mor·al·ize (*or* ·ise)
de·mor·al·iz·er (*or* ·is·er)
de·mos nation
de·mote
de·mot·ic of the people
de·mo·tion
de·mot·ist
de·mount
de·mount·able
demp·ster *variant of* deemster
de·mul·cent soothing
de·mul·si·fi·ca·tion
de·mul·si·fi·er
de·mul·si·fy (·fies, ·fy·ing, ·fied)
de·mur (·mur·ring, ·murred)
de·mure
de·mure·ness
de·mur·rable
de·mur·rage
de·mur·ral
de·mur·rer objection
demy paper size
de·mys·ti·fi·ca·tion
de·mys·ti·fy (·fies, ·fy·ing, ·fied)
de·my·tholo·gize (*or* ·gise)
den (den·ning, denned)

de·nar·ius (*plural* ·narii) coin
de·nary based on ten
de·na·tion·ali·za·tion (*or* ·sa·tion)
de·na·tion·al·ize (*or* ·ise)
de·natu·rali·za·tion (*or* ·sa·tion)
de·natu·ral·ize (*or* ·ise)
de·na·tur·ant
de·na·tura·tion
de·na·ture (*or* ·tur·ize, ·tur·ise)
de·na·zi·fy (·fies, ·fy·ing, ·fied)
Den·bigh·shire former
Welsh county
den·dri·form branching
den·drite part of nerve cell
den·drit·ic (*or* ·driti·cal)
den·driti·cal·ly
den·dro·chrono·logi·cal
den·dro·chro·nolo·gist
den·dro·chro·nol·ogy
study of tree rings
den·droid (*or* ·droi·dal)
treelike
den·dro·logi·cal (*or* ·log·ic, ·drolo·gous)
den·drolo·gist
den·drol·ogy
dene wooded valley;
compare dean
Den·eb star
de·nega·tion
den·gue viral disease
de·ni·able
de·ni·al
de·nico·tin·ize (*or* ·ise)
de·ni·er one who denies
den·ier unit of weight
deni·grate
deni·gra·tion
deni·gra·tor
den·im
de·ni·trate chemistry term
de·ni·tra·tion
de·ni·tri·fi·ca·tion
de·ni·tri·fy (·fies, ·fy·ing, ·fied)
deni·zen
Den·mark
denned
den·ning
de·nomi·nable

de·nomi·nate
de·nomi·na·tion
de·nomi·na·tion·al
de·nomi·na·tion·al·ism
de·nomi·na·tion·al·ist
de·nomi·na·tive naming
de·nomi·na·tor
de·not·able
de·no·ta·tion
de·no·ta·tive
de·note
de·note·ment
de·noue·ment
de·nounce
de·nounce·ment
de·nounc·er
dense
dense·ness
den·sim·eter
den·si·met·ric
den·sim·etry
den·si·tom·eter
den·si·to·met·ric
den·si·tom·etry
den·sity (*plural* ·sities)
dent
den·tal
den·ta·lium (*plural* ·liums *or* ·lia) mollusc
den·tate
den·ta·tion state of having teeth; *compare* dentition
den·tex fish
den·ti·cle small tooth
den·ticu·late
den·ticu·la·tion
den·ti·form
den·ti·frice
den·til architectural term
den·ti·la·bial
den·ti·lin·gual phonetics term
den·tin·al
den·tine (*or* ·tin) tooth tissue
den·tist
den·tis·try
den·ti·tion set of teeth;
compare dentation
den·toid
Den·ton Lancashire town
den·ture
de·nu·cleari·za·tion (*or* ·sa·tion)
de·nu·clear·ize (*or* ·ise)

denu·date
denu·da·tion
de·nude
de·nud·er
de·nu·mer·able
de·nun·ci·ate
de·nun·cia·tion
de·nun·cia·tor
de·nun·cia·tory
Den·ver US city
deny (de·nies, de·ny·ing, de·nied)
deo·dand legal term
deo·dar tree
de·odor·ant
de·odori·za·tion (or ·sa·tion)
de·odor·ize (or ·ise)
de·odor·iz·er (or ·is·er)
de·on·tic logic term
de·on·to·logi·cal
de·on·tolo·gist
de·on·tol·ogy branch of ethics
de·oxi·di·za·tion (or ·sa·tion)
de·oxi·dize (or ·dise)
de·oxi·diz·er (or ·dis·er)
de·oxy·cor·ti·co·ster·one (or de·oxy·cor·tone) hormone
de·oxy·gen·ate (or ·ize, ·ise)
de·oxy·gena·tion
de·oxy·ri·bo·nu·cle·ic acid (or des·)
de·oxy·ri·bose (or des·) a sugar
de·part
de·part·ment
de·part·men·tal
de·part·men·tal·ism
de·part·men·tali·za·tion (or ·sa·tion)
de·part·ment·al·ize (or ·ise)
de·part·men·tal·ly
de·par·ture
de·pas·ture
de·pend
de·pend·abil·ity (or ·able·ness)
de·pend·able
de·pend·ably
de·pend·ant (noun)

de·pend·ence (US also ·ance)
de·pend·en·cy (US also ·an·cy; plural ·cies)
de·pend·ent (US also ·ant; adj)
de·per·son·ali·za·tion (or ·sa·tion)
de·per·son·al·ize (or ·ise)
de·pict
de·pict·er (or ·pic·tor)
de·pic·tion
de·pic·tive
de·pic·ture
depi·late
depi·la·tion
depi·la·tor
de·pila·tory (plural ·tories)
de·plane
de·plet·able
de·plete
de·ple·tion
de·ple·tive (or ·tory)
de·plor·able
de·plor·able·ness (or ·abil·ity)
de·plor·ably
de·plore
de·plor·er
de·plor·ing·ly
de·ploy
de·ploy·ment
de·plu·ma·tion
de·plume deprive of feathers
de·po·lari·za·tion (or ·sa·tion)
de·po·lar·ize (or ·ise)
de·po·lar·iz·er (or ·is·er)
de·po·liti·cize (or ·cise)
de·pone Scot testify
de·po·nent linguistics term; deposition maker
de·popu·late
de·popu·la·tion
de·port
de·port·able
de·por·ta·tion
de·por·tee
de·port·ment
de·pos·able
de·pos·al
de·pose
de·pos·er

de·pos·it
de·posi·tary (plural ·taries) person; compare depository
depo·si·tion
de·posi·tor
de·posi·tory (plural ·tories) warehouse; compare depositary
de·pot
dep·ra·va·tion corruption; compare deprivation
de·prave
de·praved
de·praved·ness
de·prav·er
de·prav·ity (plural ·ities)
dep·re·cate protest against; compare depreciate
dep·re·ca·tion
dep·re·ca·tive
dep·re·ca·tor
dep·re·ca·to·ri·ly
dep·re·ca·tory
de·pre·ciable
de·pre·ci·ate lose value; compare deprecate
de·pre·cia·tion
de·pre·cia·tor
de·pre·cia·tory (or ·tive)
dep·re·date plunder
dep·re·da·tion
de·press
de·pres·sant
de·pressed
de·press·ible
de·press·ing
de·pres·sion
de·pres·sive
de·pres·so·mo·tor physiology term
de·pres·sor
de·pres·suri·za·tion (or ·sa·tion)
de·pres·sur·ize
de·priv·able
dep·ri·va·tion (or de·priv·al) loss; compare depravation
de·prive
de·prived
de·priv·er
dep·side chemistry term
depth
depu·rate purify

depu·ra·tion
depu·ra·tive purifying
depu·ra·tor
depu·ta·tion
de·pute
depu·tize (*or* ·tise)
depu·ty (*plural* ·ties)
de·rac·in·ate uproot
de·raci·na·tion
de·rail
de·rail·leur bicycle gear
de·rail·ment
de·range
de·range·ment
de·ra·tion
Der·by
Der·by·shire
de·reg·is·ter
der·elict
der·elic·tion
de·re·strict
de·re·strict·ed
de·re·stric·tion
de·ride
de·rid·er
de ri·gueur
de·ris·ible
de·ri·sion
de·ri·sive (*or* ·sory)
de·ri·sive·ness
de·riv·able
deri·va·tion
deri·va·tion·al
de·riva·tive
de·rive
de·riv·er
der·ma skin
der·mal
der·ma·ti·tis
der·mato·gen plant tissue
derma·to·glyph·ics skin
   pattern
der·ma·toid
der·ma·to·logi·cal
der·ma·tolo·gist
der·ma·tol·ogy
der·ma·tome surgical
   instrument
der·ma·tom·ic
der·ma·to·phyte parasitic
   fungus
der·ma·to·phyt·ic
der·ma·to·phy·to·sis
der·ma·to·plas·tic

der·ma·to·plas·ty skin
   grafting
der·ma·to·sis (*plural* ·ses)
   skin disease
der·mic
der·mis skin layer
der·moid
dero·gate disparage
dero·gation
de·roga·tive
de·roga·to·ri·ly
de·roga·to·ri·ness
de·roga·tory
der·rick
der·rière buttocks
derring-do bold action
der·rin·ger (*or* der·in·ger)
   pistol
der·ris plant
Der·ry Londonderry
der·ry *Austral* grudge
derv diesel oil
der·vish
Der·went river
Derwent·water lake
de·sali·nate (*or* ·nize,
   ·nise)
de·sali·na·tion (*or*
   ·ni·za·tion, ·ni·sa·tion)
de·scale
des·cant
des·cant·er
de·scend
des·cend·able
de·scend·ant (*noun*)
de·scend·ent (*adj*)
de·scend·er
de·scend·ible (*or* ·able)
de·scent
de·school
de·scrib·able
de·scribe
de·scrib·er
de·scri·er
de·scrip·tion
de·scrip·tive
de·scrip·ti·vism
de·scry (·scries, ·scry·ing,
   ·scried)
des·ecrate
des·ecra·tion
des·ecra·tor (*or* ·ter)
de·seg·re·gate
de·seg·re·ga·tion
de·seg·re·ga·tion·ist

de·sen·si·ti·za·tion (*or*
   ·sa·tion)
de·sen·si·tize (*or* ·tise)
de·sen·si·tiz·er (*or* ·tis·er)
des·ert plantless region;
   compare dessert
de·sert abandon; merit;
   compare dessert
de·sert·ed
de·sert·er
des·ert·ifi·ca·tion
de·ser·tion
de·serve
de·serv·ed·ly
de·serv·ed·ness
de·serv·er
de·serv·ing
de·sexu·ali·za·tion (*or*
   ·sa·tion)
de·sexu·al·ize (*or* ·ise)
des·ha·bille *variant spelling*
   of dishabille
des·ic·cant
des·ic·cate
des·ic·ca·ted
des·ic·ca·tion
des·ic·ca·tive
des·ic·ca·tor
de·sid·er·ate long for
de·sid·era·tion
de·sid·era·tive
de·sid·era·tum (*plural* ·ta)
   something wanted
de·sign
de·sign·able
des·ig·nate
des·ig·na·tion
des·ig·na·tive (*or* ·tory)
des·ig·na·tor
de·sign·ed·ly
de·sign·er
de·sign·ing
desi·nence word ending
desi·nent (*or* ·nen·tial)
de·sir·abil·ity (*or*
   ·sirable·ness)
de·sir·able
de·sire
de·sir·er
de·sir·ous
de·sist
de·sist·ance (*or* ·ence)
desk
des·man (*plural* ·mans)
   animal

des·mid alga
des·mid·ian
des·moid tumour
Des Moines US city
deso·late
deso·lat·er (or ·or)
deso·la·tion
de·sorb chemistry term
de·sorp·tion
des·pair
des·patch variant spelling of dispatch
des·pe·ra·do (plural ·does or ·dos)
des·per·ate
des·pera·tion
des·pi·cabil·ity (or ·cable·ness)
des·pic·able
des·pic·ably
des·pise
de·spis·er
de·spite
de·spoil
de·spoil·er
de·spoil·ment
de·spo·lia·tion
de·spond
de·spond·en·cy (or ·ence)
de·spond·ent
des·pot
des·pot·ic (or ·poti·cal)
des·poti·cal·ly
des·pot·ism
des·pu·mate clarify
des·pu·ma·tion
des·qua·mate
des·qua·ma·tion
Des·sau East German city
des·sert sweet; compare desert
dessert·spoon
des·sia·tine Russian unit
(dessicate) incorrect spelling of desiccate
des·ti·na·tion
des·tine
des·tined
des·ti·ny (plural ·nies)
des·ti·tute
des·ti·tu·tion
de·stroy
de·stroy·able
de·stroy·er
de·struct

de·struc·tibil·ity
de·struct·ible
de·struc·tion
de·struc·tion·ist
de·struc·tive
de·struc·tive·ness (or ·tiv·ity)
de·struc·tor furnace
desue·tude state of disuse
des·ul·to·ri·ly
des·ul·to·ri·ness
des·ul·tory
de·tach
de·tach·abil·ity
de·tach·able
de·tached
de·tach·er
de·tach·ment
de·tail
de·tailed
de·tain
de·tain·able
de·tainee
de·tain·er
de·tain·ment
de·tect
de·tect·able (or ·ible)
de·tec·tion
de·tec·tive
de·tec·tor
de·tent locking device
dé·tente easement
de·ten·tion
de·ter (·ter·ring, ·terred)
de·terge cleanse
de·ter·gen·cy (or ·gence)
de·ter·gent
de·terio·rate
de·terio·ra·tion
de·terio·ra·tive
de·ter·ment
de·ter·mi·nable
de·ter·mi·nant
de·ter·mi·nate
de·ter·mi·na·tion
de·ter·mi·na·tive
de·ter·mine
de·ter·mined
de·ter·mined·ly
de·ter·mined·ness
de·ter·min·er
de·ter·min·ism
de·ter·min·ist
de·ter·min·is·tic
de·ter·rence

de·ter·rent
de·ter·sive
de·test
de·test·abil·ity (or ·able·ness)
de·test·able
de·tes·ta·tion
de·test·er
de·throne
de·throne·ment
de·thron·er
deti·nue legal term
Det·mold West German city
deto·nate
deto·na·tion
deto·na·tive
deto·na·tor
de·tour
de·toxi·cant
de·toxi·cate
de·toxi·ca·tion
de·toxi·fi·ca·tion
de·toxi·fy (·fies, ·fy·ing, ·fied)
de·tract
de·trac·tion
de·trac·tive (or ·tory)
de·trac·tor
de·train
de·train·ment
de·trib·ali·za·tion (or ·sa·tion)
de·trib·al·ize (or ·ise)
det·ri·ment
det·ri·men·tal
det·ri·men·tal·ly
de·tri·tal
de·tri·tion wearing away
de·tri·tus debris
De·troit US city
de trop French superfluous
de·trude thrust out
de·trun·cate
de·trun·ca·tion
de·tru·sion
de·tu·mes·cence
Deucalion mythological character
deuce
deu·ced
deus ex machi·na Latin providential resolver
deu·ter·ago·nist drama term

deu·tera·nope

deu·tera·no·pia green
  blindness

deu·ter·an·op·ic

deu·ter·ide chemistry term

deu·ter·ium hydrogen
  isotope

deu·tero·ca·noni·cal

deu·ter·oga·mist

deu·ter·oga·my

deu·ter·on deuterium
  nucleus

Deu·ter·ono·my biblical
  book

deu·to·plasm (or
  deu·tero·) egg yolk

deu·to·plas·mic (or ·tic)

Deut·sche Mark

deut·zia shrub

Deux-Sèvres French city

deva oriental god; compare
  diva

de·valua·tion

de·value (or ·valu·ate;
  ·valu·ing, ·valu·ed or
  ·at·ing, ·ated)

De·va·na·ga·ri Indian script

dev·as·tate

dev·as·ta·tion

dev·as·ta·tive

dev·as·ta·tor

de·vel·op

de·vel·op·able

de·vel·op·er

de·vel·op·ment

de·vel·op·men·tal

de·vel·op·men·tal·ly

de·vi·ance

de·vi·ant

de·vi·ate

de·via·tion

de·via·tion·ism

de·via·tion·ist

de·via·tor

de·via·tory

de·vice contrivance; plan;
  compare devise

dev·il (·il·ling, ·illed; US
  ·il·ing, ·iled)

devil·fish (plural ·fish or
  ·fishes)

dev·il·ish

dev·il·ish·ness

dev·il·ment

dev·il·ry (plural ·ries)

de·vi·ous

de·vi·ous·ness

de·vis·able

de·vis·al act of devising

de·vise to plan; leave by
  will; a gift by will;
  compare device

de·vi·see inheritor

de·vis·er (or in legal
  contexts ·vi·sor) one
  who devises; compare
  divisor

de·vi·tali·za·tion (or
  ·sa·tion)

de·vi·tal·ize (or ·ise)

de·vit·ri·fi·ca·tion

de·vit·ri·fy (·fies, ·fy·ing,
  ·fied) chemistry term

de·vo·cal·ize (or ·ise)

de·voice phonetics term

de·void

de·voirs (plural) French
  compliments

de·vo·lu·tion

de·vo·lu·tion·ary

de·vo·lu·tion·ist

de·volve

de·volve·ment

Dev·on

De·vo·nian

Dev·on·shire

de·vote

de·vot·ed

de·vot·ed·ness

devo·tee

de·vote·ment

de·vo·tion

de·vo·tion·al

de·vo·tion·al·ity (or ·ness)

de·vour

de·vour·er

de·vour·ing·ly

de·vout

de·vout·ness

dew

de·wan Indian minister

dew·berry (plural
  ·berries)

dew·claw

dew·drop

dewi·ly

dewi·ness

dew·lap

Dews·bury Yorkshire town

dewy (dewi·er, dew·iest)

dewy-eyed

Dex·edrine (Trademark)

dex·ter

dex·ter·ity

dex·ter·ous (or dex·trous)

dex·ter·ous·ness (or
  dex·trous·ness)

dex·tral

dex·tral·ity

dex·tral·ly

dex·tran biochemical
  compound

dex·trin (or ·trine)
  adhesive gum

dextro·am·pheta·mine

dextro·glu·cose

dextro·gy·rate (or ·gyre)

dextro·ro·ta·tion

dextro·ro·ta·tory (or
  dextro·ro·ta·ry)

dex·trorse (or ·tror·sal)
  spiralling left to right

dex·trose form of glucose

dex·trous

dey Algerian ruler

Dhah·ran Saudi Arabian
  town

dhak tree

Dhaka (or Dac·ca)
  Bangladeshi capital

dhal vegetable

dhar·ma Hindu custom

dhar·na Indian sit-in

Dhau·la·gi·ri Nepalese
  mountain

dho·bi Indian washerman

dhole animal

dho·ti (or dhoo·ti,
  dhoo·tie, dhu·ti)
  loincloth

dhow boat

dia·base rock

dia·ba·sic

dia·be·tes

dia·bet·ic

dia·ble·rie devilry

dia·bol·ic

dia·boli·cal

dia·boli·cal·ly

dia·boli·cal·ness

diabo·lism

di·abo·list

di·abo·lize (or ·lise)

di·abo·lo (plural ·los)
  game

dia·caus·tic physics term
di·ac·etyl·mor·phine
di·a·chron·ic linguistics term
di·acid
dia·cid·ic
di·aco·nal of a deacon
di·aco·nate
dia·crit·ic phonetic symbol
dia·criti·cal
di·ac·tin·ic physics term
di·ac·tin·ism
dia·del·phous botany term
dia·dem
di·ad·ro·mous fan-shaped
di·aer·esis *variant spelling of*
  dieresis
di·aeret·ic *variant spelling of*
  dieretic
dia·gen·esis chemistry term
dia·geo·trop·ic
dia·geot·ro·pism response
  to gravity
di·ag·nos·able
di·ag·nose
di·ag·no·sis (*plural* ·ses)
di·ag·nos·tic
di·ag·nos·ti·cal·ly
di·ag·nos·ti·cian
di·ag·nos·tics
di·ago·nal
di·ago·nal·ly
dia·gram (·gram·ming,
  ·grammed; *US*
  ·gram·ing, ·gramed)
dia·gram·mat·ic
dia·gram·mati·cal·ly
dia·graph drawing
  instrument
dia·ki·nesis biology term
dial (dial·ling, dialled;
  US dial·ing, dialed)
dia·lect
dia·lec·tal
dia·lec·tic
dia·lec·ti·cal
dia·lec·ti·cal·ly
dia·lec·tics branch of logic
dia·lec·to·logi·cal
dia·lec·tolo·gist
dia·lec·tol·ogy
di·al·lage mineral
dial·ler
di·alo·gism philosophy term
di·alo·gist
dia·lo·gis·tic (*or* ·ti·cal)

di·alo·gize (*or* ·gise)
dia·logue (*US also* ·log)
dia·logu·er
dia·lys·abil·ity
dia·lys·able
dia·ly·sa·tion
dia·lyse (*US* ·lyze)
dia·lys·er (*US* ·lyz·)
di·aly·sis (*plural* ·ses)
dia·lyt·ic
dia·lyti·cal·ly
dia·mag·net
dia·mag·net·ic
dia·mag·neti·cal·ly
dia·mag·net·ism
dia·man·té decorated with
  sequins
dia·man·tine of diamonds
di·am·eter
di·am·etral
dia·met·ric (*or* ·ri·cal)
dia·met·ri·cal·ly
dia·mine chemistry term
dia·mond
diamond·back terrapin
di·an·drous botany term
dia·no·et·ic of thought
dia·noia philosophy term
di·an·thus (*plural* ·thuses)
  plant
dia·pa·son organ stop
dia·pa·son·al (*or* ·son·ic)
dia·pause suspended growth
dia·pede·sis medical term
dia·pedet·ic
dia·per
di·apha·nous
di·apha·nous·ness (*or*
  ·nei·ty)
dia·phone linguistics term
dia·phon·ic
di·apho·ny musical term
dia·pho·resis
dia·pho·ret·ic causing
  perspiration
dia·pho·to·trop·ic biology
  term
dia·photo·trop·ism
dia·phragm
dia·phrag·mat·ic
dia·phrag·mati·cal·ly
dia·phys·ial
di·aphy·sis bone shaft
dia·pir geological fold
di·apo·phys·ial

dia·pophy·sis (*plural* ·ses)
  anatomy term
dia·posi·tive positive
  transparency
di·arch botany term
di·ar·chic (*or* di·ar·chi·cal,
  di·ar·chal, dy·)
di·ar·chy (*or* dy·; *plural*
  ·chies) two-state
  government
dia·rist
di·ar·rhoea (*US* ·rhea)
di·ar·rhoeal (*or* ·rhoe·ic;
  US ·rheal *or* ·rhe·ic)
di·ar·thro·dial
di·ar·thro·sis (*plural* ·ses)
  movable joint
dia·ry (*plural* ·ries)
dia·scope projector
Di·as·po·ra Jews' dispersion
dia·spore mineral
dia·stal·sis (*plural* ·ses)
  physiology term
dia·stal·tic
dia·stase enzyme
dia·sta·sic
dia·sta·sis (*plural* ·ses)
  separation
dia·stat·ic
dia·ste·ma (*plural* ·ma·ta)
  fissure
di·as·ter biology term
di·as·to·le dilation of heart
di·as·tol·ic
di·as·tral biology term
dia·stroph·ic
di·as·tro·phism movement
  of earth's crust
dia·style architectural term
dia·tes·sa·ron musical term
dia·ther·man·cy (*plural*
  ·cies) heat transmission
dia·ther·man·ous
dia·ther·mic
dia·ther·my (*or* ·mia)
  medical term
diath·esis (*plural* ·eses)
  susceptibility to disease
dia·thet·ic
dia·tom alga
dia·to·ma·ceous
dia·tom·ic
di·ato·mic·ity
di·ato·mite rock
dia·ton·ic musical term
dia·toni·cal·ly

dia·toni·cism
dia·tribe
dia·trop·ic
di·at·ro·pism biology term
dia·zine (or ·zin) chemistry term
di·azo (plural ·azos or ·azoes) chemistry term
dia·zole
di·azo·methane
dia·zo·nium
dia·zo·ti·za·tion (or ·sa·tion)
dia·zo·tize (or ·tise)
dib (dib·bing, dibbed)
di·ba·sic
di·ba·sic·ity
dib·ber
dib·ble garden tool
dib·bler
di·bran·chi·ate zoology term
di·bro·mide
di·car·box·yl·ic acid
dic·ast Athenian juror
dice
di·cen·tra plant
di·cepha·lism
di·cepha·lous two-headed
di·cer
dicey (dici·er, dici·est)
di·cha·sial
di·cha·sium (plural ·sia) botany term
di·chla·myd·eous botany term
di·chlo·ride
di·chloro·di·fluoro·methane
di·chloro·di·phenyl·tri·chloro·ethane DDT
di·choga·mous (or ·cho·gam·ic)
di·choga·my botany term
di·choto·mist
di·choto·mi·za·tion (or ·sa·tion)
di·choto·mize (or ·mise)
di·choto·mous (or ·cho·tom·ic)
di·choto·my (plural ·mies)
di·chro·ic (or di·chro·it·ic)
di·chro·ism crystallography term
di·chro·ite

di·chro·mate chemistry term
di·chro·mat·ic having two colours
di·chro·mati·cism crystallography term
di·chro·ma·tism
di·chro·mic involving two colours
di·chro·scope (or ·chroi·scope, ·chroo·scope) optical instrument
di·chro·scop·ic (or ·chroi·scop·ic, ·chroo·scop·ic)
dick·ens slang term
Dick·en·sian
dick·er US barter
dicky (or dick·ey; noun, plural dickies or dick·eys; adj dicki·er, dicki·est)
di·cli·nism
di·cli·nous botany term
di·cli·ny
di·coty·ledon botany term
di·coty·ledon·ous
di·crot·ic (or ·cro·tal) having a double pulse
di·cro·tism
dic·ta plural of dictum
Dic·ta·phone (Trademark)
dic·tate
dic·ta·tion
dic·ta·tion·al
dic·ta·tor
dic·ta·tor·ial
dic·ta·tor·ial·ly
dic·ta·tor·ship
dic·ta·tress (or ·trix)
dic·tion
dic·tion·ary (plural ·aries)
Dic·to·graph (Trademark)
dic·tum (plural ·tums or ·ta)
di·cyno·dont extinct reptile
did
Dida·che treatise
di·dac·tic
di·dac·ti·cal·ly
di·dac·ti·cism
di·dac·tics teaching
did·dle

did·geri·doo musical instrument
didi·coy (or did·di·coy, dida·kai; plural ·coys or ·kais) gypsy
didn't
Dido mythological character
didst
di·dym·ium chemistry term
didy·mous in pairs
di·dyna·mous botany term
die (verb; dy·ing, died) expire; compare dye
die (noun) tool; Archaic dice; compare dye
die·back tree disease
die-cast (-casting, -cast)
di·ecious variant spelling (esp. US) of dioecious
die-hard
die-hardism
diel·drin insecticide
di·elec·tric
di·elec·tri·cal·ly
Dien Bien Phu Vietnamese battle site
di·en·cephal·ic
di·en·cepha·lon brain part
Di·eppe French port
di·er·esis (or ·aer·; plural ·eses) phonetics symbol; compare diuresis
di·eret·ic (or ·aeret·) of dieresis; compare diuretic
die·sel
diesel-electric
diesel-hydrau·lic
di·esis (plural ·eses) printing term
die·stock tool
di·estrus US spelling of dioestrus
diet
di·etary
di·et·er
di·etet·ic (or ·eteti·cal)
di·eteti·cal·ly
di·etet·ics
di·ethyl·stil·boes·trol (US ·bes·)
di·eti·tian (or ·cian)
dif·fer
dif·fer·ence
dif·fer·ent
dif·fer·en·tia (plural ·tiae) logic term

dif·fer·en·ti·abil·ity
dif·fer·en·ti·able
dif·fer·en·tial
dif·fer·en·ti·ate
dif·fer·en·tia·tion
dif·fer·en·tia·tor
dif·fi·cult
dif·fi·cul·ty (*plural* ·ties)
dif·fi·dence
dif·fi·dent
dif·fract
dif·frac·tion
dif·frac·tive
dif·frac·tom·eter
dif·fuse
dif·fuse·ness
dif·fus·er (*or* ·fu·sor)
dif·fus·ibil·ity (*or* ·ible·ness)
dif·fus·ible
dif·fu·sion
dif·fu·sive
dif·fu·siv·ity
dig (dig·ging, dug)
diga·mist
di·gam·ma obsolete Greek letter
diga·mous
diga·my (*plural* ·mies) second marriage
di·gas·tric jaw muscle
di·gen·esis zoology term
di·genet·ic
di·gest
di·gest·ant
di·gest·er
di·gest·ibil·ity (*or* ·ible·ness)
di·gest·ible
di·ges·tif *French* digestive drink
di·ges·tion
di·ges·tion·al
di·ges·tive (*or* ·tant)
dig·ger
dig·ging
dig·it
digi·tal
digi·tal·in chemical compound
digi·tal·is
digi·tal·ism
digi·tali·za·tion (*or* ·sa·tion)
digi·tal·ize (*or* ·ise)

digi·tal·ly
digi·tate (*or* ·tat·ed)
digi·ta·tion
digi·ti·form
digi·ti·grade walking on toes
dig·iti·za·tion (*or* ·sa·tion)
dig·it·ize (*or* ·ise)
digi·tox·in chemical compound
digi·tron electronics term
di·glot bilingual
di·glot·tic
dig·ni·fy (·fies, ·fy·ing, ·fied)
dig·ni·tary (*plural* ·taries)
dig·nity (*plural* ·nities)
di·graph two-letter sound
di·graph·ic
di·gress
di·gress·er
di·gres·sion
di·gres·sion·al
di·gres·sive
di·he·dral
di·he·dron
di·hy·brid
di·hy·brid·ism
Di·jon French city
dik-dik antelope
dike variant spelling of dyke
dik·tat decree
di·lapi·date
di·lapi·da·ted
di·lapi·da·tion
di·lapi·da·tor
di·lat·abil·ity (*or* ·able·ness)
di·lat·able
di·la·tan·cy physics term
di·la·tant
di·la·ta·tion
dila·ta·tion·al
dila·te
di·la·tion
di·la·tive
dila·tom·eter
dila·to·met·ric
dila·to·met·ri·cal·ly
dila·tom·etry
di·la·tor (*or* ·lat·er, di·la·ta·tor)
dila·to·ri·ness
di·la·tory

dil·do (*or* ·doe; *plural* ·dos *or* ·does) artificial penis
di·lem·ma
dil·em·mat·ic (*or* dil·em·mic)
dil·et·tante (*plural* ·tan·tes *or* ·tan·ti)
dil·et·tan·tish (*or* ·teish)
dil·et·tan·tism (*or* ·teism)
dili·gence
dili·gent
dill
dil·ly *Slang* remarkable person
dilly-dally (-dallies, -dally·ing, -dallied)
dilu·ent
di·lute
di·lu·tee
di·lut·er
di·lu·tion
di·lu·vial (*or* ·vian)
di·lu·vium (*plural* ·via) geology term
dim (*adj* dim·mer, dim·mest; *verb* dim·ming, dimmed)
dime
di·men·hy·dri·nate drug
di·men·sion
di·men·sion·al
di·men·sion·al·ity
di·men·sion·less
di·mer chemistry term
di·mer·cap·rol drug
di·mer·ic
dim·er·ism
dim·er·ous divided into two
dim·eter verse line
di·methyl·sulph·ox·ide
di·met·ric crystallography term
di·midi·ate halve; divided in halves
di·midi·ation
di·min·ish
di·min·ish·able
di·min·ish·ment
di·minu·en·do (*plural* ·dos)
dimi·nu·tion
di·minu·tive
dim·is·sory permission to depart

dim·ity (*plural* ·ities) fabric
dim·ly
dimmed
dim·mer
dim·mest
dim·ming
dim·ness
di·morph
di·mor·phism
di·mor·phous (*or* ·phic) chemistry term
dim·ple
dim·ply
dim·wit
dim-witted
dim-witted·ness
din (din·ning, dinned)
di·nar currency
dine
din·er
di·ner·ic chemistry term
di·nette
ding
ding·bat *US* unnamed object
ding·bats *Austral* delirium tremens
ding-dong
dinge
din·ghy (*or* ·gy, ·gey; *plural* ·ghies, ·gies, *or* ·geys)
din·gi·ly
din·gi·ness
din·gle dell
din·go (*plural* ·goes)
din·gy (·gi·er, ·gi·est)
di·ni·tro·ben·zene
dink *Scot* neat
Din·ka (*plural* ·kas *or* ·ka) Sudanese people
din·kum
dinky (dinki·er, dinki·est)
dinned
din·ner
din·ning
di·noc·er·as extinct mammal
di·no·flag·el·late unicellular organism
di·no·saur
di·no·saur·ian
di·no·there extinct mammal
dint

di·oc·esan
dio·cese
di·ode
di·oecious (*or esp. US* ·ecious, ·oicious) botany term
di·oestrus (*US* ·estrus) biology term
Diomedes mythological king
Dio·ny·sia ancient Greek festivals
Dio·nysi·ac
Dio·ny·sian
Dionysus Greek god
di·op·side mineral
di·op·tase mineral
di·op·tom·eter
di·op·tom·etry
di·op·tral
di·op·tre (*US* ·ter) unit
di·op·tric (*or* ·tri·cal)
di·op·tri·cal·ly
di·op·trics
dio·ra·ma display
dio·ram·ic
dio·rite rock
dio·rit·ic
di·ox·an (*or* ·ane) chemical compound
di·ox·ide
dip (dip·ping, dipped)
di·pep·tide
di·pet·al·ous having two petals
di·phase (*or* ·phas·ic) physics term
di·phenyl biphenyl
di·phenyl·amine
di·phos·gene
diph·theria
diph·therial (*or* ·therit·ic, ·ther·ic)
diph·theroid
diph·thong
diph·thon·gal
diph·thongi·za·tion (*or* ·sa·tion)
diph·thong·ize (*or* ·ise)
di·phy·cer·cal zoology term
di·phy·let·ic descent from two ancestors
di·phyl·lous having two leaves
diphy·odont dentition

di·plegia paralysis
di·plegic
di·plex electronics term
di·plex·er
dip·lo·blas·tic zoology term
dip·lo·car·di·ac zoology term
dip·lo·coc·cal (*or* ·cic)
dip·lo·coc·cus (*plural* ·coc·ci) bacterium
dip·lo·do·cus (*plural* ·cuses) dinosaur
dip·loë bone
dip·loid biology term
dip·loi·dic
dip·loidy
di·plo·ma
di·plo·ma·cy (*plural* ·cies)
dip·lo·mat
dip·lo·mate
dip·lo·mat·ic (*or* ·mati·cal)
dip·lo·mati·cal·ly
dip·lo·mat·ics study of historical documents
di·plo·ma·tist
dip·lont biology term
di·plo·pia double vision
di·plop·ic
dip·lo·pod invertebrate
di·plo·sis biology term
dip·lo·ste·mo·nous botany term
dip·lo·tene genetics term
dip·noan lungfish
dipo·dy (*plural* ·dies) metrical unit
di·po·lar
di·pole physics term
dipped
dip·per
dip·ping
dip·py *Slang* crazy
di·pro·pel·lant
di·proto·dont marsupial
dip·so·ma·nia
dip·so·ma·ni·ac
dip·so·ma·nia·cal
dip·stick
dip·ter·al architectural term
dip·ter·an (*or* ·on) two-winged insect
dip·tero·car·pa·ceous botany term
dip·ter·ous two-winged

(diptheria) *incorrect spelling of* **diphtheria**

(dipthong) *incorrect spelling of* **diphthong**

dip·tych

dire

di·rect

di·rec·tion

di·rec·tion·al

di·rec·tion·al·ity

di·rec·tion·al·ly

di·rec·tive

di·rect·ly

di·rect·ness

Di·rec·toire French Revolutionary government

di·rec·tor

di·rec·to·rate

di·rec·to·rial

di·rec·tor·ship

di·rec·tory (*plural* ·tories)

di·rec·tress

di·rect·rix (*plural* ·rixes *or* ·rices) geometry term

dire·ful

dirge

dir·ham Moroccan currency

diri·gibil·ity

di·rig·ible steerable

di·ri·ment invalidating

dirk

dirndl dress or skirt

dirt

dirti·ly

dirti·ness

dirty (*adj* dirti·er, dirti·est; *verb* dirties, dirty·ing, dirt·ied)

Dis Roman god

dis·abil·ity (*plural* ·ities)

dis·able

dis·able·ment

dis·abus·al

dis·abuse

di·sac·cha·ride (*or* ·rid)

dis·ac·cord

dis·ac·cred·it

dis·ac·cus·tom

dis·ad·vant·age

dis·ad·van·taged

dis·ad·van·ta·geous

dis·af·fect

dis·af·fect·ed·ly

dis·af·fec·tion

dis·af·fili·ate

dis·af·fili·ation

dis·af·firm

dis·af·fir·mance (*or* ·ma·tion)

dis·af·for·est legal term

dis·af·for·es·ta·tion (*or* dis·af·for·est·ment)

dis·agree (·agree·ing, ·agreed)

dis·agree·able

dis·agree·able·ness (*or* ·abil·ity)

dis·agree·ably

dis·agree·ment

dis·al·low

dis·al·low·able

dis·al·low·ance

dis·am·bigu·ate

dis·an·nul (·nul·ling, ·nulled)

dis·an·nul·ment

dis·ap·pear

dis·ap·pear·ance

dis·ap·point

dis·ap·point·ed

dis·ap·point·er

dis·ap·point·ing

dis·ap·point·ment

dis·ap·pro·ba·tion

dis·ap·prov·al

dis·ap·prove

dis·ap·prov·er

dis·arm

dis·arma·ment

dis·arm·er

dis·arm·ing

dis·ar·range

dis·ar·range·ment

dis·ar·ray

dis·ar·ticu·late

dis·ar·ticu·la·tion

dis·ar·ticu·la·tor

dis·as·sem·ble

dis·as·sem·bly

dis·as·so·ci·ate

dis·as·so·cia·tion

dis·as·ter

dis·as·trous

dis·avow

dis·avow·al

dis·avow·ed·ly

dis·avow·er

dis·band

dis·band·ment

dis·bar (·bar·ring, ·barred)

dis·bar·ment

dis·be·lief

dis·be·lieve

dis·be·liev·er

dis·be·liev·ing·ly

dis·branch

dis·bud (·bud·ding, ·bud·ded)

dis·bur·den

dis·bur·den·ment

dis·burs·able

dis·burse

dis·burse·ment (*or* ·burs·al)

dis·burs·er

disc (*US* disk) circular plate; record; *compare* disk

dis·calced barefooted

dis·card

dis·card·er

dis·cern

dis·cern·er

dis·cern·ible (*or* ·able)

dis·cern·ing

dis·cern·ment

dis·charge

dis·charge·able

dis·charg·er

dis·ci·ple

dis·ci·ple·ship

dis·ci·plin·able

dis·ci·pli·nal

dis·ci·pli·nant member of Catholic sect

dis·ci·pli·nar·ian

dis·ci·pli·nary

dis·ci·pline

dis·ci·plin·er

dis·cipu·lar of disciples

dis·claim

dis·claim·er

dis·cla·ma·tion

dis·cli·max ecology term

dis·close

dis·clos·er

dis·clo·sure

dis·co (*plural* ·cos)

dis·cobo·lus (*or* ·los; *plural* ·li) discus thrower

dis·cog·ra·pher

dis·cog·ra·phy (*plural* ·phies) record catalogue

dis·coid

dis·coi·dal
dis·col·ora·tion
dis·col·our (US ·or)
dis·col·our·ment (US ·or·)
dis·com·bobu·late confuse
dis·com·fit disconcert
dis·com·fit·er
dis·com·fi·ture
dis·com·fort
dis·com·mend
dis·com·mode
dis·com·mo·di·ous
dis·com·mod·ity (plural ·ities) economics term
dis·com·mon legal term
dis·com·pose
dis·com·pos·ed·ly
dis·com·pos·ing·ly
dis·com·po·sure
dis·con·cert
dis·con·cert·ed
dis·con·cert·ing·ly
dis·con·cer·tion (or ·cert·ment)
dis·con·form·ity (plural ·ities)
dis·con·nect
dis·con·nect·ed
dis·con·nect·er
dis·con·nec·tion (or ·nex·ion)
dis·con·nec·tive
dis·con·so·late
dis·con·so·la·tion (or ·late·ness)
dis·con·tent
dis·con·tent·ed
dis·con·tent·ed·ness
dis·con·tent·ment
dis·con·tinu·ance
dis·con·tinua·tion
dis·con·tinue (·tinu·ing, ·tinued)
dis·con·ti·nu·ity (plural ·ities)
dis·con·tinu·ous
dis·co·phile (or ·phil) record collector
dis·cord
dis·cord·ance (or ·an·cy)
dis·cord·ant
dis·co·theque
dis·count
dis·count·able

dis·coun·tenance
dis·count·er
dis·cour·age
dis·cour·age·ment
dis·cour·ag·er
dis·cour·ag·ing·ly
dis·course
dis·cours·er
dis·cour·teous
dis·cour·tesy (plural ·tesies)
dis·cov·er
dis·cov·er·able
dis·cov·er·er
dis·cov·ert legal term
dis·cov·er·ture
dis·cov·ery (plural ·eries)
dis·cred·it
dis·cred·it·able
dis·cred·it·ably
dis·creet tactful; compare discrete
dis·creet·ness
dis·crep·an·cy (plural ·cies)
dis·crep·ant
dis·crete distinct; separate; compare discreet
dis·crete·ness
dis·cre·tion
dis·cre·tion·ari·ly (or ·tion·al·ly)
dis·cre·tion·ary (or ·al)
dis·cri·mi·nant
dis·crimi·nate
dis·crimi·nat·ing
dis·crimi·na·tion
dis·crimi·na·tion·al
dis·crimi·na·tor
dis·crimi·na·to·ri·ly (or dis·crimi·na·tive·ly)
dis·crimi·na·tory (or ·tive)
dis·cur·sive
dis·cus (plural ·cuses or ·ci) disc
dis·cuss debate
dis·cus·sant (or ·cuss·er)
dis·cuss·ible (or ·able)
dis·cus·sion
dis·cus·sion·al
dis·dain
dis·dain·ful
dis·dain·ful·ly
dis·ease
dis·eased

dis·em·bark
dis·em·bar·ka·tion (or ·bark·ment)
dis·em·bar·rass
dis·em·bar·rass·ment
dis·em·bod·ied
dis·em·bodi·ment
dis·em·body (·bodies, ·body·ing, ·bod·ied)
dis·em·bogue (·bogu·ing, ·bogued) discharge
dis·em·bogue·ment
dis·em·bow·el (·el·ling, ·elled; US ·el·ing, ·eled)
dis·em·bow·el·ment
dis·em·broil
dis·en·able
dis·en·able·ment
dis·en·chant
dis·en·chant·er
dis·en·chant·ment
dis·en·cum·ber
dis·en·cum·ber·ment
dis·en·dow
dis·en·dow·er
dis·en·dow·ment
dis·en·fran·chise
dis·en·fran·chise·ment
dis·en·gage
dis·en·gage·ment
dis·en·tail
dis·en·tail·ment
dis·en·tan·gle
dis·en·tan·gle·ment
dis·en·thral (or ·thrall; ·thral·ling, ·thralled)
dis·en·thral·ment (or ·thrall·)
dis·en·ti·tle
dis·en·tomb
dis·en·twine
di·sepa·lous botany term
dis·equi·lib·rium
dis·es·tab·lish
dis·es·tab·lish·ment
dis·es·teem
di·seur (fem ·seuse) French monologue performer
dis·fa·vour (US ·vor)
dis·fea·ture
dis·fea·ture·ment
dis·fig·ure

dis·fig·ure·ment (*or* ·ura·tion)
dis·fig·ur·er
dis·fran·chise
dis·fran·chise·ment
dis·gorge
dis·gorge·ment
dis·gorg·er
dis·grace
dis·grace·ful
dis·grace·ful·ly
dis·grac·er
dis·grun·tle
dis·grun·tled
dis·grun·tle·ment
dis·guis·able
dis·guise
dis·guis·er
dis·gust
dis·gust·ed·ly
dis·gust·ing
dish
dis·ha·bille (*or* des·) half-dressed
dis·har·mo·ni·ous
dis·har·mo·ny (*plural* ·nies)
dish·cloth
dish·heart·en
dish·heart·en·ment
dished
di·shev·el (·el·ling, ·elled; *US* ·el·ing, ·eled)
di·shev·el·ment
dis·hon·est
dis·hon·es·ty (*plural* ·ties)
dis·hon·our (*US* ·or)
dis·hon·our·able (*US* ·or·)
dis·hon·our·ably (*US* ·or·)
dis·hon·our·er (*US* ·or·)
dish·washer
dish·water
dishy (dishi·er, dishi·est)
dis·il·lu·sion
dis·il·lu·sion·ment
dis·il·lu·sive
dis·in·cen·tive
dis·in·cli·na·tion
dis·in·cline
dis·in·fect
dis·in·fect·ant
dis·in·fec·tion
dis·in·fec·tor
dis·in·fest
dis·in·fes·ta·tion

dis·in·fla·tion
dis·in·genu·ous
dis·in·genu·ous·ness
dis·in·her·it
dis·in·heri·tance
dis·in·te·grable
dis·in·te·grate
dis·in·te·gra·tion
dis·in·te·gra·tive
dis·in·te·gra·tor
dis·in·ter (·ter·ring, ·terred)
dis·in·ter·est
dis·in·ter·est·ed impartial; *compare* uninterested
dis·in·ter·ment
dis·ject break apart
dis·join separate
dis·join·able
dis·joint dislocate
dis·joint·ed
dis·junct
dis·junc·tion (*or* ·ture)
dis·junc·tive
disk computer device; *US spelling of* disc
dis·lik·able (*or* ·like·)
dis·like
dis·limn efface
dis·lo·cate
dis·lo·ca·tion
dis·lodge
dis·lodg·ment (*or* ·lodge·)
dis·loy·al
dis·loy·al·ty (*plural* ·ties)
dis·mal
dis·mal·ly
dis·mal·ness
dis·man·tle
dis·man·tle·ment
dis·man·tler
dis·mast
dis·mast·ment
dis·may
dis·mem·ber
dis·mem·ber·er
dis·mem·ber·ment
dis·miss
dis·mis·sal
dis·miss·ible
dis·miss·ive
dis·mount
dis·mount·able
Dis·ney·land
dis·obedi·ence

dis·obedi·ent
dis·obey
dis·obey·er
dis·oblige
dis·oblig·ing
dis·op·era·tion ecology term
dis·or·der
dis·or·der·li·ness
dis·or·der·ly
dis·or·gani·za·tion (*or* ·sa·tion)
dis·or·gan·ize (*or* ·ise)
dis·or·gan·iz·er (*or* ·is·er)
dis·ori·en·tate (*or* dis·ori·ent)
dis·ori·en·ta·tion
dis·own
dis·own·er
dis·own·ment
dis·par·age
dis·par·age·ment
dis·par·ag·er
dis·par·ate
dis·par·ity (*plural* ·ities)
dis·pas·sion detachment
dis·pas·sion·ate
dis·pas·sion·ate·ness
dis·patch (*or* des·)
dis·patcher (*or* des·)
dis·pel (·pel·ling, ·pelled)
dis·pel·ler
dis·pen·sabil·ity (*or* ·sable·ness)
dis·pen·sable
dis·pen·sa·ry (*plural* ·ries)
dis·pen·sa·tion
dis·pen·sa·tion·al
dis·pen·sa·tory (*plural* ·tories) drug catalogue
dis·pense
dis·pens·er
di·sper·mous botany term
dis·per·sal
dis·per·sant
dis·perse
dis·pers·er
dis·per·sion
dis·per·sive
dis·per·soid chemistry term
dis·pir·it
dis·pir·it·ed
dis·pir·it·ing
dis·place
dis·place·able

dis·place·ment
dis·plac·er
dis·play
dis·play·er
dis·please
dis·pleas·ure
dis·port
dis·pos·abil·ity (or
  ·able·ness)
dis·pos·able
dis·pos·al
dis·pose
dis·posed
dis·pos·er
dis·po·si·tion
dis·po·si·tion·al
dis·pos·sess
dis·pos·ses·sion
dis·pos·ses·sor
dis·pos·ses·so·ry
dis·praise
dis·prais·er
dis·proof
dis·pro·por·tion
dis·pro·por·tion·able
dis·pro·por·tion·ate
dis·pro·por·tiona·tion
dis·prov·able
dis·prov·al
dis·prove
dis·put·abil·ity (or
  ·able·ness)
dis·put·able
dis·put·ably
dis·pu·tant
dis·pu·ta·tion
dis·pu·ta·tious (or ·tive)
dis·pute
dis·put·er
dis·quali·fi·able
dis·quali·fi·ca·tion
dis·quali·fi·er
dis·quali·fy (·fies, ·fy·ing,
  ·fied)
dis·qui·et
dis·qui·et·ed·ly (or
  dis·qui·et·ly)
dis·qui·et·ed·ness (or
  dis·qui·et·ness)
dis·qui·et·ing
dis·qui·etude
dis·qui·si·tion formal
  discourse
dis·rate reduce to lower
  rank

dis·re·gard
dis·re·gard·er
dis·re·gard·ful
dis·rel·ish
dis·re·pair
dis·repu·tabil·ity (or
  ·table·ness)
dis·repu·table
dis·repu·tably
dis·re·pute
dis·re·spect
dis·re·spect·abil·ity
dis·re·spect·able
dis·re·spect·ful
dis·re·spect·ful·ly
dis·robe
dis·robe·ment
dis·rob·er
dis·rupt
dis·rupt·er (or ·rup·tor)
dis·rup·tion
dis·rup·tive
dis·sat·is·fac·tion
dis·sat·is·fac·tory
dis·sat·is·fy (·fies, ·fy·ing,
  ·fied)
dis·sect
dis·sec·tible
dis·sec·tion
dis·sec·tor
dis·seise (or ·seize) legal
  term
dis·sei·sin (or ·zin)
dis·sei·sor (or ·zor)
dis·sem·blance
dis·sem·ble
dis·sem·bler
dis·semi·nate
dis·semi·na·tion
dis·semi·na·tive
dis·semi·na·tor
dis·semi·nule botany term
dis·sen·sion
dis·sent
dis·sent·er
dis·sen·tience (or
  ·tien·cy)
dis·sen·tient dissenting
dis·sen·tious argumentative
dis·sepi·ment dividing
  membrane
dis·sepi·men·tal
dis·ser·tate
dis·ser·ta·tion
dis·ser·ta·tion·al

dis·ser·ta·tion·ist
dis·ser·vice
dis·ser·vice·able
dis·sev·er break off
dis·sev·er·ance (or
  ·er·ment, ·era·tion)
dis·si·dence
dis·si·dent
dis·simi·lar
dis·simi·lar·ity (plural
  ·ities)
dis·simi·late phonetics
  term; compare dissimulate
dis·simi·la·tion
dis·simi·la·tive
dis·simi·la·tory
dis·si·mili·tude
dis·simu·late pretend;
  compare dissimilate
dis·simu·la·tion
dis·simu·la·tive
dis·simu·la·tor
dis·si·pate
dis·si·pat·ed
dis·si·pat·er (or ·pa·tor)
dis·si·pa·tion
dis·si·pa·tive
dis·so·ci·abil·ity (or
  ·able·ness)
dis·so·ci·able
dis·so·ci·ate
dis·so·cia·tion
dis·so·cia·tive
dis·sol·ubil·ity (or
  ·uble·ness)
dis·sol·uble
dis·so·lute
dis·so·lute·ness
dis·so·lu·tion
dis·so·lu·tive
dis·solv·abil·ity (or
  ·able·ness)
dis·solv·able
dis·solve
dis·sol·vent
dis·solv·er
dis·so·nance (or ·nan·cy)
dis·so·nant
dis·suad·able
dis·suade
dis·suad·er
dis·sua·sion
dis·sua·sive
dis·sua·sive·ness
dis·syl·lab·ic (or di·syl·)

dis·syl·la·ble (*or* di·syl·)
dis·sym·met·ric (*or* ·ri·cal)
dis·sym·me·try (*plural*
 ·tries)
dis·taff
dis·tal anatomy term
dis·tal·ly
dis·tance
dis·tant
dis·taste
dis·taste·ful
dis·taste·ful·ly
dis·tem·per
dis·tend
dis·tend·er
dis·ten·si·bil·ity
dis·ten·sible
dis·ten·sion (*or* ·tion)
dis·tich poem
dis·ti·chal
dis·ti·chous in two rows
dis·til (*US* dis·till;
 ·til·ling, ·tilled)
dis·till·able
dis·til·late
dis·til·la·tion (*or*
 dis·till·ment)
dis·til·la·tory
dis·till·er
dis·till·ery (*plural* ·eries)
dis·tinct
dis·tinc·tion
dis·tinc·tive
dis·tinc·tive·ness
dis·tinct·ness
dis·tin·gué (*fem* ·guée)
 French distinguished
dis·tin·guish
dis·tin·guish·able
dis·tin·guish·ably
dis·tin·guished
dis·tin·guish·er
dis·tort
dis·tort·ed
dis·tort·er
dis·tor·tion
dis·tor·tion·al
dis·tor·tive
dis·tract
dis·tract·ed
dis·tract·er
dis·tract·ibil·ity
dis·tract·ible
dis·trac·ting
dis·trac·tion

dis·trac·tive
dis·train
dis·train·able
dis·trainee legal term
dis·train·ment
dis·trai·nor (*or* ·train·er)
dis·traint legal term
dis·trait absent-minded
dis·traught
dis·tress
dis·tressed
dis·tress·ful
dis·tress·ful·ly
dis·tress·ing
dis·trib·ut·able
dis·tribu·tary (*plural*
 ·taries) stream
dis·trib·ute
dis·tribu·tee legal term
dis·tri·bu·tion
dis·tri·bu·tion·al
dis·tribu·tive
dis·tribu·tor (*or* ·tribut·er)
dis·trict
dis·trin·gas legal term
dis·trust
dis·trust·er
dis·trust·ful
dis·trust·ful·ly
dis·turb
dis·turb·ance
dis·turbed
dis·turb·er
di·sul·fi·ram drug
di·sul·phate (*US* ·fate)
di·sul·phide (*US* ·fide)
di·sul·phu·ric (*US* ·fu·)
dis·un·ion
dis·unite
dis·unity (*plural* ·unities)
dis·use
dis·used
dis·util·ity
dit Morse code sound
dita shrub
ditch
ditch·er
di·theism
di·theist
di·theis·tic
dith·er
dith·er·er
di·thio·nite chemical
 compound

dithy·ramb ancient Greek
 hymn
dithy·ram·bic
dithy·ram·bi·cal·ly
dit·tan·der plant
dit·ta·ny (*plural* ·nies)
 plant
dit·to (*noun, plural* ·tos;
 verb ·tos, ·to·ing, ·toed)
dit·to·graph·ic
dit·tog·ra·phy (*plural*
 ·phies) repetition
dit·ty (*plural* ·ties)
di·uresis increased
 urination; *compare* dieresis
di·uret·ic increasing
 urination; *compare* dieretic
di·ureti·cal·ly
di·ur·nal of the day
di·ur·nal·ly
div *Slang* stupid person
diva (*plural* divas *or* dive)
 prima donna; *compare*
 deva
di·va·lency
di·va·lent
di·van
di·vari·cate branching
di·vari·ca·tion
di·vari·ca·tor zoology term
dive (div·ing, dived (*US*
 dove))
dive-bomb
div·er
di·verge
di·ver·gence (*or* ·gen·cy;
 plural ·gences *or* ·cies)
di·ver·gent
di·vers *Archaic* several
di·verse varied
di·ver·si·fi·abil·ity
di·ver·si·fi·able
di·ver·si·fi·ca·tion
di·ver·si·fi·er
di·ver·si·form
di·ver·si·fy (·fies, ·fy·ing,
 ·fied)
di·ver·sion
di·ver·sion·al (*or* ·ary)
di·ver·sity
di·vert
di·vert·ed·ly
di·vert·er
di·vert·ible
di·ver·ticu·lar

di·ver·ticu·li·tis
di·ver·ticu·lo·sis
di·ver·ticu·lum (*plural* ·la) anatomical pouch
di·ver·ti·men·to (*plural* ·ti) musical work
di·vert·ing·ly
di·ver·tisse·ment brief entertainment
di·ver·tive
Dives biblical character
di·vest
di·vest·ible
di·vesti·ture (*or* ·ves·ture, ·vest·ment)
di·vid·able
di·vide
divi·dend
di·vid·er
di·vid·ers measuring compass
divi-divi (*plural* -divis *or* -divi) tree
di·vin·able
divi·na·tion
di·vina·tory
di·vine
di·vin·er
div·ing
di·vin·ing
di·vin·ity (*plural* ·ities)
divi·ni·za·tion (*or* ·sa·tion)
divi·nize (*or* ·nise) deify
di·vis·ibil·ity
di·vis·ible
di·vi·sion
di·vi·sion·al (*or* ·ary)
di·vi·sion·ism
di·vi·sion·ist
di·vi·sive
di·vi·sor maths term; *compare* deviser
di·vorce
di·vor·cé (*fem* ·cée) divorced person
di·vorce·able
di·vorce·ment
di·vorc·er
di·vor·cive
div·ot turf
di·vulge
di·vul·gence (*or* ·vulge·ment)
di·vulg·er
di·vul·sion tearing apart

di·vul·sive
div·vy (*plural* ·vies) *Slang* dividend
Dixie southern states of USA
dixie metal pot
Dixie·land jazz
Di·yar·ba·kir (*or* ·bekir) Turkish city
diz·zi·ly
diz·zi·ness
diz·zy (*adj* ·zi·er, ·zi·est; *verb* ·zies, ·zy·ing, ·zied)
Dja·ja *variant spelling of* Jaya
Dja·ja·pu·ra *variant spelling of* Jajapura
Dja·kar·ta (*or* Ja·) *variant spelling of* Jakarta
Djam·bi (*or* Jam·) *variant spelling of* Jambi
Djer·ba Tunisian island
Dji·bou·ti (*or* Ji·) African republic
djin·ni (*or* ·ny) *variant spellings of* jinni
Djok·ja·kar·ta *variant spelling of* Jogjakarta
Dne·pro·dzer·zhinsk Soviet city
Dne·pro·petrovsk Soviet city
Dnie·per (*or* Dnepr) Soviet river
Dnie·ster (*or* Dnestr) Soviet river
do (*verb* does, do·ing, did, done; *noun, plural* dos *or* do's)
doab land between rivers
do·able
dob·bin
dob·by (*plural* ·bies) loom attachment
Do·ber·man pin·scher dog
do·bla coin
Do·bro (*Trademark*; *plural* ·bros) guitar
Do·bru·ja E European region
dobson·fly (*plural* ·flies)
doc *Slang* doctor
do·cent US lecturer
do·cent·ship
Do·cetism heresy

doc·ile
do·cil·ity
dock
dock·age dock charge
dock·er
dock·et
dock·land
dock·yard
doc·tor
doc·tor·al (*or* ·to·rial)
doc·tor·ate
doc·tri·naire
doc·tri·nair·ism (*or* ·nar·ism)
doc·tri·nal
doc·tri·nal·ity
doc·tri·nar·ian
doc·trine
doc·trin·ism
docu·ment
docu·men·ta·ri·ly
docu·men·tary (*plural* ·taries)
docu·men·ta·tion
dod·der totter, tremble (*verb*); plant (*noun*)
dod·der·er
dod·der·ing
dod·dery
dod·dle
do·deca·gon 12-sided figure
do·de·cago·nal
do·deca·he·dral
do·deca·he·dron 12-faced solid
Do·deca·nese Aegean islands
do·deca·phon·ic musical term
do·deca·phon·ism
do·deca·phon·ist
do·deca·phony
dodge
Dodg·em (*Trademark*)
dodg·er
dodgy (dodgi·er, dodgi·est)
dodo (*plural* dodos *or* dodoes)
dodo·ism
Do·do·ma Tanzanian town
Do·do·na Greek town
doe (*plural* does *or* doe)
doek African headscarf
doer

does (*present tense of* **do**; *plural of* **doe**)

doe·skin

doff

doff·er

dog (**dog·ging, dogged**)

dog·bane plant

dog·berry (*plural* ·**berries**) shrub

dog·berry·ism officialdom

dog·cart

doge Venetian magistrate

dog-ear

dog-eared

dog·fight

dog·fish (*plural* ·**fish** *or* ·**fishes**)

dog·ged (*adj*)

dog·ged·ness

Dog·ger North Sea sandbank

dog·ger fishing vessel

dog·ger·el (*or* **dog·rel**)

dog·gery (*plural* ·**geries**) surly behaviour

dog·gish

dog·go *Slang* in hiding

dog·gone US slang term

dog·gy (*adj*; ·**gi·er,** ·**gi·est**)

dog·gy (*or* ·**gie**; *noun*; *plural* ·**gies**)

dog·house

do·gie *US* motherless calf

dog·leg (·**leg·ging,** ·**legged**) bend sharply

dog·leg·ged (*adj*)

dog·ma (*plural* ·**mas** *or* ·**ma·ta**)

dog·man (*plural* ·**men**) *Austral* crane-driver's assistant

dog·mat·ic (*or* ·**mati·cal**)

dog·mati·cal·ly

dog·mat·ics

dog·ma·tism

dog·ma·tist

dog·ma·ti·za·tion (*or* ·**sa·tion**)

dog·ma·tize (*or* ·**tise**)

dog·ma·tiz·er (*or* ·**tis·er**)

do-gooder

dogs·body (*plural* ·**bodies**)

dog's-tail grass

dog-tired

dog·tooth (*plural* ·**teeth**)

dog·trot

dog·vane wind vane

dog·watch nautical term

dog·wood

doh musical note

Doha capital of Qatar

doi·ly (*or* **doy·ley, doy·ly**; *plural* ·**lies** *or* ·**leys**)

do·ing

doit coin

do-it-yourself

dol unit of pain

do·lab·ri·form (*or* ·**rate**) hatchet-shaped

Dol·by (*Trademark*) recording system

dol·ce musical term

dol·ce vita *Italian* luxurious life

dol·drums

dole

dole·ful

dole·ful·ly

dole·ful·ness

dol·er·ite rock

dol·er·it·ic

doli·cho·cephal·ic (*or* **cepha·lous**) long-headed

doli·cho·cepha·lism (*or* ·**ly**)

do·li·na (*or* ·**ne**) ground depression

doll

dol·lar

dollar·bird

dollar·fish (*plural* ·**fish** *or* ·**fishes**)

doll·ish

dol·lop

dol·ly (*noun, plural* ·**lies**; *verb* ·**ly·ing,** ·**lied**)

dol·man (*plural* ·**mans**) robe

dol·mas (*or* ·**ma**) stuffed vine leaves

dol·men tomb

do·lo·mite mineral

Do·lo·mites mountain range

dolo·mit·ic

dol·or·im·etry pain measurement

do·lo·ro·so musical term

dol·or·ous

dol·our (*US* ·**or**) grief

dol·phin

dol·phin·ar·ium

dolt

dolt·ish

dom monk's title

do·main

dome

dome-like

domes·day *variant spelling of* **doomsday**

Domes·day Book (*or* **Dooms·**)

do·mes·tic

do·mes·ti·cable

do·mes·ti·cal·ly

do·mes·ti·cate

do·mes·ti·ca·tion

do·mes·ti·ca·tive

do·mes·ti·ca·tor

do·mes·ti·city (*plural* ·**cities**)

domi·cal (*or* **do·mic**) of a dome

domi·cile

domi·cili·ary

domi·cili·ate

domi·nance

domi·nant

domi·nate

domi·na·tion

domi·na·tive

domi·na·tor

do·mi·nee Afrikaner clergyman

domi·neer

Domi·ni·ca West Indian country

do·mini·cal relating to the Lord

Do·mini·can Republic; friar

domi·nie *Scot* schoolmaster

do·min·ion

do·min·ium (*or* ·**ion**) legal term

domi·no (*plural* ·**noes**)

Don Spanish title; Soviet river

don (**don·ning, donned**)

Doña Spanish woman's title

Donar Germanic god

do·nate

do·na·tion

dona·tive gift

do·na·tor

Don·bass (*or* ·**bas**) Soviet industrial region
Don·cas·ter
done
do·nee receiver of gift
Don·egal Irish county
Do·nets Soviet river
Do·netsk Soviet city
dong
don·jon castle keep
Don Juan legendary seducer
don·key
Don·na Italian woman's title
donned
don·nert *Scot* stunned
don·ning
don·nish
donny·brook rowdy brawl
do·nor
do·nor·ship
don't do not
do·nut *variant spelling (esp. US) of* **doughnut**
doo·dah
doo·dle
doodle·bug
doo·dler
doom
dooms·day (*or* **domes·**)
door
door·bell
do-or-die
door·frame
door·jamb
door·keeper
door·man (*plural* ·**men**)
door·mat
door·nail
door·post
door·sill
door·step
door·stop
door·way
door·yard *US* outside yard
do·pant chemistry term
dope
dopey (*or* **dopy**; **dopi·er**, **dopi·est**)
dopi·ness
Dop·pel·gäng·er ghost
Dop·per Afrikaner churchgoer
dor beetle

Do·ra·do constellation
Dor·ches·ter
Dor·dogne French region and river
Dor·drecht Dutch port
Do·rian ancient Greek
Dor·ic architectural term
Do·ris region of ancient Greece
Dor·king
dorm *Slang* dormitory
dor·man·cy
dor·mant
dor·mer
dor·mie (*or* ·**my**) golf term
dor·mi·tory (*plural* ·**tories**)
Dor·mo·bile (*Trademark*)
dor·mouse (*plural* ·**mice**)
dor·nick (*or* ·**neck**) cloth
do·roni·cum plant
dorp South African village
dor·sad towards the back
dor·sal of the back
dor·sal·ly
Dor·set
dor·si·grade walking on backs of toes
dor·si·ven·tral having upper and lower surfaces
dor·si·ven·tral·ity
dor·so·ven·tral from back to belly
dor·so·ven·tral·ly
dor·sum (*plural* ·**sa**) the back
Dort·mund West German city
dorty *Scot* sullen
dory (*plural* **dories**) fish; boat
dos·age
dose
dos·er
do-si-do dance figure
do·sim·eter (*or* **dose·meter**)
do·si·met·ric
do·si·metri·cian (*or* **do·sim·etrist**)
do·sim·etry
doss
dos·sal (*or* ·**sel**) church hanging
dos·ser *Slang* tramp; dosshouse

doss·house
dos·si·er
dot (**dot·ting**, **dot·ted**)
dot·age
do·tard
do·ta·tion endowment
dote
dot·er
dotted
dot·ted
dot·ter
dot·ter·el (*or* ·**trel**)
dot·ti·ly
dot·ti·ness
dot·ting
dot·tle (*or* ·**tel**) tobacco in pipe
dot·ty (·**ti·er**, ·**ti·est**)
Douai French city
Doua·la (*or* **Dua·la**) Cameroon port
Dou·ay bible
dou·ble
double-acting
double-barrelled (*US* -**barreled**)
double-bass (*adj*)
double-blind
double-breasted
double-check
double-cross
double-dealing
double-decker
double-dotted musical term
double-edged
dou·ble en·ten·dre
double-faced
double-glazing
double-header
double-hung
double-jointed
double-park
double-quick
dou·bler
double-reed
dou·bles tennis
double-space
double-stop (-**stopping**, -**stopped**)
dou·blet
double·think
dou·ble-ton bridge term
double-tongue (-**tonguing**, ·**tongued**) musical term

double·tree horizontal bar on vehicle
dou·bloon (*or* **do·blon**) coin
dou·blure lining inside book
dou·bly
Doubs French river
doubt
doubt·able
doubt·er
doubt·ful
doubt·ful·ly
doubt·ful·ness
doubt·less
douc monkey
douce *Scot* sedate
dou·ceur bribe
douche
dough
dough·boy *Slang* dumpling
dough·nut (*or esp. US* **do·nut**)
doughti·ly
dough·ty (**·ti·er**, **·ti·est**) hardy
doughy (**doughi·er**, **doughi·est**)
Doug·las Manx town
Dou·kho·bors Russian sect
doum (*or* **doom**) palm tree
dour sullen; *compare* **dower**
dou·rine horse disease
dour·ness
Dou·ro Spanish–Portuguese river
dou·rou·cou·li monkey
douse (*or* **dowse**) drench; *compare* **dowse**
dous·er (*or* **dows·**)
dove bird; *US past tense of* **dive**
dove·cote (*or* **·cot**)
dove·kie (*or* **·key**) bird
Do·ver
dove·tail
dov·ish
dow·able legal term
dowa·ger
dow·di·ly
dow·di·ness
dow·dy (*noun, plural* **·dies**; *adj* **·di·er**, **·di·est**)
dow·el
dow·er widow's inheritance; *compare* **dour**

(**dowery**) *incorrect spelling of* **dowry**
dow·itch·er bird
Dow-Jones av·er·age US stock exchange index
down
down·beat
down·bow
down·cast
down·com·er (*or* **·come**) plumbing term
down·fall
down·fallen
down·grade
down·haul nautical term
down·hearted
down·hearted·ness
down·hill
downi·ness
Down·ing Street
down·market
Down·pat·rick Irish town
down·pipe
down·pour
down·range
down·right
Downs Sussex hills
downs chalk uplands
down·side
down·spout *US* drainpipe
Down's syn·drome
down·stage
down·stairs
down·state *US* S part of state
down·stream
down·swing
down·throw
down-to-earth
down·town
down·trod·den (*or* **·trod**)
down·turn
down·ward (*adj*)
down·wards (*adv*)
down·wash
down·wind
downy (**downi·er**, **downi·est**)
dow·ry (*plural* **·ries**)
dowse to divine water; *variant spelling of* **douse**
dows·er
dows·ing
dox·as·tic logic term
doxo·logi·cal

dox·ol·ogy (*plural* **·ogies**)
doxy (*plural* **doxies**)
doy·en (*fem* **·enne**)
doze
doz·en
doz·enth
doz·er
dozy (**dozi·er**, **dozi·est**)
drab (**drab·ber**, **drab·best**)
drab·bet fabric
drab·ble make wet
drab·ly
drab·ness
dra·cae·na plant
drachm fluid dram
drach·ma (*plural* **·mas** *or* **·mae**) Greek currency
Dra·co constellation
dra·cone container towed by ship
Dra·co·nian (*or* **·con·ic**) harsh
Dra·co·ni·an·ism
dra·con·ic dragon-like
dra·coni·cal·ly
draff husks
draffy
draft sketch; military selection; money order; *US spelling of* **draught**
draftee
draft·er
drafts·man (*plural* **·men**) document drafter; *compare* **draughtsman**
drag (**drag·ging**, **dragged**)
dra·gée sweet
drag·gle trail
drag·hound
drag·line
drag·net
dra·go·man (*plural* **·mans** *or* **·men**) interpreter
drag·on
drag·on·ess
drag·on·et fish
dragon·fly (*plural* **·flies**)
dragon·head (*or* **dragon's-head**) plant
drag·on·ish
drag·on·nade persecution by dragoons
dragon·root
dra·goon
dra·goon·age

drag·rope
drail weighted hook
drain
drain·able
drain·age
drain·er
drain·pipe
drake
Dra·kens·berg African
  mountain
dram 1/16 ounce; tot;
  compare drachm
dra·ma
Dra·ma·mine
  (Trademark)
dra·mat·ic
dra·mati·cal·ly
dra·mat·ics
dra·ma·tis per·so·nae
  characters in a play
drama·tist
drama·tiz·able (or
  ·tis·able)
drama·ti·za·tion (or
  ·sa·tion)
drama·tize (or ·tise)
drama·tiz·er (or ·tis·er)
drama·turge (or ·tur·gist)
  dramatist
drama·tur·gic (or ·gi·cal)
drama·tur·gy
Drambuie (Trademark)
drank
drap·able (or drape·able)
drape
drap·er
dra·per·ied
dra·pery (plural ·peries)
drapes US curtains
dras·tic
dras·ti·cal·ly
drat
drat·ted
draught (US draft) air
  current; drink; load
  pulling; compare draft
draught·board (or
  draughts·)
draught·er (US draft·)
draughti·ness (US drafti·)
draughts game
draughts·man (US
  drafts·; plural ·men)
  plan drafter; compare
  draftsman

draughts·man·ship (US
  drafts·)
draughty (US drafty;
  draughti·er,
  draughti·est; US
  drafti·er, drafti·est)
Dra·va European river
Dra·vid·ian language group
draw (draw·ing, drew,
  drawn)
draw·able
draw·back
draw·bar
draw·bridge
drawee
draw·er
drawer·ful
drawers undergarment
draw·ing
draw·knife (or ·shave;
  plural ·knives or
  ·shaves) woodcutting tool
drawl
drawl·er
drawly
drawn
draw·plate extrusion plate
draw·string
draw·tube
dray cart; compare drey
dray·horse
dread
dread·ful
dread·fully
dread·ful·ness
dread·nought (or ·naught)
  battleship
dream (dream·ing,
  dreamt or dreamed)
dream·er
dreami·ly
dreami·ness
dream·ing·ly
dream·less
dream·like
dreamy (dreami·er,
  dreami·est)
dreari·ly
dreari·ness
dreary (dreari·er,
  dreari·est)
dredge
dredg·er
dree Scot endure
dreg

dreg·gy (·gi·er, ·gi·est)
drench
drench·er
Dren·the Dutch region
Dres·den East German city
dress
dres·sage
dressed
dress·er
dressi·ly
dressi·ness
dress·ing
dress·maker
dress·making
dressy (dressi·er,
  dressi·est)
drew
drey squirrel's nest; compare
  dray
drib·ble
drib·bler
drib·let (or ·blet) small
  amount
dried
dri·er (adj)
dri·est
drift
drift·age
drift·er
drift·wood
drifty
drill
drill·able
drill·er
drill·ing
drill·master
drill·stock tool part
dri·ly
drink (drink·ing, drank,
  drunk)
drink·able
drink·er
drip (drip·ping, dripped)
drip-dry (-dries, -dry·ing,
  -dried)
drip·ping
drip·py (·pi·er, ·pi·est)
drip·stone
driv·able (or drive·)
drive (driv·ing, drove,
  driv·en)
drive-in
driv·el (·el·ling, ·elled;
  US ·el·ing, ·eled)
driv·el·ler (US ·el·er)

driv·en

driv·er

driv·er·less

drive·way

driv·ing

driz·zle

driz·zly

drogue

droit right

droll

droll·ery (*plural* ·eries)

droll·ness

Drôme French department

drom·edary (*plural* ·edaries) camel

drom·ond sailing vessel

drone

dron·go (*plural* ·gos) bird

dron·ish

drool

droop sag; *compare* drupe

droopi·ly

droopi·ness

droopy (droopi·er, droopi·est)

drop (drop·ping, dropped)

drop·let

drop·light

drop·out

drop·per

drop·pings

drop·si·cal

drop·sied

drop·sonde meteorological device

drop·sy fluid in body

drop·wort plant

drosh·ky (*or* dros·ky; *plural* ·kies) carriage

dro·sophi·la (*plural* ·las *or* ·lae) fruit fly

dross

drossi·ness

drossy (drossi·er, drossi·est)

drought (*or* drouth)

droughty

drove

drov·er

drown

drown·er

drowse

drowsi·ly

drowsi·ness

drowsy (drowsi·er, drowsi·est)

drub (drub·bing, drubbed) beat

drub·ber

drudge

drudg·er

drudg·ery (*plural* ·eries)

druf·fen *Dialect* drunk

drug (drug·ging, drugged)

drug·get fabric

drug·gist

drug·store

dru·id (*fem* ·id·ess)

dru·id·ic (*or* ·idi·cal)

dru·id·ism

drum (drum·ming, drummed)

drum·beat

drum·fire

drum·fish (*plural* ·fish *or* ·fishes)

drum·head

drum·lin landform

drum·mer

drum·stick

drunk

drunk·ard

drunk·en

drunk·en·ness

dru·pa·ceous

drupe fruit; *compare* droop

drupe·let (*or* dru·pel) small fruit

Dru·ry Lane

Druse (*or* Druze) religious sect

druse crystals lining cavity

dry (*adj* dri·er, dri·est; *verb* dries, dry·ing, dried)

dry·able

dry·ad (*plural* ·ads *or* ·ades) wood nymph

dry·ad·ic

dry-clean

dry-cleaner

dry-cleaning

dry·er (*noun*)

dry·ness

dryo·pith·ecine extinct ape

dry-salt preserve by salting

dry-stone wall

dual two; *compare* duel

Du·ala (*plural* ·ala *or* ·alas) African people

dual·ism

dual·ist

dual·is·tic

dual·is·ti·cal·ly

dual·ity (*plural* ·ities)

dual-purpose

dub (dub·bing, dubbed)

Du·bai sheikdom

dub·bin (*or* dub·bing) leather grease

du·bi·ety (*or* du·bi·os·ity; *plural* ·ties)

du·bi·ous

du·bi·ous·ness

du·bi·table

du·bi·ta·tion doubt

Dub·lin

Du·bon·net (*Trademark*)

Du·brov·nik Yugoslav port

du·cal

duc·at coin

duce *Italian* leader

duch·ess

duchy (*plural* duchies)

duck

duck·board

duck·er

duck·ling

ducks trousers

duck·weed

ducky (*or* duckie; *plural* duckies)

duct

duc·tile

duc·til·ity (*or* ·tile·ness)

dud

dude

du·deen clay pipe

dudg·eon anger

Dud·ley English town

due

duel (duel·ling, duelled; *US* duel·ing, dueled) fight; *compare* dual

duel·ler (*or* ·list; *US* ·er *or* ·ist)

du·el·lo (*plural* ·los) duelling

du·en·na chaperon

duet (*or* du·ette)

duet·tist

duff

duf·fel (*or* ·fle)

duf·fer
dug
du·gong animal
dug·out
dui·ker (*plural* ·kers *or*
·ker) antelope
Duis·burg West German
city
duke
duke·dom
dul·cet
dul·ci·ana organ stop
dul·ci·fy (·fies, ·fying,
·fied) sweeten
dul·ci·mer musical
instrument
du·lia veneration for saints
dull
dull·ard
dull·ness (*or* dul·ness)
dulls·ville boredom
dul·ly in a dull way
du·lo·sis zoology term
dulse seaweed
Du·luth US port
duly appropriately
dumb
Dum·bar·ton Scottish town
dumb·bell
dumb·cane plant
dumb·found (*or* dum·)
dumb·found·er (*or* dum·)
dumb·ness
dumb·struck (*or*
·stricken)
dumb·waiter stand for
dishes
dum·dum bullet
Dum·fries
dum·my (*noun, plural*
·mies; *verb* ·mies,
·my·ing, ·mied)
du·mor·ti·erite mineral
dump
dump·er
dumpi·ness
dump·ling
dumpy (dumpi·er,
dumpi·est)
Dum·yat Egyptian town
dun (*verb* dun·ning,
dunned; *adj* dun·ner,
dun·nest)
Dun·bar Scottish port
dunce

Dun·dalk Irish town
Dun·dee
dunder·head
dune
Dun·edin New Zealand port
Dun·ferm·line
dung
dun·ga·ree fabric
dun·ga·rees overalls
Dun·ge·ness Kent headland
dun·geon
dung·hill
dungy
dun·ite rock
dunk
dunk·er
Dun·kirk French port
Dun Laoghaire Irish port
dun·lin bird
dun·nage cargo-packing
material
dun·na·kin *Dialect* lavatory
dunned
dun·ner
dun·nest
dun·ning
dun·nite explosive
dun·nock bird
dun·ny *Scot* cellar
Du·noon Scottish town
Dun·si·nane Scottish hill
Dun·sta·ble
dunt *Dialect* a blow
duo (*plural* duos *or* dui)
duo·deci·mal of 12
duo·deci·mo (*plural* ·mos)
book size
duo·denal
duo·dena·ry
duo·deni·tis
duo·denum (*plural* ·dena
or ·denums)
duo·logue
duo·mo (*plural* ·mos)
cathedral
duo·tone printing process
dup *Dialect* open
dup·abil·ity
dup·able
dupe
dup·er
dup·ery
du·ple musical term
du·plet chemistry term
du·plex

du·plex·ity
du·pli·cabil·ity
du·pli·cable
du·pli·cate
du·pli·ca·tion
du·pli·ca·tive
du·pli·ca·tor
du·plic·ity (*plural* ·ities)
du·pon·dius coin
du·rabil·ity (*or*
·rable·ness)
du·rable
Du·ralu·min (*Trademark*)
aluminium alloy
dura ma·ter membrane
round brain
du·ra·men wood
du·rance imprisonment
Du·ran·go Mexican state
du·ra·tion
du·ra·tion·al
du·ra·tive linguistics term
Dur·ban South African port
dur·bar African court
du·ress
Du·rex (*Trademark*)
condom
Dur·ham
du·rian (*or* ·ri·on) fruit
dur·ing
dur·mast tree
duro (*plural* duros) coin
Du·roc US pig
dur·ra (*or* dou·ra,
dou·rah) grass
durst *past tense of* dare
du·rum wheat
Du·shan·be Soviet city
dusk
duski·ness
dusky (duski·er,
duski·est)
Düs·sel·dorf West German
city
dust
dust·bin
dust·cart
dust·er
dusti·ly
dusti·ness
dust·man (*plural* ·men)
dust·pan
dust·sheet
dust-up *Slang* fight
dusty (dusti·er, dusti·est)

Dutch
Dutch·man (*plural* ·**men**)
du·teous *Archaic* dutiful
du·ti·abil·ity
du·ti·able
du·ti·ful
du·ti·ful·ly
du·ti·ful·ness
duty (*plural* **duties**)
duty-free
du·vet
du·vetyn (*or* ·**vetine**, ·**vetyne**) fabric
dux *Scot* best pupil
dvan·dva compound word
dwale deadly nightshade
dwarf (*plural* **dwarfs** *or* **dwarves**)
dwarf·ish
dwarf·ish·ness
dwarf·ism
dwell (**dwell·ing, dwelt** *or* **dwelled**)
dwell·er
dwell·ing
dwin·dle
dy·able (*or* **dye·able**)
dyad maths term
dy·ad·ic twofold
Dyak (*plural* **Dyaks** *or* **Dyak**) Malaysian people
dy·ar·chic (*or* ·**chi·cal**, ·**chal**) *variant spelling of* diarchic
dy·ar·chy (*plural* ·**chies**) *variant spelling of* **diarchy**
dyb·buk (*plural* ·**buks** *or* ·**buk·kim**) Hebrew spirit
dye (**dye·ing, dyed**) colour; *compare* **die**
dye·ing colouring; *compare* **dying**
dye·line blueprint
dy·er
dyer's-greenweed
dyer's-weed
dye·stuff

dye·wood
Dyf·ed Welsh county
dy·ing expiring; *compare* **dyeing**
dyke (*or* **dike**)
dy·nam·eter
dy·nam·ic
dy·nami·cal·ly
dy·nam·ics
dy·na·mism philosophical theory
dy·na·mist
dy·na·mis·tic
dy·na·mite
dy·na·mit·er (*or* ·**mit·ist**)
dy·na·mit·ic
dy·na·mo (*plural* ·**mos**)
dy·na·mo·elec·tric (*or* ·**tri·cal**)
dy·na·mom·eter
dy·na·mo·met·ric (*or* ·**ri·cal**)
dy·na·mom·etry
dy·na·mo·tor
dyn·ast ruler
dy·nas·tic (*or* ·**ti·cal**)
dyn·as·ty (*plural* ·**ties**)
dy·na·tron type of oscillator
dyne unit
dy·node electrode
dys·en·ter·ic
dys·en·tery
dys·func·tion
dys·gen·ic
dys·gen·ics reducing quality of race
dys·graphia impaired writing ability
dys·lexia impaired reading ability
dys·lex·ic (*or* ·**lec·tic**)
dys·men·or·rhoea (*US* ·**rhea**)
dys·men·or·rhoeal (*US* ·**rheal**)

dys·pep·sia (*or* ·**sy**) indigestion
dys·pep·tic (*or* ·**ti·cal**)
dys·pha·gia difficulty in swallowing
dys·phag·ic
dys·pha·sia impaired speech
dys·pha·sic
dys·phe·mism substitution of offensive word
dys·pho·nia impaired speech
dys·phon·ic
dys·pho·ria uneasy feeling
dys·phor·ic
dys·pla·sia abnormal organ development
dys·plas·tic
dysp·noea (*US* ·**nea**) difficulty in breathing
dysp·noeal (*or* ·**noe·ic**; *US* ·**neal** *or* ·**ne·ic**)
dys·pro·sium chemical element
dys·tel·eol·ogy philosophy term
dys·thy·mia neurotic condition
dys·thy·mic
dys·to·pia worst possible place
dys·troph·ic
dys·tro·phy (*or* ·**phia**) wasting of tissues
dys·uria painful urination
dys·uric
dy·tis·cid beetle
Dyu·la (*plural* ·**la** *or* ·**las**) African people
Dzer·zhinsk Soviet city
Dzong·ka Asian language
Dzun·ga·ria (*or* **Zun·**) Chinese region

E

each
eager keen; *compare* **eagre**
eager·ly

eager·ness
eagle
eagle-eyed

eagle·stone
eaglet
eagle·wood

eagre (*or* **eager**) tidal
bore; *compare* **eager**
eal·dor·man Anglo-Saxon
official
Ealing
ear
ear·ache
ear·bash *Austral* talk
ear·drop
ear·drum
eared
ear·flap
ear·ful
ear·ing nautical term
earl
ear·lap
earl·dom
ear·li·ness
ear·ly (**·li·er**, **·li·est**)
Ear·ly Bird satellite
ear·mark
ear·muff
earn
earn·er
ear·nest
ear·nest·ness
earn·ings
ear·phone
ear·piece
ear·plug
ear·ring
ear·shot
ear·splitting
earth
earth·born
earth·bound
earth·en
earthen·ware
earthi·ly
earthi·ness
earth·light *variant of*
earthshine
earth·li·ness
earth·ling
earth·ly (**·li·er**, **·li·est**)
earth·nut
earth·quake
earth·rise
earth·shaking
earth·shine (*or* **·light**)
earth's reflected light
earth·star fungus
earth·wards (*or esp. US*
·ward)
earth·work

earth·worm
earthy (**earthi·er**,
earthi·est)
ear·wax
ear·wig
ease
ease·ful
ease·ful·ness
easel
ease·ment
eas·er
easi·ly
easi·ness
east
East An·glia
East An·glian
East Ber·lin
East Ber·lin·er
east·bound
East·bourne
East·er
Easter-ledges plant
east·er·ly (*plural* **·lies**)
east·ern
east·ern·er
east·ern·most
East·er·tide
East Ger·man
East Ger·ma·ny
East In·dian
East In·dies
east·ing nautical term
East Kil·bride Scottish
town
East·leigh Hampshire town
east-northeast
east-southeast
east·ward (*adj*)
east·ward·ly
east·wards (*adv*)
easy (**easi·er**, **easi·est**)
easy-going
eat (**eat·ing**, **ate**, **eat·en**)
eat·able
eat·age *Dialect* grazing
rights
eat·en
eat·er
eau de Co·logne
eau de Ja·velle bleaching
solution
eau de nil greenish colour
eau de vie brandy
eaves

eaves·drop (**·drop·ping**,
·dropped)
eaves·drop·per
ebb
Ebbw Vale
ebon ebony
eb·on·ite rubber
eb·on·ize (*or* **·ise**)
eb·ony (*plural* **·onies**)
Ebora·cum *Latin* York
ebrac·te·ate
ebul·lience (*or* **·lien·cy**)
ebul·lient
ebul·li·os·co·py chemistry
term
ebul·li·tion boiling
ebur·na·tion bone condition
ecad ecology term
écar·té card game
Ec·bata·na Iranian city
ec·bol·ic medi term
ec·cen·tric
ec·cen·tri·cal·ly
ec·cen·tri·city (*plural*
·cities)
ec·chy·mo·sis (*plural* **·ses**)
skin condition
Ec·cles English town; cake
ec·cle·sia (*plural* **·siae**)
church congregation
ec·cle·si·arch sacristan
Ec·cle·si·as·tes Old
Testament book
ec·cle·si·as·tic
ec·cle·si·as·ti·cal
ec·cle·si·as·ti·cal·ly
ec·cle·si·as·ti·cism
Ec·cle·si·as·ti·cus book of
Apocrypha
ec·cle·si·ola·ter
ec·cle·si·ola·try
ecclesiastical obsession
ec·cle·sio·logi·cal (*or*
·log·ic)
ec·cle·si·olo·gist
ec·cle·si·ol·ogy study of
Church
ec·crine
ec·crin·ol·ogy study of
glands
ec·dys·ial
ec·dysi·ast striptease artist
ec·dy·sis (*plural* **·ses**)
moulting
ec·dy·sone hormone

ecesis ecology term
ec·hard biology term
eche·lon
ech·eve·ria plant
echid·na (*plural* ·nas *or* ·nae) spiny anteater
echi·nate (*or* ·nat·ed) having bristles
echi·no·coc·cus tapeworm
echi·no·derm marine animal
echi·no·der·mal (*or* ·ma·tous)
echi·noid marine animal
echi·nus (*plural* ·ni) sea urchin
echo (*noun, plural* echoes; *verb* echoes, echo·ing, ech·oed)
echo·ic
echo·ism linguistics term
echo·la·lia psychiatric term
echo·la·lic
echo·location
echo·prac·tic
echo·praxia (*or* ·prax·is) psychiatric term
echo·virus
éclair
ec·lamp·sia pregnancy condition
ec·lamp·tic
éclat acclaim
ec·lec·tic selecting the best
ec·lec·ti·cism
eclipse
eclips·er
eclip·sis linguistics term
eclip·tic astronomy term
eclip·ti·cal·ly
ec·lo·gite rock
ec·logue poem
eclo·sion emergence of insect
eco·cide environmental destruction
eco·logi·cal (*or* ·log·ic)
eco·logi·cal·ly
ecolo·gist
ecol·ogy
econo·met·ric (*or* ·ri·cal)
econo·me·tri·cian (*or* ·met·rist)
econo·met·rics economics
eco·nom·ic

eco·nomi·cal
eco·nomi·cal·ly
eco·nom·ics
econo·mist
econo·mi·za·tion (*or* ·sa·tion)
econo·mize (*or* ·mise)
econo·miz·er (*or* ·mis·er)
econo·my (*plural* ·mies)
écor·ché anatomical figure
eco·spe·cies
eco·spe·cif·ic
eco·sphere
écoss·aise dance
eco·sys·tem
eco·ton·al
eco·tone ecology term
eco·type
eco·typ·ic
eco·typi·cal·ly
écra·seur surgical device
ecru yellowish colour
ec·sta·sy (*plural* ·sies)
ec·stat·ic
ec·stati·cal·ly
ec·stat·ics
ec·thy·ma skin condition
ec·to·blast biology term
ec·to·blas·tic
ec·to·derm (*or* exo·derm) embryo part
ec·to·der·mal (*or* ·mic)
ec·to·en·zyme
ec·to·gen·esis
ec·tog·enous (*or* ·to·gen·ic) biology term
ec·to·mere embryology term
ec·to·mer·ic
ec·to·morph
ec·to·mor·phic thin
ec·to·morphy
ec·to·para·site
ec·to·para·sit·ic
ec·to·phyte parasitic plant
ec·to·pia congenital displacement
ec·top·ic in abnormal position; *compare* **entopic**
ec·to·plasm
ecto·plas·mic
ec·to·proct animal
ec·to·sarc amoeba ectoplasm
ecto·sar·cous

ec·ty·pal
ec·type copy
Ecua·dor
Ecua·do·rian (*or* ·ran)
ecu·men·ic
ecu·meni·cal (*or* oecu·)
ecu·meni·cal·ism (*or* ·cism) Christian unity
ecu·meni·cal·ly
écu·rie motor-racing team
ec·ze·ma
ec·zema·tous
eda·cious greedy
eda·cious·ness
edac·ity
Edam
edaph·ic of soil
edaphi·cal·ly
Edda Norse poems
eddo plant
eddy (*noun, plural* eddies; *verb* eddies, eddy·ing, eddied)
Ed·dy·stone rocks; lighthouse
Ede Dutch city
edel·weiss
ede·ma US spelling of oedema
edema·tous US spelling of oedematous
Eden biblical garden
eden·tate zoology term
eden·tu·lous (*or* ·late) toothless
edge
Edge·hill English battle site
edg·er
edge·ways
edgi·ly
edgi·ness
edg·ing
edgy (edgi·er, edgi·est)
edh runic character
ed·ibil·ity (*or* ·ible·ness)
ed·ible
edict
edic·tal
edi·fi·ca·tion
edifi·ca·tory
edi·fice
edi·fi·cial
edi·fi·er
edi·fy (·fies, ·fy·ing, ·fied)
edi·fy·ing·ly

edile *US variant spelling of* oedile

Ed·in·burgh

edit

edi·tion

edi·tio prin·ceps (*plural* edi·tio·nes prin·ci·pes) *Latin* first edition

edi·tor

edi·to·rial

edi·to·ri·al·ist

edi·to·ri·ali·za·tion (*or* ·sa·tion)

edi·to·ri·al·ize (*or* ·ise)

edi·to·ri·al·iz·er (*or* ·is·er)

edi·to·ri·al·ly

edi·tor·ship

Ed·mon·ton Canadian city

Edom biblical people

edu·cabil·ity (*or* educat·abil·ity)

edu·cable (*or* ·cat·able)

edu·cate

edu·cat·ed

edu·ca·tion

edu·ca·tion·al

edu·ca·tion·al·ist (*or* ·tion·ist)

edu·ca·tion·al·ly

edu·ca·tive

edu·ca·tor

edu·ca·tory

educe logic term

educ·ible

educt chemistry term

educ·tion

educ·tive

edul·co·rate wash

edul·co·ra·tion

Ed·ward·ian

eel

eel·grass

eel-like

eel·pout fish

eel·worm

e'er ever; *compare* ere

eerie (eeri·er, eeri·est) weird; *compare* eyrie

eeri·ly

eeri·ness

eff

ef·fable expressible

ef·face

ef·face·able

ef·face·ment

ef·fac·er

ef·fect (*noun*) result; (*verb*) cause; *compare* affect

ef·fect·er

ef·fect·ible

ef·fec·tive

ef·fec·tive·ly

ef·fec·tive·ness

ef·fec·tor physiology term

ef·fects

ef·fec·tual

ef·fec·tu·al·ity (*or* ·al·ness)

ef·fec·tu·al·ly

ef·fec·tu·ate bring about

ef·fec·tu·ation

ef·femi·na·cy (*or* ·nate·ness)

ef·femi·nate

ef·fen·di (*plural* ·dis) Turkish title

ef·fer·ence

ef·fer·ent conducting outwards; *compare* afferent

ef·fer·vesce

ef·fer·ves·cence

ef·fer·ves·cent

ef·fer·ves·cible

ef·fer·ves·cing·ly

ef·fete weak

ef·fi·ca·cious

ef·fi·ca·cy (*or* ·cious·ness)

ef·fi·cien·cy (*plural* ·cies)

ef·fi·cient

ef·fig·ial

ef·fi·gy (*plural* ·gies)

ef·flo·resce

ef·flo·res·cence

ef·flo·res·cent

ef·flu·ence (*or* ef·flux)

ef·flu·ent

ef·flu·vial

ef·flu·vium (*plural* ·via *or* ·viums) bad smell

ef·flux *variant of* effluence

ef·fort

ef·fort·ful

ef·fort·less

ef·fort·less·ness

ef·fron·tery (*plural* ·teries)

ef·ful·gence

ef·ful·gent radiant

ef·fuse spread out

ef·fu·si·om·eter physics apparatus

ef·fu·sion

ef·fu·sive

ef·fu·sive·ness

Efik (*plural* Efik *or* Efiks) African people

eft newt

egad

egali·tar·ian

egali·tari·an·ism

Egeria female adviser

egest excrete

eges·ta

eges·tion

eges·tive

egg

egg·beater

eg·ger (*or* ·gar) moth

egg·head

egg·nog (*or* egg-noggin)

egg·plant *US* aubergine

egg·shell

eggy

Eg·ham Surrey town

egis *US variant spelling of* aegis

eg·lan·tine plant

Eg·mont extinct volcano

ego (*plural* egos)

ego·cen·tric

ego·cen·tric·ity

ego·cen·trism

ego·ism self-interest; *compare* egotism

ego·ist

ego·is·tic (*or* ·ti·cal)

ego·ma·nia

ego·ma·ni·ac

ego·ma·nia·cal

ego·tism self-centredness; *compare* egoism

ego·tist

ego·tis·tic (*or* ·ti·cal)

ego·tis·ti·cal·ly

egre·gious bad

egre·gious·ness

egress

egres·sion

egret bird

Egypt

Egyp·tian

Egyp·to·logi·cal

Egyp·tolo·gist

Egyp·tol·ogy

eh

eider

eider·down

eidet·ic psychology term

eideti·cal·ly

eido·lon (*plural* ·la *or* ·lons) apparition

Eiffel Tower

eigen·func·tion physics term

Eiger Swiss mountain

eight

eight·een

eight·een·mo (*plural* ·mos)

eight·eenth

eight·fold

eighth

eighti·eth

eight·some

eight·vo (*plural* ·vos)

eighty (*plural* eighties)

Eilat Israeli port

Eind·ho·ven Dutch city

ein·korn wheat

Ein·stein·ian

ein·stein·ium radioactive element

Eire

eireni·con (*or* ireni·) philosophy term

eise·gesis (*plural* ·geses) text interpretation

Eisen·ach East German city

eistedd·fod (*plural* ·fods *or* ·fodau)

eistedd·fod·ic

ei·ther

ejacu·late

ejacu·la·tion

ejacu·la·tive

ejacu·la·tor

ejacu·la·tory

eject

ejec·ta volcanic material

ejec·tion

ejec·tive phonetics term

ejec·tor

eke

ekis·ti·cal (*or* ·tic)

ekis·tics human settlements

elabo·rate

elabo·rate·ness

elabo·ra·tion

elabo·ra·tive

elabo·ra·tor

el·aeop·tene *variant spelling of* eleoptene

El Ala·mein Egyptian battle site

Elam ancient kingdom

Elam·ite (*or* ·it·ic)

élan style

eland antelope

élan vital philosophy term

ela·pid snake

elapse

elas·mo·branch fish

elas·mo·saur reptile

elas·tance physics term

elas·tic

elas·ti·cal·ly

elas·ti·cate

elas·ti·ca·tion

elas·tici·ty

elas·ti·cize (*or* ·cise)

elas·tin protein

elas·to·mer rubbery material

elas·to·mer·ic

Elas·to·plast (*Trademark*)

elate

elat·ed

elat·ed·ness

ela·ter biology term

elat·er·id beetle

elat·er·in purgative

elat·er·ite bitumen

ela·terium purgative

ela·tion

ela·tive linguistics term

Elba Italian island

Elbe European river

el·bow

elbow·room

El·brus Soviet mountain

el·der

elder·berry (*plural* ·berries)

el·der·li·ness

el·der·ly

el·der·ship

eld·est

El Do·ra·do legendary city

el·dritch (*or* ·drich) unearthly

Ele·at·ic

Ele·ati·cism philosophy term

ele·cam·pane plant

elect

elect·able

elec·tion

elec·tion·eer

elec·tion·eer·er

elec·tion·eer·ing

elec·tive

elec·tiv·ity (*or* ·tive·ness)

elec·tor

elec·tor·al

elec·tor·ate

elec·tor·ship

Electra mythological character

elec·tret physics term

elec·tric

elec·tri·cal

elec·tri·cal·ly

elec·tri·cian

elec·tric·ity

elec·tri·fi·able

elec·tri·fi·ca·tion

elec·tri·fi·er

elec·tri·fy (·fies, ·fy·ing, ·fied)

elec·tro (*plural* ·tros)

elec·tro·acous·tic (*or* ·ti·cal)

elec·tro·acous·tics

elec·tro·analy·sis

elec·tro·ana·lytic (*or* ·lyti·cal)

elec·tro·car·dio·gram

elec·tro·car·dio·graph

elec·tro·car·dio·graph·ic (*or* ·graphi·cal)

elec·tro·car·di·og·ra·phy

elec·tro·chemi·cal

elec·tro·chem·ist

elec·tro·chem·is·try

elec·tro·con·vul·sive

elec·tro·cor·ti·co·gram record of brainwaves

elec·tro·cute

elec·tro·cu·tion

elec·trode

elec·tro·de·pos·it

elec·tro·depo·si·tion chemistry term

elec·tro·di·aly·sis

elec·tro·dy·nam·ic (*or* ·nami·cal)

elec·tro·dy·nam·ics

elec·tro·dy·na·mom·eter

elec·tro·en·cepha·lo·gram
elec·tro·en·cepha·lo·graph
elec·tro·en·cepha·lo·graph·ic
elec·tro·en·cepha·lo·graphi·cal·ly
elec·tro·en·cepha·log·ra·phy
elec·tro·form form by electrolysis
elec·tro·graph printing term
elec·tro·graph·ic
elec·tro·graphi·cal·ly
elec·trog·ra·phy
elec·tro·jet physics term
elec·tro·ki·net·ic
elec·tro·ki·net·ics
elec·tro·lu·mi·nes·cence
elec·tro·lu·mi·nes·cent
elec·tro·ly·sa·tion (US ·za·tion)
elec·tro·lyse (US ·lyze)
elec·tro·lys·er (US ·lyz·er)
elec·troly·sis
elec·tro·lyte
elec·tro·lyt·ic (or ·lyti·cal)
elec·tro·mag·net
elec·tro·mag·net·ic
elec·tro·mag·neti·cal·ly
elec·tro·mag·ne·tism
elec·tro·me·chani·cal
elec·tro·mer·ism chemistry term
elec·tro·met·al·lur·gi·cal
elec·tro·me·tal·lur·gist
elec·tro·met·al·lur·gy
elec·trom·eter
elec·tro·met·ric (or ·ri·cal)
elec·trom·etry
elec·tro·mo·tive current-producing
elec·tron
elec·tro·nega·tive
elec·tro·nega·tiv·ity
elec·tron·ic
elec·troni·cal·ly
elec·tron·ics
elec·tron·volt unit
elec·tro·phil·ic chemistry term
elec·tro·phone musical term

elec·tro·phon·ic
elec·tro·pho·resis physics term
elec·tro·pho·ret·ic
elec·tro·pho·rus physics apparatus
elec·tro·physio·logi·cal
elec·tro·physi·olo·gist
elec·tro·physi·ol·ogy
elec·tro·plate
elec·tro·plat·er
elec·tro·po·si·tive
elec·tro·scope
elec·tro·scop·ic
elec·tro·stat·ic
elec·tro·stati·cal·ly
elec·tro·stat·ics
elec·tro·stric·tion physics term
elec·tro·sur·gery
elec·tro·sur·gi·cal
elec·tro·thera·peu·tic (or ·ti·cal)
elec·tro·thera·peu·tics
elec·tro·thera·pist
elec·tro·thera·py
elec·tro·ther·mal
elec·tro·ton·ic
elec·troto·nus physiology term
elec·tro·type printing term
elec·tro·typ·er
elec·tro·va·len·cy (or ·lence) chemistry term
elec·tro·va·lent
elec·trum alloy
elec·tu·ary (plural ·aries) medical term
el·eemosy·nary dependent on charity
el·egance (or el·egan·cy; plural ·egances or ·cies)
el·egant
el·egi·ac
el·egist
el·egize (or ·egise)
el·egy (plural ·egies)
el·ement
el·ement·al
el·emen·ta·ri·ness
el·emen·ta·ry
el·emi (plural ·emis) resin
elen·chus (plural ·chi) logic term

elenc·tic
el·eop·tene (or ·aeop·) chemistry term
el·ephant (plural ·ephants or ·ephant)
el·ephan·ti·as·ic
el·ephan·tia·sis disease
el·ephan·tine
el·ephan·toid
elephant's-ear plant
elephant's-foot (or elephant-) plant
Eleu·sin·ian
Eleu·sis Greek town
el·evate
el·evat·ed
el·eva·tion
el·eva·tor
elev·en
eleven-plus
elev·en·ses
elev·enth
el·evon aircraft control surface
elf (plural elves)
El Fai·yum (or Al Fai·yum) Egyptian city
elfin
elf·ish (or elv·)
elf·lock
Elgin Scottish town; marbles
El Giza Egyptian city
Elia Greek department
elic·it evoke; compare illicit
elic·it·able
elici·ta·tion
elici·tor
elide linguistics term
elid·ible
eli·gibil·ity
eli·gible
eli·gibly
elimi·nable
elimi·nant
elimi·nate
elimi·na·tion
elimi·na·tive (or ·tory)
elimi·na·tor
Elis ancient Olympic Games site
eli·sion linguistics term
elite (or élite)
elit·ism
elit·ist

elix·ir
Eliza·bethan
elk
elk·hound
ell unit of length
Elles·mere Canadian Island
el·lipse flattened circle
el·lip·sis (plural ·ses)
  missing words
el·lip·soid
el·lip·soi·dal
el·lip·tic
el·lip·ti·cal
el·lip·ti·cal·ly
el·lip·ti·cal·ness
el·lip·ti·city
elm
El Man·su·ra (or Al
  Man·su·rah) Egyptian
  city
El Min·ya Egyptian port
El Mis·ti Peruvian volcano
El Obeid Sudanese city
elo·cu·tion
elo·cu·tion·ary
elo·cu·tion·ist
elon·gate
elon·ga·tion
elon·ga·tive
elope
elope·ment
elop·er
elo·quence
elo·quent
elo·quent·ness
El Paso Texan city
El Sal·va·dor
else·where
El·si·nore
elu·ant variant spelling of
  eluent
elu·ci·date
elu·ci·da·tion
elu·ci·da·tive (or ·da·tory)
elu·ci·da·tor
elude escape from; compare
  allude; illude
elud·er
elu·ate chemistry term
elu·ent (or ·ant)
elu·sion
elu·sive evasive; compare
  illusive
elu·sive·ness
elute chemistry term

elu·tri·ant
elu·tri·ate
elu·tria·tion
elu·tria·tor
elu·vial
elu·via·tion
elu·vium (plural ·via) rock
  particles; compare alluvium
el·ver eel
elves plural of elf
elv·ish variant spelling of
  elfish
Ely
Ély·sée Parisian palace
Ely·sian
Ely·sium mythological
  heaven
ely·troid (or ·trous)
ely·tron (or ·trum; plural
  ·tra) beetle's wing
em printer's measure;
  compare en
ema·ci·ate
ema·cia·ted
ema·cia·tion
ema·nate
ema·na·tion
ema·na·tion·al
ema·na·tive
ema·na·tor
ema·na·tory
eman·ci·pate
eman·ci·pa·tion
eman·ci·pa·tion·ist
eman·ci·pa·tive
eman·ci·pa·tor
eman·ci·pa·tory
emar·gi·nate (or ·nat·ed)
  notched
emar·gi·na·tion
emas·cu·late
emas·cu·la·tion
emas·cu·la·tive (or ·tory)
emas·cu·la·tor
em·balm
em·balm·er
em·balm·ment
em·bank
em·bank·ment
(embarass) incorrect
  spelling of embarrass
em·bar·go (noun, plural
  ·goes; verb ·goes,
  ·go·ing, ·goed)
em·bark

em·bar·ka·tion
em·bark·ment
em·bar·rass
em·bar·rass·ing
em·bar·rass·ment
em·bas·sy (plural ·sies)
em·bat·tle
em·bay
em·bay·ment bay-shaped
em·bed (·bed·ding,
  ·bed·ded)
em·bed·ment
em·bel·lish
em·bel·lish·er
em·bel·lish·ment
em·ber
em·bez·zle
em·bez·zle·ment
em·bez·zler
em·bit·ter
em·bit·ter·er
em·bit·ter·ment
em·bla·zon
em·bla·zon·ment
em·bla·zon·ry
em·blem
em·blem·at·ic (or ·ati·cal)
em·blem·ati·cal·ly
em·blema·tize (or ·tise,
  ·blem·ize, ·blem·ise)
em·ble·ments legal term
em·bodi·ment (or im·)
em·body (·bod·ies,
  ·body·ing, ·bod·ied)
em·bold·en
em·bo·lec·to·my (plural
  ·mies)
em·bol·ic
em·bo·lism
em·bo·lis·mic
em·bo·lus (plural ·li)
  material blocking blood
  vessel
em·bo·ly (plural ·lies)
  embryology term
em·bon·point French
  plumpness
em·boss
em·boss·er
em·boss·ment
em·bou·chure (plural
  ·chures)
em·bow architecture term
em·bow·el
em·bow·er

em·bow·ment
em·brace
em·brace·able
em·brace·ment
em·brac·er
em·brac·ery *Obsolete* jury
 bribing
em·branch·ment
em·bra·sure fortification
em·bra·sured
em·brec·to·my (*plural*
 ·mies)
em·bro·cate
em·bro·ca·tion
em·broi·der
em·broi·der·er
em·broi·dery (*plural*
 ·deries)
em·broil
em·broil·er
em·broil·ment
em·bry·ec·to·my (*plural*
 ·mies)
em·brue *variant spelling of*
 imbrue
em·bryo (*plural* ·bryos)
em·bryo·gen·ic
em·bry·og·eny
 development of embryo
em·bry·oid
em·bryo·logi·cal (*or*
 ·log·ic)
em·bry·olo·gist
em·bry·ol·ogy
em·bry·on·ic (*or*
 ·bryo·nal)
em·bry·oni·cal·ly
em·bus (·bus·ing, ·bused
 or ·bus·sing, ·bussed)
emend improve text;
 compare amend
emend·able
emen·da·tion
emen·da·tor
emen·da·tory
em·er·ald
emerge
emer·gence
emer·gen·cy (*plural* ·cies)
emer·gent
emeri·tus
emersed botany term
emer·sion emerging;
 compare immersion
em·ery mineral

em·esis vomiting
emet·ic
emeti·cal·ly
em·etine (*or* ·etin) alkaloid
emi·grant
emi·grate leave country;
 compare immigrate
emi·gra·tion
emi·gra·tion·al
emi·gra·tive
émi·gré *French* emigrant
Emilia-Romagna Italian
 region
Emi·nence (*or* ·nen·cy;
 plural ·nences *or*
 ·nen·cies) cardinal's title
emi·nence (*or* ·nen·cy;
 plural ·nences *or*
 ·nen·cies) superiority
émi·nence grise (*plural*
 emi·nences grises)
 French powerful person
emi·nent distinguished;
 compare immanent;
 imminent
emir (*or* emeer) Islamic
 ruler
emir·ate (*or* emeer·)
em·is·sary (*plural* ·saries)
emis·sion
emis·sive
emis·siv·ity physics term
emit (emit·ting, emit·ted)
emit·ter
Em·men Dutch city
em·mena·gog·ic
em·mena·gogue medical
 term
Em·men·thal (*or* ·tal,
 ·thal·er, ·tal·er) cheese
em·mer wheat
em·met *Dialect* ant
em·me·tro·pia perfect
 vision
em·me·trop·ic
Emmy television award
emol·lience
emol·lient soothing
emolu·ment salary
emote
emot·er
emo·tion
emo·tion·al
emo·tion·al·ism
emo·tion·al·ist
emo·tion·al·is·tic

emo·tion·al·ity
emo·tion·ali·za·tion (*or*
 ·sa·tion)
emo·tion·al·ize (*or* ·ise)
emo·tion·al·ly
emo·tive
emo·tive·ness (*or* ·tiv·ity)
emo·ti·vism
em·pale *less common spelling*
 of impale
em·pan·el (*US* im·;
 ·el·ling, ·elled, *US*
 ·el·ing, ·eled)
em·pan·el·ment (*US* im·)
em·path·ic (*or* ·pa·thet·ic)
em·pathi·cal·ly (*or*
 ·pa·theti·cal·ly)
em·pa·thize (*or* ·thise)
em·pa·thy
em·pen·nage aircraft tail
em·per·or
em·per·or·ship
em·pery power
em·pha·sis (*plural* ·ses)
em·pha·size (*or* ·sise)
em·phat·ic
em·phati·cal·ly
em·phati·cal·ness
em·phy·sema lung
 condition
em·phy·sema·tous
em·pire
em·pir·ic
em·piri·cal
em·piri·cal·ly
em·piri·cal·ness
em·piri·cism
em·piri·cist
em·place
em·place·ment
em·plane
em·ploy
em·ploy·abil·ity
em·ploy·able
em·ployee
em·ploy·er
em·ploy·ment
em·poi·son
em·po·rium (*plural* ·riums
 or ·ria)
em·pov·er·ish *less common*
 spelling of impoverish
em·pow·er
em·pow·er·ment
em·press

empt *Dialect* empty
emp·ti·able
emp·ti·ly
emp·ti·ness
emp·ty (*adj* ·ti·er, ·ti·est;
  verb ·ties, ·ty·ing, ·tied)
empty-handed
empty-headed
em·py·ema pus
  accumulation
em·py·emic
em·py·real
em·py·rean heavens
em·py·reu·ma burning
  smell
emu
emu·late
emu·la·tion
emu·la·tive
emu·la·tor
emu·lous competitive
emu·lous·ness
emul·si·fi·able (*or*
  emul·sible)
emul·si·fi·ca·tion
emul·si·fi·er
emul·si·fy (·fies, ·fy·ing,
  ·fied)
emul·sion
emul·sive
emul·soid chemistry term
emunc·tory (*plural*
  ·tories) excretory organ
en half an em; *compare* em
en·able
en·abler
en·act
en·ac·tion
en·ac·tive
en·act·ment
en·ac·tor
en·ac·tory
enam·el (·el·ling, ·elled;
  US ·el·ing, ·eled)
enam·el·ler (*US* ·el·er)
enam·el·list (*US* ·el·ist)
enam·el·work
en·am·our (*US* ·or)
en·am·oured (*US* ·ored)
en·antio·morph crystal
  form
en·antio·mor·phic
en·antio·morph·ism
en·ar·thro·dial

en·ar·thro·sis (*plural* ·ses)
  ball-and-socket joint
enate of the mother
enat·ic
en bloc *French* in a block
en·cae·nia festival
en·cage
en·camp
en·camp·ment
en·cap·su·late
en·cap·su·la·tion
en·case (*or* in·)
en·case·ment (*or* in·)
en·cash
en·cash·able
en·cash·ment
en·caus·tic ceramics term
en·caus·ti·cal·ly
en·ceinte pregnant
Enceladus mythological
  giant
en·cephal·ic of the brain
en·cepha·lin (*or* ·kepha·)
  brain chemical
en·cepha·li·tic
en·cepha·li·tis
en·cepha·lo·gram
en·cepha·lo·graph
en·cepha·lo·graphi·cal
en·cepha·log·ra·phy
en·cepha·lo·ma (*plural*
  ·mas *or* ·ma·ta) tumour
en·cepha·lo·my·eli·tic
en·cepha·lo·my·eli·tis
en·cepha·lon (*plural* ·la)
  brain
en·cepha·lous
en·chain
en·chain·ment
en·chant
en·chant·er
en·chant·ing
en·chant·ment
en·chant·ress
en·chase engrave
en·chi·la·da Mexican food
en·chon·dro·ma (*plural*
  ·mas *or* ·ma·ta) tumour
en·chon·droma·tous
en·cho·rial (*or* ·ric) of a
  particular country
en·ci·pher
en·ci·pher·er
en·ci·pher·ment
en·cir·cle

en·cir·cle·ment
en·clasp
en·clave
en·clit·ic linguistics term
en·cliti·cal·ly
en·clos·able (*or* in·)
en·close
en·clos·er
en·clo·sure
en·code
en·code·ment
en·cod·er
en·co·mi·ast writer of
  eulogies
en·co·mi·as·tic (*or* ·ti·cal)
en·co·mi·as·ti·cal·ly
en·co·mium (*plural*
  ·miums *or* ·mia)
en·com·pass
en·com·pass·ment
en·core
en·coun·ter
en·coun·ter·er
en·cour·age
en·cour·age·ment
en·cour·ag·er
en·cour·ag·ing·ly
en·cri·nite fossil
en·croach
en·croach·er
en·croach·ing·ly
en·croach·ment
en·crust (*or* in·)
en·crust·ant (*or* in·)
en·crus·ta·tion (*or* in·)
en·cul·tu·ra·tion
en·cul·tu·ra·tive
en·cum·ber (*or* in·)
en·cum·ber·ing·ly (*or* in·)
en·cum·brance (*or* in·)
en·cum·branc·er legal term
en·cyc·lic
en·cyc·li·cal letter from
  pope
en·cy·clo·pedia (*or*
  ·pae·dia)
en·cy·clo·pedic (*or*
  ·pae·dic)
en·cy·clo·pedi·cal·ly (*or*
  ·pae·di·)
en·cy·clo·pedism (*or*
  ·pae·dism)
en·cy·clo·pedist (*or*
  ·pae·dist)
en·cyst biology term

en·cyst·ment (*or* ·ta·tion)
end
en·dam·age
en·dam·age·ment
en·da·moeba (*US* ·meba;
  plural ·moebae *or*
  ·moebas, *US* ·mebas)
en·dan·ger
en·dan·ger·ment
end·arch botany term
end·blown music term
end·brain
en·dear
en·dear·ing
en·dear·ing·ly
en·dear·ment
en·deav·our (*US* ·or)
en·deav·our·er (*US* ·or·)
en·dem·ic (*noun*) localized
  disease; *compare* epidemic
en·dem·ic (*or* ·demi·al,
  ·demi·cal; *adj*)
en·demi·cal·ly
en·de·mism (*or* ·mic·ity)
end·er
en·der·mic absorbed
  through skin
end·game
end·ing
en·dive
end·less
end·less·ness
end·long
end·most
endo·blast embryology term
endo·blas·tic
endo·car·dial (*or* ·di·ac)
endo·car·di·tic
endo·car·di·tis
endo·car·dium (*plural*
  ·dia) heart membrane
endo·carp part of fruit
endo·car·pal (*or* ·pic)
endo·cen·tric linguistics
  term
endo·cra·nium (*plural*
  ·nia) anatomy term
endo·crin·al
endo·crine ductless;
  compare exocrine
endo·crin·ic
endo·crino·log·ic (*or*
  ·ic·al)
endo·cri·nolo·gist

endo·cri·nol·ogy study of
  hormones
endo·doc·ri·nous
endo·derm (*or* ento·) part
  of embryo
endo·der·mal (*or* ento·)
endo·der·mic (*or* ento·)
endo·derm·is botany term
endo·don·tia
endo·don·tic
endo·don·tics dentistry
  term
endo·don·tist
endo·don·tol·ogy
endo·en·zyme
endo·er·gic energy-
  absorbing; *compare*
  exoergic
en·doga·mous (*or*
  endo·gam·ic)
en·doga·my
en·dog·enous developing in
  an organism
en·dog·eny
endo·lymph fluid in ear
endo·lym·phat·ic
endo·metrial
endo·metrio·sis
endo·metrium (*plural*
  ·metria) womb lining
endo·morph
endo·mor·phic heavily built
endo·mor·phism geology
  term
endo·mor·phy
endo·neu·rium anatomy
  term
endo·para·site
endo·para·sit·ic
endo·pep·ti·dase enzyme
endo·phyte (*or* ento·)
  parasitic plant
endo·phyt·ic (*or* ento·)
endo·plasm biology term
endo·plas·mic
en·dor·phin brain chemical
en·dors·able (*or* in·)
en·dorse (*or* in·)
en·dor·see (*or* in·)
en·dorse·ment (*or* in·)
en·dors·er (*or* ·dor·sor,
  in·)
endo·scope medical
  instrument
endo·scop·ic
en·dos·co·pist

en·dos·co·py
endo·skel·etal
endo·skel·eton
en·dos·mo·sis biology term
en·dos·mot·ic
en·dos·moti·cal·ly
endo·some cell nucleus part
endo·sperm seed tissue
endo·sper·mic
endo·spore
en·dos·por·ous
en·dos·teal
en·dos·teum (*plural* ·tea)
  anatomy term
en·dos·to·sis (*plural* ·ses)
  physiology term
endo·thecial
endo·thecium (*plural*
  ·thecia) botany term
endo·thelial
endo·theli·oid
endo·thelio·ma (*plural*
  ·mata) tumour
endo·thelium (*plural*
  ·thelia) anatomy term
endo·ther·mic (*or* ·mal)
  heat-absorbing; *compare*
  exothermic
endo·ther·mi·cal·ly
endo·ther·mism
endo·tox·ic
endo·tox·in
en·dow
en·dow·er
en·dow·ment
end·paper part of book
end·plate
end·play bridge term
en·due (*or* in·; ·dues,
  ·du·ing, ·dued) endow
en·dur·abil·ity (*or*
  ·dur·able·ness)
en·dur·able
en·dur·ance
en·dure
en·dur·ing
en·dur·ing·ly
end·ways
Endymion mythological
  character
en·ema (*plural* ·emas *or*
  ·ema·ta)
en·emy (*plural* ·emies)
en·er·get·ic
en·er·geti·cal·ly

en·er·geti·cist
en·er·get·ics
en·er·gid biology term
en·er·gize (or ·gise)
en·er·giz·er (or ·gis·er)
en·er·gu·men possessed
    person
en·er·gy (plural ·gies)
en·er·vate weaken; compare
    innervate; innovate
en·er·va·tion
en·er·va·tive
en·er·va·tor
en·face
en face French facing
    forwards
en·face·ment
en fa·mille French
    informally
en·fant ter·ri·ble (plural
    en·fants ter·ri·bles)
    French indiscreet person
en·fee·ble
en·fee·ble·ment
en·fee·bler
en·feoff legal term
en·feoff·ment
En·field London borough;
    rifle
en·fi·lade military term
en·fleu·rage French
    perfume-making
en·fold (or in·)
en·fold·er (or in·)
en·fold·ment (or in·)
en·force
en·force·abil·ity
en·force·able
en·forc·ed·ly
en·force·ment
en·forc·er
en·fran·chise
en·fran·chise·ment
en·fran·chis·er
En·ga·dine Swiss region
en·gage
en·gagé French committed
en·gaged
en·gage·ment
en·gag·er
en·gag·ing
en·gag·ing·ly
en·gag·ing·ness
en garde French on guard
en·gen·der

en·gen·der·er
en·gen·der·ment
en·gine
en·gi·neer
en·gi·neer·ing
en·gine·ry (plural ·ries)
en·gla·cial
Eng·land
Eng·lish
Eng·lish·ism
English·man (plural
    ·men)
English·woman (plural
    ·women)
en·glut devour
en·gorge
en·gorge·ment
en·graft (or in·)
en·graf·ta·tion (or
    en·graft·ment, in·)
en·grail indent coin
en·grail·ment
en·grain variant spelling of
    ingrain
en·grained variant spelling
    of ingrained
en·gram psychology term
en·gram·mic (or
    ·gram·at·ic)
en·grave
en·grav·er
en·grav·ing
en·gross
en·gross·ed·ly
en·gross·er
en·gross·ing·ly
en·gross·ment
en·gulf (or in·)
en·gulf·ment
en·hance
en·hance·ment
en·hanc·er
en·hanc·ive
en·har·mon·ic
en·har·moni·cal·ly
enig·ma
en·ig·mat·ic (or ·mati·cal)
en·ig·mati·cal·ly
Eni·we·tok Pacific atoll
en·jamb·ment (or
    ·jambe·) poetry term
en·join
en·join·er
en·join·ment
en·joy

en·joy·able
en·joy·ably
en·joy·er
en·joy·ment
en·kepha·lin variant spelling
    of encephalin
en·kin·dle
en·kin·dler
en·lace
en·lace·ment
en·large
en·large·able
en·large·ment
en·larg·er
en·light·en
en·light·en·er
en·light·en·ing·ly
En·light·en·ment 18th-
    century movement
en·light·en·ment
en·list
en·list·er
en·list·ment
en·liv·en
en·liv·en·er
en·liv·en·ing·ly
en·liv·en·ment
en masse French in a mass
en·mesh (or in·, im·)
en·mity (plural ·mities)
en·nage printing term
en·nead group of nine
en·nead·ic
en·nea·gon
en·nea·he·dral
en·nea·he·dron (plural
    ·drons or ·dra)
En·nis Irish town
En·nis·kil·len (or
    In·nis·kil·ling) Northern
    Irish town
en·no·ble
en·no·ble·ment
en·no·bler
en·no·bling·ly
en·nui apathy
enol chemistry term
enol·ogy US spelling of
    aenology
enor·mity (plural ·mities)
enor·mous
eno·sis union of Greece and
    Cyprus
enough
enounce enunciate

en pas·sant *French* in
passing
en·phy·tot·ic botany term
en·plane
en·quire (*or esp. US* in·)
ask; *compare* inquire
en·quir·er (*or esp. US*
in·)
en·quiry (*or esp. US* in·;
plural ·quiries)
en·rage
en·rag·ed·ly
en·rage·ment
en rap·port *French* in
sympathy
en·rap·ture
en·rich
en·rich·er
en·rich·ment
en·robe
en·rob·er
en·rol (*US* ·roll; ·rol·ling,
·rolled)
en·rol·lee
en·rol·ler
en·rol·ment (*US* ·roll·)
en·root
en route *French* on the way
ens metaphysics term
en·san·guine stain with
blood
En·schede Dutch city
en·sconce
en·sem·ble
en·shrine (*or* in·)
en·shrine·ment
en·shroud
en·si·form sword-shaped
en·sign
en·sign·ship (*or* ·cy;
plural ·ships *or* ·cies)
en·si·labil·ity
en·si·lage
en·sile store in silo
en·slave
en·slave·ment
en·slav·er
en·snare (*or* in·)
en·snare·ment
en·snar·er
en·soul (*or* in·)
en·sphere (*or* in·)
en·sta·tite mineral
en·sue (·su·ing, ·sued)
en·su·ing·ly

en suite forming a unit
en·sure make sure; *compare*
insure
en·sur·er
en·swathe
en·tab·la·ture
en·ta·ble·ment platform
en·tail
en·tail·er
en·tail·ment
en·ta·moeba (*or* en·da·;
US ·meba; *plural*
·moebae *or* ·moebas,
US ·mebas) amoeba
en·tan·gle
en·tan·gle·ment
en·tan·gler
en·ta·sia
en·ta·sis (*plural* ·ses)
architectural term
En·teb·be Ugandan town
en·tel·echy (*plural*
·echies) philosophy term
en·tel·lus monkey
en·tente cor·diale *French*
friendly relations
en·ter
en·ter·able
en·ter·al·ly
en·ter·er
en·ter·ic (*or* ·al) intestinal
en·teri·tis
en·tero·gas·trone hormone
en·tero·ki·nase enzyme
en·ter·on (*plural* ·tera)
digestive tract
en·ter·os·to·my (*plural*
·mies)
en·ter·ot·omy (*plural*
·omies)
en·tero·vi·rus (*plural*
·ruses)
en·ter·prise
en·ter·pris·er
en·ter·pris·ing
en·ter·tain
en·ter·tain·er
en·ter·tain·ing
en·ter·tain·ing·ly
en·ter·tain·ment
en·thal·py physics term
en·thet·ic medical term
en·thral (*US* ·thrall;
·thral·ling, ·thralled)
en·thral·ler

en·thral·ling·ly
en·thral·ment (*US*
·thrall·)
en·throne
en·throne·ment
en·thuse
en·thu·si·asm
en·thu·si·ast
en·thu·si·as·tic
en·thu·si·as·ti·cal·ly
en·thy·memat·ic (*or* ·ical)
en·thy·meme logic term
en·tice
en·tice·ment
en·tic·er
en·tic·ing·ly
en·tic·ing·ness
en·tire
en·tire·ly
en·tire·ness
en·tirety (*plural* ·tireties)
en·ti·tle
en·ti·tle·ment
en·tity (*plural* ·tities)
ento·blast embryology term
ento·blas·tic
ento·derm variant of
endoderm
ento·der·mal (*or* ·mic)
en·tomb
en·tomb·ment
en·tom·ic of insects
ento·mo·logi·cal (*or*
·log·ic)
ento·molo·gist
ento·mo·lo·gize (*or* ·gise)
ento·mol·ogy study of
insects; *compare* etymology
ento·mopha·gous
ento·mophi·lous insect-
pollinated
ento·mophi·ly
ento·mos·tra·can
crustacean
ento·mos·tra·cous
ento·phyte variant of
endophyte
ento·phyt·ic variant of
endophytic
en·top·ic in normal
position; *compare* ectopic
en·tou·rage
ento·zo·ic living inside an
animal

en·to·zo·on (*or* ·an; *plural* ·zoa)

en·tr'acte *French* interval between acts

en·trails

en·train board a train

en·train·ment

en·tram·mel (·mel·ling, ·melled; *US* ·mel·ing, ·meled) obstruct

en·trance

en·trance·ment

en·tranc·ing·ly

en·trant

en·trap (·trap·ping, ·trapped)

en·trap·ment

en·trap·per

en·treat

en·treat·ing·ly

en·treat·ment

en·treaty (*plural* ·treaties)

en·tre·chat ballet movement

en·tre·côte

en·trée

en·tre·mets (*plural* ·mets) dessert

en·trench

en·trench·er

en·trench·ment

en·tre nous *French* between ourselves

en·tre·pôt trading centre

en·tre·pre·neur

en·tre·pre·neur·ial

en·tre·pre·neur·ship

en·tre·sol *French* between floors

en·tro·py (*plural* ·pies) physics term

en·trust

en·trust·ment

en·try (*plural* ·tries)

en·twine

en·twine·ment

enu·cleate remove nucleus

enu·clea·tion

enu·clea·tor

Enu·gu Nigerian city

enu·mer·able countable; *compare* innumerable

enu·mer·ate

enu·mera·tion

enu·mera·tive

enu·mera·tor

enun·ci·abil·ity

enun·ci·able

enun·ci·ate articulate; *compare* annunciate

enun·cia·tion

enun·cia·tive (*or* ·tory)

enun·cia·tor

en·ure *variant spelling of* inure

enu·resis bedwetting

enu·ret·ic

en·vel·op (*verb*)

en·velope (*noun*)

en·vel·op·ment

en·ven·om

en·ven·omed

en·vi·able

en·vi·able·ness

en·vi·ably

en·vi·er

en·vi·ous

en·vi·ous·ness

en·vi·ron (*verb*) encircle

en·vi·ron·ment

en·vi·ron·men·tal

en·vi·ron·men·tal·ism

en·vi·ron·men·tal·ist

en·vi·ron·men·tal·ly

en·vi·rons (*noun*) vicinity

en·vis·age

en·vis·age·ment

en·vi·sion

en·voy

en·vy (*noun, plural* ·vies; *verb* ·vies, ·vy·ing, ·vied)

en·vy·ing·ly

en·wind (·wind·ing, ·wound)

en·womb

en·wrap (*or* ·in; ·wrap·ping, ·wrapped)

en·wreath

en·zo·ot·ic veterinary term

en·zo·oti·cal·ly

en·zy·mat·ic (*or* ·zy·mic)

en·zyme catalyst

en·zy·mo·logi·cal

en·zy·molo·gist

en·zy·mol·ogy

en·zy·moly·sis (*or* ·mo·sis)

en·zy·mo·lyt·ic

eobi·ont biology term

Eocene geological period

Eogene geological period

eohip·pus fossil horse

eolith stone tool

Eolith·ic Stone Age period

eon *US spelling of* aeon

eonism psychiatry term

Eos Greek goddess

eosin (*or* eosine) dye

eosin·ic

eosino·phil blood cell

eosino·phil·ic (*or* eosi·nophi·lous)

Eozo·ic geological period

epact astronomy term

ep·arch Eastern bishop

ep·ar·chial

ep·ar·chy (*or* ·chate; *plural* ·chies *or* ·chates)

ep·aulet (*or* ·aulette)

épée sword

épée·ist

epei·ric (*or* epei·ro·gen·ic, epei·ro·genet·ic) of continental drift

ep·ei·rog·eny (*or* epi·rog·eny, ep·ei·ro·gen·esis)

ep·en·cephal·ic

ep·en·cepha·lon (*plural* ·la) part of brain

epen·thesis (*plural* ·theses) linguistics term

ep·en·thet·ic

epergne table ornament

ep·ex·egesis (*plural* ·egeses) linguistics term

ep·ex·eget·ic (*or* ·egeti·cal)

ep·ex·egeti·cal·ly

ephah Hebrew unit

ephebe Greek youth

ephed·rine (*or* ·rin) alkaloid

ephem·era (*plural* ·eras *or* ·erae) short-lived insect; *compare* emphemeron

ephem·er·al

ephem·er·al·ity (*or* ·al·ness)

ephem·er·id mayfly

ephem·er·is (*plural* eph·emer·ides) astronomical table

ephem·er·on (*plural* ·era
or ·er·ons*) transitory
thing; *compare* ephemera

Ephesian

Eph·esus ancient Greek city

ephod vestment

eph·or Greek magistrate

epi·blast embryology term

epi·blas·tic

epi·bol·ic

epibo·ly (*plural* ·lies)
embryology term

epic

epi·ca·lyx (*plural* ·lyxes
or ·ly·ces*) botany term

epi·can·thus (*plural* ·thi)
anatomy term

epi·car·di·ac (*or* ·dial)

epi·car·dium (*plural* ·dia)
anatomy term

epi·carp (*or* exo·) botany
term

epi·cene

epi·cen·ism

epi·cen·tral

epi·cen·tre (*US* ·ter)

epi·clesis theology term

epi·con·ti·nen·tal

epi·cot·yl botany term

epi·cri·sis medical term

epi·crit·ic anatomy term

epi·cure

Epi·cu·rean of Epicurus

epi·cu·rean devoted to
pleasure

Epi·cu·rean·ism

epi·cur·ism (*or*
·cu·rean·ism*)

epi·cy·cle

epi·cy·clic (*or* ·cli·cal)

epi·cy·cloid geometric curve

epi·cy·cloid·al

Epi·daur·us Greek port

epi·deic·tic (*or* ·dic·tic)
rhetorical term

epi·dem·ic widespread
disease; *compare* endemic

epi·demi·cal

epi·demio·logi·cal

epi·demi·olo·gist

epi·demi·ol·ogy

epi·der·mal (*or* ·mic,
·moid*)

epi·der·mis

epi·dia·scope projector

epi·didy·mal

epi·di·dy·mis (*plural*
·dymi·des*) anatomy term

epi·dote mineral

epi·dot·ic

epi·dur·al anaesthetic

epi·fo·cal geology term

epi·gas·tric (*or* ·trial)

epi·gas·trium (*plural*
·tria*) abdominal part

epi·geal (*or* ·gean,
·geous*) botany term

epi·gene formed at earth's
surface

epi·gen·esis biology theory

epi·gen·esist (*or*
epig·enist*)

epi·genet·ic

epi·geneti·cal·ly

epig·enous

epi·glot·tal (*or* ·tic)

epi·glot·tis (*plural* ·tises
or ·ti·des*) anatomy term

epi·gone (*or* ·gon) imitator

epi·gram saying

epi·gram·mat·ic

epi·gram·mati·cal·ly

epi·gram·ma·tism

epi·gram·ma·tist

epi·gram·ma·tize (*or* ·tise)

epi·graph inscription

epig·ra·pher

epi·graph·ic (*or*
·graphi·cal*)

epi·graphi·cal·ly

epig·ra·phist

epig·ra·phy

epigy·nous botany term

epigy·ny

epi·lep·sy

epi·lep·tic

epi·lep·ti·cal·ly

epi·lep·toid (*or*
·lep·ti·form*)

epi·lim·ni·on lake water

epilo·gist

epi·logue

epi·mere embryology term

epi·mor·phic

epi·mor·pho·sis zoology
term

epi·my·sium (*plural* ·sia)
anatomy term

epi·nas·tic

epi·nas·ty (*plural* ·ties)
botany term

epi·neph·rine *US*
adrenaline

epi·neu·rial

epi·neu·rium anatomy term

epi·phan·ic

Epipha·ny Christian festival

epipha·ny (*plural* ·nies)
manifestation

epi·phenom·enal

epi·phenom·enal·ism
philosophy term

epi·phenom·enal·ist

epi·phenom·enon (*plural*
·ena*)

epi·phragm shell

epi·phys·eal (*or* ·ial)

epiphy·sis (*plural* ·ses)
anatomy term

epi·phyte botany term

epi·phyt·ic (*or* ·phyti·cal)

epi·phyti·cal·ly

epi·phy·tot·ic

epi·ro·gen·ic (*or* ·genet·ic)
variants of epeirogenic

epi·rog·eny *variant spelling
of* epeirogeny

Epi·rus Greek region

epis·co·pa·cy (*plural*
·cies*) church government

epis·co·pal

epis·co·pa·lian

epis·co·pa·lian·ism

epis·co·pal·ism

epis·co·pal·ly

epis·co·pate

epi·scope projector

epi·semat·ic zoology term

epi·si·oto·my (*plural*
·mies*) medical term

epi·sode

epi·sod·ic (*or* ·sodi·cal)

epi·sodi·cal·ly

epi·some

epi·spas·tic producing a
blister

epi·sta·sis medical term

epi·stat·ic

epi·stax·is nosebleed

ep·is·tem·ic relating to
knowledge

epis·temo·logi·cal

epis·temolo·gist

epis·temol·ogy

epi·ster·num (*plural* ·na)
breastbone part

epis·tle

epis·tler (*or* ·to·ler, ·to·list)

epis·to·lary (*or* epi·stol·ic, epis·to·la·tory)

epis·to·ler

epis·tro·phe rhetorical term

epi·style architectural term

epi·taph inscription

epi·taph·ic

epi·taph·ist

epita·sis drama term

epi·tax·ial

epi·taxy (*or* ·tax·is) crystal growth

epi·tha·lam·ic

epi·tha·la·mium (*or* ·mi·on; *plural* ·mia) nuptial ode

epi·thelial (*or* ·theli·oid)

epi·thelio·ma (*plural* ·mas *or* ·ma·ta) tumour

epi·theli·oma·tous

epi·thelium (*plural* ·thelia) tissue

epi·thet

epi·thet·ic (*or* ·theti·cal)

epito·me typical example

epi·tom·ic (*or* ·tomi·cal)

epito·mist

epito·mi·za·tion (*or* ·sa·tion)

epito·mize (*or* ·mise)

epito·miz·er (*or* ·mis·er)

epi·zo·ic zoology term

epi·zo·ism

epi·zo·ite

epi·zo·on (*plural* ·zoa) animal parasite

epi·zo·ot·ic veterinary term

epi·zo·oti·cal·ly

ep·och

ep·och·al

epoch-making

ep·ode prosody term

epo·nym something named after a person

epony·mous (*or* epo·nym·ic)

epony·my

épo·pée (*or* epo·poeia) poem

epos body of poetry

epox·ide

epoxy

Ep·ping

Ep·si·lon astronomy term

ep·si·lon Greek letter

Ep·som

epyl·li·on (*plural* ·lia) poem

eq·uabil·ity (*or* ·uable·ness)

eq·uable

eq·uably

equal (equal·ling, equalled; *US* equal·ing, equaled)

equal-area cartography term

equali·tar·ian

equali·tari·an·ism

equali·ty (*plural* ·ties)

equali·za·tion (*or* ·sa·tion)

equal·ize (*or* ·ise)

equal·iz·er (*or* ·is·er)

equal·ly

equa·nim·ity

equani·mous

equat·abil·ity

equat·able

equate

equa·tion

equa·tion·al

equa·tor

equa·to·rial

Equa·to·rial Guinea African republic

eq·uer·ry (*plural* ·ries)

eques·trian

eques·tri·an·ism

eques·tri·enne

equi·an·gu·lar

equi·dis·tance

equi·dis·tant

equi·lat·eral

equili·brant

equili·brate

equi·li·bra·tion

equi·li·bra·tor

equili·brist

equili·bris·tic

equi·lib·rium (*plural* ·riums *or* ·ria)

equi·mo·lecu·lar

equine

equin·ity

equi·noc·tial

equi·nox

equip (equip·ping, equipped)

equi·page carriage

equi·par·ti·tion physics term

equip·ment

equi·poise equilibrium

equi·pol·lence (*or* ·len·cy)

equi·pol·lent equal in effect

equi·pon·der·ance (*or* ·ancy)

equi·pon·der·ant

equi·pon·der·ate counterbalance

equi·po·tent

equi·po·ten·tial physics term

equi·po·ten·ti·al·ity

equip·per

equi·setum (*plural* ·setums *or* ·seta) plant

equi·table

equi·table·ness

equi·tably

equi·tant botany term

equi·ta·tion horsemanship

equi·tes Roman cavalry

equi·ty (*plural* ·ties)

equiva·lence

equi·va·len·cy (*or* ·va·lence) chemistry term

equiva·lent

equivo·cal

equivo·cal·ity (*or* ·ca·cy)

equivo·cal·ly

equivo·cate

equivo·cat·ing·ly

equivo·ca·tion

equivo·ca·tory

equi·voque (*or* ·voke) pun

Equul·eus constellation

era

era·di·ate radiate

era·dia·tion

eradi·cable

eradi·cant

eradi·cate

eradi·ca·tion

eradi·ca·tive

eradi·ca·tor

eras·able

erase

eras·er

era·sion

Eras·ti·an·ism state
  supremacy over church
eras·ure
Er·bil (or Ir·bil, Ar·bil)
  Iraqi city
er·bium chemical element
ere Poetic before; compare
  e'er
Erebus Greek god
Erech·theum (or ·thei·on)
  Athenian temple
erect
erect·able
erect·er (or erec·tor)
erec·tile
erec·til·ity
erec·tion
erect·ness
erec·tor (or ·ter)
er·emite hermit
er·emit·ic (or ·emiti·cal)
er·emit·ism
erep·sin enzyme
er·ethism medical term
er·ethis·mic (or ·ethis·tic,
  ·ethit·ic)
Er·furt East German city
erg unit
er·ga·toc·ra·cy (plural
  ·cies) government by
  workers
ergo Latin therefore
er·go·graph muscle-
  measuring instrument
er·gom·eter dynamometer
er·go·nom·ic
er·go·nom·ics
er·gono·mist
er·gos·terol biochemical
  compound
er·got crop disease
er·got·ism human disease
eri·ca shrub
eri·ca·ceous
Erida·nus constellation
Erie Canadian lake
erig·er·on plant
Erin Archaic Ireland
eri·na·ceous of hedgehogs
Eris Greek goddess
er·is·tic logic term
er·is·ti·cal
Eri·trea Ethiopian province
Eri·trean
erk Slang aircraftsman

Er·lang unit
erl·king malevolent spirit
er·mine (plural ·mines or
  ·mine)
erne eagle
Er·nie computer lottery
erode
erod·ent
ero·genei·ty
erog·enous (or
  ero·gen·ic)
Eros
erose uneven
ero·sion
ero·sion·al
ero·sive
ero·sive·ness
ero·tema (or ·teme,
  ·tesis) rhetorical question
ero·temat·ic (or ·tet·ic)
erot·ic (or eroti·cal)
eroti·ca
eroti·cal·ly
eroti·cism (or ero·tism)
ero·to·gen·ic variant of
  erogenous
erot·ol·ogy
ero·to·ma·nia
ero·to·ma·ni·ac
err
er·ran·cy (plural ·cies)
er·rand
er·rant
er·rant·ry (plural ·tries)
er·ra·ta plural of erratum
er·rat·ic
er·rati·cal·ly
er·rati·cism
er·ra·tum (plural ·ta)
  printing error
er·rhine causing nasal
  secretion
Er Rif Moroccan region
er·ro·neous
er·ro·neous·ness
er·ror
er·satz artificial
Erse Gaelic
erst·while
eru·bes·cence redness
eru·bes·cent
eruct (or eruc·tate) belch
eruc·ta·tion
eruc·ta·tive
eru·dite

eru·di·tion (or
  eru·dite·ness)
erum·pent bursting out
erupt break out; compare
  irrupt
erupt·ible
erup·tion
erup·tion·al
erup·tive
erup·tiv·ity (or ·tive·ness)
Ery·man·thus Greek
  mountain
eryn·go (or erin·; plural
  ·goes or ·gos) plant
ery·sip·elas skin disease
ery·si·pela·tous
ery·sip·eloid
ery·thema skin redness
ery·themat·ic (or
  ·thema·tous, ·themic)
eryth·rism abnormal
  redness
ery·thris·mal
eryth·rite mineral
eryth·ri·tol (or ·rite) drug
eryth·ro·blast marrow cell
eryth·ro·blas·tic
eryth·ro·blas·to·sis blood
  disease
eryth·ro·cyte blood cell
eryth·ro·cyt·ic
eryth·ro·cy·tom·eter
eryth·ro·cy·tom·etry
eryth·ro·my·cin antibiotic
eryth·ro·poi·esis red blood
  cell formation
eryth·ro·poi·et·ic
Er·zu·rum Turkish city
Es·bjerg Danish port
es·ca·drille aircraft
  squadron; compare
  espadrille
es·ca·lade scaling walls
es·ca·lad·er
es·ca·late
es·ca·la·tion
es·ca·la·tor
es·cal·lo·nia shrub
es·cal·lope scallop
es·ca·lope veal slice
es·cap·able
es·ca·pade
es·cape
es·capee
es·cape·ment

es·cap·er
es·cap·ism
es·cap·ist
es·ca·polo·gist
es·ca·pol·ogy
es·carp fortification
es·carp·ment steep slope
escha·lot shallot
es·char scab
es·cha·rot·ic
es·cha·to·logi·cal
es·cha·tolo·gist
es·cha·tol·ogy theology
es·cheat legal term
es·chew avoid
es·chew·al
es·chew·er
es·co·lar (*plural* ·lars *or* ·lar) fish
Es·co·rial Spanish village
es·cort
es·cri·toire
es·crow legal term
es·cu·do (*plural* ·dos) Portuguese currency
es·cu·lent edible
es·cutch·eon heraldry term
es·cutch·eoned
Es·dra·elon Israeli plain
es·em·plas·tic unifying
es·er·ine alkaloid
Es·fa·han *variant spelling of* Isfahan
Esher
es·ker (*or* ·kar) glacial deposit
Eskil·stu·na Swedish city
Es·ki·mo (*plural* ·mos *or* ·mo)
Es·ki·moan
Es·ki·moid
Es·ki·sehir Turkish city
esopha·gus *US spelling of* oesophagus
eso·ter·ic abstruse; *compare* exoteric
eso·teri·cal·ly
eso·teri·cism
es·pa·drille canvas shoe; *compare* escadrille
es·pal·ier wall-trained tree
es·par·to (*plural* ·tos) grass
es·pe·cial
es·pe·cial·ly

Es·pe·ran·to artificial language
es·pial
espi·er
es·pio·nage
Es·pí·ri·to San·to Brazilian state
Es·pí·ri·tu San·to Pacific island
es·pla·nade
es·pous·al
es·pouse
es·pous·er
es·pres·so (*plural* ·sos) coffee
es·prit liveliness
es·prit de corps group pride
espy (espies, espy·ing, espied)
es·quire
es·say composition; attempt; *compare* assay
es·say·ist
Es·sen West German city
es·sence
Es·sene Jewish sect
es·sen·tial
es·sen·tial·ism philosophical doctrine
es·sen·tial·ist
es·sen·tial·ity (*or* ·ness)
es·sen·tial·ly
Es·sequi·bo South American river
Es·sex
Es·sonne French department
es·tab·lish
es·tab·lish·er
es·tab·lish·ment
es·tab·lish·men·tar·ian
es·tab·lish·men·tar·ian·ism
es·ta·mi·net French café
es·tan·cia ranch
es·tate
es·teem
es·ter chemistry term
es·ter·ase enzyme
es·teri·fi·ca·tion
es·teri·fy (·fies, ·fy·ing, ·fied)
es·ti·mable
es·ti·mable·ness
es·ti·mate

es·ti·ma·tion
es·ti·ma·tive
es·ti·ma·tor
estipu·late (*or* ex·stipu·) botany term
es·thete *US variant spelling of* aesthete
es·thetic *US variant spelling of* aesthetic
es·ti·val *US spelling of* aestival
es·ti·vate *US spelling of* aestivate
Es·to·nia Soviet republic
Es·to·nian
es·top (·top·ping, ·topped) legal term
es·top·page
es·top·pel
es·to·vers legal term
es·trade dais
es·tra·di·ol *US spelling of* oestradiol
es·tra·gon tarragon
es·trange
es·tranged
es·trange·ment
es·trang·er
es·tray
es·treat legal term
Es·tre·ma·du·ra Spanish region
es·tri·ol *US spelling of* oestriol
es·tro·gen *US spelling of* oestrogen
es·trone *US spelling of* oestrone
es·trous *US spelling of* oestrous
es·trus *US spelling of* oestrus
es·tu·ar·ial
es·tua·rine
es·tu·ary (*plural* ·aries)
esu·ri·ence (*or* ·en·cy)
esu·ri·ent greedy
eta Greek letter
etae·rio (*plural* ·rios) botany term
éta·gère *French* ornament stand
eta·lon physics device
eta·mine (*or* ·min) fabric
et cet·era and so on

et·cet·eras (*plural noun*)
extra things
etch
etch·ant etching acid
etch·er
etch·ing
eter·nal
eter·nal·ity (*or* ·ness)
eter·nali·za·tion (*or*
eter·ni·, ·sa·tion)
eter·nal·ize (*or* eter·nize,
·ise)
eter·nal·ly
eter·nity (*plural* ·nities)
ete·sian meteorology term
ethane
ethane·di·ol
etha·nol
eth·ene *variant of* ethylene
ether anaesthetic
ether (*or* aether)
hypothetical medium
ethe·real
ethe·real·ity (*or* ·ness)
ethe·reali·za·tion (*or*
·sa·tion)
ethe·real·ize (*or* ·ise)
ethe·real·ly
ether·ic
etheri·fi·ca·tion
etheri·fy (·fies, ·fy·ing,
·fied)
etheri·za·tion (*or* ·sa·tion)
ether·ize (*or* ·ise)
ether·iz·er (*or* ·is·er)
eth·ic
ethi·cal
ethi·cal·ly
ethi·cal·ness (*or* ·cali·ty)
ethi·cist
ethi·cize (*or* ·cise)
eth·ics
Ethio·pia
Ethio·pian
Ethio·pic
eth·moid facial bone
eth·moi·dal
eth·narch Roman ruler
eth·nar·chy (*plural* ·chies)
eth·nic (*or* ·ni·cal)
eth·ni·cal·ly
eth·no·bota·ny botanical
folklore
eth·no·cen·tric
eth·no·cen·tri·cal·ly

eth·no·cen·tric·ity
eth·no·cen·trism belief in
group's superiority
eth·no·gen·ic
eth·nog·enist
eth·nog·eny origin of races
eth·nog·ra·pher
eth·no·graph·ic (*or*
·graphi·cal)
eth·no·graphi·cal·ly
eth·nog·ra·phy
anthropology term
eth·no·log·ic (*or* ·logi·cal)
eth·nolo·gist
eth·nol·ogy study of races;
compare ethology
etho·log·ic (*or* ·logi·cal)
etho·logi·cal·ly
etholo·gist
ethol·ogy study of animal
behaviour; *compare*
ethnology
etho·none chemical
compound
ethos
eth·ox·ide
eth·oxy·ethane
ethyl
eth·yl·ate
eth·yla·tion
eth·yl·ene (*or* eth·ene)
eth·yl·enic
ethyl·ic
ethyne chemical compound
etio·late
etio·la·tion
eti·ol·ogy US *spelling of*
aetiology
eti·quette
Etna
Eton
Eto·nian
Etru·ria ancient Italian
country
Etrus·can (*or* Etru·rian)
étude musical composition
étui needle case
ety·mo·logi·cal (*or* ·log·ic)
ety·molo·gist
ety·mol·ogy (*plural*
·ogies) study of words;
compare entomology
ety·mon (*plural* ·mons *or*
·ma) original word form
Etzel legendary king

eubac·te·ria (*sing.* ·rium)
Euboea Greek island
Euboean
eucaine anaesthetic
euca·lyp·tol (*or* ·tole)
essential oil
euca·lyp·tus (*or* ·lypt;
plural ·tuses, ·ti *or*
·lypts)
eucha·ris plant
Eucha·rist sacrament
Eucha·ris·tic (*or* ·ti·cal)
Eucha·ris·ti·cal·ly
euchlo·rine (*or* ·rin)
explosive gas
euchre US card game
euchro·mat·ic
euchro·ma·tin chromosome
part
Euclid·ean (*or* ·ian)
eudemon benevolent spirit
eudemo·nia (*or*
eudaemo·) happiness
eudemon·ic (*or*
eudaemon·)
eudemon·ics (*or*
eudaemon·)
eudemon·ism (*or*
eudaemon·)
eudemon·is·ti·cal·ly (*or*
eudaemon·)
eudi·om·eter chemistry
term
eudio·met·ric (*or* ·ri·cal)
eudio·met·ri·cal·ly
eudi·om·etry
eugen·ic (*or* eugeni·cal)
eugeni·cal·ly
eugeni·cist
eugen·ics
eugenol essential oil
euglena protozoan
euhe·mer·ism study of
myths
euhe·mer·ist
euhe·mer·is·tic
euhe·mer·is·ti·cal·ly
euhe·mer·ize (*or* ·ise)
eula·chon (*or* ·chan;
plural ·chons, ·chon *or*
·chans, ·chan) fish
eulo·gia holy bread
eulo·gist (*or* ·giz·er,
·gis·er)
eulo·gis·tic (*or* ·ti·cal)
eulo·gis·ti·cal·ly

eulo·gize (or ·gise)
eulogy (plural eulogies)
Eumeni·des Greek Furies
eunuch
euony·mus (or evony·)
  tree
eupa·to·rium plant
eupat·rid Greek landowner
eupep·sia (or ·sy) good
  digestion
eupep·tic
euphau·si·id crustacean
euphemism inoffensive
  word; compare euphuism
euphemist
euphemis·tic (or ·ti·cal)
euphemis·ti·cal·ly
euphemize (or
  euphemise)
euphemiz·er (or
  euphemis·er)
euphon·ic (or
  euphoni·cal)
euphoni·cal·ly
eupho·ni·ous
eupho·ni·ous·ly
eupho·ni·ous·ness
eupho·nium musical
  instrument
eupho·nize (or ·nise)
eupho·ny (plural ·nies)
  pleasing sound
euphor·bia plant
euphor·bia·ceous
eupho·ria elation
eupho·ri·ant
euphor·ic
euphori·cal·ly
eupho·tic ecology term
euphra·sy (plural ·sies)
  plant
Euphra·tes Asian river
euphroe (or uphroe)
  nautical term
Euphrosyne Greek goddess
euphuism prose style;
  compare euphemism
euphu·ist
euphu·is·tic (or ·ti·cal)
euphu·is·ti·cal·ly
euplas·tic healing quickly
euploid biology term
eup·noea (US ·nea)
  normal breathing
eup·noe·ic (US ·ne·)

Eura·sia
Eura·sian
Eur·at·om European
  Atomic Energy
  Commission
Eure French department
Eure-et-Loir French
  department
eureka
eurhyth·mic (or ·mi·cal)
eurhyth·mics
eurhyth·my
euri·pus (plural ·pi)
  channel
Euroc·ly·don biblical wind
Euro·com·mun·ism
Euro·crat EEC
  administrator
Euro·dol·lar
Euro·mar·ket (or ·mart)
Eu·ro·pa satellite of Jupiter
Europa mythological
  character
Europe
Euro·pean
Euro·pean·ism
Euro·peani·za·tion (or
  ·sa·tion)
Euro·pean·ize (or ·ise)
euro·pium chemical element
Euro·poort Dutch port
Euro·vis·ion broadcasting
  network
Eurus mythological wind
Eurydice dryad
euryp·ter·id extinct animal
eury·ther·mal (or ·mic,
  ·mous) ecology term
eury·trop·ic ecology term
euspo·ran·gi·ate botany
  term
Eusta·chian tube anatomy
  term
eusta·sy
eustat·ic geology term
eustati·cal·ly
eutec·tic (or ·toid) physics
  term
Euterpe Greek Muse
eutha·na·sia
euthen·ics environmental
  study
euthen·ist
euthe·rian zoology term
eutroph·ic ecology term
eutrophi·ca·tion

eux·enite mineral
evacu·ant
evacu·ate
evacu·ation
evacu·ative
evacu·ator
evac·uee
evad·able (or ·ible)
evade
evad·er
evad·ing·ly
evagi·nate turn inside out
evagi·na·tion
evalu·ate
evalu·ation
evalu·ative
evalu·ator
eva·nesce fade gradually
eva·nes·cence
eva·nes·cent
evan·gel gospel
evan·geli·cal
evan·geli·cal·ism
evan·geli·cal·ly
evan·gelism
evan·gelist
evan·gelis·tic
evan·gelis·ti·cal·ly
evan·geli·za·tion (or
  ·sa·tion)
evan·gelize (or ·gelise)
evan·geliz·er (or ·gelis·er)
Ev·ans·ville US city
evapo·rabil·ity
evapo·rable
evapo·rate
evapo·ra·tion
evapo·ra·tive
evapo·ra·tor
evapo·rim·eter (or ·rom·)
evapo·rite rock
evapo·tran·spi·ra·tion
eva·sion
eva·sive
eva·sive·ness
eve
evec·tion astronomy term
evec·tion·al
even
even-handed
even-handed·ness
eve·ning
even·ness
evens betting term
even·song

event
even-tempered
event·ful
event·ful·ly
event·ful·ness
even·tide
even·tual
even·tu·al·ity (*plural*
·ities)
even·tu·al·ly
even·tu·ate result in
even·tua·tion
ever
Ev·er·est
Ever·glades Florida region
ever·green
ever·lasting
ever·lasting·ness
ever·more
ever·sible
ever·sion
evert turn inside out
evert·or muscle
every
every·body
every·day
Every·man medieval play
every·one
every·thing
every·where
Eve·sham
evict
evic·tion
evic·tor
evi·dence
evi·dent
evi·den·tial
evi·den·tial·ly
evi·dent·ly
evil
evil·doer
evil·doing
evil·ly
evil-minded
evil-minded·ness
evil·ness
evince
evin·cible
evin·cive
evis·cer·ate disembowel
evis·cera·tion
evis·cera·tor
evo·cable
evo·ca·tion
evoca·tive

evoca·tive·ness
evo·ca·tor biology term
evoke
evok·er
evo·lute geometry term
evo·lu·tion
evo·lu·tion·ary (*or* ·al)
evo·lu·tion·ism
evo·lu·tion·ist
evo·lu·tion·is·tic
evolv·able
evolve
evolve·ment
evolv·er
evony·mus *variant spelling*
of euonymus
ev·zone Greek soldier
ewe
ewe-neck
ewer
ex
ex·ac·er·bate aggravate
ex·ac·er·bat·ing·ly
ex·ac·er·ba·tion
ex·act
ex·act·able
ex·act·ing
ex·act·ing·ness
ex·ac·tion
ex·acti·tude
ex·act·ly
ex·act·ness
ex·ac·tor (*or* ·ter)
ex·ag·ger·ate
ex·ag·ger·at·ed
ex·ag·ger·at·ed·ly
ex·ag·ger·at·ing·ly
ex·ag·gera·tion
ex·ag·gera·tive (*or* ·tory)
ex·ag·gera·tor
ex·alt
ex·al·ta·tion
ex·alt·ed
ex·alt·ed·ly
ex·alt·ed·ness
ex·alt·er
exam
exa·men examination of
conscience
ex·am·in·able
ex·ami·na·tion
ex·ami·na·tion·al
ex·am·ine
ex·ami·nee
ex·am·in·er

ex·am·ple
ex·ani·mate
ex·ani·ma·tion
ex·an·thema (*or* ·them;
plural ·thema·ta,
·themas, *or* ·thems)
rash
ex·an·thema·tous (*or*
·themat·ic)
exa·rate entomology term
ex·arch Eastern bishop;
botany term
ex·arch·al
ex·arch·ate (*or* ·ar·chy;
plural ·ates *or* ·chies)
ex·as·per·ate
ex·as·per·at·ed·ly
ex·as·per·at·er
ex·as·per·at·ing·ly
ex·as·pera·tion
Ex·cali·bur magic sword
ex ca·thedra *Latin* with
authority
ex·cau·date tailless
ex·ca·vate
ex·ca·va·tion
ex·ca·va·tor
ex·ceed
ex·ceed·able
ex·ceed·er
ex·ceed·ing·ly
ex·cel (·cel·ling, ·celled)
ex·cel·lence
Ex·cel·len·cy (*or* ·lence;
plural ·cies *or* ·lences)
title
ex·cel·lent
ex·cel·si·or
ex·cept
ex·cept·able
ex·cept·ing
ex·cep·tion
ex·cep·tion·able
objectionable
ex·cep·tion·able·ness
ex·cep·tion·al very good
ex·cep·tion·al·ity
excep·tion·al·ly
ex·cep·tion·al·ness
ex·cep·tive
ex·cerpt book extract;
compare exert; exsert
ex·cerpt·er (*or* ·cerp·tor)
ex·cerpt·ible
ex·cerp·tion

ex·cess
ex·ces·sive
ex·ces·sive·ly
ex·ces·sive·ness
ex·change
ex·change·abil·ity
ex·change·able
ex·chang·er
Ex·cheq·uer Treasury
ex·cipi·ent medical term
ex·cis·able
ex·cise
ex·cise·man (*plural* ·men)
ex·ci·sion
ex·cit·abil·ity (*or* ·able·ness)
ex·cit·able
ex·cit·ant
ex·ci·ta·tion
ex·cita·tive (*or* ·tory)
ex·cite
ex·cit·ed
ex·cit·ed·ly
ex·cit·ed·ness
ex·cite·ment
ex·cit·er oscillator
ex·cit·ing
ex·cit·ing·ly
ex·ci·ton chemistry term
ex·ci·tor nerve
ex·claim
ex·claim·er
ex·cla·ma·tion
ex·cla·ma·tion·al
ex·clama·to·ri·ly
ex·clama·tory
ex·claus·tra·tion release of nun or monk
ex·clave
ex·clo·sure
ex·clud·abil·ity
ex·clud·able (*or* ·ible)
ex·clude
ex·clud·er
ex·clu·sion
ex·clu·sion·ary
ex·clu·sion·ist
ex·clu·sive
ex·clu·sive·ness (*or* ·sivi·ty)
ex·cogi·tate devise
ex·cog·ita·tion
ex·cogi·ta·tive
ex·cogi·ta·tor
ex·com·muni·cable

ex·com·muni·cate
ex·com·mu·ni·ca·tion
ex·com·mu·ni·ca·tive (*or* ·tory)
ex·com·mu·ni·ca·tor
ex·co·ri·ate
ex·co·ria·tion
ex·cre·ment
ex·cre·men·tal (*or* ·ti·tious)
ex·cres·cence
ex·cres·cen·cy (*plural* ·cies)
ex·cres·cent
ex·cre·ta
ex·cre·tal
ex·crete
ex·cret·er
ex·cre·tion
ex·cre·tive
ex·cre·tory
ex·cru·ci·ate
ex·cru·ci·at·ing
ex·cru·ci·at·ing·ly
ex·cru·cia·tion
ex·cul·pable
ex·cul·pate vindicate
ex·cul·pa·tion
ex·cul·pa·tory
ex·cur·rent flowing outwards
ex·cur·sion
ex·cur·sion·ist
ex·cur·sive
ex·cur·sive·ness
ex·cur·sus (*plural* ·suses *or* ·sus) digression
ex·cus·able
ex·cus·able·ness
ex·cus·ably
ex·cusa·tory
ex·cuse
ex-directory (*adj*)
ex·eat leave of absence
ex·ecrable
ex·ecrable·ness
ex·ecrate loathe
ex·ecra·tion
ex·ecra·tive (*or* ·tory)
ex·ecut·able
ex·ecu·tant
ex·ecute
ex·ecut·er one who executes something; *compare* executor

ex·ecu·tion
ex·ecu·tion·er
ex·ecu·tive
ex·ecu·tor trustee of will; *compare* executer
ex·ecu·to·rial
ex·ecu·tor·ship
ex·ecu·tory legal term
ex·ecu·trix (*plural* ·tri·ces *or* ·trixes) female executor
ex·edra continuous bench
ex·egesis (*plural* ·egeses) Bible interpretation
ex·egete (*or* ·egetist)
ex·eget·ic (*or* ·egeti·cal)
ex·egeti·cal·ly
ex·eget·ics
ex·em·plar
ex·em·pla·ri·ly
ex·em·pla·ri·ness
ex·em·pla·ry
ex·em·pli·fi·able
ex·em·pli·fi·ca·tion
ex·em·pli·fi·ca·tive
ex·em·pli·fi·er
ex·em·pli·fy (·fies, ·fy·ing, ·fied)
ex·em·pli gra·tia *Latin* for the sake of example
ex·em·plum (*plural* ·pla) example
ex·empt
ex·empt·ible
ex·emp·tion
ex·en·ter·ate remove surgically
ex·en·tera·tion
ex·equa·tur official authorization
ex·equies funeral rites
ex·er·cis·able
ex·er·cise train; use; *compare* exorcise
ex·er·cis·er
ex·ergual
ex·ergue date on coin
ex·ert make effort; *compare* excerpt; exsert
ex·er·tion
ex·er·tive
Ex·eter
ex·eunt *Latin* they leave
ex·fo·li·ate
ex·fo·lia·tion

ex·fo·lia·tive
ex gra·tia *Latin* gratuitous
ex·hal·able
ex·hal·ant
ex·ha·la·tion
ex·hale
ex·haust
ex·haust·er
ex·haust·ibil·ity
ex·haust·ible
ex·haus·tion
ex·haus·tive
ex·haust·ive·ness
ex·hib·it
ex·hi·bi·tion
ex·hi·bi·tion·er scholarship
  student
ex·hi·bi·tion·ism
ex·hi·bi·tion·ist
ex·hi·bi·tion·is·tic
ex·hibi·tive illustrative
ex·hibi·tor (*or* ·hib·it·er)
ex·hibi·tory
ex·hil·ar·ant
ex·hila·rate
ex·hil·arat·ing·ly
ex·hila·ra·tion
ex·hila·ra·tive (*or* ·tory)
ex·hila·ra·tor
ex·hort
ex·hor·ta·tion
ex·hor·ta·tive (*or* ·tory)
ex·hort·er
ex·hu·ma·tion
ex·hume
ex·hum·er
exi·gen·cy (*or* exi·gence;
  plural ·cies *or* ·gences)
exi·gent urgent
exi·gible required
exi·gu·ity (*or*
  ex·igu·ous·ness)
ex·igu·ous meagre
ex·ile
ex·il·ic (*or* ·ian)
ex·ist
ex·ist·ence
ex·ist·ent
ex·is·ten·tial
ex·is·ten·tial·ism
ex·is·ten·tial·ist
ex·is·ten·tial·ly
exit
exi·tance physics term

ex li·bris *Latin* from the
  library of
Ex·moor
exo·bi·olo·gist
exo·bi·ol·ogy astrobiology
exo·cen·tric linguistics term
exo·crine having a duct;
  compare endocrine
exo·derm *variant of*
  ectoderm
exo·don·tics dentistry
exo·don·tist
Exo·dus Old Testament
  book
exo·dus
exo·en·zyme
exo·er·gic energy-emitting;
  compare endoergic
ex of·fi·cio *Latin* by right of
  office
ex·oga·mous (*or*
  exo·gam·ic)
ex·oga·my marrying into
  another tribe
ex·og·enous
ex·on·er·ate
ex·on·era·tion
ex·on·era·tive
ex·on·era·tor
exo·nym foreigner's version
  of placename
exo·pep·ti·dase enzyme
ex·oph·thal·mic
ex·oph·thal·mos (*or* ·mus,
  ·mia) protrusion of
  eyeball
exo·rabil·ity
exo·rable moved by
  pleading
ex·or·bi·tance
ex·or·bi·tant
ex·or·cise (*or* ·cize) expel
  evil spirit; *compare*
  exercise
ex·or·cis·er (*or* ·ciz·er)
ex·or·cism
ex·or·cist
ex·or·dial
ex·or·dium (*plural* ·diums
  or ·dia) beginning of
  speech
exo·skel·etal
exo·skel·eton
ex·os·mo·sis biology term
ex·os·mot·ic (*or*
  ex·os·mic)

exo·sphere atmospheric
  layer
exo·spore botany term
exo·spor·ous
ex·os·to·sis (*plural* ·ses)
  outgrowth from bone
exo·ter·ic comprehensible;
  compare esoteric
exo·teri·cal·ly
exo·teri·cism
exo·ther·mic (*or* ·mal)
  heat-emitting; *compare*
  endothermic
exo·ther·mi·cal·ly (*or*
  ·ther·mal·ly)
ex·ot·ic
ex·oti·ca
ex·oti·cal·ly
ex·oti·cism
ex·ot·ic·ness
exo·tox·ic
exo·tox·in
ex·pand
ex·pand·able (*or* ·ible)
ex·pand·er
ex·panse
ex·pan·sibil·ity
ex·pan·sible
ex·pan·sile
ex·pan·sion
ex·pan·sion·ary
ex·pan·sion·ism
ex·pan·sion·ist
ex·pan·sion·is·tic
ex·pan·sive
ex·pan·sive·ness
ex par·te legal term
ex·pa·ti·ate enlarge upon;
  compare expiate
ex·pa·tia·tion
ex·pa·tia·tor
ex·pat·ri·ate
ex·pat·ria·tion
ex·pect
ex·pect·able
ex·pec·tan·cy (*or* ·tance;
  plural ·cies *or* ·tances)
ex·pec·tant
ex·pec·ta·tion
ex·pec·ta·tive
ex·pec·to·rant
ex·pec·to·rate
ex·pec·to·ra·tion spitting
ex·pec·to·ra·tor

ex·pedi·en·cy (*or* ·ence;
 plural ·cies *or* ·ences)
ex·pedi·ent
ex·pedi·en·tial
ex·pedite
ex·pedit·er (*or* ·pedi·tor)
ex·pedi·tion
ex·pedi·tion·ary
ex·pedi·tious
ex·pedi·tious·ness
ex·pel (·pel·ling, ·pelled)
ex·pel·lable
ex·pel·lant (*or* ·lent)
ex·pel·lee
ex·pel·ler
ex·pend
ex·pend·abil·ity
ex·pend·able
ex·pend·er
ex·pendi·ture
ex·pense
ex·pen·sive
ex·pen·sive·ness
ex·peri·ence
ex·peri·en·tial
ex·peri·ment
ex·peri·men·tal
ex·peri·men·tal·ism
ex·peri·men·tal·ist
ex·peri·men·tal·ly
ex·peri·men·ta·tion
ex·peri·ment·er
ex·pert
ex·per·tise
ex·pert·ness
ex·pi·able
ex·pi·ate atone; *compare*
 expatiate
ex·pia·tion
ex·pia·tor
ex·pia·tory
ex·pi·ra·tion
ex·pira·tory of exhalation
ex·pire
ex·pir·er
ex·pi·ry (*plural* ·ries)
ex·plain
ex·plain·able
ex·plain·er
ex·pla·na·tion
ex·plana·to·ri·ly
ex·plana·tory (*or* ·tive)
ex·plant biology term
ex·plan·ta·tion
ex·pletive swear word

ex·pli·cable
ex·pli·cate explain
ex·pli·ca·tion
ex·pli·ca·tive (*or* ·tory)
ex·pli·ca·tor
ex·plic·it
ex·plic·it·ness
ex·plode
ex·plod·er
ex·ploit
ex·ploit·able (*or*
 ·ploita·tive)
ex·ploi·ta·tion
ex·plo·ra·tion
ex·plora·tory (*or* ·tive)
ex·plore
ex·plor·er
ex·plo·sion
ex·plo·sive
ex·plo·sive·ness
ex·po·nent
ex·po·nen·tial maths term
ex·po·nen·tial·ly
ex·pon·ible needing
 explanation
ex·port
ex·port·abil·ity
ex·port·able
ex·por·ta·tion
ex·port·er
ex·pos·able
ex·pos·al
ex·pose
ex·po·sé exposure of
 scandal
ex·posed
ex·pos·ed·ness
ex·pos·er
ex·po·si·tion
ex·po·si·tion·al
ex·posi·tor expounder
ex·posi·to·ri·ly (*or*
 ·tive·ly)
ex·posi·tory (*or* ·tive)
ex post fac·to *Latin*
 retrospective
ex·pos·tu·late dissuade
ex·pos·tu·lat·ing·ly
ex·pos·tu·la·tion
ex·pos·tu·la·tor
ex·pos·tu·la·tory (*or* ·tive)
ex·po·sure
ex·pound
ex·pound·er
ex·press

ex·press·age conveyance by
 express
ex·press·er
ex·press·ible
ex·pres·sion
ex·pres·sion·al
ex·pres·sion·ism
ex·pres·sion·ist
ex·pres·sion·is·tic
ex·pres·sion·less
ex·pres·sive
ex·pres·sive·ness
ex·pres·siv·ity
(expresso) *incorrect spelling*
 of espresso
ex·press·way US motorway
ex·pro·pri·able
ex·pro·pri·ate
ex·pro·pria·tion
ex·pro·pria·tor
ex·pul·sion
ex·pul·sive
ex·punc·tion
ex·punge
ex·pung·er
ex·pur·gate
ex·pur·ga·tion
ex·pur·ga·tor
ex·pur·ga·tory (*or* ·to·rial)
ex·quis·ite
ex·quis·ite·ness
ex·san·gui·nate drain
 blood from
ex·san·guin·ation
ex·san·guine (*or*
 ·gui·nous)
ex·san·guin·ity
ex·scind (*or* ·sect) cut off
ex·sect cut out
ex·sec·tion
ex·sert protrude; *compare*
 excerpt; exert
ex·ser·tile
ex·ser·tion
ex·sic·cate dry
ex·sic·ca·tion
ex·sic·ca·tive
ex·sic·ca·tor
ex·stipu·late (*or*
 es·tipu·late) botany term
(extasy) *incorrect spelling of*
 ecstasy
ex·stro·phy medical term
ex·tant surviving

ex·tem·po·ra·neous (*or*
·po·rary)
ex·tem·po·ra·neous·ness
ex·tem·po·rari·ly
ex·tem·po·rari·ness
ex·tem·po·re impromptu
ex·tem·po·ri·za·tion (*or*
·sa·tion)
ex·tem·po·rize (*or* ·rise)
ex·tem·po·riz·er (*or*
·ris·er)
ex·tend
ex·tend·ed·ness
ex·tend·er
ex·tend·ibil·ity (*or*
·abil·ity)
ex·tend·ible (*or* ·able)
ex·ten·sibil·ity (*or*
·sible·ness)
ex·ten·sible (*or* ·sile)
ex·ten·sion
ex·ten·sion·al
ex·ten·sion·al·ity (*or* ·ism)
ex·ten·sity psychology term
ex·ten·sive
ex·ten·sive·ness
ex·ten·som·eter (*or* ·sim·)
physics term
ex·ten·sor muscle
ex·tent
ex·tenu·ate
ex·tenu·at·ing·ly
ex·tenu·ation
ex·tenu·ator
ex·tenu·atory
ex·te·ri·or
ex·te·ri·ori·za·tion (*or*
·sa·tion)
ex·te·ri·or·ize (*or* ·ise)
medical term
ex·ter·mi·nable
ex·ter·mi·nate
ex·ter·mi·na·tion
ex·ter·mi·na·tive (*or*
·tory)
ex·ter·mi·na·tor
ex·tern (*or* ·terne) US
nonresident hospital
doctor
ex·ter·nal
ex·ter·nal·ism
ex·ter·nal·ist
ex·ter·nal·ity (*plural*
·ities)
ex·ter·nali·za·tion (*or*
·sa·tion)

ex·ter·nal·ize (*or* ·ise)
ex·ter·nal·ly
ex·tero·cep·tive
ex·tero·cep·tor biology
term
ex·ter·ri·to·rial
ex·ter·ri·to·ri·al·ity
ex·tinct
ex·tinc·tion
ex·tinc·tive
ex·tine (*or* ·ine) botany
term
ex·tin·guish
ex·tin·guish·able
ex·tin·guish·ant
ex·tin·guish·er
ex·tin·guish·ment
ex·tir·pate destroy
ex·tir·pa·tion
ex·tir·pa·tive
ex·tir·pa·tor
ex·tol (*US* ·toll; ·tol·ling,
·tolled)
ex·tol·ler
ex·tol·ling·ly
ex·tol·ment
ex·tort
ex·tort·er
ex·tor·tion
ex·tor·tion·able
ex·tor·tion·ary
ex·tor·tion·ate
ex·tor·tion·ist (*or* ·er)
ex·tor·tive
ex·tra
extra·ca·noni·cal outside
scripture
extra·cel·lu·lar
ex·tract
ex·tract·abil·ity (*or*
·ibil·ity)
ex·tract·able (*or* ·ible)
ex·trac·tion
ex·trac·tive
ex·trac·tor
extra·cur·ricu·lar
extra·dit·able
extra·dite
extra·di·tion
extra·dos (*plural* ·dos *or*
·doses) architecture term
extra·ga·lac·tic
extra·ju·di·cial
extra·mari·tal

extra·mun·dane outside
the world
extra·mu·ral
extra·neous
extra·neous·ness
extra·nu·clear
extraor·di·nari·ly
extraor·di·nari·ness
ex·traor·di·nary
ex·trapo·late
ex·trapo·la·tion
ex·trapo·la·tive (*or* ·tory)
ex·trapo·la·tor
extra·po·si·tion
extra·sen·so·ry
extra·ter·res·trial
extra·ter·ri·to·rial (*or*
ex·ter·)
extra·ter·ri·to·ri·al·ity
extra·uter·ine
ex·trava·gance
ex·trava·gant
ex·trava·gan·za
ex·trava·gate *Archaic* roam
ex·trava·ga·tion
ex·trava·sate exude
ex·trava·sa·tion
extra·vas·cu·lar
extra·vehicu·lar outside a
spacecraft
extra·vert *variant spelling of*
extrovert
ex·treme
ex·treme·ly
ex·treme·ness
ex·trem·ism
ex·trem·ist
ex·trem·ity (*plural* ·ities)
ex·tri·cable
ex·tri·cate
ex·tri·ca·tion
ex·trin·sic not contained
within; *compare* intrinsic
ex·trin·si·cal·ly
(extrordinary) *incorrect
spelling of* extraordinary
ex·trorse (*or* ·tror·sal)
turned outwards
extro·ver·sion (*or* extra·)
extro·ver·sive (*or* extra·)
extro·vert (*or* extra·)
extro·vert·ed (*or* extra·)
ex·trude
ex·tru·sion
ex·tru·sive

exu·ber·ance (or ·ancy)
exu·ber·ant
exu·ber·ate
exu·da·tion
exu·da·tive
ex·ude
ex·ult
ex·ult·ant
ex·ul·ta·tion
ex·ult·ing·ly
ex·ur·bia US outside
    suburbs
exu·viae shed skin
exu·vial
exu·vi·ate
exu·via·tion
ex-works excluding delivery
    cost
eyas nestling hawk
eye (eye·ing or ey·ing,
    eyed)
eye·ball

eye·bath
eye·bolt
eye·bright plant
eye·brow
eye-catcher
eye-catching
eye·cup
eyed
eye·dropper
eye·ful
eye·glass
eye·glasses US spectacles
eye·hole
eye·ing (or ey·ing)
eye·lash
eye·less
eye·let
eye·let·eer
eye·lid
eye·liner

eye-opener
eye·piece
eye·shade
eye·shot
eye·sight
eye·sore
eye·spot
eye·stalk
eye·strain
eye·tooth (plural ·teeth)
eye·wash
eye·witness
eyra animal
Eyre Canadian lake;
    Australian peninsula
ey·rie (or aerie, aery;
    plural ey·ries or aeries)
    eagle's nest; compare eerie
ey·rir (plural aurar)
    Icelandic coin

F

fa (or fah) musical note
fab
fa·ba·ceous botany term
Fa·bian
Fa·bi·an·ism
fa·ble
fa·bled
fa·bler
fab·ric
fab·ri·cate
fab·ri·ca·tion
fab·ri·ca·tive
fab·ri·ca·tor
Fab·ri·koid (Trademark)
    waterproof fabric
fabu·list teller of fables
fabu·lous
fabu·lous·ness
fa·çade (or ·cade)
face
face·able
face·bar wrestling hold
face-centred (US
    -centered) crystallogra-
    phy term
face-harden metallurgy
    term
face·less

face·less·ness
face-lift
face-off ice hockey term
face·plate lathe part
fac·er
face-saving
fac·et (verb ·et·ing, ·et·ed
    or ·et·ting, ·et·ted)
fa·cetiae witty sayings
fa·cetious
fa·cetious·ness
fa·cia variant spelling of
    fascia
fa·cial
fa·cial·ly
fa·cies (plural ·cies)
    appearance; compare
    fasces; fascia
fac·ile
fac·ile·ly
fac·ile·ness
fa·cili·tate
fa·cili·ta·tion
fa·cili·ta·tive
fa·cili·ta·tor
fa·cil·ity (plural ·ities)
fac·ing
fac·simi·le (·le·ing, ·led)

fact
fact·ful
fac·tice rubbery material
fac·tion
fac·tion·al
fac·tion·al·ism
fac·tion·al·ist
fac·tious factional; compare
    factitious
fac·tious·ness
fac·ti·tious contrived;
    compare factious; fictitious
fac·ti·tious·ness
fac·ti·tive linguistics term
fac·tor
fac·tor·abil·ity
fac·tor·able
fac·tor·age commission paid
    to factor
fac·torial
fac·to·ri·al·ly
fac·tor·ing business term
fac·tori·za·tion (or
    ·sa·tion)
fac·tor·ize (or ·ise)
fac·tor·ship
fac·to·ry (plural ·ries)
fac·to·tum

fac·tual
fac·tu·al·ism
fac·tu·al·ist
fac·tu·al·is·tic
fac·tu·al·ly
fac·tu·al·ness (or ·ity)
facu·la (plural ·lae) sun spot
facu·lar
fac·ul·ta·tive optional
fac·ul·ty (plural ·ties)
fad
fad·able
fad·di·ness
fad·dish
fad·dism
fad·dist
fad·dy (·di·er, ·di·est)
fade
fad·ed
fad·ed·ness
fade-in
fade·less
fade-out
fad·er
fadge Dialect agree
fad·ing
fae·cal (US fe·)
fae·ces (US fe·)
Fa·en·za Italian city
fae·rie (or ·ry; plural ·ries) Archaic fairyland
Fae·roes (or Fa·roes) North Atlantic islands
Faero·ese (or Faro·; plural ·ese)
faff Slang fuss
fag (fag·ging, fagged)
fa·ga·ceous botany term
fagged
fag·ging
fag·got (or esp. US fag·ot)
fag·got·ing (or esp. US fag·ot·) needlework term
fah variant spelling of fa
fahl·band rock
Fahr·en·heit temperature scale
faï·ence (or fai·) pottery
fail
fail·ing
faille fabric
fail-safe
fail·ure

fain
fai·ne·ance (or ·an·cy)
fai·né·ant (or ·ne·) idle
faint pale; collapse; compare feint
faint·er
faint·ing
faint·ing·ly
faint·ish
faint·ly
faint·ness
faints variant spelling of feints
fair just; not dark; event; compare fare
Fair·banks Alaskan city
fair·ground
fair·ing
fair·ish
fair·lead (or ·leader) nautical term
fair·ly
fair-minded
fair-minded·ness
fair·ness
fair-spoken
fair·way
fair-weather (adj)
fairy (plural fairies)
fairy·land
fairy-like
fait ac·com·pli (plural faits accomplis) French something done
faith
faith·ful
faith·ful·ly
faith·ful·ness
faith·less
faith·less·ness
Faiza·bad Afghan city; variant spelling of Fyzabad
fake
fak·er one who fakes
fa·kir (or ·qir, ·keer) holy man
fa·la refrain
Fa·lange Spanish Fascist movement
Fa·lang·ism
Fa·lan·gist
fal·ba·la gathered frill
fal·cate (or ·ci·form) sickle-shaped
fal·chion sword

fal·con
fal·con·er
fal·con·et small falcon
fal·coni·form
fal·con·ry
fal·deral (or fal·derol, fol·derol) trifle
fald·stool bishop's seat
Fa·lerii ancient Italian city
Fa·lis·can language
Fal·kirk Scottish town
Falk·land Is·lands
fall (fall·ing, fell, fall·en)
fal·la·cious
fal·la·cious·ness
fal·la·cy (plural ·cies)
fal·lal ornament
fal·lal·ery
fall·en
fall·er
fall·fish (plural ·fish, ·fishes)
fal·libil·ity (or ·lible·ness)
fal·lible
fal·li·bly
Fal·lo·pian tube anatomy term
fall·out
fal·low
fal·low·ness
Fal·mouth Cornish port
false
false-card bridge term
false·hood
false·ly
false·ness
fal·set·to (plural ·tos)
false·work framework
fal·sies false breasts
fal·si·fi·able
fal·si·fi·ca·tion
fal·si·fi·er
fal·si·fy (·fies, ·fy·ing, ·fied)
fal·sity (plural ·sities)
falt·boat collapsible boat
fal·ter
fal·ter·er
fal·ter·ing·ly
Fa·lun Swedish city
Fa·ma·gu·sta Cypriot port
fame
fa·mil·ial
fa·mili·ar
fa·mili·ar·ity (plural ·ities)

fa·mil·iari·za·tion (*or*
·sa·tion)
fa·mil·iar·ize (*or* ·ise)
fa·mil·iar·iz·er (*or* ·is·er)
fa·mili·ar·ness
Fami·list member of sect
fa·mille Chinese porcelain
fami·ly (*plural* ·lies)
fam·ine
fam·ish
fam·ish·ment
fa·mous
fa·mous·ness
famu·lus (*plural* ·li)
sorcerer's attendant
fan (fan·ning, fanned)
Fana·ga·lo (*or* ·ka·lo)
African language
fa·nat·ic
fa·nati·cal
fa·nati·cal·ly
fa·nati·cism
fa·nati·cize (*or* ·cise)
fan·cied
fan·ci·er
fan·ci·ful
fan·ci·ful·ly
fan·ci·ful·ness
fan·ci·ly
fan·ci·ness
fan·cy (*adj* ·ci·er, ·ci·est;
noun, plural ·cies; *verb*
·cies, ·cy·ing, ·cied)
fancy-free
fancy·work
fan·dan·gle ornament
fan·dan·go (*plural* ·gos)
dance
fan·fare
fang
fanged
fan·go mud from thermal
springs
fan·ion surveyor's flag
fan·jet jet engine
fan·kle *Scot* entangle
fan·light
fanned
fan·ner
fan·ning
fan·ny (*plural* ·nies) *Slang*
female genitals
fan·on vestment
fan·tail
fan-tailed

fan-tan game
fan·ta·sia
fan·ta·size (*or* ·sise)
fan·tast visionary
fan·tas·tic (*or* ·ti·cal)
fan·ta·sy (*or* phan·; *noun,
plural* ·sies; *verb* ·sies,
·sy·ing, ·sied)
Fan·ti (*plural* ·tis *or* ·ti)
Ghanaian people
fan·toc·ci·ni marionettes
far (far·ther *or* fur·ther,
far·thest *or* fur·thest)
far·ad unit
fara·day unit
fa·rad·ic physics term
fara·dism medical use of
electricity
fara·di·za·tion (*or*
·sa·tion)
fara·dize (*or* ·dise)
fara·diz·er (*or* ·dis·er)
far·an·dole dance
far·away
farce
far·ceur (*fem* ·ceuse) farce
writer
far·ci stuffed
far·ci·cal
far·ci·cal·ity (*or* ·ness)
far·ci·cal·ly
far·cy (*plural* ·cies) animal
disease
far·del bundle
fare payment; food; to
manage; *compare* fair
Fare·ham Hampshire town
far·er
fare·well
far-fetched
far-flung
fa·ri·na flour
fari·na·ceous containing
starch
fari·nose flourlike
farl (*or* farle) cake
farm
farm·able
farm·er
farm·house
farm·ing
farm·land
farm·stead
farm·yard

Farn·bor·ough Hampshire
town
far·nesol chemical
compound
far·ness
Farn·ham Surrey town
faro card game
Fa·roes *variant spelling of*
Faeroes
Faro·ese *variant spelling of*
Faeroese
far-off
fa·rouche sullen
far·ragi·nous
far·ra·go (*plural* ·goes)
hotchpotch
far-reaching
far·ri·er
far·ri·ery (*plural* ·eries)
far·row
far-seeing
far-sighted
far-sighted·ly
far-sighted·ness
fart
far·ther (*or* fur·) more
distant; *compare* further
farther·most
far·thest (*or* fur·)
far·thing
far·thin·gale hoop under
skirt
fart·lek sports term
fas·ces (*plural noun; sing.*
·cies) Roman insignia;
compare facies
fas·cia (*or* fa·cia; *plural*
·ciae) flat surface; fibrous
tissue; *compare* facies
fas·cial (*or* fa·cial)
fas·ci·ate (*or* ·at·ed)
fas·cia·tion botany term
fas·ci·cle bundle
fas·ci·cled
fas·cicu·lar (*or* ·late)
fas·cicu·la·tion
fas·ci·cule instalment
fas·ci·cu·lus (*plural* ·li)
fas·ci·nate
fas·ci·nat·ed·ly
fas·ci·nat·ing
fas·ci·na·tion
fas·ci·na·tive
fas·cine bundle of sticks
fas·cism

fas·cist
fa·scis·tic
fa·scis·ti·cal·ly
fash *Scot* worry
fash·ion
fash·ion·able
fash·ion·ably
fash·ion·able·ness
fash·ion·er
Fa·sho·da Sudanese town
fast
fast·back car
fast-breeder nuclear reactor
fas·ten
fas·ten·er
fas·ten·ing
fast·er
fas·tidi·ous
fas·tidi·ous·ness
fas·tigi·ate (*or* ·at·ed)
 biology term
fast·ness
fat (fat·ter, fat·test)
fa·tal
fa·tal·ism
fa·tal·ist
fa·tal·is·tic
fa·tal·is·ti·cal·ly
fa·tal·ity (*plural* ·ities)
fa·tal·ly
fat·back pork fat
fate
fat·ed
fate·ful
fate·ful·ly
fate·ful·ness
Fates Greek goddesses
fat·head
fa·ther
father·hood
father-in-law (*plural*
 fathers-)
father·land
fa·ther·less
father·like
fa·ther·li·ness
fa·ther·ly
fath·om
fath·om·able
fath·om·er
Fa·thom·eter
 (*Trademark*)
fath·om·less
fa·tid·ic (*or* ·tidi·cal)
 prophetic

fati·gabil·ity (·gable·ness)
fa·tig·able
fa·tigue (·tigu·ing,
 ·tigued)
fat·ling fattened young
 animal
fat·ness
Fat·shan Chinese city
fat·so (*plural* ·sos *or*
 ·soes)
fat-soluble
fat·ted
fat·ten
fat·ten·able
fat·ten·er
fat·ti·ly
fat·ti·ness
fat·tish
fat·ty (*adj* ·ti·er, ·ti·est;
 noun, plural ·ties)
fa·tui·tous fatuous; *compare*
 fortuitous
fa·tu·ity (*plural* ·ities)
fatu·ous
fatu·ous·ness
fau·bourg French suburb
fau·cal (*or* ·cial)
fau·ces (*plural* ·ces)
 anatomy term
fau·cet *US* tap
faugh exclamation
fault
fault-finder
fault-finding
faulti·ly
faulti·ness
fault·less
fault·less·ness
faulty (faulti·er,
 faulti·est)
faun Roman deity; *compare*
 fawn
fau·na (*plural* ·nas *or*
 ·nae) animals
fau·nal
Faust (*or* Faustus)
 legendary magician
Faust·ian
faute de mieux *French*
 lacking better
fau·teuil armchair
Fauv·ism art movement
Fauv·ist
faux pas (*plural* faux
 pas)

fa·veo·late honeycombed
fa·vo·nian of the west wind
fa·vour (*US* ·vor)
fa·vour·able (*US* ·vor)
fa·vour·ably (*US* ·vor·)
fa·vour·able·ness (*US*
 ·vor·)
fa·vour·er (*US* ·vor·)
fa·vour·ing·ly (*US* ·vor·)
fa·vour·ite (*US* ·vor·)
fa·vour·it·ism (*US* ·vor·)
Fav·rile glass
fa·vus skin disease
fawn animal; colour; cringe;
 compare faun
fawn·er
fawn·ing·ly
fax facsimile transmission
fay fairy; *compare* fey
fay·al·ite mineral
faze *US* disconcert
fe·al·ty (*plural* ·ties)
 feudal loyalty
fear
fear·er
fear·ful
fear·ful·ly
fear·ful·ness
fear·less
fear·less·ness
fear·nought (*or* ·naught)
 fabric
fear·some
fear·some·ly
fear·some·ness
fea·sibil·ity (*or*
 ·sible·ness)
fea·sible
fea·sibly
feast
feast·er
feat exploit; *compare* feet
feath·er
feather·bed (·bedding,
 ·bedded)
feather·bedding
 overmanning
feather·brain
feather·brained
feather·edge
feath·er·ing
feather·stitch
feather-veined
feather-weight
feath·ery

fea·ture
feature-length (*adj*)
fea·ture·less
fea·ture·less·ness
feaze nautical term
fe·bric·ity
feb·ri·fa·cient
fe·brif·ic (*or* ·brif·er·ous)
fe·brifu·gal
feb·ri·fuge fever-reducing
  drug
fe·brile feverish
fe·bril·ity
Feb·ru·ary (*plural* ·aries)
fe·cal *US spelling of* faecal
fe·ces *US spelling of* faeces
fe·cit *Latin* made it
feck·less
feck·less·ness
fecu·la (*plural* ·lae) starch
fecu·lence
fecu·lent filthy
fe·cund fertile
fe·cun·date
fe·cun·da·tion
fe·cun·da·tor
fe·cun·da·tory
fe·cun·dity
fed
fe·da·yee (*plural* ·yeen)
  Arab commando
fed·er·al
fed·er·al·ly
fed·er·al·ism
fed·er·al·ist
fed·er·al·is·tic
fed·er·ali·za·tion (*or*
  ·sa·tion)
fed·er·al·ize (*or* ·ise)
fed·er·ate
fed·era·tion
fed·era·tive
fe·do·ra hat
fee (fee·ing, feed)
fee·ble
feeble-minded
feeble-minded·ly
feeble-minded·ness
fee·ble·ness
feed (feed·ing, fed)
feed·able
feed·back
feed·bag
feed·er
feed·lot

feel (feel·ing, felt)
feel·er
feel·ing
feet *plural of* foot; *compare*
  feat
feeze *Dialect* beat
feign
feign·er
feign·ing·ly
feint mock action; printing
  term; *compare* faint
feints (*or* faints) whisky
  residue
feld·spar (*or* fel·spar)
  mineral
feld·spath·ic (*or* fel·)
feld·spath·ose (*or* fel·)
fe·li·cif·ic making happy
fe·lici·tate
fe·lici·ta·tion
fe·lici·ta·tor
fe·lici·tous apt
fe·lici·tous·ness
fe·lic·ity (*plural* ·ities)
fe·lid animal
fe·line
fe·lin·ity (*or* ·line·ness)
fell
fell·able
fel·lah (*plural* ·lahs,
  ·la·hin, *or* ·la·heen)
  Arab peasant
fel·la·tio oral sex
fell·er
fell·monger animal skin
  dealer
fel·loe (*or* ·ly; *plural* ·loes
  or ·lies) wheel segment
fel·low
fel·low·ship
felo de se (*plural*
  fe·lo·nes de se *or* fe·los
  de se) suicide
fel·on
fe·lo·ni·ous
fe·lo·ni·ous·ness
fel·on·ry (*plural* ·ries)
felo·ny (*plural* ·nies)
fel·site (*or* ·stone) rock
fel·sit·ic
felt
felt·ing
fe·luc·ca boat
fel·wort plant
fe·male

fe·male·ness
feme woman (*in legal
  contexts*)
femi·nine
femi·nine·ly
femi·nin·ity
femi·nism
femi·nist
femi·ni·za·tion (*or*
  ·sa·tion)
femi·nize (*or* ·nise)
femme de cham·bre
  (*plural* femmes de
  cham·bre) chambermaid
femme fa·tale (*plural*
  femmes fa·tales)
  seductive woman
femo·ral of the thigh
fe·mur (*plural* ·murs *or*
  femo·ra) thigh bone
fen
fence
fenc·er
fenc·ing
fend
fend·er
fend·ered
fen·es·tel·la (*plural* ·lae)
  wall niche
fe·nes·tra (*plural* ·trae)
  biology term
fe·nes·tral
fe·nes·trat·ed (*or* ·trate)
  having windows
fen·es·tra·tion
Fe·nian Irish revolutionary
fen·nec fox
fen·nel
fennel·flower
fen·ny marshy
Fenrir (*or* Fenris,
  Fenriswolf) mythological
  wolf
Fens
fenu·greek plant
feoff *variant spelling of* fief
fe·ral (*or* ·rine) wild
fer·bam fungicide
fer-de-lance snake
fer·etory (*plural* ·etories)
  shrine
Fer·ga·na Asian region
fe·ria (*plural* ·rias *or*
  ·riae) weekday
fe·rial
fe·rine *variant of* feral

fer·ity wildness
Fer·man·agh Northern Irish county
fer·ma·ta (*plural* **·tas** *or* **·te**) musical term
fer·ment undergo fermentation; *compare* foment
fer·ment·abil·ity
fer·ment·able
fer·men·ta·tion
fer·menta·tive
fer·menta·tive·ness
fer·ment·er
fer·mi unit
fer·mi·on particle
fer·mium radioactive element
fern
fern·ery (*plural* **·eries**)
ferny
fe·ro·cious
fe·roc·ity (*or* **·ro·cious·ness**)
Fer·ra·ra Italian city
fer·rate chemistry term
fer·reous containing iron
fer·ret
fer·ret·ing silk tape
fer·ret·er
fer·rety
fer·ri·age
fer·ric chemistry term
fer·ri·cy·an·ic acid
fer·ri·cya·nide
fer·rif·er·ous producing iron
fer·ri·mag·net·ic
fer·ri·mag·net·ism
Ferris wheel fairground wheel
fer·rite ceramic
fer·ri·tin protein
fer·ro·cene chemical compound
fer·ro·chro·mium (*or* **fer·ro·chrome**)
fer·ro·con·crete
fer·ro·cy·an·ic acid
fer·ro·cya·nide
fer·ro·elec·tric
fer·ro·elec·tri·cal·ly
fer·ro·elec·tric·ity
fer·ro·mag·ne·sian
fer·ro·mag·net·ic

fer·ro·mag·net·ism
fer·ro·man·ga·nese
fer·ro·sili·con
fer·ro·type photography term
fer·rous
fer·ru·gi·nous containing iron
fer·rule (*or* **fer·ule**) metal cap; *compare* ferule
fer·ry (*noun, plural* **·ries**; *verb* **·ries**, **·ry·ing**, **·ried**)
fer·tile
fer·til·ity (*or* **·tile·ness**)
fer·ti·liz·able (*or* **·lis·able**)
fer·ti·li·za·tion (*or* **·sa·tion**)
fer·ti·lize (*or* **·lise**)
fer·ti·liz·er (*or* **·lis·er**)
feru·la (*plural* **·las** *or* **·lae**) plant
feru·la·ceous
fer·ule flat cane; *compare* ferrule
fer·ven·cy
fer·vent (*or* **·vid**)
fer·vent·ly (*or* **·vid·ly**)
fer·vid variant of fervent
fer·vour (*US* **·vor**)
fes·cue grass
fesse (*or* **fess**) heraldry term
fes·tal festive
fes·ter
fes·ti·na·tion quickening of gait
fes·ti·val
fes·tive
fes·tive·ly
fes·tive·ness
fes·tiv·ity (*plural* **·ities**)
fes·toon
fes·toon·ery
fest·schrift (*plural* **·schrift·en** *or* **·schrifts**) commemorative writings
feta cheese
fe·tal (*or* **foe·**)
fe·ta·tion (*or* **foe·**) pregnancy
fetch
fetch·er
fetch·ing
fête (*or* **fete**)

fe·tial (*plural* **fe·tia·les**) Roman herald
fet·ich variant spelling of fetish
fe·ti·cid·al (*or* **foe·**)
fe·ti·cide (*or* **foe·**) destruction of fetus
fet·id (*or* **foet·**) foul-smelling
fe·tipa·rous (*or* **foe·**) of marsupial birth
fet·ish (*or* **ich**)
fet·ish·ism (*or* **ich·**)
fet·ish·ist (*or* **ich·**)
fet·lock (*or* **fetter·**) part of horse's leg
fe·tor (*or* **foe·**) stench
fet·ter
fet·ter·er
fet·ter·less
fet·tle
fet·tling refractory material
fet·tu·ci·ne (*or* **·tuc·ci·**, **tu·ci·ni**) pasta
fe·tus (*or* **foe·**; *plural* **·tuses**)
feud
feu·dal
feu·dal·ism
feu·dal·ist
feu·dal·is·tic
feu·dal·ity (*plural* **·ities**)
feu·dali·za·tion (*or* **·sa·tion**)
feu·dal·ize (*or* **·ise**)
feu·da·tory
feud·ist
feuil·le·ton review section of paper
feuil·le·ton·ism
feuil·le·ton·ist
feuil·le·ton·is·tic
fe·ver
fe·vered
fe·ver·few plant
fe·ver·ish (*or* **·ous**)
fe·ver·ish·ness
fever·wort plant
few
few·ness
fey whimsical; *compare* fay
fez (*plural* **fez·zes**)
Fez·zan Libyan region
fezzed
fia·cre carriage

fi·an·cé (*fem* ·cée)

Fi·an·na Fail Irish political party

fi·as·co (*plural* ·cos *or* ·coes)

Fiat (*Trademark*)

fiat decree

fib (fibbed, fib·bing)

fib·ber

fi·bre (*US* ·ber)

fibre·board (*US* fiber·)

fi·bred (*US* ·bered)

fibre·fill (*US* fiber·)

fibre·glass (*US* fiber·)

fibre-optic (*adj*; *US* fiber-)

fibre optics (*noun*; *US* fiber optics)

fibre·scope (*US* fiber·)

fi·bri·form

fi·bril (*or* ·bril·la; *plural* ·brils *or* ·bril·lae) small fibre

fi·bri·lar (*or* ·bril·lar, ·bril·lose)

fi·bril·la·tion muscle twitching

fi·bril·li·form

fi·brin blood-clotting protein

fi·brino·gen

fi·brino·gen·ic (*or* ·ous)

fi·brino·geni·cal·ly

fi·bri·noly·sin enzyme

fi·bri·noly·sis

fi·bri·no·lyt·ic

fi·brin·ous

fi·bro·blast tissue cell

fi·bro·blas·tic

fi·bro·cement

fi·broid

fi·bro·in protein

fi·bro·ma (*plural* ·ma·ta *or* ·mas) tumour

fi·broma·tous

fi·bro·sis

fi·bro·si·tis

fi·brot·ic

fi·brous

fi·brous·ness

fi·bro·vas·cu·lar botany term

fibu·la (*plural* ·lae *or* ·las) leg bone

fibu·lar

fiche *short for* microfiche

fichu scarf

fick·le

fick·le·ness

fic·tile moulded from clay

fic·tion

fic·tion·al

fic·tion·ali·za·tion (*or* ·sa·tion)

fic·tion·al·ize (*or* ·ise)

fic·tion·al·ly

fic·tion·ist (*or* fic·tion·eer)

fic·ti·tious not genuine; *compare* factitious

fic·ti·tious·ness

fic·tive of fiction

fid nautical term

fid·dle

fiddle-de-dee

fiddle-faddle

fiddle-head (*or* ·neck) nautical term

fid·dler

fiddle·stick violin bow

fiddle·sticks nonsense

fiddle·wood

fid·dling

fid·dly (·dli·er, ·dli·est)

fid·ei·com·mis·sary (*plural* ·saries) legal term

fid·ei·com·mis·sum (*plural* ·sa)

fi·deism

fi·deist

fi·deis·tic

fi·del·ity (*plural* ·ities)

fidg·et

fidg·et·ing·ly

fidg·ety

fi·du·cial

fi·du·ci·ary trustee

fie exclamation

fief (*or* feoff) property granted to vassal

field

field·er

field·fare bird

field-holler Negro singing style

field·mouse

field·piece gun

fields·man (*plural* ·men)

field·stone

field·work

fiend

fiend·ish

fiend·ish·ness

fierce

fierce·ly

fierce·ness

fi·eri fa·ci·as legal term

fiery

Fie·so·le Italian town

fi·es·ta

Fife Scottish region

fife

fif·er

fif·teen

fif·teenth

fifth

fif·ti·eth

fif·ty (*plural* ·ties)

fifty-fifty

fig

fight (fight·ing, fought)

fight·er

fighter-bomber

fight·ing

fig·ment

figu·ral

figu·rant (*fem* ·rante) dancer

fig·ur·ate musical term

fig·ura·tion

fig·ura·tive

fig·ura·tive·ly

fig·ura·tive·ness

fig·ure

fig·ured

figure-ground psychology term

figure·head

fig·ur·er

figu·rine statuette

fig·wort

Fiji

Fi·jian

fil *variant of* fils

fila·gree *variant spelling of* filigree

fila·ment

fila·men·tary (*or* ·tous)

fi·lar of thread

fi·laria (*plural* ·lariae) worm

fi·lar·ial (*or* ·ian)

fila·ria·sis

fila·ture silk spinning

fil·bert nut

filch
filch·er
file
file·card
file·fish (*plural* ·fish *or* ·fishes)
fil·er
fi·let lace; meat fillet
fi·let mi·gnon (*plural* fi·lets mi·gnons) beef cut
fil·ial
fil·ial·ly
fil·ial·ness
fili·ate legal term
fili·ation lineage
fili·beg (*or* fil·li·, phili·) kilt
fili·bus·ter
fili·bus·ter·er
fili·bus·ter·ism
fili·cid·al
fili·cide killing son or daughter
fili·form threadlike
fili·gree (*or* fila·, filla·; ·gree·ing, ·greed)
fil·ings
Fili·pi·no (*plural* ·nos) inhabitant of Philippines
fill
filla·gree *variant spelling of* filigree
filled
fill·er
fil·let
fill·ing
fil·lip
fil·lis·ter (*or* fil·is·ter, fil·les·ter) wood plane
fil·ly (*plural* ·lies)
film
film·ic
filmi·ly
filmi·ness
fil·mog·ra·phy (*plural* ·phies)
film·set (·setting, ·set)
film·setter
film·setting
filmy (filmi·er, filmi·est)
filo thin pastry
filo·plume feather
fi·lose threadlike
filo·selle thread

fils (*or* fil; *plural* fils) Middle Eastern coin
fil·ter separating device; *compare* philtre
fil·ter·abil·ity (*or* ·able·ness)
fil·ter·able (*or* fil·trable)
filter-tipped
filth
filthi·ly
filthi·ness
filthy (filthi·er, filthi·est)
fil·trat·able *variant of* filterable
fil·trate
fil·tra·tion
fi·lum (*plural* ·la) anatomy term
fim·ble plant
fim·bria (*plural* ·briae) anatomy term
fim·brial
fim·bri·ate (*or* ·bri·at·ed, ·bril·late) fringed
fim·bria·tion
fin (fin·ning, finned)
fin·able (*or* fine·)
fi·na·gle use trickery
fi·na·gler
fi·nal
fi·na·le
fi·nal·ism philosophical doctrine
fi·nal·ist
fi·nal·ity (*plural* ·ities)
fi·na·li·za·tion (*or* ·sa·tion)
fi·nal·ize (*or* ·ise)
fi·nal·ly
fi·nals
fi·nance
fi·nan·cial
fi·nan·cial·ly
fi·nan·ci·er
fin·back whale
finch
find (find·ing, found)
find·able
find·er
fin de siè·cle *French* end of 19th century
find·ing
fine
fine·able *variant spelling of* finable

fine-cut
fine-draw (-drawing, -drew, -drawn)
Fine Gael Irish political party
fine-grain
fine-grained
fine·ly
fine·ness
fin·ery (*plural* ·eries)
fine·spun
fi·nesse
fine-tooth (*or* -toothed) comb
fin·foot (*plural* ·foots) bird
Fin·gal's Cave
fin·ger
finger·board
fin·gered
fin·ger·er
fin·ger·ing
fin·ger·ling young fish
finger·mark
finger·nail
finger·print
finger·stall
finger·tip
Fin·go (*plural* ·go *or* ·gos) African people
fi·nial
fi·ni·aled
fin·icky (*or* ·ick·ing)
fin·ing clarifying liquid
fin·is the end
fin·ish
fin·ish·er
Fin·is·tère French department
Fin·is·terre Spanish headland
fi·nite
fi·nite·ly
fi·nite·ness
fink *Slang* blackleg
Fin·land
Finn
fin·nan had·dock (*or* Fin·nan had·die)
finned
fin·ner whale
Finn·ic language group
fin·ning
Finn·ish

Finn·mark Norwegian
county
Finno-Ugric (or -Ugrian)
language group
fin·ny (·ni·er, ·ni·est)
fino sherry
fi·nochio (or ·noc·chio)
fennel
Fin·ster·aar·horn Swiss
mountain
fiord variant spelling of **fjord**
fio·rin grass
fip·ple mouthpiece
fir
fire
fire·able
fire-and-brimstone
fire·arm
fire·back
fire·ball
fire·bird
fire·boat
fire·bomb
fire·box
fire·brand
fire·brat insect
fire·break
fire·brick
fire·bug arsonist
fire·cracker
fire·crest bird
fire·damp
fire·dog
fire·drake dragon
fire-eater
fire-eating
fire-extinguish·er
fire·fly (plural ·flies)
beetle
fire·guard
fire·man (plural ·men)
fire·pan
fire·place
fire·proof
fir·er
fire·side
fire·stone
fire·thorn
fire·trap
fire·warden
fire·water whisky
fire·weed
fire·wood
fire·work
fir·ing

fir·kin barrel
firm
fir·ma·ment
fir·ma·men·tal
fir·mer chisel
firm·ness
firm·ware computer term
first
first-born
first-class (adj)
first-foot (or ·footer)
first-footing
first-hand
first·ling first offspring
first-nighter
first-rate
firth (or frith)
fis·cal
fish (plural fish or fishes)
fish·able
fish·bolt
fish·bowl
fish·er
fisher·man (plural ·men)
fish·ery (plural ·eries)
fish-eye camera lens
fish·finger
fish·gig pole for impaling
fish
fish-hook
fishi·ly
fishi·ness
fish·ing
fish·monger
fish·net
fish·plate metal joint
fish·tail dance step
fish·wife (plural ·wives)
fishy (fishi·er, fishi·est)
fis·sile physics term
fis·sil·ity
fis·sion
fis·sion·abil·ity
fis·sion·able
fis·si·pal·mate ornithology
term
fis·sipa·rous reproducing by
fission
fis·si·ped (or ·sip·edal)
zoology term
fis·si·ros·tral ornithology
term
fis·sure
fist
fist·ic of boxing

fisti·cuffs
fist·mele archery term
**fis·tu·la (plural ·las or
·lae)** medical term
fis·tu·lous (or ·lar, ·late)
**fit (verb fit·ting, fit·ted;
adj fit·ter, fit·test)**
fitch (or fitch·et) polecat
fit·ful
fit·ful·ly
fit·ful·ness
fit·ment
fit·ness
fit·table
fit·ted
fit·ter
fit·ting
fit·ting·ly
fit·ting·ness
five
five-finger plant
five·fold
five·penny
five·pins
fiv·er
fives ball game
five-star (adj)
fix
fix·able
fix·ate
fixa·tion
fixa·tive
fixed
fix·ed·ly
fix·ed·ness
fix·er
fix·ity (plural ·ities)
stability
fix·ture
fiz·gig
fizz
fizz·er
fizzi·ness
fiz·zle
fizzy (fizzi·er, fizzi·est)
fjeld (or field) rocky
plateau
fjord (or fiord)
flab
flab·ber·gast
flab·bi·ly
flab·bi·ness
flab·by (·bi·er, ·bi·est)
**fla·bel·late (or
·bel·li·form)** fan-shaped

fla·bel·lum (*plural* ·la)
flac·cid
flac·cid·ity (*or* ·ness)
flac·on bottle
flag (flag·ging, flagged)
flag·el·lant (*or* ·la·tor)
flag·el·lant·ism
fla·gel·lar
flag·el·late
flag·el·lat·ed
flag·el·la·tion
fla·gel·li·form
fla·gel·lum (*plural* ·la *or* ·lums) whiplike part
flageo·let musical instrument
flagged
flag·ger
flag·ging
flag·gy (·gi·er, ·gi·est) limp
fla·gi·tious wicked
flag·man (*plural* ·men)
flag·on
flag·pole
fla·gran·cy (*or* ·grance)
fla·grant
fla·gran·te de·lic·to red-handed
flag·ship
flag·staff (*plural* ·staffs *or* ·staves)
flag·stone
flag·waver
flag·waving
flail
flair talent; *compare* flare
flak (*or* flack)
flake
flak·er
flaki·ly
flaki·ness
flaky (flaki·er, flaki·est)
flam (flam·ming, flammed) *Dialect* deceive
flam·bé (*or* ·bée) cookery term
flam·beau (*plural* ·beaux *or* ·beaus) torch
Flam·bor·ough Head English promontory
flam·boy·ance (*or* ·an·cy)
flam·boy·ant
flame
flame·like

fla·men (*plural* ·mens *or* fla·mi·nes) Roman priest
fla·men·co (*plural* ·cos)
flame-of-the-forest tree
flame·out
flame·proof
flam·er
flame-thrower
flam·ing
fla·min·go (*plural* ·gos *or* ·goes)
flam·mabil·ity
flam·mable
flamy (flami·er, flami·est)
flan
Flan·ders
flâne·rie idleness
flâ·neur
flange
flang·er
flank
flank·er
flan·nel (·nel·ling, ·nelled; *US* ·nel·ing, ·neled)
flan·nel·ette
flan·nel·ly
flap (flap·ping, flapped)
flap·doodle *Slang* nonsense
flap·jack
flap·per
flare flame; widen; *compare* flair
flare-up (*noun*)
flash
flash·back
flash·board
flash·bulb
flash·cube
flash·er
flashi·ly
flashi·ness
flash·ing
flash·light
flash·over electric discharge
flashy (flashi·er, flashi·est)
flask
flask·et basket
flat (flat·ter, flat·test)
flat·boat
flat·fish (*plural* ·fish *or* ·fishes)
flat·foot
flat·footed

flat-footed·ly
flat-footed·ness
flat·head (*plural* ·head *or* ·heads) fish
flat·iron
flat·let
flat·mate
flat·ness
flat·ten
flat·ten·er
flat·ter
flat·ter·able
flat·ter·er
flat·ter·ing
flat·ter·ing·ly
flat·tery (*plural* ·teries)
flat·ting metallurgy term
flat·tish
flat·top *US* aircraft carrier
flatu·lence (*or* ·len·cy)
flatu·lent
fla·tus (*plural* ·tuses)
flat·ways
flat·worm
flaunch (*or* flaunch·ing) slope round chimney
flaunt
flaunt·er
flaunt·ing·ly
flaunty (flaunti·er, flaunti·est)
flau·tist (*US* flut·ist)
fla·ves·cent turning yellow
fla·vin (*or* ·vine) pigment
fla·vone plant pigment
fla·vo·pro·tein enzyme
fla·vo·pur·pu·rin dye
fla·vor·ous
fla·vour (*US* ·vor)
fla·vour·er (*US* ·vor·)
fla·vour·ful (*US* ·vor·)
fla·vour·ing (*US* ·vor·)
fla·vour·less (*US* ·vor·)
fla·vour·some (*US* ·vor·)
flaw
flaw·less
flaw·less·ness
flawy squally
flax
flax·en (*or* flaxy)
flax·seed
flay
flay·er
flea
flea·bag

flea·bane plant
flea·bite
flea-bitten
fleam lancet
flea·pit
flea·wort plant
flèche spire
flé·chette missile
fleck
flec·tion *variant spelling*
  (*esp. US*) *of* flexion
fled
fledge
fledg·ling (*or* fledge·)
fledgy (fledgi·er,
  fledgi·est) feathered
flee (flee·ing, fled)
fleece
fleeci·ly
fleeci·ness
fleecy (fleeci·er,
  fleeci·est)
fle·er one who flees
fleer sneer
fleet
fleet·ing
fleet·ness
Fleet·wood Lancashire port
Flem·ing native of Flanders
Flem·ish
flense (*or* flench, flinch)
  strip blubber from whale
flens·er (*or* flench·,
  flinch·)
flesh
flesh·er *Scot* butcher
fleshi·ness
flesh·ings tights
flesh·li·ness
flesh·ly (·li·er, ·li·est)
flesh·pots
fleshy (fleshi·er,
  fleshi·est)
fletch
fletch·er arrow maker
Fletch·er·ism chewing food
  thoroughly
fletch·ings arrow feathers
fleur-de-lis (*or* -lys;
  plural fleurs-de-lis *or*
  -lys)
fleu·rette (*or* ·ret)
  ornament
fleur·on ornament
fleu·ry *variant of* flory

flew
flews bloodhound's lip
flex
flexi·bil·ity (*or* ·ible·ness)
flex·ible
flex·ibly
flex·ile
flex·ion (*or esp. US*
  flection)
flex·ion·al
flexi·time
flex·or muscle
flexu·ous (*or* ·ose) having
  many bends
flex·ur·al
flex·ure
fley *Dialect* be afraid
flib·ber·ti·gib·bet
flick
flick·er
flick·er·ing·ly
flick·ery
fli·er (*or* fly·)
flies
flight
flighti·ly
flighti·ness
flight·less
flighty (flighti·er,
  flighti·est)
flim·flam (·flam·ming,
  ·flammed)
flim·si·ly
flim·si·ness
flim·sy (·si·er, ·si·est)
flinch
flinch·er
flinch·ing·ly
fling (fling·ing, flung)
fling·er
Flint Welsh town
flint quartz
flinti·ly
flinti·ness
flint·lock firearm
Flint·shire former Welsh
  county
flinty (flinti·er, flinti·est)
flip (flip·ping, flipped)
flip-flop (-flopping,
  -flopped)
flip·pan·cy
flip·pant
flip·per
flip·ping

flirt
flir·ta·tion
flir·ta·tious
flir·ta·tious·ness
flirt·er
flirt·ing·ly
flit (flit·ting, flit·ted)
flitch pork
flite (*or* flyte) *Scot* scold
flit·ter
flitter·mouse (*plural*
  ·mice) *Dialect* bat
fliv·ver old car
float
float·abil·ity
float·able
float·age *variant spelling of*
  flotage
floata·tion *variant spelling*
  of flotation
float·er
float·ing
floaty (floati·er,
  floati·est) light
floc *variant of* floccule
floc·cose tufted
floc·cu·lant anticoagulant;
  compare flocculent
floc·cu·late aggregate
floc·cu·la·tion
floc·cule (*or* floc·cu·lus,
  flock, floc) mass of
  particles
floc·cu·lence (*or* ·len·cy)
floc·cu·lent fleecy; *compare*
  flocculent
floc·cu·lus (*plural* ·li)
  marking on sun
floc·cus (*plural* ·ci) down
flock
flocky
Flod·den battlefield
floe ice; *compare* flow
flog (flog·ging, flogged)
flog·ger
flog·ging
flong printing term
flood
flood·able
flood·er
flood·gate
flood·light (·light·ing, ·lit)
floor
floor·age
floor·board

floor·ing
floo·zy (*or* ·zie, ·sy;
  plural ·zies *or* ·sies)
flop (flop·ping, flopped)
flop·pi·ly
flop·pi·ness
flop·py (·pi·er, ·pi·est)
Flora Roman goddess
flo·ra (*plural* ·ras *or* ·rae)
  plant life
flo·ral
flo·ral·ly
Flor·ence Italian city
Flor·en·tine
flo·res·cence flowering;
  compare fluorescence
flo·ret
Flo·ria·nópo·lis Brazilian
  port
flo·ri·at·ed (*or* ·reated)
  architectural term
flo·ri·bun·da rose
flo·ri·cul·tur·al
flo·ri·cul·ture
flo·ri·cul·tur·ist
flor·id
Flori·da
flo·rid·ity (*or* ·ness)
flo·ri·gen hormone
flo·ri·legium (*plural*
  ·legia) book about
  flowers
flor·in
flo·rist
flo·ris·tic
flo·ris·ti·cal·ly
flo·ris·tics branch of botany
flo·ru·it *Latin* flourished
flo·ry (*or* fleu·) heraldic
  term
flos fer·ri mineral
floss
flossy (flossi·er,
  flossi·est)
flo·tage (*or* float·age)
flo·ta·tion (*or* floata·tion)
flo·til·la
flot·sam
flounce
flounc·ing
floun·der (*plural* ·der *or*
  ·ders) fish; to struggle;
  compare founder
flour
flour·ish

flour·ish·er
floury
flout
flout·er
flout·ing·ly
flow liquid movement;
  compare floe
flow·age
flow·er
flow·er·age
flower·bed
flow·ered
flow·er·er
flow·er·et
flow·eri·ness
flow·er·ing
flow·er·less
flower-like
flower-of-an-hour plant
flower·pot
flow·ery
flown
flu illness; *compare* flue
fluc·tu·ant
fluc·tu·ate
fluc·tua·tion
flue pipe; *compare* flu
flued
flu·en·cy
flu·ent
fluff
fluffi·ly
fluffi·ness
fluffy (fluffi·er, fluffi·est)
flu·gel·horn musical
  instrument
flu·id
flu·id·al
fluid·extract
  pharmaceutical term
flu·id·ic
flu·id·ics
flu·id·ity (*or* ·ness)
flu·idi·za·tion (*or* ·sa·tion)
flu·id·ize (*or* ·ise)
flu·id·iz·er (*or* ·is·er)
flu·id·ly (*or* flu·id·al·ly)
fluke
fluki·ness
fluky (*or* fluk·ey; fluki·er,
  fluki·est)
flume ravine
flum·mery (*plural*
  ·meries)
flum·mox

flung
flunk *Slang* fail
flunky (*or* flunk·ey;
  plural flunkies *or* ·eys)
  servant
flu·or *variant of* fluorspar
fluo·rene chemical
  compound; *compare*
  fluorine
fluo·resce
fluo·res·cein (*or* ·ceine)
  chemical compound
fluo·res·cence radiation
  emission; *compare*
  florescence
fluo·res·cent
flu·or·ic of fluorine
fluori·date
fluori·da·tion
fluo·ride
fluo·rim·eter *variant of*
  fluorometer
fluori·nate treat with
  fluorine
fluori·na·tion
fluo·rine (*or* ·rin) chemical
  element; *compare* fluorene
fluo·ro·car·bon
fluo·rom·eter (*or* ·rim·)
fluo·ro·met·ric (*or* ·ri·)
fluo·rom·etry (*or* ·rim·)
fluoro·scope X-ray
  instrument
fluoro·scop·ic
fluoro·scopi·cal·ly
fluor·os·co·py
fluo·ro·sis
flu·or·spar (*or* flu·or)
  mineral
flur·ry (*noun, plural* ·ries;
  verb ·ries, ·ry·ing,
  ·ried)
flush
flush·er
Flush·ing Dutch port
flus·ter
flute
flut·ed
flut·er
flut·ing
flut·ist *US* flautist
flut·ter
flut·ter·er
flut·ter·ing·ly
flut·tery
fluty (fluti·er, fluti·est)

flu·vial (*or* ·via·tile) of a river

flu·vio·ma·rine of sea and river

flux

flux·ion change

flux·ion·al (*or* ·ary)

flux·meter

fly (*noun, plural* flies; *verb* flies, fly·ing, flew, flown)

fly·able

fly·away

fly·back physics term

fly·blow (·blow·ing, ·blew, ·blown)

fly·boat

fly·book angler's fly case

fly·by (*plural* ·bys)

fly·by·night

fly·catcher

fly·er *variant spelling of* flier

fly·fish

fly·fisher

fly·fishing

fly·ing

fly·leaf (*plural* ·leaves)

fly·over

fly·paper

fly·past

Flysch Alpine rock

fly·speck

flyte *variant spelling of* flite

fly·trap

fly·weight

fly·wheel

foal

foam

foam·flower

foami·ly

foami·ness

foam·like

foamy (foami·er, foami·est)

fob (fob·bing; fobbed)

fo·cal

fo·cali·za·tion (*or* ·sa·tion)

fo·cal·ize (*or* ·ise) focus

fo·cal·ly

fo'c's'le (*or* fo'c'sle) *variant spellings of* forecastle

fo·cus (*noun, plural* ·cuses *or* ·ci; *verb* ·cuses, ·cus·ing, ·cused)

fo·cus·able

fo·cus·er

fod·der

foe

foehn *variant spelling of* föhn

foe·man

foe·tal *variant spelling of* fetal

foe·ta·tion *variant spelling of* fetation

foe·ti·cide *variant spelling of* feticide

foet·id *variant spelling of* fetid

foe·tipa·rous *variant spelling of* fetiparous

foe·tor *variant spelling of* fetor

foe·tus *variant spelling of* fetus

fog (fog·ging, fogged)

fog·bound

fog·bow light in fog

fog·dog white spot in fog

fogged

Fog·gia Italian city

fog·gi·ly

fog·gi·ness

fog·ging

fog·gy (·gi·er, ·gi·est)

fog·horn

fogy (*or* fo·gey; *plural* fogies *or* ·geys)

fo·gy·ish (*or* ·gey·)

föhn (*or* foehn) wind

foi·ble

foil

foil·able

foils·man (*plural* ·men)

Fo·ism Chinese Buddhism

foi·son plentiful supply

Fo·ist

foist

fola·cin folic acid

fold

fold·able

fold·away

fold·boat

fold·ed

fold·er

fol·derol *variant spelling of* falderal

fold·ing

fold·out printing term

fo·lia·ceous

fo·li·age

fo·li·ar of leaves

fo·li·ate

fo·li·at·ed

fo·lia·tion

fo·lic acid vitamin

fo·lio (*noun, plural* ·lios; *verb* ·lios, ·lio·ing, ·lioed)

fo·lio·late botany term

fo·li·ose leafy

fo·lium (*plural* ·lia) geometrical curve

folk

Folke·stone

folk·ish

folk·lore

folk·lor·ic

folk·lor·ist

folk·lor·is·tic

folk·moot medieval assembly

folk-rock

folk·si·ness

folk·sy (·si·er, ·si·est)

folk·ways sociology term

fol·li·cle

fol·licu·lar

fol·licu·late (*or* ·lat·ed)

fol·licu·lin hormone

fol·low

fol·low·able

fol·low·er

fol·low·ing

follow-on (*noun*)

follow-through (*noun*)

follow-up (*noun*)

fol·ly (*plural* ·lies)

Fol·som man early man

Fo·mal·haut star

fo·ment instigate; *compare* ferment

fo·men·ta·tion

fo·ment·er

fond

fon·dant

fon·dle

fon·dler

fon·dling·ly

fond·ness

fon·due cookery term

font baptismal bowl; *variant spelling (esp. US) of* fount

Fon·taine·bleau French town

font·al

fon·ta·nelle (or ·nel)
  anatomy term

Foo·chow (or Fu·chou)
  Chinese port

food

food·stuff

fool

fool·ery (plural ·eries)

fool·har·di·ness

fool·hardy (·hardi·er,
  hardi·est)

fool·ish

fool·ish·ness

fool·proof

fools·cap

fool's-parsley

foot (plural feet)

foot·age

foot-and-mouth disease

foot·ball

foot·ball·er

foot·board

foot·boy

foot·bridge

foot-candle unit

foot·er

foot·fall

foot·gear

foot·hill

foot·hold

footie variant spelling of
  footy

foot·ing

foot-lambert unit

foot·le potter

foot·lights

foot·ling trivial

foot·loose

foot·man (plural ·men)

foot·mark

foot·note

foot·pace platform before
  altar

foot·pad highwayman

foot·path

foot·plate

foot-pound unit

foot-poundal unit

foot·print

foot·rest

foot·rope

foots dregs

foot·sie

foot·slog (·slog·ging,
  ·slogged)

foot·sore

foot·stalk

foot·stall base of column

foot·step

foot·stool

foot-ton unit

foot·wall geology term

foot·way

foot·wear

foot·work

foot·worn

footy (or footie) Slang
  football

foo yong (or foo yoong,
  foo yung, fu yung)
  Chinese omelette

foo·zle bungle golf shot

foo·zler

fop

fop·pery (plural ·peries)

fop·pish

fop·pish·ness

for

for·age

for·ag·er

fo·ra·men (plural ·rami·na
  or ·ra·mens) hole in
  bone

fo·rami·nal

fora·mini·fer protozoan

fo·rami·nif·er·al (or ·ous)

for·as·much as

for·ay

for·ay·er

for·bade (or ·bad)

for·bear (·bear·ing, ·bore,
  ·borne) to refrain; variant
  spelling of forebear

for·bear·ance

for·bear·er

for·bear·ing·ly

for·bid (·bid·ding, ·bade
  or ·bad, ·bid·den or
  ·bid)

for·bid·dance

for·bid·den

for·bid·der

for·bid·ding·ly

for·bore

for·borne

for·by Scot besides

force

force·able

forced

forc·ed·ly

forc·ed·ness

force-feed (-feeding,
  -fed)

force·ful

force·ful·ly

force·ful·ness

force ma·jeure

force·meat

for·ceps (plural ·ceps or
  ·ci·pes)

forc·er

for·cible

for·cible·ness (or
  ·cibil·ity)

for·cibly

forc·ing·ly

ford

ford·able

fore

fore-and-aft (adj)

fore-and-after vessel

fore·arm

fore·bear (or for·)
  ancestor; compare forbear

fore·bode

fore·bod·er

fore·bod·ing

fore·brain

fore·cast (·cast·ing, ·cast
  or ·cast·ed)

fore·cast·er

fore·cas·tle (or fo'c's'le,
  fo'c'sle)

fore·clos·able

fore·close

fore·clo·sure

fore·course boat's sail

fore·court

fore·deck

fore·doom

fore·father

fore·finger

fore·foot (plural ·feet)

fore·front

fore·gather variant spelling
  of forgather

fore·go (·goes, ·go·ing,
  ·went, ·gone) precede;
  variant spelling of forgo

fore·go·er

fore·going

fore·gone

fore·gone·ness

fore·ground
fore·gut
fore·hand
fore·handed
fore·head
fore·hock bacon
for·eign
for·eign·er
for·eign·ism
for·eign·ness
fore·judge prejudge; *variant spelling of* forjudge
fore·judg·ment (*or* ·judg·)
fore·know (·know·ing, ·knew, ·known)
fore·know·able
fore·know·ing·ly
fore·knowl·edge
fore·land
fore·leg
fore·limb
fore·lock
fore·man (*plural* ·men)
fore·man·ship
fore·mast
fore·most
fore·name
fore·named
fore·noon
fo·ren·sic of the law; *compare* forensics
fo·ren·si·cal·ity
fo·ren·si·cal·ly
fo·ren·sics debating; *compare* forensic
fore·or·dain
fore·or·dain·ment (*or* ·di·na·tion)
fore·part
fore·paw
fore·peak nautical term
fore·play
fore·quar·ter
fore·reach nautical term
fore·run (·run·ning, ·ran, ·run)
fore·run·ner
fore·sail
fore·see (·see·ing, ·saw, ·seen)
fore·see·able
fore·seen
fore·seer
fore·shad·ow
fore·shad·ow·er

fore·shank
fore·sheet nautical term
fore·shock *US* minor earthquake
fore·shore
fore·short·en
fore·side
fore·sight
fore·sighted
fore·sighted·ness
fore·skin
for·est
for·est·al (*or* fo·res·tial)
fore·stall
fore·stall·er
fore·stal·ment
for·esta·tion
fore·stay nautical term
forestay·sail
for·est·ed
for·est·er
forest-like
for·est·ry
fore·taste
fore·tell (·tell·ing, ·told)
fore·tell·er
fore·thought
fore·thought·ful
fore·time the past
fore·to·ken foreshadow
fore·told
fore·tooth (*plural* ·teeth)
fore·top platform on foremast
fore·topgal·lant nautical term
fore·topmast
fore·topsail
fore·tri·an·gle nautical term
for·ever
for·ever·more
fore·warn
fore·warn·er
fore·warn·ing·ly
fore·went
fore·wind
fore·wing
fore·word
fore·yard nautical term
for·feit
for·feit·able
for·feit·er
for·fei·ture
for·fend *US* protect; *Archaic* prevent

for·fi·cate forked
for·gath·er (*or* fore·) assemble
for·gave
forge
forge·able
forg·er
for·gery (*plural* ·geries)
for·get (·get·ting, ·got, ·got·ten)
for·get·ful
for·get·ful·ly
for·get·ful·ness
forget-me-not
for·get·table
for·get·ter
forg·ing
for·giv·able
for·giv·ably
for·give (·giv·ing, ·gave, ·giv·en)
for·give·ness
for·giv·er
for·giv·ing·ly
for·giv·ing·ness
for·go (*or* fore·; ·goes, ·go·ing, ·went, ·gone) give up; *compare* forego
for·go·er (*or* fore·)
for·got
for·got·ten
for·judge (*or* fore·) legal term; *compare* forejudge
for·judg·ment (*or* fore·)
fork
forked
fork·ed·ly
fork·ed·ness
fork·ful
fork-lift truck
For·lì Italian city
for·lorn
form shape, etc.; *US spelling of* forme
form·able
for·mal
for·mal·de·hyde
for·ma·lin (*or* for·mol)
for·mal·ism
for·mal·ist
for·mal·is·tic
for·mal·ity (*plural* ·ities)
for·mali·za·tion (*or* ·sa·tion)
for·mal·ize (*or* ·ise)

foundry

for·mal·iz·er (or ·is·er)

for·mal·ly in a formal way; *compare* **formerly**

for·mal·ness

for·mant acoustics term

for·mat (·mat·ting, ·mat·ted)

for·mate chemistry term

for·ma·tion

for·ma·tion·al

forma·tive

forma·tive·ly

forma·tive·ness

forme (*US* form) printing term; *compare* **form**

for·mer

for·mer·ly in the past; *compare* **formally**

for·mic of ants; acid

For·mi·ca (*Trademark*)

for·mi·cary (or ·car·ium; *plural* ·caries or ·caria) ant hill

for·mi·ca·tion skin sensation

for·mi·dabil·ity (or ·dable·ness)

for·mi·dable

for·mi·dably

form·less

form·less·ness

for·mol *variant of* **formalin**

For·mo·sa *former name of* Taiwan

for·mu·la (*plural* ·las or ·lae)

for·mu·laic

for·mu·lari·za·tion (or ·sa·tion)

for·mu·lar·ize (or ·ise)

for·mu·lar·iz·er (or ·is·er)

for·mu·lary (*plural* ·laries)

for·mu·late

for·mu·la·tion

for·mu·la·tor

for·mu·lism

for·mu·list

for·mu·lis·tic

form·work concrete mould

for·myl chemistry term

For·nax constellation

for·nenst *Scot* situated against

for·ni·cal of a fornix

for·ni·cate

for·ni·ca·tion

for·ni·ca·tor

for·nix (*plural* ·ni·ces) body structure

for·sake (·sak·ing, ·sook, ·sak·en)

for·sak·en

for·sak·en·ness

for·sak·er

for·sook

for·sooth

for·ster·ite mineral

for·swear (·swear·ing, ·swore, ·sworn)

for·swear·er

for·sworn

for·sythia

fort

For·ta·leza Brazilian port

for·ta·lice small fort

Fort-de-France Martinican capital

forte strength

for·te musical term

forte-piano musical term

forte-piano piano

Forth Scottish river

forth forward; *compare* fourth

forth·com·ing

forth·com·ing·ness

forth·right

forth·right·ness

forth·with

for·ti·eth

for·ti·fi·able

for·ti·fi·ca·tion

for·ti·fi·er

for·ti·fy (·fies, ·fy·ing, ·fied)

for·tis (*plural* ·tes) phonetics term

for·tis·si·mo (*plural* ·mos or ·mi)

for·ti·tude

for·ti·tu·di·nous

Fort Knox

fort·night

fort·night·ly

Fortran computer language

for·tress

for·tui·tism philosophy term

for·tui·tist

for·tui·tous unplanned; *compare* **fatuitous**

for·tui·tous·ness

for·tu·ity (*plural* ·ities)

Fortuna Roman goddess

for·tu·nate

for·tu·nate·ly

for·tu·nate·ness

for·tune

fortune-hunter

fortune-teller

fortune-telling

for·ty (*plural* ·ties)

forty-niner prospector

fo·rum (*plural* ·rums or ·ra)

for·ward (*adj*)

for·ward·er (*noun*)

for·ward·ness

for·wards (*adv*)

for·went

for·zan·do musical term

fos·sa (*plural* ·sae) anatomical depression

fosse (or foss) ditch

fos·sette bone depression

fos·sil

fos·sil·if·er·ous

fos·sil·iz·able (or ·is·able)

fos·sili·za·tion (or ·sa·tion)

fos·sil·ize (or ·ise)

fos·so·rial used for burrowing

fos·ter

fos·ter·age

fos·ter·er

fos·ter·ing·ly

fos·ter·ling foster child

fou·droy·ant sudden

fou·et·té ballet step

fought

foul bad; *compare* fowl

fou·lard fabric

foul·ly

foul-mouthed

Foul·ness Essex island

foul·ness

found

foun·da·tion

foun·da·tion·al

foun·da·tion·ary

found·er one who founds; to sink; *compare* flounder

found·ing

found·ling

found·ry (*plural* ·ries)

fount fountain; source
fount (or esp. US **font**)
  printing term
foun·tain
fountain·head
four
four·ball golfing term
four·chette anatomy term
four·colour (US **-color**)
  photography term
four·dimension·al
Four·drini·er paper-making
  machine
four·fold
four·handed
Fou·ri·er·ism social system
Fou·ri·er·ist (or **·ite**)
Fou·ri·er·is·tic
four-in-hand carriage
four-leaf (or **-leaved**)
  clover
four·pence
four·penny
four·poster
four·ra·gère ornamental
  cord
four·score
four·some
four·square
four-stroke en·gine
four·teen
four·teenth
fourth 4th; compare **forth**
four-way (adj)
four-wheel drive
fo·vea (plural **·veae**)
  anatomy term
fo·veal
fo·veate (or **·veat·ed**)
fo·veo·la (plural **·lae**)
  small fovea
fo·veo·lar
fo·veo·late (or **·lat·ed**)
Fowey Cornish village
fowl chicken; compare **foul**
fowl·er bird hunter
Fow·liang (or **Fou-liang**)
  Chinese city
fowl·ing
fox (plural **foxes** or **fox**)
fox·fire glow
fox·glove
fox·hole
fox·hound
fox·hunter

fox-hunting
foxi·ly
foxi·ness
fox·ing part of shoe
fox·like
fox·tail grass
fox·trot (**·trot·ting**,
  ·trot·ted)
foxy (**foxi·er**, **foxi·est**)
foy·er
Fra monk's title
fra·cas (plural **·cas**; US
  ·cases) uproar
frac·tion
frac·tion·al (or **·ary**)
frac·tion·al·ly
frac·tion·ate
frac·tiona·tion
frac·tiona·tor
frac·tioni·za·tion (or
  ·sa·tion)
frac·tion·ize (or **·ise**)
frac·tious
frac·to·cu·mu·lus (plural
  ·li)
frac·to·stra·tus (plural **·ti**)
frac·tura·ble
frac·tur·al
frac·ture
frae Scot from
frae·num (or **fre·**; plural
  ·na) fold
frag (**frag·ging**, **fragged**)
  US military slang term
frag·ile
frag·ile·ly
fra·gil·ity (or **·gile·ness**)
frag·ment
frag·men·tal
frag·men·tal·ly
frag·men·tari·ly
frag·men·tari·ness
frag·men·tary
frag·men·ta·tion
fra·grance (or **·gran·cy**;
  plural **·grances** or
  ·gran·cies)
fra·grant
frail
frail·ly
frail·ness
frail·ty (plural **·ties**)
fraise tool; neck ruff;
  rampart
Frak·tur typeface

fram·able (or **frame·**)
fram·boe·sia (US **·be·**)
  disease
fram·boise liqueur
frame
frame·less
fram·er
frame-up
frame·work
fram·ing
franc
France
Franche-Comté French
  region
fran·chise
fran·chise·ment
Fran·cis·can
fran·cium chemical element
fran·co·lin partridge
Fran·co·nian language
  group
Fran·co·phile (or **·phil**)
Fran·co·phobe
Fran·co·pho·bia
Fran·co·phone native
  French speaker
frang·er Austral condom
fran·gibil·ity (or
  ·gible·ness)
fran·gible breakable
fran·gi·pane almond pastry
fran·gi·pani (plural **·panis**
  or **·pani**) shrub
Frang·lais French with
  English words
frank
frank·able
frank·al·moign legal term
Frankenstein
frank·er
Frank·furt
frank·fur·ter
frank·in·cense
Frank·ish
Frank·lin Canadian district
frank·lin medieval
  landowner
frank·lin·ite mineral
frank·ness
frank·pledge medieval
  tithing system
fran·tic
fran·ti·cal·ly (or
  fran·tic·ly)

frap (frap·ping, frapped)
nautical term

frap·pé *French* chilled

frass insect excrement

fratchy quarrelsome

fra·ter friar

fra·ter·nal

fra·ter·nal·ly

fra·ter·nal·ism

fra·ter·nity (*plural* ·nities)

frat·er·ni·za·tion (*or* ·sa·tion)

frat·er·nize (*or* ·nise)

frat·er·niz·er (*or* ·nis·er)

frat·ri·cid·al

frat·ri·cide

Frau (*plural* Frau·en *or* Fraus) *German* woman; Mrs

fraud

fraudu·lence (*or* ·len·cy)

fraudu·lent

fraught

Fräu·lein (*plural* ·lein *or* ·leins) *German* young woman; Miss

fraxi·nel·la plant

fray

fra·zil ice spikes

fraz·zle

freak

freaki·ly

freaki·ness

freak·ish

freak·ish·ness

freaky (freaki·er, freaki·est)

freck·le

freck·led (*or* ·ly)

Fred·er·iks·berg Danish city

free (*adj* fre·er, fre·est; *verb* free·ing, freed)

free·bie *Slang* free gift

free·board

free·boot

free·booter

free·born

freed·man (*plural* ·men)

free·dom

freed·woman (*plural* ·women)

free·floater uncommitted person

free·floating

free-for-all

free-handed

free-hearted

free·hold

free·holder

free·lance

free·lancer

free-liver

free-living

free·load *US* be a sponger

free·ly

free·man (*plural* ·men)

free·martin female twin calf

Free·mason member of secret order

free·mason stonemason

Free·masonic

free·masonic

Free·masonry

free·masonry

free·range

free·sheet free newspaper

free·sia

free-spoken

free-standing

free·stone

free·style

free-swimmer

free-swimming

free·thinker

free·thinking

Free·town capital of Sierra Leone

free-trader

free·way

free·wheel

free·wheeling

freez·able

freeze (freez·ing, froze, fro·zen)

freeze-dry (-dries, -drying, -dried)

freez·er

freeze-up

freez·ing

Frei·burg West German city

freight

freight·age

freight·er

freight·liner

Fre·man·tle Australian port

fremi·tus (*plural* ·tus) medical term

Fre·mont *US* city

French

Frenchi·fy (·fies, ·fy·ing, ·fied)

French·man (*plural* ·men)

French·woman (*plural* ·women)

fre·net·ic

fre·neti·cal·ly

frenu·lum (*plural* ·la) zoology term

fre·num *variant spelling of* fraenum

fren·zied

fren·zy (*noun, plural* ·zies; *verb* ·zies, ·zy·ing, ·zied)

Fre·on (*Trademark*)

fre·quen·cy (*plural* ·cies) physics and statistics term

fre·quen·cy (*or* fre·quence) frequent occurrence

fre·quent

fre·quent·able

fre·quen·ta·tion

fre·quen·ta·tive linguistics term

fre·quent·er

fre·quent·ly

fres·co (*plural* ·coes *or* ·cos)

fresh

fresh·en

fresh·en·er

fresh·er (*or* ·man; *plural* ·ers *or* ·men)

fresh·et river overflowing

fresh·man *variant of* fresher

fresh·ness

fresh·water (*adj*)

fres·nel unit

Fres·no *US* city

fret (fret·ting, fret·ted)

fret·ful

fret·ful·ly

fret·ful·ness

fret·less

fret·ted

fret·work

Freud·ian

Freudi·an·ism

Frey Norse god

Freya Norse goddess

fri·abil·ity (*or* ·able·ness)

fri·able

fri·ar

friar·bird
fri·ary (plural ·aries)
frib·ble fritter away
frib·bler
Fri·bourg Swiss town
fric·an·deau (or ·do;
  plural ·deaus, deaux,
  or ·does) cookery term
fric·as·see (·see·ing,
  ·seed) cookery term
frica·tive phonetics term
fric·tion
fric·tion·al
Fri·day
fridge
fried
friend
friend·less
friend·less·ness
friend·li·ly
friend·li·ness
friend·ly (·li·er, ·li·est)
friend·ship
fri·er variant spelling of fryer
fries
Frie·sian cattle; variant
  spelling of Frisian
Fries·land Dutch province
frieze decorative strip
frig (frig·ging, frigged)
frig·ate
frig·ging
fright
fright·en
fright·en·able
fright·en·er
fright·en·ing
fright·en·ing·ly
fright·ful
fright·ful·ly
frig·id
Frig·id·aire (Trademark)
fri·gid·ity (or frig·id·ness)
fri·jol (plural ·joles)
  French bean
frill
frilled
frilli·ness
frilly (frilli·er, frilli·est)
fringe
frin·gil·line (or ·lid)
  ornithology term
fringy
frip·pery (plural ·peries)
frip·pet frivolous woman

Fris·bee (Trademark)
Fris·co Slang San Francisco
fri·sé fabric
fri·sette (or ·zette) fringe
fri·seur French hairdresser
Fri·sian (or Frie·)
  language; of Friesland
Fri·sian Is·lands
frisk
frisk·er
frisk·et printing term
friski·ly
friski·ness
frisky (friski·er,
  friski·est)
fris·son shiver
frit (or fritt; frit·ting,
  frit·ted) glassy material
frith variant of firth
fri·til·lary (plural ·laries)
  butterfly; plant
fritt variant spelling of frit
frit·ter
frit·ter·er
Friu·li European region
Friu·lian
Friuli-Venezia Giu·lia
  Italian region
friv·ol (·ol·ling, ·olled)
fri·vol·ity (plural ·ities)
friv·ol·ler
frivo·lous
frivo·lous·ness
fri·zette variant spelling of
  frisette
frizz
frizz·er
friz·zi·ness (or ·zli·ness)
friz·zle
friz·zler
friz·zy (or ·zly; ·zi·er,
  ·zi·est or ·zli·er,
  ·zli·est)
fro from; compare froe
frock
frock·ing coarse material
froe (or frow) tool;
  compare fro
frog (frog·ging, frogged)
frog·bit plant
frog·fish (plural ·fish or
  ·fishes)
frogged
frog·ging
frog·gy

frog·hopper insect
frog·man (plural ·men)
frog·march
frog·mouth bird
frog·spawn
frol·ic (·ick·ing, ·icked)
frol·ick·er
frol·ic·some (or frol·icky)
from
fro·men·ty variant of
  frumenty
frond
Fronde French rebellion
frond·ed
fron·des·cence botany term
fron·des·cent (or
  fron·dose, fron·dous)
Fron·deur French rebel
frons (plural fron·tes)
  entomology term
front
front·age
front·al
fron·tal·ity
fron·tal·ly
front·bencher
fron·tier
fron·tiers·man (plural
  ·men)
fron·tis·piece
front·let forehead
  decoration
fron·to·gen·esis
  meteorology term
fron·toly·sis meteorology
  term
front·runner
front·wards (or esp. US
  ·ward)
frost
frost·bite
frost·bitten
frost·ed
frosti·ly
frosti·ness
frost·ing
frost·work
frosty (frosti·er,
  frosti·est)
froth
frothi·ly
frothi·ness
frothy (frothi·er,
  frothi·est)
frott·age rubbing

frou·frou swishing sound
frow *variant spelling of* **froe**
fro·ward obstinate
frown
frown·er
frown·ing·ly
frowst
frows·ty stale
frowzi·ness (*or* **frowsi·**)
frowzy (*or* **frowsy**;
  frowzi·er, frowzi·est *or*
  frowsi·er, frows·iest)
  shabby
froze
fro·zen
fro·zen·ness
fruc·tif·er·ous fruit-bearing
fruc·ti·fi·ca·tion
fruc·ti·fi·er
fruc·ti·fy (**·fies, ·fy·ing,**
  ·fied)
fruc·tose sugar
fruc·tu·ous
fru·gal
fru·gal·ly
fru·gal·ity (*or* **·ness**)
fru·giv·or·ous fruit-eating
fruit
fruit·age
frui·tar·ian
fruit·cake
fruit·er fruit grower
fruit·er·er fruit seller
fruit·ful
fruit·ful·ly
fruit·ful·ness
fruiti·ness
frui·tion
fruit·less
fruit·less·ness
fruity (**fruiti·er, fruiti·est**)
fru·men·ta·ceous
  resembling wheat
fru·men·ty (*or* **fro·, fur·**)
  porridge
frump
frump·ish (*or* **frumpy**)
frump·ish·ness (*or*
  frumpi·ness)
Frun·ze Soviet city
frus·trate
frus·trat·er
frus·tra·tion
frus·tule botany term

frus·tum (*plural* **·tums** *or*
  ·ta) geometric solid
fru·tes·cence
fru·tes·cent (*or* **·ti·cose**)
  shrublike
fry (*noun, plural* **fries**;
  verb **fries, fry·ing,**
  fried)
fry·er (*or* **fri·**)
fry·ing
Fu-chou *variant spelling of*
  Foochow
fuch·sia shrub
fuch·sin (*or* **·sine**) dye
fuck
fuck·er
fuck·ing
fu·coid
fu·coid·al (*or* **fu·cous**)
fu·cus (*plural* **·ci** *or*
  ·cuses) seaweed
fud·dle
fuddy-duddy (*plural*
  -duddies)
fudge
Fueh·rer *variant spelling of*
  Führer
fuel (**fuel·ling, fuelled**;
  US **fuel·ing, fueled**)
fuel·ler (*US* **fuel·er**)
fug
fu·ga·cious fleeting
fu·gac·ity
fu·gal of a fugue
fu·gal·ly
fu·ga·to musical term
fu·gi·tive
fu·gi·tive·ly
fugle·man (*plural* **·men**)
  one used as example
fugue
fu·guist
Füh·rer (*or* **Fueh·**) *German*
  leader
Fuji (*or* **Fujiyama, Fuji-**
  san) Japanese mountain
Fu·kien Chinese province
Fu·kuo·ka Japanese city
Fu·ku·shi·ma Japanese city
Fula (*or* **Fu·lah**; *plural*
  Fula *or* **Fulas** *or*
  Fu·lah, Fu·lahs) African
  people
Fu·la·ni language
ful·crum (*plural* **·crums**
  or **·cra**)

ful·fil (*US* **·fill**; **·fil·ling,**
  ·filled)
ful·fil·ler
ful·fil·ment (*US* **·fill·**)
ful·gent (*or* **·gid**)
  resplendent
ful·gu·rant
ful·gu·rate flash like
  lightning
ful·gu·rat·ing painful
ful·gu·ra·tion surgical
  procedure
ful·gu·rite mineral
ful·gu·rous
Ful·ham
fu·ligi·nous smoky
full
full·back
full-blooded
full-blown
full-bodied
full·er
full-faced
full-frontal (*adj*)
full-length
full-mouthed
full·ness
full-rigged
full-sailed
full-scale
full-time (*adj*)
full-timer
ful·ly
fully-fledged
ful·mar bird
ful·mi·nant sudden
ful·mi·nate
ful·mi·na·tion
ful·mi·na·tor
ful·mi·na·tory
ful·min·ic acid
ful·some
ful·some·ly
ful·some·ness
ful·vous tawny
fu·mar·ic acid
fu·ma·role volcano vent
fu·ma·rol·ic
fu·ma·to·rium (*or* **·tory**;
  plural **·riums, ·ria,** *or*
  ·tories) fumigation
  chamber
fu·ma·tory of fumigation;
  compare **fumitory**
fum·ble

fum·bler
fum·bling·ly
fum·bling·ness
fume
fume·less
fum·er
fu·mi·gant
fu·mi·gate
fu·mi·ga·tion
fu·mi·ga·tor
fum·ing
fu·mi·tory (*plural* ·tories)
plant; *compare* fumatory
fumy (fumi·er, fumi·est)
fun (fun·ning, funned)
fu·nam·bu·lism
fu·nam·bu·list tightrope
walker
Fun·chal capital of Madeira
func·tion
func·tion·al
func·tion·al·ism
func·tion·al·ist
func·tion·al·ly
func·tion·ary (*plural*
·aries)
fund
fun·da·ment
fun·da·men·tal
fun·da·men·tal·ism
fun·da·men·tal·ist
fun·da·men·tal·is·tic
fun·da·men·tal·ity (*or*
·ness)
fun·da·men·tal·ly
fund·ed
fun·di mechanic
fun·dic
fun·dus (*plural* ·di)
anatomy term
Fun·dy Canadian bay
fu·ner·al
fu·ner·ary
fu·nereal
fun·fair
fun·gal
fun·gi *plural of* fungus
fun·gibil·ity
fun·gible legal term
fun·gic
fun·gi·cid·al
fun·gi·cide
fun·gi·form
fun·gi·stat
fun·gi·stat·ic

fun·goid
fun·gous (*adj*)
fun·gus (*noun; plural* ·gi
or ·guses)
fu·ni·cle botany term
fu·nicu·lar
fu·nicu·late
fu·nicu·lus (*plural* ·li)
anatomy term
funk
funk·er
funky (funki·er,
funki·est)
fun·nel (·nel·ling, ·nelled;
US ·nel·ing, ·neled)
fun·ni·ly
fun·ni·ness
fun·ny (·ni·er, ·ni·est)
fur (fur·ring, furred)
fur·al·de·hyde
fu·ran (*or* fur·fu·ran)
chemical compound
fur·below ornamental trim
fur·bish
fur·bish·er
fur·cate fork
fur·cat·ed
fur·ca·tion
fur·cu·la (*or* ·lum; *plural*
·lae *or* ·la) forklike organ
fur·fur (*plural* ·fures)
scaling of skin
fur·fu·ra·ceous of bran
fur·fur·al·de·hyde
fur·fu·ran *variant of* furan
fu·rio·so musical term
fu·ri·ous
fu·ri·ous·ness
furl
furl·able
furl·er
fur·long unit
fur·lough *US* leave
fur·men·ty *variant of*
frumenty
fur·nace
Fur·ness Cumbrian
peninsula
fur·nish
fur·nish·er
fur·nish·ings
fur·ni·ture
fu·ro·re (*or esp. US*
fu·ror)

fur·phy (*plural* ·phies)
Austral rumour
furred
fur·ri·er fur dealer; more
furry
fur·ri·ery (*plural* ·eries)
fur·ri·ly
fur·ri·ness
fur·ring
fur·row
fur·row·er
fur·rowy
fur·ry (·ri·er, ·ri·est)
fur·ther additional; *variant*
of farther
fur·ther·ance
fur·ther·er
further·more
further·most
fur·thest
fur·tive
fur·tive·ly
fur·tive·ness
fu·run·cle boil
fu·run·cu·lar (*or* ·lous)
fu·run·cu·lo·sis skin
condition
fury (*plural* furies)
furze gorse
furzy
fu·sain charcoal
fus·cous brownish
fuse
fu·see (*or* ·zee) clock part;
match
fu·sel oil
fu·selage
(fushia) *incorrect spelling of*
fuchsia
Fu·shun Chinese city
fu·sibil·ity (*or*
fusible·ness)
fu·sible
fu·sibly
fu·si·form spindle-shaped
fu·sil musket
fu·sile (*or* ·sil) easily
melted
fu·si·lier
fu·sil·lade rapid gunfire
fu·sion
fu·sion·ism
fu·sion·ist
fuss
fuss·er

fussi·ly
fussi·ness
fuss·pot
fussy (fussi·er, fussi·est)
fus·ta·nel·la (or ·nelle)
Greek skirt
fus·tian fabric
fus·tic tree
fus·ti·ly
fus·ti·ness
fus·ty (·ti·er, ·ti·est)
fu·thark (or ·tharc,
·thork, ·thorc) phonetic
alphabet
fu·tile

fu·tile·ly
fu·tili·tar·ian
fu·tili·tari·an·ism
fu·til·ity (plural ·ities)
fut·tock part of boat
fu·ture
fu·tur·ism
fu·tur·ist
fu·tur·is·tic
fu·tur·is·ti·cal·ly
fu·tur·ity (plural ·ities)
fu·tur·olo·gist
fu·tur·ol·ogy

fu yung variant of foo yong
fu·zee variant spelling of
fusee
fuzz
fuzzi·ly
fuzzi·ness
fuzzy (fuzzi·er, fuzzi·est)
fyke US fishing net
Fylde region of Lancashire
fyrd Anglo-Saxon militia
Fyza·bad (or Faiza·)
Indian city; compare
Faizabad

G

Ga (or Gā; plural Ga,
Gas or Gā, Gās)
African people
gab (gab·bing, gabbed)
gab·ar·dine variant spelling
of gaberdine
gab·ber
gab·ble
gab·bler
gab·bro (plural ·bros)
rock
gab·bro·ic (or ·it·ic)
gab·by (·bi·er, ·bi·est)
talkative
ga·belle French salt tax
gab·er·dine fabric
gab·er·dine (or ·ar·) cloak
Ga·bès Tunisian port
gab·fest US gathering
ga·bi·on stone-filled cylinder
ga·bi·on·ade (or ·on·nade)
ga·ble
ga·bled
ga·blet small gable
Ga·bon
Gabo·nese
Gabo·ro·ne Botswanan
capital
gaby (plural gabies)
simpleton
gad (gad·ding, gad·ded)
gad·about
gad·der
gad·fly (plural ·flies)
gadg·et

gadg·eteer lover of gadgetry
gadg·et·ry
gadg·ety
Gad·hel·ic Gaelic language
ga·did fish
ga·doid
gado·lin·ic
gado·lin·ite mineral
gado·lin·ium chemical
element
ga·droon (or go·)
decorative moulding
ga·drooned (or go·)
gad·wall (plural ·walls or
·wall) duck
Gael Gaelic speaker
Gael·ic
gaff angling pole; nautical
boom; Slang home
gaffe blunder
gaf·fer
gaff-rigged
gaff·sail
gaff-topsail
gag (gag·ging, gagged)
gaga Slang senile
Ga·gau·zi Russian language
gage pledge; greengage; US
spelling of gauge
gagged
gag·ger
gag·ging
gag·gle
gahn·ite mineral
gai·ety (plural ·eties)

gail·lar·dia plant
gai·ly
gain
gain·able
gain·er
gain·ful
gain·ful·ly
gain·ful·ness
gain·li·ness
gain·ly
gain·say (·say·ing, ·said)
gain·say·er
gait walk
gait·er
gal Slang girl; unit
gala
ga·lac·ta·gogue inducing
milk secretion
ga·lac·tic
gal·ac·tom·eter
gal·ac·tom·etry
ga·lac·to·poi·esis milk
production
ga·lac·to·poi·etic
ga·lac·tose sugar
ga·la·go (plural ·gos)
bushbaby
ga·lah bird
Galahad
ga·lan·gal plant
gal·an·tine glazed pressed
meat
Ga·lá·pa·gos Is·lands
Gala·shiels Scottish town
Ga·la·ta Turkish port

Galatea mythological character

gala·tea fabric

Ga·laţi Romanian port

Ga·la·tia ancient Asian region

Ga·la·tians New Testament book

Gal·axy solar system

gal·axy (*plural* **·axies**) any star system; distinguished gathering

gal·ba·num gum resin

gale

ga·lea (*plural* **·leae**) helmet-shaped structure

ga·leate (*or* **·leat·ed**)

ga·lei·form

ga·lena (*or* **·lenite**) mineral

Ga·len·ic of Galen's medical system

ga·leni·cal pharmacology term

Ga·len·ism

Ga·len·ist

ga·lère *French* undesirable people

Ga·li·bi (*plural* **·bi** *or* **·bis**) American Indian

Ga·li·cia European region

Ga·li·cian

Gali·lean of Galilee; of Galileo

Gali·lee Israeli region

gali·lee church porch

gal·in·gale (*or* **ga·lan·gal**) plant

gali·ot (*or* **gal·li·ot**) small galley

gali·pot (*or* **gal·li·pot**) pine resin

gall

Gal·la (*plural* **·las** *or* **·la**) African people

gal·lant

gal·lant·ness

gal·lant·ry (*plural* **·ries**)

gall blad·der

Gal·le Sri Lankan port

gal·leass (*or* **·li·ass**) warship

gal·leon

gal·ler·ied

gal·lery (*plural* **·leries**)

gal·ley

gall·fly (*plural* **·flies**)

gal·li·am·bic verse metre

gal·liard dance

Gal·lic of France or Gaul

gal·lic chemistry term; of galls

Gal·li·can

Gal·li·can·ism French Catholic movement

Gal·lice *Latin* in French

Gal·li·cism

Gal·li·ci·za·tion (*or* **·sa·tion**)

Gal·li·cize (*or* **·cise**)

Gal·li·ciz·er (*or* **·cis·er**)

gal·li·gas·kins men's breeches

gal·li·mau·fry (*plural* **·fries**) *US* hotchpotch

gal·li·na·cean

gal·li·na·ceous ornithology term

gall·ing

gal·li·nule bird

gal·li·ot *variant spelling of* galiot

Gal·lipo·li Turkish port

gal·li·pot earthenware pot; *variant spelling of* galipot

gal·lium chemical element

gal·li·vant (*or* **gali·vant**, **gala·vant**)

gal·li·wasp lizard

gall·nut (*or* **gall-apple**)

gal·lo·glass (*or* **·low·**) Irish military retainer

gal·lon

gal·lon·age

gal·loon decorative cord

gal·lop horse's gait; *compare* galop

gal·lop·er

gal·lous chemistry term

Gal·lo·way Scottish area

gal·lows (*plural* **·lowses** *or* **·lows**)

gall·stone

gal·luses *Dialect* braces

ga·loot *US* clumsy person

gal·op dance; *compare* gallop

ga·lore

ga·loshes (*or* **go·**)

ga·lumph

gal·van·ic (*or* **·vani·cal**)

gal·vani·cal·ly

gal·va·nism

gal·va·ni·za·tion (*or* **·sa·tion**)

gal·va·nize (*or* **·nise**)

gal·va·niz·er (*or* **·nis·er**)

gal·va·nom·eter

gal·va·no·met·ric (*or* **·ri·cal**)

gal·va·nom·etry

gal·va·no·scope

gal·va·no·scop·ic

gal·va·nos·co·py

gal·va·no·trop·ic

gal·va·not·ro·pism botany term

gal·vo (*plural* **·vos**) *short for* galvanometer

Gal·way Irish county

Gal·we·gian

gal·yak (*or* **·yac**) fur

gam school of whales

gam·ba·do (*plural* **·dos** *or* **·does**) leather stirrup

gam·beson medieval garment

Gam·bia

Gam·bian

gam·bier (*or* **·bir**) astringent

Gam·bier Is·lands

gam·bit

gam·ble bet; *compare* gambol

gam·bler

gam·bling

gam·boge gum resin

gam·bo·gian

gam·bol (**·bol·ling**, **·bolled**; *US* **·bol·ing**, **·boled**) frolic; *compare* gamble

gam·brel horse's hock; type of roof

game

game·cock

game·keeper

game·keeping

gam·elan oriental orchestra

game·ly

game·ness

games·man (*plural* **·men**)

games·man·ship

game·some merry

game·ster

ga·met·al (*or* **·ic**)

gam·etan·gial

gam·etan·gium (*plural* ·gia)
gam·ete reproductive cell
ga·meto·cyte
gam·eto·gen·esis (*or* ·etog·eny)
gam·eto·gen·ic (*or* ·etog·enous)
ga·meto·phore plant part
ga·meto·phor·ic
ga·meto·phyte plant producing gametes
gam·eto·phyt·ic
gam·ey *variant spelling of* gamy
gam·ic biology term
gam·in street urchin
gam·ine boyish girl
gami·ness
gam·ing
gam·ma Greek letter
gam·ma·di·on (*plural* ·dia) swastika
gam·mer *Dialect* old woman
gam·mon
gam·mon·er *Slang* deceiver
gam·my (·mi·er, ·mi·est) *Slang* lame
gamo·gen·esis biology term
gamo·genet·ic (*or* ·geneti·cal)
gamo·pet·al·ous botany term
gamo·phyl·lous
gamo·sep·al·ous
gamp umbrella
gam·ut
gamy (*or* gam·ey; gami·er, gami·est)
gan (gan·ning, ganned) *Dialect* to go
Gan·da (*plural* ·das *or* ·da) African people
gan·der
Gan·dhian
Gan·dhi·ism (*or* ·dhism)
ga·nef *US* opportunist
gang
gang·bang
ganged
gang·er labourers' foreman
Gan·ges Indian river
gang·land
gan·glial (*or* gan·gli·ar)
gan·gling (*or* ·gly)

gan·gli·on (*plural* ·glia *or* ·gli·ons) nerve tissue; cyst
gan·gli·on·ic (*or* ·at·ed)
gang·plank (*or* ·way)
gan·grene
gan·gre·nous
gang·ster
Gang·tok Indian city
gangue (*or* gang) worthless ore
gang·way
gan·is·ter (*or* gan·nis·) rock
gan·ja cannabis
gan·net
gan·oid zoology term
gan·sey *Dialect* pullover
gant·let rail track; *variant spelling of* gauntlet
gant·line nautical term
gan·try (*or* gaun·; *plural* ·tries)
Gany·mede satellite of Jupiter
Ganymede mythological character
gaol *variant spelling of* jail
gaol·er *variant spelling of* jailer
gap (gap·ping, gapped)
gape
gap·er
gapes fowl disease
gape·worm
gap·ing·ly
gapped
gap·ping grammar term
gar (*plural* gar *or* gars) fish
gar·age
Gara·mond typeface
garb
gar·bage
gar·ble
gar·bler
garb·less
gar·board nautical term
gar·çon *French* waiter
Gard *French* department
Gar·da Italian lake
gar·den
gar·den·er
gar·denia
gar·den·ing

gar·fish (*plural* ·fish *or* ·fishes)
gar·ga·ney duck
gar·gan·tuan
gar·get cattle disease
gar·gety
gar·gle
gar·gler
gar·goyle
gar·goyled
gar·ial *variant of* gavial
gari·bal·di blouse; biscuit
gar·ish
gar·ish·ness
gar·land
gar·lic
gar·licky
gar·ment
gar·ner
gar·net
gar·ni·er·ite mineral
gar·nish
gar·nishee (·nishee·ing, ·nisheed) legal term
gar·nish·er
gar·nish·ment legal notice
gar·ni·ture decoration
Ga·ronne French river
ga·rotte *variant spelling of* garrotte
gar·pike fish
gar·ret
gar·ri·son
gar·rotte (*or* gar·rote, ga·rotte) execution
gar·rott·er (*or* gar·rot·er, ga·rott·er)
gar·ru·lous
gar·ru·lous·ness (*or* gar·ru·lity)
gar·rya shrub
gar·ter
garth cloistered courtyard
Gary US port
gas (*noun, plural* gases *or* gas·ses; *verb* gases *or* gas·ses, gas·sing, gassed)
gas·bag
Gas·con of Gascony
gas·con·ade boastful talk
Gas·co·ny
gas·eous
gas·eous·ness
gases (*or* gas·ses)

gash
gas·holder
gasi·fi·able
gasi·fi·ca·tion
gasi·fi·er
gasi·form
gasi·fy (·fies, ·fy·ing,
·fied)
gas·ket
gas·kin part of horse's thigh
gas·light
gas·man (plural ·men)
gas·olier (or ·elier) fitting
for gaslights
gaso·line (or ·lene) US
petrol
gaso·lin·ic
gas·om·eter
gaso·met·ric (or ·ri·cal)
gas·ometry
gasp
Gas·pé Canadian peninsula
gasp·er
gasp·ing·ly
gassed
gas·ser
gas·si·ness
gas·sing
gas·sy (·si·er, ·si·est)
(gasteropod) incorrect
spelling of gastropod
gas·tight
gas·tight·ness
gas·tral·gia stomach pain
gas·tral·gic
gas·trec·to·my (plural
·mies)
gas·tric
gas·trin hormone
gas·trit·ic
gas·tri·tis
gas·tro·en·ter·ic
gas·tro·en·terit·ic
gas·tro·en·teri·tis
gas·tro·en·te·rolo·gist
gas·tro·en·ter·ol·ogy (or
gas·trol·ogy)
gas·tro·en·ter·os·to·my
(plural ·mies) operation
gas·tro·in·tes·ti·nal
gas·tro·lith stomach stone
gas·trol·ogy variant of
gastroenterology

gas·tro·nome (or
·trono·mer,
·trono·mist)
gas·tro·nom·ic (or
·nomi·cal)
gas·tro·nomi·cal·ly
gas·trono·mist
gas·trono·my cooking
gas·tro·pod mollusc
gas·tropo·dan
gas·tropo·dous
gas·tro·scope medical
instrument
gas·tro·scop·ic
gas·tros·co·pist
gas·tros·co·py
gas·tros·to·my (plural
·mies) artificial stomach
opening
gas·tro·to·my (plural
·mies) stomach operation
gas·tro·trich aquatic animal
gastro·vas·cu·lar
gas·tru·la (plural ·las or
·lae) embryology term
gas·tru·lar
gas·tru·la·tion
gas·works
gate
gâ·teau (or ga·; plural
·teaux)
gate-crash
gate-crasher
gated
gate·fold folded oversize
page
gate·house
gate·keeper
gate-leg (or -legged)
table
gate·post
Gates·head
gate·way
Gath biblical city
gath·er
gath·er·able
gath·er·er
gath·er·ing
Gatling gun
gauche
gauche·ly
gauche·ness
gau·cherie
gau·cho (plural ·chos)
cowboy

gaud trinket
gaud·ery (plural ·eries)
gaudi·ly
gaudi·ness
gaudy (gaudi·er,
gaudi·est)
gauf·fer variant spelling of
goffer
gauge (US also gage)
measure; compare gage
gauge·able (US also
gage·)
gauge·ably (US also
gage·)
gaug·er (US also gag·)
Gau·ha·ti Indian city
Gaul Roman province
Gau·lei·ter German
governor
Gaul·ish
Gaull·ism policies of de
Gaulle
Gaull·ist
gaul·theria shrub
gaunt
gaunt·let (or gant·)
gaunt·ness
gaun·try variant spelling of
gantry
gaur cattle
gauss (plural gauss) unit
gauss·meter
gauze
gauzi·ly
gauzi·ness
gauzy (gauzi·er,
gauzi·est)
ga·vage forced feeding
gave
gav·el hammer
gav·el·kind land tenure
ga·vial (or ghar·ial,
gar·ial) crocodile
Gäv·le Swedish port
ga·votte (or ·vot)
gawk
gawki·ly (or gawk·ish·)
gawki·ness (or gawk·ish·)
gawky (or gawk·ish;
gawki·er, gawki·est)
gawp
gay
Gay Gor·dons dance
Gaza Israeli-occupied city

Gaz·an·ku·lu South African homeland

gaze

ga·zebo (*plural* **·zebos** *or* **·zeboes**)

gaze·hound

ga·zelle (*plural* **·zelles** *or* **·zelle**)

gaz·er

ga·zette

gaz·et·teer

Ga·zi·an·tep Turkish city

gaz·pa·cho soup

ga·zump

ga·zump·er

Gdańsk Polish port

Gdy·nia Polish port

gean cherry

ge·anti·cli·nal

ge·anti·cline geology term

gear

gear·box

gear·ing

gear·shift *US* gear lever

gear·wheel

gecko (*plural* **geckos** *or* **geckoes**)

ge·dact (*or* **·deckt**) organ pipe

gee (**gee·ing, geed**)

gee-gee

geek sideshow performer

Gee·long Australian port

gee·pound unit

geese

geest German heathland

gee·zer *Slang* old man; *compare* **geyser**

ge·gen·schein glow in sky

Ge·hen·na place of torment

geh·len·ite mineral

Geiger count·er

gei·sha (*plural* **·sha** *or* **·shas**)

gel (**gel·ling, gelled**) jelly-like substance; form gel; *variant spelling of* **jell**

ge·la·da baboon

ge·län·de·sprung ski jump

gela·tin (*or* **·tine**)

ge·lati·ni·za·tion (*or* **·sa·tion**)

ge·lati·nize (*or* **·nise**)

ge·lati·niz·er (*or* **·nis·er**)

ge·lati·noid

ge·lati·nous

ge·la·tion freezing

geld (**geld·ing, geld·ed** *or* **gelt**)

Gel·der·land (*or* **Guel·**) Dutch province

gel·id very cold

ge·lid·ity (*or* **·ness**)

gel·ig·nite

gelled

gel·ling

gel·se·mium (*plural* **·miums** *or* **·mia**) shrub

Gel·sen·kir·chen West German city

gelt *Slang* money

gem (**gem·ming, gemmed**)

gemi·nate in pairs

gemi·na·tion

Gemi·ni constellation; sign of zodiac

gem·ma (*plural* **·mae**) plant structure

gem·ma·ceous

gem·mate

gem·ma·tion

gemmed

gem·ming

gem·mipa·rous reproducing by gemmae

gem·mu·la·tion

gem·mule reproductive body

gemo·logi·cal (*or* **gem·mo·**)

gem·olo·gist (*or* **gem·molo·**)

gem·ol·ogy (*or* **gem·mol·**) study of gems

ge·mot Anglo-Saxon assembly

gems·bok (*or* **·buck**; *plural* **·bok, ·boks** *or* **·buck, ·bucks**) antelope

gem·stone

ge·müt·lich *German* cosy

gen *Slang* information

ge·nappe worsted

gen·darme

gen·dar·me·rie (*or* **·ry**)

gen·der

gene

ge·nea·logi·cal (*or* **·log·ic**)

ge·nealo·gist

ge·neal·ogy (*plural* **·ogies**)

gen·era *plural of* **genus**

gen·er·able able to be generated

gen·er·al

gen·er·al·is·si·mo (*plural* **·mos**)

gen·er·al·ist

gen·er·al·ity (*plural* **·ities**)

gen·er·ali·za·tion (*or* **·sa·tion**)

gen·er·al·ize (*or* **·ise**)

gen·er·al·iz·er (*or* **·is·er**)

gen·er·al·ly

gen·er·al·ness

gen·er·al·ship

gen·er·ate

gen·era·tion

gen·era·tive

gen·era·tor

gen·era·trix (*plural* **·tri·ces**) geometry term

ge·ner·ic (*or* **·neri·cal**)

ge·neri·cal·ly

gen·er·os·ity (*plural* **·ities**)

gen·er·ous

gen·er·ous·ness

Gen·esis Old Testament book

gen·esis (*plural* **·eses**) beginning

gen·et (*or* **ge·nette**) catlike animal; *variant spelling of* **jennet**

ge·net·ic (*or* **·neti·cal**)

ge·neti·cal·ly

ge·neti·cist

ge·net·ics

Ge·neva

Ge·nevan (*or* **Gen·evese**; *plural* **·evans** *or* **·evese**)

gen·ial cheerful

ge·nial of the chin

ge·ni·al·ity (*or* **gen·ial·ness**)

ge·ni·al·ly

gen·ic of a gene

ge·nicu·late bending sharply

ge·nicu·la·tion

ge·nie (*plural* **ge·nies** *or* **ge·nii**)

geni·pap (*or* **gen·ip**) fruit

geni·tal

geni·tal·ic
geni·tals (*or* ·ta·lia)
geni·ti·val
geni·tive grammar term
geni·tor biological father
genito·uri·nary
ge·ni·us (*plural*
ge·ni·uses)
ge·ni·zah synagogue
storeroom
Genoa Italian city
genoa yacht sail
geno·cid·al
geno·cide
Geno·ese (*or* ·vese;
plural ·ese *or* ·vese)
ge·nome (*or* ·nom)
genetics term
geno·type genetics term
geno·typ·ic (*or* ·typi·cal)
geno·ty·pic·ity
gen·re
gens (*plural* gen·tes)
Roman aristocratic family
gent
gen·teel
gen·teel·ly
gen·teel·ness
gen·tian plant
gen·tia·na·ceous
gen·tian·el·la plant
Gen·tile not Jewish
gen·tile grammar term
gen·til·ity (*plural* ·ities)
gen·tle
gentle·folk
gentle·man (*plural* ·men)
gen·tleman-at-arms
(*plural* ·tlemen-)
gentle·man·li·ness
gentle·man·ly
gen·tle·ness
gentle·woman (*plural*
·women)
gen·tly
gen·tri·fi·ca·tion
gen·tri·fy (·fies, ·fy·ing,
·fied)
gen·try
genu (*plural* genua) knee
genu·flect
genu·flec·tion (*or*
·flex·ion)
genu·flec·tor
genu·ine

genu·ine·ly
genu·ine·ness
ge·nus (*plural* gen·era *or*
ge·nuses)
geo·cen·tric
geo·cen·tri·cal·ly
geo·chemi·cal
geo·chem·ist
geo·chem·is·try
geo·chrono·logi·cal
geo·chro·nol·ogy
ge·ode rock cavity
geo·des·ic
ge·od·esist
geod·esy (*or* geo·det·ics)
measurement of earth
geo·det·ic
ge·od·ic
geo·dy·nam·ic
geo·dy·nami·cist
geo·dy·nam·ics
ge·og·nos·tic
ge·og·no·sy study of earth's
structure
ge·og·ra·pher
geo·graphi·cal (*or*
·graph·ic)
geo·graphi·cal·ly
ge·og·ra·phy (*plural*
·phies)
ge·oid shape of earth
geo·logi·cal (*or* ·log·ic)
geo·logi·cal·ly
ge·olo·gist (*or* ·ger)
ge·olo·gize (*or* ·gise)
ge·ol·ogy
geo·mag·net·ic
geo·mag·ne·tism
geo·man·cer
geo·man·cy prophecy
geo·man·tic
geo·mechan·ics
ge·om·eter (*or*
ge·om·etri·cian)
geo·met·ric (*or* ·ri·cal)
geo·met·ri·cal·ly
ge·om·etrid moth
ge·om·etrize (*or* ·etrise)
ge·om·etry
geo·mor·phic of earth's
surface
geo·mor·pho·logi·cal (*or*
·log·ic)
geo·mor·pho·logi·cal·ly

geo·mor·pholo·gy (*or*
·phog·eny)
ge·opha·gist
ge·opha·gous
ge·opha·gy (*or*
geo·pha·gia,
ge·opha·gism) eating soil
geo·physi·cal
geo·physi·cist
geo·phys·ics
geo·phyte botany term
geo·phyt·ic
geo·po·liti·cal
geo·poli·ti·cian
geo·poli·tics
geo·pon·ic
geo·pon·ics agricultural
science
Geor·die Tynesider
geor·gette fabric
Geor·gia US state; Soviet
republic
Geor·gian
geor·gic poem
geo·sci·ence
geo·stat·ic
geo·stat·ics geology term
geo·strat·egy
geo·stroph·ic meteorology
term
geo·syn·chro·nous
geo·syn·cli·nal
geo·syn·cline geology term
geo·tac·tic
geo·tac·ti·cal·ly
geo·tax·is biology term
geo·tec·ton·ic of earth's
crust
geo·ther·mal (*or* ·mic)
geo·trop·ic
geo·tropi·cal·ly
ge·ot·ro·pism botany term
ge·rah Hebrew weight
ge·ra·nia·ceous botany
term
ge·ra·nial chemistry term
ge·ra·ni·ol chemical
compound
ge·ra·nium
gera·to·log·ic
gera·tol·ogy study of
elderly
ger·bil (*or* ·bille, jer·bil)
ger·ent manager
ger·enuk antelope

ger·fal·con *variant spelling of* gyrfalcon
geri·at·ric
geria·tri·cian (*or* geri·at·rist)
geri·at·rics
germ
ger·man of close relationship; *compare* germen
Ger·man
ger·man·der plant
ger·mane relevant
ger·mane·ly
ger·mane·ness
Ger·man·ic of Germany
ger·man·ic chemistry term
Ger·man·ism
ger·man·ite mineral
ger·ma·nium chemical element
Ger·mani·za·tion (*or* ·sa·tion)
Ger·man·ize (*or* ·ise)
Ger·man·iz·er (*or* ·is·er)
Ger·mano·phile (*or* ·phil)
Ger·mano·philia
Ger·mano·phobe
Ger·mano·pho·bia
ger·man·ous chemistry term
Ger·ma·ny
ger·men (*plural* ·mens *or* ·mi·na) biology term; *compare* german
ger·mi·cid·al
ger·mi·cide
ger·mi·nable (*or* ·na·tive)
ger·mi·nal embryonic
ger·mi·nal·ly
ger·mi·nant
ger·mi·nate
ger·mi·na·tion
ger·mi·na·tor
Ger·mis·ton South African city
ger·on·toc·ra·cy (*plural* ·cies) government by old men
ge·ron·to·crat·ic
ge·ron·to·logi·cal
ge·ron·tolo·gist
ge·ron·tol·ogy study of ageing
ger·ry·man·der
ger·und grammar term

ge·run·dial
ger·un·di·val
ge·run·dive grammar term
ges·so (*plural* ·soes) white plaster
ge·stalt (*plural* ·stalts *or* ·stal·ten) overall structure
Ge·sta·po
ges·tate
ges·ta·tion
ges·ta·tion·al (*or* ·tive)
ges·ta·to·ry
ges·ticu·late
ges·ticu·la·tion
ges·ticu·la·tive
ges·ticu·la·tor
ges·tur·al
ges·ture
ges·tur·er
get (get·ting, got)
get·able (*or* get·table)
get·at·able
get·away (*noun*)
Geth·sema·ne
get·out (*noun*)
get·ter
get·together
Get·tys·burg US town
get·up (*noun*)
geum plant
gew·gaw showy trinket
gey·ser hot spring; water heater; *compare* geezer
gey·ser·ite mineral
Ge·zi·ra Sudanese region
Gha·na
Gha·na·ian (*or* Gha·nian)
ghar·ial *variant of* gavial
ghar·ry (*or* ·ri; *plural* ·ries) Indian vehicle
ghast·li·ness
ghast·ly (·li·er, ·li·est)
ghat steps to river
Ghats Indian mountains
gha·zi Muslim fighter
ghee butter
Ghent Belgian port
gher·kin pickled cucumber; *compare* jerkin
ghet·to (*plural* ·tos *or* ·toes)
Ghib·el·line political faction
Ghib·el·lin·ism

ghib·li (*or* gib·) hot wind
ghil·lie laced shoe; *variant spelling of* gillie
ghost
ghost·like
ghost·li·ness
ghost·ly (·li·er, ·li·est)
ghost·write (·writ·ing, ·wrote, ·writ·ten)
ghost·writ·er
ghoul
ghoul·ish
gi·ant
gi·ant·ess
gi·ant·ism *variant of* gigantism
giaour non-Muslim
gib (gib·bing, gibbed)
gib·ber
gib·ber·el·lin plant hormone
gib·ber·ish
gib·bet
gib·bing
gib·bon
gib·bous (*or* ·bose)
gib·bous·ness
gibbs·ite mineral
gibe (*or* jibe) taunt; *compare* gybe
Gib·eon Palestinian town
gib·er (*or* jib·)
gib·ing·ly (*or* jib·)
gib·lets
gib·li *variant spelling of* ghibli
Gi·bral·tar
Gi·bral·tar·ian
Gib·son Australian desert; US cocktail
gid sheep disease
gid·di·ly
gid·di·ness
gid·dy (*adj* ·di·er, ·di·est; *verb* ·dies, ·dy·ing, ·died)
giddy-up
gidgee (*or* gidjee) tree
gie *Scot* give
gift
gift·ed
gift·ed·ness
gift·wrap (·wrap·ing, ·wrapped)
gig (gig·ging, gigged)

gi·ga·hertz (*plural* ·hertz)
physics term
gi·gan·tesque
gi·gan·tic
gi·gan·ti·cal·ly
gi·gan·tic·ness
gi·gan·tism (*or* gi·ant·ism)
gi·gan·toma·chy battle of
giants
gig·gle
gig·gler
gig·gly
gigo·lo (*plural* ·los)
gi·got leg of mutton
gigue music
Gi·jón Spanish port
gil·bert unit
Gil·ber·tian of W. S.
Gilbert
Gil·bert Is·lands *former*
name of **Kiribati**
gild (gild·ing, gild·ed *or*
gilt) cover with gold;
compare **guild**
gild·er one who gilds;
variant spelling of **guilder**
gild·ing
Gil·ead mountain region;
biblical character
gi·let bodice
gil·gai *Austral* water hole
Gilgamesh legendary king
gill
gilled
gil·lie (*or* ghil·lie, gil·ly;
plural ·lies) huntsman's
attendant; *compare* **ghillie**
Gil·ling·ham towns in Kent
and Dorset
gil·lion one thousand
million
gill-less
gil·ly·flow·er (*or* ·li·)
Gil·son·ite (*Trademark*)
asphalt
gilt covered in gold; gilding
substance; pig; *compare*
guilt
gilt-edged
gilt-head fish
gim·bals suspension device
gim·crack
gim·let
gim·mal mechanical joint
gim·me *Slang* give me
gim·mick

gim·mick·ry
gim·micky
gimp (*or* guimpe) fabric
trimming
gin (gin·ning, ginned)
gin·ger
ginger·bread
gin·ger·li·ness
gin·ger·ly
gin·gery
ging·ham
gin·gi·li (*or* ·gel·li, ·gel·ly)
sesame oil
gin·gi·va (*plural* ·vae) gum
gin·gi·val
gin·gi·vi·tis
gin·gly·mus (*plural* ·mi)
anatomy term
gink *Slang* man or boy
gink·go (*or* ging·ko;
plural ·goes *or* ·koes)
tree
gin·nel *Dialect* passageway
gin·seng
gip·py (*plural* ·pies) *Slang*
an Egyptian; gipsy
gip·sy (*or* gyp·; *plural*
·sies)
gipsy·wort
gi·raffe (*plural* ·raffes *or*
·raffe)
gir·an·dole (*or*
gi·ran·do·la) candle-
holder
gira·sol (*or* giro·sol,
gira·sole) opal
gird (gird·ing, gird·ed *or*
girt)
gird·er
gir·dle
gir·dler
girl
girl·friend
girl·hood
girlie
girl·ish
girl·ish·ness
giro (*plural* ·ros) credit
transfer; *compare* gyro
gi·ron (*or* gy·) heraldic
term
Gi·ronde French river
Gi·ron·dism
Gi·ron·dist French
revolutionary

gi·ron·ny (*or* gy·) heraldic
term
girt
girth
gi·sarme battle-axe
Gis·borne New Zealand
port
gist
git
git·tern ancient guitar
giu·sto musical term
giv·able (*or* give·able)
give (giv·ing, gave,
giv·en)
give-away (*noun*)
giv·en
giv·er
giz·zard
gla·bel·la (*plural* ·lae)
anatomy term
gla·bel·lar
gla·brous (*or* ·brate)
smooth-skinned
gla·brous·ness
gla·cé (·cé·ing, ·céed)
gla·cial
gla·ci·al·ist
gla·ci·al·ly
gla·ci·ate
gla·cia·tion
glaci·er
glacio·logi·cal (*or* ·log·ic)
glaci·olo·gist (*or*
gla·ci·al·ist)
glaci·ol·ogy
glac·is (*plural* ·ises *or* ·is)
slope
glad (glad·der, glad·dest)
glad·den
glad·den·er
glade
gladi·ate sword-shaped
gladia·tor
gladia·to·rial
gladio·lus (*plural* ·li *or*
·luses)
glad·ly
glad·ness
glad·some
Glago·lit·ic Slavic alphabet
glair bookbinding glaze
glairi·ness
glairy (*or* glair·eous)
Gla·mor·gan

glam·ori·za·tion (*or* ·sa·tion)
glam·or·ize (*or* ·ise; *US also* ·our·)
glam·or·iz·er (*or* ·is·er)
glam·or·ous (*or* ·our·)
glam·or·ous·ness (*or* ·our·)
glam·our (*US also* glam·or)
glance
glanc·ing·ly
gland
glan·dered
glan·der·ous
glan·ders disease
glan·du·lar (*or* ·lous)
glan·dule small gland
glans (*plural* glan·des) anatomy term
glare
glar·ing
glar·ing·ly
glar·ing·ness
glary
Glas·gow
glass
glass-blower
glass-blowing
glasses
glass·house
glassi·ly
glass·ine book covering
glassi·ness
glass·like
glass-maker
glass-making
glass·man (*plural* ·men)
glass·ware
glass·work
glass·worker
glass·works
glass·wort plant
glassy (glassi·er, glassi·est)
Glas·ton·bury
Glas·we·gian of Glasgow
Glauce mythological character
glau·co·ma eye disease
glau·co·ma·tous
glau·co·nite mineral
glau·co·nit·ic
glau·cous waxy
glaze

glaz·er
gla·zi·er
gla·zi·ery
glaz·ing
gleam
gleam·ing·ly
glean
glean·able
glean·er
glean·ings
glebe clergyman's benefice
glee
glee·ful
glee·ful·ly
glee·ful·ness
gleet medical term
gleety
glen
Glen·coe Scottish massacre
Glen·dale US city
glen·gar·ry (*plural* ·ries) Scottish cap
gle·noid anatomy term
Glen·roth·es Scottish town
gley soil
glia·din (*or* ·dine) protein
glib (glib·ber, glib·best)
glib·ness
glide
glid·er
glid·ing
glid·ing·ly
glim *Slang* lamp
glim·mer
glim·mer·ing
glimpse
glimps·er
glint
glio·ma (*plural* ·ma·ta *or* ·mas) tumour
glio·ma·tous
glis·sade ballet step
glis·sad·er
glis·san·do (*plural* ·di) musical term
glis·ten
glis·ten·ing·ly
glis·ter glitter
glit·ter
glit·ter·ing
glit·tery
Gli·wi·ce Polish city
gloam·ing dusk
gloat
gloat·er

gloat·ing·ly
glob
glob·al
glob·al·ly
glo·bate (*or* ·bat·ed)
globe
globe-flower
globe-trotter
globe-trotting
glo·big·eri·na (*plural* ·nas *or* ·nae) tiny animal
glo·bin protein
glo·boid
glo·bose (*or* ·bous) spherical
glo·bosi·ty (*or* ·bose·ness)
globu·lar (*or* ·lous)
glob·ule
globu·lif·er·ous
globu·lin protein
glo·chidi·ate
glo·chid·ium (*plural* ·chidia) biology term
glock·en·spiel
glogg alcoholic drink
glom·er·ate
glom·era·tion cluster
glo·meru·lar
glo·meru·late
glom·er·ule
glo·meru·lus (*plural* ·li) anatomy term
gloom
gloom·ful
gloomi·ly
gloomi·ness
gloomy (gloomi·er, gloomi·est)
Glo·ria hymn
glo·ria fabric
glo·ri·fi·able
glo·ri·fi·ca·tion
glo·ri·fi·er
glo·ri·fy (·fies, ·fy·ing, ·fied)
glo·ri·ous
glo·ri·ous·ness
glo·ry (*noun, plural* ·ries; *verb* ·ries, ·ry·ing, ·ried)
glory-of-the-snow plant
gloss
glos·sa (*plural* ·sae *or* ·sas) tongue
glos·sal

glos·sar·ial
glos·sa·rist
glos·sa·ry (*plural* ·ries)
glos·sa·tor gloss writer
glos·sec·to·my (*plural* ·mies*) removal of tongue
gloss·eme linguistics term
gloss·er
glossi·ly
glossi·ness
glos·sit·ic
glos·si·tis inflammation of tongue
glos·sog·ra·pher
glos·sog·ra·phy
glos·so·la·lia gift of tongues
glossy (*adj* glossi·er, glossi·est; *noun*, *plural* glossies)
glot·tal
glot·tic
glot·tide·an
glot·tis (*plural* ·tises or ·ti·des)
glot·to·chro·nol·ogy branch of linguistics
Glouces·ter
Glouces·ter·shire
glove
glov·er
glow
glow·er
glow·er·ing·ly
glow-worm
glox·inia plant
glu·ca·gon hormone
glu·ci·num (*or* ·cin·ium) beryllium
glu·co·cor·ti·cord biochemistry term
glu·co·gen·esis biochemistry term
glu·co·genet·ic
glu·co·neo·gen·esis
glu·co·pro·tein *variant of* glycoprotein
glu·cose
glu·cos·ic
glu·co·sid·al (*or* ·ic)
glu·co·side
glu·co·su·ria *variant of* glycosuria
glue (glu·ing, glued)
glu·er
gluey (glui·er, glui·est)

glum (glum·mer, glum·mest)
glu·ma·ceous
glume botany term
glum·ness
glu·on hypothetical physics particle
glut (glut·ting, glut·ted)
glu·ta·mate
glu·ta·mine amino acid
glu·ta·thi·one biochemical compound
glu·teal (*or* ·taeal)
glu·telin protein
glu·ten protein
glu·tenous of gluten; *compare* glutinous
glu·teus (*or* ·taeus; *plural* ·tei or ·taei) buttock muscle
glu·ti·nous sticky; *compare* glutenous
glu·ti·nous·ness (*or* ·nos·ity)
glut·ton
glut·ton·ous
glut·tony (*plural* ·tonies)
gly·cer·ic of glycerol
glyc·er·ide chemical compound
glyc·er·in (*or* ·ine)
glyc·er·ol syrupy liquid
glyc·er·yl chemistry term
gly·cine amino acid
gly·co·gen biochemical compound
gly·co·gen·esis
gly·co·genet·ic
gly·co·gen·ic
gly·col antifreeze
gly·col·ic (*or* ·col·lic)
gly·coly·sis breakdown of glucose
gly·co·pro·tein (*or* glu·co·)
gly·co·side biochemical compound
gly·co·sid·ic
gly·co·su·ria (*or* glu·) sugar in urine
gly·co·su·ric (*or* glu·)
glyph groove on frieze
glyph·ic
glypho·graph
gly·phog·ra·pher

glypho·graph·ic (*or* ·graphi·cal)
gly·phog·ra·phy printing process
glyp·tic
glyp·tics engraving gems
glyp·to·dont extinct mammal
glyp·tog·ra·pher
glyp·to·graph·ic (*or* ·graphi·cal)
glyp·tog·ra·phy engraving gems
gnarl
gnarled (*or* gnarly)
gnash
gnash·ing·ly
gnat
gnat·catcher bird
gnath·ic (*or* ·al) of the jaw
gna·thi·on anatomy term
gna·thite zoology term
gna·thon·ic deceitfully flattering
gnaw (gnaw·ing, gnawed, gnawed or gnawn)
gnaw·able
gnaw·er
gneiss rock
gneiss·ic (*or* ·oid, ·ose)
gnoc·chi dumplings
gnome
gno·mic (*or* ·mi·cal) of aphorisms
gno·mi·cal·ly
gnom·ish
gno·mon part of sundial
gno·mon·ic
gno·moni·cal·ly
gno·sis (*plural* ·ses) spiritual knowledge
gnos·tic (*or* ·ti·cal)
Gnos·ti·cism
Gnos·ti·cize (*or* ·cise)
gno·to·bi·oti·cal·ly
gno·to·bi·ot·ics biology term
gnu (*plural* gnus or gnu)
go (*verb* goes, go·ing, went, gone; *noun*, *plural* goes)
Goa Indian district
goa gazelle
goad
go-ahead (*noun*, *adj*)

goal
goalie
goal·keeper
goal·keeping
goal·less
goal·mouth
go·an·na lizard
goat
goatee beard
goat·eed
goat·herd
goat·ish
goats·beard (*or* goat's-)
plant
goat·skin
goat's-rue plant
goat·sucker bird
gob (gob·bing, gobbed)
gob·bet
gob·ble
gob·ble·de·gook (*or* ·dy·)
gob·bler
Go·belin tapestry
go-between
Gobi desert; *compare* goby
Go·bian
go·bi·oid zoology term
gob·let
gob·lin
gobo (*plural* gobos *or*
goboes) microphone
shield
gob·stopper
gobu·lar·ity (*or* ·ness)
goby (*plural* goby *or*
gobies) fish; *compare*
Gobi
god
god·child (*plural*
·children)
god·damn
god·daughter
god·dess
go·detia plant
god·father
god-fearing
god·forsaken
god·head
god·hood
god·less
god·less·ness
god·like
god·li·ness
god·ly (·li·er, ·li·est)
god·mother

go·down warehouse
god·parent
go·droon *variant spelling of*
gadroon
god·send
god·son
God·speed
Godt·haab capital of
Greenland
god·wit bird
goer
goe·thite (*or* gö·) mineral
gof·fer (*or* gauf·) to crimp;
compare gopher
Gog biblical character
go-getter
gog·gle
goggle·box
goggle-eyed
gog·gles
Goiâ·nia Brazilian city
Goi·ás Brazilian state
Goi·del Gaelic-speaking
Celt
Goi·del·ic (*or* Goi·dhel·ic,
Ga·dhel·ic)
go·ing
goi·tre (*US* ·ter) thyroid
swelling
goi·trous
go-kart
Gol·con·da ruined Indian
town
gold
gold-beater
gold-beating
gold·crest bird
gold-dig·ger
gold-digging
gold·en
golden·eye (*plural* ·eyes
or ·eye) duck
golden·rod plant
golden·seal plant
gold·eye (*plural* ·eyes *or*
·eye) fish
gold·finch
gold·fish (*plural* ·fish *or*
·fishes)
goldi·locks plant
gold-miner
gold-mining
gold-of-pleasure plant
gold-plate (*verb*)
gold·smith

gold·thread plant
go·lem resurrected being
golf
golf·er
gol·iard medieval scholar
gol·iard·ery
Goliath
gol·li·wog (*or* ·wogg)
gol·lop to eat greedily
gol·lop·er
gol·ly (*plural* ·lies)
go·loshes *variant spelling of*
galoshes
gom·broon pottery
Go·mel Soviet city
Go·mor·rah
gom·pho·sis (*plural* ·ses)
anatomy term
go·mu·ti palm tree
gon·ad sex organ
gon·ad·al (*or* go·na·dial,
go·nad·ic)
gon·ado·troph·ic (*US*
·trop·ic)
gon·ado·tro·phin (*US*
·tro·pin) hormone
Gond tribal Indian
Gon·dar Ethiopian city
Gon·di Gond language
gon·do·la
gon·do·lier
Gond·wa·na·land ancient
continent
gone
gon·er *Slang* one beyond
help; *compare* gonna
gon·fa·lon (*or* ·non)
banner
gon·fa·lon·ier magistrate
gong
Gon·go·la Nigerian state
Gon·go·rism literary style
go·nia·tite fossil
go·nid·ial (*or* ·nid·ic)
go·nid·ium (*plural* ·ia)
botany term
go·ni·om·eter angle
measurer
go·nio·met·ric (*or* ·ri·cal)
go·ni·om·etry
go·ni·on (*plural* ·nia)
anatomy term
gonk toy
gon·na *Slang* going to;
compare goner

gono·coc·cal (*or* ·cic)
gono·coc·coid
gono·coc·cus (*plural* ·coc·ci*) bacterium
gono·cyte
gono·phore biology term
gono·phor·ic (*or* go·nopho·rous)
gono·pore zoology term
gon·or·rhoea (*US* ·rhea)
gon·or·rhoeal (*or* ·rhoe·ic; *US* ·rheal *or* ·rhe·ic)
goo
goo·ber peanut
good (bet·ter, best)
good·bye
good-for-nothing
good-humoured
good-humoured·ly
good·ish
good·li·ness
good-looking
good·ly (·li·er, ·li·est)
good·man (*plural* ·men) *Archaic* husband
good-natured
good-natured·ly
good·ness
good-night
goods
good-sized
good·wife (*plural* ·wives)
Good·win Sands
goody (*plural* goodies)
goody-goody (*plural* -goodies)
goo·ey (gooi·er, gooi·est)
goof
goofi·ly
goofi·ness
goofy (goofi·er, goofi·est)
goog·ly (*plural* ·lies) cricket term
goo·gol large number
goo·gol·plex large number
Goole Humberside port
goon
goop *US* rude person
goos·an·der duck
goose (*plural* geese)
goose·berry (*plural* ·berries)
goose·foot (*plural* ·foots) plant

goose·gog *Dialect* gooseberry
goose·grass
goose·neck nautical term
goose-step (-stepping, -stepped)
goosi·ness
goosy (*or* goos·ey; goosi·er, goosi·est)
go·pak dance
go·pher animal; *compare* goffer
Go·rakh·pur Indian city
go·ral antelope
Gor·bals Glaswegian suburb
gor·cock male grouse
gore
go·reng pi·sang Malaysian dish
gorge
gorge·able
gor·geous
gor·geous·ness
gorg·er
gor·ger·in architectural term
Gor·gon mythological monster
gor·go·nian coral
Gor·gon·zo·la cheese
go·ril·la ape; *compare* guerrilla
go·ril·lian (*or* ·line)
go·ril·loid
gori·ly
gori·ness
Gor·ki (*or* ·ky) Soviet city
Gor·lov·ka Soviet city
gor·mand·ize (*or* ·ise) eat greedily; *compare* gourmandise
gor·mand·iz·er (*or* is·er)
gorm·less
Gorno-Altai Soviet region
Gorno-Badakh·shan Soviet region
gorse
Gor·sedd bardic institution
gory (gori·er, gori·est)
gosh
gos·hawk
Go·shen biblical region
gos·ling
go-slow

Gos·pel New Testament book
gos·pel truth; doctrine
gos·pel·ler (*US* ·pel·er)
Gos·plan Soviet commission
gos·po·din (*plural* ·po·da) Russian title of address
Gos·port
gos·sa·mer
gos·sip
gos·sip·er
gos·sip·ing·ly
gossip-monger
gos·sipy
gos·soon *Irish* servant
gos·ter *Dialect* laugh
got
Gö·teborg (*or* Goth·en·burg) Swedish port
Goth Germanic people
Goth·ic
Gothi·cal·ly
Gothi·cism
Got·land Swedish island
got·ten
Göt·tin·gen West German city
gouache art term
Gou·da cheese
gouge
goug·er
gou·lash
gou·ra·mi (*plural* ·mi *or* ·mis) fish
gourd
gour·mand (*or* gor·) greedy person; *compare* gourmet
gour·man·dise love of food; *compare* gormandize
gour·mand·ism
gour·met epicure; *compare* gourmand
gout
gouti·ness
gout·weed
gouty
gov·ern
gov·ern·abil·ity (*or* ·able·ness)
gov·ern·able
gov·ern·ance
gov·er·ness
gov·ern·ment

gov·ern·men·tal
gov·er·nor
gov·er·nor·ship
gow·an *Scot* daisy
Gower Welsh peninsula
gown
grab (grab·bing, grabbed)
grab·ber
grab·ble grope
grab·bler
gra·ben trough of land
grace
grace-and-favour
grace·ful
grace·ful·ly
grace·ful·ness
grace·less
Graces Greek goddesses
grac·ile slender
gra·cil·ity (*or* grac·ile·ness)
gra·cious
gra·cious·ness
grack·le bird
grad *Slang* graduate
grad·abil·ity (*or* ·able·ness)
grad·able
gra·date to cause to change
gra·da·tion
gra·da·tion·al
grade
grad·er
gra·di·ent
gra·din (*or* ·dine) step or ledge
grad·ual
gradu·al·ism
gradu·al·ist
gradu·al·is·tic
gradu·al·ly
gradu·al·ness
gradu·and person about to graduate
gradu·ate
gradua·tion
gradua·tor
gra·dus (*plural* ·dus·es) book of musical exercises
Grae·cism (*or esp. US* Gre·)
Grae·cize (*or esp. US* Gre·)
Graeco-Roman (*or esp. US* Greco·)

graf·fi·ti (*sing.* ·to)
graft
graft·er
graft·ing
Grail legendary bowl
grain
grain·er
graini·ness
grain·ing
grainy (graini·er, graini·est)
gral·la·to·rial ornithology term
gram plant
gram (*or* gramme) unit
gra·ma pasture grass
grama·rye magic
gra·mer·cy *Archaic* thanks
grami·ci·din antibiotic
gra·min·eous (*or* ·mina·ceous) of grasses
grami·nivo·rous grass-eating
gram·mar
gram·mar·ian
gram·mati·cal
gram·mati·cal·ly
gram·ma·tolo·gist
gram·ma·tol·ogy study of writing systems
gramme *variant spelling of* gram
gram-molecu·lar (*or* -molar)
Gram-negative bacteriology term
gramo·phone
Gram·pian Scottish mountains and region
Gram-positive bacteriology term
gram·pus (*plural* ·puses) dolphin
Gra·na·da Spanish city
grana·dil·la fruit
grana·ry (*plural* ·ries)
grand
grand·aunt *variant of* great-aunt
grand·child (*plural* ·children)
Grand Cou·lee US dam
grand·dad
grand·daughter
gran·dee
gran·deur

grand·father
gran·dilo·quence
gran·dilo·quent
gran·di·ose
gran·di·ose·ly
gran·di·os·ity
grandio·so musical term
grand·ma (*or* ·mama)
grand mal epilepsy
grand·master
grand·mother
grand·nephew *variant of* great-nephew
grand·niece *variant of* great-niece
grand·pa (*or* ·papa)
grand·parent
grand·son
grand·stand
grange
grang·er·ism
grang·eri·za·tion (*or* ·sa·tion)
grang·er·ize (*or* ·ise) illustrate with borrowed pictures
grang·er·iz·er (*or* ·is·er)
gran·ite
granite·ware
gra·nit·ic (*or* gran·it·oid)
gran·it·ite type of granite
grani·vore
gra·nivo·rous grain-eating
gran·ny (*or* ·nie; *plural* ·nies)
grano·dio·rite rock
grano·lith paving material
grano·lith·ic
grano·phyre rock
grano·phyr·ic
grant
Gran·ta River Cam
grant·able
grantee legal term
grant·er
grant-in-aid (*plural* grants-)
gran·tor
gran tur·is·mo touring car
granu·lar
granu·lar·ity
granu·late
granu·la·tion
granu·la·tive
granu·la·tor (*or* ·lat·er)

gran·ule

granu·lite rock

granu·lit·ic

granu·lo·cyte

granu·lo·cyt·ic

granu·lo·ma (*plural* ·mas *or* ·ma·ta) tumour

granu·loma·tous

grape

grape·fruit (*plural* ·fruit *or* ·fruits)

grapes veterinary term

grape·shot

grape·vine

grap·ey (*or* grapy)

graph

graph·eme linguistics term

gra·phemi·cal·ly

graph·ic (*or* graphi·cal)

graphi·cal·ly

graphi·cal·ness (*or* graph·ic·ness)

graph·ics

graph·ite

gra·phit·ic

graphi·ti·za·tion (*or* ·sa·tion)

graphi·tize (*or* ·tise) convert into graphite

grapho·log·ic (*or* ·logi·cal)

graph·olo·gist

graph·ol·ogy study of handwriting

grapho·mo·tor

grap·nel

grap·pa grape spirit

grap·ple

grap·pler

grap·pling

grap·to·lite fossil

grapy *variant spelling of* grapey

Gras·mere Cumbrian village

grasp

grasp·able

grasp·er

grasp·ing

grass

grass·finch

grass·hook sickle

grass·hopper

grassi·ness

grass·land

grass·quit bird

grassy (grassi·er, grassi·est)

grate

grate·ful

grate·ful·ly

grate·ful·ness

grat·er

grati·cule grid

grati·fi·ca·tion

grati·fi·er

grati·fy (·fies, ·fy·ing, ·fied)

grati·fy·ing·ly

gra·tin cookery term

grat·ing

grat·ing·ly

gra·tis free

grati·tude

gra·tui·tous

gra·tu·ity (*plural* ·ities)

Grau·bün·den Swiss canton

grau·pel hail

grav unit

gra·va·men (*plural* ·vami·na) legal term

grave burial place; accent; serious; engrave

gra·ve musical term

grav·el (·el·ling, ·elled; *US* ·el·ing, ·eled)

grav·el·ish

grav·el·ly

grav·en

grave·ly

grave·ness

grav·er engraving tool

Graves wine

Graves·end

grave·stone

Gra·vett·ian Palaeolithic culture

grave·yard

grav·id pregnant

gra·vid·ity (*or* ·ness)

gra·vim·eter

gravi·met·ric (*or* ·ri·cal)

gra·vim·etry

gravi·tate

gravi·tat·er

gravi·ta·tion

gravi·ta·tion·al

gravi·ta·tion·al·ly

gravi·ta·tive

gravi·ton physics term

grav·ity (*plural* ·ities)

gra·vure printing method

gra·vy (*plural* ·vies)

gray *US spelling of* grey; unit

gray·back *US spelling of* greyback

gray·beard *US spelling of* greybeard

gray·ling (*plural* ·ling *or* ·lings) fish

gray·wacke *US spelling of* greywacke

graze

graz·er animal

gra·zi·er farmer

graz·ing

grease

grease·paint

greas·er

grease·wood (*or* ·bush)

greasi·ly

greasi·ness

greasy (greasi·er, greasi·est)

great

great-aunt (*or* grand·)

great·coat

great·est

great·ly

great-nephew (*or* grand·)

great·ness

great-niece (*or* grand·)

Greats course at Oxford University

great-uncle (*or* grand·)

greave armour

greaves tallow residue

grebe

Gre·cian

Gre·cism *variant spelling* (*esp. US*) *of* Graecism

Gre·cize *variant spelling* (*esp. US*) *of* Graecize

Greco-Roman *variant spelling* (*esp. US*) *of* Graeco-Roman

Greece

greed

greedi·ly

greedi·ness

greedy (greedi·er, greedi·est)

Greek

green

green·back *US* currency note

green·bottle fly
green·brier
green·ery (*plural* ·eries)
green·finch
green·fly (*plural* ·flies)
green·gage
green·grocer
green·grocery (*plural*
    ·groceries)
green·head male mallard
green·heart tree
green·horn
green·house
green·ing cooking apple
green·ish
Green·land
Green·land·er
green·let bird
green·ling fish
green·ness
Green·ock Scottish port
green·ock·ite mineral
green·room
green·sand
Greens·boro US city
green·shank bird
green·stick fracture
green·stone
green·stuff
green·sward turf
Green·wich
green·wood
greet
greet·er
greet·ing
grega·rine zoology term
gre·gari·ous
gre·gari·ous·ness
Gre·go·rian
greige undyed
grei·sen rock
gre·mi·al bishop's cloth
grem·lin
Gre·na·da West Indian
    state
gre·nade
grena·dier
grena·dine fabric; syrup
Grena·dines West Indian
    islands
Grendel legendary monster
Gre·no·ble French city
gres·so·rial (*or* ·ri·ous)
    ornithology term
Gret·na Green

grew
grey (*US* gray) colour;
    compare gray
grey·back (*US* gray·)
    animal
grey·beard (*US* gray·)
grey·hen female black
    grouse
grey·hound
grey·ish (*US* gray·)
grey·lag goose
grey·ness (*US* gray·)
grey·state undyed
grey·wacke (*US* gray·)
    rock
grib·ble wood-boring animal
grid
grid·dle
griddle·cake
gride grate
grid·iron
grief
griev·ance
grieve
griev·er
griev·ing
griev·ous
griev·ous·ness
griffe architectural ornament
grif·fin (*or* grif·fon,
    gryph·on) winged
    monster
grif·fon dog; vulture; *variant
    spelling of* griffin
grig
gri·gri (*or* gris-gris,
    gree·gree; *plural* ·gris
    or ·grees) talisman
grill cooking senses; *compare*
    grille
gril·lage building term
grille (*or* grill) metal
    screen; *compare* grill
grilled
grill·er
grill·room
grilse (*plural* grilses *or*
    grilse) salmon
grim (grim·mer,
    grim·mest)
gri·mace
gri·mac·er
gri·mac·ing·ly
Gri·mal·di moon crater
gri·mal·kin old cat
grime

grim·ness
Grims·by
grimy (grim·ier,
    grim·iest)
grin (grin·ning, grinned)
grind (grind·ing, ground)
grin·de·lia plant
Grin·del·wald Swiss valley
grind·er
grind·ery (*plural* ·eries)
grind·stone
grin·go (*plural* ·gos)
grin·ner
grip (grip·ping, gripped)
gripe
grip·er complainer; *compare*
    gripper
grip·ing·ly
grippe influenza
grip·per one that grips;
    compare griper
grip·ping
grip·ping·ly
gri·saille painting term
gris·eous greyish
gri·sette French girl
gris·kin pork cut
gris·li·ness
gris·ly (·li·er, ·li·est)
    gruesome; *compare* gristly;
    grizzly
gri·son animal
grist
gris·tle
gris·tli·ness
gris·tly having gristle;
    compare grisly; grizzly
grist·mill
grit (grit·ting, grit·ted)
grith place of safety
grits coarsely ground grain
grit·ti·ly
grit·ti·ness
grit·ty (·ti·er, ·ti·est)
griv·et monkey
griz·zle become grey; *Slang*
    whine
griz·zled
griz·zler
griz·zly (*adj* ·zli·er,
    ·zli·est; *noun, plural*
    ·zlies) grey-haired; bear;
    compare grisly; gristly
groan
groan·er

groan·ing·ly
groat old coin
groats crushed grain
gro·cer
gro·cery (*plural* ·ceries)
grock·le *Dialect* tourist
Grod·no Soviet city
grog
grog·gi·ly
grog·gi·ness
grog·gy (·gi·er, ·gi·est)
grog·ram fabric
groin abdominal region; vault; *compare* groyne
Gro·li·er bookbinding style
grom·met (*or* grum·)
grom·well plant
Gro·ning·en Dutch province
groom
groom·er
groom·ing
grooms·man (*plural* ·men)
groove
groovy (groovi·er, groovi·est)
grope
grop·er
grop·ing·ly
gros·beak bird
gro·schen (*plural* ·schen) Austrian coin
gros·grain fabric
gross
gross·ness
gros·su·lar·ite gemstone
grot grotto
gro·tesque
gro·tesque·ly
gro·tesque·ness
gro·tes·query (*or* ·querie; *plural* ·queries)
grot·to (*plural* ·toes *or* ·tos)
grouch
grouchi·ly
grouchi·ness
grouchy (grouch·ier, grouch·iest)
ground
ground·age anchorage fee
ground·ing
ground·less
ground·ling

ground·mass
ground·nut
ground·sel
ground·sheet
ground·sill joist
grounds·man (*plural* ·men)
ground·speed
ground·work
group
group·er (*plural* ·er *or* ·ers) fish
groupie
group·ing
grouse (*plural* grouse *or* grouses)
grous·er complainer
grout
grout·er
grouts coffee grounds
grouty (grouti·er, grouti·est) *Dialect* muddy
grove
grov·el (·el·ling, ·elled; *US* ·el·ing, ·eled)
grov·el·ler (*US* ·el·er)
grov·el·ling·ly (*US* ·el·ing·ly)
grow (grow·ing, grew, grown)
grow·able
grow·er
growl
growl·er
grown
grown-up
growth
groyne jetty; *compare* groin
Groz·ny Soviet city
grub (grub·bing, grubbed)
grub·ber
grub·bi·ly
grub·bi·ness
grub·by (grub·bi·er, grub·bi·est)
grudge
grudg·er
grudg·ing
grudg·ing·ly
gru·el
gru·el·ling (*US* ·el·ing)
grue·some (*or* grew·)
gruff

gruff·ish
gruff·ness
gru·gru palm tree
grum·ble
grum·bler
grum·bling·ly
grum·bly
grum·met *variant spelling of* grommet
gru·mous (*or* ·mose) botany term
grump
grumpi·ly (*or* grump·ish·ly)
grumpi·ness (*or* grump·ish·ness)
grumpy (*or* grump·ish; grumpi·er, grumpi·est)
Grun·dy narrow-minded critical person
grun·ion fish
grunt
grunt·er
grunt·ing·ly
grun·tled contented
Grus constellation
Gru·yère cheese
gryph·on *variant spelling of* griffin
grys·bok antelope
gua·ca·mo·le (*or* ·cha·) avocado dish
gua·co (*plural* ·cos) plant
Gua·dal·ca·nal Pacific island
Gua·dal·qui·vir Spanish river
Gua·de·loupe
(guage) *incorrect spelling of* gauge
guaia·col medicinal liquid
guaia·cum (*or* guaio·) tree or resin
Guam Pacific island
guan bird
Gua·na·ba·ra former Brazilian state
gua·na·co (*plural* ·cos) animal
Gua·na·jua·to Mexican state
gua·nase enzyme
guani·dine (*or* ·din) biochemical compound
gua·nine biochemical compound

gua·no (*plural* ·nos) bird excrement

gua·no·sine biochemical compound

Guan·ta·na·mo Cuban city

Gua·ra·ni (*plural* ·ni *or* ·nis) Paraguayan people

gua·ra·ni (*plural* ·ni *or* ·nis) currency

guar·an·tee (·tee·ing, ·teed)

guar·an·tor

guar·an·ty (*plural* ·ties) legal term

guard

guard·able

guar·dant (*or* gar·) heraldic term

guard·ed

guard·ed·ly

guard·ed·ness

guard·er

guard·house

guard·ian

guardi·an·ship

guard·rail

guard·room

Guards regiment

guards·man (*plural* ·men)

Gua·te·ma·la

gua·va fruit

Gua·ya·quil Ecuadorian port

gua·yu·le shrub

gub·bins

gu·ber·na·to·rial of a governor

guck slimy substance

gudg·eon fish

guelder-rose

Guelph (*or* Guelf) political faction

Guelph·ic (*or* Guelf·)

Guelph·ism (*or* Guelf·)

gue·non monkey

guer·don reward

Guer·ni·ca Spanish town

Guern·sey Channel island

guern·sey sweater

Guer·rero Mexican state

guer·ril·la (*or* gue·ril·la) fighter; *compare* gorilla

guer·ril·la·ism (*or* gue·)

guess

guess·able

guess·er

guess·ti·mate

guess·work

guest

guest·house

guff *Slang* ridiculous talk

guf·faw

Gui·ana South American region

Guia·nese (*or* Gui·an·an)

guid·able

guid·ance

guide

guide·line

guide·post

guid·er

guid·ing

guid·ing·ly

gui·don flag

Gui·enne (*or* Guy·enne) former French province

guild (*or* gild) organization; *compare* gild

guil·der (*or* gild·er, gul·den; *plural* ·ders, ·der *or* ·dens, ·den) currency; *compare* gilder

Guild·ford

guild·hall (*or* gild·)

guilds·man (*or* gilds·; *plural* ·men)

guile

guile·ful

guile·ful·ly

guile·ful·ness

guile·less

guil·lemot

guil·loche architectural border

guil·lo·tine

guil·lo·tin·er

guilt guiltiness; remorse; *compare* gilt

guilti·ly

guilti·ness

guilt·less

guilty (guilti·er, guilti·est)

guimpe blouse; *variant spelling of* gimp

Guinea African republic

guinea coin

Guinea-Bissau African republic

Guin·ean

guinea pig

Guinevere legendary queen

gui·pure lace

guise

gui·tar

guitar·fish (*plural* ·fish *or* ·fishes)

gui·tar·ist

Gu·ja·rat (*or* ·je·) Indian state

Gu·ja·ra·ti (*or* ·je·)

Guj·ran·wa·la Pakistani city

Gu·lag Soviet administrative department

gu·lar of the throat

gulch *US* ravine

gul·den *variant of* guilder

gules heraldic term

gulf

gulf·weed

gull

Gul·lah (*plural* ·lahs *or* ·lah) Negro people

gul·let

gul·li·bil·ity (*or* ·la·)

gul·lible (*or* ·lable)

gul·li·bly (*or* ·la·)

gull-wing

gul·ly (*noun, plural* ·lies; *verb* ·lies, ·ly·ing, ·lied)

gulp

gulp·er

gulp·ing·ly

gum (gum·ming, gummed)

Gum·bo French patois

gum·bo (*or* gom·; *plural* ·bos) thick stew

gum·boil

gum·boot

gum·bo·til clay

gum·drop

gum·ma (*plural* ·mas *or* ·ma·ta) tumour

gum·ma·tous

gum·mi·ly

gum·mi·ness

gum·mite mineral

gum·mo·sis plant disease

gum·my (·mi·er, ·mi·est)

gump·tion

gum·shield

gum·shoe

gum·tree

gun (gun·ning, gunned)

gun·boat
gun·cotton
gun·fight
gun·fighter
gun·fire
gun·flint
gunge
gun·gy
gunk *Slang* slimy substance
gun·lock
gun·man (*plural* ·men)
gun·metal
gunned
gun·nel fish; *variant spelling of* gunwale
gun·ner
gun·nery
gun·ning
gun·ny (*plural* ·nies) *US* fabric
gun·paper
gun·play
gun·point
gun·powder
gun·runner
gun·running
gun·shot
gun·shy
gun·slinger
gun·smith
gun·smithing
gun·stock
Gun·tur Indian city
gun·wale (*or* gun·nel) nautical term
gun·yah *Austral* bush hut
Guo·min·dang *variant spelling of* Kuomintang
gup·py (*plural* ·pies) fish
Gur language
gurd·wa·ra Sikh place of worship
gur·gi·ta·tion surging movement
gur·gle
gur·gling·ly
gur·jun tree
Gur·kha (*plural* ·khas *or* ·kha)
Gur·kha·li language
Gur·mu·khi Punjabi script
gur·nard (*or* gur·net; *plural* ·nard, ·nards *or* ·net, ·nets) fish
guru (*plural* gurus)

gush
gush·er
gush·ing·ly
gushy
gus·set
gust
gus·ta·tion tasting
gus·ta·tory (*or* ·tive)
gusti·ly
gusti·ness
gus·to
gusty (gusti·er, gusti·est)
gut (gut·ting, gut·ted)
gut·bucket jazz
gut·less
gutsy (gutsi·er, gutsi·est)
gut·ta (*plural* ·tae) drop
gutta-percha
gut·tate (*or* ·tat·ed) biology term
gut·ted
gut·ter
gut·ter·ing
gutter·snipe
gut·ting
gut·tur·al
gut·tur·ali·za·tion (*or* ·sa·tion)
gut·tur·al·ize (*or* ·ise)
gut·tur·al·ly
gut·tur·al·ness (*or* ·ity, ·ism)
gut·ty (*plural* ·ties) *Irish* urchin
guv *Slang* governor
guy
Guy·ana South American republic
Guya·nese (*or* Guy·an·an)
Guy·enne *variant spelling of* Guienne
guy·ot submerged mountain
guz·zle
guz·zler
Gwa·li·or Indian city
Gwe·lo Zimbabwean town
Gwent Welsh county
Gwyn·edd Welsh county
gwyni·ad fish
gybe (*or* jibe) nautical term; *compare* gibe
gym
gym·kha·na

gym·na·si·arch Greek magistrate
gym·na·si·ast
gym·na·sium (*plural* ·siums *or* ·sia)
gym·nast
gym·nas·tic
gym·nas·ti·cal·ly
gym·nas·tics
gym·noso·phist Indian ascetic
gym·no·sperm conifer
gym·no·sper·mous
gym·slip
gy·nae·ceum (*plural* ·cea) women's apartments; *compare* gynoecium
gy·nae·cium *variant spelling of* gynoecium
gy·nae·coc·ra·cy (*US* ·ne·; *plural* ·cies) government by women
gy·nae·co·crat·ic (*US* ·ne·)
gy·nae·coid (*US* ·ne·)
gy·nae·co·logi·cal (*or* ·log·ic; *US* ·ne·)
gy·nae·co·logi·cal·ly (*US* ·ne·)
gy·nae·colo·gist (*US* ·ne·)
gy·nae·col·ogy (*US* ·ne·)
gy·nae·co·mas·tia (*US* ·ne·) male breast development
gy·nan·dro·morph biology term
gy·nan·dro·mor·phic (*or* ·phous)
gy·nan·dro·morph·ism (*or* ·mor·phy)
gy·nan·drous botany term
gy·nan·dry (*or* ·drism)
gy·narch·ic
gyn·ar·chy (*plural* ·chies) gynaecocracy
gy·noe·cium (*or* ·nae·; *US* ·ne·; *plural* ·cia) part of flower; *compare* gynaeceum
gy·no·phore botany term
gy·no·phor·ic
gyp *Slang* pain
gyp·se·ous
gyp·sif·er·ous
gyp·sophi·la plant
gyp·sum

gyp·sy *variant spelling of* gipsy
gy·ral rotating
gy·rate
gy·ra·tion
gy·ra·tor
gy·ra·tory
gyre circular movement
gyr·fal·con (*or* ger·)

gyro (*plural* **gyros**)
gyrocompass; gyroscope; *compare* giro
gy·ro·com·pass
gy·ro·mag·net·ic
gy·ro·plane
gy·ro·scope (*or* ·stat)
gy·ro·scop·ic
gy·ro·scop·ics

gy·rose botany term
gy·ro·sta·bi·liz·er (*or* ·lis·er)
gy·ro·stat·ic of rotating bodies
gy·ro·stat·ics
gy·rus (*plural* **gyri**) anatomy term
gyve *Archaic* fetter

H

ha (*or* **hah**) exclamation
haaf fishing ground
Haar·lem Dutch city; *compare* **Harlem**
haar fog
Habakkuk prophet
Ha·ba·na *Spanish* Havana
ha·ba·nera dance
ha·beas cor·pus
hab·er·dash·er
hab·er·dash·ery
hab·er·geon (*or* hau·ber·geon) coat of mail
hab·ile skilful
ha·bili·ment dress
ha·bili·tate
ha·bili·ta·tion
ha·bili·ta·tor
hab·it
hab·it·abil·ity (*or* ·able·ness)
hab·it·able
hab·it·ably
hab·it·ant
habi·tat
habi·ta·tion
habi·ta·tion·al
hab·it·ed
ha·bitu·al
ha·bitu·al·ly
ha·bitu·al·ness
ha·bitu·ate
ha·bitu·a·tion
habi·tude
habi·tu·di·nal
ha·bitué
habi·tus (*plural* ·tus) physical state
Habsburg (*or* **Hapsburg**) royal dynasty

habu snake
háček phonetic symbol
ha·chure shading
haci·en·da
hack
hacka·more *US* rope halter
hack·berry (*plural* ·berries)
hack·but (*or* hag·) gun
hack·but·eer (*or* hag·)
hack·er
hack·ing
hack·le
hack·ler
hack·les
Hack·ney London borough
hack·ney carriage; make banal
hack·neyed
hack·ney·ism
hack·saw
had
ha·dal of ocean depths
hada·way *Dialect* hurry
had·dock
hade geology term
Ha·de·an
Ha·des underworld
Ha·dhra·maut Arabian plateau
Had·ith Mohammedan tradition
hadj *variant spelling of* **hajj**
hadj·i *variant spelling of* **hajji**
hadn't
had·ron elementary particle
had·ron·ic
had·ro·saur (*or* ·saur·us)
hadst *Archaic* had
hae *Scot* have

haec·ce·ity (*plural* ·ities) philosophy term
Haeck·elian of Haeckel
haem (*US* **heme**) organic pigment
haema·chrome *variant spelling of* haemochrome
haema·cy·tom·eter (*US* hema·)
hae·mag·glu·tin·ate (*US* he·)
hae·mag·glu·ti·nin (*US* he·) antibody
haema·gogue (*US* hema·gogue *or* ·gog)
hae·mal (*US* he·)
haema·tein (*US* hema·) biological stain
haema·tem·esis (*US* hema·)
hae·mat·ic (*US* he·)
haema·tin (*US* hema·) dark pigment
haema·tin·ic (*US* hema·) medicinal drug
haema·tite (*US* hema·) mineral
haema·tit·ic (*US* hema·)
hae·mato·blast (*US* he·)
hae·mato·blas·tic (*US* he·)
haema·to·cele (*US* hema·)
haema·to·crit (*US* hema·) medical term
haema·to·cry·al (*US* hema·) zoology term
haema·to·gen·esis (*US* hema·)
haema·to·gen·ic (*US* hema·)

haema·tog·enous (*US* hema·)

haema·toid (*or* hae·moid; *US* hema· *or* he·)

haema·to·log·ic (*or* ·logi·cal; *US* hema·)

haema·tolo·gist (*US* hema·)

haema·tol·ogy (*US* hema·)

haema·toly·sis *variant of* haemolysis

haema·to·ma (*US* hema·; *plural* ·mas *or* ·mata) blood tumour

haema·to·poi·esis (*or* haemo·poi·esis; *US* hema·*or* hemo·)

haema·to·poi·et·ic (*or* haemo·poi·et·ic; *US* hema· *or* hemo·)

haema·to·sis (*US* hema·)

haema·to·ther·mal (*US* hema·) warm-blooded

haema·toxy·lin (*US* hema·) dye

haema·toxy·lon tree

haema·to·zo·on (*US* hema·; *plural* ·zoa)

haema·tu·ria (*US* hema·)

haema·tu·ric

hae·mic (*US* he·)

hae·min (*US* he·)

haemo·chrome (*or* haema·; *US* hemo· *or* hema·)

haemo·coel (*US* hemo·) zoology term

haemo·cya·nin (*US* hemo·)

haemo·cyte (*US* hemo·)

haemo·cy·tom·eter (*US* hemo·)

haemo·di·aly·sis (*US* hemo·)

haemo·flag·el·late (*US* hemo·) protozoan

haemo·glo·bin (*US* hemo·)

haemo·glo·bi·nu·ria (*US* hemo·)

hae·moid *variant of* haematoid

haemo·ly·sin (*US* hemo·)

hae·moly·sis (*or* haema·toly·sis; *US* he· *or* hema·; *plural* ·ses)

haemo·lyt·ic (*US* hemo·)

haemo·phile (*US* hemo·)

haemo·philia (*US* hemo·)

haemo·phili·ac (*US* hemo·)

haemo·phil·ic (*US* hemo·)

haemo·poi·esis *variant of* haematopoiesis

haemo·poi·et·ic *variant of* haematopoietic

haem·op·ty·sis (*US* hem·) coughing blood

haem·or·rhage (*US* hem·)

haem·or·rhag·ic (*US* hem·)

haem·or·rhoid (*US* hem·)

haem·or·rhoi·dal (*US* hem·)

haem·or·rhoid·ec·to·my (*US* hem·; *plural* ·mies)

haemo·sta·sis (*or* ·sia; *US* hemo·)

haemo·stat (*US* hemo·)

haemo·stat·ic (*US* hemo·)

hae·re·mai Maori welcome

hae·res *variant spelling of* heres

Ha-erh-pin *variant spelling of* Harbin

ha·fiz Islamic title

haf·nium chemical element

haft

Haf·ta·rah (*or* Haph·ta·rah; *plural* ·ta·roth *or* ·ta·rahs) biblical reading

haft·er

hag

Hagar biblical character

hag·but *variant spelling of* hackbut

Ha·gen West German city

Hagen legendary character

hag·fish (*plural* ·fish *or* ·fishes)

Hag·ga·dah (*or* ·da; *plural* ·dahs, ·das, *or* ·doth) Jewish literature

hag·gad·ic (*or* ·gadi·cal)

hag·ga·dist

hag·ga·dist·ic

Haggai biblical prophet

hag·gard

hag·gard·ness

hag·gis

hag·gish

hag·gish·ness

hag·gle

hag·gler

hagi·archy (*plural* ·archies) government by saints

hagi·oc·ra·cy (*plural* ·cies)

Hagi·og·ra·pha Old Testament section

hagi·og·ra·pher (*or* ·phist)

hagi·o·graph·ic (*or* ·graphi·cal)

hagi·og·ra·phy (*plural* ·phies)

hagi·ola·ter

hagi·ola·trous

hagi·ola·try veneration of saints

hagi·o·log·ic (*or* ·logi·cal)

hagi·olo·gist

hagi·ol·ogy (*plural* ·ogies) writings about saints

hagi·o·scope architectural term

hagi·o·scop·ic

hag·like

Hague

hah *variant spelling of* ha

ha-ha (*or* haw-haw) sunken fence

Hai·da (*plural* ·da *or* ·das) American Indian

Hai·dan

Hai·duk (*or* Hey·duck, Hei·duc) brigand

Hai·fa Israeli port

haik (*or* haick) Arabian garment

hai·ku (*or* hok·ku; *plural* ·ku) Japanese verse

hail frozen rain; greet; *compare* hale

hail·er

hail·stone

hail·storm

Hai·nan (*or* Hai-nan Tao) Chinese island

Hai·naut (*or* ·nault) Belgian province

Hai·phong Vietnamese port

hair
hair·ball
hair·brush
hair·cloth
hair·cut
hair·do (*plural* ·dos)
hair·dresser
hair·dressing
hair·grip
hair·if plant
hairi·ness
hair·less
hair·like
hair·line
hair·net
hair·piece
hair·pin
hair·raising
hair's-breadth
hair·splitter
hair·splitting
hair·spring
hair·streak butterfly
hair·style
hair·stylist
hair·tail fish
hair·weaving
hair·worm
hairy (hairi·er, hairi·est)
Hai·ti
Hai·tian
hajj (*or* hadj; *plural* hajjes *or* hadjes) Muslim pilgrimage
haj·ji (*or* hadji, haji)
hake (*plural* hake *or* hakes)
ha·kea shrub
ha·kim (*or* ·keem) Muslim judge or physician
Ha·ko·da·te Japanese port
Ha·la·fian Neolithic culture
Ha·la·kah (*or* ·cha) Jewish literature
Ha·lak·ic (*or* ·lach·ic)
hal·al (*or* hall·al) Muslim custom
ha·la·tion photography term
ha·la·vah *variant of* halvah
hal·berd (*or* ·bert)
hal·ber·dier
hal·cy·on
Halcyone *variant of* Alcyone

hale healthy; to haul; *compare* hail
Ha·lea·ka·la Hawaiian volcano
hale·ness
ha·ler (*plural* ·lers *or* ·leru) Czech coin
Hales·ow·en English town
half (*plural* halves)
half·back
half·baked
half·beak fish
half-caste
half-day
half-hearted
half-hearted·ly
half-hearted·ness
half-life
half-light
half-mast
half-naked
half-open
half·penny (*plural* ·pennies *or* ·pence)
half·penny·worth
half-price
half-shut
half-time
half·tone
half·way
half·wit
half·witted
half·witted·ly
half·witted·ness
hali·but (*plural* ·but *or* ·buts)
Ha·liç Turkish Golden Horn
Hali·car·nas·si·an
Hali·car·nas·sus ancient Greek city
hal·ide (*or* ·id) chemical compound
hali·dom *Archaic* holy thing
Hali·fax Canadian port; British town
hal·ite mineral
hali·to·sis
hall
hal·lah *variant spelling of* challah
hall·al *variant spelling of* halal
Hal·lel Jewish chant
hal·le·lu·jah *variant of* alleluia

hal·liard *variant spelling of* halyard
hall·mark
hal·lo *variant spelling of* halloo *or* hello
hal·loo (*or* ·lo; *noun*, *plural* ·loos *or* ·los; *verb* ·loos, ·loo·ing, ·looed; *or* ·los, ·loing, ·loed) shout; *compare* hello
hal·low
hal·lowed
hal·lowed·ness
Hal·low·e'en (*or* Hal·low·een)
hal·low·er
Hal·low·mas (*or* ·mass)
Hall·statt archaeology term
Hall·stat·tian
hal·lu·ci·nate
hal·lu·ci·na·tion
hal·lu·ci·na·tion·al (*or* ·na·tive)
hal·lu·ci·na·tor
hal·lu·ci·na·tory
hal·lu·cino·gen drug
hal·lu·ci·no·gen·ic
hal·lu·ci·no·sis mental disorder
hal·lux (*plural* ·luces) first digit on foot
hall·way
halm *variant spelling of* haulm
hal·ma
Hal·ma·he·ra Indonesian island
halo (*noun*, *plural* haloes *or* halos; *verb* haloes *or* halos, halo·ing, haloed)
ha·lo·bi·ont salt-water organism
halo·gen
halo·gen·ate
halo·gen·a·tion
halo·gen·oid
ha·log·enous
hal·oid
halo-like
halo·phyte plant
halo·phyt·ic
halo·phyt·ism
halo·thane
halt

Hal·tem·price Hull suburb
hal·ter
hal·tere zoology term
halter-like
halt·ing
halt·ing·ness
hal·vah (or hal·va, ha·la·vah) sweetmeat
halve
hal·yard (or hal·liard)
ham (ham·ming, hammed)
Hama Syrian city
Hama·dān (or Ham·edān) Iranian city
hama·dry·ad nymph
hama·dry·as baboon
ha·mal (or ham·mal, ha·maul) Oriental servant
Ha·ma·ma·tsu Japanese city
hama·meli·da·ceous botany term
ha·mate hook-shaped
Ham·ble·to·nian horse
Ham·burg
ham·burg·er
hame harness attachment
Ham·elin (or Ha·meln) West German town
Ham·ers·ley Australian mountain range
Ham·il·ton Canadian port
Ham·il·to·ni·an maths term
Ham·ite African people
Ham·it·ic
ham·let
ham·mer
ham·mer·er
hammer·head animal
hammer·headed
ham·mer·less
hammer-like
Ham·mer·smith
hammer·toe
ham·mock
hammock-like
Ham·mond US city
ham·my (ham·mi·er, ham·mi·est)
ham·per
ham·pered·ness
ham·per·er
Hamp·shire
Hamp·stead

Hamp·ton US city
ham·shack·le fetter a horse
ham·ster
ham·string (·string·ing, ·strung)
hamu·lar
hamu·lus (plural ·li) hooklike projection
ham·za (or ·zah) Arabic phonetic sign
Han Chinese dynasty; river
hana·per wickerwork basket
hance (or haunch) architectural term
hand
hand·bag
hand·ball
hand·baller
hand·barrow
hand·bell
hand·bill
hand·book
hand·brake
hand·breadth
hand·cart
hand·clasp
hand·craft
hand·cuff
hand·fast Archaic agreement
hand·fasting
hand·feed (·feed·ing, ·fed)
hand·ful
hand·grip
hand·gun
hand·hold
handi·cap (·cap·ping, ·capped)
handi·cap·per
handi·craft
handi·crafts·man (plural ·men)
handi·ly
handi·ness
handi·work
hand·ker·chief
han·dle
han·dle·able
handle·bar
han·dled
han·dle·less
han·dler
hand·less
hand·like
han·dling
hand·made

hand·maiden (or ·maid)
hand-me-down
hand·out (noun)
hand·rail
hand·saw
hand·sel (or han·) Dialect new year gift
hand·set
hand·shake
hand·some good-looking; compare hansom
hand·some·ly
hand·some·ness
hand·spike lever
hand·spring
hand·stand
hand·stroke bell-ringing term
hand·writing
hand·written
handy (handi·er, handi·est)
handy·man (plural ·men)
hang (hang·ing, hung or hanged)
hang·ar aircraft shed; compare hanger
hang·bird
Hang·chow (or Hang·chou) Chinese port
hang·dog
hanged killed; compare hung
hang·er support; one that hangs; compare hangar
hanger-on (plural hangers-on)
hang·man (plural ·men)
hang·nail
hang·over
hang-up (noun)
hank
hank·er
(hankerchief) incorrect spelling of handkerchief
hank·er·er
Han·kow (or Han-k'ou) former Chinese city
hanky (or hankie; plural hankies)
hanky-panky
Ha·noi Vietnamese capital
Hano·ver
Hano·verian
Han·sard parliamentary report

Hanse (*or* **Han·sa**)
medieval guild
Han·seat·ic
han·sel *variant spelling of*
handsel
han·som cab; *compare*
handsome
Ha·nuk·kah Jewish festival
Hanu·man monkey god
hanu·man monkey
Han·yang former Chinese
city
hap (**hap·ping, happed**)
Archaic happen; luck
ha·pax le·go·menon
(*plural* **ha·pax**
le·go·mena) nonce word
ha'·penny (*plural*
·**pennies**)
hap·haz·ard
hap·haz·ard·ness
Haph·ta·rah *variant spelling*
of Haftarah
hap·less
hap·less·ness
hap·lite *variant spelling of*
aplite
hap·lit·ic *variant spelling of*
aplitic
hap·log·ra·phy (*plural*
·**phies**) omission of letter
in writing
hap·loid biology term
hap·loidy
hap·lo·log·ic
hap·lol·ogy (*plural* ·**ogies**)
omission of syllable in
speech
hap·lo·sis biology term
hap·ly
ha'·p'orth
hap·pen
hap·pen·ing
hap·pen·stance
hap·pi·ly
hap·pi·ness
hap·py (·**pi·er**, ·**pi·est**)
happy-go-lucky
Hapsburg *variant spelling of*
Habsburg
hap·ten (*or* ·**tene**) medical
term
hap·ter·on botany term
hap·tic of touch
hap·to·trop·ism botany
term

ha·ra·ki·ri (*or* **ha·ri·ka·ri**)
Japanese suicide
ha·ram·bee African chant
ha·rangue
ha·rangu·er
Ha·rap·pa Pakistani city
Ha·rap·pan
Ha·rar (*or* **Har·rar**)
Ethiopian city
Ha·rare Zimbabwean
capital
har·ass
har·ass·er
har·ass·ing·ly
har·ass·ment
Har·bin (*or* **Ha·erh·pin**)
Chinese city
har·bin·ger
har·bour (*US* ·**bor**)
har·bour·age (*US* ·**bor·**)
har·bour·er (*US* ·**bor·**)
har·bour·less (*US* ·**bor·**)
hard
hard·back
hard·bake almond toffee
hard·board
hard·en
hard·ened
hard·en·er
hard·en·ing
hard·hack plant
hard-headed
hard-headed·ly
hard-headed·ness
hard·heads plant
hard·hearted
hard·hearted·ly
hard·hearted·ness
har·di·hood
har·di·ly
har·di·ness
hard·ly
hard·ness
hard·pan clay layer
hards (*or* **hurds**) coarse
fibres
hard·ship
hard·tack
hard·top
hard·ware
hard·wood
har·dy (·**di·er**, ·**di·est**)
hare
hare·bell
hare·brained

hare·like
hare·lip
hare·lipped
har·em (*or* ·**eem**)
Har·gei·sa Somalian city
hari·cot
(**haridan**) *incorrect spelling*
of harridan
Ha·ri·jan Indian
untouchable
ha·ri·ka·ri *variant spelling of*
harakiri
Ha·rin·gey London
borough
hark
hark·en *US variant spelling*
of hearken
harl *variant spelling of* herl
Har·lem New York district;
compare Haarlem
har·lequin
har·lequin·ade
Har·ley Street
har·lot
har·lot·ry
Har·low Essex town
harm
har·mat·tan Saharan wind
harm·er
harm·ful
harm·ful·ly
harm·ful·ness
harm·less
harm·less·ness
har·mon·ic
har·moni·ca
har·moni·cal·ly
har·mon·ics
har·mo·ni·ous
har·mo·nist
har·mo·nis·tic
har·mo·nis·ti·cal·ly
har·mo·nium
har·mo·niz·able
har·mo·ni·za·tion
har·mo·nize (*or* ·**nise**)
har·mo·niz·er
har·mo·ny (*plural* ·**nies**)
har·mo·tome
har·ness
har·ness·er
har·ness·less
harness-like
Har·ney US mountain
harp

harp·er

harp·ings (*or* ·ins) nautical term

har·poon

har·poon·er

har·poon-like

harp·si·chord

harp·si·chord·ist

har·py (*plural* ·pies)

har·que·bus *variant spelling of* arquebus

Har·rar Ethiopian city

(harrass) *incorrect spelling of* harass

har·ri·dan

har·ri·er

Har·ris Scottish island

Har·ris·burg US city

Har·ro·gate Yorkshire town

Har·ro·vian

Har·row London borough

har·row tool

har·row·er

har·row·ing

har·row·ment

har·rumph

har·ry (·ries, ·ry·ing, ·ried)

harsh

harsh·ly

harsh·ness

hars·let *variant spelling of* haslet

hart (*plural* hart *or* harts)

har·tal

har·te·beest (*or* hart·beest) antelope

Hart·ford US port

Har·tle·pool

harts·horn

harum-scarum

ha·rus·pex (*plural* ha·rus·pi·ces) Roman priest

ha·rus·pi·cal

ha·rus·pi·cy

Har·vard

har·vest

har·vest·er

har·vest·ing

har·vest·less

harvest·man (*plural* ·men)

Har·wich Essex port

Har·ya·na Indian state

Harz German mountain range

has

Ha·sa Saudi Arabian province

has-been

hash

Hash·e·mite descendant of Mohammed

hash·ish

Ha·sid·ic (*or* Has·sid·ic)

Hasi·dim (*or* Has·si·dim) Jewish sect

Has·id·ism (*or* Has·sid·ism)

hask *Dialect* cough

has·let (*or* hars·) meat loaf

hasn't

hasp

has·sle

has·sock kneeling cushion; *compare* cassock

hast

has·tate botany term

haste

haste·ful

haste·ful·ly

has·ten

has·ten·er

hasti·ly

hasti·ness

Hast·ings

has·ty (·ti·er, ·ti·est)

hat (hat·ting, hat·ted)

hat·able *variant spelling of* hateable

hat·band

hat·box

hatch

hatch·able

hatch·back

hatch·el (·el·ling, ·elled; *US* ·el·ing, ·eled) comb flax

hatch·el·ler (*US* ·el·er)

hatch·er

hatch·ery (*plural* ·eries)

hatch·et

hatchet-like

hatch·ing

hatch·ment heraldic term

hatch·way

hate

hate·able (*or* hat·)

hate·ful

hate·ful·ly

hate·ful·ness

hater

Hat·field Hertfordshire town

hath

Hath·or Egyptian goddess

Ha·thor·ic

hat·less

hat·like

hat·pin

ha·tred

hat·ter

Hat·ter·as US cape

hau·ber·geon *variant spelling of* habergeon

hau·berk coat of mail

haugh *Dialect* flat valley base

haugh·ti·ly

haugh·ti·ness

haugh·ty (·ti·er, ·ti·est)

haul

haul·age

haul·er (*or* ·ier)

haulm (*or* halm) plant stem

haunch

haunched

haunt

haunt·ed

haunt·er

haunt·ing

Hau·ra·ki New Zealand gulf

Hau·sa (*plural* ·sas *or* ·sa) African people

haus·frau

haus·tel·late

haus·tel·lum (*plural* ·la) entomology term

haus·to·ri·al

haus·to·rium (*plural* ·ria) plant organ

haut·boy strawberry

haute cou·ture

haute cui·sine

hau·teur

Ha·vana Cuban capital

Hav·ant Hampshire town

have (has, hav·ing, had)

have·lock protective cap cover

ha·ven

ha·ven·less

have-not (*noun*)

haven't
ha·ver *dither*
Ha·ver·ing *London borough*
hav·er·sack
Ha·ver·sian *anatomy term*
hav·er·sine *maths term*
hav·il·dar *Indian NCO*
hav·ing
hav·oc (·ock·ing, ·ocked)
hav·ock·er
haw
Ha·waii
Ha·wai·ian
Hawes *English lake*
haw·finch
Haw·ick *Scottish town*
hawk
hawk·bit *plant*
hawk·er
hawk·ing
hawk·ish
hawk·like
hawks·bill *turtle*
hawk·weed
Ha·worth *Yorkshire village*
hawse *nautical term*
hawse·hole
hawse·pipe
haws·er
haw·thorn
hay
hay·box
hay·cock *pile of hay*
hay·fork
hay·maker
hay·making
hay·mow
hay·rack
hay·rick
hay·seed
hay·stack
hay·ward *Obsolete parish officer*
hay·wire
haz·ard
haz·ard·able
haz·ard·free
haz·ard·ous
haz·ard·ous·ness
haze
ha·zel
hazel·hen
hazel·nut
haz·er *nautical term*

ha·zi·ly
ha·zi·ness
hazy (ha·zi·er, ha·zi·est)
he
head
head·ache
head·achy
head·band
head·board
head·cheese *US brawn*
head·dress
head·ed
head·er
head·fast *mooring rope*
head·first
head·gear
head·hunt
head·hunter
head·hunting
headi·ly
headi·ness
head·ing
head·less
head·light (*or* ·lamp)
head·like
head·line
head·lin·er
head·lock
head·long
head·man (*plural* ·men)
head·master (*fem* ·mistress)
head·master·ship (*fem* ·mistress·)
head·most
head·on
head·phones
head·piece
head·pin
head·quarters
head·race
head·rail *billiards term*
head·reach *nautical term*
head·rest
head·room
head·sail
head·scarf (*plural* ·scarves)
head·set
head·ship
head·shrinker
heads·man (*plural* ·men) *executioner*
head·spring
head·square

head·stall
head·stand
head·stock *part of machine tool*
head·stone
head·stream
head·strong
head·strong·ness
head·wards (*or esp. US* ·ward)
head·waters
head·way
head·wind
head·word
head·work
head·worker
heady (head·ier, head·iest)
heal *cure; compare* heel
heal·able
heal·er
heal·ing·ly
health
health·ful
health·ful·ly
health·ful·ness
healthi·ly
healthi·ness
healthy (health·ier, health·iest)
heap
heap·er
heap·ing
hear (hear·ing, heard)
hear·able
hear·er
heark·en (*US also* hark·)
heark·en·er
hear·say
hearse
heart
heart·ache
heart·beat
heart·break
heart·breaker
heart·breaking
heart·breaking·ly
heart·broken
heart·broken·ly
heart·broken·ness
heart·burn
heart·en
heart·en·ing·ly
heart·felt
hearth

hearth·stone
hearti·ly
hearti·ness
heart·land
heart·less
heart·less·ness
heart-rending
hearts·ease wild pansy
heart·sick
heart·sickness
heart·some
heart·some·ly
heart·some·ness
heart·strings
heart·wood
heart·worm
hearty (heart·ier,
   hearti·est)
heat
heat·ed
heat·ed·ly
heat·ed·ness
heat·er
heath
heath·berry (plural
   ·berries)
hea·then (plural ·thens or
   ·then)
hea·then·dom
hea·then·ish
hea·then·ish·ness
hea·then·ism
hea·then·ize
hea·then·ness
heath·er
heath·ered
heath·ery
heath·fowl
heath·like
heathy
heat·ing
heat·less
heat·stroke
heaume medieval helmet
heave (heav·ing, heaved
   or hove)
heav·en
heav·en·li·ness
heav·en·ly
heav·en·ward (adj)
heav·en·wards (adv)
heav·er
heaves horse disease
heavi·ly
heavi·ness

heavy (adj heavi·er,
   heavi·est; noun, plural
   heavies)
heavy-handed
heavy-handed·ly
heavy-handed·ness
heavy·weight
heb·do·mad Obsolete seven
heb·doma·dal (or ·da·ry)
   weekly
heb·doma·dal·ly
Hebe Greek goddess
he·be·phre·nia
   schizophrenia
he·be·phren·ic
heb·etate blunt
heb·eta·tion
he·bet·ic of puberty
heb·e·tude lethargy
heb·etu·di·nous
He·bra·ic (or ·brai·cal)
He·bra·i·cal·ly
He·bra·ism
He·bra·ist
He·bra·is·tic
He·bra·is·ti·cal·ly
He·bra·i·za·tion
He·bra·ize
He·bra·iz·er
He·brew
Heb·ri·dean
Heb·ri·des
Heb·ron Jordanian city
Heca·te (or Heka·te)
   Greek goddess
heca·tomb sacrifice
heck
heck·el·phone oboe
heck·le
heck·ler
hec·tare
hec·tic
hec·ti·cal·ly
hec·to·coty·lus zoology
   term
hec·to·gram
hec·to·graph copying
   process
hec·to·graph·ic
hec·to·graphi·cal·ly
hec·tog·ra·phy
hec·tor
Hec·u·ba mythological
   character
he'd

hed·dle part of loom
hedge
hedge·hog
hedge·hop (·hop·ping,
   ·hopped)
hedge·hop·per
hedg·er
hedge·row
hedgy
He·djaz Saudi Arabian
   region
he·don·ic
he·don·ics branch of
   psychology
he·don·ism
he·don·ist
heebie-jeebies
heed
heed·er
heed·ful
heed·ful·ly
heed·ful·ness
heed·less
heed·less·ly
heed·less·ness
hee-haw
heel part of foot; compare
   heal
heel·ball
heeled
heel·er
heel·less
heel·piece
heel·post
heel·tap
Heer·len Dutch city
heft
heft·er
hefti·ly
hefti·ness
hefty (hefti·er, hefti·est)
He·geli·an
He·geli·an·ism school of
   philosophy
heg·emon·ic
he·gemo·ny
Hegi·ra (or Heji·ra) flight
   of Mohammed
he·gu·men (or ·menos)
   Eastern Church leader
heh exclamation
Hei·del·berg West German
   city
Hei·duc variant spelling of
   Haiduk

heif·er

heigh-ho

height tallness; compare
hight

height·en

height·en·er

Hei·lung·kiang Chinese
province

Heim·dall (or Heim·dal,
Heim·dallr) Norse god

hei·nous

hei·nous·ness

heir

heir·dom

heir·ess

heir·less

heir·loom

heir·ship

heist

heist·er

hei·ti·ki Maori ornament

He·jaz (or Hi·jaz) Saudi
Arabian province

Heji·ra variant spelling of
Hegira

Heka·te variant spelling of
Hecate

Hek·la Icelandic volcano

Hel (or Hela) Norse
goddess

held

Hel·ena US city

Hel·go·land variant spelling
of Heligoland

he·li·a·cal astronomy term;
compare helical

he·li·an·thus (plural
·thuses) sunflower

heli·cal spiral; compare
heliacal

heli·cal·ly

heli·ces plural of helix

heli·chrysum plant

heli·cline spiral ramp

heli·co·graph

heli·coid

heli·coi·dal·ly

heli·con tuba

Heli·con Greek mountain

heli·cop·ter

Heli·go·land (or Hel·go·)
North Sea island

helio·cen·tric

helio·cen·tri·cal·ly

helio·cen·tric·i·ty (or
helio·cen·tri·cism)

Helio·chrome
(Trademark)

helio·chro·mic

helio·graph

he·li·og·ra·pher

helio·graph·ic

heliog·ra·phy

helio·gra·vure printing
term

he·li·ola·ter

he·li·ola·trous

he·li·ola·try sun worship

he·lio·lith·ic

he·li·om·eter telescope

helio·met·ric

helio·met·ri·cal·ly

he·li·om·etry

He·li·opo·lis ancient
Egyptian city

Helios sun god

helio·stat

helio·stat·ic

helio·tac·tic

helio·tax·is biology term

helio·thera·py

helio·trope plant

helio·trop·ic growing
towards sunlight

helio·trop·i·cal·ly

he·li·ot·ro·pin chemical
compound

he·li·ot·ro·pism

helio·type printing process

helio·typ·ic

helio·zo·an biology term

heli·port

he·lium chemical element

he·lix (plural heli·ces or
he·lixes)

hell

he'll he will; he shall

Hel·ladic archaeology term

Hel·las ancient Greece

hell·bender

hell·bent

hell·box

hell·cat

hell·diver bird

Hel·le mythological
character

hel·le·bore plant

hel·le·bor·ine orchid

Hel·len legendary king

Hel·lene (or Hel·le·nian)
Greek

Hel·len·ic

Hel·leni·cal·ly

Hel·len·ism

Hel·len·ist

Hel·len·is·tic

Hel·len·is·ti·cal·ly

Hel·leni·za·tion (or
·sa·tion)

Hel·len·ize (or ·ise)

Hel·len·iz·er (or ·is·er)

hel·ler (plural ·ler)
German coin

hell·ery wild behaviour

Hel·les Turkish cape

Hel·les·pont Dardanelles

hell·fire

hell·gram·mite insect larva

hell·hole

hell·hound

hel·lion

hell·ish

hell·ish·ness

hel·lo (or hal·lo, hul·lo;
plural ·los)

helm

Hel·mand Asian river

hel·met

hel·met·ed

helmet-like

hel·minth parasitic worm

hel·min·thia·sis

hel·min·thic

hel·min·thoid

hel·min·tho·logi·cal

hel·min·tholo·gist

hel·min·thol·ogy

helm·less

helms·man (plural ·men)

Helot ancient Greek class

helot serf

hel·ot·ism

hel·ot·ry

help

help·able

help·er

help·ful

help·ful·ly

help·ful·ness

help·ing

help·less

help·less·ness

help·mate

help·meet Archaic helpmate

Hel·sin·ki

helter-skelter

helve tool handle

Hel·vel·lyn English mountain

Hel·ve·tia Switzerland

Hel·ve·tian

Hel·vet·ic

Hel·vetii Celtic tribe

hem (hem·ming, hemmed)

hema· (or hemato·) US spelling of words beginning with haemo· or haemato·

he·mal US spelling of haemal

he·man (plural -men)

heme US spelling of haem

Hem·el Hemp·stead

hem·ely·tron (or hemi·; plural ·tra) zoology term

hem·era·lo·pia day blindness

hem·era·lop·ic

hemi·al·gia pain on one side

hemi·an·ops·ia sight defect

he·mic US spelling of haemic

hemi·cel·lu·lose

hemi·chor·date zoology term

hemi·cy·cle

hemi·cy·clic

hemi·demi·semi·qua·ver

hemi·ely·tron variant spelling of hemelytron

hemi·he·dral crystallography term

hemi·hy·drate

hemi·hy·drat·ed

hemi·mor·phic crystallography term

hemi·mor·phism (or ·phy)

hemi·mor·phite mineral

he·min US spelling of haemin

hemio·la musical term

hemi·ol·ic

hemi·para·site

hemi·plegia

hemi·ple·gic

hemi·pode (or ·pod) bird

he·mip·ter·an (or ·on) insect

he·mip·ter·ous

hemi·sphere

hemi·spher·ic (or ·spheri·cal)

hemi·spher·oid

hemi·spher·oi·dal

hemi·stich half line of verse

hemi·ter·pene chemistry term

hemi·trope chemistry term

hemi·trop·ic

hemi·tro·pism (or he·mit·ro·py)

hem·line

hem·lock

hem·mer

hemo· US spelling of words beginning with haemo·

hemp

hemp·en

hem·stitch

hem·stitch·er

hen

hen·bane plant

hen·bit plant

hence

hence·forth

hence·forward

hench·man (plural ·men)

hen·coop

hen·deca·gon

hen·de·cago·nal

hen·deca·he·dron

hen·deca·syl·lab·ic

hen·deca·syl·la·ble

hen·dia·dys rhetorical device

hen·equen (or hen·equin, heni·quen) fibre

henge archaeology term

Heng·yang Chinese city

hen·house

Hen·ley Oxfordshire town

hen·na

hen·nery (plural ·neries) poultry house

heno·theism worship of one deity

heno·theist

heno·theis·tic

hen·peck

hen·pecked

hen·ry (plural ·ry, ·ries, or ·rys) unit

hent Archaic seize

hep

hepa·rin biochemical substance

he·pat·ic of liver

he·pati·ca plant

hepa·ti·tis

hep·cat

Hephaestus (or Hephaistos) Greek god

hep·tad

hep·ta·deca·no·ic acid

hep·ta·gon

hep·tago·nal

hep·ta·he·dral

hep·ta·he·dron

hep·tam·er·ous

hep·tam·eter type of verse line

hep·ta·met·ri·cal

hep·tane chemical compound

hep·tan·gu·lar

hep·tarch

hep·tar·chic

hep·tar·chy (plural ·chies)

hep·ta·stich

Hep·ta·teuch Old Testament books

hep·tava·lent

hep·tose

her

Hera (or Here) Greek goddess

Hera·clea ancient Greek colony

Hera·clean

Heracles (or Herakles) variants of Hercules

Hera·cli·dan

Hera·clid (or ·klid) descendant of Hercules

her·ald

he·ral·dic

he·ral·di·cal·ly

her·ald·ist

her·ald·ry

He·rat Afghan city

herb

her·ba·ceous

herb·age

herb·al

herb·al·ist

her·bar·ial

her·bar·ium (plural ·iums or ·ia)

her·bi·cid·al

herbi·cide

her·bi·vore

her·bivo·rous

her·bivo·rous·ness

herb·like

herby (herbi·er,
herbi·est)
Her·cego·vi·na (*or* ·zego·)
Yugoslav region
Her·cu·la·neum ancient
Italian city
her·cu·lean
Her·cu·les constellation
Hercules (*or* Heracles,
Herakles) mythological
hero
Her·cyn·ian geology term
herd
herd·er
her·dic *US* small carriage
herds·man (*plural* ·men)
Herd·wick sheep
here
here·abouts
here·after
here·at
here·by
he·redes *plural of* heres
he·redi·tabil·ity
he·redi·table
he·redi·tably
her·edita·ment legal term
he·redi·tari·an·ism
psychology term
he·redi·tari·ly
he·redi·tari·ness
he·redi·tary
he·redi·tist
he·red·ity (*plural* ·ities)
Her·eford
here·in
here·in·after
here·in·before
here·into
here·of
here·on
He·rero (*plural* ·rero *or*
·reros) African people
he·res (*or* hae·; *plural*
·redes) heir
he·resi·arch heretical leader
her·esy (*plural* ·esies)
her·etic
he·reti·cal
he·reti·cal·ly
here·to
here·to·fore
here·under
here·unto
here·upon

here·with
heri·ot medieval death duty
her·it·abil·ity
her·it·able
her·it·ably
her·it·age
heri·tor (*fem* ·tress)
herl (*or* harl) angling term
herm
her·maph·ro·dite
her·maph·ro·dit·ic
her·maph·ro·diti·cal·ly
her·maph·ro·dit·ism
Hermaphroditus
mythological character
her·meneu·tic
her·meneu·ti·cal·ly
her·meneu·tics
her·meneu·tist
Hermes Greek god
Her·mes asteroid
her·met·ic air-tight;
compare hermitic
her·meti·cal·ly
her·mit
her·mit·age
Her·mit·ian maths term
her·mit·ic hermit-like;
compare hermetic
her·miti·cal·ly
her·mit-like
Her·mon mountain
Her·mou·po·lis Greek port
hern *Dialect* heron
her·nia
her·nial
her·ni·at·ed
her·ni·or·rha·phy (*plural*
·phies) hernia surgery
Hero mythological character
hero (*plural* heroes)
Herodias mother of Salome
he·ro·ic
he·roi·cal·ly
he·ro·ics
hero·in drug
hero·ine heroic female
hero·ism
her·on
her·on·ry (*plural* ·ries)
her·pes
her·pes sim·plex
her·pes zos·ter
her·pet·ic

her·pe·to·log·ic (*or*
·logi·cal)
her·pe·to·logi·cal·ly
her·pe·tolo·gist
her·pe·tol·ogy study of
reptiles
Herr (*plural* Her·ren)
German title of address
her·ring (*plural* ·rings *or*
·ring)
herring·bone
hers of her
her·self
Herst·mon·ceux (*or*
Hurst·)
Hert·ford
Hert·ford·shire
hertz (*plural* hertz) unit
Hertz·ian physics term
Hertzsprung-Russell
diagram
Her·zego·vi·na *variant
spelling of* Hercegovina
he's he is; he has
Hesi·od·ic of Hesiod
Hesione mythological
princess
hesi·tan·cy
hesi·tant
hesi·tant·ly
hesi·tate
hesi·tat·er
hesi·tat·ing·ly
hesi·ta·tion
hesi·ta·tive
Hes·per·ia western land
Hes·pe·rian
Hesperides mythological
characters
Hes·per·id·ian (*or* ·ean)
hes·peri·din biochemical
compound
hes·per·id·ium botany term
Hes·per·us evening star
Hesse West German state
Hes·sian of Hesse
hes·sian fibre
hes·site mineral
hes·so·nite gemstone
hest behest
Hestia Greek goddess
Hesy·chast Greek
Orthodox mystic
Hesy·chast·ic
het *Archaic* heated

he·tae·ra (*or* ·tai·; *plural*
·tae·rae *or* ·tai·rai)
Greek prostitute
he·tae·ric (*or* ·tai·)
he·tae·rism (*or* ·tai·)
he·tae·rist (*or* ·tai·)
he·tae·ris·tic (*or* ·tai·)
hetero·cer·cal zoology term
hetero·chro·mat·ic
hetero·chro·ma·tin
hetero·chro·ma·tism
hetero·chro·mo·some
hetero·chro·mous
hetero·clite grammar term
hetero·clit·ic
hetero·cy·clic
hetero·dac·tyl ornithology
term
hetero·dont zoology term
hetero·dox
hetero·doxy
hetero·dyne electronics
term
het·er·oecious botany term
het·er·oecism
hetero·gam·ete
heteroga·mous
het·er·oga·my botany term
hetero·geneity
hetero·geneous of different
parts; *compare*
heterogenous
hetero·gen·esis
hetero·genet·ic
hetero·genetical·ly
hetero·gen·ous of different
origin; *compare*
heterogeneous
heter·ogeny
het·er·ogo·nous
heter·ogo·ny biology term
hetero·graft
hetero·graph·ic
het·er·og·ra·phy grammar
term
het·er·ogy·nous
hetero·leci·thal
het·er·olo·gous
het·er·ol·ogy
het·er·oly·sis
hetero·lyt·ic
het·er·om·er·ous
hetero·mor·phic
hetero·mor·phism
het·er·ono·mous

het·er·ono·my
hetero·nym grammar term
het·er·ony·mous
Hetero·ousian Christian
sect
het·er·opho·ny musical
term
hetero·phyl·lous
hetero·phyl·ly
hetero·phyte
hetero·plas·tic
hetero·plas·ty (*plural*
·ties) surgical transplant
hetero·po·lar
hetero·po·larity
het·er·op·ter·ous zoology
term
hetero·scedas·tic·ity
statistics term
hetero·sex·ism
hetero·sex·ist
hetero·sex·ual
hetero·sexu·al·ity
hetero·sexu·al·ly
hetero·sis
het·er·os·po·rous
het·er·os·po·ry
hetero·sty·lous
hetero·sty·ly botany term
hetero·tac·tic
hetero·tax·is
hetero·thal·lic botany term
hetero·to·pia (*or*
het·er·oto·py)
displacement of body part
hetero·top·ic
hetero·troph·ic biology
term
hetero·typ·ic (*or* ·typi·cal)
biology term
hetero·zy·go·sis
hetero·zy·gote
hetero·zy·gous genetics
term
heth (*or* cheth) Hebrew
letter
het·man (*plural* ·men)
Cossack leader
heu·land·ite mineral
heu·ris·tic
heu·ris·ti·cal·ly
hew (hew·ing, hewed,
hewed *or* hewn) cut;
compare hue
hew·er
hex *US* bewitch

hexa·chloro·cyclo·hex·ane
hexa·chloro·ethane
hexa·chloro·phene
hexa·chord musical term
hexa·co·sa·no·ic acid
hex·ad six
hexa·decane
hexa·deci·mal
hex·adic
hexa·em·er·ic
hexa·em·er·on (*or*
·hem·er·on) the Creation
hexa·gon
hex·ago·nal
hex·ag·o·nal·ly
hexa·gram
hexa·gram·moid
hexa·he·dral
hexa·he·dron
hexa·hy·drate
hexa·hy·drat·ed
hex·am·er·ism
hex·am·er·ous (*or* ·eral)
hex·am·eter
hexa·methylene·tetramine
hexa·met·ric
hex·ane
hex·an·gu·lar
hexa·no·ic acid
hexa·pla Old Testament
edition
hexa·plar (*or* ·plar·ic)
hexa·pod insect
hexa·pod·ic
hex·apo·dy (*plural* ·dies)
verse form
hexa·stich (*or*
hex·as·ti·chon) six-line
poem
hexa·stich·ic
hexa·style architecture term
Hexa·teuch Old Testament
books
Hexa·teu·chal
hexa·va·lent
hex·one chemical
compound
hexo·san biochemical
compound
hex·ose sugar
hex·yl
hexyl·resor·cin·ol
hey exclamation
hey·day

Hey·duck *variant spelling of* Haiduk

Hey·sham Lancashire port

Hey·wood English town

Hezekiah biblical character

hi

Hia·leah US city

hia·tal

hia·tus (*plural* ·tuses *or* ·tus)

hi·ba·chi brazier

hi·ber·nacu·lum (*or* ·nac·le; *plural* ·ula *or* ·les)

hi·ber·nal

hi·ber·nate

hi·ber·na·tion

hi·ber·na·tor

Hi·ber·nia Ireland

Hi·ber·nian

Hi·ber·ni·an·ism

Hi·ber·ni·cism

hi·bis·cus

hic·cup (·cup·ing, ·cuped *or* ·cup·ping, ·cupped)

hick

hick·ey US gadget

hicko·ry (*plural* ·ries)

hid

hid·able

hi·dal·go (*plural* ·gos) Spanish nobleman

Hi·dal·go Mexican state

hid·den

hid·den·ite gemstone

hid·den·ness

hide (hid·ing, hid, hid·den *or* hid)

hide-and-seek

hide·away

hide·bound

hide·less

hid·eous

hid·eous·ly

hid·eous·ness (*or* hid·eos·ity)

hid·er

hid·ing

hi·dro·sis sweating

hi·drot·ic

hie (hie·ing *or* hy·ing, hied) hurry

hie·land *Scot* easily tricked

hi·emal of winter

hi·era·co·sphinx (*plural* ·sphinxes *or* ·sphin·ges)

hi·er·arch

hi·er·ar·chal

hi·er·ar·chi·cal

hi·er·ar·chi·cal·ly

hi·er·arch·ism

hi·er·ar·chy (*plural* ·chies)

hi·er·at·ic of priests

hi·er·ati·cal·ly

hi·er·oc·ra·cy (*plural* ·cies)

hi·ero·crat·ic

hi·ero·dule Greek slave

hi·ero·du·lic

hi·ero·glyph

hi·ero·glyph·ic

hi·ero·glyphi·cal·ly

hi·ero·glyph·ics

hi·ero·glyph·ist

hi·ero·gram sacred symbol

hi·ero·log·ic

hi·er·olo·gist

hi·er·ol·ogy (*plural* ·ogies) sacred literature

hi·ero·phant ancient Greek priest

hi·ero·phant·ic

hi·ero·phan·ti·cal·ly

hi·fa·lu·tin *variant spelling of* highfalutin

hi-fi

hig·gle

higgledy-piggle·dy

high

high·ball

high·bind·er US gangster

high·born

high·boy US tallboy

high·brow

high·chair

high·fa·lu·tin (*or* hi·)

high-flier (*or* -flyer)

high-flown

high-handed

high-handed·ly

high-handed·ness

high·jack *less common spelling of* hijack

high·jack·er *less common spelling of* hijacker

High·land of Scottish Highlands

high·land

high·land·er

High·lander

High·lands

high·life

high·light

high·ly

highly-strung

high-minded

high-minded·ness

high·ness high condition

High·ness title for royalty

high-rise

high·road

high-spirit·ed

high-spirit·ed·ness

hight *Archaic* named; *compare* height

high·tail

high-tech (*or* hi-)

High·veld South African region

high·way

highway·man (*plural* ·men)

High Wy·combe

hi·jack (*or* high·)

hi·jack·er (*or* high·)

Hi·jaz *variant spelling of* Hejaz

hike

hik·er

hi·lar anatomy term

hi·lari·ous

hi·lari·ous·ness

hi·lar·ity

hill

Hil·la Iraqi town

hill·bil·ly (*plural* ·lies)

hill·er

hill·fort

Hil·ling·don London borough

hill·ock

hill·ocked (*or* ·ocky)

hill·side

hilly (hilli·er, hilli·est)

hilt

hi·lum (*plural* ·la) botany term

hi·lus (*plural* ·li) anatomy term

Hil·ver·sum Dutch city

him

Hi·ma·chal Pra·desh Indian state

Hima·la·yan
Hima·la·yas
hi·mati·on (*plural* ·matia)
Greek cloak
Hi·meji Japanese city
Hims *variant of* Homs
him·self
Him·yar·ite Arabian people
Him·yar·it·ic language
group
hin Hebrew unit
Hi·na·ya·na Buddhism
Hi·na·ya·nist
Hi·na·ya·nis·tic
Hinck·ley English town
hind (*adj* hind·er,
hind·most *or*
hinder·most; *noun*,
plural hinds *or* hind)
hind·brain
hin·der obstruct
hind·er at the rear
hin·der·er
hin·der·ing·ly
hind·gut
Hin·di language; *compare*
Hindu
hind·most (*or*
hinder·most)
Hin·doo *former spelling of*
Hindu
Hin·doo·ism *former spelling*
of Hinduism
hind·quarter
hin·drance
hind·sight
Hin·du (*plural* ·dus)
people; *compare* Hindi
Hin·du·ism
Hin·du Kush Asian
mountains
Hin·du·stan
Hin·du·sta·ni
hinge
hinge·like
hing·er
hin·ny (*noun, plural*
·nies; *verb* ·nies,
·ny·ing, ·nied)
hint
hint·er
hinter·land
hip
hip·bone
hip·less
hip·like

hip·parch ancient Greek
cavalry commander
Hip·par·chus moon crater
hip·pe·as·trum plant
hipped
hip·pie (*or* ·py; *plural*
·pies)
hip·po (*plural* ·pos)
hippo·campal
hippo·campus (*plural*
·campi)
hip·po·cras wine
Hip·po·crat·ic of
Hippocrates
Hip·po·crene ancient
Greek spring
Hip·po·crenian
hippo·drome
hip·po·griff mythological
monster
Hippolyta (*or* Hippolyte)
Amazonian queen
Hippolytus son of Theseus
Hippomenes mythological
character
hippo·pota·mus (*plural*
·muses *or* ·mi)
Hip·po Re·gius ancient
African city
hip·py *variant spelling of*
hippie
hip·sters trousers
hir·able (*or* hire·)
hi·ra·ga·na Japanese writing
Hi·ram biblical character
hir·cine lascivious
hire
hire·ling
hir·er
Hi·ro·shi·ma
hir·sute
hir·sute·ness
hiru·din anticoagulant
hi·run·dine of swallows
his
His·pania Iberia
His·pan·ic
His·pani·cism
His·pani·cist
His·pani·ci·za·tion (*or*
·sa·tion)
His·pani·cize (*or* ·cise)
His·panio·la West Indian
island
his·pid bristly
his·pid·ity

hiss
hiss·er
hist
his·tami·nase enzyme
his·ta·mine
his·ta·min·ic
his·ti·dine amino acid
his·tio·cyte
his·tio·cyt·ic
his·to·chemi·cal
his·to·chem·is·try
his·to·gen plant tissue
his·to·gen·esis (*or*
his·tog·eny)
his·to·genet·ic (*or* ·gen·ic)
his·to·geneti·cal·ly (*or*
·geni·cal·ly
his·to·gram
his·toid
his·to·logi·cal
(his·to·log·ic)
his·to·logi·cal·ly
his·tolo·gist
his·tol·ogy study of tissues
his·toly·sis
his·to·lyt·ic
his·to·lyti·cal·ly
his·tone protein
his·to·patho·logi·cal
his·to·pa·thol·ogy
his·to·plas·mo·sis
his·to·rian
his·to·ri·at·ed decorated
his·tor·ic
his·tori·cal
his·tori·cal·ly
his·tor·i·cal·ness
his·tori·cism
his·tori·cist
his·to·ric·ity
his·to·ri·og·ra·pher
his·to·rio·graph·ic
his·to·ri·og·ra·phy
his·to·ry (*plural* ·ries)
his·tri·on·ic (*or* ·oni·cal)
his·tri·oni·cal·ly
histrionics
hit (hit·ting, hit)
hitch
hitch·er
hitch·hike
hitch·hik·er
hi-tech *variant spelling of*
high-tech
hith·er

hither·most
hither·to
Hit·ler·ism
hit·ter
Hit·tite
hive
hive·like
hives nettle rash
ho exclamation; compare hoe
ho·act·zin variant spelling of hoatzin
hoar
hoard store; compare horde
hoard·er
hoard·ing
hoar·frost
hoar·hound variant spelling of horehound
hoari·ly
hoari·ness
hoarse grating; compare horse
hoarse·ly
hoars·en
hoarse·ness
hoary (hoari·er, hoari·est)
hoatch·ing Scot infested
ho·at·zin (or ·act·) bird
hoax
hoax·er
hob (hob·bing, hobbed)
Ho·bart Tasmanian capital
Hobbes·ian
Hob·bism political philosophy
Hob·bist
hob·ble
hobble·dehoy
hob·bler
hob·by (plural ·bies)
hobby·horse
hob·byist
hob·goblin
hob·like
hob·nail
hob·nailed
hob·nob (·nob·bing, ·nobbed)
hobo (plural hobos or hoboes) vagrant
hobo·ism
Ho·bo·ken Belgian city
hobson-jobson folk etymology

Hoch·hei·mer wine
hock
hock·er
hock·ey
Hock·tide former festival
ho·cus (·cus·ing, cused, or ·cus·sing, ·cussed)
hocus-pocus (·pocusing, -pocused or -pocussing, -pocussed)
hod
hod·den coarse cloth
hod·din
Ho·dei·da Yemeni port
hodge·podge US hotchpotch
hod·man (plural ·men)
ho·dom·eter variant of odometer
hodo·scope
hoe (hoe·ing, hoed) gardening tool; compare ho
hoe·down dance
Hoek van Hol·land Hook of Holland
hoe·like
hoer
Ho·fei Chinese city
hog (hog·ging, hogged)
ho·gan American Indian dwelling
Ho·garth·ian
hog·back narrow ridge
hog·fish plural ·fish or ·fishes
hogged
hog·ger
hog·ging
hog·gish
hog·gish·ly
hog·gish·ness
hog·like
Hog·ma·nay
hog·nose snake
hog·nut
hogs·head
hog·tie (·ty·ing, ·tied) US tie limbs
hog·wash
hog·weed
hoick
hoi·den variant spelling of hoyden
hoi pol·loi
hoist

hoist·er
hoity-toity
hoke overact
hokey cokey song and dance
ho·key-pokey hocus-pocus
Hok·kai·do Japanese island
hok·ku variant spelling of haiku
ho·kum
Hol·arc·tic zoogeographical term
hold (hold·ing, held)
hold·able
hold·all
hold·er
hold·er·ship
hold·fast
hold·ing
hole
holey
holi·day
ho·li·ly
Ho·li·ness pope's title
ho·li·ness
ho·lism
ho·lis·tic
ho·lis·ti·cal·ly
hol·la variant of hollo
hol·land cloth
Hol·land
hol·lan·daise sauce
Hol·land·er
Hol·lands Dutch gin
hol·ler Slang shout
hol·lo (or ·la; plural ·los or ·las) shout
hol·low
hol·low·ly
hol·low·ness
hol·ly (plural ·lies)
hol·ly·hock
Hol·ly·wood
holm Dialect river island
hol·mic
hol·mium chemical element
holo·blas·tic
holo·blas·ti·cal·ly
holo·caust
hol·o·caus·tal (or ·caus·tic)
Holo·cene geological period
holo·crine physiology term
holo·en·zyme

holo·gram handwritten document
holo·graph three-dimensional image
holo·graph·ic
hol·o·graphi·cal·ly
ho·log·ra·phy
holo·he·dral
holo·he·drism
holo·mor·phic
holo·phras·tic
holo·phyte
holo·phyt·ic
holo·plank·ton
holo·thu·rian zoology term
holo·type
holo·typ·ic
holo·zo·ic
hol·pen Archaic helped
Hol·stein West German region; cattle
hol·ster
hol·stered
holt Archaic woodland
holus-bolus Slang all at once
holy (adj **ho·li·er**, **ho·li·est**; noun, plural **holies**)
Holy·head
ho·ly·stone
holy·tide
hom (or **homa**) sacred plant
hom·age
hom·bre US man
hom·burg hat
home
home·bred
home·coming
home·land
home·less
home·less·ness
home·like
home·li·ness
home·ly (**·li·er**, **·li·est**) unpretentious; US ugly; compare **homy**
home·mak·ing
homeo·mor·phic (or **homoeo·**)
homeo·mor·phism (or **homoeo·**)
homeo·path·ic (or **homoeo·**)

homeo·pathi·cal·ly (or **homoeo·**)
homeopa·thist (or **homoepa·**)
homeopa·thy (or **homoeopa·**)
homeo·sta·sis (or **homoeo·**)
homeo·stat·ic (or **homoeo·**)
homeo·typ·ic (or **·typi·cal**, **homoeo·**) biology term
hom·er
Ho·merian
Ho·mer·ic
Ho·meri·cal·ly
home·sick
home·sick·ness
home·spun
home·stead
home·stead·er
home·ward (adj)
home·wards (adv)
home·work
homey variant spelling of **homy**
homey·ness variant spelling of **hominess**
homi·ci·dal
homi·ci·dal·ly
homi·cide
homi·let·ic (or **homi·leti·cal**)
homi·leti·cal·ly
homi·let·ics art of preaching sermons
homi·list
homi·ly (plural **·lies**)
homi·ness (or **homey·ness**)
hom·ing
homi·nid
homi·noid
homi·ny US ground maize
homo (plural **homos**) Slang homosexual
homo·cen·tric
homo·cen·tri·cal·ly
homo·cer·cal zoology term
homo·chro·mat·ic
homo·chro·ma·tism
homo·chro·mous
homo·cy·clic
homo·dont
homoeo· variant spelling of words beginning **homeo·**

homo·erotic
homo·eroti·cism
homo·ero·tism
ho·moga·mous
ho·moga·my botany term
ho·mog·enate
homo·genei·ty
homo·geneous uniform; compare **homogenous**
homo·geneous·ness
ho·mog·eni·za·tion (or **·sa·tion**)
ho·mog·enize (or **·enise**)
ho·mog·eniz·er (or **·enis·er**)
ho·mog·enous similar through common ancestry; compare **homogeneous**
ho·mog·eny
ho·mogo·nous
ho·mog·ony botany term
homo·graft
homo·graph
homo·graph·ic
ho·moio·ther·mic warm-blooded
ho·moio·ther·my
Ho·moi·ou·sian
Ho·moi·ou·si·an·ism Christian sect
homo·log US variant spelling of **homologue**
ho·molo·gate ratify
ho·molo·ga·tion
homo·logi·cal homologous
homo·logi·cal·ly
ho·molo·gize (or **·gise**)
ho·molo·giz·er (or **·gis·er**)
ho·molo·gous
ho·molo·graph·ic
homo·logue (US also **·log**)
ho·mol·ogy (plural **·ogies**)
ho·mol·o·sine cartography term
ho·moly·sis
homo·lyt·ic
homo·mor·phic (or **·phous**)
homo·mor·phism
homo·nym
homo·nym·ic
homo·nym·ity
Homo·ou·sian

Homo·ou·si·an·ism
Christian sect
homo·phile
homo·phone
homo·phon·ic
homo·phoni·cal·ly
ho·mopho·nous
ho·mopho·ny linguistics
term
homo·phyl·lic
ho·mophy·ly biology term
homo·plas·tic
homo·plas·ti·cal·ly
homo·plas·ty
homo·po·lar chemistry term
homo·po·lar·ity
ho·mop·ter·ous entomology
term
ho·mor·gan·ic linguistics
term
Homo sa·pi·ens
homo·scedas·tic·ity
statistics term
homo·sex·ual
homo·sex·ual·ity
homo·sex·ual·ly
ho·mos·po·rous botany
term
ho·mos·po·ry
homo·taxi·al·ly
homo·tax·ic
homo·tax·is
homo·thal·lic
homo·thal·lism botany
term
homo·zy·go·sis
homo·zy·gote
homo·zy·got·ic
homo·zy·gous genetics
term
Homs (or Hims, Hums)
Syrian city
ho·mun·cu·lar
ho·mun·cu·lus (plural ·li)
miniature man
homy (or homey;
homi·er, homi·est)
cosy; compare homely
ho·nan fabric
Honda (Trademark)
Hon·do variant of Honshu
Hon·du·ran
Hon·du·ras
hone
hon·est

hon·est·ly
hon·est·ness
hon·es·ty (plural ·ties)
hone·wort plant
hon·ey
honey·bee
honey·bunch
honey·comb
honey·dew
hon·ey·dewed
honey-eater bird
hon·eyed (or ·ied)
hon·eyed·ly (or ·ied·)
honey-like
honey·moon
honey·moon·er
honey·sucker bird
honey·suckle
hong Chinese factory
Hong Kong
Ho·nia·ra capital of
Solomon Islands
hon·ied variant spelling of
honeyed
Honi·ton lace
honk
honk·er
honky (plural honkies)
US slang white man
honky-tonk
Hono·lu·lu
hon·or US spelling of honour
hono·rar·ium (plural
·rar·iums or ·raria)
hon·or·ary
hon·or·if·ic
hon·or·ifi·cal·ly
hon·our (US ·or)
Hon·our·able title of
respect
hon·our·able (US ·or·)
hon·our·able·ness (US
·or·)
hon·our·ably (US ·or·)
hon·our·er (US ·or·)
hon·our·less (US ·or·)
Hon·shu (or Hon·do)
hooch
hood
hood·ed
hoodie crow
hood·less
hood·like
hood·lum
hood·lum·ism

hoo·doo (plural ·doos)
hoo·doo·ism
hood·wink
hood·wink·er
hoo·ey
hoof (plural hoofs or
hooves)
hoof·bound veterinary term
hoofed
hoof·er
hoof·less
hoof·like
Hoogh·ly Indian river
hoo-ha
hook
hook·ah oriental pipe
hooked
hook·ed·ness
hook·er
hook·less
hook·like
hook·nose
hook·nosed
hook·worm
hooky (or hookey)
hoo·li·gan
hoo·li·gan·ism
hoop
hooped
hoop·er
hoop·la
hoop·like
hoo·poe bird
hoo·rah (or ·ray) variants
of hurrah
hoose·gow US jail
hoot
hoot·en·an·ny (or
hoot·nan·ny; plural
·nies) US folksinging
hoot·er
Hoo·ver (Trademark)
hoo·ver (verb)
hooves
hop (hop·ping, hopped)
hope
hope·ful
hope·ful·ly
hope·ful·ness
Ho·peh Chinese province
hope·less
hope·less·ly
hope·less·ness
hop·er
hop·head Slang drug addict

Hopi (*plural* Hopis *or* Hopi) American Indian
hop·lite Greek soldier
hop·lit·ic
hop·lol·ogist
hop·lol·ogy study of weapons
hop·per
hop·ping
hop·ple hobble
hop·pler
Hop·pus foot unit
hop·sack
hop·scotch
hora dance
Horae Roman goddesses
ho·ral hourly
ho·ra·ry *Archaic* hourly
Ho·ra·tian of the poet Horace
Horatius legendary Roman hero
horde mob; *compare* hoard
hor·dein protein
Ho·reb biblical mountain
hore·hound (*or* hoar·) plant
ho·ri·zon
ho·ri·zon·less
hori·zon·tal
hori·zon·tal·ly
hori·zon·tal·ness
hor·me psychology term
hor·mic
hor·mo·nal
hor·mone
Hor·muz (*or* Or·muz) Iranian island
horn
horn·beam
horn·bill
horn·blende mineral
horn·blen·dic
horn·book
horned
horn·ed·ness
hor·net
horn·fels rock
horni·ly
horni·ness
horn·less
horn·like
horn·pipe
horn-rimmed
horn·stone

horns·wog·gle *Slang* cheat
horn·tail insect
horn·wort plant
horny (horni·er, horni·est)
horo·loge timepiece
horo·log·ic
ho·rol·o·gist (*or* ho·rolo·ger)
horo·lo·gium (*plural* ·gia) clock tower
ho·rol·ogy
horo·scope
horo·scop·ic
ho·ros·co·py (*plural* ·pies)
hor·ren·dous
hor·ri·ble
hor·ri·ble·ness
hor·ri·bly
hor·rid
hor·rid·ness
hor·rif·ic
hor·rifi·cal·ly
hor·ri·fi·ca·tion
hor·ri·fy (·fies, ·fy·ing, ·fied)
hor·ri·fy·ing·ly
hor·ripi·la·tion gooseflesh
hor·ror
horror-stricken (*or* -struck)
hors de com·bat *French* injured
hors d'oeu·vre (*plural* hors d'oeu·vre *or* hors d'oeu·vres)
horse animal; *compare* hoarse
horse·back
horse·box
horse·flesh
horse·fly (*plural* ·flies)
horse·hair
horse·hide
horse·leech
horse·less
horse·like
horse·man (*plural* ·men)
horse·man·ship
horse·mint
horse·play
horse·power (*plural* horse·power) unit
horse·radish

horse·shoe (·shoe·ing, ·shoed)
horse·tail plant
horse·weed
horse·whip (·whip·ping, ·whipped)
horse·whip·per
horse·woman (*plural* ·women)
horsi·ly
horsi·ness
horst ridge
horsy (*or* horsey; horsi·er, horsi·est)
hor·ta·to·ri·ly
hor·ta·tory (*or* ·tive) urging
hor·ti·cul·tur·al
hor·ti·cul·tur·al·ly
hor·ti·cul·ture
hor·ti·cul·tur·ist
hor·tus sic·cus collection of dried plants
Horus Egyptian god
ho·san·na
hose
Hosea biblical character
ho·sier
ho·siery
hos·pice
hos·pi·table
hos·pi·table·ness
hos·pi·tably
hos·pi·tal
hos·pi·tal·ity
hos·pi·tali·za·tion (*or* ·sa·tion)
hos·pi·tal·ize (*or* ·ise)
Hos·pi·tal·ler religious knight
hos·pi·tal·ler (*US* ·tal·er) hospital worker
hos·pit·ium (*plural* ·ia) travellers' refuge
hos·po·dar Ottoman ruler
host
hos·ta plant
hos·tage
hos·tel
hos·tel·ler (*US* ·tel·er)
hos·tel·ling (*US* ·tel·ing)
hos·tel·ry (*plural* ·ries)
host·ess
hos·tile
hos·tile·ly

hos·til·ity (*plural* ·ities)
host·ler *variant of* ostler
hot (*adj* hot·ter, hot·test; *verb* hot·ting, hot·ted)
hot·bed
hot-blooded
hot-blooded·ness
hotch·pot *legal term*
hotch·potch (*US* hodge·podge)
ho·tel
ho·tel·ier
hot·foot
hot·head
hot-headed
hot-headed·ly
hot-headed·ness
hot·house
Ho·tien (*or* Ho-t'ien, Kho-tan) *Chinese oasis*
hot·ly
hot·ness
hot·plate
hot·pot
hot·spur *impetuous person*
Hot·ten·tot (*plural* ·tot *or* ·tots)
hot·tish
Hou·dan *fowl*
hough *hock*
Houghton-le-Spring *Tyneside town*
hou·mous (*or* ·mus) *variant of* hummus
hound
hound·er
Houns·low
hour
hour·glass
hou·ri (*plural* ·ris) *Muslim nymph*
hour·ly
house
house·boat
house·bound
house·boy
house·break·er
house·break·ing
house·carl *medieval servant*
house·coat
house·fath·er
house·fly (*plural* ·flies)
house·hold
house·holder
house·holder·ship

house·keeper
house·keeping
hou·sel *Archaic Eucharist*
house·leek
house·less
house·line *nautical term*
house·maid
house·man (*plural* ·men)
house·master
house·mistress
house·moth·er
house-proud
house·room
house·top
house·wife (*plural* ·wives)
house·wife·li·ness
house·wife·ly
house·wif·ery
house·work
house·worker
housey-housey
hous·ing
Hou·ston *Texan port*
hous·to·nia *plant*
hout·ing *fish*
hove
Hove *Sussex town*
hov·el (·el·ling, ·elled; *US* ·el·ing, ·eled)
hov·er
hover·craft
hov·er·er
hov·er·ing·ly
hover·port
hover·train
how
how-be·it
how·dah *seat on elephant*
how·dy *US hello*
howe'er
how·ever
howf *Scot public house*
how·itz·er
howl
How·land *Pacific island*
howl·er
how·let *owl*
howl·ing
How·rah *Indian city*
how·so·ever
how·tow·die *Scottish chicken dish*
hoy
hoya *plant*
hoy·den (*or* hoi·)

hoy·den·ish (*or* hoi·)
hoy·den·ish·ness (*or* hoi·)
Hoy·lake *English town*
Hsi *variant spelling of* Si
Hsian *variant spelling of* Sian
Hsiang *variant spelling of* Siang
Hsin-hai-lien *variant spelling of* Sinhailien
Hsi·ning *variant spelling of* Sining
Hsü-chou *variant spelling of* Süchow
Huai-nan *Chinese city*
Huang Hai *variant spelling of* Hwang Hai
Huang Ho *variant spelling of* Hwang Ho
hub
hubble-bubble
hub·bub
hub·by (*plural* ·bies)
hub·cap
Hub·li *Indian city*
hu·bris (*or* hy·bris)
hu·bris·tic
hucka·back *fabric*
huck·le
huck·le·berry (*plural* ·berries)
huck·le·bone *Archaic anklebone*
huck·ster
huck·ster·ism
Hud·ders·field
hud·dle
hud·dler
hu·di·bras·tic *mock-heroic*
Hud·son *Canadian bay; US river*
hue *colour; compare* hew
hued
huff
huffi·ly
huffi·ness
huff·ish
huffy (huffi·er, huffi·est)
hug (hug·ging, hugged)
huge
huge·ly
huge·ness
hug·gable
hug·ger
hug·ger-mug·ger

Hu·gue·not
Hu·gue·not·ic
Hu·gue·not·ism
huh exclamation
Hu·he·hot (or Hu-ho-hao-t'e) Chinese town
hula (or hula-hula) Hawaiian dance
hulk
hulk·ing
hull
Hull English port; Canadian city
hul·la·ba·loo (or ·bal·loo; plural ·loos)
hull·er
hull-less
hul·lo variant spelling of hello
hum (hum·ming, hummed)
hu·man
hu·mane
hu·mane·ly
hu·mane·ness
hu·man·ism
hu·man·ist
hu·man·ist·ic
hu·mani·tar·ian
hu·mani·tari·an·ism
hu·mani·tari·an·ist
hu·man·ity (plural ·ities)
hu·mani·za·tion (or ·sa·tion)
hu·man·ize (or ·ise)
hu·man·iz·er (or ·is·er)
human·kind
hu·man·like
hu·man·ly
hu·man·ness
hu·man·oid
Hum·ber
Humber·side
hum·ble
hum·ble·bee
hum·ble·ness
hum·bler
hum·bling·ly
hum·bly
Hum·boldt cur·rent
hum·bug (·bug·ging, ·bugged)
hum·bug·ger
hum·bug·gery
hum·ding·er

hum·drum
hum·drum·ness
hu·mec·tant
hu·mer·al
hu·mer·us (plural ·meri) arm bone; compare humorous
hu·mic
hu·mid
hu·midi·fi·ca·tion
hu·midi·fi·er
hu·midi·fy (·fies, ·fy·ing, ·fied)
hu·midi·stat
hu·mid·ity
hu·mid·ness
hu·mi·dor tobacco container
hu·mili·ate
hu·mili·at·ing·ly
hu·milia·tion
hu·mil·ia·tive
hu·mili·a·tor
hu·mil·ia·tory
hu·mil·ity (plural ·ities)
hummed
hum·mel Scot hornless
hum·mer
hum·ming
humming·bird
hum·mock
hum·mocky
hum·mus (or hou·mus, ·mous) Middle Eastern food
hu·mor US spelling of humour
hu·mor·al of body fluids
hu·mor·esque
hu·mor·ist
hu·mor·is·tic
hu·mor·ous funny; compare humerus
hu·mor·ous·ness
hu·mour (US ·mor)
hu·mour·ful (US ·mor·)
hu·mour·less (US ·mor·)
hu·mour·less·ness (US ·mor·)
hu·mour·some (US ·mor·)
hump
hump·back
hump·backed
humph
humpi·ness

hump·like
hump·ty (plural ·ties) padded seat
humpy (humpi·er, humpi·est)
Hums variant of Homs
hu·mus
Hun
Hu·nan Chinese province
hunch
hunch·back
hunch·backed
hun·dred (plural ·dreds or ·dred)
hun·dredth
hundred·weight (plural ·weights or ·weight)
hung suspended; compare hanged
Hun·gar·ian
Hun·ga·ry
hun·ger
Hung·nam North Korean port
hun·gri·ly
hun·gri·ness
hun·gry (·gri·er, ·gri·est)
hunk
hunk·ers Dialect haunches
hunky-dory
Hun·like
Hun·nish
Hun·nish·ly
Hun·nish·ness
hunt
hunt·ed
hunt·er
hunt·ing
Hun·ting·don Cambridgeshire town
Hun·ting·don·shire former English county
hunts·man (plural ·men)
Hunts·ville US city
Huon Tasmanian river
Hu·peh (or ·pei) Chinese province
hup·pah Jewish wedding ceremony
hur·dle
hur·dler
hurds variant of hards
hurdy-gurdy (plural -gurdies)
hurl

hurl·er
hur·ley hurling stick
hurl·ing
hurly-burly (*plural*
 -burlies)
Hu·ron (*plural* ·rons *or*
 ·ron) American Indian
Hu·ron (Lake)
hur·rah (*or* hoo·ray,
 hoo·rah)
hur·ri·cane
hur·ried
hur·ried·ly
hur·ried·ness
hur·ry (*verb* ·ries, ·ry·ing,
 ·ried; *noun, plural*
 ·ries)
hur·ry·ing·ly
hurst *Archaic* wood
Hurst·mon·ceux *variant*
 spelling of Herstmonceux
hurt (hurt·ing, hurt)
hur·ter
hurt·ful
hurt·ful·ly
hurt·ful·ness
hurt·le
hus·band
hus·band·er
hus·band·less
husband·man (*plural*
 ·men)
hus·band·ry
hush
husha·by
husk
husk·er
huski·ly
huski·ness
husk·like
husky (*adj* huski·er,
 huski·est; *noun, plural*
 huskies)
huss dogfish
hus·sar
Huss·ism (*or* Huss·it·ism)
Huss·ite heretical Christian
hus·sy (*plural* ·sies)
hus·tings
hus·tle
hus·tler
hut
hutch
hut·like
hut·ment

Hu·tu (*plural* ·tu *or* ·tus)
 African people
huz·zah *Archaic* hurrah
hwan *variant of* won
Hwang Hai (*or* Huang
 Hai) Chinese sea
Hwang Ho (*or* Huang
 Ho) Chinese river
hwyl poetic fervour
hya·cinth
hya·cin·thine
Hyacinthus mythological
 character
Hya·des (*or* Hy·ads) star
 cluster
hy·aena *variant spelling of*
 hyena
hya·lin biochemical
 substance
hya·line translucent
hya·lite variety of opal
hya·loid transparent
hya·lu·ron·ic acid
hya·lu·roni·dase enzyme
hy·brid
hy·brid·ism
hy·brid·ity
hy·brid·iz·able (*or*
 ·is·able)
hy·bridi·za·tion (*or*
 ·sa·tion)
hy·brid·ize (*or* ·ise)
hy·brid·iz·er (*or* ·is·er)
hy·bris *variant spelling of*
 hubris
hy·dan·to·in crystalline
 substance
hy·da·thode botany term
hy·da·tid tapeworm cyst
Hyde English town
Hy·dera·bad
hyd·no·car·pate
hyd·no·car·pic acid
hy·dra (*plural* ·dras *or*
 ·drae) marine animal
Hy·dra mythological
 character
hy·drac·id acid without
 oxygen
hy·dran·gea
hy·drant
hy·dranth zoology term
hy·drar·gy·ric
hy·drar·gy·rum mercury
hy·dras·tine biochemical
 compound

hy·dras·ti·nine biochemical
 compound
hy·dras·tis plant
hy·drate
hy·drat·ed
hy·dra·tion
hy·dra·tor
hy·drau·lic
hy·drau·li·cal·ly
hy·drau·lics
hy·dra·zine
hy·dra·zo·ic acid
hy·dria ancient Greek jar
hy·dric
hy·dride
hy·dri·od·ic
hy·dro (*plural* ·dros)
hydro·bro·mic
hydro·car·bon
hydro·cele pathology term
hydro·cel·lu·lose
hydro·cephal·ic
hydro·cepha·lus (*or*
 ·cephaly)
hydro·chlo·ric
hydro·chlo·ride
hy·dro·cor·al (*or*
 ·cor·al·line) zoology term
hydro·cor·ti·sone
hydro·cy·an·ic
hydro·dy·nam·ic
hydro·dy·nami·cal·ly
hydro·dy·nam·ics
hydro·elec·tric
hydro·elec·tric·ity
hydro·flu·or·ic
hydro·foil
hydro·gen
hydro·gen·ate
hydro·gena·tion
hydro·gena·tor
hydro·geni·za·tion (*or*
 ·sa·tion)
hydro·gen·ize (*or* ·ise)
hydro·gen·oly·sis
hy·drog·enous
hydro·graph
hy·drog·ra·pher
hydro·graph·ic (*or*
 ·graphi·cal)
hydro·graphi·cal·ly
hy·drog·ra·phy mapping
 oceans and rivers
hy·droid

hydro·ki·net·ic (*or* ·neti·cal)
hydro·ki·net·ics
hydro·log·ic (*or* ·logi·cal)
hydro·logi·cal·ly
hy·drol·o·gist
hy·drol·ogy
hydro·lys·able (*US* ·lyz·)
hy·droly·sate
hy·dro·ly·sa·tion (*US* ·za·tion)
hydro·lyse (*US* ·lyze)
hydro·lys·er (*US* ·lyz·er)
hy·droly·sis
hydro·lyte
hydro·lyt·ic
hydro·mag·net·ics
hydro·manc·er
hydro·man·cy divination by water
hydro·man·tic
hydro·mechani·cal
hydro·mechan·ics
hydro·medu·sa (*plural* ·sas *or* ·sae) zoology term
hydro·medu·san
hydro·mel mead
hydro·met·al·lur·gi·cal
hydro·met·al·lur·gy
hydro·meteor
hydro·meteoro·logi·cal
hydro·meteor·ol·ogy
hy·drom·eter
hydro·met·ric (*or* ·met·ri·cal)
hy·drom·etry
hydro·path·ic (*or* ·pathi·cal)
hy·dropa·thist (*or* hydro·path)
hy·dropa·thy water cure
hydro·phane variety of opal
hydro·phil·ic
hy·drophi·lous botany term
hy·drophi·ly
hydro·pho·bia
hydro·pho·bic
hydro·phone underwater microphone
hydro·phyte
hydro·plane
hydro·poni·cal·ly
hydro·pon·ics
hydro·pow·er

hydro·scope
hydro·ski hydrofoil on seaplane
hydro·sphere
hydro·stat
hydro·stat·ic
hydro·stat·ics
hydro·sul·phide (*US* ·fide)
hydro·thera·peu·tic
hydro·thera·pist
hydro·thera·py
hydro·trop·ic growing towards water
hy·drous
hy·drox·ide
hy·droxy chemistry term
hy·droxyl
hydro·zoan zoology term
Hy·drus constellation
hy·ena (*or* ·aena)
hy·eto·graph rainfall chart
hy·eto·graph·ic (*or* ·graphi·cal)
hy·eto·graphi·cal·ly
hy·etog·ra·phy
Hygeia Greek goddess
hy·giene
hy·gien·ic
hy·gieni·cal·ly
hy·gien·ics
hy·gien·ist
hygro·graph
hy·grom·eter humidity measurer
hygro·met·ric
hygro·met·ri·cal·ly
hy·grom·etry
hygro·phi·lous botany term
hygro·scope
hygro·scop·ic
hygro·scopi·cal·ly
Hyk·sos (*plural* ·sos) Asian nomad
hyla tree frog
hy·lo·zo·ism philosophical doctrine
hy·lo·zo·ist
Hymen god of marriage
hy·men anatomical membrane
hy·men·al of the hymen
hy·meneal of marriage
hy·menium (*plural* ·menia) fungal tissue

hy·menop·ter·an (*plural* ·ter·ans *or* ·tera) insect
hymn
hym·nal
hym·nic
hym·nist (*or* hym·no·dist)
hym·no·dy
hym·nolo·gist
hym·nol·ogy
hy·oid bone
hy·os·cine
hy·os·cya·mine
hype
hyper·ac·id (*adj*)
hyper·acid·ity
hyper·ac·tive
hyper·ac·tiv·ity
hyper·aemia (*US* ·emia) pathology term
hyper·aemic (*US* ·emic)
hyper·aes·the·sia (*US* ·es·) increased sensitivity
hyper·aes·thet·ic (*US* ·es·)
hyper·bar·ic of high pressure
hyper·ba·ton reversed word order
hyper·bo·la (*plural* ·las *or* ·lae) geometrical curve
hyper·bo·le exaggeration
hyper·bol·ic (*or* ·boli·cal)
hyper·bo·lize (*or* ·lise) exaggerate
hyper·bo·loid
Hyper·bo·rean mythological character
hyper·bo·rean of extreme north
hyper·charge
hyper·criti·cal
hyper·criti·cal·ly
hyper·criti·cism
hyper·du·lia veneration for Virgin Mary
hyper·du·lic (*or* hyper·du·li·cal)
hyper·gly·cae·mia (*US* ·cemia) excess blood sugar
hyper·gly·cae·mic (*US* ·cemic)
hyper·gol·ic spontaneously flammable
hyper·icum plant
hyper·in·fla·tion

hyper·in·su·lin·ism
Hyperion Greek god
hyper·ki·nesia (or ·nesis)
hyper·ki·net·ic
hyper·mar·ket
hyper·meter verse line
hyper·met·ric (or
　·metri·cal)
hyper·metro·pia (US
　hyper·opia) long-
　sightedness
hyper·metrop·ic
hy·perm·ne·sia psychology
　term
hyper·on elementary
　particle
hyper·opia US
　hypermetropia
hyper·plasia enlargement of
　body part
hyper·plas·tic
hy·perp·noea (US ·nea)
　increased breathing rate
hyper·py·rexia high fever
hyper·sen·si·tive
hyper·sen·si·tiv·ity
hyper·sen·si·tize (or ·tise)
　photography term
hyper·son·ic
hyper·space
hyper·spa·tial
hyper·ten·sion
hyper·ten·sive
hyper·ther·mia (or
　·ther·my)
hyper·thy·roid
hyper·thy·roid·ism
hyper·ton·ic
hyper·troph·ic
hyper·tro·phy (noun,
　plural ·phies; verb
　·phies, ·phy·ing, ·phied)
hyper·ven·ti·la·tion
hyper·vita·mi·no·sis
hy·pha (plural ·phae) part
　of fungus
hy·phen
hy·phen·ate
hy·phena·tion
hyp·na·gog·ic psychology
　term
hyp·noid
hyp·nol·ogy study of sleep

hyp·no·pae·dia
hyp·no·sis (plural ·ses)
hyp·no·thera·py
hyp·not·ic
hyp·noti·cal·ly
hyp·no·tism
hyp·no·tist
hyp·no·tize (or ·tise)
hypo (plural hypos)
　photographic fixer; syringe
hypo·acid·ity
hypo·caust Roman heating
　system
hypo·cen·tre (US ·ter)
hypo·chlor·ite
hypo·chlor·ous
hypo·chon·dria
hypo·chon·dri·ac
hypo·chon·dria·cal·ly
hypo·chon·drium (plural
　·dria) anatomy term
hy·poco·rism pet name
hy·poc·ri·sy (plural ·sies)
hypo·crite
hypo·criti·cal
hypo·criti·cal·ly
hypo·cy·cloid geometric
　curve
hypo·cy·cloi·dal
hypo·der·mic
hypo·der·mis biology term
Hy·po·do·rian musical term
hypo·gas·tric
hypo·gas·trium (plural
　·tria) anatomy term
hypo·geal (or ·geous)
　botany term
hypo·gene geology term
hy·pog·enous botany term
hypo·gen·ic
hypo·geum (plural ·gea)
　burial vault
hypo·glos·sal anatomy term
hypo·gly·cae·mia (US
　·cemia) low blood sugar
hypo·gly·caem·ic (US
　·cemic)
hy·poid
hypo·lim·nion bottom layer
　in lake
hypo·ma·nia

hypo·man·ic
hypo·nas·tic
hypo·nas·ty botany term
hypo·phys·eal
hy·pophy·sis (plural ·ses)
　pituitary gland
hypo·plasia (or ·plas·ty)
hypo·sen·si·tize (or ·tise)
hypo·stat·ic
hypos·ta·sis (plural ·ses)
hy·pos·ta·tize (or ·tise)
hypo·style architectural
　term
hypo·ten·sion
hypo·ten·sive
hy·pot·enuse
hypo·thala·mus (plural
　·mi)
hy·poth·ecate legal term
hy·poth·eca·tion
hy·poth·eca·tor
hypo·ther·mia
hy·poth·esis (plural ·eses)
hy·poth·esize (or ·esise)
hypo·theti·cal
hypo·theti·cal·ly
hypo·thy·roid
hypo·thy·roid·ism
hypo·ton·ic
hy·poxia oxygen deficiency
hy·pox·ic
hyp·so·met·ric (or ·ri·cal)
hyp·som·etry altitude
　measurement
hy·rax animal
hy·son Chinese tea
hys·sop herb
hys·ter·ec·to·my (plural
　·mies)
hys·te·re·sis physics term
hys·te·ria
hys·ter·ic
hys·teri·cal
hys·teri·cal·ly
hys·ter·ics
hys·tero·gen·ic
hys·ter·oid (or ·teroi·dal)
hys·ter·oto·my (plural
　·mies) incision into uterus
hys·tri·co·morph rodent

I

I
iamb (*or* iam·bus; *plural*
iambs, iam·bi, *or*
iam·buses) metrical foot
iam·bic
iam·bi·cal·ly
Iap·etus satellite of Saturn
iat·ric (*or* ·ri·cal) of
medicine
iat·ro·gen·ic
iat·ro·genic·ity
Iba·dan Nigerian city
Iba·gué Colombian city
I-beam girder
Iberia
Iberian
ibex (*plural* ibexes,
ibi·ces, *or* ibex) goat
Ibibio (*plural* Ibibio *or*
Ibibios) Nigerian people
ibis (*plural* ibises *or* ibis)
bird
Ibi·za (*or* Ivi·za) Spanish
island
Ibo (*or* Igbo; *plural* Ibos,
Ibo *or* Igbos, Igbo)
African people
Icaria Greek island
Icar·ian
Icarus mythological
character
ice
ice·berg
ice·blink
ice·bound
ice·box
ice·breaker
ice·cap
ice cream
ice·fall
Ice·land
Ice·land·er
Ice·land·ic
Iceni ancient British tribe
Ichang (*or* I-ch'ang)
Chinese port
I Ching Chinese book of
divination
Ichi·no·mi·ya Japanese
town

ich·neu·mon mongoose;
insect
ich·nite (*or* ·no·lite) fossil
footprint
ich·no·graph·ic (*or*
·graphi·cal)
ich·no·graphi·cal·ly
ich·nog·ra·phy ground-plan
drawing
ich·no·logi·cal
ich·nol·ogy study of fossil
footprints
ichor
ichor·ous
ich·thy·ic of fishes
ich·thy·oid (*or* ·oid·al)
ich·thyo·log·ic (*or*
·logi·cal)
ich·thyo·logi·cal·ly
ich·thy·olo·gist
ich·thy·ol·ogy
ich·thy·opha·gous
ich·thy·opha·gy
ich·thy·or·nis extinct bird
ich·thyo·saur (*or* ·saur·us;
plural ·saurs,
·saur·uses, *or* ·sau·ri)
ich·thyo·sis skin disease
ich·thy·ot·ic
ici·cle
ici·cled
ici·ly
ici·ness
ic·ing
icon (*or* ikon)
icon·ic (*or* iconi·cal)
icono·clasm
icono·clast
icono·clas·tic
icono·clas·ti·cal·ly
ico·nog·ra·pher
icono·graph·ic (*or*
·graphi·cal)
ico·nog·ra·phy (*plural*
·phies)
ico·nola·ter
ico·nola·trous
ico·nola·try
icono·logi·cal
ico·nolo·gist

ico·nol·ogy
icono·mat·ic representing
sounds with pictures
icono·mati·cism
icono·scope
ico·sa·he·dral
ico·sa·he·dron (*plural*
·drons *or* ·dra)
ic·ter·ic
ic·ter·us jaundice
ic·tus (*plural* ·tuses *or*
·tus) poetry term
icy (ici·er, ici·est)
I'd I had; I would
id
Ida Cretan mountain
Ida·ho
ide fish
idea
ideal
ideal·ism
ideal·ist
ideal·is·tic
ideal·is·ti·cal·ly
ideal·ity (*plural* ·ities)
ideali·za·tion (*or* ·sa·tion)
ideal·ize (*or* ·ise)
ideal·iz·er (*or* ·is·er)
ideal·ly
ideate imagine
idea·tion
idea·tion·al
idea·tive
idea·tum (*plural* ·ta)
philosophy term
idée fixe (*plural* idées
fixes)
idem·po·tent maths term
iden·tic diplomacy term
iden·ti·cal
iden·ti·cal·ly
iden·ti·cal·ness
iden·ti·fi·able
iden·ti·fi·able·ness
iden·ti·fi·ca·tion
iden·ti·fi·er
iden·ti·fy (·fies, ·fy·ing,
·fied)
Iden·ti·kit (*Trademark*)
iden·tity (*plural* ·tities)

ideo·gram (*or* ·graph)
symbol
id·eog·ra·phy
ideo·logi·cal (*or* ·log·ic)
ideo·logi·cal·ly
ideolo·gist (*or* ideo·logue)
ideol·ogy (*plural* ·ogies)
ideo·mo·tor physiology
term
ides day in Roman calendar
idio·blast plant cell
idio·blas·tic
idio·cy (*plural* ·cies)
idio·graph·ic
idio·lect individual's
language
idio·lect·al (*or* ·ic)
idi·om
idio·mat·ic (*or* ·mati·cal)
idio·mati·cal·ly
idio·mor·phic mineralogy
term
idio·mor·phi·cal·ly
idio·mor·phism
idio·path·ic
idi·opa·thy (*plural* ·thies)
disease of unknown cause
idio·phone musical
instrument
idio·phon·ic
idio·syn·cra·sy (*plural*
·sies)
idio·syn·crat·ic
idio·syn·crati·cal·ly
idi·ot
idi·ot·ic
idi·oti·cal·ly
idle lazy; *compare* idol
idle·ness
idler
idly
idol image; *compare* idle
idola·ter (*fem* ·tress)
idola·trize (*or* ·trise)
idola·triz·er (*or* ·tris·er)
idola·trous
idola·try
idoli·za·tion (*or* ·sa·tion)
idol·ize (*or* ·ise)
idol·iz·er (*or* ·is·er)
idyll (*or* idyl)
idyl·lic
idyl·li·cal·ly
idyl·list
if

Ife Nigerian town
Igbo *variant spelling of* Ibo
ig·loo (*or* iglu; *plural*
·loos *or* iglus)
ig·ne·ous geology term
ig·nes·cent giving off sparks
ig·nit·abil·ity (*or* ·ibil·ity)
ig·nit·able (*or* ·ible)
ig·nite
ig·nit·er
ig·ni·tion
ig·ni·tron physics term
ig·no·bil·ity (*or* ·ble·ness)
ig·no·ble
ig·no·bly
ig·no·mini·ous
ig·no·miny (*plural*
·minies)
ig·nor·able
ig·no·ra·mus (*plural*
·muses)
ig·no·rance
ig·no·rant
ig·no·ra·tio elen·chi logic
term
ig·nore
ig·nor·er
Igraine (*or* Ygerne) King
Arthur's mother
Igua·çú (*or* Iguas·sú)
South American river
igua·na lizard
igua·nian
iguano·don dinosaur
ih·ram Muslim pilgrim's
robes
IJs·sel·meer (*or* Ys·)
Dutch lake
ikeba·na Japanese flower
arranging
ikon *variant spelling of* icon
il·eac (*or* ·eal) of ileum;
compare iliac
Île-de-France
il·ei·tis intestinal disorder
il·eos·to·my (*plural* ·mies)
abdominal operation
Ilesha Nigerian town
il·eum small intestine;
compare ilium
il·eus intestinal obstruction
ilex tree
ili·ac of ilium; *compare* ileac
Ili·ad
Ili·ad·ic

Il·ium Troy
il·ium (*plural* ·ia) hip
bone; *compare* ileum
ilk
Il·kes·ton Derbyshire town
I'll I will; I shall
ill
ill-advised
ill-assorted
il·la·tive linguistics term
Il·la·war·ra Australian
district
ill-bred
ill-breed·ing
ill-considered
Ille-et-Vilaine French
department
il·legal
il·legal·ity (*plural* ·ities)
il·legali·za·tion (*or*
·sa·tion)
il·legal·ize (*or* ·ise)
il·legal·ly
il·leg·ibil·ity (*or*
·ible·ness)
il·leg·ible
il·leg·ibly
il·legiti·ma·cy (*or*
·mate·ness)
il·legiti·mate
il·legiti·mate·ly
ill-fated
ill-favou·red (*US*
·favored)
ill-gotten
il·lib·er·al
il·lib·er·al·ity (*or* ·ness,
·ism)
il·lic·it illegal; *compare* elicit
il·lim·it·abil·ity (*or*
·able·ness)
il·lim·it·able
Il·li·nois
Il·li·nois·an (*or* ·noian,
·nois·ian)
il·liq·uid
il·lit·era·cy (*plural* ·cies)
il·lit·er·ate
ill-mannered
ill-natured
ill·ness
il·locu·tion philosophy term
il·lo·cu·tion·ary
il·logi·cal
il·logi·cal·ity (*or* ·ness)

il·logi·cal·ly
ill-omened
ill-starred
ill-timed
ill-treat
ill-treatment
il·lude deceive; *compare* allude; elude
il·lume
il·lu·mi·nance
il·lu·mi·nant
il·lu·mi·nate
il·lu·mi·na·ti (*sing.* ·to) enlightened people
il·lu·mi·na·tion
il·lu·mi·na·tive
il·lu·mi·na·tor
il·lu·mine
il·lu·mi·nism belief in enlightenment
il·lu·mi·nist
ill-use (*verb*)
ill-use (*or* -usage)
il·lu·sion delusion; *compare* allusion
il·lu·sion·ary (*or* ·al)
il·lu·sion·ism
il·lu·sion·ist
il·lu·sion·is·tic
il·lu·sive illusory; *compare* elusive
il·lu·so·ri·ly
il·lu·so·ri·ness
il·lu·sory
il·lus·trat·able
il·lus·trate
il·lus·tra·tion
il·lus·tra·tion·al
il·lus·tra·tive
il·lus·tra·tor
il·lus·tri·ous
il·lu·via·tion
Il·lyria Adriatic region
Il·lyr·ian
il·men·ite mineral
Iloi·lo Philippine port
Ilor·in Nigerian city
I'm
(imaculate) *incorrect spelling of* immaculate
im·age
im·age·ry (*plural* ·ries)
im·agi·nable
im·agi·nably

im·agi·nal of an image or imago
im·agi·nari·ly
im·agi·nary
im·agi·na·tion
im·agi·na·tive
im·ag·ine
im·ag·in·er
im·ag·ism poetic movement
im·ag·ist
im·ag·is·tic
im·ag·is·ti·cal·ly
ima·go (*plural* ·gos, ·goes, *or* ·gi·nes) adult insect; psychiatry term
imam (*or* imaum) Islamic priest
imam·ate
ima·ret Turkish hospice
im·bal·ance
im·becile
im·becil·ity (*plural* ·ities)
im·bed *less common spelling of* embed
im·bibe
im·bib·er
im·bi·bi·tion
im·bri·cate (*or* ·cat·ed)
im·bri·ca·tion
im·bro·glio (*plural* ·glios)
im·brue (*or* em·; ·bru·ing, ·brued) to stain; *compare* imbue
im·bue (·bu·ing, ·bued) instil; *compare* imbrue
im·id·az·ole
im·ide chemistry term
im·id·ic
(imigrate) *incorrect spelling of* immigrate
imine chemistry term
imi·tabil·ity (*or* ·table·ness)
imi·table
imi·tate
imi·ta·tion
imi·ta·tion·al
imi·ta·tive
imi·ta·tor
im·macu·la·cy (*or* ·late·ness)
im·macu·late
im·ma·nence (*or* ·nen·cy)
im·ma·nent existing within; *compare* eminent; imminent

im·ma·nent·ism religious belief
im·ma·terial
im·ma·teri·al·ism
im·ma·teri·al·ist
im·ma·terial·ity (*or* ·teri·al·ness)
im·ma·teri·al·ize (*or* ·ise)
im·ma·ture
im·ma·tu·rity (*or* ·ture·ness)
im·meas·ur·abil·ity (*or* ·able·ness)
im·meas·ur·able
im·meas·ur·ably
im·media·cy (*or* ·medi·ate·ness)
im·medi·ate
im·medi·ate·ly
im·medi·cable
im·memo·ri·able
im·memo·rial
im·memo·ri·al·ly
im·mense
im·mense·ly
im·men·si·ty (*plural* ·ties)
im·men·su·rable
im·merse
im·mers·ible
im·mer·sion immersing; *compare* emersion
im·mer·sion·ism Christian doctrine
im·mer·sion·ist
im·methodi·cal
im·methodi·cal·ly
im·mi·grant
im·mi·grate enter country; *compare* emigrate
im·mi·gra·tion
im·mi·gra·tory
im·mi·gra·tor
im·mi·nence
im·mi·nent impending; *compare* eminent; immanent
Im·ming·ham Humberside port
im·mis·cibil·ity
im·mis·cible
im·mis·cibly
im·mo·bile
im·mo·bil·ism political policy
im·mo·bil·ity

im·mo·bi·li·za·tion (or ·sa·tion)
im·mo·bi·lize (or ·lise)
im·mo·bi·liz·er (or ·lis·er)
im·mo·der·ate
im·mo·der·ate·ly
im·mod·era·tion (or ·er·ate·ness)
im·mod·est
im·mod·es·ty
im·mo·late sacrifice
im·mo·la·tion
im·mo·la·tor
im·mor·al morally bad; compare amoral
im·mor·al·ist
im·mo·ral·ity (plural ·ities)
im·mor·al·ly
im·mor·tal
im·mor·tal·ity
im·mor·tali·za·tion (or ·sa·tion)
im·mor·tal·ize (or ·ise)
im·mor·tal·iz·er (or ·is·er)
im·mor·tal·ly
im·mor·telle everlasting flower
im·mo·tile
im·mo·til·ity
im·mov·abil·ity (or ·mov·able·ness)
im·mov·able (or in legal contexts ·move·)
im·mov·ably
im·mune
im·mu·nity (plural ·nities)
im·mu·ni·za·tion (or ·sa·tion)
im·mu·nize (or ·nise)
im·mu·niz·er (or ·nis·er)
im·mu·no·as·say
im·mu·no·chem·is·try
im·mu·no·genet·ic (or ·geneti·cal)
im·mu·no·genet·ics
im·mu·no·gen·ic
im·mu·no·geni·cal·ly
im·mu·no·globu·lin
im·mu·no·log·ic (or ·logi·cal)
im·mu·no·logi·cal·ly
im·mu·nolo·gist
im·mu·nol·ogy
im·mu·no·reac·tion

im·mu·no·sup·pres·sion
im·mu·no·sup·pres·sive
im·mu·no·thera·py
im·mure
im·mu·tabil·ity (or ·table·ness)
im·mu·table
im·mu·tably
Imo Nigerian state
imp
im·pact
im·pact·ed
im·pac·tion
im·pair
im·pair·er
im·pair·ment
im·pa·la (plural ·las or ·la) antelope
im·pale
im·pale·ment
im·pal·er
im·pal·pa·bil·ity
im·pal·pable
im·pal·pably
im·pa·na·tion Christian ritual
im·pan·el US spelling of empanel
im·pari·pin·nate botany term
im·pari·syl·la·bic
im·par·ity (plural ·ities) disparity
im·part
im·par·ta·tion (or ·part·ment)
im·part·er
im·par·tial
im·par·ti·al·ity (or ·ness)
im·par·tial·ly
im·part·ibil·ity
im·part·ible legal term
im·pass·abil·ity (or ·able·ness)
im·pass·able
im·pass·ably
im·passe
im·pas·sion
im·pas·sioned
im·pas·sioned·ly
im·pas·sive
im·pas·sive·ness (or ·siv·ity)
im·pas·ta·tion
im·paste paint thickly

im·pas·to paint applied thickly
im·pa·tience
im·pa·ti·ens (plural ·ens) plant
im·pa·tient
im·peach
im·peach·abil·ity
im·peach·able
im·peach·er
im·peach·ment
im·pearl
im·pec·cabil·ity
im·pec·cable
im·pec·cably
im·pec·cant sinless
im·pecu·ni·ous
im·pecu·ni·ous·ness (or ·os·ity)
im·ped·ance physics term
im·pede
im·ped·er
im·pedi·ment
im·pedi·men·ta impeding objects
im·pedi·men·tal (or ·tary)
im·ped·ing·ly
im·pel (·pel·ling, ·pelled)
im·pel·lent
im·pel·ler
im·pend
im·pend·ence (or ·en·cy)
im·pend·ing
im·pen·etrabil·ity
im·pen·etrable
im·pen·etrably
im·peni·tence (or ·ten·cy, ·tent·ness)
im·peni·tent
im·pera·tive
im·pera·tor
im·per·cep·tibil·ity (or ·tible·ness)
im·per·cep·tible
im·per·cep·tibly
im·per·cep·tion
im·per·cep·tive
im·per·cep·tiv·ity (or ·tive·ness)
im·per·cipi·ent
im·per·cipi·ence
im·per·fect
im·per·fec·tion
im·per·fec·tive
im·per·fo·rate

im·per·fo·ra·tion
im·perial
im·peri·al·ism
im·peri·al·ist
im·peri·al·is·tic
im·peri·al·is·ti·cal·ly
im·peri·al·ly
im·per·il (·il·ling, ·illed;
  US also ·il·ing, ·iled)
im·peri·ous
im·per·ish·abil·ity (*or*
  ·able·ness)
im·per·ish·able
im·perium (*plural* ·peria)
  ancient Roman supreme
  power
im·per·ma·nence (*or*
  ·nen·cy)
im·per·ma·nent
im·per·meabil·ity (*or*
  ·meable·ness)
im·per·meable
im·per·mis·sibil·ity
im·per·mis·sible
im·per·son·al
im·per·son·al·ity
im·per·son·ali·za·tion (*or*
  ·sa·tion)
im·per·son·al·ize (*or* ·ise)
im·per·son·al·ly
im·per·son·ate
im·per·sona·tion
im·per·sona·tor
im·per·ti·nence (*or*
  ·nen·cy)
im·per·ti·nent
im·per·turb·abil·ity (*or*
  ·able·ness)
im·per·turb·able
im·per·turb·ably
im·per·tur·ba·tion
im·per·vi·ous
im·petigi·nous
im·peti·go skin disease
im·petrate obtain by prayer
im·petra·tion
im·petra·tive
im·petra·tor
im·petu·os·ity (*or*
  ·ous·ness)
im·petu·ous
im·petus (*plural* ·petuses)
Im·phal Indian city

impi (*plural* impi *or*
  impies) Bantu warrior
  group
im·pi·ety (*plural* ·eties)
im·pinge
im·pinge·ment
im·ping·er
im·pi·ous
imp·ish
im·plac·abil·ity (*or*
  ·able·ness)
im·plac·able
im·plac·ably
im·plant
im·plan·ta·tion
im·plant·er
im·plau·sibil·ity (*or*
  ·sible·ness)
im·plau·sible
im·plau·sibly
im·plead prosecute
im·plead·able
im·plead·er
im·ple·ment tool; to carry
  out
im·ple·men·tal
im·ple·men·ta·tion
im·ple·ment·er (*or* ·or)
im·pli·cate
im·pli·ca·tion
im·plica·tive
im·plic·it
im·plic·it·ness (*or*
  ·plic·ity)
(impliment) *incorrect
  spelling of* implement
im·plode
im·plo·ra·tion
im·plo·ra·tory
im·plore
im·plor·er
im·plor·ing·ly
im·plo·sion
im·plo·sive phonetics term
im·ply (·plies, ·ply·ing,
  ·plied)
im·poli·cy (*plural* ·cies)
im·po·lite
im·po·lite·ness
im·poli·tic
im·poli·tic·ly
im·pon·dera·bilia
im·pon·der·abil·ity (*or*
  ·able·ness)
im·pon·der·able

im·pon·der·ably
im·po·nent
im·port
im·port·able
im·por·tance
im·por·tant
im·por·ta·tion
im·port·er
im·por·tu·nate
im·por·tune
im·por·tun·er
im·por·tu·nity (*plural*
  ·nities)
im·pos·able
im·pose
im·pos·er
im·pos·ing
im·pos·ing·ly
im·po·si·tion
im·pos·sibil·ity (*plural*
  ·ities)
im·pos·sible
im·pos·sibly
im·post customs duty
im·pos·tor (*or* ·post·er)
im·pos·trous (*or* ·tur·ous)
im·pos·ture
im·po·tence (*or* ·ten·cy,
  ·tent·ness)
im·po·tent
im·pound
im·pound·age (*or* ·ment)
im·pound·er
im·pov·er·ish
im·pov·er·ish·er
im·pov·er·ish·ment
im·prac·ti·cabil·ity (*or*
  ·cable·ness)
im·prac·ti·cable not
  feasible
im·prac·ti·cably
im·prac·ti·cal not practical
im·prac·ti·cal·ity (*or*
  ·ness)
im·prac·ti·cal·ly
im·pre·cate
im·pre·ca·tion
im·pre·ca·tory
im·pre·cise
im·pre·ci·sion (*or*
  ·cise·ness)
im·preg·nabil·ity (*or*
  ·nable·ness)
im·preg·nable (*or*
  im·preg·na·table)

im·preg·nate
im·preg·na·tion
im·preg·na·tor
im·pre·sa (*or* im·prese) emblem
im·pre·sa·rio (*plural* ·rios)
im·pre·scrip·tibil·ity
im·pre·scrip·tible legal term
im·press
im·press·er
im·press·ible
im·pres·sion
im·pres·sion·abil·ity (*or* ·able·ness)
im·pres·sion·able
im·pres·sion·al
im·pres·sion·al·ly
im·pres·sion·ism
im·pres·sion·ist
im·pres·sion·is·tic
im·pres·sive
im·pres·sive·ness
im·press·ment conscription
im·prest
im·pri·ma·tur sanction
im·print
im·print·er
im·print·ing
im·pris·on
im·pris·on·er
im·pris·on·ment
im·prob·abil·ity (*or* ·able·ness)
im·prob·able
im·pro·bity (*plural* ·bities)
im·promp·tu
im·prop·er
im·pro·pri·ate transfer to laity
im·pro·pria·tion
im·pro·pria·tor
im·pro·pri·ety (*plural* ·eties)
im·prov·abil·ity (*or* ·able·ness)
im·prov·able
im·prove
im·prove·ment
im·prov·er
im·provi·dence
im·provi·dent
im·prov·ing·ly
im·provi·sa·tion
im·provi·sa·tion·al

im·pro·vise
im·pro·vis·er
im·pru·dence
im·pru·dent unwise; *compare* impudent
im·pu·dence (*or* ·den·cy)
im·pu·dent impertinent; *compare* imprudent
im·pugn
im·pug·na·tion (*or* ·pugn·ment)
im·pugn·er
im·pu·is·sance
im·pu·is·sant
im·pulse
im·pul·sion
im·pul·sive
im·pul·sive·ness
im·pu·nity (*plural* ·nities)
im·pure
im·pu·rity (*plural* ·rities)
im·put·abil·ity (*or* ·able·ness)
im·put·able
im·pu·ta·tion
im·pu·ta·tive
im·pute
im·put·er
in
in·abil·ity (*plural* ·ities)
in ab·sen·tia *Latin* in the absence of
in·ac·ces·sibil·ity (*or* ·sible·ness)
in·ac·ces·sible
in·ac·ces·sibly
in·ac·cu·ra·cy (*plural* ·cies)
in·ac·cu·rate
in·ac·tion
in·ac·ti·vate
in·ac·ti·va·tion
in·ac·tive
in·ac·tiv·ity (*or* ·tive·ness)
in·ad·equa·cy (*plural* ·cies)
in·ad·equate
in·ad·mis·sibil·ity
in·ad·mis·si·ble
in·ad·mis·sibly
in·ad·vert·ence (*or* ·en·cy)
in·ad·vert·ent
in·ad·vis·abil·ity (*or* ·able·ness)
in·ad·vis·able

in·ad·vis·ably
in·al·ien·abil·ity (*or* ·able·ness)
in·al·ien·able
in·al·ien·ably
in·al·ter·abil·ity (*or* ·able·ness)
in·al·ter·able
in·al·ter·ably
in·amo·ra·ta (*masc* ·to; *plural* ·tas *or* ·tos) lover
in·ane
in·ani·mate
ina·ni·tion
in·ani·mate·ness (*or* ·ma·tion)
in·an·ity (*plural* ·ities)
in·ap·pli·cabil·ity (*or* ·cable·ness)
in·ap·pli·cable
in·ap·po·site
in·ap·pre·ciable
in·ap·pre·cia·tive
in·ap·pre·hen·sive
in·ap·proach·abil·ity
in·ap·proach·able
in·ap·pro·pri·ate
in·ap·pro·pri·ate·ness
in·apt inappropriate; *compare* inept
in·ap·ti·tude (*or* ·apt·ness)
in·arch botany term
in·ar·ticu·late
in·ar·tis·tic
in·ar·tis·ti·cal·ly
in·as·much
in·at·ten·tion (*or* ·tive·ness)
in·at·ten·tive
in·audibil·ity (*or* ·audible·ness)
in·audible
in·audibly
in·augu·ral
in·augu·rate
in·augu·ra·tion
in·augu·ra·tor
in·augu·ra·tory
in·aus·pi·cious
in·board
in·born
in·bound
in·bred
in·breed (·breed·ing, ·bred)

Inca (*plural* **Inca** *or*
 Incas)
In·caic
in·cal·cu·labil·ity (*or*
 ·lable·ness)
in·cal·cu·lable
in·cal·cu·lably
in·ca·les·cence
in·ca·les·cent chemistry
 term
in cam·era *Latin* in private
In·can
in·can·desce
in·can·des·cence (*or*
 ·cen·cy)
in·can·des·cent
in·can·ta·tion
in·can·ta·tion·al (*or*
 ·ta·tory)
in·ca·pabil·ity (*plural*
 ·ities)
in·ca·pable
in·ca·pably
in·ca·paci·tate
in·ca·paci·ta·tion
in·ca·pac·ity (*plural* ·ities)
in·cap·su·late *less common*
 spelling of encapsulate
in·car·cer·ate
in·car·cera·tion
in·car·cera·tor
in·car·di·nate
in·car·di·na·tion
in·car·nate
in·car·na·tion
in·cau·tious
in·cau·tious·ness (*or*
 ·cau·tion)
in·cen·dia·rism
in·cen·di·ary (*plural*
 ·aries)
in·cense
in·cen·so·ry (*plural* ·ries)
 incense-burner
in·cen·tive
in·cept
in·cep·tion
in·cep·tive
in·cept·or
in·cer·ti·tude
in·ces·san·cy (*or*
 ·sant·ness)
in·ces·sant
in·cest
in·ces·tu·ous

inch
inch·meal inch by inch
in·cho·ate
in·choa·tion
in·choa·tive
In·chon (*or* ·cheon) South
 Korean port
inch·worm
in·ci·dence
in·ci·dent
in·ci·den·tal
in·ci·den·tal·ly
in·cin·er·ate
in·cin·era·tion
in·cin·era·tor
in·cipi·ence (*or* ·en·cy)
in·cipi·ent
in·ci·pit *Latin* here begins
in·cise
in·ci·sion
in·ci·sive
in·ci·sor
in·ci·sur·al
in·ci·sure
in·ci·ta·tion
in·cite
in·cite·ment
in·cit·er
in·cit·ing·ly
in·ci·vil·ity (*plural* ·ities)
in·clem·en·cy (*or*
 ·ent·ness)
in·clem·ent
in·clin·able
in·cli·na·tion
in·cli·na·tion·al
in·cline
in·clin·er
in·cli·nom·eter
in·close *less common spelling*
 of enclose
in·clos·ure *less common*
 spelling of enclosure
in·clud·able (*or* ·ible)
in·clude
in·clu·sion
in·clu·sive
in·co·er·cible
in·cog·ni·to (*fem* ·ta;
 plural ·tos *or* ·tas)
in·cog·ni·zance
in·cog·ni·zant
in·co·her·ence (*or* ·en·cy,
 ·ent·ness)
in·co·her·ent

in·com·bus·tibil·ity (*or*
 ·tible·ness)
in·com·bus·tible
in·com·bus·tibly
in·come
in·com·ing
in·com·men·su·rabil·ity
 (*or* ·rable·ness)
in·com·men·su·rable
in·com·men·su·rably
in·com·men·su·rate
in·com·mode
in·com·mo·di·ous
in·com·mod·ity (*plural*
 ·ities)
in·com·mu·ni·cabil·ity (*or*
 ·cable·ness)
in·com·mu·ni·cable
in·com·mu·ni·cably
in·com·mu·ni·ca·do
in·com·mu·ni·ca·tive
in·com·mut·abil·ity (*or*
 ·able·ness)
in·com·mut·able
in·com·mut·ably
in·com·pa·rabil·ity (*or*
 ·rable·ness)
in·com·pa·rable
in·com·pa·rably
in·com·pat·ibil·ity (*or*
 ·ible·ness)
in·com·pat·ible
in·com·pat·ibly
in·com·pe·tence (*or*
 ·ten·cy)
in·com·pe·tent
in·com·plete
in·com·plete·ness (*or*
 ·ple·tion)
in·com·pli·ance (*or*
 ·an·cy)
in·com·pli·ant
in·com·pre·hen·sibil·ity
 (*or* ·sible·ness)
in·com·pre·hen·sible
in·com·pre·hen·sibly
in·com·pre·hen·sion
in·com·pre·hen·sive
in·com·press·ibil·ity (*or*
 ·ible·ness)
in·com·press·ible
in·com·press·ibly
in·com·put·abil·ity
in·com·put·able
in·con·ceiv·abil·ity (*or*
 ·able·ness)

in·con·ceiv·able
in·con·ceiv·ably
in·con·clu·sive
in·con·den·sabil·ity (or ·sibil·)
in·con·den·sable (or ·sible)
in·con·form·ity
in·con·gru·ity (plural ·ities)
in·con·gru·ous (or ·ent)
in·con·gru·ous·ness (or ·gru·ence)
in·con·sequence (or ·sequent·ness)
in·con·sequen·tial (or ·sequent)
in·con·sequen·ti·al·ity (or ·tial·ness)
in·con·sequen·tial·ly
in·con·sid·er·able
in·con·sid·er·ate
in·con·sid·era·tion
in·con·sist·en·cy (plural ·cies)
in·con·sist·ent
in·con·sol·abil·ity (or ·able·ness)
in·con·sol·able
in·con·sol·ably
in·con·so·nance
in·con·so·nant
in·con·spicu·ous
in·con·stan·cy (plural ·cies)
in·con·stant
in·con·sum·able
in·con·sum·ably
in·con·test·abil·ity (or ·able·ness)
in·con·test·able
in·con·test·ably
in·con·ti·nence (or ·nen·cy)
in·con·ti·nent
in·con·tro·vert·ibil·ity (or ·ible·ness)
in·con·tro·vert·ible
in·con·tro·vert·ibly
in·con·ven·ience
in·con·ven·ient
in·con·vert·ibil·ity (or ·ible·ness)
in·con·vert·ible
in·con·vert·ibly

in·con·vin·cibil·ity (or ·cible·ness)
in·con·vin·cible
in·co·ordi·nate
in·co·ordi·na·tion
in·cor·po·rable
in·cor·po·rate
in·cor·po·rat·ed
in·cor·po·ra·tion
in·cor·po·ra·tive
in·cor·po·ra·tor
in·cor·po·real
in·cor·po·real·ly
in·cor·po·reity (or ·real·ity)
in·cor·rect
in·cor·rect·ness
in·cor·ri·gibil·ity (or ·gible·ness)
in·cor·ri·gible
in·cor·ri·gibly
in·cor·rupt
in·cor·rupt·ibil·ity (or ·ible·ness)
in·cor·rupt·ible
in·cor·rupt·ibly
in·cras·sate (or ·sat·ed) thickened
in·cras·sa·tion
in·creas·able
in·crease
in·creas·ing·ly
in·creas·er
in·cred·ibil·ity (or ·ible·ness)
in·cred·ible
in·cred·ibly
in·cre·du·lity
in·credu·lous
in·cre·ment
in·cre·men·tal
in·cres·cent
in·cre·tion secretion into bloodstream
in·cre·tion·ary (or ·tory)
in·crimi·nate
in·crimi·na·tion
in·crimi·na·tor
in·crimi·na·tory
in·cross inbreed
in·crust variant spelling of encrust
in·cu·bate
in·cu·ba·tion
in·cu·ba·tion·al

in·cu·ba·tive (or ·tory)
in·cu·ba·tor
in·cu·bus (plural ·bi or ·buses) male demon
in·cu·date (or ·dal) of incus
in·cul·cate
in·cul·ca·tion
in·cul·ca·tor
in·cul·pabil·ity (or ·pable·ness)
in·cul·pable
in·cul·pate
in·cul·pa·tion
in·cul·pa·tive (or in·cul·pa·to·ry)
in·cum·ben·cy (plural ·cies)
in·cum·bent
in·cu·nabu·la (sing. ·lum) early books
in·cu·nabu·lar
in·cur (·cur·ring, ·curred)
in·cur·abil·ity (or ·able·ness)
in·cur·able not curable; compare incurrable
in·cu·ri·os·ity (or ·ous·ness)
in·cu·ri·ous
in·cur·rable liable to incur; compare incurable
in·cur·rence
in·cur·rent
in·cur·sion
in·cur·sive
in·cur·vate
in·cur·va·tion
in·cur·va·ture
in·curve
in·cus (plural ·cu·des) ear bone
in·cuse design on coin
Ind India
in·da·mine chemical compound
in·debt·ed
in·debt·ed·ness
in·de·cen·cy (plural ·cies)
in·de·cent
in·de·cidu·ous
in·de·ci·pher·abil·ity (or ·able·ness)
in·de·ci·pher·able
in·de·ci·sion
in·de·ci·sive

in·de·clin·able
in·deco·rous
in·de·co·rum
in·deed
in·de·fati·gabil·ity (*or* ·gable·ness)
in·de·fati·gable
in·de·fati·gably
in·de·fea·sibil·ity (*or* ·sible·ness)
in·de·fea·sible
in·de·fea·sibly
in·de·fen·sibil·ity (*or* ·sible·ness)
in·de·fen·sible
in·de·fin·able
in·de·fin·ably
in·defi·nite
in·de·his·cence
in·de·his·cent botany term
in·del·ibil·ity (*or* ·ible·ness)
in·del·ible
in·del·ibly
in·deli·ca·cy (*plural* ·cies)
in·deli·cate
in·dem·ni·fi·ca·tion
in·dem·ni·fi·er
in·dem·ni·fy (·fies, ·fy·ing, ·fied)
in·dem·nity (*plural* ·nities)
in·de·mon·strable
in·dene chemical compound
in·dent
in·den·ta·tion
in·dent·er (*or* den·tor)
in·den·tion indentation
in·den·ture
in·den·ture·ship
in·de·pend·ence
in·de·pend·en·cy (*plural* ·cies)
in·de·pend·ent
in·de·scrib·abil·ity (*or* ·able·ness)
in·de·scrib·able
in·de·scrib·ably
in·de·struct·ibil·ity (*or* ·ible·ness)
in·de·struct·ible
in·de·struct·ibly
in·de·ter·mi·nable
in·de·ter·mi·na·cy (*or* ·na·tion, ·nate·ness)

in·de·ter·mi·nate
in·de·ter·min·ism philosophy term
in·de·ter·min·ist
in·de·ter·min·is·tic
in·dex (*plural* ·dexes *or esp. in mathematical contexts* ·di·ces)
in·dex·er
in·dexi·cal
index-linked
In·dia
In·dian
In·di·ana US state
In·di·an·apo·lis US city
In·dic language group
in·di·can chemical compound
in·di·cant
in·di·cat·able
in·di·cate
in·di·ca·tion
in·dica·tive
in·di·ca·tor
in·dica·tory
in·di·ces *plural of* index
in·di·cia (*sing.* ·cium) distinguishing markings
in·di·cial
in·dict accuse; *compare* indite
in·dict·able
in·dictee
in·dict·er (*or* ·dic·tor)
in·dict·ment
In·dies
in·dif·fer·ence
in·dif·fer·ent
in·dif·fer·ent·ism indifference to religion
in·dif·fer·ent·ist
in·di·gence
in·di·gene (*or* ·gen) a native
in·dig·enous
in·dig·enous·ness (*or* in·di·gen·ity)
in·di·gent
in·di·gest·ibil·ity (*or* ·ible·ness)
in·di·gest·ible
in·di·ges·tion
in·di·ges·tive
in·dign undeserving
in·dig·nant

in·dig·na·tion
in·dig·nity (*plural* ·nities)
in·di·go (*plural* ·gos *or* ·goes)
in·di·goid
in·di·got·ic
in·di·rect
in·di·rec·tion
in·di·rect·ness
in·dis·cern·ible
in·dis·cern·ibly
in·dis·ci·pline
in·dis·creet tactless
in·dis·crete undivided
in·dis·cre·tion
in·dis·cre·tion·ary
in·dis·crimi·nate
in·dis·crimi·na·tion
in·dis·crimi·na·tive
in·dis·pen·sabil·ity (*or* ·sable·ness)
in·dis·pen·sable
in·dis·pen·sably
in·dis·pose
in·dis·posed
in·dis·po·si·tion
in·dis·put·abil·ity (*or* ·able·ness)
in·dis·put·able
in·dis·put·ably
in·dis·sol·ubil·ity (*or* ·uble·ness)
in·dis·sol·uble
in·dis·sol·ubly
in·dis·tinct
in·dis·tinc·tive
in·dis·tin·guish·abil·ity (*or* ·able·ness)
in·dis·tin·guish·able
in·dis·tin·guish·ably
in·dite *Archaic* write; *compare* indict
in·dium chemical element
in·di·vid·ual
in·di·vidu·al·ism
in·di·vidu·al·ist
in·di·vidu·al·is·tic
in·di·vidu·al·is·ti·cal·ly
in·di·vidu·al·ity (*plural* ·ities)
in·di·vidu·ali·za·tion (*or* ·sa·tion)
in·di·vidu·al·ize (*or* ·ise)
in·di·vidu·al·iz·er (*or* ·is·er)

in·di·vid·ual·ly
in·di·vidu·ate
in·di·vidu·ation
in·di·vid·ua·tor
in·di·vis·ibil·ity (*or*
·ible·ness)
in·di·vis·ible
in·di·vis·ibly
Indo·china (*or* Indo-
China)
Indo·chinese (*or* Indo-
Chinese)
in·do·cile
in·do·cil·ity
in·doc·tri·nate
in·doc·tri·na·tion
in·doc·tri·na·tor
Indo-European
in·dole (*or* ·dol) chemical
compound
in·dole·acetic acid
in·dole·bu·tyr·ic acid
in·do·lence
in·do·lent
In·dolo·gist
In·dol·ogy
in·do·metha·cin
in·domi·tabil·ity (*or*
·table·ness)
in·domi·table
in·domi·tably
In·do·nesia
In·do·nesian
in·door (*adj*)
in·doors (*adv*)
Indo-Pacific
in·do·phenol
In·dore Indian city
in·dorse *variant spelling of*
endorse
in·dox·yl chemical
compound
in·draught (*US* ·draft)
in·drawn
Indre French department
Indre-et-Loire French
department
in·dris (*or* ·dri) animal
in·du·bi·tabil·ity (*or*
·table·ness)
in·du·bi·table
in·du·bi·tably
in·duce
in·duce·ment
in·duc·er

in·duc·ible
in·duct
in·duct·ance electrical
property
in·duc·tee *US* military
conscript
(inducter) *incorrect spelling
of* inductor
in·duc·tile not pliant
in·duc·til·ity
in·duc·tion
in·duc·tion·al
in·duc·tive
in·duc·tor
in·dulge
in·dul·gence
in·dul·gent
in·dulg·er
in·dulg·ing·ly
in·du·line (*or* ·lin) dye
in·dult Catholic dispensation
in·du·pli·cate (*or* ·cat·ed)
in·du·pli·ca·tion
in·du·rate
in·du·ra·tion
in·du·ra·tive
In·dus Asian river
in·du·sial
in·du·sium (*plural* ·sia)
membrane
in·dus·trial
in·dus·tri·al·ism
in·dus·tri·al·ist
in·dus·tri·ali·za·tion (*or*
·sa·tion)
in·dus·tri·al·ize (*or* ·ise)
in·dus·tri·al·ly
in·dus·tri·ous
in·dus·try (*plural* ·tries)
in·dwell (·dwell·ing,
·dwelt)
in·earth bury
in·ebri·ant
in·ebri·ate
in·ebri·at·ed
in·ebria·tion
in·ebri·ety
in·ed·ibil·ity
in·ed·ible
in·ed·it·ed
in·edu·cabil·ity
in·edu·cable
in·ef·fabil·ity (*or*
·fable·ness)
in·ef·fable

in·ef·fably
in·ef·face·abil·ity
in·ef·face·able
in·ef·fec·tive
in·ef·fec·tual
in·ef·fec·tu·al·ity (*or*
·ness)
in·ef·fec·tual·ly
in·ef·fi·ca·cious
in·ef·fi·ca·cy (*or*
·ca·cious·ness)
in·ef·fi·cien·cy
in·ef·fi·cient
in·elas·tic
in·elas·tic·al·ly
in·elas·tic·ity
in·el·egance (*or* ·egan·cy)
in·el·egant
in·eli·gibil·ity (*or*
·gible·ness)
in·eli·gible
in·elo·quence
in·elo·quent
in·eluc·tabil·ity
in·eluc·table
in·eluc·tably
in·ept incompetent; *compare*
inapt
in·epti·tude
in·equal·ity (*plural* ·ities)
in·equi·table
in·equi·tably
in·equi·ty (*plural* ·ties)
in·eradi·cable
in·eradi·cably
in·ert
in·er·tia
in·er·tial
in·es·cap·able
in·es·cap·ably
in·es·cutch·eon heraldic
term
in esse *Latin* actually
existing
in·es·sen·tial
in·es·sen·ti·al·ity
in·es·sive linguistics term
in·es·ti·mabil·ity (*or*
·mable·ness)
in·es·ti·mable
in·es·ti·mably
in·evi·tabil·ity (*or*
·table·ness)
in·evi·table
in·evi·tably

in·ex·act
in·ex·acti·tude
in·ex·cus·abil·ity (or
·able·ness)
in·ex·cus·able
in·ex·cus·ably
in·ex·haust·ibil·ity (or
·ible·ness)
in·ex·haust·ible
in·ex·haust·ibly
in·ex·ist·ence (or ·en·cy)
in·ex·ist·ent
in·exo·rabil·ity (or
·rable·ness)
in·exo·rable
in·exo·rably
in·ex·pe·di·ence (or
·en·cy)
in·ex·pe·di·ent
in·ex·pen·sive
in·ex·pe·ri·ence
in·ex·pe·ri·enced
in·ex·pert
in·ex·pi·able
in·ex·pi·ably
in·ex·pli·cabil·ity (or
·cable·ness)
in·ex·pli·cable
in·ex·pli·cably
in·ex·plic·it
in·ex·press·ibil·ity (or
·ible·ness)
in·ex·press·ible
in·ex·press·ibly
in·ex·pres·sive
in·ex·ten·sibil·ity
in·ex·ten·sible
in·ex·tin·guish·able
in·ex·tir·pable
in ex·tre·mis *Latin* in
extremity
in·ex·tri·cabil·ity (or
·cable·ness)
in·ex·tri·cable
in·ex·tri·cably
in·fal·libil·ity (or
·lible·ness)
in·fal·lible
in·fal·libly
in·fam·ize (or ·ise) make
infamous
in·fa·mous
in·fa·my (*plural* ·mies)
in·fan·cy (*plural* ·cies)
in·fant

in·fan·ta Spanish princess
in·fan·te Spanish prince
in·fan·ti·cid·al
in·fan·ti·cide
in·fan·tile
in·fan·ti·lism
in·fan·til·ity
in·fan·try (*plural* ·tries)
in·fantry·man (*plural*
·men)
in·farct dead tissue
in·farct·ed
in·farc·tion
in·fare *Dialect* wedding
reception
in·fatu·ate
in·fatu·at·ed
in·fatu·at·ed·ly
in·fat·ua·tion
in·fect
in·fec·tion
in·fec·tious
in·fec·tious·ness
in·fec·tive
in·fec·tive·ness (or
·tiv·ity)
in·fec·tor (or ·fect·er)
in·fe·cund
in·fe·cun·dity
in·fe·lici·tous
in·fe·lic·ity (*plural* ·ities)
in·fer (·fer·ring, ·ferred)
in·fer·able (or ·ible,
·rable, ·rible)
in·fer·ence
in·fer·en·tial
in·fe·ri·or
in·fe·ri·or·ity
in·fer·nal
in·fer·nal·ity
in·fer·nal·ly
in·fer·no (*plural* ·nos)
in·ferred
in·fer·rer
in·fer·ring
in·fer·tile
in·fer·til·ity
in·fest
in·fes·ta·tion
in·fest·er
in·fi·del
in·fi·del·ity (*plural* ·ities)
in·field
in·fielder
in·fighter

in·fighting
in·fil·trate
in·fil·tra·tion
in·fil·tra·tive
in·fil·tra·tor
in·fi·nite
in·fi·nite·ly
in·fini·tesi·mal
in·fini·tesi·mal·ly
in·fini·ti·val
in·fini·tive
in·fini·tude
in·fin·ity (*plural* ·ities)
in·firm
in·fir·ma·ry (*plural* ·ries)
in·fir·mity (*plural* ·mities)
in·fix
in·fix·ion
in·flame
in·flam·er
in·flam·ing·ly
in·flam·mabil·ity (or
·mable·ness)
in·flam·mable
in·flam·ma·tion
in·flam·ma·to·ri·ly
in·flam·ma·tory
in·flat·able
in·flate
in·flat·ed·ly
in·flat·er (or ·fla·tor)
in·fla·tion
in·fla·tion·ary
in·fla·tion·ism
in·fla·tion·ist
in·flect
in·flect·ed·ness
in·flec·tion (or ·flex·ion)
in·flec·tion·al (or
·flex·ion·)
in·flec·tive
in·flec·tor
in·flexed botany term
in·flex·ibil·ity (or
·ible·ness)
in·flex·ible
in·flex·ibly
in·flex·ion *variant spelling of*
inflection
in·flict
in·flict·er (or ·flic·tor)
in·flic·tion
in·flic·tive
in·flo·res·cence
in·flo·res·cent

in·flow
in·flu·ence
in·flu·ence·able
in·flu·enc·er
in·flu·ent flowing in
in·flu·en·tial
in·flu·en·tial·ly
in·flu·en·za
in·flu·en·zal
in·flux
info *Slang* information
in·fold *variant spelling of* enfold
(inforce) *incorrect spelling of* enforce
in·form
in·for·mal
in·for·mal·ity (*plural* ·ities)
in·for·mal·ly
in·form·ant
in·for·ma·tion
in·for·ma·tion·al
in·forma·tive (*or* ·tory)
in·forma·tive·ly
in·form·ed·ly
in·form·er
in·form·ing·ly
infra·cos·tal *anatomy term*
in·fract *violate*
in·frac·tion
in·frac·tor
in·fra dig
infra·lap·sar·ian *theology term*
infra·lap·sari·an·ism
in·fran·gibil·ity (*or* ·gible·ness)
in·fran·gible
infra·red
infra·son·ic
infra·soni·cal·ly
infra·sound
infra·struc·ture
in·fre·quen·cy (*or* ·quence)
in·fre·quent
in·fringe
in·fringe·ment
in·fring·er
in·fu·lae (*sing.* ·la) ribbons on bishop's mitre
in·fun·dibu·lar (*or* ·late)
in·fun·dibu·li·form

in·fun·dibu·lum (*plural* ·la) anatomical part
in·furi·ate
in·furi·at·ing·ly
in·furia·tion
in·fus·cate (*or* ·cat·ed) tinged with brown
in·fuse
in·fus·er
in·fu·sibil·ity (*or* ·sible·ness)
in·fu·sible
in·fu·sion
in·fu·sion·ism *theology term*
in·fu·sion·ist
in·fu·sive
in·fu·so·rial
in·gath·er
in·gen·ious *skilful; compare* ingenuous
in·gé·nue *naive girl*
in·genu·ity (*plural* ·ities)
in·genu·ous *naive; compare* ingenious
in·gest
in·ges·ta (*plural*) food
in·gest·ible
in·ges·tion
in·ges·tive
in·gle
ingle·nook
in·glo·ri·ous
in·go·ing
in·got
in·graft *variant spelling of* engraft
in·grain (*or* en·)
in·grained (*or* en·)
in·grain·ed·ly (*or* en·)
in·grain·ed·ness (*or* en·)
in·grate
in·gra·ti·ate
in·gra·ti·at·ing (*or* in·gra·tia·tory)
in·gra·tia·tion
in·grati·tude
in·gra·ves·cence
in·gra·ves·cent *becoming worse*
in·gre·di·ent
in·gress
in·gres·sion
in·gres·sive
in·group

in·grow·ing
in·grown
in·growth
in·gui·nal *of the groin*
in·gur·gi·tate *to gorge*
in·gur·gi·ta·tion
In·gush (*plural* ·gushes *or* ·gush) *Soviet people*
in·hab·it
in·hab·it·abil·ity
in·hab·it·able
in·hab·it·an·cy (*or* ·ance)
in·hab·it·ant
in·habi·ta·tion
in·hal·ant
in·ha·la·tion
in·ha·la·tor *device aiding breathing*
in·hale
in·hal·er
in·har·mon·ic
in·har·mo·ni·ous
in·har·mo·ny
in·haul (*or* ·haul·er) *nautical term*
in·here
in·her·ence (*or* ·en·cy)
in·her·ent
in·her·it
in·her·it·abil·ity (*or* ·able·ness)
in·her·it·able
in·her·it·ance
in·heri·tor (*fem* ·tress *or* ·trix; *plural* ·tors, ·tresses, *or* ·tri·ces)
in·he·sion *inherence*
in·hib·it
in·hib·it·able
in·hib·it·er (*or* ·hibi·tor)
in·hi·bi·tion
in·hibi·tive (*or* ·tory)
in·hibi·tor
in·hos·pi·table
in·hos·pi·tably
in·hos·pi·tal·ity
in·house
in·hu·man
in·hu·mane
in·hu·man·ity (*plural* ·ities)
in·hu·ma·tion
in·hume *inter*
in·hum·er
in·imi·cal

in·imi·cal·ly
in·imi·cal·ness (*or* ·ity)
in·imi·tabil·ity (*or*
 ·table·ness)
in·imi·table
in·imi·tably
ini·on anatomy term
in·iqui·tous
in·iquity (*plural* ·iquities)
ini·tial (·tial·ling, ·tialled;
 US ·tial·ing, ·tialed)
ini·tial·er (*or* ·tial·ler)
ini·tiali·za·tion (*or*
 ·sa·tion)
ini·tial·ize (*or* ·ise)
 computer term
ini·tial·ly
ini·ti·ate
ini·tia·tion
ini·tia·tive
ini·tia·tor
ini·tia·tory
ini·tia·tress (*or* ·trix)
in·ject
in·ject·able
in·jec·tion
in·jec·tive
in·jec·tor
in·ju·di·cious
In·jun *US* American Indian
in·junc·tion
in·junc·tive
in·jur·able
in·jure
in·jur·er
in·ju·ri·ous
in·ju·ry (*plural* ·ries)
in·jus·tice
ink
ink·berry (*plural* ·berries)
ink·blot
ink-cap fungus
In·ker·man Crimean battle
ink·horn
inki·ness
in·kle linen tape
ink·ling
ink·stand
ink·well
inky (inki·er, inki·est)
in·laid
in·land
in·land·er
in-law
in·lay (·lay·ing, ·laid)

in·lay·er
in·let (·let·ting, ·let)
in·li·er geology term
in loco pa·ren·tis
in·mate
in me·mo·ri·am
in·mi·grant immigrant
in·most
inn
in·nards
in·nate
in·ner
inner·most
in·ner·vate supply with
 nerves; *compare* enervate;
 innovate
in·ner·va·tion
in·nerve stimulate
in·ning baseball term
in·nings (*plural* ·nings)
inn·keeper
in·no·cence
in·no·cent
(innoculate) *incorrect
 spelling of* inoculate
in·nocu·ous
in·nomi·nate
in nomi·ne musical term
in·no·vate introduce new
 ideas; *compare* enervate;
 innervate
in·no·va·tion
in·no·va·tion·al
in·no·va·tion·ist
in·no·va·tive (*or* ·tory)
in·no·va·tor
in·nox·ious harmless
Inns·bruck Austrian city
in·nu·en·do (*plural* ·dos
 or ·does)
In·nu·it (*or* Inu·it; *plural*
 ·it *or* ·its) Eskimo
in·nu·mer·abil·ity (*or*
 ·able·ness)
in·nu·mer·able (*or* ·ous)
in·nu·mer·ably
in·nu·mer·ate
in·nu·tri·tion
in·nu·tri·tious
in·ob·serv·ance
in·ob·serv·ant
in·ocu·labil·ity
in·ocu·lable
in·ocu·late
in·ocu·la·tion

in·ocu·la·tive
in·ocu·la·tor
in·ocu·lum (*or* ·lant;
 plural ·la *or* ·lants)
in·odor·ous
in·of·fen·sive
in·of·fi·cious contrary to
 moral duty
in·op·er·abil·ity (*or*
 ·able·ness)
in·op·er·able
in·op·era·tive
in·op·por·tune
in·op·por·tune·ness (*or*
 ·tun·ity)
in·or·di·na·cy (*or*
 ·nate·ness)
in·or·di·nate
in·or·gan·ic
in·or·gani·cal·ly
in·os·cu·late
in·os·cu·la·tion
ino·si·tol chemical
 compound
ino·trop·ic physiology term
in·pa·tient
in per·pe·tuum
in pos·se *Latin* possible
in·put (·put·ting, ·put)
in·qi·lab Indian revolution
in·quest
in·qui·et
in·qui·etude
in·qui·line biology term
in·qui·lin·ism (*or* ·ity)
in·qui·li·nous
in·quire formally
 investigate; *US* spelling of
 enquire
in·quir·er
in·quiry (*plural* ·quiries)
 formal investigation; *US
 spelling of* enquiry
in·qui·si·tion
in·qui·si·tion·al
in·qui·si·tion·ist
in·quisi·tive
in·quisi·tive·ness
in·quisi·tor
in·quisi·to·rial
in·quisi·to·rial·ly
in re legal term
in rem legal term
in·road
in·rush

in·sali·vate
in·sali·va·tion
in·sa·lu·bri·ous
in·sa·lu·bri·ty
in·sane
in·sani·tari·ness (or
 ·ta·tion)
in·sani·tary
in·san·ity (plural ·ities)
in·sa·tiabil·ity (or
 ·tiable·ness,
 ·ti·ate·ness)
in·sa·tiable (or ·ti·ate)
in·sa·tiably (or ·ti·ate·ly)
in·scape person's nature
in·scrib·able
in·scribe
in·scrib·er
in·scrip·tion
in·scrip·tion·al
in·scrip·tive
in·scru·tabil·ity (or
 ·table·ness)
in·scru·table
in·sect
in·sec·tar·ium (or ·tary;
 plural ·tar·iums, ·tar·ia,
 or ·taries)
in·sec·tean (or ·tan, ·tile)
in·sec·ti·cid·al
in·sec·ti·cide
in·sec·ti·vore
in·sec·tivo·rous
in·secure
in·secu·rity (plural ·rities)
in·sel·berg rocky hill
in·semi·nate
in·semi·na·tion
in·semi·na·tor
in·sen·sate
in·sen·sibil·ity (or
 ·sible·ness)
in·sen·sible
in·sen·sibly
in·sen·si·tive
in·sen·si·tiv·ity
in·sen·ti·ence (or ·en·cy)
in·sen·ti·ent
in·sepa·rabil·ity (or
 ·rable·ness)
in·sepa·rable
in·sepa·rably
in·sert
in·sert·able
in·sert·er

in·ser·tion
in·ser·tion·al
in·ses·so·rial ornithology
 term
in·set (·set·ting, ·set)
in·set·ter
in·shore
in·side
in·sid·er
in·sidi·ous
in·sight
in·sight·ful
in·sig·nia (plural ·nias or
 ·nia)
in·sig·nifi·cance (or
 ·can·cy)
in·sig·nifi·cant
in·sin·cere
in·sin·cere·ly
in·sin·cer·ity (plural
 ·ities)
in·sinu·ate
in·sinu·a·tion
in·sinua·tive (or ·tory)
in·sinua·tor
in·sip·id
in·si·pid·ity (or ·ness)
in·sist
in·sist·ence (or ·en·cy)
in·sist·ent
in·sist·er
in situ
in·so·bri·ety
in so far (US in·so·far)
in·so·late expose to sun;
 compare insulate
in·so·la·tion
in·sole
in·so·lence
in·so·lent
in·sol·ubil·ity (or
 ·uble·ness)
in·sol·uble
in·sol·ubly
in·solv·abil·ity
in·solv·able
in·sol·ven·cy
in·sol·vent
in·som·nia
in·som·ni·ac
in·som·ni·ous
in·so·much
in·sou·ci·ance
in·sou·ci·ant

in·span (·span·ning,
 ·spanned) harness
in·spect
in·spect·able
in·spec·tion
in·spec·tion·al
in·spec·tive
in·spec·tor
in·spec·to·ral (or ·rial)
in·spec·tor·ate
in·spec·tor·ship
in·spir·able
in·spi·ra·tion
in·spi·ra·tion·al
in·spira·tive
in·spira·tory
in·spire
in·spir·er
in·spir·ing
in·spir·it
in·spir·it·er
in·spir·it·ing·ly
in·spir·it·ment
in·stabil·ity (plural ·ities)
in·stall (or ·stal; ·stall·ing,
 ·stalled or ·stal·ling,
 ·stalled)
in·stal·la·tion
in·stall·er
in·stal·ment (US ·stall·)
in·stance
in·stant
in·stan·ta·neous
in·stan·ta·neous·ness (or
 ·neity)
in·stan·ter without delay
in·stan·ti·ate represent by
 example
in·stant·ly
in·star zoology term
in·state
in·state·ment
in·stead
in·step
in·sti·gate
in·sti·ga·tion
in·sti·ga·tive
in·sti·ga·tor
in·stil (or ·still; ·stil·ling,
 ·stilled or ·still·ing,
 ·stilled)
in·stil·la·tion
in·still·er
in·stil·ment (or ·still·)
in·stinct

in·stinc·tive (*or* ·tual)
in·sti·tute
in·sti·tu·tion
in·sti·tu·tion·al
in·sti·tu·tion·al·ism
in·sti·tu·tion·al·ist
in·sti·tu·tion·ali·za·tion
  (*or* ·sa·tion)
in·sti·tu·tion·al·ize (*or*
  ·ise)
in·sti·tu·tion·ary
in·sti·tu·tive
in·sti·tu·tor (*or* ·tut·er)
in·struct
in·struct·ible
in·struc·tion
in·struc·tion·al
in·struc·tive
in·struc·tor
in·struc·tor·ship
in·struc·tress
in·stru·ment
in·stru·men·tal
in·stru·men·tal·ism
  philosophy term
in·stru·men·tal·ist
in·stru·men·tal·ity
in·stru·men·tal·ly
in·stru·men·ta·tion
in·sub·or·di·nate
in·sub·or·di·na·tion
in·sub·stan·tial
in·sub·stan·ti·al·ity
in·sub·stan·tial·ly
in·suf·fer·able
in·suf·fer·ably
in·suf·fi·cien·cy (*or*
  ·cience)
in·suf·fi·cient
in·suf·flate
in·suf·fla·tion
in·suf·fla·tor
in·su·la (*plural* ·lae)
  anatomy term
in·sul·ant
in·su·lar
in·su·lar·ity (*or* ·ism)
in·su·late isolate; *compare*
  insolate
in·su·la·tion
in·su·la·tor
in·su·lin hormone; *compare*
  inulin
in·sult
in·sult·er

in·su·per·abil·ity (*or*
  ·able·ness)
in·su·per·able
in·su·per·ably
in·sup·port·able
in·sup·port·ably
in·sup·press·ible
in·sur·abil·ity
in·sur·able
in·sur·ance financial
  protection; *insurance
  against death is* life
  assurance
in·sure protect against loss;
  compare ensure
in·sured
in·sur·er
in·sur·gence
in·sur·gen·cy (*plural*
  ·cies)
in·sur·gent
in·sur·mount·abil·ity (*or*
  ·able·ness)
in·sur·mount·able
in·sur·mount·ably
in·sur·rec·tion
in·sur·rec·tion·al
in·sur·rec·tion·ary
in·sur·rec·tion·ism
in·sur·rec·tion·ist
in·sus·cep·tibil·ity
in·sus·cep·tible
in·swing cricket term
in·swinger
in·tact
in·tag·li·at·ed
in·tag·lio (*plural* ·lios *or*
  ·li) engraving
in·take
in·tan·gibil·ity (*or*
  ·gible·ness)
in·tan·gible
in·tan·gibly
in·tar·sia mosaic of wood
in·te·ger
in·te·gral
in·te·gral·ly
in·te·grand maths term
in·te·grant part of whole
in·te·grate
in·te·gra·tion
in·te·gra·tion·ist
in·te·gra·tive
in·te·gra·tor
in·teg·rity

in·tegu·ment
in·tegu·men·tary (*or*
  ·men·tal)
in·tel·lect
in·tel·lec·tion thought
in·tel·lec·tive
in·tel·lec·tual
in·tel·lec·tu·al·ism
in·tel·lec·tu·al·ist
in·tel·lec·tu·al·is·tic
in·tel·lec·tu·al·is·ti·cal·ly
in·tel·lec·tu·al·ity (*or*
  ·ness)
in·tel·lec·tu·ali·za·tion (*or*
  ·sa·tion)
in·tel·lec·tu·al·ize (*or* ·ise)
in·tel·lec·tu·al·iz·er (*or*
  ·is·er)
in·tel·lec·tu·al·ly
in·tel·li·gence
in·tel·li·gent
in·tel·li·gent·sia
in·tel·li·gibil·ity (*or*
  ·gible·ness)
in·tel·li·gi·ble
in·tel·li·gibly
In·tel·sat communications
  satellite
in·tem·per·ance
in·tem·per·ate
in·tend
in·tend·ance French public
  department
in·tend·an·cy
in·tend·ant provincial
  official
in·tend·ed
in·tend·er
in·tend·ment legal term
in·ten·er·ate make tender
in·tense
in·ten·si·fi·ca·tion
in·ten·si·fi·er
in·ten·si·fy (·fies, ·fy·ing,
  ·fied)
in·ten·sion logic term;
  compare intention
in·ten·sion·al
in·ten·si·ty (*plural* ·sities)
in·ten·sive
in·tent
in·ten·tion purpose;
  compare intension
in·ten·tion·al
in·ten·tion·al·ity

in·ten·tion·al·ly
in·tent·ly
in·ter (·ter·ring, ·terred)
inter·act
inter·ac·tion
inter·ac·tion·al
inter·ac·tive
in·ter·ac·tiv·ity
in·ter alia *Latin* among
   other things
in·ter ali·os *Latin* among
   other people
inter·atom·ic
inter·bed·ded
inter·brain
inter·breed (·breed·ing,
   ·bred)
inter·ca·lari·ly
inter·ca·lary
inter·ca·late
inter·ca·la·tion
inter·ca·la·tive
inter·cede
inter·ced·er
inter·cel·lu·lar
inter·cept
inter·cep·tion
inter·cep·tive
inter·cep·tor (*or* ·cept·er)
inter·ces·sion
inter·ces·sion·al (*or*
   inter·ces·sory)
inter·ces·sor
inter·ces·so·ri·al
inter·change
inter·change·abil·ity (*or*
   ·able·ness)
inter·change·able
inter·change·ably
inter·city
inter·clavi·cle
inter·cla·vicu·lar
inter·col·legi·ate
inter·co·lum·nar
inter·co·lum·nia·tion
inter·com
inter·com·mu·ni·cabil·ity
inter·com·mu·ni·cable
inter·com·mu·ni·cate
inter·com·mu·ni·ca·tion
inter·com·mu·ni·ca·tive
inter·com·mu·ni·ca·tor
inter·com·mun·ion
inter·con·nect
inter·con·nec·tion

inter·con·ti·nen·tal
inter·cos·tal anatomy term
inter·course
inter·crop (·crop·ping,
   ·cropped)
inter·cross crossbreed
inter·cur·rence
inter·cur·rent
inter·denomi·na·tion·al
inter·denomi·na·tion·al·
   ism
inter·den·tal
inter·de·part·men·tal
inter·de·pend·ence (*or*
   ·en·cy)
inter·de·pend·ent
inter·dict
inter·dic·tion
inter·dic·tive (*or* ·tory)
inter·dic·tor
inter·dis·ci·pli·nary
in·ter·est
in·ter·est·ed
in·ter·est·ed·ly
in·ter·est·ing
inter·face
inter·fa·cial
inter·fa·cial·ly
inter·fac·ing
inter·fere
inter·fer·ence
inter·feren·tial
inter·fer·er
inter·fer·ing
inter·fer·om·eter physics
   instrument
inter·fero·met·ric
inter·fero·met·ri·cal·ly
inter·fer·om·etry
inter·fer·on biochemical
   substance
inter·fer·tile
inter·fer·til·ity
inter·file
inter·flu·ent flowing
   together
inter·fluve land between
   rivers
inter·flu·vial
inter·fuse
inter·fu·sion
inter·ga·lac·tic
inter·gla·cial
inter·gov·ern·men·tal
inter·gra·da·tion

inter·gra·da·tion·al
inter·grade
inter·gra·di·ent
inter·group
in·ter·im
in·te·ri·or
inter·ject
inter·jec·tion
inter·jec·tion·al (*or*
   ·tion·ary, ·tur·al)
inter·jec·tor
inter·jec·tory
inter·lace
inter·lace·ment
In·ter·la·ken Swiss town
inter·lami·nar
inter·lami·nate
inter·lami·na·tion
inter·lard
inter·lay (·lay·ing, ·laid)
inter·leaf (noun; *plural*
   ·leaves)
inter·leave (*verb*)
inter·line
inter·lin·ear (*or* ·eal)
inter·lin·eate
inter·line·ation
inter·lin·er
Inter·lin·gua language
inter·lin·ing
inter·link
inter·lock
inter·lock·er
inter·lo·cu·tion
inter·locu·tor
inter·locu·to·ri·ly
inter·locu·tory
inter·locu·tress (*or* ·trice,
   ·trix)
inter·lope
inter·lop·er
inter·lude
inter·lu·nar
inter·lu·na·tion period of
   moon's invisibility
inter·mar·riage
inter·mar·ry (·ries,
   ·ry·ing, ·ried)
inter·media·cy
inter·medi·ary (*plural*
   ·aries)
inter·medi·ate
inter·media·tor
in·ter·ment burial; *compare*
   internment

inter·mez·zo (*plural* ·zos
  or ·zi)
inter·mi·gra·tion
in·ter·mi·nable
in·ter·mi·nable·ness (*or*
  ·nabil·ity)
in·ter·mi·nably
inter·min·gle
inter·mis·sion
inter·mis·sive
inter·mit (·mit·ting,
  ·mit·ted)
inter·mit·tence (*or*
  ·ten·cy)
inter·mit·tent sporadic;
  compare intromittent
inter·mit·tor
inter·mix
inter·mix·able
inter·mix·ture
inter·mo·lecu·lar
in·tern
in·ter·nal
in·ter·nal·ity (*or* ·ness)
in·ter·nali·za·tion (*or*
  ·sa·tion)
in·ter·nal·ize (*or* ·ise)
in·ter·nal·ly
inter·na·tion·al
inter·na·tion·al·ism
inter·na·tion·al·ist
inter·na·tion·al·ity
inter·na·tion·ali·za·tion
  (*or* ·sa·tion)
inter·na·tion·al·ize (*or*
  ·ise)
inter·na·tion·al·ly
inter·necine
in·ternee
inter·neu·rone (*or* ·ron)
in·tern·ist
in·tern·ment confinement;
  compare interment
inter·nod·al
inter·node part of plant
  stem
in·tern·ship
inter·nun·cial
inter·nun·cio (*plural*
  ·cios) papal ambassador
intero·cep·tive
intero·cep·tor physiology
  term
inter·os·cu·late biology
  term
inter·os·cu·la·tion

inter·page
inter·pel·lant
inter·pel·late question in
  parliament; *compare*
  interpolate
in·ter·pel·la·tion
in·ter·pel·la·tor
inter·pen·etrable
inter·pen·etrant
inter·pen·etrate
inter·pen·etra·tion
inter·pen·etra·tive
inter·per·son·al
inter·phase
inter·phone
inter·plan·etary
inter·play
inter·plead (·plead·ing,
  ·plead·ed, ·plead *or*
  ·pled) legal term
inter·plead·er
Inter·pol
in·ter·po·late insert;
  compare interpellate
in·ter·po·lat·er (*or* ·la·tor)
in·ter·po·la·tion
in·ter·po·la·tive
inter·pos·able
inter·pos·al
inter·pose
inter·pos·er
inter·po·si·tion
in·ter·pret
in·ter·pret·abil·ity (*or*
  ·able·ness)
in·ter·pret·able
in·ter·pre·ta·tion
in·ter·pre·ta·tion·al
in·ter·pre·ta·tive
in·ter·pret·er
in·ter·pre·tive
inter·ra·cial
inter·ra·cial·ly
inter·ra·di·al
inter·reg·nal
inter·reg·num (*plural*
  ·nums *or* ·na)
inter·re·late
inter·re·la·tion
inter·re·la·tion·ship
inter·rex (*plural* ·re·ges)
  interim ruler
in·ter·ro·bang (*or*
  ·tera·bang) punctuation
  mark

in·ter·ro·gate
in·ter·ro·gat·ing·ly
in·ter·ro·ga·tion
in·ter·ro·ga·tion·al
in·ter·rogative
in·ter·ro·ga·tor
in·ter·roga·to·ri·ly
in·ter·roga·tory (*plural*
  ·tories)
in·ter·rupt
in·ter·rupt·er (*or* ·rup·tor)
in·ter·rupt·ible
in·ter·rup·tion
in·ter·rup·tive
inter·scho·las·tic
inter·sect
inter·sec·tion
inter·sec·tion·al
inter·sex
inter·sex·ual
inter·sexu·al·ity (*or* ·ism)
inter·sex·ual·ly
inter·space
inter·spa·tial
inter·sperse
inter·sper·sion (*or* ·sal)
inter·sta·dial interglacial
inter·state
inter·stel·lar
in·ter·stice
in·ter·sti·tial
inter·strati·fi·ca·tion
inter·strati·fy (·fies,
  ·fy·ing, ·fied) geology
  term
inter·tex·ture
inter·tid·al
inter·trib·al
inter·tri·go (*plural* ·gos)
  chafed skin
inter·tropi·cal
inter·twine
in·ter·val
inter·vene
inter·ven·er (*or* ·ve·nor)
inter·ven·tion
inter·ven·tion·al
inter·ven·tion·ism
inter·ven·tion·ist
inter·view
inter·viewee
inter·view·er
in·ter vivos legal term
inter·vo·cal·ic between
  vowels

inter·vo·cali·cal·ly
inter·weave (·weav·ing,
·wove *or* ·weaved,
·woven *or* ·weaved)
inter·weav·er
inter·wind (·wind·ing,
·wound)
inter·woven
in·tes·ta·cy
in·tes·tate
in·tes·ti·nal
in·tes·tine
in·ti·ma (*plural* ·mae)
anatomy term
in·ti·ma·cy (*plural* ·cies)
in·ti·mal
in·ti·mate
in·ti·ma·tion
in·timi·date
in·timi·da·tion
in·timi·da·tor
in·tinc·tion part of
Communion
in·tine botany term
into
in·tol·er·abil·ity (*or*
·able·ness)
in·tol·er·able
in·tol·er·ably
in·tol·er·ance
in·tol·er·ant
in·to·nate
in·to·na·tion
in·to·na·tion·al
in·tone
in·ton·er
in·tor·sion botany term
in toto *Latin* entirely
in·toxi·cable
in·toxi·cant
in·toxi·cate
in·toxi·cat·ing·ly
in·toxi·ca·tion
in·toxi·ca·tive
in·toxi·ca·tor
intra-atomic
intra·car·di·ac
intra·cel·lu·lar
intra·cos·tal anatomy term
intra·cra·nial
in·trac·tabil·ity (*or*
·table·ness)
in·trac·table
in·trac·tably
intra·cu·ta·neous

intra·der·mal (*or* ·mic)
in·tra·dos (*plural* ·dos *or*
·doses) inner curve of
arch
intra·mo·lecu·lar
intra·mu·ral
intra·mus·cu·lar
in·tran·si·gence (*or*
·gen·cy)
in·tran·si·gent
in·tran·si·gent·ist
in·tran·si·tive
intra·nu·clear
intra·state
intra·tel·lu·ric
intra·uter·ine
in·trava·sa·tion
intra·venous
(intravert) *incorrect spelling
of* introvert
in·treat *Archaic* entreat
in·trench *less common
spelling of* entrench
in·trep·id
in·tre·pid·ity (*or*
·trep·id·ness)
in·tri·ca·cy (*plural* ·cies)
in·tri·cate
in·tri·cate·ness
in·trigue (·trigu·ing,
·trigued)
in·tri·guer
intrigu·ing
in·trin·sic (*or* ·si·cal)
in·trin·si·cal·ly
in·tro (*plural* ·tros)
intro·duce
intro·duc·er
intro·duc·ible
intro·duc·tion
intro·duc·to·ri·ly
intro·duc·tory
in·tro·gres·sion
in·troit prayer
in·troi·tal
intro·ject
intro·jec·tion psychology
term
intro·jec·tive
intro·mis·sion insertion
intro·mit·tent insertable;
compare intermittent
in·trorse turned inwards
intro·spect
intro·spec·tion

intro·spec·tion·al
intro·spec·tion·ist
intro·spec·tive
intro·ver·sion
intro·ver·sive (*or* ·tive)
intro·vert
in·trude
in·trud·er
in·trud·ing·ly
in·tru·sion
in·tru·sion·al
in·tru·sive
in·trust *less common spelling
of* entrust
in·tu·bate
in·tu·ba·tion
in·tu·it
in·tu·it·able
in·tui·tion
in·tui·tion·al
in·tui·tion·ism (*or*
·tion·al·ism)
in·tui·tion·ist (*or*
tion·al·ist)
in·tui·tive
in·tui·tiv·ism
in·tui·tiv·ist
in·tu·mesce
in·tu·mes·cence (*or*
·cen·cy)
in·tu·mes·cent
in·tus·sus·cept
in·tus·sus·cep·tion medical
and biology term
in·tus·sus·cep·tive
in·twine *less common
spelling of* entwine
inu·lin plant compound;
compare insulin
in·unc·tion
in·un·dant (*or* ·da·tory)
in·un·date
in·un·da·tion
in·un·da·tor
in·ure (*or* en·)
in·ur·ed·ness (*or* en·)
in·urn
in ut·ero *Latin* in the womb
in·utile
in·util·ity
in va·cuo *Latin* in a vacuum
in·vad·able
in·vade
in·vad·er
in·vagi·nable

in·vagi·nate
in·vagi·na·tion
in·va·lid disabled person
in·val·id not valid
in·vali·date
in·vali·da·tion
in·vali·da·tor
in·va·lid·ism being an invalid
in·va·lid·ity (or ·val·id·ness) being not valid
in·valu·able
in·valu·ably
In·var (Trademark)
in·vari·abil·ity (or ·able·ness)
in·vari·able
in·vari·ably
in·vari·ance (or ·an·cy)
in·vari·ant
in·va·sion
in·va·sive
in·vec·tive
in·veigh rail against
in·veigh·er
in·vei·gle cajole
in·vei·gle·ment
in·vei·gler
in·vent
in·vent·ible (or ·able)
in·ven·tion
in·ven·tion·al
in·ven·tive
in·ven·tive·ness
in·ven·tor
in·ven·to·ri·able
in·ven·to·ri·al
in·ven·tory (noun, plural ·tories; verb ·tories, ·tory·ing, ·toried)
in·ve·rac·ity (plural ·ities)
In·ver·car·gill New Zealand city
In·ver·ness
in·verse
in·ver·sion
in·ver·sive
in·vert
in·vert·ase enzyme
in·ver·te·bra·cy (or ·tebrate·ness)
in·ver·te·bral
in·ver·tebrate
in·vert·er (or ·ver·tor)

in·vert·ibil·ity
in·vert·ible
in·vest
in·vest·able (or ·ible)
in·ves·ti·gable
in·ves·ti·gate
in·ves·ti·ga·tion
in·ves·ti·ga·tion·al
in·ves·ti·gative (or ·ga·tory)
in·ves·ti·ga·tor
in·ves·ti·tive
in·ves·ti·ture
in·vest·ment
in·ves·tor
in·vet·era·cy (or ·er·ate·ness)
in·vet·er·ate
in·vi·abil·ity (or ·able·ness)
in·vi·able
in·vidi·ous
in·vigi·late
in·vigi·la·tion
in·vigi·la·tor
in·vig·or·ate
in·vig·or·at·ing·ly
in·vig·ora·tion
in·vig·ora·tive
in·vig·ora·tor
in·vin·cibil·ity (or ·cible·ness)
in·vin·cible
in·vin·cibly
in·vio·labil·ity (or ·lable·ness)
in·vio·lable
in·vio·lably
in·vio·la·cy (or ·late·ness)
in·vio·late
in·vis·ibil·ity (or ·ible·ness)
in·vis·ible
in·vis·ibly
in·vi·ta·tion
in·vi·ta·tory
in·vite
in·vit·er
in·vit·ing
in vi·tro outside the body
in vivo within the body
in·vo·cable
in·vo·ca·tion
in·vo·ca·tion·al
in·voca·tory

in·voice
in·voke
in·vok·er
in·volu·cel (or ·cel·lum; plural ·cels or ·cel·la)
in·volu·cel·ate (or ·at·ed)
in·vo·lu·cral
in·vo·lu·crate
in·vo·lu·cre (or ·crum; plural ·cres or ·cra) botany term
in·vol·un·tari·ly
in·vol·un·tari·ness
in·vol·un·tary
in·vo·lute (or ·lut·ed)
in·vo·lu·tion
in·vo·lu·tion·al
in·volve
in·volved
in·volve·ment
in·volv·er
in·vul·ner·abil·ity (or ·able·ness)
in·vul·ner·able
in·vul·ner·ably
in·vul·tua·tion making images for witchcraft
in·ward (adj)
in·ward·ly
in·wards (adv)
in·weave (·weav·ing, ·wove or ·weaved, ·wo·ven or ·weaved)
in·wrought
Io satellite of Jupiter
iodate chemistry term
ioda·tion
iod·ic chemistry term
iodide
iodine
iodism iodine poisoning
iodi·za·tion (or ·sa·tion)
iodize (or iodise)
iodiz·er (or iodis·)
iodo·form antiseptic
iodo·met·ric (or ·ri·cal)
iodo·met·ri·cal·ly
iodom·etry chemistry term
iodop·sin retinal pigment
iodous chemistry term
ion
Io·na Scottish island
Ionia Aegean region
Ionian

Ion·ic architecture term
ion·ic of ions
ioni·za·tion (or **·sa·tion**)
ion·ize (or **·ise**)
ionone plant extract
iono·pause
iono·sphere
iono·spher·ic
ion·to·pho·resis
  biochemical technique
iota
iota·cism
IOU (plural **IOUs**)
Iowa
ip·ecac (or **·ecacu·an·ha**)
  purgative
Ipoh Malaysian city
ipo·moea plant
ipso facto
Ips·wich
ira·cund easily angered
Irá·kli·on Cretan port
Iran
Ira·nian
Iraq
Ira·qi
iras·cibil·ity (or
  ·cible·ness)
iras·cible
iras·cibly
irate
Ir·bid Jordanian town
ire
Ire·land
iren·ic (or **ireni·cal**)
  conciliatory
ireni·cal·ly
iren·ics branch of theology
iri·da·ceous botany term
iri·dec·to·my (plural
  ·mies) eye surgery
iri·des·cence
iri·des·cent
irid·ic
irid·ium chemical element
iri·doto·my (plural **·mies**)
  eye surgery
iris (plural **irises**) flowers
iris (plural **iri·des** or
  irises) part of eye
Irish
Irish·ism
Irish·man (plural **·men**)
Irish·woman (plural
  ·women)

irit·ic
iri·tis eye disease
irk
irk·some
Ir·ku·tsk Soviet city
iron
iron·bark tree
iron·bound unyielding
iron·clad
iron·er
iron·ic (or **ironi·cal**)
ironi·cal·ly
iron·ing
iro·nist
iro·nize indulge in irony
iron·monger
iron·mongery
Ironsides Cromwell's
  cavalry
iron·stone
iron·ware
iron·wood
iron·work
iro·ny (plural **·nies**)
  sarcasm
irony containing iron
Iro·quoi·an
Iro·quois (plural **·quois**)
  American Indian
ir·ra·di·ance
ir·ra·di·ant
ir·ra·di·ate
ir·ra·dia·tion
ir·ra·dia·tive
ir·ra·dia·tor
ir·ra·tion·al
ir·ra·tion·al·ity (or **·ism**)
ir·ra·tion·al·ly
Ir·ra·wad·dy Burmese river
ir·re·claim·abil·ity (or
  ·able·ness)
ir·re·claim·able
ir·re·claim·ably
ir·rec·on·cil·abil·ity (or
  ·able·ness)
ir·rec·on·cil·able
ir·rec·on·cil·ably
ir·re·cov·er·able
ir·re·cov·er·ably
ir·re·cu·sable unable to be
  rejected
ir·re·deem·abil·ity (or
  ·able·ness)
ir·re·deem·able
ir·re·deem·ably

ir·re·den·tism
ir·re·den·tist territorial
  claimant
ir·re·duc·ibil·ity (or
  ·ible·ness)
ir·re·duc·ible
ir·re·duc·ibly
ir·ref·ra·gabil·ity (or
  ·gable·ness)
ir·ref·ra·gable indisputable
ir·ref·ra·gably
ir·re·fran·gibil·ity (or
  ·gible·ness)
ir·re·fran·gible inviolable
ir·refu·tabil·ity (or
  ·table·ness)
ir·refu·table
ir·refu·tably
ir·regu·lar
ir·regu·lar·ity (plural
  ·ities)
ir·rela·tive unrelated
ir·rel·evance (or **·evan·cy**;
  plural **·evances** or
  ·cies)
ir·rel·evant
ir·re·liev·able
ir·re·li·gion
ir·re·li·gion·ist
ir·re·li·gious
ir·re·medi·able
ir·re·medi·ably
ir·re·mis·sibil·ity (or
  ·sible·ness)
ir·re·mis·sible
ir·re·mis·sibly
ir·re·mov·abil·ity (or
  ·able·ness)
ir·re·mov·able
ir·re·mov·ably
ir·repa·rabil·ity (or
  ·rable·ness)
ir·repa·rable
ir·repa·rably
ir·re·place·able
ir·re·plevi·able (or **·sable**)
  legal term
ir·re·press·ibil·ity (or
  ·ible·ness)
ir·re·press·ible
ir·re·press·ibly
ir·re·proach·abil·ity (or
  ·able·ness)
ir·re·proach·able
ir·re·proach·ably

ir·re·sist·ibil·ity (*or*
  ·ible·ness)
ir·re·sist·ible
ir·re·sist·ibly
ir·reso·lubil·ity
ir·reso·luble
ir·reso·lute
ir·reso·lu·tion
ir·re·solv·abil·ity (*or*
  ·able·ness)
ir·re·solv·able
ir·re·spec·tive
ir·re·spir·able
ir·re·spon·sibil·ity (*or*
  ·sible·ness)
ir·re·spon·sible
ir·re·spon·sibly
ir·re·spon·sive
ir·re·ten·tive
ir·re·triev·abil·ity (*or*
  ·able·ness)
ir·re·triev·able
ir·re·triev·ably
ir·rev·er·ence
ir·rev·er·ent (*or* ·eren·tial)
ir·re·vers·ibil·ity (*or*
  ·ible·ness)
ir·re·vers·ible
ir·re·vers·ibly
ir·revo·cabil·ity (*or*
  ·cable·ness)
ir·revo·cable
ir·revo·cably
(irridescent) *incorrect*
  spelling of iridescent
ir·ri·gable
ir·ri·gate
ir·ri·ga·tion
ir·ri·ga·tion·al
ir·ri·ga·tive
ir·ri·ga·tor
ir·ri·tabil·ity
ir·ri·table
ir·ri·tably
ir·ri·tant
ir·ri·tate
ir·ri·ta·tion
ir·ri·ta·tive
ir·ri·ta·tor
ir·rupt *enter or increase*
  suddenly; compare erupt
ir·rup·tion
ir·rup·tive
Ir·tysh (*or* Ir·tish) Asian
  river

Ir·vine Scottish town
is
isa·go·ge
isa·gog·ic
isa·gog·ics introductory
  studies
is·al·lo·bar line on map
Isar European river
isa·tin (*or* ·tine)
isa·tin·ic
Iscariot biblical character
is·chae·mia (*US* ·che·)
  inadequate blood supply
is·chaem·ic (*US* ·chem·)
Is·chia Mediterranean island
is·chial
is·chium (*plural* ·chia) hip
  bone
is·en·trop·ic physics term
Isère French river
Is·fa·han (*or* Es·) Iranian
  city
Ishmael biblical character
isin·glass
Isis Thames at Oxford;
  Egyptian goddess
Is·ken·de·run Turkish port
Is·lam
Is·lama·bad Pakistani
  capital
Is·lam·ic
Is·lam·ize
is·land
is·land·er
Is·lay Scottish island
isle
Isle of Wight
is·let
Is·ling·ton
ism
Is·mai·li Muslim sect
Is·mai·lia Egyptian city
isn't
iso·ag·glu·ti·na·tion
iso·ag·glu·ti·na·tive
iso·ag·glu·ti·nin
iso·anti·gen
iso·bar
iso·bar·ic
iso·bar·ism
iso·bath line on map
iso·bath·ic
iso·cheim (*or* ·chime) line
  on map

iso·chei·mal (*or* ·menal,
  ·chi·mal)
iso·chor (*or* ·chore) line
  on graph
iso·chor·ic
iso·chro·mat·ic
isoch·ro·nal (*or* ·nous)
isoch·ro·nize (*or* ·nise)
isoch·ro·ous of uniform
  colour
iso·cli·nal (*or* ·clin·ic)
iso·cline geology term
isoc·ra·cy (*plural* ·cies)
  political equality
iso·crat·ic
iso·cya·nide
iso·dia·met·ric
iso·dia·phere physics term
iso·di·mor·phism chemistry
  term
iso·di·mor·phous (*or*
  ·phic)
iso·dy·nam·ic
iso·elec·tric
iso·elec·tron·ic
iso·gam·ete biology term
iso·ga·met·ic
isoga·mous
isoga·my
isog·enous genetically
  uniform
isog·eny
iso·geo·therm
iso·geo·ther·mal (*or* ·mic)
iso·gloss linguistics term
iso·glos·sal
iso·glot·tic
iso·gon maths term
iso·gon·ic (*or* isogo·nal)
iso·hel line on map
iso·hy·et line on map
iso·labil·ity
iso·lable
iso·late
iso·la·tion
iso·la·tion·ism
iso·la·tion·ist
iso·la·tive
iso·la·tor
iso·leci·thal biology term
iso·leu·cine amino acid
iso·lex linguistics term
iso·line isopleth
isolo·gous chemistry term
iso·logue

iso·mag·net·ic
iso·mer
iso·mer·ic
isom·er·ism
isom·eri·za·tion (*or* ·sa·tion)
isom·er·ize (*or* ·ise)
isom·er·ous
iso·met·ric
iso·met·ri·cal
iso·met·rics exercises
iso·metro·pia physiology term
isom·etry maths term
iso·morph
iso·mor·phic (*or* ·phous)
iso·mor·phism
iso·nia·zid medicinal drug
isono·my equality before the law
iso·octane chemical compound
iso·phone linguistics term
iso·pi·es·tic having equal atmospheric pressure
iso·pi·es·ti·cal·ly
iso·pleth line on map
iso·pod crustacean
isopo·dan (*or* ·dous)
iso·prene chemical compound
iso·pro·pyl
iso·rhyth·mic musical term
isos·celes geometry term
iso·seis·mal
is·os·mot·ic
iso·spon·dy·lous zoology term
isos·ta·sy (*plural* ·sies) geological theory
iso·stat·ic
iso·ster·ic chemistry term
iso·tac·tic

isoth·er·al
iso·there line on map
iso·therm
iso·ther·mal
iso·tone chemistry term
iso·ton·ic
iso·to·nic·ity
iso·tope
iso·top·ic
iso·topi·cal·ly
isoto·py
iso·tron physics apparatus
iso·trop·ic
iso·tropi·cal·ly
isot·ro·pous
isot·ro·py
Is·ra·el
Is·rae·li (*plural* ·lis *or* ·li)
Is·rael·ite
Is·ra·fil Islamic archangel
is·su·able
is·su·ance
is·su·ant
is·sue (·su·ing, ·sued)
is·su·er
Is·sus battle
Is·tan·bul
isth·mi·an
isth·moid
isth·mus (*plural* ·muses *or* ·mi)
is·tle (*or* ix·) fibre
Is·tria Adriatic peninsula
Is·trian
it
ita·colu·mite sandstone
Ital·ian
Ital·ian·ate
Ital·ian·esque
Ital·ian·ism
Ital·ian·ize
Ital·ic language

ital·ic type or print
Itali·cism
itali·ci·za·tion (*or* ·sa·tion)
itali·cize (*or* ·cise)
Ita·ly
itch
itchi·ness
itch·ing
itchy (itchi·er, itchi·est)
item
itemi·za·tion (*or* ·sa·tion)
item·ize (*or* ·ise)
it·er·ant
it·er·ate
it·era·tion (*or* ·er·ance)
it·era·tive
Itha·ca Greek island
Itha·can
ithy·phal·lic poetry term
itin·er·an·cy (*or* ·era·cy; *plural* ·cies)
itin·er·ant
itin·er·ary (*plural* ·aries)
itin·er·ate travel about
itin·era·tion
it'll it will; it shall
its of it
it's it is
it·self
Iva·no·vo Soviet city
I've I have
ivied
ivo·ry (*plural* ·ries)
ivy (*plural* ivies)
Iwo Jima Pacific island
ixia plant
ix·tle *variant spelling of* istle
izard chamois
Izhevsk Soviet city
Iz·mir Turkish port
Iz·mit Turkish town

J

jab (jab·bing, jabbed)
Jab·al·pur (*or* Jub·bul·pore) Indian city
jabbed
jab·ber
jab·ber·er

jab·ber·wocky nonsense verse
jab·bing
jabi·ru bird
jabo·ran·di shrub
ja·bot frill
jaca·mar bird

ja·ça·na bird
jaca·ran·da tree
ja·cinth gemstone
jack
jack·al
jacka·napes
jack·ass

jack·boot
jack·daw
jack·eroo (*or* jacka·roo; *plural* ·roos) *Austral* trainee sheep-station manager
jack·et
jack·et·ed
jack·fish (*plural* ·fish *or* ·fishes)
jack·fruit
jack·hammer
jack·knife (*plural* ·knives)
jack·pot
jacks game
jack·shaft
jack·smelt (*plural* ·smelts *or* ·smelt) fish
jack·snipe (*plural* ·snipe *or* ·snipes) bird
Jack·son US city
Jack·son·ville US port
jack·stay nautical term
jack·straws game
Jaco·bean of James I
Ja·co·bian maths term
Jaco·bin French radical
Jaco·bin·ic (*or* ·bini·cal)
Jaco·bin·ism
Jaco·bite of James II
Jaco·bit·ic
Jaco·bit·ism
ja·co·bus (*plural* ·buses) coin
jaco·net fabric
Jac·quard fabric; loom
jac·ti·ta·tion boasting
Ja·cuzzi (*Trademark*)
jade
jad·ed
jade·ite mineral
jae·ger marksman; bird
Jael biblical character
Jaf·fa Israeli port
Jaff·na Sri Lankan port
jag (jag·ging, jagged)
jag·ged
jag·ged·ly
jag·ged·ness
jag·gery (*or* ·gary, ·ghery) date sugar
jag·ging
jag·gy (·gi·er, ·gi·est)
jagu·ar

ja·gua·ron·di (*or* ·run·; *plural* ·dis) feline
jai alai Spanish game
jail (*or* gaol)
jail·bird (*or* gaol·)
jail·break (*or* gaol·)
jail·er (*or* ·or, gaol·er)
jail·house
Jain (*or* Jai·na) Hindu
Jain·ism
Jain·ist
Jai·pur Indian city
Ja·ja·pu·ra (*or* Dja·) Indonesian port
Ja·kar·ta (*or* Dja·) Indonesian capital
jal·ap (*or* ·op) purgative
ja·lap·ic
Ja·lis·co Mexican state
ja·lopy (*or* ·lop·py; *plural* ·lopies *or* ·lop·pies)
jalou·sie shutter
jam (jam·ming, jammed) crowd; preserve; *compare* jamb
Ja·mai·ca
Ja·mai·can
jamb (*or* jambe) part of frame; *compare* jam
jam·ba·laya Creole dish
jam·bart (*or* jam·beau, jam·ber; *plural* ·barts, ·beaux, *or* ·bers) armour
Jam·bi (*or* Djam·) Indonesian port
jam·bo·ree
jammed
jam·mer
jam·ming
Jam·mu Indian city
jam·my (·mi·er, ·mi·est)
Jam·na·gar Indian city
jam·pan sedan chair
Jam·shed·pur Indian city
Jamshid (*or* Jamshyd) mythological king
Ja·na·ta Indian political party
jan·gle
jan·gler
Ja·nicu·lum Roman hill
jan·is·sary (*or* jani·zary; *plural* ·saries *or* ·zaries) Turkish guard
jani·tor (*fem* ·tress)

jani·to·ri·al
Jan·sen·ism Catholic doctrine
Jan·sen·ist
Jan·sen·is·tic (*or* ·ti·cal)
Janu·ary (*plural* ·aries)
Janus Roman god
Ja·pan
ja·pan (·pan·ning, ·panned) lacquer
Japa·nese
jape
jap·er
jap·ery
Japheth biblical character
jap·ing·ly
ja·poni·ca shrub
Ja·pu·rá South American river
jar (jar·ring, jarred)
jar·di·nière plant holder
jar·ful
jar·gon language
jar·gon (*or* ·goon) gemstone
jar·goni·za·tion (*or* ·sa·tion)
jar·gon·ize (*or* ·ise)
jarl Scandinavian chieftain
jaro·site mineral
jarp (*or* jaup) *Dialect* to smash
jar·rah tree
jarred
jar·ring
jar·ring·ly
Jar·row English port
jar·vey (*or* ·vie) coachman
jas·mine
jas·pé variegated
jas·per
Jat (*plural* Jat *or* Jats) Indo-European people
jato (*plural* ·tos) jet-assisted takeoff
jaun·dice
jaunt
jaun·ti·ly
jaun·ty (·ti·er, ·ti·est)
Java
Java·nese (*or* Ja·van)
jave·lin
jaw
Ja·wan Indian soldier
jaw·bone

jaw·breaker
jay
Jaya (*or* Dja·ja)
 Indonesian mountain
jay·walk
jay·walk·er
jay·walk·ing
jazz
jazzi·ly
jazzi·ness
jazzy (jazzi·er, jazzi·est)
jeal·ous
jeal·ous·ly
jeal·ousy (*plural* ·ousies)
jeans
jeb·el (*or* djeb·) Arab hill
Jeb·el Musa Moroccan
 mountain
Jed·da *variant spelling of*
 Jidda
jeep
jeer
jeer·er
jeer·ing·ly
je·had *variant spelling of*
 jihad
Je·hol Chinese region
Je·ho·vah
Je·ho·vian (*or* ·vic)
je·ju·nal
je·june naive
je·june·ly
je·june·ness (*or* je·jun·ity)
je·ju·num small intestine
Jekyll and Hyde
jell (*or* gel; jel·ling, jelled
 or gel·ling, gelled)
 congeal; *compare* gel
jel·laba (*or* ·lab·ah) cloak
jel·lied
jel·li·fi·ca·tion
jel·li·fy (·fies, ·fy·ing,
 ·fied)
jello *US* jelly
jel·ly (*noun, plural* ·lies;
 verb ·lies, ·ly·ing, ·lied)
jelly·bean
jelly·fish (*plural* ·fish *or*
 ·fishes)
jem·my (*noun, plural*
 ·mies; *verb* ·mies,
 ·my·ing, ·mied)
jen·net (*or* gen·et,
 gen·net) female donkey;
 compare genet

jen·ny (*plural* ·nies)
 machine; female animal
jeop·ard·ize (*or* ·ise)
jeop·ardy
je·quir·ity (*or* ·quer·;
 plural ·ties) plant
jer·bil *variant spelling of*
 gerbil
jer·boa
jer·emi·ad lamentation
Je·rez Spanish town
Jeri·cho
je·rid javelin
jerk
jerk·er
jerki·ly
jer·kin jacket; *compare*
 gherkin
jerky (jerki·er, jerki·est)
jero·bo·am wine bottle
Jer·ry (*plural* ·ries) *Slang*
 German
jer·ry (*plural* ·ries) *Slang*
 chamber pot
jerry-build (-building,
 -built)
Jer·sey island; cattle
jer·sey garment
Je·ru·sa·lem
jess falconry term
jes·sa·mine *Archaic* jasmine
jest
jes·ter
Jesu
Jesu·it
Jesu·it·ic (*or* ·iti·cal)
Jesu·it·ism (*or* ·it·ry)
Jesus
jet (jet·ting, jet·ted)
jeté ballet step
jet·liner
jet·port
jet-propelled
jet·sam (*or* ·som)
jet·setter
jet·ti·ness
jet·ti·son
jet·ton gambling token
jet·ty (*plural* ·ties)
Jew
jew·el (·ell·ing, ·elled; *US*
 ·el·ing, ·eled)
jewel·fish (*plural* ·fish *or*
 ·fishes)
jew·el·ler (*US* ·el·er)

jew·el·lery (*US* ·el·ry)
Jew·ess
jew·fish (*plural* ·fish *or*
 ·fishes)
Jew·ish
Jew·ish·ness
Jew·ry (*plural* ·ries)
jew's-ear fungus
jew's-harp
Jezebel biblical character
jezebel shameless woman
Jhan·si Indian city
jib (jib·bing, jibbed)
jib·ber
jib·bons *Dialect* spring
 onions
jibe *variant spelling of* gibe *or*
 gybe
jib-headed
Ji·bou·ti *variant spelling of*
 Djibouti
Jid·da (*or* ·dah, Jed·)
 Saudi Arabian port
jif·fy (*or* jiff; *plural*
 jif·fies *or* jiffs)
jig (jig·ging, jigged)
jig·ger
jig·gered
jigger·mast
jiggery-pokery
jig·ging
jig·gle
jig·gly
jig·saw
ji·had (*or* je·) Islamic holy
 war
jil·lion large number
jil·lionth
jilt
jilt·er
jin·gle
jin·gler
jin·gly (·gli·er, ·gli·est)
jin·go (*plural* ·goes)
jin·go·ism
jin·go·ist
jin·go·is·tic
jin·go·is·ti·cal·ly
Jin·ja Ugandan town
jink
jinks high spirits; *compare*
 jinx
jin·ni (*or* ·nee, djin·ni,
 djin·ny; *plural* jinn *or*
 djinn) Muslim spirit

jinx bad luck; *compare* jinks
ji·pi·ja·pa plant
jit·ter
jitter·bug (·bug·ging,
·bugged)
jit·tery
jive
Joab biblical character
Job biblical character
job (job·bing, jobbed)
job·ber
job·bery corruption
job·bing
Job·cen·tre
job·less
job·less·ness
Jocasta mother of Oedipus
Jock *Slang* Scot
jock·ey
jock·strap
jo·cose
jo·cose·ly
jo·cose·ness (or
    jo·cos·ity)
jocu·lar
jocu·lar·ity
joc·und
jo·cun·dity (or
    joc·und·ness)
Jodh·pur Indian city
jodh·purs riding trousers
Jodo Buddhist sect
joey *Austral* young kangaroo
jog (jog·ging, jogged)
jog·ger
jog·gle
jog·gler
Jog·ja·kar·ta *variant
    spelling of* Yokyakarta
jog-trot (-trot·ting,
    -trot·ted)
jo·han·nes (or ·an·; *plural*
    ·nes) Portuguese coin
Jo·han·nes·burg
John Dory fish
john·ny (*plural* ·nies)
    Slang man; condom
John o'Groats
John·so·nian of Samuel
    Johnson
Jo·hore Malaysian state
joie de vivre
join
join·der legal term
join·er

join·ery
joint
joint·ed
joint·er
joint·ly
joint·ress legal term
join·ture legal term
joint·worm
joist
jo·joba tree; oil
joke
jok·er
jok·ey (or joky; joki·er,
    joki·est)
jok·ing·ly
jol·li·fi·ca·tion
jol·li·fy (·fies, ·fy·ing,
    ·fied)
jol·lity (*plural* ·lities)
jol·ly (*adj* ·li·er, ·li·est;
    verb ·lies, ·ly·ing, ·lied)
Jolo Philippine island
jolt
jolt·er
jolt·ing·ly
jolty
Jön·kö·ping Swedish city
jon·nock *Dialect* genuine
jon·quil
Jop·pa biblical Jaffa
Jor·dan
Jor·da·nian
jo·rum drinking bowl
Jos Nigerian city
josh *US* tease
joss Chinese deity
jos·tle
jos·tler
jot (jot·ting, jot·ted)
jot·ter
joual Canadian French
    dialect
joule unit of energy
jounce jolt
jour·nal
jour·nal·ese
jour·nal·ism
jour·nal·ist
jour·nal·is·tic
jour·nal·is·ti·cal·ly
jour·nali·za·tion (or
    ·sa·tion)
jour·nal·ize (or ·ise)
    record in journal
jour·nal·iz·er (or ·is·er)

jour·ney
jour·ney·er
journey·man (*plural*
    ·men) craftsman
journo (*plural* journos)
    Austral journalist
joust
joust·er
Jove Roman god
jo·vial
jo·vi·al·ity (or ·ness)
jo·vi·al·ly
Jo·vian
jowl
joy
joy·ful
joy·ful·ly
joy·ful·ness
joy·less
joy·less·ness
joy·ous
joy·ous·ness
joy·pop (·pop·ping,
    ·popped) *Slang* take
    drugs
joy-ride (-riding, -rode,
    -ridden)
joy·rider
Juan de Fuca US–
    Canadian strait
juba Negro dance
Ju·bal biblical character
Jub·bul·pore *variant
    spelling of* Jabalpur
jube church gallery
ju·bi·lance (or ·lan·cy)
ju·bi·lant
ju·bi·late
ju·bi·la·tion
ju·bi·lee
Ju·daea (or ·dea)
Ju·daean (or ·dean)
Ju·da·ic (or ·dai·cal)
Ju·dai·ca Jewish literature
Ju·da·ism
Ju·da·ist
Ju·da·is·tic
Ju·dai·za·tion (or
    ·sa·tion)
Ju·da·ize (or ·ise)
Ju·da·iz·er (or ·is·er)
Judas traitor
ju·das peephole
jud·der
judge

judge·able
judg·er
judge·ship
judg·ing·ly
judg·ment (*or* judge·)
judg·men·tal (*or* judge·)
ju·di·cable
ju·di·ca·tive
ju·di·ca·tor judge
ju·di·ca·to·rial
ju·di·ca·tory
ju·di·ca·ture
ju·di·cial
ju·di·cial·ly
ju·di·ci·ary (*plural* ·aries)
ju·di·cious
ju·di·cious·ly
ju·di·cious·ness
judo
ju·do·gi judo costume
ju·do·ist
ju·do·ka judo expert
Judy (*or* judy; *plural* Judies *or* judies) *Slang* girl
jug (jug·ging, jugged)
ju·gal cheekbone
ju·gate botany term
jug·ful (*plural* ·fuls)
jugged
Jug·ger·naut Hindu idol
jug·ger·naut vehicle; destructive force
jug·ging
jug·gins silly fellow
jug·gle
jug·gler
jug·glery
jug·gling
ju·glan·da·ceous botany term
Ju·go·sla·via *variant spelling of* Yugoslavia
jugu·lar
ju·gum biology term
juice
juici·ly
juici·ness
juicy (juici·er, juici·est)
ju·jit·su (*or* ju·jut·su, jiu·)
juju African fetish
ju·ju·ism
ju·ju·ist
ju·jube plant; sweet
juke·box

ju·lep drink
Jul·ian of Julius Caesar
ju·li·enne cookery term
Jul·lun·dur Indian city
July (*plural* Julies)
jum·ble
jum·bler
jum·bly (·bli·er, ·bli·est)
jum·bo (*plural* ·bos)
jum·buck *Austral* sheep
Jum·na Indian river
jump
jump·able
jump·er
jumpi·ly
jumpi·ness
jump-off (*noun*)
jump-start
jumpy (jumpi·er, jumpi·est)
jun·ca·ceous botany term
jun·co (*plural* ·cos) bird
junc·tion
junc·tion·al
junc·ture
Jun·diaí Brazilian city
June
Ju·neau Alaskan capital
Jung·frau Swiss mountain
Jung·ian psychiatry term
jun·gle
jun·gly (·gli·er, ·gli·est)
jun·ior
ju·ni·per
junk
Jun·ker Prussian landowner
jun·ket
jun·ket·er (*or* ·ket·ter, ·ke·teer)
junkie (*or* junky; *plural* junkies)
junk·yard
Juno Roman goddess; asteroid
Ju·no·esque
jun·ta
Ju·pi·ter planet
Jupiter Roman god
ju·pon garment
Jura European mountains; Scottish island
jura *plural of* jus
ju·ral of the law
Ju·ras·sic geological period
ju·rat legal term

ju·ra·tory
ju·rel fish
ju·ridi·cal (*or* ·rid·ic)
ju·ris·con·sult legal advisor
ju·ris·dic·tion
ju·ris·dic·tion·al
ju·ris·dic·tion·al·ly
ju·ris·dic·tive
ju·ris·pru·dence
ju·ris·pru·dent
ju·ris·pru·den·tial
ju·ris·pru·den·tial·ly
ju·rist
ju·ris·tic (*or* ·ti·cal)
ju·ror
Ju·ruá South American river
jury (*plural* juries)
jury·man (*plural* ·men)
jury-rigged nautical term
jury·woman (*plural* ·women)
jus (*plural* jura) legal right
jus ci·vi·le civil law
jus di·vi·num divine law
jus na·tu·ra·le natural law
jus·sive grammar term
jus soli legal term
just
jus·tice
jus·tice·ship
jus·ti·ci·abil·ity
jus·ti·ci·able subject to jurisdiction
jus·ti·ci·ar medieval legal officer
jus·ti·ci·ar·ship
jus·ti·ci·ary (*plural* ·aries)
jus·ti·fi·abil·ity (*or* ·able·ness)
jus·ti·fi·able
jus·ti·fi·ably
jus·ti·fi·ca·tion
jus·ti·fi·ca·tory (*or* ·tive)
jus·ti·fi·er
jus·ti·fy (·fies, ·fy·ing, ·fied)
jus·ti·fy·ing·ly
jus·tle jostle
just·ly
just·ness
jut (jut·ting, jut·ted)
Jute Germanic tribe
jute fibre
Jut·ish
Jut·land Danish peninsula

Jut·land·er
jut·ted
jut·ting
ju·venes·cence youth

ju·venes·cent
ju·venile
ju·venilia
ju·venil·ity (*plural* ·ities)

jux·ta·pose
jux·ta·po·si·tion
jux·ta·po·si·tion·al

K

kab·ba·la (*or* ka·ba·la)
  variant spellings of cabbala
ka·ba·ra·go·ya lizard
Ka·bardino-Balkar Soviet
  republic
ka·bu·ki Japanese drama
Ka·bul Afghan capital
Ka·byle (*plural* ·byles *or*
  ·byle) Berber people
ka·chang pu·teh Malaysian
  dish
ka·chi·na American Indian
  spirit
Kad·dish (*plural*
  kad·di·shim) Jewish
  prayer
Ka·di·yev·ka Soviet city
Ka·du·na Nigerian state
Kaf·fir (*plural* ·firs *or* ·fir)
  S African people
kaf·fir sorghum
Kaf·ir (*plural* ·irs *or* ·ir)
  Afghan people
kaf·tan (*or* caf·)
Ka·gera African river
Ka·go·shi·ma Japanese port
kai·ak *variant spelling of*
  kayak
Kai·feng Chinese city
kail *variant spelling of* kale
kai·nite mineral
kai·no·gen·esis *variant*
  spelling of caenogenesis
Kai·ser
kai·ser·dom (*or* ·ism)
Kai·sers·lau·tern West
  German city
kaka parrot
ka·ka·po (*plural* ·pos)
  parrot
ka·kemo·no (*plural* ·nos)
  Japanese wall hanging
kaki (*plural* kakis) fruit
kala-azar disease
Ka·la·ha·ri African desert
Kala·ma·zoo US city

Ka·lat (*or* Khe·) Pakistani
  region
kale (*or* kail) cabbage
ka·lei·do·scope
ka·lei·do·scop·ic
ka·lei·do·scopi·cal·ly
kal·ends *variant spelling of*
  calends
kale·yard (*or* kail·) Scot
  vegetable garden
Kal·goor·lie Australian city
Kali Hindu goddess
kali plant
kal·ian hookah
ka·lif (*or* kha·) *variant*
  spellings of caliph
Ka·li·nin Soviet city
Ka·li·nin·grad Soviet port
kal·mia shrub
Kal·muck (*or* ·myk;
  plural ·mucks, ·muck
  or ·myks, ·myk)
  Mongoloid people
ka·long fruit bat
kal·so·mine *variant spelling*
  of calcimine
Ka·lu·ga Soviet city
Kama Soviet river; Hindu
  god
kama·cite alloy
Kama·ku·ra Japanese city
ka·ma·la tree
Ka·ma·su·tra Hindu text
Kam·chat·ka Soviet
  peninsula
kame mound
Kamensk-Uralski Soviet
  city
Ka·met Indian mountain
kami (*plural* kami)
  Japanese spirit
ka·mi·ka·ze
Kam·pa·la Ugandan capital
kam·pong Malaysian village
Kampuchea
Kampuchean

kana Japanese writing
kana·my·cin antibiotic
Ka·nan·ga Zaïrian city
Ka·na·ra (*or* Ca·) Indian
  region
Ka·na·rese (*or* Ca·; *plural*
  ·rese)
Kana·za·wa Japanese port
Kan·chi·pu·ram Indian city
Kan·da·har Afghan city
Kan·dy Sri Lankan city
kan·ga (*or* khan·) African
  garment
kan·ga·roo (*plural* ·roos)
Kang·chen·jun·ga (*or*
  Kan·chen·) Himalayan
  mountain
Ka·Ngwa·ne South African
  homeland
Kan·na·da Indian language
Kano Nigerian state
Kan·pur Indian city
Kan·sas
Kan·su Chinese province
kan·tar unit of weight
Kant·ian
Kant·ian·ism (*or*
  Kant·ism) philosophy
Kao·hsiung (*or* Kao·
  hsiung) Chinese port
kao·li·ang sorghum
kao·lin (*or* ·line)
kao·lin·ic
kao·lin·ite mineral
kaon physics particle
ka·pell·meis·ter (*plural*
  ·ter)
ka·pok
kap·pa Greek letter
ka·put *Slang* not
  functioning; *compare* caput
kara·bi·ner mountaineering
  clip
Karachai-Cherkess Soviet
  region
Ka·ra·chi Pakistani city

Ka·ra·gan·da Soviet city
Kara·ite Jewish sect
Kara-Kalpak Soviet republic
Ka·ra·ko·ram mountain range
Ka·ra·ko·rum Mongolian city
kara·kul (*or* **cara·**) sheep; *compare* caracul
ka·ra·te
Kar·ba·la (*or* **Ker·be·**) Iraqi town
Ka·relia Soviet republic
Ka·relian
Ka·ren (*plural* **·rens** *or* **·ren**) Thai language and people
Ka·ri·ba African lake and dam
Karl-Marx-Stadt East German city
Karls·ruhe West German city
kar·ma destiny
kar·mic
Kar·na·taka Indian state
Ka·roo (*or* **Kar·roo**) South African plateau
ka·roo (*or* **kar·roo**; *plural* **·roos**) plateau
ka·ross African garment
kar·ri tree
karst limestone scenery
karst·ic
karyo·gam·ic
kary·oga·my biology term
karyo·ki·nesis
karyo·ki·net·ic
karyo·lymph
kary·oly·sis
karyo·lyt·ic
karyo·plasm
karyo·plas·mic (*or* **·mat·ic**)
karyo·some
karyo·type
karyo·typ·ic (*or* **·typi·cal**)
Ka·sai African river
kas·bah (*or* **cas·**)
ka·sher *variant spelling of* kosher
Kash·gar Chinese city
Kash·mir
Kash·miri (*plural* **·miris** *or* **·miri**)

Kash·mir·ian
Kas·sa·la Sudanese city
Kas·sel West German city
kat (*or* **khat**) narcotic
kata·bat·ic meteorology term
ka·ta·ka·na Japanese writing
Ka·tan·ga Zaïrian province
Kat·an·gese
Ka·thia·war Indian peninsula
Kat·mai Alaskan volcano
Kat·man·du (*or* **Kath·**) Nepalese capital
Ka·to·wi·ce Polish city
Kat·si·na Nigerian city
Kat·te·gat Scandinavian strait
ka·ty·did insect
Ka·uai Hawaiian island
Kau·nas Soviet city
kau·ri (*or* **·ry**; *plural* **·ris** *or* **·ries**) tree
kava drink
Ka·wa·sa·ki Japanese port
kay·ak (*or* **kai·**) canoe
Kay·seri Turkish city
ka·za·chok dance
Ka·zakh (*or* **·zak**; *plural* **·zakhs** *or* **·zaks**) Soviet people
Ka·zan Soviet city
Kaz·bek Soviet volcano
ka·zoo (*plural* **·zoos**) musical instrument
ke·bab
keck retch
Ked·ah Malaysian state
ked·dah *variant spelling of* kheda
kedge nautical term
ked·geree
Ke·di·ri Indonesian city
keek *Scot* peep
keel
keel·haul
keel·son (*or* **kel·**)
keen
keen·ness
keep (**keep·ing, kept**)
keep·er
keep·net
keep·sake

kees·hond (*plural* **·honds** *or* **·honden**) dog
Kee·wa·tin Canadian district
keg
Keigh·ley Yorkshire town
keis·ter (*or* **kees·**) *US* buttocks
keit·loa rhinoceros
Ke·lan·tan Malaysian state
ke·loid (*or* **che·**) scar tissue
ke·loi·dal (*or* **che·**)
kelp seaweed
kel·pie (*or* **·py**; *plural* **·pies**) sheepdog
kel·son *variant spelling of* keelson
Kelt *variant spelling of* Celt
kelt salmon
kel·ter (*or esp. US* **kil·**)
Kelt·ic *variant spelling of* Celtic
kel·vin unit
Ke·mero·vo Soviet city
kempt tidy
ken (**ken·ning, kenned** *or* **kent**)
ke·naf fibre
Ken·dal Cumbrian town
ken·do Japanese sport
Ken·il·worth Warwickshire town
kenned (*or* **kent**)
ken·nel (**·nel·ling, ·nelled;** *US* **·nel·ing, ·neled**)
ke·no (*or* **kee·no, ki·no, qui·no**) US game
ke·no·sis theology term
ke·not·ic
Ken·sing·ton
ken·speckle *Scot* easily recognized
Kent
ken·te fabric
Kent·ish
kent·ledge ship's ballast
Ken·tuck·ian
Ken·tucky
Ken·ya
Ken·yan
Keos Greek island
kep *Dialect* to catch
kepi (*plural* **kepis**) military cap
kept

Kera·la Indian state
kera·tin protein
ke·rat·ini·za·tion (*or* ·sa·tion)
ke·rat·in·ize (*or* ·ise)
kera·ti·tis eye disease
kera·tog·enous
kera·toid horny
kera·to·plas·tic
kera·to·plas·ty (*plural* ·ties) eye surgery
kera·tose zoology term
kera·to·sis skin condition
kerb (*US* **curb**) pavement edge; *compare* **curb**
Ker·be·la *variant spelling of* Karbala
kerb·ing (*US* **curb·**)
kerb·stone (*US* **curb·**)
Kerch Soviet port
ker·chief
ker·chiefed
kerf saw cut
ker·fuf·fle
Ker·gue·len Is·lands
Ker·man Iranian city
Ker·man·shah Iranian city
ker·mes insect; dye
ker·mis Dutch carnival
kern (*or* **kerne**) printing term
ker·nel
ker·nite mineral
kero·sene (*or* ·sine)
Ker·ry Irish county
Ker·ry (*plural* ·ries) cattle
ker·sey woollen cloth
ker·sey·mere woollen cloth
Kes·te·ven Lincolnshire region
kes·trel
Kes·wick
ketch sailing vessel
ketch·up (*US also* **catch·up, cat·sup**)
ke·tene toxic gas
keto chemistry term
ke·tone
ke·ton·ic
ke·to·nu·ria
ke·tose sugar
ke·to·sis medical term
ke·tox·ime
Ket·ter·ing Northamptonshire town

ket·tle
kettle·drum
kettle·drummer
kettle·ful
kev·el nautical term
Kew
kex plant
key
key·board
key·hole
Keynes·ian·ism economic theory
key·note
key·stone
key·stroke
key·way
Kha·ba·rovsk Soviet port
khad·dar (*or* **kha·di**) Indian cloth
Kha·kass Soviet region
kha·ki (*plural* ·kis)
Khal·kha Mongolian language
kham·sin (*or* **kam·seen,** ·sin) wind
khan
khan·ate
khan·ga *variant spelling of* kanga
kha·rif Indian crop
Khar·kov Soviet city
Khar·toum (*or* ·tum)
khat *variant spelling of* kat
kha·yal Indian music
kheda (*or* **khed·ah,** **ked·dah**) elephant enclosure
khe·dive viceroy of Egypt
Kher·son Soviet port
Khmer Cambodian people
Khmer·ian
Khoi·khoi language group
Khoi·san language
Kho·tan *variant of* Hotien
Khul·na Bangladeshi city
khus·khus grass
Khy·ber Pass
ki·aat tree
ki·ang wild ass
Kiang·si Chinese province
Kiang·su Chinese province
Kiao·chow Chinese territory
kib·ble
kib·butz (*plural* ·but·zim)
kib·butz·nik

kibe chilblain
kib·itz *US* interfere
kib·lah (*or* ·la) direction of Mecca
ki·bosh
kick
kick·able
kick·back
kick·er
kick·off
kick·shaw trinket
kick·sorter physics apparatus
kick·stand
kick·start
kid (**kid·ding, kid·ded**)
kid·der
Kid·der·min·ster
kid·ding
kid·dle device for catching fish
Kid·dush Jewish blessing
kid·dy (*or* ·die; *plural* ·dies)
kid·nap (·nap·ping, ·napped; *US* ·nap·ing, ·naped)
kid·nap·per (*US* ·nap·er)
kid·ney
kid·skin
Kiel West German port
Kiel·ce Polish city
kier bleaching vat
kie·sel·guhr soft rock
kie·ser·ite mineral
Kiev
kif (*or* **kaif, keef, kef, kief**) marijuana
ki·koi cloth
kiku·mon Japanese emblem
Ki·ku·yu (*plural* ·yus or ·yu) African people
Kil·dare
Kili·man·ja·ro
Kil·ken·ny
kill
Kil·lar·ney
kill·deer (*plural* ·deer or ·deers) bird
kill·er
kil·lick (*or* ·lock) anchor
Kil·lie·cran·kie Scottish battle site
kil·li·fish (*plural* ·fish or ·fishes)

kill·ing
kill·ing·ly
kill-joy
Kil·mar·nock
kiln
kilo (*plural* kilos)
kilo·calo·rie
kilo·cycle
kilo·gram (*or* ·gramme)
kilo·hertz
kilo·metre (*US* ·meter)
kilo·met·ric (*or* ·ri·cal)
kilo·ton
kilo·volt
kilo·watt
kilowatt-hour
kilt
kilt·ed
kil·ter *variant spelling* (*esp.
US*) *of* kelter
Kim·ber·ley South African
city
kim·ber·lite rock
ki·mo·no (*plural* ·nos)
ki·mo·noed
kin
Kina·ba·lu Malaysian
mountain
kin·aes·the·sia (*or* ·sis;
US ·es·) physiology term
kin·aes·thet·ic (*US* ·es·)
ki·nase biochemical agent
Kin·car·dine (*or*
Kin·car·dine·shire)
former Scottish county
kin·cob fabric
kind
kin·der·gar·ten
kin·der·gar·ten·er
kind-hearted
kind-hearted·ly
kind-hearted·ness
kin·dle
kin·dler
kind·less *Archaic* heartless
kind·li·ness
kin·dling
kind·ly (·li·er, ·li·est)
kind·ness
kin·dred
kin·dred·ness (*or*
kin·dred·ship)
kine cattle
kin·emat·ic
kin·emati·cal·ly

kin·emat·ics branch of
physics
ki·nesics study of body
language
ki·net·ic
ki·neti·cal·ly
ki·net·ics branch of
mechanics
ki·neto·nu·cle·us
ki·neto·plast
king
king·bird
king·bolt
king·cup
king·dom
king·fish (*plural* ·fish *or*
·fishes)
king·fisher
king·let
king·li·ness
king·ly
king·maker
king-of-arms (*plural*
kings-)
king·pin
king·ship
king-size (*or* -sized)
King's Lynn
King·ston Jamaican capital;
Canadian port
Kingston upon Thames
Kings·town West Indian
port
King·wa·na African
language
king·wood
ki·nin protein
kink
kin·ka·jou animal
kinki·ly
kinki·ness
kinky (kinki·er, kinki·est)
kin·ni·kin·nick (*or* ·ki·nic)
mixture for smoking
kino resin
Kin·ross former Scottish
county
kins·folk
Kin·sha·sa Zaïrian capital
kin·ship
kins·man (*plural* ·men)
kins·woman (*plural*
·women)
ki·osk
kip (kip·ping, kipped)

kip·per
Kir·ghiz (*or* ·giz; *plural*
·ghiz *or* ·giz) Soviet
people
Kir·ghi·zia (*or* ·gi·)
Ki·ri·ba·ti island republic
kiri·gami paper cutting
Ki·rin Chinese province
kirk
Kirk·by Merseyside town
Kirk·cal·dy Scottish port
Kirk·cud·bright Scottish
county
kirk·man (*plural* ·men)
Scot church member
Kirk·patrick Antarctic
mountain
Kir·kuk Iraqi city
Kirk·wall Scottish town
Kir·man Persian carpet
Ki·rov Soviet city
Ki·ro·va·bad Soviet city
Ki·ro·vo·grad Soviet city
Kirsch (*or*
Kirsch·was·ser) cherry
brandy
Ki·run·di African language
Kis·an·ga·ni Zaïrian city
kish graphite
Ki·shi·nev Soviet city
kis·met
kiss
kiss·able
kis·sel Russian dessert
kiss·er
kiss·ing
kist *Dialect* large coffer
kit (kit·ting, kit·ted)
Ki·ta·kyu·shu Japanese
port
kit·bag
kitch·en
Kitch·ener Canadian town
kitch·en·ette (*or* ·et)
kitchen·ware
kite
kith
kitsch
kit·ten
kit·ten·ish
kit·ten·ish·ness
kit·ti·wake
kit·tle *Scot* capricious
kit·ty (*plural* ·ties)
Kit·we Zambian city

kiva underground room
Ki·wa·nis US organization
kiwi (*plural* kiwis)
Klai·pe·da Soviet port
klang·far·be musical term
Klans·man (*plural* ·men)
  Ku Klux Klan member
klax·on
Kleen·ex (*Trademark*;
  plural ·ex *or* ·exes)
klepht Greek brigand
kleph·tic
klep·to·ma·nia (*or* clep·)
klep·to·ma·ni·ac (*or* clep·)
klip·spring·er antelope
Klon·dike Canadian region
kloof mountain pass
klys·tron electronics
  apparatus
knack
knack·er
knack·ery
knack·wurst (*or* knock·)
  sausage
knag knot in wood
knap (knap·ping,
  knapped) *Dialect* hill
  crest; to hit
knap·per
knap·sack
knap·weed
knar *variant spelling of* knur
knave
knav·ery (*plural* ·eries)
knav·ish
knav·ish·ness
knaw·el plant
knead
knead·er
knee (knee·ing, kneed)
knee·cap (·cap·ping,
  ·capped)
knee-deep
knee·hole
kneel (kneel·ing, knelt *or*
  kneeled)
kneel·er
knee·pad
knee·pan kneecap
knees-up
knell
knelt
Knes·set Israeli parliament
knew

Knickerbocker *US* New
  Yorker
knick·er·bock·ers
knick·ers
knick·knack (*or*
  nick·nack)
knick·point
knife (*plural* knives)
knif·er
knife·rest
knight
knight-errant (*plural*
  knights-)
knight-errantry
knight·head nautical term
knight·hood
knight·li·ness
knight·ly
knish dumpling
knit (knit·ting, knit·ted *or*
  knit)
knit·table
knit·ter
knit·ting
knit·wear
knob (knob·bing,
  knobbed) projection;
  compare nob
knob·bly (·bli·er, ·bli·est)
knob·by (·bi·er, ·bi·est)
knob·ker·rie stick
knock
knock·down (*adj*)
knock·er
knock-kneed
knock-on
knock·out
knoll
Knos·sos (*or* Cnos·sus)
  Cretan city
knot (knot·ting, knot·ted)
knot·grass
knot·hole
knot·ted
knot·ter
knot·ti·ly
knot·ti·ness
knot·ting
knot·ty (·ti·er, ·ti·est)
knot·weed
knout whip
know (know·ing, knew,
  known)
know·able
know-all

know·er
know-how
know·ing
know·ing·ly
know·ing·ness
knowl·edge
knowl·edge·able (*or*
  ·edg·able)
knowl·edge·ably
known
Knox·ville US city
knuck·le
knuckle·bone
knuckle-duster
knuckle·head
knuck·ly
knur (*or* knurr, knar)
  knot in wood
knurl (*or* nurl) ridge
knurled
KO (*verb* KO's, KO'ing,
  KO'ed; *noun, plural*
  KO's)
koa tree
koa·la
koan Buddhist riddle
kob antelope
Kobe Japanese port
Ko·blenz (*or* Co·) West
  German city
kob·old mythological spirit
Ko·chi Japanese port
Kodak (*Trademark*)
Ko·di·ak bear; Alaskan
  island
Ko·dok Sudanese town
kof·ta Indian food
koft·gar Indian goldsmith
Ko·hi·ma Indian city
Kohi·noor (*or* ·nor, ·nur)
  diamond
kohl cosmetic
kohl·ra·bi (*plural* ·bies)
  cabbage
Ko·hou·tek comet
koi·ne common language
Ko·kand Soviet city
ko·kanee salmon
Koko Nor (*or* Kuka Nor)
  Chinese lake
kola *variant spelling of* cola
Kol·ha·pur Indian city
ko·lin·sky (*plural* ·skies)
  mink

kol·khoz (*or* ·**khos**, ·**koz**) collective farm

Kol Ni·dre Jewish prayer

kolo (*plural* **kolos**) dance

Ko·lom·na Soviet city

Ko·ly·ma Soviet river

Ko·ma·ti African river

ko·mat·ik Eskimo sledge

Komi (*plural* ·**mi** *or* ·**mis**) Finnish people

Kom·mu·narsk Soviet city

Ko·mo·do Indonesian island

Kom·so·mol Soviet association

Kom·so·molsk Soviet city

Kon·go (*plural* ·**gos** *or* ·**go**) African people

kon·go·ni animal

ko·ni·ol·ogy (*or* ·**co**·)

Kon·stanz *variant spelling of* **Constance**

Kon·ya (*or* **Konia**) Turkish city

koo·doo *variant spelling of* **kudu**

kook *US* eccentric person

kooka·bur·ra

kooky (*or* **kookie**; **kooki·er**, **kooki·est**) *US* crazy

Koo·te·nay (*or* ·**nai**) US river

kop hill

ko·peck (*or* ·**pek**, **co·peck**) Soviet coin

Ko·peisk (*or* ·**peysk**) Soviet city

kop·je (*or* ·**pie**) hill

Ko·ran

Ko·ran·ic

Kor·do·fan Sudanese province

Ko·rea

Ko·rean

kor·ma food

ko·ru·na Czech coin

Kos Greek island

kos (*plural* **kos**) Indian unit of distance

Kos·ci·us·ko Australian mountain

ko·sher (*or* **ka·**)

Koši·ce Czech city

Kosovo-Metohi·ja Yugoslav region

Ko·stro·ma Soviet city

Kota (*or* **Ko·tah**) Indian city

koto (*plural* **kotos**) musical instrument

kou·li·bia·ca (*or* **cou·**) food

kou·mis (*or* ·**miss**) *variant spellings of* **kumiss**

Kov·rov Soviet city

kow·hai tree

Kow·loon part of Hong Kong

kow·tow

kow·tow·er

Ko·zhi·kode Indian port

Kra Thai isthmus

kraal (*or* **craal**) African village

kraft wrapping paper; *compare* **craft**

krait snake

Kra·ka·toa (*or* ·**tau**) Indonesian island

kra·ken sea monster

Kra·ma·torsk Soviet city

kra·meria shrub

Kras·no·dar Soviet city

Kras·no·yarsk Soviet city

Kre·feld West German city

Kre·men·chug Soviet city

Krem·lin

krieg·spiel war game

krill (*plural* **krill**)

krim·mer (*or* **crim·**) lambswool

Krio African language

kris knife

Krish·na

Krish·naism

Kriss Krin·gle *US* Santa Claus

Kris·tian·sand Norwegian port

Kris·tian·stad Swedish town

kro·mes·ky savoury dish

kró·na (*plural* ·**nur**) Icelandic or Swedish coin

kro·ne (*plural* ·**ner**) Danish or Norwegian coin

Kron·stadt Soviet port

kroon (*plural* **kroons** *or* **krooni**) former Estonian coin

Kru·gers·dorp South African city

kryp·ton

Kua·la Lum·pur

Ku·ching Malaysian port

ku·dos prestige

kudu (*or* **koo·doo**) antelope

kud·zu plant

Ku·fic (*or* **Cu·**) Arabic script

Kui·by·shev (*or* **Kuy·**) Soviet port

Ku Klux Klan

Ku Klux·er (*or* **Ku Klux Klan·ner**)

kuk·ri (*plural* ·**ris**) Gurkha knife

kula Pacific island ceremony

ku·lak wealthy Russian peasant

Ku·ma·mo·to Japanese city

Ku·masi Ghanaian city

kum·ba·loi worry beads

ku·miss (*or* **kou·miss**, **kou·mis**, **kou·myss**) drink

küm·mel German liqueur

kum·quat (*or* **cum·**) fruit

kung fu

Kun·gur Chinese mountain

Kun·lun (*or* **Kuen·**, **Kwen·**) Chinese mountains

Kun·ming (*or* **K'un·ming**) Chinese city

kunz·ite gemstone

Kuo·min·tang (*or* **Guo·min·dang**) political party

Ku·ra Asian river

Kurd Turkic people

Kurd·ish

Kur·di·stan (*or* **Kur·destan**, **Kor·destan**)

Kure Japanese port

Kur·gan Soviet city

Ku·ril Is·lands

kur·ra·jong (*or* **cur·**) tree

kur·saal building at health resort

Kursk Soviet city

kur·to·sis statistics term

Kus·ko·kwim Alaskan river

Ku·tai·si Soviet city

Kutch (*or* **Cutch**) former Indian state

Ku·wait
Ku·wai·ti
Kuz·netsk Ba·sin Soviet
region
kvass (*or* kvas, quass)
drink
Kwa language group
kwa·cha Zambian currency
Kwa·ja·lein Pacific atoll
Kwa·ki·utl (*plural* ·utl *or*
·utls*) American Indian
Kwang·chow·an Chinese
region
Kwang·ju Korean city
Kwangsi-Chuang Chinese
region
Kwang·tung Chinese
province

kwan·za Angolan currency
kwashi·or·kor protein
deficiency
Kwa·zu·lu South African
homeland
Kwei·chow (*or*
Kuei·chou*) Chinese
province
Kwei·lin (*or* Kuei-lin)
Chinese city
Kwei·yang (*or* Kuei-
yang*) Chinese city
kwe·la African music
ky·ani·za·tion (*or*
·sa·tion*)
ky·an·ize (*or* ·ise) treat
timber
kyat Burmese currency

kyle *Scot* narrow strait
ky·lix (*or* cy·lix; *plural*
·li·kes*) drinking vessel
ky·loe cattle
ky·mo·graph (*or* cy·*)
medical instrument
ky·mo·graph·ic (*or* cy·)
Kyo·to (*or* Kio·) Japanese
city
ky·pho·sis (*plural* ·ses)
spinal curvature
ky·phot·ic
Kyrie elei·son
kyu judo grade
Kyu·shu (*or* Kiu·)
Japanese island

L

laa·ger (*or* la·) African
camp; *compare* lager
lab
laba·rum (*plural* ·ra)
Christian banner
lab·da·num (*or* la·) plant
resin
la·bel (·bel·ling, ·belled;
US ·bel·ing, ·beled)
la·bel·ler (*US* ·bel·er)
la·bel·loid
la·bel·lum (*plural* ·la)
biology term
la·bia *plural of* labium
la·bial
la·bi·al·ism
la·bi·al·ity
la·bi·ali·za·tion (*or*
·sa·tion*)
la·bi·al·ize (*or* ·ise)
la·bial·ly
la·bi·ate plant
la·bile
la·bil·ity
la·bio·den·tal
la·bio·na·sal
la·bio·velar
la·bium (*plural* ·bia)
lab·lab bean
la·bora·tory (*plural*
·tories*)

La·bor Australian political
party
la·bor *US spelling of* labour
la·bo·ri·ous
la·bo·ri·ous·ly
la·bo·ri·ous·ness
La·bour British political
party
la·bour (*US* ·bor)
la·boured (*US* ·bored)
la·boured·ly (*US* ·bored·)
la·bour·er (*US* ·bor·)
la·bour·ism (*US* ·bor·)
la·bour·ist (*US* ·bor·)
La·bour·ite Labour Party
supporter
Lab·ra·dor Canadian
peninsula; dog
lab·ra·dor·ite mineral
la·bret lip ornament
lab·roid (*or* ·rid) fish
la·brum (*plural* ·bra) lip
La·buan Malaysian island
la·bur·num
Laby·rinth mythological
maze
laby·rinth
laby·rin·thi·cal·ly
laby·rin·thine (*or* ·thian,
·thic*)
lac resin; *variant spelling of*
lakh

lac·co·lith (*or* ·lite)
geology term
lac·co·lith·ic (*or* ·lit·ic)
lace
Lac·edae·mon Sparta
Lac·edae·mo·nian
lac·er
lac·er·abil·ity
lac·er·able
lac·er·ant distressing
lac·er·ate
lac·era·tion
lac·era·tive
La·cer·ta constellation
lac·er·til·ian lizard
lace-up (*adj, noun*)
lace·wing insect
(lacey) *incorrect spelling of*
lacy
lach·es (*sing.*) legal term
lach·ry·mal *variant spelling*
of lacrimal
lach·ry·ma·tory (*plural*
·tories*) vessel; *variant*
spelling of lacrimatory
lach·ry·mose
lach·ry·mose·ly
lach·ry·mos·ity
laci·ly
laci·ness
lac·ing

la·cini·ate (*or* ·cinia·ted) jagged

la·cinia·tion

lack

lacka·dai·si·cal

lacka·dai·si·cal·ly

lacka·dai·si·cal·ness

lack·ey

lack·lustre (*US* ·luster)

La·co·nia ancient Greek country

La·co·nian

la·con·ic (*or* ·coni·cal) of few words

la·coni·cal·ly

La Co·ru·ña (*or* Co·run·na) Spanish port

lac·quer

lac·quer·er

lac·ri·mal (*or* lach·ry·, lac·ry·)

lac·ri·ma·tion

lac·ri·ma·tor (*or* lach·ry·, lac·ry·) substance causing tear flow

lac·ri·ma·tory (*or* lach·ry·, lac·ry·; *adj*) of tears; *compare* lachrymatory

la·crosse

lac·tal·bu·min

lac·tam chemical group

lac·ta·ry of milk

lac·tase enzyme

lac·tate

lac·ta·tion

lac·ta·tion·al

lac·ta·tion·al·ly

lac·teal

lac·teal·ly

lac·tes·cence

lac·tes·cent

lac·tic

lac·tif·er·ous

lac·to·ba·cil·lus (*plural* ·li)

lac·to·gen·ic

lac·tom·eter

lac·tone chemical compound

lac·ton·ic

lac·to·pro·tein

lac·to·scope

lac·tose milk sugar

la·cu·na (*plural* ·nae *or* ·nas)

la·cu·nar (*plural* ·nars *or* ·nar·ia) ceiling panel; of lacunae

la·cu·nose (*or* ·nal, ·nary)

lacu·nos·ity

la·cus·trine

lacy (laci·er, laci·est)

lad

lad·der

lad·die

lade (lad·ing, lad·ed, lad·en *or* lad·ed) load cargo; *compare* laid

lad·er

la·di·da (*or* lah-di-dah)

la·dies *plural of* lady

la·dies' man

lad·ing cargo

La·di·no language

la·di·no (*plural* ·nos) clover

la·dle

ladle·ful

la·dler

lady (*plural* la·dies)

lady·bird

la·dy·fy (*or* ·di·; ·fy·ing, ·fied)

lady-in-waiting (*plural* ladies-)

lady-killer

lady·like

lady·love

la·dy·ship

lady's maid (*plural* la·dies' maids)

La·dy·smith South African city

lady's-slipper orchid

lady's-smock plant

Laertes mythological character

lae·vo·ro·ta·tion (*US* le·)

lae·vo·ro·ta·tory (*or* ·ro·ta·ry; *US* le·)

laevu·lin (*US* levu·)

laevu·lose (*US* levu·) a sugar

lag (lag·ging, lagged)

lag·an (*or* li·gan) wreckage

la·gena bottle

la·ger beer; *compare* laager

lag·gard

lag·gard·ly

lag·gard·ness

lagged

lag·ging

la·gniappe (*or* ·gnappe) *US* small gift

lago·morph type of mammal

lago·mor·phic (*or* ·phous)

la·goon

La·gos Nigerian port

lah musical note

lah-di-dah *variant spelling of* la-di-da

Lahn·da language

La·hore Pakistani city

Lah·ti Finnish town

laic (*or* lai·cal) secular

lai·cal·ly

lai·cism

lai·ci·za·tion (*or* ·sa·tion)

lai·cize (*or* ·cise)

laid *past tense and past participle of* lay; *compare* lade; lain

laik *Dialect* to play

lain *past participle of* lie; *compare* laid

lair

laird

lairy (lairi·er, lairi·est) *Austral* gaudy

lais·sez faire (*or* lais·ser faire)

laissez-faireism (*or* laisser-)

lais·sez pas·ser

la·ity

lake

Lake·land the Lake District

lak·er lake cargo boat

lakh (*or* lac) 100 000 Indian rupees

Lak·shad·weep Indian islands

laky (laki·er, laki·est) reddish

Lala Indian form of address

la·lang grass

Lal·lans (*or* ·lan) Scottish dialect

lal·la·tion speech defect

lal·ly·gag (·gag·ging, ·gagged) *US* loiter

lam (lam·ming, lammed)

lama Tibetan priest; *compare* llama

La·ma·ism form of Buddhism

La·ma·ist

La·ma·is·tic

La·marck·ian

La·marck·ism theory of evolution

la·ma·sery (*plural* **·series**)

lamb

lam·baste (*or* **·bast**) *Slang* beat severely

lamb·da Greek letter

lamb·da·cism phonetics term

lamb·doid (*or* **·doi·dal**)

lam·ben·cy

lam·bent

lam·bert unit of illumination

Lam·beth

lamb·kin

lam·bre·quin ornamental hanging

lamb·skin

lamé fabric

lame

la·mel·la (*plural* **·lae** *or* **·las**) thin layer

la·mel·lar (*or* **lam·el·late, la·mel·lose**)

lam·el·lat·ed

lam·el·la·tion

la·mel·li·branch mollusc

la·mel·li·bran·chi·ate

la·mel·li·corn beetle

la·mel·li·form

la·mel·li·ros·tral (*or* **·trate**) zoology term

lam·el·los·ity

lame·ly

lame·ness

la·ment

lam·en·table

lam·en·table·ness

lam·en·tably

la·men·ta·tion

La·men·ta·tions biblical book

la·ment·ed

la·ment·er

la·mia (*plural* **·mias** *or* **·miae**) mythological monster

lami·na (*plural* **·nae** *or* **·nas**) thin plate

lami·nable

lami·nar (*or* **·nose**)

lami·naria seaweed

lami·nate

lami·na·ted

lami·na·tion

lami·na·tor

lami·ni·tis horse disease

Lam·mas religious feast

lam·mer·gei·er (*or* **·gey·er**) vulture

lamp

lam·pas animal disease; fabric

lamp·black

Lam·pedu·sa Mediterranean island

lam·pern lamprey

lam·pion oil lamp

lamp·lighter

lam·poon

lam·poon·er (*or* **·ist**)

lam·poon·ery

lamp·post

lam·prey

lam·pro·phyre rock

La·nai Hawaiian island

la·nai veranda

Lan·ark Scottish town

la·nate (*or* **·nose**) woolly

Lan·ca·shire

Lan·cas·ter

Lan·cas·trian

lance

lance·let tiny animal

lan·ceo·late tapering

lanc·er

lan·cers dance

lan·cet surgical knife

lan·cet·ed architectural term

lance·wood

Lan·chow (*or* **Lan·chou**) Chinese city

lan·cin·ate

lan·ci·na·tion

Land (*plural* **Län·der**) German state

land

land·am·mann Swiss official

lan·dau

lan·dau·let (*or* **·lette**)

land·ed

Landes French region

Lan·des·haupt·mann Austrian governor

land·fall

land·form

land·grave German ruler

land·gra·vine landgrave's wife

land·ing

land·lady (*plural* **·ladies**)

land·locked

land·lop·er *Scot* vagrant

land·lord

land·lub·ber

land·mark

land·mass

land·owner

land·owner·ship

land·owning

land·race pig breed

land·scape

land·scap·ist

Land's End

land·shark land profiteer

land·side part of plough

lands·knecht a mercenary

land·slide

lands·man (*plural* **·men**)

Land·tag German assembly

land·ward

lane

lang *Scot* long

lang·lauf cross-country skiing

lang·läuf·er

lan·gouste spiny lobster

lang·syne *Scot* long ago; *compare* **auld lang syne**

lan·guage

langue linguistics term

langue de chat biscuit

Langue·doc French region

langue d'oc language

lan·guid

lan·guid·ness

lan·guish

lan·guish·er

lan·guish·ment

lan·guor weariness; *compare* **langur**

lan·guor·ous

lan·guor·ous·ness

lan·gur monkey; *compare* **languor**

lan·iard *variant spelling of* **lanyard**

la·ni·ary (*plural* **·aries**) tooth

la·nif·er·ous (or ·nig·) wool-bearing
lank
lanki·ly
lanki·ness
lank·ly
lank·ness
lanky (lanki·er, lanki·est)
lan·ner falcon
lan·ner·et male lanner
lano·lat·ed
lano·lin (or ·line)
Lan·sing US city
lans·que·net gambling game
lan·ta·na shrub
lan·tern
lan·tha·nide (or ·non) chemistry term
lan·tha·num chemical element
la·nu·go (plural ·gos) fine hair
lan·yard (or ·iard)
Lao (plural Lao or Laos) Asian people
Laoag Philippine city
Laocoon mythological priest
La·odi·cea ancient Greek city
La·odi·cean
la·odi·cean indifferent
Laoigh·is Irish county
Laos
Lao·tian
lap (lap·ping, lapped)
lapa·rot·omy (plural ·omies) abdominal surgery
La Paz Bolivian capital
lap·board
lap-chart
la·pel
la·pelled
lapi·dar·ian
lapi·dary (plural ·daries)
lapi·date to stone
lapi·da·tion
la·pidi·fy (·fy·ing, ·fied) change into stone
la·pil·lus (plural ·li) piece of lava
lap·is lazu·li
Lap·land

Lap·land·er
Lapp
lapped
lap·per
lap·pet
lap·pet·ed
lap·ping
Lapp·ish
laps·able (or ·ible)
lapse
laps·er
lap·strake nautical term
lap·sus (plural ·sus) error
lap·wing
lar·board
lar·cenist (or ·cener)
lar·cenous
lar·ceny (plural ·cenies)
larch
lard
lar·der
lar·don (or ·doon) strip of fat
lardy
lares Roman gods
large
large·ly
large-minded
larg·en
large·ness
large-scale
lar·gess (or ·gesse)
lar·ghet·to (plural ·tos) music term
larg·ish
lar·go (plural ·gos)
lari·at lasso
lar·ine of gulls
Lá·ri·sa (or La·ris·sa) Greek city
lark
lark·er
lark·ish·ness
lark·some
lark·spur
lar·nax terracotta coffin
La Ro·chelle French port
lar·ri·gan leather boot
lar·ri·kin Austral hooligan
lar·rup Dialect to beat
lar·va (plural ·vae) preadult animal; compare lava
lar·val
lar·vi·cid·al

lar·vi·cide
lar·yn·geal (or la·ryn·gal)
la·ryn·ges plural of larynx
lar·yn·git·ic
lar·yn·gi·tis
la·ryn·go·logi·cal (or ·log·ic)
lar·yn·golo·gist
lar·yn·gol·ogy
la·ryn·go·scope
la·ryn·go·scop·ic
la·ryn·gos·co·pist
la·ryn·gos·co·py
lar·yn·got·omy (plural ·omies)
lar·ynx (plural la·ryn·ges or lar·ynxes)
la·sa·gne (or ·gna)
La Salle Canadian city
las·car (or lash·kar) East Indian sailor
Las·caux French cave
las·civi·ous
las·civi·ous·ly
las·civi·ous·ness
lase act as laser
la·ser
lash
lash·er
lash·ing
Lashio Burmese town
lash·kar variant spelling of las·car
lash-up (noun)
las·ket nautical term
Las Pal·mas
La Spe·zia Italian port
lass
Las·sa fe·ver
las·sie
las·si·tude
las·so (noun, plural ·sos or ·soes; verb ·sos or ·soes, ·so·ing, ·soed)
las·so·er
last
last·er
last·ing
last·ing·ly
last·ly
Las Ve·gas
lat (plural lats, latu, or lati) Latvian currency
Lata·kia Syrian port
latch

latch·et *Archaic* shoelace
latch·key
late
late·comer
la·teen nautical term
lateen-rigged
(lateish) *incorrect spelling of* latish
late·ly
la·ten·cy
late·ness
la·tent
lat·er
lat·er·al
lat·er·al·ly
Lat·er·an Roman palace
lat·er·ite clay
lat·er·it·ic
lat·ero·ver·sion
lat·est
la·tex (*plural* ·texes *or* lati·ces)
lath (*plural* laths) wood strip
lathe machine
lath·er
lath·ery
la·thi Indian stick
lati·cif·er·ous botany term
lati·meria fish
Lat·in
Lat·in·ate
Lat·in·ism
Lat·in·ist
La·tin·ity
Lat·ini·za·tion (*or* ·sa·tion)
Lat·in·ize (*or* ·ise)
Lat·in·iz·er (*or* ·is·er)
La·ti·no (*plural* ·nos) *US* Latin American
lat·ish
lati·tude
lati·tu·di·nal
lati·tu·di·nal·ly
lati·tu·di·nar·ian
lati·tu·di·nari·an·ism
La·tium Italian region
la·tria Catholic worship
la·trine
lat·ten sheet metal
lat·ter
latter-day
lat·ter·ly
latter·most

lat·tice
lat·ticed
Lat·via
Lat·vian
laud
laud·abil·ity (*or* ·able·ness)
laud·able
laud·ably
lau·da·num
lau·da·tion praise
lauda·tory (*or* ·tive)
laud·er
laugh
laugh·able
laugh·able·ness
laugh·ably
laugh·er
laugh·ing·ly
laugh·ter
launch
launch·er
laun·der
laun·der·er
Laun·der·ette (*Trademark*)
laun·dress
Laun·dro·mat (*Trademark*)
laun·dry (*plural* ·dries)
laundry·man (*plural* ·men)
laundry·woman (*plural* ·women)
lau·ra·ceous botany term
Laura·sia ancient continent
lau·reate
lau·reate·ship
lau·rea·tion
lau·rel (·rel·ling, ·relled; *US* ·rel·ing, ·reled)
Lau·ren·tian of St Lawrence river; *compare* Lawrentian
lau·rus·ti·nus shrub
Lau·sanne
lav *short for* lavatory
lava molten rock; *compare* larva
lava·bo (*plural* ·boes *or* ·bos)
lav·age medical procedure
La·val Canadian city
la·va·tion washing
la·va·tion·al

lava·tory (*plural* ·tories)
lav·en·der
la·ver seaweed; font
lav·er·ock *Dialect* skylark
lav·ish
lav·ish·er
lav·ish·ly
lav·ish·ness
law
law-abiding
law·breaker
law·breaking
law·ful
law·ful·ly
law·ful·ness
law·giver
law·giving
law·less
law·less·ly
law·less·ness
law·man (*plural* ·men)
lawn
lawny
law·ren·cium chemical element
Law·ren·tian of D. H. Lawrence; *compare* Laurentian
law·suit
law·yer
lax
laxa·tion defecation
laxa·tive
lax·ity (*or* lax·ness)
lax·ly
lay (lay·ing, laid)
lay·about
lay-by
(layed) *incorrect spelling of* laid
lay·er
lay·er·ing
lay·ette
lay·ing
lay·man (*plural* ·men)
lay·shaft
lay·woman (*plural* ·women)
laz·ar leper
laza·ret·to (*or* ·ret, ·rette; *plural* ·tos, ·rets, ·rettes) ship's locker; leper hospital
laze
la·zi·ly

la·zi·ness
lazu·lite mineral
lazu·rite lapis lazuli
lazy (la·zi·er, la·zi·est)
lazy·bones
L-dopa
lea meadow; unit of length; compare lee; ley
leach percolate; compare leech
leach·er
lead (lead·ing, led) guide
lead (lead·ing, lead·ed) metal
lead·en
lead·en·ly
lead·en·ness
lead·er
lead·er·ship
lead-in (noun)
lead·ing
leads·man (plural ·men)
lead·wort shrub
leady
leaf (plural leaves)
leaf·age
leaf-climber
leaf·cutter ant
leaf-hopper insect
leafi·ness
leaf·let
leaf·stalk
leafy (leafi·er, leafi·est)
league (leagu·ing, leagued)
leak hole; escape; compare leek
leak·age
leak·er
leaki·ness
leaky (leaki·er, leaki·est)
leal Scot loyal
Leam·ing·ton
lean (lean·ing, leant or leaned)
Leander mythological character
lean·ness
leant
lean-to (plural -tos)
leap (leap·ing, leapt or leaped)
leap·er
leap·frog (·frog·ging, ·frogged)

leapt
learn (learning, learnt or learned)
learn·able
learn·ed wise
learn·ed·ly
learn·ed·ness
learn·er
learn·ing
learnt
leary variant spelling of leery
leas·able
lease
lease·back property transaction
lease·hold
lease·holder
leas·er
leash
least
least·ways
leat trench
leath·er
leather·back turtle
Leath·er·ette (Trademark)
Leath·er·head Surrey town
leather·head bird
leath·eri·ness
leather·jacket fish; insect
leath·ern
leather·neck Slang US marine
leather·wood
leath·ery
leave (leav·ing, left)
leaved with leaves
leav·en
leav·en·ing
leav·er
leaves plural of leaf or leave; present tense of leave
leave-taking
leav·ing
Leba·nese
Leba·non
leb·en curdled milk
Le·bens·raum German territory
leb·ku·chen (plural ·chen) biscuit
Lech European river
lech lust
lech·er
lech·er·ous

lech·ery (plural ·eries)
leci·thin biochemical compound
le·cithi·nase enzyme
lec·tern
lec·tion variant reading
lec·tion·ary (plural ·aries) book of church readings
lec·tor lecturer
lec·tor·ate (or ·ship)
lec·ture
lec·tur·er
lec·ture·ship
lecy·thus (plural ·thi) Greek vase
led
Leda mythological character
le·der·ho·sen leather shorts
ledge
ledged
ledg·er
ledg·er line (or leg·) musical term
ledgy
lee sheltered side; compare lea; ley
lee·board
leech bloodsucker; compare leach
leech (or leach) nautical term; compare leach
Leeds
leek vegetable; compare leak
leer
leer·ing·ly
leery (or leary; leeri·er, leeri·est or leari·er, leari·est)
lees sediment
leet manorial court
lee·ward
Lee·ward Is·lands
lee·way
left
left-hand (adj)
left-handed
left-handed·ly
left-handed·ness
left-hander
left·ism
left·ist
left·over
left·wards
left-winger
lefty (plural lefties)

leg (leg·ging, legged)
lega·cy (*plural* ·cies)
le·gal
le·gal·ese legal jargon
le·gal·ism
le·gal·ist
le·gal·is·tic
le·gal·is·ti·cal·ly
le·gal·ity (*plural* ·ities)
le·gali·za·tion (*or* ·sa·tion)
le·gal·ize (*or* ·ise)
le·gal·ly
leg·ate envoy
lega·tee recipient of legacy
leg·ate·ship
lega·tine
le·ga·tion
le·ga·tion·ary
le·ga·to (*plural* ·tos) music term
lega·tor bequeather
lega·to·rial
leg·end
leg·end·ary (*adj*)
leg·end·ry (*noun*)
leg·er·demain
leg·er·demain·ist
leg·er line *variant spelling of* ledger line
legged *past tense of* leg
leg·ged having legs
leg·gi·ness
leg·ginged
leg·gings
leg·gy (·gi·er, ·gi·est)
Leg·horn Livorno; domestic fowl
leg·horn straw hat
leg·ibil·ity (*or* ·ible·ness)
leg·ible
leg·ibly
le·gion
le·gion·ary (*plural* ·aries)
le·gion·naire
leg·is·late
leg·is·la·tion
leg·is·la·tive
leg·is·la·tor
leg·is·la·to·rial
leg·is·la·tress
leg·is·la·ture
le·gist legal expert
le·git *Slang* legitimate
le·giti·ma·cy (*or* ·mate·ness)

le·giti·mate
le·giti·mate·ly
le·giti·ma·tion
le·giti·ma·ti·za·tion (*or* ·sa·tion) legitimization
le·giti·ma·tize (*or* ·tise) legitimize
le·giti·mism
le·giti·mist supporter of legitimate ruler
le·giti·mis·tic
le·giti·mi·za·tion (*or* ·sa·tion)
le·giti·mize (*or* ·mise)
leg·less
leg·man (*plural* ·men) *US* newspaper reporter
leg·room
leg·ume pod
le·gu·min protein
le·gu·mi·nous botany term
leg·work
Le Ha·vre French port
lei Hawaiian garland
Leices·ter
Leices·ter·shire
Lei·den (*or* Ley·) Dutch city
Leigh English town
Lein·ster Irish province
Leip·zig East German city
leish·ma·nia protozoan
leish·mania·sis (*or* ·ma·nio·sis) infection
leis·ter fishing spear
lei·sure
lei·sured
lei·sure·li·ness
lei·sure·ly
Leith Scottish port
leit·mo·tiv (*or* ·tif)
Lei·trim Irish county
lek Albanian currency
Le Mans French city
lem·ma (*plural* ·mas *or* ·ma·ta) logic term
lem·ming
lem·nis·cate maths term
lem·nis·cus (*plural* ·nis·ci) anatomy term
Lem·nos (*or* Lím·) Greek island
lem·on
lem·on·ade
lem·ony

lem·pi·ra Honduran currency
le·mur
lemu·roid (*or* ·rine)
Lena Soviet river
lend (lend·ing, lent)
lend·er
lend-lease
length
length·en
length·en·er
lengthi·ly
lengthi·ness
length·ways (*or* ·wise)
lengthy (lengthi·er, lengthi·est)
le·ni·en·cy (*or* ·ni·ence)
le·ni·ent
le·ni·ent·ly
Le·ni·na·bad Soviet town
Le·ni·na·kan Armenian city
Le·nin·grad
Len·in·ism political theory
Len·in·ist (*or* ·ite)
le·nis (*plural* le·nes) linguistics term
leni·tive soothing pain
len·ity (*plural* ·ities)
leno (*plural* lenos) fabric weave
lens
Lent
lent
len·ta·men·te musical term
Len·ten of Lent
len·tic ecology term
len·ti·cel botany term
len·ti·cel·late
len·ticu·lar (*or* ·ti·form)
len·ti·form
len·tigi·nous (*or* ·nose)
len·ti·go (*plural* ·tigi·nes) freckle
len·til
len·tis·si·mo music term
len·to (*plural* ·tos) music term
Leo constellation
León cities in Spain, Mexico, and Nicaragua
Leo·nid (*plural* Leo·nids *or* Le·oni·des) meteor shower
leo·nine
leop·ard

leop·ard·ess
leopard's-bane plant
leo·tard
lep·er
le·pido·lite mineral
lepi·dop·ter·an (*plural*
·ter·ans *or* ·tera)
lepi·dop·ter·ist
lepi·dop·ter·ous
lepi·do·si·ren fish
lepi·dote biology term
lepo·rid hare
lepo·rine of hares
lep·re·chaun
lep·ro·sar·ium (*plural* ·ia)
leper hospital
lep·rose
lep·ro·sy
lep·rous
lep·rous·ness
lep·to·cepha·lus (*plural*
·li) eel larva
lep·ton (*plural* ·ta) Greek
currency
lep·ton (*plural* ·tons)
physics particle
lep·to·phyl·lous botany
term
lep·tor·rhine zoology term
lep·to·some slender person
lep·to·so·mic (*or* ·mat·ic)
lep·to·spi·ro·sis disease
lep·to·tene biology term
le·quear ceiling panel
Ler·wick Scottish town
Les·bian of Lesbos
les·bian female homosexual
les·bi·an·ism
Les·bos Greek island
Les Cayes Haitian port
lese-majesty (*or* lèse-
majesté)
le·sion
Le·so·tho African kingdom
less
les·see one to whom lease is
granted
les·see·ship
less·en
less·er less great; *compare*
lessor
les·son
les·sor one who grants lease;
compare lesser
lest

let (let·ting, let)
le·thal
le·thal·ity
le·thal·ly
le·thar·gic (*or* ·gi·cal)
le·thar·gi·cal·ly
leth·ar·gy (*plural* ·gies)
Leth·bridge Canadian city
Le·the mythological river
Leto mother of Apollo
let's
Lett a Latvian
let·ter
let·tered
let·ter·er
letter·head
let·ter·ing
letter·press
let·ter·set
let·ting
Let·tish Latvian
let·tuce
leu·cine (*or* ·cin) amino
acid
leu·cite mineral
leu·cit·ic
leu·co·crat·ic geology term
leu·co·cyte (*US* ·ko·)
leu·co·cyt·ic (*US* ·ko·)
leu·co·cy·to·sis (*US* ·ko·)
leu·co·cy·tot·ic (*US* ·ko·)
leu·co·der·ma (*US* ·ko·)
unpigmented skin
leu·co·der·mal (*or* ·mic;
US ·ko·)
leu·co·ma corneal scar
leu·co·maine biochemical
compound
leu·co·penia (*US* ·ko·)
leu·co·penic (*US* ·ko·)
leu·co·plast (*or* ·plas·tid)
structure in plant cell
leu·co·poi·esis (*US* ·ko·)
leu·co·poi·et·ic (*US* ·ko·)
leu·cor·rhoea (*US*
·kor·rhea) vaginal
discharge
leu·cor·rhoeal (*US*
·kor·rheal)
leu·cot·omy brain surgery
leu·kae·mia (*US* ·ke·mia)
leuko *US spelling of some*
words beginning with leuco
lev (*plural* leva) Bulgarian
currency

Le·val·loi·sian (*or* ·lois)
Palaeolithic culture
Le·vant Middle Eastern
region
le·vant leather
le·vant·er wind
Le·van·tine of Levant
le·van·tine silk cloth
le·va·tor
levee
lev·el (·el·ling, ·elled; *US*
·el·ing, ·eled)
level-headed
level-headed·ly
level-headed·ness
Lev·el·ler radical
Parliamentarian
lev·el·ler (*US* ·el·er)
lev·el·ly
Le·ven Scottish loch
lev·er
lev·er·age
lev·er·et young hare
Le·ver·ku·sen West
German town
levi·able
le·via·than biblical monster
levi·er
levi·gate grind into powder
levi·ga·tion
levi·ga·tor
levi·rate marrying brother's
widow
Le·vis (*Trademark*) jeans
levi·tate
levi·ta·tion
levi·ta·tor
Le·vite priest
Le·viti·cal (*or* Le·vit·ic)
Le·viti·cus biblical book
lev·ity (*plural* ·ities)
le·vo·ro·ta·tion *US spelling*
of laevorotation
le·vo·ro·ta·tory *US spelling*
of laevorotatory
levu·lin *US spelling of*
laevulin
levu·lose *US spelling of*
laevulose
levy (*verb* levies, levy·ing,
levied; *noun, plural*
levies)
lewd
lewd·ly
lewd·ness

Lew·es Sussex town
Lew·is Scottish island
lew·is (or lew·is·son) lifting device
Lewi·sham
lew·is·ite war gas
lex (plural leges) body of laws
lex·eme linguistics term
lexi·cal
lexi·cal·ity
lexi·cal·ly
lexi·cog·ra·pher
lexi·co·graph·ic (or ·graphi·cal)
lexi·co·graphi·cal·ly
lexi·cog·ra·phy
lexi·co·logi·cal
lexi·co·logi·cal·ly
lexi·colo·gist
lexi·col·ogy
lexi·con
lexi·co·sta·tis·tics
lexi·gra·phy
Lex·ing·ton US city
lex·is vocabulary
lex loci law of the place
ley prehistoric track; compare lea; lee
Ley·den variant spelling of Leiden
Ley·te Philippine island
Lha·sa Tibetan capital
li unit of length
lia·bil·ity (plural ·ities)
lia·ble
li·aise
liai·son
lia·na (or li·ane) plant
lia·noid
Liao·ning Chinese province
Liao·tung (or ·dong) Chinese peninsula
Liao·yang Chinese city
liar
Li·ard Canadian river
li·ard coin
Lias rock series
lias blue limestone
Li·as·sic
lib Slang liberation
li·ba·tion
li·ba·tion·al (or ·ary)
li·bec·cio (or ·chio) Corsican wind

li·bel (·bel·ling, ·belled; US ·bel·ing, ·beled)
li·bel·lant (US ·bel·ant)
li·bel·lee (US ·bel·ee)
li·bel·ler (or li·bel·ist; US ·bel·er or ·bel·ist)
li·bel·lous (US ·bel·ous)
Lib·er·al political party
lib·er·al progressive; abundant
lib·er·al·ism
lib·er·al·ist
lib·er·al·is·tic
lib·er·al·ity (plural ·ities)
lib·er·ali·za·tion (or ·sa·tion)
lib·er·al·ize (or ·ise)
lib·er·al·iz·er (or ·is·er)
lib·er·al·ly
lib·er·al·ness
lib·er·ate
lib·era·tion
lib·era·tor (fem ·tress)
Li·beria
Li·berian
lib·er·tar·ian freethinker; compare libertine
lib·er·tari·an·ism
li·ber·ti·cid·al
li·ber·ti·cide destruction of freedom
lib·er·tine dissolute person; compare libertarian
lib·er·tin·ism (or ·age)
lib·er·ty (plural ·ties)
li·bidi·nal
li·bidi·nous
li·bi·do (plural ·dos)
Li·bra constellation; sign of zodiac
Lib·ran
li·brar·ian
li·brar·ian·ship
li·brary (plural ·braries)
li·brate waver
li·bra·tion
li·bra·tion·al
li·bra·tory
li·bret·tist
li·bret·to (plural ·tos or ·ti)
Li·breville Gabonese capital
li·bri·form botany term
Lib·rium (Trademark)

Libya
Liby·an
lice
li·cence (US ·cense) a permit
li·cens·able
li·cense to grant licence; US spelling of licence
li·cen·see
li·cens·er (or ·cen·sor)
li·cen·ti·ate licence holder; compare licentious
li·cen·ti·ate·ship
li·cen·tia·tion
li·cen·tious promiscuous; compare licentiate
li·cen·tious·ness
li·chee (or ·chi) variant spelling of litchi
li·chen
li·chen·in chemical compound
li·chen·oid
li·chen·ol·ogy
li·chen·ous (or ·ose)
Lich·field Staffordshire city
lich gate (or lych gate)
lic·it lawful
lick
lick·er
lick·er·ish Archaic lustful; compare liquorice
lickety-split US very quickly
lick·ing
lick·spit·tle
lico·rice US spelling of liquorice
lic·tor Roman official
lid
lid·ded
lid·less
lido (plural lidos)
lie (ly·ing, lied) tell untruth; compare lye
lie (ly·ing, lay, lain) recline; compare lye
Lieb·frau·milch (or ·frau·en·milch) wine
Liech·ten·stein
lied (plural lied·er) song
lief Archaic willingly
Li·ège Belgian city
liege owed allegiance
liege·man (plural ·men)

lien legal term
lien·al
li·en·ter·ic
li·en·tery medical term
li·erne architectural term
Li·etu·va Lithuania
lieu
lieu·ten·an·cy
lieu·ten·ant
life (*plural* lives)
life·blood
life·boat
life·guard
life·less
life·less·ly
life·less·ness
life·like
life·line
life·long for life; *compare*
   livelong
lif·er
life-saver
life-saving
life-size (*or* -sized)
life·time
Lif·fey Irish river
lift
lift·able
lift·boy
lift·er
lift·off
liga·ment
liga·men·tous (*or* ·tal,
   ·ta·ry)
li·gan *variant spelling of*
   lagan
lig·and chemistry term
li·gate constrict with ligature
li·ga·tion
liga·tive
liga·ture
li·ger animal
light (light·ing, light·ed *or*
   lit)
light·en
light·en·er
light·en·ing making lighter;
   compare lightning
light·er
light·er·age
lighter·man (*plural* ·men)
light-fast
light-fingered
light-footed
light-headed

light-headed·ly
light-headed·ness
light-hearted
light-hearted·ly
light-hearted·ness
light·house
light·ing
light·ish
light·ly
light·ness
light·ning light flash;
   compare lightening
light·ship
light·some
light·weight
lign·al·oes tree
lig·ne·ous
lig·ni·fi·ca·tion
lig·ni·form
lig·ni·fy (·fies, ·fy·ing,
   ·fied) make woody
lig·nin plant tissue
lig·nite brown coal
lig·nit·ic
lig·no·caine anaesthetic
lig·no·cel·lu·lose
lig·num vi·tae wood
lig·ro·in chemical compound
ligu·la (*plural* ·lae *or* ·las)
   part of insect's lip
ligu·lar
ligu·late
lig·ule plant part
ligu·loid
lig·ure biblical gem
Li·gu·ria Italian region
Li·gu·ri·an
lik·able (*or* like·)
lik·able·ness (*or* like·)
Li·ka·si Zaïrian city
like
like·li·hood (*or* ·ness)
like·ly (·li·er, ·li·est)
like-minded
like-minded·ly
like-minded·ness
lik·en
like·ness
like·wise
lik·ing
li·lac
lilia·ceous
lil·ied
Lilith biblical demon
Lille French city

Lil·li·pu·tian tiny person
lilly-pilly tree
Lilo (*Trademark*; *plural*
   Lilos)
Li·long·we Malawian
   capital
lilt
lilting
lily (*plural* lilies)
lily-livered
Lima Peruvian capital
lima bean
lima·cine of slugs
li·ma·çon maths term
Li·mas·sol Cypriot port
limb
lim·bate botany term
lim·ber
lim·bic anatomy term
limb·less
lim·bo (*plural* ·bos)
Lim·burg (*or* ·bourg)
   Belgian or Dutch province
Lim·burg·er cheese
lim·bus (*plural* ·bi)
   anatomy term
lime
lime·ade
lime-kiln
lime·light
li·men (*plural* ·mens *or*
   limi·na) psychology term
Lim·er·ick Irish port and
   county
lim·er·ick comic verse
li·mes (*plural* limi·tes)
   boundary of Roman
   empire
lime·stone
lime·water
lim·ey *US* Briton; *compare*
   limy
li·mico·line ornithology
   term
li·mico·lous living in mud
limi·nal psychology term
limi·ness
lim·it
lim·it·able
limi·tar·ian
limi·tary
limi·ta·tion
lim·it·ed
lim·it·er
lim·it·less

lim·it·less·ly
lim·it·less·ness
limi·trophe near a frontier
limn to draw
lim·ner
lim·net·ic ecology term
lim·no·logi·cal (or ·log·ic)
lim·nolo·gist
lim·nol·ogy study of lakes
Lim·nos variant spelling of Lemnos
Li·moges French city
limo·nene chemical compound
li·mo·nite mineral
Li·mou·sin French region
lim·ou·sine car
limp
limp·er
lim·pet
lim·pid
lim·pid·ity (or ·ness)
limp·ing·ly
limp·kin bird
limp·ness
Lim·po·po African river
limu·lus (plural ·li) crab
limy (limi·er, limi·est) of lime; compare limey
lin·able (or line·)
lin·age (or line·) number of lines; compare lineage
lin·alo·ol (or ·alol)
linch·pin pin for wheel; compare lynch
Lin·coln
Lin·coln·shire
lin·crus·ta embossed wallpaper
linc·tus (plural ·tuses)
lin·dane pesticide
lin·den
Lin·dis·farne
line (lin·ing, lined)
lin·eage descent from ancestor; variant spelling of linage
lin·eal
lin·eal·ly directly; compare linearly
linea·ment facial feature; compare liniment
linea·men·tal
lin·ear
lin·ear·ity

lin·ear·ly in a line; compare lineally
lin·eate (or ·eat·ed)
lin·ea·tion
line·caster
line·engrav·er
line·engrav·ing
line·man (plural ·men) US footballer; rail worker; compare linesman
lin·en fabric; compare linin
lineo·late (or ·lat·ed)
line·out
lin·er
lines·man (plural ·men) sporting official; rail worker; compare lineman
line·up (noun)
ling heather
ling (plural ling or lings) fish
ling·cod (plural ·cod or ·cods) fish
lin·ger
lin·ger·er
lin·gerie
lin·ger·ing·ly
lin·go (plural ·goes)
lin·gua (plural ·guae) the tongue
lin·gua fran·ca (plural lin·gua fran·cas or lin·guae fran·cae) common language
lin·gual
lin·gual·ly
lin·gui·form
lin·gui·ni pasta
lin·guist
lin·guis·tic
lin·guis·ti·cal·ly
lin·guis·tics
lin·gu·late (or ·lat·ed)
lin·hay Dialect farm building
lini·ment topical medicine; compare lineament
li·nin biology term; compare linen
lin·ing
link
link·able
link·age
link·boy torch carrier
link·man (plural ·men) broadcaster
Lin·kö·ping Swedish city

link·up (noun)
link·work
Lin·lith·gow Scottish town
linn Scot waterfall
Lin·nean (or ·naean) of Linnaeus; note Linnean Society
lin·net
Lin·nhe Scottish loch
lino (plural linos)
li·no·cut
li·no·leate
li·no·leum
Li·no·type (Trademark)
Li·no·typ·er (or ·ist)
lin·sang animal
lin·seed
linsey-woolsey fabric
lin·stock
lint
lin·tel
lin·telled (US ·teled)
lint·er
lint·white Scot linnet
linty
Linz Austrian port
lion
li·on·ess
lion·fish (plural ·fish or ·fishes)
lion-hearted
li·oni·za·tion (or ·sa·tion)
li·on·ize (or ·ise)
li·on·iz·er (or ·is·er)
lip (lip·ping, lipped)
li·pase enzyme
Li·petsk Soviet city
li·pid
lip·oid fatty
lip·oi·dal
li·poly·sis
lipo·lyt·ic
li·po·ma (plural ·mas or ·mata) tumour
li·poma·tous
lipo·phil·ic (or lipo·trop·ic) chemistry term
lipo·pro·tein
Lip·pe German river
Lip·pi·zan·er horse
lip·py (·pi·er, ·pi·est) US insolent
lip-read (-reading, -read)
lip-reader

lip·stick

li·quate separate by melting

li·qua·tion

liq·ue·fa·cient

liq·ue·fac·tion (*or* ·ui·)

liq·ue·fac·tive (*or* ·ui·)

liq·ue·fi·able (*or* ·ui·)

liq·ue·fi·er (*or* ·ui·)

liq·ue·fy (*or* ·ui·; ·fies, ·fy·ing, ·fied)

li·quesce

li·ques·cence (*or* ·cen·cy)

li·ques·cent

li·queur

liq·uid

liq·uid·am·bar balsam

liq·ui·date

liq·ui·da·tion

liq·ui·da·tor

li·quid·ity

liq·uid·ize (*or* ·ise)

liq·uid·iz·er (*or* ·is·er)

liq·ui·fy *variant spelling of* liquefy

liq·uor

liquo·rice (*US* lico·) confectionery; *compare* lickerish

lira (*plural* lire *or* liras)

lirio·den·dron (*plural* ·drons *or* ·dra) tree

liri·pipe (*or* ·poop) tip of graduate's hood

Lis·bon

lisle

lisp

lis pen·dens legal term

lisp·er

lis·som (*or* ·some)

lis·som·ness (*or* ·some·)

list

list·able

list·ed

lis·tel architectural term

lis·ten

lis·ten·er

lis·ter plough

lis·teri·osis food poisoning

list·ing

list·less

list·less·ness

lit

lita·ny (*plural* ·nies)

li·tchi (*or* ·chee, ·chi, ly·chee; *plural* ·tchis, ·chees, ·chis, *or* ·chees)

li·ter *US spelling of* litre

lit·era·cy

lit·er·al of words or letters; *compare* littoral

lit·er·al·ism

lit·er·al·ist

lit·er·al·is·tic

lit·er·al·is·ti·cal·ly

lit·er·al·ly

lit·er·al·ness (*or* ·ity)

lit·er·ari·ly

lit·er·ari·ness

lit·er·ary

lit·er·ate

lit·era·ti scholarly people

lit·era·tim letter for letter

lit·era·tion

lit·era·tor *variant of* littérateur

lit·era·ture

lith·arge lead compound

lithe

lithe·ly

lithe·ness

lithe·some

lithia lithium compound

li·thia·sis medical term

lith·ic of stone

lith·ium

li·tho (*plural* ·thos) lithograph

litho·graph

li·thog·ra·pher

litho·graph·ic (*or* ·graphi·cal)

litho·graphi·cal·ly

li·thog·ra·phy

lith·oid (*or* li·thoi·dal)

litho·log·ic (*or* ·logi·cal)

litho·logi·cal·ly

li·tholo·gist

li·thol·ogy study of rocks

litho·marge kaolin

litho·meteor

litho·phyte

litho·phyt·ic

litho·pone pigment

litho·sol soil

litho·sphere

litho·tom·ic (*or* ·tomi·cal)

li·thoto·mist

li·thoto·my (*plural* ·mies) removal of bladder stone

li·thot·rity (*plural* ·rities) crushing of bladder stone

Lithua·nia

Lithua·nian

liti·gable

liti·gant

liti·gate

liti·ga·tion

liti·ga·tor

li·ti·gious

lit·mus

li·to·tes (*plural* ·tes) understatement

li·tre (*US* ·ter)

lit·ter

lit·té·ra·teur (*or* lit·era·tor) professional writer

litter·bug

lit·tle

lit·to·ral of the shore; *compare* literal

li·tur·gi·cal (*or* ·gic)

li·tur·gi·cal·ly

li·tur·gics study of liturgies

lit·ur·gism

lit·ur·gist

lit·ur·gis·tic

lit·ur·gy (*plural* ·gies)

liv·abil·ity (*or* live·)

liv·able (*or* live·)

liv·able·ness (*or* live·)

live

live·able *variant spelling of* livable

live·li·hood

live·li·ness

live·long very long; entire; *compare* lifelong

live·ly (·li·er, ·li·est)

liv·en

liv·en·er

liv·er

liv·er·ied

liv·er·ish

liv·er·ish·ness

Liv·er·pool

Liv·er·pud·lian

liver·wort plant

liver·wurst sausage

liv·ery (*plural* ·eries)

liv·ery·man (*plural* ·men)

live·stock

live·trap (·trap·ping,
·trapped)
live·ware computer workers
liv·id
liv·id·ly
liv·id·ness (or li·vid·ity)
liv·ing
Li·vo·nia former Russian
province; US city
Li·vo·nian
Li·vor·no Italian port
lix·ivi·ate chemistry term
lix·ivia·tion
lix·iv·ium (plural ·iums or
·ivia) alkaline solution
liz·ard
Lju·blja·na Yugoslav city
lla·ma animal; compare lama
Llan·daff Cardiff suburb
Llan·dud·no Welsh town
Llan·elli (or ·elly) Welsh
town
lla·no (plural ·nos)
grassland
Lla·no Es·ta·ca·do Texan
region
Lloyd's underwriters
lo exclamation
loach
load burden, etc.; compare
lode
load·ed
load·er
load·ing
load·star variant spelling of
lodestar
load·stone variant spelling
of lodestone
loaf (plural loaves)
loaf·er
loam
loami·ness
loamy (loami·er,
loami·est)
loan
loan·able
loan·er
loath (or loth) reluctant
loathe to hate
loath·er
loath·ing
loath·ly
loath·some
loath·some·ness
loaves plural of loaf

lob (lob·bing, lobbed)
lo·bar
lo·bate (or ·bat·ed)
lobbed
lob·bing
lob·by (noun, plural ·bies;
verb ·bies, ·by·ing,
·bied)
lob·by·er
lob·by·ism
lob·by·ist
lobe
lo·bec·to·my (plural
·mies)
lo·belia
lo·beline alkaloid
Lo·bi·to Angolan port
lob·lol·ly (plural ·lies) tree
lo·boto·my (plural ·mies)
lob·scouse sailor's stew
lob·ster (plural ·sters or
·ster)
lobu·lar (or ·late, ·lat·ed,
·lose)
lobu·la·tion
lob·ule
lo·cal
lo·cale (noun)
lo·cal·ism
lo·cal·ist
lo·cal·is·tic
lo·cal·ity (plural ·ities)
lo·cal·iz·able (or ·is·able)
lo·cali·za·tion (or ·sa·tion)
lo·cal·ize (or ·ise)
lo·cal·iz·er (or ·is·er)
lo·cal·ly
lo·cat·able
lo·cate
lo·cat·er
lo·ca·tion
loca·tive
loch
lochia vaginal discharge
loch·ial
loci plural of locus
lock
lock·able
lock·age canal locks
lock·er
lock·et
lock·jaw
lock·nut
lock·out (noun)
lock·smith

lock·smithery (or
·smithing)
lock·up (noun)
loco (plural locos) Slang
locomotive; US insane
lo·co·ism cattle disease
lo·co·man (plural ·men)
engine driver
lo·co·mo·tion
lo·co·mo·tive
lo·co·mo·tor of locomotion
lo·co·weed
locu·lar (or ·late) biology
term
locu·la·tion
locu·ule (or locu·lus;
plural ·ules or ·li)
biology term
lo·cum short for locum
tenens
lo·cum te·nens (plural
lo·cum te·nen·tes)
professional stand-in
lo·cus (plural loci)
lo·cust
lo·cu·tion
Lód Israeli town
lode ore deposit; compare
load
lo·den wool
lode·star (or load·)
lode·stone (or load·)
lodge
lodge·able
lodg·er
lodg·ing
lodg·ings
lodg·ment (or lodge·)
lodi·cule botany term
Lódź Polish city
lo·ess soil
lo·ess·ial (or ·al)
Lo·fo·ten Is·lands
loft
loft·er golf club
lofti·ly
lofti·ness
lofty (lofti·er, lofti·est)
log (log·ging, logged)
Lo·gan Canadian mountain
logan·berry (plural
·berries)
lo·ga·nia·ceous botany
term
loga·oedic verse form

loga·rithm
loga·rith·mic (or ·mi·cal)
loga·rith·mi·cal·ly
log·book
loge theatre box
logged
log·ger
log·ger·head
log·gia (plural ·gias or
·gie) roofed gallery;
compare logia
log·ging
logia plural of logion;
compare loggia
log·ic
logi·cal
logi·cal·ity (or ·ness)
logi·cal·ly
lo·gi·cian
logi·cism
logi·on (plural logia)
saying of Christ
lo·gis·tic
lo·gis·ti·cal
lo·gis·ti·cal·ly
log·is·ti·cian
lo·gis·tics
log·log maths term
logo (plural logos)
logo·gram (or ·graph)
logo·gram·mat·ic (or
·graph·ic, ·graphi·cal)
logo·gram·mati·cal·ly (or
·graphi·cal·ly)
lo·gog·ra·pher
lo·gog·ra·phy
logo·griph word puzzle
logo·griph·ic
lo·goma·chist
lo·goma·chy (plural
·chies) word argument
logo·paedic (US ·pedic)
logo·paedics (US ·pedics)
speech therapy
log·or·rhoea (US ·rhea)
talkativeness
Log·os second person of
Trinity
log·os reason
logo·type printing term
lo·go·typy
log·wood
logy (logi·er, logi·est) US
dull or listless

Lohengrin legendary
character
loin
loin·cloth
Loire French river
Loire-Atlantique French
department
Loi·ret French department
Loir-et-Cher French
department
loi·ter
loi·ter·er
loi·ter·ing·ly
Loki Norse god
loll
Lol·lard
Lol·lardy (or ·lard·ry,
·lard·ism)
loll·er
loll·ing·ly
lol·li·pop
lol·lop
lol·ly (plural ·lies)
Lom·bard
Lom·bar·dic
Lom·bardy
Lom·bok Indonesian island
Lomé capital of Togo
lo·ment (or ·men·tum;
plural ·ments or
·men·ta) plant pod
lo·men·ta·ceous
Lo·mond Scottish lake
Lon·don
Lon·don·der·ry
Lon·don·er
Lon·dri·na Brazilian city
lone
lone·li·ness
lone·ly (·li·er, ·li·est)
lone·ness
lon·er
lone·some
lone·some·ly
lone·some·ness
long
lon·gan fruit
lon·ga·nim·ity patience
lon·gani·mous
long·boat
long·bow
long·cloth
long-distance (adj)
long-drawn-out
lon·geron part of aircraft

lon·gev·ity
lon·gevous
Long·ford Irish county
long-haired
long·hand
long-headed shrewd
long·horn cattle
lon·gi·corn beetle
long·ing
long·ing·ly
long·ish
lon·gi·tude
lon·gi·tu·di·nal
lon·gi·tu·di·nal·ly
long johns underpants
long-lived
long-range (adj)
long·ship
long·shore
long·shore·man (plural
·men)
long-sighted
long-sighted·ly
long-sighted·ness
long·spur bird
long-standing
long-suffer·ance
long-suffer·ing
long-term
long·time (adj)
Lon·gueuil Canadian city
lon·gueur French boredom
long·ways (US ·wise)
long-winded
long-winded·ly
long-winded·ness
Long·year·byen
Norwegian village
lo·nic·era honeysuckle
loo (plural loos)
loo·by (plural ·bies) fool
loo·fah (US also ·fa,
luf·fa)
look
look·alike
look·er
looker-on (plural
lookers-)
look-in (noun)
look·out
loom
loom-state undyed
loon
looni·ness

loony (*or* **looney**; *adj*
  looni·er, looni·est;
  noun, plural **loonies**)
loop
loop·er caterpillar
loop·hole
loopi·ness
loopy (**loopi·er, loopi·est**)
loose
loose·box
loose-jointed
loose-leaf (*adj*)
loose·ly
loos·en
loos·en·er
loose·ness
loose·strife plant
loose-tongued
loos·ish
loot
loot·er
lop (**lop·ping, lopped**)
lope
lop-eared
lop·er
lo·pho·branch fish
lopho·bran·chi·ate
lo·pho·phor·ate
lo·pho·phore zoology term
lop·ing
lopped
lop·per
lop·ping
lop·sided
lop·sided·ly
lop·sided·ness
lo·qua·cious
lo·quac·ity (*or*
  lo·qua·cious·ness)
lo·quat fruit
lo·qui·tur *Latin* he or she
  speaks
lor exclamation
lo·ran navigation system
Lord God
lord nobleman
lord·li·ness
lord·ling
lord·ly (**·li·er, ·li·est**)
lor·do·sis spinal curvature
lor·dot·ic
lord·ship
lordy exclamation
lore knowledge; zoology
  term; *compare* **law**

Lo·relei siren
lor·gnette
lor·gnon
lo·ri·ca (*plural* **·cae**) shell
lori·cate (*or* **·cat·ed**)
lori·keet parrot
lori·mer (*or* **·ner**)
  metalworker
lo·ris (*plural* **·ris**) animal
lorn forsaken
Lor·raine
lor·ry (*plural* **·ries**) vehicle
lory (*plural* **lories**) parrot
los·able
Los An·ge·les
lose (**los·ing, lost**)
lo·sel *Dialect* worthless
  person
los·er
los·ing
loss
los·sy dissipating energy
lost
lot (**lot·ting, lot·ted**)
lota (*or* **lo·tah**) water
  container
Lot-et-Garonne French
  department
loth *variant spelling of* **loath**
Lo·thario (*plural* **·tharios**)
  libertine
Lo·thian Scottish region
lo·tic ecology term
lo·tion
lot·ted
lot·tery (*plural* **·teries**)
lot·ting
lot·to
lo·tus (*or* **lo·tos**)
lotus-eater
louche shifty
loud
loud·en
loud-hailer
loud·ish
loud·ly
loud·mouth
loud·ness
loud·speaker
lough
Lough·bor·ough
  Leicestershire town
lou·is (*or* **lou·is d'or;**
  plural **lou·is** *or* **lou·is**
  d'or) coin

Lou·is·burg (*or* **·bourg**)
  Canadian fortress
Loui·si·ana
Lou·is·ville US port
lounge
loung·er
loupe magnifying glass
lour (*or* **low·er**) look
  menacing
Lourdes French town
lour·ing·ly (*or* **low·er·**)
louse (*plural* **lice**)
louse·wort
lousi·ly
lousi·ness
lousy (**lousi·er, lousi·est**)
lout
Louth Irish county
lout·ish
lout·ish·ly
lout·ish·ness
Lou·vain Belgian town
lou·var fish
Lou·vre French museum
lou·vre (*US* **·ver**) slat
lou·vred (*US* **·vered**)
lov·abil·ity (*or* **love·**)
lov·able (*or* **love·**)
lov·ably (*or* **love·**)
lov·age plant
lov·at fabric
love
love·bird
love·less
love·li·ness
love·lock
love·lorn
love·ly (*adj* **·li·er, ·li·est;**
  noun, plural **·lies**)
love·making
lov·er
love·sick
love·sick·ness
lov·ey
lovey-dovey
lov·ing
lov·ing·ly
lov·ing·ness
low
low·an bird
low-born (*or* **·bred**)
low·boy *US* table with
  drawers
low·bred
low·brow

low·brow·ism
low-down (*noun*)
low-down (*adj*)
low·er less high; *variant spelling of* lour
low·er·able
low·er·ing·ly *variant spelling of* louringly
lower·most
low·est
Lowes·toft
low-key (*or* -keyed)
Low·land of Lowlands
low·land flat ground
Low·land·er
low·land·er
Low·lands Scottish region
low·li·ness
low·ly (·li·er, ·li·est)
low-minded
low·ness
low-pitched
low-rise (*adj*)
low-spirit·ed
lox smoked salmon
loxo·drom·ic (*or* ·dromi·cal)
loxo·dromi·cal·ly
loxo·drom·ics (*or* lox·od·ro·my) navigation technique
loy·al
loy·al·ism
Loy·al·ist Northern Irish Protestant
loy·al·ist
loy·al·ly
loy·al·ty (*plural* ·ties)
Lo·yang Chinese city
loz·enge
loz·engy heraldic term
Lo·zère French department
Lozi Zambian language
Lu·an·da Angolan capital
Luba (*plural* Luba) African people
lub·ber clumsy person
Lub·bock Texan city
Lü·beck West German port
Lu·blin Polish city
lub·ri·cant
lu·bri·cate
lu·bri·ca·tion
lu·bri·ca·tion·al
lu·bri·ca·tive

lu·bri·ca·tor
lu·bric·ity lewdness
lu·bri·cous (*or* ·cious)
Lu·bum·ba·shi Zaïrian city
lu·carne dormer window
lu·cen·cy
lu·cent
Lu·cerne Swiss town
lu·cerne plant
lu·cid
lu·cid·ity (*or* ·cid·ness)
Lu·ci·fer
lu·cif·er·in biochemical compound
Lucina Roman goddess
luck
lucki·ly
lucki·ness
luck·less
luck·less·ness
Luck·now Indian city
lucky (lucki·er, lucki·est)
luc·ra·tive
lu·cra·tive·ly
lu·cre
lu·cu·brate to study
lu·cu·bra·tion
lu·cu·bra·tor
Lud·dite
Lu·dhia·na Indian city
lu·di·crous
Lud·low Shropshire town
ludo
Lud·wigs·ha·fen West German city
luff nautical term
luf·fa *US variant spelling of* loofah
Luft·waf·fe German Air Force
lug (lug·ging, lugged)
Lu·gan·da African language
luge toboggan
Lu·ger (*Trademark*)
lug·gage
lugged
lug·ger
lug·ging
lug·sail
lu·gu·bri·ous
lug·worm
luke·warm
lull

lulla·by (*noun, plural* ·bies; *verb* ·bies, ·by·ing, ·bied)
lull·ing·ly
lulu *US* wonderful person or thing
lum·ba·go
lum·bar of loin
lum·ber timber; move awkwardly
lum·ber·er
lum·ber·ing
lum·ber·ing·ly
lumber·jack
lumber·jacket
lumber·yard
lum·bri·cal
lum·bri·ca·lis muscle
lum·bri·coid wormlike
lu·men (*plural* ·mens) unit
lu·men (*plural* ·mina) anatomical duct
lu·men·al (*or* ·min·)
lu·mi·nance
lu·mi·nary (*plural* ·naries)
lu·mi·nesce
lu·mi·nes·cence
lu·mi·nes·cent
lu·mi·nos·ity (*plural* ·ities)
lu·mi·nous
lu·mi·nous·ly
lu·mis·te·rol biochemical compound
lum·me exclamation
lum·mox clumsy person
lump
lump·en stupid
lum·pen·pro·le·tari·at
lum·per *US* stevedore
lump·fish (*plural* ·fish *or* ·fishes)
lumpi·ly
lumpi·ness
lump·ish
lumpy (lumpi·er, lumpi·est)
Luna Roman goddess
luna moth; *compare* lunar
lu·na·cy (*plural* ·cies)
lu·nar of the moon; *compare* luna
lu·nate (*or* ·nat·ed)
lu·na·tic (*or* lu·nati·cal)
lu·na·tion lunar month

lunch
lunch·eon
lunch·eon·ette *US* café
lunch·er
Lund Swedish city
Lun·dy island
lune maths term
Lü·ne·burg West German city
lu·nette
lung
lunge
lung·er
lung·fish (*plural* ·fish *or* ·fishes)
lung·ful
lun·gi (*or* ·gee) Indian cloth
lung·worm
lung·wort plant
lu·ni·so·lar
lu·ni·tid·al
lu·nu·la (*or* ·nule; *plural* ·lae *or* ·nules)
lu·nu·late (*or* ·lat·ed)
luny (*adj* luni·er, luni·est; *noun, plural* lunies)
Lu·per·ca·lia (*plural* ·lia *or* ·lias) Roman festival
lu·pin (*US* ·pine) plant
lu·pine wolflike; *US spelling of* lupin
lu·pu·lin sedative
Lu·pus constellation
lu·pus skin disease
lur (*or* lure; *plural* lures) musical horn
lurch
lurch·er
lurch·ing·ly
lur·dan stupid
lure
lur·er
Lu·rex (*Trademark*)
lu·rid
lu·rid·ness
lur·ing·ly
lurk
lurk·er
lurk·ing·ly
Lu·sa·ka Zambian capital
Lu·sa·tia East German region
Lu·sa·tian
lus·cious

lus·cious·ness
lush
lush·ly
lush·ness
Lü·shun Chinese port
Lu·si·ta·nia ship
lust
lus·ter *US spelling of* lustre
lust·ful
lust·ful·ly
lust·ful·ness
lusti·ly
lusti·ness
lus·tral
lus·trate purify
lus·tra·tion
lus·tra·tive
lus·tre (*US* ·ter)
lus·tre·less (*US* ·ter·)
lustre·ware (*US* luster·)
lus·trous
lus·trum (*plural* ·trums *or* ·tra) five years
lusty (lusti·er, lusti·est)
lute
lu·teal biology term
lu·tein·iz·ing hor·mone
lu·tenist lute player
lu·teo·lin plant compound
lu·teous greenish-yellow
Lu·tetia *Latin* Paris
lu·tetium (*or* ·tecium) chemical element
Lu·ther·an
Lu·ther·an·ism
Lu·ther·ism
lu·thern dormer window
Lu·tine bell
Lu·ton
lux (*plural* lux) unit
lux·ate dislocate
luxa·tion
Lux·em·bourg
Lux·or Egyptian town
lux·ulia·nite (*or* ·ul·lia·nite) granite
luxu·ri·ance
luxu·ri·ant
luxu·ri·ate
luxu·ria·tion
luxu·ri·ous
luxu·ry (*plural* ·ries)
Lu·zon Philippine island
Ly·all·pur Pakistani city
ly·can·thrope werewolf

ly·can·thro·py
ly·cée (*plural* ·cées) French school
Ly·ceum Athenian school
ly·ceum public building
ly·chee *variant spelling of* litchi
lych gate *variant spelling of* lich gate
lych·nis plant
ly·co·pod club moss
ly·co·po·dium type of club moss
lydd·ite explosive
Lydia ancient Asian region
Lyd·ian
lye alkaline solution; *compare* lie
ly·ing
lying-in (*plural* lyings-in)
lyke-wake vigil over corpse
Lyme Re·gis
Lym·ing·ton Hampshire town
lymph
lym·phad·eni·tis
lym·phan·gial
lym·phan·git·ic
lym·phan·gi·tis (*plural* ·gi·des)
lym·phat·ic
lym·phati·cal·ly
lym·pho·blast blood cell
lym·pho·blas·tic
lym·pho·cyte blood cell
lym·pho·cyt·ic
lym·pho·cy·to·sis
lym·pho·cy·tot·ic
lym·phoid
lym·pho·ma (*plural* ·ma·ta *or* ·mas) tumour
lym·pho·ma·toid
lym·pho·poi·esis (*plural* ·eses)
lym·pho·poi·et·ic
lyn·cean resembling a lynx
lynch kill; *compare* linchpin
lynch·er
lynch·ing
lynx (*plural* lynxes *or* lynx)
Lyon French city
Lyon·nais former French province
ly·on·naise cookery term

Ly·on·nesse legendary place
lyo·phil·ic
ly·ophi·lize (*or* ·**lise**) freeze-dry
lyo·pho·bic
Lyra constellation
ly·rate (*or* **rat·ed**)
lyre
lyre·bird
lyr·ic

lyri·cal
lyri·cal·ly
lyri·cism
lyri·cist
lyr·ist
lyse biology term
ly·ser·gic acid
ly·sim·eter
ly·sin substance that destroys cells
ly·sine amino acid

ly·sis (*plural* ·**ses**) biology term
Ly·sol (*Trademark*)
ly·so·so·mal
ly·so·some cell particle
ly·so·zyme enzyme
Lyth·am St. Anne's
lyth·ra·ceous botany term
lyt·ic biology term
lyt·ta (*plural* ·**tas** *or* ·**tae**) zoology term

M

ma *Slang* mother
Ma'am title of address for royalty
maar (*plural* **maars** *or* **maare**) volcanic crater
Maas·tricht (*or* **Maes·**) Dutch city
Mab fairy queen
ma·bela ground corn
mac
ma·ca·bre
ma·ca·co (*plural* ·**cos**) lemur; *compare* **macaque**
mac·ad·am road surface
maca·da·mia tree
mac·ad·ami·za·tion (*or* ·**sa·tion**)
mac·ad·am·ize (*or* ·**ise**)
mac·ad·am·iz·er (*or* ·**is·er**)
Ma·cao Chinese city
ma·caque monkey; *compare* **macaco**
maca·ro·ni (*plural* ·**nis**) pasta
maca·ro·ni (*plural* ·**nies**) dandy
maca·ron·ic type of verse
maca·roni·cal·ly
maca·roon
Ma·cas·sar *variant spelling of* Makassar
ma·caw
Mac·ca·bean
Mac·ca·bees Apocryphal book
mac·ca·boy (*or* ·**co·boy**, ·**ca·baw**) snuff
Mac·cles·field

mace
mace·bearer
ma·cedoine diced vegetables
Mac·edon (*or* ·**edo·nia**) former kingdom
Mac·edo·nia Yugoslav republic; division of Greece
Mac·edo·nian
Ma·ceió Brazilian port
mac·er macebearer
mac·er·ate
mac·er·at·er (*or* ·**era·tor**)
mac·era·tion
mac·era·tive
ma·chan tiger-hunting platform
ma·chete
Machia·vel·lian (*or* ·**vel·ian**)
ma·chico·late fortifications term
ma·chico·la·tion
ma·chin·abil·ity
ma·chin·able (*or* ·**chine·**)
machi·nate
machi·na·tion
machi·na·tor
ma·chine
machine-gun (*verb*; -**gunning**, -**gunned**)
ma·chin·ery (*plural* ·**eries**)
ma·chin·ist
ma·chis·mo
Mach·meter physics term

Mach num·ber physics term
macho
ma·chree *Irish* my dear
Ma·chu Pic·chu Incan city
Ma·cí·as Ngue·ma Guinean island
Mac·kay Australian port
Mac·ken·zie Canadian district or river
macke·rel (*plural* ·**rel** *or* ·**rels**)
Macki·naw coat
mack·in·tosh (*or* **mac·in·**)
mack·le (*or* **mac·ule**) printing term; *compare* **macle**
Maclaurin's se·ries maths term
ma·cle mineral; *compare* **mackle**
Mâ·con French city; wine
mac·ra·mé
mac·ren·cepha·ly (*or* ·**lia**) abnormally large brain
macro·bi·ot·ic
macro·cephal·ic (*or* **mega·**, **mega·lo·**)
macro·cepha·ly (*or* **mega·**, **mega·lo·**) abnormally large head
macro·cli·mate
macro·cli·mat·ic
macro·cli·mati·cal·ly
macro·cosm
macro·cos·mic
macro·cos·mi·cal·ly
macro·cyst

macro·cyte blood cell
macro·cyt·ic
macro·cy·to·sis
macro·eco·nom·ic
macro·eco·nom·ics
macro·evo·lu·tion
macro·evo·lu·tion·ary
macro·gam·ete (or mega·)
macro·graph
macro·graph·ic
macro·mo·lecu·lar
macro·mol·ecule
mac·ron phonetic symbol
macro·nu·cleus (plural ·clei)
macro·nu·tri·ent
macro·phage cell
macro·phag·ic
macro·phys·ics
mac·rop·ter·ous having large wings
macro·scop·ic (or ·scopi·cal)
macro·scopi·cal·ly
macro·spo·ran·gium (plural ·gia) botany term
macro·spore
ma·cru·ral (or ·roid, ·rous)
ma·cru·ran crustacean
macu·la (or mac·ule; plural ·lae or ·ules) anatomy term
macu·la lu·tea (plural macu·lae lu·teae) spot on retina
macu·lar
macu·la·tion
mac·ule variant of mackle or macula
mad (mad·der, mad·dest)
Mada·gas·can
Mada·gas·car
mad·am term of address; conceited girl; brothel keeper
mad·ame (plural mes·dames) French lady; Mrs
mad·cap
mad·den
mad·den·ing
mad·der plant; dye; more mad
mad·dest

mad·ding Archaic mad or maddening
made
Ma·dei·ra
mad·eleine cake
mad·emoi·selle (plural mes·de·moi·selles)
mad·house
Madh·ya Pra·desh Indian state
Madi·son US city and avenue
mad·ly
mad·man (plural ·men)
mad·ness
Ma·don·na Virgin Mary
Ma·dras Indian port
mad·ras fabric
mad·re·por·al (or ·por·ic, ·por·it·ic, ·po·rian)
mad·re·pore coral
Ma·drid
mad·ri·gal
mad·ri·gal·esque
mad·ri·gal·ian
mad·ri·gal·ist
mad·ri·lène consommé
ma·dro·ña (or ·ño, ·ne; plural ·ñas, ·ños, or ·nes) tree
Ma·du·ra Indonesian island
Ma·du·rai Indian city
Ma·du·rese of Madura
ma·du·ro cigar
mad·woman (plural ·women)
mad·wort plant
Ma·eba·shi Japanese city
Mael·strom Norwegian whirlpool
mael·strom whirlpool; confusion
mae·nad (or me·nad)
mae·nad·ic
maes·to·so musical term
maes·tro (plural ·tros or ·tri)
Maf·eking South African town
Ma·fia (or Maf·fia)
ma·fio·so (plural ·sos or ·si)
mag
maga·zine
mag·da·len reformed prostitute

Mag·da·lena Colombian river
Mag·da·lenian Palaeolithic culture
Mag·de·burg East German city
Ma·gel·lan strait
ma·gen·ta
mag·got fly larva; compare magot
mag·goti·ness
mag·goty
Ma·ghreb (or ·ghrib)
Ma·ghre·bi (or ·ghri·)
Magi (sing. Magus) biblical wise men
magi plural of magus
ma·gian
mag·ic (·ick·ing, ·icked)
magi·cal
magi·cal·ly
ma·gi·cian
ma·gilp variant spelling of megilp
Ma·gi·not line
mag·is·te·rial
mag·is·te·rial·ly
mag·is·tery (plural ·teries) alchemical substance
mag·is·tra·cy (or ·ture; plural ·cies or ·tures)
mag·is·tral pharmacology term
mag·is·tral·ly (or mag·is·trati·cal·ly)
mag·is·trate
mag·is·trate·ship
mag·is·tra·ture variant of magistracy
Mag·le·mo·sian (or ·sean) Mesolithic culture
mag·ma (plural ·mas or ·ma·ta) molten rock
mag·mat·ic
mag·ma·tism
Mag·na Car·ta (or Char·ta)
mag·na·nim·ity (plural ·ities)
mag·nani·mous
mag·nani·mous·ness
mag·nate
mag·ne·sia magnesium oxide

mag·ne·sian (*or* ·ne·sic,
　·ne·sial)
mag·ne·site mineral
mag·ne·sium
mag·net
mag·net·ic
mag·neti·cal·ly
mag·net·ics
mag·net·ism
mag·net·ite mineral
mag·net·it·ic
mag·net·iz·able (*or*
　·is·able)
mag·neti·za·tion (*or*
　·sa·tion)
mag·net·ize (*or* ·ise)
mag·net·iz·er (*or* ·is·er)
mag·ne·to (*plural* ·tos)
mag·ne·to·chemi·cal
mag·ne·to·chem·is·try
mag·ne·to·elec·tric (*or*
　·tri·cal)
mag·ne·to·elec·tric·ity
mag·ne·to·graph
mag·ne·to·hy·dro·dy·
　nam·ic
mag·ne·to·hy·dro·dy·
　nam·ics
mag·ne·tom·eter
mag·ne·to·met·ric
mag·ne·tom·etry
mag·ne·to·mo·tive
mag·ne·ton physics unit;
　compare magnetron
mag·ne·to·sphere
mag·ne·to·stric·tion
mag·ne·to·stric·tive
mag·ne·tron microwave
　generator; *compare*
　magneton
mag·ni·fi·able
Mag·nifi·cat canticle
mag·nifi·ca·tion
mag·nifi·cence
mag·nifi·cent
mag·nifi·co (*plural* ·coes)
　grandee
mag·ni·fi·er
mag·ni·fy (·fies, ·fy·ing,
　·fied)
mag·nilo·quence
mag·nilo·quent
Mag·ni·to·gorsk Soviet city
mag·ni·tude
mag·ni·tu·di·nous
mag·no·lia

mag·no·lia·ceous
mag·num (*plural* ·nums)
　wine bottle
mag·num opus
mag·nus hitchknot
Magog biblical character
ma·got oriental figurine;
　compare maggot
mag·pie
mag·uey fibre
Magus (*sing. of* Magi)
magus (*plural* magi)
　Zoroastrian priest;
　sorcerer
Mag·yar Hungarian
Ma·ha·bha·ra·ta (*or* ·tam,
　·tum) Indian poem
Ma·hal·la el Ku·bra
　Egyptian city
Ma·ha·na·di Indian river
ma·ha·ra·jah (*or* ·ja)
ma·ha·ra·ni (*or* ·nee)
　maharajah's wife
Ma·ha·rash·tra Indian
　state
ma·ha·ri·shi Hindu teacher
ma·hat·ma Brahman sage
Ma·ha·ya·na Buddhist
　school
Mahé Seychelles island
Ma·hi·can (*or* Mo·;
　plural ·cans *or* ·can)
　American Indian
mah·jong (*or* mah·jongg)
mahl·stick *variant spelling*
　of maulstick
ma·hoga·ny (*plural* ·nies)
Ma·hom·etan Muslim
ma·ho·nia shrub
ma·hout elephant keeper
Mah·rat·ta *variant spelling*
　of Maratha
mah·seer fish
Maia mythological character
maid
mai·dan meeting place
maid·en young girl
maiden·hair fern
Maid·en·head Berkshire
　town
maid·en·head virginity
maid·en·hood
maid·en·li·ness
maid·en·ly
maid·servant
Maid·stone Kent town

maieu·tic (*or* ·ti·cal)
　philosophy term
Mai·kop Soviet city
mail
mail·able
mail·bag
mail·box
mail·coach
mail·er
mail·sack
mail·shot
maim
maim·er
main
main·brace
Maine US state
Maine-et-Loire French
　department
Main·land Scottish island
main·land
main·line (*adj, verb*)
main·ly
main·mast
main·sail
main·sheet
main·spring
main·stay
main·stream
main·tain
main·tain·able
main·tain·er
main·te·nance
main·top
main·topmast
main·top·sail
Mainz West German port
ma·ioli·ca *variant spelling of*
　majolica
mai·son·ette (*or*
　·son·nette)
maî·tre d'hô·tel (*plural*
　maî·tres d'hô·tel)
maize cereal; *compare* maze
ma·jes·tic (*or* ·ti·cal)
ma·jes·ti·cal·ly
Maj·es·ty (*plural* ·ties)
　title for royalty
maj·es·ty dignity
ma·joli·ca (*or* ·ioli·)
　pottery
ma·jor
Ma·jor·ca
major-domo (*plural*
　-domos)
ma·jor·ette

ma·jor·ity (*plural* ·ities)
ma·jus·cu·lar
ma·jus·cule printing term
Ma·ka·lu Himalayan
   mountain range
Ma·kas·ar (*or* ·kas·sar,
   ·cas·sar) Indonesian port
make (mak·ing, made)
make-believe (*noun*)
make·fast
mak·er
make·shift
make-up (*noun*)
make·weight (*noun*)
Ma·ke·yev·ka Soviet city
Ma·khach·ka·la Soviet port
mak·ing
mako (*plural* makos)
   shark; tree
Ma·kur·di Nigerian port
Mala·bar Indian region
Ma·la·bo capital of
   Equatorial Guinea
mal·ab·sorp·tion
Ma·lac·ca Malaysian state
ma·lac·ca walking stick
mala·chite mineral
mala·co·logi·cal
mala·colo·gist
mala·col·ogy study of
   molluscs
mala·coph·yl·lous having
   fleshy leaves
mala·cop·te·ryg·ian fish
mala·cos·tra·can
   crustacean
mala·cos·tra·cous
mal·ad·dress awkwardness
mal·ad·just·ed
mal·ad·just·ment
mal·ad·min·is·ter
mal·ad·min·is·tra·tion
mal·ad·min·is·tra·tor
mala·droit
mala·droit·ness
mala·dy (*plural* ·dies)
mala fide *Latin* in bad faith
Má·la·ga Spanish port;
   wine
Mala·gasy Madagascan
   language
ma·la·gueña dance
ma·laise
mala·mute (*or*
   mal·emute) Eskimo dog

mal·an·ders (*or* mal·lan·,
   mal·len·) horse disease
Ma·lang Indonesian city
mala·pert saucy
mala·prop·ian
mala·prop·ism
mal·ap·ro·pos
ma·lar of the cheek
ma·laria
ma·lar·ial (*or* ·lar·ian,
   ·lari·ous)
ma·lar·key (*or* ·ky)
mal·as·simi·la·tion
mal·ate chemistry term
Mala·thi·on (*Trademark*)
Ma·la·tya Turkish city
Ma·la·wi
Ma·la·wian
Ma·lay
Ma·laya
Mala·ya·lam (*or* ·laam)
   language
Ma·lay·an
Ma·lay·sia
Ma·lay·sian
mal·con·tent
mal de mer *French* sea
   sickness
Mal·dives
Mal·div·ian (*or* ·di·van)
male
Malé capital of the
   Maldives
ma·leate chemistry term
mal·edict
mal·edic·tion
mal·edic·tive (*or* ·tory)
mal·efac·tion
mal·efac·tor (*fem* ·tress)
ma·lef·ic
ma·lefi·cence
ma·lefi·cent
ma·leic acid
male·ness
ma·levo·lence
ma·levo·lent
mal·fea·sance illegal act
mal·fea·sant
mal·for·ma·tion
mal·formed
mal·func·tion
mal·gré lui *French* in spite
   of himself
Mali African republic
Malian

mal·ic acid
mal·ice
ma·li·cious
ma·li·cious·ness
ma·lign
ma·lig·nan·cy (*plural*
   ·cies)
ma·lig·nant
ma·lign·er
ma·lig·nity (*plural* ·nities)
mal·im·print·ed
mal·im·print·ing
ma·lines fabric
ma·lin·ger
ma·lin·ger·er
Ma·lin·ke (*or* ·nin·ke;
   plural ·ke *or* ·kes)
   African people
mali·son curse
mall
mal·lam (*or* mal·am)
   Islamic scholar
mal·lard (*plural* ·lard *or*
   ·lards)
mal·le·abil·ity (*or*
   ·able·ness)
mal·le·able
mal·lee tree
mal·le·muck bird
mal·leo·lar
mal·leo·lus (*plural* ·li)
   ankle bone
mal·let
mal·le·us (*plural* ·lei) ear
   bone
mal·low
malm limestone
Malmö Swedish port
malm·sey wine
mal·nour·ished
mal·nu·tri·tion
mal·oc·clud·ed
mal·oc·clu·sion dentistry
   term
mal·odor·ous
ma·lo·nic acid
mal·pighia·ceous botany
   term
Mal·pigh·ian anatomy term
mal·posed
mal·po·si·tion
mal·prac·tice
mal·prac·ti·tion·er
malt
Mal·ta

malt·ase enzyme
malt·ed
Mal·tese (*plural* ·tese)
mal·tha mineral tar
Mal·thu·sian
Mal·thu·si·an·ism
   population theory
malti·ness
malt·ing
malt·ose sugar
mal·treat
mal·treat·er
mal·treat·ment
malt·ster
malty (malti·er, malti·est)
mal·va·ceous botany term
mal·va·sia wine
Mal·vern
mal·voi·sie wine
mam *Slang* mother
mama (*or* mam·ma)
   mother; *compare* mamma
mam·ba snake
mam·bo (*plural* ·bos)
   dance
mam·elon hillock
Mam·eluke (*or*
   Mama·luke) Egyptian
   ruler
ma·mey (*or* mam·mee)
   fruit; *compare* mammy
ma·mil·la (*US* mam·mil·;
   plural ·lae) nipple
ma·mil·lary (*US*
   mam·mil·)
ma·mil·late (*or* ·lat·ed;
   US mam·mil·)
mam·ma (*plural* ·mae)
   breast; *compare* mama
mam·ma *variant spelling of*
   mama
mam·mal
mam·ma·lian
mam·ma·logi·cal
mam·malo·gist
mam·mal·ogy
mam·ma·ry
mam·mee *variant spelling of*
   mamey
mam·mif·er·ous
mam·mil·la *US spelling of*
   mamilla
mam·mock *Dialect* shred
mam·mo·gram
mam·mog·ra·phy
mam·mon

mam·mon·ism
mam·mon·ist (*or* ·ite)
mam·mon·is·tic
mam·moth
mam·my (*or* ·mie; *plural*
   ·mies) mother; *compare*
   mamey
Man (Isle of)
man (*noun, plural* men;
   verb man·ning,
   manned)
mana power; *compare*
   manna
mana·cle
Ma·na·do *variant spelling of*
   Menado
man·age
man·age·abil·ity (*or*
   ·able·ness)
man·age·able
man·age·ably
man·age·ment
man·ag·er
man·ag·er·ess
mana·gerial
mana·geri·al·ly
man·ag·ing
Ma·na·gua Nicaraguan
   capital
mana·kin bird; *compare*
   manikin; mannequin
Ma·na·ma capital of
   Bahrain
ma·ña·na *Spanish* tomorrow
Ma·nas·sas US town
man-at-arms (*plural*
   men-)
mana·tee sea mammal
mana·toid
Ma·naus (*or* Ma·náos)
   Brazilian port
Manche French department
Man·ches·ter
man·chi·neel tree
Man·chu (*plural* ·chus *or*
   ·chu) Chinese dynasty
Man·chu·ria
Man·chu·rian
man·ci·ple steward
Man·cu·nian native of
   Manchester
Man·daean
Man·dae·an·ism Iraqi sect
Man·da·lay Burmese city
man·da·mus (*plural*
   ·muses) legal term

Man·da·rin language
man·da·rin official; fruit;
   duck
man·da·tary *variant spelling*
   of mandatory (*noun*)
man·date
man·da·to·ri·ly
man·da·tory obligatory
man·da·tory (*or* ·tary;
   plural ·tories *or* ·taries)
   mandate holder
Man·de (*plural* ·de *or*
   ·des) language group
man·di Indian market
man·di·ble
man·dibu·lar
man·dir Hindu temple
man·do·la mandolin
man·do·lin (*or* ·line)
man·do·lin·ist
man·dor·la art term
man·drake (*or*
   man·drago·ra)
man·drel (*or* ·dril) spindle
man·drill monkey
man·du·cate eat or chew
mane
man-eater
maned
ma·nège (*or* ·nege) riding
   school; *compare* ménage
ma·nes Roman deities
ma·neu·ver *US spelling of*
   manoeuvre
man·ful
man·ful·ly
man·ful·ness
man·ga·bey monkey
Man·ga·lore Indian port
man·ga·nate
man·ga·nese
man·gan·ic
Man·gan·in (*Trademark*)
man·ga·nite mineral
man·ga·nous
mange skin disease
man·gel-wur·zel (*or*
   ·gold-)
man·ger
mange-tout pea
man·gi·ly
man·gi·ness
man·gle
man·gler

man·go (*plural* ·goes *or* ·gos)

man·go·nel war engine

man·go·steen fruit

man·grove

man·gy (*or* ·gey; ·gi·er, ·gi·est)

man·handle

Man·hat·tan

man·hole

man·hood

man·hour

man·hunt

man·hunter

ma·nia

ma·ni·ac

ma·nia·cal

ma·nia·cal·ly

man·ic

manic-depres·sive

Mani·chae·ism (*or* ·che·) religion

Mani·chee

ma·ni·cot·ti stuffed noodles

mani·cure

mani·cur·ist

mani·fest

mani·fest·able

mani·fes·ta·tion

mani·fes·ta·tion·al

mani·fes·to (*plural* ·toes *or* ·tos)

mani·fold

mani·fold·er

mani·kin (*or* mana·kin, man·ni·kin) dwarf; *compare* manakin; mannequin

Ma·nila Philippine port

ma·nil·la African currency

ma·nille card trump

mani·oc (*or* manio·ca) plant

mani·ple

ma·nipu·labil·ity

ma·nipu·lar

ma·nipu·lat·able (*or* ·lable)

ma·nipu·late

ma·nipu·la·tion

ma·nipu·la·tive

ma·nipu·la·tor

ma·nipu·la·tory

Ma·ni·pur Indian region

Ma·ni·sa Turkish city

Mani·to·ba Canadian province

mani·tou (*or* ·tu; *plural* ·tous, tou, *or* ·tus, ·tu) American Indian spirit

Mani·tou·lin Canadian island

Mani·za·les Colombian city

man·kind

manky (manki·er, manki·est) *Scot* dirty

man·like

man·li·ness

man·ly (·li·er, ·li·est)

man-made

man·na celestial food; *compare* mana

manned

man·ne·quin model; *compare* manakin; manikin

man·ner

man·nered

man·ner·ism

man·ner·ist

man·ner·is·tic (*or* ·ti·cal)

man·ner·is·ti·cal·ly

man·ner·less

man·ner·less·ness

man·ner·li·ness

man·ner·ly

Mann·heim West German city

man·nish

man·nish·ness

man·nit·ic

man·ni·tol plant compound

man·nose sugar

ma·noeu·vrabil·ity (*US* ·neu·)

ma·noeu·vrable (*US* ·neu·)

ma·noeu·vre (*US* ·neu·ver)

ma·noeu·vrer (*US* ·neu·ver·er)

man-of-war (*plural* men-)

ma·nom·eter

mano·met·ric (*or* ·ri·cal)

mano·met·ri·cal·ly

ma·nom·etry

man·or

ma·no·rial

man·power

man·qué unfulfilled

man·rope ship railing

man·sard roof

manse

man·servant (*plural* men·servants)

Mans·field Nottinghamshire town

man·sion

man-sized

man·slaughter

man·sue·tude gentleness

man·ta fish; fabric

man·teau (*plural* ·teaus *or* ·teaux) cloak

man·tel (*or* ·tle) frame round fireplace; *compare* mantle

man·tel·et woman's mantle

man·tel·let·ta vestment

mantel·piece

mantel·shelf (*plural* ·shelves)

mantel·tree lintel over fireplace

man·tic of prophecy

man·ti·cal·ly

man·til·la Spanish scarf

man·tis (*plural* ·tises *or* ·tes)

man·tis·sa maths term

man·tle cloak; *compare* mantle

man·tling

man·tra Hindu psalm

man·trap

Man·tua Italian city

man·tua gown

manu·al

manu·al·ly

ma·nu·brial

ma·nu·brium (*plural* ·bria *or* ·briums) zoology term

manu·fac·tory (*plural* ·tories)

manu·fac·tur·able

manu·fac·tur·al

manu·fac·ture

manu·fac·tur·er

manu·fac·tur·ing

ma·nu·ka tree

Ma·nu·kau New Zealand city

manu·mis·sion

manu·mit (·mit·ting, ·mit·ted) free from slavery

ma·nure

ma·nur·er
ma·nus (*plural* ·nus) hand
manu·script
Manx
Manx·man (*plural* ·men)
many
many·plies cow's stomach
many-sided
many-sided·ness
man·za·nil·la sherry
Mao·ism
Mao·ist
Mao·ri (*plural* ·ris *or* ·ri)
map (map·ping, **mapped**)
ma·ple
map·pable
Ma·pu·to capital of
   Mozambique
ma·quette sculptor's model
Ma·quis French Resistance
ma·quis (*plural* ·quis)
   shrubby vegetation
mar (mar·ring, **marred**)
mara rodent
mara·bou stork
mara·bout Muslim holy
   man
ma·ra·bun·ta wasp
ma·raca percussion
   instrument
Mara·cai·bo Venezuelan
   port and lake
Ma·ra·cay Venezuelan city
mar·ag·ing steel
Ma·ra·nhão Brazilian state
ma·ras·ca cherry tree
mara·schi·no (*plural* ·nos)
   liqueur; cherry
ma·ras·mic
ma·ras·mus
Ma·ra·tha (*or* Mah·rat·ta)
   Indian people
Ma·ra·thi (*or* Mah·rat·ti)
Mara·thon Greek plain
mara·thon race
ma·raud
ma·raud·er
mara·vedi (*plural* ·vedis)
   coin
mar·ble
mar·bled
mar·bler
mar·bling
mar·bly

Mar·burg West German
   city
marc brandy
mar·ca·site mineral
mar·ca·siti·cal
mar·cel (·cel·ling, ·celled)
   hair style
mar·ces·cence
mar·ces·cent botany term
March month; *compare*
   Marche
march
Marche former French
   province; *compare* **March**
march·er
Marches border country
mar·che·sa (*plural* ·se)
   wife of marchese
mar·che·se (*plural* ·si)
   Italian nobleman
mar·chion·ess wife of
   marquis or marquess
Mar del Pla·ta Argentine
   city
Mar·di Gras Shrove
   Tuesday
mardy *Dialect* spoilt or
   irritable
mare (*plural* mares)
   female horse
mare (*plural* ma·ria) lunar
   plain
mare clau·sum legal term
mare li·be·rum legal term
ma·rem·ma (*plural* ·me)
   marsh
mare's-tail cloud; plant
marg (*or* marge) *short for*
   margarine
mar·gar·ic (*or* ·it·ic) of
   pearl
mar·ga·rine (*or* ·rin)
mar·ga·ri·ta cocktail
mar·ga·rite mineral;
   compare marguerite
Mar·gate
Mar·gaux wine
mar·gay animal
mar·gin
mar·gin·al
mar·gi·na·lia
mar·gin·al·ity
mar·gin·al·ly
mar·gin·ate
mar·gina·tion
mar·gra·vate

mar·grave German
   nobleman
mar·gra·vine wife of
   margrave
mar·gue·rite flower;
   compare margarite
mari·achi Mexican street
   musicians
Mar·ian of the Virgin Mary
Ma·ria·nao Cuban city
Ma·ri·bor Yugoslav city
mari·cul·ture
mari·gold
ma·ri·jua·na (*or* ·hua·)
ma·rim·ba percussion
   instrument
ma·ri·na
mari·nade (*noun*, *verb*)
mari·nate (*verb*)
mari·na·tion
Ma·rin·du·que Philippine
   island
ma·rine
Mari·ner US space probe
mari·ner seaman
Mari·ola·try (*or* Mary·)
   veneration of Virgin Mary
Mari·ol·ogy (*or* Mary·)
mari·on·ette
mari·po·sa plant
Mar·ist member of
   Christian sect
mar·it·age feudal right
mari·tal
mari·time
Mari·time Alps; Provinces
Mari·tim·er
mar·jo·ram
mark
mark·down (*noun*)
marked
mark·ed·ly
mark·ed·ness
mark·er
mar·ket
mar·ket·abil·ity (*or*
   ·able·ness)
mar·ket·able
mar·ket·ably
mar·ket·er
mar·ket·ing
market·place
mar·khor (*or* ·khoor;
   plural ·khors, ·khor *or*
   ·khoors, ·khoor) goat

mark·ing

mark·ka (*plural* ·kaa)
Finnish currency

marks·man (*plural* ·men)

marks·man·ship

marks·woman (*plural*
·women)

mark-up (*noun*)

marl

mar·la·cious (*or* marly)

Marl·bor·ough

mar·lin (*plural* ·lin *or*
·lins) fish

mar·line (*or* ·lin, ·ling)
nautical rope

mar·line·spike (*or* ·lin·,
·ling·)

mar·lite (*or* marl·stone)

marly

mar·ma·lade

Mar·ma·ra (*or* ·mo·)
Turkish sea

Mar·mite (*Trademark*)
food

mar·mite cooking pot

mar·mo·real (*or* ·rean) of
marble

mar·mo·set

mar·mot animal

Marne French river

maro·cain fabric

Maro·nite Syrian Christian

ma·roon

ma·rooned

maro·quin leather

Marprelate tracts

marque brand of car

mar·quee

mar·quess British nobleman

mar·quess·ate

mar·que·try (*or*
·que·te·rie; *plural* ·tries
or ·ries)

mar·quis (*plural* ·quises
or ·quis) foreign
nobleman

mar·quis·ate

mar·quise gemstone; wife of
marquis

mar·qui·sette fabric

Mar·ra·kech (*or* ·kesh)
Moroccan city

mar·ram grass

Mar·ra·no (*plural* ·nos)
Iberian Jew

marred

mar·rer

mar·riage

mar·riage·abil·ity (*or*
·able·ness)

mar·riage·able

mar·ried

mar·ri·er

mar·ring

mar·ron chestnut

mar·ron gla·cé (*plural*
mar·rons gla·cés) glazed
chestnut

mar·row

marrow·bone

marrow·fat pea

mar·ry (·ries, ·ry·ing,
·ried)

Mars

Mar·sa·la Sicilian port;
wine

Mar·seil·laise French
national anthem

Mar·seille (*or* ·seilles)
French port

mar·seille (*or* ·seilles)
fabric

marsh

mar·shal (·shal·ling,
·shalled; *US* ·shal·ling,
·shaled)

mar·shal·cy (*or* ·shal·ship)

mar·shal·ler (*US* ·shal·er)

Mar·shal·sea former prison

marshi·ness

marsh·land

marsh·mal·low sweet

marsh mal·low plant

marshy (marshi·er,
marshi·est)

mar·su·pial

mar·su·pia·lian (*or*
·su·pian)

mar·su·pium (*plural* ·pia)
pouch

mart

mar·ta·gon lily

mar·tel·la·to (*or* ·lan·do)
music term

Mar·tel·lo tower

mar·ten (*plural* ·tens *or*
·ten) mammal; *compare*
martin

mar·ten·site metallurgy
term

mar·ten·sit·ic

mar·tial

mar·tial·ism

mar·tial·ist

mar·tial·ly

Mar·tian

mar·tin bird; *compare*
marten

mar·ti·net

mar·ti·net·ish

mar·ti·net·ism

mar·tin·gale

Mar·ti·ni (*Trademark*)
vermouth

mar·ti·ni (*plural* ·nis)
cocktail

Mar·ti·ni·can

Mar·ti·nique

Mar·tin·mas

mart·let heraldic swallow

mar·tyr

mar·tyr·dom

mar·tyr·ize (*or* ·ise)

mar·tyri·za·tion (*or*
·sa·tion)

mar·tyro·logi·cal (*or*
·log·ic)

mar·tyr·olo·gist

mar·tyr·ol·ogy (*plural*
·ogies)

mar·tyry (*plural* ·tyries)
martyr's shrine

mar·vel (·vel·ling, ·veled;
US ·vel·ing, ·veled)

mar·vel·lous (*US*
·vel·ous)

mar·vel·ment

Marx·ian

Marxi·an·ism

Marx·ism

Marxism-Leninism

Marx·ist

Marxist-Leninist

Mary·land

mar·zi·pan

Ma·sai (*plural* ·sais *or*
·sai) African people

Ma·san Korean port

Mas·ba·te Philippine island

mas·cara

mas·cle heraldic term

mas·con lunar region

mas·cot

mas·cu·line

mas·cu·lin·ity (*or*
·line·ness)

mas·cu·li·ni·za·tion (*or* ·sa·tion)

mas·cu·lin·ize (*or* ·ise)

ma·ser microwave laser; *compare* mazer

Ma·se·ru capital of Lesotho

mash

mash·er

Mash·had (*or* Me·shed) Iranian city

mashie (*or* mashy; *plural* mashies) golf club

mas·jid (*or* mus·) mosque

mask face covering, etc.; *variant spelling of* masque

mas·ka·nonge (*or* ·ki·) *variants of* muskellunge

masked

mask·er

maso·chism

maso·chist

maso·chis·tic

Ma·son freemason

ma·son stone worker

Mason-Dixon Line

Ma·son·ic

ma·son·ic

ma·soni·cal·ly

ma·son·ry (*plural* ·ries)

Ma·so·ra (*or* Ma·so·rah, Mas·so·ra, Mas·so·rah) Hebrew text

Maso·rete (*or* Mas·so·rete, Maso·rite) Hebrew scholar

masque (*or* mask) entertainment; *compare* mask

mas·quer (*or* mask·er)

mas·quer·ade

mas·quer·ad·er

Mass church service

mass

Mas·sa·chu·set (*or* ·setts; *plural* ·sets, ·set, *or* ·setts) American Indian

Mas·sa·chu·setts US state

mas·sa·cre

mas·sa·crer

mas·sage

mas·sag·er (*or* ·ist)

mas·sa·sau·ga snake

mas·sé billiards stroke

mass·edly

mas·se·ter muscle

mas·se·ter·ic

mas·seur (*fem* ·seuse)

mas·si·cot mineral

mas·sif landform; *compare* massive

Mas·sif Cen·tral French plateau

mas·sive huge; *compare* massif

mas·sive·ness (*or* ·siv·ity)

Mas·so·ra (*or* ·rah) *variant spellings of* Masora

mas·so·thera·peu·tic

mas·so·thera·pist

mas·so·thera·py massage

mass-produce

mass-produc·er

mass-pro·duc·tion

massy (massi·er, massi·est) massive

mast

mas·ta·ba (*or* ·bah) pyramid prototype

mas·tec·to·my (*plural* ·mies)

mas·ter

master-at-arms (*plural* masters-)

mas·ter·dom

mas·ter·ful

mas·ter·ful·ly

mas·ter·ful·ness

mas·ter·hood

mas·ter·li·ness

mas·ter·ly

master·mind

master·piece

mas·ter·ship

master·stroke

master·work

mas·tery (*plural* ·teries)

mast·head

mas·tic resin

mas·ti·cable chewable

mas·ti·cate

mas·ti·ca·tion

mas·ti·ca·tor

mas·ti·ca·tory (*plural* ·tories)

mas·tiff

mas·ti·gopho·ran (*or* ·go·phore) protozoan

mas·ti·tis breast inflammation

mas·to·don extinct elephant

mas·toid ear bone

mas·toid·ec·to·my (*plural* ·mies)

mas·toid·itis ear inflammation

mas·tur·bate

mas·tur·ba·tion

mas·tur·ba·tor

Ma·su·ria Polish region

Ma·su·rian

mat (mat·ting, mat·ted) floor covering; tangle; *compare* matte

mat (*or* matt, matte; mat·ting, mat·ted) lacking gloss; *compare* matte

Mata·be·le (*plural* ·les *or* ·le) African people

Mata·be·le·land

Ma·ta·di Zaïrian port

mata·dor

Mata·mo·ros Mexican port

Mata·pan Greek cape

match

match·board

match·box

match·less

match·less·ness

match·maker

match·mark

match·stick

match·wood

mate

maté (*or* mate) tea

matelas·sé embossed

mate·lot (*or* ·lo, ·low) *Slang* sailor

mat·elote (*or* ·elotte) fish stew

ma·ter *Slang* mother

ma·ter·fa·mili·as

ma·terial

ma·teri·al·ism

ma·teri·al·ist

ma·teri·al·is·tic

ma·teri·al·ity (*plural* ·ities)

ma·teri·ali·za·tion (*or* ·sa·tion)

ma·teri·al·ize (*or* ·ise)

ma·teri·al·iz·er (*or* ·is·er)

ma·teri·al·ly

ma·teria medi·ca study of drugs

ma·teri·el (or ·**téri·**) materials and equipment
ma·ter·nal
ma·ter·nal·ism
ma·ter·nal·is·tic
ma·ter·nal·ly
ma·ter·nity
matey (**mati·er, mati·est**)
matey·ness (or **mati·ness**)
math·emati·cal (or ·**emat·ic**)
math·emati·cal·ly
math·ema·ti·cian
math·emat·ics
Ma·thu·ra Indian city
mati·er
mati·est
Ma·til·da Austral bushman's swag
mat·in (or **mat·tin, mat·in·al**) of matins
mati·née
mati·ness variant spelling of mateyness
mat·ins (or **mat·tins**)
Mat·lock Derbyshire town
Mato Gros·so (or **Mat·to Gros·so**) Brazilian plateau
ma·tri·arch
ma·tri·ar·chal (or ·**chic**)
ma·tri·ar·chate
ma·tri·ar·chy (plural ·**chies**)
ma·tri·ces plural of matrix
mat·ri·cid·al
mat·ri·cide
mat·ri·cli·nous (or **mat·ro·cli·nous, mat·ro·cli·nal**) biology term
ma·tricu·lant
ma·tricu·late
ma·tricu·la·tion
ma·tricu·la·tor
mat·ri·lin·eal
mat·ri·lin·eal·ly
mat·ri·lo·cal living with wife's family
mat·ri·lo·cal·ity
mat·ri·mo·nial
mat·ri·mo·nial·ly
mat·ri·mo·ny (plural ·**nies**)
ma·trix (plural ·**tri·ces**)

mat·ro·cli·nous (or ·**nal**) variants of matriclinous
ma·tron
ma·tron·age
ma·tron·al
ma·tron·li·ness
ma·tron·ly
mat·ro·nym·ic variant spelling of metronymic
Ma·tsu·ya·ma Japanese port
matt variant spelling of mat
mat·ta·more subterranean storehouse
matte smelting material; variant spelling of mat
mat·ted
mat·ter
Mat·ter·horn
matter-of-fact (adj)
mat·ting
mat·tock agricultural tool
mat·tress
matu·rate
matu·ra·tion
matu·ra·tion·al
ma·tura·tive
ma·ture
ma·tur·ity
ma·tu·ti·nal of morning
(maty) incorrect spelling of matey
mat·zo (or ·**zoh**; plural ·**zos, ·zohs,** or ·**zoth**) Jewish biscuit
mat·zoon (or **mad·**) fermented milk
maud plaid shawl
maud·lin
maud·lin·ism
maud·lin·ness
maul
maul·er
maul·stick (or **mahl·**) artist's stick
Mau Mau (plural **Mau Maus** or **Mau Mau**) Kenyan terrorist
Mau·na Kea Hawaiian volcano
Mau·na Loa Hawaiian volcano
maund unit of weight
maun·der behave aimlessly
maun·der·er
Maun·dy money; Thursday

Mau·rist French monk
Mau·ri·ta·nia African republic
Mau·ri·ta·nian
Mau·ri·tian
Mau·ri·tius island state
Mau·ser (Trademark) gun
mau·so·lean
mau·so·leum (plural ·**leums** or ·**lea**)
mauve
mav·er·ick
ma·vis Dialect thrush
ma·vour·neen Irish term of endearment
maw
mawk·ish
mawk·ish·ness
maw·sie Scot jersey
maxi (plural **maxis**) long garment
max·il·la (plural ·**lae**) upper jaw
max·il·lar (or ·**lary**)
max·il·li·ped (or ·**pede**) zoology term
max·il·li·ped·ary
max·im
maxi·ma (plural of maximum)
maxi·mal
Maxi·mal·ist Soviet radical
maxi·mal·ist activist
maxi·mal·ly
maxi·min maths term
maxi·mi·za·tion (or ·**sa·tion**)
max·im·ize (or ·**ise**)
maxi·miz·er (or ·**mis·er**)
maxi·mum (plural ·**mums** or ·**ma**)
maxi·mus bell-ringing term
maxi·sin·gle
ma·xixe dance
max·well unit
May
may (might)
Maya (plural **Maya** or **Mayas**) American Indian
maya Hindu concept
Ma·yan
may·be (adv)
May·day signal
May Day 1 May

Ma·yenne French
department
May·fair
May·flower ship
may·flower plant
may·fly (*plural* **·flies**)
may·hem (*or* **mai·**)
May·ing May Day
celebration
mayn't may not
Mayo Irish county
Ma·yon Philippine volcano
may·on·naise
mayor
mayor·al
mayor·al·ty (*plural* **·ties**)
mayor·ess
mayor·ship
may·pole
may·weed
Ma·zat·lán Mexican port
Maz·da·ism (*or*
Maz·deism) religion
maze confusing network;
compare **maize**
ma·zer (*or* **·zard,**
maz·zard) bowl; *compare*
maser
ma·zi·ly
ma·zi·ness
ma·zu·ma *US* money
ma·zur·ka (*or* **·zour·**)
mazy (**·zi·er, ·zi·est**)
perplexing
maz·zard (*or* **ma·zard**)
variants of **mazer**
Mba·ba·ne capital of
Swaziland
Mbu·ji·ma·yi Zaïrian city
McCar·thy·ism
anticommunism
McCoy *Slang* genuine thing
McNaughten Rules (*or*
McNaghten Rules)
me pronoun; *variant spelling*
of **mi**
mea cul·pa *Latin* my fault
mead drink; *compare* **meed**
mead·ow
meadow·lark
meadow·sweet
mea·gre (*US* **·ger**)
meal
meal·worm
mealy (**meali·er,**
meali·est)

mealy-mouthed
mean (**mean·ing, meant**)
intend; miserly; midpoint;
compare **mien**
me·ander
me·ander·er
me·ander·ing·ly
me·androus
mean·ing
mean·ing·ful
mean·ing·ful·ly
mean·ing·ful·ness
mean·ing·less
mean·ing·less·ness
mean·ness
means (*plural* **means**)
method
meant
mean·time
mean·while
meany (*plural* **meanies**)
Slang miserly person
mea·sled
mea·sles
mea·sly (**·sli·er, ·sli·est**)
meas·ur·abil·ity (*or*
·able·ness)
meas·ur·able
meas·ur·ably
meas·ure
meas·ured
meas·ured·ly
meas·ure·less
meas·ure·ment
meas·ur·er
meas·ur·ing
meat
meat·ball
Meath Irish county
meati·ly
meati·ness
mea·tus (*plural* **·tuses** *or*
·tus) anatomy term
meaty (**meati·er,**
meati·est)
Mec·ca
Mec·ca·no (*Trademark*)
me·chan·ic
me·chani·cal
me·chani·cal·ly
mecha·ni·cian
me·chan·ics
mecha·nism
mecha·nist
mecha·nis·tic

mecha·nis·ti·cal·ly
mecha·ni·za·tion (*or*
·sa·tion)
mecha·nize (*or* **·nise**)
mecha·niz·er (*or* **·nis·er**)
mecha·no·thera·py
Mech·elen (*or* **·lin**)
Belgian city
meck *Dialect* small coin
Meck·len·burg German
region
me·co·nium
Med short for **Mediterranean**
med·al (*verb* **·al·ling,**
·alled; *US* **·al·ing,**
·aled) award; *compare*
meddle
me·dal·lic
me·dal·lion
me·dal·lion·ist
med·al·list (*US* **·al·ist**)
Me·dan Indonesian city
med·dle interfere; *compare*
medal
med·dler interferer; *compare*
medlar
med·dle·some
med·dle·some·ness
med·dling·ly
Mede inhabitant of Media
Medea mythological
princess
Me·del·lín Colombian city
Me·dia ancient country
me·dia *plural of* **medium,**
esp. in communications
sense
me·dia (*plural* **·diae**)
anatomy and phonetics
term
me·dia·cy
me·di·aeval *variant spelling*
of **medieval**
me·dial
me·dial·ly
Me·dian of Medes or Media
me·dian
me·di·ant music term
me·di·as·ti·nal
me·di·as·ti·num (*plural*
·na) anatomy term
me·di·ate
me·dia·tion
me·dia·tive (*or* **·tory,**
·to·rial)

me·dia·ti·za·tion (*or* ·sa·tion)

me·dia·tize (*or* ·tise) annex a state

me·dia·tor

me·dia·to·ri·al·ly

me·dia·trix (*or* ·trice)

med·ic *Slang* doctor; *US* spelling of medick

medi·cable

medi·ca·bly

Medi·caid US health assistance

medi·cal

medi·cal·ly

me·dica·ment

medi·ca·men·tal (*or* ·tary)

Medi·care US health insurance

medi·cate

medi·ca·tion

medi·ca·tive

me·dici·nal

me·dici·nal·ly

medi·cine

med·ick (*US* ·ic) plant; *compare* medic

medi·co (*plural* ·cos)

me·di·eval (*or* ·aeval)

me·di·eval·ism (*or* ·aeval·)

me·di·eval·ist (*or* ·aeval·)

me·di·eval·is·tic (*or* ·aeval·)

me·di·eval·ly (*or* ·aeval·)

Me·di·na Saudi Arabian city

me·dio·cre

me·di·oc·ri·ty (*plural* ·rities)

medi·tate

medi·tat·ing·ly

medi·ta·tion

medi·ta·tive

medi·ta·tive·ness

medi·ta·tor

Medi·ter·ra·nean

me·dium (*plural* ·dia *or* ·diums)

med·lar fruit; *compare* meddler

med·ley

Mé·doc French region; wine

me·dul·la (*plural* ·las *or* ·lae)

me·dul·lary (*or* ·lar)

med·ul·lat·ed

Medusa mythological character

me·du·sa (*plural* ·sas *or* ·sae) jellyfish

me·du·san

me·du·soid

Med·way

mee Malaysian noodles

meed *Archaic* reward; *compare* mead

meek

meek·ly

meek·ness

meer·kat mongoose

meer·schaum

Mee·rut Indian city

meet (meet·ing, met) come together; *compare* mete

meet (*adj*) *Archaic* fitting; *compare* mete

meet·er

meet·ing

mega·cephal·ic *variant of* macrocephalic

mega·cepha·ly *variant of* macrocephaly

mega·cy·cle

mega·death

mega·ga·mete *variant of* macrogamete

mega·lith

mega·lith·ic

mega·lo·blast blood cell

mega·lo·blast·ic

mega·lo·car·dia abnormally large heart

mega·lo·cephal·ic *variant of* macrocephalic

mega·lo·cepha·ly *variant of* macrocephaly

mega·lo·ma·nia

mega·lo·ma·ni·ac

mega·lo·ma·nia·cal

mega·lopo·lis

mega·lo·poli·tan

mega·lo·saur dinosaur

mega·phone

mega·phon·ic

mega·phoni·cal·ly

mega·pode bird

Mega·ra Greek town

mega·ron (*plural* ·ra) room

mega·spore botany term

mega·spor·ic

mega·spo·ro·phyll

me·gass (*or* ·gasse) paper

mega·there (*or* ·ther·ium; *plural* ·theres *or* ·ther·ia) extinct sloth

mega·ton

mega·volt

mega·watt

me·gil·lah (*plural* ·lahs *or* ·loth) Hebrew scroll

me·gilp (*or* ma·) oil-painting medium

meg·ohm

me·grim *Archaic* migraine

Mei·ji period in Japanese history

meio·sis (*plural* ·ses) cell division; rhetorical device; *compare* miosis

mei·ot·ic

mei·oti·cal·ly

Meis·sen East German town

Meis·ter·sing·er (*plural* ·er *or* ·ers)

Mek·nès Moroccan city

Me·kong Asian river

mel honey

mela·leu·ca shrub

mela·mine

mel·an·cho·lia

mel·an·cho·li·ac

mel·an·chol·ic

mel·an·choli·cal·ly

mel·an·choli·ly

mel·an·choli·ness

mel·an·choly (*plural* ·cholies)

Mela·nesia

Mela·nesian

mé·lange *French* mixture

me·lan·ic

mela·nin pigment

mela·nism dark pigmentation; *variant of* melanosis

mela·nis·tic

mela·nite gemstone

mela·no·cyte melanin cell

mela·noid

mela·no·ma (*plural* ·mas *or* ·ma·ta) tumour

mela·no·sis (*or* ·nism) skin disease

mela·nos·ity

mela·not·ic
mela·nous
mela·phyre rock
mela·to·nin hormone
Melba sauce; toast
Mel·bourne
Mel·bur·nian
Mel·chite Eastern Church member
meld
me·lee (or mê·lée)
me·lia·ceous botany term
mel·ic to be sung
meli·lot plant
meli·nite explosive
me·lio·rate ameliorate
me·lio·ra·tion
me·lio·rism
me·lis·ma (plural ·ma·ta or ·mas) musical term
mel·is·mat·ic
Me·li·to·pol Soviet city
mel·lif·er·ous (or ·lif·ic) producing honey
mel·lif·lu·ous (or ·lu·ent) sweet-sounding
mel·lif·lu·ous·ness (or ·lu·ence)
mel·lo·phone brass instrument
mel·low
mel·low·ness
me·lo·deon accordion
me·lod·ic
me·lodi·cal·ly
me·lo·dious
me·lo·di·ous·ness
melo·dist
melo·dize (or ·dise)
melo·diz·er (or ·dis·er)
melo·dra·ma
melo·dra·mat·ic
melo·dra·mati·cal·ly
melo·drama·tist
melo·drama·tize (or ·tise)
melo·dy (plural ·dies)
mel·oid beetle
mel·on
Me·los Greek island
melt (melt·ing, melt·ed, melt·ed or mol·ten)
melt·abil·ity
melt·able
melt·age
melt·down

melt·er
melt·ing·ly
mel·ton fabric
Mel·ton Mow·bray
melt·water
Mem·ber an MP
mem·ber
mem·ber·ship
mem·brane
mem·bra·nous (or ·bra·na·ceous)
me·men·to (plural ·tos or ·toes)
me·men·to mori
memo (plural memos)
mem·oir
memo·ra·bilia (sing. ·rabi·le)
memo·rabil·ity (or ·rable·ness)
memo·rable
memo·rably
memo·ran·dum (plural ·dums or ·da)
me·mo·rial
me·mo·ri·al·ist
me·mo·ri·ali·za·tion (or ·sa·tion)
me·mo·ri·al·ize (or ·ise)
me·mo·ri·al·iz·er (or ·is·er)
memo·riz·able (or ·ris·able)
memo·ri·za·tion (or ·sa·tion)
memo·rize (or ·rise)
memo·riz·er (or ·ris·er)
memo·ry (plural ·ries)
Mem·phis
Mem·phre·ma·gog North American lake
mem·sa·hib
men
men·ace
men·ac·er
men·ac·ing·ly
me·nad variant spelling of maenad
mena·di·one vitamin
Me·na·do (or Ma·) Indonesian port
mé·nage household; compare manège
mé·nage à trois (plural mé·nage à trois)
me·nag·erie

Menai Strait
Me·nam Thai river
mena·qui·none vitamin
men·ar·che start of menstruation
men·ar·cheal (or ·chial)
mend
mend·able
men·da·cious
men·da·cious·ness
men·dac·ity (plural ·ities) untruthfulness; compare mendicancy
men·de·levium chemical element
Men·de·lian
Men·del·ism (or ·de·li·an·ism) science of heredity
mend·er
men·di·can·cy (or men·dic·ity) begging; compare mendacity
men·di·cant
mend·ing
Men·dips
Men·do·za Argentine city
Menelaus mythological king
men·folk
men·ha·den (plural ·den) fish
men·hir Bronze Age stone
me·nial
me·nial·ly
me·nin·geal
me·nin·ges (sing. me·ninx) brain membranes
men·in·git·ic
men·in·gi·tis
me·nis·coid
me·nis·cus (plural ·ci or ·cuses)
meni·sper·ma·ceous botany term
meno musical term
me·nol·ogy (plural ·ogies) ecclesiastical calendar
meno·pau·sal (or ·sic)
meno·pause
me·no·rah Jewish candelabrum
men·or·rha·gia excessive menstruation
men·or·rhag·ic

Men·sa constellation
men·ses (*plural* ·ses)
    menstruation
Men·she·vik Russian
    socialist
mens rea legal term
men·strual
men·stru·ate
men·strua·tion
men·struous
men·struum (*plural*
    ·struums *or* ·strua)
    solvent
men·sur·able
men·su·ral
men·su·ra·tion measuring;
    compare menstruation
men·su·ra·tion·al
men·su·ra·tive
mens·wear
men·tal
men·tal·ism philosophy
    term
men·tal·is·tic
men·tal·is·ti·cal·ly
men·tal·ity (*plural* ·ities)
men·tal·ly
men·tha·ceous botany term
men·thol
men·tho·la·ted
men·tion
men·tion·able
men·tion·er
Men·ton French town
men·tor
men·to·rial
menu
meow (*or* miaou, miaow)
mepa·crine drug
Meph·is·to·phelean (*or*
    ·phelian)
Mephistopheles (*or*
    Mephisto)
me·phit·ic (*or* ·phiti·cal)
    poisonous
me·phiti·cal·ly
me·phi·tis foul stench
me·pro·ba·mate
    tranquillizer
mer·bro·min antiseptic
mer·can·tile
mer·can·til·ism
mer·can·til·ist
mer·cap·tan chemical
    compound

mer·cap·tide chemical
    compound
mer·cap·to·pu·rine drug
mer·ce·nari·ly
mer·ce·nari·ness
mer·ce·nary (*plural*
    ·naries)
mer·cer
mer·ceri·za·tion (*or*
    ·sa·tion)
mer·cer·ize (*or* ·ise)
mer·chan·dise
mer·chan·dis·er
mer·chant
mer·chant·able
mer·chant·man (*plural*
    ·men) ship
Mer·cia Anglo-Saxon
    kingdom
Mer·cian
mer·ci·ful
mer·ci·ful·ly
mer·ci·ful·ness
mer·ci·less
mer·ci·less·ness
mer·cu·rate treat with
    mercury
mer·cu·ra·tion
mer·cu·rial
mer·cu·ri·al·ism mercury
    poisoning
mer·cu·ri·ali·za·tion (*or*
    ·sa·tion)
mer·cu·ri·al·ize (*or* ·ise)
mer·cu·rial·ly
mer·cu·ri·al·ness (*or*
    ·ri·al·ity)
mer·cu·ric
Mer·cu·ro·chrome
    (*Trademark*)
mer·cu·rous
Mer·cu·ry planet
Mercury Roman god
mer·cu·ry (*or* ·ries)
mer·cy (*plural* ·cies)
mere
mere·ly
me·ren·gue dance
mer·etri·cious insincere;
    compare meritorious
mer·gan·ser (*plural* ·sers
    or ·ser) duck
merge
mer·gence
mer·ger

me·rid·ian
me·ridio·nal
me·ringue
me·ri·no (*plural* ·nos)
Meri·on·eth·shire former
    Welsh county
me·ri·stem plant tissue
meri·ste·mat·ic
me·ris·tic biology term
mer·it
mer·it·ed·ly
mer·it·less
meri·toc·ra·cy (*plural*
    ·cies)
meri·to·ri·ous
    praiseworthy; *compare*
    meretricious
mer·kin pubic wig
merle *Scot* blackbird
mer·lin falcon
mer·lon part of battlement
mer·maid
mer·man (*plural* ·men)
mero·blas·tic biology term
mero·blas·ti·cal·ly
mero·crine physiology term
Meroë ancient Sudanese
    city
mero·plank·ton
Mero·vin·gian Frankish
    dynasty
mero·zo·ite biology term
mer·ri·ly
mer·ri·ment
mer·ri·ness
mer·ry (·ri·er, ·ri·est)
merry-go-round
merry·maker
merry·making
merry·thought wishbone
Merse Scottish area
Mer·se·burg East German
    city
Mer·sey
Mer·sey·side
Mer·sin Turkish port
Mer·thyr Tyd·fil
Mer·ton London borough
mesa tableland
mé·sal·li·ance *French*
    unsuitable marriage;
    compare misalliance
mes·arch botany term
Mesa Verde Colorado
    plateau

mes·cal cactus; alcohol
mes·ca·line (*or* ·lin) drug
mes·dames *plural of*
madame
mes·de·moi·selles *plural of*
mademoiselle
mes·em·bry·an·themum
plant
mes·en·cephal·ic
mes·en·cepha·lon part of
brain
mes·en·chy·mal (*or*
·chyma·tous)
mes·en·chyme embryology
term
mes·en·ter·ic
mes·en·teri·tis
mes·en·ter·on (*plural*
·tera) zoology term
mes·en·ter·on·ic
mes·en·tery (*plural*
·teries)
mesh
Meshach biblical character
Me·shed *variant spelling of*
Mashhad
meshy
me·sial anatomy term
me·sial·ly
me·sic ecology term; of a
meson
mesi·cal·ly
me·sity·lene chemical
compound
mes·mer·ic
mes·meri·cal·ly
mes·mer·ism
mes·mer·ist
mes·meri·za·tion (*or*
sa·tion)
mes·mer·ize (*or* ·ise)
mes·mer·iz·er (*or* ·is·er)
mesne legal term
meso·ben·thos
meso·blast embryonic tissue
meso·carp botany term
meso·ce·phal·ic
meso·ceph·aly
meso·crat·ic geology term
meso·derm
meso·der·mal (*or* ·mic)
meso·gas·tric
meso·gas·trium
meso·glea (*or* ·gloea)
me·sog·na·thism (*or* ·thy)

me·sog·na·thous
Meso·lith·ic archaeological
period
meso·morph
meso·mor·phic of muscular
build
meso·mor·phism
meso·mor·phous
meso·mor·phy
me·son elementary particle
meso·neph·ric
meso·neph·ros
meso·pause meteorology
term
meso·phyll
meso·phyl·lic (*or* ·lous)
meso·phyte
meso·phyt·ic
Meso·po·ta·mia
Meso·po·ta·mian
meso·sphere
meso·spher·ic
meso·thelial
meso·thelium
meso·tho·rac·ic
meso·tho·rax (*plural*
·raxes *or* ·races)
Meso·zo·ic geological
period
mes·quite (*or* ·quit) tree
mess
mes·sage
mes·sa·line fabric
Mes·sene ancient Greek
city
mes·sen·ger
Mes·senia Greek region
Mes·si·ah
mes·si·an·ic (*or* Mes·)
mes·sieurs *plural of*
monsieur
messi·ly
Mes·si·na Sicilian port
messi·ness
mess·mate
Messrs *plural of* Mr
mes·suage legal term
messy (messi·er,
messi·est)
mes·ter *Dialect* master
mes·ti·zo (*fem* ·za; *plural*
·zos *or* ·zoes, ·zas) one
of mixed parentage
mes·tra·nol synthetic
hormone

met
Meta Colombian river
meta·bol·ic
meta·boli·cal·ly
me·tabo·lism
me·tabo·lite
me·tabo·liz·abil·ity (*or*
·lis·abil·ity)
me·tabo·liz·able (*or*
·lis·able)
me·tabo·lize (*or* ·lise)
meta·car·pal
meta·car·pus (*plural* ·pi)
hand bones; *compare*
metatarsus
meta·cen·tre (*US* ·ter)
physics term
meta·cen·tric
meta·chro·mat·ic
meta·chro·ma·tism
meta·cin·nab·a·rite
mercury ore
meta·female genetics term
meta·ga·lac·tic
meta·gal·axy (*plural*
·axies)
met·age official measuring
of goods
meta·gen·esis
meta·ge·net·ic (*or* ·gen·ic)
meta·geneti·cal·ly
me·tag·na·thism
me·tag·na·thous
met·al (*verb* ·al·ling,
·alled; *US* ·al·ing,
·aled) substance; *compare*
mettle
meta·lan·guage
me·tal·lic
me·tal·li·cal·ly
met·al·lif·er·ous
met·al·line of metals
met·al·list (*US* ·al·ist)
met·al·li·za·tion (*or*
·sa·tion; *US*
met·ali·za·tion)
met·al·lize (*or* ·lise; *US*
·al·ize)
me·tal·lo·cene chemical
compound
met·al·log·ra·pher (*or*
·phist)
me·tal·lo·graph·ic
me·tal·lo·graphi·cal·ly
met·al·log·ra·phy
met·al·loid

met·al·loi·dal
met·al·lur·gic (*or* ·gi·cal)
met·al·lur·gi·cal·ly
met·al·lur·gist
met·al·lur·gy
metal·work
metal·worker
metal·working
meta·male genetics term
meta·math·emati·cal
meta·math·ema·ti·cian
meta·math·emat·ics
meta·mer chemistry term
me·tam·er·al
meta·mere zoology term
meta·mer·ic
meta·meri·cal·ly
me·tam·er·ism
meta·mor·phic (*or* ·phous)
meta·mor·phism geology term
meta·mor·phose
meta·mor·pho·sis (*plural* ·ses)
meta·neph·ros
meta·phase biology term
meta·phor
meta·phor·ic (*or* ·phori·cal)
meta·phori·cal·ly
meta·phori·cal·ness
meta·phos·phate
meta·phrase literal translation
meta·phrast
meta·phras·tic (*or* ·ti·cal)
meta·phras·ti·cal·ly
meta·phys·ic
Meta·physi·cal denoting poetic group
meta·physi·cal of metaphysics
meta·physi·cal·ly
meta·phy·si·cian (*or* ·physi·cist)
meta·phys·ics
meta·pla·sia
meta·plasm
meta·plas·mic
meta·psy·cho·logi·cal
meta·psy·chol·ogy
meta·so·ma·tism (*or* ·ma·to·sis) geology term
meta·sta·bil·ity

meta·sta·ble
me·tas·ta·sis (*plural* ·ses) medical term
me·tas·ta·size (*or* ·sise)
meta·stat·ic
meta·stati·cal·ly
meta·tar·sal
meta·tar·sus (*plural* ·si) foot bones; *compare* meta carpus
meta·theo·ry study of philosophy
meta·therian marsupial
me·tath·esis (*plural* ·eses) linguistics term
me·tath·esize (*or* ·esise)
meta·thet·ic (*or* ·theti·cal)
meta·tho·rac·ic
meta·tho·rax (*plural* ·raxes *or* ·races)
meta·xy·lem
meta·zo·an
meta·zo·ic
mete allot; *compare* meet
met·em·piri·cal (*or* ·pir·ic)
met·em·piri·cist
met·em·pir·ics
me·tem·psy·cho·sis (*plural* ·ses)
met·en·cephal·ic
met·en·cepha·lon (*plural* ·lons *or* ·la) embryology term
me·teor
me·teor·ic
me·teori·cal·ly
me·teor·ite
me·teor·it·ic
me·teoro·graph
me·teoro·graph·ic (*or* ·graphi·cal)
me·teor·oid
me·teoro·logi·cal (*or* ·log·ic)
me·teoro·logi·cal·ly
me·teor·olo·gist
me·teor·ol·ogy study of weather; *compare* metrology
me·ter instrument; *US spelling of* metre
met·es·trus *US spelling of* metoestrus
meth·ac·ry·late
metha·done (*or* ·don) drug

met·haemo·glo·bin (*US* ·hemo·)
me·thane
metha·nol
me·thinks
me·thio·nine amino acid
meth·od
me·thodi·cal (*or* ·thod·ic)
me·thodi·cal·ly
me·thodi·cal·ness
Meth·od·ism
Meth·od·ist
Meth·od·is·ti·cal·ly
meth·odi·za·tion (*or* ·sa·tion)
meth·od·ize (*or* ·ise)
meth·od·iz·er (*or* ·is·er)
meth·odo·logi·cal
meth·odo·logi·cal·ly
meth·od·olo·gist
meth·od·ol·ogy (*plural* ·ogies)
metho·trex·ate drug
me·thought
meth·ox·ide
Me·thu·se·lah
me·thyl
meth·yl·al chemical compound
me·thyla·mine
meth·yl·ate
meth·yla·tion
meth·yla·tor
me·thyl·do·pa
meth·yl·ene
me·thyl·ic
me·thyl·naph·tha·lene
met·ic ancient Greek alien
me·ticu·lous
me·ticu·lous·ness (*or* ·los·ity)
mé·ti·er profession
Mé·tis (*or* ·tif; *plural* ·tis *or* ·tifs) one of mixed parentage
met·oes·trus (*US* ·es·)
me·tol chemical compound
Me·ton·ic cy·cle
meto·nym
meto·nymi·cal (*or* ·nym·ic)
me·tony·my (*plural* ·mies) linguistics term
met·ope architectural term
me·top·ic of the forehead

me·tral·gia womb pain
me·tre (*US* ·ter) unit;
 verse rhythm; *compare*
 meter
met·ric
met·ri·cal
met·ri·cal·ly
met·ri·cate
met·ri·ca·tion
met·rics use of poetic metre
met·ri·fi·er
met·ri·fy (·fies, ·fy·ing,
 ·fied)
met·rist
me·tri·tis inflammation of
 womb
met·ro (*or* mét·; *plural*
 ·ros)
met·ro·logi·cal
me·trolo·gist
me·trol·ogy (*plural*
 ·ogies) study of
 measurement; *compare*
 meteorology
met·ro·ni·da·zole
met·ro·nome
met·ro·nom·ic of a
 metronome
met·ro·nym·ic (*or* mat·)
 maternal name
me·tropo·lis (*plural* ·lises)
met·ro·poli·tan
met·ro·poli·tan·ism
me·tror·rha·gia abnormal
 bleeding from womb
met·tle courage; *compare*
 metal
met·tle·some
Metz French city
meu plant
meu·nière cookery term
Meurthe-et-Moselle
 French department
Meuse European river
mew
mewl
mewl·er
mews (*plural* mews)
Mexi·cali Mexican city
Mexi·can
Mexi·co
me·zereon shrub
me·zereum (*or* ·zereon)
 drug
Me·zières French town

me·zu·zah (*plural* ·zahs
 or ·zoth)
mez·za·nine
mez·zo (*plural* ·zos)
 musical term
mezzo-relievo (*or*
 -rilievo; *plural*
 -relievos *or* -rilievos)
mezzo-soprano (*plural*
 -sopranos)
mez·zo·tint
mi (*or* me) musical term
Mi·ami
miaou (*or* miaow) *variant*
 spellings of meow
mi·as·ma (*plural* ·ma·ta
 or ·mas)
mi·as·mal (*or* ·mat·ic,
 ·mati·cal, ·mic)
mica
mi·ca·ceous
Mi·caw·ber feckless person
Mi·caw·ber·ish
mice
mi·cel·lar
mi·celle (*or* ·cell, ·cel·la)
Mich·ael·mas
Michi·gan
Michi·gan·der
Michi·gan·ite
Mi·choa·cán Mexican state
mick·ery pool in river bed
mick·ey (*or* micky; *as in*
 take the mickey)
Mick·ey Finn
mick·le *Dialect* much
Mic·mac (*plural* ·macs *or*
 ·mac) American Indian
micro·analy·sis (*plural*
 ·ses)
micro·ana·lyst
micro·ana·lyt·ic (*or*
 ·lyti·cal)
micro·bal·ance
micro·baro·graph
mi·crobe
mi·cro·bial (*or* ·bic, ·bian)
micro·bio·logi·cal (*or*
 ·log·ic)
micro·bi·olo·gist
micro·bi·ol·ogy
micro·cephal·ic
micro·cepha·lous
micro·cepha·ly abnormally
 small skull
micro·chemi·cal

micro·chem·is·try
micro·chip
micro·cir·cuit
micro·cir·cuit·ry
micro·cli·mate
micro·cli·mat·ic
micro·cli·mati·cal·ly
micro·cli·ma·to·log·ic (*or*
 ·logi·cal)
micro·cli·ma·tolo·gist
micro·cli·ma·tol·ogy
micro·cline mineral
micro·coc·cus (*plural*
 ·coc·ci)
micro·com·put·er
micro·copy (*plural*
 ·copies) reduced
 photographic copy
micro·cosm (*or* ·cos·mos)
micro·cos·mic (*or*
 ·cos·mi·cal)
micro·crys·tal·line
micro·cyte blood cell
micro·cyt·ic
micro·detec·tor
micro·dont (*or* ·don·tous)
micro·dot
micro·eco·nom·ic
micro·eco·nom·ics
micro·elec·tron·ic
micro·elec·tron·ics
micro·fiche
micro·film
micro·gam·ete
micro·graph
mi·crog·ra·pher
micro·graph·ic
micro·graphi·cal·ly
mi·crog·ra·phy
micro·groove
micro·habi·tat
micro·light
micro·lith
micro·meteor·ite
micro·meteor·ol·ogy
mi·crom·eter measuring
 instrument
micro·metre (*US* ·meter)
 unit of length
micro·met·ric (*or* ·ri·cal)
mi·crom·etry
micro·minia·turi·za·tion
 (*or* ·sa·tion)
mi·cron (*plural* ·crons *or*
 ·cra) unit of length

Micro·nesia

Micro·nesian

micro·nu·cleus (*plural* ·clei)

micro·nu·tri·ent

micro·or·gan·ism

micro·palae·on·to·logi·cal (*or* ·log·ic; *US* ·pale·)

micro·palae·on·tolo·gist (*US* ·pale·)

micro·palae·on·tol·ogy (*US* ·pale·)

micro·para·site

micro·para·sit·ic

micro·phone

micro·phon·ic

micro·pho·to·graph

micro·pho·to·graph·ic

micro·pho·tog·ra·phy

micro·physi·cal

micro·phys·ics

micro·phyte microscopic plant

micro·phyt·ic

micro·print

micro·pro·ces·sor

micro·py·lar

micro·pyle biology term

micro·py·rom·eter

micro·read·er

micro·scope

micro·scop·ic (*or* ·scopi·cal)

micro·scopi·cal·ly

mi·cros·co·pist

mi·cros·co·py

micro·sec·ond

micro·seism

micro·seis·mic (*or* ·mi·cal)

micro·so·mal (*or* ·so·mial, ·so·mic)

micro·some biology term

micro·spo·ran·gium (*plural* ·gia)

micro·spore

micro·spor·ic (*or* ·spo·rous)

micro·sporo·phyll

micro·stoma·tous (*or* mi·cros·to·mous) having small mouth

micro·struc·ture

icro·tome cutting instrument

micro·tom·ic (*or* ·tomi·cal)

mi·croto·mist

mi·croto·my (*plural* ·mies)

micro·ton·al

micro·to·nal·ity

micro·tone musical term

micro·wave

mi·crurgy microscopy technique

mic·tu·rate

mic·tu·ri·tion

mid *Archaic* amid

mid- *prefix denoting* middle

mid·air

Midas legendary king

mid·brain

mid·day

Mid·del·burg Dutch city

mid·den

mid·dle

middle-aged

middle·brow

middle·browism

middle-class (*adj*)

middle-distance (*adj*)

middle·man (*plural* ·men)

Mid·dles·brough

Mid·dle·sex

Mid·dle·ton English town

middle·weight

mid·dling

mid·dy (*plural* ·dies) midshipman

mid·field

Mid·gard Norse mythological place

midge

midg·et

Mid Gla·mor·gan Welsh county

mid·gut

Mid·heav·en astrology term

Midi S France

midi skirt length

Mid·ian biblical character

Midi·an·ite

midi·nette Parisian salesgirl

mid·iron golf club

mid·land inland region

Mid·lands central England

mid·line

Mid·lo·thian former Scottish county

mid·most

mid·night

mid·off

mid·on

mid·point

mid·rash (*plural* ·ra·shim) Jewish biblical commentaries

mid·rib leaf vein

mid·riff

mid·sec·tion

mid·ship

mid·ship·man (*plural* ·men)

mid·ships

midst

mid·sum·mer

mid·term

mid·town *US* town centre

mid·way

mid·week

Mid·west (*or* Mid·dle West) US region

Mid·west·ern

Mid·west·ern·er

mid·wicket

mid·wife (*plural* ·wives)

mid·wife·ry

mid·win·ter

mid·year

mien bearing; *compare* mean

miff *Slang* take offence

mif·fi·ness

mif·fy (·fi·er, ·fi·est)

might

mighti·ly

mighti·ness

mighty (mighti·er, mighti·est)

mi·gnon *French* dainty

mi·gnon·ette plant

mi·graine

mi·grain·ous

mi·grant

mi·grate

mi·gra·tion

mi·gra·tion·al

mi·gra·tor

mi·gra·tory

mih·rab niche in mosque

mi·ka·do (*plural* ·dos)

mike *Slang* microphone

mil unit of length

mi·la·dy (*or* ·la·di; *plural* ·dies)

mil·age *variant spelling of* mileage

Mi·lan

Mil·an·ese (*plural* ·ese)

milch

mild

mil·dew

mil·dewy

mild·ness

mile

mile·age (*or* mil·age)

mile·om·eter (*or* mi·lom·eter)

mile·post

mil·er

Mi·lesian

mile·stone

Mi·letus old Asian city

mil·foil plant

mili·aria heat rash

mil·iary

mi·lieu (*plural* ·lieus *or* ·lieux)

mili·tan·cy (*or* ·tant·ness)

mili·tant

mili·tari·ly

mili·ta·rism

mili·ta·rist

mili·ta·ris·tic

mili·ta·ris·ti·cal·ly

mili·ta·ri·za·tion (*or* ·sa·tion)

mili·ta·rize (*or* ·rise)

mili·tary (*plural* ·taries)

mili·tate

mili·ta·tion

mi·li·tia

mi·li·tia·man (*plural* ·men)

mil·ium (*plural* milia) skin nodule

milk

milk·er

milk·fish (*plural* ·fish *or* ·fishes)

milki·ly

milki·ness

milk·maid

milk·man (*plural* ·men)

milko *Austral* milkman

milk·sop

milk·weed

milk·wort

milky (milki·er, milki·est)

Milky Way

mill

mill·able

mill·board

mill·dam

milled

mille·feuille pastry

mille·fleurs textile design

mil·le·nar·ian (*or* ·nary)

mil·le·nari·an·ism Christian belief

mil·le·nary (*plural* ·naries) a thousand; *compare* millinery

mil·len·nial

mil·len·ni·al·ist

mil·len·nium (*plural* ·niums *or* ·nia)

mil·le·pede *variant spelling of* millipede

mil·le·pore coral-like organism

mil·ler

mil·ler·ite mineral

mil·lesi·mal denoting a thousandth

mil·let

mil·li·ard thousand million

mil·liary denoting Roman mile

mil·li·bar

mil·lieme Tunisian coin

mil·li·gram (*or* ·gramme)

mil·li·li·tre (*US* ·ter)

mil·li·metre (*US* ·meter)

mil·line unit of advertising copy

mil·li·ner

mil·li·nery hat making; *compare* millenary

mill·ing

mil·lion (*plural* ·lions *or* ·lion)

mil·lion·aire (*or* ·lion·naire)

mil·lion·air·ess

mil·lionth

mil·li·pede (*or* ·le·pede, ·le·ped)

mil·li·sec·ond

mill·pond

mill·race

mill·run

mill·stone

mill·stream

mill·wheel

mill·wright

mi·lord

mi·lom·eter *variant spelling of* mileometer

milque·toast *US* timid person

milt

mil·ter

Mil·ton·ic (*or* ·to·nian) of John Milton

Mil·ton Keynes

Mil·wau·kee *US* port

mim *Dialect* prim

Mi·mas satellite of Saturn

mime

Mimeo·graph (*Trademark*)

mim·er

mi·mesis

mi·met·ic

mi·meti·cal·ly

mim·etite mineral

mim·ic (·ick·ing, ·icked)

mim·ick·er

mim·ic·ry (*plural* ·ries)

miminy-piminy *variant of* niminy-piminy

Mimir Norse giant

mi·mo·sa

mimo·sa·ceous

Min Chinese dialect

mina (*plural* minae *or* minas) ancient unit

mina *variant spelling of* myna

min·able (*or* mine·able)

mi·na·cious threatening

mi·nac·ity

Mina Has·san Tani Moroccan port

mina·ret

mina·ret·ed

Mi·nas Ge·rais Brazilian state

mina·to·ri·ly (*or* ·ri·al·ly)

mina·tory (*or* ·to·rial)

mince

mince·meat

minc·er

Minch Atlantic channel

minc·ing

minc·ing·ly

mind

Min·dan·ao Philippine island

mind·ed

Min·del glaciation period

mind·er

mind·ful

mind·ful·ly

mind·ful·ness

mind·less

mind·less·ness

mind-reader

mind-reading

mine

mine-field

mine·lay·er

min·er one who mines;
compare minor

min·er·al

min·er·ali·za·tion (or
·sa·tion)

min·er·al·ize (or ·ise)

min·er·al·iz·er (or ·is·er)

min·er·alo·cor·ti·coid
hormone

min·er·alo·gi·cal (or
·og·ic)

min·er·alo·gist

min·er·al·ogy

min·estro·ne

mine·sweeper

mine·sweeping

Ming

min·gle

Min·gre·lian (or
Min·grel) Georgian
people

min·gy (·gi·er, ·gi·est)

mini (plural minis)

minia·ture

minia·tur·ist

minia·turi·za·tion (or
·sa·tion)

minia·tur·ize (or ·ise)

mini·bus

mini·cab

mini·com·put·er

mini·dress

mini·fi·ca·tion

mini·fy (·fies, ·fy·ing,
·fied)

min·im

mini·ma (plural of
minimum)

mini·mal

Mini·mal·ist Russian
revolutionary

mini·mal·ist advocate of
minimal policy

mini·mal·ly

mini·max maths term

mini·mi·za·tion (or
·sa·tion)

mini·mize (or ·mise)

mini·miz·er (or ·mis·er)

mini·mum (plural ·mums
or ·ma)

mini·mus youngest

min·ing

min·ion

mini·pill

(miniscule) incorrect
spelling of minuscule

mini·skirt

mini·skirted

min·is·ter

min·is·terial

min·is·terial·ly

min·is·te·rium (plural
·ria) Lutheran ministers

min·is·trant

mini·stra·tion

min·is·tra·tive

min·is·try (plural ·tries)

Mini·track (Trademark)

(miniture) incorrect spelling
of miniature

min·ium red lead

mini·ver fur

mini·vet bird

mink

minke whale

Min·na Nigerian city

Min·ne·apo·lis

min·neo·la hybrid fruit

min·ne·sing·er German
minstrel

Min·ne·so·ta

Min·ne·so·tan

min·now (plural ·nows or
·now)

Mi·no·an of Cretan culture

mi·nor lesser; compare miner

Mi·nor·ca

Mi·nor·can

Mi·no·rite friar

mi·nor·ity (plural ·ities)

Minos legendary king

Minotaur legendary
monster

Minsk Soviet city

min·ster

min·strel

min·strel·sy (plural ·sies)

mint

mint·age

mint·er

Min·ton porcelain

minty (minti·er,
minti·est)

minu·end maths term

minu·et

mi·nus

mi·nus·cu·lar

mi·nus·cule

min·ute 60 seconds

mi·nute very small

min·ute·ly every minute

mi·nute·ly in great detail

Min·ute·man (plural
·men)

mi·nute·ness

min·utes record of
proceedings

mi·nu·tiae (sing. ·tia)
trifling details

minx

minx·ish

Mio·cene geological period

mio·sis (or myo·)
constriction of pupil;
compare meiosis

mi·ot·ic (or my·)

Mi·que·lon French island

mi·ra·bi·le dic·tu Latin
wonderful to relate

Mira Ceti star

mi·ra·cid·ial

mi·ra·cid·ium (plural ·iia)
fluke larva

mira·cle

mi·racu·lous

mira·dor balcony or turret

mi·rage

Mi·ran·da satellite of
Uranus

mire

mire·poix vegetable mixture

mir·ky variant spelling of
murky

mir·ror

mirth

mirth·ful

mirth·ful·ly

mirth·ful·ness

mirth·less

mirth·less·ness

miry

mis·ad·ven·ture

mis·ad·vise

mis·align·ment
mis·al·li·ance unsuitable
    alliance; *compare*
    mésalliance
mis·an·thrope (*or*
    ·thro·pist)
mis·an·throp·ic (*or*
    ·thropi·cal)
mis·an·thropi·cal·ly
mis·an·thro·pist *variant of*
    misanthrope
mis·an·thro·py
mis·ap·pli·ca·tion
mis·ap·ply (·plies,
    ·ply·ing, ·plied)
mis·ap·pre·hend
mis·ap·pre·hend·ing·ly
mis·ap·pre·hen·sion
mis·ap·pre·hen·sive
mis·ap·pro·pri·ate
mis·ap·pro·pria·tion
mis·be·come (·com·ing,
    ·came) be unsuitable for
mis·be·got·ten
mis·be·have
mis·be·hav·er
mis·be·hav·iour (*US* ·ior)
mis·be·lief
mis·cal·cu·late
mis·cal·cu·la·tion
mis·call
mis·car·riage
mis·car·ry (·ries, ·ry·ing,
    ·ried)
mis·cast (·cast·ing, ·cast)
mis·ce·gena·tion
    interbreeding
mis·ce·genet·ic
mis·cel·la·nea (*plural*)
mis·cel·la·neous
mis·cel·la·nist
mis·cel·la·ny (*plural*
    ·nies)
mis·chance
mis·chief
mis·chie·vous
mis·chiev·ous·ness
misch met·al
mis·cibil·ity
mis·cible capable of mixing;
    compare missable
mis·con·ceive
mis·con·ceiv·er
mis·con·cep·tion
mis·con·duct

mis·con·struc·tion
mis·con·strue (·stru·ing,
    ·strued)
mis·copy (·copies,
    ·copy·ing, ·cop·ied)
mis·count
mis·cre·ance (*or* ·an·cy)
mis·cre·ant wrongdoer
mis·cre·ate create badly
mis·crea·tion
mis·cue (·cu·ing, ·cued)
mis·date
mis·deal (·deal·ing,
    ·dealt)
mis·deal·er
mis·deed
mis·de·mean·ant
mis·de·mean·our (*US* ·or)
mis·di·rect
mis·di·rec·tion
mis·doubt
mise legal term
mise en scène scenery
mi·ser
mis·er·able
mis·er·able·ness
mis·er·ably
mi·sère call in solo whist
Mis·erere 51st psalm
mis·erere misericord
mis·eri·cord (*or* ·corde)
    part of church
mi·ser·li·ness
mi·ser·ly
mis·ery (*plural* ·eries)
mis·fea·sance legal term
mis·file
mis·fire
mis·fit (·fit·ting, ·fit·ted)
mis·for·tune
mis·give (·giv·ing, ·gave,
    ·giv·en)
mis·giv·ing
mis·gov·ern
mis·gov·ern·ment
mis·gov·er·nor
mis·guid·ance
mis·guide
mis·guid·ed
mis·guid·er
mis·han·dle
mis·hap
mis·hear (·hear·ing,
    ·heard)
mis·hit (·hit·ting, ·hit)

mish·mash
Mish·nah (*or* ·na) Jewish
    precepts
Mish·na·ic
mis·in·form
mis·in·form·ant (*or*
    ·form·er)
mis·in·for·ma·tion
mis·in·ter·pret
mis·in·ter·pre·ta·tion
mis·in·ter·pret·er
mis·join·der legal term
mis·judge
mis·judg·er
mis·judg·ment (*or*
    ·judge·)
Mis·kolc Hungarian city
mis·lay (·lay·ing, ·laid)
mis·lay·er
mis·lead (·lead·ing, ·led)
mis·lead·er
mis·man·age
mis·man·age·ment
mis·man·ag·er
mis·match
mis·no·mer
mi·soga·mist marriage
    hater
mi·soga·my
mi·sogy·nist woman hater
mi·sogy·nous
mi·sogy·ny
mi·solo·gist
mi·sol·ogy hatred of
    reasoning
miso·neism hatred of
    anything new
miso·neist
miso·neis·tic
mis·pick·el mineral
mis·place
mis·place·ment
mis·play
mis·plead (·plead·ing,
    ·plead·ed, ·plead, *or*
    ·pled)
mis·plead·ing
mis·print
mis·pri·sion concealment of
    treason
mis·prize (*or* ·prise)
    undervalue
mis·pro·nounce
mis·pro·nun·cia·tion
mis·pro·por·tion

mis·quo·ta·tion
mis·quote
mis·read (·read·ing,
·read)
mis·re·mem·ber
mis·re·port
mis·rep·re·sent
mis·rep·re·sen·ta·tion
mis·rep·re·sen·ta·tive
mis·rep·re·sent·er
mis·rule
Miss title of address
miss
miss·able able to be missed;
compare miscible
mis·sal prayer book
mis·sel thrush variant
spelling of mistle thrush
mis·shape (·shap·ing,
·shaped or ·shap·en)
mis·sile
mis·sile·ry (or ·sil·ry)
mis·sing
mis·sion
mis·sion·ary (plural
·aries)
mis·sion·er
mis·sis
miss·ish
Mis·sis·sau·ga Canadian
town
Mis·sis·sip·pi
Mis·sis·sip·pian
mis·sive
Mis·souri
Mis·sou·rian
mis·spell (·spell·ing,
·spelt or ·spelled)
mis·spend (·spend·ing,
·spent)
mis·state
mis·state·ment
mis·sup·pose
missy (plural missies)
mist
mis·tak·able (or ·take·)
mis·tak·ably (or ·take·)
mis·take (·tak·ing, ·took
or ·tak·en)
mis·tal Scot cowshed
Mis·tas·si·ni Canadian lake
mis·teach (·teach·ing,
·taught)
mis·ter
mis·ti·gris joker in poker

misti·ly
mis·time
misti·ness
mis·tle thrush (or mis·sel
thrush)
mis·tle·toe
mis·took
mis·tral wind; compare
mistrial
mis·treat
mis·treat·ment
mis·tress
mis·tri·al void trial; compare
mistral
mis·trust
mis·trust·er
mis·trust·ful
mis·trust·ful·ly
mis·trust·ful·ness
mis·trust·ing·ly
misty (misti·er, misti·est)
mis·under·stand
(·stand·ing, ·stood)
mis·us·age
mis·use
mis·us·er
mitch Dialect play truant
mite
mi·ter US spelling of mitre
Mith·ra·ic
Mith·ra·ism (or ·rai·cism)
Mith·ra·ist
Mith·ras (or ·ra) Persian
god
mith·ri·dat·ic
mith·ri·da·tism immunity
to poison
miti·cid·al
miti·cide mite-killing
substance
miti·gable
miti·gate
miti·gat·ing
miti·ga·tion
miti·ga·tive (or ·tory)
miti·ga·tor
mi·tis malleable iron
mi·to·chon·drial
mi·to·chon·drion (plural
·dria) biology term
mi·to·sis (plural ·ses) cell
division
mi·tot·ic
mi·toti·cal·ly
mi·trail·leuse machine gun

mi·tral
mi·tre (US ·ter)
mitre·wort (US miter·)
plant
mitt
mit·ten
mit·ti·mus (plural ·muses)
legal term
mitz·vah (plural ·vahs or
·voth)
mix
mix·abil·ity
mix·able
mixed
mix·er
mix·ing
mixo·lyd·ian music term
Mix·tec (plural ·tecs or
·tec) American Indian
mix·ture
mix-up (noun)
Mi·zar star
Mi·zo·ram Indian state
miz·zen (or miz·en)
nautical term
miz·zen·mast (or miz·en·)
miz·zle Dialect drizzle
m'lud
mne·mon·ic memory aid
mne·moni·cal·ly
mne·mon·ics
Mnemosyne Greek
goddess
mo (plural mos) Slang
moment
moa extinct bird
Moab biblical kingdom
Mo·ab·ite
moan
moan·er
moan·ing·ly
moat ditch; compare mote
mob (mob·bing, mobbed)
mob·ber
mob·cap
Mo·bile US port
mo·bile
mo·bil·ity
mo·bi·liz·able (or
·lis·able)
mo·bi·li·za·tion (or
·sa·tion)
mo·bi·lize (or ·lise)
mob·oc·ra·cy (plural
·cies)

mobo·crat

mobo·crat·ic (*or* ·crati·cal)

mob·ster

Mo·bu·tu African lake

moc·ca·sin

Mo·cha Yemeni port

mo·cha coffee

mock

mock·able

mock·er

mock·ery (*plural* ·eries)

mock-heroic

mock-heroical·ly

mocking·bird

mock·ing·ly

mock-up (*noun*)

mod

mod·al

mo·dal·ity

mo·dal·ly

mode

mod·el (·el·ling, ·elled; *US* ·el·ing, ·eled)

mod·el·ler (*US* ·el·er)

mo·dem computer term

Mo·dena Italian city

mod·er·ate

mod·er·ate·ly

mod·er·ate·ness

mod·era·tion

mod·era·to music term

mod·era·tor

mod·era·tor·ship

mod·ern

mo·derne architectural style

mod·ern·ism

mod·ern·ist

mod·ern·is·tic

mod·ern·is·ti·cal·ly

mo·der·nity (*plural* ·nities)

mod·erni·za·tion (*or* ·sa·tion)

mod·ern·ize (*or* ·ise)

mod·ern·iz·er (*or* ·is·er)

mod·ern·ness

mod·est

mod·est·ly

mod·es·ty (*plural* ·ties)

modge *Dialect* to botch

modi·cum

modi·fi·abil·ity (*or* ·able·ness)

modi·fi·able

modi·fi·ca·tion

modi·fi·ca·tory (*or* ·tive)

modi·fi·er

modi·fy (·fies, ·fy·ing, ·fied)

mo·dil·lion architectural ornament

mo·dio·lus (*plural* ·li) anatomy term

mod·ish

mod·ish·ness

mo·diste (*plural* ·distes) fashionable dressmaker

modu·la·bil·ity

modu·lar

modu·late

modu·la·tion

modu·la·tive (*or* ·tory)

modu·la·tor

mod·ule

modu·lus (*plural* ·li) physics term

mo·dus op·eran·di (*plural* modi op·eran·di) method of working

mo·dus vi·ven·di (*plural* modi vi·ven·di) practical compromise

mo·fette opening in volcano

mog *Slang* cat

Moga·dishu (*or* ·discio) Somali capital

Moga·don (*Trademark*) drug

Moga·dor Moroccan port

mog·gy (*or* ·gie; *plural* ·gies) *Slang* cat

Mo·gi·lev (*or* ·hi·) Soviet city

Mo·gul Muslim ruler

mo·gul important person

mo·hair

Mo·ham·med·an Muslim

Mo·ha·ve (*or* ·ja·; *plural* ·ves *or* ·ve) American Indian

Mo·ha·ve Des·ert (*or* Mo·ja·ve Des·ert)

Mo·hawk (*plural* ·hawks *or* ·hawk) American Indian

Mo·hi·can *variant spelling of* Mahican

Mo·hock ruffian

Mo·hole geological project

moi·der *Dialect* to bother

moi·dore coin

moi·ety (*plural* ·eties) half

moire (*noun*) fabric

moi·ré (*adj*) having watered pattern

moist

mois·ten

moist·en·er

moist·ness

mois·ture

mois·tur·ize (*or* ·ise)

mois·tur·iz·er (*or* ·is·er)

Mo·ja·ve *variant spelling of* Mohave

moke *Slang* donkey

Mok·po South Korean port

mola (*plural* mola *or* molas) fish

mo·lal

mo·lal·ity (*plural* ·ities) chemistry term

mo·lar tooth; chemistry term

mo·lar·ity

mo·las·ses

mold *US spelling of* mould

Mol·da·via

Mol·da·vian

mol·da·vite glass

mold·er *US spelling of* moulder

mole

mo·lecu·lar

mol·ecule

mole·hill

mole·skin

mo·lest

mo·les·ta·tion

mo·lest·er

mo·line heraldic term

Mo·li·se Italian region

moll

mol·li·fi·able

mol·li·fi·ca·tion

mol·li·fi·er

mol·li·fy (·fies, ·fy·ing, ·fied)

mol·li·fy·ing·ly

mol·lusc (*US* ·lusk)

mol·lus·can (*US* ·kan)

mol·lus·coid (*or* ·coi·dal) zoology term

mol·ly (*plural* ·lies) fish

molly·coddle

molly·coddler

Molly Maguire Irish secret
society member
Mo·loch Semitic god
mo·loch lizard
Mo·lo·kai Hawaiian island
molt *US spelling of* moult
mol·ten
mol·to musical term
Mo·luc·cas Indonesian
islands
moly (*plural* **molies**)
mythological herb; flower
mo·lyb·date
mo·lyb·de·nite mineral
mo·lyb·de·nous
mo·lyb·de·num chemical
element
mo·lyb·dic
mo·lyb·dous
mom *US* mother
Mom·ba·sa Kenyan port
mo·ment
mo·men·tari·ly
mo·men·tary
mo·men·tous
mo·men·tum (*plural* ·ta
or ·tums)
Momus Greek god
mona monkey
Mona·can
mona·chal monastic
mona·chism
Mona·co
mon·ad (*plural* ·ads *or*
mona·des)
mona·del·phous botany
term
mo·nad·ic (*or* ·nadi·cal)
mon·ad·ism (*or*
·ad·ol·ogy) philosophy
mon·ad·is·tic
mo·nad·nock hill
mon·ad·ol·ogy *variant of*
monadism
Mona·ghan Irish county
mon·al (*or* ·aul) pheasant
mo·nan·drous botany term
mo·nan·dry
mo·nan·thous botany term
mon·arch
mo·nar·chal (*or* ·chi·al)
mo·nar·chic (*or* ·chi·cal)
mon·ar·chism
mon·ar·chist
mon·ar·chis·tic

mon·ar·chy (*plural* ·chies)
mo·nar·da plant
mon·as·te·rial
mon·as·tery (*plural*
·teries)
mo·nas·tic (*or* ·ti·cal)
mo·nas·ti·cal·ly
mo·nas·ti·cism
mon·atom·ic (*or* mono·)
mon·aural
mona·zite mineral
Mönchen-Gladbach West
German city
Mon·day
mondi·al of the world
Mon·egasque citizen of
Monaco
Monel metal
(*Trademark*)
mon·etar·ism
mon·etar·ist
mon·etary
mon·eti·za·tion (*or*
·sa·tion)
mon·etize (*or* ·etise)
mon·ey (*plural* ·eys *or*
·ies)
money·changer
mon·eyed (*or* mon·ied)
money·lender
money·lending
money·maker
money·making
money·spinner
money·wort
mon·ger
mon·ger·ing
mon·go (*or* goe; *plural*
·gos *or* ·goes)
Mongolian currency
Mon·gol
Mon·go·lia
Mon·go·lian
Mon·gol·ic
mon·go·lism *former name of*
Down's syndrome
Mon·gol·oid
mon·goose (*plural*
·gooses)
mon·grel
mon·grel·ism (*or* ·ness)
mon·greli·za·tion (*or*
·sa·tion)
mon·grel·ize (*or* ·ise)
mon·grel·ly

moni·ker (*or* mon·ick·er)
Slang nickname
mo·nili·form
mon·ism
mon·ist
mo·nis·tic
mo·nis·ti·cal·ly
mo·ni·tion warning
moni·tor
moni·to·rial
moni·tor·ship
moni·tory (*or* ·to·rial)
warning
moni·tress
monk
mon·key
monkey·pot tree
monk·fish (*plural* ·fish *or*
·fishes)
Mon-Khmer language
monk·hood being a monk
monk·ish
monks·hood plant
Mon·mouth
Mon·mouth·shire former
Welsh county
mono (*plural* **monos**)
mono·ac·id (*or* mon·ac·id,
mono·acid·ic,
mona·cid·ic)
mono·atom·ic *variant of*
monatomic
mono·ba·sic
mono·carp botany term
mono·car·pel·lary
mono·car·pic (*or* ·pous)
Mo·noc·er·os constellation
mono·cha·sial
mono·cha·sium (*plural*
·sia) botany term
mono·chlo·ride
mono·chord acoustic
instrument
mono·chro·mat (*or* ·mate)
mono·chro·mat·ic (*or*
mono·chro·ic)
mono·chro·mati·cal·ly
mono·chro·ma·tism visual
defect
mono·chrome
mono·chro·mic (*or*
·mi·cal)
mono·chrom·ist
mono·cle
mono·cli·nal

monotrichous

mono·cline geology term
mono·clin·ic
  crystallography term
mono·cli·nism botany term
mono·cli·nous
mono·coque car or aircraft
  body
mono·coty·ledon botany
  term
mono·coty·ledon·ous
mo·noc·ra·cy (*plural*
  ·cies)
mono·crat
mono·crat·ic
mo·noc·u·lar
mono·cul·ture
mono·cy·clic
mono·cyte blood cell
mono·cyt·ic
mo·nod·ic (*or* ·nodi·cal)
mono·dist
mono·dra·ma
mono·dra·mat·ic
mono·dy (*plural* ·dies)
mo·noecious (*or* ·necious,
  ·noi·cous) botany term
mono·fila·ment (*or* ·fil)
mo·noga·mist
mo·noga·mis·tic
mo·noga·mous
mo·noga·my having one
  spouse; *compare* monogyny
mono·gen·esis biology
  term
mono·genet·ic
mono·gen·ic genetics term
mo·nog·enous
mo·nog·eny
mono·gram
mono·gram·matic
mono·grammed
mono·graph
mo·nog·ra·pher
mono·graph·ic
mono·graphi·cal·ly
mo·nogy·nist
mo·nogy·nous
mo·nogy·ny having one
  female partner; *compare*
  monogamy
mono·hull
mono·hy·brid
mono·hy·drate
mono·hy·droxy
mo·nola·ter (*or* ·trist)

mo·nola·trous
mo·nola·try worship of one
  god
mono·lay·er
mono·lin·gual
mono·lith
mono·lith·ic
mono·lithi·cal·ly
mono·log·ic (*or* ·logi·cal)
mono·log·ist
mono·logue (*US also*
  ·log)
mo·nol·ogy
mono·ma·nia
mono·ma·ni·ac
mono·ma·nia·cal
mono·mark
mono·mer chemistry term
mono·mer·ic
mo·nom·er·ous botany
  term
mono·me·tal·lic
mono·met·al·lism
mono·met·al·list
mo·nom·eter verse line
mono·met·ri·cal (*or*
  ·met·ric)
mo·no·mial
mono·mo·lecu·lar
mono·mor·phic (*or*
  ·phous)
mono·mor·phism
mono·nu·clear
mono·nu·cleo·sis
mono·pet·al·ous
mo·nopha·gous
mo·nopha·gy
mono·pho·bia
mono·pho·bic
mono·phon·ic
mo·nopho·ny
mon·oph·thong
mon·oph·thon·gal
mono·phy·let·ic genetics
  term
mono·phyl·lous botany
  term
mono·plane
mono·plegia
mono·plegic
mono·po·dial
mono·po·dium (*plural*
  ·dia) botany term
mo·nopo·lism
mo·nopo·list

mo·nopo·lis·tic
mo·nopo·lis·ti·cal·ly
mo·nopo·li·za·tion (*or*
  ·sa·tion)
mo·nopo·lize (*or* ·lise)
mo·nopo·liz·er (*or* ·lis·er)
Mo·nopo·ly (*Trádemark*)
  game
mo·nopo·ly (*plural* ·lies)
mono·pro·pel·lant
mo·nop·so·nis·tic
mo·nop·so·ny (*plural*
  ·nies) economics term
mon·op·te·ros (*or* ·ron;
  plural ·roi *or* ·ra)
  architectural term
mono·rail
mono·sac·cha·ride
mono·semy having only
  one meaning
mono·sepa·lous
mono·so·dium
  glu·ta·mate
mono·some chromosome
mono·so·mic
mono·sper·mous (*or*
  ·sper·mal)
mono·stich single-line poem
mono·stich·ic
mono·stich·ous botany
  term
mono·stome (*or*
  mo·nos·to·mous) having
  one mouth
mo·nos·tro·phe poem
mono·stroph·ic
mono·sty·lous botany term
mono·syl·lab·ic
mono·syl·labi·cal·ly
mono·syl·la·bism
mono·syl·la·ble
mono·theism
mono·theist
mono·theis·tic
mono·theis·ti·cal·ly
mono·tint
mono·tone
mono·ton·ic
mo·noto·nous
mo·noto·ny (*plural* ·nies)
mono·trema·tous
mono·treme mammal
mo·no·tri·chous (*or*
  ·trich·ic) bacteriology
  term

Mono·type (*Trademark*) typesetting machine

mono·type

mono·typ·ic

mono·va·lence (*or* ·len·cy)

mono·va·lent

mon·ox·ide

Mon·ro·via Liberian capital

Mons Belgian town

mons (*plural* mon·tes) anatomy term

Mon·sei·gneur (*plural* Mes·sei·gneurs) French title

mon·sieur (*plural* mes·sieurs) *French* gentleman; Mr

Mon·sig·nor (*plural* ·nors *or* ·nori) ecclesiastical title

mon·soon

mon·ster

mon·strance receptacle for consecrated Host

mon·stros·ity (*plural* ·ities)

mon·strous

mon·strous·ness

mon·tage

Mon·ta·gnard (*plural* ·gnards *or* ·gnard) mountain people

Mon·tana

mon·tane of mountainous regions

Mon·tau·ban French city

Mont Blanc

mont·bre·tia plant

mon·te gambling game

Mon·te Car·lo

Mon·te·go Bay Jamaican port

mon·teith bowl for cooling wineglasses

Mon·te·ne·grin

Mon·te·ne·gro Yugoslav republic

Mon·te·rey Californian city

mon·te·ro (*plural* ·ros) hunting cap

Mon·ter·rey Mexican city

Montessori meth·od

Mon·te·vi·deo Uruguayan capital

mont·gol·fier hot-air balloon

Mont·gom·ery US city

month

month·ly (*plural* ·lies)

mon·ti·cule small hill

Mont·mar·tre

Mont·par·nasse

Mont·pel·lier

Mon·treal

Mon·treuil Parisian suburb

monu·ment

monu·men·tal

monu·men·tal·ly

monu·men·tal·ity

Mon·za Italian city

mon·zo·nite rock

mon·zo·nit·ic

moo

mooch

mooch·er

mood

moodi·ly

moodi·ness

moody (moodi·er, moodi·est)

Moog syn·the·siz·er (*Trademark*)

moo·lah *Slang* money

mool·vie (*or* ·vi) Muslim learned man

moon

moon·beam

moon·calf (*plural* ·calves)

moon·eye fish

moon·faced

moon·fish (*plural* ·fishes *or* ·fish)

moon·flower

mooni·ly

mooni·ness

moon·less

moon·light

moon·lighter

moon·light·ing

moon·lit

moon·quake

moon·raker sail

moon·rise

moon·scape

moon·seed

moon·set

moon·shine

moon·shiner *US* whisky smuggler

moon·shot

moon·stone

moon·struck (*or* ·stricken)

moon·wort

moony (mooni·er, mooni·est)

Moor African Muslim

moor open ground; attach boat; *compare* more

moor·age

moor·cock

moor·fowl

moor·hen

moor·ing

moor·ings

Moor·ish

moor·land

moor·wort shrub

moose (*plural* moose)

moot

moot·er

mop (mop·ping, mopped)

mope

moped *past tense of* mope

mo·ped motorcycle

mop·er

mop·ing·ly

mo·poke owl

mopped

mop·pet

mop·ping

mo·quette fabric

mor humus

mora (*plural* morae *or* moras) prosody term

mo·ra·ceous botany term

Mo·ra·da·bad Indian city

mo·rain·al (*or* ·ic)

mo·raine glacier debris; *compare* murrain

mor·al

mo·rale confidence

mor·al·ism

mor·al·ist

mor·al·is·tic

mor·al·is·ti·cal·ly

mo·ral·ity (*plural* ·ities)

mor·ali·za·tion (*or* ·sa·tion)

mor·al·ize (*or* ·ise)

mor·al·iz·er (*or* ·is·er)

mor·al·iz·ing·ly (*or* ·is·ing·ly)

mor·al·ly

Mor·ar Scottish loch

mo·rass

mora·to·rium (*plural* ·ria *or* ·riums*)

mora·tory

Mo·ra·va Czech river

Mo·ra·via

Mo·ra·vian

Mo·ra·vi·an·ism religious movement

Mor·ay former Scottish county

mo·ray (*plural* ·rays) eel

mor·bid

mor·bid·ity

mor·bid·ness

mor·bif·ic causing disease

mor·bifi·cal·ly

Mor·bi·han French department

mor·bil·li measles

mor·ceau (*plural* ·ceaux) *French* morsel

mor·cha Indian demonstration

mor·da·cious sarcastic

mor·dac·ity (*or* ·da·cious·ness)

mor·dan·cy

mor·dant sarcastic; dye fixer

mor·dent musical ornament

Mord·vin (*plural* ·vin *or* ·vins) Finnish people

Mor·dvin·ian

more *comparative of* **much**; *compare* **moor**

More·cambe Lancashire town

mo·reen fabric

more·ish (*or* mor·ish)

mo·rel edible fungus

Mo·relia Mexican city

mo·rel·lo (*plural* ·los) cherry

Mo·relos Mexican state

more·over

mo·res customs

Mo·res·co *variant spelling of* Morisco

Mo·resque Moorish

Mor·gan horse

mor·ga·nat·ic

mor·ga·nati·cal·ly

mor·gan·ite gemstone

Morgan le Fay legendary character

morgue

mori·bund

mori·bun·dity

mo·ri·on helmet

Mo·ris·co (*or* ·res·; *plural* ·coes *or* ·cos) Spanish Moor

mor·ish *variant spelling of* moreish

Mor·mon

Mor·mon·ism

morn morning; *compare* mourn

mor·nay cookery term

morn·ing

morning-glory (*plural* -glories)

Moro (*plural* **Moros** *or* **Moro**) Muslim people

Mo·roc·can

Mo·roc·co

mo·roc·co leather

mor·on

Mo·ro·ni capital of Comoro Islands

mo·ron·ic

mo·roni·cal·ly

mo·ron·ism (*or* ·ity)

mo·rose

mo·rose·ly

mo·rose·ness

morph linguistics term

mor·phal·lax·is (*plural* ·laxes) zoology term

mor·pheme grammatical unit

mor·phem·ic

mor·phemi·cal·ly

Morpheus Greek god

mor·phine (*or* ·phia)

mor·phin·ism

mor·pho·gen·esis

mor·pho·genet·ic (*or* ·gen·ic)

mor·pho·log·ic (*or* ·logi·cal)

mor·pho·logi·cal·ly

mor·pholo·gist

mor·phol·ogy

mor·pho·pho·neme linguistics term

mor·pho·pho·nemic

mor·pho·pho·nemics

mor·pho·sis (*plural* ·ses) biology term

mor·ris dance

mor·ro (*plural* ·ros) hill

mor·row

Mors Roman god

Morse code

morse cloak fastening

mor·sel

mort hunting term

mor·tal

mor·tal·ity (*plural* ·ities)

mor·tal·ly

mor·tar

mortar·board

mort·gage

mort·gage·able

mort·ga·gee

mort·gag·or (*or* ·er)

mor·tice *variant spelling of* mortise

mor·ti·cian *US* undertaker

mor·ti·fi·ca·tion

mor·ti·fi·er

mor·ti·fy (·fies, ·fy·ing, ·fied)

mor·ti·fy·ing·ly

mor·tise (*or* ·tice)

mor·tis·er

mort·main legal term

mor·tu·ary (*plural* ·aries)

moru·la (*plural* ·las *or* ·lae) biology term

moru·lar

mor·wong fish

Mo·sa·ic (*or* ·sai·cal) of Moses

mo·sa·ic (·ick·ing, ·icked)

mo·sai·cist

mos·cha·tel plant

Mos·cow

Mo·selle European river; wine

mo·sey

Mos·lem *variant spelling of* Muslim

Mo·so·tho (*plural* ·tho *or* ·thos) African people

mosque

mos·qui·to (*plural* ·toes *or* ·tos)

moss

moss·back *US* conservative

moss·bunk·er fish

Mos·si (*plural* ·**sis** *or* ·**si**)
African people
mos·sie bird
mossi·ness
mos·so musical term
moss·trooper
mossy (**mossi·er,**
mossi·est)
most
most·ly
Mosul Iraqi city
mote tiny speck; *compare*
moat
mo·tel
mo·tet
moth
moth·ball
moth-eaten
moth·er
moth·er·hood
mother-in-law (*plural*
mothers-)
mother·land
moth·er·less
moth·er·li·ness
moth·er·ly
mother-of-pearl
mother·wort plant
moth·proof
mothy (**mothi·er,**
mothi·est)
mo·tif theme; *compare*
motive
mo·tile
mo·til·ity
mo·tion
mo·tion·er
mo·tion·less
mo·tion·less·ness
mo·ti·vate
mo·ti·va·tion
mo·ti·va·tion·al
mo·ti·va·tive
mo·tive reason; causing
motion; *compare* motif
mo·tive·less
mo·tive·less·ness
mo·tiv·ity
mot juste (*plural* **mots**
justes)
mot·ley
mot·mot bird
mo·to·cross motorcycle
race
mo·to·neu·ron nerve cell

mo·tor
motor·bike
motor·boat
motor·bus
motor·cade
motor·car
motor·coach
motor·cycle
motor·cyclist
mo·tor·ist
mo·tori·za·tion (*or*
·**sa·tion**)
mo·tor·ize (*or* ·**ise**)
motor·man (*plural* ·**men**)
motor·way
motte castle mound
mott·le
mot·to (*plural* ·**toes** *or*
·**tos**)
mouf·lon (*or* **mouf·flon**)
wild sheep
mouil·lé phonetics term
mould (*US* **mold**)
mould·abil·ity (*US* **mold·**)
mould·able (*US* **mold·**)
mould·board (*US* **mold·**)
curved blade of plough
mould·er (*US* **mold·**)
crumble; one who moulds
mouldi·ness (*US* **moldi·**)
mould·ing (*US* **mold·**)
mould·warp *Dialect* mole
mouldy (*US* **moldy;**
mouldi·er, mouldi·est,
US **moldi·er,**
moldi·est)
mou·lin glacier shift
Moul·mein (*or*
Maul·main) Burmese
port
moult (*US* **molt**)
moult·er (*US* **molt·**)
mound
mount
mount·able
moun·tain
moun·tain·eer
moun·tain·eer·ing
moun·tain·ous
mountain·top
moun·tebank
moun·tebank·ery
mount·ed
mount·er

Mountie Canadian
policeman
mount·ing
Mount Rush·more
mourn grieve; *compare* morn
mourn·er
mourn·ful
mourn·ful·ly
mourn·ful·ness
mourn·ing
mouse (*plural* **mice**)
mous·er
mouse·tail plant
mouse·trap
mousi·ness
mous·ing nautical term
mous·sa·ka (*or* **mou·sa·**)
mousse
mousse·line fabric; cookery
term
mous·tache (*US* **mus·**)
mousy (*or* **mous·ey;**
mousi·er, mousi·est)
mouth
mouth·brooder (*or*
·**breeder**) fish
(**mouthe**) *incorrect spelling*
of mouth (*verb*)
mouth·er
mouth·ful (*plural* ·**fuls**)
mouth·part
mouth·piece
mouth-to-mouth
mouth·wash
mouth·water·ing
mou·ton processed
sheepskin
mov·abil·ity (*or*
·**able·ness**)
mov·able (*or in legal*
contexts **move·**)
mov·ably
move (**mov·ing, moved**)
move·ables legal term
move·ment
mov·er
movie
Movie·tone (*Trademark*)
mov·ing
mov·ing·ly
Mo·vio·la (*Trademark*)
mow (**mow·ing, mowed,**
mowed *or* **mown**)
mow·burnt agricultural
term

mow·er
moxa medicinal substance
moxie US courage
Mo·zam·bi·can
Mo·zam·bique (or
  Mo·çam·)
moz·za·rel·la cheese
moz·zet·ta (or mo·zet·ta)
  clerical cape
Mr (plural Messrs)
Mrs
Ms
much (more, most)
much·ness
mu·cic acid
mu·cid mouldy
mu·ci·lage
mu·ci·lagi·nous
mu·cin biochemical
  compound
mu·cin·ous
muck
muck·er
mucki·ly
mucki·ness
muck·le Scot much
muck·rake
muck·rak·er
muck·worm
mucky (mucki·er,
  mucki·est)
mu·coid (or ·coi·dal)
mu·co·mem·bra·nous
mu·co·poly·sac·cha·ride
mu·co·pro·tein
mu·co·pu·ru·lent
mu·co·sa (plural ·sae)
  mucous membrane
mu·cos·ity
mu·cous (or ·cose; adj)
mu·cro (plural
  mu·cro·nes) biology
  term
mu·cro·nate (or ·nat·ed)
mu·cro·na·tion
mu·cus (noun)
mud (mud·ding, mud·ded)
mud·cat fish
mud·died
mud·di·ly
mud·di·ness
mud·dle
mud·dled·ness
muddle·headed
muddle·headed·ness

mud·dle·ment
mud·dler
mud·dling·ly
mud·dy (adj ·di·er,
  ·di·est; verb ·dies,
  ·dy·ing, ·died)
mud·fish (plural ·fish or
  ·fishes)
mud·guard
mu·dir governor
mud·lark
mud·pack
mu·dra Hindu dance
  movement
mud·skipper fish
mud·slinger
mud·slinging
mud·stone
muen·ster cheese
mues·li
mu·ez·zin mosque official
muff
muf·fin
muf·fle
muf·fler
Muf·ti (plural ·tis) Muslim
  legal adviser
muf·ti (plural ·tis) civilian
  dress
Mu·fu·li·ra Zambian town
mug (mug·ging, mugged)
mug·ger street robber
mug·ger (or ·gar, ·gur)
  crocodile
mug·gi·ly
mug·gi·ness
mug·gins
mug·gy (·gi·er, ·gi·est)
mug·wort
mug·wump politically
  neutral person
Mu·ham·mad·an Muslim
Mühl·hau·sen West
  German city
muk·luk Eskimo boot
mu·lat·to (plural ·tos or
  ·toes)
mul·berry (plural
  ·berries)
mulch soil enricher
mulct cheat
mule
mu·leta matador's cape
mu·leteer mule driver

mul·ey (or mul·ley)
  hornless cattle
mul·ga tree
Mül·heim an der Ruhr
  West German city
mu·li·eb·rity womanhood
mul·ish
mul·ish·ness
Mull Scottish island
mull
mul·lah (or mul·la)
  Muslim leader
mul·lein (or ·len) plant
mul·ler
mul·let
mul·ley variant spelling of
  muley
mul·li·gan stew
mul·li·ga·taw·ny
mul·li·on
mul·li·oned
mul·lite mineral
mul·lock Dialect mess
mullo·way fish
Mul·tan Pakistani city
mul·tan·gu·lar (or
  multi·an·)
mul·teity manifoldness
multi·birth
multi·cel·lu·lar
multi·chan·nel
multi·cide mass murder
multi·col·lin·ear·ity
  statistics term
multi·col·oured (US
  ·ored)
multi·di·rec·tion·al
multi·dis·ci·pli·nary
multi·fac·et·ed
multi·fac·to·rial
multi·fari·ous
multi·fid (or
  mul·tifi·dous)
multi·foil looped design
multi·fold
multi·fo·li·ate
multi·form
multi·for·mity
multi·gravi·da obstetrics
  term
multi·hull
multi·lami·nar
multi·lat·er·al
multi·lin·gual
multi·media

multi·mil·lion·aire

multi·na·tion·al

multi·no·mial

multi·nu·clear (*or* ·cleate)

mul·tipa·ra (*plural* ·rae)
obstetrics term

multi·par·ity

mul·tipa·rous

multi·par·tite

multi·plane multi-winged
aircraft

multi·ple

multiple-choice

multiple-poind·ing Scottish
legal term

multi·plet physics term

multi·plex electronics term

multi·plex·er

multi·pli·able

multi·pli·cand number
multiplied

multi·pli·cate manifold

multi·pli·ca·tion

multi·pli·ca·tion·al

multi·pli·ca·tive

multi·plic·ity (*plural*
·ities)

multi·pli·er

multi·ply (·plies, ·ply·ing,
·plied)

multi·pro·gram·ming

multi·pur·pose

multi·racial

multi·role

multi·screen

multi·stage

multi·sto·rey

multi·tude

multi·tu·di·nous

multi·va·len·cy

multi·va·lent

multi·vi·bra·tor

mul·ture miller's fee

mum mother; silent

mum (*or* mumm;
mum·ming, mummed)
act in mummer's play

mum·ble

mum·bler

mum·bling·ly

mum·bo jum·bo (*plural*
mum·bo jum·bos)

mum·chance dumbstruck

mum·mer

mum·mery (*plural*
·meries)

mum·mi·fi·ca·tion

mum·mi·fy (·fies, ·fy·ing,
·fied)

mum·my (*plural* ·mies)

mumps

munch

munch·er

mun·dane

mun·dane·ness

mung bean

munga *Austral* food

mun·go (*or* mon·go,
mon·goe; *plural* ·gos
or ·goes) fabric

Mu·nich

mu·nici·pal

mu·nici·pal·ity (*plural*
·ities)

mu·nici·pali·za·tion (*or*
·sa·tion)

mu·nici·pal·ize (*or* ·ise)

mu·nici·pal·ly

mu·nifi·cence (*or*
·cent·ness)

mu·nifi·cent

mu·ni·ment means of
defence

mu·ni·ments title deeds

mu·ni·tion

Mun·ster Irish province

Mün·ster West German city

munt·jac (*or* ·jak) deer

muon elementary particle

mu·ral

mu·ral·ist

mur·der

mur·der·er (*fem* ·ess)

mur·der·ous

mur·der·ous·ness

Mu·reş European river

mu·rex (*plural* mu·ri·ces)
mollusc

mu·ri·cate (*or* ·cat·ed)
biology term

mu·rine of rats and mice

murk (*or* mirk)

murki·ly (*or* mirki·)

murki·ness (*or* mirki·)

murky (*or* mirky;
murki·er, murki·est *or*
mirki·er, mirki·est)

Mur·mansk Soviet port

mur·mur

mur·mur·er

mur·mur·ing

mur·mur·ous

mur·phy (*plural* ·phies)
Dialect potato

mur·rain cattle disease;
compare moraine

Mur·ray Australian river

murre guillemot

murre·let bird

mur·rhine (*or* ·rine)
Roman vase material

Mur·rum·bidgee
Australian river

mur·ther *Archaic* murder

mu·sa·ceous botany term

Mus·ca constellation

mus·ca·del (*or* ·delle)
variants of muscatel

mus·ca·dine US grape

mus·ca·rine poisonous
alkaloid

Mus·cat capital of Oman

mus·cat grape

mus·ca·tel (*or* ·del, ·delle)
wine

mus·cid fly

mus·cle

muscle-bound

mus·cle·man (*plural*
·men)

mus·cly

mus·co·va·do (*or* mus·ca·)
raw sugar

Mus·co·vite native of
Moscow

mus·co·vite mineral

Mus·co·vy Russian
principality; duck

mus·cu·lar

mus·cu·lar·ity

mus·cu·la·ture

muse

muse·ful

mus·eol·ogy museum
organization; *compare*
musicology

mus·er

mu·sette bagpipe

mu·seum

mush

mushi·ly

mushi·ness

mush·room

mushy (mushi·er,
mushi·est)

mu·sic
mu·si·cal
mu·si·cale *US* musical
evening
mu·si·cal·ly
mu·si·cal·ness (*or* ·ity)
mu·si·cian
mu·si·cian·ship
mu·si·co·logi·cal
mu·si·colo·gist
mu·si·col·ogy study of
music; *compare* museology
mus·jid *variant spelling of*
masjid
musk
mus·keg bog
mus·kel·lunge (*or*
mas·ka·nonge, ·ki·) fish
mus·ket
mus·ket·eer
mus·ket·ry
muski·ness
musk·melon
musk·rat (*plural* ·rats *or*
·rat)
musky (muski·er,
muski·est)
Mus·lim (*or* Mos·lem;
plural ·lims, ·lim *or*
·lems, ·lem)
Mus·lim·ism (*or*
Mos·lem·)
mus·lin
muso *Austral* musician
mus·quash
muss *US* rumple
mus·sel mollusc; *compare*
muscle
must
mus·tache *US spelling of*
moustache
mus·ta·chio (*plural*
·chi·os)
mus·ta·chi·oed
mus·tang
mus·tard
mus·tee (*or* mes·) person
of mixed parentage
mus·te·line of badger
family
mus·ter
musth (*or* must) sexual
heat in animals
musti·ly
musti·ness
mus·ty (·ti·er, ·ti·est)

mu·tabil·ity (*or*
·table·ness)
mu·table
mu·tably
mu·ta·gen substance
causing mutation
mu·ta·gen·ic
mu·tant
mu·tate
mu·ta·tion
mu·ta·tion·al
mu·ta·tis mu·tan·dis
mutch linen cap
mute
mute·ness
mu·ti·cous botany term
mu·ti·late
mu·ti·la·tion
mu·ti·la·tive
mu·ti·la·tor
mu·ti·neer
mu·ti·nous
mu·ti·ny (*noun, plural*
·nies; *verb* ·nies,
·ny·ing, ·nied)
mut·ism
mutt *Slang* fool; cur
mut·ter
mut·ter·er
mut·ter·ing·ly
mut·ton
mutton·chops side whiskers
mut·tony
mu·tu·al
mu·tu·al·ity (*or* ·ness)
mu·tu·al·ize (*or* ·ise)
mu·tu·al·ly
mu·tule architecture term
Mu·zak (*Trademark*)
mu·zhik (*or* mou·jik,
mu·jik) Russian peasant
muzz make muzzy
muz·zi·ly
muz·zi·ness
muz·zle
muz·zler
muz·zy (·zi·er, ·zi·est)
my
my·al·gia muscle pain
my·al·gic
mya·lism witchcraft
my·all tree
my·as·thenia muscular
weakness
my·as·then·ic

my·celial
my·celium (*plural* ·celia)
fungal body
my·celoid
My·cenae ancient Greek
city
My·cenaean
my·ceto·ma (*plural* ·mas
or ·ma·ta) fungal
infection
my·ceto·zoan fungus
my·co·bac·te·rium (*plural*
·ria)
my·co·logi·cal (*or* ·log·ic)
my·colo·gist
my·col·ogy study of fungi
my·cor·rhi·za (*or* ·co·rhi·;
plural ·zae *or* ·zas)
botany term
my·cor·rhi·zal (*or* ·co·rhi·)
my·co·sis fungal disease
my·cot·ic
my·dria·sis pupil dilation
myd·ri·at·ic
my·elen·cephal·ic
my·elen·cepha·lon (*plural*
·lons *or* ·la) embryology
term
my·elin (*or* ·eline) nerve
sheath
my·elin·ic
my·eli·tis
my·eloid
my·elo·ma tumour
my·elo·ma·toid
myia·sis (*plural* ·ses)
infestation by fly larvae
my·lo·nite rock
myna (*or* my·nah, mina)
bird
Myn·heer Dutch title of
address
myo·car·dial
myo·car·dio·graph
myo·car·di·tis
myo·car·dium (*plural*
·dia) heart muscle
myo·gen·ic
myo·glo·bin protein
myo·graph
myo·graph·ic
myo·graphi·cal·ly
my·og·ra·phy
myo·log·ic (*or* ·logi·cal)
my·olo·gist

my·ol·ogy study of muscle
   diseases
myo·ma (*plural* ·mas *or*
   ·ma·ta) tumour
my·ope
myo·pia
my·op·ic
my·opi·cal·ly
myo·sin protein
myo·sis *variant spelling of*
   miosis
myo·so·tis (*or* ·sote) plant
myo·tome anatomy term
myo·to·nia lack of muscle
   tone
myo·ton·ic
myri·ad
myria·pod invertebrate
myri·apo·dan
myri·apo·dous
my·ri·ca medicinal bark
myr·meco·logi·cal
myr·mecolo·gist
myr·mecol·ogy study of
   ants
myr·mecopha·gous
myr·meco·phile
myr·mecophi·lous
Myr·mi·don (*plural*
   mi·dons *or* mido·nes)
   mythological race
my·roba·lan fruit
myrrh

myr·ta·ceous
myr·tle
my·self
My·sore Indian city
mys·ta·gog·ic (*or*
   ·gogi·cal)
mys·ta·gogi·cal·ly
mys·ta·gogue mystic
   teacher
mys·ta·go·gy
mys·teri·ous
mys·teri·ous·ness
mys·tery (*plural* ·teries)
mys·tic
mys·ti·cal
mys·ti·cal·ly
mys·ti·cism
mys·ti·fi·ca·tion
mys·ti·fi·er
mys·ti·fy (·fies, ·fy·ing,
   ·fied)
mys·ti·fy·ing·ly
mys·tique
myth
mythi·cal
mythi·cal·ly
mythi·cist (*or* ·ciz·er,
   ·cis·er)
mythi·ci·za·tion (*or*
   ·sa·tion)
mythi·cize (*or* ·cise)
mytho·logi·cal

my·tholo·gist
my·tholo·gi·za·tion (*or*
   ·sa·tion)
my·tholo·gize (*or* ·gise)
my·tholo·giz·er (*or*
   ·gis·er)
my·thol·ogy (*plural*
   ·ogies)
mytho·ma·nia psychiatric
   term
mytho·ma·ni·ac
mytho·poeia (*or* ·po·esis)
   myth making
mytho·poe·ic
mytho·poe·ism
mytho·poe·ist
my·thos (*plural* ·thoi)
   group of beliefs
(myxamatosis) *incorrect
   spelling of* myxomatosis
myx·oedema (*US*
   ·edema) thyroid disease
myx·oedem·ic (*US*
   ·edem·)
myxo·ma (*plural* ·mas *or*
   ·ma·ta) tumour
myxo·ma·to·sis
myx·oma·tous
myxo·my·cete fungus
myxo·my·cetous
myxo·vi·rus

N

Naafi (*or* NAAFI)
nab (nab·bing, nabbed)
Na·blus (*or* Nabu·lus)
   Jordanian town
na·bob
na·bob·ery (*or* ·ism)
Nabonidus biblical
   character
Naboth biblical character
na·celle part of aircraft
na·cre mother-of-pearl
na·cred
na·cre·ous
Na-Dene (*or* -Déné)
   language group
na·dir
nae *Scot* no
nae·void (*US* ne·)

nae·vus (*US* ne·; *plural*
   ·vi) birthmark
nag (nag·ging, nagged)
Naga (*plural* Nagas *or*
   Naga) Indian people
Na·ga·land
na·ga·na (*or* n'ga·na)
   animal disease
Na·ga·no Japanese city
Na·ga·ri Indian script
Na·ga·sa·ki Japanese port
nagged
nag·ger
nag·ging
na·gor antelope
Nagorno-Karabakh Soviet
   region
Na·go·ya Japanese city

Nag·pur Indian city
Na·huatl (*plural* ·huatl *or*
   ·huatls) American Indian
Na·hua·tlan
nai·ad (*plural* ·ads *or*
   ·ades)
na·ïf *variant spelling of* naive
nail
nail·brush
nail·er
nail·file
nail·head decorative device
nain·sook fabric
nai·ra Nigerian currency
Nairn former Scottish
   county
Nai·ro·bi
nais·sant heraldry term

na·ive (*or* ·ïve, ·if)
na·ive·ty (*or* ·ive·té, ·ïve·té)
Najd *variant spelling of* Nejd
na·ked
na·ked·ness
na·ker kettledrum
Na·khi·che·van Soviet city
Nal·chik Soviet city
Nama (*or* Na·ma·qua; *plural* Nama, Namas *or* ·qua, ·quas) Hottentot people
nam·able (*or* name·)
Na·man·gan Soviet city
namby-pamby (*plural* -pambies)
nam·dah *variant spelling of* numdah
name
name-dropper
name-dropping
name·less
name·ly
name·plate
name·sake
name·tape
Nam·hoi Chinese city
Na·mibia
Na·mib·ian
Na·mur Belgian province
nan (*or* nanna) *Slang* grandmother
Nan·chang (*or* Nan-ch'ang) Chinese city
Nan·cy French city
nan·cy (*plural* ·cies) effeminate man
Nan·da Devi Himalayan mountain
Nan·ga Par·bat Himalayan mountain
nan·keen (*or* ·kin) fabric
Nan·king (*or* Nan-ching) Chinese port
nanna *variant of* nan
Nan·ning (*or* Nan-ning) Chinese port
nan·ny (*plural* ·nies)
na·no·metre (*US* ·meter)
na·no·plank·ton (*or* nan·no·)
na·no·sec·ond
Nan Shan Chinese mountain range
Nantes French port
Nan·tuck·et US island

Nan·tung Chinese city
Naoise Irish mythological character
nap (nap·ping, napped)
na·palm
nape
naph·tha
naph·tha·lene (*or* ·line, ·lin)
naph·thene
naph·thol
naph·thyl
Na·pier New Zealand port
Na·pier·ian loga·ri·thm
na·pi·form turnip-shaped
nap·kin
Na·ples
na·po·le·on coin
Na·po·leon·ic
nap·pa leather
nappe rock fold
napped
nap·per *Slang* head
nap·pi·ness
nap·ping
nap·py (*noun, plural* ·pies; *adj* ·pi·er, ·pi·est)
Nara Japanese city
Na·ra·yan·ganj Bangladeshi city
nar·ceine (*or* ·ceen) alkaloid
nar·cis·sism (*or* nar·cism)
nar·cis·sist
nar·cis·sis·tic
nar·cis·sus (*plural* ·si *or* ·suses)
nar·co·analy·sis
nar·co·lep·sy
nar·co·lep·tic
nar·co·sis (*plural* ·ses)
nar·co·syn·thesis medical treatment
nar·cot·ic
nar·coti·cal·ly
nar·co·tism
nar·co·ti·za·tion (*or* ·sa·tion)
nar·co·tize (*or* ·tise)
nard medicinal plant
nar·es (*sing.* ·is) nostrils
nar·ghi·le hookah
nar·ial (*or* ·ine)
nark
Nar·ra·gan·set (*or* ·sett; *plural* ·set, ·sets *or*

·sett, ·setts) American Indian
nar·rat·able
nar·rate
nar·ra·tion
nar·ra·tive
nar·ra·tor (*or* ·rat·er)
nar·row
narrow-minded
narrow-minded·ness
nar·row·ness
nar·thex church portico
Nar·vik Norwegian port
nar·whal (*or* ·wal, ·whale) whale
nary *Dialect* not
na·sal
na·sal·ity
na·sali·za·tion (*or* ·sa·tion)
na·sal·ize (*or* ·ise)
na·sal·ly
nas·cence (*or* ·cen·cy)
nas·cent
Nash·ville US city
na·sial
na·si·on anatomy term
na·so·fron·tal
na·so·pha·ryn·geal
na·so·phar·ynx (*plural* ·pha·ryn·ges *or* ·phar·ynxes)
Nas·sau West German region; Bahamian capital
nas·tic botany term
nas·ti·ly
nas·ti·ness
na·stur·tium
nas·ty (*adj* ·ti·er, ·ti·est; *noun, plural* ·ties)
Na·tal South African province; Brazilian port
na·tal of birth
na·tal·ity
na·tant floating
na·ta·tion swimming
na·ta·tion·al
na·ta·tory
na·tes (*sing.* ·tis) buttocks
na·tion
na·tion·al
na·tion·al·ism
na·tion·al·ist
na·tion·al·is·tic
na·tion·al·ity (*plural* ·ities)

na·tion·ali·za·tion (*or* ·sa·tion)
na·tion·al·ize (*or* ·ise)
na·tion·al·ly
na·tion·hood
nation·wide
na·tive American Indian
na·tiv·ism
na·tiv·ist
na·tiv·is·tic
Na·tiv·ity Christ's birth
na·tiv·ity (*plural* ·ities) birth or origin
NATO
nat·ro·lite mineral
na·tron mineral
nat·ter
nat·ter·jack toad
nat·ti·ly
nat·ti·ness
nat·ty (·ti·er, ·ti·est)
natu·ral
natu·ral·ism artistic movement; *compare* naturism
natu·ral·ist
natu·ral·is·tic
natu·ral·is·ti·cal·ly
natu·rali·za·tion (*or* ·sa·tion)
natu·ral·ize (*or* ·ise)
natu·ral·ly
natu·ral·ness
na·ture
na·tur·ism nudism; *compare* naturalism
na·tur·ist
na·turo·path
na·turo·path·ic
na·tur·opa·thy nature cure
naught *Archaic* nothing; *US spelling of* nought
naugh·ti·ly
naugh·ti·ness
naugh·ty (·ti·er, ·ti·est)
nau·plius (*plural* ·plii) crustacean larva
Nau·ru island republic
Nau·ruan
nau·sea
nau·seate
nau·sea·tion
nau·seous
nau·seous·ness
nautch (*or* nauch) Indian dance
nau·ti·cal

nau·ti·cal·ly
nau·ti·loid
nau·ti·lus (*plural* ·luses *or* ·li) mollusc
Nava·ho (*or* ·jo; *plural* ·ho, ·hos *or* ·jo, ·jos) American Indian
na·val of ships; *compare* navel
na·val·ly
nav·ar navigation system
nava·rin mutton stew
Na·varre
nave
na·vel umbilicus; *compare* naval
navi·cert cargo certificate
na·vicu·lar boat-shaped
navi·gabil·ity (*or* ·gable·ness)
navi·gable
navi·gably
navi·gate
navi·ga·tion
navi·ga·tion·al
navi·ga·tor
nav·vy (*plural* ·vies) labourer
navy (*plural* navies)
na·wab Indian prince
Nax·os Greek island
nay no; *compare* neigh
Na·ya·rit Mexican state
Naza·rene inhabitant of Nazareth; Syrian Christian
Naza·reth
Naza·rite (*or* Nazi·) Old Testament ascetic
Naze Essex headland
Nazi (*plural* Nazis)
Na·zi·fy (·fies, ·fy·ing, ·fied)
Na·zism
Ndja·me·na capital of Chad
Ndo·la Zambian city
Neagh Northern Irish lake
Ne·an·der·thal
neap tide
Nea·poli·tan
near
near·by
Ne·arc·tic zoogeographical term
near·ly
near·ness
near·side
near·sighted

near-sighted·ness
neat
neat·en
neath *Archaic* beneath
neat·ness
neat's-foot oil
neb *Dialect* projecting part
Ne·bras·ka
nebu·chad·nez·zar wine bottle
nebu·la (*plural* ·lae *or* ·las)
nebu·lar
nebu·li·za·tion (*or* ·sa·tion)
nebu·lize (*or* ·lise) atomize
nebu·liz·er (*or* ·lis·er)
nebu·los·ity (*plural* ·ities)
nebu·lous
nebu·lous·ness
ne·ces·saries
nec·es·sari·ly
nec·es·sary
ne·ces·si·tar·ian (*or* nec·es·sar·ian)
ne·ces·si·tari·an·ism (*or* nec·es·sari·an·ism) philosophy term
ne·ces·si·tate
ne·ces·sita·tion
ne·ces·si·ta·tive
ne·ces·si·tous
ne·ces·sity (*plural* ·sities)
neck
Neck·ar West German river
neck·band
neck·cloth
neck·er
neck·er·chief
neck·lace
neck·line
neck·piece
neck·tie
neck·wear
nec·ro·bio·sis death of cells
nec·ro·bi·ot·ic
ne·crola·try worship of the dead
nec·ro·logi·cal
ne·crolo·gist
ne·crol·ogy (*plural* ·ogies) list of dead people
nec·ro·man·cer
nec·ro·man·cy
nec·ro·man·tic
nec·ro·philia (*or* ne·crophi·lism)

nec·ro·phili·ac (*or* ·phile)
nec·ro·phil·ic
nec·ro·phobe
nec·ro·pho·bia
nec·ro·pho·bic
ne·cropo·lis (*plural* ·lises *or* ·leis)
nec·rop·sy (*plural* ·sies)
ne·crose (*verb*)
ne·cro·sis
ne·crot·ic
ne·croto·my (*plural* ·mies) dissection of corpse
nec·tar
nec·tar·eous (*or* ·ous)
nec·tar·ine
nec·ta·ry (*plural* ·ries)
ned·dy (*plural* ·dies)
née (*or* nee) indicating maiden name
need
need·ful
need·ful·ness
needi·ness
nee·dle
needle·cord
needle·craft
needle·fish (*plural* ·fish *or* ·fishes)
needle·ful
needle·point
need·less
need·less·ness
needle·woman (*plural* ·women)
needle·work
need·ments
needn't
needy (needi·er, needi·est)
neep *Dialect* turnip
ne'er
ne'er-do-well
ne·fari·ous
nefari·ous·ness
ne·gate
ne·ga·tion
nega·tive
nega·tive·ness
negative-raising grammar term
nega·ti·vism
nega·tiv·ist
nega·tiv·is·tic
nega·tiv·ity
ne·ga·tor (*or* ·gat·er)

ne·ga·to·ry
Neg·ev (*or* ·eb) Israeli desert
ne·glect
ne·glect·er (*or* ·glec·tor)
ne·glect·ful
ne·glect·ful·ly
ne·glect·ful·ness
neg·li·gee (*or* ·gée, ·gé)
neg·li·gence
neg·li·gent
neg·li·gibil·ity (*or* ·gible·ness)
neg·li·gible
neg·li·gibly
ne·go·tiabil·ity
ne·go·tiable
ne·go·ti·ant
ne·go·ti·ate
ne·go·tia·tion
ne·go·tia·tor
Ne·gress
Ne·gril·lo (*plural* ·los *or* ·loes) African Negroid people
Neg·ri Sem·bi·lan Malaysian state
Ne·grit·ic of Negroes or Negritos
Ne·gri·to (*plural* ·tos *or* ·toes) Asian Negroid people
ne·gri·tude
Ne·gro (*plural* ·groes)
Ne·groid
Ne·gro·ism
Ne·gro·phile (*or* ·phil)
Ne·gro·phobe
Ne·gro·pho·bia
Neg·ro·pont Greek island
Ne·gros Philippine island
ne·gus (*plural* ·guses) spiced drink
neigh sound of a horse; *compare* nay
neigh·bour (*US* ·bor)
neigh·bour·hood (*US* ·bor·)
neigh·bour·ing (*US* ·bor·)
neigh·bour·li·ness (*US* ·bor·)
neigh·bour·ly (*US* ·bor·)
Neis·se Polish river
nei·ther
Nejd (*or* Najd) Saudi Arabian province
nek mountain pass

nek·ton minute marine organisms
nek·ton·ic
nel·ly (*plural* ·lies)
Nel·son Lancashire town; New Zealand port
nel·son wrestling hold
ne·lum·bo (*plural* ·bos) plant
nema·thel·minth worm
ne·mat·ic chemistry term
nema·to·cyst
nema·to·cys·tic
nema·tode
Nem·bu·tal (*Trademark*)
Ne·mea ancient Greek valley
Ne·mean
ne·mer·tean (*or* nem·er·tine) marine worm
ne·mesia plant
Nemesis Greek goddess
nem·esis (*plural* ·eses) retribution
(nemonic) *incorrect spelling of* mnemonic
nene goose
neo·an·throp·ic
neo·ars·phena·mine
Neo·cene geological term
neo·clas·si·cal (*or* ·sic)
neo·clas·si·cism
neo·clas·si·cist
neo·co·lo·nial
neo·co·lo·ni·al·ism
neo·co·lo·ni·al·ist
neo·dym·ium chemical element
Neo·gaea zoogeographical area
Neo·gaean
Neo·gene geological term
neo·im·pres·sion·ism
neo·lith
Neo·lith·ic
neo·logi·cal
neo·logi·cal·ly
ne·olo·gism (*or* ne·ol·ogy; *plural* ·gisms *or* ·ogies)
ne·olo·gist
ne·olo·gis·tic (*or* ·ti·cal)
ne·olo·gis·ti·cal·ly
ne·olo·gize (*or* ·gise)
ne·ol·ogy *variant of* neologism
neo·my·cin antibiotic

neon
neo·na·tal
neo·nate newborn child
neo·phyte novice
neo·phyt·ic
neo·plasm tumour
neo·plas·tic
neo·plas·ti·cism style of
   painting
neo·plas·ty plastic surgery
Neo-Platonism philosophy
Neo-Platonist
neo·prene synthetic rubber
ne·ot·enous
ne·ot·eny zoology term
neo·ter·ic modern
neo·teri·cal·ly
Neo·tropi·cal
   zoogeographical term
neo·type
Neo·zo·ic geological term
Ne·pal
Nepa·lese (plural ·lese)
Ne·pali
ne·pen·the
ne·pen·thean
ne·per unit
neph·eline (or ·elite)
   mineral
neph·elin·ite rock
neph·elom·eter chemistry
   apparatus
neph·elom·etry
neph·ew
nepho·gram
nepho·graph
nepho·logi·cal
ne·pholo·gist
ne·phol·ogy study of clouds
nepho·scope
ne·phral·gia kidney pain
ne·phral·gic
ne·phrec·to·my (plural
   ·mies) removal of kidney
ne·phrid·ial
ne·phrid·ium (plural
   ·phridia) excretory organ
neph·rite mineral
ne·phrit·ic of the kidneys
ne·phri·tis
ne·phrol·ogy
neph·ron
ne·phro·sis
ne·phrot·ic
ne·phroto·my (plural
   ·mies)

ne plus ul·tra Latin the
   perfect state
ne·pot·ic (or ·tis·tic)
nepo·tism
nepo·tist
Nep·tune planet
Neptune Roman god
Nep·tu·nian
nep·tu·nium chemical
   element
ne·ral chemistry term
Ne·reid (plural ·rei·des)
   Greek nymph
ne·reis worm
ne·rit·ic ecology term
nero·li oil
ner·vate having leaf veins
nerve
nerve·less
nerve·less·ness
nerve-racking (or
   -wracking)
nervi·ly
nerv·ine soothing the nerves
nervi·ness
nerv·ous
nerv·ous·ness
ner·vure biology term
nervy (nervi·er, nervi·est)
nes·ci·ence ignorance
nes·ci·ent
nesh Dialect timid
Ness Scottish lake
ness promontory
nes·sel·rode pudding
nest
nest·er
nes·tle
nes·tler
nest·ling
Nestor mythological
   character
Nes·to·ri·an·ism
   theological doctrine
net (net·ting, net·ted)
   mesh
net (or nett; net·ting,
   net·ted) remaining; earn
   as profit
net·ball
neth·er
Neth·er·land·er
Neth·er·lands
nether·most
net·su·ke

nett variant spelling of net
net·ted
net·ting
net·tle
net·tle·some causing
   irritation
net·tly
net·ty Dialect lavatory
net·work
Neu·châ·tel Swiss city and
   lake
Neuf·châ·tel French town;
   cheese
neume (or neum) musical
   symbol
neu·ral
neu·ral·gia
neu·ral·gic
neu·ras·the·nia
neu·ras·then·ic
neu·ras·theni·cal·ly
neu·rec·to·my (plural
   ·mies)
neu·rit·ic
neu·ri·tis
neu·ro·blast embryonic cell
neu·ro·coele embryology
   term
neu·ro·fi·bril
neu·ro·fi·bril·lar
neu·ro·gen·ic
neu·rog·lia nerve tissue
neu·ro·hy·pophy·sis
   (plural ·ses)
neu·ro·lem·ma (or
   neu·ri·) nerve sheath
neu·ro·logi·cal
neu·rolo·gist
neu·rol·ogy
neu·ro·ma (plural ·ma·ta
   or ·mas) tumour
neu·roma·tous
neu·ro·mus·cu·lar
neu·rone (or ·ron) nerve
   cell
neu·ron·ic
neu·ro·path person with
   nervous disorder
neu·ro·path·ic
neu·ro·pathi·cal·ly
neu·ro·pa·tholo·gist
neu·ro·pa·thol·ogy
neu·ropa·thy disease of
   nervous system
neu·ro·physio·logi·cal

neu·ro·physio·logi·cal·ly
neu·ro·physi·olo·gist
neu·ro·physi·ol·ogy
neu·ro·psy·chi·at·ric
neu·ro·psy·chia·trist
neu·ro·psy·chia·try
neu·rop·ter·an (or ·on;
  plural ·ter·ans or ·tera)
  insect
neu·rop·ter·ous (or
  ·ter·an)
neu·ro·sci·ence
neu·ro·sis (plural ·ses)
neu·ro·sur·geon
neu·ro·sur·gery
neu·ro·sur·gi·cal
neu·ro·sur·gi·cal·ly
neu·rot·ic
neu·roti·cal·ly
neu·roti·cism
neu·roto·mist
neu·roto·my (plural
  ·mies) nerve surgery
neu·ro·vas·cu·lar
Neuss West German city
neu·ter
neu·tral
neu·tral·ism
neu·tral·ist
neu·tral·ity
neu·trali·za·tion (or
  ·sa·tion)
neu·tral·ize (or ·ise)
neu·tral·iz·er (or ·is·er)
neu·tral·ly
neu·tret·to (plural ·tos)
  physics term
neu·tri·no (plural ·nos)
  elementary particle
neu·tron
neu·tro·phil (or ·phile)
  blood cell
Neva Soviet river
Ne·va·da
névé mass of ice
nev·er
never·more
never·never
never·the·less
Ne·vis West Indian island
ne·vus US spelling of naevus
new
New·ark English town; US
  port
new·born

New Bruns·wick
New·burg cookery term
New·bury
New·cas·tle Australian port
New·castle-under-Lyme
New·castle-upon-Tyne
new·comer
new·el
new·fan·gled
New·fie Slang inhabitant of
  Newfoundland
New·found·land
New·found·land·er
New·gate former prison
New·ham London borough
New·ha·ven
new·ish
new·ly
newly·wed
New·mar·ket
new·mar·ket gambling
  game; riding coat
new·ness
New Or·le·ans
New·port Isle of Wight
  town; Welsh port
news
news·agent
news·cast US news
  broadcast
news·caster
news·hawk
newsi·ness
news·letter
news·paper
news·paper·man (plural
  ·men)
new·speak
news·print
news·reel
news·stand
news·worthi·ness
news·worthy
newsy (newsi·er,
  newsi·est)
newt
New·ton Welsh town
new·ton unit
Newton·abbey Northern
  Irish town
New·to·nian of Isaac
  Newton
New Zea·land
New Zea·land·er
next

next-door (adj)
nex·us (plural nex·us or
  nex·uses)
ngaio (plural ngaios) tree
ngo·ma African drum
Ngu·ni language
ngwee Zambian coin
nia·cin vitamin
Ni·aga·ra
Nia·mey capital of Niger
nib (nib·bing, nibbed)
nib·ble
nib·bler
nib·lick golf club
Nica·ra·gua
Nica·ra·guan
nic·co·lite mineral
Nice French city
nice
Ni·cene Creed
nice·ness
ni·cety (plural ·ceties)
niche
Ni·chrome (Trademark)
nic·ish
nick
nick·el (·el·ling, ·elled;
  US ·el·ing, ·eled)
nick·el·ic
nick·el·if·er·ous
nickel·odeon
nick·el·ous
nick·er
nick·nack variant spelling of
  knickknack
nick·name
Nico·bar Indian islands
Nicol prism
Nico·sia Cypriot capital
ni·co·tia·na plant
nico·tina·mide vitamin
nico·tine
nico·tin·ic
nico·tin·ism
nic·ti·tate (or nic·tate) to
  blink
nic·ti·ta·tion (or
  nic·ta·tion)
ni·dal
niddle-noddle nod rapidly
nide variant of nye
ni·dico·lous ornithology
  term
nidi·fi·cate build nest
nidi·fi·ca·tion

ni·di·fu·gous ornithology
  term
nidi·fy (·fies, ·fy·ing,
  ·fied) build nest
nid-nod (-nod·ding,
  -nod·ded)
ni·dus (plural ·di)
niece
ni·el·list
ni·el·lo (noun, plural ·li or
  ·los; verb ·lo·ing, ·loed)
  engraving term
Nier·stein·er wine
Nie·tzschean
Nie·tzsche·ism (or
  ·tzschean·ism)
  philosophy
nieve Dialect fist
Niè·vre French department
niff
niffy (niffi·er, niffi·est)
nif·ti·ly
nif·ti·ness
nif·ty (·ti·er, ·ti·est)
Ni·ger
Ni·geria
Ni·gerian
nig·gard
nig·gard·li·ness
nig·gard·ly
nig·ger
nig·gle
nig·gler
nig·gling
nig·gly
nigh
night
night·cap
night·club
night·dress
night·fall
night·gown
night·hawk
nightie (or nighty; plural
  nighties)
night·in·gale
night·jar
night·life
night-light
night·long
night·ly
night·mare
night·mar·ish
night·rider
night·shade

night·shirt
night·spot
night-time
night·wear
ni·gres·cence
ni·gres·cent blackish
ni·gro·sine (or ·sin)
  pigment
ni·hil Latin nothing
ni·hil·ism
ni·hil·ist
ni·hil·is·tic
ni·hil·ity
Nii·ga·ta Japanese port
Nij·megen Dutch town
Nik·ko Japanese town
Ni·ko·la·yev Soviet city
nil
nil de·spe·ran·dum Latin
  never despair
Nile
nil·gai (or ·ghau; plural
  ·gai, ·gais, or ·ghau,
  ·ghaus) antelope
Ni·lot·ic
nim game
nim·ble
nim·ble·ness
nimble·wit US clever
  person
nim·bly
nim·bo·stra·tus (plural ·ti)
nim·bus (plural ·bi or
  ·buses)
Nîmes French city
niminy-piminy (or
  miminy-)
Nimrod biblical hunter
nin·com·poop
nine
nine·fold
nine·pins
nine·teen
nine·teenth
nine·ti·eth
nine·ty (plural ·ties)
Ni·neveh Assyrian capital
Ning·po Chinese port
Ning·sia Hui Chinese
  region
nin·ny (plural ·nies)
ni·non fabric
ninth
nio·bic
nio·bite

nio·bium chemical element
nio·bous
nip (nip·ping, nipped)
nipa palm tree
Nipi·gon Canadian lake
Nip·is·sing Canadian lake
nip·per
nip·pi·ly
nip·ple
nipple·wort plant
Nip·pon
Nip·pon·ese (plural ·ese)
Nip·pur Babylonian city
nip·py (·pi·er, ·pi·est)
nir·va·na
nir·va·nic
Niš Yugoslav town
Ni·sha·pur Iranian town
Ni·shi·no·mi·ya Japanese
  city
nisi legal term
nisi pri·us legal term
ni·sus (plural ·sus) striving
nit
ni·ter US spelling of nitre
Ni·terói Brazilian port
ni·tid bright
ni·tra·mine
ni·trate
ni·tra·tion
ni·tre (US ·ter)
ni·tric containing nitrogen
ni·tride chemical compound
ni·trid·ing metallurgy term
ni·tri·fi·able
ni·tri·fi·ca·tion
ni·tri·fy (·fies, ·fy·ing,
  ·fied)
ni·trile
ni·trite
ni·tro·bac·te·ria (sing.
  ·rium)
ni·tro·ben·zene
ni·tro·cel·lu·lose
ni·tro·chlo·ro·form
ni·tro·gen
ni·trog·eni·za·tion (or
  ·sa·tion)
ni·trog·en·ize (or ·ise)
ni·trog·enous
ni·tro·glyc·er·in (or ·ine)
ni·trom·eter
ni·tro·methane
ni·tro·met·ric
ni·tro·par·af·fin

ni·trosa·mine
ni·tro·so (or ·syl)
ni·trous
nit·ty (·ti·er, ·ti·est)
nitty-gritty
nit·wit
Niue Pacific island
ni·val of snow
ni·va·tion geology term
niv·eous resembling snow
Ni·ver·nais former French
   province
nix (fem nixie) water
   sprite
nix·er Irish spare-time job
Ni·zam Indian title
ni·zam former Turkish
   soldier
Njord (or Njorth) Norse
   god
no (plural noes or nos)
No (or Noh) Japanese
   drama
Noa·chian (or No·ach·ic)
   of Noah
nob Slang wealthy person;
   cribbage term; compare
   knob
no-ball
nob·ble
nob·bler
nob·but Dialect nothing but
no·belium chemical element
no·bili·ary
no·bil·ity (plural ·ities)
no·ble
no·ble·man (plural ·men)
no·ble·ness
no·blesse oblige French
   nobility obliges
noble·woman (plural
   ·women)
no·bly
no·body (plural ·bodies)
no·ci·cep·tive causing pain
nock notch on arrow
noc·tam·bu·lism (or
   ·la·tion)
noc·tam·bu·list
noc·ti·lu·ca (plural ·cae)
   protozoan
noc·ti·lu·cence
noc·ti·lu·cent
noc·tu·id moth
noc·tule bat

noc·turn part of Catholic
   matins; compare nocturne
noc·tur·nal
noc·tur·nal·ity
noc·tur·nal·ly
noc·turne musical piece;
   compare nocturn
nocu·ous
nod (nod·ding, nod·ded)
no·dal
no·dal·ity
nod·dle
nod·dy (plural ·dies) bird;
   fool
node
nodi·cal astronomy term
no·dose (or ·dous)
no·dos·ity
nodu·lar (or ·lose, ·lous)
nod·ule
no·dus (plural ·di)
   problematic situation
Noel (or Noël)
no·esis intellectual
   functioning
no·et·ic
nog
nog·gin measure of spirits
nog·ging building term
Noh variant spelling of No
noil textile fibres
noise
noise·less
noise·less·ness
noi·sette
noisi·ly
noisi·ness
noi·some offensive
noi·some·ness
noisy (noisi·er, noisi·est)
no·lens vo·lens Latin
   willing or unwilling
noli-me-tangere warning;
   plant
nol·le pros·equi legal term
nolo con·ten·de·re legal
   term
noma medical term
no·mad
no·mad·ic
no·madi·cal·ly
no·mad·ism
no-man's-land
nom·arch

nom·ar·chy (or nome;
   plural ·chies or nomes)
   Greek province
nom·bril heraldic term
nom de guerre (plural
   noms de guerre)
   assumed name
nom de plume (plural
   noms de plume) pen
   name
nome variant of nomarchy
no·men (plural nomi·na)
   ancient Roman's name
no·men·cla·tor inventor of
   names
no·men·cla·ture
nomi·nal
nomi·nal·ism
nomi·nal·ist
nomi·nal·is·tic
nomi·nal·ly
nomi·nate
nomi·na·tion
nomi·na·tive
nomi·na·tor
nomi·nee
no·mism theology term
no·mis·tic
no·moc·ra·cy (plural
   ·cies) government based
   on law
nomo·gram (or ·graph)
   type of graph
no·mog·ra·pher
nomo·graph·ic
nomo·graphi·cal
no·mo·graphi·cal·ly
no·mog·ra·phy (plural
   ·phies)
no·mo·logi·cal
no·mo·logi·cal·ly
no·molo·gist
no·mol·ogy science of law
nomo·thet·ic (or
   ·theti·cal) giving laws
no·nage
no·na·genar·ian
nona·gon
non-ago·nal
non-aligned
non-ap·pear·ance
non-at·tend·ance
non-at·tribu·tive
nonce
non·cha·lance
non·cha·lant

non·com *Slang*
  noncommissioned officer
non·com·bat·ant
non·com·mis·sioned
non·com·mit·tal
non·com·mit·tal·ly
non·com·pli·ance
non com·pos men·tis
  Latin of unsound mind
non·con·cur·rent
non·con·duc·tor
non·con·form·ism
Non·con·form·ist
  dissenting Protestant
non·con·form·ist one who
  does not conform
Non·con·form·ity (*or*
  ·ism)
non·con·form·ity
non·con·sti·tu·tion·al
non·con·ta·gious
non·con·tribu·ting
non·con·tribu·tory
non·co·op·era·tion
non·co·op·era·tive
non·co·op·era·tor
non·cor·rod·ing
non·crea·tive
non·de·nomi·na·tion·al
non·de·script
non·dis·junc·tion
non·drink·er
none
non·ed·ible
non·ego philosophy term
non·en·tity (*plural* ·tities)
non·equiva·lence
nones Roman date;
  canonical hour
non·es·sen·tial
none·such (*or* non·)
non·et
none·the·less
non·ethi·cal
non·event
non·ex·ist·ence
non·ex·ist·ent
non·ex·plo·sive
non·fac·tual
non·fea·sance legal term
non·fer·rous
non·fic·tion
non·fic·tion·al
non·flam·mable
nong *Austral* stupid person

non·har·mon·ic
non·iden·ti·cal
non·idio·mat·ic
no·nil·lion 10^{54}
no·nil·lionth
non·in·dus·trial
non·in·fec·tious
non·in·flam·mable
non·inter·ven·tion
non·inter·ven·tion·al
non·inter·ven·tion·ist
non·in·toxi·cat·ing
non·ir·ri·tant
non·join·der legal term
non·judg·men·tal (*or*
  ·judge·)
non·ju·ror one refusing to
  take oath
non li·cet *Latin* unlawful
non·ma·lig·nant
non·medi·cal
non·mem·ber
non·met·al
non·met·al·lic
non·op·er·able
non·op·era·tive
non·pa·reil unsurpassed
non·par·ous never having
  given birth
non·par·tici·pat·ing
non·par·ti·san (*or* ·zan)
non·par·ty
non·plus (*noun, plural*
  ·pluses; *verb* ·plusses,
  ·plus·sing, ·plussed;
  US ·pluses, ·plus·ing,
  ·plused)
non·poi·son·ous
non·po·liti·cal
non·pro·duc·tive
non·pro·duc·tive·ness
non·pro·duc·tiv·ity
non·pro·gres·sive
non·pro·lif·era·tion
non·pros (-prosses,
  -prossing, -prossed) legal term
non pro·sequi·tur legal
  term
non·rep·re·sen·ta·tion·al
non·resi·dence (*or*
  ·den·cy)
non·resi·dent
non·resi·den·tial
non·re·sis·tant

non·re·stric·tive
non·re·turn·able
non·rig·id
non·sched·uled
non·sec·ta·rian
non·sense
non·sen·si·cal
non·sen·si·cal·ly
non·sen·si·cal·ness (*or*
  ·ity)
non se·qui·tur
non·slip
non·smok·er
non·spe·cif·ic
non·stand·ard
non·stand·ard·ized (*or*
  ·ised)
non·start·er
non·sta·tive linguistics term
non·stick
non·stimu·lat·ing
non·stop
non·stra·te·gic
non·striker
non·such *variant spelling of*
  nonesuch
non·suit
non·swim·mer
non·tech·ni·cal
non·tox·ic
non·typi·cal
non-U
non·un·ion
non·un·ion·ism
non·ver·bal
non·vio·lence
non·vio·lent
non·vot·er
non-White
noo·dle
nook
noon
noon·day
no-one (*or* no one)
noon·ing *US* midday break
noon·time (*or* ·tide)
noose
no·pal cactus
no-par (*adj*)
nope *Slang* no
nor
nor·adrena·line
Nor·dic
Nor·folk
no·ria waterwheel

Nori·cum Celtic Alpine
  kingdom
nor·ite rock
nork *Austral* breast
norm
Nor·ma constellation
nor·mal
nor·mal·ity (*or esp. US*
  ·cy)
nor·mali·za·tion (*or*
  ·sa·tion)
nor·mal·ize (*or* ·ise)
nor·mal·ly
Nor·man
Nor·man·dy
nor·ma·tive
Norn Norse goddess
Norr·kö·ping Swedish port
Norse
Norse·man (*plural* ·men)
north
North·al·ler·ton Yorkshire
  town
North·amp·ton
North·amp·ton·shire
north·bound
north·country·man
  (*plural* ·men)
north·east
north·easter
north·easter·ly (*plural*
  ·lies)
north·eastern
north·eastward
nor·ther·ly (*plural* ·lies)
north·ern
north·ern·er
north·ern·most
north·ing navigation term
north·northeast
north·northwest
North Pole
North·um·ber·land county
North·um·bria region
North·um·brian
north·ward (*adj*)
north·wards (*adv*)
north·west
north·wester
north·wester·ly (*plural*
  ·lies)
north·western
north·westward
North·wich Cheshire town
Nor·way

Nor·we·gian
Nor·wich
nose
nose·bag
nose·band
nose·bleed
nose·dive (*verb*)
nose·gay
nos·ey *variant spelling of*
  nosy
nosh
no·side rugby term
nosi·ly
nosi·ness
nos·ing
no·so·co·mial medical term
no·sog·ra·pher
no·so·graph·ic
no·sog·ra·phy written
  description of disease
noso·logi·cal
noso·logi·cal·ly
no·solo·gist
no·sol·ogy classification of
  diseases
nos·tal·gia
nos·tal·gic
nos·tal·gi·cal·ly
nos·toc alga
nos·to·log·ic
nos·tol·ogy study of senility
nos·tril
nos·trum quack medicine
nosy (*or* nos·ey; nosi·er,
  nosi·est)
nosy-parker
not
nota bene *Latin* note well
no·tabil·ity (*plural* ·ities)
no·table
no·table·ness
no·tably
no·tar·ial
no·ta·rize (*or* ·rise)
no·ta·ry (*plural* ·ries)
no·tate
no·ta·tion
no·ta·tion·al
notch
note
note·book
note·case
not·ed
note·let
note·paper
note·worthi·ly

note·worthi·ness
note·worthy
noth·ing
noth·ing·ness
no·tice
no·tice·abil·ity
no·tice·able
no·tice·ably
no·ti·fi·able
no·ti·fi·ca·tion
no·ti·fi·er
no·ti·fy (·fies, ·fy·ing,
  ·fied)
no·tillage farming system
not·ing
no·tion
no·tion·al
no·tion·al·ly
no·titia ecclesiastical register
no·to·chord zoology term
no·to·chord·al
No·to·gaea zoogeographical
  term
No·to·gaean
no·to·ri·ety (*or*
  no·to·ri·ous·ness)
no·to·ri·ous
no·tor·nis bird
no·to·ther·ium (*plural*
  ·theria) extinct marsupial
no·tour legal term
No·tre Dame
no-trump bridge term
Not·ting·ham
Not·ting·ham·shire
no·tum (*plural* ·ta)
  entomology term
No·tus mythological wind
not·with·stand·ing
nou·gat
nought (*US* naught) zero;
  compare naught
nou·menon (*plural*
  ·mena) philosophy term
noun
noun·al
nour·ish
nour·ish·er
nour·ish·ing·ly
nour·ish·ment
nous *Slang* common sense
nou·veau riche (*plural*
  nou·veaux riches)
nova (*plural* novae *or*
  novas) star
no·vacu·lite rock
No·va·ra Italian city

Nova Sco·tia

no·va·tion legal term

nov·el

nov·el·ese

nov·el·ette

nov·el·et·tish

nov·el·ist

nov·el·is·tic·

nov·eli·za·tion (or ·sa·tion)

nov·el·ize (or ·ise)

no·vel·la (plural ·las or ·le)

nov·el·ty (plural ·ties)

No·vem·ber

no·vena (plural ·venae) Catholic devotion

Nov·go·rod Soviet city

nov·ice

no·vi·ti·ate (or ·ci·ate)

No·vo·caine (Trademark)

No·vo·kuz·netsk Soviet city

No·vo·si·birsk Soviet city

now

nowa·days

no·way

Now·el (or ·ell) Archaic Noel

no·where

nowt Dialect nothing

Nox Roman goddess

nox·ious

nox·ious·ness

no·yade execution by drowning

noy·au (plural ·aux) liqueur

noz·zle

nth

nu·ance

nub

Nuba (plural Nubas or Nuba) Sudanese people

nub·bin US undeveloped fruit

nub·ble

nub·bly (or ·by)

nu·becu·la (plural ·lae) small galaxy

Nu·bia

Nu·bian

nu·bile

nu·bil·ity

nu·cel·lar

nu·cel·lus (plural ·li) botany term

nu·cha (plural ·chae) nape of neck

nu·chal

nu·clear

nu·clease enzyme

nu·cleate

nu·clea·tion

nu·clea·tor

nu·clei plural of nucleus

nu·cleic

nu·clein protein

nu·cleo·lar (or ·late, ·lat·ed, ·loid)

nu·cleo·lus (plural ·li) part of cell nucleus

nu·cleon

nu·cleon·ic

nu·cleoni·cal·ly

nu·cleon·ics branch of physics

nu·cleo·phile

nu·cleo·phil·ic

nu·cleo·plasm

nu·cleo·plas·mic (or ·mat·ic)

nu·cleo·pro·tein

nu·cleo·side biochemical compound

nu·cleo·tide biochemical compound

nu·cleus (plural ·clei or ·cleuses)

nu·clide type of atom

nude

nude·ness

nudge

nudg·er

nu·di·branch mollusc

nu·di·caul (or ·cau·lous) botany term

nud·ism

nud·ist

nu·dity (plural ·dities)

Nue·vo León Mexican state

nu·ga·tory

nug·gar sailing boat

nug·get

nug·gety

nui·sance

nuke Slang nuclear bomb

Nu·ku'a·lo·fa Tongan capital

null

nul·lah Indian stream

nulla-nulla Aboriginal club

nul·li·fi·ca·tion

nul·li·fi·ca·tion·ist

nul·li·fid·ian sceptic

nul·li·fi·er

nul·li·fy (·fies, ·fy·ing, ·fied)

nul·lipa·ra (plural ·rae) obstetrics term

nul·lipa·rous

nul·li·pore seaweed

nul·lity (plural ·lities)

Nu·man·tia ancient Spanish city

numb

num·bat marsupial

num·ber numeral

numb·er more numb

num·ber·less

number·plate

numb·fish (plural ·fish or ·fishes)

numb·ness

numb·skull variant spelling of numskull

num·dah (or nam·) Indian fabric

nu·men (plural ·mi·na) Roman deity

nu·mer·able

nu·mer·ably

nu·mera·cy

nu·mer·al

nu·mer·ary of numbers; compare nummary

nu·mer·ate

nu·mera·tion

nu·mera·tive

nu·mera·tor

nu·meri·cal (or ·mer·ic)

nu·meri·cal·ly

nu·mero·logi·cal

nu·mer·ol·ogy divination by numbers

nu·mer·ous

nu·mer·ous·ness

Nu·midia ancient African country

Nu·mid·ian

nu·mi·nous awe-inspiring

nu·mis·mat·ic

nu·mis·mat·ics (or ·ma·tol·ogy)

nu·mis·ma·tist (or ·tolo·gist)

num·ma·ry of coins; compare numerary

num·mu·lar

num·mu·lite fossil

num·mu·lit·ic
num·skull (*or* numb·)
nun
nuna·tak mountain peak
Nunc Di·mit·tis canticle
nun·cia·ture
nun·cio (*plural* ·cios)
nun·cle *Dialect* uncle
nun·cu·pa·tive legal term
Nun·eaton
nun·hood
nun·like
nun·nery (*plural* ·neries)
Nupe (*plural* Nupe *or*
Nupes) Nigerian people
nup·tial
Nu·rem·berg
Nuri (*plural* Nuris *or*
Nuri) Indo-European
people
Nu·ri·stan Afghan region
nurse
nurse·maid
nurse·ry (*plural* ·ries)
nursery·man (*plural*
·men)
nurs·ing
nurs·ling (*or* nurse·)
nursed child
nur·tur·able
nur·ture
nur·tur·er
nut (nut·ting, nut·ted)
nu·tant botany term

nu·ta·tion
nu·ta·tion·al
nut·brown
nut·case
nut·cracker
nut·gall
nut·hatch
nut·let
nut·meg
nu·tria coypu fur
nu·tri·ent
nu·tri·ment
nu·tri·tion
nu·tri·tion·al (*or* ·ary)
nu·tri·tion·ist
nu·tri·tious
nu·tri·tious·ness
nu·tri·tive
nut·shell
nut·ted
nut·ter
nut·ti·ly
nut·ti·ness
nut·ting
nut·ty (·ti·er, ·ti·est)
nut·wood
nux vomi·ca
nuz·zle
nya·la (*plural* ·la *or* ·las)
antelope
Nyan·ja (*plural* ·ja *or*
·jas) African people
Ny·asa·land *former name of*
Malawi

nyc·ta·gi·na·ceous botany
term
nyc·ta·lo·pia night
blindness
nyc·ti·nas·tic
nyc·ti·nas·ty botany term
nyc·ti·trop·ic
nyc·tit·ro·pism botany term
nyc·to·pho·bia
nyc·to·pho·bic
nye (*or* nide) flock of
pheasants
ny·lon
nymph
nym·pha (*plural* ·phae)
anatomy term
nym·phaea·ceous botany
term
nym·phal (*or* ·phean)
nym·pha·lid butterfly
nymph·et
nymph·like
nym·pho (*plural* ·phos)
nym·pho·lep·sy (*plural*
·sies) violent emotion
nym·pho·lept
nym·pho·lep·tic
nym·pho·ma·nia
nym·pho·ma·ni·ac
nym·pho·ma·nia·cal
nys·tag·mic
nys·tag·mus eye condition
nys·ta·tin antibiotic
Nyx Greek goddess

O

O exclamation; *used chiefly
in religious and poetic
contexts*
oaf (*plural* oafs)
oaf·ish
oaf·ish·ness
oak
oak·en
Oak·ham Leicestershire
town
Oak·land US port
oakum fibre
oar
oared
oar·fish (*plural* ·fish *or*
·fishes)
oar·lock

oars·man (*plural* ·men)
oars·man·ship
oasis (*plural* oases)
oast
oast·house
oat
oat·cake
oat·en
oath (*plural* oaths)
oat·meal
Oaxa·ca Mexican state
oba African chief
Oban Scottish port
ob·bli·ga·to (*or* ob·li·;
plural ·tos *or* ·ti)
musical term
ob·con·ic botany term

ob·cor·date botany term
ob·du·ra·cy (*or* ·rate·ness)
ob·du·rate
obeah *variant of* obi
obedi·ence
obedi·ent
obedi·en·tia·ry (*plural*
·ries) holder of monastic
office
obei·sance
obei·sant
ob·elis·cal
ob·elisk
ob·elis·koid
ob·elize (*or* ·elise)
ob·elus (*plural* ·eli) text
symbol

Ober·am·mer·gau West
German village
Ober·hau·sen West
German city
Ober·land Swiss region
Ober·on satellite of Uranus
Oberon fairy king
obese
obesity (or obese·ness)
obey
obey·er
ob·fus·cate
ob·fus·ca·tion
ob·fus·ca·tory
obi (plural obis or obi)
Japanese sash
obi (or obeah; plural obis
or obeahs) witchcraft
obit obituary; memorial
service
obi·ter dic·tum (plural
obi·ter dic·ta) Latin
something said in passing
obi·tu·ar·ist
obi·tu·ary (plural ·aries)
ob·ject
ob·jec·ti·fi·ca·tion
ob·jec·ti·fy (·fies, ·fy·ing,
·fied)
ob·jec·tion
ob·jec·tion·abil·ity (or
·able·ness)
ob·jec·tion·able
ob·jec·tion·ably
ob·jec·tive
ob·jec·tiv·ism
ob·jec·tiv·ist
ob·jec·tiv·is·tic
ob·jec·tiv·is·ti·cal·ly
ob·jec·tiv·ity (or
·tive·ness)
ob·jet d'art (plural ob·jets
d'art)
ob·jet trou·vé (plural
ob·jets trou·vés) French
object considered
aesthetically
ob·jur·gate scold
ob·jur·ga·tion
ob·jur·ga·tor
ob·jur·ga·tory (or ·tive)
ob·lan·ceo·late botany term
ob·last Soviet administrative
division
ob·late
ob·la·tion
ob·la·tory (or ·tion·al)

ob·li·gable
ob·li·gate
ob·li·ga·tion
ob·li·ga·tion·al
ob·liga·tive
ob·li·ga·to variant spelling of
obbligato
ob·li·ga·tor
ob·liga·to·ri·ly
ob·liga·tory
oblige
ob·li·gee creditor
oblig·er
oblig·ing
ob·li·gor debtor
oblique
oblique·ness
obliqui·tous
obliqui·ty (plural ·ties)
oblit·erate
oblit·era·tion
oblit·era·tive
oblit·era·tor
oblivi·on
oblivi·ous
ob·livi·ous·ness
ob·long
ob·lo·quy (plural ·quies)
ob·nox·ious
ob·nox·ious·ness
ob·nu·bil·ate to darken
oboe
obo·ist
obo·lus (or obol; plural
·li or obols) Greek unit;
coin
ob·ovate botany term
ob·ovoid botany term
ob·rep·tion obtaining by
deceit
ob·scene
ob·scen·ity (plural ·ities)
ob·scur·ant
ob·scu·rant·ism
ob·scu·rant·ist
ob·scu·ra·tion
ob·scure
ob·scu·rity (plural ·rities)
ob·se·quent
ob·se·quies (sing. ·quy)
ob·se·qui·ous
ob·se·qui·ous·ness
ob·serv·able
ob·serv·able·ness (or
·abil·ity)
ob·serv·ably
ob·ser·vance

ob·ser·vant
ob·ser·va·tion
ob·ser·va·tion·al
ob·ser·va·tion·al·ly
ob·ser·va·tory (plural
·tories)
ob·serve
ob·serv·er
ob·sess
ob·ses·sion
ob·ses·sion·al
ob·ses·sive
ob·ses·sive·ness
ob·sid·ian
ob·so·lesce
ob·so·les·cence
ob·so·les·cent
ob·so·lete
ob·so·lete·ness
ob·sta·cle
ob·stet·ric (or ·ri·cal)
ob·stet·ri·cal·ly
ob·ste·tri·cian
ob·stet·rics
ob·sti·na·cy (plural ·cies)
ob·sti·nate
ob·sti·pa·tion
ob·strep·er·ous
ob·strep·er·ous·ness
ob·struct
ob·struct·er (or ·struc·tor)
ob·struc·tion
ob·struc·tion·al
ob·struc·tion·ism
ob·struc·tion·ist
ob·struc·tive
ob·struc·tive·ness
ob·stru·ent medical term
ob·tain
ob·tain·abil·ity
ob·tain·able
ob·tain·er
ob·tain·ment
ob·tect entomology term
ob·trude
ob·trud·er
ob·tru·sion
ob·tru·sive
ob·tru·sive·ness
ob·tund deaden
ob·tu·rate block up
ob·tu·ra·tion
ob·tu·ra·tor
ob·tuse
ob·tuse·ness
ob·verse
ob·ver·sion

ob·vert logic term
ob·vi·ate
ob·vi·a·tion
ob·vi·ous
ob·vi·ous·ly
ob·vi·ous·ness
ob·vo·lute
ob·vo·lu·tion
ob·vo·lu·tive
oca plant
oca·ri·na musical
instrument
oc·ca·sion
oc·ca·sion·al
oc·ca·sion·al·ism
philosophical theory
oc·ca·sion·al·ly
Oc·ci·dent Europe and
America
oc·ci·dent the west
Oc·ci·den·tal (noun)
oc·ci·den·tal (or Oc·; adj)
Oc·ci·den·tal·ism
Oc·ci·den·tal·ist
oc·ci·den·tali·za·tion (or
Oc·, ·sa·tion)
oc·ci·den·tal·ize (or Oc·,
·ise)
oc·ci·den·tal·ly (or Oc·)
oc·cipi·tal
oc·ci·put (plural ·puts or
·cipi·ta) anatomy term
oc·clude
oc·clud·ent
oc·clu·sal
oc·clu·sion
oc·clu·sive
oc·clu·sive·ness
oc·cult
oc·cul·ta·tion astronomy
term
oc·cult·ism
oc·cult·ist
oc·cu·pan·cy (plural ·cies)
oc·cu·pant
oc·cu·pa·tion
oc·cu·pa·tion·al
oc·cu·pi·er
oc·cu·py (·pies, ·py·ing,
·pied)
oc·cur (·cur·ring, ·curred)
oc·cur·rence
oc·cur·rent
ocean
ocean·ar·ium (plural
·ar·iums or ·aria)
ocean-going

Oceania Pacific islands
Oce·an·ian
Ocean·ic of Oceania
ocean·ic of the ocean
Ocea·nid (plural
Ocea·nids or
Oceani·des) Greek
nymph
ocean·og·ra·pher
oceano·graph·ic (or
·graphi·cal)
oceano·graphi·cal·ly
ocean·og·ra·phy
ocean·ol·ogy
ocel·lar
oc·el·late (or ·lated)
having ocelli; compare
oscillate; osculate
oc·el·la·tion
ocel·lus (plural ·li) simple
eye
oc·elot
och Scot exclamation
ocher US spelling of ochre
och·loc·ra·cy (plural
·cies) mob rule
och·lo·crat
och·lo·crat·ic
och·lo·pho·bia fear of
crowds
ochre (US ocher)
ochre·ous (or ochrous,
ochry; US ocher·ous
or ochery)
ochroid
ock·er Austral boorish
person
o'clock
oco·til·lo (plural ·los) tree
oc·rea (or och·; plural
·reae) sheath
oc·re·ate
oc·ta·chord musical
instrument
oc·tad
oc·tad·ic
oc·ta·gon (or ·tan·gle)
oc·tago·nal
oc·tago·nal·ly
oc·ta·he·dral
oc·ta·he·drite
oc·ta·he·dron (plural
·drons or ·dra)
oc·tal number system
oc·tam·er·ous
oc·tam·eter
oc·tane

oc·tan·gu·lar
Oc·tans constellation
oc·tant eighth part of circle
oc·tar·chy (plural ·chies)
(octaroon) incorrect spelling
of octoroon
oc·ta·va·lent
oc·tave
oc·ta·vo (plural ·vos) book
size
oc·ten·nial
oc·ten·nial·ly
oc·tet
oc·til·lion 10^{48}
oc·til·lionth
Oc·to·ber
oc·to·deci·mo (plural
·mos)
oc·to·genar·ian (or
oc·tog·enary; plural
·ians or ·enaries)
(octogon) incorrect spelling
of octagon
(octohedral) incorrect
spelling of octahedral
oc·to·pod
oc·to·pus (plural ·puses)
oc·to·roon
oc·to·syl·lab·ic
oc·to·syl·la·ble
oc·troi duty on goods
oc·tu·ple
ocu·lar
ocu·lar·ist artificial-eye
maker
ocu·list ophthalmologist
ocu·lo·mo·tor
oda·lisque (or ·lisk)
odd
odd·ball
odd·ity (plural ·ities)
odd·ly
odd·ment
odd·ness
odd-pinnate botany term
odds-on
ode
Oden·se Danish port
Oder European river
Odes·sa Soviet port
odeum (plural odea)
(building for musical
performances; compare
odium; oidium
Odin (or Othin) Norse god
odi·ous
odi·ous·ness

odium hatred; *compare*
odeum; oidium
odom·eter (*or* ho·dom·)
US mileometer
od·on·tal·gia toothache
od·on·tal·gic
odon·to·blast
odon·to·blas·tic
odon·to·glos·sum orchid
odon·to·graph gear-tooth
marking aid
odon·to·graph·ic
od·on·tog·ra·phy
odon·toid
odon·to·logi·cal
od·on·tolo·gist
od·on·tol·ogy science of
teeth
od·on·topho·ral (*or*
·toph·or·ous)
odon·to·phore zoology
term
odor *US spelling of* odour
odor·if·er·ous
odor·ous
odor·ous·ness
odour (*US* odor)
odour·less (*US* odor·)
Od·ys·sean
Odysseus mythological
hero
Od·ys·sey poem
oede·ma (*US* ede·; *plural*
·ma·ta)
oedema·tous (*or* ·tose;
US edema·)
oedi·pal (*or* ·pean)
Oedipus mythological
character
oeil·lade suggestive glance
oeno·logi·cal (*US* eno·)
oenolo·gist (*US* enolo·)
oenol·ogy (*US* enol·)
study of wine
oeno·mel drink
Oenone Greek nymph
o'er over
oer·sted unit
oesopha·geal (*US*
esopha·)
oesopha·gus (*US*
esopha·; *plural* ·gi)
oes·tra·di·ol (*US* es·)
hormone
oes·tri·ol (*US* es·)
hormone
oes·tro·gen (*US* es·)

oes·tro·gen·ic (*US* es·)
oes·tro·geni·cal·ly (*US*
es·)
oes·trone (*US* es·)
hormone
oes·trous (*adj*; *US* es·)
oes·trus (*noun*; *US* es·)
oeuvre work of art
of
off
of·fal
Of·fa·ly Irish county
off·beat
off·centre
off·drive (·driving, ·drove,
·driven)
Of·fen·bach West German
city
of·fence (*US* ·fense)
of·fend
of·fend·er
of·fen·sive
of·fen·sive·ness
of·fer
of·fer·er (*or* ·fe·ror)
of·fer·ing
of·fer·tory (*plural* ·tories)
off·glide
off·hand
off·handed
off·handed·ly
off·hand·ed·ness
of·fice
of·fic·er
of·fi·cial
of·fi·cial·dom
of·fi·cial·ese
of·fi·cial·ly
of·fi·ci·ant
of·fi·ci·ary (*plural* ·aries)
body of officials
of·fi·ci·ate
of·fi·cia·tion
of·fi·cia·tor
of·fi·cious
of·fi·cious·ness
of·fing
of·fish
off·key (*adj*)
off·licence
off·line (*adj*)
off·load
off·peak
off·print
off·putting
off·season (*adj*)
off·set (·set·ting, ·set)

off·shoot
off·shore
off·side
off·spring
off·stage
off·white
oft
of·ten
Oga·den Ethiopian region
Og·bo·mo·sho Nigerian
city
og·do·ad group of eight
ogee architectural moulding
og·ham (*or* ogam) ancient
writing
ogiv·al
ogive architectural term
ogle
ogler
Ogo·oué (*or* ·we) African
river
ogre (*fem* ogress)
ogre·ish
Ogyg·ian prehistoric
oh
Ohio
ohm
ohm·age
ohm·meter
oid·ium (*plural* ·ia) fungal
spore
oil
oil·bird
oil·can
oil·cloth
oil·cup
oil·er
oil·field
oil·fired
oili·ly
oili·ness
oil·man (*plural* ·men)
oil·skin
oil·stone
oily (oili·er, oili·est)
oint·ment
Oi·reach·tas Irish
parliament
Oita Japanese city
OK (*or* okay; *noun*,
plural OK's *or* okays;
verb OK'ing, OK'ed *or*
okay·ing, okayed)
oka (*or* oke) Turkish
weight
oka·pi (*plural* ·pis *or* ·pi)
okay *variant of* OK

Oka·ya·ma Japanese city
Okee·cho·bee Florida lake
okey-doke (or -dokey)
Oki·na·wa Japanese island
Ok·la·ho·ma
Okla·ho·man
okra vegetable
okta meteorological unit
old
Old Bai·ley
old·en
Ol·den·burg West German
  city
old·er
old·fangled
old-fashioned
Old·ham English town
oldie
old·ness
old-time
old-timer
Ol·du·vai Tanzanian gorge
old·wife (plural ·wives)
  duck; fish
old-world
olé Spanish exclamation
olea·ceous botany term
oleagi·nous oily
olean·der shrub
oleas·ter shrub
oleate chemistry term
olec·ra·nal
olec·ra·non anatomy term
olefine (or olefin)
olefin·ic
oleic acid
oleo·graph
oleo·graph·ic
oleog·ra·phy
oleo·res·in
oleo·res·in·ous
oleum (plural olea or
  oleums) chemistry term
ol·fac·tion
ol·fac·tory (plural ·tories)
oliba·num frankincense
olid foul-smelling
oli·garch
oli·gar·chic (or ·chi·cal)
oli·gar·chi·cal·ly
oli·gar·chy (plural ·chies)
Oli·go·cene geological
  period
oli·go·chaete worm
oli·go·clase mineral
oli·gopo·lis·tic

oli·gopo·ly (plural ·lies)
  economics term
oli·gop·so·nis·tic
oli·gop·so·ny (plural
  ·nies) economics term
oli·go·sac·cha·ride
oli·go·troph·ic ecology term
oli·got·ro·phy
oli·gu·ret·ic
oli·gu·ria (or ·resis)
  medical term
olio (plural olios)
  miscellany
oli·va·ceous
oli·vary
ol·ive
oliv·en·ite mineral
oli·vine mineral
olla cooking pot
olla po·dri·da Spanish stew
ol·ogy (plural ·ogies)
  Slang branch of
  knowledge
olo·ro·so (plural ·sos)
  sherry
Olym·pia
Olym·pi·ad
Olym·pian
Olym·pic
Olym·pus Greek mountain
Om Hindu syllable
oma·dhaun Irish fool
Omagh Irish town
Oma·ha US city
Oman Arabian sultanate
Omani
oma·sum (plural ·sa)
  cow's stomach
Omay·yad (or Umay·;
  plural ·yads or ·ya·des)
  caliph
om·bre (US ·ber) card
  game
om·buds·man (plural
  ·men)
Om·dur·man Sudanese city
omega
ome·lette (or esp. US
  ome·let)
omen
omen·tal
omen·tum (plural ·ta)
  anatomy term
omer Hebrew unit
omi·cron Greek letter
omi·nous
omi·nous·ness

omis·sible
omis·sion
omit (omit·ting, omit·ted)
omit·ter
om·ma·tid·ial
om·ma·tid·ium (plural
  ·tidia) zoology term
om·mato·phore zoology
  term
om·ma·topho·rous
om·ni·bus (plural ·buses)
om·ni·com·pe·tence
om·ni·com·pe·tent
om·ni·di·rec·tion·al
om·ni·fari·ous of all sorts
om·nif·ic (or om·nifi·cent)
om·nipo·tence
om·nipo·tent
om·ni·pres·ence
om·ni·pres·ent
om·ni·range navigation
  system
om·nis·ci·ence
om·nis·ci·ent
omnium-gather·um
  assortment
om·ni·vore
om·niv·or·ous
omo·pha·gia (or
  omoph·agy) eating raw
  food
omo·phag·ic (or
  omopha·gous)
Omphale mythological
  queen
om·pha·los sacred object
Omu·ta Japanese city
on
ona·ger (plural ·gri or
  ·gers) wild ass
ona·gra·ceous botany term
onan·ism
onan·ist
once
once-over
onco·gene
on·co·gen·ic (or
  on·cog·enous)
on·co·logi·cal
on·colo·gist
on·col·ogy study of tumours
on·coming
on·cost
on·do·gram
on·do·graph
on·dom·eter
one

Onei·da (*plural* ·**das** *or*
·**da**) US city and lake;
American Indian
onei·ric of dreams
onei·ro·crit·ic
onei·ro·criti·cal
one·ness
one-off
oner *Slang* something
outstanding
on·er·ous
on·er·ous·ness
one·self
one-sided
one-sidedness
one-step
one-time
one-to-one
one-track
one-upmanship
one-way
on-glide
on·going
on·ion
onion·skin paper
on·iony
Onit·sha Nigerian port
on·looker
on·looking
only
ono·ma·si·ol·ogy
ono·mas·tic
ono·mas·tics study of
proper names
ono·mato·poeia
ono·mato·poe·ic (*or*
·**po·et·ic**)
ono·mato·poei·cal·ly (*or*
·**po·eti·cal·ly**)
on·rush
on·set
on·shore
on·side sports term
on·slaught
on·stage
On·tario
onto
on·to·gen·ic (*or* ·**ge·net·ic**)
on·to·geni·cal·ly (*or*
·**ge·neti·cal·ly**)
on·tog·eny (*or*
·**to·gen·esis**) biology
term
on·to·logi·cal
on·to·logi·cal·ly
on·tol·ogy philosophy term
onus (*plural* **onuses**)

onus pro·ban·di burden of
proof
on·ward
on·wards
ony·chopho·ran zoology
term
ony·mous bearing author's
name
onyx gemstone; *compare*
oryx
oocyte biology term
oodles
oof *Slang* money
ooga·mous
oog·amy biology term
oogen·esis
ooge·net·ic
oogo·nial
oogo·nium (*plural* ·**nia** *or*
·**niums**) biology term
ooh exclamation
oolite rock
oolit·ic
oologi·cal
oolo·gist
ool·ogy study of birds' eggs
oolong tea
oomi·ak *variant spelling of*
umiak
oom·pah
oopho·rec·to·my (*plural*
·**mies**) removal of ovary
oopho·rit·ic
oopho·ri·tis
oophyte botany term
oophyt·ic
oosperm
oosphere botany term
oospore
oo·spor·ic (*or* ·**ous**)
ootheca (*plural* **oothecae**)
zoology term
oothecal
ootid zoology term
ooze
oozi·ly
oozi·ness
oozy (**oozi·er, oozi·est**)
opac·ity (*plural* ·**ities**)
opah fish
opal
opa·lesce
opal·es·cence
opal·es·cent
opal·ine
opaque (**opaqu·ing,**
opaqued)

opaque·ness
open
open-and-shut
open·cast
open-ended
open·er
open-eyed
open-faced
open-handed
open-handed·ness
open-hearted
open-hearted·ness
open·ing
open-minded
open-minded·ness
open-mouthed
open·ness
open·work
op·era
op·er·abil·ity
op·er·able
op·er·and maths term
op·er·ant
op·er·ate
op·er·at·ic
op·er·ati·cal·ly
op·er·at·ics
op·era·tion
op·era·tion·al
op·era·tion·al·ism (*or*
·**tion·ism**) science term
op·era·tion·al·ist·ic
op·era·tion·al·ly
op·era·tive
op·era·tive·ness (*or*
·**tiv·ity**)
op·era·tize (*or* ·**tise**) make
into an opera
op·era·tor
oper·cu·lar (*or* ·**late**)
oper·cu·lum (*plural* ·**la** *or*
·**lums**) biology term
op·er·et·ta
op·er·et·tist
op·er·on genetics term
ophi·cleide musical
instrument
ophid·ian
ophio·logi·cal
ophi·olo·gist
ophi·ol·ogy study of snakes
Ophir biblical region
ophite rock
ophit·ic
Ophiu·chus constellation
oph·thal·mia
oph·thal·mic

oph·thal·mi·tis
oph·thal·mo·logi·cal
oph·thal·molo·gist
oph·thal·mol·ogy
oph·thal·mo·scope
oph·thal·mo·scop·ic
oph·thal·mos·co·py
opi·ate
opine
opin·ion
opin·ion·at·ed (*or*
　opin·iona·tive)
opin·ion·at·ed·ness
opis·tho·branch zoology
　term
op·is·thog·na·thism
op·is·thog·na·thous
opium
opi·um·ism
Opor·to Portuguese port
opos·sum (*plural* ·sums
　or ·sum)
op·pi·dan urban
op·pi·late to block
op·pi·la·tion
op·po·nen·cy
op·po·nent
op·por·tune
op·por·tune·ness
op·por·tun·ism
op·por·tun·ist
op·por·tun·is·tic
op·por·tu·nity (*plural*
　·nities)
op·pos·abil·ity
op·pos·able
op·pos·ably
op·pose
op·pos·er
op·pos·ing·ly
op·po·site on the other side
　of; *compare* apposite
op·po·site·ness
Op·po·si·tion parliamentary
　party
op·po·si·tion
op·po·si·tion·al
op·po·si·tion·ist
op·press
op·pres·sing·ly
op·pres·sion
op·pres·sive
op·pres·sive·ness
op·pres·sor
op·pro·bri·ous
op·pro·brium
op·pugn to dispute

op·pug·nant
op·pugn·er
Ops Roman goddess
op·son·ic
op·so·nin
op·so·ni·za·tion (*or*
　·sa·tion,
　·soni·fi·ca·tion)
op·so·nize (*or* ·nise,
　·soni·fy) medical term
opt
op·ta·tive expressing a wish
(opthalmic) *incorrect*
　spelling of ophthalmic
(opthalmology) *incorrect*
　spelling of ophthalmology
op·tic
op·ti·cal
op·ti·cal·ly
op·ti·cian
op·tics
op·ti·mal
op·ti·mal·ly
op·ti·mism
op·ti·mist
op·ti·mis·tic (*or* ·ti·cal)
op·ti·mis·ti·cal·ly
op·ti·mi·za·tion (*or*
　·sa·tion)
op·ti·mize (*or* ·mise)
op·ti·mum (*plural* ·ma *or*
　·mums)
op·tion
op·tion·al
op·tion·al·ly
op·tom·eter
op·to·met·ric
op·tom·etrist ophthalmic
　optician
op·tom·etry
opu·lence (*or* ·len·cy)
opu·lent
opun·tia plant
opus (*plural* opuses *or*
　opera)
or
or·ache (*or esp. US*
　or·ach) plant
ora·cle
oracu·lar
ora·cy
Ora·dea Romanian city
oral of the mouth; *compare*
　aural
oral·ly
Oran Algerian port
or·ange

or·ange·ade
Or·ange·ism
Orange·man (*plural*
　·men) Irish Protestant
or·ang·ery (*plural* ·eries)
orange·wood
orang-utan (*or* -outang)
orate
ora·tion
ora·tor
ora·tori·cal
ora·to·rio (*plural* ·rios)
ora·tory (*plural* ·tories)
orb
or·bicu·lar (*or* ·late,
　·lat·ed)
or·bicu·lar·ity
or·bit
or·bit·al
orc whale
Or·cad·ian of the Orkneys
or·cein dye
or·chard
or·ches·tra
or·ches·tral
or·ches·tral·ly
or·ches·trate
or·ches·tra·tion
or·ches·tra·tor
or·ches·tri·na (*or* ·on)
　musical instrument
or·chid
or·chi·da·ceous
or·chil (*or* ar·) lichen; dye
or·chis orchid
or·chit·ic
or·chi·tis inflammation of
　testicle
or·ci·nol (*or* or·cin)
　chemical compound
Or·cus Roman god
or·dain
or·dain·er
or·dain·ment
or·deal
or·der
or·der·er
or·der·li·ness
or·der·ly (*plural* ·lies)
or·di·nal
or·di·nance decree; *compare*
　ordnance; ordonnance
or·di·nand
or·di·nari·ly
or·di·nari·ness
or·di·nary (*plural* ·naries)
or·di·nate

or·di·na·tion

ord·nance weaponry; *compare* ordinance; ordonnance

or·don·nance systematic arrangement; *compare* ordnance; ordinance

Or·do·vi·cian geological period

or·dure excrement

Or·dzho·ni·ki·dze (*or* Or·jo·) Soviet city

ore mineral

öre (*plural* öre) Swedish currency

øre (*plural* øre) Danish or Norwegian currency

oread Greek nymph

Örebro Swedish town

orec·tic of desire

orega·no

Or·egon

Oren·burg Soviet city

Orestes mythological character

orfe fish

or·fray *variant spelling of* orphrey

or·gan

or·gan·die (*US* ·dy; *plural* ·dies)

or·ga·nelle

or·gan·ic

or·gani·cal·ly

or·gani·cism biological theory

or·gani·cist

or·gani·cis·tic

or·gan·ism

or·gan·is·mal (*or* ·mic)

or·gan·ist

or·gani·za·tion (*or* ·sa·tion)

or·gani·za·tion·al (*or* ·sa·tion·al)

or·gan·ize (*or* ·ise)

or·gan·iz·er (*or* ·is·er)

or·gano·gen·esis

or·gano·genet·ic

or·gano·geneti·cal·ly

or·gano·graph·ic (*or* ·graphi·cal)

or·gan·og·ra·phist

or·gan·og·ra·phy

or·gano·lep·tic

or·gano·logi·cal

or·gan·olo·gist

or·gan·ol·ogy

or·gano·metal·lic

or·ga·non (*or* ·num; *plural* ·na, ·nons, *or* ·nums) philosophy term

or·gano·thera·peu·tic

or·gano·thera·py

or·ga·num (*plural* ·na *or* ·nums) music; *variant spelling of* organon

or·gan·za fabric

or·gan·zine silk thread

or·gasm

or·gas·mic (*or* ·tic)

or·geat barley drink

or·gi·as·tic

orgy (*plural* orgies)

ori·bi (*plural* ·bi *or* ·bis) antelope

ori·el window; *compare* oriole

Ori·ent eastern countries

ori·ent the east; *variant of* orientate

Ori·en·tal (*noun*)

ori·en·tal (*or* Ori·; *adj*)

Ori·en·tal·ism

Ori·en·tal·ist

ori·en·tali·za·tion (*or* Ori·, ·sa·tion)

ori·en·tal·ize (*or* Ori·, ·ise)

ori·en·tal·ly (*or* Ori·)

ori·en·tate (*or* ori·ent)

ori·en·ta·tion

ori·en·ta·tion·al

Ori·en·te Cuban province

ori·en·teer·ing

ori·fice

ori·flamme flag

ori·ga·mi paper folding

ori·ga·num marjoram or oregano

ori·gin

origi·nal

origi·nal·ity (*plural* ·ities)

origi·nal·ly

origi·nate

origi·na·tion

origi·na·tor

ori·na·sal phonetics term; *compare* oronasal

Ori·no·co South American river

ori·ole bird; *compare* oriel

Ori·on constellation

Orion mythological character

ori·son prayer

Oris·sa Indian state

Ori·ya (*plural* ·ya) Indian people

Ori·za·ba Mexican city

Ork·ney Is·lands (*or* Ork·neys)

orle heraldic term

Or·lé·ans French city

Or·lon (*Trademark*)

or·lop nautical term

Orly Parisian suburb

or·mer mollusc

or·mo·lu decoration

Or·muz *variant spelling of* Hormuz

or·na·ment

or·na·men·tal

or·na·men·tal·ly

or·na·men·ta·tion

or·nate

or·nate·ness

or·nith·ic of birds

or·ni·thine amino acid

or·ni·this·chian zoology term

or·ni·tho·logi·cal

or·ni·tho·logi·cal·ly

or·ni·tholo·gist

or·ni·thol·ogy

or·ni·tho·man·cy divination from bird behaviour

or·ni·tho·pod dinosaur

or·ni·thop·ter (*or* or·thop·ter) aircraft

or·ni·tho·rhyn·chus platypus

or·ni·thos·co·py divination by bird observation

or·ni·tho·sis

oro·ban·cha·ceous botany term

oro·gen·ic (*or* ·ge·net·ic)

oro·geni·cal·ly (*or* ·geneti·cal·ly)

orog·eny (*or* oro·gen·esis) mountain formation

orog·ra·pher (*or* orolo·gist)

oro·graph·ic (*or* oro·logi·cal)

oro·graphi·cal·ly (*or* oro·logi·cal·ly)

orog·ra·phy (*or* orol·ogy)
　mapping mountain relief
oro·ide alloy
orom·eter
Oron·tes Asian river
oro·tund resonant;
　pompous; *compare* **rotund**
or·phan
or·phan·age
or·phari·on lute
Or·phean
Orpheus
Or·phic
Or·phism ancient Greek
　religion
or·phrey (*or* ·fray) border
　on vestment
or·pi·ment mineral
or·pine (*or* ·pin) plant
or·re·ry (*plural* ·ries)
　model of solar system
or·ris (*or* ·rice) plant
or·ta·nique fruit
or·thi·con electronic device
ortho·cen·tre (*US* ·ter)
　maths term
ortho·cephal·ic (*or*
　·cepha·lous) anatomy
　term
ortho·cepha·ly
ortho·chro·mat·ic
ortho·chro·ma·tism
ortho·clase mineral
ortho·don·tic
ortho·don·tics (*or*
　·don·tia)
or·tho·don·tist
Ortho·dox religion
ortho·dox conforming
ortho·doxy (*plural*
　·doxies)
ortho·ep·ic
ortho·epi·cal·ly
ortho·epy correct
　pronunciation
ortho·gen·esis
ortho·ge·net·ic
ortho·geneti·cal·ly
ortho·gen·ic medical term
ortho·geni·cal·ly
or·thog·na·thism (*or* ·thy)
or·thog·na·thous anatomy
　term
or·thogo·nal
or·thogo·nal·ly
or·thog·ra·pher (*or* ·phist)

ortho·graph·ic (*or*
　·graphi·cal)
ortho·graphi·cal·ly
or·thog·ra·phy (*plural*
　·phies)
ortho·hy·dro·gen
ortho·mor·phic
ortho·paedic (*US* ·pedic)
ortho·paedics (*US*
　·pedics)
ortho·paedist (*US*
　·pedist)
ortho·phos·phate
ortho·psy·chi·at·ric
ortho·psy·chia·trist
ortho·psy·chia·try
or·thop·ter variant of
　ornithopter
or·thop·ter·an (*or* ·on;
　plural ·ans *or* ·tera)
　insect
or·thop·ter·ous (*or* ·an)
or·thop·tic
or·thop·tics
or·thop·tist
ortho·rhom·bic
　crystallography term
ortho·scop·ic
or·thos·ti·chous
or·thos·ti·chy (*plural*
　·chies) botany term
ortho·trop·ic
or·thot·ro·pism
or·thot·ro·pous botany
　term
or·to·lan bird
orts *Dialect* scraps
Oru·ro Bolivian city
Or·vie·to Italian town; wine
Or·wel·lian
oryx (*plural* or·yxes *or*
　oryx) antelope; *compare*
　onyx
os (*plural* ossa) bone
os (*plural* ora) mouth
Osage (*plural* Osages *or*
　Osage) American Indian
Osa·ka Japanese port
Os·car film award
os·cil·late fluctuate
　regularly; *compare*
　ocellate; osculate
os·cil·la·tion
os·cil·la·tor
os·cil·la·tory
os·cil·lo·gram
os·cil·lo·graph

os·cil·lo·graph·ic
os·cil·log·ra·phy
os·cil·lo·scope
os·cine ornithology term
os·ci·tan·cy (*or* ·tance;
　plural ·tan·cies *or*
　·tances)
os·ci·tant drowsy
os·cu·lant biology term
os·cu·lar
os·cu·late kiss; maths term;
　compare ocellate; oscillate
os·cu·la·tion
os·cu·la·tory
os·cu·lum (*plural* ·la)
　mouthlike part
Osha·wa Canadian city
Oshog·bo Nigerian city
osier willow tree
Osiris Egyptian god
Oslo
Os·man·li of Ottoman
　Empire
os·mic
os·mi·ous *variant of* osmous
os·mi·rid·ium alloy
os·mium metal
os·mom·eter
os·mo·met·ric
os·mo·met·ri·cal·ly
os·mom·etry
os·mose undergo osmosis
os·mo·sis (*plural* ·ses)
os·mot·ic
os·moti·cal·ly
os·mous (*or* ·mi·ous)
os·mun·da (*or* ·mund) fern
Os·na·brück West German
　city
os·na·burg fabric
os·prey
Ossa Greek mountain
os·sein protein
os·seous bony
Os·setia Soviet region
Os·set·ic (*or* ·se·tian)
Ossian legendary Irish bard
os·si·cle small bone
os·sicu·lar
os·sif·er·ous
os·si·fi·ca·tion
os·si·fi·er
os·si·frage bird
os·si·fy (·fies, ·fy·ing,
　·fied)
os·su·ary (*plural* ·aries)
　urn for bones

os·teal
os·tei·tic
os·tei·tis
Os·tend Belgian port
os·ten·sibil·ity
os·ten·sible
os·ten·sibly
os·ten·sive
os·ten·sory (*plural* ·sories*) container for Host
os·ten·ta·tion
os·ten·ta·tious
os·teo·ar·thrit·ic
os·teo·ar·thri·tis
os·teo·blast bone cell
os·teo·blas·tic
os·teoc·la·sis medical term
os·teo·clast
os·teo·clas·tic
os·teo·gen·esis
os·teoid
os·teo·logi·cal
os·teo·logi·cal·ly
os·teolo·gist
os·teol·ogy study of bones
os·teo·ma (*plural* ·ma·ta or ·mas*) tumour
os·teo·ma·la·cia
os·teo·ma·la·cial (*or* ·lac·ic)
os·teo·my·eli·tis
os·teo·path (*or* ·teopa·thist)
os·teo·path·ic
os·teo·pathi·cal·ly
os·teopa·thy
os·teo·phyte bony outgrowth
os·teo·phyt·ic
os·teo·plas·tic
os·teo·plas·ty (*plural* ·ties*) bone grafting
os·teo·por·o·sis
os·teo·tome surgical instrument
os·teoto·my (*plural* ·mies*)
Os·tia ancient Italian town
os·ti·ary (*plural* ·aries*) Catholic official
os·ti·na·to (*plural* ·tos*) musical term
os·tio·lar
os·ti·ole pore
os·tium (*plural* ·tia*) biology term
ost·ler (*or* host·ler*)

ost·mark East German currency
os·to·sis formation of bone
os·tra·cism
os·tra·ciz·able (*or* ·cis·)
os·tra·cize (*or* ·cise*)
os·tra·ciz·er (*or* ·cis·er*)
os·tra·cod tiny animal
os·tra·co·dan (*or* ·dous*)
os·tra·co·derm extinct fish
Os·tra·va Czech city
os·trich (*plural* ·triches or ·trich*)
Os·tro·goth
otal·gia earache
oth·er
other-direct·ed
other·gates *Archaic* otherwise
oth·er·ness
other·where *Archaic* elsewhere
other·wise
other·worldli·ness
other·worldly
otic of the ear
oti·ose futile
oti·os·ity (*or* ·ose·ness*)
oti·tis
oto·cyst
oto·cys·tic
oto·la·ryn·go·logi·cal
oto·lar·yn·golo·gist
oto·lar·yn·gol·ogy
oto·lith
oto·lith·ic
oto·logi·cal
otolo·gist
otol·ogy
oto·scope
oto·scop·ic
ot·ta·va octave
Ot·ta·wa
ot·ter (*plural* ·ters or ·ter*)
Ot·to·man (*or* **Oth·man**; *plural* ·mans*) Turk; Turkish
ot·to·man (*plural* ·mans*) sofa
oua·ba·in drug
Ouachi·ta (*or* **Washi·ta**) US river
Oua·ga·dou·gou capital of Burkina Faso
oua·na·niche salmon
oubli·ette dungeon
ouch

Oudh Indian region
ought should; *variant spelling of* aught
Oui·ja (*Trademark*)
Ouj·da Moroccan city
ounce
our
ours of us
our·selves
Ouse English river
ousel *variant spelling of* ouzel
oust
out
out·age missing goods
out-and-out
out·back
out·bal·ance
out·bid (·bid·ding, ·bid, ·bid·den or ·bid*)
out·bluff
out·board
out·bound
out·brave
out·break
out·breed (·breed·ing, ·bred*)
out·build·ing
out·burst
out·cast one cast out
out·caste one with no caste
out·class
out·come
out·crop (·crop·ping, ·cropped*)
out·cross
out·cry (*noun, plural* ·cries; *verb* ·cries, ·cry·ing, ·cried*)
out·date
out·dat·ed
out·dis·tance
out·do (·does, ·do·ing, ·did, ·done*)
out·door (*adj*)
out·doors (*adv*)
out·er
outer·most
out·face
out·fall
out·field
out·field·er
out·fit (·fit·ting, ·fit·ted*)
out·fit·ter
out·flank
out·flow
out·foot

out·fox
out·gas (·gas·ses, ·gas·sing, ·gassed)
out·go (·goes, ·go·ing, ·went, ·gone)
out·go·ing (*adj*)
out·go·ings
out-group
out·grow (·grow·ing, ·grew, ·grown)
out·growth
out·gun (·gun·ning, ·gunned)
out·haul
out·house
out·ing
out·jockey
out·land·er
out·land·ish
out·last
out·law
out·law·ry (*plural* ·ries)
out·lay (·lay·ing, ·laid)
out·let
out·li·er
out·line
out·live
out·look
out·ly·ing
out·man (·man·ning, ·manned)
out·ma·noeu·vre (*US* ·ver)
out·match
out·mod·ed
out·num·ber
out-of-doors
out-of-the-way
out·pa·tient
out·point
out·port
out·post
out·pour
out·pour·ing
out·put (·put·ting, **put** *or* ·put·ted)
out·rage
out·ra·geous
out·ra·geous·ness
out·rank
ou·tré unconventional
out·reach
out·ride (·rid·ing, ·rode, ·rid·den)
out·rid·er
out·rig·ger
out·right

out·ri·val (·val·ling, ·valled; *US* ·val·ing, ·valed)
out·run (·run·ning, ·ran, ·run)
out·run·ner
out·rush
out·sell (·sell·ing, ·sold)
out·sert printing term
out·set
out·shine (·shin·ing, ·shone)
out·shoot (·shoot·ing, ·shot)
out·side
out·sid·er
out·size
out·skirts
out·smart
out·sole
out·spo·ken
out·spread (·spread·ing, ·spread)
out·stand (·stand·ing, ·stood)
out·stand·ing (*adj*)
out·stare
out·sta·tion
out·stay
out·stretch
out·strip (·strip·ping, ·stripped)
out·swing
out·swing·er
out·talk
out·think (·think·ing, ·thought)
out·vote
out·ward (*adj*)
out·ward·ly
out·wards (*adv*)
out·wash glacial deposit
out·wear (·wear·ing, ·wore, ·worn)
out·weigh
out·wit (·wit·ting, ·wit·ted)
out·work (·work·ing, ·worked *or* ·wrought)
out·work·er
ouzel (*or* ousel) bird
ouzo (*plural* ouzos) drink
ova *plural of* ovum
oval
oval·ness (*or* ·ity)
ovar·ian
ovari·ec·to·my

ovari·oto·my (*plural* ·mies)
ova·ri·tis
ova·ry (*plural* ·ries)
ovate
ova·tion
ova·tion·al
oven
oven·bird
oven-ready
oven·ware
over
over·abun·dance
over·achieve
over·act
over·ac·tive
over·age
over·all
over·alls
over·am·bi·tious
over·anx·ious
over·arch
over·arm
over·awe
over·bal·ance
over·bear (·bear·ing, ·bore, ·borne)
over·bear·ing·ly
over·bid (·bid·ding, ·bid, ·bid·den *or* ·bid)
over·blown
over·board
over·book
over·boot
over·build (·build·ing, ·built)
over·bur·den
over·call
over·came
over·ca·pac·ity
over·capi·tali·za·tion (*or* ·sa·tion)
over·capi·tal·ize (*or* ·ise)
over·cast
over·cau·tious
over·charge
over·check
over·cloud
over·coat
over·come (·com·ing, ·came, ·come)
over·com·pen·sate
over·com·pen·sa·tion
over·com·pen·sa·tory
over·con·fi·dent
over·cook
over·criti·cal

over·criti·cize (*or* ·cise)
over·crop (·crop·ping, ·cropped)
over·crowd
over·crowd·ing
over·cul·ti·vate
over·devel·op
over·devel·op·ment
over·do (·does, ·do·ing, ·did, ·done)
over·dos·age
over·dose
over·draft money
over·draught air current
over·draw (·draw·ing, ·drew, ·drawn)
over·dress
over·drive (·driv·ing, ·drove, ·driv·en)
over·due
over·dye
over·eat (·eat·ing, ·ate, ·eat·en)
over·elabo·rate
over·em·pha·size (*or* ·sise)
over·em·phat·ic
over·en·thu·si·asm
over·en·thu·si·as·tic
over·es·ti·mate
over·es·ti·ma·tion
over·ex·cite
over·ex·pose
over·ex·po·sure
over·feed (·feed·ing, ·fed)
over·fill
over·flight
over·flow (·flow·ing, ·flowed, ·flown)
over·fly (·flies, ·fly·ing, ·flew, ·flown)
over·fold geology term
over·gar·ment
over·gen·er·ous
over·glaze
over·ground
over·grow (·grow·ing, ·grew, ·grown)
over·growth
over·hand
over·hang (·hang·ing, ·hung)
over·haul
over·head
over·heads
over·hear (·hear·ing, ·heard)

over·heat
over·hung
Over·ijs·sel Dutch province
over·in·dulge
over·in·dul·gence
over·in·dul·gent
over·is·sue (·sues, ·su·ing, ·sued)
over·joyed
over·kill
over·land
over·lap (·lap·ping, ·lapped)
over·lay (·lay·ing, ·laid)
over·leaf
over·lie (·ly·ing, ·lay, ·lain)
over·load
over·long
over·look
over·lord
over·ly
over·man (·man·ning, ·manned)
over·man·tel
over·master
over·mat·ter
over·much
over·nice
over·night
over·pass (·pas·sing, ·passed, ·past)
over·pay (·pay·ing, ·paid)
over·pitch —
over·play
over·plus excess
over·popu·late
over·popu·la·tion
over·pow·er
over·pow·er·ing
over·print
over·pro·duce
over·pro·duc·tion
over·pro·tect
over·pro·tec·tion
over·pro·tec·tive
over·quali·fied
over·ran
over·rate
over·reach
over·react
over·reac·tion
over·ride (·rid·ing, ·rode, ·rid·den)
over·rid·er
over·riding (*adj*)
over·ripe

over·rode
over·rule
over·run (·run·ning, ·ran, ·run)
over·score cross out
over·seas
over·see (·see·ing, ·saw, ·seen)
over·seer
over·sell (·sell·ing, ·sold)
over·set (·set·ting, ·set) disturb
over·sew (·sew·ing, ·sewed, ·sewn)
over·sexed
over·shad·ow
over·shoe
over·shoot (·shoot·ing, ·shot)
over·side
over·sight
over·sim·pli·fi·ca·tion
over·sim·pli·fy (·fies, fy·ing, ·fied)
over·size
over·sized
over·skirt
over·slaugh military term
over·sleep (·sleep·ing, ·slept)
over·soul spiritual essence
over·spend (·spend·ing, ·spent)
over·spill (·spill·ing, ·spilt *or* ·spilled)
over·staff
over·state
over·state·ment
over·stay
over·steer
over·step (·step·ping, ·stepped)
over·strung
over·stuff
over·sub·scribe
overt
over·take (·tak·ing, ·took, ·tak·en)
over·task
over·tax
over-the-counter (*adj*)
over·throw (·throw·ing, ·threw, ·thrown)
over·thrust geological fault
over·time
over·tire
over·tired

over·tone
over·took
over·top (·top·ping, ·topped)
over·trade
over·trick bridge term
over·trump
over·ture
over·turn
over·use
over·view
over·watch
over·ween·ing
over·weigh
over·weight
over·whelm
over·whelm·ing
over·wind (·wind·ing, ·wound)
over·win·ter
over·word repeated word
over·work
over·write (·writ·ing, ·wrote, ·writ·ten)
over·wrought
ovi·du·cal (or ·duc·tal)
ovi·duct
Ovie·do Spanish city
ovif·er·ous
ovi·form egg-shaped
ovine sheeplike
ovi·par·ity
ovipa·rous egg-laying
ovi·pos·it
ovi·po·si·tion
ovi·posi·tor
ovi·sac egg sac
ovoid
ovo·lo (plural ·li) architectural term
ovo·tes·tis (plural ·tes)
ovo·vi·vi·par·ity
ovo·vi·vipa·rous
ovu·lar
ovu·late
ovu·la·tion

ovule
ovum (plural ova)
ow exclamation
owe
ow·el·ty (plural ·ties) legal term
Ower·ri Nigerian town
ow·ing
owl
owl·et
owl·ish
own
own·er
owner-occupier
own·er·ship
owt Dialect anything
ox (plural oxen)
oxa·late chemistry term
ox·al·ic acid
oxa·lis plant
oxa·zine
ox·blood
ox·bow lake
Ox·bridge
oxen plural of ox
ox·eye plant
Ox·fam
Ox·ford
Ox·ford·shire
ox·heart cherry
ox·hide
oxi·dant
oxi·dase enzyme
oxi·date oxidize
oxi·da·tion
oxi·da·tion·al
oxi·da·tion-reduction
oxi·da·tive
ox·ide
oxi·di·met·ric
oxi·dim·etry
oxi·diz·able chemistry term
oxi·di·za·tion (or ·sa·tion)
oxi·dize (or ·dise)
oxi·diz·er (or ·dis·er)
ox·ime chemical compound

ox·lip plant
Oxo·nian
ox·pecker bird
ox·tail
ox·tongue
oxy·acety·lene
oxy·acid
oxy·cephal·ic (or ·cepha·lous) anatomy term
oxy·cepha·ly
oxy·gen
oxy·gen·ate (or ·ize, ·ise)
oxy·gena·tion
oxy·gen·ic (or ox·yg·enous)
oxy·gen·iz·able (or ·is·able)
oxy·ge·niz·er (or ·is·er)
oxy·hae·mo·glo·bin (US ·he·)
oxy·hy·dro·gen
oxy·mo·ron (plural ·mo·ra) rhetoric term
oxy·salt
oxy·sul·phide (US ·fide)
oxy·tet·ra·cy·cline
oxy·to·cic
oxy·to·cin hormone
oxy·tone linguistics term
oyer legal term
oyez (or oyes) interjection
Oyo Nigerian state
oys·ter
oyster·catcher
Oz Austral Australia
Oza·lid (Trademark)
ozo·cerite (or ·kerite) wax
ozone
ozon·ic (or ozo·nous)
ozo·nif·er·ous
ozo·ni·za·tion (or ·sa·tion)
ozo·nize (or ·nise)
ozo·niz·er (or ·nis·er)
ozo·noly·sis
ozo·no·sphere ozone layer

P

pa Slang father
paca animal
pace
pace·maker
pac·er

pace·setter
pace·way Austral racecourse
pa·cha variant spelling of pasha
pa·chi·si board game

pachy·derm animal
pachy·der·ma·tous
pachy·tene genetics term
Pa·cif·ic ocean, etc.
pa·cif·ic conciliatory

pa·cifi·cal·ly
paci·fi·ca·tion
paci·fi·er
paci·fism
paci·fist
paci·fy (·fies, ·fy·ing, ·fied)
pack
pack·able
pack·age
pack·ag·er
pack·ag·ing
pack·er
pack·et
pack·horse
pack·ing
pack·saddle
pack·thread
pact
pad (pad·ding, pad·ded)
pa·dang Malaysian field
pa·dauk (or ·douk) tree
pad·ding
pad·dle
paddle·fish (plural ·fish or ·fishes)
pad·dler
pad·dock
Pad·dy (plural ·dies) Slang Irishman
pad·dy (plural ·dies) rice field; temper
pad·dy·whack
pad·emel·on (or pad·dy·mel·on) wallaby
pad·lock
pa·dre
pa·dro·ne Italian innkeeper
Pad·ua
padua·soy fabric
paean (US also pean) song of praise; compare paeon; pean; peon
pae·di·at·ric (US pe·)
pae·dia·tri·cian (US pe·)
pae·di·at·rics (US pe·)
pae·do·gen·esis biology term
pae·do·genet·ic (or ·gen·ic)
pae·do·logi·cal (US pe·)
pae·dolo·gist (US pe·)
pae·dol·ogy (US pe·)
pae·do·mor·pho·sis biology term
pae·do·phile (US pe·)
pae·do·philia (US pe·)

pa·el·la (plural ·las)
pae·on metrical foot; compare paean; pean; peon
(paeony) incorrect spelling of peony
pa·gan
pa·gan·ism
pa·gan·ist
pa·gan·ist·ic
pa·gan·isti·cal·ly
pa·gani·za·tion (or ·sa·tion)
pa·gan·ize (or ·ise)
pa·gan·iz·er (or ·is·er)
page
pag·eant
pag·eant·ry (plural ·ries)
page·boy
pagi·nal
pagi·nate
pagi·na·tion
pa·go·da
pa·gu·rian (or ·rid) zoology term
Pa·hang Malaysian state
Pa·ha·ri language group
Pah·la·vi Persian language
paid
pai·gle Dialect cowslip
Paign·ton
pail bucket; compare pale
pail·lette sequin
pain hurt; compare pane
pained
pain·ful
pain·ful·ly
pain·ful·ness
pain·killer
pain·less
pain·less·ness
pains·taking
pains·taking·ness
paint
paint·box
paint·brush
paint·er
paint·er·ly
paint·ing
paint·work
painty
pair two similar things; compare pare
pair-oar
pai·sa (plural ·se) Indian coin
Pais·ley Scottish town
pais·ley fabric; pattern

pa·jam·as US spelling of pyjamas
pa·keha non-Maori
Pa·ki·stan
Pa·ki·stani
pal (pal·ling, palled) Slang friend; to befriend; compare pall
pal·ace
pala·din
palae·an·throp·ic (US pale·)
Palae·arc·tic zoogeographical region
palae·eth·no·logi·cal (US pale·)
palae·eth·nolo·gist (US pale·)
palae·eth·nol·ogy (US pale·)
palaeo·an·thro·pol·ogy (US paleo·)
palaeo·bo·tani·cal (or ·tan·ic; US paleo·)
palaeo·bota·nist (US paleo·)
palaeo·bota·ny (US paleo·)
Palaeo·cene (US Paleo·) geological epoch
palaeo·cli·ma·tol·ogy (US paleo·)
palaeo·eth·no·bota·ny (US paleo·)
Palaeo·gene (US Paleo·) geology term
palaeo·graph·ic (US paleo·)
palaeo·graphi·cal (US paleo·)
palae·og·ra·phy (US paleo·) study of ancient handwriting
palaeo·lith (US paleo·)
Palaeo·lith·ic (US Paleo·)
palae·on·to·graph·ic (or ·graphi·cal; US pale·)
palae·on·tog·ra·phy (US pale·) description of fossils
palae·on·to·logi·cal (US pale·)
palae·on·tolo·gist (US pale·)
palae·on·tol·ogy (US pale·)

Palaeo·zo·ic (*US* **Paleo·**) geological era

palaeo·zoo·logi·cal (*US* paleo·)

palaeo·zo·olo·gist (*US* paleo·)

palaeo·zo·ol·ogy (*US* paleo·)

pal·aes·tra (*plural* **·tras** *or* **·trae**)

pal·ais dance

pal·an·quin (*or* **·keen**)

pal·at·abil·ity (*or* **·able·ness**)

pal·at·able

pal·at·ably

pala·tal

pala·tali·za·tion (*or* **·sa·tion**)

pala·tal·ize (*or* **·ise**) phonetics term

pal·ate roof of mouth; *compare* **palette; pallet**

pa·la·tial

pa·la·tial·ly

pa·la·tial·ness

Pa·lati·nate German region

pa·lati·nate territory of palatine prince

Pala·tine of the Palatinate; Roman hill

pala·tine

pa·la·ver

pale lacking colour; wooden post; *compare* **pail**

pa·lea (*plural* **·leae**) botany term

pa·lea·ceous

pale·face

pale·ly in a pale way; *compare* **paly**

Pa·lem·bang Indonesian port

pale·ness

paleo· *US spelling of words beginning with* **palaeo·**

Pa·ler·mo Sicilian capital

Pal·es·tine

Pal·es·tin·ian

pal·ette (*or* **pal·let**) artist's board; *compare* **palate; pallet**

pal·ette knife (*plural* **pal·ette knives**)

pal·frey

pal·imp·sest manuscript

pal·in·drome

pal·in·drom·ic

pal·ing

pal·in·gen·esis (*plural* **·eses**) theology term

pal·in·genet·ic

palin·geneti·cal·ly

pali·node poem

pali·sade

pal·ish

pall coffin cover; to be boring; *compare* **pal; pawl**

Pal·la·dian architectural term

pal·lad·ic chemistry term

Pal·la·dium statue of Athena

pal·la·dium chemical element

pal·la·dous chemistry term

Pallas Athena; asteroid

pall·bearer

palled *past tense of* **pal** *or* **pall**

pal·let straw bed; potter's knife; machine part; *variant spelling of* **palette**; *compare* **palate**

pal·leti·za·tion (*or* **·sa·tion**)

pal·let·ize (*or* **·ise**)

pal·li·asse (*or* **pail·lasse**)

pal·li·ate

pal·lia·tion

pal·lia·tive

pal·lia·tor

pal·lid

pal·lium (*plural* **·lia** *or* **·liums**) vestment; anatomy term

Pall Mall

pal·lor

pal·ly (**·li·er, ·li·est**)

palm

Pal·ma Spanish resort; *compare* **Parma**

pal·ma·ceous botany term

pal·mar

pal·mate (*or* **·mat·ed**)

pal·ma·tion

palm·er pilgrim

pal·mette archaeological ornament

pal·met·to (*plural* **·tos** *or* **·toes**) palm tree

Pal·mi·ra Colombian city

palm·ist

palm·is·try

pal·mi·tate chemistry term

pal·mi·tin chemical compound

palmy (**palmi·er, palmi·est**)

pal·my·ra palm tree

pa·lo·lo (*plural* **·los**) worm

Palo·mar Californian mountain

palo·mi·no (*plural* **·nos**) horse

pa·loo·ka *US* clumsy person

palp (*or* **pal·pus**; *plural* **palps** *or* **pal·pi**)

pal·pabil·ity (*or* **·pable·ness**)

pal·pable

pal·pably

pal·pate examine medically; of palps; *compare* **palpitate**

pal·pa·tion

pal·pe·bral of the eyelid

pal·pe·brate

pal·pi·tate beat rapidly; *compare* **palpate**

pal·pi·ta·tion

pal·sied

pal·sy (*noun, plural* **·sies**; *verb* **·sies, ·sy·ing, ·sied**)

pal·ter be insincere

pal·ter·er

pal·tri·ly

pal·tri·ness

pal·try (**·tri·er, ·tri·est**)

paly heraldic term; *compare* **palely**

paly·no·logi·cal

paly·nolo·gist

paly·nol·ogy study of pollen

Pa·mirs Asian mountains

pam·pas

pam·pean

pam·per

pam·per·er

pam·pero (*plural* **·peros**) wind

pam·phlet

pam·phlet·eer

Pam·phylia ancient Asian region

Pam·plo·na Spanish city

Pan Greek god

pan (**pan·ning, panned**)

pana·cea

pana·cean

panache

pa·nache
pa·na·da thick sauce
Pana·ma
pana·ma
Pana·ma·nian
Pan-Ameri·can
Pan-Ameri·can·ism
Pan-Arab (or -Arabic)
Pan-Arabism
pana·tela (or pana·tel·la)
Pa·nay Philippine island
pan·cake
pan·chax fish
Pan·chen Lama
pan·chro·mat·ic
pan·chro·ma·tism
pan·cre·as
pan·cre·at·ic
pan·crea·tin
pan·da animal; compare
  pander
(pandamonium) incorrect
  spelling of pandemonium
pan·da·na·ceous botany
  term
pan·da·nus (plural ·nuses)
  plant
Pandarus mythological
  character
Pan·dean of Pan
pan·dect treatise
pan·dem·ic
pan·de·mo·ni·ac (or
  ·mon·ic)
pan·de·mo·nium
pan·der gratify weakness;
  pimp; compare panda
pan·der·er
pan·dit less common spelling
  of pundit except as Indian
  title, as in Pandit Nehru
Pandora mythological
  character
pan·dora variant of bandora
pan·dour Croatian soldier
pan·dow·dy (plural ·dies)
  US fruit pie
pan·du·rate (or
  ·du·ri·form) botany term
pan·dy (plural ·dies)
  school punishment
pane sheet of glass; compare
  pain
pan·egyr·ic praise; compare
  paregoric
pan·egyri·cal
pan·egyr·ist

pan·egy·rize (or ·rise)
pan·el (·el·ling, ·elled;
  US ·el·ing, ·eled)
pan·el·list
pan·et·to·ne spiced bread
pan·ful (plural ·fuls)
pang
pan·ga knife
Pan·gaea ancient continent
pan·gen·esis heredity
  theory
pan·genet·ic
pan·geneti·cal·ly
pan·go·lin animal
pan·han·dle
Pan·hel·len·ic
Pan·hel·len·ism
Pan·hel·len·ist
Pan·hel·len·is·tic
pan·ic (·ick·ing, ·icked)
pan·icky
pani·cle botany term
pani·cled
panic-stricken (or
  -struck)
pa·nicu·late (or ·lat·ed)
pan·jan·drum
pan·mix·is (or ·mixia)
  genetics term
Pan·mun·jom Korean
  village
pan·nage pig pasturage
panne fabric
pan·ni·er
pan·ni·kin
pa·no·cha (or pe·nu·che)
  sugar
pano·plied
pano·ply (plural ·plies)
pan·op·tic (or ·ti·cal)
pan·op·ti·cal·ly
pano·ra·ma
pano·ram·ic
pano·rami·cal·ly
pan·pipes
pan·soph·ic (or ·sophi·cal)
pan·sophi·cal·ly
pan·so·phy universal
  knowledge
pan·sy (plural ·sies)
pant
pan·ta·lets (or ·lettes)
  women's drawers
pan·ta·loon pantomime
  character
pan·ta·loons men's trousers
pan·tech·ni·con

pan·theism
pan·theist
pan·theis·tic (or ·ti·cal)
pan·theis·ti·cal·ly
Pan·the·on Roman temple
pan·the·on temple to all
  gods
pan·ther (plural ·thers or
  ·ther)
panties
pan·ti·hose
pan·tile
pan·ti·soc·ra·cy community
  ruled by all
pan·to (plural ·tos) Slang
  pantomime
pan·to·graph
pan·tog·ra·pher
pan·to·graph·ic
pan·to·graphi·cal·ly
pan·tog·ra·phy
pan·to·mime
pan·to·mim·ic
pan·to·mim·ist
pan·to·then·ic acid
pan·toum verse form
pan·try (plural ·tries)
pants
pant·suit US trouser suit
panty·waist US childish
  person
pan·zer
Pao·ting (or Pao-ting)
  Chinese city
Pao·tow Chinese city
pap
papa
pa·pa·cy (plural ·cies)
pa·pa·in enzyme
pa·pal
pa·pal·ly
pa·pa·vera·ceous botany
  term
pa·pa·ver·ine alkaloid
pa·paw (or paw·) American
  fruit
pa·pa·ya West Indian fruit
Pa·pe·ete Tahitian capital
pa·per
paper·back
paper·bark tree
paper·board
paper·boy
paper·clip
paper·cutter
pa·per·er
paper·girl

paper·hanger
paper·hanging
pa·peri·ness
paper·knife (*plural* ·knives)
paper·weight
paper·work
pa·pery
pap·eterie box for papers
Paph·la·go·nia Roman province
Pa·phos Cypriot village
papier-mâché
pa·pil·la (*plural* ·lae)
pa·pil·lary (*or* ·late, ·lose)
pap·il·lo·ma (*plural* ·ma·ta *or* ·mas) tumour
pap·il·lo·ma·to·sis
pap·il·lo·ma·tous
pap·il·lon dog
pap·il·lote paper frill in cookery
pa·pist
pa·pis·ti·cal (*or* ·pis·tic)
pa·pist·ry
pa·poose (*or* pap·poose) American Indian baby
pap·pose (*or* ·pous)
pap·pus (*plural* ·pi) plant hairs
pap·py (·pi·er, ·pi·est) mushy
pap·ri·ka
Pa·puan
Pa·pua New Guinea
papu·lar
pap·ule (*or* papu·la; *plural* ·ules *or* ·lae)
papu·lif·er·ous
papy·ra·ceous
papy·rol·o·gist
papy·rol·ogy
pa·py·rus (*plural* ·ri *or* ·ruses)
par accepted standard; *compare* parr
para (*plural* paras *or* para) Yugoslav coin
para (*plural* paras) paratrooper; paragraph
Pará Brazilian state
pa·raba·sis (*pluras* ·ses) speech of Greek chorus
para·bio·sis (*plural* ·ses) union of two individuals
para·bi·ot·ic
para·blast biology term

para·blas·tic
para·ble religious story
pa·rabo·la maths term
para·bol·ic of a parabola
para·bol·ic (*or* ·boli·cal) of parables
para·boli·cal·ly
pa·rabo·list
pa·rabo·li·za·tion (*or* ·sa·tion)
pa·rabo·lize (*or* ·lise)
para·rabo·loid maths term
pa·rabo·loi·dal
para·brake
pa·ra·ceta·mol
pa·rach·ro·nism error in dating
para·chute
para·chut·ist
Para·clete Holy Ghost
para·clete mediator
pa·rade
pa·rad·er
para·digm
para·dig·mat·ic
para·dise
para·di·sia·cal (*or* ·disi·ac)
para·dos bank behind trench
para·dox
para·doxi·cal
para·doxi·cal·ly
para·drop
par·aes·thesia (*US* ·es·; *plural* ·thesiae) medical term
par·aes·thet·ic (*US* ·es·)
par·af·fin (*or* ·fine)
para·form·al·de·hyde (*or* para·form)
para·gen·esis (*or* ·genesia) geology term
para·genet·ic
para·geneti·cal·ly
para·go·ge (*or* para·gogue) linguistics term
para·gog·ic (*or* ·gogi·cal)
para·gogi·cal·ly
para·gon
para·graph
para·graphia psychiatric term
para·graph·ic (*or* ·graphi·cal)
para·graphi·cal·ly
Para·guay

Para·guay·an
para·hy·dro·gen
Pa·raí·ba Brazilian state
para·keet (*or* par·ra·keet)
para·lan·guage
par·al·de·hyde
para·leip·sis (*or* ·lip·sis; *plural* ·ses) rhetorical device
pa·ra·li·pom·ena supplementary writings
par·al·lac·tic
par·al·lac·ti·cal·ly
par·al·lax
par·al·lel (·lel·ing, ·leled)
par·al·lel·epi·ped (*or* ·lelo·pi·ped)
par·al·lel·ism
par·al·lel·ist
par·al·lelo·gram
pa·ralo·gism invalid argument
pa·ralo·gist
pa·ralo·gis·tic
para·ly·sa·tion (*US* ·za·tion)
para·lyse (*US* ·lyze)
para·lys·er (*US* ·lyz·er)
pa·raly·sis (*plural* ·ses)
para·lyt·ic
para·lyti·cal·ly
para·mag·net·ic
para·mag·net·ism
Para·mari·bo capital of Surinam
para·mat·ta (*or* par·ra·mat·ta) fabric
para·mecium (*plural* ·mecia) protozoan
para·med·ic
para·medi·cal
para·ment (*plural* ·ments *or* ·men·ta) vestment
pa·ram·eter
para·met·ric (*or* ·ri·cal)
para·mili·tary
par·am·ne·sia
para·mo (*plural* ·mos) Andean plateau
para·morph mineralogy term
para·mor·phic (*or* ·phous)
para·mor·phism
para·mount
par·amour
Pa·ra·ná Brazilian state, river, and city

pa·rang knife
para·noia
para·noi·ac
para·noid
para·nor·mal
para·pet
para·pet·ed
par·aph flourish after
  signature
para·pher·na·lia
para·phrase
para·phras·tic
pa·raphy·sis (*plural* ·ses)
  botany term
para·plegia
para·plegic
para·po·dium (*plural* ·dia)
  zoology term
para·prax·is psychology
  term
para·psy·chol·ogy
Para·quat (*Trademark*)
para·sang Persian unit
para·sele·ne (*plural* ·nae)
  astronomy term
Pa·ra·shah (*plural* ·shoth)
  synagogue reading
para·site
para·sit·ic
para·siti·cal·ly
para·siti·cid·al
para·siti·cide
para·sit·ism
para·si·tize (*or* ·tise)
para·si·to·logi·cal
para·sit·olo·gist
para·sit·ol·ogy
para·sol
pa·ras·ti·chy (*plural*
  ·chies) botany term
para·sym·pa·thet·ic
para·syn·the·sis linguistics
  term
para·syn·the·ton (*plural*
  ·ta)
para·tac·tic
para·tac·ti·cal·ly
para·tax·is linguistics term
para·thi·on insecticide
para·thy·roid
para·troop·er
para·troops
para·ty·phoid
para·vane device on
  minesweeper
par avion *French* by plane

para·zo·an (*plural* ·zoans
  or ·zoa) zoology term
par·boil
par·buck·le rope sling
par·cel (·cel·ling, ·celled;
  US ·cel·ing, ·celed)
par·cenary joint heirship
par·cener
parch
parch·ment
par·close church screen
pard *Archaic* leopard
par·da·lote bird
pard·ner *US* partner
par·don
par·don·able
par·don·ably
par·don·er
pare trim; *compare* pair
par·egor·ic medicine;
  compare panegyric
pa·rei·ra medicinal root
pa·ren·chy·ma tissue
par·en·chyma·tous
par·ent
par·ent·age
pa·ren·tal
par·en·ter·al medical term
par·en·ter·ally
pa·ren·thesis (*plural*
  ·theses)
pa·ren·thesize (*or*
  ·thesise)
par·en·thet·ic (*or*
  ·theti·cal)
par·en·theti·cal·ly
par·ent·hood
par·er
par·er·gon (*plural* ·ga)
  additional work
pa·resis paralysis
par·es·thesia *US spelling of*
  paraesthesia
pa·ret·ic
par ex·cel·lence *French*
  beyond comparison
par·fait dessert
par·fleche rawhide
par·get
par·get·ing
par·he·lic (*or* ·he·lia·cal)
par·he·li·on (*plural* ·lia)
  astronomy term
pa·ri·ah
Parian marble
pari·es (*plural* pa·ri·etes)
  anatomy term

pa·ri·etal
pari-mutuel (*plural* pari-
  mutuels *or* paris-
  mutuels) betting system
par·ing
pari pas·su *Latin* legal term
pari·pin·nate botany term
Par·is French capital
Paris mythological character
par·ish
pa·rish·ion·er
Pa·ris·ian
Pa·risi·enne Parisian
  woman
pari·son glass mass
pari·syl·lab·ic
par·ity (*plural* ·ities)
park
par·ka coat
par·kin cake
park·ing
par·kin·son·ism
park·land
park·way
parky (parki·er,
  parki·est)
par·lance
par·lan·do music term
par·lay *US* double up in
  betting
par·ley discuss
par·ley·er
par·lia·ment (*or* Par·)
Par·lia·men·tar·ian
  parliamentary supporter in
  Civil War
par·lia·men·tar·ian
par·lia·men·tari·an·ism
  (*or* ·tar·ism)
par·lia·men·ta·ry
par·lour (*US* ·lor)
par·lous dangerous
Par·ma Italian city; *compare*
  Palma
Par·men·tier cookery term
Par·me·san cheese
Par·nas·sian
Par·nas·sus
pa·ro·chial
pa·ro·chi·al·ism
pa·ro·chi·al·ly
pa·rod·ic (*or* ·rodi·cal)
paro·dy (*noun, plural*
  ·dies; *verb* ·dies,
  ·dy·ing, ·died)
pa·roi·cous (*or* ·roe·cious)
  botany term

pa·rol oral
pa·rol·able
pa·role conditional release
pa·rolee
paro·no·ma·sia play on
  words
paro·no·mas·ti·cal·ly
paro·nym linguistics term
paro·nym·ic (or
  pa·rony·mous)
Pár·os Greek island
pa·rot·ic near the ear
pa·rot·id gland
paro·ti·tis (or
  pa·roti·di·tis) mumps
pa·ro·toid poison gland on
  toad
par·ox·ysm
par·ox·ys·mal (or ·mic)
par·quet
par·quet·ry
parr (plural parrs or
  parr) salmon; compare
  par
par·rel (or ·ral) nautical
  term
par·ri·cid·al
par·ri·cide killing of parent;
  compare patricide
par·rot
parrot·fashion
parrot·fish (plural ·fish or
  ·fishes)
par·ry (verb ·ries, ·ry·ing,
  ·ried; noun, plural
  ·ries)
pars·able
parse
par·sec unit
Par·see
Par·see·ism Indian religion
pars·er
par·si·mo·ni·ous
par·si·mo·ny
pars·ley
pars·nip
par·son
par·son·age
part
par·take (·tak·ing, ·took,
  ·tak·en)
par·tak·er
par·tan Scot crab
part·ed
par·terre garden
par·theno·car·pic (or
  ·pous)

par·theno·car·py botany
  term
par·theno·genesis
par·theno·genet·ic
par·theno·geneti·cal·ly
Par·the·non Greek temple
Parthenope mythological
  character
Par·thia ancient Asian
  country
Par·thian
par·tial
par·tial·ity (plural ·ities)
par·tial·ly
par·tial·ness
part·ible
par·tici·pant
par·tici·pate
par·tici·pa·tion (or
  ·tici·pance)
par·tici·pa·tor
par·ti·cipi·al
par·ti·ci·ple
par·ti·cle
parti·coloured (US
  ·colored)
par·ticu·lar
par·ticu·lar·ism
par·ticu·lar·ist
par·ticu·lar·is·tic
par·ticu·lar·ity (plural
  ·ities)
par·ticu·lari·za·tion (or
  ·sa·tion)
par·ticu·lar·ize (or ·ise)
par·ticu·lar·iz·er (or
  ·is·er)
par·ticu·late (adj)
part·ing
par·ti pris French
  preconceived opinion
par·ti·san (or ·zan)
par·ti·san·ship (or
  ·zan·ship)
par·ti·ta musical piece
par·tite divided
par·ti·tion
par·ti·tion·er (or ·ist)
par·ti·tive
part·let shawl
part·ly
part·ner
part·ner·ship
par·ton physics term
par·took
par·tridge (plural ·tridges
  or ·tridge)

part-time (adj)
part-timer
par·tu·ri·ent of childbirth
par·tu·ri·fa·cient
par·tu·ri·tion
par·ty (plural ·ties)
pa·ru·lis (plural ·li·des)
  gumboil
pa·rure set of jewels
par·venu (fem ·venue)
par·vis (or ·vise) church
  porch
Pasa·dena US city
Pa·sar·ga·dae ancient
  Persian city
Pa·say Philippine city
pas·cal unit
pas·chal of Easter
Pas-de-Calais French
  department
pas de deux (plural pas
  de deux) ballet sequence
pash Slang infatuation
Pa·sha Turkish title
pa·sha (or ·cha) Ottoman
  governor
pa·sha·lik (or ·lic) province
  of pasha
Pash·to (or Push·tu)
  language
paso do·ble (plural paso
  do·bles or pasos
  do·bles) dance
pasque·flow·er
pas·quin·ade (or pas·quil)
  satire
pas·quin·ad·er
pass
pass·able able to be passed;
  compare passible
pass·ably
pas·sa·ca·glia musical piece
pas·sade dressage term
pas·sage
passage·way
pas·sant heraldic term
pass·book
pas·sé out-of-date
passed past tense of pass;
  compare past
passe·men·terie decorative
  trimming
pas·sen·ger
passe-partout picture
  mounting
passe·pied dance

passer-by (*plural* **passers-by**)

pas·ser·ine ornithology term

pas seul dance sequence

pas·sibil·ity

pas·sible sensitive; *compare* passable

pas·si·flo·ra·ceous botany term

pas·sim *Latin* throughout

pass·ing

Pas·sion Christ's sufferings

pas·sion

pas·sion·al

pas·sion·ate

pas·sion·ate·ness

passion·flower

pas·sion·less

pas·sion·less·ness

Passion·tide

pas·sive

pas·sive·ness (*or* pas·siv·ity)

pas·siv·ism

pas·siv·ist

pass·key

Pass·over

pass·port

(passtime) *incorrect spelling of* pastime

pas·sus (*plural* ·sus *or* ·suses) part of poem

pass·word

past

pas·ta

paste

paste·board

pas·tel drawing crayon; *compare* pastille

pas·tel·list (*or* ·tel·ist)

pas·tern part of horse's foot

paste-up

pas·teur·ism rabies treatment

pas·teuri·za·tion (*or* ·sa·tion)

pas·teur·ize (*or* ·ise)

pas·teur·iz·er (*or* ·is·er)

pas·tic·cio (*plural* ·cios) pastiche

pas·tiche artistic medley; *compare* postiche

pas·tille (*or* ·til) lozenge; *compare* pastel

pasti·ly

pas·time

pasti·ness

pas·tis alcoholic drink

pas·tor

pas·to·ral of shepherds or pastors

pas·to·rale (*plural* ·rales *or* ·ra·li) musical piece

pas·to·ral·ly

pas·tor·ate

pas·tra·mi smoked beef

pas·try (*plural* ·tries)

pas·tur·age

pas·ture

(pasturize) *incorrect spelling of* pasteurize

pasty (*noun*, *plural* pasties; *adj* pasti·er, pasti·est) a pastry; pale

pat (pat·ting, pat·ted)

pa·ta·gium (*plural* ·gia) zoology term

Pata·go·nia South American region

patch

patch·able

patch·er

patchi·ly

patchi·ness

patchou·li (*or* pachou·li, patchou·ly) perfume

patch·work

patchy (patchi·er, patchi·est)

pate the head

pâté food; *compare* pattée

pâté de foie gras (*plural* pâtés de foie gras)

pa·tel·la (*plural* ·lae) kneecap

pa·tel·lar

pa·tel·late

pa·tel·li·form

pat·en (*or* ·in, ·ine) plate for Eucharist; *compare* patten

pa·ten·cy

pa·tent

pa·tent·able

pa·tentee

pa·tent·ly

pa·ten·tor

pa·ter *Slang* father

pa·ter·fa·mili·as (*plural* pa·tres·fa·mili·as) male head of family

pa·ter·nal

pa·ter·nal·ism

pa·ter·nal·ist

pa·ter·nal·is·tic

pa·ter·nal·is·ti·cal·ly

pa·ter·nal·ly

pa·ter·nity

Pat·er·nos·ter Lord's Prayer

pat·er·nos·ter rosary beads; fishing tackle; lift

Pat·er·son US city

path

Pa·than Afghan or Pakistani Muslim

pa·thet·ic

pa·theti·cal·ly

path·finder

path·finding

patho·gen (*or* ·gene)

patho·gen·esis (*or* pa·thog·eny)

patho·genet·ic of disease

patho·gen·ic causing disease

path·og·no·mon·ic indicating disease

path·og·no·moni·cal·ly

path·og·no·my study of emotions

patho·logi·cal (*or* ·log·ic)

patho·logi·cal·ly

pa·tholo·gist

pa·thol·ogy (*plural* ·ogies)

pa·thos

path·way .

Pa·tia·la Indian city

pa·tience

pa·tient

pa·tient·ly

pati·na

pa·tio (*plural* ·tios)

pa·tis·serie

Pat·mos Greek island

Pat·na Indian city; rice

pat·ois (*plural* pat·ois) dialect

Pa·tras Greek port

pa·trial

pa·tri·arch

pa·tri·ar·chal

pa·tri·ar·chate

pa·tri·ar·chy (*plural* ·chies)

pa·tri·cian

pa·tri·ci·ate rank of patrician

pat·ri·cid·al

pat·ri·cide killing one's father; *compare* parricide

pat·ri·cli·nous (*or* ·ro·cli·nous, ·ro·cli·nal) resembling male parent

pat·ri·lin·eal (*or* ·ear)

pat·ri·lo·cal living with husband's family

pat·ri·mo·nial

pat·ri·mo·ny (*plural* ·nies)

pa·tri·ot

pat·ri·ot·ic

pat·ri·ot·ism

pa·tris·tic (*or* ·ti·cal)

pa·tris·ti·cal·ly

pa·trol (·trol·ling, ·trolled)

pa·trol·ler

patrol·man (*plural* ·men)

pa·trol·ogy writings of Church Fathers

pa·tron

pat·ron·age

pa·tron·al

pa·tron·ess

pat·ron·ize (*or* ·ise)

pat·ron·iz·er (*or* ·is·er)

pat·ron·iz·ing·ly (*or* ·is·ing·ly)

pat·ro·nym·ic

pat·ted

pat·tée type of cross; *compare* pâté

pat·ten wooden clog; *compare* paten

pat·ter

pat·tern

pat·ting

pat·ty (*plural* ·ties)

patu·lous

paua shellfish

pau·cal linguistics term

pau·city

paul·dron armour plate

Paul·ine of St Paul

pau·low·nia tree

paunch

paunchi·ness

paunchy (paunchi·er, paunchi·est)

pau·per

pau·per·ism

pau·per·ize (*or* ·ise)

pause

paus·er

paus·ing·ly

pav·age paving tax

pa·vane (*or* pa·van) dance

pave

pavé paved surface

pave·ment

pa·vil·ion

pav·ing

pav·ior (*or* ·iour) one who paves

pav·is (*or* ·ise) shield

Pav·lo·va meringue cake

pavo·nine of peacocks

paw

pawky (pawki·er, pawki·est) *Scot* drily witty

pawl part of ratchet; *compare* pall

pawn

pawn·age

pawn·broker

pawn·broking

Paw·nee (*plural* ·nees *or* ·nee) American Indian

pawn·shop

paw·paw *variant spelling of* papaw

pax

pax·wax *Dialect* ligament

pay (pay·ing, paid)

pay·able

pay·day

payee

pay·er

pay·load

pay·master

pay·ment

pay·nim *Archaic* heathen

pay·off (*noun*)

pay·ola *US* bribe

pay·phone

pay·roll

pea

peace

peace·able

peace·able·ness

peace·ful

peace·ful·ly

peace·ful·ness

peace·maker

peace·time

peach

peachi·ness

peachy (peachi·er, peachi·est)

pea·cock (*plural* ·cocks *or* ·cock)

pea·fowl (*plural* ·fowls *or* ·fowl)

pea·hen

peak summit; to sicken; *compare* peek; peke

peaked

peaky (peaki·er, peaki·est)

peal loud sound; *compare* peel

pean heraldic term; *US variant spelling of* paean; *compare* paeon; peon

pea·nut

pear

pearl jewel; *compare* purl

pearl·er

pearl·ite steel constituent; *variant spelling of* perlite

pearl·it·ic

pearl·ized (*or* ·ised)

pearly (*adj* pearli·er, pearli·est; *noun, plural* pearlies)

pear·main apple

peas·ant

peas·ant·ry

pease *Dialect* pea

pea·shooter

pea·soup·er *Slang* fog

peat

peaty

peau de soie fabric

peb·ble

pebble-dash

peb·bling

peb·bly

pe·can nut; *compare* pekan

pec·ca·bil·ity

pec·cable liable to sin

pec·ca·dil·lo (*plural* ·los *or* ·loes)

pec·can·cy

pec·cant

pec·ca·ry (*plural* ·ries *or* ·ry) piglike animal

pec·ca·vi (*plural* ·vis) confession of guilt

peck

peck·er

peck·ing

peck·ish

pec·tase enzyme

pec·tate

pec·ten (*plural* ·tens *or* ·ti·nes) zoology term; *compare* pectin

pec·tic of pectin; *compare* peptic

pec·tin gelling substance; *compare* pecten

pec·ti·nate (*or* ·nat·ed) comb-shaped

pec·ti·na·tion

pec·tin·ous

pec·tiz·able (*or* ·tis·able)

pec·ti·za·tion (*or* ·sa·tion)

pec·tize (*or* ·tise) jellify

pec·to·ral

pecu·late embezzle

pecu·la·tion

pecu·la·tor

pe·cu·liar

pe·cu·li·ar·ity (*plural* ·ities)

pe·cu·ni·ari·ly

pe·cu·ni·ary

peda·gog·ic (*or* ·gogi·cal)

peda·gogi·cal·ly

peda·gog·ics

peda·gog·ism (*or* ·gogu·ism)

peda·gogue (*or* ·gog)

peda·go·gy

ped·al (·al·ling, ·alled; *US* ·dal·ing, ·daled) foot lever; operate pedals; *compare* peddle

pe·dal of the foot

pe·dal·fer soil

ped·al·ler (*US* ·al·er) one who pedals; *compare* peddler; pedlar

peda·lo (*plural* ·los *or* ·loes) pedal boat

ped·ant

pe·dan·tic

ped·ant·ry (*plural* ·ries)

ped·ate biology term

pe·dati·fid botany term

ped·dle sell; *compare* pedal

ped·dler drugs seller; *US spelling of* pedlar

ped·er·ast (*or* paed·)

ped·er·as·tic (*or* paed·)

ped·er·as·ty (*or* paed·)

ped·es·tal

pe·des·trian

pe·des·tria·ni·za·tion (*or* ·sa·tion)

pe·des·tri·an·ize (*or* ·ise)

Pedi African people

pe·di·at·rics *US spelling of* paediatrics

pedi·cab tricycle cab

pedi·cel flower stalk

pedi·cle small stalk

pe·dicu·lar of lice or pedicles

pe·dicu·late zoology term

pe·dicu·lo·sis infestation with lice

pe·dicu·lous

pedi·cure

pedi·form

pedi·gree

pedi·greed

pedi·ment

pedi·ment·al

pedi·palp zoology term

ped·lar (*US* ped·dler) hawker; *compare* peddler

pedo·cal soil

pe·do·logi·cal

pe·dolo·gist

pe·dol·ogy study of soils

pe·dom·eter

pe·dun·cle flower stalk

pe·dun·cu·lar

pe·dun·cu·late (*or* ·lat·ed)

pe·dun·cu·la·tion

pee (pee·ing, peed)

Pee·bles former Scottish county

peek peep; *compare* peak; peke

peeka·boo

peel rind; to be shed; fortified tower; *compare* peal

peel·er

peelie-wally *Scot* unwell

peel·ing

peen part of hammer

peep

peep·er

peep·hole

peep·show

pee·pul (*or* pi·pal) sacred tree

peer a noble; an equal; to look; *compare* pier

peer·age

peer·ess

peer·less

peeve *Slang* irritate

peev·ers *Scot* hopscotch

peev·ish

peev·ish·ness

pee·wee *variant spelling of* pewee

pee·wit (*or* pe·wit) lapwing

peg (peg·ging, pegged)

Pega·sus mythological horse; constellation

peg·board

peg·ma·tite rock

peg·ma·tit·ic

peign·oir

pejo·ra·tion

pe·jo·ra·tive

pek·an animal; *compare* pecan

peke *Slang* Pekingese dog; *compare* peak; peek

Pe·kin duck

Pe·king Chinese capital

Pe·king·ese (*or* ·kin·) dog; of Peking

pe·koe tea

pel·age

Pe·la·gi·an·ism Christian doctrine

pe·lag·ic of open sea

pel·ar·go·nium

Pe·lée West Indian volcano

pel·er·ine cape

Peleus mythological character

pelf *Slang* money

pel·ham horse's bit

peli·can

Pe·li·on Greek mountain

pe·lisse

pe·lite rock

pe·lit·ic

Pel·la ancient Greek city

pel·la·gra

pel·la·grous

pel·let

pel·li·cle

pel·licu·lar

pel·li·tory (*plural* ·tories) plant

pell-mell

pel·lu·cid

pel·lu·cid·ity (*or* ·ness)

Pel·man·ism memory training

pel·man·ism card game

pel·met

Pelo·pon·nese

Pelo·pon·ne·sian

Pelops mythological character

pe·lo·ria botany term

pe·lo·rus (*plural* ·ruses) gyrocompass

pe·lo·ta ball game
Pe·lo·tas Brazilian port
pelt
pel·tast ancient Greek
 soldier
pel·tate botany term
pel·ta·tion
pelt·er
Peltier ef·fect
pelt·ry (*plural* ·ries)
 animal pelts
pel·vic
pel·vis (*plural* ·vises *or*
 ·ves)
Pem·ba Tanzanian island
Pem·broke
Pem·broke·shire former
 Welsh county
pem·mi·can (*or* pemi·can)
 food
pem·phi·gus skin disease
pen (pen·ning, penned)
 writing tool; write
pen (pen·ning, penned *or*
 pent) enclosure; enclose
pe·nal
pe·nali·za·tion (*or*
 ·sa·tion)
pe·nal·ize (*or* ·ise)
pen·al·ty (*plural* ·ties)
pen·ance
Pe·nang Malaysian state
pe·na·tes Roman gods
pence
pen·cel (*or* ·sel, ·sil) small
 flag; *compare* pencil
pen·chant
Pen·chi (*or* ·ki) Chinese
 city
pen·cil (·cil·ling, ·cilled;
 US ·cil·ing, ·ciled)
 writing tool, etc.; *compare*
 pencel
pen·cil·ler (*US* ·cil·er)
pend
pen·dant necklace
pen·dent dangling
pen·den·te lite legal term
pen·den·tive architectural
 term
pend·ing
pen·dragon leader of
 ancient Britons
pen·du·lous
pen·du·lum
pe·neplain (*or* ·neplane)
 flat land

pe·ne·pla·na·tion
pen·etrabil·ity
pen·etrable
pen·etra·lia innermost parts
pen·etra·lian
pen·etrance
pen·etrant
pen·etrate
pen·etra·tion
pen·etra·tor
Peng·pu (*or* Pang-fou)
 Chinese city
pen·guin
peni·cil·late biology term
peni·cil·la·tion
peni·cil·lin antibiotic
peni·cil·lium (*plural*
 ·liums *or* ·lia) mould
pe·nile of the penis
pe·nil·li·on (*sing.* pe·nill)
 Welsh sung poetry
pen·in·su·la
pen·in·su·lar
pe·nis (*plural* ·nises *or*
 ·nes)
peni·tence
peni·tent
peni·ten·tial
peni·ten·tia·ry (*plural*
 ·ries)
pen·knife (*plural* ·knives)
pen·man (*plural* ·men)
pen·man·ship
pen·na (*plural* ·nae)
 feather
pen·nant ship's flag;
 compare pennon
pen·nate (*or* ·nat·ed)
penned
pen·nies
pen·ni·less
pen·ni·less·ness
Pen·nine
Pen·nines
pen·ning
pen·ni·nite mineral
pen·non long flag; *compare*
 pennant
Penn·syl·va·nia
Penn·syl·va·nian
pen·nul·ti·mate
pen·ny (*plural* pen·nies *or*
 pence)
pen·ny·cress
penny-pincher
penny-pinching
penny·royal plant

penny·weight
penny-wise
penny·wort plant
penny·worth
pe·no·logi·cal (*or* poe·)
pe·nolo·gist (*or* poe·)
pe·nol·ogy (*or* poe·)
Pen·rith Cumbrian town
pen·sile ornithology term
pen·sil·ity (*or* ·sile·ness)
pen·sion
pen·sion·able
pen·sion·ary (*plural*
 ·aries)
pen·sion·er
pen·sive
pen·sive·ness
pen·stock water channel
pent
pen·ta·chlo·ro·phe·nol
pen·ta·cle *variant of*
 pentagram
pen·tad group of five
pen·ta·dac·tyl
Pen·ta·gon US defence
 headquarters
pen·ta·gon five-sided
 polygon
pen·tago·nal
pen·ta·gram (*or* ·cle)
 magical symbol
pen·ta·he·dron (*plural*
 ·drons *or* ·dra)
pen·tam·er·ous botany
 term
pen·tam·eter verse line
pen·tane organic compound
pen·tan·gu·lar
pen·ta·no·ic acid
pen·ta·prism
pen·ta·quine drug
pen·tar·chi·cal
pen·tar·chy (*plural* ·chies)
 government by five
pen·ta·stich five-line poem
Pen·ta·teuch Old
 Testament books
pen·tath·lete
pen·tath·lon
pen·ta·ton·ic musical term
pen·ta·va·lent
Pen·tecost
Pen·tecos·tal
pen·tene organic compound
pent·house
pen·ti·men·to (*plural* ·ti)
 art term

pent·land·ite mineral
pen·to·bar·bi·tone (*US* ·tal)
pen·tode electronic valve
pen·tom·ic military term
pen·to·san biochemical compound
pen·tose sugar
Pen·to·thal (*Trademark*)
pent·ox·ide
pent·ste·mon (*or* pen·ste·mon) plant
pent-up
pen·tyl chemistry term
pentylene·tetrazol
pe·nu·che *variant of* panocha
pen·ult (*or* pe·nul·ti·ma)
pe·nul·ti·mate
pe·num·bra (*plural* ·brae *or* ·bras)
pe·num·bral (*or* ·brous)
pe·nu·ri·ous
penu·ry
Pen·za Soviet city
Pen·zance
peon Indian worker; debtor; *compare* paean; paeon; pean
pe·on·age (*or* pe·on·ism)
peo·ny (*plural* ·nies)
peo·ple
Peo·ria US port
pep (pep·ping, pepped)
pep·lum (*plural* ·lums *or* ·la) ruffle
pepo (*plural* pepos) botany term
pep·per
pepper·corn
pepper·grass
pepper·mint
pepper·wort
pep·pery
pep·py (·pi·er, ·pi·est)
pep·sin (*or* ·sine) enzyme
pep·si·nate
pep·sino·gen enzyme
pep·tic of digestion; *compare* pectic
pep·ti·dase enzyme
pep·tide protein
pep·tiz·able (*or* ·tis·able)
pep·ti·za·tion (*or* ·sa·tion)
pep·tize (*or* ·tise)
pep·tiz·er (*or* ·tis·er)

pep·tone product of digestion
pep·to·ni·za·tion (*or* ·sa·tion)
pep·to·nize (*or* ·nise)
pep·to·niz·er (*or* ·nis·er)
Pe·quot (*plural* ·quot *or* ·quots) American Indian
per
per·acid
pera·cid·ity
per·ad·ven·ture *Archaic* by chance
Pe·raea ancient Palestinian region
Pe·rak Malaysian state
per·am·bu·late
per·am·bu·la·tion
per·am·bu·la·tor
per·am·bu·la·tory
per an·num
per·bo·rate chemistry term
per·cale sheet fabric
per·ca·line lining fabric
per capi·ta
per·ceiv·abil·ity
per·ceiv·able
per·ceive
per·ceiv·er
per cent
per·cent·age
per·cen·tile
per·cept object of perception
per·cep·tibil·ity (*or* ·tible·ness)
per·cep·tible
per·cep·tibly
per·cep·tion
per·cep·tion·al
per·cep·tive
per·cep·tivi·ty (*or* ·tive·ness)
per·cep·tual
perch (*plural (for fish)* perch *or* perches)
per·chance
perch·er
Per·cheron horse
per·chlo·rate
per·chlo·ride
per·cipi·ence
per·cipi·ent
per·coid (*or* ·coi·dean) zoology term
per·co·late
per·co·la·tion

per·co·la·tive
per·co·la·tor
per·cuss
per·cus·sion
per·cus·sion·ist
per·cus·sive
per·cus·sor
per·cu·ta·neous
per diem *Latin* every day
per·di·tion
per·egri·nate
per·egri·na·tion
per·egri·na·tor
per·egrine
Pe·rei·ra Colombian city
pe·rei·ra medicinal bark
per·emp·to·ri·ly
per·emp·to·ri·ness
per·emp·tory
pe·ren·nate botany term
pe·ren·na·tion
per·en·nial
per·en·nial·ly
per·fect
per·fect·er
per·fect·ibil·ity
per·fect·ible
per·fec·tion
per·fec·tion·ism
per·fec·tion·ist
per·fec·tive
per·fec·to (*plural* ·tos) cigar
per·fer·vid ardent
per·fidi·ous
per·fidi·ous·ness
per·fi·dy (*plural* ·dies)
per·fo·li·ate botany term
per·fo·li·a·tion
per·fo·rable
per·fo·rate
per·fo·ra·tion
per·fo·ra·tive (*or* ·tory)
per·fo·ra·tor
per·force
per·form
per·form·able
per·for·mance
per·for·ma·tive
per·form·er
per·form·ing
per·fume
per·fum·er
per·fum·ery (*plural* ·eries)
per·func·to·ri·ly
per·func·to·ri·ness

per·func·tory
per·fuse
per·fu·sion
per·fu·sive
Per·ga·mum ancient Asian
    city
per·go·la
per·haps
peri (*plural* peris) fairy
peri·anth petals of flower
peri·apt amulet
peri·blem plant tissue
peri·car·dit·ic
peri·car·di·tis
peri·car·dium (*plural* ·dia)
peri·carp botany term
peri·car·pial (*or* ·pic)
peri·chon·drium (*plural*
    ·dria) anatomy term
peri·clase mineral
peri·clas·tic
peri·cli·nal botany term
peri·cline mineral
pe·rico·pe church reading
peri·cra·nial
peri·cra·nium (*plural* ·nia)
peri·cy·cle plant tissue
peri·cy·clic
peri·cyn·thi·on point in
    lunar orbit
peri·derm botany term
peri·derm·al (*or* ·ic)
pe·rid·ium (*plural* ·ridia)
    botany term
peri·dot gemstone
peri·do·tite rock
peri·do·tit·ic
peri·gean (*or* ·geal)
peri·gee point in lunar orbit
peri·gon maths term
Peri·gor·dian Palaeolithic
    culture
pe·rigy·nous botany term
pe·rigy·ny
peri·he·lion (*plural* ·lia)
    point in planet's orbit
per·il
peri·lous
peri·lous·ness
peri·lune point in lunar
    orbit
peri·lymph anatomy term
pe·rim·eter
peri·met·ric (*or* ·ri·cal,
    pe·rim·etral)
peri·met·ri·cal·ly
pe·rim·etry

peri·morph mineralogy
    term
peri·mor·phic (*or* ·phous)
peri·mor·phism
peri·mys·ium anatomy term
peri·na·tal
peri·neal
peri·neph·rium (*plural*
    ·ria) anatomy term
peri·neum (*plural* ·nea)
    vaginal area
peri·neu·ri·tic
peri·neu·ri·tis
peri·neu·rium nerve tissue
pe·ri·od
pe·rio·date chemistry term
pe·ri·od·ic
peri·od·ic acid
pe·ri·odi·cal
pe·ri·odi·cal·ly
pe·rio·dic·ity (*plural*
    ·ities)
perio·don·tal
perio·don·tic
perio·don·ti·cal·ly
perio·don·tics
perio·don·tol·ogy branch
    of dentistry
peri·onych·ium (*plural*
    ·onychia) anatomy term
peri·os·teum (*plural* ·tea)
    bone tissue
peri·os·tit·ic
peri·os·ti·tis
peri·otic around the ear
peri·pa·tet·ic
peri·pa·teti·cal·ly
peri·peteia (*or* ·petia,
    pe·rip·ety) drama term
peri·peteian (*or* ·petian)
pe·riph·er·al
pe·riph·er·al·ly
pe·riph·ery (*plural* ·eries)
pe·riph·ra·sis (*plural* ·ses)
    circumlocution
peri·phras·tic
peri·phras·ti·cal·ly
pe·riphy·ton aquatic
    organisms
pe·rip·teral
pe·rique tobacco
peri·sarc zoology term
peri·sar·cal (*or* ·cous)
peri·scope
peri·scop·ic
peri·scopi·cal·ly
per·ish

per·ish·abil·ity (*or*
    ·able·ness)
per·ish·able
per·ish·er
per·ish·ing
peri·sperm botany term
peri·sperm·al
peri·spo·menon linguistics
    term
pe·ris·so·dac·tyl (*or* ·tyle)
    zoology term
pe·ris·so·dac·ty·lous
peri·stal·sis (*plural* ·ses)
peri·stal·tic
peri·stal·ti·cal·ly
peri·sto·mal (*or* ·mial)
peri·stome botany term
peri·sty·lar
peri·style colonnade
peri·thecium (*plural*
    ·thecia) botany term
peri·to·neal
peri·to·neum (*plural* ·nea
    or ·niums)
peri·to·nit·ic
peri·to·ni·tis
peri·track taxiway
pe·rit·ri·cha (*sing.*
    peri·trich) biology term
pe·rit·ri·chous
peri·wig
peri·win·kle
(perjorative) *incorrect
    spelling of* pejorative
per·jure
per·jur·er
per·jury (*plural* ·juries)
perk
perki·ly
perki·ness
perky (perki·er,
    perki·est)
Per·lis Malaysian state
per·lite (*or* pearl·) filler
    and soil-conditioner;
    compare pearlite
per·lit·ic (*or* pearl·)
per·lo·cu·tion
per·lo·cu·tion·ary
Perm Soviet port
perm
per·ma·frost
perm·al·loy
per·ma·nence
per·ma·nen·cy (*plural*
    ·cies)
per·ma·nent

per·man·ga·nate
per·me·abil·ity (*plural* ·ities)
per·me·able
per·me·ance
per·me·ant
per·me·ate
per·mea·tion
per·mea·tive
per·mea·tor
per men·sem *Latin* every month
Per·mian geological period
per·mis·sibil·ity
per·mis·sible
per·mis·sion
per·mis·sive
per·mis·sive·ness
per·mit (·mit·ting, ·mit·ted)
per·mit·ter
per·mit·tiv·ity (*plural* ·ities) physics term
per·mu·ta·tion
per·mu·ta·tion·al
per·mute
Per·nam·bu·co Brazilian state
per·ni·cious
per·ni·cious·ness
per·nick·eti·ness
per·nick·ety
Per·nod (*Trademark*)
pe·ro·neal of the outer leg
pero·rate
pero·ra·tion
pe·roxi·dase enzyme
per·ox·ide
per·pend (*or* ·pent) wall stone
per·pen·dicu·lar
per·pen·dicu·lar·ity
per·pe·trate
per·pe·tra·tion
per·pe·tra·tor
per·pet·ual
per·pet·ual·ly
per·petu·ate
per·petua·tion
per·pe·tu·ity (*plural* ·ities)
Per·pi·gnan French town
per·plex
per·plex·ity (*plural* ·ities)
per·qui·site
Per·rier (*Trademark*)
per·ron flight of steps

per·ry (*plural* ·ries) pear wine
per·salt chemical compound
per se *Latin* in itself
perse greyish-blue
per·secute
per·secu·tion
per·secu·tive (*or* ·tory)
per·secu·tor
Per·seid meteor shower
Persephone mythological character
Per·sepo·lis capital of ancient Persia
Perseus mythological character
Per·seus constellation
per·sever·ance
per·se·ver·ant
per·sev·era·tion psychology term
per·severe
Per·sia
Per·sian
per·si·caria plant
per·si·ennes Persian blinds
per·si·flage
per·sim·mon fruit
Per·sis ancient Persian region
per·sist
per·sis·tence (*or* ·ten·cy)
per·sis·tent
per·sist·er
per·son (*plural* ·sons)
per·so·na (*plural* ·nae)
per·son·able
per·son·able·ness
per·son·age
per·so·na gra·ta (*plural* per·so·nae gra·tae)
per·son·al
per·son·al·ism
per·son·al·ist
per·son·al·is·tic
per·son·al·ity (*plural* ·ities)
per·son·ali·za·tion (*or* ·sa·tion)
per·son·al·ize (*or* ·ise)
per·son·al·ly
per·son·al·ty (*plural* ·ties) personal property
per·so·na non gra·ta (*plural* per·so·nae non gra·tae)
per·son·ate

per·sona·tion
per·sona·tive
per·sona·tor
per·soni·fi·able
per·soni·fi·ca·tion
per·soni·fy (·fies, ·fy·ing, ·fied)
per·son·nel
per·spec·tive
Per·spec·tiv·ism philosophical doctrine
Per·spex (*Trademark*)
per·spi·ca·cious perceptive; *compare* perspicuous
per·spi·cac·ity (*or* ·ca·cious·ness)
per·spi·cu·ity (*or* ·spicu·ous·ness)
per·spicu·ous lucid; *compare* perspicacious
per·spi·ra·tion
per·spir·atory
per·spire
per·spir·ing·ly
per·suad·abil·ity (*or* per·sua·si·bil·ity)
per·suad·able (*or* per·sua·sible)
per·suade
per·suad·er
per·sua·sion
per·sua·sive
per·sua·sive·ness
(persue) *incorrect spelling of* pursue
pert
per·tain
Perth
per·ti·na·cious
per·ti·nac·ity (*or* ·na·cious·ness)
per·ti·nence
per·ti·nent
pert·ness
per·turb
per·turb·able
per·turb·ably
per·tur·ba·tion
per·turb·ing·ly
per·tus·sis whooping cough
Peru
Pe·ru·gia Italian city
pe·ruke wig
pe·rus·al
pe·ruse
pe·rus·er
Pe·ru·vian

per·vade
per·vad·er
per·va·sion
per·va·sive
per·va·sive·ness
per·verse
per·verse·ness
per·ver·sion
per·ver·sity (*plural* ·sities)
per·ver·sive
per·vert
per·vert·ed
per·vert·ed·ly
per·vert·ed·ness
per·vert·er
per·ver·tible
per·vi·ous
per·vi·ous·ness
pes (*plural* pedes) foot
Pe·sach (*or* ·sah) Passover
pe·sade dressage term
Pe·sca·ra Italian city
pe·seta Spanish currency
pe·sewa Ghanaian currency
Pesha·war Pakistani city
Pe·shit·ta (*or* ·shi·to)
  Syriac Bible
pesky (peski·er,
  peski·est)
peso (*plural* pesos) coin
pe·soni·fi·er
pes·sa·ry (*plural* ·ries)
pes·si·mism
pes·si·mist
pes·si·mis·tic (*or* ·ti·cal)
pes·si·mis·ti·cal·ly
pest
pes·ter
pes·ter·er
pes·ter·ing·ly
pest·hole
pes·ti·cid·al
pes·ti·cide
pes·tif·er·ous
pes·ti·lence
pes·ti·lent
pes·ti·len·tial
pes·tle
pet (pet·ting, petted)
pet·al
pet·al·if·er·ous (*or* ·al·ous)
pet·al·ine
pet·alled (*US* ·aled)
petal-like
peta·lod·ic
pet·alo·dy botany term
pet·al·oid

pe·tard
pet·cock valve on steam
  boiler
pe·techia (*plural* ·techiae)
  red spot on skin
pe·techial
pe·ter
Pe·ter·bor·ough
Pe·ter·lee Durham town
Pe·ter·loo massacre
peter·man (*plural* ·men)
  Slang safe-breaker
Pe·ters·burg US city;
  compare St Petersburg
pe·ter·sham ribbon
pethi·dine
petio·late (*or* ·la·ted)
peti·ole leaf stalk
pe·tio·lule
pet·it of lesser importance;
  small; *compare* petite
pe·tit bour·geois (*plural*
  pe·tits bour·geois)
pe·tite small and dainty;
  compare petit
pet·ite bour·geoisie
pet·it four (*plural* pet·its
  fours) small cake
pe·ti·tion
pe·ti·tion·ary
pe·ti·tion·er
pet·it mal epilepsy
pet·it point needlework
  stitch
pe·tits pois *French* peas
Pet·ra ancient city
pet·rel bird; *compare* petrol
Pe·tri dish
pet·ri·fac·tion (*or*
  pet·ri·fi·ca·tion)
pe·tri·fi·er
pet·ri·fy (·fies, ·fy·ing,
  ·fied)
Pe·trine of St Peter
pet·ro·chemi·cal
pet·ro·chem·is·try
pet·ro·dol·lar
pet·ro·glyph prehistoric
  rock carving
Pet·ro·grad *former name of*
  Leningrad
pe·trog·ra·pher
pet·ro·graph·ic (*or*
  ·graphi·cal)
pet·ro·graphi·cal·ly
pe·trog·ra·phy classification
  of rocks

pet·rol fuel; *compare* petrel
pet·ro·la·tum petroleum
  jelly
pe·tro·leum
pe·trol·ic of petroleum
pet·ro·logi·cal
pe·trolo·gist
pe·trol·ogy (*plural* ·ogies)
  study of rocks
pet·ro·nel firearm
Pe·tro·pav·lovsk Soviet
  city
Pe·tró·po·lis Brazilian city
pe·tro·sal anatomy term
pet·rous
Pe·tro·za·vodsk Soviet city
pet·ter
pet·ti·coat
pet·ti·fog (·fog·ging,
  ·fogged)
pet·ti·fog·ger
pet·ti·fog·gery
pet·ti·ly
pet·ting
pet·tish
pet·tish·ness
pet·ti·toes pigs' trotters
pet·ty (·ti·er, ·ti·est)
petu·lance (*or* ·lan·cy)
petu·lant
pe·tu·nia
pe·tun·tse (*or* ·tze) mineral
pew
pe·wee (*or* pee·) bird
pe·wit *variant spelling of*
  peewit
pew·ter
pew·ter·er
pe·yo·te cactus
pfen·nig (*plural* ·nigs or
  ·ni·ge) German coin
Pforz·heim West German
  city
Phaedra wife of Theseus
Phaëthon mythological
  character
phae·ton horse-drawn
  carriage
phage virus
phag·edae·na (*or esp. US*
  ·edena) ulcer
phago·cyte
phago·cyt·ic
phago·cy·to·sis
phago·ma·nia compulsive
  eating
phago·ma·ni·ac

phago·pho·bia
phago·pho·bic
phal·ange variant of phalanx
pha·lan·geal anatomy term
pha·lan·ger marsupial
pha·lan·ges plural of phalanx
phal·an·stery (plural ·steries)
phal·anx (plural phal·anxes or pha·lan·ges) battle formation; compact group
phal·anx (or ·ange; plural pha·lan·ges) finger or toe bone
phala·rope bird
phal·lic
phal·li·cism (or phal·lism)
phal·li·cist (or phal·list)
phal·lus (plural ·li or ·luses)
phan·ero·crys·tal·line
phan·ero·gam botany term
phan·ero·gam·ic (or ·er·oga·mous)
pha·nero·phyte botany term
Pha·nero·zo·ic biology term
phan·tasm
phan·tas·ma·go·ria (or ·gory)
phan·tas·ma·go·ric (or ·ri·cal)
phan·tas·ma·go·ri·cal·ly
phan·tas·mal (or ·mic)
phan·tom
phar·aoh (or Phar·)
phar·aon·ic (or Phar·)
Phari·sa·ic (or ·sai·cal)
Phari·see
phar·ma·ceu·ti·cal (or ·tic)
phar·ma·ceu·tics
phar·ma·cist (or ·ma·ceu·tist)
phar·ma·co·dy·nam·ic
phar·ma·co·dy·nam·ics
phar·ma·cog·no·sist
phar·ma·cog·nos·tic
phar·ma·cog·no·sy branch of pharmacology
phar·ma·co·logi·cal
phar·ma·colo·gist
phar·ma·col·ogy
phar·ma·co·poeia

phar·ma·co·poe·ial (or ·poe·ic)
phar·ma·co·poe·ist
phar·ma·cy (plural ·cies)
Pha·ros Greek lighthouse
phar·yn·geal (or pha·ryn·gal)
phar·yn·gi·tis
phar·yn·go·logi·cal
phar·yn·golo·gist
phar·yn·gol·ogy
pha·ryn·go·scope
pha·ryn·go·scop·ic
phar·yn·gos·co·py
phar·yn·goto·my (plural ·mies)
phar·ynx (plural pha·ryn·ges or phar·ynxes)
phase
pha·sic (or phaseal)
phas·mid insect
phat·ic of conversation
pheas·ant
phel·lem
phel·lo·derm
phel·lo·der·mal
phel·lo·gen
phel·lo·genet·ic (or ·gen·ic)
phe·na·caine anaesthetic
phe·nac·etin analgesic
phena·cite (or ·kite) mineral
phe·nan·threne
phena·zine
phe·net·ic biology term
phe·neti·dine
phen·etole
phen·for·min drug
phe·no·bar·bi·tone (US ·tal)
phe·no·copy (plural ·copies) biology term
phe·no·cryst geology term
phe·nol
phe·no·late disinfect
phe·nol·ic
phe·no·logi·cal
phe·nolo·gist
phe·nol·ogy study of phenomena
phenol·phthalein
phe·nom·ena plural of phenomenon
phe·nom·enal
phe·nom·enal·ism

phe·nom·enal·ist
phe·nom·enal·is·ti·cal·ly
phe·nom·enal·ly
phe·nom·eno·logi·cal
phe·nom·enol·ogy
phe·nom·enon (plural ·ena or ·enons)
phe·no·thia·zine
phe·no·type biology term
phe·no·typ·ic (or ·typi·cal)
phe·no·typi·cal·ly
phe·nox·ide
phe·nyl
phenyl·alanine
phenyl·keton·uria
phero·mone chemical in animals
phew
phial
Phi Beta Kap·pa US academic society
Phila·del·phia
phila·del·phus shrub
Phi·lae Egyptian island
phi·lan·der
phi·lan·der·er
phil·an·throp·ic (or ·thropi·cal)
phi·lan·thro·pist (or phil·an·thrope)
phi·lan·thro·py (plural ·pies)
phil·an·thropi·cal·ly
phila·tel·ic
phila·teli·cal·ly
phi·lat·elist
phi·lat·ely
phil·har·mon·ic
phil·hel·lene (or ·len·ist) lover of Greece
phil·hel·len·ism
Phi·lip·pi ancient Macedonian city
phi·lip·pic bitter speech
Phil·ip·pine
Phil·ip·pines
Phil·is·tine
Phil·is·tin·ism
phil·lu·men·ist collector of matchbox labels
philo·den·dron (plural ·drons or ·dra) plant
phi·logy·ny fondness for women
philo·logi·cal
phi·lolo·gist (or ·ger)
phi·lol·ogy

philo·mel (*or* ·mela)
  nightingale
Philomela mythological
  princess
phi·loso·pher
philo·soph·ic
philo·sophi·cal (*or*
  ·soph·ic)
philo·sophi·cal·ly
philo·sophi·cal·ness
phi·loso·phi·za·tion (*or*
  ·sa·tion)
phi·loso·phize (*or* ·phise)
phi·loso·phiz·er (*or*
  ·phis·er)
phi·loso·phy (*plural*
  ·phies)
phil·tre (*US* ·ter) love
  potion; *compare* filter
phi·mo·sis medical term
phi·phenom·enon (*plural*
  ·ena) psychology term
phiz *Slang* face
phle·bit·ic
phle·bi·tis
phlebo·scle·ro·sis
phlebo·tom·ic (*or*
  ·tomi·cal)
phle·boto·mist
phle·boto·mize
phle·boto·my (*plural*
  ·mies) incision into vein
phlegm
phleg·mat·ic (*or* ·mati·cal)
phleg·mati·cal·ly
phleg·mati·cal·ness (*or*
  ·mat·ic·ness)
phlo·em plant tissue
phlo·gis·tic
phlo·gis·ton
phlogo·pite mineral
phlox (*plural* phlox *or*
  phloxes)
phlyc·ten (*or* ·te·na;
  plural ·tens *or* ·nae)
  blister
Phnom Penh (*or* Pnom
  Penh) Cambodian capital
pho·bia
pho·bic
Pho·bos satellite of Mars
pho·cine of seals
Pho·cis region of ancient
  Greece
pho·co·melia (*or*
  ·com·ely)
Phoe·be satellite of Saturn

phoe·be bird
Phoebus Apollo
Phoe·ni·cia
Phoe·ni·cian
Phoe·nix US city
phoe·nix legendary bird
phon unit
pho·nate utter speech
pho·na·tion
pho·na·tory
phone
phone-in (*noun*)
pho·neme linguistics term
pho·nemic
pho·nemi·cal·ly
pho·nemics
pho·net·ic
pho·neti·cal·ly
pho·neti·cian
pho·net·ics
pho·net·ist
pho·ney (*or* ·ny; *adj*
  ·ni·er, ·ni·est; *noun,*
  plural ·neys *or* ·nies)
pho·ney·ness (*or* ·ni·)
phon·ic
phoni·cal·ly
phon·ics teaching method
pho·ni·ness *variant spelling*
  of phoneyness
pho·no·gram
pho·no·gram·ic (*or*
  ·gram·mic)
pho·no·graph
pho·nog·ra·pher (*or*
  ·phist)
pho·nog·ra·phy
pho·no·lite rock
pho·no·lit·ic
pho·no·logi·cal
pho·nolo·gist
pho·nol·ogy (*plural*
  ·ogies)
pho·nom·eter
pho·no·met·ric (*or* ·ri·cal)
pho·non physics term
pho·no·scope
pho·no·tac·tics branch of
  linguistics
pho·no·type
pho·no·typ·ic (*or*
  ·typi·cal)
pho·no·typ·ist (*or* ·typ·er)
pho·no·typy phonetic
  transcription
pho·ny *variant spelling of*
  phoney

phoo·ey
phos·gene poisonous gas
phos·ge·nite mineral
phos·pha·tase enzyme
phos·phate
phos·phat·ic
phos·pha·tide biochemical
  compound
phos·pha·ti·za·tion (*or*
  ·sa·tion)
phos·pha·tize (*or* ·tise)
phos·pha·tu·ria
phos·pha·tu·ric
phos·phene physiology
  term; *compare* phosphine
phos·phide
phos·phine gas; *compare*
  phosphene
phos·phite
phos·pho·crea·tine (*or*
  ·tin)
phos·pho·lip·id
phos·pho·pro·tein
phos·phor
phos·pho·rate
phos·pho·resce
phos·pho·res·cence
phos·pho·res·cent
phos·phor·ic
phos·pho·rism
phos·pho·rite mineral
phos·pho·rit·ic
phos·phoro·scope
phos·pho·rous (*adj*)
phos·pho·rus (*noun*)
phos·phory·lase enzyme
phot unit
pho·tic of light
pho·to (*plural* ·tos)
photo·ac·tin·ic
photo·ac·tive
photo·auto·troph·ic
  biology term
photo·bath·ic biology term
photo·cath·ode
photo·cell
photo·chemi·cal
photo·chem·ist
photo·chem·is·try
photo·com·pose
photo·com·pos·er
photo·com·po·si·tion
photo·con·duc·tion
photo·con·duc·tiv·ity
photo·con·duc·tor
photo·copi·er

photo·copy (noun, plural ·copies; verb ·copies, ·copy·ing, ·cop·ied)
photo·cur·rent
photo·dis·in·te·gra·tion
photo·dy·nam·ic
photo·dy·nam·ics
photo·elas·tic·ity
photo·elec·tric (or ·tri·cal)
photo·elec·tri·cal·ly
photo·elec·tric·ity
photo·elec·tron
photo·elec·tro·type
photo·emis·sion
photo·emis·sive
photo·en·grave
photo·en·grav·er
photo·en·grav·ing
Photo·fit (Trademark)
photo·flash
photo·flood tungsten lamp
photo·fluo·rog·ra·phy
photo·gen·ic
photo·geni·cal·ly
photo·geol·ogy
photo·gram type of photograph
photo·gram·met·ric
photo·gram·metrist
photo·gram·metry
photo·graph
pho·tog·ra·pher
photo·graph·ic
photo·graphi·cal·ly
pho·tog·ra·phy
photo·gra·vure
photo·jour·nal·ism
photo·jour·na·list
photo·jour·na·lis·tic
photo·ki·nesis
photo·ki·net·ic
photo·ki·neti·cal·ly
photo·litho·graph
photo·li·thog·ra·pher
photo·li·thog·ra·phy
pho·to·lu·mi·nes·cence
pho·to·lu·mi·nes·cent
pho·toly·sis
photo·lyt·ic
photo·map (·map·ping, ·mapped)
photo·mechani·cal
pho·tom·eter
photo·met·ric
photo·met·ri·cal·ly
pho·tom·etrist
pho·tom·etry

photo·micro·graph
photo·mi·crog·ra·pher
photo·micro·graph·ic
photo·micro·graphi·cal·ly
photo·mi·crog·ra·phy
photo·mon·tage
photo·multi·pli·er
photo·mu·ral
pho·ton
photo·nas·tic
photo·nas·ty botany term
photo·neu·tron
photo·nu·cle·ar
photo-offset
photo·peri·od
photo·peri·od·ic
photo·peri·odi·cal·ly
photo·peri·od·ism biology term
pho·tophi·lous botany term
pho·tophi·ly
photo·pho·bia
photo·pho·bic
photo·phore light-producing organ
photo·pia day vision
pho·top·ic
photo·poly·mer
photo·recep·tor
photo·recon·nais·sance
photo·sen·si·tive
photo·sen·si·tiv·ity
photo·sen·si·ti·za·tion (or ·sa·tion)
photo·sen·si·tize (or ·tise)
photo·set (·set·ting, ·set)
photo·set·ter
photo·sphere surface of sun
photo·spher·ic
Photo·stat (Trademark) machine
photo·stat (noun, verb) photocopy
photo·stat·ic
photo·syn·the·sis
photo·syn·the·size
photo·syn·thet·ic
photo·syn·theti·cal·ly
photo·tac·tic
photo·tax·is (or ·taxy) biology term
photo·tele·graph·ic
photo·tele·graphi·cal·ly
photo·teleg·ra·phy
photo·thera·peu·tic
photo·thera·peu·ti·cal·ly

photo·thera·py (or ·peu·tics)
photo·ther·mic (or ·mal)
photo·ther·mi·cal·ly (or ·mal·ly)
photo·ton·ic
pho·toto·nus botany term
photo·to·pog·ra·phy
photo·tran·sis·tor
photo·trop·ic
pho·tot·ro·pism botany term
photo·tube
photo·type
photo·type·set·ting
photo·typ·ic
photo·typi·cal·ly
photo·ty·pog·ra·phy
photo·vol·ta·ic
photo·zin·co·graph
photo·zin·cog·ra·phy
phras·al
phrase
phra·seo·gram symbol
phra·seo·graph phrase
phra·seo·graph·ic
phra·seog·ra·phy
phra·seo·logi·cal
phra·seolo·gist
phra·seol·ogy (plural ·ogies)
phras·ing
phra·tric anthropology term
phra·try (plural ·tries)
phre·at·ic geography term
phren·ic of the diaphragm
phre·net·ic obsolete spelling of frenetic
phreno·logi·cal
phre·nolo·gist
phre·nol·ogy study of head bumps
Phrygia ancient Asian country
Phryg·ian
phtha·lein
phthal·ic acid
phthalo·cya·nine
phthi·ria·sis infestation with lice; compare pthisis
phthi·sic
phthisi·cal
phthi·sis wasting disease; compare phthiriasis
phut
phy·co·logi·cal
phy·colo·gist

phy·col·ogy study of algae
phy·co·my·cete fungus
phy·co·my·cetous
phy·lac·tery (*plural*
·teries) case for Hebrew
texts
phy·le (*plural* ·lae) ancient
Greek tribe
phy·let·ic (*or*
phy·lo·genet·ic) biology
term
phy·leti·cal·ly (*or*
phy·lo·geneti·cal·ly)
phyl·lite rock
phyl·lit·ic
phyl·lo·clade (*or* ·clad)
botany term
phyl·lode botany term
phyl·lo·dial
phyl·loid leaflike
phyl·lome botany term
phyl·lom·ic
phyl·lo·qui·none vitamin
phyl·lo·tax·is (*or* ·taxy;
plural ·taxes *or* taxies)
phyl·lox·era (*plural* ·erae
or ·eras) vine pest
phy·lo·gen·ic (*or*
·genet·ic)
phy·log·eny (*or*
·lo·gen·esis; *plural*
·nies *or* ·eses) biology
term
phylo·tac·tic
phy·lum (*plural* ·la)
physi·at·ric (*or* ·ri·cal)
physi·at·rics *US*
physiotherapy
phys·ic (·ick·ing, ·icked)
physi·cal
physi·cal·ism philosophical
doctrine
physi·cal·ist
physi·cal·is·tic
physi·cal·ly
physi·cal·ness
phy·si·cian
physi·cist
physi·co·chemi·cal
phys·ics
physio·crat
physio·crat·ic
physi·og·nom·ic (*or*
·nomi·cal)
physi·og·nomi·cal·ly
physi·og·no·mist

physi·og·no·my (*plural*
·mies)
physi·og·ra·pher
physio·graph·ic (*or*
·graphi·cal)
physi·og·ra·phy physical
geography
physio·logi·cal
physio·logi·cal·ly
physi·olo·gist
physi·ol·ogy
(physionomy) *incorrect
spelling of* physiognomy
physio·thera·pist
physio·thera·py
phy·sique
phy·so·clis·tous zoology
term
phy·so·stig·mine (*or* ·min)
drug
phy·sos·to·mous zoology
term
phyto·gen·esis (*or*
phy·tog·eny) botany
term
phyto·genet·ic
phyto·geneti·cal·ly
phyto·gen·ic
phyto·geog·ra·pher
phyto·geog·ra·phy
phy·tog·ra·phy
phyto·hor·mone
phy·tol·ogy
phy·ton botany term
phyto·patho·logi·cal
phyto·pa·tholo·gist
phyto·pa·thol·ogy
phy·topha·gous
phy·topha·gy
phyto·plank·ton
phyto·plank·ton·ic
phyto·so·cio·logi·cal
phyto·so·ci·olo·gist
phyto·so·ci·ol·ogy
phyto·tox·in
phyto·tron botanical
apparatus
pi (*plural* pis) Greek letter
Pia·cen·za Italian town
pi·acu·lar making
atonement
pi·affe dressage term
pia ma·ter brain membrane
pia·nism
pia·nis·si·mo
pia·nist
pia·nis·tic

pi·ano (*plural* ·anos)
pi·ano·for·te
Pia·no·la (*Trademark*)
pi·as·sa·va (*or* ·ba) palm
tree
pi·as·tre (*or esp. US* ·ter)
currency
Piauí Brazilian state
pi·az·za
pi·broch bagpipe music
pica printer's measure;
eating dirt; *compare* pika
pica·dor
Pic·ar·dy French region
pica·resque of type of
fiction; *compare*
picturesque
pica·roon (*or* picka·)
adventurer
pica·yune *US* of little value
Pic·ca·dil·ly
pic·ca·lil·li pickle
pic·ca·nin·ny (*or* picka·;
plural ·nies) Negro child
pic·co·lo (*plural* ·los)
pice (*plural* pice) coin
pic·eous of pitch
pichi·ci·ego (*plural* ·egos)
animal
pick
picka·back *variant of*
piggyback
pick·able
pick·axe (*US* ·ax)
pick·er
pick·er·el (*plural* ·el *or*
·els) fish
pickerel·weed
pick·et
pick·et·er
pick·et·ing
pick·ings
pick·le
pick·led
pick·ler
pick·lock
pick-me-up
pick·pocket
pick-up (*noun*)
Pick·wick·ian
picky
pic·nic (·nick·ing,
·nicked)
pic·nick·er
pico·line chemical
compound
pico·lin·ic

pi·cot pattern of loops
pico·tee carnation
pic·rate chemistry term
pic·ric acid
pic·rite rock
pic·ro·tox·in
Pict
Pict·ish
pic·to·graph
pic·to·rial
pic·to·rial·ly
pic·ture
pic·tur·esque strikingly
  pleasing; *compare*
  picaresque
pic·tur·esque·ness
pic·ul unit
pid·dle
pid·dling
pid·dock mollusc
pidg·in language; *compare*
  pigeon
pie
pie·bald
piece
pièce de ré·sis·tance
  (*plural* **pièces de**
  ré·sis·tance)
piece-dyed
piece·meal
piec·er
piece·work
pie·crust
pied multi-coloured
pied-à-terre (*plural*
  pieds-à-terre)
Pied·mont Italian region
pied·mont at mountain base
pied·mont·ite mineral
pie-eyed
pie·man (*plural* **·men**)
pier landing place; pillar;
  compare **peer**
pierc·able
pierce
pierc·er
pierc·ing
pierc·ing·ly
Pi·erian
Pi·eri·des Muses
pi·eri·dine zoology term
Pi·er·rot pantomime clown
pi·età religious painting
Pie·ter·mar·itz·burg South
  African city
pi·ety (*plural* **·eties**)
pi·ezo·chem·is·try

pi·ezo·elec·tric
pi·ezo·elec·tri·cal·ly
pi·ezo·elec·tric·ity
pi·ezom·eter
pi·ezo·met·ric
pi·ezo·met·ri·cal·ly
pif·fle
pig (**pig·ging**, **pigged**)
pi·geon bird; *compare* **pidgin**
pigeon·hole
pigeon-toed
pig·face plant
pig·fish (*plural* **·fish** *or*
  ·fishes)
pig·gery (*plural* **·geries**)
pig·gin small bucket
pig·gish
pig·gish·ness
pig·gy (*noun*, *plural* **·gies**;
  adj **·gi·er**, **·gi·est**)
piggy·back (*or*
  picka·back)
pig·headed
pig·headed·ness
pig·let
pig·like
pig·meat
pig·ment
pig·men·tary
pig·men·ta·tion
pig·ment·ed
pig·my *variant spelling of*
  pygmy
pig·nut
pig·skin
pig·stick
pig·stick·er
pig·stick·ing
pig·sty (*plural* **·sties**)
pig·swill
pig·tail
pig·tailed
pig·weed
pika animal; *compare* **pica**
pike
pike·let crumpet
pike·perch (*plural* **·perch**
  or **·perches**) fish
pik·er
pike·staff
pil·af (*or* **·aff**) *variant of*
  pilau
pi·las·ter
pi·lau (*or* **·af**, **pil·af**, **pil·aff**)
  rice dish
pilch *Archaic* infant's
  garment

pil·chard
pile
pi·leate (*or* **·leat·ed**)
  biology term
pile-driver
pi·leous of hair
piles
pi·leum (*plural* **·lea**) top of
  bird's head
pile-up (*noun*)
pi·leus (*plural* **·lei**)
  mushroom cap
pile·wort
pil·fer
pil·fer·age
pil·fer·er
pil·garlic *Dialect* pitiful
  person
pil·grim
pil·grim·age
pili (*plural* **pilis**) tree
pi·li *plural of* **pilus**
pi·lif·er·ous
pili·form
pil·ing
pill
pil·lage
pil·lag·er
pil·lar
pill·box
pil·lion
pil·li·winks instrument of
  torture
pil·lo·ry (*noun*, *plural*
  ·ries; *verb* **·ries**, **·ry·ing**,
  ·ried)
pil·low
pillow·case (*or* **·slip**)
pi·lo·car·pine (*or* **·pin**)
  drug
pi·lose biology term
pi·lot
pi·lot·age
Pils·ner (*or* **Pil·sen·er**)
  beer
Pilt·down man
pilu·lar
pil·ule
pi·lus (*plural* **·li**) a hair
pi·men·to (*plural* **·tos**)
  spice
pi·mien·to (*plural* **·tos**)
  sweet pepper
pimp
pim·per·nel
pim·ple
pim·pled

pim·pli·ness
pim·ply (·pli·er, ·pli·est)
pin (pin·ning, pinned)
pi·na·ceous botany term
pina·fore
pi·nas·ter pine tree
pin·ball
pince-nez (*plural* pince-nez)
pin·cer
pin·cers tool
pinch
pinch·beck imitation gold
pinch·cock clamp
pinch·penny (*plural* ·pennies)
pin·cushion
Pin·dar·ic ode
pind·ling *Dialect* peevish
Pin·dus Greek mountain range
pine
pin·eal gland
pine·apple
pi·nene chemical compound
pi·nery (*plural* ·neries)
pi·netum (*plural* ·neta) plantation
pin·feather
pin·fish (*plural* ·fish or ·fishes)
pin·fold
ping
ping·er
pin·go (*plural* ·gos) landform
Ping-Pong (*Trademark*) (*or* ping-pong)
pin·guid fatty
pin·guid·ity (*or* ·ness)
pin·head
pin·hole
pin·ion
pin·ite mineral
pink
pink·eye
pinkie (*or* pinky) *US* little finger
pink·ish
pink·root
pinky pinkish; *variant spelling of* pinkie
pin·na (*plural* ·nae or ·nas) biology term
pin·nace boat
pin·na·cle

pin·nate (*or* ·nat·ed) feather-like
pin·nati·fid botany term
pin·na·tion
pin·nati·par·tite botany term
pin·nati·ped ornithology term
pin·nati·sect botany term
pinned
pin·ner
pin·ning
pin·ni·ped (*or* ·pedian) zoology term
pin·nu·lar
pin·nule (*or* ·nu·la; *plural* ·nules or ·nu·lae)
pin·ny (*plural* ·nies) *Slang* pinafore
pi·noch·le (*or* ·nuch·le, ·noc·le) card game
pi·no·le flour
pin·point
pin·prick
pin·stripe
pint
pin·ta skin disease
pin·ta·dera Neolithic stamp
pin·tail (*plural* ·tails or ·tail) duck
pin·tle hinge pin
pin·to (*plural* ·tos) piebald horse
pin-up (*noun*)
pin·wheel
pin·work
pin·worm
pinx·it *Latin* painted (*inscription on painting*)
piny (*or* piney; pini·er, pini·est)
pio·let ice axe
pion physics term
pio·neer
pi·ous
pi·ous·ness
pip (pip·ping, pipped)
pipa toad
pip·age
pi·pal *variant spelling of* peepul
pipe
pipe·clay
pipe·fish (*plural* ·fish or ·fishes)
pipe·fitting
pipe·line

pip·er
pip·era·ceous botany term
pi·pera·zine drug
pi·peri·dine organic compound
pip·er·ine alkaloid
pip·ero·nal fragrant compound
pipe·stone
pi·pette
pipe·wort
pip·ing
pipi·strelle bat
pip·it bird
pip·kin small pot
pipped
pip·pin apple
pip·ping
pip·sis·sewa plant
pip·squeak
pi·quan·cy (*or* ·quant·ness)
pi·quant
pique (piqu·ing, piqued)
pi·qué fabric
pi·quet card game
pi·ra·cy (*plural* ·cies)
Pi·rae·us (*or* Pei·) Greek port
pi·ra·nha (*or* ·na)
pi·rate
pi·rat·ic (*or* ·rati·cal)
pi·rati·cal·ly
pirn fishing rod
pi·rog (*plural* ·ro·gi) pie
pi·rogue (*or* pi·ra·gua) canoe
pirou·ette
Pisa
pis al·ler *French* a last resort
pis·ca·ry (*plural* ·ries) fishing place
pis·ca·to·rial (*or* ·tory)
Pi·sces constellation; sign of zodiac
pis·ci·cul·tur·al
pis·ci·cul·ture
pis·ci·cul·tur·ist
pis·ci·na (*plural* ·nae or ·nas) basin in church
pis·cine
pis·civo·rous
pi·shogue *Irish* sorcery
pisi·form pealike
pis·mire *Dialect* ant
pi·so·lite rock

piss

pis·ta·chio (*plural* ·chios)

pis·ta·reen coin

piste skiing slope

pis·til flower part; *compare* pistol

pis·til·late

pis·tol (·tol·ling, ·tolled; US ·tol·ing, ·toled) gun; *compare* pistil

pis·tole coin

pis·to·leer soldier

pis·ton

pit (pit·ting, pit·ted)

pita fibre; *compare* pitta

pita·pat (·pat·ting, ·pat·ted)

Pit·cairn Pacific island

pitch

pitch·black

pitch·blende mineral

pitch·dark

pitch·er

pitch·fork

pitchi·ness

pitch·om·eter nautical term

pitch·stone

pitchy (pitchi·er, pitchi·est)

pit·eous

pit·eous·ness

pit·fall

pith

pit·head

pith·ecan·thro·pine (*or* ·poid)

pith·ecan·thro·pus (*plural* ·pi) apelike man

pithi·ly

pithi·ness

pi·thos (*plural* ·thoi) oil container

pithy (pithi·er, pithi·est)

piti·able

piti·able·ness

piti·ably

piti·ful

piti·ful·ly

piti·ful·ness

piti·less

piti·less·ness

pit·man (*plural* ·men)

pi·ton mountaineering spike

pit·saw

pit·ta flat bread; *compare* pita

pit·tance

pitter-patter

Pitts·burgh US port

pi·tui·tary (*plural* ·taries)

pitu·ri shrub

pity (*noun, plural* pities; *verb* pities, pity·ing, pit·ied)

pity·ing·ly

pity·ria·sis (*plural* ·ses) skin disease

Piu·ra Peruvian city

piv·ot

piv·ot·al

pix *Slang* pictures; *compare* pyx

pixie (*or* pixy; *plural* pixies)

pixi·lat·ed *US* eccentric

pize *Dialect* to hit

piz·za

piz·ze·ria

piz·zi·ca·to (*plural* ·ti *or* ·tos)

plac·abil·ity (*or* ·able·ness)

plac·able easily placated; *compare* placeable

plac·ard

pla·cate

pla·ca·tion

placa·tory (*or* ·tive)

place position; *compare* plaice

place·able easily placed; *compare* placable

pla·cebo (*plural* ·cebos *or* ·ceboes)

place·ment

pla·cen·ta (*plural* ·tas *or* ·tae)

pla·cen·tal (*or* ·tate)

plac·en·ta·tion

plac·er

pla·cet vote of assent

plac·id

pla·cid·ity (*or* ·ness)

plac·ing

plack·et dressmaking term

placo·derm extinct fish

plac·oid platelike

(plad) *incorrect spelling of* plaid

pla·fond ceiling; card game

pla·gal musical term

plage astronomy term

pla·gia·rism

pla·gia·rist

pla·gia·ris·tic

pla·gia·rize (*or* ·rise)

pla·gia·riz·er (*or* ·ris·er)

pla·gio·clase mineral

pla·gio·cli·max ecology term

pla·gi·ot·ro·pism botany term

plague (plagu·ing, plagued)

plagu·er

pla·gui·ly

pla·guy (*or* ·guey)

plaice (*plural* plaice *or* plaices) fish; *compare* place

plaid tartan cloth

plain simple; unattractive; treeless region; *compare* plane

plain·chant

plain·ish rather plain; *compare* planish

plain·laid describing rope

plain·ness

plains·man (*plural* ·men)

plain·song

plain·spoken

plaint

plain·tiff legal term

plain·tive melancholy

plain·tive·ness

plait braid; *compare* plat

plan (plan·ning, planned)

pla·nar

pla·nar·ian flatworm

pla·na·tion erosion of land

planch·et blank coin

plan·chette board for spirit messages

plane aircraft; level; tool; tree; *compare* plain

plan·er

plan·et

plan·etar·ium (*plural* ·iums *or* ·taria)

plan·etary (*plural* ·etaries)

plan·etesi·mal small planetary body

plan·et·oid asteroid

plan·etoid·al

plan·form silhouette

plan·gen·cy

plan·gent

pla·nim·eter

pla·ni·met·ric (*or* ·ri·cal)

pla·nim·etry
plan·ish to smooth; *compare* plainish
plan·ish·er
plani·sphere
plani·spher·ic
plank
plank·ing
plank-sheer nautical term
plank·ton
plank·ton·ic
planned
plan·ner
plan·ning
plano-concave
plano-convex
plano·gam·ete
pla·no·graph·ic
pla·no·graphi·cal·ly
pla·nog·ra·phy printing process
pla·nom·eter
pla·no·met·ric
pla·nom·etry
pla·no·sol soil
plant
plant·able
plan·tain weed; cooking banana
plan·tar of sole of foot
plan·ta·tion
plant·er
plan·ti·grade zoology term
planu·la (*plural* ·lae) larva
planu·lar
plaque
plash
plashy (plashi·er, plashi·est)
plasm protoplasm
plas·ma blood fluid; physics term
plas·ma·gel jelly-like protoplasm
plas·ma·gene
plas·ma·gen·ic
plas·ma·sol fluid protoplasm
plas·min enzyme
plas·mo·des·ma (*or* ·desm; *plural* ·des·ma·ta *or* ·desms) botany term
plas·mo·dium (*plural* ·dia) biology term; malaria parasite
plas·mo·lyse (*US* ·lyze)

plas·moly·sis
plas·mo·lyt·ic
plas·mo·lyti·cal·ly
plas·mon biology term
plas·mo·some
Plas·sey Indian battle site
plas·ter
plaster·board
plas·tered
plas·ter·er
plas·ter·ing
plas·tic
plas·ti·cal·ly
Plas·ti·cine (*Trademark*)
plas·tic·ity
plas·ti·ci·za·tion (*or* ·sa·tion)
plas·ti·cize (*or* ·cise)
plas·ti·ciz·er (*or* ·cis·er)
plas·tid cell structure
plas·tom·eter plasticity measurer
plas·to·met·ric
plas·tom·etry
plas·tral
plas·tron
plat small plot; *compare* plait
plat·an plane tree; *compare* platen
plat du jour (*plural* plats du jour)
plate
plat·eau (*plural* ·eaus *or* ·eaux)
plat·ed
plate·ful (*plural* ·fuls)
plate·layer
plate·let
plate·mark hallmark
plat·en printing plate; typewriter roller; *compare* platan
plat·er
plat·form
plati·na alloy
plat·ing
pla·tin·ic
plati·nif·er·ous
plat·ini·rid·ium alloy
plati·ni·za·tion (*or* ·sa·tion)
plati·nize (*or* ·nise)
plati·no·cya·nide
plati·noid
plati·no·type photographic process
plati·nous

plati·num
platinum-blond (*fem* -blonde)
plati·tude
plati·tu·di·nize (*or* ·nise)
plati·tu·di·niz·er (*or* ·nis·er)
plati·tu·di·nous
Pla·ton·ic of Plato
pla·ton·ic nonerotic
pla·toni·cal·ly
Pla·to·nism
Pla·to·nize (*or* ·nise)
pla·toon
Platte US river
plat·ter
platy (plati·er, plati·est)
platy (*plural* platy, platys, *or* platies) fish
platy·hel·minth flatworm
platy·hel·min·thic
platy·pus (*plural* ·puses)
plat·yr·rhine (*or* ·rhin·ian) zoology term
plau·dit
plau·sibil·ity (*or* ·sible·ness)
plau·sible
plau·sibly
plau·sive approving
play
pla·ya lake
play·able
play·act
play·actor
play·back
play·bill
play·boy
play·er
play·fellow
play·ful
play·ful·ly
play·ful·ness
play·goer
play·ground
play·group
play·house
play·let
play·mate
play-off (*noun*)
play·pen
play·room
play·school
play·suit
play·thing
play·time
play·wright

pla·za
plea
pleach make hedge
plead (plead·ing,
  plead·ed, plead *or*
  pled)
plead·able
plead·er
pleas·able
pleas·ance secluded garden
pleas·ant
pleas·ant·ness
pleas·ant·ry (*plural* ·ries)
please
pleased
pleas·ed·ly
pleas·er
pleas·ing
pleas·ing·ness
pleas·ur·able
pleas·ur·able·ness
pleas·ur·ably
pleas·ure
pleas·ure·ful
pleas·ure·less
pleat
pleat·er
pleb
pleb·by (·bi·er, ·bi·est)
ple·beian
ple·beian·ism
plebi·scite
plec·tog·nath fish
plec·trum (*or* ·tron;
  plural ·tra, ·trums, *or*
  ·trons)
pledge
pledgee
pledg·er (*or esp. in legal*
  contexts ·or)
pledg·et bandaging pad
plei·ad talented group
Pleia·des constellation
Pleiades (*sing.* Pleiad)
  mythological characters
plein-air art term
plei·ot·ro·pism genetics
  term
Pleis·to·cene geological
  epoch
ple·na·ri·ly
ple·na·ry
ple·nipo·tent
pleni·po·ten·ti·ary (*plural*
  ·aries)
pleni·tude abundance
plen·teous

plen·teous·ness
plen·ti·ful
plen·ti·ful·ly
plen·ti·ful·ness
plen·ty (*plural* ·ties)
ple·num (*plural* ·nums *or*
  ·na)
pleo·chro·ic
ple·och·ro·ism chemistry
  term
pleo·mor·phic
pleo·mor·phism (*or* ·phy)
  biology term
pleo·nasm use of
  superfluous words
pleo·nas·tic
pleo·nas·ti·cal·ly
ple·sio·saur
ples·sor *variant of* plexor
pletho·ra
ple·thys·mo·graph
pleu·ra (*plural* ·rae)
  membrane round lungs;
  plural of pleuron
pleu·ral
pleu·ri·sy
pleu·rit·ic
pleu·ro·dont zoology term
pleu·ro·dy·nia pain between
  ribs
pleu·ron (*plural* ·ra)
  zoology term; *compare*
  pleura
pleu·ro·pneu·mo·nia
pleu·roto·my (*plural*
  ·mies)
pleus·ton floating algae
plew (*or* plue, plu) beaver
  skin
plexi·form
Plexi·glass (*Trademark*)
plex·or (*or* ples·sor)
  medical hammer
plex·us (*plural* ·uses *or*
  ·us) network
pli·abil·ity (*or* able·ness)
pli·able
pli·an·cy (*or* ·ant·ness)
pli·ant
pli·ca (*plural* ·cae)
  anatomy term
pli·cal
pli·cate (*or* ·cat·ed)
  pleated
pli·cate·ness
pli·ca·tion (*or* plica·ture)
plié ballet posture

pli·er (*or* ply·) one who
  plies
pli·ers tool
plight
plight·er
plim·soll (*or* ·sole)
Plim·soll line
plinth
Plio·cene (*or* Pleio·cene)
  geological epoch
plis·sé fabric with wrinkled
  finish
ploat *Dialect* thrash
plod (plod·ding, plod·ded)
plod·der
plod·ding·ly
plod·ding·ness
plodge *Dialect* wade
Plo·eş·ti Romanian city
plonk
plonk·er *Slang* idiot
plonko *Austral* alcoholic
plop (plop·ping, plopped)
plo·sion phonetics term
plo·sive phonetics term
plot (plot·ting, plot·ted)
plot·ter
Plough group of stars
plough (*US* plow)
plough·boy (*US* plow·)
plough·er (*US* plow·)
plough·man (*US* plow·;
  plural ·men)
plough·man·ship (*US*
  plow·)
plough·share (*US* plow·)
plough·staff (*US* plow·)
Plov·div Bulgarian city
plov·er
plow *US spelling of* plough
ploy
pluck
pluck·er
plucki·ly
plucki·ness
plucky (plucki·er,
  plucki·est)
plug (plug·ging, plugged)
plug·board
plum fruit; *compare* plumb
plum·age
plu·mate (*or* ·mose)
plumb work as plumber;
  experience misery;
  compare plum
plumb·able

plum·bagi·na·ceous botany
term
plum·ba·go (*plural* ·gos)
graphite; plant
plum·beous of lead
plumb·er
plumb·ery (*plural* ·eries)
plum·bic chemistry term
plum·bi·con TV camera
tube
plum·bif·er·ous
plumb·ing
plum·bism lead poisoning
plum·bous chemistry term
plum·bum lead
plume
plum·met
plum·my (·mi·er, ·mi·est)
plump
plump·er
plump·ness
plu·mule
plumy (plumi·er,
plumi·est)
plun·der
plun·der·able
plun·der·age
plun·der·er
plun·der·ous
plunge
plung·er
plunk
plu·per·fect grammar term
plu·ral
plu·ral·ism
plu·ral·ist
plu·ral·ity (*plural* ·ities)
plu·rali·za·tion (or
·sa·tion)
plu·ral·ize (or ·ise)
plu·ral·iz·er (or ·is·er)
plu·ral·ly
plus
plush
plush·ness
plushy (plushi·er,
plushi·est)
Pluto Greek god
Plu·to planet
plu·toc·ra·cy (*plural* ·cies)
plu·to·crat
plu·to·crat·ic (or
·crati·cal)
plu·to·crati·cal·ly
plu·ton geology term
Plu·to·nian infernal
plu·ton·ic geology term

plu·to·nium
plu·vial of rain
plu·vi·om·eter
plu·vio·met·ric
plu·vio·met·ri·cal·ly
plu·vi·om·etry
plu·vi·ous (or ·ose)
ply (*verb* plies, ply·ing,
plied; *noun, plural*
plies)
ply·er *variant spelling of* plier
Plym·outh
ply·wood
Plzeň Czech city
pneu·ma philosophy term
pneu·mat·ic
pneu·mati·cal·ly
pneu·mat·ics branch of
physics
pneu·ma·tol·ogy branch of
theology
pneu·ma·toly·sis geology
term
pneu·ma·tom·eter
pneu·ma·tom·etry
pneu·mato·phore biology
term
pneu·mo·ba·cil·lus (*plural*
·li)
pneu·mo·coc·cus (*plural*
·coc·ci)
pneu·mo·co·nio·sis
pneu·mo·dy·nam·ics
pneumatics
pneu·mo·en·cepha·lo·gram
pneu·mo·gas·tric
pneu·mo·graph
pneu·mo·nec·to·my (or
pneu·mec·to·my; *plural*
·mies)
pneu·mo·nia
pneu·mon·ic
pneu·mon·it·is
pneu·mo·tho·rax
Po Italian river
po (*plural* pos) chamber
pot
poa·ceous botany term
poach
poach·er
poach·ing
po·chard (*plural* ·chards
or ·chard) duck
pock
pock·et
pock·et·able
pocket·book

pock·et·ful (*plural* ·fuls)
pocket·knife (*plural*
·knives)
pock·mark
poco musical term
po·co·cu·ran·te indifferent
pod (pod·ding, pod·ded)
po·dag·ra gout
po·dag·ral (or ·ric, ·ri·cal,
·rous)
pod·dy (*plural* ·dies)
Austral hand-fed calf
po·des·ta Italian magistrate
podgi·ly
podgi·ness
podgy (podgi·er,
podgi·est)
po·dia·try *US* chiropody
po·dium (*plural* ·diums or
·dia)
Po·dolsk Soviet city
podo·phyl·lin medicinal
resin
pod·zol (or ·sol)
pod·zol·ic (or ·sol·ic)
poem
po·esy (*plural* ·esies)
poet
po·et·as·ter inferior poet
po·et·ess
po·et·ic (or ·eti·cal)
po·eti·cal·ly
po·eti·cize (or po·et·ize,
po·eti·cise, po·et·ise)
po·et·ics
poet lau·reate (*plural*
poets lau·reate)
po·et·ry
po-faced
pogge fish
po·go·nia orchid
pog·rom
Po·hai inlet of Yellow Sea
poi Hawaiian food
poign·an·cy
poign·ant
poi·ki·lo·ther·mic (or
·mal) cold-blooded
poi·ki·lo·ther·mism (or
·my)
poi·lu French soldier
poin·cia·na tree
poin·set·tia house plant
point
point-blank
pointe ballet term
point·ed

point·ed·ly
point·ed·ness
Pointe-Noire Congolese
  port
point·er
poin·til·lism painting
  technique
poin·til·list
point·ing
point·less
point·less·ness
points·man (*plural* ·men)
point-to-point
poise
poised
poi·son
poi·son·er
poi·son·ous
poi·son·ous·ness
Poi·tiers French town
Poi·tou former French
  province
poke
poke·berry (*plural*
  ·berries)
pok·er
poke·weed
poki·ly
poki·ness
poky (poki·er, poki·est)
Po·land
po·lar
po·lar·im·eter
po·lari·met·ric
Po·la·ris North Star; missile
po·lari·scope
po·lar·ity (*plural* ·ities)
po·lar·iz·able (*or* ·is·able)
po·lari·za·tion (*or*
  ·sa·tion)
po·lar·ize (*or* ·ise)
po·lar·iz·er (*or* ·is·er)
po·lar·og·ra·phy
Po·lar·oid (*Trademark*)
pol·der reclaimed land
Pole Polish native; star
pole
pole-axe (*US* ·ax)
pole·cat (*plural* ·cats *or*
  ·cat)
pol·emarch ancient Greek
  official
po·lem·ic
po·lemi·cal
po·lemi·cal·ly
po·lemi·cist (*or* ·emist)

po·lem·ics
pol·emo·nia·ceous botany
  term
po·len·ta Italian porridge
pol·er
pole-vault (*verb*)
po·leyn armour
po·lice
police·man (*plural* ·men)
police·woman (*plural*
  ·women)
poli·cy (*plural* ·cies)
policy·holder
po·lio
po·lio·my·eli·tis
pol·is (*plural* ·eis) Greek
  city-state
Po·lish
pol·ish
pol·ish·er
Pol·it·bu·ro
po·lite
po·lite·ness
poli·tesse *French* formal
  politeness
poli·tic shrewd
po·liti·cal of politics
po·liti·cal·ly
poli·ti·cian
po·liti·cize (*or* ·cise)
poli·tick·ing political
  canvassing
po·liti·co (*plural* ·cos)
  Slang politician
poli·tics
pol·ity (*plural* ·ities)
pol·je geography term
pol·ka (*noun, plural* ·kas;
  verb ·kas, ·ka·ing,
  ·kaed)
poll
pol·lack (*or* ·lock; *plural*
  ·lacks, ·lack *or* ·locks,
  ·lock) fish
pol·lan fish; *compare* pollen
pol·lard
polled
pol·len plant product;
  compare pollan
pol·lex (*plural* ·li·ces)
  thumb
pol·li·cal
pol·li·nate (*or* ·lenate)
pol·li·na·tion (*or*
  ·lena·tion)
pol·li·na·tor (*or* ·lena·tor)
poll·ing

pol·lin·ic of pollen
pol·li·nif·er·ous (*or*
  ·lenif·er·ous)
pol·lin·ium (*plural* ·linia)
pol·lino·sis (*or* ·leno·) hay
  fever
pol·li·wog (*or* ·ly·) *Slang*
  sailor; tadpole
poll·ster
pol·lu·cite mineral
pol·lu·tant
pol·lute
pol·lut·er
pol·lu·tion
Pollux star; mythological
  character
polo
polo·naise
po·lo·nium radioactive
  element
po·lo·ny (*plural* ·nies)
  sausage
Pol·ta·va Soviet city
pol·ter·geist
pol·troon
poly (*plural* polys) *Slang*
  polytechnic
polya·del·phous botany
  term
poly·am·ide
poly·an·drous
poly·an·dry
poly·an·thus (*plural*
  ·thuses)
poly·atom·ic
poly·ba·sic
poly·ba·site mineral
poly·car·pel·lary
poly·car·pic (*or* ·pous)
  botany term
poly·carpy
poly·cen·trism political
  theory
poly·chaete worm
poly·chae·tous
poly·cha·sium (*plural*
  ·sia) botany term
poly·chro·mat·ic (*or* ·mic,
  ·mous)
poly·chro·ma·tism
poly·chrome
poly·chro·my
poly·clin·ic hospital
poly·con·ic maths term
poly·coty·ledon
poly·coty·ledon·ous
poly·cy·clic

poly·cy·thae·mia (*US* ·themia)
poly·dac·tyl
poly·dac·ty·lous
poly·dem·ic ecology term
poly·dip·sia
poly·dip·sic
poly·em·bry·on·ic
poly·em·bry·ony
poly·es·ter
po·lyga·la plant
po·lyga·la·ceous
po·lyga·mist
po·lyga·mous
po·lyga·my
poly·gene genetics term
poly·gen·ic
poly·gen·esis biology term
poly·genet·ic
poly·geneti·cal·ly
poly·glot
poly·glot·ism (*or* ·glot·tism)
poly·gon
poly·go·naceous botany term
po·lygo·nal
po·lygo·num plant
poly·graph lie detector
poly·graph·ic
poly·graphi·cal·ly
po·lygy·nist
po·lygy·nous
po·lygy·ny
poly·he·dral
poly·he·dron (*plural* ·drons *or* ·dra)
poly·hy·droxy (*or* ·dric)
poly·iso·prene
poly·math
poly·math·ic
poly·mer
poly·mer·ic
po·lym·er·ism
po·lym·eri·za·tion (*or* ·sa·tion)
poly·mer·ize (*or* ·ise)
po·lym·er·ous
poly·morph
poly·mor·phism
poly·mor·pho·nu·clear
poly·mor·phous (*or* ·phic)
poly·myx·in antibiotic
Poly·nesia
Poly·nesian
poly·neu·ri·tis

Polynices mythological character
poly·no·mial
poly·nu·clear (*or* ·cleate)
poly·nu·cleo·tide
po·lyn·ya arctic water
poly·ony·mous having several names
pol·yp
poly·pary (*or* ·par·ium; *plural* ·paries *or* ·paria) zoology term
poly·pep·tide
poly·pet·al·ous
poly·pha·gia
pol·ypha·gous
poly·phase
poly·phone linguistics term
poly·phon·ic
poly·phoni·cal·ly
po·lypho·nous
po·lypho·ny (*plural* ·nies) musical term
poly·phy·let·ic biology term
poly·phy·leti·cal·ly
poly·phyo·dont zoology term
poly·ploid genetics term; *compare* polypoid
poly·ploi·dal (*or* ·dic)
poly·ploi·dy
poly·pod many-legged animal
po·lypo·dous
poly·po·dy (*plural* ·dies) fern
poly·poid of a polyp; *compare* polyploid
poly·pro·pyl·ene
poly·pro·to·dont zoology term
pol·yp·tych altarpiece
poly·pus (*plural* ·pi) pathological polyp
poly·rhythm
poly·rhyth·mic
poly·sac·cha·ride (*or* ·rose)
poly·semous
poly·semy ambiguity
poly·sep·al·ous
poly·so·mic genetics term
poly·sty·rene
poly·sul·phide (*US* ·fide)
poly·syl·lab·ic (*or* ·labi·cal)
poly·syl·labi·cal·ly

poly·syl·la·ble
poly·syl·lo·gism
poly·syn·deton grammar term
poly·syn·the·sis
poly·syn·the·sism
poly·syn·thet·ic
poly·tech·nic
poly·tet·ra·fluo·ro·ethy·lene
poly·theism
poly·theist
poly·theis·tic
poly·theis·ti·cal·ly
poly·thene
poly·to·nal
poly·to·nal·ist
poly·to·nal·ity (*or* ·ism)
poly·troph·ic biology term
poly·typ·ic (*or* ·typi·cal)
poly·un·satu·rat·ed
poly·urethane (*or* ·urethan)
poly·uria
poly·ur·ic
poly·va·len·cy
poly·va·lent
poly·vi·nyl
Polyxena mythological princess
poly·zoan aquatic organism
poly·zo·ar·ium (*plural* ·aria)
poly·zo·ic
pom *short for* pommy
pom·ace pulped apples
po·ma·ceous botany term
po·made hair oil
po·man·der
pome fruit of apple
pom·egran·ate
pom·elo (*plural* ·elos) grapefruit
Pom·era·nia European region
Pom·era·nian
pom·fret liquorice sweet
pomi·cul·ture
pom·if·er·ous
pom·mel part of saddle; *less common spelling of* pummel
pom·my (*plural* ·mies) *Austral* English person
pomo·logi·cal
pom·olo·gist
pom·ol·ogy fruit cultivation
Po·mo·na Roman goddess
pomp

pom·pa·dour hairstyle
pom·pa·no (*plural* ·no *or* ·nos) fish
Pom·peii
Pom·pei·ian
Pom·pey *Slang* Portsmouth
pom-pom cannon
pom·pon (*or* ·pom) globular tuft, flower, etc.
pom·pos·ity (*plural* ·ities)
pomp·ous
pomp·ous·ness
Pon·ce Puerto Rican port
ponce
pon·cho (*plural* ·chos)
pond
pon·der
pon·der·abil·ity
pon·der·able
pon·der·er
pon·der·ous
Pon·di·cher·ry Indian territory
Pon·do·land South African region
pond-skater insect
pond·weed
pone maize bread
pong
pon·gee fabric
pon·gid ape
pon·iard dagger
pons (*plural* pon·tes) anatomy term
pons asi·no·rum geometry theorem
pons Va·ro·lii (*plural* pon·tes Va·ro·lii) part of brain
pont river ferry
Pont·char·train US lake
Pon·te·fract
Pon·tia·nak Indonesian port
Pon·tic of the Black Sea
pon·ti·fex (*plural* ·tifi·ces)
pon·tiff
pon·tifi·cal
pon·tifi·cals bishop's robes
pon·tifi·cate
pon·tine of bridges
pon·to·nier bridge builder
pon·toon
Pon·ty·pool Welsh town
Pon·ty·pridd Welsh town
pony (*plural* ponies)
pony·tail

pooch
pood unit of weight
poo·dle
poof (*or* poove) *Slang* homosexual; *compare* pouf
pooh
Pooh-Bah pompous official
pooh-pooh
pool
Poole Dorset port
pools gambling system
poon tree
Poo·na (*or* Pune) Indian city
poop
poor needy; unfortunate; *compare* pore; pour
poor·house
poor·ly
poor·ness
pop (pop·ping, popped)
pop·corn
pope
pope·dom
pop·ery
pop·eyed
pop·gun
pop·in·jay
pop·ish
pop·ish·ness
pop·lar
pop·lin
pop·lit·eal anatomy term
Po·po·ca·té·petl Mexican volcano
pop·over
pop·pa·dom (*or* ·dum) Indian bread
popped
pop·per
pop·pet
pop·ping
pop·ple
pop·py (*plural* ·pies)
poppy·cock
poppy·head
Pop·si·cle (*Trademark*)
pop·sy (*plural* ·sies)
popu·lace
popu·lar
popu·lar·ity
popu·lari·za·tion (*or* ·sa·tion)
popu·lar·ize (*or* ·ise)
popu·lar·iz·er (*or* ·is·er)
popu·late
popu·la·tion

Popu·list member of US political party
popu·lous
popu·lous·ness
por·bea·gle shark
porce·lain
por·cel·la·neous
porch
por·cine
por·cu·pine
pore examine; small hole; *compare* poor; pour
por·gy (*plural* ·gy *or* ·gies) fish
po·rif·er·an a sponge
po·rif·er·ous
Po·ri·rua New Zealand city
po·rism mathematical proposition
pork
pork·er
porki·ness
pork·pie
porky (porki·er, porki·est)
por·noc·ra·cy (*plural* ·cies) government by prostitutes
por·nog·ra·pher
por·no·graph·ic
por·no·graphi·cal·ly
por·nog·ra·phy
poro·mer·ic chemistry term
po·ros·ity (*plural* ·ities)
po·rous
po·rous·ness
por·phy·ria disease
por·phy·rin pigment
por·phy·rit·ic geology term
por·phy·rog·enite prince
por·phy·roid geology term
por·phy·rop·sin pigment
por·phy·ry (*plural* ·ries) rock
por·poise (*plural* ·poise *or* ·poises)
por·ridge
por·rin·ger dish
Porsena legendary king
port
port·abil·ity (*or* ·able·ness)
port·able
Por·ta·down Northern Irish town
por·tage
por·tal

por·ta·men·to (*plural* ·ti) musical term
por·ta·tive portable
Port-au-Prince Haitian capital
port·cul·lis
porte-cochere covered entrance
por·tend
por·tent
por·ten·tous
por·ten·tous·ness
por·ter
por·ter·age
porter·house
port·fire
port·fo·lio (*plural* ·lios)
Port Har·court Nigerian port
port·hole
por·ti·co (*plural* ·coes *or* ·cos)
por·ti·ère door curtain
por·tion
Port·land
Port·laoise Irish town
port·li·ness
port·ly (·li·er, ·li·est)
port·man·teau (*plural* ·teaus *or* ·teaux)
Port Mores·by capital of New Guinea
Pôr·to Ale·gre Brazilian port
Por·to Novo capital of Benin
por·trait
por·trait·ist
por·trai·ture
por·tray
por·tray·able
por·tray·al
por·tray·er
port·ress
Port Said Egyptian port
Port-Salut cheese
Ports·mouth
Port Tal·bot Welsh port
Por·tu·gal
Por·tu·guese (*plural* ·guese)
por·tu·laca plant
por·tu·la·ca·ceous
pose
Poseidon Greek god
pos·er one who poses; problem

po·seur affected person
posh
pos·it postulate; *compare* posset
posi·tif organ keyboard
po·si·tion
po·si·tion·al
posi·tive
posi·tive·ly
posi·tive·ness
posi·tiv·ism
posi·tiv·ist
posi·tiv·is·tic
posi·tiv·is·ti·cal·ly
posi·tron physics term
posi·tro·nium physics term
po·sol·ogy branch of medicine
pos·se
pos·sess
pos·sessed
pos·ses·sion
pos·ses·sive
pos·ses·sive·ness
pos·ses·sor
pos·ses·so·ry
pos·set hot drink; *compare* posit
pos·sibil·ity (*plural* ·ities)
pos·sible
pos·sibly
pos·sum *Slang* opossum; phalanger
post
post·age
post·al
post·ax·ial
post·bag
post-bellum after war
post·box
post·boy
post·card
post·ca·val anatomy term
post chaise
post·code
post·coit·al
post·date
post·di·lu·vial
post·di·lu·vian
post·doc·tor·al
post·er
poste res·tante
pos·teri·or
pos·ter·ity
pos·tern
post·fix add to the end
post·free

post·gla·cial
post·gradu·ate
post·haste
post·hu·mous
post·hyp·not·ic
pos·tiche architectural term; *compare* pastiche
pos·ti·cous posterior
pos·til marginal note
pos·til·ion (*or* ·til·lion)
post·im·pres·sion·ism
post·im·pres·sion·ist
post·ing
post·limi·ny (*or* ·li·min·ium; *plural* ·nies *or* ·minia) legal term
post·lude concluding music
post·man (*plural* ·men)
post·mark
post·master
post·me·rid·ian (*adj*)
post me·rid·iem *Latin* after noon
post·mil·len·nial
post·mor·tem
post·na·tal
post·nup·tial
post-obit legal term
post·op·era·tive
post·paid
post·par·tum after childbirth
post·pon·able
post·pone
post·pone·ment
post·pon·er
post·po·si·tion
post·po·si·tion·al
post·posi·tive
post·pran·dial
post·script
po·tu·lan·cy (*or* ·lant·ship)
pos·tu·lant
pos·tu·late
pos·tu·la·tion
pos·tu·la·tor
pos·tur·al
pos·ture
pos·tur·er
post·war
posy (*plural* posies)
pot (pot·ting, pot·ted)
pot·abil·ity (*or* ·able·ness)
po·table drinkable
po·tage *French* soup; *compare* pottage

po·tam·ic
po·ta·mol·ogy study of
  rivers
pot·ash
po·tas·sic
po·tas·sium
po·ta·tion drinking
po·ta·to (*plural* ·toes)
pot-au-feu French stew
pot·bel·lied
pot·belly (*plural* ·bellies)
pot·boiler
pot·boy (*or* pot·man;
  plural ·boys *or* ·men)
potch *Austral* inferior opal
po·teen *Irish* illicit whiskey
po·ten·cy (*or* ·tence;
  plural ·ten·cies *or*
  ·tences)
po·tent
po·ten·tate ruler; *compare*
  potentiate
po·ten·tial
po·ten·ti·al·ity (*plural*
  ·ities)
po·ten·tial·ly
po·ten·ti·ate increase
  effectiveness; *compare*
  potentate
po·ten·til·la
po·ten·ti·om·eter
po·tent·ness
pot·ful (*plural* ·fuls)
pot·head *Slang* cannabis
  user
poth·er
pot·herb
pot·hole
pot·holer
pot·hol·ing
pot·hook
pot·house
pot·hunter
po·tiche (*plural* ·tiches)
  tall vase
po·tion
Potiphar biblical character
pot·latch ceremonial feast
pot·luck
Po·to·mac US river
pot·pie stew pie
pot·pour·ri (*plural* ·ris)
Pots·dam East German city
pot·sherd (*or* ·shard)
pot·stone
pot·tage thick soup;
  compare potage

pot·ted
pot·ter
pot·ter·er
Pot·teries Staffordshire
  region
pot·tery (*plural* ·teries)
pot·ting
pot·to (*plural* ·tos) animal
pot·ty (*adj* ·ti·er, ·ti·est;
  noun, plural ·ties)
pouch
pouched
pouchy
pouf (*or* pouffe) cushion
  seat; *compare* poof
pou·lard (*or* ·larde) spayed
  hen
poult young chicken
poul·ter·er
poul·tice
poul·try
poultry·man (*plural*
  ·men)
pounce
pound
pound·age
pound·al unit
pound·er
pour flow; *compare* poor;
  pore
pour·boire French tip
pour·er
pour·par·ler French
  informal conference
pour·point doublet
pous·sette country dance
pous·sin spring chicken
pout
pout·er
pout·ing·ly
pov·er·ty
poverty-stricken
pow exclamation
pow·an fish
pow·der
pow·der·er
pow·dery
pow·er
power·boat
pow·er·ful
pow·er·ful·ly
pow·er·ful·ness
power·house
pow·er·less
pow·er·less·ness
pow·wow
Pow·ys Welsh county

pox
poxy
Po·yang Chinese lake
Poz·nań Polish city
poz·zuo·la·na (*or* ·zo·)
  volcanic ash
prac·ti·cabil·ity (*or*
  ·cable·ness)
prac·ti·cable
prac·ti·cably
prac·ti·cal
prac·ti·cal·ity (*or*
  ·cal·ness)
prac·ti·cal·ly
prac·tice (*noun*)
prac·tise (*US* ·tice; *verb*)
prac·tised (*US* ·ticed)
prac·ti·tion·er
prae·dial (*or* pre·) of land
prae·di·al·ity (*or* pre·)
prae·mu·ni·re legal term
prae·no·men Roman's first
  name
Prae·se·pe star cluster
prae·sid·ium *variant spelling*
  of presidium
prae·tor (*or* pre·) Roman
  magistrate
prag·mat·ic
prag·mati·cal·ly
prag·mat·ics (*sing.*)
prag·ma·tism
prag·ma·tist
prag·ma·tis·tic
Prague
prai·rie
praise acclaim; *compare*
  prase
prais·er
praise·worthi·ly
praise·worthi·ness
praise·worthy
pra·line
prall·triller musical term
pram
prance
pranc·er
pranc·ing·ly
pran·dial
prang
prank
prank·ish
prank·ster
prase quartz; *compare* praise
pra·seo·dym·ium chemical
  element
prat *Slang* idiot

prate chatter
prat·er
prat·in·cole bird
prat·ing·ly
pra·tique permission to use
port
Pra·to Italian city
prat·tle
prat·tler
prat·tling·ly
prau variant of proa
prawn
prawn·er
prax·is (plural prax·ises
or praxes) practice
pray utter prayer; compare
prey
prayer petition
pray·er one who prays
prayer·ful
prayer·ful·ly
preach
preach·er
preachi·fi·ca·tion
preachi·fy (·fies, ·fy·ing,
·fied)
preach·ment
pre·ad·am·ite
pre·ad·ap·ta·tion
pre·ado·les·cence
pre·ado·les·cent
pre·am·ble
pre·am·bu·lar (or ·la·tory,
·lary)
pre·am·pli·fi·er
pre·ar·range
pre·ar·ranged
pre·ar·range·ment
pre·ar·rang·er
pre·ax·ial
preb·end
pre·ben·dal
preb·en·dary (plural
·daries)
Pre·cam·brian geological
term
pre·can·cel (·cel·ling,
·celled; US ·cel·ing,
·celed)
pre·can·cel·la·tion
pre·cari·ous
pre·cari·ous·ness
pre·cast (·cast·ing, ·cast)
preca·tory (or ·tive)
pre·cau·tion
pre·cau·tion·ary (or
·tion·al)

pre·cau·tious
pre·cede come before;
compare proceed
prec·edence
prec·edent
prec·eden·tial
pre·ced·ing
pre·cen·tor cleric; compare
preceptor
pre·cen·to·rial
pre·cept
pre·cep·tive
pre·cep·tor teacher;
compare precentor
pre·cep·tor·ate
pre·cep·to·rial (or ·to·ral)
pre·cep·tor·ship
pre·cep·tress
pre·cess
pre·ces·sion rotation;
motion of equinoxes;
compare procession
pre·ces·sion·al
pre·cinct
pre·ci·os·ity (plural ·ities)
affectation
pre·cious
pre·cious·ness
preci·pice
preci·piced
pre·cipi·tance (or ·tan·cy)
pre·cipi·tant
pre·cipi·tate
pre·cipi·ta·tion
pre·cipi·ta·tive
pre·cipi·ta·tor
pre·cipi·tin antibody
pre·cipi·tous
pre·cipi·tous·ness
pre·cis (or pré·; plural
·cis)
pre·cise
pre·cise·ness
pre·ci·sian strict observer of
rules; compare precision
pre·ci·sian·ism
pre·ci·sion accuracy;
compare precisian
pre·ci·sion·ism
pre·ci·sion·ist
pre·clini·cal
pre·clud·able
pre·clude
pre·clu·sion
pre·clu·sive
pre·co·cial ornithological term
pre·co·cious

pre·co·cious·ness (or
pre·coc·ity)
pre·cog·ni·tion
pre·cog·ni·tive
pre·con·ceive
pre·con·cep·tion
pre·con·cert
pre·con·demn
pre·con·di·tion
pre·co·ni·za·tion (or
·sa·tion)
pre·co·nize (or ·nise)
announce publicly
pre·con·scious
pre·con·scious·ness
pre·con·tract
pre·cook
pre·criti·cal
pre·cur·sor
pre·cur·sory (or ·sive)
pre·da·cious (or ·ceous)
predatory
pre·da·cious·ness (or
·ceous·ness,
pre·dac·ity)
pre·date precede
pre·da·tion predatory action
preda·tor
preda·to·ri·ly
preda·to·ri·ness
preda·tory
pre·de·cease
pre·de·ces·sor
pre·del·la (plural ·le) altar
platform; painting
pre·des·ti·nar·ian
pre·des·ti·nari·an·ism
pre·des·ti·nate predestined;
variant of predestine
pre·des·ti·na·tion
pre·des·tine (or ·ti·nate)
pre·de·ter·mi·nate
pre·de·ter·mi·na·tion
pre·de·ter·mi·na·tive
pre·de·ter·mine
pre·de·ter·min·er
pre·dial variant spelling of
praedial
predi·cabil·ity (or
·cable·ness)
predi·cable affirmable
pre·dica·ment
predi·cant of preaching
predi·cate
predi·ca·tion
pre·dica·tive
predi·ca·tory of preaching

pre·dict
pre·dict·abil·ity (or
   ·able·ness)
pre·dict·able
pre·dict·ably
pre·dic·tion
pre·dic·tive
pre·dic·tive·ly
pre·dic·tor
pre·di·gest
pre·di·ges·tion
pre·di·lec·tion
pre·dis·pos·al
pre·dis·pose
pre·dis·po·si·tion
pred·ni·sone drug
pre·domi·nance (or
   ·nan·cy)
pre·domi·nant
pre·domi·nate
pre·domi·na·tion
pre·domi·na·tor
pre-eclamp·sia
pree·mie (or pre·mie) US
   premature baby
pre-eminence
pre-eminent
pre-empt
pre-emption
pre-emptive
pre-emptor
pre-emptory
preen
preen·er
pre-exist
pre-exist·ence
pre·fab
pre·fab·ri·cate
pre·fab·ri·ca·tion
pre·fab·ri·ca·tor
pref·ace
pref·ac·er
prefa·to·ri·ly (or ·ri·al·ly)
prefa·tory (or ·to·rial)
pre·fect
pre·fec·to·rial
pre·fec·tur·al
pre·fec·ture
pre·fer (·fer·ring, ·ferred)
pref·er·abil·ity (or
   ·able·ness)
pref·er·able
pref·er·ably
pref·er·ence
pref·er·en·tial
pref·er·en·tial·ly
pref·er·en·ti·al·ity

pre·fer·ment
pre·fer·rer
pre·figu·ra·tion
pre·figu·ra·tive
pre·figu·ra·tive·ness
pre·fig·ure
pre·fig·ure·ment
pre·fix
pre·fix·al
pre·flight
pre·form
pre·for·ma·tion
pre·fron·tal anatomy term
pre·gla·cial
preg·nabil·ity
preg·nable
preg·nan·cy (plural ·cies)
preg·nant
pre·heat
pre·hen·sile
pre·hen·sion
pre·his·to·rian
pre·his·tor·ic (or ·tori·cal)
pre·his·tori·cal·ly
pre·his·to·ry (plural ·ries)
pre·homi·nid
pre·ignition
pre·judge
pre·judg·er
pre·judg·ment (or
   ·judge·ment)
preju·dice
preju·di·cial
prela·cy (plural ·cies)
prel·ate
pre·lat·ic
prela·tism
prela·tist
prela·ture
pre·lect to lecture
pre·lec·tion
pre·lec·tor
pre·lexi·cal grammar term
pre·limi·nari·ly
pre·limi·nary (plural
   ·naries)
pre·lims front matter of
   book; first exams
pre·lit·era·cy
pre·lit·er·ate
prel·ude
pre·lud·er
pre·lu·di·al
pre·lu·sion
pre·lu·sive (or ·so·ry)
pre·mari·tal
prema·ture

prema·tur·ity (or
   ·ture·ness)
pre·max·il·la (plural ·lae)
   bone
pre·max·il·lary
pre·med short for
   premedical; premedication
pre·medi·cal
pre·medi·ca·tion
pre·medi·tate
pre·medi·tat·ed·ly
pre·medi·ta·tion
pre·medi·ta·tive
pre·medi·ta·tor
pre·men·stru·al
prem·ier first in importance
premi·ere first performance
prem·ier·ship
prem·ise state as premiss;
   variant spelling of premiss
prem·ises land and
   buildings
prem·iss (or ·ise) logical
   statement
pre·mium
pre·mo·lar
premo·ni·tion
pre·moni·tory
pre·morse biology term
pre·mu·ni·tion immunity
pre·na·tal
pre·nomi·nal
pre·oc·cu·pa·tion (or
   ·pan·cy)
pre·oc·cu·py (·pies,
   ·py·ing, ·pied)
pre·or·dain
pre·or·di·na·tion
prep Slang homework;
   preparatory school
pre·pack
pre·pack·age
prepaid
prepa·ra·tion
pre·para·tive
pre·para·to·ri·ly
pre·para·tory
pre·pare
pre·par·ed·ly
pre·par·ed·ness
pre·pay (·pay·ing, ·paid)
pre·pay·able
pre·pay·ment
pre·pense premeditated
pre·pon·der·ance (or
   ·an·cy)
pre·pon·der·ant

pre·pon·der·ate
pre·pon·der·at·ing·ly
pre·pon·dera·tion
prepo·si·tion
prepo·si·tion·al
pre·posi·tive linguistics
term
pre·posi·tor (*or* ·pos·tor)
prefect
pre·pos·sess
pre·pos·sess·ing
pre·pos·sess·ing·ness
pre·pos·ses·sion
pre·pos·ter·ous
pre·pos·ter·ous·ness
pre·po·ten·cy
pre·po·tent
pre·puce foreskin
pre·pu·tial
Pre-Raphael·ite
pre·re·cord
pre·requi·site
pre·roga·tive
pre·sa (*plural* ·se) musical
term
pres·age
pre·sage·ful
pre·sag·er
pres·byo·pia
pres·by·op·ic
pres·by·ter church elder
pres·by·ter·al
pres·byt·er·ate
pres·by·ter·ial
Pres·by·ter·ian Church
pres·by·ter·ian of
government by presbyters
Pres·by·teri·an·ism
pres·by·teri·an·is·tic
pres·by·tery (*plural*
·teries)
pre·school
pres·ci·ence foreknowledge
pres·ci·ent
pre·scribe give ruling; order
use of drug; *compare*
proscribe
pre·scrib·er
pre·script
pre·scrip·tibil·ity
pre·scrip·tible
pre·scrip·tion
pre·scrip·tive
pre·scrip·tiv·ism
pres·ence
pres·ent the time now; in
existence now

pre·sent gift; to give
pre·sent·able
pre·sent·ably
pre·sent·able·ness (*or*
·abil·ity)
pres·en·ta·tion
pres·en·ta·tion·al
pres·en·ta·tion·ism
philosophy term
pres·en·ta·tion·ist
pre·senta·tive
pre·senta·tive·ness
present-day (*adj*)
pres·en·tee
pre·sent·er
pre·sen·tient
pre·sen·ti·ment
pres·ent·ly
pre·sent·ment
pre·serv·abil·ity
pre·serv·able
pres·er·va·tion
pre·serva·tive
pre·serve
pre·serv·er
pre·set (·set·ting, ·set)
pre·set·ter
pre·shrunk
pre·side
presi·den·cy (*plural* ·cies)
presi·dent
president-elect
presi·den·tial
pre·sid·er
pre·sidio (*plural* ·sidios)
military establishment
pre·sid·ium (*or* prae·;
plural ·iums *or* ·ia)
Communist committee
pre·sig·ni·fy (·fies, ·fy·ing,
·fied)
press
press·er one that presses;
compare pressor
press-gang (*verb*)
press·ing
press·ing·ness
press·man (*plural* ·men)
press·mark code on library
book
pres·sor (*adj*) increasing
blood pressure; *compare*
presser
press·room
press-up (*noun*)
pres·sure

pres·suri·za·tion (*or*
·sa·tion)
pres·sur·ize (*or* ·ise)
pres·sur·iz·er (*or* ·is·er)
press·work
pres·ti·digi·ta·tion
pres·ti·digi·ta·tor
pres·tige
pres·tig·ious
pres·tig·ious·ness
pres·tis·si·mo (*plural*
·mos) musical term
pres·to (*plural* ·tos)
Pres·ton Lancashire town
Pres·ton·pans Scottish
battle site
pre·stress
Prest·wich Scottish town
pre·sum·able
pre·sum·ably
pre·sume
pre·sum·ed·ly
pre·sum·er
pre·sum·ing·ly
pre·sump·tion
pre·sump·tive
pre·sump·tive·ness
pre·sump·tu·ous
pre·sump·tu·ous·ness
pre·sup·pose
pre·sup·po·si·tion
pre·tence (*US* ·tense)
pre·tend
pre·tend·ed·ly
pre·tend·er
pre·ten·sion
pre·ten·tious
pre·ten·tious·ness
pret·er·ite (*or* ·it) grammar
term
pret·eri·tion act of omitting
pre·teri·tive grammar term
pre·ter·natu·ral
pre·ter·natu·ral·ism
pre·ter·natu·ral·ness (*or*
·ral·ity)
pre·test
pre·text
Pre·to·ria
pret·ti·fy (·fies, ·fy·ing,
·fied)
pret·ti·ly
pret·ti·ness
pret·ty (*adj* ·ti·er, ·ti·est;
verb ·ties, ·ty·ing, ·tied)
pret·zel biscuit
pre·vail

pre·vail·er
pre·vail·ing
pre·vail·ing·ly
preva·lence (*or* ·lent·ness)
preva·lent
pre·vari·cate
pre·vari·ca·tion
pre·vari·ca·tor
pre·ve·ni·ent preceding
pre·vent
pre·vent·able
pre·vent·ably
pre·ven·ta·tive *variant of* preventive
pre·vent·er
pre·ven·tion
pre·ven·tive (*or* ·ta·tive)
pre·ven·tive·ness (*or* ·ta·tive·ness)
pre·view (*or* ·vue)
pre·vi·ous
pre·vi·ous·ly
pre·vi·ous·ness
pre·vi·sion
pre·vo·cal·ic coming before a vowel
pre·war
prey victim; to hunt; victimize; *compare* pray
prey·er
Priam mythological king
pri·ap·ic of Priapus
pria·pism medical term
Priapus fertility god
price
price·less
price·less·ness
pricey (*or* pricy; prici·er, prici·est)
prick
prick·er
prick·et
prick·le
prick·li·ness
prick·ly (·li·er, ·li·est)
pricy *variant spelling of* pricey
pride
pride·ful
prie-dieu kneeling desk
pri·er (*or* pry·) one who pries; *compare* prior
priest
priest·craft
priest·ess
priest-hole

priest·hood
priest·li·ness
priest·ly (·li·er, ·li·est)
priest-ridden
prig
prig·gery (*or* prig·gish·ness)
prig·gish
prig·gism
prill
prim (*adj* prim·mer, prim·mest; *verb* prim·ming, primmed)
pri·ma bal·leri·na
pri·ma·cy (*plural* ·cies)
pri·ma don·na (*plural* pri·ma don·nas)
pri·mae·val *variant spelling of* primeval
pri·ma fa·cie
pri·mal
pri·ma·quine drug
pri·mari·ly
pri·ma·ry (*plural* ·ries)
pri·mate
pri·ma·tial
pri·ma·tol·ogy branch of zoology
prime
prime·ness
pri·mer introductory text
prim·er one that primes
pri·mero card game
pri·meval (*or* ·mae·val)
pri·meval·ly
primi·gravi·da (*plural* ·das *or* ·dae) obstetrics term
pri·mine botany term
prim·ing
pri·mipa·ra (*or* uni·; *plural* ·ras *or* ·rae) obstetrics term
primi·par·ity
pri·mipa·rous
primi·tive
primi·tive·ness
primi·tiv·ism
primi·tiv·ist
primi·tiv·is·tic
prim·ness
pri·mo (*plural* ·mos *or* ·mi)
pri·mo·geni·tary
pri·mo·geni·tor
pri·mo·geni·ture
pri·mor·dial
pri·mor·dium (*plural* ·dia)

primp
prim·rose
primu·la
primu·la·ceous
pri·mum mo·bi·le *Latin* prime mover
Pri·mus (*Trademark*) stove
pri·mus presiding bishop
prince
prince·dom
prince·li·ness
prince·ling
prince·ly (·li·er, ·li·est)
prin·cess
Prince·ton US town
prin·ci·pal foremost; head person; *compare* principle
prin·ci·pal·ity (*plural* ·ities)
prin·ci·pal·ly
Prín·ci·pe island
prin·cip·ium (*plural* ·cipia) fundamental principle
prin·ci·ple standard; *compare* principal
prin·ci·pled
prink
prink·er
print
print·abil·ity (*or* ·able·ness)
print·able
print·er
print·ing
print·maker
print·out
pri·or abbot's deputy; *compare* prier
pri·or·ate
pri·or·ess
pri·or·ity (*plural* ·ities)
pri·ory (*plural* ·ories)
pris·age duty on wine
prise (*or* prize) force open; *compare* prize
prism
pris·mat·ic
pris·ma·toid geometric solid
pris·ma·toid·al
pris·moid
pris·moid·al
pris·on
pris·on·er
pris·si·ly
pris·si·ness

pris·sy (·si·er,~si·est)
pris·tine
prithee
pri·va·cy (*plural* ·cies)
pri·vate
pri·va·teer
pri·va·tion
priva·tive
priv·et
privi·lege
privi·leged
privi·ly
priv·ity (*plural* ·ities) legal
    relationship
privy (*noun, plural*
    privies; *adj* privi·er,
    privi·est) lavatory; secret
prize award; *variant spelling
    of* prise
prize·fight
prize·fighter
pro (*plural* pros)
proa (*or* prau) boat
pro·ac·tive
pro·am professional and
    amateur
proba·bil·ism
prob·abil·ist
prob·abil·is·tic
prob·abil·ity (*plural* ·ities)
prob·able
prob·ably
pro·band person in
    genealogical study
pro·bang surgical
    instrument
pro·bate
pro·ba·tion
pro·ba·tion·al (*or*
    ·tion·ary)
pro·ba·tion·er
pro·ba·tive (*or* ·tory)
probe
probe·able
prob·er
pro·bity
prob·lem
prob·lem·at·ic (*or* ·ati·cal)
prob·lem·ati·cal·ly
pro bono pub·li·co *Latin*
    for the public good
pro·bos·cid·ean (*or* ·ian)
    zoology term
pro·bos·cis (*plural* ·cises
    or ·ci·des)
pro·caine
pro·cam·bial

pro·cam·bium botany term
pro·carp botany term
pro·ca·thedral church
pro·cedur·al
pro·cedure
pro·ceed carry on; *compare*
    precede
pro·ceed·er
pro·ceed·ing
pro·ceed·ings
pro·ceeds (*noun*)
proc·eleus·mat·ic prosody
    term
pro·cephal·ic anatomy term
pro·cess
pro·ces·sion
pro·ces·sion·al
pro·ces·sor
process-server
pro·chro·nism dating error
pro·claim
proc·la·ma·tion
pro·clama·tory
pro·clit·ic linguistics term
pro·cliv·ity (*plural* ·ities)
Procne mythological
    princess
pro·con·sul
pro·con·su·lar
pro·con·su·late (*or*
    ·sul·ship)
pro·cras·ti·nate
pro·cras·ti·na·tion
pro·cras·ti·na·tor
pro·creant (*or* ·crea·tive)
pro·cre·ate
pro·crea·tion
pro·crea·tor
Pro·crus·tean
Procrustes mythological
    robber
pro·cryp·tic zoology term
pro·cryp·ti·cal·ly
proc·to·logi·cal
proc·tolo·gist
proc·tol·ogy branch of
    medicine
proc·tor
proc·to·rial
proc·to·scope
proc·to·scop·ic
proc·tos·co·py
pro·cum·bent
pro·cur·able
procu·ra·tion
procu·ra·tor

procu·ra·tor fis·cal
    Scottish legal officer
procu·ra·tory
pro·cure
pro·cure·ment (*or*
    ·cur·ance, ·cur·al)
pro·cur·er (*fem* ·ess)
prod (prod·ding,
    prod·ded)
prod·der
prodi·gal
prodi·gal·ity (*plural* ·ities)
prodi·gal·ly
pro·di·gious
pro·di·gious·ness
prodi·gy (*plural* ·gies)
pro·dro·mal (*or* ·drom·ic)
pro·drome symptom of
    disease
pro·duce
pro·duc·er
pro·duc·ibil·ity
pro·duc·ible
prod·uct
pro·duc·tion
pro·duc·tion·al
pro·duc·tive
prod·uc·tiv·ity (*or*
    ·tive·ness)
pro·em preface
pro·emial
prof *Slang* professor
profa·na·tion
pro·fana·to·ry
pro·fane
pro·fane·ness
pro·fan·er
pro·fan·ity (*plural* ·ities)
pro·fess
pro·fess·ed·ly
pro·fes·sion
pro·fes·sion·al
pro·fes·sion·al·ism
pro·fes·sion·al·ist
pro·fes·sion·al·ly
pro·fes·sor
prof·es·so·rial
prof·es·sor·iate (*or*
    ·so·rate)
pro·fes·sor·ship
prof·fer
prof·fer·er
pro·fi·cien·cy (*plural*
    ·cies)
pro·fi·cient
pro·file
prof·it

prof·it·abil·ity
prof·it·able
prof·it·ably
profi·teer
prof·it·er
pro·fit·er·ole
prof·it·less
profit-sharing
prof·li·ga·cy
prof·li·gate
prof·lu·ent flowing
  smoothly
pro-form grammar term
pro for·ma *Latin* as
  prescribed
pro·found
pro·found·ly
pro·found·ness
pro·fun·dity (*plural*
  ·dities)
pro·fuse
pro·fuse·ly
pro·fuse·ness
pro·fu·sion
prog (prog·ging, progged)
  Slang prowl
pro·geni·tive
pro·geni·tive·ness
pro·geni·tor
prog·eny (*plural* ·enies)
pro·ges·ta·tion·al before
  pregnancy
pro·ges·ter·one hormone
pro·ges·to·gen (*or*
  pro·ges·tin) synthetic
  progesterone
pro·glot·tis (*or* ·tid; *plural*
  ·glot·ti·des) tapeworm
  segment
prog·na·thism
prog·na·thous (*or*
  ·nath·ic)
prog·no·sis (*plural* ·ses)
prog·nos·tic
prog·nos·ti·cate
prog·nos·ti·ca·tion
prog·nos·ti·ca·tive
prog·nos·ti·ca·tor
pro·gram *US spelling of*
  programme
pro·gram (·gram·ming,
  ·grammed) computer
  term
pro·gram·ma·ble
pro·gram·mat·ic
pro·gramme (*US* ·gram;
  ·gram·ming,

·grammed; *US*
  ·gram·ing, ·gramed)
pro·gram·mer
pro·gress
pro·gres·sion
pro·gres·sion·al
Pro·gres·sive political party
pro·gres·sive
pro·gres·sive·ness
pro·gres·siv·ism
pro·gres·siv·ist
pro·hib·it
pro·hib·it·er (*or* ·hibi·tor)
pro·hi·bi·tion
pro·hi·bi·tion·ary
pro·hi·bi·tion·ism
pro·hi·bi·tion·ist
pro·hibi·tive (*or* ·tory)
pro·hibi·tive·ness
proj·ect
pro·jec·tile
pro·jec·tion
pro·jec·tion·al
pro·jec·tion·ist
pro·jec·tive
pro·jec·tor
pro·jet draft treaty
Pro·kop·yevsk Soviet city
pro·lac·tin hormone
pro·la·mine plant protein
pro·lapse
pro·late spheroidal
pro·late·ness
prole
pro·leg zoology term
pro·legom·enal
pro·legom·enon (*plural*
  ·ena) critical introduction
pro·lep·sis (*plural* ·ses)
  rhetorical device
pro·lep·tic
pro·lep·ti·cal·ly
pro·letar·ian (*or* ·letary;
  plural ·ians *or*
  ·letaries)
pro·letar·ian·ism
pro·letar·ian·ness
pro·letari·at
pro·lif·er·ate
pro·lif·era·tion
pro·lif·era·tive
pro·lif·er·ous
pro·lif·ic
pro·lifi·cal·ly
pro·lif·ic·ness (*or*
  ·lifi·ca·cy)
pro·line amino acid

pro·lix long-winded
pro·lix·ity (*or* ·ness)
pro·locu·tor Anglican
  official
pro·logue (*US also* ·log;
  ·logu·ing, ·logued; *US
  also* ·log·ing, ·loged)
pro·long
pro·lon·ga·tion
pro·long·er
pro·long·ment
pro·lu·sion preliminary
  essay
pro·lu·so·ry
prom
prom·enade
prom·enad·er
Pro·methean
Prometheus mythological
  character
pro·methium radioactive
  element
promi·nence
promi·nent
promi·nent·ness
promis·cu·ity (*plural*
  ·ities)
pro·mis·cu·ous
pro·mis·cu·ous·ness
prom·ise
promi·see
prom·is·er (*or in legal
  contexts* promi·sor)
prom·is·ing
prom·is·sory
prom·on·tory (*plural*
  ·tories)
pro·mot·able
pro·mote
pro·mot·er
pro·mo·tion
pro·mo·tion·al
pro·mo·tive
pro·mo·tive·ness
prompt
prompt·book
prompt·er
promp·ti·tude
prompt·ness
prom·ul·gate
prom·ul·ga·tion
prom·ul·ga·tor
pro·my·celium (*plural*
  ·celia) botany term
pro·nate
pro·na·tion
pro·na·tor muscle

proselytizer

prone
prone·ness
pro·neph·ric
pro·neph·ros (*plural* ·roi
or ·ra) zoology term
prong
prong·horn deer
pro·nomi·nal of a pronoun
pro·nomi·nali·za·tion (*or*
·sa·tion)
pro·nomi·nal·ize (*or* ·ise)
pro·noun
pro·nounce
pro·nounce·able
pro·nounced
pro·nounc·ed·ly
pro·nounce·ment
pro·nounc·er
pron·to
pro·nu·clear
pro·nu·cleus (*plural* ·clei)
pro·nun·cia·men·to
(*plural* ·tos) manifesto
pro·nun·cia·tion
pro-oestrus (*US*
pro·es·trus)
proof
proof·read (·read·ing,
·read)
proof·reader
prop (prop·ping,
propped)
pro·pae·deu·tic preparatory
instruction
pro·pae·deu·ti·cal
propa·gabil·ity (*or*
·gable·ness)
propa·gable
propa·gan·da
propa·gan·dism
propa·gan·dist
propa·gan·dize (*or* ·dise)
propa·gate
propa·ga·tion
propa·ga·tion·al
propa·ga·tive
propa·ga·tor
propa·gule (*or*
pro·pagu·lum; *plural*
·gules *or* ·la) botany
term
pro·pane
pro·pa·roxy·tone grammar
term
pro pa·tria *Latin* for one's
country
pro·pel (·pel·ling, ·pelled)

pro·pel·lant (*or* ·lent;
noun)
pro·pel·lent (*adj*)
pro·pel·ler
pro·pene chemical
compound
pro·pen·sity (*plural*
·sities)
prop·er
prop·er·ly
prop·er·ness
prop·er·tied
prop·er·ty (*plural* ·ties)
pro·phage virus
pro·phase biology term
proph·ecy (*plural* ·ecies)
proph·esi·able
proph·esi·er
proph·esy (·esies,
·esy·ing, ·esied)
proph·et (*fem* ·et·ess)
pro·phet·ic
pro·pheti·cal·ly
prophy·lac·tic
prophy·lax·is
pro·pin·quity
pro·pio·nate
pro·pi·on·ic acid
pro·pi·ti·able
pro·pi·ti·ate
pro·pi·tia·tion
pro·pi·tia·tious appeasing;
compare propitious
pro·pi·tia·tive
pro·pi·tia·tor
pro·pi·tious favourable;
compare propipiatious
pro·pi·tious·ness
prop·jet
propo·lis substance
collected by bees
pro·po·nent
pro·por·tion
pro·por·tion·abil·ity
pro·por·tion·able
pro·por·tion·al
pro·por·tion·al·ity
pro·por·tion·al·ly
pro·por·tion·ate
pro·por·tion·ate·ness
pro·por·tion·ment
pro·po·sable
pro·po·sal
pro·pose
pro·pos·er
propo·si·tion
propo·si·tion·al

pro·posi·tus (*plural* ·ti)
legal term
pro·pound
pro·pound·er
pro·prae·tor provincial
praetor
pro·prano·lol
pro·pri·etari·ly
pro·pri·etary
pro·pri·etor (*fem* ·etress)
pro·pri·etor·ial
pro·pri·ety (*plural* ·eties)
pro·prio·cep·tive
pro·prio·cep·tor nerve
ending
prop·to·sis (*plural* ·ses)
medical term
pro·pul·sion
pro·pul·sive (*or* ·sory)
pro·pyl chemistry term
propy·laeum (*or* ·lon;
plural ·laea *or* ·lons,
·la) temple portico
pro·pyl·ene propene
propy·lite geology term
pro rata
pro·rate
pro·ra·tion
pro·ro·ga·tion
pro·rogue
pro·sa·ic
pro·sai·cal·ly
pro·sa·ic·ness
pro·sa·ism (*or* ·sai·cism)
prosaic style
pro·scenium (*plural*
·scenia *or* ·sceniums)
pro·sciut·to Italian ham
pro·scribe prohibit;
compare prescribe
pro·scrip·tion
pro·scrip·tive
pro·scrip·tive·ness
prose
pro·sec·tor dissector
pros·ecut·able
pros·ecute
pros·ecu·tion
pros·ecu·tor
pros·elyte
pros·elyt·ic
pros·elyt·ism
pros·elyti·za·tion (*or*
·sa·tion)
pros·elyt·ize (*or* ·ise)
pros·elyt·iz·er (*or* ·is·er)

pros·en·cepha·lon (*plural* ·la) anatomy term

pros·en·chy·ma plant tissue

pros·en·chy·ma·tous

Proserpina Roman goddess

prosi·ly

pro·sim·ian zoology term

prosi·ness

pro·sod·ic

proso·dist

proso·dy

proso·po·poeia (*or* ·peia) rhetorical device

proso·po·poeial (*or* ·peial)

pros·pect

pro·spec·tive

pro·spec·tor

pro·spec·tus (*plural* ·tuses)

pros·per

pros·per·ity (*plural* ·ities)

pros·per·ous

pros·per·ous·ness

pros·ta·glan·din hormone-like compound

pros·tate gland; *compare* prostrate

pros·ta·tec·to·my (*plural* ·mies)

pros·tat·ic

pros·ta·ti·tis

pros·the·sis (*plural* ·ses) artificial body part; *compare* prothesis

pros·thet·ic

pros·theti·cal·ly

pros·thet·ics

pros·tho·don·tics branch of dentistry

pros·tho·don·tist

pros·ti·tute

pros·ti·tu·tion

pros·ti·tu·tor

pro·sto·mium (*plural* ·mia) zoology term

pros·trate face down; *compare* prostate

pros·tra·tion

pro·style architectural term

prosy (prosi·er, prosi·est)

pro·tac·tin·ium radioactive element

pro·tago·nism

pro·tago·nist

pro·ta·mine protein

pro·tan·drous botany term

pro·tan·dry

pro·ta·no·pia red blindness

pro·ta·nop·ic

prota·sis (*plural* ·ses) conditional clause

pro·tea shrub

pro·tean variable

pro·tease enzyme

pro·tect

pro·tec·tion

pro·tec·tion·ism

pro·tec·tion·ist

pro·tec·tive

pro·tec·tive·ness

pro·tec·tor

pro·tec·to·ral

pro·tec·tor·ate

pro·tec·tory (*plural* ·tories) institution for children

pro·tec·tress

pro·té·gé (*fem* ·gée)

pro·tein

pro·teina·ceous (*or* ·tein·ic, ·tei·nous)

pro·tein·ase enzyme

pro tem (*or* pro tem·po·re) temporarily

pro·teoly·sis

pro·teo·lyt·ic

pro·teose biochemical compound

Pro·tero·zo·ic geology term

pro·test

Prot·es·tant religion

pro·test·ant protester

Prot·es·tant·ism

pro·tes·ta·tion

pro·test·er

pro·test·ing·ly

Proteus Greek god

pro·tha·la·mi·on (*or* ·mium; *plural* ·mia) marriage song

pro·thal·lic (*or* ·lial)

pro·thal·lus (*or* ·lium; *plural* ·li *or* ·lia) botany term

proth·esis linguistics term; *compare* prosthesis

pro·thet·ic

pro·theti·cal·ly

pro·thono·tar·ial (*or* pro·tono·)

pro·tho·no·tary (*or* proto·no·tary; *plural* ·taries)

pro·tho·rax (*plural* ·raxes *or* ·ra·ces)

pro·throm·bin

pro·tist microscopic organism

pro·tium isotope of hydrogen

proto·chor·date zoology term

proto·col

pro·togy·nous

pro·togy·ny biology term

proto·his·tor·ic

proto·his·to·ry

proto·hu·man

proto·lan·guage

proto·lith·ic of the Stone Age

proto·mor·phic primitive

pro·ton

proto·nema (*plural* ·ne·ma·ta) botany term

proto·ne·mal (*or* ·nema·tal)

proto·path·ic

pro·topa·thy physiology term

proto·plasm

proto·plas·mic (*or* ·mal, ·mat·ic)

proto·plast

proto·plas·tic

Proto·semit·ic language

proto·star

proto·stele botany term

proto·stelic

proto·therian zoology term

proto·troph·ic biology term

proto·ty·pal (*or* ·typ·ic, ·typi·cal)

proto·type

pro·tox·ide

proto·xy·lem

proto·zoan (*or* ·zo·on; *plural* ·zoans *or* ·zoa)

proto·zoo·logi·cal

proto·zo·olo·gist

proto·zo·ol·ogy

pro·tract

pro·tract·ed·ly

pro·tract·ed·ness

pro·trac·tile (*or* ·tract·ible)

pro·trac·tion

pro·trac·tive

pro·trac·tor

pro·trud·able

pro·trude
pro·tru·dent
pro·tru·sile
pro·tru·sion
pro·tru·sive
pro·tru·sive·ness
pro·tu·ber·ance (or
·an·cy; *plural* ·ances or
·an·cies)
pro·tu·ber·ant
pro·tyle (or ·tyl) chemistry
term
proud
proud·ness
proust·ite mineral
prov·abil·ity
prov·able
prove (prov·ing, proved,
proved *or* prov·en)
prov·enance (or
·veni·ence)
Pro·ven·çal of Provence
Pro·ven·çale cookery term
Pro·vence
prov·en·der
prov·en·ly
pro·ven·tricu·lar
pro·ven·tricu·lus (*plural*
·li) zoology term
prov·erb
pro·ver·bial
pro·ver·bial·ly
pro·vide
Provi·dence US port
provi·dence
provi·dent
provi·den·tial
provi·den·tial·ly
pro·vid·er
prov·ince
pro·vin·cial
pro·vin·cial·ism
pro·vin·ci·al·ity
pro·virus
pro·vi·sion
pro·vi·sion·al (or ·ary)
pro·vi·sion·al·ly
pro·vi·sion·er
pro·vi·sions
pro·vi·so (*plural* ·sos or
·soes)
pro·vi·so·ri·ly
pro·vi·sory
pro·vita·min
Pro·vo (*plural* ·vos)
Provisional IRA member
provo·ca·tion

pro·voca·tive
pro·voca·tive·ness
pro·voke
pro·vok·ing·ly
pro·vo·lo·ne cheese
prov·ost
prow
prow·ess
prowl
prowl·er
Proxi·ma star
proxi·mal anatomy term
proxi·mal·ly
proxi·mate nearest
proxi·mate·ness
proxi·ma·tion
prox·im·ity
proxi·mo next month
proxy (*plural* proxies)
prude
pru·dence
pru·dent
pru·den·tial
pru·dent·ness
prud·ery (*plural* ·eries)
prud·ish
prud·ish·ness
prui·nose botany term
prun·able
prune
pru·nel·la (or ·nelle,
·nel·lo) fabric
pru·nelle liqueur
prun·er
pru·ri·ence
pru·ri·ent lewd; *compare*
purulent
pru·ri·go skin disease
pru·rit·ic
pru·ri·tus itching
Prus·sia
Prus·sian
prus·si·ate cyanide
prus·sic acid
pry (*verb* pries, pry·ing,
pried; *noun, plural*
pries)
pry·er *variant spelling of*
prier
pryta·neum (*plural* ·nea)
ancient Greek town hall
psalm
psalm·ic
psalm·ist
psalm·od·ic
psalmo·dist
psalmo·dy (*plural* ·dies)

Psalms Old Testament book
Psal·ter (or psal·) psalm
book
psal·ter·ium (*plural* ·teria)
cow's stomach
psal·tery (*plural* ·teries)
musical instrument
pse·phite rock
pse·phit·ic
psepho·logi·cal
psepho·logi·cal·ly
pse·pholo·gist
pse·phol·ogy study of
elections
pseud *Slang* pretentious
person
pseud·axis botany term
Pseud·epig·ra·pha Jewish
writings
pseu·do *Slang* pretended
pseudo·carp botany term
pseudo·morph geology
term
pseudo·mor·phic (or
·phous)
pseudo·mor·phism
pseudo·mu·tu·al·ity
(*plural* ·ities) psychology
term
pseudo·nym
pseudo·nym·ity
pseu·dony·mous
pseudo·po·dium (*plural*
·dia) biology term
pshaw exclamation
psi Greek letter
psilo·cy·bin hallucinogen
psi·lom·elane mineral
psit·ta·cine of parrots
psit·ta·co·sis
Pskov Soviet city
pso·as muscle
pso·ra·lea plant
pso·ria·sis skin disease
pso·ri·at·ic
psych *Slang* deduce; prepare
Psyche mythological
character
psy·che human mind
psychedelia
psychedel·ic (or psycho·)
psychedeli·cal·ly (or
psycho·deli·)
psy·chi·at·ric
psy·chi·at·ri·cal·ly
psy·chia·trist
psy·chia·try

psy·chic telepathic
psy·chi·cal
psy·cho (*plural* **·chos**) *Slang* psychopath
psycho·acous·tics
psycho·ac·tive
psycho·ana·lyse (*US* **·lyze**)
psycho·analy·sis
psycho·ana·lyst
psycho·ana·lyt·ic (*or* **·lyti·cal**)
psycho·ana·lyti·cal·ly
psycho·bio·logi·cal
psycho·bi·olo·gist
psycho·bi·ol·ogy
psycho·chemi·cal
psycho·dra·ma
psycho·dra·mat·ic
psycho·dy·nam·ic
psycho·dy·nami·cal·ly
psycho·dy·nam·ics
psycho·gen·esis
psycho·genet·ic
psycho·geneti·cal·ly
psycho·gen·ic
psycho·geni·cal·ly
psy·chog·no·sis
psy·chog·nos·tic
psycho·graph
psycho·graph·ic
psy·chog·ra·phy
psycho·his·to·ry (*plural* **·ries**)
psycho·ki·nesis
psycho·ki·net·ic
psycho·lin·guist
psycho·lin·guis·tic
psycho·lin·guis·tics
psycho·logi·cal
psycho·logi·cal·ly
psy·cholo·gism belief in psychology
psy·cholo·gist
psy·cholo·gist·ic
psy·cholo·gize (*or* **·gise**)
psy·chol·ogy (*plural* **·ogies**)
psycho·met·ric (*or* **·ri·cal**)
psycho·met·ri·cal·ly
psycho·metri·cian (*or* **psy·chom·etrist**)
psycho·met·rics (*or* **psy·chom·etry**) testing mental processes
psycho·mo·tor

psycho·neu·ro·sis (*plural* **·ses**)
psycho·neu·rot·ic
psycho·path
psycho·path·ic
psycho·path·ical·ly
psycho·patho·logi·cal
psycho·pa·tholo·gist
psycho·pa·thol·ogy
psy·chopa·thy
psycho·phar·ma·co·logi·cal
psycho·phar·ma·colo·gist
psycho·phar·ma·col·ogy
psycho·physi·cal
psycho·phys·ics
psycho·physio·logi·cal
psycho·physi·olo·gist
psycho·physi·ol·ogy
psycho·sex·ual
psycho·sexu·al·ity
psy·cho·sis (*plural* **·ses**)
psycho·so·cial
psycho·so·mat·ic
psycho·sur·gery
psycho·sur·gi·cal
psycho·tech·ni·cal
psycho·tech·ni·cian
psycho·tech·nics
psycho·thera·peu·tic
psycho·thera·peu·ti·cal·ly
psycho·thera·pist
psycho·thera·py
psycho·trop·ic
psy·chot·ic
psy·choti·cal·ly
psy·choto·mi·met·ic
psy·chrom·eter humidity meter
psy·chro·phil·ic biology term
psyl·lid (*or* **·la**) insect
Ptah Egyptian god
ptar·mi·gan (*plural* **·gans** *or* **·gan**) bird
pteri·do·logi·cal
pteri·dolo·gist
pteri·dol·ogy study of ferns
pteri·do·phyte
pteri·do·phyt·ic (*or* **·dophy·tous**)
pteri·do·sperm extinct plant
ptero·dac·tyl
ptero·pod mollusc
ptero·saur
ptery·goid anatomy term

ptery·la (*plural* **·lae**) ornithology term
pti·san grape juice
pto·choc·ra·cy (*plural* **·cies**) government by the poor
Ptol·emae·us moon crater
Ptol·ema·ic
Ptol·ema·ist
pto·maine (*or* **·main**) chemical compound
pto·sis (*plural* **·ses**) drooping of eyelid
ptya·lin enzyme
ptya·lism excessive salivation
pub (**pub·bing, pubbed**)
pu·ber·ty
pu·beru·lent downy
pu·bes (*plural* **·bes**) pubic region; *plural of* **pubis**
pu·bes·cence
pu·bes·cent
pu·bic
pu·bis (*plural* **·bes**) hip bone
pub·lic
pub·li·can
pub·li·ca·tion
pub·li·cist
pub·lic·ity
pub·li·cize (*or* **·cise**)
pub·lic·ly
public-spirit·ed
pub·lish
pub·lish·able
pub·lish·er
puc·coon plant
puce
puck
puck·er
puck·ish
puck·ish·ness
pud·ding
pud·dle
pud·dler
pud·dling
pud·dly
pu·den·cy modesty
pu·den·dal
pu·den·dum (*plural* **·da**)
pudgi·ly
pudgi·ness
pudgy (**pudgi·er, pudgi·est**)
Pue·bla Mexican city

Pueb·lo (*plural* ·lo *or*
 ·los) American Indian
pueb·lo (*plural* ·los)
 village
pu·er·ile
pu·er·il·ism
pu·er·il·ity (*plural* ·ities)
pu·er·per·al
pu·er·per·ium period after
 childbirth
Puer·to Ri·can
Puer·to Rico
puff
puff·ball
puff·bird
puff·er
puff·ery (*plural* ·eries)
 exaggerated praise
puffi·ly
puf·fin
puffi·ness
puffy (puffi·er, puffi·est)
pug (pug·ging, pugged)
 dog; knead clay
pug·gish
pu·gi·lism
pu·gi·list
pu·gi·lis·tic
pu·gi·lis·ti·cal·ly
pug·na·cious
pug·nac·ity (*or*
 ·na·cious·ness)
pug-nosed
puis·ne legal term
pu·is·sance *Archaic* power;
 showjumping event
pu·is·sant
puke
puk·ka
pul (*plural* puls *or* puli)
 Afghan coin
pul·chri·tude
pul·chri·tudi·nous
pule to whimper
pul·er
pull
pul·let
pul·ley
pull-in (*noun*)
Pull·man (*plural* ·mans)
 rail coach
pull-out (*noun*)
pull-over
pul·lu·late breed rapidly
pul·lu·la·tion
pul·mo·nary
pul·mo·nate

pul·mon·ic
Pul·motor (*Trademark*)
pulp
pulpi·ness
pul·pit
pulp·wood
pulpy (pulpi·er, pulpi·est)
pul·que alcoholic drink
pul·sar star
pul·sate
pul·sa·tile
pul·sa·til·ity
pul·sa·tion
pul·sa·tive
pul·sa·tor
pul·sa·tory
pulse
pulse·jet
pul·sim·eter (*or* ·som·)
pul·ver·able
pul·veri·za·tion (*or*
 ·sa·tion)
pul·ver·ize (*or* ·ise)
pul·ver·iz·er (*or* ·is·er)
pul·veru·lence
pul·veru·lent of dust
pul·vil·lus (*plural* ·li)
 zoology term
pul·vi·nate (*or* ·nat·ed)
pul·vi·nus (*plural* ·ni)
 botany term
puma
pum·ice
pu·mi·ceous
pum·mel (*or* pom·;
 ·mel·ling, ·melled; *US*
 ·mel·ing, ·meled) to
 pound; *compare* pommel
pump
pum·per·nick·el
pump·kin
pumpkin·seed
pun (pun·ning, punned)
punce *Dialect* kick
punch
punch·ball
punch·board
punch·bowl
punch-drunk
pun·cheon
punch·er
Pun·chi·nel·lo (*plural* ·los
 or ·loes) clown
punch-up (*noun*)
punchy (punchi·er,
 punchi·est)
punc·tate (*or* ·tat·ed)

punc·ta·tion
punc·tilio (*plural* ·tilios)
 etiquette
punc·tili·ous
punc·tili·ous·ness
punc·tu·al
punc·tu·al·ity
punc·tu·al·ly
punc·tu·ate
punc·tua·tion
punc·tua·tor
punc·tum (*plural* ·ta)
 anatomy term
punc·tur·able
punc·ture
punc·tur·er
pun·dit (*or* pan·) expert;
 learned Hindu; *compare*
 pandit
pung *US* sleigh
pun·gen·cy
pun·gent
Pu·nic of Carthage
puni·ness
pun·ish
pun·ish·abil·ity
pun·ish·able
pun·ish·er
pun·ish·ing·ly
pun·ish·ment
pu·ni·tive (*or* ·tory)
pu·ni·tive·ness
Pun·jab
Pun·ja·bi (*or* Pan·)
punk
pun·ka (*or* ·kah) palm-leaf
 fan
punned
pun·ner
pun·net
pun·ning
pun·ster
punt
punt·er
pun·ty (*plural* ·ties) glass-
 blowing rod
puny (pu·ni·er, pu·ni·est)
pup (pup·ping, pupped)
pupa (*plural* pupae *or*
 pupas)
pu·pal
pu·par·ial
pu·par·ium (*plural* ·paria)
pu·pate
pu·pa·tion
pu·pil
pu·pil·lage (*US* ·pil·age)

pu·pil·lary (*or* ·pil·lary)

pu·pipa·rous entomology
    term

pup·pet

pup·pet·eer

pup·pet·ry

pup·ping

Pup·pis constellation

pup·py (*plural* ·pies)

pup·py·hood

pup·py·ish

Pu·ra·na Sanskrit writings

Pur·beck Dorset peninsula;
    marble

pur·blind

pur·chasa·bil·ity

pur·chas·able

pur·chase

pur·chas·er

pur·dah (*or* pur·da,
    par·dah)

pure

pure·bred

pu·ree (*or* puri) Indian
    bread

pu·rée (·rée·ing, ·réed)
    pulped food

pure·ly

pure·ness

pur·fle ornamental band

pur·ga·tion

pur·ga·tive

pur·ga·to·rial

pur·ga·tory

purge

purg·er

Puri Indian port

pu·ri·fi·ca·tion

pu·ri·fi·ca·tor Communion
    cloth

pu·rifi·ca·tory

pu·ri·fi·er

pu·ri·fy (·fies, ·fy·ing,
    ·fied)

Pu·rim Jewish holiday

pu·rine (*or* ·rin)
    biochemical compound

pur·ism

pur·ist

pu·rist·ic

pu·ris·ti·cal·ly

Pu·ri·tan extreme Protestant

pu·ri·tan strictly moral
    person

pu·ri·tani·cal (*or* ·tan·ic)

pu·ri·tani·cal·ness

Pu·ri·tan·ism

pu·ri·tan·ism

pu·rity

purl knitting stitch; *compare*
    pearl

pur·ler headlong fall

pur·lieu outlying area

pur·lin (*or* ·line) roof beam

pur·loin

pur·loin·er

pur·ple

pur·ple·ness

pur·plish

pur·port

pur·pose

pur·pose·ful

pur·pose·ful·ly
    determinedly; *compare*
    purposely

pur·pose·ful·ness

pur·pose·less

pur·pose·less·ness

pur·pose·ly intentionally;
    compare purposefully

pur·pos·ive

pur·pos·ive·ness

pur·pu·ra disease

pur·pure heraldic purple

pur·pu·rin biological dye

purr

purse

purs·er

purs·lane plant

pur·su·ance

pur·su·ant

pur·sue (·su·ing, ·sued)

pur·su·er

pur·suit

pur·sui·vant heraldic officer

pursy short-winded

pu·ru·lence (*or* ·len·cy)

pu·ru·lent of pus; *compare*
    prurient

pur·vey

pur·vey·ance

pur·vey·or

pur·view scope

pus matter from wound;
    compare puss

Pu·san South Korean port

push

push·chair

push·er

pushi·ly

pushi·ness

push·ing

push·ing·ly

push·ing·ness

push·over

push·pull

push·rod

Push·tu *variant of* Pashto

push·up *US* press·up

pushy (pushi·er,
    pushi·est)

pu·sil·la·nim·ity

pu·sil·lani·mous

puss *Slang* cat; *compare* pus

pus·sy (·si·er, ·si·est) full
    of pus

pussy (*or* pussy·cat;
    plural pussies *or* ·cats)

pussy·foot

pus·tu·lant

pus·tu·lar

pus·tu·late

pus·tu·la·tion

pus·tule

put (put·ting, put) to
    place, etc.; *compare* putt

pu·ta·men (*plural*
    ·tami·na) botany term

pu·ta·tive

put·down (*noun*)

put·log (*or* ·lock) scaffold
    beam

put·on (*noun*)

pu·tre·fac·tion

pu·tre·fac·tive (*or*
    ·fa·cient)

pu·tre·fi·able

pu·tre·fi·er

pu·tre·fy (·fies, ·fy·ing,
    ·fied)

pu·tres·cence

pu·tres·cent

pu·tres·cine organic
    compound

pu·trid

pu·trid·ity (*or* ·trid·ness)

(putrify) *incorrect spelling of*
    putrefy

Putsch *German* uprising

putt golf stroke; *compare* put

put·tee (*or* ·ty; *plural*
    ·tees *or* ·ties) leg cloth

putt·er golf club

put·ter placer

putt·ing golf stroke

put·ting placing

put·to (*plural* ·ti) boy
    cupid

put·ty (*noun, plural* ·ties;
    verb ·ties, ·ty·ing, ·tied)

putty·root

put-up (*adj*)
Puy de Dôme French
  department
puz·zle
puz·zle·ment
puz·zler
puz·zling·ly
pya Burmese coin
py·aemia (*US* ·emia)
  blood poisoning
py·aemic (*US* ·emic)
pyc·nid·ium (*plural*
  ·nidia) botany term
pyc·nom·eter density
  measurer
pyc·no·met·ric
Pyd·na ancient Macedonian
  town
pye-dog (*or* pie-)
py·elit·ic
py·eli·tis kidney disease
py·elo·gram
py·elo·graph·ic
py·elog·ra·phy
py·elo·nephri·tis
py·emia *US spelling of*
  pyaemia
py·gid·ial
py·gid·ium (*plural* ·gidia)
  zoology term
Pygmalion mythological
  king
Pyg·my (*or* Pig·; *plural*
  ·mies) African race
pyg·my (*or* pig·; *plural*
  ·mies) dwarf
py·ja·ma (*US* pa·; *adj*)
py·ja·mas (*US* pa·)
pyk·nic squat
py·lon
py·lo·rec·to·my (*plural*
  ·mies)
py·lo·ric
py·lo·rus (*plural* ·ri)
  stomach opening
pyo·der·ma skin disease
pyo·gen·esis
pyo·gen·ic causing pus;
  compare pyrogenic
py·oid
Pyong·yang capital of
  North Korea
py·or·rhoea (*US* ·rhea)
  gum disease
py·or·rhoeal (*or* ·rhoe·ic;
  US ·rheal *or* ·rhe·ic)
pyo·sis pus formation

py·ra·can·tha shrub
pyra·lid moth
pyra·mid
py·rami·dal (*or*
  pyra·midi·cal,
  pyra·mid·ic)
Pyramus legendary lover
py·ran chemical compound
py·ra·nom·eter solarimeter
py·rar·gy·rite mineral
py·ra·zole chemical
  compound
pyre
py·rene chemical
  compound; botany term
Pyr·enean
Pyr·enees
Py·ré·nées At·lan·tiques
  French department
Py·ré·nées-Orientales
  French department
pyr·enoid protein granule
py·rethrin insecticide
py·rethrum plant
py·ret·ic of fever
Py·rex (*Trademark*)
py·rexia fever
py·rex·ial (*or* ·rex·ic)
pyr·he·li·om·eter
pyr·he·lio·met·ric
pyri·dine chemical
  compound
pyri·dox·al biochemical
  compound
pyri·doxa·mine
pyri·dox·ine
pyri·form pear-shaped
py·rimi·dine biochemical
  compound
py·rite mineral
py·ri·tes (*plural* ·tes)
  mineral
py·rit·ic (*or* ·ti·tous)
pyro·cat·echol (*or* ·echin)
pyro·chemi·cal
pyro·clas·tic geology term
pyro·con·duc·tiv·ity
pyro·elec·tric
pyro·elec·tric·ity
pyro·gal·late
pyro·gal·lic
pyro·gal·lol
pyro·gen
pyro·gen·ic (*or*
  py·rog·enous) causing
  heat or fever; *compare*
  pyogenic

py·rog·nos·tics
py·rog·ra·pher
pyro·graph·ic
py·rog·ra·phy (*plural*
  ·phies) design by burning
pyro·lig·ne·ous (*or*
  ·lig·nic)
pyro·lit·ic
pyro·lu·site mineral
py·roly·sis chemical
  reaction
pyro·man·cer
pyro·man·cy divination by
  fire
pyro·ma·nia
pyro·ma·ni·ac
pyro·ma·nia·cal
pyro·man·tic
pyro·met·al·lur·gy
py·rom·eter
pyro·met·ric (*or*
  ·met·ri·cal)
pyro·met·ri·cal·ly
py·rom·etry
pyro·mor·phite mineral
py·rone chemical compound
py·rope garnet
pyro·phor·ic
pyro·phos·phate
pyro·pho·tom·eter
pyro·pho·tom·etry
pyro·phyl·lite mineral
pyro·sis heartburn
pyro·stat
pyro·stat·ic
pyro·sul·phate (*US* ·fate)
pyro·tech·nic (*or* ·ni·cal)
pyro·tech·nics
py·rox·ene mineral
py·rox·en·ic
py·rox·enite rock
py·roxy·lin constituent of
  plastics
Pyrrha mythological
  character
Pyr·rhic of Pyrrhus
pyr·rhic prosody term
pyr·rho·tite (*or* ·tine)
  mineral
pyr·rhu·loxia bird
pyr·role biochemical
  compound
pyr·rol·ic
pyr·roli·dine
pyr·ru·vic acid
Py·thago·rean

Pythia mythological
 priestess
Pyth·ian
py·thon
py·thon·ess female
 soothsayer

py·thon·ic
pyu·ria medical term
pyx container for Eucharist;
 compare pix
pyx·id·ium (*plural* ·idia)
 botany term

pyxie shrub
pyx·is (*plural* **pyxi·des**)
 box

Q

Qair·wan Tunisian city
Qa·tar Arabian state
Qa·ta·ri
Qeshm (*or* **Qishm**)
 Iranian island
qin·tar (*or* ·**dar**) Albanian
 coin
qua in the capacity of
quack
quack·ery (*plural* ·**eries**)
quack·sal·ver quack doctor
quad quadrangle;
 quadruplet; *compare* quod
quad·ra·ge·nar·ian
Quad·ra·gesi·ma
Quad·ra·gesi·mal
quad·ran·gle
quad·ran·gu·lar
quad·rant
quad·ran·tal
quad·ra·phon·ic (*or* ·**ro**·)
quad·ra·phon·ics (*or* ·**ro**·)
quad·rat ecology term
quad·rate cube; bone
quad·rat·ic
quad·rat·ics branch of
 algebra
quad·ra·ture maths term
quad·ren·nial
quad·ren·nial·ly
quad·ren·nium (*plural*
 ·**niums** *or* ·**nia**)
quad·ric maths term
quad·ri·cen·ten·nial
quad·ri·ceps (*plural*
 ·**cepses**) muscle
quad·ri·cipi·tal
quad·ri·fid botany term
quad·ri·ga (*plural* ·**gas** *or*
 ·**gae**) chariot
quad·ri·lat·er·al
quad·rille dance
quad·ril·lion 10^{24}
quad·ril·lionth
quad·ri·no·mial

quad·ri·par·tite
quad·ri·plegia
quad·ri·plegic
quad·ri·sect
quad·ri·sec·tion
quad·ri·va·len·cy (*or*
 ·**lence**)
quad·ri·va·lent
quad·riv·ial having four
 roads meeting
quad·riv·ium medieval
 branch of learning
quad·roon
quad·ru·ma·nous zoology
 term
quad·ru·ped
quad·ru·ped·al
quad·ru·ple
quad·ru·plet
quad·ru·plex fourfold
quad·ru·pli·cate
quad·ru·pli·ca·tion
quad·ru·plic·ity (*plural*
 ·**ities**)
quaes·tor (*or* **ques**·)
 Roman magistrate
quaff
quaff·er
quag·ga (*plural* ·**gas** *or*
 ·**ga**) extinct horse
quag·gy (·**gi·er**, ·**gi·est**)
 marshy
quag·mire
qua·hog clam
quail (*plural* **quails** *or*
 quail)
quaint
quaint·ness
quake
Quak·er
Quak·er·ism
quaki·ly
quaki·ness
quaky (**quaki·er**,
 quaki·est)

qua·le (*plural* ·**lia**)
 philosophy term
quali·fi·able
quali·fi·ca·tion
quali·fi·ca·tory
quali·fied
quali·fi·er
quali·fy (·**fies**, ·**fy·ing**,
 ·**fied**)
quali·fy·ing·ly
quali·ta·tive
qual·ity (*plural* ·**ities**)
qualm
qualm·ish
quam·ash plant
quan·da·ry (*plural* ·**ries**)
quan·dong (*or* ·**dang**,
 ·**tong**) fruit tree
quango (*plural* **quangos**)
quant punting pole
quan·tal
quan·tic maths term
quan·ti·fi·able
quan·ti·fi·ca·tion
quan·ti·fi·er
quan·ti·fy (·**fies**, ·**fy·ing**,
 ·**fied**)
quan·ti·ta·tive (*or*
 quan·ti·tive)
quan·tity (*plural* ·**tities**)
quan·ti·za·tion (*or*
 ·**sa·tion**)
quan·tize (*or* ·**tise**)
quan·tum (*plural* ·**ta**)
qua·qua·ver·sal geology
 term
quar·an·tine
quare *Irish* remarkable
quark
quar·rel (·**rel·ling**, ·**relled**;
 US ·**rel·ing**, ·**reled**)
quar·rel·ler (*US* ·**rel·er**)
quar·rel·some
quar·rian bird

quincentenary

quar·ri·er (*or*
  quarry·man; *plural* ·ers
  or ·men)
quar·ry (*noun, plural*
  ·ries; *verb* ·ries, ·ry·ing,
  ·ried)
quart
quar·tan every third day
quar·ter
quar·ter·age quarterly
  payment
quarter·back
quarter·bound
quarter·deck
quar·tered
quarter·final
quarter·hour
quar·ter·ing
quarter·light window
quar·ter·ly (*plural* ·lies)
quarter·master
quar·tern measure of weight
quar·ters
quarter·saw (·saw·ing,
  ·sawed, ·sawed *or*
  ·sawn)
quarter·staff (*plural*
  ·staves)
quar·tet (*or* ·tette)
quar·tic maths term
quar·tile
quar·to (*plural* ·tos)
quartz
quartz·if·er·ous
quartz·ite
qua·sar
quash
quas·sia tree
qua·ter·cen·te·nary
  (*plural* ·naries)
Qua·ter·nary geological
  period
qua·ter·nary (*plural*
  ·naries) of four; fourth
qua·ter·ni·on maths term
qua·ter·ni·ty (*plural* ·ties)
  group of four
quat·rain
qua·tre playing card
quatre·foil
quat·tro·cen·to 15th
  century
qua·ver
qua·ver·er
qua·ver·ing·ly
qua·very (*or* ·ver·ous)
quay

quay·age
quay·side
quea·si·ly
quea·si·ness
quea·sy (·si·er, ·si·est)
Que·bec
Qué·be·cois (*plural* ·cois)
que·bra·cho (*plural* ·chos)
  tree
Quech·ua (*or* Kech·ua;
  plural ·uas *or* ·ua)
  American Indian
Quech·uan (*or* Kech·)
queen
queen·cake
queen·dom
queen·li·ness
queen·ly (·li·er, ·li·est)
Queens New York borough
Queens·ber·ry rules
Queens·land
queer
queer·ness
quell
quell·er
quel·que·chose
  insignificant thing
quench
quench·able
quench·er
que·nelle dumpling
quer·cetin (*or* ·ci·tin)
  pigment
quer·cine of the oak
Que·réta·ro Mexican state
que·rist questioner
quern stone hand mill
queru·lous
queru·lous·ness
que·ry (*noun, plural* ·ries;
  verb ·ries, ·ry·ing,
  ·ried)
quest
quest·er
quest·ing·ly
ques·tion
ques·tion·able
ques·tion·able·ness (*or*
  ·abil·ity)
ques·tion·ably
ques·tion·ary
ques·tion·er
ques·tion·ing
ques·tion·less
ques·tion·naire
Quet·ta Pakistani city
quet·zal bird

Quet·zal·coa·tl Aztec god
queue (queu·ing, queued)
  line; pigtail; *compare* cue
Que·zon City Philippine
  capital
quib·ble
quib·bler
quib·bling·ly
Qui·beron French
  peninsula
quiche
quick
quick·en
quick-freeze (-freezing,
  -froze, -frozen)
quickie
quick·lime
quick·ly
quick·ness
quick·sand
quick·set hedge
quick·silver
quick·step (·step·ping,
  ·stepped)
quick-tempered
quick-witted
quick-witted·ness
quid
quid·dity (*plural* ·dities)
quid·nunc gossipmonger
quid pro quo (*plural* quid
  pro quos)
qui·es·cence (*or* ·cen·cy)
qui·es·cent
qui·et
qui·et·en
qui·et·ism form of
  mysticism
qui·et·ness
qui·etude
qui·etus (*plural* ·etuses)
quiff
quill
quil·lai tree
quill·wort
Quil·mes Argentine city
quilt
quilt·er
quilt·ing
quin
qui·na·ry (*noun, plural*
  ·ries) consisting of five
qui·nate composed of five
  parts
quince
quin·cen·te·nary (*plural*
  ·naries)

quin·cun·cial

quin·cunx arrangement of five

quin·deca·gon 15-sided figure

quin·deca·plet group of 15

quin·de·cen·nial

Qui Nhong Vietnamese port

quini·dine

qui·nine

quin·ol

quino·line

qui·none

quino·noid (or quin·oid)

quin·qua·genar·ian

Quin·qua·gesi·ma

quin·que·fo·li·ate

quin·quen·nial

quin·quen·nial·ly

quin·quen·nium (plural ·nia)

quin·que·par·tite

quin·que·reme ship

quin·que·va·len·cy (or ·lence)

quin·que·va·lent

quin·sy

quint organ stop; piquet term

quin·tain tilting target

quin·tal unit of weight

quin·tan recurring every fourth day

quin·tes·sence

quin·tes·sen·tial

quin·tes·sen·tial·ly

quin·tet (or ·tette)

quin·tic maths term

quin·tile astrology term

quin·til·lion (plural ·lions or ·lion) 10^{30}

quin·til·lionth

quin·tu·ple

quin·tu·plet

quin·tu·pli·cate

quin·tu·pli·ca·tion

quip (·quip·ping, ·quipped)

quip·ster

quire set of paper; compare choir

Quiri·nal Roman hill

Quirinus Roman god

quirk

quirki·ly

quirki·ness

quirky (quirki·er, quirki·est)

quirt whip

quis·ling

quist Dialect wood pigeon

quit (quit·ting, quit·ted or quit)

quitch grass

quit·claim legal term

quite

Qui·to Ecuadorian capital

quits

quit·tance

quit·ter one that quits

quit·tor horse's foot infection

quiv·er

quiv·er·er

quiv·er·ful

quiv·er·ing·ly

quiv·ery

qui vive French attentive

quix·ot·ic (or ·oti·cal)

quix·oti·cal·ly

quixo·tism

quiz (noun, plural quiz·zes; verb quiz·zes, quiz·zing, quizzed)

quiz·master

quiz·zer

quiz·zi·cal

quiz·zi·cal·ity

quiz·zi·cal·ly

quod Slang jail; compare quad

quod erat de·mon·stran·dum Latin which was to be proved

quod·li·bet piece of music

quod·li·beti·cal

quod·li·beti·cal·ly

quoin (or coign, coigne) cornerstone

quoit

quoits

quok·ka wallaby

quon·dam former

quor·um

quo·ta

quot·abil·ity

quot·able

quo·ta·tion

quote

quoth Archaic said

quo·tid·ian daily

quo·tient

quo war·ran·to legal term

R

Ra (or Re) Egyptian god

Ra·bat Moroccan capital

ra·ba·to (or re·; plural ·tos) collar

rab·bet variant of rebate

rab·bi (or ·bin; plural ·bis or ·bins)

rab·bin·ate office of rabbi

Rab·bin·ic language

rab·bini·cal (or ·bin·ic)

rab·bin·ism

rab·bit note Welsh rabbit (or rarebit)

rab·bit·er

rabbit·fish (plural ·fish or ·fishes)

rab·bit·ry (plural ·ries)

rab·bity

rab·ble

rab·bler

rabble-rouser

rabble-rousing

Rab·elai·sian

rabi Indian crop

rab·id

ra·bid·ity (or rab·id·ness)

ra·bies

rac·coon (or ra·coon)

race

race·card

race·course

race·go·er

race·horse

ra·ceme botany term

ra·cemic chemistry term

rac·emism

rac·emi·za·tion (or ·sa·tion)

rac·emize

rac·emose (*or* ·emous) botany term

rac·er

race·track

ra·chial (*or* ·chid·ial, rha·)

ra·chis (*or* rha·; *plural* ·chises *or* ·chi·des) biology term

ra·chit·ic

ra·chi·tis rickets

Rach·man·ism exploitation of tenants

ra·cial

ra·cial·ly

raci·ly

raci·ness

rac·ing

rac·ism (*or* ra·cial·ism)

rac·ist (*or* ra·cial·ist)

rack frame; toothed bar; to strain; etc.; *compare* wrack

rack (*or* wrack) destruction, *esp. in* rack and ruin

rack-and-pinion

rack·er

rack·et disturbance; dishonest practice

rack·et (*or* rac·quet) bat

rack·et·eer

rack·ets game

rack·ety

rack-rent

rack-renter

rac·on·teur

ra·coon *variant spelling of* raccoon

rac·quet *variant spelling of* racket

racy (raci·er, raci·est)

rad unit

ra·dar

radar·scope

rad·dle

rad·dled

ra·dial

ra·dial·ly

radial-ply

ra·dian unit

ra·di·ance (*or* ·an·cy; *plural* ·ances *or* ·an·cies)

ra·di·ant

ra·di·ate

ra·dia·tion

ra·dia·tion·al

ra·dia·tive (*or* ·tory)

ra·dia·tor

radi·cal basic; extreme; chemistry term; *compare* radicle

radi·cal·ism

radi·cal·is·tic

radi·cal·is·ti·cal·ly

radi·cal·ly

radi·cal·ness

radi·cand maths term

radi·cel tiny root

radi·ces *plural of* radix

radi·cle embryonic plant root; *compare* radical

ra·dii *plural of* radius

ra·dio (*noun, plural* ·dios; *verb* ·dios, ·dio·ing, ·di·oed)

radio·ac·ti·vate

radio·ac·ti·va·tion

radio·ac·tive

radio·ac·tiv·ity

radio·bio·logi·cal

radio·bi·olo·gist

radio·bi·ol·ogy

radio·car·bon

radio·chemi·cal

radio·chem·ist

radio·chem·is·try

radio·com·mu·ni·ca·tion

radio·el·ement

radio·gen·ic

radio·gram

radio·graph

ra·di·og·ra·pher

radio·graph·ic

ra·di·og·ra·phy

radio·iso·tope

radio·iso·top·ic

radio·lar·ian marine organism

radio·lo·ca·tion·al

radio·logi·cal

ra·di·olo·gist

ra·di·ol·ogy

radio·lu·cent

radio·lu·mi·nes·cence

radio·lu·mi·nes·cent

ra·di·oly·sis

ra·di·om·eter

radio·met·ric

ra·di·om·etry

ra·dio·mi·crom·eter

radio·nu·clide

radio·pac·ity (*or* radio-opacity)

radio·paque (*or* radio-opaque) impervious to X-rays

radio·phone

radio·phon·ic

radio·phoni·cal·ly

ra·di·opho·ny

radio·scope

radio·scop·ic

radio·scopi·cal·ly

ra·di·os·co·py

radio·sen·si·tive

radio·sen·si·tiv·ity

radio·sonde meteorological device

radio·tele·gram

radio·tele·graph

radio·tele·graph·ic

radio·tele·graphi·cal·ly

radio·teleg·ra·phy

radio·telem·etry

radio·tele·phone

radio·tele·phon·ic

radio·telepho·ny

radio·tele·type

radio·thera·peu·tic

radio·thera·peu·ti·cal·ly

radio·thera·pist

radio·thera·py

radio·thermy

radio·tox·ic

rad·ish

ra·dium radioactive element

ra·dius (*plural* ·dii *or* ·di·uses)

ra·dix (*plural* ·di·ces *or* ·dixes) maths or biology term

Rad·nor·shire former Welsh county

Ra·dom Polish city

ra·dome radar antenna's housing

ra·don radioactive element

radu·la (*plural* ·lae) zoology term

radu·lar

raff *Dialect* rubbish

raf·fia (*or* raphia)

raf·fi·nate chemistry term

raf·fi·nose sugar

raff·ish

raff·ish·ness

raf·fle

raf·fler

raf·fle·sia plant

raft

raft·er

rag (rag·ging, ragged)

raga musical term

raga·muf·fin

rag·bag

rage

ragged teased

rag·ged tattered

rag·ged·ness

rag·gedy

raggle-taggle

ragi (or rag·gee, rag·gy) cereal

rag·lan

rag·man (plural ·men)

ra·gout stew

rag·tag

rag·time

rag·weed

rag·worm

rag·wort

raid

raid·er

rail

rail·car

rail·er

rail·head

rail·ing

rail·lery (plural ·leries)

rail·road

rail·way

rail·way·man (plural ·men)

rai·ment

rain

rain·band

rain·bird

rain·bow

rain·check

rain·coat

rain·drop

rain·fall

Rai·ni·er US mountain

raini·ly

raini·ness

rain·maker

rain·making

rain·out radioactive fallout

rain·proof

rain·storm

rain·water

rain·wear

rainy (raini·er, raini·est)

rais·able (or raise·)

raise elevate; compare raze

rais·er

rai·sin

rais·ing

rai·siny

rai·son d'être (plural rai·sons d'être)

raj

ra·jah (or raja)

Ra·ja·sthan Indian state

Raj·kot Indian city

Raj·put (or ·poot) Indian clan

Ra·jya Sa·bha chamber of Indian parliament

rake

rake-off (noun)

rak·er

raki (or ra·kee) drink

rak·ish

rak·ish·ly

rak·ish·ness

rale (or râle) medical term

Ra·leigh US city

ral·len·tan·do musical term

ral·li·er

ral·line ornithology term

ral·ly (verb ·lies, ·ly·ing, ·lied; noun, plural ·lies)

ral·ly·cross

ram (ram·ming, rammed)

Rama Hindu hero

Ramachandra mythological character

Rama·dan (or Rhama·dhan, Rama·zan) period in Muslim year

Ra·mat Gan Israeli city

ram·ble

ram·bler

ram·bling

Ram·bouil·let sheep

ram·bunc·tious Slang boisterous

ram·bu·tan fruit

ram·ekin (or ·equin)

ram·en·ta·ceous

ra·men·tum (plural ·ta) fern scale

ramie (or ramee) fibre

rami·fi·ca·tion

rami·form

rami·fy (·fies, ·fy·ing, ·fied)

Ra·mil·lies Belgian battle site

ram·jet

rammed

ram·mer

ram·ming

ram·mish (or ram·my)

ra·mose (or ·mous) branched

ra·mos·ity

ramp

ram·page

ram·pa·geous

ram·pa·geous·ness

ram·pag·er

ram·pan·cy

ram·pant

ram·part

ram·pi·on plant

Ram·pur Indian city

ram·rod

Rams·gate

ram·shack·le

ram·sons plant

ram·til plant

ramu·lose (or ·lous)

ra·mus (plural rami) biology term

rance marble

ranch

ranch·er

ran·che·ro (plural ·ros) US rancher

Ran·chi Indian city

ran·cid

ran·cid·ness (or ·ity)

ran·cor·ous

ran·cor·ous·ness

ran·cour (US ·cor)

rand

ran·dan boat

randi·ly

randi·ness

ran·dom

ran·domi·za·tion (or ·sa·tion)

ran·dom·ize (or ·ise)

ran·dom·ness

randy (randi·er, randi·est)

rang

range

range·finder

Rang·er senior Guide

rang·er

rangi·ly

rangi·ness

Ran·goon Burmese capital

rangy (rangi·er, rangi·est)

rani (or ra·nee) Indian queen or princess

rank

rank·er

Rankine scale

rank·ing

ran·kle

rank·ness

ran·sack

ran·sack·er

ran·som

ran·som·er

rant

rant·er

rant·ing·ly

ra·nun·cu·la·ceous botany term

ra·nun·cu·lus (*plural* ·luses *or* ·li) plant

rap (rap·ping, rapped) strike; *compare* wrap

ra·pa·cious

ra·pac·ity (*or* ·pa·cious·ness)

Rapa Nui Easter Island

rape

rape·seed

Rapha·el·esque

ra·phe (*plural* ·phae) botany term

raphia *variant spelling of* raffia

ra·phide (*or* ra·phis; *plural* raphi·des) botany term

rap·id

ra·pid·ity (*or* rap·id·ness)

rap·ids

ra·pi·er

rap·ine (*noun*)

rap·ist

rap·pa·ree Irish soldier

rapped *past tense of* rap; *compare* rapt

rap·pee snuff

rap·pel (·pel·ling, ·pelled) mountaineering technique

rap·per

rap·ping

rap·port harmony

rap·por·teur preparer of report

rap·proche·ment

rap·scal·lion

rapt engrossed; *compare* rapped

rap·tor bird of prey

rap·to·rial

rap·ture

rap·tur·ous

rap·tur·ous·ness

rara avis (*plural* ra·rae aves) *Latin* unusual person or thing

rare

rare·bit *variant of* (Welsh) rabbit

rar·efac·tion (*or* ·efi·ca·tion)

rar·efac·tion·al (*or* ·efac·tive)

rar·efi·able

rar·efi·er

rar·efy (·fies, ·fy·ing, ·fied)

rare·ly

rare·ripe *US* ripening early

rar·ing

rar·ity (*plural* ·ities)

Ra·ro·ton·ga Pacific island

ras·bo·ra fish

ras·cal

ras·cal·ity (*plural* ·ities)

ras·cal·ly

rase *variant spelling of* raze

rash

rash·er

rash·ness

Rasht (*or* **Resht**) Iranian city

ra·so·rial zoology term

rasp

ras·pa·tory (*plural* ·tories) surgical instrument

rasp·berry (*plural* ·berries)

rasp·er

rasp·ing (*or* raspy)

rasse civet; *compare* wrasse

Ras·ta·far·ian (*or* **Ras·ta**)

ras·ter electronics term

rat (rat·ting, rat·ted)

ra·ta tree

rat·abil·ity (*or* ·able·ness, rate·)

rat·able (*or* rate·)

rat·ably (*or* rate·)

rata·fia (*or* ·fee) liqueur; biscuit

ra·tal ratable value

ra·tan *variant spelling of* rattan

rata·tat-tat (*or* rata·tat)

ra·ta·touille vegetable stew

rat·bag

ratch·et

rate

rate·able *variant spelling of* ratable

ra·tel animal

rate·payer

rat·fink

rat·fish (*plural* ·fish *or* ·fishes)

rathe (*or* rath) *Archaic* blossoming early

ra·ther

rati·fi·able

rati·fi·ca·tion

rati·fi·er

rati·fy (·fies, ·fy·ing, ·fied)

ra·tine (*or* ra·teen, rat·teen, rati·né) cloth

rat·ing

ra·tio (*plural* ·tios)

ra·ti·oci·nate argue logically

ra·ti·oci·na·tion

ra·ti·oci·na·tor

ra·tion

ra·tion·al using reason

ra·tion·ale basis

ra·tion·al·ism

ra·tion·al·ist

ra·tion·al·is·tic

ra·tion·al·is·ti·cal·ly

ra·tion·al·ity (*plural* ·ities)

ra·tion·ali·za·tion (*or* ·sa·tion)

ra·tion·al·ize (*or* ·ise)

ra·tion·al·iz·er (*or* ·is·er)

ra·tion·al·ly

ra·tions

Rat·is·bon Regensburg

rat·ite flightless bird

Rat·lam Indian city

rat·line (*or* ·lin) nautical term

ra·toon (*or* rat·toon) new shoot

rats·bane

rat·tail fish; horse; file

rat·tan (*or* ra·tan)

rat·ted

rat·ter

rat·ti·ly

rat·ti·ness

rat·ting

rat·tish

rat·tle

rattle·box

rat·tler

rattle·snake

rattle·trap

rat·tling
rat·tly (·tli·er, ·tli·est)
rat·trap
rat·ty (·ti·er, ·ti·est)
rau·cous
rau·cous·ness (or rau·city)
raun·chy (·chi·er, ·chi·est)
rau·wol·fia drug
rav·age
rav·age·ment
rav·ag·er
rave
rav·el (·el·ling, ·elled; US ·el·ing, ·eled)
rave·lin fortification
rav·el·ler (US ·el·er)
rav·el·ly
ra·ven bird
rav·en to plunder
rav·en·er
rav·en·ing
Ra·ven·na Italian city
rav·en·ous
rav·en·ous·ness
rav·er
rave-up
ra·vine
rav·ing
ra·vio·li
rav·ish
rav·ish·er
rav·ish·ing
rav·ish·ment
raw
Ra·wal·pin·di
raw·boned
raw·hide
ra·win·sonde meteorological balloon
raw·ness
ray
ray·less
ray·let
ray·on
raze (or rase) destroy; compare raise
razee ship
raz·er (or ras·) demolisher; compare razor
ra·zoo Austral small sum of money
ra·zor shaver; compare razer
razor·back whale
razor·bill
razor-cut (-cutting, -cut)
razz Slang deride

razz·ma·tazz (or razzle-dazzle)
re concerning
re·ab·sorb
reach
reach·able
reach·er
re·act act in response
re·act act again
re·ac·tance physics term
re·ac·tant
re·ac·tion
re·ac·tion·al
re·ac·tion·ary (plural ·aries)
re·ac·tion·ism
re·ac·ti·vate
re·ac·ti·va·tion
re·ac·tive
re·ac·tiv·ity (or ·tive·ness)
re·ac·tor
read (read·ing, read)
read·abil·ity (or ·able·ness)
read·able
read·ably
re·ad·dress
read·er
read·er·ship
read·ily
readi·ness
Read·ing
re·adjust
re·adjust·able
re·adjust·er
re·adjust·ment
re·admis·sion
re·admit (·admit·ting, ·admit·ted)
re·admit·tance
read-out (noun)
ready (adj readi·er, readi·est; verb readies, ready·ing, readied)
ready-made
ready-mix
ready-to-wear
ready-witted
re·affirm
re·affir·ma·tion (or ·affirm·ance)
re·affor·est (or ·for·est)
re·affor·esta·tion (or ·for·esta·tion)
re·agent
real actual

real (plural reals or rea·les) Spanish coin
real (plural reis) Portuguese coin
re·al·gar mineral
re·align
re·align·ment
re·al·ism
re·al·ist
re·al·is·tic
re·al·is·ti·cal·ly
re·al·ity (plural ·ities)
re·al·iz·able (or ·is·able)
re·al·iz·ably (or ·is·ably)
re·ali·za·tion (or ·sa·tion)
re·al·ize (or ·ise)
re·al·iz·er (or ·is·er)
re·allo·cate
re·allo·ca·tion
re·al·ly
realm
Re·al·po·li·tik German opportunistic politics
re·al·tor US estate agent
re·al·ty real property
ream
ream·er
re·ani·mate
re·ani·ma·tion
reap
reap·able
reap·er
re·appear
re·appear·ance
re·apply (·applies, ·apply·ing, ·applied)
re·appoint
re·appoint·ment
re·appor·tion
re·apprais·al
re·appraise
rear
rear·er
rear-guard
re·arm
rear·most
re·arrange
re·arrange·ment
re·arrang·er
rear·ward (adj)
rear·wards (adv)
rea·son
rea·son·able
rea·son·able·ness (or ·abil·ity)
rea·son·ably
rea·soned

rea·son·er
rea·son·ing
re·as·sem·ble
re·assur·ance
re·assure
re·assur·er
re·assur·ing
rea·ta *variant spelling of* riata
re·awak·en
reb *US* Confederate soldier
re·bar·ba·tive
re·bat·able (*or* ·bate·)
re·bate refund
re·bate (*or* rab·bet)
  carpentry term
re·bat·er
re·bec (*or* ·beck) musical
  instrument
re·bel (·bel·ling, ·belled)
re·bel·lion
re·bel·lious
re·bel·lious·ness
re·birth
re·born
re·bound
re·buff
re·build (·build·ing, ·built)
re·buk·able
re·buke
re·buk·er
re·buk·ing·ly
re·bus (*plural* ·buses)
  picture puzzle
re·but (·but·ting, ·but·ted)
re·but·table
re·but·tal
re·but·ter
rec *Slang* recreation ground
re·cal·ci·trance (*or*
  ·tran·cy)
re·cal·ci·trant
re·cal·esce
re·ca·les·cence chemistry
  term
re·ca·les·cent
re·call
re·call·able
re·cant
re·can·ta·tion
re·cant·er
re·cap (·cap·ping,
  ·capped)
re·capi·tali·za·tion (*or*
  ·sa·tion)
re·capi·tal·ize (*or* ·ise)
re·ca·pitu·late
re·ca·pitu·la·tion

re·ca·pitu·la·tive (*or* ·tory)
re·cap·tion legal term
re·cap·ture
re·cast (·cast·ing, ·cast)
rec·ce (·ce·ing, ·ced *or*
  ·ceed) *Slang* reconnoitre;
  reconnaissance
re·cede withdraw
re·cede restore
re·ceipt
re·ceipt·or
re·ceiv·able
re·ceive
re·ceiv·er
re·ceiv·er·ship
re·cen·sion literary revision
re·cent
re·cent·ness (*or* ·cen·cy)
re·cept psychology term
re·cep·ta·cle
re·cep·tion
re·cep·tion·ist
re·cep·tive
re·cep·tiv·ity (*or*
  ·tive·ness)
re·cep·tor
re·cess
re·ces·sion
re·ces·sion·al
re·ces·sive
re·ces·sive·ness
Rech·abite teetotaller
re·charge
ré·chauf·fé warmed-up food
re·cher·ché exquisite; rare
re·chris·ten
re·cidi·vism
re·cidi·vist
re·cidi·vis·tic (*or*
  ·cidi·vous)
(recieve) *incorrect spelling of*
  receive
Re·ci·fe Brazilian port
reci·pe
re·cipi·ence
re·cipi·ent
re·cip·ro·cal
re·cip·ro·cal·ity (*or* ·ness)
re·cip·ro·cal·ly
re·cip·ro·cate
re·cip·ro·ca·tion
re·cip·ro·ca·tive (*or* ·tory)
re·cip·ro·ca·tor
reci·proc·ity
re·ci·sion cancellation
re·cit·able
re·cit·al

reci·ta·tion
reci·ta·tive (*or* ·ta·ti·vo)
re·cite
re·cit·er
reck·less
reck·less·ness
Reck·ling·hau·sen West
  German city
reck·on
reck·on·er
reck·on·ing
re·claim
re·claim·able
re·claim·ant (*or* ·er)
rec·la·ma·tion
ré·clame acclaim
re·clin·able
rec·li·nate bent backwards
rec·li·na·tion
re·cline
re·clin·er
re·clothe
re·cluse
re·clu·sion
re·clu·sive
rec·og·ni·tion
rec·og·ni·tion·al (*or*
  ·ni·tive, ·ni·tory)
rec·og·niz·abil·ity (*or*
  ·nis·)
rec·og·niz·able (*or* ·nis·)
rec·og·niz·ably (*or* ·nis·)
re·cog·ni·zance (*or*
  ·sance)
rec·og·nize (*or* ·nise)
rec·og·ni·zee (*or* ·see)
rec·og·niz·er (*or* ·nis·er *or*
  in legal contexts
  ·ni·zor, ·ni·sor)
re·coil
re·coil·er
re·coil·ing·ly
re·coil·less
rec·ol·lect
rec·ol·lec·tion
rec·ol·lec·tive
re·com·bi·nant
re·com·bi·na·tion
re·com·bine
re·com·mence
re·com·mence·ment
rec·om·mend
rec·om·mend·able
rec·om·men·da·tion
rec·om·menda·tory
rec·om·mend·er

re·com·mit (·mit·ting,
·mit·ted)
re·com·mit·ment (or
·mit·tal)
rec·om·pen·sable
rec·om·pense
rec·om·pens·er
re·com·pose
re·com·po·si·tion
rec·on·cil·abil·ity (or
·able·ness)
rec·on·cil·able
rec·on·cil·ably
rec·on·cile
rec·on·cile·ment
rec·on·cil·er
rec·on·cilia·tion
rec·on·cilia·tory
rec·on·cil·ing·ly
re·con·dite
re·con·dite·ness
re·con·di·tion
re·con·di·tion·er
re·con·nais·sance (or
·nois·sance)
rec·on·noi·tre (US ·ter)
rec·on·noi·trer (US
·ter·er)
re·con·sid·er
re·con·sid·era·tion
re·con·stitu·ent
re·con·sti·tute
re·con·sti·tut·ed
re·con·sti·tu·tion
re·con·struct
re·con·struc·tible
re·con·struc·tion
re·con·struc·tive (or
·tion·al)
re·con·struc·tor
re·con·vene
re·con·ver·sion
re·con·vert
rec·ord (noun)
re·cord (verb)
re·cord·able
record-changer
re·cord·er
re·cord·ing
record-player
re·count relate
re·count count again
re·count·al
re·coup
re·coup·able
re·coup·ment
re·course

re·cov·er regain
re-cover cover again
re·cov·er·abil·ity
re·cov·er·able
re·cov·er·er
re·cov·ery (plural ·eries)
re·create
re-creation new creation
rec·rea·tion enjoyment
rec·rea·tion·al
re-creator
rec·re·ment waste matter
rec·re·men·tal
re·crimi·nate
re·crimi·na·tion
re·crimi·na·tive (or ·tory)
re·crimi·na·tor
re·cru·desce
re·cru·des·cence
re·cruit
re·cruit·able
re·cruit·er
re·cruit·ment
re·crys·tal·li·za·tion (or
·sa·tion)
re·crys·tal·lize (or ·lise)
rec·ta plural of rectum
rec·tal
rec·tan·gle
rec·tan·gu·lar
rec·tan·gu·lar·ity
rec·ti plural of rectus
rec·ti·fi·able
rec·ti·fi·ca·tion
rec·ti·fi·er
rec·ti·fy (·fies, ·fy·ing,
·fied)
rec·ti·lin·ear (or ·eal)
rec·ti·tude
rec·to (plural ·tos) right-
hand page
rec·to·cele hernia
rec·tor
rec·tor·ate
rec·tor·ial
rec·tor·ship
rec·tory (plural ·tories)
rec·trix (plural ·tri·ces)
tail feather
rec·tum (plural ·tums or
·ta) part of intestine
rec·tus (plural ·ti) muscle
re·cum·bence (or ·ben·cy)
re·cum·bent
re·cu·per·ate
re·cu·pera·tion
re·cu·pera·tive

re·cu·pera·tor
re·cur (·cur·ring, ·curred)
re·cur·rence
re·cur·rent
re·cur·ring·ly
re·cur·sion returning
re·curve
recu·sance (or ·san·cy)
recu·sant insubordinate
re·cy·cle
red (red·der, red·dest)
colour; variant spelling of
redd
re·dact prepare for
publication
re·dac·tion
re·dac·tion·al
re·dac·tor
re·dan fortification
red-blooded
red·breast
red·brick
red·bud tree
red·bug
red·cap
red·coat
red·cur·rant
redd (or red; red·ding,
redd or red·ded) Dialect
to tidy
red·den
red·dish
Red·ditch
red·dle variant spelling of
ruddle
re·deco·rate
re·deem
re·deem·abil·ity
re·deem·able (or
re·demp·tible)
re·deem·ably
re·deem·er
re·deem·ing
re·deliv·er
re·deliv·ery
re·demand
re·demand·able
re·demp·tion
re·demp·tion·al (or ·tive,
·tory)
re·demp·tion·er emigrant
to America
Re·demp·tor·ist Catholic
missionary
re·deploy
re·deploy·ment
re·de·sign

re·devel·op
re·devel·op·er
re·devel·op·ment
red·eye
red·faced
red·fin fish
red·fish (*plural* ·fish *or*
·fishes)
red·handed
red·head
red·headed
red·hot
re·dia (*plural* ·diae)
zoology term
re·dial (·dial·ling, ·dialled;
US ·dial·ing, ·dialed)
Re·dif·fu·sion
(*Trademark*)
red·in·gote overcoat
red·in·te·grate renew
red·in·te·gra·tion
red·in·te·gra·tive
re·di·rect
re·di·rec·tion
re·dis·count
re·dis·cov·er
re·dis·cov·ery (*plural*
·eries)
re·dis·trib·ute
re·dis·tri·bu·tion
red·neck
red·ness
redo (re·does, ·do·ing,
·did, ·done)
redo·lence (*or* ·len·cy)
redo·lent
re·dou·ble
re·doubt fortification
re·doubt·able
re·doubt·able·ness
re·doubt·ably
re·dound affect
redo·wa folk dance
re·dox chemistry term
red·poll bird
re·draft
re·draw (·drawing, ·drew,
·drawn)
re·dress put right
re·dress dress again
re·dress·able (*or* ·ible)
re·dress·er (*or* ·dres·sor)
red·root plant
red·shank bird
red·skin
red·start bird
re·duce

re·duc·er
re·duc·ibil·ity
re·duc·ible
re·duc·tase enzyme
re·duc·tio ad ab·sur·dum
re·duc·tion
re·duc·tion·al (*or* ·tive)
re·dun·dan·cy (*plural*
·cies)
re·dun·dant
re·du·pli·cate
re·du·pli·ca·tion
re·du·pli·ca·tive
re·du·vi·id insect
red·ware seaweed
red·wing bird
red·wood
re·echo (·echoes,
·echoing, ·echoed)
reed
reed·buck (*plural* ·bucks
or ·buck) antelope
reedi·ness
reed·ing moulding
reed·ling bird
re·educate
re·education
reedy (reedi·er, reedi·est)
reef
reef·er
reek
reek·ing·ly
reeky
reel
reel·able
reel·ably
re·elect
re·election
reel·er
re·em·ploy
re·em·ploy·ment
reen (*or* rean) *Dialect* ditch
re·enact
re·enforce enforce again;
compare reinforce
re·enforce·ment
re·enforc·er
re·enter
re·entrance
re·entrant
re·entry (*plural* -entries)
reeve (reev·ing, reeved *or*
rove) nautical term; bird;
medieval official
re·examin·able
re·examina·tion
re·examine

re·examin·er
re·export
re·exporta·tion
re·export·er
ref *Slang* referee
re·face
re·fash·ion
re·fec·tion
re·fec·tory (*plural* ·tories)
re·fer (·fer·ring, ·ferred)
ref·er·able (*or*
re·fer·rable)
ref·eree (·eree·ing,
·ereed)
ref·er·ence
ref·er·enc·er
ref·er·en·dum (*plural*
·dums *or* ·da)
ref·er·ent
ref·er·en·tial of a reference;
compare reverential
re·fer·ral
re·fer·rer
re·fill
re·fill·able
re·fin·able
re·fi·nance
re·fine
re·fined
re·fine·ment
re·fin·er
re·fin·ery (*plural* ·eries)
re·fin·ish
re·fin·ish·er
re·fit (·fit·ting, ·fit·ted)
re·flate
re·fla·tion
re·flect
re·flec·tance
re·flect·ing·ly
re·flec·tion (*or* ·flex·ion)
re·flec·tion·al (*or*
·flex·ion·al)
re·flec·tive contemplative;
able to reflect; *compare*
reflexive
re·flec·tive·ness (*or*
·tiv·ity)
re·flec·tor
re·flet lustre
re·flex
re·flex·ion *variant spelling*
of reflection
re·flex·ive grammar term;
compare reflective
re·flex·ive·ness (*or* ·iv·ity)
re·flex·ol·ogy therapy

re·flux
re·form improve
re·form form again
re·form·able
Ref·or·ma·tion religious movement
ref·or·ma·tion
re·formation
ref·or·ma·tion·al
re·forma·tive
re·forma·tory (*plural* ·tories)
re·formed
re·form·er
re·form·ism
re·form·ist
re·fract
re·fract·able
re·frac·tion
re·frac·tion·al
re·frac·tive
re·frac·tive·ness (*or* ·tiv·ity)
re·frac·tom·eter
re·frac·to·met·ric
re·frac·tom·etry
re·frac·tor
re·frac·to·ri·ly
re·frac·to·ri·ness
re·frac·tory (*plural* ·tories)
re·frain
re·frain·er
re·frain·ment
re·fran·gibil·ity (*or* ·gible·ness)
re·fran·gible
re·freeze (·freez·ing, ·froze, ·fro·zen)
re·fresh (*or* ·fresh·en)
re·fresh·er
re·fresh·ful
re·fresh·ing
re·fresh·ment
re·frig·er·ant
re·frig·er·ate
re·frig·era·tion
re·frig·era·tive (*or* ·tory)
re·frig·era·tor
re·frin·gen·cy (*or* ·gence)
re·frin·gent
re·froze
re·fu·el (·el·ling, ·elled; *US* ·el·ing, ·eled)
ref·uge
refu·gee
refu·gee·ism

re·fu·gium (*plural* ·gia)
re·ful·gence (*or* ·gen·cy)
re·ful·gent shining
re·fund give back money
re·fund replace bond issue
re·fund·able
re·fund·er
re·fur·bish
re·fur·bish·ment
re·fus·able
re·fus·al
re·fuse decline
ref·use rubbish
re·fus·er
refu·tabil·ity
refu·table
refu·ta·tion
re·fute
re·fut·er
re·gain
re·gain·able
re·gain·er
re·gal royal
re·gale amuse
re·gale·ment
re·ga·lia
re·gal·ity (*plural* ·ities)
re·gal·ly
re·gard
re·gard·able
re·gar·dant heraldic term
re·gard·ful
re·gard·ing
re·gard·less
re·gards
re·gat·ta
re·ge·late
re·ge·la·tion physics term
Re·gen·cy historical period
re·gen·cy (*plural* ·cies) rule by regent
re·gen·er·able
re·gen·era·cy
re·gen·er·ate
re·gen·era·tion
re·gen·era·tive
re·gen·era·tor
Re·gens·burg West German city
re·gent
re·gent·al
re·gent·ship
reg·gae
Reg·gio di Ca·la·bria Italian port
Reg·gio nell'Emilia Italian city

regi·cid·al
regi·cide
re·gime (*or* ré·gime) administration
regi·men course of treatment
regi·ment
regi·men·tal
regi·men·tals military dress
regi·men·ta·tion
Re·gi·na the queen; Canadian city
re·gion
re·gion·al
re·gion·al·ism
re·gion·al·ist
re·gion·al·ly
reg·is·ter
reg·is·ter·er
reg·is·trable
reg·is·trant
reg·is·trar
reg·is·trar·ship
reg·is·tra·tion
reg·is·tra·tion·al
reg·is·try (*plural* ·tries)
Re·gius pro·fes·sor
reg·let
reg·nal of a sovereign
reg·nant reigning
rego·lith
re·gorge
rego·sol soil
re·grate buy up for profit
re·grat·er
re·gress
re·gres·sion
re·gres·sive
re·gres·sive·ness
re·gres·sor
re·gret (·gret·ting, ·gret·ted)
re·gret·ful
re·gret·ful·ly
re·gret·ful·ness
re·gret·table
re·gret·tably
re·gret·ter
re·group
re·growth
regu·lable
regu·lar
regu·lar·ity (*plural* ·ities)
regu·lari·za·tion (*or* ·sa·tion)
regu·lar·ize (*or* ·ise)
regu·late

relive

regu·la·tion
regu·la·tive (*or* ·tory)
regu·la·tor
regu·line
regu·lus (*plural* ·luses *or*
·li) impure metal
re·gur·gi·tant
re·gur·gi·tate
re·gur·gi·ta·tion
re·ha·bili·tate
re·ha·bili·ta·tion
re·ha·bili·ta·tive
re·hash
re·hear (·hear·ing, ·heard)
re·hears·al
re·hearse
re·hears·er
re·heat
re·heat·er
re·ho·bo·am wine bottle
re·house
Reich *German* kingdom or
republic
Reichs·mark (*plural*
·marks *or* ·mark)
currency
Reichs·tag *German*
assembly
rei·fi·ca·tion
rei·fier
rei·fy (·fies, ·fy·ing, ·fied)
make real
Rei·gate
reign rule; *compare* rein
re·im·burs·able
re·im·burse
re·im·burse·ment
re·im·burs·er
re·im·port
re·im·por·ta·tion
re·im·pose
re·im·po·si·tion
re·im·pres·sion
Reims (*or* Rheims)
French city
rein long strap; *compare*
reign
re·incar·nate
re·incar·na·tion
re·incar·na·tion·ist
rein·deer (*plural* ·deer *or*
·deers)
re·inforce strengthen;
compare re-enforce
re·inforce·ment
re·install
re·in·stal·la·tion

re·instate
re·instate·ment
re·insta·tor
re·insur·ance
re·insure
re·insur·er
re·intro·duce
re·intro·duc·tion
re·invest
re·invest·ment
re·issu·able
re·issue (·issu·ing,
·issued)
re·issu·er
re·it·er·ant
re·it·er·ate
re·it·era·tion
re·it·era·tive
re·ject
re·ject·able
re·ject·er (*or* ·jec·tor)
re·jec·tion
re·jec·tive
re·jig (·jig·ging, ·jigged)
re-equip
re·joice
re·joic·er
re·joic·ing
re·join
re·join·der
re·ju·venate (*or* ·venize,
·venise)
re·ju·vena·tion
re·ju·vena·tor
re·ju·venesce
re·ju·venes·cence
re·ju·venes·cent
re·kin·dle
re·la·bel (·bel·ling,
·belled; *US* ·bel·ing,
·beled)
re·lapse
re·laps·er
re·lat·able
re·late
re·lat·ed
re·lat·ed·ness
re·lat·er one that relates;
compare relator
re·la·tion
re·la·tion·al
re·la·tion·ship
rela·tive
rela·tive·ly
rela·tiv·ism
rela·tiv·ist
rela·tiv·is·tic

rela·tiv·is·ti·cal·ly
rela·tiv·ity
re·la·tor legal term; *compare*
relater
re·la·tum (*plural* ·ta) logic
term
re·lax
re·lax·able
re·lax·ant
re·laxa·tion
re·lax·ed·ly
re·lax·er
re·lax·in hormone
re·lay convey
re·lay (-laying, -laid) lay
again
re·lease
re·leas·er
rel·ega·table
rel·egate
rel·ega·tion
re·lent
re·lent·less
re·lent·less·ness
re·let (·let·ting, ·let)
rel·evance (*or* ·evan·cy)
rel·evant
re·li·abil·ity (*or*
·able·ness)
re·li·able
re·li·ably
re·li·ance
re·li·ant
rel·ic object from past
rel·ict biology term; widow
re·lief
re·liev·able
re·lieve
re·liev·er
re·li·gion
re·li·gion·ism
re·ligi·ose
re·ligi·os·ity
re·li·gious
re·li·gious·ness
re·line
re·lin·quish
re·lin·quish·er
re·lin·quish·ment
reli·quary (*plural*
·quaries)
re·liquiae fossil remains
rel·ish
rel·ish·able
rel·ish·ing·ly
re·liv·able
re·live

re·load
re·lo·cate
re·lo·ca·tion
re·luc·tance (*or* ·tan·cy)
re·luc·tant
rel·uc·tiv·ity (*plural* ·ities)
 physics term
rely (re·lies, rely·ing,
 re·lied)
re·made
re·main
re·main·der
remainder·man (*plural*
 ·men) legal term
re·mains
re·make (·mak·ing,
 ·made)
re·mand
re·mand·ment
rema·nence physics term
re·mark
re·mark·able
re·mark·able·ness (*or*
 ·abil·ity)
re·mark·ably
re·mark·er
re·marque (*or* ·mark)
 mark on engraved plate
re·mar·riage
re·mar·ry (·ries, ·ry·ing,
 ·ried)
re·match
re·medi·able
re·medi·ably
re·medial
re·medial·ly
rem·edi·less
rem·edy (*noun, plural*
 ·edies; *verb* ·edies,
 ·edy·ing, ·edied)
re·mem·ber
re·mem·ber·er
re·mem·brance
Re·mem·branc·er
 Exchequer official
re·mex (*plural* remi·ges)
 flight feather
re·mig·ial
re·mind
re·mind·er
re·mind·ful
remi·nisce
remi·nis·cence
remi·nis·cent
re·mise legal term
re·miss negligent

re·mis·sibil·ity (*or*
 ·sible·ness)
re·mis·sible
re·mis·sion (*or* ·mit·tal)
re·mis·sive
re·miss·ness
re·mit (·mit·ting, ·mit·ted)
re·mit·table
re·mit·tal
re·mit·tance payment
re·mit·tee
re·mit·tence (*or* ·ten·cy)
 diminution
re·mit·tent
re·mit·ter (*or* ·tor)
rem·nant
re·mod·el (·el·ling, ·elled)
re·mod·el·ler
re·mon·eti·za·tion (*or*
 ·sa·tion)
re·mon·etize (*or* ·etise)
re·mon·strance
re·mon·strant
re·mon·strate
re·mon·stra·tion
re·mon·stra·tive
re·mon·stra·tor
re·mon·tant
rem·on·toir (*or* ·toire)
 device in clock
remo·ra fish
re·morse
re·morse·ful
re·morse·ful·ly
re·morse·ful·ness
re·morse·less
re·morse·less·ness
re·mote
remote-controlled
re·mote·ness
re·mould (*US* ·mold)
re·mount
re·mov·abil·ity (*or*
 ·able·ness)
re·mov·able
re·mov·ably
re·mov·al
re·mov·al·ist *Austral*
 furniture remover
re·move
re·mov·er
Rem·scheid West German
 city
re·mu·ner·abil·ity
re·mu·ner·able
re·mu·ner·ate
re·mu·nera·tion

re·mu·nera·tive
re·mu·nera·tor
Re·nais·sance historical
 period
re·nais·sance (*or*
 ·nas·cence) revival
re·nal
re·name
re·nas·cent
Ren·ault (*Trademark*)
rend (rend·ing, rent)
rend·er (*noun*)
ren·der (*verb*)
rend·er·able submittable;
 compare rendible
rend·er·er
ren·der·ing
ren·dez·vous (*plural*
 ·vous)
rend·ible tearable; *compare*
 renderable
ren·di·tion
ren·dzi·na soil
ren·egade
re·nege (*or* ·negue)
re·neg·er (*or* ·negu·er)
re·nego·ti·able
re·nego·ti·ate
re·nego·tia·tion
re·new
re·new·abil·ity
re·new·able
re·new·al
re·new·edly
re·new·er
Ren·frew Scottish town
reni·form kidney-shaped
re·nin kidney enzyme;
 compare rennin
Rennes French city
ren·net
ren·nin milk-coagulating
 enzyme; *compare* renin
Reno US city
re·nounce
re·nounce·ment
re·nounc·er
reno·vate
reno·va·tion
reno·va·tive
reno·va·tor
re·nown
re·nowned
re·nown·edly
rens·selaer·ite mineral
rent
rent·abil·ity

rent·able
rent·al
rente *French* type of income
rent·er
rent-free
ren·tier one living on rentes
rent-roll
re·num·ber
re·nun·cia·tion
re·nun·cia·tive (*or* ·tory)
ren·voi legal term
re·oc·cu·pa·tion
re·oc·cu·py (·pies, ·py·ing,
   ·pied)
re·open
re·or·der
re·or·gani·za·tion (*or*
   ·sa·tion)
re·or·gan·ize (*or* ·ise)
re·or·gan·iz·er (*or* ·is·er)
rep *Slang* representative;
   repertory
rep (*or* repp) fabric
re·paint
re·pair
re·pair·able able to be
   repaired; *compare*
   reparable
re·pair·er
re·pair·man (*plural* ·men)
re·pand having a wavy
   margin
repa·rabil·ity
repa·rable able to be made
   good; *compare* repairable
repa·rably
repa·ra·tion
re·para·tive (*or* ·tory)
rep·ar·tee
rep·ar·ti·tion
re·past
re·pat·ri·ate
re·pat·ria·tion
re·pay (·pay·ing, ·paid)
re·pay·able
re·pay·ment
re·peal
re·peal·able
re·peal·er
re·peat
re·peat·abil·ity
re·peat·able
re·peat·ed
re·peat·ed·ly
re·peat·er
rep·echage contest for
   runners-up

re·pel (·pel·ling, ·pelled)
re·pel·lence (*or* ·len·cy)
re·pel·lent
re·pel·ler
re·pel·ling·ly
re·pel·ling·ness
re·pent
re·pent·ance
re·pent·ant
re·pent·er
re·peo·ple
re·per·cus·sion
re·per·cus·sive
rep·er·toire
rep·er·to·rial
rep·er·tory (*plural* ·tories)
rep·etend repeated digit
ré·pé·ti·teur opera-singer
   coach
rep·eti·tion
rep·eti·tious
rep·eti·tious·ness
re·peti·tive
re·peti·tive·ness
re·phrase
re·pine
re·place
re·place·abil·ity
re·place·able
re·place·ment
re·plac·er
re·plan (·plan·ning,
   ·planned)
re·plant
re·play
re·plen·ish
re·plen·ish·er
re·plen·ish·ment
re·plete
re·plete·ness
re·ple·tion
re·ple·tive
re·plevi·able (*or*
   ·plev·is·able)
re·plev·in legal term
re·plevy (*verb* ·plevies,
   ·plevy·ing, ·plev·ied;
   noun, plural ·plevies)
   legal term
rep·li·ca
rep·li·cate
rep·li·ca·tion
rep·li·ca·tive
re·pli·er
re·ply (*verb* ·plies,
   ·ply·ing, ·plied; *noun,
   plural* ·plies)

re·point
re·pone legal term
re·port
re·port·able
re·port·age
re·port·ed·ly
re·port·er
re·pos·al
re·pose
re·pos·ed·ly
re·pose·ful
re·pose·ful·ly
re·pose·ful·ness
re·pos·er
re·pos·it put away
re·po·si·tion
re·posi·tory (*plural*
   ·tories)
re·pos·sess
re·pos·ses·sion
re·pos·ses·sor
re·pot (·pot·ting, ·pot·ted)
re·pous·sé raised design
repp *variant spelling of* rep
rep·re·hend
rep·re·hend·able
rep·re·hend·er
rep·re·hen·sibil·ity (*or*
   ·sible·ness)
rep·re·hen·sible
rep·re·hen·sibly
rep·re·hen·sion
rep·re·hen·sive
rep·re·hen·sory
rep·re·sent correspond to
re-present present again
rep·re·sent·abil·ity
rep·re·sent·able
rep·re·sen·ta·tion
rep·re·sen·ta·tion·al
rep·re·sen·ta·tion·al·ism
   philosophy term
rep·re·sen·ta·tion·al·is·tic
rep·re·senta·tive
rep·re·senta·tive·ness
re·press restrain
re-press press again
re·press·er (*or* ·pres·sor)
re·press·ible
re·pres·sion
re·pres·sive
re·pres·sive·ness
re·priev·able
re·prieve
re·priev·er
rep·ri·mand
rep·ri·mand·er

rep·ri·mand·ing·ly
re·print
re·print·er
re·pris·al
re·prise
re·pro (*plural* ·pros)
re·proach
re·proach·able
re·proach·ably
re·proach·er
re·proach·ful
re·proach·ful·ly
re·proach·ful·ness
re·proach·ing·ly
rep·ro·ba·cy (*or*
·bate·ness)
rep·ro·bate
rep·ro·bat·er
rep·ro·ba·tion
rep·ro·ba·tive (*or*
·tion·ary)
re·pro·duce
re·pro·duc·er
re·pro·duc·ibil·ity
re·pro·duc·ible
re·pro·duc·tion
re·pro·duc·tive
re·pro·duc·tive·ness
rep·ro·graph·ic
re·prog·ra·phy
re·proof rebuke
re·proof renew texture
re·prov·able
re·prov·al
re·prove
re·prov·er
re·prov·ing·ly
re·pro·vi·sion
rep·tant
rep·tile
rep·til·ian
rep·ti·loid
re·pub·lic
Re·pub·li·can political
party
re·pub·li·can of a republic
re·pub·li·can·ism
re·pub·li·cani·za·tion (*or*
·sa·tion)
re·pub·li·can·ize (*or* ·ise)
re·pub·li·ca·tion
re·pub·lish
re·pub·lish·able
re·pub·lish·er
re·pu·di·able
re·pu·di·ate
re·pu·di·a·tion

re·pu·dia·tive
re·pu·dia·tor
re·pu·dia·tory
re·pugn oppose
re·pug·nance (*or* ·nan·cy;
plural ·nances *or*
·nan·cies)
re·pug·nant
re·pulse
re·puls·er
re·pul·sion
re·pul·sive
re·pul·sive·ness
repu·tabil·ity (*or*
·table·ness)
repu·table
repu·tably
repu·ta·tion
re·pute
re·put·ed
re·put·ed·ly
re·quest
re·quest·er
requi·em
requi·es·cat prayer
re·quir·able
re·quire
re·quire·ment
re·quir·er
requi·site
requi·si·tion
requi·si·tion·ary
requi·si·tion·er (*or* ·ist)
re·quit·able
re·quit·al
re·quite
re·quite·ment
re·quit·er
re·ra·dia·tion
re·read (·read·ing, ·read)
rere·dos
rere·mouse *Dialect* bat
re·route (·route·ing *or*
·rout·ing, ·routed)
re·run (·run·ning, ·ran,
·run)
re·sal·able (*or* ·sale·)
re·sale
re·scind
re·scind·able
re·scind·er
re·scind·ment
re·scis·sible rescindable
re·scis·sion
re·scis·sory able to rescind
re·script
res·cu·able

res·cue (·cu·ing, ·cued)
res·cu·er
re·search
re·search·able
re·search·er
re·seat
re·seau (*plural* ·seaux *or*
·seaus) lace mesh
re·sect remove surgically
re·sec·tion
re·sec·tion·al
res·eda plant
re·sell (·sell·ing, ·sold)
re·sem·blance
re·sem·blant
re·sem·ble
re·sem·bler
re·sent
re·sent·ful
re·sent·ful·ly
re·sent·ful·ness
re·sent·ment
re·ser·pine drug
re·serv·able
res·er·va·tion
re·servable
re·serve set aside, etc.
re·serve serve again
re·served
re·serv·ed·ly
re·serv·ed·ness
re·serv·er
re·serv·ist
res·er·voir
re·set (·set·ting, ·set)
re·set·ter
re·set·tle
re·set·tle·ment
re·shape
re·ship (·ship·ping,
·shipped)
re·ship·ment
Resht *variant spelling of*
Rasht
re·shuf·fle
re·side
resi·dence
resi·den·cy (*plural* ·cies)
resi·dent
resi·den·tial
resi·den·tiary (*plural*
·tiaries)
resi·dent·ship
re·sid·er
re·sid·ual
re·sidu·ary
resi·due

re·sid·uum (*plural* ·sidua)
re·sign give up
re·sign sign again
res·ig·na·tion
re·signed
re·sign·ed·ly
re·sign·ed·ness
re·sign·er
re·sile spring back
re·sile·ment
re·sili·ence (*or* ·en·cy)
re·sili·ent
res·in gumlike substance;
  compare rosin
res·in·ate
res·in·if·er·ous
res·in·oid
res·in·ous
res·in·ous·ness
resi·pis·cence
  acknowledgment of error
re·sist
Re·sist·ance French
  organization
re·sist·ance
re·sist·ant (*or* ·sis·tive)
Re·sis·ten·cia Argentine
  city
re·sist·er opposer; *compare*
  resistor
re·sist·ibil·ity (*or*
  ·ible·ness)
re·sist·ible
re·sist·ibly
re·sist·ing·ly
re·sis·tive·ness (*or*
  ·tiv·ity)
re·sis·tiv·ity electrical
  property
re·sist·less
re·sis·tor electrical
  component; *compare*
  resister
re·sit (·sit·ting, ·sat)
res·na·tron electronic valve
re·sole
re·sol·ubil·ity (*or*
  ·uble·ness)
re·sol·uble resolvable
re·soluble able to be
  dissolved again
reso·lute
reso·lute·ness
reso·lu·tion
reso·lu·tion·er (*or* ·ist)
re·solv·abil·ity (*or*
  ·able·ness)

re·solv·able
re·solve
re·solved
re·solv·ed·ness
re·sol·vent
re·solv·er
reso·nance
reso·nant
reso·nate
reso·na·tion
reso·na·tor
re·sorb
re·sorb·ent
res·or·cin·ol chemical
  compound
re·sorp·tion
re·sorp·tive
re·sort holiday town; to use
re·sort sort again
re·sort·er
re·sound echo
re·sound sound again
re·sound
re·sound·ing
re·sound·ing·ly
re·source .
re·source·ful
re·source·ful·ly
re·source·ful·ness
re·source·less
re·spect
re·spect·abil·ity (*plural*
  ·ities)
re·spect·able
re·spect·ably
re·spect·er
re·spect·ful
re·spect·ful·ly
re·spect·ful·ness
re·spect·ing
re·spec·tive
re·spec·tive·ly
re·spir·abil·ity
res·pir·able
res·pi·ra·tion
res·pi·ra·tion·al
res·pi·ra·tor
re·spira·tory
re·spire
res·pite
re·splend·ence (*or* ·en·cy)
re·splend·ent
re·spond
re·spond·ence (*or* ·en·cy)
re·spond·ent legal term
re·spond·er
re·sponse

re·spons·er (*or* ·spon·sor)
  radio receiver
re·spon·sibil·ity (*plural*
  ·ities)
re·spon·sible
re·spon·sible·ness
re·spon·sibly
re·spon·sive
re·spon·sive·ly
re·spon·sive·ness
re·spon·so·ry (*plural*
  ·ries)
re·spray
res pu·bli·ca *Latin* the state
rest
re·state
re·state·ment
res·tau·rant
res·tau·ra·teur
rest·er
rest·ful
rest·ful·ly
rest·ful·ness
rest·harrow plant
res·ti·form
rest·ing
res·ti·tu·tion
res·ti·tu·tive (*or* ·tory)
res·tive
res·tive·ly
res·tive·ness
rest·less
rest·less·ly
rest·less·ness
re·stock
re·stor·able
Res·to·ra·tion historical
  period
res·to·ra·tion
res·to·ra·tion·ism
  theological belief
re·stora·tive
re·store
re·stor·er
re·strain
re·strain·able
re·strain·ed·ly
re·strain·er
re·strain·ing·ly
re·straint
re·strict
re·strict·ed·ly
re·strict·ed·ness
re·stric·tion
re·stric·tion·ist
re·stric·tive
re·stric·tive·ly

re·stric·tive·ness
re·struc·ture
re·style
re·sult
re·sult·ant
re·sum·able
re·sume restart
ré·su·mé summary
re·sump·tion
re·sump·tive
re·su·pi·nate botany term
re·su·pi·na·tion
re·sur·face
re·surge
re·sur·gence
re·sur·gent
res·ur·rect
Res·ur·rec·tion rising of
  Christ
res·ur·rec·tion revival
res·ur·rec·tion·al
res·ur·rec·tion·ary
res·ur·rec·tion·ism
res·ur·rec·tion·ist
re·sus·ci·table
re·sus·ci·tate
re·sus·ci·ta·tion
re·sus·ci·ta·tive
re·sus·ci·ta·tor
ret (ret·ting, ret·ted) soak
  fibre
re·ta·ble altar screen
re·tail
re·tail·er
re·tain
re·tain·abil·ity (or
  ·able·ness)
re·tain·able
re·tain·er
re·tain·ment
re·take (·tak·ing, ·took,
  ·tak·en)
re·tak·er
re·tali·ate
re·talia·tion
re·talia·tive (or ·tory)
re·talia·tor
re·tard
re·tard·ant
re·tard·ate retarded person
re·tar·da·tion (or
  ·tard·ment)
re·tarda·tive (or ·tory)
re·tard·ed
re·tard·er

retch vomit; compare wretch
rete (plural re·tia)
  anatomy term
re·tell (·tell·ing, ·told)
re·tene chemical compound
re·ten·tion
re·ten·tive
re·ten·tive·ly
re·ten·tive·ness
re·ten·tiv·ity
re·think (·think·ing,
  ·thought)
re·tial of a rete
re·ti·ar·ius (plural ·arii)
  gladiator
reti·cence
reti·cent
reti·cle (or ·cule) grid;
  compare reticule
re·ticu·lar
re·ticu·late
re·ticu·la·tion
reti·cule woman's bag;
  variant of reticle
re·ticu·lo·cyte
re·ticu·lo·en·do·the·lial
  anatomy term
re·ticu·lum (plural ·la)
  network; cow's stomach
reti·na (plural ·nas or
  ·nae)
reti·nacu·lar
reti·nacu·lum (plural ·la)
  biology term
reti·nal
reti·nene biochemical
  compound
reti·nite resin
reti·ni·tis
reti·nol biochemical
  compound
reti·no·scop·ic
reti·no·scopi·cal·ly
reti·nos·co·pist
reti·nos·co·py ophthalmic
  procedure
reti·nue
reti·nued
re·tire
re·tire·ment
re·tir·er
re·tir·ing
re·tir·ing·ly
re·tool

re·tor·sion reprisal
re·tort
re·tort·er
re·tor·tion retorting
re·touch
re·touch·able
re·touch·er
re·trace
re·trace·able
re·trace·ment
re·tract
re·tract·abil·ity (or ·ibil·)
re·tract·able (or ·ible)
re·trac·tile
re·trac·til·ity
re·trac·tion
re·trac·tive
re·trac·tor
re·train
re·tread (·tread·ing,
  ·tread·ed) remould
re·tread (·tread·ing,
  -trod, -trod·den or
  -trod) tread again
re·treat
re·treat·al
re·trench
re·trench·able
re·trench·ment
re·tri·al
ret·ri·bu·tion
re·tribu·tive (or ·tory)
re·tribu·tive·ly
re·triev·abil·ity
re·triev·able
re·triev·ably
re·triev·al
re·trieve
re·triev·er
ret·ro (plural ·ros) Slang
  retrorocket
retro·act
retro·ac·tion
retro·ac·tive
retro·ac·tive·ly
retro·ac·tiv·ity (or
  ·tive·ness)
retro·cede give back
retro·ces·sion (or
  ·ced·ence)
retro·ces·sive (or
  ·ced·ent)
retro·choir space behind
  altar
retro·fire

retro·fit (·fit·ting, ·fit·ted)
  equip with extra parts
retro·flex (or ·flexed)
retro·flex·ion (or
  ·flec·tion)
retro·gra·da·tion
retro·gra·da·tory
retro·grade
retro·gress
retro·gres·sion
retro·gres·sive
retro·gres·sive·ly
retro·ject throw backwards
retro·len·tal anatomy term
retro·operative
retro·pack
retro·rock·et
re·trorse pointing
  backwards
retro·spect
retro·spec·tion
retro·spec·tive
retro·spec·tive·ly
retro·spec·tive·ness
re·trous·sé
retro·verse
retro·ver·sion
retro·vert·ed
re·try (·tries, ·try·ing,
  ·tried)
ret·si·na
re·turn
re·turn·abil·ity
re·turn·able
re·turn·er
re·tuse botany term
re·type
re·uni·fi·ca·tion
re·uni·fy (·fies, ·fy·ing,
  ·fied)
Réu·nion French island
re·union
re·union·ism
re·union·ist
re·union·is·tic
re·unit·able
re·unite
re·unit·er
re·up·hol·ster
re·us·abil·ity (or
  ·able·ness)
re·us·able
re·use
re·uti·li·za·tion (or
  ·sa·tion)

re·uti·lize (or ·lise)
rev (rev·ving, revved)
re·val·ori·za·tion (or
  ·sa·tion)
re·val·or·ize (or ·ise)
  revalue
re·valua·tion
re·value (·valu·ing,
  ·valued)
re·vamp
re·vamp·er
re·vamp·ing
re·vanch·ism foreign policy
re·vanch·ist
re·veal
re·veal·abil·ity
re·veal·able
re·veal·ed·ly
re·veal·er
re·veal·ing
re·veal·ing·ly
re·veal·ment
re·veg·etate grow again
re·veg·eta·tion
re·veil·le
rev·el (·el·ling, ·elled; US
  ·el·ing, ·eled)
rev·ela·tion
rev·ela·tion·al
rev·ela·tion·ist believer in
  divine revelation
rev·el·ler (US ·el·er)
rev·el·ment
rev·el·rous
rev·el·ry (plural ·ries)
rev·enant
re·venge
re·venge·ful
re·venge·ful·ly
re·veng·er
re·veng·ing·ly
rev·enue
rev·enued
rev·enu·er US revenue
  officer
re·ver·able
re·ver·ber·ant
re·ver·ber·ate
re·ver·bera·tion
re·ver·bera·tive
re·ver·bera·tor
re·ver·bera·tory (plural
  ·tories)
re·vere
rev·er·ence

rev·er·enc·er
rev·er·end deserving
  reverence; clergyman
rev·er·ent feeling reverence
rev·er·en·tial showing
  reverence; compare
  referential
rev·er·en·tial·ly
rev·er·ent·ly
rev·er·ent·ness
re·ver·er
rev·erie (or ·ery; plural
  ·eries)
re·vers (plural ·vers) lapel
re·ver·sal
re·verse
re·vers·er
re·ver·si board game
re·vers·ibil·ity (or
  ·ible·ness)
re·vers·ible
re·vers·ibly
re·ver·sion
re·ver·sion·ary (or ·al)
re·ver·sion·er legal term
re·vert
re·vert·er
re·vert·ible
re·ver·tive
re·vest restore power
re·vet (·vet·ting, ·vet·ted)
  face with stones
re·vet·ment
re·view survey; critical
  opinion; compare revue
re·view·able
re·view·al
re·view·er
re·vile
re·vile·ment
re·vil·er
re·vil·ing·ly
re·vis·abil·ity
re·vis·able
re·vis·al
re·vise
re·vis·er (or ·or)
re·vi·sion
re·vi·sion·al (or ·ary)
re·vi·sion·ism
re·vi·sion·ist
re·vi·so·ry
re·vi·tali·za·tion (or
  ·sa·tion)
re·vi·tal·ize (or ·ise)

re·viv·abil·ity
re·viv·able
re·viv·ably
re·viv·al
re·viv·al·ism
re·viv·al·ist
re·viv·al·is·tic
re·vive
re·viv·er
re·vivi·fi·ca·tion
re·vivi·fy (·fies, ·fy·ing,
·fied)
re·viv·ing·ly
revi·vis·cence revival
revi·vis·cent
revo·cabil·ity (or
·cable·ness)
revo·cable (or
re·vok·able)
revo·cably
revo·ca·tion
re·voca·tive (or
revo·ca·tory)
re·voice
re·vok·able variant spelling
of revocable
re·voke
re·vok·er
re·vok·ing·ly
re·volt
re·volt·er
re·volt·ing
re·volt·ing·ly
revo·lute botany term
revo·lu·tion
revo·lu·tion·ari·ly
revo·lu·tion·ary (plural
·aries)
revo·lu·tion·ist
revo·lu·tion·ize (or ·ise)
revo·lu·tion·iz·er (or
·is·er)
re·volv·able
re·volve
re·volv·er
re·volv·ing
re·volv·ing·ly
re·vue entertainment;
compare review
re·vul·sion
re·vul·sion·ary
re·vul·sive
re·ward
re·ward·able
re·ward·er

re·ward·ing
re·wind (·wind·ing,
·wound)
re·wind·er
re·wir·able
re·wire
re·word
re·work
re·write (·writ·ing, ·wrote,
·writ·ten)
Rex the king
Rey·kja·vik Icelandic
capital
Rey·no·sa Mexican city
rhab·do·man·cy water
divining
rhab·do·man·tist (or
·man·cer)
rhab·do·myo·ma (plural
·mas or ·ma·ta) tumour
Rhae·tia Roman province
Rhae·tian
Rhae·tic (or **Rhe·tic**)
geology term
rham·na·ceous botany term
rhap·sod·ic
rhap·sodi·cal·ly
rhap·so·dist
rhap·so·dis·tic
rhap·so·dize (or ·dise)
rhap·so·dy (plural ·dies)
rhata·ny (plural ·nies)
shrub
rhea bird
rhe·bok (or ree·; plural
·boks or ·bok) antelope
Rheims variant spelling of
Reims
Rhe·mish of Reims
Rhen·ish of the Rhine
rhe·nium chemical element
rheo·base physiology term
rheo·logi·cal
rhe·olo·gist
rhe·ol·ogy branch of
physics
rhe·om·eter
rheo·met·ric
rhe·om·etry
rheo·stat
rheo·stat·ic
rheo·tac·tic
rheo·tax·is biology term
rheo·trop·ic
rhe·ot·ro·pism botany term

rhe·sus
rhe·tor teacher of rhetoric
rheto·ric
rhe·tori·cal
rhe·tori·cal·ly
rhe·tori·cian
rheum
rheu·mat·ic
rheu·mati·cal·ly
rheu·mat·ics
rheu·ma·tism
rheu·ma·toid (or ·toi·dal)
rheu·ma·tolo·gist
rheu·ma·tol·ogy
rheumy
Rheydt West German town
rhigo·lene anaesthetic
rhi·nal of the nose
Rhine
Rhine·land
Rhineland-Palati·nate
rhi·nen·cephal·ic
rhi·nen·cepha·lon (plural
·lons or ·la) anatomy
term
rhine·stone
rhi·ni·tis
rhi·no (plural ·nos or ·no)
rhi·noc·er·os (plural ·oses
or ·os)
rhi·no·cerot·ic
rhi·no·logi·cal
rhi·nolo·gist
rhi·nol·ogy branch of
medicine
rhi·no·plas·tic
rhi·no·plas·ty plastic
surgery of nose
rhi·no·scop·ic
rhi·nos·co·py
rhi·zo·bium (plural ·bia)
bacterium
rhi·zo·car·pous botany
term
rhi·zo·cepha·lan zoology
term
rhi·zo·cepha·lous
rhi·zo·gen·ic (or
·zo·genet·ic,
·zog·enous)
rhi·zoid rootlike part
rhi·zoi·dal
rhi·zoma·tous
rhi·zome

rhi·zo·morph
rhi·zo·mor·phous
rhi·zo·pod protozoan
rhi·zopo·dan
rhi·zopo·dous
rhi·zo·pus fungus
rhi·zo·sphere
rhi·zoto·my (*plural* ·mies)
  surgery
rho Greek letter
rho·da·mine dye
Rhode Is·land
Rhodes
Rho·desia
Rho·desian
Rho·dian of Rhodes
rho·dic
rho·di·nal oil
rho·dium chemical element
rho·do·chro·site mineral
rho·do·den·dron
rhodo·lite gemstone
rhodo·nite mineral
rho·dop·sin retinal pigment
rhomb rhombus; *compare*
  rhumb
rhom·ben·cepha·lon
  anatomy term
rhom·bic (*or* ·bi·cal)
rhom·bo·he·dral
rhom·bo·he·dron (*plural*
  ·drons *or* ·dra)
rhom·boid
rhom·boi·dal
rhom·bus (*plural* ·buses
  or ·bi) geometric figure
rhon·chal (*or* ·chial)
rhon·chus (*plural* ·chi)
  breathing sound
Rhon·dda
Rhône
rho·ta·cism phonetics term
rho·ta·cist
rho·ta·cis·tic
rho·tic
rhu·barb
rhumb navigation term;
  compare rhomb; rum
rhum·ba *variant spelling of*
  rumba
rhum·ba·tron
rhyme identical-sounding
  word; verse; *compare* rime
rhyme·ster (*or* rhym·er)

rhyn·cho·cephal·ian
  zoology term
rhyo·lite rock
rhyo·lit·ic
rhythm
rhyth·mic (*or* ·mi·cal)
rhyth·mi·cal·ly
rhyth·mic·ity
rhyth·mics
rhy·ton (*plural* ·ta)
  drinking vessel
ria inlet
rial currency
Ri·al·to Venetian island
ri·al·to (*plural* ·tos) market
ria·ta (*or* rea·ta) lasso
rib (rib·bing, ribbed)
rib·ald
rib·ald·ry
rib·and (*or* rib·band)
  award
Rib·ble English river
rib·bon
ribbon·fish (*plural* ·fish *or*
  ·fishes)
ribbon·wood
Ri·bei·rão Pré·to Brazilian
  city
ri·bo·fla·vin (*or* ·vine)
  vitamin
ri·bo·nu·clease enzyme
ri·bo·nu·cleic acid
ri·bose sugar
ri·bo·so·mal
ri·bo·some part of cell
rib·wort
rice
rice·bird
ric·er *US* sieve
ri·cer·ca·re (*or* ri·cer·car;
  plural ·ca·ri *or* ·cars)
  musical term
rich
riches
Rich·mond
rich·ness
Richter scale
ri·cin protein
ric·ino·leic acid
rick
rick·eti·ness
rick·ets
rick·ett·sia (*plural* ·siae
  or ·sias) pathogenic
  microorganism

rick·ett·sial
rick·ety
rick·rack (*or* ric·rac) braid
rick·shaw (*or* ·sha)
rico·chet (·chet·ing,
  ·chet·ed *or* ·chet·ting,
  ·chet·ted)
ri·cot·ta cheese
ric·tal
ric·tus (*plural* ·tus *or*
  ·tuses) gape
rid (rid·ding, rid *or*
  rid·ded)
rid·able (*or* ride·)
rid·dance
rid·den
rid·der
rid·dle
rid·dler
ride (rid·ing, rode,
  rid·den)
ride·able *variant spelling of*
  ridable
rid·er
rid·er·less
ridge
ridge·ling (*or* ridg·ling,
  rid·gel) veterinary term
ridge·pole (*or* ·tree) roof
  timber
ridge·way
ridgy
ridi·cule
ridi·cul·er
ri·dicu·lous
ri·dicu·lous·ly
ri·dicu·lous·ness
rid·ing
ri·dot·to (*plural* ·tos)
  musical entertainment
ries·ling wine
Rif (*or* Riff; *plural* Rifs,
  Riffs, Rifis *or* Rif,
  Riff) Moroccan people
rife
rife·ness
riff jazz term
rif·fle
rif·fler
riff·raff
ri·fle
rifle·bird
rifle·man (*plural* ·men)
ri·fler
ri·fle·ry

ri·fling
rift
rig (rig·ging, rigged)
Riga Soviet port
riga·doon (*or* ri·gau·don)
  dance
ri·ga·to·ni pasta
rig·ger
rig·ging
right
right·able
right-angled
right·en
right·eous
right·eous·ly
right·eous·ness
right·er
right·ful
right·ful·ly
right·ful·ness
right-hand (*adj*)
right-handed
right-handed·ness
right-hander
right·ish
right·ism
right·ist
right·ly
right-minded
right-minded·ly
right-minded·ness
right·ness
right·ward (*adj*)
right·wards (*adv*)
right-winger
rig·id
ri·gidi·fy (·fy·ing, ·fied)
ri·gid·ity (*or* ·ness)
rig·id·ly
rig·ma·role (*or* riga·)
ri·gor medical term; *compare*
  rigour
rig·or *US spelling of* rigour
rig·or·ism
rig·or·ist
rig·or·is·tic
rig·or mor·tis
rig·or·ous
rig·or·ous·ly
rig·or·ous·ness
rig·our (*US* ·or) harshness;
  compare rigor
Rig-Veda Hindu poetry
Ri·je·ka Yugoslav port
Rijks·museum

rile
rill stream; channel
rill (*or* rille) moon valley
ril·let
rim (rim·ming, rimmed)
rime frost; *less common*
  spelling of rhyme
rim-fire
Ri·mi·ni
rimmed
rim·ming
ri·mose botany term
ri·mos·ity
rim·rock
rimy (rimi·er, rimi·est)
rind
rinder·pest
ring (ring·ing, rang, rung)
  produce sound
ring (ring·ing, ringed)
  circular band; to encircle
ring-bolt
ring·bone
ring-dove
ring-dyke
rin·gent botany term
ring·er
ring·git Malaysian currency
ring·hals (*plural* ·hals *or*
  ·halses) snake
ring·ing
ring·leader
ring·let
ring·master
ring-necked
ring·side
ring-tail animal
ring-tailed
ring·worm
rink
rins·abil·ity (*or* ·ibil·ity)
rins·able (*or* ·ible)
rinse
rins·er
Rio de Ja·nei·ro
Rio Grande
Rio Gran·de do Nor·te
  Brazilian state
Rio Gran·de do Sul
  Brazilian state
riot
ri·ot·er
ri·ot·ous
ri·ot·ous·ly
ri·ot·ous·ness

rip (rip·ping, ripped)
ri·par·ian of a river bank
rip·cord
ripe
ripe·ly
rip·en
rip·en·er
ripe·ness
ri·pieno (*plural* ·pienos)
  musical term
rip-off (*noun*)
Rip·on
ri·poste (*or* ·post)
rip·pable
ripped
rip·per
rip·ping
rip·ple
rip·pler
rip·plet
rip·pling·ly
rip·ply
rip-roaring
rip·saw
rip-snorter
rip·tide
rise (ris·ing, rose, ris·en)
ris·er
ris·ibil·ity (*plural* ·ities)
ris·ible laughable
ris·ibly
ris·ing
risk
risk·er
risk·ily
riski·ness
risky (riski·er, riski·est)
  involving risk; *compare*
  risqué
Ri·sor·gi·men·to political
  movement
ri·sot·to (*plural* ·tos)
ris·qué improper; *compare*
  risky
Riss glaciation
ris·sole
ri·tar·dan·do musical term
rite
ri·tenu·to musical term
ri·tor·nel·lo musical term
ritu·al
ritu·al·ism
ritu·al·ist
ritu·al·is·tic
ritu·al·is·ti·cal·ly

ritu·al·ize (*or* ·ise)
ritu·al·ly
ritzy (ritzi·er, ritzi·est)
ri·val (·val·ling, ·valled;
 US ·val·ing ·valed)
ri·val·rous
ri·val·ry (*plural* ·ries)
rive (riv·ing, rived, rived
 or riv·en)
riv·er
river·bed
river·head
riv·er·ine
River·side US city
river·side
riv·et
riv·et·er
Rivi·era
ri·vi·ère necklace
rivu·let
rix-dollar
Ri·yadh Saudi Arabian
 capital
ri·yal currency
roach nautical term; *Slang*
 cockroach
roach (*plural* roach *or*
 roaches) fish
road
road·bed
road·block
road·holding
road·house
road·roller
road·runner bird
road·stead
road·ster
road·way
road·work sports training
road·works road repairs
road·worthi·ness
road·worthy
roam
roam·er
roan
Roa·noke US island
roar
roar·er
roar·ing
roast
roast·er
roast·ing
rob (rob·bing, robbed)
roba·lo (*plural* ·los *or* ·lo)
 fish

rob·and (*or* rob·bin)
 nautical term
rob·ber
rob·bery (*plural* ·beries)
rob·bin *variant of* roband;
 compare robin
rob·bing
robe
rob·in bird; *compare* robbin
ro·binia tree
ro·ble oak
ro·bor·ant fortifying
ro·bot
ro·bot·ics
ro·bot·ism (*or* ·bot·ry)
ro·bust
ro·bust·ness
roc legendary bird; *compare*
 rock
ro·caille decorative work
roc·am·bole plant
Roch·dale Lancashire town
Roch·es·ter Kent city; US
 city
roch·et bishop's surplice
rock hard mass; sway;
 compare roc
rocka·bil·ly
rock-and-roll (*or* rock-
 'n'- roll)
rock-and-roller (*or* rock-
 'n'-roller)
rock-bottom (*adj*)
rock-bound
rock·er
rock·ery (*plural* ·eries)
rock·et
rock·et·eer (*or* ·er) rocket
 engineer
rock·et·ry
rock·fish (*plural* ·fish *or*
 ·fishes)
Rock·ford US city
Rockies Rocky Mountains
rocki·ly
rocki·ness
rock·like
rock·ling (*plural* ·lings *or*
 ·ling) fish
rock·oon exploratory rocket
rock·rose
rock·shaft
rock·weed
rocky (rocki·er, rocki·est)
Rocky Moun·tains

ro·co·co
rod
rode
ro·dent
ro·denti·cide
ro·deo (*plural* ·deos)
rod·like
rodo·mon·tade boastful
 talk
roe fish ovary or testis; deer;
 compare row
roe·buck (*plural* ·bucks
 or ·buck)
roent·gen (*or* rönt·)
 radiation unit
roent·geno·gram (*or*
 ·graph, rönt·) *US* X-ray
 photograph
roent·gen·ol·ogy (*or*
 rönt·) radiology
ro·ga·tion
roga·tory
rog·er
rogue
ro·guery (*plural* ·gueries)
ro·guish
ro·guish·ly
ro·guish·ness
roil
roily (roili·er, roili·est)
 cloudy
rois·ter
roist·er·er
roist·er·ous
role (*or* rôle)
role-playing
roll
roll·away mounted on
 rollers
roll·bar
roll·er
rol·lick
rol·lick·ing
rol·lick·some (*or* ·licky)
roll·ing
roll·mop
roll·neck
roll-on (*noun, adj*)
Rolls Royce
 (*Trademark*)
roll-top
roll·way
roly-poly (*plural* -polies)
Rom (*plural* Roma) male
 gipsy

Ro·ma·gna Italian region
Ro·ma·ic language
ro·maine US cos lettuce
ro·ma·ji alphabet
Ro·man of Rome
ro·man type style
Ro·mance language
ro·mance love affair
Roma·nes Romany
　language
Ro·man·esque art style
Ro·ma·nia (or Ru·)
Ro·ma·nian (or Ru·)
Ro·man·ism Roman
　Catholicism
Ro·man·ist
Ro·man·ize (or ·ise)
Ro·ma·no cheese
Romanov Russian dynasty
Ro·mansch (or ·mansh)
　Swiss language
ro·man·tic
ro·man·ti·cal·ly
ro·man·ti·cism
ro·man·ti·cist
ro·man·ti·ci·za·tion (or
　·sa·tion)
ro·man·ti·cize (or ·cise)
Roma·ny (or Rom·ma·ny;
　plural ·nies)
Rome
Romeo (plural Romeos)
romp
romp·er
romp·ers baby garment
romp·ing·ly
ron·deau (plural ·deaux)
　poem; compare rondo
ron·del (or roun·del)
　poem
ron·delet poem
ron·do (plural ·dos)
　musical work; compare
　rondeau
ron·dure curvature
rone Scot drainpipe
Ro·neo (Trademark; verb
　·neos, ·neo·ing, ·neod;
　noun, plural ·neos)
rong·geng Malay dance
rönt·gen variant spelling of
　roentgen
roo Austral kangaroo
rood
Roo·depoort South African
　city

roof (plural roofs)
roof·ing
roof·less
roof·tree
rook
rook·ery (plural ·eries)
rookie Slang new recruit
room
room·er
room·ette US rail sleeper
room·ful (plural ·fuls)
roomi·ly
roomi·ness
room·mate
roomy (roomi·er,
　roomi·est)
roor·back US false report
roose Dialect to praise
roost
roost·er
root
root·age
root·er
rooti·ness
root·le
root·less
root·let
root·like
root·stock
rooty
rop·able (or rope·)
rope
rope·walk
ropi·ly
ropi·ness
ropy (ropi·er, ropi·est)
roque US game
Roque·fort cheese
roque·laure cloak
ro·quet croquet term
ror·qual whale
Rorschach test
rort Austral party
rorty
ros·ace rose window
ro·sa·ceous botany term
ro·sani·line (or ·lin) dye
ro·sar·ian rose grower
Ro·sa·rio Argentine port
ro·sar·ium (plural
　·sar·iums or ·saria) rose
　garden
ro·sary (plural ·saries)
　prayer beads; compare
　rosery

Ros·com·mon Irish county
rosé wine
rose
ro·seate
rose·bay plant
rose·bud
rose·bush
rose·fish (plural ·fish or
　·fishes)
rose·hip
ro·sel·la parrot
ro·sema·ling decoration
rose·mary (plural
　·maries)
ro·seo·la skin rash
ro·seo·lar
rose-root plant
ro·sery (plural ·series)
　rose garden; compare
　rosary
Ro·set·ta Egyptian town
ro·sette
rose·wood
Rosh Ha·sha·nah (or
　Rosh Ha·sha·na) Jewish
　New Year
Ro·si·cru·cian
Ro·si·cru·cian·ism
rosi·ly
ros·in type of resin
Ros·in·ante old horse
rosi·ness
rosin·weed
ros·iny
ros·tel·late (or ·lar)
ros·tel·lum (plural ·la)
　biology term
ros·ter
Ros·tock East German port
Ros·tov Soviet port
ros·tral (or ·trate,
　·trat·ed)
ros·trum (plural ·trums or
　·tra)
rosy (rosi·er, rosi·est)
rot (rot·ting, rot·ted)
rota
Ro·ta·me·ter
　(Trademark)
Ro·tar·ian
Ro·ta·ry association
ro·ta·ry (plural ·ries)
ro·tat·able
ro·tate
ro·ta·tion

ro·ta·tion·al
ro·ta·tive
ro·ta·tor
ro·ta·tory
rote
ro·tenone insecticide
rot·gut
Roth·er·ham Yorkshire town
Rothe·say Scottish town
roti bread
ro·ti·fer minute organism
ro·tif·er·al (*or* ·ous)
ro·tis·serie
rotl (*plural* rotls *or* ar·tal) unit of weight
ro·to·gra·vure printing process
ro·tor
Ro·to·rua New Zealand city
rot·ted
rot·ten
rot·ten·ly
rot·ten·ness
rotten·stone
rot·ter
Rot·ter·dam
rot·ting
Rott·wei·ler dog
ro·tund stout; *compare* orotund
ro·tun·da building
ro·tun·dity (*or* ·tund·ness)
Rou·baix French city
rou·ble (*or* ru·)
rouche *variant spelling of* ruche
roué
Rou·en French city
rouge
rouge et noir card game
rough
rough·age
rough-and-readi·ness
rough-and-ready
rough-and-tumble
rough·cast (cast·ing, ·cast)
rough·cast·er
rough-dry (-dries, -dry·ing, -dried)
rough·en
rough-hew (-hewing, -hewed, -hewed *or* -hewn)

rough·house
rough·ish
rough·ly
rough·neck
rough·ness
rough·rider
rough·shod
rough-spoken
rou·lade
rou·leau (*plural* ·leaux *or* ·leaus)
rou·lette
round
round·about (*noun, adj*)
round-arm cricketing term
round·ed
round·ed·ness
roun·del
roun·de·lay dance
round·er
round·ers
Round·head Parliamentarian
round·house
round·ish
round·ly
round·ness
round-shouldered
rounds·man (*plural* ·men)
round·up (*noun*)
round·worm
roup *Dialect* auction; bird disease
roupy
rouse
rous·edness
rous·er
rous·ing
rous·ing·ly
Rous·sil·lon former French province
roust
roust·about
rout defeat
route road; course
route·march
rout·er
rou·tine
rou·tine·ly
rou·tin·ism
rou·tin·ist
roux (*plural* roux) fat-and-flour paste; *compare* rue
rove

rove-over prosody term
rov·er
row line; propel boat; *compare* roe
ro·wan
row·boat
row·di·ly
row·di·ness (*or* ·dy·ism)
row·dy (·di·er, ·di·est)
row·el (·el·ling, ·elled; *US* ·el·ing, ·eled) spur wheel
row·er
row·lock
roy·al
roy·al·ism
roy·al·ist
roy·al·is·tic
roy·al·ly
roy·al·ty (*plural* ·ties)
roz·zer *Slang* policeman
rub (rub·bing, rubbed)
ru·bái·yát Persian verse form
Rub' al Kha·li Arabian desert
ru·ba·to (*plural* ·tos) musical term
rubbed
rub·ber
rub·ber·ize (*or* ·ise)
rubber·neck *Slang* inquisitive person
rubber-stamp (*verb*)
rub·bery
rub·bing
rub·bish
rub·bishy
rub·ble
rubble·work
rub·bly
rube *US* country bumpkin
ru·befa·cient
ru·befac·tion
ru·befy (·befies, ·befy·ing, ·befied) make red
ru·bel·la German measles; *compare* rubeola
ru·bel·lite gemstone
ru·beo·la measles; *compare* rubella
ru·beo·lar
ru·bes·cence
ru·bes·cent
ru·bia·ceous botany term

Ru·bi·con
ru·bi·cund
ru·bi·cun·dity
ru·bid·ic
ru·bid·ium radioactive
element
ru·bigi·nous (*or* ·**nose**)
rust-coloured
ru·bi·ous dark red
ru·bric
ru·bri·cal
ru·bri·cate
ru·bri·ca·tion
ru·bri·ca·tor
ru·bri·cian
ruby (*plural* **rubies**)
ruche (*or* **rouche**)
ruch·ing
ruck
ruck·sack
ruck·us (*plural* ·**uses**)
uproar
ruc·tion
ru·da·ceous geology term
rud·beckia plant
rudd (*plural* **rudd** *or*
rudds) fish
rud·der
rudder·head
rudder·less
rudder·post
rud·di·ly
rud·di·ness
rud·dle (*or* **rad·**, **red·**) red
dye
rud·dock *Dialect* robin
rud·dy (·**di·er**, ·**di·est**)
rude
rude·ly
rude·ness (*or* **ru·dery**)
ru·deral botany term
Ru·des·heim·er wine
ru·di·ment
ru·di·men·ta·ril·ly (*or*
·**men·tal·ly**)
ru·di·men·ta·ry (*or*
·**men·tal**)
rud·ish
rue (**ru·ing**, **rued**) regret;
plant; *compare* **roux**
rue·ful
rue·ful·ly
rue·ful·ness
ru·fes·cence
ru·fes·cent

ruff raised collar; bird; cards
term
ruffe (*or* **ruff**) fish
ruf·fian
ruf·fi·an·ism
ruf·fi·an·ly
ruf·fle
ruf·fler
ruf·fly
ru·fous
rug
ruga (*plural* **rugae**)
anatomy term
Rug·by Warwickshire town
rug·by football
rug·ged
rug·ged·ize (*or* ·**ise**) make
durable
rug·ged·ly
rug·ged·ness
rug·ger
ru·gose (*or* ·**gous**, ·**gate**)
ru·gos·ity
Ruhr West German river
ruin
ru·in·able
ru·ina·tion
ru·in·er
ru·ing
ru·in·ous
Ruis·lip
rul·able
rule
rul·er
rul·ing
rum (**rum·mer**, **rum·mest**)
spirit; *Slang* odd; *compare*
rhumb
Ru·ma·nia *variant spelling*
of **Romania**
rum·ba (*or* **rhum·**)
rum·ble
rum·bler
rum·bling·ly
rum·bly
rum·bus·tious
rum·bus·tious·ly
rum·bus·tious·ness
Ru·melia part of Ottoman
empire
ru·men (*plural* ·**mens** *or*
·**mi·na**) cow's stomach
ru·mi·nant
ru·mi·nate
ru·mi·nat·ing·ly

ru·mi·na·tion
ru·mi·na·tive
ru·mi·na·tor
rum·mage
rum·mag·er
rum·mer drinking glass
rum·my
ru·mour (*US* ·**mor**)
rump
rum·ple
rum·ply
rum·pus (*plural* ·**puses**)
run (**run·ning**, **ran**, **run**)
run·about (*noun*)
run·away (*noun*, *adj*)
runch plant
run·ci·nate botany term
Run·corn Cheshire town
run·dle ladder rung
run-down (*noun*)
run-down (*adj*)
rune
rung
ru·nic
run·nel (*or* ·**let**)
run·ner
runner-up (*plural*
runners-up)
run·ning
run·ny (·**ni·er**, ·**ni·est**)
Run·ny·mede
run-off (*noun*)
run-of-the-mill
run-on (*noun*)
runt
runti·ness
runt·ish
runt·ish·ness
runty
run-up (*noun*)
run·way
ru·pee
ru·pi·ah (*plural* ·**ah** *or*
·**ahs**) Indonesian currency
rup·tur·able
rup·ture
ru·ral
ru·ral·ism
ru·ral·ist (*or* ·**ite**)
ru·ral·ity
ru·rali·za·tion (*or* ·**sa·tion**)
ru·ral·ize (*or* ·**ise**)
ru·ral·ly
Ru·ri·ta·nia fictional
kingdom

Ru·ri·ta·nian
Ruse Bulgarian city
ruse
rush
rush·er
rushi·ness
rushy (rushi·er, rushi·est)
rusk
rus·set
rus·set·ish (or ·sety)
Rus·sia
Rus·sian
Rus·sian·ize (or ·ise)
Russ·ky (or ·ki; plural ·kies or ·kis) Slang a Russian
Rus·so·phile (or ·phil)
Rus·so·phobe
Rus·so·pho·bia
Rus·so·pho·bic
rust
rus·tic
rus·ti·cal·ly
rus·ti·cate
rus·ti·ca·tion

rus·ti·ca·tor
rus·tic·ity
rusti·ly
rusti·ness
rus·tle
rus·tler
rus·tling·ly
rust·proof
rusty (rusti·er, rusti·est)
rut (rut·ting, rut·ted)
ru·ta·ba·ga US swede
ru·ta·ceous botany term
Ru·the·nia Soviet region
Ru·the·nian
ru·then·ic
ru·the·nious
ru·the·nium chemical element
ruth·er·ford unit
ruth·ful
ruth·less
ruth·less·ly
ruth·less·ness

ru·ti·lat·ed mineralogy term
ru·tile mineral
Rut·land former English county
rut·ted
rut·ti·ly
rut·ti·ness
rut·ting
rut·tish of an animal in rut
rut·tish·ness
rut·ty (·ti·er, ·ti·est) full of ruts
Ru·wen·zo·ri African mountains
Rwan·da African republic
Rya·zan Soviet city
Ry·binsk Soviet city
Ry·dal Cumbrian village
rye
rye-brome plant
rye-grass
ryo·kan Japanese inn
ryot Indian peasant

S

Saab (Trademark)
Saar European river
Saar·brück·en West German city
Saar·land West German state
Saba West Indian island
Sa·ba·dell Spanish town
saba·dil·la plant
Sa·bah Malaysian state
sa·ba·yon dessert
Sab·ba·tar·ian observer of Sabbath
Sab·bath seventh day
sab·bath (or ·bat) rest period
Sab·bati·cal (or ·bat·ic) of the Sabbath
sab·bati·cal (noun) academic leave
Sa·bel·lian language
sa·ber US spelling of sabre
sa·bin unit
Sab·ine

sa·ble (plural ·bles or ·ble)
sab·ot
sabo·tage
sabo·teur
sa·bra Israeli-born Jew
sa·bre (US ·ber)
sa·bre·tache (US ·ber·) leather case
sabu·los·ity
sabu·lous (or ·lose) gritty
sac biological pouch; compare sack
saca·ton grass
sac·cate
sac·cha·rase enzyme
sac·cha·rate chemical compound
sac·cha·ride sugar
sac·chari·fi·ca·tion
sac·chari·fy (·fies, ·fy·ing, ·fied)
sac·cha·rim·eter
sac·cha·rin sugar
sac·cha·rine sugary

sac·cha·rin·ity
sac·cha·ri·za·tion (or ·sa·tion)
sac·cha·rize (or ·rise)
sac·cha·roid (or ·roi·dal) geology term
sac·cha·rom·eter
sac·cha·rose
sac·cu·late (or ·lat·ed, ·lar)
sac·cu·la·tion
sac·cule (or ·cu·lus)
sac·er·do·tal
sac·er·do·tal·ism
sa·chet
sack bag; to plunder, etc.; compare sac
sack·but
sack·cloth
sack·er
sack·ful (plural ·fuls)
sack·ing
sack·like
sa·cral of sacred rites or the sacrum

sac·ra·ment
sac·ra·men·tal
sac·ra·men·tal·ism
sac·ra·men·tal·ist
sac·ra·men·tal·ity (or ·ness)
sac·ra·men·tal·ly
Sac·ra·men·tar·ian theology term
Sac·ra·men·to US port
sa·crar·ium (plural ·craria) church sanctuary
sa·cred
sa·cred·ness
sac·ri·fice
sac·ri·fice·able
sac·ri·fic·er
sac·ri·fi·cial
sac·ri·fi·cial·ly
sac·ri·fic·ing
sac·ri·lege
sac·ri·legious
sac·ri·legious·ness
sac·ri·legist
sac·ris·tan (or sac·rist)
sac·ris·ty (plural ·ties)
sa·cro·ili·ac anatomy term
sac·ro·sanct
sac·ro·sanc·tity (or ·sanct·ness)
sa·crum (plural ·cra) bone
sad (sad·der, sad·dest)
sad·den
sad·den·ing
sad·der
sad·dest
sad·dle
saddle·back
saddle·bag
saddle·bill
saddle·bow
saddle·cloth
sad·dler
sad·dlery (plural ·dleries)
saddle·tree saddle frame
Sad·du·cean
Sad·du·cees
sad·iron heavy iron
sad·ism
sad·ist
sa·dis·tic
sa·dis·ti·cal·ly
sad·ly
sad·ness
sado·maso·chism

sado·maso·chist
sado·maso·chis·tic
Sa·do·wa battle site
sa·fa·ri (plural ·ris)
safe
safe-conduct
safe-deposit (or safety-)
safe·guard
safe·keeping
safe·light photography term
safe·ness
safe·ty (plural ·ties)
saf·fian tanned leather
saf·flow·er
saf·fron
Sa·fid Rud Iranian river
saf·ra·nine (or ·nin) dye
saf·role plant oil
sag (sag·ging, sagged)
saga
sa·ga·cious
sa·ga·cious·ness
sa·gac·ity
saga·more American Indian chief
sage
sage·brush shrub
sag·gar (or ·ger) pottery-firing box
sagged
sag·ging
Sa·git·ta constellation
sag·it·tal
Sag·it·ta·rian
Sag·it·ta·rius
sag·it·tate (or sa·git·ti·form)
sago (plural sagos)
Sa·guache US mountain range
sa·gua·ro (or ·hua·; plural ·ros) cactus
Sa·hap·tin (or ·tan; plural ·tins, ·tin or ·tans, ·tan) American Indian
Sa·ha·ra
Sa·har·an
Sa·ha·ran·pur Indian town
Sa·hel African region
sa·hib (or ·heb)
said
Sai·da Lebanese port
sai·ga antelope
Sai·gon
sail

sail·able
sail·cloth
sail·er sailing vessel; compare sailor
sail·fish (plural ·fish or ·fishes)
sail·ing
sail·or seaman; compare sailer
sail·or·ly
sail·plane
sain·foin plant
saint
St Al·bans
St An·drews
St Aus·tell Cornish town
St Ber·nard dog
saint·ed
Sainte Foy suburb of Quebec
Saint-Émilion wine
St-Étienne French town
St Gall Swiss town
St George's capital of Grenada
St He·le·na Atlantic island
St Hel·ens Merseyside town
St Hel·ier Jersey town
saint·hood
St Ives
St John Canadian city
St John's Canadian city; Antiguan port
St Kil·da Hebridean island
St Kitts West Indian island
St Law·rence North American river
St Leg·er horse race
saint·li·ly
saint·li·ness
St Lou·is US city
St Lu·cia West Indian island
saint·ly
St Mo·ritz Swiss resort
St Paul US city
saint·pau·lia plant
St Pe·ters·burg former name of Leningrad; compare Pe·ters·burg
St Vitus's dance
Sai·pan Pacific island
Saïs Egyptian city
saithe fish

Sai·va Hindu
Sa·kai Japanese port
sake benefit
sake (or saké, saki) Japanese liquor; compare saki
sa·ker falcon
Sa·kha·lin (or ·ghal·ien) Soviet island
saki monkey; compare sake
Sak·tas Hindu sect
Sa·kya·mu·ni title of Buddha
sal salt
sa·laam Muslim greeting
sal·able variant spelling (esp. US) of saleable
sa·la·cious
sa·la·cious·ness (or ·lac·ity)
sal·ad
Sala·man·ca Spanish city
sala·man·der amphibian
sala·man·drine
Sa·lam·bria Greek river
sa·la·mi sausage; compare salmi
Sala·mis Greek island
sala·ried
sala·ry (noun, plural ·ries; verb ·ries, ·ry·ing, ·ried)
sal·chow ice-skating jump
sale
sale·abil·ity (or ·able·ness)
sale·able (or esp. US sal·able)
sale·ably
Sa·lem Indian city; US city
sal·ep dried orchid tuber
sal·era·tus sodium bicarbonate
Sa·ler·no Italian port
sale·room
sales·clerk
sales·man (plural ·men)
sales·man·ship
sales·room
sales·woman (plural ·women)
Sal·ford
Sa·lian Frankish
Sal·ic of Frankish law
sal·ic geology term
sali·ca·ceous botany term

sa·li·cin (or ·cine) drug
sa·li·cion·al (or sa·li·cet) organ stop
sali·cor·nia plant
sa·licy·late
sali·cyl·ic acid
sa·li·ence (or ·en·cy)
sa·li·ent
sa·li·en·tian amphibian
sa·li·ent·ness
sa·lif·er·ous containing salt
sali·fi·able
sali·fi·ca·tion
sali·fy (·fies, ·fy·ing, ·fied) mix with salt
sal·im·eter
sali·met·ric
sal·im·etry
sa·lina salt lake
sa·line containing salt
sa·lin·ity
sali·nom·eter
sali·no·met·ric
sali·nom·etry
Salis·bury
Sa·lish (or ·lish·an) language
sa·li·va
sali·vary
sali·vate
sali·va·tion
sal·lee tree
sal·let (or sal·et, sa·lade) helmet
sal·li·er
sal·low
sal·low·ness
sal·ly (noun, plural ·lies; verb ·lies, ·ly·ing, ·lied)
Sal·ly Lunn cake
sal·ma·gun·di salad
sal·ma·naz·ar wine bottle
sal·mi (or ·mis; plural ·mis) French stew; compare salami
salm·on (plural ·ons or ·on)
salmon·berry (plural ·berries)
sal·mo·nel·la (plural ·lae) bacterium
sal·mo·nel·lo·sis
sal·mo·noid
sal·ol chemical compound

sa·lon reception room; beauty establishment, etc.; compare saloon
Sa·lo·ni·ka Greek port
sa·loon large room; pub bar; compare salon
sa·loop aromatic infusion
salo·pette skiing garment
sal·pa (plural ·pas or ·pae) marine organism
sal·pi·con chopped food
sal·pi·form
sal·pi·glos·sis plant
sal·pin·gec·to·my (plural ·mies)
sal·pin·gian
sal·pin·gi·tic
sal·pin·git·is
sal·pinx (plural ·pin·ges) Fallopian tube
sal·si·fy (plural ·fies) vegetable
salt
Sal·ta Argentine city
sal·tant biology term
sal·ta·rel·lo (plural ·li or ·los) dance
sal·ta·tion biology term
sal·ta·to·rial (or sal·ta·tory) adapted for jumping
salt·box
salt·bush
salt·cellar
salt·ed
salt·er
salt·ern saltworks
salt·fish
sal·ti·grade moving by jumps
Sal·til·lo Mexican state
salti·ly
salti·ness
sal·tire (or ·tier) heraldic term
salt·ness
salt·pan
salt·pe·tre (US ·ter)
salt·pot
sal·tus (plural ·tuses) break in sequence
salt·water
salt·works
salt·wort
salty (salti·er, salti·est)
sa·lu·bri·ous

sa·lu·bri·ous·ness (*or* ·bri·ty)
Sa·lu·ki dog
salu·tari·ly
salu·tari·ness
salu·tary beneficial; *compare* salutatory
salu·ta·tion
sa·lu·ta·to·ri·ly
sa·lu·ta·tory welcoming; *compare* salutary
sa·lute
sa·lut·er
sal·vabil·ity (*or* ·vable·ness)
salv·able
sal·vably
Sal·va·dor Brazilian port
Sal·va·do·rian
sal·vage rescue; *compare* selvage
sal·vage·able
sal·vag·er
sal·va·tion
sal·va·tion·al
sal·va·tion·ism
sal·va·tion·ist member of evangelical sect
salve
sal·ver tray; *compare* salvor
sal·ver·form botany term
sal·via plant
sal·vo (*plural* ·vos *or* ·voes*) gun fire
sal·vo (*plural* ·vos) provisos
sal vola·ti·le
sal·vor one who salvages; *compare* salver
Sal·ween Asian river
Sal·yut Soviet space station
Salz·burg
Salz·git·ter West German city
sa·ma·ra botany term
Sa·maria Palestinian region
Sa·mari·tan
Sa·mari·tan·ism
sa·mar·ium chemical element
Sa·mar·kand
sa·mar·skite mineral
sam·ba (*plural* ·bas) dance
sam·bar (*or* ·bur; *plural* ·bars, ·bar *or* ·burs, ·bur) deer

same
same·ness
Sa·mian of Samos
sami·sen musical instrument
sam·ite fabric
sa·mi·ti (*or* ·thi) Indian political association
Sam·nite
Sam·ni·um ancient Italian city
Sa·moa Pacific islands
Sa·mo·an
Sa·mos Greek island
Samo·thrace Greek island
samo·var
Samo·yed (*plural* ·yed *or* ·yeds) Siberian people; dog
sam·pan boat
sam·phire plant
sam·ple
sam·pler
sam·pling
Sam·sun Turkish port
samu·rai (*plural* ·rai)
San language group
San'a (*or* Sa·naa) capital of North Yemen
San An·to·nian
San An·to·nio US city
sana·to·rium (*US* sani·ta·; *plural* ·riums *or* ·ria)
san·be·ni·to (*plural* ·tos) garment
San Ber·nar·di·no US city
sanc·ti·fi·able
sanc·ti·fi·ca·tion
sanc·ti·fi·er
sanc·ti·fy (·fies, ·fy·ing, ·fied)
sanc·ti·mo·ni·ous
sanc·ti·mo·ni·ous·ness
sanc·ti·mo·ny
sanc·tion
sanc·tion·able
sanc·tion·er
sanc·ti·tude
sanc·tity (*plural* ·tities)
sanc·tu·ary (*plural* ·aries)
sanc·tum (*plural* ·tums *or* ·ta)
Sanc·tus hymn
sand

san·dal
san·dalled (*US* ·daled)
sandal·wood
san·da·rac (*or* ·rach) tree
sand·bag (*verb* ·bag·ging, ·bagged)
sand·bag·ger
sand·bank
sand·blast
sand·blast·er
sand·blind
sand·blindness
sand·box
sand·cast (-casting, -cast)
sand·er
sand·er·ling bird
sand·fly (*plural* ·flies)
sand·grouse
san·dhi (*plural* ·dhis) linguistics term
sand·hog *US* underground worker
Sand·hurst
San Di·ego US port
sandi·ness
sand·man (*plural* ·men)
sand·paper
sand·piper
sand·pit
San·dring·ham
sand·soap
sand·stone
sand·storm
sand·wich
sand·worm
sand·wort
sandy (sandi·er, sandi·est)
sane
sane·ness
San Fernando Trinidadian port
San·for·ize (*or* ·ise; *Trademark*)
San Fran·cis·can
San Fran·cis·co
sang
san·ga·ree spiced drink
sang-froid
San·graal (*or* ·greal) Holy Grail
san·gria drink
san·gui·naria drug; plant
san·gui·nari·ly
san·gui·nari·ness

san·gui·nary
san·guine
san·guine·ness (*or* ·guin·ity)
san·guin·eous
san·guino·len·cy
san·guino·lent containing blood
San·hed·rin Jewish tribunal
sani·cle plant
sa·ni·es discharge from wound
sani·tar·ian of sanitation
san·itari·ly
sani·tari·ness
sani·ta·rium *US spelling of* sanatorium
sani·tary
sani·ta·tion
sani·tize (*or* ·tise)
san·ity
San Jose Californian city
San José Costa Rican capital
San Juan Puerto Rican capital
sank
San Luis Po·to·sí Mexican state
San Mari·nese (*or* Sam·mari·nese)
San Ma·ri·no European republic
sann·ya·si Brahman mendicant
San Sal·va·dor capital of El Salvador
sans-culotte
San Se·bas·tián Spanish port
san·ser·if (*or* sans serif)
san·se·vieria plant
San·skrit
San·skrit·ic
San·skrit·ist
sans ser·if *variant spelling of* san·ser·if
San Ste·fa·no Turkish village
San·ta Ana El Salvador city; Californian city
San·ta Ca·ta·ri·na Brazilian state
San·ta Cla·ra Cuban city
Santa Claus

San·ta Cruz Argentine province; Bolivian city
San·ta Cruz de Te·ne·rife Tenerife port
San·ta Fe Mexican city; Argentine port
san·ta·la·ceous botany term
San·ta Maria Brazilian city
San·ta Mar·ta Colombian port
San·tan·der Spanish port
San·ta·rém Brazilian port
San·tee US river
San·tia·go Chilean capital
San·tia·go de Cuba Cuban port
San·tia·go del Es·te·ro Argentine city
San·to Do·min·go capital of Dominican Republic
san·toni·ca plant
san·to·nin
San·tos Brazilian port
São Luís (*or* São Luíz) Brazilian port
Saône-et-Loire French department
São Pau·lo Brazilian port
São Tomé e Prín·ci·pe island republic
sap (sap·ping, sapped)
sapa·jou monkey
sa·pele tree
sa·phe·na (*plural* ·nae) vein
sa·phe·nous
(saphire) *incorrect spelling of* sapphire
sap·id palatable
sa·pid·ity (*or* ·ness)
sa·pi·ence (*or* ·en·cy) wisdom
sa·pi·ent
sa·pi·en·tial
sap·in·da·ceous botany term
sap·less
sap·ling
sapo·dil·la fruit
sapo·na·ceous soapy
sa·poni·fi·able
sa·poni·fi·ca·tion
sa·poni·fi·er
sa·poni·fy (·fies, ·fy·ing, ·fied)

sapo·nin plant compound
sapo·nite mineral
sa·po·ta fruit
sapo·ta·ceous
sap·pan·wood (*or* sap·an·)
sapped
sap·per
Sap·phic verse form; of Sappho
sap·phire
sap·phir·ine mineral
sap·pi·ly
sap·pi·ness
sap·ping
Sap·po·ro Japanese city
sap·py (·pi·er, ·pi·est)
sa·prae·mia (*US* ·pre·) blood poisoning
sa·prae·mic (*US* ·pre·)
sap·robe organism inhabiting foul water
sap·ro·bic
sap·ro·gen·ic (*or* ·ous)
sap·ro·genic·ity
sap·ro·lite geological deposit
sap·ro·lit·ic
sap·ro·pel sludge
sap·ro·pel·ic
sa·propha·gous feeding on decaying matter
sap·ro·phyte
sap·ro·phyt·ic
sap·ro·phyti·cal·ly
sap·ro·zo·ic
sap·sa·go cheese
sap·sucker bird
sap·wood
sara·band (*or* ·bande)
Sara·cen
Sara·cen·ic (*or* ·ceni·cal)
Sara·gos·sa Spanish city
Sa·ra·jevo (*or* Se·) Yugoslav city
sa·ran resin
Sa·ransk Soviet city
Sa·ra·tov Soviet city
Sa·ra·wak Malaysian state
sar·casm
sar·cas·tic
sar·cas·ti·cal·ly
sar·co·carp botany term
sar·coid
sar·co·ma (*plural* ·mas *or* ·ma·ta)

sar·co·ma·toid (*or* ·tous)
sar·co·ma·to·sis
sar·copha·gus (*plural* ·gi *or* ·guses)
sar·cous muscular or fleshy
sard gemstone
sar·dine (*plural* ·dine *or* ·dines)
Sar·dinia
Sar·din·ian
Sar·dis (*or* ·des) ancient Asian city
sar·di·us biblical gemstone
sar·don·ic
sar·doni·cal·ly
sar·doni·cism
sar·don·yx gemstone
Sar·gas·so sea
sar·gas·so (*plural* ·sos) seaweed
sar·gas·sum seaweed
sarge *Slang* sergeant
Sar·go·dha Pakistani city
sari (*plural* ·ris)
Sark Channel island
sar·men·tose (*or* ·tous, ·ta·ceous) botany term
Sar·nia Canadian port
sa·rong
sa·ron·ic
sa·ros cycle of eclipses
sar·panch Indian leader
sar·ra·cenia plant
sar·ra·cenia·ceous
sar·sa·pa·ril·la
sar·sen boulder
Sarthe French department
sar·tor tailor
sar·to·rial
sar·to·rius (*plural* ·to·rii) muscle
Sar·um Salisbury
Sa·sebo Japanese port
sash
Sas·katch·ewan
Sas·ka·toon Canadian city
sas·ka·toon fruit
(sarsparilla) *incorrect spelling of* **sarsaparilla**
sass *US* insolent
sas·sa·by (*plural* ·bies) antelope
sas·sa·fras tree; oil

Sas·sa·nid (*plural* ·sa·nids *or* ·sani·dae) member of Persian dynasty
Sas·sa·ri Sardinian city
Sas·se·nach
sas·si·ly
sas·si·ness
sas·sy (·si·er, ·si·est) saucy
sas·sy (*or* sass·wood, sas·sy wood) tree
sa·stru·ga (*or* zas·tru·) ridge on snowfield
sat
sa·tai (*or* ·tay) Indonesian food
Satan
sa·tang (*plural* ·tang) Thai coin
sa·tan·ic (*or* ·tani·cal)
sa·tani·cal·ly
sa·tani·cal·ness
Sa·tan·ism
Sa·tan·ist
satch·el
sate
sa·teen imitation satin
sat·el·lite
sat·el·lit·ium astrology term
sa·tem linguistics term
sa·ti·abil·ity (*or* ·able·ness)
sa·ti·able
sa·ti·ably
sa·ti·ate
sa·tia·tion
sa·ti·ety
sat·in
sati·net (*or* ·nette) imitation satin
satin·wood
sat·iny
sat·ire parody; *compare* satyr
sa·tir·ic
sa·tiri·cal (*or* ·tir·ic)
sa·tiri·cal·ly
sa·tiri·cal·ness
sati·rist
sati·ri·za·tion (*or* ·sa·tion)
sati·rize (*or* ·rise)
sati·riz·er (*or* ·ris·er)
sat·is·fac·tion
sat·is·fac·tion·al
sat·is·fac·to·ri·ly
sat·is·fac·to·ri·ness

sat·is·fac·tory
sat·is·fi·able
sat·is·fi·er
sat·is·fy (·fies, ·fy·ing, ·fied)
sat·is·fy·ing·ly
sa·trap Persian governor
sa·trapy (*plural* ·trapies)
Sa·tsu·ma Japanese province; porcelain
sat·su·ma fruit
satu·rabil·ity
satu·rable
satu·rant
satu·rate
satu·rat·ed
satu·rat·er (*or* ·ra·tor)
satu·ra·tion
Sat·ur·day
Sat·urn planet
Saturn Roman god
Sat·ur·na·lia (*plural* ·lia *or* ·lias) ancient festival
Sa·tur·nian
sa·tur·ni·id moth
sat·ur·nine
sat·ur·nine·ness (*or* ·nin·ity)
sat·ur·nism lead poisoning
sat·ya·gra·hi nonviolent protester
sa·tyr goatlike deity; lustful man; *compare* satire
saty·ria·sis (*or* sa·tyro·ma·nia)
sa·tyr·ic (*or* ·tyri·cal)
sa·ty·rid butterfly
sauce
sauce·pan
sau·cer
sau·cer·ful (*plural* ·fuls)
sau·ci·ly
sau·ci·ness
saucy (·ci·er, ·ci·est)
Sau·di (*or* Sau·di Ara·bian)
Sau·di Ara·bia
sau·er·bra·ten beef dish
sau·er·kraut
sau·ger fish
Sault Ste Ma·rie Canadian city; US city
sau·na
saun·ter
saun·ter·er

sau·rian lizard-like
saur·is·chian dinosaur
sau·ro·pod dinosaur
sau·ropo·dous
sau·ry (*plural* ·ries) fish
sau·sage
sau·té (·té·ing *or* ·tée·ing, ·téed)
Sau·ternes wine
Sava (*or* Save) Yugoslav river
sav·able (*or* save·able)
sav·able·ness (*or* save·)
sav·age
sav·age·ness
sav·age·ry (*plural* ·ries)
Sa·vaii Samoan island
sa·van·na (*or* ·nah)
Sa·van·nah US port
sa·vant (*fem* ·vante) learned person
sa·vate form of boxing
save
save·able *variant spelling of* savable
save-all
sav·eloy
sav·er
sav·in (*or* ·ine) shrub
sav·ing
sav·ings
Sav·iour (*US* ·ior) Christ
sav·iour (*US* ·ior) rescuer
Sa·voie French department
savoir-faire
sa·vor·ous
sa·vory (*plural* ·vories) plant; *US spelling of* savoury
sa·vour (*US* ·vor)
sa·vouri·ness (*US* ·vori·)
sa·vour·ing·ly (*US* ·vor·)
sa·voury (*US* ·vory; *plural* ·vouries)
Sa·voy French region
sa·voy cabbage
Sa·voy·ard of Savoy
sav·vy (·vies, ·vy·ing, ·vied)
saw (saw·ing, sawed, sawed *or* sawn)
saw·bill
saw·bones
saw·der flatter
saw·dust

sawed
saw·er one that saws; *compare* sawyer
saw·fish (*plural* ·fish *or* ·fishes)
saw·fly (*plural* ·flies)
saw·horse
saw·ing
saw·mill
sawn
sawn-off
saw·tooth
saw·yer professional timber sawer; *compare* sawer
sax axe
saxe blue
sax·horn
sax·ico·lous (*or* saxa·tile) biology term
saxi·fra·ga·ceous
saxi·frage
Sax·on
Saxo·ny German region
saxo·ny yarn
saxo·phone
saxo·phon·ic
sax·opho·nist
sax·tuba
say (say·ing, said)
say·er
say-so
say·yid (*or* say·id, said) Muslim title
saz·erac cocktail
scab (scab·bing, scabbed)
scab·bard
scab·bi·ly
scab·bi·ness
scab·ble shape roughly
scab·by (·bi·er, ·bi·est)
sca·bies
sca·bi·et·ic
sca·bi·ous scabby; plant
sca·brous scaly; salacious
scad fish
scads *US* many
Sca·fell Pike Cumbrian mountain
scaf·fold
scaf·fold·er
scaf·fold·ing
scag (scag·ging, scagged) *Dialect* to tear
scaglio·la imitation marble
scal·able

scal·able·ness
scal·ably
scal·age *US* price reduction
sca·lar maths term; *compare* scaler
sca·lare fish
sca·lari·form
scala·wag *variant spelling of* scallywag
scald
scald·fish (*plural* ·fish *or* ·fishes)
scale
scale·board veneer
sca·lene maths term
sca·lenus (*plural* ·leni) muscle
scal·er one that scales; *compare* scalar
scales
scali·ness
scall scalp disease
scal·lion small onion
scal·lop
scal·lop·er
scal·ly·wag (*or* scala·wag)
sca·lop·pi·ne (*or* ·ni) Italian dish
scalp
scal·pel
scal·pel·lic
scalp·er
scalp·ing
scaly (scali·er, scali·est)
scam·mo·ni·ate
scam·mo·ny (*plural* ·nies) plant; medicinal resin
scamp
scamp·er
scam·per·er
scam·pi
scamp·ish
scan (scan·ning, scanned)
scan·dal
scan·dali·za·tion (*or* ·sa·tion)
scan·dal·ize (*or* ·ise)
scan·dal·iz·er (*or* ·is·er)
scandal·monger
scan·dal·ous
scan·dal·ous·ness
Scan·da·roon pigeon
scan·dent climbing
Scan·dian Scandinavian
scan·dic of scandium

Scan·di·na·via

Scan·di·na·vian

scan·dium chemical element

scan·ner

scan·sion

scan·so·rial adapted for
climbing

scant

scanti·ly

scanti·ness

scant·ling rafter

scant·ness

scanty (scanti·er,
scanti·est)

Scapa Flow naval base

scape biology term

scape·goat

scape·grace

scapho·pod mollusc

scapo·lite mineral

scap·ose botany term

scapu·la (*plural* ·lae or
·las) shoulder bone

scapu·lar of scapula; part of
monk's habit

scar (scar·ring, scarred)

scar·ab beetle

scara·bae·id (*or* ·baean)

scara·bae·oid (*or*
scara·boid)

scara·bae·us (*plural*
·bae·uses or ·baei)
scarab

Scar·borough

scarce

scarce·ly

scarce·ment wall ledge

scarce·ness

scar·city (*plural* ·cities)

scare

scare·crow

scare·monger

scar·er

scarf (*plural* scarfs or
scarves)

scarf·skin outer skin layer

scari·fi·ca·tion

scari·fi·ca·tor surgical
instrument

scari·fi·er

scari·fy (·fies, ·fy·ing,
·fied)

scar·ing·ly

scari·ous (*or* ·ose) botany
term

scar·la·ti·na scarlet fever

scar·la·ti·nal (*or* ·nous)

scar·let

scarp

scarp·er

scary (scari·er, scari·est)

scat (scat·ting, scat·ted)

scathe

scath·ing

scato·logi·cal (*or* ·log·ic)

sca·tolo·gist

sca·tol·ogy study of
excrement

scat·ter

scat·ter·able

scatter·brain

scatter·brained

scat·ter·er

scatter-gun

scat·ter·ing

scat·ti·ly

scat·ti·ness

scat·ty (·ti·er, ·ti·est)

scaup duck

scav·enge

scav·en·ger

sce·nario (*plural* ·narios)

sce·nar·ist

scend (*or* send;
scend·ing, scend·ed or
send·ing, sent) nautical
term

scene

scen·ery (*plural* ·eries)

sce·nic

sce·ni·cal·ly

sce·nog·raph·er

sce·no·graph·ic (*or*
·graphi·cal)

sce·no·graphi·cal·ly

sce·nog·ra·phy depicting in
perspective

scent

scented

scent·less

scep·tic (*US* skep·)
doubter; *compare* septic

scep·ti·cal (*US* skep·)

scep·ti·cal·ly (*US* skep·)

scep·ti·cal·ness (*US*
skep·)

scep·ti·cism (*US* skep·)

scep·tre (*US* ·ter)

scep·tred (*US* ·tered)

Schaer·beek Belgian city

Schaff·hau·sen Swiss town

schap·pe yarn or fabric

schedu·lar

sched·ule

scheel·ite mineral

Scheldt European river

sche·ma (*plural* ·ma·ta)

sche·mat·ic

sche·mati·cal·ly

sche·ma·tism

sche·ma·ti·za·tion (*or*
·sa·tion)

sche·ma·tize (*or* ·tise)

scheme

schem·er

schem·ing

schem·ing·ly

scher·zan·do (*plural* ·di or
·dos) musical term

scher·zo (*plural* ·zos or
·zi)

schil·ler metallic lustre

schil·ling Austrian currency

schip·per·ke dog

schism

schis·mat·ic (*or* ·mati·cal)

schis·mati·cal·ly

schis·mati·cal·ness

schist rock

schis·tose

schis·tos·ity

schis·to·some blood
parasite

schis·to·so·mia·sis

schizo (*plural* schizos)

schizo·carp botany term

schizo·car·pous (*or* ·pic)

schizo·gen·esis biology
term

schizo·genet·ic

schi·zogo·ny zoology term

schiz·oid

schizo·my·cete biology
term

schizo·my·cet·ic

schizo·my·cetous

schi·zont zoology term

schizo·phre·nia

schizo·phren·ic

schizo·phy·ceous

schizo·phyte

schizo·phyt·ic

schizo·pod crustacean

schizo·thy·mia psychology
term

schizo·thy·mic

schle·miel *US* clumsy

schlep (schlep·ping, schlepped) *US* drag

Schleswig-Holstein West German state

schlie·ren physics term

schlie·ric

schlock *US* inferior goods

schmaltz (*or* **schmalz**) sentimentality

schmaltzy

schmooze *US* chat

schnapps (*or* **schnaps**)

schnau·zer dog

schnecke (*plural* schneck·en) *US* bread roll

schnit·zel

schnook *US* stupid person

schnor·rer *US* professional beggar

schnoz·zle *Slang* nose

scho·la can·to·rum (*plural* schol·ae can·to·rum) choir

schol·ar

schol·ar·li·ness

schol·ar·ly

schol·ar·ship

scho·las·tic

scho·las·ti·cal

scho·las·ti·cal·ly

scho·las·ti·cate Jesuit's probation period

scho·las·ti·cism

scho·li·ast

scho·li·as·tic

scho·lium (*plural* ·lia) marginal note

school

school·boy

school·child (*plural* ·children)

school·girl

school·fellow

school·house

schoolie *Austral* schoolteacher

school·ing

school·marm

school·marm·ish

school·master

school·master·ship

school·mate

school·mistress

school·mistressy

school·teacher

schoon·er

schorl mineral

schor·la·ceous

schot·tische dance

schuss ski run

schwa (*or* **shwa**) unstressed vowel sound

Schwa·ben West German region

Schwe·rin East German city

Schwyz Swiss town

sci·aenid (*or* ·aenoid) fish

sci·ama·chy (*or* ·oma·, ski·) fight with imaginary enemy

sci·at·ic

sci·ati·ca

sci·ence

sci·en·ter legal term

sci·en·tial knowledgeable

sci·en·tif·ic

sci·en·tifi·cal·ly

sci·en·tism

sci·en·tist

sci·en·tis·tic

Sci·en·tolo·gist

Sci·en·tol·ogy religious cult

sci-fi

scili·cet that is

scil·la plant

Scil·lo·nian

Scil·ly Isles (*or* Scil·lies)

scimi·tar (*or* simi·)

scin·coid (*or* ·coid·ian) skinklike

scin·tig·ra·phy medical technique

scin·til·la minute amount

scin·til·late

scin·til·lat·ing·ly

scin·til·la·tion

scin·til·la·tor physics term

scin·til·lom·eter

scio·man·cer

scio·man·cy divination through ghosts

scio·man·tic

sci·on descendant; plant graft

scir·rhoid

scir·rhos·ity

scir·rhous (*adj*)

scir·rhus (*plural* ·rhi *or* ·rhuses) cancerous growth; *compare* **cirrus**

scis·sel waste metal

scis·sile divisible

scis·sion

scis·sor

scis·sors

sciu·rine of squirrels

sciu·roid

sclaff golf stroke

sclaff·er

scle·ra eyeball covering

scle·ren·chy·ma plant tissue

scle·ren·chyma·tous

scle·rite zoology term

scle·rit·ic

scle·ri·tis (*or* ·ro·ti·tis) eye inflammation

scle·ro·der·ma skin disease

scle·ro·der·ma·tous

scle·roid

scle·ro·ma (*plural* ·ma·ta) hard tissue

scle·rom·eter geology apparatus

sclero·met·ric

scle·ro·phyll botany term

scle·ro·pro·tein

scle·ro·sal

scle·rosed

scle·ro·sis (*plural* ·ses)

scle·rot·ic

scle·ro·ti·oid (*or* ·ro·tial)

scle·ro·tium (*plural* ·tia) fungal tissue

scle·roto·my (*plural* ·mies) eye surgery

scle·rous

scoff

scoff·er

scoff·ing·ly

scoff·law *US* habitual lawbreaker

scold

scold·able

scold·er

scold·ing

scold·ing·ly

scol·ecite mineral

sco·lex (*plural* sco·leces *or* scoli·ces) tapeworm head

sco·lio·sis (*or* **·lio·ma**)
  spinal curvature
sco·li·ot·ic
(scollop) *incorrect spelling of*
  scallop
scolo·pen·drid centipede
scolo·pen·drine
scom·broid fish
sconce
Scone Scottish site of
  coronation stone
scone cake
scoop
scoop·er
scoot
scoot·er
scop Anglo-Saxon minstrel
scope
sco·pola·mine drug
sco·po·line sedative
scopu·la (*plural* **·las** *or*
  ·lae) zoology term
scopu·late
scor·bu·tic (*or* **·ti·cal**)
  having scurvy
scorch
scorch·er
scorch·ing
score
score·board
score·card
scor·er
sco·ria (*plural* **·riae**) solid
  lava; slag
sco·ria·ceous
sco·ri·fi·ca·tion
sco·ri·fi·er
sco·ri·fy (**·fies**, **·fy·ing**,
  ·fied)
scorn
scorn·er
scorn·ful
scorn·ful·ly
scorn·ful·ness
scorn·ing·ly
scor·pae·nid fish
scor·pae·noid
scor·per (*or* **scau·**) chisel
Scor·pi·an of Scorpio
Scor·pio sign of zodiac
scor·pi·oid
Scor·pi·on Scorpius
scor·pi·on arachnid
Scor·pius constellation
Scot

Scotch whisky; eggs; broth;
  its use as a synonym for
  Scottish *or* Scots *is*
  regarded as incorrect
scotch
sco·ter (*plural* **·ters** *or*
  ·ter) duck
scot-free
sco·tia architectural
  moulding
Scot·land
sco·to·ma (*plural* **·mas** *or*
  ·ma·ta) visual defect
sco·toma·tous
sco·to·pia night vision
sco·top·ic
Scots
Scots·man (*plural* **·men**)
Scots·woman (*plural*
  ·women)
Scot·ti·cism
Scot·tie (*or* **Scot·ty**;
  plural **·ties**)
Scot·tish
scoun·drel
scoun·drel·ly
scour
scour·er
scourge
scourg·er
scourg·ing·ly
Scouse Liverpudlian
scouse *Dialect* stew
scout
scout·er
scout·master
scow boat
scowl
scowl·er
scowl·ing·ly
Scrab·ble (*Trademark*)
  game
scrab·ble
scrab·bler
scrag (**scrag·ging**,
  scragged)
scrag·gi·ly
scrag·gi·ness
scrag·gly (**·gli·er**, **·gli·est**)
  untidy
scrag·gy (**·gi·er**, **·gi·est**)
  scrawny
scram (**scram·ming**,
  scrammed)
scramb (*or* **scram**) *Dialect*
  scratch

scram·ble
scram·bler
scran *Slang* food
Scran·ton US city
scrap (**scrap·ping**,
  scrapped)
scrap·able
scrap·book
scrape
scrap·er
scrap·er·board
scrap·heap
scrap·pi·ly
scrap·pi·ness
scrap·py (**·pi·er**, **·pi·est**)
scratch
scratch·er
scratchi·ly
scratchi·ness
scratchy (**scratchi·er**,
  scratchi·est)
scrawl
scrawl·er
scrawly
scrawni·ly
scrawni·ness
scrawny (**scrawni·er**,
  scrawni·est)
screak *Dialect* screech
scream
scream·er
scree
screech
screech·er
screechy
screed
screen
screen·able
screen·er
screen·ings sifted refuse
screen·play
screw
screw·ball
screw·driver
screw·er
screw·worm
screwy (**screwi·er**,
  screwi·est)
scrib·al of scribes
scrib·ble
scrib·bler
scrib·bly
scribe
scrib·er tool
scrim fabric

scrim·mage struggle; compare scrummage

scrim·mag·er

scrimp

scrimpi·ly

scrimpi·ness

scrimpy (scrimpi·er, scrimpi·est)

scrim·shank Slang shirk work

scrim·shaw sailors' carving

scrip certificate

script

scrip·to·rium (plural ·riums or ·ria)

scrip·tur·al

scrip·ture sacred book

Scrip·tures Bible

script·writer

script·writing

scrive·ner

scro·bicu·late (or ·lat·ed) biology term

scrod US young cod

scrofu·la

scrofu·lous

scroll

scroll·work

scroop Dialect creak

scrophu·laria·ceous botany term

scro·tal

scro·tum (plural ·ta or ·tums)

scrouge Dialect to crowd

scrounge

scroung·er

scrub (scrub·bing, scrubbed)

scrub·ber

scrub·bi·ness

scrub·by (·bi·er, ·bi·est)

scrub·land

scruff

scruffi·ly

scruffi·ness

scruffy (scruffi·er, scruffi·est)

scrum (scrum·ming, scrummed)

scrum·mage rugby scrum; compare scrimmage

scrum·mag·er

scrump Dialect steal apples

scrump·tious

scrump·tious·ness

scrumpy cider

scrunch

scru·ple

scru·pu·lous

scru·pu·lous·ness

scru·ta·tor examiner

scru·ti·neer

scru·ti·nize (or ·nise)

scru·ti·niz·er (or ·nis·er)

scru·ti·niz·ing·ly (or ·nis·ing·ly)

scru·ti·ny (plural ·nies)

scry (scry·ing, scried) crystal-gaze

scu·ba

scud (scud·ding, scud·ded)

scuff

scuf·fle

scull oar; compare skull

scull·er

scul·lery (plural ·leries)

scul·lion

scul·pin (plural ·pin or ·pins) fish

sculp·sit Latin sculptured (inscription on sculpture)

sculpt

sculp·tor (fem ·tress)

sculp·tur·al

sculp·tur·al·ly

sculp·ture

sculp·tur·esque

scum (scum·ming, scummed)

scum·ble art term

scum·mer

scum·my (·mi·er, ·mi·est)

scun·cheon part of door jamb; compare scutcheon

scunge Austral borrow

scungy (scungi·er, scungi·est) Austral miserable

scun·ner Scot aversion

Scun·thorpe

scup fish

scup·per ship's drain

scup·per·nong wine

scurf

scurfy

scur·ril·ity

scur·ril·ous

scur·ri·lous·ness

scur·ry (verb ·ries, ·ry·ing, ·ried; noun, plural ·ries)

scur·vi·ly

scur·vi·ness

scur·vy (·vi·er, ·vi·est)

scut tail

scu·tage feudal payment

Scu·ta·ri Albanian town; Turkish town

scu·tate biology term

scu·ta·tion

scutch separate fibres

scutch·eon escutcheon; compare scuncheon

scute zoology term

scu·tel·lar

scu·tel·late

scu·tel·la·tion

scu·tel·lum (plural ·la) biology term

scu·ti·form shield-shaped

scut·ter

scut·tle

scuttle·butt ship's drinking fountain

scu·tum (plural ·ta) zoology term; Roman shield

Scylla sea monster

scy·phi·form cup-shaped

scy·phis·to·ma (plural ·mae or ·mas) zoology term

scy·pho·zo·an jellyfish

scy·phus (plural ·phi) drinking cup

scythe

Scythia ancient Asian region

Scyth·ian

sea

sea·bed

sea·board

sea·borne

sea·coast

sea·cock

sea·dog

sea·farer

sea·faring

sea·food

sea·front

sea·girt

sea·going

sea·gull

seal device; to close; animal;
  compare seel
seal·able
sea-lane
seal·ant
sealed-beam
seal·er
seal·ery (*plural* ·eries)
sea·lion
seal-point Siamese cat
seal·skin
Sealy·ham terrier
seam
sea·man (*plural* ·men)
  sailor; *compare* semen
sea·man·ly
sea·man·ship
sea·mark
seam·er
seami·ness
seam·less
sea·mount underwater
  mountain
seam·stress (*or* semp·)
seamy (seami·er,
  seami·est)
Sean·ad Éire·ann Irish
  parliament
se·ance
sea·plane
sea·port
sea·quake
sear scorch; gun part;
  compare seer; sere
search
search·able
search·er
search·ing
search·ing·ly
search·light
sear·ing
sea·scape
sea·shell
sea·shore
sea·sick
sea·sick·ness
sea·side
sea·son
sea·son·able
sea·son·able·ness
sea·son·ably
sea·son·al
sea·son·al·ly
sea·son·al·ness
sea·soned·ly

sea·son·er
sea·son·ing
seat
seat·ed
seat·er
seat·ing
Se·at·tle
sea·wan (*or* se·wan) shell
  beads
sea·ward (*adj*)
sea·wards (*adv*)
sea·ware seaweed
sea·water
sea·way
sea·weed
sea·worthiness
sea·worthy
se·ba·ceous
Se·bas·to·pol *variant*
  spelling of Sevastopol
se·bif·er·ous biology term
seb·or·rhoea (*US* ·rhea)
seb·or·rhoeal (*or* ·rhoe·ic;
  US ·rheal *or* ·rhe·ic)
se·bum oily secretion
sec *short for* second *or*
  secant; dry (*of wine*)
se·cant
seca·teurs
sec·co (*plural* ·cos) wall
  painting
se·cede withdraw
se·ced·er
se·ces·sion
se·ces·sion·al
se·ces·sion·ism
se·ces·sion·ist
se·clude
se·clud·ed sheltered;
  compare seclusive
se·clud·ed·ness
se·clu·sion
se·clu·sive reclusive;
  compare secluded
se·clu·sive·ness
sec·ond unit of time;
  following first
se·cond transfer
sec·ond·ari·ly
sec·ond·ari·ness
sec·ond·ary (*plural* ·aries)
second-best (*adj*)
second-class (*adj*)
se·conde fencing position
sec·ond·er

second-floor (*adj*)
second-hand
se·cond·ment
se·con·do (*plural* ·di) part
  in piano duet
second-rate
second-rater
second-sighted
se·cre·cy (*plural* ·cies)
se·cret
sec·re·taire writing desk
sec·re·tar·ial
sec·re·tari·at
sec·re·tary (*plural* ·taries)
sec·retary-general (*plural*
  sec·re·taries-general)
sec·re·tary·ship
se·crete
se·cre·tin hormone
se·cre·tion
se·cre·tion·ary
se·cre·tive
se·cre·tive·ness
se·cre·tory
sect
sec·tar·ian
sec·tari·an·ism
sec·tary (*plural* ·taries)
  member of sect
sec·tile easily sliced
sec·til·ity
sec·tion
sec·tion·al
sec·tion·al·ism
sec·tion·al·ist
sec·tion·ali·za·tion (*or*
  ·sa·tion)
sec·tion·al·ize (*or* ·ise)
sec·tion·al·ly
sec·tor
sec·tor·al
sec·to·rial
secu·lar
secu·lar·ism
secu·lar·ist
secu·lar·is·tic
secu·lar·ity (*plural* ·ities)
secu·lari·za·tion (*or*
  ·sa·tion)
secu·lar·ize (*or* ·ise)
secu·lar·iz·er (*or* ·is·er)
se·cund botany term
sec·un·dine botany term
sec·un·dines (*plural*)
  afterbirth

se·cur·able
se·cure
se·cure·ment
se·cure·ness
se·cur·er
se·cu·ri·ty (*plural* ·rities)
se·dan
se·date
se·date·ness
se·da·tion
seda·tive
sed·en·tari·ly
sed·en·tari·ness
sed·en·tary
Se·der Jewish meal
sedge
Sedge·moor English battle
  site
sedgy
se·di·lia (*sing.* ·le) church
  seats
sedi·ment
sedi·men·tari·ly
sedi·men·tary (*or* ·tal)
sedi·men·ta·tion
sedi·men·tol·ogy
sedi·men·tous
se·di·tion
se·di·tion·ary (*plural*
  ·aries)
se·di·tious
se·di·tious·ness
se·duce
se·duc·er
se·duc·ible (*or* ·duce·able)
se·duc·ing·ly
se·duc·tion
se·duc·tive
se·duc·tive·ness
se·duc·tress
se·du·lity
sedu·lous
sedu·lous·ness
se·dum plant
see (see·ing, saw, seen)
see·able
See·beck philately term
seed
seed·bed
seed·cake
seed·case
seed·er
seedi·ly
seedi·ness
seed·less

seed·ling
seedy (seedi·er, seedi·est)
see·ing
seek (seek·ing, sought)
seek·er
seel falconry term; *compare*
  seal
seem
seem·er
seem·ing
seem·ing·ly
seem·li·ness
seem·ly (·li·er, ·li·est)
seen
seep
seep·age
seer prophet; *compare* sear;
  sere
seer·sucker
see·saw
seethe
seeth·ing·ly
seg·ment
seg·men·tal
seg·men·tary
seg·men·ta·tion
se·gno (*plural* ·gni)
  musical term
Se·go·via Spanish town
seg·re·gable
seg·re·gate
seg·re·ga·tion
seg·re·ga·tion·al
seg·re·ga·tion·ist
seg·re·ga·tive
seg·re·ga·tor
se·gui·dil·la dance
seiche water movement
(seige) *incorrect spelling of*
  siege
sei·gneur
sei·gneu·rial
sei·gneury (*plural*
  ·gneuries)
sei·gnior·age
Seine French river
seine fishing net
Seine-et-Marne French
  department
Seine-Maritime French
  department
Seine-Saint-Denis French
  department
seis·able

seise legal term; *compare*
  seize
seis·er
sei·sin legal term
seism earthquake
seis·mic (*or* ·mal, ·mi·cal)
seis·mi·cal·ly
seis·mism
seis·mo·gram
seis·mo·graph
seis·mog·ra·pher
seis·mo·graph·ic
seis·mog·ra·phy
seis·mo·log·ic (*or*
  ·logi·cal)
seis·molo·gist
seis·mol·ogy
seis·mo·scope
seis·mo·scop·ic
(seive) *incorrect spelling of*
  sieve
seiz·able
seize grasp; *compare* seise
seiz·er
seiz·ing
sei·zure
se·jant (*or* ·jeant) heraldic
  term
Sejm Polish legislature
Sek·on·di Ghanaian port
se·la·chian zoology term
sela·gi·nel·la moss
Se·lan·gor Malaysian state
sel·dom
se·lect
se·lec·tion
se·lec·tive
se·lec·tive·ness
se·lec·tiv·ity
se·lect·ness
se·lec·tor
sel·enate
se·lenic
se·leni·ous (*or* ·lenous)
sel·enite mineral
se·lenium chemical element
se·leno·graph
se·lenog·ra·pher (*or*
  ·phist)
se·leno·graph·ic (*or*
  ·graphi·cal)
se·leno·graphi·cal·ly
se·lenog·ra·phy mapping
  moon's surface
se·lenolo·gist

se·lenol·ogy study of moon
se·leno·mor·phol·ogy
Se·leu·cid (*plural* ·cids *or*
·cidae) member of
Hellenistic dynasty
self (*plural* selves)
self-abasement
self-abnega·tion
self-absorbed
self-absorp·tion
self-abuse
self-action
self-actuali·za·tion
self-addressed
self-aggran·dize·ment
self-analy·sis
self-analyti·cal
self-anneal·ing
self-annihi·la·tion
self-appoint·ed
self-assertion
self-assertive
self-assurance
self-assured
self-aware
self-aware·ness
self-cater·ing
self-centred (*US*
·centered)
self-centred·ness (*US*
·centered·ness)
self-coloured (*US*
·colored)
self-concept
self-confessed
self-confidence
self-confident
self-conscious
self-conscious·ness
self-contained
self-contra·dic·tion
self-contra·dic·tory
self-control
self-controlled
self-deception (*or*
·deceit)
self-deceptive
self-defence
self-denial
self-denying
self-discipline
self-disciplined
self-educat·ed
self-employed
self-efface·ment

self-effacing
self-esteem
self-evident
self-evidence
self-feeder
self-fertile
self-fertili·za·tion (*or*
·sa·tion)
self-fertilized (*or*
-fertilised)
self-govern·ment
self-heal plant
self-help
self-hood
self-image
self-import·ance
self-import·ant
self-imposed
self-improve·ment
self-induced
self-induct·ance
self-induction
self-inductive
self-indulgence
self-indulgent
self-inflict·ed
self-inflic·tion
self-interest
self·ish
self·ish·ness
self-justifi·ca·tion
self-justify·ing
self-knowledge
self·less
self·less·ness
self-liquidat·ing
self-loading
self-made
self-opin·ion·at·ed (*or*
-opinioned)
self-pity
self-pitying
self-pollinat·ed
self-pollina·tion
self-portrait
self-possessed
self-posses·sion
self-preser·va·tion
self-propelled
self-protec·tion
self-raising
self-regard
self-reliance
self-reliant
self-reproach

self-reproach·ful
self-respect
self-respect·ing
self-restraint
self-righteous
self-righteous·ness
self-rule
self-sacrifice
self-sacrific·ing
self·same
self-satisfac·tion
self-satisfied
self-sealing
self-seeker
self-seeking
self-service
self-starter
self-styled
self-sufficiency
self-sufficient (*or*
-suffic·ing)
self-taught
self-willed
self-winding
Sel·juk (*or* ·ju·kian)
member of Turkish
dynasty
Sel·kirk former Scottish
county
sell (sell·ing, sold)
sell·er
selling-plater type of
racehorse
Sel·lo·tape (*Trademark*)
sell·out (*noun*)
Selt·zer mineral water
sel·va forest
sel·vage (*or* ·vedge) edge
of fabric; *compare* salvage
selves *plural of* self
se·man·tic
se·man·ti·cal·ly
se·man·ti·cist
se·man·tics
sema·phore
sema·phor·ic (*or*
·phori·cal)
sema·phori·cal·ly
Se·ma·rang (*or* Sa·)
Indonesian port
se·ma·sio·logi·cal
se·ma·sio·logi·cal·ly
se·ma·si·olo·gist
se·ma·siol·ogy semantics
se·mat·ic zoology term

sema·tol·ogy semantics
sem·blance
semé (or se·mée) heraldry
  term
sem·eme linguistics term
se·men ejaculated fluid;
  compare seaman
se·mes·ter
se·mes·tral
semi (plural semis)
semi·an·nual
semi·an·nu·al·ly
semi·aquat·ic
semi·ar·id
semi·arid·ity
semi·auto·mat·ic
semi·auto·mati·cal·ly
Semi-Bantu African
  language
semi·bold printing term
semi·breve
semi·cen·ten·nial
semi·cir·cle
semi·cir·cu·lar
semi·co·lon
semi·con·duc·tion
semi·con·duc·tor
semi·con·scious
semi·con·scious·ness
semi·de·tached
semi·di·am·eter
semi·di·ur·nal
semi·dome
semi·el·lip·ti·cal
semi·fi·nal
semi·fi·nal·ist
semi·flu·id
semi·flu·id·ic
semi·flu·id·ity
semi·lit·er·ate
semi·lu·nar
semi·month·ly
semi·nal
semi·nal·ity
semi·nal·ly
semi·nar
semi·nar·ial
semi·nar·ian student at
  seminary
semi·nary (plural ·naries)
semi·nif·er·ous
  transporting semen
Semi·nole (plural ·noles
  or ·nole) American
  Indian

se·mi·ol·ogy (or ·mei·)
se·mi·ot·ic (or ·mei·)
se·mi·ot·ics (or ·mei·)
  study of symbols
Se·mi·pa·la·tinsk Soviet
  city
semi·pal·mate (or
  ·mat·ed) zoology term
semi·para·sit·ic
semi·para·sit·ism
semi·per·meabil·ity
semi·per·meable
semi·porce·lain
semi·precious
semi·pro (plural ·pros)
semi·pro·fes·sion·al
semi·qua·ver
Se·mira·mis legendary
  queen
semi·rig·id
semi·skilled
semi·sol·id
Se·mite (or Shem·ite)
Se·mit·ic (or She·)
Se·mit·ics study of Semitic
  languages
Semi·tist
semi·ton·al·ly
semi·tone
semi·ton·ic
semi·trail·er
semi·tropi·cal
semi·trop·ics
semi·vit·reous
semi·vo·cal (or ·cal·ic)
semi·vow·el
semi·week·ly
semi·year·ly
semo·li·na
sem·per fi·de·lis Latin
  always faithful
sem·per pa·ra·tus Latin
  always prepared
sem·pi·ter·nal everlasting
sem·pi·ter·nity
sem·pli·ce musical term
sem·pre musical term
semp·stress variant spelling
  of seamstress
sen (plural sen) Oriental
  currency
sen·ar·mon·tite mineral
sen·ary of six
Sen·ate senate of USA,
  ancient Rome, etc.

sen·ate legislative body
sena·tor
sena·to·rial
send (send·ing, sent)
send·able
Sen·dai Japanese city
sen·dal fabric
send·er
send·off
send·up (noun)
Sen·eca (plural ·ecas or
  ·eca) American Indian
sen·ega plant
Sen·egal
Sen·ega·lese
Sen·egam·bia African
  region
se·nes·cence
se·nes·cent
sen·eschal medieval
  steward
sen·hor (plural ·hors or
  ·hores) Portuguese man;
  Mr
sen·hora Portuguese
  woman; Mrs
sen·hor·ita Portuguese
  young woman; Miss
se·nile
se·nil·ity
sen·ior
sen·ior·ity (plural ·ities)
Sen·lac battle site
sen·na
Sen·nar Sudanese region
sen·net fanfare
sen·nit braided cordage
se·ñor (plural ·ñors or
  ·ñores) Spanish man; Mr
se·ño·ra Spanish woman;
  Mrs
se·ño·ri·ta Spanish young
  woman; Miss
sen·sate (·sat·ed)
sen·sa·tion
sen·sa·tion·al
sen·sa·tion·al·ly
sen·sa·tion·al·ism
sen·sa·tion·al·ist
sen·sa·tion·al·is·tic
sense
sense·less
sense·less·ness
sen·si·bilia what can be
  sensed

sen·sibil·ity (*plural* ·ities)
sen·sible
sen·sible·ness
sen·sibly
sen·sil·lum (*plural* ·la) zoology term
sen·si·tive
sen·si·tive·ness
sen·si·tiv·ity (*plural* ·ities)
sen·si·ti·za·tion (*or* ·sa·tion)
sen·si·tize (*or* ·tise)
sen·si·tiz·er (*or* ·tis·er)
sen·si·tom·eter
sen·si·tom·etry
sen·sor sensing device; *compare* censor
sen·so·ri·mo·tor (*or* sen·so·mo·tor) physiology term
sen·so·rium area of brain
sen·so·ry (*or* ·rial)
sen·sual gratifying the senses; *compare* censual; sensuous
sen·su·al·ism
sen·su·al·ist
sen·su·al·ity (*plural* ·ities)
sen·su·al·ly
sen·su·al·ness
sen·su·ous pleasing to the senses; *compare* sensual
sen·su·ous·ness
sent
sen·tence
sen·ten·tial
sen·ten·tious
sen·ten·tious·ness
sen·tience (*or* ·tien·cy)
sen·ti·ent
sen·ti·ment
sen·ti·ment·al
sen·ti·men·tal·ism
sen·ti·men·tal·ist
sen·ti·men·tal·ity (*plural* ·ities)
sen·ti·men·tali·za·tion (*or* ·sa·tion)
sen·ti·men·tal·ize (*or* ·ise)
sen·ti·men·tal·ly
sen·ti·nel
sen·try (*plural* ·tries)
Se·nus·si (*or* ·nu·si; *plural* ·sis) member of Muslim sect

sen·za musical term
Seoul capital of South Korea
sep·al
se·palled (*or* ·pal·ous)
se·pa·loid (*or* ·line)
sepa·rabil·ity (*or* ·rable·ness)
sepa·rable
sepa·rate
sepa·rate·ness
sepa·ra·tion
sepa·ra·tism
sepa·ra·tist (*or* ·ra·tion·ist)
sepa·ra·tis·tic
sepa·ra·tive
sepa·ra·tive·ness
sepa·ra·tor
sepa·ra·trix (*plural* ·trices) oblique stroke
Se·phar·di (*plural* ·dim) Iberian Jew
Se·phar·dic
se·pia
se·pio·lite mineral
se·poy Indian soldier
sep·sis
sept clan
sep·ta *plural of* septum
sep·tal
sep·tar·ian
sep·tar·ium (*plural* ·ia) geology term
sep·tate
sep·ta·va·lent *variant spelling of* septivalent
Sep·tem·ber
Sep·tem·brist French revolutionary
sep·te·nary (*plural* ·naries)
sep·ten·nial
sep·ten·nium (*plural* ·niums *or* ·nia)
sep·tet (*or* ·tette)
sep·tic putrefying; *compare* sceptic
sep·ti·cae·mia (*US* ·cemia)
sep·ti·cae·mic (*US* ·cemic)
sep·ti·cal·ly
sep·ti·cid·al botany term
sep·tic·ity
sep·tif·ra·gal botany term

sep·ti·lat·er·al
sep·til·lion (*plural* ·lion *or* ·lions) 10^{42}
sep·til·lionth
sep·time fencing position
sep·ti·va·lent (*or* ·ta·)
sep·tua·genar·ian
Sep·tua·gesi·ma third Sunday before Lent
Sep·tua·gint Greek Old Testament
sep·tum (*plural* ·ta)
sep·tu·ple
sep·tup·let
sep·tu·pli·cate
se·pul·chral
se·pul·chral·ly
sep·ul·chre (*US* ·cher)
sep·ul·ture burial
se·qua·cious in sequence
se·quac·ity
se·quel
se·quela (*plural* ·quelae) medical term
se·quence
se·quenc·er electronic device
se·quent
se·quen·tial
se·quen·ti·al·ity
se·quen·tial·ly
se·ques·ter
se·ques·trable
se·ques·tral
se·ques·trant
se·ques·trate
se·ques·tra·tion
se·ques·tra·tor
se·ques·trum (*plural* ·tra) medical term
se·quin
se·quined
se·quoia
ser (*or* seer) Indian unit
sera *plural of* serum
sé·rac ice pinnacle
se·ra·glio (*plural* ·glios)
se·rail harem
Se·rang Indonesian island
ser·aph (*plural* ·aphs *or* ·aphim) angel; *compare* serif
Sera·pis Egyptian god
Serb a Serbian

Ser·bia Yugoslav republic
Ser·bian
Serbo-Croat (*or*
-Croa·tian) language
ser·dab chamber in
Egyptian tomb
sere ecology term; *compare*
cere; sear; seer
sere (*or* sear) withered;
compare cere; sear; seer
se·rein tropical rain
ser·enade
ser·enad·er
se·rena·ta cantata
ser·en·dip·ity
se·rene
se·rene·ness
se·ren·ity (*plural* ·ities)
serf medieval peasant;
compare surf
serf·dom (*or* ·hood)
serge fabric; *compare* surge
ser·gean·cy (*or*
·geant·ship)
ser·geant
Ser·gi·pe Brazilian state
se·rial story in instalments;
in series; *compare* cereal
se·rial·ism
se·riali·za·tion (*or*
·sa·tion)
se·rial·ize (*or* ·ise)
se·rial·ly
se·ri·ate
se·ria·tim in a series
se·ri·ceous
seri·cin protein in silk
seri·cul·tur·al
seri·cul·ture silkworm
rearing
seri·cul·tur·ist
seri·ema bird
se·ries (*plural* ·ries)
series-wound electrical
term
ser·if (*or* ·iph) printing
term; *compare* seraph
seri·graph silk-screen print
se·rig·ra·phy
ser·in bird
ser·ine amino acid
se·rin·ga rubber tree;
compare syringa
se·rio·com·ic (*or*
·comi·cal)
se·rio·comi·cal·ly

se·ri·ous grave; *compare*
serous
se·ri·ous·ly
se·ri·ous·ness
ser·jeant at law
ser·mon
ser·mon·ic
ser·moni·cal
ser·mon·ize (*or* ·ise)
ser·mon·iz·er (*or* ·is·er)
se·ro·log·ic (*or* ·logi·cal)
se·rolo·gist
se·rol·ogy study of serums
se·ro·sa membrane
se·rosi·ty (*or* ·rous·ness)
se·roti·nal (*or* ·nous)
sero·tine bat
sero·to·nin biochemical
compound
se·rous of serum; *compare*
serious
ser·ow antelope
ser·pent
ser·pen·tine
ser·pigi·nous
ser·pi·go skin disease
ser·pu·lid worm
ser·ra·nid (*or* ·noid) fish
ser·rate
ser·rat·ed
ser·ra·tion (*or* ·ture)
ser·ried
ser·ri·form
ser·ru·late (*or* ·lat·ed)
ser·ru·la·tion notch
ser·tu·lar·ian zoology term
se·rum (*plural* ·rums *or*
·ra)
serv·able (*or* serve·)
ser·val (*plural* ·vals *or*
·val) animal
serv·ant
serve
serv·er
serv·ery (*plural* ·eries)
ser·vice
ser·vice·abil·ity (*or*
·able·ness)
ser·vice·able
ser·vice·ably
ser·vice·berry (*plural*
·berries)
ser·vice·man (*plural*
·men)
ser·vi·ette

ser·vile
ser·vil·ity (*or* ·vile·ness)
serv·ing
ser·vi·tor
ser·vi·tude
ser·vo (*plural* ·vos)
ser·vo·mechani·cal
ser·vo·mecha·nism
ser·vo·mo·tor
sesa·me
sesa·moid bone
Se·so·tho language
ses·qui·al·te·ra organ stop
ses·qui·car·bon·ate
ses·qui·cen·ten·nial
ses·qui·ox·ide
ses·qui·peda·lian (*or*
·quip·edal) using long
words
ses·qui·peda·li·an·ism
ses·sile
ses·sil·ity
ses·sion meeting; *compare*
cession
ses·sion·al
ses·sion·al·ly
ses·terce (*or* ·ter·tius;
plural ·terces *or* ·tia)
Roman coin
ses·ter·tium (*plural* ·tia)
Roman coin
ses·tet six-line verse;
compare sextet
ses·ti·na verse form
Ses·tos ancient Turkish
town
set (set·ting, set)
seta (*plural* setae) small
bristle
se·ta·ceous
se·tal
set·back
se·ti·form
set·line
set-off printing term
se·tose bristly
set·screw
sett (*or* set) paving slab;
badger's den
set·tee
set·ter
set·ting
set·tle
set·tle·able
set·tle·ment

set·tler (*or in legal contexts* ·tlor)
set-to (*noun, plural* -tos)
set-up (*noun*)
Se·van Soviet lake
Se·vas·to·pol (*or* ·bas·) Soviet port
sev·en
sev·en·fold
sev·en·teen
sev·en·teenth
sev·enth
sev·en·ti·eth
sev·en·ty (*plural* ·ties)
sev·er
sev·er·able
sev·er·al
sev·er·al·ly
sev·er·al·ty (*plural* ·ties) separateness
sev·er·ance
se·vere
se·vere·ness
se·ver·ity (*plural* ·ities)
Sev·ern British river
Se·ville Spanish port
Sèvres porcelain
sew (sew·ing, sewed, sewn *or* sewed) to stitch; *compare* sow
sew·age waste matter
sew·er sewage drain; one who sews; *compare* suer
sew·er·age system of sewers
sew·ing
sewn
sex
sexa·genar·ian
sex·ag·enary (*plural* ·enaries)
Sexa·gesi·ma second Sunday before Lent
sexa·gesi·mal of 60
sex·cen·te·nary (*plural* ·naries)
sex·en·nial
sexi·ly
sexi·ness
sex·ism
sex·ist
sexi·va·lent (*or* sexa·)
sex·less
sex·less·ness
sex·olo·gist
sex·ol·ogy

sex·par·tite
sex·pot
sext canonical hour
sex·tant
sex·tet (*or* ·tette) group of six; *compare* sestet
sex·tile
sex·til·lion (*plural* ·lions *or* ·lion) 10^{36}
sex·til·lionth
sex·to·deci·mo (*plural* ·mos)
sex·ton
sex·tu·ple
sex·tup·let
sex·tu·pli·cate
sex·ual
sexu·al·ity
sex·ual·ly
sexy (sexi·er, sexi·est)
Sey·chelles
Sfax Tunisian port
sfor·zan·do (*or* ·za·to) musical term
sfu·ma·to art term
sgraf·fi·to (*plural* ·ti) art term
shab·bi·ly
shab·bi·ness
shab·by (·bi·er, ·bi·est)
shack
shack·le
shack·ler
shad (*plural* shad *or* shads) fish
shad·bush
shad·dock fruit
shade
shadi·ly
shadi·ness
shad·ing
sha·doof (*or* ·duf) water-raising device
shad·ow
shadow-box
shadow-boxing
shad·ow·er
shad·ow·graph
shad·owi·ness
shad·owy
Shadrach biblical character
shady (shadi·er, shadi·est)
shaft
shaft·ing

shag (shag·ging, shagged)
shag·bark (*or* shell·bark)
shag·gi·ly
shag·gi·ness
shag·gy (·gi·er, ·gi·est)
sha·green
shah
shah·dom
Shah·ja·han·pur Indian city
shak·able (*or* shake·)
shake (shak·ing, shook, shak·en)
shake·down (*noun*)
shak·er
Shak·ers US sect
Shake·spear·ean (*or* ·ian)
Shake·spear·ea·na
shake-up (*noun*)
Shakh·ty Soviet city
shaki·ly
shaki·ness
shako (*or* shacko; *plural* shakos *or* shackos) military headdress
shaky (shaki·er, shaki·est)
shale
shall (should)
shal·loon fabric
shal·lop boat
shal·lot
shal·low
shal·low·ness
sha·lom Jewish greeting; *compare* slalom
shalt
shaly
sham (sham·ming, shammed)
sham·able (*or* shame·)
sham·an priest
sham·an·ism
Sha·mash Assyrian god
sham·ble
sham·bles
sham·bol·ic
shame
shame·faced
shame·faced·ness
shame·ful
shame·ful·ly
shame·ful·ness
shame·less
shame·less·ness

sham·mer
sham·my (*plural* ·mies) leather
sham·poo (*noun, plural* ·poos; *verb* ·poos, ·poo·ing, ·pooed)
sham·poo·er
sham·rock
Shan (*plural* Shans *or* Shan) Mongoloid people
shan·dry·dan cart
shan·dy (*plural* ·dies)
shan·dy·gaff *US* shandy
Shang Chinese dynasty
Shang·hai Chinese port
shang·hai (·hais, ·hai·ing, ·haied) kidnap
Shangri-la
shank
Shan·non Irish river
shan·ny (*plural* ·nies) fish
Shan·si Chinese province
shan't shall not
Shan·tung Chinese province
shan·tung silk
shan·ty (*plural* ·ties) hut
shan·ty (*or* shan·tey, chan·ty; *US* chan·tey; *plural* ·ties *or* ·teys) sea song
shanty·town
shap·able (*or* shape·)
shape
shape·less
shape·less·ness
shape·li·ness
shape·ly (·li·er, ·li·est)
shap·er
shar·able (*or* share·)
shard (*or* sherd)
share
share·crop (·crop·ping, ·cropped)
share·crop·per
share·holder
share-out (*noun*)
shar·er
sha·ria (*or* she·) Islamic doctrines
shark
shark·skin
Sha·ron Israeli plain
sharp
sharp·en
sharp·en·er

sharp·er
sharp-eyed
sharp·ish
sharp·ness
sharp-set
sharp·shooter
sharp-sighted
sharp-sighted·ness
sharp-tongued
sharp-witted
sharp-witted·ness
shash·lik (*or* ·lick) kebab
shat·ter
shat·ter·er
shat·ter·ing·ly
shatter·proof
shav·able (*or* shave·)
shave (shav·ing, shaved, shaved *or* shav·en)
shav·er
Sha·vian of G. B. Shaw
shav·ing
shawl
shawm musical instrument
Shaw·nee (*plural* ·nees *or* ·nee) American Indian
she
shea tree
shead·ing Manx region
sheaf (*plural* sheaves)
shear (shear·ing, sheared, sheared *or* shorn) cut; deformation; *compare* sheer
shear·er
shear·legs *variant spelling of* sheerlegs
shear·ling
shears
shear·water bird
sheat·fish (*plural* ·fish *or* ·fishes)
sheath (*noun; plural* sheaths)
sheath·bill
sheathe (*verb*)
sheath·ing
sheave bind in sheaves; grooved wheel
She·ba ancient kingdom
she·bang *Slang* situation
she·been (*or* ·bean) illegal drinking place
She·chem ancient Jordanian town

shed (shed·ding, shed)
she'd she had; she would
shed·able (*or* shed·dable)
shed·der
sheen
sheeny
sheep (*plural* sheep)
sheep·cote
sheep-dip
sheep·dog
sheep·fold
sheep·ish
sheep·ish·ness
sheep·shank knot
sheeps·head (*plural* ·head *or* ·heads) fish
sheep·shearer
sheep·shearing
sheep·skin
sheep·walk grazing land
sheer steep; transparent; absolutely; deviate; *compare* shear
sheer·legs (*or* shear·) lifting device
Sheer·ness English port
sheer·ness
sheet
sheet·ing
Shef·field
sheik (*or* sheikh)
sheik·dom (*or* sheikh·)
shei·la *Austral* girl
shek·el
shel·duck (*or* ·drake; *plural* ·ducks, ·duck *or* ·drakes, ·drake)
shelf (*plural* shelves)
shell
she'll she will
shel·lac (·lack·ing, ·lacked)
shell·back experienced sailor
shell·fire
shell·fish (*plural* ·fish *or* ·fishes)
shell·less
shell·like
shell·proof
shell-shocked
Shel·ta tinkers' language
shel·ter
shel·ter·er

shel·tie (or ·ty; plural
·ties) dog; pony
shelve (verb)
shelv·er
shelv·ing
She·ma Jewish doctrine
she·moz·zle
Shen·an·do·ah US river;
national park
she·nani·gan
Shen·si Chinese province
Shen·yang Chinese city
She·ol abode of the dead
shep·herd
shep·herd·ess
shepherd's-purse
Shep·pey (Isle of)
sher·ardi·za·tion (or
·sa·tion)
sher·ard·ize (or ·ise)
Sheraton furniture
sher·bet
Sher·brooke Canadian city
sherd variant spelling of
shard
she·rif (or ·reef) Muslim
ruler
sher·iff officer
Sher·pa (plural ·pas or
·pa)
sher·ry (plural ·ries)
sher·wa·ni Indian coat
she's she is
Shet·land
shew·bread (or show·)
biblical bread
Shi·ah Muslim sect
shiai judo contest
shib·bo·leth
shick·er Austral alcoholic
drink
shied
shield
shield·er
shiel·ing Scot hut; pasture
shi·er (adj) variant spelling
of shyer
shi·est variant spelling of
shyest
shift
shift·er
shifti·ly
shifti·ness
shift·ing·ly
shift·less

shift·less·ness
shifty (shifti·er, shifti·est)
shi·gel·la bacterium
Shih·chia·chuang (or
·kia·chwang) Chinese
city
shih-tzu dog
Shi·ism
Shi·ite adherent of Shiah
shi·kar (·kar·ring,
·karred) hunt game
shi·ka·ri (or ·ree; plural
·ris or ·rees) hunter
Shi·ko·ku Japanese island
shil·lelagh (or shil·la·la)
Irish cudgel
shil·ling
Shil·long Indian city
shilly-shalli·er
shilly-shally (·shallies,
·shally·ing, ·shallied)
Shi·loh biblical city
shi·ly less common spelling of
shyly
shim (shim·ming,
shimmed)
shim·mer
shim·mer·ing·ly
shim·mery
shim·my (noun, plural
·mies; verb ·mies,
·my·ing, ·mied) dance
Shi·mo·no·seki Japanese
port
shin (shin·ning, shinned)
shin·bone
shin·dig (or ·dy; plural
·digs or ·dies)
shine (shin·ing, shone)
shin·er
shin·gle
shin·gler
shin·gles
shin·gly
shini·ness
Shin·to Japanese religion
Shin·to·ism
Shin·to·ist
shin·ty (US ·ny; plural
·ties or ·nies) hockey
shiny (shini·er, shini·est)
ship (ship·ping, shipped)
ship·able
ship·board
ship·builder
ship·building

ship·load
ship·master (or ·man;
plural ·masters or
·men)
ship·mate
ship·ment
ship·owner
ship·per
ship·ping
ship-rigged
ship·shape
ship·way
ship·worm
ship·wreck
ship·wright
ship·yard
shi·ra·lee Austral swagman's
bundle
Shi·raz Iranian city
Shi·ré African river
shire
shirk
shirk·er
shirr
shirr·ing
shirt
shirti·ly
shirti·ness
shirt·ing
shirt·sleeve
shirt-tail
shirt·waister
shirty (shirti·er,
shirti·est)
shit (shit·ting, shit·ted or
shit)
shit·tah (plural ·tim or
·tahs) biblical tree
Shit·tim biblical place
shit·ty
Shiva variant spelling of Siva
shive cork
shiv·er
shiv·er·er
shiv·er·ing·ly
shiv·ery
Shi·zuo·ka Japanese city
Shluh (plural Shluhs or
Shluh) African people
Shoa Ethiopian province
shoal
shoali·ness
shoaly
shoat (or shote) weaned
piglet

shock
shock·abil·ity
shock·able
shock·er
shock·headed
shock·ing
shock·ing·ness
shock·proof
shod
shod·di·ly
shod·di·ness
shod·dy (·di·er, ·di·est)
shoe (shoe·ing, shod)
  footwear; *compare* shoo
shoe·bill
shoe·black
shoe·horn
shoe·lace
shoe·maker
shoe·making
shoe·shine
shoe·string
shoe·tree
sho·far (*or* ·phar; *plural*
  ·fars, ·phars *or* ·froth,
  ·phroth) Jewish horn
sho·gun Japanese leader
sho·gun·ate
sho·ji (*plural* ·ji *or* ·jis)
  paper screen
Sho·la·pur Indian city
Sho·na (*plural* ·na *or*
  ·nas) African people
shone
shoo (shoos, shoo·ing,
  shooed) chase off;
  compare shoe
shook
shoon *Scot* shoes
shoot (shoot·ing, shot)
shoot·er
shoot-out (*noun*)
shop (shop·ping,
  shopped)
shop·girl
shop·keeper
shop·keeping
shop·lifter
shop·lifting
shop·per
shop·ping
shop·soiled (*US* ·worn)
shop·talk
shop·walker
shop·worn *US* shopsoiled

shor·an radar system
shore
shore·less
shore·line
shore·ward (*adj*)
shore·wards (*adv*)
shor·ing
shorn
short
short·age
short·bread
short·cake
short-change
short-changer
short-circuit (*verb*)
short·coming
short·en
short·en·er
short·en·ing
short·fall
short-haired
short·hand
short-handed
short-handed·ness
short·horn cattle
shortie (*or* shorty; *plural*
  shorties)
short·ish
short-list (*verb*)
short-lived
short·ly
short·ness
short-range
shorts
short-sighted
short-sighted·ness
short-spoken
short-tempered
short-term (*adj*)
short-waisted
short-winded
shorty *variant spelling of*
  shortie
Sho·sho·ne (*or* ·ni; *plural*
  ·nes, ·ne *or* ·nis, ·ni)
  American Indian
Sho·sho·nean (*or* ·nian)
shot
shote *variant spelling of*
  shoat
shot·gun (·gun·ning,
  ·gunned)
shot-putter
shott (*or* chott) salt lake
shot·ten recently spawned

should
shoul·der
shouldn't
shouse *Austral* lavatory
shout
shout·er
shove
shov·el (·el·ling, ·elled;
  US ·el·ing, ·eled)
shov·el·er duck; *compare*
  shoveller
shovel·ful (*plural* ·fuls)
shovel·head shark
shov·el·ler (*US* ·el·er) one
  who shovels; *compare*
  shoveler
shovel·nose fish
shov·er
show (show·ing, showed,
  shown *or* showed)
show·biz
show·boat
show·case
showd *Scot* rock
show·down
show·er
shower·proof
show·ery
show·girl
showi·ly
showi·ness
show·ing
show·jumper
show·jumping
show·man (*plural* ·men)
show·man·ship
shown
show-off (*noun*)
show·piece
show·place
show·room
showy (showi·er,
  showi·est)
shrank
shrap·nel
shred (shred·ding,
  shred·ded *or* shred)
shred·der
Shreve·port US city
shrew
shrewd
shrewdie *Austral* shrewd
  person
shrewd·ness
shrew·ish

shrew·ish·ness
Shrews·bury
shriek
shriek·er
shrie·val of a sheriff
shriev·al·ty (plural ·ties)
shrift
shrike
shrill
shrill·ness
shrilly
shrimp
shrimp·er
shrine
shrink (shrink·ing,
    shrank or shrunk,
    shrunk or shrunk·en)
shrink·able
shrink·age
shrink·er
shrink·ing·ly
shrink-wrap (-wrapping,
    -wrapped)
shrive (shriv·ing, shrove
    or shrived, shriv·en or
    shrived)
shriv·el (·el·ling, ·elled;
    US ·el·ing, ·eled)
shriv·er
shroff detector of counterfeit
    money
Shrop·shire
shroud
shroud-laid
shrove
Shrove·tide
shrub
shrub·bery (plural
    ·beries)
shrub·bi·ness
shrub·by (·bi·er, ·bi·est)
shrug (shrug·ging,
    shrugged)
shrunk
shrunk·en
shuck
shuck·er
shucks exclamation
shud·der
shud·der·ing·ly
shud·dery
shuf·fle
shuffle·board
shuf·fler

shug·gy (plural ·gies)
    Dialect swing
shul (or schul; plural
    shuln or schuln)
    synagogue
shun (shun·ning,
    shunned)
shun·nable
shun·ner
shunt
shunt·er
shunt-wound electrical
    term
shush
shut (shut·ting, shut)
shut·down (noun)
shut·eye
shut-off (noun)
shut·out (noun)
shut·ter
shut·ter·ing
shut·tle
shuttle·cock
shy (adj shy·er, shy·est or
    shi·er, shi·est; verb
    shies, shy·ing, shied;
    noun, plural shies)
shy·er (noun)
Shy·lock heartless creditor
shy·ly
shy·ness
shy·ster
Si (or Hsi) Chinese river
sial part of earth's crust
si·ala·gog·ic (or ·alo·)
    stimulating salivation
si·ala·gogue (or ·alo·)
si·al·ic
Si·al·kot Pakistani city
sia·loid saliva-like
Siam former name of
    Thailand
sia·mang ape
Sia·mese (plural ·mese)
Sian (or Hsian) Chinese
    city
Siang (or Hsiang) Chinese
    river
Siang·tan Chinese city
sib (or sibb) kin
Si·beria
Si·berian
sibi·lance (or ·lan·cy)
sibi·lant
sibi·late

sibi·la·tion
Si·biu Romanian town
sib·ling
sib·yl prophetess
sib·yl·line (or si·byl·lic)
sic Latin thus; indicates the
    deliberate inclusion of a
    questionable word in text
sic·ca·tive drying agent
sice variant spelling of syce
Si·cil·ian
Sici·ly
sick
sick·bay
sick·bed
sick·en
sick·en·er
sick·en·ing
sick·en·ing·ly
sick·le
sickle·bill
sick·li·ness
sick·ly (·li·er, ·li·est)
sick·ness
sic pas·sim Latin thus
    everywhere; indicates a
    word in text is the same
    throughout
Sicy·on ancient Greek city
side
side·band electronics term
side·board
side·boards (or esp. US
    ·burns)
side·car
side·dress
side·kick
side·light
side·line
side·long
si·dereal of stars
si·der·ite mineral
si·der·it·ic
si·dero·lite meteorite
si·der·osis disease
si·dero·stat astronomical
    instrument
si·dero·stat·ic
sid·er·ot·ic
side·saddle
side·show
side·slip (·slip·ping,
    ·slipped)
sides·man (plural ·men)
side-splitting

side·step (·step·ping,
  ·stepped)
side·step·per
side·stroke
side·swipe
side·swip·er
side·track
side·walk *US* pavement
side·wall
side·ward (*adj*)
side·wards (*adv*)
side·ways
side·wheel
side·wheeler boat
side·winder snake
Sidi-bel-Abbès Algerian
  city
sid·ing
si·dle
si·dler
Si·don Phoenician city
siè·cle *French* century
siege
sie·mens (*plural* ·mens)
  unit
Si·ena Italian city
si·en·na pigment
si·er·ra
Si·er·ra Leo·ne
Si·er·ra Le·on·ean
Si·er·ra Ma·dre Mexican
  mountains
si·er·ran
Si·er·ra Ne·va·da US
  mountains
si·es·ta
sieve
(sieze) *incorrect spelling of*
  seize
si·fa·ka animal
sift
sift·er
sift·ings
sigh
sigh·er
sight vision; *compare* site
sight·able
sight·ed
sight·er
sight·less
sight·less·ness
sight·li·ness
sight·ly (·li·er, ·li·est)
sight-read (-reading,
  -read)

sight-reader
sight-screen
sight-see (·see·ing, ·saw,
  ·seen)
sight·seer
sig·la list of symbols
sig·los (*plural* ·loi) coin
sig·ma Greek letter
sig·mate
sig·ma·tion
sig·moid (*or* ·moi·dal)
sig·moido·scope medical
  instrument
sig·moido·scop·ic
sig·moid·os·co·py
sign
sig·nal (·nal·ling, ·nalled;
  US ·nal·ing, ·naled)
sig·nal·ize (*or* ·ise)
sig·nal·ler (*US* ·nal·er)
sig·nal·ly
sig·nal·man (*plural* ·men)
sig·na·tory (*plural* ·tories)
sig·na·ture
sign·board
sign·er
sig·net seal on ring; *compare*
  cygnet
sig·ni·fi·able
sig·nifi·cance
sig·nifi·cant
sig·nifi·cant·ly
sig·ni·fi·ca·tion
sig·nifi·ca·tive
sig·nifi·ca·tive·ness
sig·ni·fi·er
sig·ni·fy (·fies, ·fy·ing,
  ·fied)
si·gnor (*plural* ·gnors *or*
  ·gnori) *Italian* man; Mr
si·gno·ra (*plural* ·ras *or*
  ·re) *Italian* woman; Mrs
si·gno·re (*plural* ·ri)
  Italian man; Sir
si·gnori·na (*plural* ·nas *or*
  ·ne) *Italian* young
  woman; Miss
sign·post
Sigurd Norse hero
sika deer
sike *Dialect* small stream
Sikh
Sikh·ism
Sik·kim Indian state
Sik·ki·mese

si·lage
Si·las·tic (*Trademark*)
sild fish
sile *Dialect* rain
si·lence
si·lenc·er
si·lent
si·lent·ly
si·lent·ness
Silenus Greek satyr
Si·lesia European region
si·lesia fabric
si·lex heat-resistant glass
sil·hou·ette
sili·ca mineral; *compare*
  silicon; silicone
sili·cate
si·li·ceous (*or* ·cious)
si·lic·ic
sili·cide chemical compound
sili·cif·er·ous
si·lici·fi·ca·tion
si·lici·fy (·fies, ·fy·ing,
  ·fied)
sili·cle (*or* si·licu·la,
  sili·cule) botany term
sili·con chemical element;
  compare silica; silicone
sili·cone polymer; *compare*
  silica; silicon
sili·co·sis disease
si·licu·lose
si·li·qua (*or* ·lique; *plural*
  ·li·quae, ·li·quas, *or*
  ·liques) botany term
sili·qua·ceous
silk
silka·line (*or* ·lene) fabric
silk·en
silki·ly
silki·ness
silk·worm
silky (silki·er, silki·est)
sill
sil·la·bub *variant spelling of*
  syllabub
sil·li·ly
sil·li·ma·nite mineral
sil·li·ness
sil·ly (*adj* ·li·er, ·li·est;
  noun, plural ·lies)
silo (*plural* silos)
si·lox·ane
silt
sil·ta·tion

silty
Si·lu·res ancient Britons
Si·lu·rian geological period;
of Silures
si·lu·rid fish
sil·va *variant spelling of* sylva
sil·van *variant spelling of*
sylvan
Silvanus (*or* Sylvanus)
Roman god
sil·ver
sil·ver·er
silver·fish (*plural* ·fish *or*
·fishes)
sil·veri·ness
sil·ver·ing
silver·point drawing
technique
silver·side
silver·smith
silver·ware
silver·weed
sil·very
sil·vi·cul·tur·al
sil·vi·cul·ture tree
cultivation
sil·vi·cul·tur·ist
s'il vous plaît *French* please
sima layer of earth's crust
sima·rou·ba (*or* ·ru·) tree
sima·rou·ba·ceous (*or*
·ru·)
Sim·fero·pol Soviet city
sim·ian (*or* simi·ous)
simi·lar
simi·lar·ity (*plural* ·ities)
simi·lar·ly
simi·le (*plural* ·les)
si·mili·tude
simi·ous *variant of* simian
sim·mer
sim·mer·ing·ly
sim·nel cake
si·mo·ni·ac practiser of
simony
si·mo·nia·cal
si·mo·nia·cal·ly
si·mon·ist
si·mo·ny
si·moom (*or* ·moon) wind
simp *US* simpleton
sim·pa·ti·co
sim·per
sim·per·er
sim·per·ing·ly

sim·ple
simple-minded
simple-minded·ly
simple-minded·ness
sim·ple·ness
sim·ple·ton
sim·plex
sim·pli·ci·den·tate zoology
term
sim·plic·ity (*plural* ·ities)
sim·pli·fi·ca·tion
sim·pli·fi·ca·tive
sim·pli·fi·er
sim·pli·fy (·fies, ·fy·ing,
·fied)
sim·plism
sim·plis·tic
sim·plis·ti·cal·ly
Sim·plon Pass
simp·ly
Simp·son Australian desert
simu·la·crum (*plural* ·cra)
simu·lant
simu·lar
simu·late
simu·lated
simu·la·tion
simu·la·tive
simu·la·tor
sim·ul·cast radio–TV
broadcast
sim·ul·ta·neous
sim·ul·ta·neous·ly
sim·ul·ta·neous·ness (*or*
·ta·neity)
sin (sin·ning, sinned)
Si·nai Egyptian peninsula
Si·na·it·ic (*or* Si·na·ic)
Si·na·loa Mexican state
sin·an·thro·pus primitive
man
sina·pism mustard plaster
Sin·ar·quist Mexican fascist
since
sin·cere
sin·cere·ly
sin·cer·ity (*or* ·cere·ness)
sin·cipi·tal
sin·ci·put (*plural* ·ci·puts
or ·cipi·ta) part of skull
Sind Pakistani province
Sin·dhi (*plural* ·dhi *or*
·dhis)
sine trigonometry term;
Latin without

si·necure
si·necur·ism
si·necur·ist
sine die *Latin* without a day
fixed
sine qua non *Latin*
essential requirement
sin·ew
sin·ewi·ness
sin·ewy
sin·fo·nia (*plural* ·nie)
symphony
sin·fo·niet·ta
sin·ful
sin·ful·ly
sin·ful·ness
sing (sing·ing, sang,
sung)
sing·able
Sin·ga·pore
Sin·ga·po·rean
singe (singe·ing, singed)
sing·er
sing·ing·ly
sin·gle
single-acting
single-action
single-blind
single-breasted
single-cross
single-decker
single-handed
single-minded
single-minded·ness
single·ness
single-phase
sin·gles tennis match
single-space (*verb*)
single·stick wooden sword
sin·glet
sin·gle·ton
single-track (*adj*)
sin·gly
sing·song
sin·gu·lar
sin·gu·lar·ity (*plural*
·ities)
sin·gu·lari·za·tion (*or*
·sa·tion)
sin·gu·lar·ize (*or* ·ise)
sin·gu·lar·ly
sin·gu·lar·ness
sin·gul·tus hiccup
sinh trigonometry term

skate

Sin·hai·lien (*or* Hsin-hai-
   lien) Chinese city
Sin·ha·lese (*or* ·gha·;
   plural ·leses *or* ·lese)
   Sri Lankan
Si·ning (*or* Hsi·ning)
   Chinese city
sin·is·ter
sin·is·ter·ly
sin·is·ter·ness
sin·is·tral of the left side
sin·is·tral·ly
sin·is·tro·dex·tral
sin·is·tror·sal
sin·is·trorse spiralling right
   to left
sin·is·trous
Si·nit·ic language group
sink (sink·ing, sank *or*
   sunk, sunk *or* sunk·en)
sink·able
sink·er
sink·hole
Sinkiang-Uighur Chinese
   region
sink·ing
sin·less
sin·less·ness
sinned
sin·ner
Sinn Fein
Sinn Fein·er
Sinn Fein·ism
sin·ning
Si·no·logi·cal
Si·nolo·gist
Si·no·logue
Si·nol·ogy study of Chinese
Sino-Tibetan
sin·ter silicaceous deposit
sinu·ate (*or* ·at·ed) botany
   term
Si·nŭi·ju North Korean port
sinu·os·ity (*or* sinua·tion;
   plural ·ities *or* ·tions)
sinu·ous
sinu·ous·ly
sinu·ous·ness
si·nus (*plural* ·nuses)
si·nusi·tis
si·nus·oid maths term
si·nusoi·dal
Siouan
Sioux (*plural* Sioux)
sip (sip·ping, sipped)

si·phon (*or* sy·)
si·phon·age
si·phon·al (*or* ·ic)
si·pho·no·phore marine
   animal
si·pho·nopho·rous
si·phono·stele botany term
si·pho·no·stelic
Si·ple Antarctic mountain
sipped
sip·per
sip·pet small piece
sip·ping
sir
sir·dar leader
sire
si·ren
si·renian zoology term
Si·ret European river
Sir·ius star
sir·loin
si·roc·co (*plural* ·cos)
   wind
sir·rah archaic term of
   address
sir·ree US exclamation
sir·up US variant spelling of
   syrup
sir·vente verse form
sis
si·sal
Sisera biblical character
sis·kin bird
sis·sy (*plural* ·sies)
sis·sy·ish
sis·ter
sis·ter·hood
sister-in-law (*plural*
   sisters-)
sis·ter·li·ness
sis·ter·ly
Sis·tine chapel
sis·troid maths term
sis·trum (*plural* ·tra)
   musical instrument
Sisy·phean
Sisyphus mythological king
sit (sit·ting, sat)
si·tar musical instrument
si·tar·ist
sit·com
site place; *compare* sight
sit·fast sore on horse
sit-in (*noun*)
si·tol·ogy study of nutrition

si·tos·ter·ol soya-bean
   extract
sit·ter
sit·ting
situ·ated (*or* esp. *in legal*
   contexts ·ate)
situa·tion
situa·tion·al
situ·la (*plural* ·lae) Iron
   Age container
si·tus (*plural* ·tus)
   anatomical location
sitz·kreig
sitz·mark skiing term
Siva (*or* Shiva) Hindu god
Si·va·ism
Si·va·ist
Si·vas Turkish city
si·wash Canadian sweater
six
six·ain six-line poem
six·fold
six-footer
six·mo (*plural* ·mos) book
   size
six·pence
six·penny
sixte fencing position
six·teen
six·teen·mo (*plural* ·mos)
   book size
six·teenth
sixth
sixth-former
six·ti·eth
six·ty (*plural* ·ties)
siz·able (*or* size·)
siz·able·ness (*or* size·)
siz·ably (*or* size·)
siz·ar maintained student
si·zar·ship
size
sized
siz·er
siz·zle
siz·zler
sjam·bok whip
Ska·gen *variant of* Skaw
Skag·er·rak Scandinavian
   channel
skald (*or* scald)
   Scandinavian bard
skat card game
skate (*noun, verb*) sport

skate (*plural* skate *or* skates) fish
skate·board
skate·board·er
skat·er
skat·ing
skat·ole organic compound
Skaw (*or* Ska·gen) Danish cape
skean dagger
ske·dad·dle
skeet clay-pigeon shooting
skeg nautical term
skein
skel·etal
skel·etal·ly
skel·eton
skel·eton·ize (*or* ·ise)
skelf *Dialect* wood splinter
skel·ly (*plural* ·lies) fish
Skel·mers·dale Merseyside town
skelp *Dialect* slap; metal tube
sken (sken·ing, skenned) *Dialect* squint
skep beehive
skep·tic *US spelling of* sceptic
sker·rick *US* small fragment
sker·ry (*plural* ·ries) *Scot* small island
sket (sket·ting, sket·ted) *Welsh* splash
sketch
sketch·able
sketch·book
sketch·er
sketchi·ly
sketchi·ness
sketchy (sketchi·er, sketchi·est)
skew
skew·back
skew·bald
skew·er long pin; *compare* skua
skew·ness
skew·whiff
ski (*verb* skis, ski·ing, skied *or* ski'd; *noun, plural* skis)
ski·able
skia·scope eye-examining instrument
ski·as·co·py

ski·bob
ski·bob·ber
ski·bob·bing
skid (skid·ding, skid·ded)
skid·lid *Slang* crash helmet
skid·pan
skid·proof
skid·way *US* platform for logs
skied
ski·er one who skis; *compare* skyer
skiff
skif·fle
ski·ing
ski·jor·er
ski·jor·ing snow sport
skil·ful (*US* skill·)
skil·ful·ly (*US* skill·)
skil·ful·ness (*US* skill·)
skill
skilled
skil·let
skill·ful *US spelling of* skilful
skil·ling coin
skil·lion *Austral* lean-to
skil·ly thin soup
skim (skim·ming, skimmed)
skim·mer
skim·mia shrub
skim·mings
skimp
skimpi·ly
skimpi·ness
skimpy (skimpi·er, skimpi·est)
skin (skin·ning, skinned)
skin-deep
skin-diver
skin·flint
skin·ful
skin·head
skink lizard
skin·less
skinned
skin·ner
skin·ni·ness
skin·ning
skin·ny (·ni·er, ·ni·est)
skint
skin·tight
skip (skip·ping, skipped)
skip·jack (*plural* ·jacks *or* ·jack) fish

ski·plane
skip·per
skip·pet box for document
skip·ping
skipping-rope
Skip·ton Yorkshire town
skirl *Dialect* play bagpipes
skir·mish
skir·mish·er
skirr move rapidly
skir·ret plant
skirt
skirt·er *Austral* fleece trimmer
skirt·ing
skit
skite *Austral* boast
skit·ter
skit·tish
skit·tish·ly
skit·tish·ness
skit·tle
skive
skiv·er
skiv·vy (*noun, plural* ·vies; *verb* ·vies, ·vy·ing, ·vied)
skoal drinking toast
skoki·aan South African liquor
Skop·je Yugoslav city
(skrimshank) *incorrect spelling of* scrimshank
skua bird; *compare* skewer
skul·dug·gery
skulk
skulk·er
skull head bones; *compare* scull
skull·cap
skunk (*plural* skunk *or* skunks)
sky (*noun, plural* skies; *verb* skies, sky·ing, skied)
sky-dive (·div·ing, ·dived (*US* dove), dived)
sky-div·er
Skye Scottish island
sky·er one who skies; *compare* skier
sky-high
sky·jack
sky·jack·er
Sky·lab *US* space station

sky·lark
sky·lark·er
sky·light
sky·line
sky·rocket
Sky·ros (*or* Scy·) Greek
  island
sky·sail
sky·scape
sky·scraper
sky·wards (*or esp. US*
  ·ward)
sky·writer
sky·writing
slab (slab·bing, slabbed)
slab·ber *Dialect* slobber
slack
slack·en
slack·er
slack·ness
slacks
slag (slag·ging, slagged)
slag·gy
slain
slais·ter *Scot* confused mess
slak·able (*or* slake·)
slake
slak·er
sla·lom skiing race; *compare*
  shalom
slam (slam·ming,
  slammed)
slan·der
slan·der·er
slan·der·ous
slan·der·ous·ness
slang
slangi·ly
slangi·ness
slangy
slant
slant·ing
slant·ing·ly (*or* slant·ly)
slant·wise (*or* ·ways)
slap (slap·ping, slapped)
slap-bang
slap·dash
slap·happy (·happier,
  ·happiest)
slap·jack card game
slap·per
slap·shot ice hockey shot
slap·stick
slap-up (*adj*)
slash

slash·er
slash·ing·ly
slat (slat·ting, slat·ted)
slate
slat·er
slath·er *Slang* large quantity
slati·ness
slat·ing
slat·tern
slat·tern·li·ness
slat·tern·ly
slaty (slati·er, slati·est)
slaugh·ter
slaugh·ter·er
slaughter·house
slaughter·man (*plural*
  ·men)
slaugh·ter·ous
Slav
slave
slave-drive (-driving,
  -drove, -driven)
slave-driver
slav·er
slav·er·er
slav·ery
slav·ey servant
Slav·ic *variant of* Slavonic
slav·ish
slav·ish·ly
slav·ish·ness
slav·oc·ra·cy (*plural* ·cies)
  domination by
  slaveholders
Sla·vo·nia Yugoslav region
Sla·vo·nian
Sla·von·ic (*or* Slav·ic)
  language
Slavo·phile (*or* ·phil)
Sla·vophi·lism
slay (slay·ing, slew, slain)
  kill; *compare* sleigh
slay·er
sleave tangled thread;
  compare sleeve
slea·zi·ly
slea·zi·ness
slea·zy (·zi·er, ·zi·est)
sled (sled·ding, sled·ded)
  variant (*esp. US*) *of* sledge
sled·der
sledge (*or esp. US* sled)
sledge·hammer
sleek
sleek·ness

sleep (sleep·ing, slept)
sleep·er
sleepi·ly
sleepi·ness
sleep·less
sleep·less·ly
sleep·less·ness
sleep·walk
sleep·walk·er
sleep·walk·ing
sleepy (sleepi·er,
  sleepi·est)
sleepy·head
sleet
sleety
sleeve covering; *compare*
  sleave
sleeve·less
sleev·ing wire insulation
sleigh sledge; *compare* slay
sleigh·er
sleight trick; *compare* slight
slen·der
slen·der·ize (*or* ·ise)
slen·der·ness
slept
sleuth
sleuth·hound
slew *past tense of* slay
slew (*US also* slue) twist
slice
slice·able
slic·er
slick
slick·en·side geology term
slick·er
slick·ly
slick·ness
slid
slid·able
slide (slid·ing, slid *or*
  slid·den)
slide-action
slid·er
slid·ing
sli·er *variant spelling of* slyer
sli·est *variant spelling of*
  slyest
slight small; snub; *compare*
  sleight
slight·ing
slight·ing·ly
slight·ly
slight·ness
Sli·go Irish county

sli·ly *variant spelling of* **slyly**
slim (*adj* **slim·mer,**
  slim·mest; *verb*
  slim·ming, slimmed)
slime
slimi·ly
slimi·ness
slim·mer
slim·ming
slim·ness
slim·sy *US* frail
slimy (**slimi·er, slimi·est**)
sling (**sling·ing, slung**)
sling·back
sling·er
sling·shot
slink (**slink·ing, slunk**)
slinki·ly
slinki·ness
slink·ing·ly
slinky (**slinki·er,**
  slinki·est)
slip (**slip·ping, slipped**)
slip·case
slip·knot
slip·noose
slip-on (*adj, noun*)
slip·over
slip·page
slip·per
slip·pered
slip·peri·ness
slipper·wort
slip·pery
slip·pi·ness
slip·ping·ly
slip·py (**·pi·er, ·pi·est**)
slip·sheet
slip·shod
slip·shoddi·ness (*or*
  ·shod·ness)
slip·slop
slip·stream
slip-up (*noun*)
slip·way
slit (**slit·ting, slit**)
slith·er
slith·ery
slit·ter
sliv·er
sliv·er·er
slivo·vitz plum brandy
slob
slob·ber
slob·ber·er

slob·bery
sloe fruit; *compare* **slow**
sloe-eyed
slog (**slog·ging, slogged**)
slo·gan
slo·gan·eer
slog·ger
sloop
sloop-rigged
sloot ditch
slop (**slop·ping, slopped**)
slope
slop·er
slop·ing
slop·ing·ly
slop·pi·ly
slop·pi·ness
slop·py (**·pi·er, ·pi·est**)
slops
slop·work
slop·worker
slosh
sloshy
slot (**slot·ting, slot·ted**)
sloth
sloth·ful
sloth·ful·ly
sloth·ful·ness
slot·ter
slouch
slouch·er
slouchi·ly
slouchi·ness
slouch·ing·ly
slouchy
Slough Berkshire town
slough bog; to shed
sloughy
Slo·vak (*or* **·vak·ian**)
Slo·vakia Czech region
slov·en
Slo·vene (*or* **·venian**)
Slo·venia Yugoslav republic
slov·en·li·ness
slov·en·ly
slow not fast, etc.; *compare*
  sloe
slow·coach
slow·down
slow·ly
slow·ness
slow·poke *US* slowcoach
slow-witted
slow·worm

slub (**slub·bing, slubbed**)
  lump in yarn; twist fibre
slub·ber·de·gul·lion
  slovenly person
sludge
sludgy
slue (**slu·ing, slued**) *US*
  variant spelling of **slew**
slug (**slug·ging, slugged**)
sluga·bed
slug·gard
slug·gard·li·ness
slug·gard·ly
slug·ger
slug·gish
slug·gish·ness
sluice
sluice-gate
slum (**slum·ming,**
  slummed)
slum·ber
slum·ber·er
slum·ber·ing·ly
slum·ber·less
slum·ber·ous
slum·ber·ous·ness
slum·mer
slum·my (**·mi·er, ·mi·est**)
slump
slung
slunk
slur (**slur·ring, slurred**)
slurp
slur·ry (*plural* **·ries**)
slush
slushi·ness
slushy
slut
slut·tish
slut·tish·ness
sly (**sly·er, sly·est** *or*
  sli·er, sli·est)
sly·ly (*or* **sli·**)
sly·ness
slype passageway in
  cathedral
smack
smack·er
small
small·boy steward's
  assistant
small·holder
small·holding
small·ish
small-minded

small-minded·ly
small-minded·ness
small·ness
small·pox
smalls underwear
small-scale
smalt blue glass; pigment
smalt·ite mineral
smal·to (*plural* ·tos *or* ·ti)
    mosaic pieces
sma·rag·dite mineral
smarm
smarmy (smarmi·er,
    smarmi·est)
smart
smart·en
smartie clever person
smart·ing·ly
smart·ish
smart·ness
smash
smash·able
smash·er
smash·ing
smash-up (*noun*)
smat·ter
smat·ter·er
smat·ter·ing
smaze *US* smoky haze
smear
smear·er
smeari·ness
smeary (smeari·er,
    smeari·est)
smec·tic chemistry term
smeg·ma sebum
smell (smell·ing, smelt *or*
    smelled)
smelli·ness
smelly (smelli·er,
    smelli·est)
smelt (*plural* smelt *or*
    smelts) extract metal;
    fish
smel·ter
smelt·ery (*plural* ·eries)
smew duck
smid·gen (*or* ·gin)
smi·la·ca·ceous botany
    term
smi·lax shrub
smile
smil·er
smil·ing·ly
smil·ing·ness

smirch
smirch·er
smirk
smirk·er
smirk·ing·ly
smit (*or* smit·tle) *Dialect*
    infection
smite (smit·ing, smote,
    smit·ten *or* smit)
smit·er
smith
smith·er·eens
smith·ery (*plural* ·eries)
Smith·so·nian *US* museum
smith·son·ite mineral
smithy (*plural* smithies)
smit·ten
smock
smock·ing
smog
smog·gy
smok·able (*or* smoke·)
smoke
smoke·house
smoke·jack spit-turning
    device
smoke·less
smok·er
smoke·stack
smoki·ly
smoki·ness
smok·ing
smo·ko (*or* smoke·ho;
    plural ·kos *or* ·hos)
    Austral teabreak
smoky (smoki·er,
    smoki·est)
smol·der *US spelling of*
    smoulder
Smo·lensk Soviet city
smolt young salmon
smooch
smoodge *Austral* smooch
smooth
smooth·able
smooth·bore
smooth·en
smooth·er
smooth-faced
smoothie
smooth·ness
smooth-spoken
smooth-tongued

smor·gas·bord
    Scandinavian hors
    d'oeuvres
smote
smoth·er
smoth·ery
smoul·der (*US* smol·)
smri·ti Hindu literature
smudge
smudgi·ly (*or*
    smudg·ed·ly)
smudgi·ness
smudgy (smudgi·er,
    smudgi·est)
smug (smug·ger,
    smug·gest)
smug·gle
smug·gler
smug·gling
smug·ly
smug·ness
smut (smut·ting,
    smut·ted)
smutch smudge
smutchy
smut·ti·ly
smut·ti·ness
smut·ty (·ti·er, ·ti·est)
Smyr·na ancient Asian city
snack
snack·ette snack bar
snaf·fle
sna·fu (·fues, ·fu·ing,
    ·fued) *US* chaos; make
    chaotic
snag (snag·ging, snagged)
snaggle-tooth (*plural*
    ·teeth)
snag·gy
snail
snail-like
snake
snake·bite
snake·like
snake-mouth orchid
snake·root
snake·skin
snaki·ly
snaki·ness
snaky (snaki·er,
    snaki·est)
snap (snap·ping,
    snapped)
snap·back
snap·dragon

snap·pable
snap·per
snap·pi·ly
snap·pi·ness
snap·ping·ly
snap·py (·pi·er, ·pi·est)
snap·shot
snare
snar·er
snar·ing·ly
snarl
snarl·er
snarl·ing·ly
snarl-up (*noun*)
snarly
snatch
snatch·er
snatchi·ly
snatchy (snatchi·er,
  snatchi·est) spasmodic
snath (*or* snathe) scythe
  handle
snaz·zi·ly
snaz·zi·ness
snaz·zy (·zi·er, ·zi·est)
sneak
sneak·ers shoes
sneaki·ly
sneaki·ness
sneak·ing
sneak·ing·ly
sneak·ing·ness
sneaky (sneaki·er,
  sneaki·est)
sneck wall stone; latch
sned (sned·ding,
  sned·ded) *Dialect* to
  prune
sneer
sneer·er
sneer·ing
sneer·ing·ly
sneeze
sneez·er
sneeze-wort
sneezy
snib *Scot* door fastening
snick
snick·er
snick·et *Dialect* passageway
snide
snide·ness
sniff
sniff·er
sniffi·ly

sniffi·ness
sniff·ing·ly
snif·fle
snif·fler
snif·fy (·fi·er, ·fi·est)
snif·ter
snig·ger
snig·ger·ing·ly
snig·gle catch eels
snig·gler
snip (snip·ping, snipped)
snipe (*plural* snipe *or*
  snipes) bird; to attack
snipe-fish (*plural* ·fish *or*
  ·fishes)
snip·er
sniper·scope
snip·pet
snip·pi·ly
snip·pi·ness (*or*
  ·peti·ness)
snip·py (·pi·er, ·pi·est)
snips shears
snitch
sniv·el (·el·ling, ·elled;
  US ·el·ing, ·eled)
sniv·el·ler (*US* ·el·er)
sniv·el·ly
snob
snob·bery
snob·bish
snob·bish·ness (*or* ·bism)
Sno-Cat (*Trademark*)
snog (snog·ging,
  snogged)
snood
snook rude gesture
snook (*plural* snook *or*
  snooks) fish
snook·er
snoop
snoop·er
snooper·scope
snoopy
snoot *Slang* nose
snooti·ly
snooti·ness
snooty (snooti·er,
  snooti·est)
snooze
snooz·er
snoozy
snore
snor·er
snor·kel

snort
snort·er
snort·ing·ly
snot
snot·ti·ly
snot·ti·ness
snot·ty (*noun, plural*
  ·ties; *adj* ·ti·er, ·ti·est)
snout
snout·ed
snout·like
snow
snow·ball
snow·ball·ing
snow·berry (*plural*
  ·berries)
snow·bird
snow·blind
snow·blind·ness
snow·blink reflection from
  snow
snow·bound
snow·cap
snow·capped
Snow·don
Snow·donia
snow·drift
snow·drop
snow·fall
snow·field
snow·flake
snowi·ly
snowi·ness
snow·man (*plural* ·men)
snow·mobile
snow·plough
snow·shed
snow·shoe (·shoe·ing,
  ·shoed)
snow·sho·er
snow·storm
snow-white
snowy (snowi·er,
  snowi·est)
snub (snub·bing,
  snubbed)
snub·ber
snub·bing·ly
snub·by
snub-nosed
snuff
snuff·box
snuf·fer
snuffi·ness
snuff·ing·ly

snuf·fle
snuf·fler
snuf·fly
snuffy (snuffi·er, snuffi·est) unpleasant
snug (*adj* snug·ger, snug·gest; *verb* snug·ging, snugged)
snug·gery (*plural* ·geries)
snug·gle
snug·ness
snye river channel
so
soak
soak·age
soak·er
soak·ing
soak·ing·ly
so-and-so (*plural* so-and-sos)
soap
soap·bark
soap·berry (*plural* ·berries)
soap·box
soapi·ly
soapi·ness
soap·less
soapo·lal·lie drink
soap·stone (*or* ·rock)
soap·suds
soap·sudsy
soap·wort
soapy (soapi·er, soapi·est)
soar
soar·er
soar·ing·ly
sob (sob·bing, sobbed)
sob·ber
sob·bing·ly
so·beit *Archaic* provided that
so·ber
so·ber·ing·ly
so·ber·ness
so·bri·ety
so·bri·quet (*or* sou·)
soc·age legal term
soc·ag·er
so-called (*adj*)
soc·cer
So·che (*or* So-ch'e) Chinese town
So·chi Soviet city

so·cia·bil·ity (*or* ·ble·ness)
so·cia·ble
so·cia·bly
so·cial
so·cial·ism
so·cial·ist
so·cial·is·tic
so·cial·is·ti·cal·ly
so·cial·ite
so·ci·al·ity (*plural* ·ities)
so·cial·iz·able (*or* ·is·able)
so·ciali·za·tion (*or* ·sa·tion)
so·cial·ize (*or* ·ise)
so·cial·iz·er (*or* ·is·er)
so·cial·ly
so·cial·ness
so·ci·etal
so·ci·ety (*plural* ·eties)
So·cin·ian
So·cini·an·ism religious doctrine
so·cio·biolo·gy
so·cio·eco·nom·ic
so·cio·eco·nomi·cal·ly
so·cio·lin·guist
so·cio·lin·guis·tic
so·cio·lin·guis·tics
so·cio·logi·cal
so·ci·olo·gist
so·ci·ol·ogy
so·cio·met·ric
so·ci·om·etrist
so·ci·om·etry
so·cio·path
so·cio·path·ic
so·cio·pa·thy
so·cio·po·liti·cal
sock
sock·dolo·ger (*or* ·dola·) *US* decisive blow
sock·et
sock·eye salmon
so·cle plinth
soc·man (*or* soke·; *plural* ·men) tenant
So·crat·ic (*or* ·crati·cal)
sod (sod·ding, sod·ded)
soda
so·da·lite mineral
so·dal·ity (*plural* ·ities) Catholic society
so·da·mide chemical compound
sod·den

sod·den·ness
sod·ding
so·dium
Sod·om biblical city
sodo·mite
sodo·mize (*or* ·mise)
sodo·my
so·ever
sofa
so·far marine locating system
sof·fit architectural term
So·fia Bulgarian capital
soft
sof·ta Muslim student
soft·ball
soft-boiled
sof·ten
sof·ten·er
soft-finned
soft-headed
soft-hearted
soft-hearted·ness
softie *variant spelling of* softy
soft·ness
soft-pedal (-pedalling, -pedalled; *US* -pedaling, -pedaled)
soft-soap (*verb*)
soft-spoken
soft·ware
soft·wood
softy (*or* softie; *plural* softies)
sog·gi·ly
sog·gi·ness
sog·gy (·gi·er, ·gi·est)
soh (*or* so) musical note
Soho
soi-disant *French* so-called
soi·gné (*fem* ·gnée) well-groomed
soil
soil·age green fodder
soil·less
soi·ree
so·journ
so·journ·er
soke legal term
sol colloid
sol (*plural* sols *or* so·les) Peruvian currency
sol·ace
sol·ac·er
sola·na·ceous botany term

so·lan·der botanical box
so·la·num plant
so·lar
so·lar·im·eter
so·lar·ium (plural ·laria or ·lar·iums)
so·lari·za·tion (or ·sa·tion)
so·lar·ize (or ·ise)
sold
sol·dan Archaic sultan
sol·der
sol·der·able
sol·der·er
sol·dier
sol·dier·li·ness
sol·dier·ly
sol·diery (plural ·dieries)
sole only; underside of foot or shoe; compare soul
sole (plural sole or soles) fish; compare soul
sol·ecism
sol·ecist
sol·ecis·tic (or ·ti·cal)
sole·ly
sol·emn
so·lem·ni·fi·ca·tion
so·lem·ni·fy (·fies, ·fy·ing, ·fied)
so·lem·nity (plural ·nities)
sol·em·ni·za·tion (or ·sa·tion)
sol·em·nize (or ·nise)
sol·em·niz·er (or ·nis·er)
sol·emn·ness (or ·em·ness)
so·leno·don animal
so·lenoid
so·lenoi·dal
So·lent English strait
sol·fa musical system
sol·fa·ta·ra volcanic vent
sol·fa·ta·ric
sol·feg·gio (or ·fège; plural ·feg·gi, ·feg·gios, or ·fèges) musical term
sol·fe·ri·no reddish-purple
soli musical term
so·lic·it
so·lici·ta·tion
so·lici·tor

So·lici·tor Gen·er·al (plural So·lici·tors Gen·er·al)
so·lici·tor·ship
so·lici·tous
so·lici·tous·ly
so·lici·tous·ness
so·lici·tude
sol·id
soli·da·go (plural ·gos) plant
soli·dar·ity (plural ·ities)
soli·dary united by interests
so·lidi·fi·able
so·lidi·fi·ca·tion
so·lidi·fi·er
so·lidi·fy (·fies, ·fy·ing, ·fied)
so·lid·ity
sol·id·ness
solid-state (adj)
soli·dus (plural ·di) oblique stroke in text
soli·fid·ian religious term
soli·fluc·tion (or ·flux·ion) soil movement
So·li·hull English town
so·lilo·quist (or ·quiz·er, ·quis·er)
so·lilo·quize (or ·quise)
so·lilo·quy (plural ·quies)
So·ling·en West German city
sol·ip·sism
sol·ip·sist
sol·ip·sis·tic
soli·taire game; gem
soli·tari·ly
soli·tari·ness
soli·tary (plural ·taries)
soli·tude
soli·tu·di·nous
sol·ler·et part of armour
sol·mi·za·tion (or ·sa·tion) musical term
solo (plural solos or soli)
so·lo·ist
Solo·mon Is·lands
sol·on·chak soil
solo·netz (or ·nets) soil
So·lo·thurn Swiss town
sol·stice
sol·sti·tial
sol·ubil·ity (plural ·ities)
solu·bil·ize (or ·ise)

sol·uble
sol·uble·ness
sol·ubly
so·lum (plural ·lums or ·la) soil layer
so·lute
so·lu·tion
So·lu·trean Palaeolithic culture
solv·abil·ity (or ·able·ness)
solv·able
solv·ate
solva·tion
Solvay pro·cess
solve
sol·ven·cy
sol·vent
solv·er
sol·voly·sis chemistry term
Sol·way Firth
soma (plural soma·ta or somas) biology term
So·ma·li (plural ·lis or ·li)
So·ma·lia African republic
So·ma·lian
So·ma·li·land former African region
so·mat·ic of the body
so·mati·cal·ly
so·ma·to·log·ic (or ·logi·cal)
so·ma·tolo·gist
so·ma·tol·ogy
so·ma·to·plasm
so·ma·to·plas·tic
so·ma·to·pleu·ral (or ·ric)
so·ma·to·pleure embryonic tissue
so·ma·to·type
som·bre (US ·ber)
som·bre·ly (US ·ber·)
som·bre·ness (US ·ber·)
som·brero (plural ·breros)
som·brous
some
some·body (plural ·bodies)
some·day
some·how
some·one
some·place
som·er·sault (or sum·mer·sault)

Som·er·set
some·thing
some·time (*adv, adj*)
some·times
some·way
some·what
some·where
some·wise somehow
so·mi·tal (*or* ·mit·ic)
so·mite embryonic tissue
Somme French river
som·melier wine steward
som·nam·bu·lance
som·nam·bu·lant
som·nam·bu·late
som·nam·bu·la·tion
som·nam·bu·la·tor
som·nam·bu·lism
som·nam·bu·list
som·nam·bu·lis·tic
som·nilo·quy (*plural* ·quies*) talking in one's sleep
som·no·lence (*or* ·len·cy)
som·no·lent
son
so·nance
so·nant phonetics term
so·nant·al (*or* ·nan·tic)
so·nar
so·na·ta
sona·ti·na
son·dage archaeological trench
sonde observing device
sone unit
son et lu·mi·ère
song
song·bird
song·ful
song·ful·ly
song·ful·ness
Son·ghai (*plural* ·ghai *or* ·ghais*) African people
song·ster (*fem* ·stress*)
song·writer
son·ic
so·nif·er·ous
son-in-law (*plural* sons-)
son·net
son·net·eer
son·ny (*plural* ·nies*)
so·no·buoy
So·no·ra Mexican state
son·or·ant phonetics term

so·nor·ity
so·no·rous
so·no·rous·ness
Soo·chow (*or* Su·chou*) Chinese city
sook *Dialect* coward
soon
soon·er
soot
sooth *Archaic* truth
soothe
sooth·er
sooth·ing
sooth·ing·ly
sooth·say (·say·ing, ·said*)
sooth·say·er
sooti·ly
sooti·ness
sooty (sooti·er, sooti·est*)
sop (sop·ping, sopped*)
soph·ism
soph·ist
soph·ist·er second-year undergraduate
so·phis·tic (*or* ·ti·cal*)
so·phis·ti·cal·ly
so·phis·ti·cate
so·phis·ti·cat·ed
so·phis·ti·ca·tion
so·phis·ti·ca·tor
soph·ist·ry (*plural* ·ries*)
sopho·more *US* second-year student
So·phy (*or* So·phi; *plural* ·phies*) title of Persian kings
so·por stupor
sopo·rif·er·ous
sopo·rif·ic
sopo·rifi·cal·ly
sopped
sop·pi·ly
sop·pi·ness
sop·ping
sop·py (·pi·er, ·pi·est*)
so·pra·ni·no (*plural* ·nos*)
so·pra·no (*plural* ·nos *or* ·ni*)
sora bird
sorb tree
sor·befa·cient causing absorption
sor·bet
sorb·ic acid
sor·bi·tol

Sor·bonne French university
sor·bose sugar
sor·cer·er (*fem* ·ess*)
sor·cer·ous
sor·cery (*plural* ·ceries*)
sor·did
sor·did·ness
sor·di·no (*plural* ·ni*) musical term
sore
so·redium (*plural* ·redia*) botany term
sore·head *US* peevish person
sore·ly
sore·ness
sor·ghum cereal crop
sor·go (*or* ·gho; *plural* ·gos *or* ·ghos*) fodder crop
sori *plural of* sorus
sori·cine shrewlike
so·ri·tes logic term
so·riti·cal (*or* ·rit·ic*)
sorn *Scot* scrounge hospitality
So·ro·ca·ba Brazilian city
so·ror·ate marriage custom
so·rori·cid·al
so·rori·cide
so·ror·ity (*plural* ·ities*)
so·ro·sis (*plural* ·ses*) botany term
sorp·tion adsorption or absorption
sor·rel
Sor·ren·to Italian port
sor·ri·ly
sor·ri·ness
sor·row
sor·row·er
sor·row·ful
sor·row·ful·ly
sor·row·ful·ness
sor·ry (·ri·er, ·ri·est*)
sort
sort·able
sort·er
sor·tie (·tie·ing, ·tied*)
sor·ti·lege divination by drawing lots
sor·ti·tion casting lots
so·rus (*plural* ·ri*) spore-producing structure

Sos·no·wiec Polish town
so-so
sos·te·nu·to musical term
sot
so·te·ri·ol·ogy doctrine of
salvation
So·thic of Sirius
So·tho (*plural* ·tho *or*
·thos) African people
sot·tish
sot·to voce
sou coin
sou·bise onion sauce
sou·brette pert girl
sou·bri·quet *variant spelling
of* sobriquet
sou·chong tea
Sou·dan *French* Sudan
souf·fle medical term
souf·flé light dish
sough sighing sound
sought
soul spirit; *compare* sole
soul-destroy·ing
soul·ful
soul·ful·ly
soul·ful·ness
soul·less
soul·less·ly
soul·less·ness
soul-searching
sound
sound·able
sound·box
sound·er
sound·ing
sound·less
sound·less·ness
sound·ly
sound·ness
sound·post musical term
sound·proof
sound·track
soup
soup·çon *French* slight
amount
soup·fin shark
soupy (soupi·er,
soupi·est)
sour
source
sour·dine organ stop
sour·ish
sour·ly
sour·ness

sour·puss
sour·sop fruit
sou·sa·phone
sou·sa·phon·ist
souse
sous·lik (*or* sus·) animal
Sousse Tunisian port
sou·tache braid
sou·tane cassock
sout·er *Scot* cobbler
sou·ter·rain underground
chamber
south
South·amp·ton
south·bound
South·down sheep
south·east
south·easter
south·easter·ly (*plural*
·lies)
south·eastern
south·eastern·most
south·eastward (*adj*)
south·eastwards (*adv*)
South·end
south·er
south·er·li·ness
south·er·ly (*plural* ·lies)
south·ern
south·ern·er
south·ern·most
southern·wood
south·ing navigation term
south·paw
South Pole
South·port
south-southeast
south-southwest
south·ward (*adj*)
south·wards (*adv*)
South·wark London
borough
south·west
south·wester strong wind
south·wester·ly (*plural*
·lies)
south·western
south·western·most
south·westward (*adj*)
south·westwards (*adv*)
sou·venir
sou'·west·er hat
sov·er·eign
sov·er·eign·ty (*plural*
·ties)

So·vi·et of the USSR
so·vi·et a Soviet council
so·vi·et·ism
so·vi·et·ist
so·vi·et·is·tic
so·vi·eti·za·tion (*or*
·sa·tion)
so·vi·eti·ize (*or* ·ise)
sov·khoz (*plural* ·kho·zy)
state farm
sov·ran *Poetic* sovereign
sow female pig
sow (sow·ing, sowed,
sown *or* sowed) plant
seed; *compare* sew
sow·bread plant
sow·er
So·we·to South African
suburb
sow·ing
sown
soya bean (*US* soy·bean)
soy sauce
So·yuz Soviet spacecraft
soz·zled
spa mineral spring; *compare*
spar
space
space·band printing term
space-bar
space·craft
space·less
space·man (*plural* ·men)
space·port
spac·er
space·ship
space·suit
space-time physics term
space·walk
space·woman (*plural*
·women)
spac·ing
spa·cious roomy; *compare*
specious
spa·cious·ness
spade
spade·fish (*plural* ·fish *or*
·fishes)
spade·ful (*plural* ·fuls)
spad·er
spade·work
spa·di·ceous
spa·dix (*plural* ·di·ces)
botany term
spae *Scot* foretell

spa·ghet·ti
Spain
spake
spall rock splinter
spalla·tion nuclear reaction
spal·peen Irish rascal
Spam (Trademark)
span (span·ning,
  spanned)
span·cel (·cel·ling,
  ·celled; US ·cel·ing,
  ·celed) fettering rope
span·drel (or ·dril)
  architectural term
spang US exactly
span·gle
span·gly
Span·iard
span·iel
Span·ish
Spanish-American
spank
spank·er
spank·ing
span·ner
spar (spar·ring, sparred)
  fight; nautical gear;
  mineral; compare spa
spar·able small nail
spare
spare·ly
spare·ness
spar·er
spare·rib
sparge sprinkle
spar·id (or ·oid) fish
spar·ing frugal; compare
  sparring
spar·ing·ly
spar·ing·ness
spark
spar·kle
spar·kler
spar·ling (plural ·lings or
  ·ling) fish
spar·ring fighting; compare
  sparing
spar·row
sparrow·grass Dialect
  asparagus
sparrow·hawk
spar·ry geology term
sparse
sparse·ly
sparse·ness (or spar·sity)

Spar·ta
Spar·tan
Spar·tan·ism
spar·teine alkaloid
spasm
spas·mod·ic (or ·modi·cal)
spas·modi·cal·ly
spas·tic
spas·ti·cal·ly
spat past tense of spit
spat (spat·ting, spat·ted)
  quarrel
spatch·cock
spate
spa·tha·ceous
spathe botany term
spathed
spath·ic (or ·ose)
  mineralogy term
spa·tial (or ·cial)
spa·ti·al·ity
spa·tial·ly
spa·tio·tem·por·al
spat·ter
spatu·la
spatu·lar
spatu·late
spav·in
spav·ined
spawn
spawn·er
spay
speak (speak·ing, spoke,
  spo·ken)
speak·able
speak·easy (plural
  ·easies)
speak·er
speak·er·ship
speak·ing
spear
spear·er
spear·head
spear·mint
spear·wort
spec speculation
spe·cial
spe·cial·ism
spe·cial·ist
spe·cial·is·tic
spe·ci·al·ity (US ·ty;
  plural ·ities) special
  skill; compare specialty
spe·ciali·za·tion (or
  ·sa·tion)

spe·cial·ize (or ·ise)
spe·cial·ly
spe·cial·ness
spe·cial·ty (plural ·ties)
  legal term; medical
  speciality; US spelling of
  speciality
spe·cia·tion biology term
spe·cie coin money
spe·cies (plural ·cies)
speci·fi·able
spe·cif·ic
spe·cifi·cal·ly
speci·fi·ca·tion
speci·fi·ca·tive
speci·fic·ity
speci·fi·er
speci·fy (·fies, ·fy·ing,
  ·fied)
speci·men
spe·ci·os·ity (plural ·ities)
spe·cious deceptively
  plausible; compare
  spacious
spe·cious·ly
spe·cious·ness
speck
speck·le
specs Slang spectacles
spec·ta·cle
spec·ta·cled
spec·ta·cles
spec·tacu·lar
spec·tacu·lar·ly
spec·ta·tor
spec·tra plural of spectrum
spec·tral
spec·tral·ity (or ·tral·ness)
spec·tral·ly
spec·tre (US ·ter)
spec·tro·bo·lom·eter
spec·tro·bolo·met·ric
spec·tro·graph
spec·tro·graph·ic
spec·tro·graphi·cal·ly
spec·trog·ra·phy
spec·tro·he·lio·graph
spec·tro·he·lio·graph·ic
spec·tro·he·lio·scope
spec·tro·he·lio·scop·ic
spec·trom·eter
spec·tro·met·ric
spec·trom·etry
spec·tro·pho·tom·eter
spec·tro·photo·met·ric

spec·tro·pho·tom·etry
spec·tro·scope
spec·tro·scop·ic (or ·scopi·cal)
spec·tro·scopi·cal·ly
spec·tros·co·pist
spec·tros·co·py
spec·trum (plural ·tra)
specu·lar
specu·late
specu·la·tion
specu·la·tive
specu·la·tive·ly
specu·la·tive·ness
specu·la·tor
specu·lum (plural ·la or ·lums)
sped
speech
speechi·fi·ca·tion
speechi·fi·er
speechi·fy (·fies, ·fy·ing, ·fied)
speech·less
speech·less·ly
speech·less·ness
speed (speed·ing, sped or speed·ed)
speed·boat
speed·er
speedi·ly
speedi·ness
speedo (plural speedos) Slang speedometer
speed·om·eter
speed·ster
speed·way
speed·well
Speed·writing (Trademark)
speedy (speedi·er, speedi·est)
speel Dialect wood splinter; compare spiel
speiss smelting term
spe·laean (or ·lean) of caves
spe·leo·logi·cal (or ·laeo·)
spe·leolo·gist (or ·laeolo·)
spe·leol·ogy (or ·laeol·) study of caves
spelk Dialect wood splinter
spell (spell·ing, spelt or spelled)
spell·able

spell·bind (·bind·ing, ·bound)
spell·bind·er
spell·bound
spell·er
spell·ing
spelt wheat; past tense of spell
spel·ter impure zinc
spe·lunk·er cave explorer
spe·lunk·ing
spence Dialect larder
spen·cer short coat; vest
Spen·cer Gulf
spend (spend·ing, spent)
spend·able
spend·er
spend·thrift
Spen·serian of the poet Spenser
spent
spe·os temple
sperm (plural sperm or sperms)
sper·ma·ceti waxy substance
sper·mary (plural ·maries) sperm-producing organ
sper·ma·the·ca
sper·ma·the·cal
sper·mat·ic
sper·ma·tid immature sperm
sper·ma·tium (plural ·tia)
sper·mato·cyte
sper·mato·gen·esis
sper·ma·to·genet·ic
sper·mato·go·nial
sper·mato·go·nium (plural ·nia)
sper·ma·topho·ral
sper·mato·phore
sper·ma·to·phyte seed plant
sper·ma·to·phyt·ic
sper·ma·tor·rhoea (US ·rhea)
sper·ma·to·zo·al (or ·an, ·ic)
sper·ma·to·zo·id botany term
sper·ma·to·zo·on (plural ·zoa)
sper·mic
sper·mi·ci·dal

sper·mi·cide
sperm·ine biochemical compound
sper·mio·gen·esis
sper·mio·genet·ic
sper·mo·go·nium (plural ·nia)
sper·mo·phile animal
sper·mous
sperry·lite mineral
spes·sar·tite mineral
spew
spew·er
Spey Scottish river
sphag·nous
sphag·num
sphal·er·ite mineral
sphene mineral
sphe·nic wedge-shaped
sphe·no·don lizard
sphe·noid (noun) bone
sphe·noid (or ·noi·dal; adj) wedge-shaped
spher·al
sphere
spheri·cal (or spher·ic)
spheri·cal·ly
spheri·cal·ness
sphe·ric·ity
spher·ics (US sfer·ics) atmospherics
sphe·roid
sphe·roi·dal
sphe·roi·dic·ity
sphe·rom·eter
spheru·lar
spher·ule tiny sphere
spheru·lite geology term
spheru·lit·ic
sphery Poetic spherelike; starlike
sphinc·ter
sphinc·ter·al
sphin·go·my·elin
sphin·go·sine
Sphinx mythological monster
sphinx (plural sphinxes or sphin·ges) Egyptian statue
sphra·gis·tic
sphra·gis·tics study of seals
sphyg·mic of the pulse
sphyg·mo·graph
sphyg·mo·graph·ic

sphyg·mog·ra·phy
sphyg·moid
sphyg·mo·ma·nom·eter
Spi·ca star
spi·ca (*plural* ·cae *or* ·cas)
spiral bandage
spi·cate botany term
spic·ca·to musical term
spice
spice·berry (*plural*
·berries)
spice·bush
spic·er
spic·ery (*plural* ·eries)
spici·ly
spici·ness
spick-and-span (*or* spic-)
spicu·late
spic·ule
spicu·lum (*plural* ·la)
spicy (spici·er, spici·est)
spi·der
spider·man (*plural* ·men)
spider·wort
spi·dery
spied
spie·gelei·sen pig iron
spiel *Slang* glib talk;
compare speel
spiel·er
spif·fing
spif·fy (·fi·er, ·fi·est) *US*
smart
spif·li·cate *Slang* destroy
spig·nel plant
spig·ot cask stopper
spike
spike·let grass flower
spike·nard plant
spike-rush plant
spiki·ly
spiki·ness
spiky (spiki·er, spiki·est)
spile heavy stake
spill (spill·ing, spilt *or*
spilled)
spill·age
spill·er
spil·li·kin (*or* spili·) thin
strip
spil·li·kins game
spill·way
spilt
spin (spin·ning, spun)
spi·na bi·fi·da

spin·ach
spi·nal
spi·nal·ly
spin·dle
spin·dling
spin·dly (·dli·er, ·dli·est)
spin·drift (*or* spoon·) sea
spray
spin-dry (-dries, -drying,
-dried)
spin-dryer
spine
spine-chiller
spine-chilling
spi·nel mineral
spine·less
spine·less·ness
spi·nes·cence
spi·nes·cent
spin·et
spi·nif·er·ous (*or* ·nig·)
spini·fex plant
spini·ness
spin·na·ker racing sail
spin·ner
spin·ner·et zoology term
spin·ney
spin·ning
spin-off
spi·nose
spi·nos·ity
spi·nous
Spi·no·zism philosophical
system
spin·ster
spin·ster·hood
spin·ster·ish
spin·tha·ri·scope physics
apparatus
spi·nule
spi·nu·lose
spiny (spini·er, spini·est)
spiny-finned
spira·cle respiratory
aperture
spi·racu·lar
spi·racu·late
spi·raea shrub
spi·ral (·ral·ling, ·ralled;
US ·ral·ing, ·ralled)
spi·ral·ly
spi·rant phonetics term
spire
spi·reme cytology term
spi·rif·er·ous

spi·ril·lar
spi·ril·lum (*plural* ·la)
bacterium
spir·it
spir·it·ed
spir·it·ed·ly
spir·it·ed·ness
spir·it·less
spir·it·less·ness
spi·ri·to·so musical term
spiri·tous *variant of*
spirituous
spir·itu·al
spir·itu·al·ism
spir·itu·al·ist
spir·itu·al·ity (*plural*
·ities)
spir·itu·ali·za·tion (*or*
·sa·tion)
spir·itu·al·ize (*or* ·ise)
spir·itu·al·iz·er (*or* ·is·er)
spir·itu·al·ly
spir·itu·al·ness
spir·itu·el (*fem* ·elle) witty
spir·itu·os·ity (*or*
·ous·ness)
spir·itu·ous (*or* spiri·tous)
alcoholic
spir·ket·ting nautical term
spi·ro·chaete bacterium
spi·ro·chae·to·sis
spi·ro·graph medical
apparatus
spi·ro·graph·ic
spi·ro·gy·ra alga
spi·roid
spi·rom·eter
spi·ro·met·ric
spi·rom·etry
spi·ro·no·lac·tone drug
spirt *variant spelling of* spurt
spiru·la mollusc
spiry
spit (spit·ting, spat *or*
spit) expectorate
spit (spit·ting, spit·ted)
pointed rod; pierce
spitch·cock
spite
spite·ful
spite·ful·ly
spite·ful·ness
spit·fire
Spit·head

spit·sticker wood-engraving tool

spit·ter

spit·tle

spittle·bug

spit·toon

spitz dog

spiv

spiv·vy

splake trout

splanch·nic visceral

splash

splash·back

splash·board

splash·down

splash·er

splashi·ly

splashi·ness

splashy (splashi·er, splashi·est)

splat

splat·ter

splay

splay·foot

splay·footed·ly

spleen

spleen·ish (or spleeny)

spleen·wort

splen·did

splen·did·ness

splen·dif·er·ous

splen·dor·ous (or ·drous)

splen·dour (US ·dor)

sple·nec·to·my (plural ·mies) removal of spleen

sple·net·ic (or ·neti·cal) peevish

sple·neti·cal·ly

sple·nial of the splenius

splen·ic of the spleen

sple·ni·tis

sple·nius (plural ·nii) muscle

sple·no·mega·ly

splice

splic·er

spline machine part

splint

splin·ter

splin·tery

Split Yugoslav port

split (split·ting, split)

split-level

splits gymnastic act

split·ter

split·ting

splodge

splodgy

splore Scot revel

splotch

splotchy

splurge

splut·ter

splut·ter·er

splut·tery

spode porcelain

spodu·mene mineral

spoil (spoil·ing, spoilt or spoiled)

spoil·age

spoil·er

spoil·five card game

spoils

spoil·sport

Spo·kane US city

spoke

spo·ken

spoke·shave

spokes·man (plural ·men)

spokes·woman (plural ·women)

spo·li·ate despoil

spo·lia·tion

spo·lia·tory

spon·da·ic (or ·dai·cal)

spon·dee metrical foot

spon·du·lix (or ·licks) Slang money

spon·dy·li·tis spinal disorder

sponge

sponge·able

spong·er

spon·gi·ly

spon·gin

spon·gi·ness

spon·gio·blast nerve cell

spon·gio·blas·tic

spon·gy (·gi·er, ·gi·est)

spon·sion sponsorship

spon·son support on boat

spon·sor

spon·so·rial

spon·sor·ship

spon·ta·neity (plural ·neities)

spon·ta·neous

spon·ta·neous·ly

spon·ta·neous·ness

spon·toon short pike

spoof

spoof·er

spook

spooki·ly

spooki·ness

spook·ish

spooky (spooki·er, spooki·est)

spool

spoon

spoon·bill

spoon·er·ism

spoon-feed (-feeding, -fed)

spoon·ful (plural ·fuls)

spoony (spooni·er, spooni·est) amorous

spoor animal trail; compare spore

spoor·er

Spora·des Greek islands

spo·rad·ic (or ·radi·cal)

spo·radi·cal·ly

spo·radi·cal·ness

spo·ran·gial

spo·ran·gium (plural ·gia)

spore reproductive body; compare spoor

spo·ro·carp

spo·ro·cyst

spo·ro·cyte

spo·ro·gen·esis

spo·rog·enous

spo·ro·go·nial

spo·ro·go·nium (plural ·nia)

spo·rogo·ny

spo·ro·phore

spo·ro·phyll (or ·phyl)

spo·ro·phyte

spo·ro·phyt·ic

spo·ro·zo·an

spo·ro·zo·ite

spor·ran

sport

sport·er

sporti·ly

sporti·ness

sport·ing

sport·ing·ly

spor·tive

spor·tive·ly

spor·tive·ness

sports·cast

sports·caster

sports·man (*plural* ·men)
sportsman-like
sports·man·ly
sports·man·ship
sports·wear
sports·woman (*plural* ·women)
sporty (sporti·er, sporti·est)
sporu·late produce spores
sporu·la·tion
spor·ule
spot (spot·ting, spot·ted)
spot·less
spot·less·ness
spot·light (·light·ing, ·lit or ·light·ed)
spot-on
spot·table
spot·ted
spot·ter
spot·ti·ly
spot·ti·ness
spot·ty (·ti·er, ·ti·est)
spot-weld
spot-welder
spous·al marriage ceremony
spouse
spout
spout·er
sprag
sprain
sprang
sprat
sprawl
sprawl·er
sprawl·ing
sprawly
spray
spray·er
spread (spread·ing, spread)
spread-able
spread-eagle
spread·er
sprech·stimme *German* musical term
spree
sprig (sprig·ging, sprigged)
sprig·ger
sprig·gy
spright·li·ness
spright·ly (·li·er, ·li·est)

spring (spring·ing, sprang *or* sprung, sprung)
spring·board
Spring·bok South African athlete
spring·bok (*or* ·buck; *plural* ·bok, boks *or* ·buck, ·bucks) antelope
spring-clean
spring-cleaning
springe snare
spring·er
Spring·field US city
spring·haas (*plural* ·haas, ·ha·se) animal
spring·head
springi·ly
springi·ness
spring·ing
spring·let
Springs South African city
spring·tail
spring·time
spring·wood
springy (springi·er, springi·est)
sprin·kle
sprin·kler
sprin·kling
sprint
sprint·er
sprit nautical term
sprite
sprit·sail
sprock·et
sprout
spruce
spruce·ly
spruce·ness
sprue disease
spru·ik *Austral* speak in public
sprung
spry (spri·er, spri·est)
spry·ly
spry·ness
spud (spud·ding, spud·ded)
spume froth
spu·mes·cence
spu·mes·cent
spu·mo·ne (*or* ·ni; *plural* ·ni) ice cream
spu·mous (*or* spumy)
spun

spunk
spunki·ly
spunki·ness
spunky (spunki·er, spunki·est)
spur (spur·ring, spurred)
spurge plant
spu·ri·ous
spu·ri·ous·ly
spu·ri·ous·ness
spurn
spurn·er
spur·ri·er spur maker
spur·ry (*or* ·rey; *plural* ·ries) plant
spurt (*or* spirt)
sput·nik Soviet satellite
sput·ter
sput·ter·er
spu·tum (*plural* ·ta)
spy (*noun, plural* spies; *verb* spies, spy·ing, spied)
spy·glass
spy·ing
squab (*plural* squabs *or* squab) young pigeon
squab·ble
squab·bler
squab·by (·bi·er, ·bi·est)
squac·co (*plural* ·cos) heron
squad
squad·die (*or* ·dy; *plural* ·dies) *Slang* soldier
squad·ron
squa·lene biochemical compound
squal·id
squa·lid·ity (*or* squal·id·ness)
squall
squall·er
squal·ly
squal·or
squa·ma (*plural* ·mae) scale
squa·mate
squa·ma·tion
squa·mo·sal bone
squa·mous (*or* ·mose)
squa·mous·ness (*or* ·mose)
squamu·lose covered with small scales

squander

squan·der
squan·der·er
squan·der·ing·ly
square
square·ly
square·ness
squar·er
square-rigger
squar·ish
squar·rose biology term
squash
squash·er
squashi·ly
squashi·ness
squashy (squashi·er, squashi·est)
squat (squat·ting, squat·ted)
squat·ness
squat·ter
squat·toc·ra·cy Austral rich farmers
squaw
squawk
squawk·er
squeak
squeak·er
squeaki·ly
squeaki·ness
squeaky
squeal
squeal·er
squeam·ish
squeam·ish·ness
squee·gee (or squil·; ·gee·ing, ·geed)
squeez·able
squeeze
squeez·er
squelch
squelch·er
squelch·ing·ly
sque·teague (plural ·teague or ·teagues) fish
squib (squib·bing, squibbed)
squid (plural squid or squids)
squif·fy (·fi·er, ·fi·est)
squig·gle
squig·gler
squig·gly
squill plant

squil·la (plural ·las or ·lae) shrimp
squinch architectural support
squint
squint·er
squinty
squire
squire·ar·chy (or squir·ar·chy; plural ·chies)
squirm
squirm·er
squirm·ing·ly
squirmy
squir·rel
squirrel·fish (plural ·fish or ·fishes)
squirt
squirt·er
squish
squishy (squishi·er, squishi·est)
squit Slang insignificant person
squiz (plural squizzes) Austral inquisitive glance
Sri Lan·ka
Sri Lan·kan
Sri·na·gar Indian city
St abbrev. for Saint; all entries preceded by St are listed in the section of this dictionary following the entry saint
stab (stab·bing, stabbed)
Sta·bat Ma·ter hymn
stab·ber
sta·bile arts term
sta·bil·ity (plural ·ities)
sta·bi·li·za·tion (or ·sa·tion)
sta·bi·lize (or ·lise)
sta·bi·li·zer (or ·ser)
sta·ble
stable·boy
stable·man (plural ·men)
sta·ble·ness
sta·bling
sta·bly
stac·ca·to
stack
stack·er
stac·te biblical spice
stad·dle prop
staddle·stone

stad·hold·er (or stadt·) Dutch ruler
sta·di·om·eter
sta·dium (plural ·diums or ·dia)
staff (plural staffs) personnel
staff (plural staffs or staves) pole
staff (or stave; plural staffs or staves) musical term
Staf·fa Scottish island
staff·er Slang staff member
staff·man (plural ·men)
Staf·ford
Staf·ford·shire
stag
stage
stage·coach
stage·craft
stage·hand
stage-manage
stag·er
stag·fla·tion economics term
stag·gard deer
stag·ger
stagger·bush
stag·ger·er
stag·ger·ing
stag·ger·ing·ly
stag·gers horse disease
stag·hound
stagi·ly
stagi·ness
stag·ing
Sta·gi·ra ancient Macedonian city
stag·nan·cy (or ·nance)
stag·nant
stag·nate
stag·na·tion
stagy (stagi·er, stagi·est) theatrical
staid sedate; compare stayed
staid·ness
stain
stain·abil·ity
stain·able
stain·er
Staines Surrey town
stain·less
stair step; compare stare
stair·case

stair·head

stairs

stair·way

stair·well

stake stick; money; *compare* steak

stake·out

sta·lac·ti·form

stal·ac·tite downward projection in cave

stal·ac·tit·ic (*or* ·titi·cal)

sta·lag German prison camp

stal·ag·mite upward projection in cave

stal·ag·mit·ic (*or* ·miti·cal)

stale

stale·ly

stale·mate

stale·ness

Sta·lin·ism

Sta·lin·ist

stalk

stalked

stalk·er

stalki·ly

stalki·ness

stalk·like

stalky (stalki·er, stalki·est)

stall

stall-feed (-feeding, -fed)

stal·lion

stal·wart

stal·wart·ness

Stam·bul (*or* ·boul) part of Istanbul

sta·men (*plural* sta·mens *or* stami·na)

Stam·ford US city

stami·na

stami·nal

stami·nate having stamens

stami·nif·er·ous

stami·node (*or* ·no·dium; *plural* ·nodes *or* ·no·dia) botany term

stami·no·dy

stam·mel fabric

stam·mer

stam·mer·er

stam·mer·ing·ly

stamp

stam·pede

stam·ped·er

stamp·er

stance

stanch (*or* staunch) check blood flow; *compare* staunch

stanch·able (*or* staunch·)

stanch·er (*or* staunch·)

stan·chion

stand (stand·ing, stood)

stand·ard

standard-bearer

stand·ardi·za·tion (*or* ·sa·tion)

stand·ard·ize (*or* ·ise)

stand·ard·iz·er (*or* ·is·er)

stand-by (*noun*; *plural* -bys)

standee one who stands

stand·er

stand-in (*noun*)

stand·ing

stand·ish inkstand

stand-offish

stand·pipe

stand·point

stand·still

stang *Dialect* throb with pain

stan·hope carriage

stank

Stan·ley capital of Falkland Islands

Stan·na·ries English district

stan·na·ry (*plural* ·ries) tin mine

stan·nic chemistry term

stan·nif·er·ous

stan·nite mineral

stan·nous chemistry term

stan·za

stan·zaed

stan·za·ic

sta·pedial

sta·pelia plant

sta·pes (*plural* ·pes *or* ·pedes) ear bone

staphy·lo·coc·cal

staphy·lo·coc·cus (*plural* ·coc·ci)

staphy·lo·plas·tic

staphy·lo·plas·ty palate surgery

staphy·lor·rhaph·ic

staphy·lor·rha·phy repair of cleft palate

sta·ple

sta·pler

star (star·ring, starred)

star-apple

Sta·ra Za·go·ra Bulgarian city

star·board

starch

starch·er

starchi·ly

starchi·ness

starch-reduced

starchy (starchi·er, starchi·est)

star-crossed

star·dom

star·dust

stare look at; *compare* stair

star·er

star·fish (*plural* ·fish *or* ·fishes)

star·flower

star·gaze

star·gaz·er

star·gaz·ing

stark

stark·ness

star·less

star·let

star·light

star·like

star·ling

star·lit

star-of-Bethlehem plant

starred

star·ri·ly

star·ri·ness

star·ry (·ri·er, ·ri·est)

starry-eyed

star-spangled

start

start·er

star·tle

star·tler

star·tling

star·tling·ly

star·va·tion

starve

starve·ling

starv·er

starv·ing

star·wort

stash

sta·sis stagnation

stat·able (*or* state·)

sta·tant heraldic term

state
state·craft
state·hood
State·house *US* state
 capitol
state·less
state·less·ness
state·li·ness
state·ly (·li·er, ·li·est)
state·ment
Stat·en Is·land
sta·ter one who states;
 ancient coin; *compare*
 stator
state·room
States the USA
state·side
states·man (*plural* ·men)
statesman-like (*or*
 states·man·ly)
states·man·ship
states·woman (*plural*
 ·women)
stat·ic
stati·cal
stati·cal·ly
stat·ice plant
stat·ics
sta·tion
sta·tion·ari·ly
sta·tion·ari·ness
sta·tion·ary not moving;
 compare stationery
sta·tion·er
sta·tion·ery writing
 materials; *compare*
 stationary
station·master
stat·ism state control
stat·ist
sta·tis·tic
sta·tis·ti·cal
sta·tis·ti·cal·ly
stat·is·ti·cian
sta·tis·tics
sta·tive linguistics term
stato·blast zoology term
stato·cyst zoology term
stato·lith biology term
stato·lith·ic
sta·tor part of machine;
 compare stater
stato·scope aircraft
 instrument
statu·ary (*plural* ·aries)

statue
stat·ued
statu·esque
statu·esque·ly
statu·esque·ness
statu·ette
stat·ure
sta·tus (*plural* ·tuses)
sta·tus quo
statu·table
stat·ute
statu·to·ri·ly
statu·tory
staunch loyal; *variant
 spelling of* stanch
staunch·ness
stau·ro·lite mineral
stau·ro·lit·ic
stau·ro·scope
stau·ro·scopi·cal·ly
Sta·vang·er Norwegian port
stave (stav·ing, staved *or*
 stove) wooden strip; to
 crush; *variant spelling of*
 staff
staves (*noun*) plural of staff
 or stave
staves·acre plant
Stav·ro·pol Soviet city
stay
stayed *past tense of* stay;
 compare staid
stay·er
stays boned corsets
stay·sail
stead
stead·fast (*or* sted·)
stead·fast·ness (*or* sted·)
steadi·ly
steadi·ness
steady (*adj* steadi·er,
 steadi·est; *verb*
 stead·ies, steady·ing,
 stead·ied)
steady·ing·ly
steak meat; *compare* stake
steak·house
steal (steal·ing, stole,
 sto·len)
steal·er
stealth
stealth·ful
stealthi·ly
stealthi·ness

stealthy (stealthi·er,
 stealthi·est)
steam
steam·boat
steam-boiler
steam-chest
steam-engine
steam·er
steamie *Scot* public
 washhouse
steami·ly
steami·ness
steam·roller
steam·ship
steam-shovel
steam-tight
steam-tight·ness
steamy (steami·er,
 steami·est)
ste·ap·sin enzyme
stea·rate
ste·aric
stea·rin (*or* ·rine)
 biochemical compound
stea·rop·tene
stea·tite mineral
stea·tit·ic
stea·toly·sis digestive
 process
stea·to·py·gia (*or* ·ga)
 excessively fat buttocks
stea·to·pyg·ic (*or*
 ·py·gous)
stea·tor·rhoea (*US* ·rhea)
steed
steel alloy; *compare* stele
steel·head (*plural* ·heads
 or ·head) fish
steeli·ness
steel·work
steel·worker
steel·working
steel·works
steely (steeli·er,
 steeli·est)
steel·yard
steen·bok *variant spelling of*
 steinbok
steep
steep·en
steep·er
steep·ish
stee·ple
steeple·chase
steeple·chas·er

steeple·jack
steep·ness
steer guide; bullock;
   compare stere
steer·able
steer·age
steer·age·way
steer·er
steer·ing
steers·man (*plural* ·men)
steeve nautical term
stego·don (*or* ·dont)
   extinct mammal
stego·myia mosquito
stego·saur (*or* ·saur·us)
stein beer mug
stein·bok (*or* steen·;
   plural ·boks *or* ·bok)
   antelope
ste·lar of a stele; *compare*
   stellar
ste·le (*or* ·la; *plural* ·lae
   or ·les) stone slab
stele plant tissue; *compare*
   steel
stel·lar of stars; *compare*
   stelar
stel·lara·tor physics
   apparatus
stel·late (*or* ·lat·ed)
stel·lif·er·ous
stel·li·form
stel·li·fy (·fies, ·fy·ing,
   ·fied) change into a star
Stel·lite (*Trademark*)
stel·lu·lar
stem (stem·ming,
   stemmed)
stem·head
stem·ma family tree
stem·mer
stem·son nautical term
stem·ware stemmed glasses
stem-winder
stench
sten·cil (·cil·ling, ·cilled;
   US ·cil·ing, ·ciled)
sten·cil·ler (*US* ·cil·er)
Sten gun
steno (*plural* stenos) *US*
   shorthand typist
steno·graph
ste·nog·ra·pher *US*
   shorthand typist
steno·graph·ic (*or*
   ·graphi·cal)

ste·nog·ra·phy
steno·ha·line
steno·pet·al·ous
ste·nopha·gous
steno·phyl·lous
ste·no·sis (*plural* ·ses)
steno·ther·mal
ste·not·ic
steno·trop·ic (*or* ·top·)
   ecology term
Steno·type (*Trademark*)
steno·typ·ic
steno·typ·ist
steno·typy form of
   shorthand
sten·tor loud person;
   microscopic animal
sten·to·rian
step (step·ping, stepped)
   motion of foot; stage; etc.;
   compare steppe
step·brother
step·child (*plural*
   ·children)
step·daughter
step·father
stepha·no·tis
step·ladder
step·mother
step-parent
steppe grassy plain; *compare*
   step
step·per
Steppes Eurasian grasslands
step·sister
step·son
step·wise
ste·ra·dian unit
ster·co·ra·ceous of dung
ster·co·rico·lous
ster·cu·lia·ceous botany
   term
stere unit; *compare* steer
ste·reo (*plural* ·reos)
ste·reo·bate foundation of
   building
ste·reo·chem·is·try
ste·reo·chrome
ste·reo·chro·my wall
   painting
ste·reo·gram
ste·reo·graph
ste·reo·graph·ic (*or*
   ·graphi·cal)
ste·reog·ra·phy

ste·reo·iso·mer
ste·reo·isom·er·ism
ste·reo·iso·met·ric
ste·reo·met·ric
ste·reo·met·ri·cal
ste·reom·etry
ste·reo·phon·ic
ste·reo·phoni·cal·ly
ste·reoph·ony
ste·reop·sis stereoscopic
   vision
ste·reop·ti·con type of
   projector
ste·reo·scope
ste·reo·scop·ic (*or*
   ·scopi·cal)
ste·reo·scopi·cal·ly
ste·reos·co·pist
ste·reos·co·py
ste·reo·spe·cif·ic
ste·reo·tac·tic (*or* ·ti·cal)
ste·reo·tac·ti·cal·ly
ste·reo·tax·is biology term
ste·reot·omy
ste·reo·trop·ic
ste·reot·ro·pism botany
   term
ste·reo·type
ste·reo·typ·er (*or* ·ist)
ste·reo·typ·ic (*or*
   ·typi·cal)
ste·reo·typy
ste·reo·vi·sion
ste·ric (*or* ·ri·cal)
   chemistry term
ste·ri·cal·ly
ster·ig·ma (*plural* ·ma·ta)
   botany term
steri·lant
ster·ile
ste·ril·ity
steri·liz·able (*or* ·lis·able)
steri·li·za·tion (*or*
   ·sa·tion)
steri·lize (*or* ·lise)
steri·liz·er (*or* ·lis·er)
ster·let fish
ster·ling
stern
ster·nal of the sternum
stern·most
stern·ness
stern·post
stern·son nautical term

ster·num (*plural* ·na *or* ·nums) breastbone
ster·nu·ta·tion sneezing
ster·nu·ta·tive
ster·nu·ta·tor
ster·nu·ta·tory (*plural* ·tories)
stern·wards (*or esp. US* ·ward)
stern·way
ster·oid
ster·oi·dal
ster·ol biochemical compound
ster·tor noisy breathing
ster·to·rous
ster·to·rous·ness
stet (stet·ting, stet·ted)
stetho·scope
stetho·scop·ic
ste·thos·co·py
stet·son
ste·vedore
Ste·ven·age Hertfordshire town
Ste·ven·graph (*or* ·vens·) silk picture
stew
stew·ard
stew·ard·ess
stew·ard·ship
stewed
sthen·ic strong
stib·ine poisonous gas
stib·nite mineral
stich line of poetry; *compare* stitch
stich·ic
stichi·cal·ly
sticho·met·ric (*or* ·ri·cal)
sti·chom·etry
sticho·mythia (*or* sti·chomy·thy) drama term
stick (stick·ing, stuck)
stick·er
stick·ful (*plural* ·fuls)
sticki·ly
sticki·ness
stick·le argue
stickle·back
stick·ler
stick·seed
stick·tight plant
stick-up (*noun*)

stick·weed
sticky (sticki·er, sticki·est)
sticky·beak *Austral* inquisitive person
stiff
stiff·en
stiff·en·er
stiff·ness
sti·fle
sti·fler
sti·fling
sti·fling·ly
stig·ma (*plural* ·mas) mark; flower part
stig·ma (*plural* ·ma·ta) crucifixion mark
stig·mas·ter·ol biochemical compound
stig·mat·ic (*or* ·mati·cal)
stig·ma·tism
stig·ma·tist
stig·ma·ti·za·tion (*or* ·sa·tion)
stig·ma·tize (*or* ·tise)
stig·ma·tiz·er (*or* ·tis·er)
stil·bene
stil·bite mineral
stil·boes·trol (*US* ·bes·)
stile steps over fence; *compare* style
sti·let·to (*noun, plural* ·tos; *verb* ·toes, ·toe·ing, ·toed)
still
stil·lage platform
still·birth
still·born
still life (*plural* still lifes) picture
stil·li·cide legal term
still·ness
stilt
stilt·ed
stilt·ed·ness
Stil·ton cheese
stimu·lable
stimu·lant
stimu·late
stimu·lat·ing·ly
stimu·la·tion
stimu·la·tive
stimu·la·tor (*or* ·lat·er)
stimu·lus (*plural* ·li)
sting (sting·ing, stung)

sting·er
stin·gi·ly
stin·gi·ness
sting·ing·ly
stin·go beer
sting·ray
stin·gy (·gi·er, ·gi·est)
stink (stink·ing, stank *or* stunk)
stink·er
stink·horn fungus
stink·ing·ly
stink·ing·ness
stink·pot
stink·stone
stink·weed
stink·wood
stint
stint·er
stipe plant stalk
sti·pel small leaflike structure; *compare* stipple
sti·pel·late
sti·pend
sti·pen·di·ary (*plural* ·aries)
sti·pes (*plural* stipi·tes) zoology term
sti·pi·form (*or* stipi·ti·)
stipi·tate
stip·ple dot or fleck; *compare* stipel
stip·pler
stip·pling
stipu·lable
stipu·lar
stipu·late
stipu·la·tion
stipu·la·tor
stipu·la·tory
stip·ule leaflike structure
stir (stir·ring, stirred)
stirk heifer
Stir·ling Scottish town
stirps (*plural* stir·pes) line of descendants
stir·rable
stir·rer
stir·ring
stir·ring·ly
stir·rup
stitch needlework link; *compare* stich
stitch·er
stitch·ing

stitch·wort

stithy (*plural* **stithies**)
  Dialect forge

sti·ver coin

stoa (*plural* **stoae** *or*
  stoas) covered walk

stoat

stob *Dialect* stump

sto·chas·tic statistics term

sto·chas·ti·cal·ly

stock

stock·ade

stock·breeder

stock·breeding

stock·broker

stock·bro·ker·age (*or*
  ·broking)

stock·er

stock·fish (*plural* ·fish *or*
  ·fishes)

stock·holder

stock·holding

Stock·holm

stocki·ly

stocki·ness

stocki·net

stock·ing

stock·inged

stock·ish stupid

stock·ist

stock·jobber

stock·jobbery (*or*
  ·jobbing)

stock·man (*plural* ·men)

stock·pile

stock·pil·er

Stock·port English town

stock·pot

stock·room

stocks instrument of
  punishment

stock·still

stock·taking

Stock·ton English town;
  US port

stocky (stocki·er,
  stocki·est)

stock·yard

stodge

stodgi·ly

stodgi·ness

stodgy (stodgi·er,
  stodgi·est)

sto·gy (*or* sto·gey; *plural*
  ·gies) US cigar

Sto·ic philosopher

sto·ic self-controlled person

stoi·cal

stoi·cal·ly

stoi·cal·ness

stoi·chio·logi·cal

stoi·chi·ol·ogy branch of
  biology

stoi·chio·met·ric

stoi·chi·om·etry branch of
  chemistry

stoi·cism

stoke

stoke·hold

stoke·hole

Stoke Mandeville
  Buckinghamshire town

stok·er

stokes (*or* stoke; *plural*
  stokes) unit

stole long shawl; *past tense*
  of steal

stol·en

stol·id

sto·lid·ity (*or* stol·id·ness)

stol·len bread

sto·lon stem

sto·loni·fer·ous

sto·ma (*plural* ·ma·ta)

stom·ach

stomach·ache

stom·ach·er

sto·mach·ic

sto·machi·cal

stom·achy

sto·ma·tal (*or* stoma·tous)

sto·mat·ic of the mouth

sto·ma·ti·tic

sto·ma·ti·tis

sto·ma·tol·ogy

stoma·to·plas·ty

stoma·to·pod crustacean

sto·mo·daeal (*or* ·deal)

sto·mo·daeum (*or* ·deum)
  embryonic mouth cavity

stomp

stomp·er

ston·able (*or* stone·)

stone

stone-blind

stone-chat bird

stone-crop plant

stone-cutter

stone-cutting

stoned

stone-fish (*plural* ·fish *or*
  ·fishes)

stone-fly (*plural* ·flies)

stone-ground

Stone·henge

stone·less

stone-lily fossil

stone·mason

stone·mason·ry

ston·er

stone·wall

stone·wall·er

stone·ware

stone·work

stone·worker

stone·wort alga

stoni·ly

stoni·ness

stonk bombard with artillery

stony (*or* stoney;
  stoni·er, stoni·est)

stony-broke

stony-hearted

stony-hearted·ness

stood

stooge

stook

stook·er

stool

stoop bend body; *compare*
  stoup; stupe

stoop·er

stoop·ing·ly

stop (stop·ping, stopped)

stop·cock

stope mine excavation

stop·gap

stop-go economics term

stop·ing geology term

stop·light

stop·over (*noun*)

stop·pable

stop·page

stop·per

stop·ping

stops card game

stop·watch

stor·able

stor·age

sto·rax plant; drug

store

store·house

store·keeper

store·keeping

store·room

sto·rey (*plural* ·reys *or* ·ries) level; *compare* story

sto·reyed multilevelled

sto·ried recorded

stork

storks·bill plant

storm

storm·bound

stormi·ly

stormi·ness

storm·proof

storm-trooper

stormy (stormi·er, stormi·est)

Stor·no·way Scottish port

Stor·ting (*or* ·thing) Norwegian parliament

sto·ry (*plural* ·ries) tale; *compare* storey

story·book

story·teller

story·telling

stoss geology term

stot (stot·ting, stot·ted) *Scot* bounce

sto·tin·ka (*plural* ·ki) Bulgarian coin

sto·tious *Irish* drunk

stot·ter *Scot* good-looking woman

stound *Dialect* short period

stoup basin for holy water; drinking mug; *compare* stoop; stupe

stour *Dialect* turmoil

Stour·bridge English town

stout

stout·hearted

stout·hearted·ness

stout·ish

stout·ness

stove

stove·pipe

stove·pipes tight trousers

stov·er

stow

stow·age

stow·away

stra·bis·mal (*or* ·mic, ·mi·cal)

stra·bis·mus squint

strad·dle

strad·dler

Stradi·var·ius violin

strafe

straf·er

strag·gle

strag·gler

strag·gling·ly

strag·gly (·gli·er, ·gli·est)

straight not curved; directly; *compare* strait

straight·away

straight·edge

straight·en put straight; *compare* straiten

straight·en·er

straight-faced

straight·forward

straight·forward·ness

straight·ness

strain

strained

strained·ness

strain·er

strain·ing·ly

strait sea channel; difficulty; *compare* straight

strait·en embarrass financially; *compare* straighten

strait·jacket (*or* straight·)

strait-laced (*or* straight-)

strait·ness

strake metal part of wheel

stra·mo·nium drug

Strand London street

strand

stranded

strange

strange·ness

stran·ger

stran·gle

strangle·hold

stran·gler

stran·gles horse disease

stran·gu·late

stran·gu·la·tion

stran·gu·ry painful urination

Stran·raer Scottish port

strap (strap·ping, strapped)

strap·hanger

strap·hanging

strap·less

strap·pa·do (*plural* ·does) torture

strap·per

strap·ping

Stras·bourg French city

strass imitation gem

stra·ta *plural of* stratum

strata·gem

stra·tal

stra·tegic (*or* ·tegi·cal)

stra·tegi·cal·ly

stra·tegics military strategy

strat·egist

strat·egy (*plural* ·egies)

Stratford-on-Avon

strath *Scot* glen

Strath·clyde Scottish region

strath·spey dance

stra·ticu·late geology term

stra·ticu·la·tion

strati·fi·ca·tion

strati·form

strati·fy (·fies, ·fy·ing, ·fied)

stra·tig·ra·pher (*or* ·phist)

strati·graph·ic (*or* ·graphi·cal)

stra·tig·ra·phy study of rock strata

stra·toc·ra·cy (*plural* ·cies) military rule

strato·crat

strato·crat·ic

strato·cu·mu·lus (*plural* ·li)

strato·pause meteorology term

strato·sphere

strato·spher·ic (*or* ·spheri·cal)

stra·tum (*plural* ·ta *or* ·tums) layer

stra·tus (*plural* ·ti) cloud

stra·vaig *Scot* wander

straw

straw·berry (*plural* ·berries)

straw·board

straw·flower

strawy

stray

stray·er

strays electronics term

streak

streaked

streak·er

streaki·ly

streaki·ness

streak·ing

streaky (streaki·er,
  streaki·est)

stream

stream·er

stream·line

stream·lined

street

street·car

street·light (*or* ·lamp)

street·walker

street·walking

stre·lit·zia plant

strength

strength·en

strength·en·er

strenu·os·ity (*or*
  ·ous·ness)

strenu·ous

strep·to·coc·cal (*or* ·cic)

strep·to·coc·cus (*plural*
  ·coc·ci)

strep·to·ki·nase drug

strep·to·my·cin antibiotic

strep·to·thri·cin antibiotic

stress

stress·ful

stress·ful·ly

stretch

stretch·abil·ity

stretch·able

stretch·er

stretcher-bearer

stretchi·ness

stretchy (stretchi·er,
  stretchi·est)

stret·to (*plural* ·tos *or* ·ti)
  musical term

streu·sel pastry topping

strew (strew·ing, strewed,
  strewn *or* strewed)

strew·er

strewth exclamation

stria (*plural* striae)

stri·ate (*or* ·at·ed)

stria·tion

strick textile fibres

strick·en

strick·le

strict

strict·ness

stric·ture

stride (strid·ing, strode,
  strid·den)

stri·dence (*or* ·den·cy)

stri·dent

stri·dor wheezing sound

stridu·late zoology term

stridu·la·tion

stridu·la·tor

stridu·la·tory

stridu·lous (*or* ·lant)

stridu·lous·ness (*or*
  stridu·lance)

strife

strigi·form ornithology term

strig·il body scraper

stri·gose biology term

strik·able

strike (strik·ing, struck)

strike·bound

strike·breaker

strike·breaking

strik·er

strik·ing

strik·ing·ness

string (string·ing, strung)

string·board

stringed

strin·gen·cy

strin·gen·do musical term

strin·gent

string·er

string·halt veterinary term

stringi·ly

stringi·ness

string·piece

stringy (stringi·er,
  stringi·est)

strip (strip·ping, stripped)

stripe

strip·er

strip·ling lad

strip·per

strip·tease

stripy (stripi·er stripi·est)

strive (striv·ing, strove,
  striv·en)

striv·er

strobe lighting

stro·bic spinning

stro·bi·la (*plural* ·lae)
  body of tapeworm

stro·bi·la·ceous

stro·bi·la·tion

stro·bi·lus (*or* stro·bile;
  plural ·li, ·luses *or*
  ·biles) plant cone

stro·bo·scope

stro·bo·scop·ic (*or*
  ·scopi·cal)

stro·bo·scopi·cal·ly

strode

stroga·noff

stroke

stroll

stroll·er

stro·ma (*plural* ·ma·ta)
  biology term

stro·mat·ic (*or* ·ma·tous)

stro·mato·lite rock

stro·mato·lit·ic

Strom·bo·li volcanic island

strong

strong-arm

strong·box

strong·hold

strong·ly

strong·man (*plural* ·men)

strong-minded

strong-minded·ness

strong·ness

strong·room

strong-willed

stron·gyle (*or* ·gyl)
  parasitic worm

strontia strontium
  compound

stron·ti·an·ite (*or*
  stron·tian) mineral

stron·tium chemical
  element

strop (strop·ping,
  stropped)

stro·phan·thin drug

stro·phan·thus tree

stro·phe prosody term

stroph·ic (*or* strophi·cal)

strop·pi·ly

strop·pi·ness

strop·py (·pi·er, ·pi·est)

Stroud English town

stroud fabric

strove

struck

struc·tur·al

struc·tur·al·ism

struc·tur·al·ist

struc·tur·al·ly

struc·ture

struc·ture·less

stru·del

strug·gle

strug·gler

strug·gling·ly

strum (strum·ming, strummed)

stru·ma (*plural* ·mae) swelling

stru·mat·ic (*or* stru·mous, stru·mose)

strum·mer

strum·pet

strung

strut (strut·ting, strut·ted)

stru·thi·ous ostrich-like

strut·ter

strut·ting·ly

strych·nic

strych·nine

strych·nin·ism

stub (stub·bing, stubbed)

stub·bi·ly

stub·bi·ness

stub·ble

stub·bled

stub·bly

stub·born

stub·born·ness

stub·by (·bi·er, ·bi·est)

stuc·co (*noun, plural* ·coes *or* ·cos; *verb* ·coes *or* ·cos, ·co·ing, ·coed)

stuck

stud (stud·ding, stud·ded)

stud·book

stud·ding

studding·sail

stu·dent

stu·dent·ship

stud·horse

stud·ied

stud·ied·ly

stud·ied·ness

stu·dio (*plural* ·dios)

stu·di·ous

stu·di·ous·ness

stud·work

study (*noun, plural* studies, *verb* stud·ies, study·ing, stud·ied)

stuff

stuffed

stuff·er

stuf·fi·ly

stuffi·ness

stuff·ing

stuffy (stuffi·er, stuffi·est)

stull mining prop

stul·ti·fi·ca·tion

stul·ti·fi·er

stul·ti·fy (·fies, ·fy·ing, ·fied)

stum (stum·ming, stummed) wine-making term

stum·ble

stum·bler

stum·bling·ly

stu·mer *Slang* forgery

stump

stump·er

stumpi·ness

stumpy (stumpi·er, stumpi·est)

stun (stun·ning, stunned)

stung

stunk

stun·ner

stun·ning

stun·ning·ly

stunt

stunt·ed

stunt·ed·ness

stupe medical compress; *compare* stoop; stoup

stu·pefa·ci·ent (*or* ·pefac·tive)

stu·pefac·tion

stu·pefi·er

stu·pefy (·pefies, ·pefy·ing, ·pefied)

stu·pefy·ing·ly

stu·pen·dous

stu·pen·dous·ness

stu·pid

stu·pid·ity (*plural* ·ities)

stu·pid·ness

stu·por

stu·por·ous

stur·di·ly

stur·di·ness

stur·dy (·di·er, ·di·est)

stur·geon

Stur·mer apple

stut·ter

stut·ter·er

stut·ter·ing·ly

Stutt·gart West German city

sty (*noun, plural* sties, *verb* sties, sty·ing, stied) pig's pen

sty (*or* stye; *plural* sties *or* styes) inflamed eye spot

Styg·ian of the Styx

stylar

style form; elegance; flower part; *compare* stile

style·book

styl·er

sty·let

sty·li·form

styl·ish

styl·ish·ness

styl·ist

sty·lis·tic

sty·lis·ti·cal·ly

sty·lite recluse

styli·za·tion (*or* ·sa·tion)

styl·ize (*or* ·ise)

styl·iz·er (*or* ·is·er)

sty·lo·bate architectural term

sty·lo·graph

sty·lo·graph·ic (*or* ·graphi·cal)

sty·lo·graphi·cal·ly

sty·log·ra·phy engraving

sty·loid

sty·lo·lite geology term

sty·lo·lit·ic

sty·lo·pize (*or* ·pise) parasitize with stylops

sty·lo·po·dium (*plural* ·dia) botany term

sty·lops (*plural* ·lo·pes) insect

sty·lo·stix·is acupuncture

sty·lus (*plural* ·li *or* ·luses)

sty·mie (*or* ·my; *verb* ·mies, ·mie·ing, ·mied *or* ·mies, ·my·ing, ·mied; *noun, plural* ·mies)

styp·sis

styp·tic

styp·ti·cal

styp·tic·ity

sty·ra·ca·ceous

sty·rax tree

sty·rene organic compound

Styria Austrian province

Styx mythological river

su·abil·ity

su·able

Sua·kin Sudanese port

suave
suave·ly
suav·ity (*or* suave·ness)
sub (sub·bing, subbed)
sub·ac·etate
sub·acid
sub·acid·ity (*or*
·acid·ness)
sub·acute medical term
sub·acute·ly
sub·agent
su·bah Mogul province
sub·al·pine
sub·al·tern
sub·al·ter·nate botany term
sub·al·ter·na·tion
sub·ant·arc·tic
sub·aquat·ic
sub·aque·ous
sub·arc·tic
sub·ar·id
sub·as·sem·bly (*plural*
·blies)
sub·atom·ic
sub·audi·tion
sub·auricu·lar
sub·ax·il·la·ry
sub·base pedestal base
sub·base·ment
sub·bass (*or* ·base) organ
stop
sub·cali·bre
sub·car·ti·lagi·nous
sub·ce·les·tial
sub·cep·tion subliminal
perception
sub·chlo·ride
sub·class
sub·cla·vian
sub·cli·mac·tic
sub·cli·max
sub·com·mit·tee
sub·con·scious
sub·con·scious·ness
sub·con·ti·nent
sub·con·ti·nen·tal
sub·con·tract
sub·con·trac·tor
sub·con·tra·ry (*plural*
·ries)
sub·cor·tex (*plural* ·tices)
sub·cor·ti·cal
sub·cul·tur·al
sub·cul·ture
sub·cu·ta·neous

sub·dea·con
sub·dea·con·ate
sub·de·lir·ium (*plural*
·lir·iums *or* ·liria)
sub·di·aco·nal
sub·di·aco·nate
subdeacon's rank
sub·di·vide
sub·di·vid·er
sub·di·vi·sion
sub·di·vi·sion·al
sub·domi·nant
sub·du·able
sub·du·al
sub·duct
sub·duc·tion
sub·due (·dues, ·du·ing,
·dued)
sub·dued·ly
sub·dued·ness
sub·edit
sub·edi·tor
sub·equa·to·rial
su·ber·in plant substance
su·beri·za·tion (*or*
·sa·tion)
su·ber·ize (*or* ·ise)
su·ber·ose (*or* ·bereous,
·ber·ic) of cork
sub·fami·ly (*plural* ·lies)
sub·floor
sub·fusc drab; academic
dress
sub·ge·ner·ic
sub·ge·nus (*plural*
·gen·era *or* ·ge·nuses)
sub·gla·cial
sub·gla·cial·ly
sub·group
sub·head·ing (*or* ·head)
sub·hu·man
sub·in·dex (*plural* ·dices
or ·dexes)
sub·in·feu·date
sub·in·feu·da·tion
sub·in·feu·da·tory (*plural*
·tories)
sub·ir·ri·gate
sub·ir·ri·ga·tion
su·bi·to musical term
sub·ja·cen·cy
sub·ja·cent
sub·ject
sub·ject·abil·ity
sub·ject·able

sub·jec·ti·fi·ca·tion
sub·jec·ti·fy (·fies, ·fy·ing,
·fied)
sub·jec·tion
sub·jec·tive
sub·jec·tive·ly
sub·jec·tiv·ism
sub·jec·tiv·ist
sub·jec·ti·vis·tic
sub·jec·ti·vis·ti·cal·ly
sub·jec·tiv·ity (*or*
·tive·ness)
subject-raising
sub·join
sub·join·der
sub ju·di·ce
sub·ju·gable
sub·ju·gate
sub·ju·ga·tion
sub·ju·ga·tor
sub·junc·tion
sub·junc·tive
sub·king·dom
sub·lease
sub·les·see
sub·les·sor
sub·let (·let·ting, ·let)
sub·lieu·ten·an·cy
sub·lieu·ten·ant
sub·li·mable
sub·li·mate
sub·li·ma·tion
sub·lime
sub·lime·ly
sub·limi·nal
sub·limi·nal·ly
sub·lim·ity (*plural* ·ities)
sub·lin·gual
sub·lit·to·ral near seashore
sub·lu·nary between moon
and earth
sub·machine-gun
sub·mar·gin·al
sub·ma·rine
sub·ma·rin·er
sub·max·il·lary of lower
jaw
sub·me·di·ant musical term
sub·men·tal beneath the
chin
sub·merge (*or* ·merse)
sub·mers·ibil·ity (*or*
·merg·)
sub·mers·ible (*or* ·merg·)

sub·mer·sion (or
·merg·ence)
sub·micro·scop·ic
sub·micro·scopi·cal·ly
sub·miss *Archaic* docile
sub·mis·sion
sub·mis·sive
sub·mis·sive·ly
sub·mis·sive·ness
sub·mit (·mit·ting,
·mit·ted)
sub·mit·table (or
·mis·sible)
sub·mit·tal
sub·mit·ter
sub·mit·ting·ly
sub·mon·tane
sub·mu·co·sa (*plural* ·sae)
sub·mul·ti·ple
sub·nor·mal
sub·nor·mal·ity
sub·nor·mal·ly
sub·ocean·ic
sub·or·bi·tal
sub·or·der
sub·or·di·nal
sub·or·di·nary (*plural*
·naries) heraldic term
sub·or·di·nate
sub·or·di·nate·ly
sub·or·di·nate·ness
sub·or·di·na·tion
sub·or·di·na·tive
sub·orn
sub·or·na·tion
sub·or·na·tive
sub·orn·er
sub·ox·ide
sub·phy·lar
sub·phy·lum (*plural* ·la)
sub·plot
sub·poe·na (·nas, ·na·ing,
·naed)
sub·popu·la·tion
sub·prin·ci·pal
sub·re·gion
sub·re·gion·al
sub·rep·tion concealment of
facts
sub·rep·ti·tious
sub·ro·gate legal term
sub·ro·ga·tion
sub rosa *Latin* in secret
sub·rou·tine
sub·scapu·lar

sub·scribe
sub·scrib·er
sub·script
sub·scrip·tion
sub·scrip·tive
sub·sec·tion
sub·se·quence
sub·se·quent
sub·serve
sub·ser·vience (or
·vi·en·cy)
sub·ser·vi·ent
sub·set
sub·shrub
sub·side
sub·sid·ence
sub·sid·er
sub·sidi·ari·ly
sub·sidi·ari·ness
sub·sidi·ary (*plural* ·aries)
sub·si·diz·able (or
·dis·able)
sub·si·di·za·tion (or
·sa·tion)
sub·si·dize (or ·dise)
sub·si·diz·er (or ·dis·er)
sub·si·dy (*plural* ·dies)
sub·sist
sub·sist·ence
sub·sist·ent
sub·sist·er
sub·sist·ing·ly
sub·so·cial
sub·soil
sub·soil·er
sub·so·lar
sub·son·ic
sub·soni·cally
sub·spe·cies (*plural* ·cies)
sub·spe·cif·ic
sub·spe·cifi·cal·ly
sub·stage
sub·stance
sub·stand·ard
sub·stan·tial
sub·stan·tial·ism
sub·stan·tial·ist
sub·stan·ti·al·ity (or
·tial·ness)
sub·stan·tial·ly
sub·stan·ti·ate
sub·stan·tia·tion
sub·stan·tia·tive
sub·stan·tia·tor

sub·stan·ti·val grammar
term
sub·stan·ti·val·ly
sub·stan·tive
sub·stan·tive·ly
sub·stan·tive·ness
sub·stan·ti·vi·za·tion (or
·sa·tion)
sub·stan·tiv·ize (or ·ise)
sub·sta·tion
sub·stitu·ent
sub·sti·tuta·bil·ity
sub·sti·tut·able
sub·sti·tute
sub·sti·tu·tion
sub·sti·tu·tive
sub·strate
sub·stra·tive (or ·tal)
sub·stra·tum (*plural*
·stra·ta)
sub·struc·tur·al (or
·tion·al)
sub·struc·ture (or ·tion)
sub·sum·able
sub·sume
sub·sump·tion
sub·sump·tive
sub·tan·gent
sub·tem·per·ate
sub·ten·an·cy (*plural*
·cies)
sub·ten·ant
sub·tend
sub·ter·fuge
sub·ter·ra·nean
sub·ter·res·trial
sub·tili·za·tion (or
·sa·tion)
sub·til·ize (or ·ise) refine
sub·til·iz·er (or ·is·er)
sub·ti·tle
sub·titu·lar
sub·tle
sub·tle·ness
sub·tler more subtle;
compare sutler
sub·tle·ty (*plural* ·ties)
sub·tly
sub·ton·ic musical note
sub·tor·rid
sub·to·tal (·tal·ling,
·talled; *US* ·tal·ing,
·taled)
sub·tract
sub·tract·er

sub·trac·tion
sub·trac·tive
sub·tra·hend number subtracted
sub·tropi·cal
sub·trop·ics
sub·type
sub·typi·cal
su·bu·late awl-shaped
sub·urb
sub·ur·ban
sub·ur·ban·ite
sub·ur·bani·za·tion (or ·sa·tion)
sub·ur·ban·ize (or ·ise)
sub·ur·bia
sub·vene
sub·ven·tion
sub·ven·tion·ary
sub·ver·sion
sub·ver·sive
sub·ver·sive·ly
sub·ver·sive·ness
sub·vert
sub·vert·er
sub·way
sub·zero
suc·ce·da·neous
suc·ce·da·neum (plural ·nea) substitute drug
suc·ceed
suc·ceed·able
suc·ceed·er
suc·ceed·ing·ly
suc·cen·tor cathedral cleric
suc·cess
suc·cess·ful
suc·cess·ful·ly
suc·cess·ful·ness
suc·ces·sion
suc·ces·sion·al
suc·ces·sive
suc·ces·sive·ly
suc·ces·sive·ness
suc·ces·sor
suc·ces·sor·al
suc·cin·ate chemical compound
suc·cinct
suc·cinct·ness
suc·cin·ic of amber; chemistry term
suc·cory (plural ·cories) chicory

suc·co·tash US mixed vegetables
suc·cour (US ·cor)
suc·cour·able (US ·cor·)
suc·cour·er (US ·cor·)
suc·cu·bus (plural ·bi) female demon
suc·cu·lence (or ·len·cy)
suc·cu·lent
suc·cumb
suc·cumb·er
suc·cur·sal subsidiary
suc·cuss
suc·cus·sion
suc·cus·sive
such
such·like
Su·chou variant spelling of Soochow
Sü·chow (or Hsü·chou) Chinese city
suck
suck·er
sucker·fish (or suck·fish; plural ·fish or ·fishes)
suck·le
suck·ler
suck·ling
su·crase enzyme
su·crose sugar
suc·tion
suc·tion·al
suc·to·rial
Su·dan
Su·da·nese (plural ·nese)
Su·dan·ic
su·dar·ium (plural ·daria) face cloth
su·da·to·rium (or ·tory; plural ·to·ria or ·tories) steam-bath room
Sud·bury Canadian city
sudd water weed
sud·den
sud·den·ness
Su·deten·land Czech region
Su·detes (or Su·deten) European mountains
su·dor sweat
su·dor·al
su·dor·if·er·ous
su·dor·if·ic
suds
sudsy
sue (su·ing, sued)

(sueable) incorrect spelling of suable
suede
suer one who sues; compare sewer
suet
su·ety
Suez
suf·fer
suf·fer·able
suf·fer·ance
suf·fer·er
suf·fer·ing
suf·fice
suf·fic·er
suf·fi·cien·cy (plural ·cies)
suf·fi·cient
suf·fix
suf·fix·al
suf·fix·ion
suf·fo·cate
suf·fo·cat·ing·ly
suf·fo·ca·tion
suf·fo·ca·tive
Suf·folk
suf·fra·gan assistant bishop
suf·fra·gan·ship
suf·frage
suf·fra·gette
suf·fra·get·tism
suf·fra·gism
suf·fra·gist
suf·fru·ti·cose botany term
suf·fu·mi·gate
suf·fu·mi·ga·tion
suf·fuse
suf·fu·sion
suf·fu·sive
Sufi (plural Sufis) Muslim mystic
Su·fic
Su·fism
Su·fis·tic
sug·ar
sug·ari·ness
sugar·plum
sug·ary
sug·gest
sug·gest·er
sug·gest·ibil·ity
sug·gest·ible
sug·gest·ible·ness
sug·gest·ing·ly
sug·ges·tion

sug·ges·tive
sug·ges·tive·ly
sug·ges·tive·ness
sui·cid·al
sui·cid·al·ly
sui·cide
sui gen·eris unique
su·int substance in fleece
suit clothes; set of cards;
 petition; to be
 appropriate; *compare* suite
suit·abil·ity (*or*
 ·able·ness)
suit·able
suit·ably
suit·case
suite set of rooms; furniture;
 musical piece; *compare*
 suit
suit·ing
suit·or
Su·khu·mi Soviet port
su·ki·ya·ki Japanese dish
Su·la·we·si Indonesian
 island
sul·cate
sul·ca·tion
sul·cus (*plural* ·ci) groove
sul·fur US *spelling of*
 sulphur; *note all words*
 starting sulph- *have the US*
 spelling sulf-
sulk
sulk·er
sulki·ly
sulki·ness
sulky (*adj* sulki·er,
 sulki·est; *noun, plural*
 sulkies) sullen; vehicle
sul·lage sewage
sul·len
sul·len·ness
sul·li·able
sul·ly (·lies, ·ly·ing, ·lied)
sul·pha (US ·fa) class of
 drugs; *compare* sulphur
sul·pha·dia·zine (US ·fa·)
sul·pha·nila·mide (US
 ·fa·)
sul·phate (US ·fate)
sul·pha·thia·zole (US ·fa·)
sul·pha·tion (US ·fa·)
sul·phide (US ·fide)
sul·phi·soxa·zole (US ·fi·)
sul·phite (US ·fite)
sul·phit·ic (US ·fit·)

sul·phona·mide (US
 ·fona·) sulpha drug
sul·pho·nate (US ·fo·)
sul·phone (US ·fone)
sul·phon·me·thane (US
 ·fon·)
sul·phur (US ·fur)
 chemical element; *compare*
 sulpha
sul·phur·ate (US ·fur·)
sul·phu·ra·tion (US ·fu·)
sul·phu·reous (US ·fu·)
sul·phu·reous·ness (US
 ·fu·)
sul·phu·ret (US ·fu·;
 ·ret·ting, ·ret·ted, US
 ·ret·ing, ·ret·ed)
sul·phu·ric (US ·fu·)
sul·phu·ri·za·tion (*or*
 ·sa·tion; US
 ·fu·ri·za·tion)
sul·phu·rize (*or* ·rise; US
 ·fu·rize)
sul·phur·ous (US ·fur·)
sul·phur·ous·ness (US
 ·fur·)
sul·phur·yl (US ·fur·)
sul·tan
sul·tana
sul·tan·ate
sul·tan·ic
sul·tri·ly
sul·tri·ness
sul·try (·tri·er, ·tri·est)
Sulu Philippine archipelago
sum (sum·ming, summed)
su·mach (*or* ·mac) shrub
Su·ma·tra
Su·ma·tran
Su·mer Babylonian region
Su·me·rian
sum·ma (*plural* ·mae)
 medieval compendium
sum·ma cum lau·de
 highest achievement in
 examination
sum·mand part of a sum
sum·mari·ly
sum·mari·ness
sum·ma·riz·able (*or*
 ·ris·able)
sum·ma·ri·za·tion (*or*
 ·sa·tion)
sum·ma·rize (*or* ·rise)
sum·ma·riz·er (*or* ·ris·er)

sum·mary (*plural*
 ·maries) brief account;
 compare summery
sum·ma·tion
sum·ma·tion·al
sum·mer
summer·house
sum·meri·ness
sum·mer·sault *variant*
 spelling of somersault
summer·time
summer·wood
sum·mery like summer;
 compare summary
summing-up (*plural*
 summings-)
sum·mit
sum·mit·al
sum·mit·ry
sum·mon (*verb*)
sum·mon·able
sum·mons (*noun, plural*
 ·monses; *verb* ·mons,
 ·mons·ing, ·monsed)
sum·mum bon·um *Latin*
 highest good
Sumo wrestling
sump
sump·tua·ry
sump·tu·ous
sump·tu·ous·ness (*or*
 ·tu·os·ity)
sun (sun·ning, sunned)
sun·bake *Austral*
 sunbathing
sun·baked
sun·bathe
sun·bather
sun·beam
sun·bird
sun·bonnet
sun·bow
sun·burn
sun·burnt (*or* ·burned)
sun·burst
sun·dae dessert
Sun·da Is·lands
Sun·day
sun·der
sun·der·able
sun·der·ance
sun·der·er
Sun·der·land
sun·dew
sun·dial

sun·dog small rainbow
sun·down
sun·dress
sun-dried
sun·dry (*plural* ·dries)
sun·fast
sun·fish (*plural* ·fish *or* ·fishes)
sun·flower
sung
Sun·ga·ri Chinese river
sun·glass burning glass
sun·glasses spectacles
sun·glow
sun·god
sun·grebe bird
sun·hat
sunk
sunk·en
sun·less
sun·less·ness
sun·light
sun·lit
sunn fibre
Sun·na Islamic law
sunned
Sun·ni (*plural* ·ni) Muslim sect
sun·ni·ly
sun·ni·ness
sun·ning
Sun·nite Muslim
sun·ny (·ni·er, ·ni·est)
sun·ray pleats
sun·rise
sun·roof
sun·set
sun·shade
sun·shine
sun·shiny
sun·spot
sun·spotted
sun·star starfish
sun·stroke
sun·suit
sun·tan
sun·tanned
sun·trap
sun·wards (*or esp. US* ·ward)
sun·wise
sup (sup·ping, supped)
su·per
super·abil·ity (*or* ·able·ness)

super·able
super·ably
super·abound
super·abun·dance
supera·bun·dant
super·add
super·ad·di·tion
super·ad·di·tion·al
super·an·nu·ate
super·an·nu·at·ed
super·an·nua·tion
su·perb
super·ba·zaar Indian store
su·perb·ness
super·cal·en·der
super·car·go (*plural* ·goes)
(supercede) *incorrect spelling of* **supersede**
super·charge
super·char·ger
super·cili·ary of the eyebrow
super·cili·ous
super·cili·ous·ness
super·class
super·co·lum·nar
super·con·duc·tion
super·con·duc·tive (*or* ·duct·ing)
super·con·duc·tiv·ity
super·con·duc·tor
super·cool (*verb*)
super-duper
super·ego (*plural* ·egos)
super·el·eva·tion
super·emi·nence
super·emi·nent
super·eroga·tory superfluous
super·fami·ly (*plural* ·lies)
super·fe·cun·da·tion
super·fe·tate
super·fe·ta·tion physiology term
super·fi·cial
super·fi·ci·al·ity (*or* ·cial·ness)
super·fi·cial·ly
super·fine
super·fix linguistics term
super·fluid
super·flu·id·ity
super·flu·ity
super·flu·ous

super·flu·ous·ness
super·gi·ant
super·gla·cial
super·heat (*verb*)
super·he·ro (*plural* ·roes)
super·het·ero·dyne radio receiver
super·high·way US fast dual carriageway
super·hu·man
super·hu·man·ity (*or* ·man·ness)
super·im·pose
super·im·po·si·tion
super·in·cum·bence (*or* ·ben·cy)
super·in·cum·bent
super·in·duce
super·induce·ment
super·in·duc·tion
super·in·tend
super·in·tend·ence
super·in·tend·en·cy (*plural* ·cies) office of superintendent
super·in·ten·dent
Su·peri·or US lake
su·peri·or
su·peri·or·ity
super·ja·cent
super·la·tive
super·la·tive·ly
super·la·tive·ness
super·lun·ar
super·lun·ary
super·man (*plural* ·men)
super·mar·ket
super·nal celestial
super·nal·ly
super·na·tant
super·na·ta·tion
super·natu·ral
super·natu·ral·ism
super·natu·ral·ist
super·natu·ral·is·tic
super·natu·ral·ly
super·natu·ral·ness
super·nor·mal
super·nor·mal·ity (*or* ·ness)
super·nor·mal·ly
super·no·va (*plural* ·vae *or* ·vas)
super·nu·mer·ary (*plural* ·aries)

super·or·der
super·ordi·nal
super·or·di·nate
super·ox·ide
super·phos·phate
super·physi·cal
super·pos·able
super·pose
super·po·si·tion
super·pow·er
super·satu·rat·ed chemistry term
super·satu·ra·tion
super·scribe
super·script
super·scrip·tion
super·sed·able
super·sede
super·sed·ence
super·sed·er
super·se·dure
super·sen·sible (*or* ·sory)
super·ses·sion
super·sex genetics term
super·son·ic
super·soni·cal·ly
super·son·ics
super·star
super·sti·tion
super·sti·tious
super·sti·tious·ness
super·store
super·stra·tum (*plural* ·ta *or* ·tums)
super·struct build on another structure
super·struc·tur·al
super·struc·ture
super·tank·er
super·tax
super·ton·ic musical note
super·vene
super·veni·ent
super·ven·tion (*or* ·veni·ence)
super·vise
super·vi·sion
super·vi·sor
super·vi·sory
su·pi·nate
su·pi·na·tion
su·pi·na·tor muscle
su·pine
su·pine·ly
su·pine·ness

su·plex wrestling hold
supped
sup·per
sup·ping
sup·plant
sup·plan·ta·tion
sup·plant·er
sup·ple
supple·jack plant
sup·ple·ly *variant spelling of* supply
sup·plement
sup·plemen·tal
sup·ple·men·ta·ri·ly (*or* ·tal·ly)
sup·plemen·ta·ry (*plural* ·ries)
sup·plemen·ta·tion
sup·plement·er
sup·ple·ness
sup·pletion linguistics term
sup·pletive
sup·pleto·ri·ly
sup·pletory
sup·pli·able
sup·pli·ance (*or* ·an·cy)
sup·pli·ant
sup·pli·cant (*or* ·pli·ant)
sup·pli·cate
sup·pli·ca·tion
sup·pli·ca·tory
sup·pli·er
sup·ply (*noun, plural* ·plies; *verb* ·plies, ·ply·ing, ·plied)
sup·ply (*or* sup·ple·ly) in a supple way
sup·port
sup·port·abil·ity (*or* ·able·ness)
sup·port·ably
sup·port·able
sup·port·er
sup·port·ing
sup·port·ive
sup·pos·able
sup·pose
sup·posed
sup·pos·ed·ly
sup·pos·er
sup·po·si·tion
sup·po·si·tion·al
sup·po·si·tious (*or* ·posi·ti·tious)

sup·po·si·tious·ness (*or* ·posi·ti·tious·ness)
sup·posi·tive involving supposition
sup·posi·tory (*plural* ·tories)
sup·press
sup·press·ible
sup·pres·sion
sup·pres·sive
sup·pres·sor (*or* ·press·er)
sup·pu·rate
sup·pu·ra·tion
sup·pu·ra·tive
su·pra above
supra·glot·tal
supra·lap·sar·ian theology term
supra·limi·nal
supra·mo·lecu·lar
supra·na·tion·al
supra·na·tion·al·ism
supra·or·bit·al
supra·re·nal
supra·seg·men·tal
su·prema·cist
su·prema·cy
Su·prema·tism cubist art
su·prema·tism
Su·prema·tist
su·preme
su·prême cookery term
su·preme·ly
su·preme·ness
su·prem·ity
su·pre·mo (*plural* ·mos)
sura Koran chapter
Su·ra·ba·ya (*or* ·ja, Soe·ra·ba·ja) Indonesian port
su·rah fabric
Su·ra·kar·ta Indonesian town
su·ral anatomy term
Su·rat Indian port
su·rat fabric
sur·base architectural term
sur·base·ment
sur·cease
sur·charge
sur·charg·er
sur·cin·gle horse's girth; cassock belt
sur·coat
sur·cu·lose bearing suckers

surd maths term
sure
sure-fire
sure-footed
sure-footed·ly
sure-footed·ness
sure·ly
sure·ness
sure·ty (*plural* ·ties)
surf breaking waves;
  compare serf
surf·able
sur·face
surface-active
sur·fac·er
sur·fac·tant
surf·bird
surf·board
surf·boat
surf·caster
surf·casting shore-fishing
sur·feit
sur·feit·er
surf·er
surfie *Austral* surfer
surf·ing
surf·like
surf·perch fish
surf·rider
surfy
surge rush; *compare* serge
sur·geon
sur·geon·cy (*plural* ·cies)
surgeon·fish (*plural* ·fish
  or ·fishes)
surg·er
sur·gery (*plural* ·geries)
sur·gi·cal
sur·gi·cal·ly
su·ri·cate animal
Su·ri·nam South American
  republic
sur·jec·tion
sur·jec·tive
sur·li·ly
sur·li·ness
sur·ly (·li·er, ·li·est)
sur·mis·able
sur·mise
sur·mis·ed·ly
sur·mis·er
sur·mount
sur·mount·able
sur·mount·able·ness
sur·mount·er

sur·name
sur·pass
sur·pass·able
sur·pas·sing
sur·pass·ing·ly
sur·pass·ing·ness
sur·plice vestment
sur·pliced
sur·plus (*plural* ·pluses)
  excess
sur·plus·age
sur·print overprint
sur·prise
sur·pris·ed·ly
sur·pris·er
sur·pris·ing
sur·pris·ing·ly
sur·pris·ing·ness
sur·ra animal disease
sur·re·al
sur·re·al·ism
sur·re·al·ist
sur·re·al·is·tic
sur·re·al·is·ti·cal·ly
sur·re·but·tal
sur·re·but·ter
sur·re·join·der
sur·ren·der
sur·ren·der·er
sur·rep·ti·tious
sur·rep·ti·tious·ness
Sur·rey English county
sur·rey carriage
sur·ro·gate
sur·ro·gate·ship
sur·ro·ga·tion
sur·round
sur·round·ing
sur·round·ings
sur·tax
sur·tout overcoat
sur·veil·lance
sur·veil·lant
sur·vey
sur·vey·able
sur·vey·ing
sur·vey·or
sur·vey·or·ship
sur·viv·abil·ity
sur·viv·able
sur·viv·al
sur·vive
sur·vi·vor
Susa ancient Persian city

sus·cep·tance magnetic
  property
sus·cep·tibil·ity (*plural*
  ·ities)
sus·cep·tible
sus·cep·tibly
sus·cep·tible·ness
sus·cep·tive
sus·cep·tiv·ity (*or*
  ·tive·ness)
su·shi Japanese food
sus·lik *variant spelling of*
  souslik
sus·pect
sus·pect·er
sus·pend
sus·pend·er
sus·pend·ibil·ity
sus·pend·ible (*or* ·pens·)
sus·pense
sus·pense·ful
sus·pen·sion
sus·pen·sive
sus·pen·sive·ness
sus·pen·soid chemistry term
sus·pen·sor
sus·pen·so·ry (*plural*
  ·ries)
sus·pi·cion
sus·pi·cion·al
sus·pi·cious
sus·pi·cious·ness
sus·pi·ra·tion
sus·pire sigh
Sus·que·han·na US river
suss
Sus·sex
sus·tain
sus·tain·able
sus·tain·ed·ly
sus·tain·er
sus·tain·ing·ly
sus·tain·ment
sus·te·nance
sus·ten·tacu·lar supporting
sus·ten·ta·tion nourishment
sus·ten·tion
su·sur·rant
su·sur·rate
su·sur·ra·tion (*or*
  su·sur·rus)
Suth·er·land former
  Scottish county
Sut·lej Asian river

sut·ler provisioner; *compare* subtler

su·tra Sanskrit sayings

sut·tee Hindu custom

Sut·ton Cold·field English town

su·tur·al

su·ture

Suva Fijian capital

Su·wan·nee (*or* Swa·nee) US river

su·ze·rain

su·ze·rain·ty (*plural* ·ties)

Sval·bard Norwegian archipelago

svelte

Sverd·lovsk Soviet city

swab (swab·bing, swabbed)

swab·ber

Swa·bia former German duchy

Swa·bian

swacked *Slang* intoxicated

swad·dle

swag (swag·ging, swagged)

swage tool

swag·er

swag·ger

swag·ger·er

swag·ger·ing·ly

swag·man (*plural* ·men)

Swa·hi·li (*plural* ·lis *or* ·li)

Swa·hi·lian

swain

swal·low

swal·low·able

swal·low·er

swallow·tail

swallow·wort

swam

swa·mi (*plural* ·mies *or* ·mis) Hindu title

swamp

swamp·land

swampy (swampi·er, swampi·est)

swan (swan·ning, swanned)

Swa·nee *variant spelling of* Suwannee

swan·herd

swank

swanki·ly

swanki·ness

swanky (swanki·er, swanki·est)

swan·like

swan·nery (*plural* ·neries)

swan's-down

Swan·sea

swan·skin

swan-upping

swap (*or* swop; swap·ping, swapped *or* swop·ping, swopped)

swap·per (*or* swop·)

swa·raj Indian self-government

sward (*or* swarth) turf; *compare* sword

swarf metal off-cuttings

swarm

swarthi·ly

swarthi·ness

swarthy (swarthi·er, swarthi·est)

swash splash

swash·buck·ler

swash·buck·ling

swash·ing·ly

swas·ti·ka

swat (swat·ting, swat·ted) hit; *compare* swot

swatch

swath (*or* swathe; *noun*)

swath·able (*or* swathe·)

swathe (*verb*)

Swa·tow Chinese port

swats *Dialect* beer

swat·ter

sway

sway·able

sway-back

sway·er

sway·ing·ly

Swa·zi (*plural* ·zis *or* ·zi)

Swa·zi·land

swear (swear·ing, swore, sworn)

swear·er

swear·ing·ly

swear·word

sweat (sweat·ing, sweat *or* sweat·ed)

sweat·band

sweat·box

sweat·er

sweati·ly

sweati·ness

sweat·shop

sweaty (sweati·er, sweati·est)

Swede native of Sweden

swede vegetable

Swe·den

Swe·den·bor·gi·an·ism (*or* ·bor·gism) religious movement

Swe·dish

swee·ny veterinary term

sweep (sweep·ing, swept)

sweep·back

sweep·er

sweep·ing

sweep·ing·ly

sweep·ing·ness

sweep·ings

sweep·stake

sweet

sweet·bread

sweet·brier

sweet·en

sweet·en·er

sweet·en·ing

sweet·heart

sweetie

sweetie·wife (*plural* ·wives) *Scot* talkative woman

sweet·ish

sweet·meal

sweet·meat

sweet·ness

sweet·shop

sweet·sop fruit

swell (swell·ing, swelled, swol·len *or* swelled)

swell·fish (*plural* ·fish *or* ·fishes)

swell·ing

swel·ter

swel·ter·ing

swel·ter·ing·ly

swept

swept·back

swept·wing

swerv·able

swerve

swerv·er

swerv·ing·ly

swift

swift·er nautical term

swiftie *Austral* a trick

swift·let bird
swift·ness
swig (swig·ging, swigged)
swig·ger
swill
swill·er
swim (swim·ming, swam,
    swum)
swim·mable
swim·mer
swim·mer·et zoology term
swim·ming·ly
swim·suit
swin·dle
swin·dler
swin·dling·ly
Swin·don
swine (plural swines)
swine·herd
swine·pox
swing (swing·ing, swung)
swing·boat
swinge (swinge·ing,
    swinged) punish
swing·er
swing·ing
swin·gle flax-beating
    instrument
swing·om·eter
swing-wing
swin·ish
swin·ish·ness
swink Dialect toil
swipe
swipes Slang beer
swip·ple (or swi·ple) part
    of flail
swirl
swirl·ing·ly
swirly
swish
swish·er
swish·ing·ly
swishy
Swiss
switch
switch·back
switch·board
switch·er
switch·eroo US unexpected
    change
switch·girl Austral
    switchboard operator
switch-over (noun)
swith·er Scot hesitate

Switz·er a Swiss
Swit·zer·land
swiv·el (·el·ling, ·elled;
    US ·el·ing, ·eled)
swiv·et Dialect excitement
swizz Slang disappointment
swiz·zle
swol·len
swol·len·ness
swoon
swoon·ing·ly
swoop
swoosh
swop variant spelling of swap
sword weapon; compare
    sward
sword·bill
sword·craft
sword·fish (plural ·fish or
    ·fishes)
sword·like
sword·play
swords·man (plural ·men)
swords·man·ship
sword·stick
sword·tail fish
swore
sworn
swot (swot·ting, swot·ted)
    study; compare swat
swound Dialect swoon
swum
swung
swy Austral gambling game
Syba·ris ancient Greek
    colony
Syba·rite
syba·rite lover of luxury
syba·rit·ic (or ·riti·cal)
syba·riti·cal·ly
(sybil) incorrect spelling of
    sibyl
syca·mine mulberry
syca·more
syce (or sice, saice)
    Indian servant
sy·cee silver ingots
sy·co·nium (plural ·nia)
    botany term
syco·phan·cy
syco·phant
syco·phan·tic
syco·phan·ti·cal·ly
sy·co·sis skin disease

Syd·ney Australian city;
    Canadian port
Sy·ene ancient Egyptian
    town
sy·enite rock
sy·enit·ic
Syk·tyv·kar Soviet city
syl·la·bary (plural ·baries)
syl·lab·ic
syl·labi·cal·ly
syl·labi·cate syllabify
syl·labi·fi·ca·tion (or
    ·labi·ca·tion)
syl·labi·fy (·fies, ·fy·ing,
    ·fied)
syl·la·bism
syl·la·ble
syl·labo·gram
syl·lab·og·ra·phy
syl·la·bub (or sil·)
syl·la·bus (plural ·buses
    or ·bi)
syl·lep·sis (plural ·ses)
    linguistics term
syl·lep·tic
syl·lep·ti·cal·ly
syl·lo·gism
syl·lo·gis·tic
syl·lo·gis·ti·cal
syl·lo·gis·ti·cal·ly
syl·lo·gi·za·tion (or
    ·sa·tion)
syl·lo·gize (or ·gise)
syl·lo·giz·er (or ·gis·er)
sylph
sylph·ic (or ·id)
sylph-like (or ·ish)
syl·va (or sil·; plural ·vas
    or ·vae) trees
syl·van (or sil·)
syl·van·ite mineral
Sylvanus variant spelling of
    Silvanus
syl·vat·ic (or ·ves·tral)
    occurring in a wood
syl·vite (or ·vine) mineral
sym·bi·ont
sym·bi·on·tic
sym·bio·sis
sym·bi·ot·ic (or ·oti·cal)
sym·bi·oti·cal·ly
sym·bol (·bol·ling,
    ·bolled; US ·bol·ing,
    ·boled) thing representing
    something; compare
    cymbal

sym·bol·ic (*or* ·boli·cal)
sym·boli·cal·ly
sym·boli·cal·ness
sym·bol·ism
sym·bol·ist
sym·bol·is·tic (*or* ·ti·cal)
sym·bol·is·ti·cal·ly
sym·boli·za·tion (*or* ·sa·tion)
sym·bol·ize (*or* ·ise)
sym·bo·logi·cal
sym·bolo·gist
sym·bol·ogy
sym·met·al·lism economic doctrine
sym·met·ri·cal
sym·met·ri·cal·ly
sym·met·ri·cal·ness
sym·me·tri·za·tion (*or* ·sa·tion)
sym·me·trize (*or* ·trise)
sym·me·try (*plural* ·tries)
sym·pa·thec·to·my (*plural* ·mies) nerve surgery
sym·pa·thet·ic (*or* ·theti·cal)
sym·pa·theti·cal·ly
sym·pa·thin hormone
sym·pa·thize (*or* ·thise)
sym·pa·thiz·er (*or* ·this·er)
sym·pa·thiz·ing·ly (*or* ·this·ing·ly)
sym·pa·tho·lyt·ic pharmacology term
sym·pa·tho·mi·met·ic pharmacology term
sym·pa·thy (*plural* ·thies)
sym·pat·ric biology term
sym·pat·ri·cal·ly
sym·pet·al·ous
sym·phile entomology term
sym·phon·ic
sym·phoni·cal·ly
sym·pho·ni·ous
sym·pho·nist
sym·pho·ny (*plural* ·nies)
sym·phys·ial (*or* ·eal)
sym·physi·cal·ly (*or* ·phyti·)
sym·phy·sis (*plural* ·ses) anatomy term
sym·phys·tic (*or* ·phyt·ic)
sym·po·dial

sym·po·dium (*plural* ·dia) botany term
sym·po·si·ac
sym·po·sium (*plural* ·siums *or* ·sia)
symp·tom
symp·to·mat·ic (*or* ·mati·cal)
symp·to·mati·cal·ly
symp·toma·tol·ogy
syn·aer·esis *variant spelling of* syneresis
syn·aes·the·sia (*US* ·es·) medical term
syn·aes·thet·ic (*US* ·es·)
syna·gogi·cal (*or* ·gog·al)
syna·gogue
syna·lepha (*or* ·loepha) linguistics term
syn·apse nerve-cell junction
syn·ap·sis (*plural* ·ses) stage of meiosis
syn·ap·tic (*or* ·ti·cal)
syn·ap·ti·cal·ly
syn·ar·chy (*plural* ·chies) joint rule
syn·ar·thro·dial
syn·ar·thro·sis (*plural* ·ses) anatomy term
sync *Slang* synchronize; synchrony
syn·carp botany term
syn·car·pous
syn·car·py
syn·chro (*plural* ·chros) electrical device
syn·chro·cy·clo·tron
syn·chro·flash camera mechanism
syn·chro·mesh
syn·chron·ic
syn·chroni·cal·ly
syn·chro·nism
syn·chro·nis·tic (*or* ·ti·cal)
syn·chro·nis·ti·cal·ly
syn·chro·ni·za·tion (*or* ·sa·tion)
syn·chro·nize (*or* ·nise)
syn·chro·niz·er (*or* ·nis·er)
syn·chro·nous
syn·chro·nous·ness
syn·chrony
syn·chro·scope (*or* ·chrono·)
syn·chro·tron

syn·clas·tic maths term
syn·cli·nal
syn·cline geology term
syn·cli·no·rium (*plural* ·ria)
Syn·com communications satellite
syn·co·pate
syn·co·pa·tion
syn·co·pa·tor
syn·co·pe
syn·cop·ic (*or* ·co·pal)
syn·cret·ic (*or* ·cre·tis·tic)
syn·cre·tism
syn·cre·tist
syn·cre·ti·za·tion (*or* ·sa·tion)
syn·cre·tize (*or* ·tise) combine differing beliefs
syn·cyt·ial
syn·cyt·ium (*plural* ·cytia) zoology term
syn·dac·tyl
syn·dac·tyly (*or* ·tyl·ism)
syn·de·sis linguistics term
syn·des·mo·sis (*plural* ·ses) anatomy term
syn·des·mot·ic
syn·det·ic (*or* ·deti·cal)
syn·deti·cal·ly
syn·de·ton
syn·dic business agent
syn·di·cal
syn·di·cal·ism
syn·di·cal·ist
syn·di·cal·is·tic
syn·di·cate
syn·di·ca·tion
syn·dic·ship
syn·dio·tac·tic chemistry term
syn·drome
syn·drom·ic
syne *Scot* since
syn·ec·do·che figure of speech
syn·ec·doch·ic (*or* ·dochi·cal)
syn·ec·dochi·cal·ly
syn·eco·log·ic (*or* ·logi·cal)
syn·eco·logi·cal·ly
syn·ecol·ogy
syn·ec·tics problem solving

syn·er·esis (*or* ·aer·)
  chemistry or phonetics
  term
syn·er·get·ic (*or* ·gis·tic)
syn·er·geti·cal·ly (*or*
  ·gis·ti·)
syn·er·gic
syn·er·gism acting together
syn·er·gist
syn·er·gis·tic
syn·er·gy (*plural* ·gies)
syn·esis linguistics term
syn·es·the·sia *US spelling*
  of synaesthesia
syn·gam·ic (*or* ·ga·mous)
syn·ga·my (*or* ·gen·esis)
  biology term
syni·zesis phonetics or
  biology term
syn·kary·on biology term
syn·kary·on·ic
syn·od
syn·od·al (*or* ·odi·cal)
syn·od·ic
syn·oecious (*or*
  syn·ecious, synoi·cous)
  botany term
syn·oekete (*or* ·oecete)
  zoology term
syno·nym
syno·nym·ic (*or*
  ·nymi·cal)
syno·nym·ity
syn·ony·mize (*or* ·mise)
syn·ony·mous
syn·ony·mous·ness
syn·ony·my (*plural* ·mies)
syn·op·sis (*plural* ·ses)
syn·op·tic
syn·op·ti·cal·ly
syn·op·tist
syno·via fluid in joint
syno·vial
syno·vit·ic
syno·vi·tis

syn·sep·al·ous botany term
syn·tac·tic (*or* ·ti·cal)
syn·tac·ti·cal·ly
syn·tac·tics study of
  symbols
syn·tag·ma (*or* syn·tagm;
  plural ·tag·ma·ta *or*
  ·tagms) linguistics term
syn·tax
syn·the·sis (*plural* ·ses)
syn·the·sist
syn·the·si·za·tion (*or*
  ·sa·tion)
syn·the·size (*or* ·sise)
syn·the·siz·er (*or* ·sis·er)
syn·thet·ic
syn·theti·cal
syn·theti·cal·ly
syn·the·tism art term
syn·the·tist
syn·ton·ic psychology term
syn·toni·cal·ly
sy·pher woodworking term;
  compare cipher
sy·pher·ing
syphi·lis
syphi·lit·ic
syphi·liti·cal·ly
syphi·loid
syphi·lolo·gist
syphi·lol·ogy
syphi·lo·ma (*plural* ·mas
  or ·ma·ta) tumour
sy·phon *variant spelling of*
  siphon
Sy·ra·cuse Italian port; US
  city
Syria
Syri·ac
Syr·ian
sy·rin·ga ornamental shrub;
  compare seringa
sy·ringe
sy·rin·geal

sy·rin·go·my·elia disease
sy·rin·go·my·el·ic
syr·inx (*plural* sy·rin·ges
  or syr·inx·es) zoology
  term
syr·phid fly
syr·up (*US also* sir·)
syr·upy
sys·sar·co·sis (*plural* ·ses)
  anatomy term
sys·sar·cot·ic
sys·tal·tic of heartbeat
sys·tem
sys·tem·at·ic methodical;
  compare systemic
sys·tem·ati·cal·ly
sys·tem·ati·cal·ness
sys·tem·at·ics
sys·tema·tism
sys·tema·tist
sys·tema·ti·za·tion (*or*
  ·sa·tion)
sys·tema·tize (*or* ·tise)
sys·tema·tiz·er (*or* ·tis·er)
sys·tema·tol·ogy
sys·tem·ic affecting whole
  body; *compare* systematic
sys·temi·cal·ly
sys·temi·za·tion (*or*
  ·sa·tion) systematization
sys·tem·iz·er (*or* ·is·er)
sys·to·le
sys·tol·ic
Syz·ran Soviet port
syzy·geti·cal·ly
sy·zyg·ial (*or* syzy·get·ic,
  syzy·gal)
syzy·gy (*plural* ·gies)
  astronomy term
Szcze·cin Polish port
Sze·chwan Chinese
  province
Sze·ged Hungarian city

T

ta *Slang* thank you
Taal Philippine volcano
tab (tab·bing, tabbed)
taba·nid fly
tab·ard

taba·ret fabric
Ta·bas·co Mexican state;
  (*Trademark*) sauce
tabbed
tab·bing

tab·by (*plural* ·bies)
tab·er·nac·le
tab·er·nacu·lar
ta·bes wasting
ta·bes·cence

ta·bes·cent

tab·la·ture musical notation

ta·ble

tab·leau (*plural* ·leaux *or* ·leaus)

table·cloth

ta·ble d'hôte (*plural* ta·bles d'hôte)

table·land

table·spoon

table·spoon·ful (*plural* ·fuls)

tab·let

table-turning

table·ware

tab·loid

ta·boo (*or* tabu; *plural* ·boos *or* ·bus)

ta·bor (*or* ·bour) drum

tabo·ret (*or* tabou·) stool

tabo·rin (*or* tabou·) drum

Ta·briz Iranian city

tabu·lable

tabu·lar

tabu·lar·ize

tabu·late

tabu·la·tion

tabu·la·tor

taca·ma·hac (*or* tac·ma·hack) gum

ta·cet musical term

tache *Archaic* buckle; *Slang* moustache

tach·eom·eter (*or* ta·chym·) surveying instrument; *compare* tachometer

tacheo·met·ric (*or* ·ri·cal, tachy·)

tacheo·met·ri·cal·ly (*or* tachy·)

tach·eom·etry (*or* ta·chym·)

tachi·na fly

ta·chis·to·scope

ta·chis·to·scop·ic

ta·chis·to·scopi·cal·ly

tacho·graph speed-recording device

ta·chom·eter speed-measuring device; *compare* tacheometer

tacho·met·ric (*or* ·ri·cal)

tacho·met·ri·cal·ly

ta·chom·etry

tachy·car·dia rapid heartbeat

tachy·car·di·ac

ta·chyg·ra·pher (*or* ·phist)

tachy·graph·ic (*or* ·graphi·cal)

ta·chyg·ra·phy shorthand

tachy·lyte (*or* ·lite) basalt

tachy·lyt·ic (*or* ·lit·)

ta·chym·eter *variant of* tacheometer

ta·chym·etry *variant of* tacheometry

tachy·on physics term

tachy·phy·lax·is medical term

tac·it

tac·it·ness

taci·turn

taci·tur·nity

tack

tack·er

tack·et *Dialect* hobnail

tacki·ly

tacki·ness

tack·le

tack·ler

tacky (tacki·er, tacki·est)

tac·node maths term

taco (*plural* tacos) Mexican food

Ta·co·ma US port

taco·nite rock

tact

tact·ful

tact·ful·ly

tact·ful·ness

tac·tic

tac·ti·cal

tac·ti·cal·ly

tac·ti·cian

tac·tics

tac·tile

tac·til·ity

tact·less

tact·less·ness

tac·tual

tad *US* boy

tad·pole

Ta·dzhik (*plural* ·dzhiks *or* ·dzhik) Muslim people

Ta·dzhiki·stan Soviet republic

Tae·gu South Korean city

Tae·jon South Korean city

tae·nia (*or esp. US* te·; *plural* ·niae) band; architectural term; *compare* tinea

tae·nia (*US also* te·; *plural* ·niae) tapeworm; *compare* tinea

tae·nia·cide (*US also* te·)

tae·nia·fuge (*US also* te·)

tae·nia·sis (*US also* te·)

taf·fe·ta

taff·rail ship's rail

Taf·fy (*plural* ·fies) *Slang* Welshman

taf·fy (*plural* ·fies) *US* sweet

tafia (*or* taf·fia) rum

Ta·fi·lelt (*or* Ta·fi·la·let) oasis

tag (tag·ging, tagged)

Ta·ga·log (*plural* ·logs *or* ·log) Philippine people

Ta·gan·rog Soviet port

tag·gers tin-coated iron sheet

tag·ging

ta·glia·tel·le pasta

tag·meme linguistics term

tag·mem·ic

tag·mem·ics

Ta·gus European river

ta·hi·na sesame paste

Ta·hi·ti

Ta·hi·tian

tahr animal

tah·sil·dar Indian tax collector

Tai·chung (*or* T'ai-chung) Chinese city

tai·ga subarctic forests

tail appendage; *compare* tale

tail·back

tail·board

tail-ender

tail·gate

tail·ing

taille (*plural* tailles) French tax

tail·less

tail·light (*or* ·lamp)

tail-like

tai·lor

tailor·bird

tailor-made

tail·piece

tail·pipe

tail·plane
tail·race
tails tail coat
tail·skid
tail·spin
tail·stock
tail·wind
tain mirror backing
Tai·nan (or T'ai-nan)
  Chinese city
taint
tai·pan snake
Tai·pei (or T'ai-pei)
  Taiwanese capital
Tai·wan
Tai·wan·ese
Tai·yuan (or T'ai-yüan)
  Chinese city
taj Muslim cap
Taj Ma·hal
taka Bangladeshi currency
tak·able (or take·able)
ta·ka·he bird
Taka·mat·su Japanese port
take (tak·ing, took,
  tak·en)
take·away
tak·en
take·off
take·over
tak·er
tak·in animal
tak·ing
tak·ing·ness
tak·ings
Ta·ko·ra·di Ghanaian port
tala·poin monkey
ta·laria winged sandals
talc (talck·ing, talcked or
  talc·ing, talced)
Tal·ca·hua·no Chilean city
talc·ose (or tal·cous)
tal·cum
tale story; compare tail
tal·ent
tal·ent·ed
ta·les legal term
ta·les·man (plural ·men)
tali·grade zoology term
tali·on legal term
tali·ped
tali·pes club foot
tali·pot palm tree
tal·is·man (plural ·mans)
tal·is·man·ic

talk
talka·bil·ity
talk·able
talka·tive
talka·tive·ly
talka·tive·ness
talk·er
talkie
talking-to (plural -tos)
tall
tal·lage historical tax
Tal·la·has·see US city
tall·boy
tal·li·er
Tal·linn (or ·lin) Soviet
  port
tall·ish
tal·lith (plural ·lai·sim,
  ·lithes or ·li·toth) prayer
  shawl
tall·ness
tal·low
tally-ho (verb -hos,
  -hoing, -hoed; noun,
  plural -hos)
  hoing, -hoed; noun,
  plural -hos)
tally·man (plural ·men)
Tal·mud Jewish literature
Tal·mud·ic (or ·mudi·cal)
Tal·mud·ism
Tal·mud·ist
tal·on
ta·loned
ta·luk (or ·lu·ka, ·loo·ka)
  Indian district
ta·lus (plural ·li) anklebone
ta·lus (plural ·luses) scree
tam·abil·ity (or tame·)
tam·able (or tame·)
tam·able·ness (or tame·)
ta·ma·le Mexican food
ta·man·dua (or ·du) animal
tama·rack tree
ta·ma·rau (or ·rao) cattle
tama·rin monkey
tama·rind (or ·rin·do;
  plural ·rinds or
  ·rin·dos) tree, fruit
tama·risk tree
ta·ma·sha Indian
  entertainment
Ta·mau·li·pas Mexican
  state

Tam·bo·ra Indonesian
  volcano
tam·bour
tam·boura musical
  instrument
tam·bou·rin dance
tam·bou·rine musical
  instrument
tam·bou·rin·ist
Tam·bov Soviet city
tame
tame·able variant spelling of
  tamable
tame·ness
tam·er
Tam·il (plural ·ils or ·il)
  Asian people
Tam·il Nadu Indian state
tam·is (plural ·ises)
  straining cloth
Tam·ma·ny Hall US
  political party
  organization
tam·my (plural ·mies)
tam-o'-shanter
tamp
Tam·pa Florida resort
tam·per
Tam·pe·re Finnish city
tam·per·er
Tam·pi·co Mexican port
tamp·ing Welsh angry
tam·pi·on (or tom·) gun
  plug
tam·pon medical plug
tam·pon·ade
tam-tam gong; compare
  tom-tom
tan (tan·ning, tanned)
Tana Ethiopian lake
tana lemur
tana·ger bird
Tana·na Alaskan river
tan·bark
tan·dem
tan·doori
Tang Chinese dynasty
tang
Tan·ga Tanzanian port
Tan·gan·yi·ka African lake
tan·ge·lo (plural ·los)
  hybrid fruit
tan·gen·cy
tan·gent
tan·gen·tial

tan·gen·ti·al·i·ty
tan·gen·tial·ly (*or* ·tal·ly)
Tan·ge·rine of Tangier
tan·ge·rine fruit
tan·gibil·ity (*or*
  ·gible·ness)
tan·gible
Tan·gier Moroccan port
tangi·ness
tan·gle
tan·gle·ment
tan·gler
tan·gly
tan·go (*noun, plural* ·tos;
  verb ·goes, ·go·ing,
  ·goed)
tan·go·ist
tan·gram puzzle
Tang·shan Chinese city
tangy (tangi·er, tangi·est)
tanh maths term
Ta·nis ancient Egyptian city
tan·ist heir of Celtic
  chieftain
Tan·jore Indian city
tank
tan·ka (*plural* ·kas *or* ·ka)
  Japanese verse
tank·age
tank·ard
tank·er
tank·ful (*plural* ·fuls)
tan·nage
tan·nate
tanned
tan·ner
tan·nery (*plural* ·neries)
tan·nic
tan·nin
tan·ning
Tan·noy (*Trademark*)
tan·sy (*plural* ·sies) plant
Tan·ta Egyptian city
tan·ta·late
tan·tal·ic
tan·ta·lite mineral
tan·ta·li·za·tion (*or*
  ·sa·tion)
tan·ta·lize (*or* ·lise)
tan·ta·liz·er (*or* ·lis·er)
tan·ta·liz·ing·ly (*or*
  ·lis·ing·ly)
tan·ta·lous chemistry term;
  compare tantalus
tan·ta·lum chemical element

Tantalus mythological king
tan·ta·lus case for bottles;
  compare tantalous
tan·ta·mount
tan·ta·ra fanfare
tan·tivy (*plural* ·tivies)
  hunting cry
tan·to musical term
Tan·tra Sanskrit books
Tan·tric
Tan·trism
Tan·trist
tan·trum
Tan·za·nia
Tan·za·nian
Tao·ism Chinese philosophy
Tao·ist
tap (tap·ping, tapped)
tapa mulberry bark
tap-dance (*verb*)
tap-dancer
tapa·der·a stirrup covering
tape
ta·per
ta·per·er
ta·per·ing·ly
tap·es·tried
tap·es·try (*plural* ·tries)
ta·petal
ta·petum (*plural* ·peta)
  biology term
tape·worm
tap·hole
tapio·ca
ta·pir (*plural* ·pirs *or* ·pir)
  animal
tap·is (*plural* tap·is) carpet
tap·pable
tapped
tap·per
tap·pet
tap·ping
tappit-hen
tap·room
tap·root
tap·ster
tar (tar·ring, tarred)
ta·ra·did·dle *variant spelling
  of* tarradiddle
ta·ra·ma·sa·la·ta
ta·ran·tass Russian carriage
tar·an·tel·la dance; *compare*
  tarantula
tar·ant·ism nervous disorder
Ta·ran·to Italian port

ta·ran·tu·la (*plural* ·las *or*
  ·lae) spider; *compare*
  tarantella
ta·raxa·cum plant
tar·boosh (*or* ·bush,
  ·bouche) Muslim cap
Tar·de·noi·sian Mesolithic
  culture
tar·di·grade minute animal
tar·di·ly
tar·di·ness
tar·dy (·di·er, ·di·est)
tare plant; weight of goods
  container; *compare* tear
tar·get
tar·iff
Ta·rim Chinese river
tar·la·tan fabric
tar·mac (·mack·ing,
  ·macked)
tarn lake
tar·nal *US* damned
tar·na·tion
Tarn-et-Garonne French
  department
tar·nish
tar·nish·able
tar·nish·er
taro (*plural* taros) plant
ta·rot card
tarp *Austral* tarpaulin
tar·pan extinct horse
tar·pau·lin
Tar·pe·ian Rock
tar·pon (*plural* ·pons *or*
  ·pon) fish
tar·ra·did·dle (*or* ta·ra·)
tar·ra·gon
Tar·ra·sa Spanish city
tarred
tar·ri·ness
tar·ring
tar·ry (*verb* ·ries, ·ry·ing,
  ·ried; *adj* ·ri·er, ·ri·est)
tar·sal
tar·si·er animal
tar·so·meta·tar·sal
tar·so·meta·tar·sus (*plural*
  ·si)
Tar·sus Turkish city
tar·sus (*plural* ·si) ankle
  bones
tart
tar·tan

Tar·tar *variant spelling of*
Tatar

tar·tar deposit on teeth;
fearsome person; sauce;
chemical substance

tar·tar·ic

tar·tari·za·tion (*or*
·sa·tion)

tar·tar·ize (*or* ·ise)

tar·tar·ous of tartar

Tar·ta·rus Hades

Tar·ta·ry *variant spelling of*
Tatary

tart·let

tart·ness

tar·trate

tarty

Tar·zan

Tash·kent Soviet city

ta·sim·eter temperature-
change measurer

tasi·met·ric

ta·sim·etry

task

task·er

task·master (*fem*
·mistress)

task·work

Tas·ma·nia

Tas·ma·nian

Tas·man Sea

Tass Soviet news agency

tass *Dialect* cup

tas·sel (·sel·ling, ·selled;
US ·sel·ing, ·seled)

tas·sel·ly

tas·set piece of armour

tast·able

taste

taste·ful

taste·ful·ly

taste·ful·ness

taste·less

taste·less·ness

tast·er

tasti·ly

tasti·ness

tasty (tasti·er, tasti·est)

tat (tat·ting, tat·ted)

ta-ta *Slang* goodbye

Ta·tar (*or* Tar·tar)
Mongoloid people

Ta·tar·ian (*or* Tar·tar·ian,
Ta·tar·ic, Tar·tar·ic)

Ta·ta·ry (*or* Tar·ta·ry)
historical region

ta·ter *Dialect* potato

Tat·ler journal; *compare*
tattler

tatou·ay armadillo

Ta·tra mountain range

tat·ted

tat·ter

tat·ter·de·mal·ion

tat·ter·sall fabric

tat·ting

tat·tle

tat·tler one who tattles;
compare Tatler

tattle·tale

tat·tling·ly

tat·too (*noun, plural*
·toos; *verb* toos,
·too·ing, ·tooed)

tat·too·ist (*or* ·er)

tat·ty (·ti·er, ·ti·est)

tatty-peelin *Scot*
pretentious

tau Greek letter; *compare*
taw

taught past tense of teach;
compare taut

taunt

taunt·er

taunt·ing·ly

Taun·ton Somerset town

taupe brownish grey

Tau·ranga New Zealand
port

Tau·rean

tau·rine bull-like;
biochemical compound

tau·ro·ma·chian

tau·roma·chy bullfighting

Tau·rus constellation; sign
of zodiac

taut tight; *compare* taught

taut·en

taut·ness

tau·tog fish

tau·to·logi·cal (*or*
·to·log·ic, ·tolo·gous)

tau·to·logi·cal·ly

tau·tolo·gize (*or* ·gise)

tau·tol·ogy (*plural* ·gies)

tau·to·mer chemistry term

tau·to·mer·ic

tau·tom·er·ism

tau·to·nym biology term

tau·to·nym·ic (*or*
·tony·mous)

tau·tony·my

Ta·vel wine

tav·ern

tav·ern·er

taw marble; tanning term;
compare tau

taw·dri·ly

taw·dri·ness

taw·dry (·dri·er, ·dri·est)

taw·er

taw·ny (*or* ·ney)

tawse (*or* taws) leather
strap

tax

tax·abil·ity (*or* ·able·ness)

tax·able

taxa·ceous botany term

taxa·tion

taxa·tion·al

tax-deduct·ible

tax·eme linguistics term

tax·er

taxi (*noun, plural* taxis *or*
taxies; *verb* taxies,
taxi·ing, tax·ied)

taxi·cab

taxi·der·mal (*or* ·mic)

taxi·der·mist

taxi·der·my

taxi·meter

tax·ing·ly

taxi·plane

tax·is biology term; surgical
process

taxis (*or* taxies) *plural of*
taxi

taxi·way

tax·man (*plural* ·men)

tax·on (*plural* taxa)
biology term

taxo·nom·ic (*or*
·nomi·cal)

taxo·nomi·cal·ly

tax·ono·mist (*or* ·mer)

tax·ono·my

tax·payer

tax·paying

Tay Scottish river

tay *Irish* tea

tay·ra animal

Tay·side Scottish region

taz·za wine cup

Tbi·li·si (*or* **Tif·lis**) Soviet city

te (*or* **ti**) musical term; *compare* **tea**; **tee**

tea beverage; *compare* **te**; **tee**

tea·berry (*plural* **·berries**)

tea·cake

tea·cart

teach (**teach·es, teach·ing, taught**)

teach·able

teach·er

teach·in

teach·ing

tea·cup

tea·cup·ful (*plural* **·fuls**)

tea·house

teak

tea·kettle

teal (*plural* **teals** *or* **teal**) duck

team group; *compare* **teem**

tea·maker

team·mate

team·ster

team·work

tea·pot

tea·poy table with tripod base

tear (**tear·ing, tore, torn**) rip; *compare* **tare**

tear drop from eye; *compare* **tier**

tear·able

tear·er

tear·ful

tear·ful·ly

tear·ful·ness

tear·ing

tear·ing·ly

tear·jerker

tear·less

tea·room

tease

tea·sel (*or* **·zel, ·zle; ·sel·ling, ·selled;** *US* **·sel·ing, ·seled**)

teas·er

tea·shop

teas·ing·ly

tea·spoon

tea·spoon·ful (*plural* **·fuls**)

teat

techi·ly *variant spelling of* **tetchily**

techi·ness *variant spelling of* **tetchiness**

tech·ne·tium chemical element

tech·nic *variant of* **technique**

tech·ni·cal

tech·ni·cal·ity (*plural* **·ities**)

tech·ni·cal·ly

tech·ni·cian

Tech·ni·col·or (*Trademark*)

tech·nics study of industry

tech·nique (*or* **·nic**)

tech·noc·ra·cy (*plural* **·cies**)

tech·no·crat

tech·no·crat·ic

tech·nog·ra·phy

tech·no·logi·cal

tech·no·logi·cal·ly

tech·nolo·gist

tech·nol·ogy (*plural* **·ogies**)

tech·no·struc·ture

techy *variant spelling of* **tetchy**

tec·ton·ic

tec·toni·cal·ly

tec·ton·ics

tec·tri·cial

tec·trix (*plural* **·tri·ces**) feather

ted (**ted·ding, ted·ded**) shake out hay

ted·der

ted·dy (*plural* **·dies**)

Te De·um

te·di·ous

te·di·ous·ness

te·dium

tee (**tee·ing, teed**) golf term; T-shaped part; *compare* **te**; **tea**

teem abound; *compare* **team**

teem·ing

teen

teen·age

teen·aged

teen·ager

tee·ny (**·ni·er, ·ni·est**)

teeny·bopper

Tees English river

Tees·side

tee·ter

teeth *plural of* **tooth**

teethe (*verb*)

teeth·ing

tee·to·tal

tee·to·tal·ism

tee·to·tal·ler (*US* **·tal·er**)

tee·to·tum spinning top

tef (*or* **teff**) grass

Tef·lon (*Trademark*)

teg sheep

teg·men (*plural* **·mi·na**) zoology term

teg·mi·nal

Te·gu·ci·gal·pa Honduran capital

tegu·lar of a tile

tegu·lar·ly

Teh·ran (*or* **Te·he·ran**)

Te·huan·tepec Mexican region

tek·tite

tela (*plural* **telae**) weblike structure

tel·aes·the·sia (*US* **·es·**) paranormal perception

tel·aes·thet·ic (*US* **·es·**)

tela·mon (*plural* **·mones**) supporting pillar

tel·an·gi·ec·ta·sis (*or* **·sia;** *plural* **·ses**) medical term

tel·an·gi·ec·tat·ic

Tel·auto·graph (*Trademark*)

tel·auto·graph·ic

tel·autog·ra·phy

Tel Aviv

tele·cast (**·cast·ing, ·cast** *or* **·cast·ed**)

tele·cast·er

tele·com·mu·ni·ca·tion

tele·com·mu·ni·ca·tions

tel·edu badger

te·le·ga cart

tele·gen·ic

tel·eg·no·sis parapsychology term

tel·eg·nos·tic

tel·egon·ic

Telegonus son of Odysseus

te·lego·ny genetics term

tele·gram

tele·graph

te·leg·ra·pher (*or* **·phist**)

tele·graph·ic
tele·graphi·cal·ly
te·leg·ra·phy
tele·ki·ne·sis
tele·ki·net·ic
Telemachus son of
  Odysseus
tel·emark skiing term
te·lem·eter
tele·met·ric (or ·ri·cal)
tele·met·ri·cal·ly
te·lem·etry
tel·en·cephal·ic
tel·en·cepha·lon anatomy
  term
teleo·logi·cal (or ·log·ic)
teleo·logi·cal·ly
tele·olo·gism
tele·olo·gist
tele·ol·ogy
tel·eost fish
tele·path·ic
tele·pathi·cal·ly
te·lepa·thist
te·lepa·thize (or ·thise)
te·lepa·thy
tele·phone
tele·phon·er
tele·phon·ic
te·lepho·nist
te·lepho·ny
tele·photo·graph·ic
tele·pho·tog·ra·phy
tele·photo
tele·play
tele·print·er
tele·prompt·er
Tele·ran (*Trademark*)
  navigational aid
tele·scope
tele·scop·ic
tele·scopi·cal·ly
te·les·co·py
tele·script
tele·sis
tele·spec·tro·scope
tele·ste·reo·scope
tel·es·the·sia *US spelling of*
  telaesthesia
te·les·tich poem
tele·thon
tele·tran·scrip·tion
tele·tube *short for* television
  tube
Tele·type (*Trademark*)

Tele·type·set·ter
  (*Trademark*)
tele·type·set·ting
te·leu·to·spore
te·leu·to·spor·ic
tele·vise
tele·vi·sion
tele·vi·sion·al
tele·vi·sion·ary
tele·writ·er
tel·ex
Tel·ford Shropshire town
tel·geni·cal·ly
te·lial
tel·ic purposeful
te·lio·spore
te·lium (*plural* ·lia) fungal
  structure
tell (tell·ing, told)
tell·able
Tell el Amar·na Egyptian
  ruins
tell·er
tell·ing
tell·ing·ly
tell·tale
tel·lu·rate chemistry term
tel·lu·rian of the earth
tel·lu·ric
tel·lu·ride chemical
  compound
tel·lu·ri·on (or ·lu·rian)
  model of earth
tel·lu·rite
tel·lu·rium chemical
  element
tel·lu·rize (or ·rise)
tel·lu·rom·eter surveying
  instrument
tel·lu·rous
tel·ly (*plural* tel·lies)
telo·phase biology term
telo·pha·sic
tel·pher (or ·fer)
tel·pher·age (or ·fer·)
  transport system
tel·pher·ic (or ·fer·)
tel·son zoology term
tel·son·ic
Tel·star satellite
Te·luk·be·tung (or
  Te·loek·be·toeng)
  Indonesian port
Tema Ghanaian port
tem·er·ari·ous

te·mer·ity
temp
tem·per
tem·pera painting medium
tem·per·abil·ity
tem·per·able
tem·pera·ment
tem·pera·men·tal
tem·pera·men·tal·ly
tem·per·ance
tem·per·ate
tem·per·ate·ly
tem·per·ate·ness
tem·pera·ture
tem·per·er
tem·pest
tem·pes·tu·ous
tem·pes·tu·ous·ness
Tem·plar member of
  religious order
tem·plate (or ·plet)
tem·ple
tem·po (*plural* ·pos *or* ·pi)
tem·po·ral of time or the
  temples
tem·po·ral·ity
tem·po·ral·ly of time
tem·po·rari·ly not
  permanently
tem·po·rari·ness
tem·po·rary (*plural*
  ·raries)
tem·po·ri·za·tion (or
  ·sa·tion)
tem·po·rize (or ·rise)
tem·po·riz·er (or ·ris·er)
tempt
tempt·able
temp·ta·tion
tempt·er
tempt·ing
tempt·ing·ly
tempt·ress
tem·pu·ra Japanese food
Te·mu·co Chilean city
ten
ten·abil·ity (or ·able·ness)
ten·able
ten·ably
ten·ace bridge term
te·na·cious
te·na·cious·ness
te·nac·ity
te·nacu·lum (*plural* ·la)
  surgical instrument

te·naille fortification
ten·an·cy (*plural* ·cies)
ten·ant
ten·ant·able
ten·ant·ry
tench (*plural* tench)
tend
ten·den·cy (*plural* ·cies)
ten·den·tious (*or* ·cious)
ten·den·tious·ness (*or* ·cious·)
ten·der
ten·der·able
ten·der·er
tender·foot (*plural* ·foots *or* ·feet)
tender·hearted
tender·hearted·ness
ten·deri·za·tion (*or* ·sa·tion)
ten·der·ize (*or* ·ise)
ten·der·iz·er (*or* ·is·er)
ten·der·loin
ten·der·ness
ten·din·itis inflammation of tendon
ten·di·nous of tendons
ten·don
ten·dril
ten·dril·lar (*or* ·ous)
ten·ebrism style of painting
ten·ebrist
ten·ebros·ity
ten·ebrous (*or* te·neb·ri·ous)
Ten·edos Greek island
ten·ement
ten·emen·tal (*or* ·tary)
ten·ement·ed
Ten·erife
te·nes·mic
te·nes·mus medical term
ten·et belief
ten·fold
Ten·gri Nor Chinese lake
te·nia *variant spelling* (*esp.* US) *of* taenia
ten·ner
Ten·nes·sean
Ten·nes·see
ten·nis
ten·no (*plural* ·no *or* ·nos) Japanese emperor
ten·on
ten·on·er

ten·or
teno·rite mineral
te·nor·rha·phy (*plural* ·phies) tendon surgery
te·noto·mist
te·noto·my (*plural* ·mies) incision into tendon
ten·pin
ten·pins
ten·rec animal
tense
tense·ly
tense·ness
ten·sibil·ity (*or* ·sible·ness)
ten·sible
ten·sile
ten·sil·ity (*or* ·sile·ness)
ten·sim·eter device measuring vapour pressure
ten·si·om·eter device measuring tensile strength
ten·sion
ten·sion·al
ten·sive
ten·sor
ten·so·rial
tent
ten·ta·cle
ten·ta·cled
ten·tacu·lar
tent·age tents
ten·ta·tion mechanical process
ten·ta·tive
ten·ta·tive·ness
tent·ed
ten·ter
tenter·hook
tenth
tenu·ity
tenu·ous
tenu·ous·ness
ten·ure
tenu·rial
te·nu·to musical term
teo·cal·li (*plural* ·lis) Aztec pyramid
teo·sin·te grass
te·pal botany term
te·pee (*or* tee·) tent
tep·efac·tion
tep·efy (·efies, ·efy·ing, ·efied) make tepid
teph·rite rock

teph·rit·ic
Te·pic Mexican city
tep·id
te·pid·ity (*or* tep·id·ness)
te·qui·la
Te·rai Indian marshland
ter·aph (*plural* ·aphim) biblical god
tera·tism malformed fetus
tera·to·gen
tera·to·gen·ic causing fetal deformity
tera·toid
tera·to·log·ic (*or* ·logi·cal)
tera·tolo·gist
tera·tol·ogy study of fetal abnormalities
tera·to·ma (*plural* ·mas *or* ·ma·ta)
ter·bic
ter·bium chemical element
terce (*or* tierce) canonical hour
ter·cel (*or* tier·cel) male falcon
ter·cen·te·nary (*or* ·cen·ten·nial; *plural* ·naries *or* ·nials)
ter·cet verse
ter·ebene
te·reb·ic acid
ter·ebinth tree
ter·ebin·thine
te·re·do (*plural* ·dos *or* ·di·nes) mollusc
Te·re·si·na Brazilian port
te·rete botany term
ter·gal
ter·gi·ver·sate
ter·gi·ver·sa·tion
ter·gi·ver·sa·tor (*or* ·ver·sant)
ter·gi·ver·sa·tory
ter·gum (*plural* ·ga) zoology term
teri·ya·ki Japanese food
term
ter·ma·gan·cy
ter·ma·gant
ter·mi·nabil·ity (*or* ·nable·ness)
ter·mi·nable
ter·mi·nal
ter·mi·nal·ly
ter·mi·nate

tetchiness

ter·mi·na·tion
ter·mi·na·tion·al
ter·mi·na·tive
ter·mi·na·tor
ter·mi·na·tory
ter·mi·no·logi·cal
ter·mi·nolo·gist
ter·mi·nol·ogy (*plural* ·ogies*)
ter·mi·nus (*plural* ·ni *or* ·nuses*)
ter·mi·tar·ium (*plural* ·taria*) termite nest
ter·mite
ter·mit·ic
term·less
ter·mor (*or* ·mer*) legal term
tern bird; compare terne; turn
ter·na·ry (*plural* ·ries*)
ter·nate botany term
terne alloy; *compare* tern; turn
Ter·ni Italian city
ter·pene
ter·pe·nic
ter·pin·eol
Terpsichore Greek Muse
Terp·si·cho·rean (*or* ·real*)
ter·ra land
ter·race
ter·ra·cot·ta
ter·ra fir·ma
ter·rain surroundings; *compare* terrane
Ter·ra·my·cin (*Trademark*)
ter·rane rock formation; *compare* terrain
ter·ra·pin
ter·rar·ium (*plural* ·rar·iums *or* ·raria*) biological container
ter·raz·zo
ter·rene earthly; *compare* terrine; tureen
terre·plein top of rampart
ter·res·trial
ter·res·tri·al·ly
ter·ret harness ring
terre-verte painting pigment
ter·ri·ble
ter·ri·ble·ness

ter·ri·bly
ter·rico·lous living in soil
ter·ri·er
ter·rif·ic
ter·rifi·cal·ly
ter·ri·fi·er
ter·ri·fy (·fies, ·fy·ing, ·fied*)
ter·ri·fy·ing·ly
ter·rig·enous of the earth
ter·rine dish; food; *compare* terrene; tureen
ter·ri·to·rial
ter·ri·to·ri·al·ism
ter·ri·to·ri·al·ist
ter·ri·to·ri·al·ity
ter·ri·to·ri·ali·za·tion (*or* ·sa·tion*)
ter·ri·to·ri·al·ize (*or* ·ise*)
ter·ri·to·rial·ly
ter·ri·tory (*plural* ·tories*)
ter·ror
ter·ror·ful
ter·ror·ism
ter·ror·ist
ter·ror·is·tic
ter·rori·za·tion (*or* ·sa·tion*)
ter·ror·ize (*or* ·ise*)
ter·ror·iz·er (*or* ·is·er*)
terror-stricken (*or* -struck*)
ter·ry (*plural* ·ries*) towelling
terse
terse·ly
terse·ness
ter·tial ornithology term
ter·tian recurring every other day
Ter·tiary geological period
ter·tiary (*plural* ·tiaries*)
ter·tium quid a third unknown thing
ter·va·lent *variant of* trivalent
Tery·lene (*Trademark*)
ter·zet·to (*plural* ·tos *or* ·ti*) vocal trio
tes·la unit; coil
tes·sel·late
tes·sel·la·tion
tes·sera (*plural* ·serae*) mosaic tile

tes·ser·act four-dimensional figure
tes·ser·al
tes·si·tu·ra musical term
test
tes·ta (*plural* ·tae*) seed coat
test·abil·ity
test·able
tes·ta·ceous
tes·ta·cy
tes·ta·ment
tes·ta·men·tal
tes·ta·men·tary
tes·tate
tes·ta·tor (*fem* ·trix*)
test-drive (*verb* -driving, -drove, -driven*)
test·er one who tests
tes·ter canopy; coin
tes·tes *plural of* testis
tes·ti·cle
tes·ticu·lar
tes·ticu·late
tes·ti·fi·ca·tion
tes·ti·fi·er
tes·ti·fy (·fies, ·fy·ing, ·fied*)
testi·ly
tes·ti·mo·nial
tes·ti·mo·ny (*plural* ·nies*)
testi·ness
test·ing
test·ing·ly
tes·tis (*plural* ·tes*)
tes·ton (*or* ·toon*) coin
tes·tos·ter·one hormone
tes·tu·di·nal (*or* ·nary*) of tortoises
tes·tu·do (*plural* ·di·nes*) Roman military manoeuvre
tes·ty (·ti·er, ·ti·est*)
te·tan·ic
te·tani·cal·ly
teta·ni·za·tion (*or* ·sa·tion*)
teta·nize (*or* ·nise*)
teta·nus
teta·ny
te·tar·to·he·dral·ism (*or* te·to·he·drism*)
te·tar·to·he·dral
tetchi·ly (*or* techi·*)
tetchi·ness (*or* techi·*)

tetchy (or techy;
  tetchi·er, tetchi·est or
  techi·er, techi·est)
tête-à-tête (plural -têtes
  or -tête)
tête-bêche philately term
teth·er
tet·ra (plural ·ra or ·ras)
  fish
tetra·ba·sic
tetra·ba·sic·ity
tetra·brach metrical foot
tetra·bran·chi·ate zoology
  term
tetra·chlo·ride
tetra·chord musical term
tetra·chor·dal
te·trac·id chemistry term
tetra·cy·cline
tet·rad
te·trady·mite mineral
tetra·dy·na·mous botany
  term
tetra·ethyl
te·trago·nal
tetra·gram
tetra·he·dral
tetra·he·drite mineral
tetra·he·dron (plural
  ·drons or ·dra)
te·tral·ogy (plural ·ogies)
  set of four
te·tram·er·ism
te·tram·er·ous biology term
tetra·methyl·diar·sine
tetra·ple·gia
tetra·ploid genetics term
tetra·ploidy
tetra·pod
tetra·pod·ic
te·trapo·dy (plural ·dies)
  metrical unit
te·trap·ter·ous four-winged
te·trarch
te·trarch·ate
te·trar·chic (or ·chi·cal)
te·trar·chy (plural ·chies)
tetra·spore
tetra·spor·ic (or ·ous)
tetra·stich four-line poem
tetra·stich·ic (or
  tetras·ti·chal)
te·tras·ti·chous botany
  term

tetra·syl·lab·ic (or
  ·labi·cal)
tetra·syl·la·ble
tetra·tom·ic
tetra·va·len·cy
tetra·va·lent
tet·rode electronic valve
te·trox·ide
tet·ryl
tet·ter skin eruption
Te·tuán Moroccan city
Teucer mythological
  character
Teu·ton ancient German
Teu·ton·ic
Teu·ton·ism
Teu·ton·ize (or ·ise)
Tewkes·bury
Tex·an
Tex·as
text
text·book
tex·tile
tex·tu·al of text; compare
  textural
tex·tu·al·ism
tex·tu·al·ist
tex·tu·al·ly
tex·tu·ary (plural ·aries)
tex·tur·al of texture;
  compare textual
tex·tur·al·ly
tex·ture
Thai (plural Thais or
  Thai)
Thai·land
thala·men·cephal·ic
thala·men·cepha·lon
  (plural ·lons or ·la)
  anatomy term
tha·lam·ic
tha·lami·cal·ly
thala·mus (plural ·mi)
  part of brain
tha·las·sic of the sea
thal·as·soc·ra·cy (or
  ·at·toc·)
tha·ler (or ta·; plural ·ler
  or ·lers) coin
tha·lido·mide
thal·lic
thal·lium chemical element
thal·loid
thal·lo·phyte
thal·lo·phyt·ic

thal·lous of thallium
thal·lus (plural ·li or
  ·luses) botany term
thal·weg (or tal·)
  geography term
Thames
than
thana·top·sis
Thanatos personification of
  death
thane (or thegn)
Than·et
Than·ja·vur Indian city
thank
thank·ful
thank·ful·ly
thank·ful·ness
thank·less
thank·less·ness
thanks·giving
Thap·sus battle site
Thá·sos Greek island
that
thatch
thatch·er
Thatch·er·ism
Thatch·er·ite supporter of
  Margaret Thatcher
thatch·ing
thau·ma·tol·ogy study of
  miracles
thau·ma·trope
thau·ma·tropi·cal
thau·ma·turge miracle
  performer
thau·ma·tur·gic
thau·ma·tur·gy
thaw
thaw·er
thea·ceous botany term
the·an·throp·ic
the·an·thro·pism
the·an·thro·pist
the·ar·chic
the·ar·chy (plural ·chies)
  government by gods
thea·tre (US ·ter)
theatre·goer (US
  theater·)
the·at·ri·cal
the·at·ri·cal·ity (or
  ·cal·ness)
the·at·ri·cal·ly
the·at·ri·cals dramatic
  entertainments

the·at·rics exaggerated mannerisms

the·ba·ine drug

The·ban

Thebes

the·ca (plural ·cae) biology term

the·cal (or ·cate)

the·co·dont extinct reptile

thee

theft

thegn variant spelling of thane

the·ine stimulant in tea

their of them; compare there; they're

theirs

the·ism

the·ist

the·is·tic (or ·ti·cal)

the·is·ti·cal·ly

them

the·mat·ic

the·mati·cal·ly

theme

Themis Greek goddess

them·selves

then

the·nar palm of hand

the·nard·ite mineral

thence

thence·forth

thence·forward (or ·forwards)

theo·bro·mine

theo·cen·tric theology term

theo·cen·tric·ity

theo·cen·trism (or ·tri·cism)

the·oc·ra·cy (plural ·cies)

the·oc·ra·sy mingling of deities

theo·crat

theo·crat·ic (or ·crati·cal)

theo·crati·cal·ly

the·odi·cy (plural ·cies) branch of theology

the·odo·lite

the·odo·lit·ic

the·ogo·ny (plural ·nies) origin of the gods

theo·lo·gian

theo·logi·cal

theo·logi·cal·ly

the·olo·gist

the·olo·gi·za·tion (or ·sa·tion)

the·olo·gize (or ·gise)

the·olo·giz·er (or ·gis·er)

the·ol·ogy (plural ·ogies)

the·oma·chy (plural ·chies) battle among the gods

theo·man·cy

theo·ma·nia

theo·ma·niac

the·ono·my being governed by God

the·opa·thy religious emotion

the·opha·gy (plural ·gies)

the·opha·ny (plural ·nies) manifestation of deity

Theophi·lus moon crater

theo·pho·bia

theo·pho·bi·ac

theo·phyl·line

the·or·bo (plural ·bos) musical instrument

theo·rem

theo·remat·ic (or ·rem·ic)

theo·remati·cal·ly

theo·reti·cal (or ·ret·ic)

theo·reti·cal·ly

theo·reti·cian

theo·ret·ics

theo·rist

theo·ri·za·tion (or ·sa·tion)

theo·rize (or ·rise)

theo·riz·er (or r·is·er)

theo·ry (plural ·ries)

theo·soph·ic (or ·sophi·cal)

theo·sophi·cal·ly

the·oso·phism

the·oso·phist

the·oso·phy

thera·peu·tic

thera·peu·ti·cal·ly

thera·peu·tics

thera·pist

the·rap·sid extinct reptile

thera·py (plural ·pies)

there in that place; compare their; they're

there·abouts (or ·about)

there·after

there·at

there·by

there·fore

there·from

there·in

there·in·after

there·into

there·of

there·on

there·to

there·to·fore

there·under

there·upon

there·with (or ·with·al)

the·ri·an·throp·ic part animal, part human

the·rian·thro·pism

the·rio·morph

the·rio·mor·phic (or ·phous) in animal form

therm unit

ther·mae public baths

therm·aes·the·sia (US ·es·) sensitivity to temperature

ther·mal

ther·mal·ly

ther·mal·ize (or ·ise)

ther·mic

ther·mi·on

ther·mi·on·ic

ther·mi·on·ics

ther·mis·tor

Ther·mit (or ·mite; Trademark)

ther·mite pro·cess

ther·mo·baro·graph

ther·mo·chemi·cal

ther·mo·chemi·cal·ly

ther·mo·chem·ist

ther·mo·chem·is·try

ther·mo·cline

ther·mo·cou·ple

ther·mo·dy·nam·ic (or ·nami·cal)

ther·mo·dy·nami·cal·ly

ther·mo·dy·nam·ics

ther·mo·elec·tric (or ·tri·cal)

ther·mo·elec·tri·cal·ly

ther·mo·elec·tric·ity

ther·mo·elec·tron

ther·mo·gen·esis

ther·mog·enous (or ·mo·genet·ic)

ther·mo·gram

ther·mo·graph

ther·mog·ra·pher
ther·mo·graph·ic
ther·mog·ra·phy
ther·mo·junc·tion
ther·mo·la·bile
ther·mo·lu·mi·nes·cence
ther·mo·lu·mi·nes·cent
ther·moly·sis
ther·mo·lyt·ic
ther·mo·mag·net·ic
ther·mom·eter
ther·mo·met·ric (*or* ·ri·cal)
ther·mo·met·ri·cal·ly
ther·mom·etry
ther·mo·nu·clear
ther·mo·phile (*or* ·phil) organism thriving in warmth
ther·mo·phil·ic (*or* ·phil·ous)
ther·mo·pile radiant-energy detector
ther·mo·plas·tic
ther·mo·plas·tic·ity
Ther·mopy·lae battle site
Ther·mos (*Trademark*)
ther·mo·scope
ther·mo·scop·ic (*or* ·scopi·cal)
ther·mo·scopi·cal·ly
ther·mo·set·ting
ther·mo·si·phon
ther·mo·sphere atmospheric layer
ther·mo·sta·bil·ity
ther·mo·stable
ther·mo·stat
ther·mo·stat·ic
ther·mo·stati·cal·ly
ther·mo·stat·ics
ther·mo·tac·tic
ther·mo·tax·is biology term
ther·mo·ten·sile
ther·mo·thera·py
ther·mo·trop·ic
ther·mo·tro·pism botany term
the·roid beastlike
the·ro·pod dinosaur
the·ropo·dan
the·sau·rus (*plural* ·ri *or* ·ruses)
these

Theseus mythological character
the·sis (*plural* ·ses)
Thespian
Thes·sa·li·an
Thes·sa·lo·nian
Thes·sa·lo·ni·ca ancient Thessaloníki
Thes·sa·lo·ní·ki Greek port
Thes·sa·ly Greek region
the·ta
thet·ic of metrical stress
theti·cal·ly
Thetis Greek goddess
the·urg·ic (*or* ·ur·gi·cal)
the·ur·gi·cal·ly
the·ur·gist
the·ur·gy (*plural* ·gies) divine intervention
thew muscle
they
they'd they would; they had
they'll they will; they shall
they're they are; *compare* their; there
they've they have
thia·mine (*or* ·min) vitamin
thia·zine
thia·zole (*or* ·zol)
thick
thick-and-thin
thick·en
thick·en·er
thick·en·ing
thick·et
thick·head
thick·headed·ness
thick·leaf (*plural* ·leaves) plant
thick·ly
thick·ness
thick·set
thick-skinned
thick-witted
thick-witted·ness
thief (*plural* thieves)
thieve
thiev·ery (*plural* ·eries)
thiev·ing
thiev·ing·ly
thiev·ish
thiev·ish·ness
thigh
thigh·bone

thig·mo·tac·tic
thig·mo·tax·is biology term
thig·mo·trop·ic
thig·mot·ro·pism botany term
thim·ble
thim·ble·ful (*plural* ·fuls)
thimble·rig game
thimble·weed
thimble·wit *US* dunce
thi·mero·sal antiseptic
thin (*adj* thin·ner, thin·nest; *verb* thin·ning, thinned)
thine
thin-film electronics term
thing
thingu·ma·bob (*or* thinga·)
thingu·ma·jig (*or* thinga·)
think (think·ing, thought)
think·able
think·er
think·ing
think-tank
thin·ner
thin·ness
thin·nish
thin-skinned
thio·cya·nate
thio·cy·an·ic acid
thio·ether
thiol
thi·on·ic of sulphur
thio·nine (*or* ·nin)
thio·nyl
thio·pen·tone (*US* ·tal)
thio·phen (*or* ·phene)
thio·sina·mine
thio·sul·phate (*US* ·fate)
thio·sul·phur·ic acid (*US* ·fur·)
thio·ura·cil
thio·urea
third
third-rate
third·stream jazz
thirl *Dialect* to drill
Thirl·mere Cumbrian lake
thirst
thirst·er
thirsti·ly
thirsti·ness
thirsty (thirsti·er, thirsti·est)

thir·teen
thir·teenth
thir·ti·eth
thir·ty (*plural* ·ties)
this
this·tle
thistle·down
this·tly
thith·er (*or* ·er·ward)
thither·to
thixo·trop·ic
thix·ot·ro·py chemistry
    term
thole (*or* thole·pin)
tho·los (*plural* ·loi) tomb
Tho·mism doctrine of
    Thomas Aquinas
Tho·mist
Thon·bu·ri Thai city
thong
Thor Norse god
tho·rac·ic (*or* ·ra·cal)
tho·ra·co·plas·ty (*plural*
    ·ties) surgery
thora·coto·my (*plural*
    ·mies)
thor·ax (*plural* thor·axes
    or tho·ra·ces)
tho·ria chemical compound
tho·ria·nite mineral
tho·ric
tho·rite mineral
tho·rium radioactive
    element
thorn
thorn·back fish
thorn·bill
thorni·ly
thorni·ness
thorny (thorni·er,
    thorni·est)
tho·ron radioisotope of
    radon
thor·ough
Thorough·bred horse
thorough·bred purebred
thorough·fare
thorough·going
thor·ough·ly
thor·ough·ness
thorough·paced
thorough·pin swollen hock
those
Thoth Egyptian god
thou

though
thought
thought·ful
thought·ful·ly
thought·ful·ness
thought·less
thought·less·ness
thought-out
thou·sand
thou·sandth
Thrace Balkan region
thrall
thrall·dom
thrash
thrash·er
thrash·ing
thrawn *Dialect* crooked
thread
thread·bare
thread·er
thread·fin (*plural* ·fin *or*
    ·fins) fish
threadi·ness
Thread·needle Street
thread·worm
thready (threadi·er,
    threadi·est)
threap (*or* threep) *Dialect*
    to scold
threat
threat·en
threat·en·er
threat·en·ing
three
three-dimension·al
three·fold
three-legged
three-phase
three-piece
three-ply
three-quarter (*adj*)
three-quarters
three·score
three·some
three-wheeler
threm·ma·tol·ogy science
    of breeding
threno·dy (*or* thre·node;
    plural ·dies *or* ·nodes)
    ode of lamentation
threo·nine amino acid
thresh
thresh·er
thresh·old
threw

thrice
thrift
thrifti·ly
thrifti·ness
thrift·less
thrift·less·ness
thrifty (thrifti·er,
    thrifti·est)
thrill
thrill·er
thrill·ing
thrips (*plural* thrips)
    insect
thrive (thriv·ing, thrived
    or throve, thrived *or*
    thriv·en)
throat
throati·ly
throati·ness
throat·lash (*or* ·latch)
    bridle strap
throaty (throati·er,
    throati·est)
throb (throb·bing,
    throbbed)
throe violent pang; *compare*
    throw
throm·bin enzyme
throm·bo·cyte
throm·bo·cyt·ic
throm·bo·em·bo·lism
throm·bo·gen protein
throm·bo·phle·bi·tis
throm·bo·plas·tic
throm·bo·plas·tin
throm·bose (*verb*)
throm·bo·sis
throm·bot·ic
throm·bus (*plural* ·bi)
    blood clot
throne
throng
thros·tle thrush
throt·tle
throt·tler
through
through·out
through·put
through·way
throw (throw·ing, threw,
    thrown) cast; *compare*
    throe
throw·away (*adj, noun*)
throw·back
throw·er

thrown

throw·ster yarn spinner

thrum (thrum·ming, thrummed)

thrum·mer

thrush

thrust

thrust·er

thud (thud·ding, thud·ded)

Thug Indian assassin

thug

thug·gee practices of Thugs

thug·gery

thug·gish

thu·ja (or ·ya) tree

Thule ancient northern land; Eskimo settlement

thu·lium chemical element

thumb

thumb·nail

thumb·nut

thumb·print

thumb·screw

thumb·stall

thumb·tack US drawing pin

thump

thump·er

thump·ing

thun·der

thunder·bird

thunder·bolt

thunder·clap

thunder·cloud

thun·der·er

thunder·head cloud

thun·der·ing

thun·der·ous

thunder·shower

thunder·stone

thunder·storm

thunder·struck (or ·stricken)

thun·dery

Thur·gau Swiss canton

thu·ri·ble incense container

thu·ri·fer thurible carrier

Thu·rin·gia German region

Thu·rin·gian

Thurs·day

thus

thwack

thwack·er

thwart

thwart·er

thy

Thyestes mythological character

thy·la·cine animal

thyme herb

thym·elaea·ceous botany term

thym·ic

thy·mi·dine

thy·mine

thy·mol

thy·mus (plural ·muses or ·mi)

thymy of thyme

thy·ra·tron

thy·ris·tor

thy·ro·cal·ci·ton·in hormone

thy·roid

thy·roid·ec·to·my (plural ·mies)

thy·roidi·tis

thy·ro·toxi·co·sis

thy·ro·tro·pin (or ·phin) hormone

thy·rox·ine (or ·in) hormone

thyrse (plural therses) botany term

thyr·soid

thyr·sus (plural ·si) Bacchus' staff

thysa·nu·ran insect

thy·self

ti plant; variant spelling of te

Tia Ma·ria (Trademark)

ti·ara

ti·ar·aed

Ti·ber

Ti·bes·ti African mountains

Ti·bet

Ti·bet·an

tibia (plural tibiae or tibias)

tib·ial

tic twitch; compare tick

ti·cal (plural ·cals or ·cal)

tic dou·lou·reux neuralgia

Ti·ci·no Swiss canton; river

tick parasite; compare tic

tick·er

tick·et

tick·ing

tick·le

tick·ler

tick·lish

tick·lish·ness

tick·ly

tick·tack

tick-tack-toe US noughts and crosses

tick·tock

Ti·con·dero·ga US battle site

tid·al

tid·al·ly

tid·bit US spelling of titbit

tid·dler

tid·dly

tiddly·winks

tide

tide·mark

tide·water

tide·way

ti·di·ly

ti·di·ness

tid·ings

tidy (adj tidi·er, tidi·est; verb ti·dies, tidy·ing, ti·died; noun, plural ti·dies)

tie (ty·ing, tied)

tie·back US curtain fastening

tie·breaker (or ·break)

tied

tie-dyeing

tie-dyed

tie·man·nite mineral

Tien·tsin (or T'ien-ching) Chinese city

tie·pin

tier layer; compare tear

tierce fencing position; variant spelling of terce

tiered

Tier·ra del Fue·go South American archipelago

tiff

tif·fa·ny (plural ·nies) fabric

tif·fin meal

Tif·lis variant spelling of Tbilisi

ti·ger

ti·ger·ish

tiger's-eye (or tiger·eye) gemstone

tight

tight·en

tight·en·er
tight·fisted
tight·knit
tight·lipped
tight·ness
tight·rope
tights
tight·wad
tig·lic acid
ti·gon (or tig·lon) animal
Ti·gré Ethiopian province
ti·gress
Ti·gri·nya Ethiopian language
Ti·gris Asian river
Ti·jua·na Mexican city
tike variant spelling of tyke
tiki Maori amulet
ti·lapia fish
Til·burg Dutch city
Til·bury Essex region
til·bury (plural ·buries) carriage
til·de phonetic symbol
tile
tile·fish (plural ·fish or ·fishes)
til·er
tilia·ceous botany term
til·ing
till
till·able
till·age
til·land·sia plant
till·er
til·li·cum US friend
Til·sit Soviet town
tilt
tilt·er
tilth
tilt·yard
Tima·ru New Zealand port
tim·bal (or tym·) kettledrum
tim·bale pie
tim·ber wood; compare timbre
timber·head
tim·ber·ing
timber·land
timber·work
timber·yard
tim·bre tone quality; compare timber
tim·brel tambourine

Tim·buk·tu Malian town
time
time·able
time·card
time-consum·ing
time-honoured
time·keeper
time·keeping
time·lag
time·less
time·less·ness
time·li·ness
time·ly (·li·er, ·li·est)
time·ous Scot timely
time·piece
tim·er
time·saver
time·saving
time·server
time·serving
time·table
time·work
time·worker
time·worn
tim·id
ti·mid·ity (or tim·id·ness)
tim·ing
Ti·mi·şoa·ra Romanian city
ti·moc·ra·cy (plural ·cies) political system
Ti·mor Indonesian island
tim·or·ous
tim·or·ous·ness
timo·thy grass
tim·pa·ni (or tym·; sing. ·no) kettledrums; compare tympanum
tim·pa·nist (or tym·)
timps short for timpani
tin (tin·ning, tinned)
tina·mou bird
tin·cal borax
tinct tinted
tinc·to·rial of dyeing
tinc·ture
tin·der
tinder·box
tin·dery
tine
tinea ringworm; compare taenia
tin·eal
tin·eid moth
tin·foil
ting

ting-a-ling
tinge (tinge·ing or ting·ing, tinged)
tin·gle
tin·gler
tin·gling·ly
tin·gly
ti·ni·ly
ti·ni·ness
tink·er
tink·er·er
tin·kle
tin·kling
tin·kly
tin liz·zie Slang decrepit car
tinned
tin·ni·ly
tin·ni·ness
tin·ning
tin·ni·tus ringing in ears
tin·ny (·ni·er, ·ni·est)
tin-plate (verb)
tin·pot Slang inferior
tin·sel (·sel·ling, ·selled; US ·sel·ing, ·seled)
tin·smith
tint
Tin·tag·el
tint·ed
tin·tin·nabu·lar (or ·lary, ·lous)
tin·tin·nabu·la·tion
tin·tin·nabu·lum (plural ·la) bell
tin·type photographic print
tin·ware
tin·work
tiny (tini·er, tini·est)
tip (tip·ping, tipped)
tip·cat game
tip-off (noun)
tip·pable
tipped
tip·per
Tip·per·ary
tip·pet cape
tip·ping
tip·ple
tip·pler
tip·si·ly
tip·si·ness
tip·staff
tip·ster
tip·sy (·si·er, ·si·est)
tip·toe (·toe·ing, ·toed)

tip·top
ti·rade
Ti·ra·na (or ·në) Albanian capital
tire exhaust; US spelling of tyre
tire·less
tire·less·ness
tire·some
tire·some·ness
Ti·rich Mir Pakistani mountain
tir·ing
tiro variant spelling of tyro
Ti·rol variant spelling of Tyrol
Ti·ros US satellite
Ti·ru·nel·veli Indian city
'tis
ti·sane
tis·sue
tit
Ti·tan Greek god; satellite of Saturn
ti·tan·ate chemistry term
Ti·tan·esque
Ti·ta·nia satellite of Uranus
ti·tan·ic huge; chemistry term
ti·tani·cal·ly
ti·tan·if·er·ous
Ti·tan·ism spirit of rebellion
ti·tan·ite mineral
ti·ta·nium chemical element
ti·tano·saur
ti·tano·there extinct mammal
ti·tan·ous
tit·bit (US tid·)
ti·ter US spelling of titre
tith·able
tithe
tith·er
tith·ing
Tithonus mythological character
titi (plural titis) monkey
tit·il·late
tit·il·lat·ing
tit·il·la·tion
tit·il·la·tive
titi·vate (or tit·ti·)
titi·va·tion (or tit·ti·)
titi·va·tor (or tit·ti·)
tit·lark

ti·tle
ti·tled
title·holder
tit·man (plural ·men) small piglet
tit·mouse (plural ·mice)
Ti·to·grad Yugoslav city
Ti·to·ism
Ti·to·ist
ti·trant chemistry term
ti·trat·able
ti·trate
ti·tra·tion
ti·tre (US ·ter)
tit·ter
tit·ter·er
tit·tle
tittle-tattle
tittle-tattler
tit·tup (·tup·ping, ·tupped)
titu·ba·tion medical term
titu·lar (or ·lary; plural ·lars or ·laries)
Tiv (plural Tivs or Tiv) African people
Tivo·li Italian town
tiz·zy (plural ·zies)
Tlax·ca·la Mexican state
Tlin·git (plural ·gits or ·git) American Indian
tme·sis linguistics term
to
toad
toad·fish (plural ·fish or ·fishes)
toad·flax
toad·ish (or ·like)
toad·stone
toad·stool
toady (noun, plural toadies; verb toadies, toady·ing, toad·ied)
toady·ism
to-and-fro (adj)
toast
toast·er
toast·master (fem ·mistress)
to·bac·co (plural ·cos or ·coes)
to·bac·co·nist
To·ba·go West Indian island
to·bog·gan
to·bog·gan·er (or ·ist)

To·bruk Libyan port
toby jug
toc·ca·ta
To·char·ian (or ·khar·) language
to·col·ogy (or ·kol·) obstetrics
to·coph·er·ol vitamin
toc·sin alarm bell; compare toxin
tod
to·day
tod·dle
tod·dler
tod·dy (plural ·dies)
to-do (plural ·dos)
tody (plural todies) bird
toe (toe·ing, toed)
toea coin
toe·cap
toed
toe·hold
toe-in
toe·ing
toe·nail
toey Austral nervous
toff
tof·fee (or ·fy; plural ·fees or ·fies)
toft homestead
tog (tog·ging, togged)
toga
to·geth·er
to·geth·er·ness
togged
tog·gery clothes
tog·ging
tog·gle
Tog·li·at·ti Soviet city
Togo African republic
To·go·lese
to·he·roa mollusc
toil
toile fabric
toil·er
toi·let lavatory
toi·let·ry (plural ·ries)
toi·lette act of dressing
toil·some (or ·ful)
toil·some·ness
To·kay wine
to·kay lizard
to·ken
to·ken·ism

toko·loshe mythical creature

To·kyo

tola unit of weight

to·lan (or ·lane) organic compound

tol·bu·ta·mide drug

told

tole metal ware

To·ledo Spanish city; US city

tol·er·able

tol·er·able·ness (or ·abil·ity)

tol·er·ably

tol·er·ance

tol·er·ant

tol·er·ate

tol·era·tion

tol·era·tion·ism

tol·era·tion·ist

tol·era·tive

tol·era·tor

toli·dine

toll

toll·booth (or tol·)

toll·gate

toll·house

Tol·pud·dle Dorset town; martyrs

Tol·tec (plural ·tecs or ·tec) American Indian

tolu·ate chemical compound

To·lu·ca Mexican city

tolu·ene

to·lu·ic acid

to·lui·dine

tolu·yl

tol·yl

tom male animal

toma·hawk

tom·al·ley lobster liver

to·man coin

to·ma·to (plural ·toes)

tomb

tom·bac (or tam·) alloy

tomb·like

tom·bo·la lottery

tom·bo·lo (plural ·los) sand bar

tom·boy

tom·boy·ish

tomb·stone

tom·cat

tome book

to·men·tose

to·men·tum (plural ·ta) biology term

tom·fool

tom·fool·ery (plural ·eries)

tom·my (plural ·mies)

tommy·rot

tomo·gram

to·mog·ra·phy X-ray technique

to·mor·row

tom·pi·on variant spelling of tampion

Tomsk Soviet city

tom·tit

tom-tom drum; compare tam-tam

ton imperial weight; compare tonne; tun

ton·al

to·nal·ity (plural ·ities)

ton·al·ly

Ton·bridge Kent town; compare Tunbridge Wells

ton·do (plural ·di) circular painting

tone

tone-deaf

tone·less

tone·less·ness

ton·eme linguistics term

ton·er

to·net·ic linguistics term

tong

Tonga Pacific kingdom

Ton·ga (plural ·gas or ·ga) African people

Tong·an

tongs

tongue (tongu·ing, tongued)

tongue-tied

ton·ic

toni·cal·ly

to·nic·ity

to·night

ton·ing

tonk Austral effeminate man

ton·ka tree; bean

Ton·kin (or Tong·king) Chinese gulf

Ton·le Sap Cambodian lake

ton·nage (or tun·)

tonne metric weight; compare ton; tun

ton·neau (plural ·neaus or ·neaux)

to·nom·eter

tono·met·ric

to·nom·etry

ton·sil

ton·sil·lar (or ·lary)

ton·sil·lec·to·my (plural ·mies)

ton·sil·lit·ic

ton·sil·li·tis

ton·sil·loto·my (plural ·mies)

ton·so·rial

ton·sure

ton·tine annuity scheme

to·nus muscle tone

too

toodle-oo

took

tool

tool·er

tool·ing

tool·less

tool-maker

tool-making

toon tree

toot

toot·er

tooth (plural teeth)

tooth·ache

tooth·brush

toothed

toothi·ly

toothi·ness

tooth·less

tooth·paste

tooth·pick

tooth·some

tooth·some·ness

tooth·wort

toothy (tooth·ier, toothi·est)

too·tle

too·tler

toots (or toot·sie) term of endearment

toot·sy (or tootsy-wootsy; plural ·sies or -wootsies) Slang foot

top (top·ping, topped)

top·arch ruler

top·ar·chy

to·paz
to·pazo·lite gemstone
top·coat
top·dress (*verb*)
tope
to·pee (*or* topi; *plural* ·pees *or* topis) tropical helmet
To·pe·ka US city
top·er
top·flight (*adj*)
top·gal·lant ship's mast
top·heavily
top·heaviness
top·heavy
To·phet (*or* ·pheth) biblical place
to·phus (*plural* ·phi) gout stone
topi *variant spelling of* topee
to·pi·ar·ian
to·pia·rist
to·pi·ary
top·ic
topi·cal
topi·cal·ity
topi·cal·ly
top·knot
top·less
top·less·ness
top·level (*adj*)
top·lofty haughty
top·mast
top·min·now (*plural* ·now *or* ·nows) fish
top·most
top·notch
top·notcher
to·pog·ra·pher
topo·graph·ic (*or* ·graphi·cal)
topo·graphi·cal·ly
to·pog·ra·phy (*plural* ·phies) mapping; *compare* topology
topo·logic (*or* ·logi·cal)
topo·logi·cal·ly
to·polo·gist
to·pol·ogy branch of geometry; *compare* topography
topo·nym
topo·nym·ic (*or* ·nymi·cal)
to·pony·my

top·os (*plural* ·oi) basic concept
topo·type
topped
top·per
top·ping
top·ple
top·sail
top·secret (*adj*)
top·shell mollusc
top·side
top·soil
top·spin
topsy-turvy
toque (*or* to·quet) hat
tor hill; *compare* torr
To·rah Jewish writings
Tor·bay Devon town
tor·bern·ite mineral
torch
torch·bearer
tor·chère candelabrum stand
tor·chier (*or* ·chiere) lamp
torch·light
torch·lit
tor·chon lace
torch·wood
tore
torea·dor
to·re·ro (*plural* ·ros) bullfighter
to·reu·tic
to·reu·tics metalworking
tori *plural of* torus
tor·ic
to·rii (*plural* ·rii) gateway
tor·ment
tor·ment·ed·ly
tor·men·til plant
tor·ment·ing·ly
tor·men·tor (*or* ·ment·er)
torn
tor·nad·ic
tor·na·do (*plural* ·does *or* ·dos) storm; *compare* tournedos
to·roid geometry term
to·roi·dal
to·roi·dal·ly
To·ron·to
To·ron·to·nian
to·rose (*or* ·rous) biology term

tor·pe·do (*noun, plural* ·does; *verb* ·does, ·do·ing, ·doed)
tor·pid
tor·pid·ity (*or* ·ness)
tor·por
tor·por·if·ic
tor·quate
Tor·quay
torque metal collar; mechanical force
tor·ques zoology term
torr unit; *compare* tor
Tor·rance US city
tor·re·fac·tion (*or* ·ri·)
tor·re·fy (*or* ·ri·; ·fies, ·fy·ing, ·fied) roast
tor·rent
tor·ren·tial
tor·ren·tial·ly
Tor·re·ón Mexican city
Tor·ri·cel·lian physics term
tor·rid
tor·rid·ity (*or* ·ness)
tor·sade ornament on hat
tor·si·bil·ity
tor·sion
tor·sion·al
torsk (*plural* torsks *or* torsk) fish
tor·so (*plural* ·sos *or* ·si)
tort legal term
torte cake
tor·tel·li·ni pasta
tort·feasor legal term
tor·ti·col·lar
tor·ti·col·lis wryneck
tor·til·la Mexican pancake
tor·tious legal term; *compare* tortuous; torturous
tor·toise
tortoise·shell
tor·to·ni ice cream
tor·tri·cid moth
tor·tu·os·ity (*plural* ·ities)
tor·tu·ous twisting; devious; *compare* tortious; torturous
tor·tu·ous·ness
tor·ture
tor·tured·ly
tor·tur·er
tor·ture·some
tor·tur·ing·ly

tor·tur·ous causing pain;
　compare tortious; tortuous
To·ruń Polish city
to·rus (*plural* ·ri)
Tory (*plural* Tories)
To·ry·ism
tosh
toss
toss·er
toss·pot *Archaic* drinker
tot (tot·ting, tot·ted)
to·tal (·tal·ling, ·talled;
　US ·tal·ing, ·taled)
to·tali·tar·ian
to·tali·tar·ian·ism
to·tal·ity (*plural* ·ities)
to·tali·za·tion (*or* ·sa·tion)
to·tali·za·tor (*or* ·sa·tor)
　betting machine
to·tal·ize (*or* ·ise)
to·tal·iz·er (*or* ·is·er)
to·tal·ly
to·ta·quine drug
tote
to·tem
to·tem·ic
to·temi·cal·ly
to·tem·ism
to·tem·ist
to·tem·is·tic
tot·er
to·ti·pal·mate
to·ti·pal·ma·tion
to·tipo·ten·cy
to·tipo·tent zoology term
tot·ted
tot·ter
tot·ter·er
tot·tery
tot·ting
tou·can
touch
touch·able
touch·down
tou·ché acknowledgment
touch·er
touchi·ly
touchi·ness
touch·ing
touch·ing·ly
touch·line
touch·mark
touch·stone
touch·type
touch·typist

touch·wood
touchy (touchi·er,
　touchi·est)
tough
tough·en
tough·en·er
toughie
tough·ish
tough·ness
Tou·lon French town
Tou·louse French city
tou·pee hairpiece
tour
tou·ra·co (*or* tu·; *plural*
　·cos) bird
Tou·raine French region
Tou·rane Vietnamese port
tour·bil·lion whirlwind
tour de force (*plural*
　tours de force)
tour·er
tour·ism
tour·ist
tour·is·tic
tour·isty
tour·ma·line
tour·ma·lin·ic
tour·na·ment
tour·nedos (*plural*
　·nedos) steak; *compare*
　tornado
tour·ney
tour·ni·quet
Tours French town
tou·sle
tous-les-mois plant
tout *Slang* solicit
tout à fait *French*
　completely
tout en·sem·ble *French* all
　in all
tout le monde *French*
　everyone
to·va·risch (·rich *or* ·rish)
　Russian term of address
tow
tow·age
to·ward (*adj*)
to·wards (*prep.*)
tow·bar
tow·boat
tow·el (·el·ling, ·elled;
　US ·el·ing, ·eled)
tow·el·ling (*US* ·el·ing)
tow·er

tow·er·ing
tow-haired
tow·head
tow·hee bird
tow·line
town
townee
town·hall
town·scape
town·ship
towns·man (*plural* ·men)
towns·people (*or* ·folk)
towns·woman (*plural*
　·women)
tow·path
tow·rope
tox·aemia (*US* ·emia)
tox·aemic (*US* ·emic)
tox·al·bu·min
toxa·phene
tox·ic
toxi·cal·ly
toxi·cant poison
tox·ic·ity
toxi·co·gen·ic
toxi·co·logi·cal (*or* ·log·ic)
toxi·co·logi·cal·ly
toxi·colo·gist
toxi·col·ogy
toxi·co·sis
tox·in poison; *compare*
　tocsin
tox·oid
tox·ophi·lite archer
tox·ophi·lit·ic
tox·ophi·ly
toxo·plas·mic
toxo·plas·mo·sis
toy
To·ya·ma Japanese city
toy·er
tra·beated (*or* ·beate)
　architectural term
tra·bea·tion
tra·becu·la (*plural* ·lae)
　anatomy term
tra·becu·lar (*or* ·late)
Trab·zon Turkish port
trace
trace·abil·ity (*or*
　·able·ness)
trace·able
trace·less
trac·er
trac·ery (*plural* ·eries)

tra·chea (*plural* ·cheae)
tra·cheal
tra·cheate
tra·che·id (*or* ·ide) plant cell
tra·chei·dal
tra·che·itis
tra·cheo·phyte botany term
tra·che·osto·my (*plural* ·mies)
tra·che·oto·mist
tra·che·oto·my (*plural* ·mies)
tra·cho·ma eye disease
tra·choma·tous
tra·chyte rock
tra·chyt·ic
trachy·toid
trac·ing
track
track·able
track·er
track·less
track·suit
tract
trac·tabil·ity (*or* ·table·ness)
trac·table
trac·tably
Trac·tar·ian
Trac·tari·an·ism religious movement
trac·tate treatise
trac·tile ductile
trac·til·ity
trac·tion
trac·tion·al
trac·tive
trac·tor
trad *Slang* traditional jazz
trad·able (*or* trade·)
trade
trade-in (*noun*)
trade·mark
trade-off (*noun*)
trad·er
trad·es·can·tia plant
trades·man (*plural* ·men)
trades·people (*or* ·folk)
trades·woman (*plural* ·women)
trade union (*plural* trade unions) note Trades Union Congress
trad·ing

tra·di·tion
tra·di·tion·al
tra·di·tion·al·ism
tra·di·tion·al·ist
tra·di·tion·al·is·tic
tra·di·tion·ally
tra·di·tion·ist
tradi·tor (*plural* ·to·res *or* ·tors) Christian betrayer
tra·duce
tra·duce·ment
tra·duc·er
tra·du·cian·ism theology term
tra·du·cian·ist (*or* ·du·cian)
tra·du·cian·is·tic
tra·duc·ible
Tra·fal·gar
traf·fic (·fick·ing, ·ficked)
traf·fi·ca·tor car indicator
traf·fick·er
traga·canth plant
tra·gal
tra·gedian (*fem* ·gedi·enne)
trag·edy (*plural* ·edies)
trag·ic (*or* tragi·cal)
tragi·cal·ly
tragi·com·edy (*plural* ·edies)
tragi·com·ic (*or* ·comi·cal)
tragi·comi·cal·ly
trago·pan bird
tra·gus (*plural* ·gi) part of ear
trail
trail·blazer
trail·blazing
trail·er
trail·ing·ly
trail·less
train
train·able
train·band English militia
train·bearer
trainee
train·er
train·ing
traipse
trait characteristic
trai·tor
trai·tor·ous
trai·tor·ous·ness
trai·tress

tra·ject *Archaic* transport
tra·jec·tile
tra·jec·tion
tra·jec·tory (*plural* ·tories)
tra·la
Tra·lee Irish town
tram (tram·ming, trammed)
tram·car
tram·line
tram·mel (·el·ling, ·elled; *US* ·el·ing, ·eled)
tram·mel·ler (*US* ·mel·er)
tram·mie *Austral* tram driver
tra·mon·tane (*or* trans·) across mountains
tramp
tramp·er
tramp·ish
tramp·ish·ness
tram·ple
tram·pler
tram·po·line
tram·po·lin·er (*or* ·ist)
tram·way
trance
trance·like
tranche
tran·nie *Slang* transistor radio
tran·quil
tran·quil·lity
tran·quil·li·za·tion (*or* ·sa·tion; *US* ·quili·za·tion)
tran·quil·lize (*or* ·lise; *US* ·quil·ize)
tran·quil·liz·er (*US* ·quil·iz·er)
tran·quil·ly
tran·quil·ness
trans·act
trans·ac·ti·nide
trans·ac·tion
trans·ac·tion·al
trans·ac·tor
trans·al·pine
trans·at·lan·tic
Trans·cau·ca·sia Soviet region
Trans·cau·ca·sian
trans·ceiv·er
trans·cend

tran·scend·ence (*or*
  ·en·cy)
trans·cend·ent
tran·scen·den·tal
tran·scen·den·tal·ism
tran·scen·den·tal·ist
tran·scen·den·tal·ity
tran·scen·den·tal·ly
tran·scend·ent·ness
trans·con·ti·nen·tal
trans·con·ti·nen·tal·ly
tran·scrib·able
tran·scribe
tran·scrib·er
tran·script
tran·scrip·tion
tran·scrip·tion·al (*or*
  ·scrip·tive)
trans·cul·tura·tion
trans·cur·rent
trans·duc·er
trans·duc·tion
tran·sect
tran·sec·tion
tran·sept
tran·sep·tal
trans·eunt philosophy term
trans·fer (·fer·ring,
  ·ferred)
trans·fer·abil·ity
trans·fer·able (*or*
  ·fer·rable)
trans·fer·ase enzyme
trans·feree
trans·fer·ence
trans·fer·en·tial
trans·fer·rer (*or in legal
  contexts* ·fer·or)
trans·fer·rin biochemical
  compound
trans·figu·ra·tion
trans·fig·ure
trans·fig·ure·ment
trans·fi·nite
trans·fix (·fix·ing, fixed
  or ·fixt)
trans·fix·ion
trans·form
trans·form·able
trans·for·ma·tion
trans·for·ma·tion·al
trans·forma·tive
trans·form·er
trans·form·ism
  evolutionary theory

trans·form·ist
trans·fuse
trans·fus·er
trans·fus·ible (*or* ·able)
trans·fu·sion
trans·fu·sive
trans·gress
trans·gress·ible
trans·gress·ing·ly
trans·gres·sion
trans·gres·sive
trans·gres·sor
tran·ship *variant spelling of*
  transship
trans·hu·mance migration
  of livestock
trans·hu·mant
tran·si·ence (*or* ·en·cy,
  ·ent·ness)
tran·si·ent
trans·il·lu·mi·nate
trans·il·lu·mi·na·tion
trans·il·lu·mi·na·tor
tran·sis·tor
tran·sis·tori·za·tion (*or*
  ·sa·tion)
tran·sis·tor·ize (*or* ·ise)
trans·it
tran·sit·able
tran·si·tion
tran·si·tion·al (*or* ·ary)
tran·si·tion·al·ly
tran·si·tive
tran·si·tive·ness (*or*
  ·tiv·ity)
tran·si·to·ri·ly
tran·si·to·ri·ness
tran·si·tory
Trans-Jordan
Trans-Jordanian
Trans·kei South African
  republic
Trans·kei·an
trans·lat·abil·ity (*or*
  ·able·ness)
trans·lat·able
trans·late
trans·la·tion
trans·la·tion·al
trans·la·tor
trans·la·to·rial
trans·lit·er·ate
trans·lit·era·tion
trans·lit·era·tor
trans·lo·cate

trans·lo·ca·tion
trans·lu·cence (*or*
  ·cen·cy)
trans·lu·cent
trans·lu·nar (*or* ·nary)
trans·mi·grant
trans·mi·grate
trans·mi·gra·tion
trans·mi·gra·tion·al
trans·mi·gra·tive
trans·mi·gra·tor
trans·mi·gra·tory
trans·mis·sibil·ity
trans·mis·sible
trans·mis·sion
trans·mis·sive
trans·mis·sive·ness
trans·mis·siv·ity
trans·mit (·mit·ting,
  ·mit·ted)
trans·mit·table (*or* ·tible)
trans·mit·tal
trans·mit·tance
trans·mit·tan·cy physics
  term
trans·mit·ter
trans·mog·ri·fi·ca·tion
trans·mog·ri·fy (·fies,
  ·fy·ing, ·fied)
trans·mon·tane *variant of*
  tramontane
trans·mun·dane beyond
  this world
trans·mut·able
trans·mut·ably
trans·mu·ta·tion
trans·mu·ta·tion·al (*or*
  ·ta·tive)
trans·mu·ta·tion·ist
trans·mute
trans·mut·er
trans·ocean·ic
tran·som
tran·son·ic of the sound
  barrier
trans·pa·cif·ic
trans·pa·dane
trans·par·en·cy (*plural*
  ·cies)
trans·par·ent
trans·par·ent·ness
tran·spicu·ous transparent
trans·pierce
tran·spir·able
tran·spi·ra·tion

tran·spira·tory
tran·spire
trans·plant
trans·plant·able
trans·plan·ta·tion
trans·plant·er
trans·po·lar
tran·spond·er (or
·spon·dor)
trans·pon·tine across a
bridge
trans·port
trans·port·abil·ity
trans·port·able
trans·por·ta·tion
trans·port·ed·ly
trans·port·er
trans·port·ive
trans·pos·abil·ity
trans·pos·able
trans·pos·al
trans·pose
trans·pos·er
trans·po·si·tion
trans·po·si·tion·al (or
·posi·tive)
trans·sexu·al
trans·sex·ual·ism
trans·ship (or tran·ship;
·ship·ping, ·shipped)
trans·ship·ment (or
tran·ship·)
Trans-Siberian Rail·way
tran·sub·stan·tial
tran·sub·stan·ti·ate
tran·sub·stan·tia·tion
tran·sub·stan·tia·tion·al·ist
tran·su·date
tran·su·da·tion
tran·su·da·tory
tran·sude
transu·ran·ic (or ra·nian,
·ra·nium) chemistry term
Trans·vaal
Trans·vaal·er
Trans·vaal·ian
trans·valu·ation
trans·value (·valu·ing,
·valued)
trans·valu·er
trans·ver·sal
trans·ver·sal·ly
trans·verse
trans·verse·ly
trans·verse·ness

trans·ves·tism (or ·ti·tism)
trans·ves·tite
Transylvania
Transylvanian
trap (trap·ping, trapped)
tra·peze
tra·pezial
tra·pezium (plural
·peziums or ·pezia)
tra·pezius (plural
·peziuses) muscle
tra·pezo·he·dral
tra·pezo·he·dron (plural
·drons or ·dra)
trap·ezoid
trap·per
trap·pings
Trap·pist monk
trap·rock
traps belongings
trap·shooter
trap·shooting
tra·pun·to (plural ·tos)
quilting
trash
trashi·ly
trashi·ness
trashy (trashi·er,
trashi·est)
trass rock
trat·to·ria
trau·ma (plural ·mas,
·ma·ta)
trau·mat·ic
trau·mati·cal·ly
trau·ma·tism
trau·ma·ti·za·tion (or
·sa·tion)
trau·ma·tize (or ·tise)
trav·ail
trave horse-shoeing cage;
crossbeam
trav·el (·el·ling, ·elled;
US ·el·ing, ·eled)
trav·el·ler (US ·el·er)
trav·elogue (US also
·elog)
tra·vers·able
tra·vers·al
trav·erse
tra·vers·er
trav·er·tine (or ·tin) rock
trav·es·ty (noun, plural
·ties; verb ·ties, ·ty·ing,
·tied)

tra·vois (plural ·vois)
sledge
trawl
trawl·er
tray receptacle; compare trey
tray·mobile Austral trolley
treach·er·ous
treach·er·ous·ness
treach·ery (plural ·eries)
trea·cle
trea·cli·ness
trea·cly
tread (tread·ing, trod,
trod·den or trod)
tread·er
trea·dle
trea·dler
tread·mill
trea·son
trea·son·able (or ·ous)
trea·son·able·ness
trea·son·ably
treas·ur·able
treas·ure
treas·ur·er
treas·ur·er·ship
treasure-trove
Treas·ury government
department
treas·ury (plural ·uries)
treat
treat·able
treat·er
trea·tise
treat·ment
trea·ty (plural ·ties)
Trebi·zond former name of
Trabzon
tre·ble
Tre·blin·ka concentration
camp
tre·bly
trebu·chet (or
tre·buck·et) weapon
tre·cen·tist
tre·cen·to 14th century
tree (tree·ing, treed)
tree·hopper insect
tree·less
tree·less·ness
tre·en wooden
tree·nail (or tre·nail,
trun·nel) dowel
treen·ware
tre·foil

tre·ha·la sugary substance
tre·ha·lose
treil·lage trellis
trek (trek·king, trekked)
trek·ker
trel·lis
trellis·work
trema·tode parasite
trem·ble
trem·bler
trem·bling·ly
trem·bly
tre·men·dous
tre·men·dous·ness
tremo·lite mineral
tremo·lo (plural ·los)
trem·or
trem·or·ous
tremu·lant musical term
tremu·lous
tremu·lous·ness
trench
trench·an·cy
trench·ant
trench·er
trencher·man (plural
    ·men) hearty eater
trend
trendi·ly
trendi·ness
trendy (adj trendi·er,
    trendi·est; noun, plural
    trendies)
Treng·ga·nu Malaysian
    state
Trent English river
Trentino-Alto Adi·ge
    Italian region
Tren·ton US city
tre·pan (·pan·ning,
    panned) surgical
    instrument
tre·pang sea cucumber
trephi·na·tion
tre·phine surgical
    instrument
trepi·da·tion
trepo·nema (or ·neme;
    plural ·nemas,
    ·nema·ta, or ·nemes)
    bacterium
trepo·nema·tous
tres·pass
tres·pass·er
tress

tres·sure heraldic term
tressy
tres·tle
trestle·tree
trestle·work
tret commerce term
tre·val·ly fish
trews trousers
trey card or dice thrown;
    compare tray
tri·able
tri·able·ness
tri·ac·id
Tri·ad Chinese secret society
tri·ad
tri·ad·ic
tri·ad·ism
tri·age
tri·al
tri·an·gle
tri·an·gu·lar
tri·an·gu·lar·ity
tri·an·gu·late
tri·an·gu·la·tion
Tri·an·gu·lum constellation
tri·ar·chy (plural ·chies)
Trias geology term
Tri·as·sic
tri·ath·lon
tri·atom·ic
tri·atomi·cal·ly
tri·ax·ial
tria·zine (or ·zin)
tria·zole
tria·zol·ic
trib·ade lesbian
tri·bad·ic
trib·ad·ism
trib·al
trib·al·ism
trib·al·ist
trib·al·ly
tri·ba·sic
tribe
tribes·man (plural ·men)
trib·let spindle
tri·bo·elec·tric
tri·bo·elec·tric·ity
tri·bol·ogy study of friction
tri·bo·lu·mi·nes·cence
tri·bo·lu·mi·nes·cent
tri·brach metrical foot
tri·brach·ic (or ·brach·ial)
tri·bro·mo·etha·nol
tribu·la·tion

tri·bu·nal
tribu·nary
tribu·nate (or
    trib·une·ship)
trib·une
tribu·tari·ly
tribu·tary (plural ·taries)
trib·ute
trice
tri·cen·ten·ary (plural
    ·aries)
tri·cen·ten·nial
tri·ceps (plural ·cepses or
    ·ceps)
tri·cera·tops
tri·chia·sis eye condition
tri·chi·na (plural ·nae)
    parasite
trichi·nia·sis variant of
    trichinosis
trichi·ni·za·tion (or
    ·sa·tion)
trichi·nize (or ·nise)
Trichi·nopo·ly Indian city
trichi·no·sis (or ·nia·)
    parasitic disease
trichi·nous
trich·ite crystal
tri·chit·ic
tri·chlo·ride
tri·chlo·ro·acetic acid
tri·chlo·ro·phenoxy·acetic
    acid
tricho·cyst zoology term
tricho·cys·tic
tricho·gyne botany term
tricho·gyn·ial (or ·ic)
trich·oid
tri·cholo·gist
tri·chol·ogy study of hair
tri·chome plant structure
tri·chom·ic
tricho·mon·ad parasite
tricho·mona·dal (or
    ·mon·al)
tricho·mo·nia·sis
tri·chop·ter·an insect
tri·cho·sis hair disease
tricho·tom·ic (or
    ·choto·mous)
tri·choto·my (plural
    ·mies)
tri·chro·ic
tri·chro·ism crystallography
    term

tri·chro·mat
tri·chro·mat·ic (*or* ·chro·mic)
tri·chro·ma·tism
trick
trick·er
trick·ery (*plural* ·eries)
tricki·ly
tricki·ness
trick·ing·ly
trick·le
trick·ling·ly
trick·ly
trick·si·ness
trick·ster
trick·sy (·si·er, ·si·est) mischievous
tricky (tricki·er, tricki·est)
tri·clin·ic crystallography term
tri·clin·ium (*plural* ·ia) Roman dining room
tri·col·our (*US* ·or)
tri·col·oured (*US* ·ored)
tri·corn (*or* ·corne) hat
tri·cos·tate biology term
tri·cot fabric
tri·co·tine fabric
tri·crot·ic medical term
tri·crot·ism
tric·trac (*or* trick·track) board game
tri·cus·pid
tri·cus·pi·dal
tri·cy·cle
tri·cy·clic chemistry term
tri·cy·clist
tri·dac·tyl (*or* ·tyl·ous)
tri·dent
tri·den·tate (*or* ·tal)
Tri·den·tine of Council of Trent
tri·di·men·sion·al
tri·di·men·sion·al·ity
trid·uum prayer days
tried
tri·en·nial
tri·en·nial·ly
tri·en·nium (*plural* ·niums *or* ·nia)
Trier West German city
tri·er one who tries
tri·er·ar·chy (·chies)
Tri·este Italian port

trif·fid fictional plant
tri·fid three-lobed
tri·fle
tri·fler
tri·fling
tri·fo·cal
tri·fo·li·ate (*or* ·at·ed)
tri·fo·lium plant
tri·fo·rial
tri·fo·rium (*plural* ·ria) part of church
tri·fur·cate (*or* ·cat·ed)
tri·fur·ca·tion
trig (trig·ging, trigged)
    Dialect neat; wedge
tri·gemi·nal anatomy term
trig·ger
trigger·fish (*plural* ·fish *or* ·fishes)
tri·glyc·er·ide
tri·glyph architectural term
tri·glyph·ic
tri·gon harp
trigo·nal crystallography term
trigo·no·met·ric (*or* ·ri·cal)
trigo·no·met·ri·cal·ly
trigo·nom·etry
trigo·nous botany term
tri·graph phonetics term
tri·graph·ic
tri·he·dral
tri·he·dron (*plural* ·drons *or* ·dra)
tri·hy·drate
tri·hy·dric (*or* ·droxy)
tri·io·do·thy·ro·nine
trike *Slang* tricycle
tri·lat·er·al
tri·lat·er·al·ly
tri·lat·era·tion surveying method
tril·by (*plural* ·bies)
tri·lem·ma
tri·lin·ear
tri·lin·gual
tri·lin·gual·ism
tri·lin·gual·ly
tri·lit·er·al
tri·lith·ic
tri·lith·on (*or* tri·lith)
trill
tril·lion
tril·lionth

tril·lium plant
tri·lo·bate three-lobed
tri·lo·bite fossil
tri·locu·lar
tril·ogy (*plural* ·gies)
trim (*adj* trim·mer, trim·mest; *verb* trim·ming, trimmed)
tri·ma·ran
tri·mer chemistry term
trim·er·ous
tri·mes·ter
tri·mes·tral (*or* ·trial)
trim·eter verse line
tri·metha·di·one
tri·met·ric (*or* ·ri·cal)
tri·met·ro·gon aerial photography
trim·ly
trim·mer
trim·ming
trim·ness
tri·mo·lecu·lar
tri·month·ly
tri·morph
tri·mor·phic (*or* ·phous)
tri·mor·phism
Tri·mur·ti Hindu gods
tri·nal
tri·na·ry consisting of three
Trin·co·ma·lee Sri Lankan port
trine astrology term
Trini·dad
Trini·dad·ian
Trini·tar·ian believer in the Trinity
Trini·tar·ian·ism
tri·ni·tro·ben·zene
tri·ni·tro·cre·sol
tri·ni·tro·glyc·er·in
tri·ni·tro·phe·nol
tri·ni·tro·tolu·ene (*or* ·ol)
Trin·ity God
trini·ty (*plural* ·ities)
trin·ket
trin·ket·ry
tri·nocu·lar
tri·no·mial
trio (*plural* trios)
tri·ode electronic valve
tri·oecious (*or* ·ecious) botany term
trio·elein
tri·ol

trio·let verse form
tri·ose
tri·ox·ide
trip (trip·ping, tripped)
tri·pal·mi·tin
tri·par·tite
tri·par·tite·ly
tri·par·ti·tion
tripe
trip·hammer
tri·phe·nyl·me·thane
tri·phibi·ous
triph·thong vowel sound
triph·thong·al
triphy·lite mineral
tri·pin·nate botany term
tri·plane
tri·ple
tri·plet
triple·tail (plural ·tail or
   ·tails) fish
triple-tongue musical term
Tri·plex (Trademark)
trip·li·cate
trip·li·ca·tion
tri·plic·ity (plural ·ities)
   group of three
trip·lo·blas·tic
trip·loid biology term
trip·loidy
triply
tri·pod
tripo·dal
tripo·dy (plural ·dies)
   metrical unit
Tripo·li Libyan capital
tripo·li rock
Tripo·li·ta·nia Libyan
   region
Tripo·li·ta·nian
tri·pos
trip·per
trip·pet
trip·ping·ly
trip·tane
trip·ter·ous
Triptolemus mythological
   character
trip·tych altarpiece; compare
   tryptic
trip·tyque customs permit
Tripu·ra Indian state
trip·wire
tri·que·trous
tri·ra·di·ate

tri·reme
tri·sac·cha·ride
tri·sect
tri·sec·tion
tri·sec·tor
tri·se·rial
tris·kai·deka·pho·bia fear
   of number 13
tris·kai·deka·pho·bic
tris·keli·on (or ·kele)
   symbol
tris·mic
tris·mus lockjaw
tris·oc·ta·he·dral
tris·oc·ta·he·dron (plural
   ·drons or ·dra)
tri·some genetics term
tri·so·mic
tri·somy
Tris·tan da Cu·nha South
   Atlantic islands
tris·tich three-line poem
tris·tich·ic
tris·ti·chous
tri·sul·phide
tri·syl·la·ble
tri·syl·lab·ic (or ·labi·cal)
tri·tano·pia blue blindness
tri·tan·op·ic
trite
trite·ly
trite·ness
tri·the·ism belief in Trinity
tri·the·ist
triti·ate chemistry term
tritia·tion
triti·ca·le hybrid cereal
triti·cum cereal grass
trit·ium isotope of hydrogen
Tri·ton satellite of Neptune
Triton Greek god
tri·ton mollusc
tri·tone musical term
tritu·rable
tritu·rate grind
tritu·ra·tion
tritu·ra·tor
tri·umph
tri·um·phal
tri·um·phal·ly
tri·um·phant
tri·umph·er
tri·um·vir (plural ·virs or
   ·vi·ri)

tri·um·vi·ral
tri·um·vi·rate
tri·une three in one
tri·unity
tri·va·len·cy
tri·va·lent (or ter·)
Tri·van·drum Indian city
triv·et
trivia (plural)
triv·ial
trivi·al·ity (plural ·ities)
trivi·ali·za·tion (or
   ·sa·tion)
trivi·al·ize (or ·ise)
trivi·al·ly
trivi·al·ness
tri·week·ly (plural ·lies)
Tro·as Trojan region
troat bellow
tro·car surgical instrument
tro·cha·ic of a trochee
tro·chai·cal·ly
tro·chal zoology term
tro·chan·ter anatomy term
troche lozenge
tro·chee metrical foot
trochi·lus hummingbird
troch·lea (plural ·leae)
   anatomy term
troch·le·ar
tro·choid
tro·choi·dal
trocho·phore (or ·sphere)
   zoology term
trod
trod·den
trog (trog·ging, trogged)
   stroll
trog·lo·dyte
trog·lo·dyt·ic (or ·dyti·cal)
tro·gon bird
troi·ka
Troilus mythological
   character
Tro·jan
troll
trol·ley
trol·lop
trom·bi·dia·sis mite
   infestation
trom·bone
trom·bon·ist
trom·mel
trompe forge apparatus

trompe l'oeil (*plural* **trompe l'oeils**) painting illusion

tro·na mineral

Trond·heim Norwegian port

troop large group; move in group; *compare* **troupe**

troop·er

troops

troop·ship

troost·ite mineral

tro·paeo·lin

tro·paeo·lum (*plural* ·**lums** *or* ·**la**) plant

trope figure of speech; liturgical interpolation

troph·al·lac·tic

troph·al·lax·is

troph·ic of nutrition

trophi·cal·ly

tropho·blast embryonic membrane

tropho·blas·tic

tropho·zo·ite zoology term

tro·phy (*plural* ·**phies**)

trop·ic line of latitude

tro·pic of a tropism

tropi·cal

tropi·cal·ity

tropi·cali·za·tion (*or* ·**sa·tion**)

tropi·cal·ize (*or* ·**ise**)

tropi·cal·ly

tropic·bird

trop·ics

tro·pism biology term

tropo·log·ic (*or* ·**logi·cal**)

tro·pol·ogy (*plural* ·**ogies**) use of tropes

tropo·pause atmospheric layer

tro·pophi·lous

tropo·phyte

tropo·phyt·ic

tropo·sphere atmospheric layer

tropo·spher·ic

trop·po musical term

Tros·sachs Scottish valley

trot (**trot·ting, trot·ted**)

troth

trot·line

Trot·sky·ism

Trot·sky·ite (*or* ·**ist**)

trot·ter

tro·tyl TNT

trou·ba·dour

trou·ble

trou·bled·ly

trouble·maker

trouble·making

trou·bler

trouble·shooter

trou·ble·some

trou·ble·some·ness

trou·bling·ly

trou·blous

trou·de·loup (*plural* **trous·de·loup**) pit for defence

trough

trounce

troupe group of performers; *compare* **troop**

troup·er

trou·pial bird

trouse Irish breeches

trou·sered

trou·sers

trous·seau (*plural* ·**seaux** *or* ·**seaus**)

trout (*plural* **trout** *or* **trouts**)

trou·vère (*or* ·**veur**) medieval poet

trove

tro·ver legal term

Trow·bridge Wiltshire town

trow·el (·**el·ling,** ·**elled;** *US* ·**el·ing,** ·**eled**)

trow·el·ler (*US* ·**el·er**)

Troy

tru·an·cy

tru·ant

truce

Tru·cial States

truck

truck·age *US* conveyance by lorry

truck·er

truckie *Austral* truck driver

truck·ing

truck·le

truck·ler

truck·load

trucu·lence (*or* ·**len·cy**)

trucu·lent

trudge

trudg·en swimming stroke

trudg·er

true (*adj* **tru·er, tru·est;** *verb* **tru·ing, trued**)

true-blue

true-born

true-life (*adj*)

true·love

true·ness

truf·fle

trug

tru·ism

tru·is·tic (*or* ·**ti·cal**)

Trujillo Peruvian city

tru·ly

tru·meau (*plural* ·**meaux**) architectural term

trump

trump·ery (*plural* ·**eries**)

trum·pet

trum·pet·er

trumpet·weed

trun·cate

trun·cat·ed

trun·ca·tion

trun·cheon

trun·dle

trunk

trunk·fish (*plural* ·**fish** *or* ·**fishes**)

trunk·ful (*plural* ·**fuls**)

trunks

trun·nion pivot

Tru·ro Cornish town

truss

truss·er

truss·ing

trust

trust·abil·ity

trust·able

trus·tee (·**tee·ing,** ·**teed**)

trus·tee·ship

trust·er

trust·ful (*or* ·**ing**)

trust·ful·ly (*or* ·**ing·ly**)

trust·ful·ness (*or* ·**ing·**)

trusti·ly

trusti·ness

trust·worthi·ly

trust·worthi·ness

trust·worthy

trusty (**trusti·er, trusti·est**)

truth

truth·ful

truth·ful·ly

truth·ful·ness
truth-function *logic term*
truth-value *logic term*
try (*verb* tries, try·ing, tried; *noun, plural* tries)
(tryer) *incorrect spelling of* trier
try·ing·ly
try·ing·ness
try·ma (*plural* ·ma·ta) *botany term*
try-on (*noun*)
try-out (*noun*)
trypa·no·so·mal (*or* ·som·ic)
trypa·no·some *parasite*
trypa·no·so·mia·sis *sleeping sickness*
try·par·sa·mide
tryp·sin *enzyme*
tryp·sino·gen *enzyme*
tryp·tic *of trypsin; compare* triptych
tryp·to·phan *amino acid*
try·sail
tryst
tryst·er
tsar (*or* czar)
tsar·dom (*or* czar·)
tsar·evitch (*or* czar·)
tsa·ri·na (*or* ·rit·sa, cza·)
tsar·ism (*or* czar·)
tsar·ist (*or* czar·)
Tse·li·no·grad *Soviet city*
tset·se (*or* tzet·ze)
Tshi·lu·ba *African language*
Tsi·nan (*or* Chi·nan, Chi·nan) *Chinese city*
Tsing·hai (*or* Ching·hai, Ch'ing-hai) *Chinese province*
Tsing·tao (*or* Ching·tao, Ch'ing-tao) *Chinese port*
Tson·ga (*plural* ·ga *or* ·gas) *African people*
tsu·na·mi *tidal wave*
Tsu·shi·ma *Japanese islands*
tsu·tsu·ga·mu·shi dis·ease
Tswa·na (*plural* ·na *or* ·nas) *African people*
Tua·reg (*plural* ·reg *or* ·regs) *Berber people*
tuart *tree*
tua·ta·ra *reptile*
tub (tub·bing, tubbed)

tuba (*plural* tubas *or* tubae) *musical instrument; compare* tuber
tu·bal
Tubal-cain *biblical character*
tu·bate
tubbed
tub·bi·ness
tub·bing
tub·by (·bi·er, ·bi·est)
tube
tube·less
tu·ber *underground plant stem; compare* tuba
tu·ber·cle
tu·ber·cu·lar
tu·ber·cu·late *covered with nodules*
tu·ber·cu·la·tion
tu·ber·cu·lin
tu·ber·cu·lo·sis
tu·ber·cu·lous
tu·ber·ose *plant; compare* tuberous
tu·ber·os·ity (*plural* ·ities)
tu·ber·ous (*or* ·ose) *having tubers; compare* tuberose
tu·bi·fex (*plural* ·fex *or* ·fexes) *worm*
tu·bi·form
tub·ing
tub-thumper
tubu·lar
tu·bu·lar·ity
tu·bu·late
tu·bu·la·tion
tu·bu·la·tor
tu·bule
tu·bu·li·flo·rous *botany term*
tu·bu·lous
Tu·ca·na *constellation*
tu·chun *Chinese governor*
tuck
tuck·er
tuck·et *flourish on trumpet*
tu·co·tu·co (*or* tu·cu·tu·cu) *animal*
Tuc·son *US city*
Tu·cu·mán *Argentine city*
Tu·dor
Tues·day
tufa *soft rock*
tuff *hard rock*

tuffa·ceous
tuf·fet
tuft
tuft·ed
tuft·er
tufty
tug (tug·ging, tugged)
tug·ger
tu·grik (*or* ·ghrik) *Mongolian currency*
tui *bird*
Tui·ler·ies *French palace*
tui·tion
tui·tion·al (*or* ·ary)
tu·la·rae·mia (*US* ·re·) *disease*
tu·la·rae·mic (*US* ·remic)
tu·lip
tulip·wood
tulle *fabric*
Tul·sa *US city*
tum *Slang stomach*
tum·ble
tumble-down
tumble-drier
tumble·home *nautical term*
tum·bler
tum·bler·ful (*plural* ·fuls)
tumble·weed
tum·brel (*or* ·bril)
tu·mefa·ci·ent
tu·mefac·tion
tu·mefy (·mefies, ·mefy·ing, ·mefied) *swell*
tu·mes·cence
tu·mes·cent
tu·mid
tu·mid·ity (*or* ·ness)
tum·my (*plural* ·mies)
tu·mor·ous (*or* ·mor·al)
tu·mour (*US* ·mor)
tump *Dialect small mound*
tu·mu·lar
tu·mu·lose (*or* ·lous)
tu·mu·los·ity
tu·mult
tu·mul·tu·ous
tu·mul·tu·ous·ness
tu·mu·lus (*plural* ·li) *burial mound*
tun (tun·ning, tunned) *cask; compare* ton; tonne
tuna (*plural* tuna *or* tunas)

tun·able (*or* tune·)
Tun·bridge Wells Kent town; *compare* Tonbridge
tun·dra
tune
tune·ful
tune·ful·ly
tune·ful·ness
tune·less
tune·less·ness
tun·er
tune·smith
tung·sten
tung·stic
tung·stite mineral
Tun·gus (*plural* ·guses *or* ·gus) Mongoloid people
Tun·gu·sian
Tun·gus·ic language
tu·nic
tu·ni·ca (*plural* ·cae) anatomy term
tu·ni·cate marine animal
tu·ni·cle vestment
tun·ing musical term
Tu·nis Tunisian capital
Tu·ni·sia
Tu·ni·sian
tun·nage *variant spelling of* tonnage
tun·nel (·nel·ling, ·nelled; *US* ·nel·ing, ·neled)
tun·nel·ler (*US* ·nel·er)
tun·ny (*plural* ·nies *or* ·ny) tuna fish
tup (tup·ping, tupped)
tu·pelo (*plural* ·pelos) tree
Tupi (*plural* ·pis *or* ·pi) South American Indian
tupped
tup·pence *variant spelling of* twopence
tup·pen·ny *variant spelling of* twopenny
tup·ping
tuque cap
tur·ban
tur·baned
tur·ba·ry (*plural* ·ries) peat-cutting area
tur·bel·lar·ian flatworm
tur·bid opaque; muddy; *compare* turgid
tur·bi·dim·eter
tur·bid·ity (*or* ·ness)

tur·bi·nate (*or* ·nal) scroll-shaped
tur·bi·na·tion
tur·bine
tur·bit pigeon
tur·bo·car
tur·bo·charg·er
turbo-electric
tur·bo·fan
tur·bo·gen·era·tor
tur·bo·jet
tur·bo·prop
tur·bo·super·charg·er
tur·bot (*plural* ·bot *or* ·bots)
tur·bu·lence (*or* ·len·cy)
tur·bu·lent
turd
tur·dine of thrushes
tu·reen soup dish; *compare* terrene; terrine
turf (*plural* turfs *or* turves)
turfi·ness
turfy (turfi·er, turfi·est)
tur·ges·cence (*or* ·cen·cy)
tur·ges·cent
tur·gid swollen; pompous; *compare* turbid
tur·gid·ity (*or* ·ness)
tur·gite mineral
tur·gor biology term
Tu·rin Italian city
Turing ma·chine
turi·on plant bud
Turk
Tur·ke·stan *variant spelling of* Turkistan
Tur·key
tur·key (*plural* ·keys *or* ·key)
Tur·ki of Turkic
Tur·kic language
Turk·ish
Tur·ki·stan (*or* ·ke·) Asian region
Turk·men language
Turk·meni·stan Soviet republic
Turko·man (*or* Turk·man; *plural* ·mans *or* ·men) Asian people
Tur·ku Finnish city
tur·mer·ic

tur·moil
turn move; *compare* tern; terne
turn·able
turn·about
turn·around
turn·buckle
turn·coat
turn·er
turn·ery (*plural* ·eries) lathe work
turn·ing
tur·nip
turn·key
turn-off (*noun*)
turn-on (*noun*)
turn-out (*noun*)
turn·over (*noun*)
turn·pike
turn·round (*noun*)
turn·sole plant
turn·stile
turn·stone bird
turn·table
turn-up (*noun*)
tur·pen·tine
tur·peth plant
tur·pi·tude
turps turpentine
tur·quoise
tur·ret
tur·ret·ed
tur·ricu·late (*or* ·la·ted)
tur·tle
turtle·back part of ship
turtle·dove
turtle·neck
tur·tler
Tus·can
Tus·ca·ny
Tus·ca·ro·ra (*plural* ·ras *or* ·ra) American Indian
tusche lithographic substance
Tus·cu·lum ancient city
tush
tusk
tusk·er
tusk·like
tus·sah (*or* tus·sore) silk
tus·sal
tus·sis cough
tus·sive
tus·sle
tus·sock

tus·socky

tus·sore *variant spelling of* tussah

tut (**tut·ting, tut·ted**)

tu·tee

tu·telage

tu·telary (*or* ·**telar**; *plural* ·**telaries** *or* ·**telars**)

tu·ti·or·ism Catholic doctrine

tu·ti·or·ist

tu·tor

tu·tor·age (*or* ·**ship**)

tu·to·rial

tu·to·rial·ly

tut·san shrub

tut·ti musical term

tutti-frutti ice cream

tut·ty polishing powder

tutu ballet skirt

Tuvalu Pacific state

tu-whit tu-whoo

tux·edo (*plural* ·**dos**)

tu·yère (*or* **twy·er**) blast-furnace nozzle

twad·dle

twad·dler

twain

twang

twangy

'twas

tway·blade orchid

tweak

twee

Tweed Scottish river

tweed fabric

tweedy (**tweedi·er, tweedi·est**)

tweeny (*plural* **tweenies**) *Slang* maid

tweet

tweet·er loudspeaker

tweeze

twee·zers

twelfth

Twelfth·tide Epiphany

twelve

twelve·mo (*plural* ·**mos**) paper size

twelve·month

twelve-tone musical term

twen·ti·eth

twen·ty (*plural* ·**ties**)

'twere

twerp

Twi (*plural* **Twi** *or* **Twis**) language or people

twi·bill (*or* ·**bil**) tool

twice

twice-laid

Twick·en·ham

twid·dle

twid·dler

twig (**twig·ging, twigged**)

twig·gy (·**gi·er,** ·**gi·est**)

twi·light

twi·lit

twill

twin (**twin·ning, twinned**)

twine

twin·er

twin·flower

twinge (**twinge·ing** *or* **twing·ing, twinged**)

twink

twin·kle

twin·kler

twin·kling·ly

twirl

twirl·er

twist

twist·abil·ity

twist·able

twist·ed·ly

twist·er

twist·ing·ly

twisty (**twisti·er, twisti·est**)

twit (**twit·ting, twit·ted**)

twitch

twitch·er

twitchi·ly

twitchi·ness

twitch·ing·ly

twitchy (**twitchi·er, twitchi·est**)

twite bird

twit·ter

twit·ter·er

twit·tery

twixt

two (*plural* **twos**)

two-by-four

two-dimen·sion·al

two-dimen·sion·al·ity

two-dimen·sion·al·ly

two-edged

two-faced

two-facedly

two-facedness

two·fold

two-handed

two-handed·ly

two·pence (*or* **tup·pence**)

two·pen·ny (*or* **tup·pen·ny**)

two-phase

two-piece

two-ply (*plural* -**plies**)

two-seater

two-sided

two·some

two-step

two-stroke

two-time

two-timer

two-tone

two-way

Ty·burn

Tyche Greek goddess

tych·ism philosophy term

Ty·cho moon crater

ty·coon

ty·ing

tyke (*or* **tike**)

ty·lo·pod zoology term

ty·lo·sis botany term

tym·pan printing term

tym·pa·ni *variant spelling of* timpani

tym·pan·ic

tym·pa·nist *variant spelling of* timpanist

tym·pa·ni·tes (*or* ·**pa·ny**) abdominal distension

tym·pa·nit·ic

tym·pa·ni·tis

tym·pa·num (*plural* ·**nums** *or* ·**na**) part of ear; architectural term; *compare* timpani

tym·pa·ny *variant of* tympanites

Tyne English river

Tyne and Wear English county

Tyne·side

Tyn·wald Manx Parliament

type

type·bar

type·case

type·cast (·**cast·ing,** ·**cast**)

type·cast·er

type·face

type-high

type·script
type·set (·set·ting, ·set)
type·set·ter
type·write (·writ·ing, ·wrote, ·writ·ten)
type·writ·er
typh·li·tic
typh·li·tis intestinal disorder
typh·lol·og·y study of blindness
ty·pho·gen·ic causing typhoid
ty·phoid
ty·phoi·dal
ty·phoi·din
ty·phon·ic
ty·phoon
ty·phous (*adj*)
ty·phus (*noun*)
typi·cal (*or* typ·ic)
typi·cal·ly
typi·cal·ness (*or* ·ity)
typi·fi·ca·tion
typi·fi·er
typi·fy (·fies, ·fy·ing, ·fied)
typ·ing

typ·ist
typo (*plural* typos)
ty·pog·ra·pher
ty·po·graphi·cal (*or* ·graph·ic)
ty·po·graphi·cal·ly
ty·pog·ra·phy
ty·po·logi·cal (*or* ·log·ic)
ty·polo·gist
ty·pol·og·y theology term
ty·poth·etae *US* printers
ty·ra·mine
ty·ran·ni·cal (*or* ran·nic)
ty·ran·ni·cal·ly
ty·ran·ni·cal·ness
ty·ran·ni·cid·al
ty·ran·ni·cide
tyr·an·nize (*or* ·nise)
tyr·an·niz·er (*or* ·nis·er)
tyr·an·niz·ing·ly (*or* ·nis·ing·ly)
ty·ran·no·saur (*or* ·saur·us)
tyr·an·nous
tyr·an·nous·ness
tyr·an·ny (*plural* ·nies)

ty·rant
Tyre Lebanese port
tyre (*US* tire) wheel ring; *compare* tire
Tyr·ian
tyro (*or* tiro; *plural* tyros *or* tiros) novice
ty·ro·ci·dine antibiotic
Ty·rol (*or* Ti·) Austrian province
Tyro·lese (*or* ·lean)
Ty·ro·li·enne dance
Ty·rone Irish county
ty·ron·ic (*or* ti·)
ty·ro·si·nase enzyme
ty·ro·sine amino acid
ty·ro·thri·cin antibiotic
Tyr·rhe·nian Sea
Tyu·men Soviet port
tzar *less common spelling of* tsar
Tzi·gane gipsy
tzet·ze variant spelling of tsetse
Tzu·po (*or* Tze·po) Chinese city

U

ubi·ety being in particular place
ubiqui·tar·ian Lutheran
ubiqui·tous
ubiquity (*or* ubiqui·tous·ness)
ubi su·pra *Latin* where mentioned above
U-boat
Udai·pur Indian city
udal legal term
ud·der
Udi·ne Italian city
udo (*plural* udos) plant
Uf·fizi Italian art gallery
UFO (*plural* UFOs)
ufol·og·y study of UFOs
Ugan·da
Ugan·dan
Uga·rit·ic language
ugli (*plural* uglis *or* uglies) fruit
ug·li·fi·ca·tion

ug·li·fi·er
ug·li·fy (·fies, ·fy·ing, ·fied)
ug·li·ly
ug·li·ness
ugly (ug·li·er, ug·li·est)
Ugrian Asian people
Ugric language
uh·lan Polish lancer
uhu·ru African national independence
Uigur (*or* Uighur; *plural* Uigur, Uigurs *or* Uighur, Uighurs) Mongoloid people
Uigu·rian (*or* ·ric, Uighu·)
uin·ta·there extinct mammal
uit·land·er *South African* foreigner
Uj·jain Indian city
ukase tsar's edict

uke·lele *variant spelling of* ukulele
uki·yoe (*or* ukiyo-e) Japanese art
Ukraine
Ukrain·ian
uku·lele (*or* uke·)
Ulan Ba·tor Mongolian capital
Ulan-Ude Soviet city
ul·cer
ul·cer·ate
ul·cera·tion
ul·cera·tive
ul·cer·ous
ulema Muslim scholar
ul·lage
ul·laged
Ulls·wa·ter
ul·ma·ceous botany term
ulna (*plural* ulnae *or* ulnas) arm bone
ul·nar

ulot·ri·chous curly haired
ulot·ri·chy
Ul·ster Northern Ireland
ul·ster overcoat
Ul·ster·man (*plural* ·men)
ul·te·ri·or
ul·ti·ma final syllable
ul·ti·mate
ul·ti·mate·ly
ul·ti·ma·tum (*plural* ·tums
    or ·ta)
ul·ti·mo last month
ul·ti·mo·geni·ture legal
    term
ul·tra
ultra·cen·trifu·gal
ultra·cen·trifu·ga·tion
ultra·cen·tri·fuge
ultra·con·ser·va·tive
ultra·fiche
ultra·fil·ter
ultra·fil·tra·tion
ultra·high
ultra·ism extreme
    philosophy
ultra·ist
ultra·is·tic
ultra·ma·rine colour
ultra·mi·crom·eter
ultra·micro·scope
ultra·micro·scop·ic
ultra·mi·cros·co·py
ultra·mod·ern
ultra·mod·ern·ism
ultra·mod·ern·ist
ultra·mod·ern·is·tic
ultra·mon·tane beyond the
    mountains
ultra·mon·ta·nism religious
    doctrine
ultra·mon·tan·ist
ultra·mun·dane beyond
    this world
ultra·na·tion·al
ultra·na·tion·al·ism
ultra·na·tion·al·ist
ultra·na·tion·al·is·tic
ultra·short
ultra·son·ic
ultra·soni·cal·ly
ultra·son·ics
ultra·sound
ultra·struc·tur·al
ultra·struc·ture
ultra·vio·let

ul·tra vi·res legal term
ultra·vi·rus
ulu·lant
ulu·late wail
ulu·la·tion
Ul·ya·novsk Soviet city
Umay·yad *variant spelling of*
    Omayyad
um·bel botany term
um·bel·late (*or* ·lar,
    ·lat·ed)
um·bel·lif·er·ous
um·bel·lu·late
um·bel·lule
um·ber pigment
um·bili·cal
um·bili·cate
um·bili·ca·tion
um·bili·cus (*plural* ·ci)
    navel
um·bili·form
umbo (*plural* um·bo·nes
    or umbos) small hump
um·bo·nate (*or* ·bo·nal,
    ·bon·ic)
um·bra (*plural* ·brae)
    shadow
um·brage
um·bra·geous shady
um·bral
um·brel·la
Um·bria Italian region
Um·brian
Um·bri·el satellite of
    Uranus
umi·ak (*or* oomi·) Eskimo
    boat
um·laut
um·pire
um·pire·ship (*or* ·pir·age)
ump·teen
ump·teenth
Um·ta·li Zimbabwean city
un·abashed
un·abat·ed
un·able
un·abridged
un·ab·sorbed
un·ac·cent·ed
un·ac·cep·table
un·ac·claimed
un·ac·com·mo·dat·ed
un·ac·com·mo·dat·ing
un·ac·com·pa·nied
un·ac·com·plished

un·ac·count·able
un·ac·count·able·ness (*or*
    ·abil·ity)
un·ac·count·ably
un·ac·count·ed
un·ac·counted-for
un·ac·cus·tomed
un·ack·nowl·edged
un·ac·quaint·ed
un·ad·mit·ted
un·adopt·ed
un·adorned
un·adul·ter·at·ed
un·ad·ven·tur·ous
un·ad·vised
un·ad·vis·ed·ly
un·ad·vis·ed·ness
un·af·fect·ed
un·afraid
un·aid·ed
un·aimed
un·aired
un·al·loyed pure
un·al·ter·able
un·al·ter·ably
un·al·tered
un·am·bigu·ous
un·am·bi·tious
un-Ameri·can
una·nim·ity (*or*
    unani·mous·ness)
unani·mous
un·an·nounced
un·an·swer·able
un·an·swered
un·ap·peal·able legal term
un·ap·peased
un·ap·pre·ciat·ed
un·ap·pre·cia·tive
un·ap·proach·able
un·ap·pro·pri·at·ed
un·apt inapt
un·apt·ness
un·argu·able
un·arm
un·armed
unary consisting of single
    element
un·ashamed
un·asham·ed·ly
un·asham·ed·ness
un·asked
un·as·sail·able
un·as·sist·ed
un·as·sumed

un·as·sum·ing
un·atoned
un·at·tached
un·at·tain·able
un·at·tend·ed
un·at·test·ed
un·at·trac·tive
un·authen·ti·cat·ed
un·author·ized
un·avail·able
un·avail·ing
un·avoid·abil·ity (*or*
·able·ness)
un·avoid·able
un·avoid·ably
un·aware
un·aware·ness
un·awares (*adv*)
un·backed
un·bal·ance
un·bal·anced
un·bal·las·ted
un·bar (·bar·ring, ·barred)
un·bear·able
un·bear·able·ness
un·bear·ably
un·beat·able
un·beat·en
un·be·com·ing
un·be·com·ing·ness
un·be·fit·ting
un·be·known (*or*
·knownst)
un·be·lief
un·be·liev·abil·ity (*or*
·able·ness)
un·be·liev·able
un·be·liev·ably
un·be·liev·er
un·be·liev·ing
un·be·liev·ing·ly
un·belt
un·bend (·bend·ing,
·bent)
un·bend·able
un·bend·ing
un·bend·ing·ness
un·bent
un·bi·ased (*or* ·assed)
un·bi·ased·ly (*or* ·assed·)
un·bi·ased·ness (*or*
·assed·)
un·bid·den
un·bind (·bind·ing,
·bound)

un·birth·day
un·blem·ished
un·blessed
un·bless·ed·ness
un·blink·ing
un·block
un·blush·ing
un·bolt
un·bolt·ed
un·boned
un·bon·net remove hat
un·born
un·bos·om relieve by
disclosing
un·bound released
un·bound·ed unlimited
un·bowed
un·brace relax
un·break·able
un·bred
un·bri·dle
un·bri·dled
un-Brit·ish
un·bro·ken
un·brushed
un·buck·le
un·bur·den
un·bur·ied
un·but·ton
un·caged
uncalled-for
un·can·ni·ly
un·can·ny (·ni·er, ·ni·est)
un·cap (·cap·ping,
·capped)
uncared-for
un·car·ing
un·ceas·ing
un·ceas·ing·ness
un·cer·emo·ni·ous
un·cer·emo·ni·ous·ness
un·cer·tain
un·cer·tain·ness
un·cer·tain·ty (*plural*
·ties)
un·chain
un·chal·lenge·able
un·chal·lenged
un·changed
un·chang·ing
un·chap·er·oned
un·charged
un·chari·table
un·chari·tably
un·chari·table·ness

un·chart·ed not mapped
un·char·tered not
authorized
un·chaste
un·chaste·ness (*or*
·chas·tity)
un·checked
un·chris·tian
un·church excommunicate
un·cial type of capital letter
un·ci·form hook-shaped
un·ci·na·ria·sis hookworm
disease
un·ci·nate
un·ci·nus (*plural* ·ni) small
hook
un·cir·cum·cised
un·civ·il
un·ci·vil·ity (*or*
·civ·il·ness)
un·civi·lized (*or* ·lised)
un·civil·ly
un·clad
un·claimed
un·clasp
un·clas·si·fied
un·cle
un·clean
un·cleaned
un·clean·li·ness
un·clean·ly
un·clean·ness
un·clear
un·clench
un·clip (·clip·ping,
·clipped)
un·cloak
un·clog (·clog·ging,
·clogged)
un·close
un·clothe (·cloth·ing,
·clothed *or* ·clad)
un·clothed
un·cloud·ed
un·clut·tered
unco *Scot* strange
un·coil
un·coined
un·com·fort·able
un·com·fort·ably
un·com·mer·cial
un·com·mit·ted
un·com·mon
un·com·mon·ly
un·com·mon·ness

un·com·mu·ni·ca·tive
un·com·pen·sat·ed
un·com·peti·tive
un·com·plain·ing
un·com·plet·ed
un·com·pli·cat·ed
un·com·pli·men·ta·ry
un·com·pro·mis·ing
un·com·pro·mis·ing·ness
un·con·cealed
un·con·cern
un·con·cerned
un·con·cern·ed·ly
un·con·cern·ed·ness
un·con·clud·ed
un·con·di·tion·al
un·con·di·tion·al·ly
un·con·di·tion·al·ness (or
·ity)
un·con·di·tioned
un·con·fined
un·con·firmed
un·con·form·abil·ity (or
·able·ness)
un·con·form·able
un·con·form·ity (plural
·ities)
un·con·gen·ial
un·con·gen·ial·ly
un·con·nect·ed
un·con·nect·ed·ness
un·con·quer·able
un·con·quered
un·con·scion·able
unscrupulous; excessive
un·con·scious
un·con·scious·ness
un·con·sent·ing
un·con·sti·tu·tion·al
un·con·sti·tu·tion·al·ity
un·con·sti·tu·tion·al·ly
un·con·strained
un·con·sum·mat·ed
un·con·tami·nat·ed
un·con·test·ed
un·con·trol·labil·ity (or
·lable·ness)
un·con·trol·lable
un·con·trol·lably
un·con·ven·tion·al
un·con·ven·tion·al·ity
un·con·ven·tion·al·ly
un·con·vert·ed
un·con·vinced
un·con·vinc·ing

un·cooked
un·co·opera·tive
un·co·ordi·nat·ed
un·cork
un·cor·rected
un·cor·robo·rat·ed
un·cor·rupt·ed
un·count·able
un·count·ed
un·cou·ple
un·couth
un·cov·enant·ed
un·cov·er
un·cov·ered
un·criti·cal
un·criti·cal·ly
un·cross
un·crowned
unc·tion
unc·tu·os·ity (or
·tu·ous·ness)
unc·tu·ous
un·cul·ti·vat·ed
un·curbed
un·cured
un·curl
un·curt·ained
un·cus (plural unci)
hooked structure
un·cut
un·dam·aged
un·damped
un·dat·ed
un·daunt·ed
un·deca·gon eleven-sided
polygon
un·de·ceiv·able
un·de·ceive
un·de·ceiv·er
un·de·cid·ed
un·de·cid·ed·ness
un·de·clared
un·de·feat·ed
un·de·fend·ed
un·de·filed
un·de·mand·ing
un·demo·crat·ic
un·demo·crati·cal·ly
un·de·mon·stra·tive
un·de·ni·able
un·de·ni·ably
un·der
under·achieve
under·achieve·ment
under·achiev·er

under·act
under·age
under·arm
under·belly (plural
·bellies)
under·bid (·bid·ding, ·bid)
under·bid·der
under·body (plural
·bodies)
under·bred
under·breeding
under·brush US
undergrowth
under·buy (·buy·ing,
·bought)
under·capi·tal·ize (or ·ise)
under·carriage
under·cart undercarriage
under·charge
under·clay
under·clothes (or
·cloth·ing)
under·coat
under·cook
under·cov·er
under·croft underground
chamber
under·cur·rent
under·cut (·cut·ting, ·cut)
under·de·vel·op
under·de·vel·op·ment
under·do (·does, ·do·ing,
·did, ·done)
under·dog
under·done
under·drain
under·drain·age
under·dressed
under·em·ployed
under·em·ploy·ment
under·es·ti·mate
under·es·ti·ma·tion
under·ex·pose
under·ex·po·sure
under·feed (·feed·ing,
·fed)
under·felt
under·floor
under·foot
under·fur
under·gar·ment
under·gird (·gird·ing,
·gird·ed or ·girt)
strengthen from below
under·glaze

under·go (·goes, ·go·ing, ·went, ·gone)
under·go·er
under·gone
under·gradu·ate
under·ground
under·grown
under·growth
under·hand
under·hand·ed
under·hand·ed·ly
under·hand·ed·ness
under·hung
under·laid
under·lain
under·lay (·lay·ing, ·laid) to place under
under·let (·let·ting, ·let)
under·let·ter
under·lie (·ly·ing, ·lay, ·lain) to lie under
under·li·er
under·line
under·ling
under·ly·ing
under·manned
under·men·tioned
under·mine
under·min·er
under·min·ing·ly
under·most
under·named
under·neath
under·nour·ish
under·nour·ished
under·nour·ish·ment
under·paid
under·paint·ing
under·pants
under·pass
under·pay (·pay·ing, ·paid)
under·pay·ment
under·pin (·pin·ning, ·pinned)
under·pin·nings
under·play
under·plot subplot
under·price
under·privi·leged
under·pro·duc·tion
under·proof less than proof spirit
under·prop (·prop·ping, ·propped)

under·quote
under·rate
under·ripe
under·score
under·sea
under·seal
under·sec·re·tary (plural ·taries)
under·sec·re·tary·ship
under·sell (·sel·ling, ·sold)
under·sell·er
under·set (·set·ting, ·set)
under·sexed
under·sher·iff
under·shirt
under·shoot (·shoot·ing, ·shot)
under·side
under·signed
under·sized
under·skirt
under·slung
under·soil
under·sold
under·spend (·spend·ing, ·spent)
under·staffed
under·stand (·stand·ing, ·stood)
under·stand·able
under·stand·ably
under·stand·ing
under·stand·ing·ly
under·state
under·state·ment
under·stock
under·stood
under·study (noun, plural ·studies; verb ·studies, ·study·ing, ·stud·ied)
under·sur·face
under·take (·tak·ing, ·took, ·tak·en)
under·tak·er
under·tak·ing
under·thrust geological fault
under·tint
under·tone
under·took
under·tow
under·trick bridge term
under·trump
under·valu·ation

under·value (·valu·ing, ·val·ued)
under·valu·er
under·vest
under·wa·ter
under·wear
under·weight
under·went
under·wing moth
under·world
under·write (·writ·ing, ·wrote, ·writ·ten)
under·writ·er
un·des·cend·ed
un·de·served
un·de·serv·ing
un·de·sign·ing
un·de·sir·abil·ity (or ·able·ness)
un·de·sir·able
un·de·sir·ably
un·de·sired
un·de·tect·ed
un·de·ter·mined
un·de·terred
un·de·vel·oped
un·de·vi·at·ing
un·di·ag·nosed
un·did
un·dies
un·dif·fer·en·ti·at·ed
un·di·gest·ed
un·dig·ni·fied
un·di·lut·ed
un·dim·in·ished
un·dimmed
un·dine water spirit
un·di·rect·ed
un·dis·ci·plined
un·dis·closed
un·dis·cov·ered
un·dis·crimi·nat·ing
un·dis·guised
un·dis·put·ed
un·dis·solved
un·dis·tin·guished
un·dis·trib·ut·ed logic term
un·dis·turbed
un·di·vid·ed
undo (un·does, un·do·ing, un·did, un·done)
un·do·er
un·do·ing
un·done
un·doubt·ed

un·doubt·ed·ly
un·dreamed (or ·dreamt)
un·dress
un·drink·able
un·due
un·du·lance
un·du·lant
un·du·late
un·du·la·tion
un·du·la·tor
un·du·la·tory
un·du·ly
un·dy·ing
un·earned
un·earth
un·earth·li·ness
un·earth·ly
un·ease
un·easi·ly
un·easi·ness
un·easy
un·eat·able
un·eat·en
un·eco·nom·ic
un·eco·nomi·cal
un·eco·nomi·cal·ly
un·ed·it·ed
un·edu·cat·ed
un·elect·able
un·emo·tion·al
un·emo·tion·al·ly
un·em·ploy·abil·ity
un·em·ploy·able
un·em·ployed
un·em·ploy·ment
un·end·ing
un·en·gaged
un·Eng·lish
un·en·light·ened
un·en·ter·pris·ing
un·en·thu·si·as·tic
un·en·thu·si·asti·cal·ly
un·en·vi·able
un·equal
un·equalled (US
  ·equaled)
un·equal·ly
un·equivo·cal
un·equivo·cal·ly
un·equivo·cal·ness
un·err·ing
un·err·ing·ly
un·es·sen·tial less common
  word for inessential
un·ethi·cal

un·ethi·cal·ly
un·even
un·even·ness
un·event·ful
un·event·ful·ly
un·ex·am·pled
un·ex·cep·tion·able
  beyond criticism
un·ex·cep·tion·able·ness
  (or ·abil·ity)
un·ex·cep·tion·al ordinary
un·ex·cit·ing
un·ex·pec·ted
un·ex·pec·ted·ly
un·ex·pect·ed·ness
un·ex·pe·ri·enced
un·ex·pired
un·ex·plain·able less
  common word for
  inexplicable
un·ex·plained
un·ex·plod·ed
un·ex·plored
un·ex·posed
un·ex·pressed
un·ex·pres·sive
un·ex·pres·sive·ness
un·ex·pur·gat·ed
un·fad·ing
un·fail·ing
un·fair
un·fair·ness
un·faith·ful
un·faith·ful·ly
un·faith·ful·ness
un·fa·mil·iar
un·fa·mili·ar·ity
un·fash·ion·able
un·fash·ion·ably
un·fas·ten
un·fa·thered
un·fath·om·able
un·fath·omed
un·fa·vour·able (US ·vor·)
un·fa·vour·able·ness (US
  ·vor·)
un·fa·vour·ably (US ·vor·)
un·fed
un·feel·ing
un·feel·ing·ness
un·feigned
un·feigned·ly
un·femi·nine
un·fenced
un·fer·til·ized (or ·ised)

un·fet·ter
un·fil·ial
un·filled
un·fin·ished
un·fit
un·fit·ness
un·fit·ted
un·fit·ting
un·fix
un·flag·ging
un·flap·pabil·ity (or
  ·pable·ness)
un·flap·pable
un·flat·ter·ing
un·fledged
un·flinch·ing
un·flinch·ing·ness
un·flust·ered
un·fo·cused
un·fold
un·fold·er
un·forced
un·fore·see·able
un·fore·seen
un·for·get·table
un·for·giv·able
un·for·giv·en
un·for·giv·ing
un·for·got·ten
un·formed
un·for·tu·nate
un·for·tu·nate·ly
un·for·tu·nate·ness
un·found·ed
un·found·ed·ness
un·framed
un·freeze (·freez·ing,
  ·froze, ·fro·zen)
un·fre·quent·ed
un·friend·li·ness
un·friend·ly (·li·er, ·li·est)
un·frock
un·froze
un·fro·zen
un·fruit·ful
un·fruit·ful·ly
un·fruit·ful·ness
un·ful·filled
un·furl
un·fur·nished
un·gain·li·ness
un·gain·ly (·li·er, ·li·est)
Un·ga·va Canadian region
un·gen·er·ous
un·gen·tle·man·ly

un·get·at·able
un·glazed
un·god·li·ness
un·god·ly (·li·er, ·li·est)
un·gov·ern·able
un·gov·ern·able·ness
un·gov·ern·ably
un·grace·ful
un·grace·ful·ly
un·gra·cious
un·gram·mati·cal
un·grate·ful
un·grate·ful·ly
un·grate·ful·ness
un·grudg·ing
un·gual (*or* ·gu·lar) of
   finger- or toenails
un·guard·ed
un·guard·ed·ness
un·guent ointment
un·guen·tary
un·guicu·late biology term
un·gui·nous greasy
un·guis (*plural* ·gues) claw
   or hoof
un·gu·la (*plural* ·lae)
   maths term
un·gu·lar
un·gu·late hoofed mammal
un·gu·li·grade walking on
   hooves
un·hair
un·hal·lowed
un·ham·pered
un·hand
un·hand·some
un·hand·some·ness
un·hap·pi·ly
un·hap·pi·ness
un·hap·py (·pi·er, ·pi·est)
un·harmed
un·har·ness
un·healthi·ly
un·healthi·ness
un·healthy (·healthi·er,
   ·healthi·est)
un·heard
unheard-of
un·heed·ed
un·heed·ing
un·helm remove the helmet
   of
un·help·ful
un·help·ful·ly
un·her·ald·ed

un·hesi·tat·ing
un·hid·den
un·hinge
un·ho·li·ness
un·ho·ly (·li·er, ·li·est)
un·hon·oured (*US* ·ored)
un·hook
unhoped-for
un·horse
un·hur·ried
un·hurt
un·hy·gien·ic
un·hy·gieni·cal·ly
un·hy·phen·at·ed
uni *Austral* university
Uni·at (*or* ·ate) Eastern
   Church
Uni·at·ism
uni·ax·ial
uni·cam·er·al
uni·cam·er·al·ism
uni·cam·er·al·ist
uni·cel·lu·lar
uni·cel·lu·lar·ity
uni·col·our (*or* ·oured;
   US ·or *or* ·ored)
uni·corn
uni·cos·tate having one rib
uni·cy·cle
uni·cy·clist
un·iden·ti·fi·able
un·iden·ti·fied
uni·di·rec·tion·al
uni·fi·able
uni·fi·ca·tion
uni·fied
uni·fi·er
uni·fo·li·ate botany term
uni·fo·lio·late botany term
uni·form
uni·formi·tar·ian
uni·formi·tari·an·ism
   geological theory
uni·form·ity (*plural* ·ities)
uni·form·ly
uni·form·ness
uni·fy (·fies, ·fy·ing, ·fied)
uni·ju·gate botany term
uni·lat·er·al
uni·lat·er·al·ism (*or* ·ity)
uni·lat·er·al·ly
un·il·lus·trat·ed
uni·locu·lar botany term
un·im·agi·nable
un·im·agi·nably

un·im·agi·na·tive
un·im·ag·ined
un·im·paired
un·im·peach·abil·ity (*or*
   ·able·ness)
un·im·peach·able
un·im·ped·ed
un·im·por·tant
un·im·pos·ing
un·im·pressed
un·im·pres·sive
un·im·proved
un·in·cor·po·ra·ted
un·in·flu·enced
un·in·formed
un·in·hab·it·able
un·in·hab·it·ed
un·in·hib·it·ed
un·in·jured
un·in·spired
un·in·spir·ing
un·in·sur·able
un·in·sured
un·in·tel·li·gence
un·in·tel·li·gent
un·in·tel·li·gibie
un·in·tel·li·gibly
un·in·tend·ed
un·in·ten·tion·al
un·in·ten·tion·ally
un·in·ter·est·ed not
   interested; *compare*
   disinterested
un·in·ter·est·ed·ly
un·in·ter·est·ed·ness
un·in·ter·est·ing
un·in·ter·rupt·ed
uni·nu·cleate
un·in·vit·ed
un·in·vit·ing
un·ion
un·ion·ism
un·ion·ist
un·ion·is·tic
un·ioni·za·tion (*or*
   ·sa·tion)
un·ion·ize (*or* ·ise) join
   trade union
un·ionized not ionized
uni·para *variant of* primipara
unip·ar·ous biology term
uni·per·son·al
uni·per·son·al·ity
uni·pla·nar
uni·pod one-legged support

uni·po·lar
uni·po·lar·ity
unique
unique·ly
unique·ness
uni·ra·mous undivided
uni·sep·tate biology term
uni·sex
uni·sexu·al
uni·sexu·al·ity
uni·son
uniso·nous (or ·nal,
·nant)
unit
Uni·tar·ian
uni·tar·ian
Uni·tari·an·ism Christian
belief
uni·tari·an·ism centralized
government
uni·tary
unite
unit·ed
unit·ed·ly
unit·ed·ness
unit·er
uni·tive
unity (plural unities)
uni·va·len·cy
uni·va·lent
uni·valve zoology term
uni·ver·sal
uni·ver·sal·ism
uni·ver·sal·ist
uni·ver·sal·is·tic
uni·ver·sal·ity (plural
·ities)
uni·ver·sali·za·tion (or
·sa·tion)
uni·ver·sal·ize (or ·ise)
uni·ver·sal·ly
uni·ver·sal·ness
uni·verse
uni·ver·sity (plural ·sities)
uni·vo·cal unambiguous
un·just
un·jus·ti·fi·able
un·jus·ti·fied
un·just·ness
un·kempt
un·kempt·ness
un·kenned Dialect unknown
un·ken·nel (·nel·ling,
·nelled; US ·nel·ing,
·neled)

un·kind
un·kind·li·ness
un·kind·ness
un·knit (·knit·ting,
·knit·ted or ·knit)
un·know·able
un·know·able·ness (or
·abil·ity)
un·know·ing
un·know·ing·ly
un·known
un·known·ness
un·la·belled (US ·beled)
un·lace
un·lade unload
un·la·den
un·lady·like
un·laid
un·lam·ent·ed
un·lash
un·latch
un·law·ful
un·law·ful·ly
un·law·ful·ness
un·lay (·lay·ing, ·laid)
untwist
un·lead printing term
un·lead·ed
un·learn (·learn·ing,
·learnt or ·learned)
un·learn·ed ignorant
un·leash
un·leav·ened
un·less
un·let·tered
un·li·censed
un·like
un·like·li·ness (or
·li·hood)
un·like·ly
un·lim·ber prepare for use
un·lim·it·ed
un·lined
un·list·ed
un·lit
un·live
un·lived-in
un·load
un·load·er
un·lock
un·lock·able
unlooked-for
un·loose (or ·loos·en)
un·lov·able
un·loved

un·love·ly
un·lov·ing
un·lucki·ly
un·lucki·ness
un·lucky (·lucki·er,
·lucki·est)
un·made
un·make (·mak·ing,
·made)
un·mak·er
un·man (·man·ning,
·manned)
un·man·age·able
un·man·li·ness
un·man·ly
un·manned
un·man·nered
un·man·ner·li·ness
un·man·ner·ly
un·marked
un·mar·riage·able
un·mar·ried
un·mask
un·mask·er
un·matched
un·mean·ing
un·meant
un·meas·ur·able unable to
be measured; compare
immeasurable
un·meas·ured
un·meet unsuitable
un·men·tion·able
un·men·tion·ables
un·mer·ci·ful
un·mer·ci·ful·ly
un·mer·it·ed
un·mind·ful
un·mis·tak·able (or
·take·)
un·mis·tak·ably (or
·take·)
un·miti·gat·ed
un·mixed
un·mo·lest·ed
un·moor
un·mor·al amoral
un·mo·ral·ity
un·mount·ed
un·mourned
un·moved
un·mu·si·cal
un·mu·si·cal·ly
un·mu·si·cal·ness
un·muz·zle

un·name·able
un·named
un·natu·ral
un·natu·ral·ly
un·natu·ral·ness
un·navi·gable
un·nec·es·sari·ly
un·nec·es·sary
un·neigh·bour·ly (*US* ·bor·)
un·nerve
un·nerv·ing
un·no·ticed
un·num·bered
un·ob·jec·tion·able
un·ob·scured
un·ob·ser·vant
un·ob·served
un·ob·struct·ed
un·ob·tain·able
un·ob·tru·sive
un·ob·tru·sive·ly
un·ob·tru·sive·ness
un·oc·cu·pied
un·of·fend·ing
un·of·fi·cial
un·of·fi·cial·ly
un·opened
un·op·posed
un·or·gan·ized (*or* ·ised)
un·origi·nal
un·ortho·dox
un·owned
un·pack
un·pack·er
un·paged
un·paid
un·paint·ed
un·pained
un·pal·at·able
un·par·al·leled
un·par·don·able
un·par·lia·men·ta·ry
un·pat·ent·ed
un·pat·ri·ot·ic
un·paved
un·peeled
un·peg (·peg·ging, ·pegged)
un·peo·ple (*verb*)
un·per·ceived
un·per·fo·rat·ed
un·per·son
un·per·turbed
un·pick

un·pin (·pin·ning, ·pinned)
un·pity·ing
un·place·able
un·placed
un·planned
un·play·able
un·pleas·ant
un·pleas·ant·ness
un·pleas·ing
un·plug (·plug·ging, ·plugged)
un·plumbed
un·poli·tic
un·po·liti·cal
un·polled
un·pol·lut·ed
un·popu·lar
un·popu·lar·ity
un·posed
un·prac·ti·cal impractical
un·prac·ti·cal·ity (*or* ·ness)
un·prac·tised (*US* ·ticed)
un·prec·edent·ed
un·pre·dict·abil·ity (*or* ·able·ness)
un·pre·dict·able
un·pre·dict·ably
un·preju·diced
un·pre·medi·tat·ed
un·pre·medi·ta·tion
un·pre·pared
un·pre·par·ed·ness
un·pre·pos·sess·ing
un·pre·sent·able
un·pre·ten·tious
un·pre·ten·tious·ness
un·pre·vent·able
un·priced
un·prin·ci·pled
un·print·able
un·pro·duc·tive
un·pro·fessed
un·pro·fes·sion·al
un·pro·fes·sion·al·ly
un·prof·it·abil·ity (*or* ·able·ness)
un·prof·it·able
un·prof·it·ably
un·prom·is·ing
un·prompt·ed
un·pro·nounce·able
un·pro·tect·ed
un·prov·able

un·proved
un·prov·en
un·pro·vid·ed
un·pub·lished
un·punc·tual
un·pun·ished
un·put·down·able
un·quali·fi·able
un·quali·fied
un·quench·able
un·ques·tion·abil·ity (*or* ·able·ness)
un·ques·tion·able
un·ques·tion·ably
un·ques·tioned
un·ques·tion·ing
un·qui·et
un·quote
un·rav·el (·el·ling, ·elled; *US* ·el·ing, ·eled)
un·rav·el·ler (*US* ·el·er)
un·rav·el·ment
un·reach·able
un·read
un·read·abil·ity (*or* ·able·ness)
un·read·able
un·readi·ness
un·ready
un·real
un·re·al·is·tic
un·re·al·isti·cal·ly
un·re·al·ity
un·re·al·ized (*or* ·ised)
un·rea·son
un·rea·son·able
un·rea·son·able·ness
un·rea·son·ably
un·rea·son·ing
un·reck·on·able
un·rec·og·niz·able (*or* ·nis·able)
un·rec·og·nized (*or* ·nised)
un·rec·on·ciled
un·re·con·struct·ed
un·re·cord·ed
un·reeve (·reev·ing, ·rove *or* ·reeved) nautical term
un·re·fined
un·re·flect·ed
un·re·flec·tive
un·re·gard·ed
un·re·gen·era·cy

un·re·gen·er·ate
  unrepentant
un·reg·is·tered
un·re·hearsed
un·re·lat·ed
un·re·lent·ing
un·re·li·abil·ity (or
  ·able·ness)
un·re·li·able
un·re·li·ably
un·re·mit·ting
un·re·paired
un·re·peat·able
un·re·pent·ant
un·re·port·ed
un·rep·re·senta·tive
un·rep·re·sent·ed
un·re·quit·ed
un·re·served
un·re·serv·ed·ly
un·re·serv·ed·ness
un·re·sist·ing
un·re·solved
un·re·spon·sive
un·rest
un·re·strained
un·re·strict·ed
un·re·ward·ed
un·re·ward·ing
un·rhymed
un·rid·able
un·rid·dle solve
un·rid·dler
un·ri·fled
un·rig (·rig·ging, ·rigged)
un·right·eous
un·rip (·rip·ping, ·ripped)
un·ripe (or ·rip·ened)
un·ri·valled (US ·valed)
un·roll
un·root
un·round·ed
un·rove nautical term
un·ruf·fled
un·ruf·fled·ness
un·ruled
un·ru·li·ness
un·ru·ly (·li·er, ·li·est)
un·sad·dle
un·safe
un·said
un·sale·able (US
  ·sal·able)
un·salt·ed
un·sanc·tioned

un·sani·tary
un·sat·is·fac·tori·ly
un·sat·is·fac·tory
un·sat·is·fied
un·sat·is·fy·ing
un·satu·rat·ed
un·satu·ra·tion
un·saved
un·sa·vouri·ly (US ·vori·)
un·sa·vouri·ness (US
  ·vori·)
un·sa·voury (US ·vory)
un·say (·say·ing, ·said)
un·scal·able
un·scarred
un·scathed
un·scent·ed
un·sched·uled
un·schooled
un·sci·en·tif·ic
un·sci·en·tifi·cal·ly
un·scram·ble
un·scram·bler
un·scratched
un·screened
un·screw
un·script·ed
un·scru·pu·lous
un·scru·pu·lous·ness (or
  ·los·ity)
un·seal
un·seal·able
un·seam
un·search·able
un·sea·son·able
un·sea·son·ably
un·sea·soned
un·seat
un·sea·worthy
un·secured
un·seed·ed
un·seem·li·ness
un·seem·ly
un·seen
un·seg·re·gat·ed
un·self·con·scious
un·self·ish
un·self·ish·ness
un·sepa·rat·ed
un·ser·vice·able
un·set
un·set·tle
un·set·tled
un·set·tle·ment
un·sex

un·shack·le
un·shad·ed
un·shak·able (or ·shake·)
un·shak·en
un·shap·en
un·shav·en
un·sheathe
un·shed
un·ship (·ship·ping,
  ·shipped)
un·shock·able
un·sight·ed
un·sight·li·ness
un·sight·ly
un·signed
un·sink·able
un·skil·ful (US ·skill·ful)
un·skilled
un·slaked
un·sling (·sling·ing,
  ·slung)
un·smil·ing
un·smoked
un·snap (·snap·ping,
  ·snapped)
un·snarl
un·so·ciabil·ity (or
  ·ciable·ness)
un·so·ciable
un·so·ciably
un·so·cial
un·sold
un·so·lic·it·ed
un·solv·able
un·solved
un·so·phis·ti·cat·ed
un·so·phis·ti·cat·ed·ness
  (or ·ca·tion)
un·sort·ed
un·sought
un·sound
un·spar·ing
un·speak·able
un·speak·ably
un·spe·cif·ic
un·speci·fied
un·spent
un·spoiled (or ·spoilt)
un·spo·ken
un·sport·ing
un·spot·ted
un·sta·ble
un·stamped
un·steadi·ly
un·steadi·ness

un·steady (*adj* ·steadi·er,
 ·steadi·est; *verb*
 ·steadies, ·steady·ing,
 ·stead·ied)
un·step (·step·ping,
 ·stepped) nautical term
un·stick (·stick·ing,
 ·stuck)
un·stint·ing
un·stop (·stop·ping,
 ·stopped)
un·stop·pable
un·stopped
un·strained
un·strap (·strap·ping,
 ·strapped)
un·strati·fied
un·stressed
un·stri·at·ed
un·string (·string·ing,
 ·strung)
un·striped
un·struc·tured
un·strung
un·stuck
un·stud·ied
un·sub·stan·tial
un·sub·stan·ti·al·ity
un·sub·stan·ti·at·ed
un·suc·cess·ful
un·suc·cess·ful·ly
un·sug·ared
un·suit·abil·ity (*or*
 ·able·ness)
un·suit·able
un·suit·ably
un·suit·ed
un·sul·ied
un·sung
un·sure
un·sur·passed
un·sus·pect·ed
un·sus·pect·ing
un·swathe
un·swear (·swear·ing,
 ·swore, ·sworn) retract
un·sweet·ened
un·swept
un·swerv·ing
un·sym·pa·thet·ic
un·sym·pa·theti·cal·ly
un·sys·tem·at·ic
un·taint·ed
un·tame·able
un·tamed

un·tan·gle
un·tapped
un·tast·ed
un·taught
un·teach (·teach·ing,
 ·taught)
un·teach·able
un·tear·able
un·ten·abil·ity (*or*
 ·able·ness)
un·ten·able
un·ten·ant·ed
Un·ter·wal·den Swiss
 canton
un·test·ed
un·thanked
un·thank·ful
un·thank·ful·ness
un·think (·think·ing,
 ·thought)
un·think·abil·ity (*or*
 ·able·ness)
un·think·able
un·think·ably
un·think·ing
un·thought-of
un·thread
un·ti·di·ly
un·ti·di·ness
un·ti·dy (*adj* ·di·er,
 ·di·est; *verb* ·dies,
 ·dy·ing, ·died)
un·tie (·ty·ing, ·tied)
un·til
un·time·ly
un·tinged
un·tir·ing
un·tit·led
unto
un·told
un·touch·abil·ity
un·touch·able
un·touched
un·to·ward
un·trace·able
un·trained
un·tram·melled (*US*
 ·meled)
un·trans·lat·able
un·trav·elled (*US* ·eled)
un·treat·able
un·treat·ed
un·tried
un·trod·den
un·true

un·truss
un·trust·worthy
un·truth
un·truth·ful
un·truth·ful·ly
un·truth·ful·ness
un·tuck
un·turned
un·tu·tored
un·typi·cal
un·us·able
un·used
un·usual
un·usu·al·ly
un·ut·ter·able
un·ut·tered
un·val·ued
un·var·ied
un·var·nished
un·vary·ing
un·veil
un·veil·ing
un·versed
un·voice phonetics term
un·voiced
un·want·ed
un·war·rant·able
un·war·rant·ed
un·wari·ly
un·wari·ness
un·wary
un·washed
un·watched
un·wat·ered
un·wa·ver·ing
un·wear·able
un·wea·ried
un·weary·ing
un·wed
un·weighed
un·wel·come
un·well
un·wept
un·whole·some
un·whole·some·ly
un·whole·some·ness
un·wieldi·ly (*or*
 ·wield·li·ly)
un·wieldi·ness (*or*
 ·wield·li·ness)
un·wieldy (*or* ·wield·ly)
un·willed
un·will·ing
un·will·ing·ness

un·wind (·wind·ing, ·wound)
un·wind·able
un·wind·er
un·wink·ing
un·wise
un·wise·ly
un·wish
un·wished
un·wit·nessed
un·wit·ting
un·wont·ed
un·work·able
un·world·li·ness
un·world·ly
un·worn
un·worthi·ly
un·worthi·ness
un·wor·thy (·thi·er, thi·est)
un·wound
un·wrap (·wrap·ping, ·wrapped)
un·writ·ten
un·yield·ing
un·yoke
un·zip (·zip·ping, ·zipped)
up (up·ping, upped)
up-anchor
up-and-coming
up-and-under
Upani·shad Hindu treatise
upas tree
up·beat
up·bow musical term
up·braid
up·braid·er
up·bring·ing
up·build (·build·ing, ·built)
up·build·er
up·cast (·cast·ing, ·cast)
up·country
up·date
up·dat·er
up·draught (US ·draft)
up·end
up·grade
up·grad·er
up·growth
up·heav·al
up·heave (·heav·ing, ·heaved or ·hove)
up·held
up·hill

up·hold (·hold·ing, ·held)
up·hold·er
up·hol·ster
up·hol·ster·er
up·hol·stery (plural ·steries)
up·hove variant of upheaved
uphroe variant spelling of euphroe
up·keep
up·land
up·lift
up·lift·er
up·lift·ing
up·most variant of uppermost
upon
up·per
upper-case (adj, verb)
upper-class (adj)
upper·cut (·cut·ting, ·cut)
upper·most (or up·most)
up·pish
up·pish·ness
up·pi·ty
Upp·sa·la (or Up·sa·la) Swedish city
up·raise
up·rais·er
up·rear
up·right
up·right·ness
up·rise (·ris·ing, ·rose, ·ris·en)
up·ris·er
up·ris·ing
up·river
up·roar
up·roari·ous
up·root
up·root·er
up·rose
up·rush
Up·sa·la variant spelling of Uppsala
up·set (·set·ting, ·set)
up·set·table
up·set·ter
up·set·ting
up·shot
up·side
upside-down
upside-downness
up·si·lon Greek letter
up·stage

up·stairs
up·stand·ing
up·stand·ing·ness
up·start
up·state
up·stream
up·stretched
up·stroke
up·surge
up·sweep (·sweep·ing, ·swept)
up·swing (·swing·ing, ·swung)
upsy-daisy
up·take
up·throw
up·thrust
up·tight
up·tilt
up-to-date
up-to-dateness
up·town
up·turn
up·ward (adj)
up·ward·ly
up·ward·ness
up·wards (adv)
up·wind
Ur Sumerian city
ura·cil biochemical compound
urae·mia (US ure·)
urae·mic (US ure·)
urae·us (plural ·uses) sacred serpent
Ural Soviet river
Ural-Altaic language group
Ural·ic (or Ura·lian)
ural·ite mineral
ural·it·ic
Urals Soviet mountains
ura·naly·sis variant of urinalysis
Ura·nian of Uranus; celestial
uran·ic chemistry term
ura·nide chemical element
urani·nite mineral
ura·nite mineral
ura·nit·ic
ura·nium
ura·nog·ra·pher (or ·phist)
ura·no·graph·ic (or ·graphi·cal)

ura·nog·ra·phy star mapping
ura·nous chemistry term
Ura·nus planet
Uranus Greek god
ura·nyl chemical group
ura·nyl·ic
urate
urat·ic
ur·ban
ur·bane
ur·bane·ly
ur·bane·ness
ur·ban·ite
ur·ban·ity (*plural* ·ities)
ur·bani·za·tion (*or* ·sa·tion)
ur·ban·ize (*or* ·ise)
urbi et orbi papal blessing
ur·ceo·late pitcher-shaped
ur·chin
urd bean plant
urdé heraldic term
Urdu
urea
ureal (*or* ureic)
urease enzyme
ure·dial
uredium (*or* uredin·ium; *plural* uredia *or* uredinia) fungal structure
uredo (*plural* uredi·nes) urticaria
uredo·so·rus (*plural* ·so·ri) uredium
uredo·spore
ureic *variant of* ureal
ureide chemical compound
ure·mia *US spelling of* uraemia
ureter
ureter·al (*or* ·ic)
urethane (*or* urethan) chemistry term
urethra (*plural* urethrae *or* urethras)
urethral
urethrit·ic
urethri·tis
urethro·scope
urethro·scop·ic
urethros·co·py
uret·ic of urine
urge
ur·gen·cy

ur·gent
urg·er
urg·ing·ly
uric
uri·dine biochemical compound
uri·nal
uri·naly·sis (*or* ura·; *plural* ·ses)
uri·nant heraldic term
uri·nary (*plural* ·naries)
uri·nate
uri·na·tion
uri·na·tive
urine
uri·nif·er·ous transporting urine
uri·no·geni·tal *variant of* urogenital
uri·nous (*or* ·nose)
Ur·mia Iranian lake
urn
urn·field cemetery
urn·like
uro·chord zoology term
uro·chor·dal
uro·chor·date marine animal
uro·chrome pigment
uro·dele type of amphibian
uro·geni·tal (*or* uri·no·)
urog·enous producing urine
uro·lith stone in urinary tract
uro·lith·ic
uro·log·ic (*or* ·logi·cal)
urolo·gist
urol·ogy branch of medicine
uro·pod crustacean appendage
uropo·dal (*or* ·dous)
uro·pyg·ial
uro·pyg·ium base of bird's tail
uro·scop·ic
uros·co·pist
uros·co·py examination of urine
uro·style zoology term
ur·sine of bears
Ur·su·line nun
Ur·text *German* original text
ur·ti·ca·ceous botany term
ur·ti·caria nettle rash
ur·ti·car·ial (*or* ·cari·ous)

ur·ti·cate medical term
ur·ti·ca·tion
Urua·pan Mexican city
Uru·guay
Uru·guay·an
Urum·chi (*or* Wu·lu·mu·ch'i) Chinese city
uru·shi·ol poisonous liquid
us
us·abil·ity (*or* ·able·ness, use·)
us·able (*or* use·)
us·age
us·ance commerce term
use
use·abil·ity (*or* ·able·ness) *variants of* usability
use·able *variant spelling of* usable
used
use·ful
use·ful·ly
use·ful·ness
use·less
use·less·ness
user
Ush·ant French island
ush·er
ush·er·ette
Usk Welsh river
Üs·kü·dar Turkish town
us·que·baugh Irish liqueur
Usta·shi terrorist organization
Ust-Kameno·gorsk Soviet city
us·tu·la·tion burning
usu·al
usu·al·ly
usu·al·ness
usu·fruct legal term
usu·fruc·tu·ary (*plural* ·aries)
usu·rer
usu·ri·ous
usu·ri·ous·ness
usurp
usur·pa·tion
usur·pa·tive (*or* ·tory)
usurp·er
usurp·ing·ly
usu·ry (*plural* ·ries)
Utah
Utah·an

Ute (*plural* **Utes** *or* **Ute**)
American Indian
uten·sil
uter·ine
uter·us (*plural* **uteri**)
Ut·gard Norse mythological
place
Uti·ca ancient African city
utili·tar·ian
utili·tari·an·ism
util·ity (*plural* ·ities)
uti·liz·able (*or* ·lis·able)
uti·li·za·tion (*or* ·sa·tion)
uti·lize (*or* ·lise)
uti·liz·er (*or* ·lis·er)
ut in·fra *Latin* as below
uti pos·si·detis legal term
ut·most (*or* utter·)
Uto-Aztecan language
Uto·pia

Uto·pian (*or* uto·)
Uto·pi·an·ism (*or* uto·)
Utrecht Dutch province
utri·cle (*or* utricu·lus;
plural utri·cles *or*
utricu·li) part of ear
utricu·lar (*or* ·late)
utricu·li·tis
ut su·pra *Latin* as above
Ut·tar Pra·desh Indian
state
ut·ter
ut·ter·able
ut·ter·able·ness
ut·ter·ance
ut·ter·er
ut·ter·ly
utter·most *variant of* **utmost**
U-turn

uva·rov·ite green garnet
uvea part of eye
uveal (*or* uveous)
uveit·ic
uveitis
uvu·la (*plural* ·las *or* ·lae)
uvu·lar
uvu·li·tis
Ux·bridge
uxo·rial wifely
uxo·ri·cid·al
uxo·ri·cide
uxo·ri·ous wife-loving
uxo·ri·ous·ness
Uz·bek (*plural* ·beks *or*
·bek)
Uz·beki·stan Soviet
republic

V

Vaal South African river
vac *Slang* vacation
va·can·cy (*plural* ·cies)
va·cant
va·cant·ness
va·cat·able
va·cate
va·ca·tion
va·ca·tion·ist (*or* ·er)
vac·ci·nal
vac·ci·nate
vac·ci·na·tion
vac·ci·na·tor
vac·cine
vac·cinia cowpox
vac·cin·ial
vac·il·lant
vac·il·late
vac·il·lat·ing
vac·il·lat·ing·ly
vac·il·la·tion
vac·il·la·tor
vacua *plural of* **vacuum**
va·cu·ity (*plural* ·ities)
vacuo·lar
vacuo·late
vacuo·la·tion
vacu·ole cell cavity
vacu·ous
vacu·ous·ness

vacuum (*plural* **vacuums**
or **vacua**)
vacuum-packed
vade me·cum handbook
Va·do·da·ra Indian city
va·dose geology term
Va·duz Liechtenstein capital
vag *Austral* vagrant
vaga·bond
vaga·bond·age
vaga·bond·ism
va·gal of the vagus
va·gary (*plural* ·garies)
va·gi·na (*plural* ·nas *or*
·nae)
vagi·nal
vagi·nate botany term
vagi·nec·tomy (*plural*
·tomies)
vagi·nis·mus vaginal spasm
vagi·ni·tis
va·goto·my (*plural* ·mies)
surgery of the vagus
va·go·to·nia overactivity of
the vagus
va·go·trop·ic affecting the
vagus
va·gran·cy (*plural* ·cies)
va·grant
va·grant·ness

vague
vague·ly
vague·ness
va·gus (*plural* ·gi) nerve
va·hana mythological
vehicle
vain conceited; *compare* **vane**
vain·glo·ri·ous
vain·glo·ry
vain·ly
vain·ness
vair fur trimming
Va·lais Swiss canton
val·ance drapery; *compare*
valence
val·anced
Val-de-Marne French
department
Val-d'Oise French
department
vale *Latin* farewell
vale valley; *compare* **veil**
val·edic·tion
val·edic·tory (*plural*
·tories)
va·lence (*or* ·len·cy;
plural ·lences *or* ·cies)
chemistry term; *compare*
valance
Va·len·cia Spanish port

Va·len·ci·ennes French
town; lace
va·len·cy *variant of* valence
val·en·tine
va·lerian plant
va·leria·na·ceous
va·ler·ic
val·et
va·leta *variant spelling of*
veleta
Va·let·ta *variant spelling of*
Valletta
val·etu·di·nar·ian (*or*
·nary; *plural* ·ians *or*
·naries)
val·etu·di·nar·ian·ism
val·gus medical term
Val·hal·la
val·iance (*or* ·ian·cy,
·iant·ness)
val·iant
val·id
vali·date
vali·da·tion
vali·da·tory
va·lid·ity
val·id·ness
va·line amino acid
va·lise
Valium (*Trademark*)
Val·kyrie (*or* Wal·kyrie,
Val·kyr)
Va·lla·do·lid Spanish city
val·la·tion building
fortifications
val·lecu·la (*plural* ·lae)
biology term
val·lecu·lar (*or* ·late)
Val·le d'Ao·sta Italian
region
Val·let·ta (*or* Va·let·ta)
Maltese capital
val·ley
va·lo·nia acorns used in
tanning
val·ori·za·tion (*or*
·sa·tion)
val·or·ize (*or* ·ise) fix price
for
val·or·ous
val·our (*US* ·or)
Val·pa·rai·so Chilean port
valse *French* waltz
valu·able
valu·able·ness
valu·ably

valu·ate
valua·tion
valua·tion·al
valua·tor
value (valu·ing, valued)
value·less
value·less·ness
valu·er
valu·ta currency exchange
rate
val·vate
valve
valve·less
val·vu·lar
val·vule (*or* valve·let)
val·vu·li·tis heart-valve
inflammation
vam·brace armour
va·moose
vamp
vam·pire
vam·pir·ic (*or* ·ish)
vam·pir·ism
Van Turkish city
van
vana·date chemical
compound
va·nad·ic
va·nadi·nite mineral
va·na·dium chemical
element
vana·dous
va·na·spa·ti vegetable fat
Van·cou·ver
van·da orchid
Van·dal Germanic invader
van·dal destroyer
van·dal·ism
van·dal·is·tic (*or* ·dal·ish)
van·dal·ize (*or* ·ise)
Van·dyke beard; collar
vane flat blade; *compare*
vain
vang nautical term
van·guard
va·nil·la
va·nil·lic
van·il·lin
van·ish
van·ish·er
van·ish·ing·ly
van·ish·ment
van·ity (*plural* ·ities)
van·quish
van·quish·able

van·quish·er
van·quish·ment
van·tage
Vanu·atu island republic
van·ward
vap·id
va·pid·ity
vap·id·ness
va·por·es·cence
va·por·es·cent
va·po·ret·to (*plural* ·ti *or*
·tos) steamboat
va·por·if·ic
va·por·im·eter
va·por·iz·able (*or* ·is·able)
va·pori·za·tion (*or*
·sa·tion)
va·por·ize (*or* ·ise)
va·por·iz·er (*or* ·is·er)
va·por·ous
va·por·ous·ness (*or*
·os·ity)
va·pour (*US* ·por)
va·pour·abil·ity (*US*
·por·)
va·pour·able (*US* ·por·)
va·pour·er (*US* ·por·)
va·pour·ish (*US* ·por·)
va·pour·ish·ness (*US*
·por·)
var unit of power
vara unit of length
va·rac·tor electronic device
Va·ra·na·si Indian city
Va·ran·gian medieval
Scandinavian
var·ec seaweed
varia literary miscellany
vari·abil·ity (*or*
·able·ness)
vari·able
vari·ably
vari·ance
vari·ant
vari·ate a random variable
vari·ation
vari·ation·al (*or* ·ative)
vari·cel·la chickenpox
vari·cel·lar
vari·cel·late ridged
vari·cel·loid
vari·ces *plural of* varix
vari·co·cele medical term
vari·col·oured (*US* ·ored)
vari·cose

velate

vari·co·sis
vari·cos·ity (*plural* ·ities)
vari·coto·my (*plural*
·mies) varicose-vein
surgery
var·ied
var·ied·ness
varie·gate
varie·gat·ed
varie·ga·tion
va·ri·etal
va·ri·ety (*plural* ·eties)
vari·form
va·rio·la smallpox
va·rio·lar
va·rio·late inoculate
va·rio·la·tion
vari·ole geology term
vari·olite rock
vario·lit·ic
vario·loid mild smallpox
va·rio·lous of smallpox
vari·om·eter
vario·rum annotated text
vari·ous
vari·ous·ly
vari·ous·ness
var·is·cite mineral
var·is·tor electronic
component
vari·type
Vari·typ·er (*Trademark*)
justifying typewriter
vari·typ·ist
var·ix (*plural* vari·ces)
varicose vein
var·let
var·mint
Var·na Bulgarian port
var·na Hindu caste
var·nish
var·nish·er
var·sity (*plural* ·sities)
Slang university
var·us medical term
varve geology term
vary (varies, vary·ing,
var·ied)
vary·ing·ly
vas·al of vas deferens;
compare vassal
vas·cu·lar conducting fluids
vas·cu·lar·ity
vas·cu·lari·za·tion (*or*
·sa·tion) medical term

vas·cu·lum (*plural* ·la *or*
·lums) plant-specimen
container
vas de·fe·rens (*plural*
vasa de·fe·ren·tia)
anatomy term
vase
vas·ec·to·mize (*or* ·mise)
vas·ec·to·my (*plural*
·mies)
Vas·eline (*Trademark*)
vaso·active affecting blood
vessels
vaso·con·stric·tion
vaso·con·stric·tive
vaso·con·stric·tor
vaso·di·la·tion
vaso·di·la·tor
vaso·in·hibi·tor
vaso·in·hibi·tory
vaso·mo·tor
vaso·pres·sin hormone
vas·sal feudal tenant;
compare vasal
vas·sal·age
vas·sal·ize (*or* ·ise)
vast
Väs·ter·ås Swedish city
vas·tity
vast·ness
vasty (vasti·er, vasti·est)
Archaic vast
vat (vat·ting, vat·ted)
vat·ic of a prophet
Vati·can
Vati·can·ism
Vau·cluse French
department
Vaud Swiss canton
vau·de·ville
vau·de·vil·lian
vau·de·vil·list
Vau·dois (*plural* ·dois) of
Vaud; Waldenses
vault
vault·ed
vault·er
vault·ing
vaunt
vaunt·er
vaunt·ing·ly
vava·sor (*or* ·sour) vassal
veal
veal·er veal calf
vec·tor

vec·to·rial
Veda Hindu scriptures
ve·da·lia ladybird
Ve·dan·ta Hindu school of
philosophy
Ve·dan·tic
Ved·da (*or* ·dah; *plural*
·da, ·das *or* ·dah, ·dahs)
Sri Lankan people
Ved·doid
ve·dette
Ve·dic of the Veda
veer
veer·ing·ly
veery (*plural* veeries) bird
veg *Slang* vegetables
Vega star
ve·gan
veg·eta·ble
veg·etal of plants;
nonsexual
veg·etar·ian
veg·etari·an·ism
veg·etate
veg·eta·tion
veg·eta·tion·al
veg·eta·tive
veg·eta·tive·ness
ve·he·mence
ve·he·ment
ve·hi·cle
ve·hicu·lar
Veii Etruscan city
veil head covering; *compare*
vale
veiled
veil·ed·ly
veil·er
veil·ing
vein
vein·ing
vein·let
vein·stone ore material
veiny (veini·er, veini·est)
ve·la·men (*plural*
·lami·na) biology term
ve·lar biology or phonetics
term
ve·lar·ium (*plural* ·laria)
awning in Roman theatre
ve·lari·za·tion (*or*
·sa·tion)
ve·lar·ize (*or* ·ise)
phonetics term
ve·late biology term

Vel·cro (*Trademark*)
veld (*or* **veldt**)
ve·leta (*or* **va·**) dance
veli·ger mollusc larva
ve·li·tes Roman troops
vel·le·ity (*plural* **·ities**) a
  wish
Vel·lore Indian town
vel·lum parchment; *compare*
  velum
ve·lo·ce musical term
ve·loci·pede early bicycle
ve·loc·ity (*plural* **·ities**)
ve·lo·drome cycle-racing
  arena
ve·lours (*or* **·lour**) fabric
ve·lou·té sauce
ve·lum (*plural* **·la**) biology
  term; *compare* **vellum**
ve·lure velvet
ve·lu·ti·nous covered with
  hairs
vel·vet
vel·vet·een
vel·vety
vena (*plural* **venae**) vein
vena cava (*plural* **venae**
  cavae)
ve·nal open to bribery;
  compare venial
ve·nal·ity
ve·nal·ly
ve·nat·ic (*or* **·nati·cal**) of
  hunting
ve·na·tion arrangement of
  veins; *compare* vernation
ve·na·tion·al
vend
Ven·da (*plural* **·da** *or*
  ·das) African people
ven·dace (*plural* **·daces** *or*
  ·dace) fish
Ven·dée French department
ven·dee buyer
vend·er *variant spelling of*
  vendor
ven·det·ta
ven·det·tist
vend·ibil·ity (*or*
  ·ible·ness)
vend·ible
vend·ing
ven·di·tion
ven·dor (*or* **vend·er**)
ven·due *US* public sale
ve·neer

ve·neer·er
ve·neer·ing
ven·epunc·ture *variant*
  spelling of **venipuncture**
ven·er·abil·ity (*or*
  ·able·ness)
ven·er·able
ven·er·ably
ven·er·ate
ven·era·tion
ven·era·tion·al (*or*
  ·era·tive)
ven·era·tor
ve·nereal
ve·nere·olo·gist
ve·nere·ol·ogy
ven·ery hunting; sexual
  gratification
ven·esec·tion incision into
  vein
Ve·netia ancient Italian
  region
Ve·netian
Ve·net·ic language
Ve·neto Italian region
Ven·ezue·la
Ven·ezue·lan
venge·ance
venge·ful
venge·ful·ly
venge·ful·ness
ve·nial easily forgiven;
  compare venal
ve·ni·al·ity (*or* **·al·ness**)
ve·nial·ly
Ven·ice
ven·in poison
veni·punc·ture (*or*
  ven·epunc·ture)
ve·ni·re fa·ci·as legal term
veni·son
Ve·ni·te 95th psalm
Venn dia·gram
ven·om
ven·om·ous
ve·nose
ve·nos·ity
ve·nous
ve·nous·ness
vent
vent·age small hole
ven·tail armour
ven·ter biology or legal term
ven·ti·lable
ven·ti·late

ven·ti·la·tion
ven·ti·la·tive
ven·ti·la·tor
ven·ti·la·tory
ven·tral
ven·tral·ly
ven·tri·cle
ven·tri·cose biology term
ven·tri·cos·ity
ven·tricu·lar
ven·tricu·lus (*plural* **·li**)
  zoology term
ven·tri·lo·quial (*or* **·qual**)
ven·trilo·quism (*or* **·quy**)
ven·trilo·quist
ven·trilo·quis·tic
ven·trilo·quize (*or* **·quise**)
ven·trilo·quy *variant of*
  ventriloquism
ven·ture
ven·tur·er
ven·ture·some (*or*
  ·tu·rous)
ven·ture·some·ness
Venturi tube
venue
venu·lar
ven·ule small vein
Ve·nus planet
Venus Roman goddess
Ve·nu·sian
ve·ra·cious truthful;
  compare voracious
ve·ra·cious·ness
ve·rac·ity (*plural* **·ities**)
Vera·cruz Mexican state
ve·ran·da (*or* **·dah**)
ve·ran·daed (*or* **·dahed**)
ve·ra·tri·dine chemical
  compound
vera·trine (*or* **·trin**) former
  medicine
verb
ver·bal
ver·bal·ism
ver·bal·ist
ver·bali·za·tion (*or*
  ·sa·tion)
ver·bal·ize (*or* **·ise**)
ver·bal·iz·er (*or* **·is·er**)
ver·bal·ly
ver·ba·tim
ver·be·na
ver·be·na·ceous botany
  term

ver·bi·age
ver·bid linguistics term
ver·bi·fi·ca·tion
ver·bi·fy (·fies, ·fy·ing, ·fied)
ver·bose
ver·bose·ly
ver·bos·ity (or ·bose·ness)
ver·bo·ten German forbidden
ver·dan·cy
ver·dant
ver·der·er
ver·dict
ver·di·gris
ver·din bird
ver·dure
ver·dur·ous
Ve·ree·ni·ging South African city
verge
ver·ger
ver·glas (plural ·glases) thin ice
ve·ridi·cal truthful
ve·ridi·cal·ity
veri·fi·able
veri·fi·ca·tion
veri·fi·ca·tive (or ·tory)
veri·fi·er
veri·fy (·fies, ·fy·ing, ·fied)
veri·ly
veri·simi·lar likely
veri·si·mili·tude
ver·ism extreme realism
ve·ris·mo type of opera
ver·ist
ve·ris·tic
veri·table
veri·table·ness
veri·tably
ver·ity (plural ·ities)
ver·juice
ver·kramp·te Afrikaner nationalist
ver·lig·te South African liberal
ver·meil gilded metal
ver·mi·cel·li
ver·mi·cid·al
ver·mi·cide
ver·micu·lar wormlike
ver·micu·late
ver·micu·la·tion

ver·micu·lite mineral
ver·mi·form
ver·mi·fuge worm-expelling drug
ver·mil·ion (or ·mil·lion)
ver·min
ver·mi·na·tion infestation with vermin
ver·mi·nous
ver·min·ous·ness
ver·mis (plural ·mes) part of brain
ver·mivo·rous worm-eating
Ver·mont
Ver·mont·er
ver·mouth
ver·nacu·lar
ver·nacu·lar·ism
ver·nal
ver·nali·za·tion (or ·sa·tion)
ver·nal·ize (or ·ise) botany term
ver·nal·ly
ver·na·tion leaf arrangement in bud; compare venation
ver·ni·er measuring scale
ver·nis·sage opening of art exhibition
Ve·ro·na Italian city
Vero·nal (Trademark) drug
ve·roni·ca shrub
ver·ru·ca (plural ·cae or ·cas)
ver·ru·cose (or ·cous)
ver·ru·cos·ity
Ver·sailles
ver·sant mountain side
ver·sa·tile
ver·sa·til·ity (or ·tile·ness)
verse
versed
ver·si·cle
ver·si·col·our (US ·or)
ver·si·fi·ca·tion
ver·si·fi·er
ver·si·fy (·fies, ·fy·ing, ·fied)
ver·sion
ver·sion·al
vers li·bre French free verse
ver·so (plural ·sos) left-hand page

ver·sus against
vert heraldry term
ver·te·bra (plural ·brae or ·bras)
ver·te·bral
ver·te·brate
ver·te·bra·tion
ver·tex (plural ·texes or ·tices) apex; compare vortex
ver·ti·cal
ver·ti·cal·ity (or ·ness)
ver·ti·cal·ly
ver·ti·ces plural of vertex
ver·ti·cil biology term
ver·ti·cil·las·ter botany term
ver·ti·cil·las·trate
ver·tic·il·late
ver·tic·il·la·tion
ver·tigi·nous of vertigo
ver·tigi·nous·ness
ver·ti·go (plural ·ti·goes or ·tigi·nes)
ver·tu variant spelling of virtu
Vertumnus Roman god
(verucca) incorrect spelling of verruca
Veru·la·mium Latin St Albans
ver·vain plant
verve
ver·vet monkey
very
Very light
vesi·ca (plural ·cae) bladder
vesi·cal of the bladder; compare vesicle
vesi·cant (or ·ca·tory; plural ·cants or ·ca·tories) blistering substance
vesi·cate
vesi·ca·tion
vesi·cle small cavity; compare vesical
ve·sicu·lar
ve·sicu·late
ve·sicu·la·tion
ves·per evening prayer
ves·per·al prayer book
ves·pers canonical hour
ves·per·tilio·nid zoology term
ves·per·tilio·nine

ves·per·tine occurring in the evening
ves·pi·ary (*plural* ·**aries**) wasps' nest
ves·pid entomology term
ves·pine of wasps
ves·sel
vest
Ves·ta asteroid
Vesta Roman goddess
ves·ta wooden match
ves·tal virgin
vest·ed
ves·ti·ary (*plural* ·**aries**) room for clothes
ves·tibu·lar
ves·ti·bule
ves·tige
ves·tig·ial
vest·ment
vest·ment·al
vest·ment·ed
ves·tral
ves·try (*plural* ·**tries**)
vestry·man (*plural* ·**men**)
ves·tur·al
ves·ture garment
ve·su·vi·an·ite mineral
Ve·su·vi·us
vet (**vet·ting**, **vet·ted**)
vetch
vetch·ling
vet·er·an
vet·eri·nar·ian
vet·eri·nary
veti·ver a grass
veto (*noun, plural* **vetoes**; *verb* **vetoes**, **ve·to·ing**, **ve·toed**)
ve·to·er
vet·ted
vet·ting
vex
vexa·tion
vexa·tious
vexa·tious·ness
vex·ed·ly
vex·ed·ness
vex·er
vex·il·lary (*or* ·**lar**)
vex·il·late
vex·il·lolo·gist
vex·il·lol·ogy study of flags
vex·il·lum (*plural* ·**la**) biology term

vex·ing·ly
via
vi·abil·ity
vi·able
Via Dolo·ro·sa road to Calvary
via·duct
vial *less common spelling of* **phial**
via me·dia *Latin* compromise
vi·and a food
vi·ands provisions
vi·ati·cum (*plural* ·**ca** *or* ·**cums**)
vibes *Slang* vibrations; vibraphone
vib·ist vibraphone player
vi·bracu·lar
vi·bracu·loid
vi·bracu·lum (*plural* ·**la**) zoology term
vi·bra·harp musical instrument
vi·bran·cy
vi·brant
vi·bra·phone
vi·bra·phon·ist
vi·brate
vi·bra·tile
vi·bra·til·ity
vi·brat·ing·ly
vi·bra·tion
vi·bra·tion·al
vi·bra·tive
vi·bra·to (*plural* ·**tos**)
vi·bra·tor
vi·bra·tory
vib·rio (*plural* ·**rios**) bacterium
vib·ri·oid
vi·bris·sa (*plural* ·**sae**) whisker
vi·bris·sal
vi·bron·ic physics term
vi·bur·num
vic·ar
vic·ar·age
vi·car·ial
vi·cari·ate (*or* **vic·ar·ship**)
vi·cari·ous
vi·cari·ous·ness
vice sin; deputy; in place of
vice (*US* **vise**) tool
vice ad·mi·ral

vice-admiral·ty
vice-chairman (*plural* -**chairmen**)
vice-chairman·ship
vice chan·cel·lor
vice-chancellor·ship
vice·ge·ral
vice·ge·ren·cy (*plural* ·**cies**)
vice·ge·rent deputy
vice·like (*US* **vise·**)
vic·enary of 20
vi·cen·nial 20 years
Vi·cen·za Italian city
vice-presiden·cy (*plural* ·**cies**)
vice presi·dent
vice-presiden·tial
vice-re·gal of viceroy
vice·reine viceroy's wife
vice·roy
vice·roy·al·ty (*plural* ·**ties**)
vice·roy·ship
vice ver·sa
Vi·chy French town
vi·chy·ssoise soup
vici·nal
vi·cin·ity (*plural* ·**ities**)
vi·cious
vi·cious·ness
vi·cis·si·tude
vi·cis·si·tu·di·nary (*or* ·**di·nous**)
Vicks·burg US city
vi·comte (*fem* ·**com·tesse**) French noble
vic·tim
vic·timi·za·tion (*or* ·**sa·tion**)
vic·tim·ize (*or* ·**ise**)
vic·tim·iz·er (*or* ·**is·er**)
vic·tor
Vic·to·ria place name
vic·to·ria carriage; plum; water lily
Vic·to·rian
Vic·to·ri·ana
Vic·to·ri·an·ism
vic·to·ri·ous
vic·to·ri·ous·ness
vic·to·ry (*plural* ·**ries**)
vict·ual (·**ual·ling**, ·**ualled**; *US* ·**ual·ing**, ·**ualed**)
vict·ual·ler (*US also* ·**ual·er**)

vict·uals
vi·cu·ña
vide *Latin* see
vi·deli·cet *Latin* namely
video (*noun, plural*
  videos; *verb* videos,
  video·ing, videoed)
vid·eo·phone
vid·eo·phon·ic
video-tape (*verb*)
vidi·con small television
  camera tube
vie (vying, vied)
Vi·en·na Austrian capital
Vienne French river;
  department
Vi·en·nese (*plural* ·nese)
Vien·ti·ane Laotian capital
Vi·et·cong (*or* Viet Cong)
Vi·et·minh (*or* Viet
  Minh)
Vi·et·nam
Vi·et·nam·ese (*plural*
  ·ese)
view
view·able
view·er
view·finder
view·ing
view·less
view·point
vi·gesi·mal of 20
vig·il
vigi·lance
vigi·lant
vigi·lan·te
vi·gnette
vi·gnet·ting photography
  term
vi·gnet·tist
Vigo Spanish port
vi·go·ro·so musical term
vig·or·ous
vig·or·ous·ness
vig·our (*US* ·or)
Vi·jaya·wa·da Indian town
Vi·king
vi·la·yet Turkish
  administrative division
vile
vile·ly
vile·ness
vili·fi·ca·tion
vili·fi·er
vili·fy (·fies, ·fy·ing, ·fied)

vili·pend treat with
  contempt
vil·la
vil·lage
vil·lag·er
Vil·la·her·mo·sa Mexican
  town
vil·lain (*fem* ·lain·ess)
  wicked person; *compare*
  villein
vil·lain·ous
vil·lain·ous·ness
vil·lainy (*plural* ·lainies)
vil·la·nel·la (*plural* ·las)
  song
vil·la·nelle verse form
Vil·la·no·van archaeology
  term
vil·lat·ic rustic
vil·lein serf; *compare* villain
Ville·ur·banne French
  town
vil·li *plural of* villus
vil·li·form
vil·los·ity (*plural* ·ities)
vil·lous
vil·lus (*plural* ·li)
Vil·ni·us (*or* ·ny·) Soviet
  city
vim *Slang* vigour
vi·men (*plural* vimi·na)
  plant shoot
Vimi·nal Roman hill
vi·min·eous
vina musical instrument
vi·na·ceous
Viña del Mar Chilean city
vinai·grette
vi·nasse residue in a still
vin·cible
vin·cu·lum (*plural* ·la)
  maths symbol; anatomy
  term
vin·di·cabil·ity
vin·di·cable
vin·di·cate
vin·di·ca·tion
vin·di·ca·tor
vin·di·ca·tory
vin·dic·tive
vin·dic·tive·ly
vin·dic·tive·ness
vine
vine·dresser
vin·egar

vin·egar·roon arachnid
vin·egary
vin·ery (*plural* ·eries)
  place for growing grapes
vine·yard
vine·yard·ist
vingt-et-un card game
vi·nic of wine
vini·cul·tur·al
vini·cul·ture
vini·cul·tur·ist
vi·nif·er·ous
vi·nifi·ca·tion
vi·nifi·ca·tor wine-making
  apparatus
Vin·land *Viking name for*
  NE America
Vin·ni·tsa Soviet city
vino (*plural* vinos) *Slang*
  wine
vin or·di·naire (*plural*
  vins or·di·naires)
vi·nos·ity
vi·nous
vin·tage
vin·tag·er grape harvester
vint·ner
viny
(vinyard) *incorrect spelling
  of* vineyard
vi·nyl
vi·nyli·dene chemistry term
viol
vio·la
vio·labil·ity (*or*
  ·lable·ness)
vio·lable
vio·la·ceous botany term
vio·la da gam·ba
vio·la d'amo·re
vio·late
vio·la·tion
vio·la·tive
vio·la·tor (*or* ·lat·er)
vio·lence
vio·lent
vio·let
vio·lin
vio·lin·ist
vi·ol·ist
vio·lon·cel·list
vio·lon·cel·lo (*plural* ·los)
  cello
vio·lone musical instrument
vi·per

vi·per·ine

vi·per·ous (*or* ·ish)

vi·ragi·nous

vi·ra·go (*plural* ·goes *or* ·gos)

vi·ral

vir·elay poem

vireo (*plural* vireos) bird

vi·res·cence

vi·res·cent becoming green

vir·ga meteorology term

vir·gate rod-shaped; obsolete land measure

vir·gin

vir·gin·al

vir·gin·al·ly

Vir·ginia

Vir·gin·ian

vir·gin·ity

virgin's-bower plant

Vir·go constellation; sign of zodiac

Vir·goan

vir·go in·tac·ta virgin

vir·gu·late rod-shaped

vir·gule printing term

viri·des·cence

viri·des·cent becoming green

vi·rid·ian green pigment

vi·rid·ity greenness

vir·ile

viri·lism medical term

vi·ril·ity

vi·ro·logi·cal

vi·rolo·gist

vi·rol·ogy

vir·tu (*or* ver·) connoisseurship

vir·tual

vir·tu·al·ity

vir·tu·al·ly

vir·tue

vir·tu·os·ic

vir·tu·os·ity

vir·tuo·so (*plural* ·sos *or* ·si)

vir·tu·ous

vir·tu·ous·ness

viru·lence

viru·lent

vi·rus (*plural* ·ruses) bird

visa (vi·sa·ing, vi·saed)

vis·age

Vi·sa·kha·pat·nam *variant of* Vishakhapatnam

vis-à-vis

Vi·sa·yan (*plural* ·yans *or* ·yan) Philippine people

vis·ca·cha (*or* viz·) animal

vis·cera (*sing.* ·cus) internal organs

vis·cer·al

vis·ce·ro·mo·tor physiology term

vis·cid

vis·cid·ity (*or* ·ness)

vis·coid (*or* ·coi·dal)

vis·com·eter (*or* ·co·sim·eter)

vis·co·met·ric (*or* ·ri·cal)

vis·com·etry

vis·cose

vis·cos·ity (*plural* ·ities)

vis·count

vis·count·cy (*or* ·county; *plural* ·cies *or* ·counties)

vis·count·ess

vis·cous thick; *compare* viscus

vis·cous·ness

vis·cus *sing. of* viscera; *compare* viscous

vise *US spelling of* vice

Vi·sha·kha·pat·nam (*or* Vi·sa·kha·pat·nam, Vi·za·ga·pa·tam) Indian port

Vishnu Hindu god

vis·ibil·ity

vis·ible

vis·ible·ness

vis·ibly

Visi·goth

vi·sion

vi·sion·al

vi·sion·ari·ness

vi·sion·ary (*plural* ·aries)

vis·it

vis·it·able

visi·tant

vis·ita·tion

vis·ita·tion·al

vis·ita·to·rial of official visitation

visi·tor

visi·to·rial

vi·sor (*or* ·zor)

vi·sored (*or* ·zored)

vis·ta

vis·taed

Vis·tu·la Polish river

vis·ual

visu·ali·za·tion (*or* ·sa·tion)

visu·al·ize (*or* ·ise)

visu·al·iz·er (*or* ·is·er)

visu·al·ly

vi·ta·ceous botany term

vi·tal

vi·tal·ism philosophical doctrine

vi·tal·ist

vi·tal·is·tic

vi·tal·ity (*plural* ·ities)

vi·tali·za·tion (*or* ·sa·tion)

vi·tal·ize (*or* ·ise)

vi·tal·iz·er (*or* ·is·er)

vi·tal·ly

vi·tals

vita·min

vita·min·ic

Vi·tebsk Soviet city

vi·tel·lin protein

vi·tel·line of egg yolk

vi·ti·able

vi·ti·ate

vi·tia·tion

vi·tia·tor

viti·cul·tur·al

viti·cul·ture grape cultivation

viti·cul·tur·er (*or* ·ist)

viti·li·go unpigmented skin

Vi·to·ria Spanish city

Vi·tó·ria Brazilian port

vit·rain coal

vit·re·ous

vit·re·ous·ness (*or* ·os·ity)

vi·tres·cence

vi·tres·cent

vit·ric of glass

vit·ri·fi·abil·ity

vit·ri·fi·able

vit·ri·fi·ca·tion

vit·ri·form

vit·ri·fy (·fies, ·fy·ing, ·fied)

vit·rine glass display case

vit·ri·ol (·ol·ing, ·oled *or* ·ol·ling, ·olled)

vit·ri·ol·ic

vit·ri·oli·za·tion (*or* ·sa·tion)

vit·ri·ol·ize (or ·ise)
vit·ta (plural ·tae) biology
  term
vit·tate
vi·tu·line of calves
vi·tu·per·ate
vi·tu·pera·tion
vi·tu·pera·tive
vi·tu·pera·tor
viva (vi·va·ing, vi·vaed)
  short for viva voce
vi·va·ce musical term
vi·va·cious
vi·va·vious·ly
vi·va·cious·ness
vi·vac·ity (plural ·ities)
vi·var·ium (plural ·iums
  or ·ia)
viva voce oral exam
vi·ver·rine zoology term
viv·id
viv·id·ness
vivi·fi·ca·tion
vivi·fi·er
vivi·fy (·fies, ·fy·ing, ·fied)
vivi·par·ity (or
  vi·vipa·rism,
  vi·vipa·rous·ness)
vi·vip·ar·ous
vivi·sect
vivi·sec·tion
vivi·sec·tion·al
vivi·sec·tion·ist
vivi·sec·tor
vix·en
vix·en·ish
vix·en·ish·ness
Vi·yel·la (Trademark)
Vi·za·ga·pa·tam variant
  spelling of Vishakhapatnam
viz·ard mask
viz·ca·cha variant spelling of
  viscacha
vi·zier
vi·zier·ate
vi·zor variant spelling of visor
Vlach (or Wa·lach)
  medieval European people
Vla·di·mir Soviet port
Vla·di·vos·tok Soviet port
vo·cab short for vocabulary
vo·cable vocal sound
vo·cabu·lary (plural
  ·laries)
vo·cal

vo·cal·ic
vo·cal·ise vocal exercise;
  variant spelling of vocalize
vo·cal·ism
vo·cal·ist
vo·cal·ity (or ·ness)
vo·cali·za·tion (or
  ·sa·tion)
vo·cal·ize (or ·ise)
vo·cal·iz·er (or ·is·er)
vo·cal·ly
vo·ca·tion
vo·ca·tion·al
voca·tive
vo·cif·er·ance
vo·cif·er·ant
vo·cif·er·ate
vo·cif·era·tion
vo·cif·era·tor
vo·cif·er·ous
vo·cif·er·ous·ness
vod·ka
vogue
voguish
Vo·gul (plural ·gul or
  ·guls) Siberian people
voice
voiced
voice·ful
voice·less
voice·less·ness
voice-over
voice·print
voic·er
void
void·able
void·able·ness
void·ance annulment
void·ed
void·er
voile fabric
Voio·tia Greek department
voir dire legal term
Voj·vo·di·na (or Voi·)
  Yugoslav region
Vo·lans constellation
vo·lant
Vola·puk artificial language
Vola·puk·ist
vo·lar anatomy term
vola·tile
vola·til·ity
vo·lati·liz·able (or
  ·lis·able)

vo·lati·liza·tion (or
  ·lisa·tion)
vo·lati·lize (or ·lise)
vol-au-vent
vol·can·ic
vol·cani·cal·ly
vol·can·ic·ity
vol·can·ism (or vul·)
vol·cani·za·tion (or
  ·sa·tion)
vol·can·ize (or ·ise)
vol·ca·no (plural ·noes or
  ·nos)
vol·cano·logi·cal (or vul·)
vol·cano·olo·gist (or vul·)
vol·can·ol·ogy (or vul·)
vole
Vol·ga Soviet river
Vol·go·grad Soviet port
voli·tant moving rapidly
vo·li·tion
vo·li·tion·al (or ·ary)
voli·tive of the will
vol·ley
volley·ball
vol·ley·er
Vo·log·da Soviet city
vo·lost peasant community
vol·plane glide without
  power
Vol·sci Latin people
volt
Vol·ta African river or lake
vol·ta (plural ·te) dance
volt·age
vol·ta·ic
vol·ta·ism
vol·tam·eter instrument
  measuring electric charge;
  compare voltmeter
volt·am·meter instrument
  measuring volts or
  amperes; compare
  voltmeter
volt-ampere unit
Vol·ta Re·don·da Brazilian
  city
volte-face (plural volte-
  face) reversal of opinion
volt·me·ter instrument
  measuring volts; compare
  voltameter; voltammeter
vol·ubil·ity (or ·uble·ness)
vol·uble
vol·ubly
vol·ume

vol·umed

vo·lu·meter

volu·met·ric

volu·met·ri·cal·ly

vo·lu·metry

vo·lu·mi·nos·ity (*or* ·nous·ness)

vo·lu·mi·nous

vol·un·tar·ily

vol·un·tari·ness

vol·un·ta·rism (*or* ·tary·)

vol·un·ta·rist (*or* ·tary·)

vol·un·ta·ris·tic

vol·un·tary (*plural* ·aries)

vol·un·teer

vo·lup·tu·ary (*plural* ·aries)

vo·lup·tu·ous

vo·lup·tu·ous·ness (*or* ·os·ity)

vol·ute

vo·lu·tion

vol·va (*plural* ·vae *or* ·vas) mushroom sheath; *compare* vulva

vol·vate

Volvo (*Trademark*)

vol·vox microscopic animal

vol·vu·lus (*plural* ·luses) intestinal disorder

vo·mer bone

vo·mer·ine

vom·it

vom·it·er

vomi·tive

vomi·tory (*plural* ·tories)

vomi·tu·ri·tion retching

vomi·tus (*plural* ·tuses) vomited matter

voo·doo (*noun, plural* ·doos; *verb* ·doos, ·doo·ing, ·dooed)

voo·doo·ism

voo·doo·ist

voo·doo·is·tic

Voor·trek·ker Afrikaner settler

vo·ra·cious greedy; *compare* veracious

vo·rac·ity (*or* ·ra·cious·ness)

Vor·arl·berg Austrian province

vor·la·ge skiing position

Vo·ro·nezh Soviet city

Vo·ro·shi·lov·grad Soviet city

vor·tex (*plural* ·texes *or* ·ti·ces) whirling mass; *compare* vertex

vor·ti·cal

vor·ti·cel·la (*plural* ·lae) protozoan

vor·ti·ces *plural of* vortex

vor·ti·cism art movement

vor·ti·cist

vor·tigi·nous

Vosges French mountain range

Vos·tok Soviet spacecraft

vot·able (*or* vote·)

vo·tar·ess (*or* vo·tress)

vo·ta·rist

vo·ta·ry (*plural* ·ries)

vote

vote·able *variant spelling of* votable

vot·er

vo·tive

vo·tive·ness

vo·tress *variant of* votaress

Vo·ty·ak (*plural* ·aks *or* ·ak) Finnish people

vouch

vouch·er

vouch·safe

vouch·safe·ment

vouge weapon

vous·soir wedge-shaped stone

Vou·vray wine

vow

vow·el

vow·eli·za·tion (*or* ·sa·tion)

vow·el·ize (*or* ·ise)

vowel·less

vow·er

vox (*plural* vo·ces) voice

vox hu·ma·na organ stop

vox po·pu·li public opinion

voy·age

voy·ag·er

vo·ya·geur Canadian woodsman

vo·yeur

vo·yeur·ism

vo·yeur·is·tic

vo·yeur·is·ti·cal·ly

vrai·sem·blance verisimilitude

vroom exclamation

vug mining term

Vulcan Roman god

vul·ca·nian volcanic

vul·can·ism *variant spelling of* volcanism

vul·can·ite hard rubber

vul·can·iz·able (*or* ·is·able)

vul·cani·za·tion (*or* ·sa·tion)

vul·can·ize (*or* ·ise)

vul·can·iz·er (*or* ·is·er)

vul·can·ol·ogy *variant spelling of* volcanology

vul·gar

vul·gar·ian

vul·gar·ism

vul·gar·ity (*plural* ·ities)

vul·gari·za·tion (*or* ·sa·tion)

vul·gar·ize (*or* ·ise)

vul·gar·iz·er (*or* ·is·er)

vul·gar·ness

Vul·gate Latin Bible

vul·gate commonly accepted text

vul·ner·abil·ity (*or* ·able·ness)

vul·ner·able

vul·ner·ably

vul·ner·ary (*plural* ·aries) wound-healing drug

Vul·pecu·la constellation

vul·pine (*or* ·pecu·lar) of foxes

vul·ture

vul·tur·ine

vul·tur·ous

vul·va (*plural* ·vae *or* ·vas) female external genitals; *compare* volva

vul·val (*or* ·var, ·vate)

vul·vi·form

vul·vi·tis

vul·vo·vagi·ni·tis

vy·ing

W

Wa·bash US river
wacky (wacki·er, wacki·est)
wad (wad·ding, wad·ded)
wad·able (or wade·)
wad·ding
wad·dle
wad·dler
wad·dling·ly
wad·dy (noun, plural ·dies; verb ·dies, ·dy·ing, ·died) Aboriginal club; compare wadi
wade
wade·able variant spelling of wadable
wad·er
wad·ers
wadi (or wady; plural wadis or wa·dies) watercourse; compare waddy
Wadi Hal·fa Sudanese town
Wad Me·da·ni Sudanese town
wad·set (·set·ting, ·set·ted) Scot mortgage
wady variant spelling of wadi
wae Dialect woe
wa·fer
wa·fery
waff Dialect gust
waf·fle
waft
waft·age
waft·er
wag (wag·ging, wagged)
wage
wa·ger
wa·ger·er
wages
wag·ga Austral blanket
Wag·ga Wag·ga Australian city
wagged
wag·gery
wag·ging
wag·gish

wag·gish·ness
wag·gle
wag·gling·ly
wag·gly
Wag·ne·rian
wag·on (or wag·gon)
wag·on·er (or wag·gon·)
wag·on·ette (or wag·gon·)
wagon-lit (plural wagons-lits) sleeping car
wagon·load (or waggon·)
wag·tail
Wah·ha·bi (or Wa·ha·bi; plural ·bis) conservative Muslim
wa·hi·ne Polynesian woman
wa·hoo (plural ·hoos) tree; fish
waif
Wai·ka·to New Zealand river
Wai·ki·ki Hawaiian resort
wail
wail·er
wail·ful
wail·ing·ly
wain farm wagon; compare wane
wain·scot
wain·scot·ed
wain·scot·ing (or ·scot·ting)
wain·wright
waist
waist·band
waist·coat
waist·ed
waist·less
waist·line
wait
wait·er
wait·ress
waive relinquish; compare wave
waiv·er relinquishment; compare waver
Wa·kash·an American Indian language
Wa·ka·ya·ma Japanese city

wake (wak·ing, woke, wok·en)
Wake·field
wake·ful
wake·ful·ly
wake·ful·ness
wake·less
wak·en
wak·en·er
wak·er
wake·rife Dialect wakeful
wake-robin plant
wak·ing
Wa·lach variant of Vlach
Wa·la·chia (or Wal·la·chia) former European principality
Wał·brzych Polish city
Wal·che·ren Dutch island
Wal·den·ses Catholic sect
wald·grave medieval German forest officer
Wal·dorf sal·ad
wale weal; ridge
Wa·ler horse; compare whaler
Wales
walk
walk·able
walk·about
walk·er
walkie-talkie (or walky-talky; plural -talkies)
walk-in (adj)
walk·ing
walk-on (noun, adj)
walk·out (noun)
walk·over (noun)
walk·way
Wal·kyrie variant spelling of Valkyrie
walky-talky variant spelling of walkie-talkie
wall
wal·la·by (plural ·bies or ·by)
Wal·la·chia variant spelling of Walachia
wal·lah (or wal·la) Slang person in charge

wal·la·roo (*plural* ·roos *or* ·roo) large kangaroo

Wal·la·sey Merseyside town

wall·board

walled

wal·let

wall·eye (*plural* ·eyes *or* ·eye)

wall·eyed

wall·flower

wall·like

Wal·loon French-speaking Belgian

wal·lop

wal·lop·er

wal·lop·ing

wal·low

wal·low·er

wall·paper

Walls·end English town

wall-to-wall

wal·ly *Slang* idiot; *Scot* made of china

wal·nut

Wal·pur·gis Night

wal·rus (*plural* ·ruses *or* ·rus)

Wal·sall

waltz

waltz·er

wame *Dialect* belly; womb

wam·pum shell money

wan (*adj* wan·ner, wan·nest; *verb* wan·ning, wanned)

wand

wan·der

wan·der·er

wan·der·ing

wan·der·ing·ly

wan·der·lust

wan·deroo (*plural* ·deroos) monkey

wan·doo (*plural* ·doos) tree

Wands·worth

wane decrease; *compare* wain

waney (*or* wany; wani·er, wani·est)

Wan·ga·nui New Zealand port

wan·gle

wan·gler

wank

wan·na *Slang* want to

wanned

wan·ner

wan·nest

wan·ning

want

want·er

want·ing

wan·ton

wan·ton·ness

wap·en·take former county division

wapi·ti (*plural* ·tis) deer

wap·pen·shaw gathering of clans

war (war·ring, warred)

Wa·ran·gal Indian city

wa·ra·tah shrub

warb *Austral* dirty person

war·ble

war·bler

ward

ward·ed

war·den

war·den·ry

war·der (*fem* ·dress)

ward·robe

ward·room

ward·ship

ware *Archaic* beware

ware·house

ware·house·man (*plural* ·men)

wares goods

war·fare

war·fa·rin

war·head

war·horse

wari·ly

wari·ness

wari·son bugle note

War·ley English town

war·like

war·lock

war·lord

warm

warm-blooded

warm-blooded·ness

warm·er

warm-hearted

warm-hearted·ness

warm·ish

warm·ness

war·monger

warmth

warm-up (*noun*)

warn

warn·er

warn·ing

warp

warp·age

war·path

warp·er

war·plane

war·rant

war·rant·abil·ity

war·rant·able

war·rant·ably

war·rant·ee

war·rant·er one who warrants

war·ran·tor warranty giver

war·ran·ty (*plural* ·ties)

warred

war·ren

war·rig·al *Austral* dingo

war·ring

War·ring·ton Cheshire town

war·ri·or

War·saw

war·ship

war·sle *Dialect* wrestle

wart

wart·ed

war·time

warty (warti·er, warti·est)

War·wick

War·wick·shire

wary (wari·er, wari·est)

was

wash

wash·abil·ity

wash·able

wash·basin

wash·board

wash·bowl

wash·day

wash·er

washer·man (*plural* ·men)

washer·woman (*or* wash·woman; *plural* ·women)

wash·ery (*plural* ·eries)

wash-house

washi·ly

wash-in aeronautics term

washi·ness

wash·ing

Wash·ing·ton

Wash·ing·to·nian
washing-up
wash·out (*noun*)
wash·rag *US* face cloth
wash·room
wash·stand
wash·tub
wash·woman *variant of*
    washerwoman
washy (washi·er,
    washi·est)
wasn't
wasp
waspi·ly
waspi·ness
wasp·ish
wasp·ish·ness
waspy
was·sail
was·sail·er
wast·able
wast·age
waste
waste·ful
waste·ful·ly
waste·ful·ness
waste·land
waste·paper
wast·er
waste·weir water channel
wast·rel
wat Thai monastery
wa·tap American Indian
    thread
watch
watch·case
watch·dog
watch·er
watch·ful
watch·ful·ly
watch·ful·ness
watch·glass
watch·maker
watch·making
watch·man (*plural* ·men)
watch·strap
watch·tower
watch·word
wa·ter
wa·ter·age transportation
    by ship
water·bed
water·borne
water·buck antelope
water·colour (*US* ·color)

water·colour·ist (*US*
    ·color·)
water·cool
water·cooled
water·course
water·craft
water·cress
wa·ter·er
water·fall
Wa·ter·ford
water·fowl
water·front
Water·gate
wa·teri·ness
wa·ter·less
water·logged
Wa·ter·loo
water·man (*plural* ·men)
water·man·ship
water·mark
water·melon
water·proof
water·proof·ness
water·repellent
water·resistant
water·scape
water·shed
water·sick excessively
    irrigated
water·side
water·ski (*noun, plural*
    -skis; *verb* -skis,
    -skiing, -skied *or* ski'd)
water·skier
water·spout
water·tight
water·tightness
water·way
water·weed
water·works
water·worn
wa·tery
Wat·ford
watt unit
watt·age
watt·hour
wat·tle
wattle·bird
watt·meter
Wa·tu·si (*or* ·tut·; *plural*
    ·sis *or* ·si) African people
waul (*or* wawl) wail
wave undulation, etc.; move
    to and fro; *compare* waive
wave·band

wave·form physics term
wave·guide electronics term
wave·length
wave·let
wave·like
wa·vell·ite mineral
wave·meter
wave·off signal to aircraft
wa·ver hesitate; one who
    waves; *compare* waiver
wa·ver·er
wa·ver·ing·ly
wavi·ly
wavi·ness
wavy (wavi·er, wavi·est)
wawl *variant spelling of* waul
wax
wax·berry (*plural*
    ·berries)
wax·bill bird
wax·en
wax·er
waxi·ly
waxi·ness
wax·like
wax·plant
wax·wing bird
wax·work object
wax·work·er
wax·works exhibition
waxy (waxi·er, waxi·est)
way
way·bill document
way·farer
way·faring
Way·land legendary smith
way·lay (·lay·ing, ·laid)
way·lay·er
way·out
way·side
way·ward
way·ward·ness
wayz·goose printers' annual
    outing
Wa·ziri·stan Asian region
we
weak
weak·en
weak·en·er
weak·fish (*plural* ·fish *or*
    ·fishes)
weak·kneed
weak·li·ness
weak·ling
weak·ly (·li·er, ·li·est)

weak-minded

506

weak-minded
weak-minded·ness
weak·ness
weak-willed
weal prosperity
weal (or wheal) mark on skin
Weald English region
weald open country; compare wield
wealth
wealthi·ly
wealthi·ness
wealthy (wealthi·er, wealthi·est)
wean
wean·er
wean·ling
weap·on
weap·oned
weap·on·eer
wea·pon·ry
Wear English river
wear (wear·ing, wore, worn)
wear·abil·ity
wear·able
wear·er
wea·ri·ful variant of wearisome
wea·ri·less
wea·ri·ly
wea·ri·ness
wear·ing
wear·ing·ly
wea·ri·some (or ·ful)
wea·ri·some·ness (or ·ful·ness)
wear·proof
wea·ry (adj ·ri·er, ·ri·est; verb ·ries, ry·ing, ·ried)
wea·ry·ing·ly
wea·sand Dialect windpipe
wea·sel (plural ·sel or ·sels)
wea·sel·ly
weath·er climatic conditions; compare wether; whether
weath·er·abil·ity
weather-beaten
weather·board
weather·boarding
weather-bound
weather·cock

weath·er·er
weather·glass
weath·er·ing
weath·er·ly nautical term
weather·man (plural ·men)
weather·proof
weather-wise
weather·worn
weave (weav·ing, wove or weaved, wo·ven or weaved)
weav·er one who weaves; compare weever
weav·ing
web (web·bing, webbed)
web·bing
web·by (·bi·er, ·bi·est)
we·ber unit
web·foot
web-footed
web-toed
wed (wed·ding, wed·ded or wed)
we'd we had; we would
wed·ding
wed·el·ing skiing turn
wedge
Wedg·wood (Trademark) pottery
wedgy
wed·lock
Wednes·day
wee (wee·ing, wee'd) Slang tiny; to urinate
weed
weed·er
weedi·ly
weedi·ness
weed·killer
weedy (weedi·er, weedi·est)
week
week·day
week·end
week·end·er
week·ly (plural ·lies)
week·night
wee·ny (or ween·sy; ·ni·er, ·ni·est or ·si·er, ·si·est)
weep (weep·ing, wept)
weep·er
weepi·ness

weep·ing
weep·ing·ly
weepy (adj weepi·er, weepi·est; noun, plural weepies)
wee·ver fish; compare weaver
wee·vil
wee·vily
weft
Wehr·macht German armed service
wei·ge·la shrub
weigh
weigh·able
weigh·bridge
weigh·er
weight
weight·er
weighti·ly
weighti·ness
weight·ing
weight·less
weight·less·ness
weight-lifter
weight-lifting
weighty (weighti·er, weighti·est)
Wei·hai Chinese port
Wei·mar East German city
Wei·mar·an·er dog
(Weir) incorrect spelling of Wear
weir
weird
weir·die (or ·do; plural ·dies or ·dos)
weird·ness
Weis·mann·ism biological theory
weka bird
Welch variant spelling of Welsh, now obsolete except in regimental names, esp. Royal Welch Fusiliers
welch variant spelling of welsh
wel·come
wel·come·ly
wel·come·ness
wel·com·er
weld
weld·abil·ity
weld·able
weld·er (or wel·dor)

wel·fare

(welk) *incorrect spelling of*
 whelk

Wel·kom South African
 town

well

we'll we will; we shall

well-accustomed

well-acquaint·ed

well-acted

well-adapted

well-advised

well-appoint·ed

well-argued

well-assort·ed

well-attend·ed

well-aware

well-balanced

well-behaved

well·being

well·bred

well·built

well-connect·ed

well-construct·ed

well-defined

well-deserved

well-developed

well-disposed

well-document·ed

well-done

well-dressed

well-educat·ed

well-endowed

well-equipped

well-established

well-favoured (*US*
 ·favored)

well-fed

well-found

well-founded

well-groomed

well-grounded

well·head

well-heeled

well-hung

wel·lies *Slang* Wellington
 boots

well-informed

Wel·ling·ton New Zealand
 capital; boot

well-intentioned

well-judged

well-knit

well-known

well-mannered

well-matched

well-meaning

well-nigh

well-off

well-oiled

well-organized (*or*
 -organised)

well-paid

well-pleased

well-preserved

well-propor·tioned

well-provid·ed

well-qualified

well-read

well-received

well-rounded

Wells Somerset city

well-situat·ed

well-spent

well-spoken

well·spring

well-support·ed

well-tempered

well-thought-of

well-timed

well-to-do

well-tried

well-turned

well-wisher

well-wishing

well-worded

well-worn

Welsh

welsh (*or* welch) fail in
 obligation

Welsh·man (*plural* ·men)

Welsh·woman (*plural*
 ·women)

welt

wel·ter

wel·ter·weight

wel·witschia plant

Wel·wyn Gar·den City

Wem·bley

wen cyst

wench

wench·er

Wend Slavonic people

wend

Wend·ish

Wen·dy house

Wens·ley·dale Yorkshire
 town; cheese

went

wen·tle·trap mollusc

wept

were

we're we are

weren't were not

were·wolf (*plural* ·wolves)

wer·gild (*or* were·gild,
 wer·geld) price on life

wer·ner·ite mineral

Wes·ley·an

Wes·ley·an·ism

Wes·sex

west

west·bound

West Brom·wich

west·er to move towards
 west

west·er·ing

west·er·li·ness

west·er·ly (*plural* ·lies)

west·ern

west·ern·er

west·ern·ism

west·erni·za·tion (*or*
 ·sa·tion)

west·ern·ize (*or* ·ise)

west·ern·most

West Ger·man

West Ger·many

West In·dian

West In·dies

west·ing westerly movement

West·meath Irish county

West·min·ster

West·mor·land former
 English county

west-northwest

Weston-super-Mare

West·pha·lia

West·pha·lian

west-southwest

west·ward (*adj*)

west·wards (*adv*)

wet (*adj* wet·ter, wet·test;
 verb wet·ting, wet *or*
 wet·ted) not dry; make
 wet; *compare* whet

weth·er male sheep;
 compare weather; whether

wet·lands

wet·ness

wet-nurse (*verb*)

wet·tabil·ity

wet·table

wet·ted

wet·ter

wet·test
wet·ting
wet·tish
we've we have
Wex·ford Irish county
Wey·mouth
whack
whack·er
whack·ing
whacko exclamation
whale (*plural* **whales** *or* whale)
whale·boat
whale·bone
whal·er whale catcher; whaleboat; *compare* **Waler**
whal·ing
wham (wham·ming, whammed)
whang
Whan·ga·rei New Zealand port
whangee bamboo grass
whare Maori hut
wharf (*plural* **wharves** *or* wharfs)
wharf·age
wharf·in·ger
wharve flywheel; pulley
what
what·ev·er
what·not
what·sit
what·so·ev·er
whaup *Scot* curlew
wheal *variant spelling of* **weal**
wheat
wheat·ear bird
wheat·en
wheat·worm
whee·dle
whee·dler
whee·dling·ly
wheel
wheel·bar·row
wheel·base
wheel·chair
wheel·er
wheeler-dealer
wheel·house
wheelie skateboarding manoeuvre
wheel·less
wheel·work
wheel·wright

wheen *Dialect* few
wheeze
wheez·er
wheezi·ly
wheezi·ness
wheez·ing·ly
wheezy (wheezi·er, wheezi·est)
whelk
whelp
when
whence
whene'er
when·ever
when·so·ever
where
where·abouts
where·as
where·at
where·by
where'er
where·fore
where·from
where·in
where·into
where·of
where·on
where·so·ever
where·to
where·upon
wher·ever
where·with
where·with·al
wher·rit worry
wher·ry (*plural* **·ries**) boat
wherry·man (*plural* **·men**)
whet (whet·ting, whet·ted) sharpen; stimulate; *compare* wet
wheth·er (*conj*) *compare* weather; wether
whet·stone
whet·ter
whey watery liquid
whey·ey (*or* **·ish, ·like**)
whey·face
whey·faced
which
which·ever
whick·er whinny; *compare* wicker
whid·ah *variant spelling of* whydah
whiff
whiff·er

whif·fle
whif·fler
whif·fle·tree crossbar in harness
Whig political party
Whig·gery (*or* **·gism**)
Whig·gish
Whig·gish·ness
while during the time that; *note* while away; *compare* wile
whilst
whim
whim·brel bird
whim·per
whim·per·er
whim·per·ing·ly
whim·si·cal
whim·si·cal·ity (*plural* **·ities**)
whim·si·cal·ly
whim·si·cal·ness
whim·sy (*or* **·sey;** *noun,* *plural* **·sies** *or* **·seys;** *adj* **·si·er, ·si·est**)
whin gorse
whin·chat bird
whine
whin·er
whinge
whin·ing·ly
whin·ny (*verb* **·nies,** **·ny·ing, ·nied;** *noun,* *plural* **·nies**)
whin·stone
whiny (whini·er, whini·est) peevish; *compare* winy
whip (whip·ping, whipped)
whip·cord
whip·lash
whip·like
whip·per
whipper-in (*plural* whippers-in)
whip·per·snap·per
whip·pet
whip·ping
whip·poor·will
whippy (whip·pier, whip·piest)
whip-round (*noun*)
whip·saw
whip·stall aeronautics term
whip·stitch

whip·stock whip handle
whip·worm
whir (*or* whirr; whir·ring, whirred)
whirl spin; confusion; *compare* whorl
whirl·about
whirl·er
whirli·gig
whirl·ing·ly
whirl·pool
whirl·wind
whirly·bird
whirr *variant spelling of* whir
whish swish
whisk
whisk·er
whisk·ered
whisk·ers
whisk·ery
whis·key Irish or US whisky
whis·ky (*plural* ·kies)
whis·per
whis·per·er
whist
whis·tle
whis·tler
whis·tling
Whit Christian festival
whit iota
white
white·bait
white·beam tree
white·cap white-crested wave
White·chapel
white-collar (*adj*)
white-damp mine gas
whit·ed sep·ul·chre
white-eye bird
white·fish (*plural* ·fish *or* ·fishes)
white·fly (*plural* ·flies)
White·hall
white-hot
white-livered
whit·en
whit·en·er
white·ness
whit·en·ing
white·out
whites
white-slaver
white·smith metal polisher
white·throat bird

white·wall tyre
white·wash
white·wash·er
white·wood
whit·ey (*or* wity; *plural* ·eys *or* wities)
whith·er
whit·ing (*plural* ·ing *or* ·ings) fish
whit·ing (*or* ·en·ing) ground chalk
whit·ish
whit·low
Whit·sun
Whit·sun·tide
whit·tle
whit·tler
whit·tlings wood shavings
whity whitish; *variant spelling of* whitey
whiz (*or* whizz; whiz·zing, whizzed)
whiz-bang (*or* whizz-)
whiz·zer
who
whoa
who'd who had; who would
who·dun·it (*or* ·dun·nit)
who·ever
whole
whole·food
whole·hearted
whole·hearted·ness
whole·meal
whole·ness
whole·sale
whole·sal·er
whole·some
whole·some·ly
whole·some·ness
who'll who will; who shall
whol·ly
whom
whom·ever
whom·so·ever
whoop
whoo·pee
whoop·er swan
whoop·ing cough
whoops exclamation
whoosh (*or* woosh)
whop (*or* wop; whop·ping, whopped *or* wop·ping, wopped) hit
whop·per

whop·ping
whore
whore·dom
whore·house
whore·monger
whore·son
whor·ish
whorl spiral pattern or arrangement; *compare* whirl
whorled
whortle·berry (*plural* ·berries)
who's who is
whose of who
who·so·ever (*or* who·so)
why (*plural* whys)
Why·al·la Australian port
whyd·ah (*or* whid·) bird
Wichi·ta US city
Wick Scottish town
wick
wick·ed
wick·ed·ness
wick·er flexible twig; *compare* whicker
wicker·work
wick·et
wicket·keeper
wick·ing
wicki·up American Indian hut
Wick·low Irish county
wico·py plant
wid·der·shins *variant spelling of* withershins
wide
wide-awake
wide-awakeness
wide-eyed
wide·ly
wid·en
wid·en·er
wide·ness
wide-open
wide-ranging
wide-screen (*adj*)
wide·spread
widg·eon *variant spelling of* wigeon
widg·et
widgie *Austral* unruly woman
wid·ish
Wid·nes Cheshire town

wid·ow

wid·ow·er

wid·ow·hood

width

width·wise (*or* ·ways)

wield manipulate; *compare* weald

wield·able

wield·er

wieldy (wieldi·er, wieldi·est)

Wie·ner schnit·zel

(wier) *incorrect spelling of* weir

(wierd) *incorrect spelling of* weird

Wies·ba·den West German city

wife (*plural* wives)

wife·li·ness

wife·ly

wig (wig·ging, wigged)

Wig·an

wig·eon (*or* widg·) duck

wigged

wig·ging

wig·gle

wig·gler

wig·gly

Wight (Isle of)

wig·wag (·wag·ging, ·wagged)

wig·wag·ger

wig·wam

wil·co signalling expression

wild

wild·cat (·cat·ting, ·cat·ted)

wild·cat·ter

wil·de·beest (*plural* ·beests *or* ·beest)

wil·der·ness

wild-eyed

wild·fire

wild·fowl

wild·fowl·er

wild·fowl·ing

wild-goose chase

wild·ing (*or* ·ling)

wild·life

wild·ness

wile craftiness; trick; *compare* while

wil·ful (*US* will·)

wil·ful·ly (*US* will·)

wil·ful·ness (*US* will·)

Wil·helms·ha·ven West German port

wili·ly

wili·ness

will

will·able

wil·lem·ite mineral

will·er

wil·let bird

will·ful *US spelling of* wilful

Wil·liams·burg US city

wil·lies *Slang* fright

will·ing

will·ing·ness

wil·li·waw *US* turmoil

will-o'-the-wisp

wil·low

wil·low·herb

wil·lowy

will·power

willy-nilly

wilt

Wil·ton carpet

Wilt·shire

wily (wili·er, wili·est)

wim·ble tool

Wim·ble·don

wimp

wimp·ish

wim·ple

Wim·py (*Trademark*) hamburger

win (win·ning, won)

wince

winc·er

win·cey fabric

win·cey·ette

winch

winch·er

Win·ches·ter English city; rifle

win·ches·ter large bottle

winc·ing·ly

wind (wind·ing, wound) coil

wind (wind·ing, wind·ed) air current, etc.

wind·able

wind·age

wind·bag

wind·blown

wind-borne

wind-bound

wind·break

wind-broken asthmatic

wind·burn

wind·burnt (*or* ·burned)

wind-cheater

wind·ed

wind·er

Win·der·mere

wind·fall

wind·flower

wind·gall fetlock swelling

wind·galled

Wind·hoek Namibian capital

wind·hover *Dialect* kestrel

windi·ly

windi·ness

wind·ing

wind·ing·ly

wind·jam·mer

wind·lass

win·dle·straw *Dialect* dried grass

wind·mill

win·dow

window-dresser

window-dressing

window·pane

window-shop (-shopping, -shopped)

window-shopper

window·sill

wind·pipe

wind-pollinat·ed

wind-pollina·tion

wind·row line of hay

wind·row·er

wind·sail

wind·screen

wind·shield

wind·sock

Wind·sor

wind·storm

wind·sucker

wind-sucking

wind·swept

wind-up (*noun*)

wind·ward

windy (windi·er, windi·est)

wine

wine-bibber

wine-bibbing

wine·glass

wine·glass·ful

wine·press

win·ery (*plural* ·eries)
wine·skin
wing
wing·ding *US* party
winged
wing·er
wing·less
wing·less·ness
wing·let
wing·like
wing·over aircraft
    manoeuvre
wing·span (*or* ·spread)
wink
wink·er
win·kle
win·nable
Win·ne·ba·go (*plural* ·gos
    or ·go) *US* lake;
    American Indian
win·ner
win·ning
win·ning·ness
win·nings
Win·ni·peg
Win·ni·peg·ger
Win·ni·pego·sis Canadian
    lake
win·now
win·now·er
wino (*plural* winos) *Slang*
    wine drinker
win·some
win·some·ly
win·some·ness
Winston-Salem *US* city
win·ter
winter·bourne stream
win·ter·er
winter·feed (·feeding,
    ·fed)
winter·green shrub
winter·kill
winter·time
win·tri·er
win·tri·est
win·tri·ly
win·tri·ness (*or* ·teri·ness)
win·try (*or* ·tery; ·tri·er,
    ·tri·est)
winy (wini·er, wini·est)
    like wine; *compare* whiny
winze mining shaft
wipe
wipe·out (*noun*)

wip·er
wire
wire·draw (·draw·ing,
    ·drew, ·drawn)
wire·gauge
wire·haired
wire·less
wire·man (*plural* ·men)
    US electrician
wir·er
wire·work
wire·worker
wire·works
wire·worm
wire·wove
wiri·ly
wiri·ness
wir·ing
wir·ra Irish exclamation
Wir·ral English peninsula
wiry (wiri·er, wiri·est)
Wis·con·sin
Wis·con·sin·ite
wis·dom
wise
wisea·cre
wise·crack
wise·crack·er
wise·ly
wise·ness
wi·sent European bison
wish
wish·bone
wish·er
wish·ful
wish·ful·ly
wish·ful·ness
wishy-washy
wisp
wispi·ly
wispi·ness
wispy (wispi·er, wispi·est)
wis·te·ria
wist·ful
wist·ful·ly
wist·ful·ness
wit
wit·an Anglo-Saxon council
witch
witch·craft
witch elm *variant spelling of*
    wych elm
witch·ery (*plural* ·eries)
witch·et·ty edible grub

witch ha·zel (*or* wych
    hazel)
witch-hunt
witch-hunter
witch-hunting
witch·ing
witch·like
wite *Scot* blame
wit·ena·gamot witan
with
with·al
with·draw (·draw·ing,
    ·drew, ·drawn)
with·draw·able
with·draw·al
with·draw·er
with·drawn
with·drawn·ness
with·drew
withe (*or* withy; *plural*
    withes *or* withies)
    flexible twig
with·er
with·ered·ness
with·er·er
with·er·ing·ly
with·er·ite mineral
with·ers
with·er·shins (*or* wid·der·)
with·hold (·hold·ing,
    ·held)
with·hold·er
with·in
with·out
with·stand (·stand·ing,
    ·stood)
with·stand·er
with·stood
withy (*plural* withies)
    willow tree; *variant
    spelling of* withe
wit·less
wit·less·ness
wit·loof Belgian chicory
wit·ness
wit·ness·able
wit·ness·er
wits
wit·ter
wit·ti·cism
wit·ti·ly
wit·ti·ness
wit·ting·ly intentional
wit·ty (·ti·er, ·ti·est)

Wit·wa·ters·rand South African region

wive *Archaic* to marry

wi·vern *variant spelling of* wyvern

wives *plural of* wife

wiz·ard

wiz·ard·ry

wiz·en

wiz·ened

woad

woad·ed

wob·be·gong shark

wob·ble

wob·bler

wob·bli·ness

wob·bly (·bli·er, ·bli·est)

Woden (*or* **Wodan**) Anglo-Saxon god

wodge

woe

woe·be·gone

woe·ful

woe·ful·ly

woe·ful·ness

wog·gle

wok

woke

wok·en

Wo·king

wold upland

wolf (*plural* **wolves**)

wolf·bane (*or* **wolfs·bane**, **wolf's-bane**) plant

wolf·er *variant of* wolver

wolf·fish (*plural* ·fish *or* ·fishes)

wolf·hound

wolf·ish

wolf·ish·ness

wolf·like

wolf·ram tungsten

wolf·ram·ite mineral

wolfs·bane (*or* **wolf's-bane**) *variants of* wolfbane

wolf-whistle (*verb*)

wol·las·ton·ite mineral

Wol·lon·gong Australian city

wol·ly (*plural* ·lies) *Dialect* pickled cucumber; *compare* wally

Wol·of (*plural* ·of *or* ·ofs) African people

wolv·er (*or* **wolf·**) wolf hunter

Wol·ver·hamp·ton

wol·ver·ine animal

wolves *plural of* wolf

wom·an (*plural* ·en)

wom·an·hood

wom·an·ish

wom·an·ish·ness

wom·an·ize (*or* ·ise)

wom·an·iz·er (*or* ·is·er)

wom·an·kind

woman-like

wom·an·li·ness

wom·an·ly

womb

wom·bat

womb·like

wom·en

women·folk

wom·era *variant spelling of* woomera

won *past tense of* win

won (*or* **hwan**; *plural* **won** *or* **hwan**) North Korean currency

won·der

won·der·er

won·der·ful

won·der·ful·ly

won·der·ful·ness

wonder·land

won·der·ment

wonder·work miracle

wonder-worker

wonder-working

won·drous

won·drous·ness

won·ky (·ki·er, ·ki·est)

Won·san North Korean port

wont accustomed; custom

won't will not

wont·ed

won ton Chinese food

woo (**woos, woo·ing, wooed**)

wood

wood·bine

wood·borer beetle larva

wood·carver

wood·carving

wood·chat bird

wood·chuck

wood·cock

wood·craft

wood·crafts·man (*plural* ·men)

wood·cut

wood·cut·ter

wood·cutting

wood·ed

wood·en

wooden·head

wood·en·ness

wood·grouse

woodi·ness

wood·land

wood·lander

wood·lark

wood·louse (*plural* ·lice)

wood·man (*plural* ·men)

wood·note natural song

wood·pecker

wood·pile

wood·print

wood·ruff plant

wood·rush

wood·screw

wood·shed

wood·sia fern

woods·man (*plural* ·men)

wood·wind

wood·work

wood·worker

wood·working

wood·worm

woody (**woodi·er, woodi·est**)

wooed

woo·er

woof weft; bark of dog

woof·er loudspeaker

woo·ing

wool

wool·gather·er

wool·gather·ing

wool·grower

wool·growing

wool·len (*US* **wool·en**)

wool·li·ly

wool·li·ness

wool·ly (*US also* **wooly**; *adj* ·li·er, ·li·est; *noun*, *plural* ·lies)

wool·pack

wool·sack

Woom·era Australian town

woom·era (*or* **wom·era**) Aboriginal spear thrower

Woop Woop *Austral*
  remote town
woosh *variant spelling of*
  whoosh
woozi·ly
woozi·ness
woozy (woozi·er,
  woozi·est)
wop *variant spelling of* **whop;**
  Slang Italian
Worces·ter
Worces·ter·shire former
  county; *note*
  Worcestershire sauce
word
word·age
word·blind
word·book
word·break
word·deaf
wordi·ly
wordi·ness
word·ing
word·less
word·less·ness
word·perfect
word·play
word·smith
wordy (wordi·er,
  wordi·est)
wore
work
work·abil·ity (or
  ·able·ness)
work·able
worka·day
worka·hol·ic
work·bag
work·bench
work·book
work·box
work·day
work·er
worker-priest
work·folk
work-harden
work-harden·ing
work·horse
work·house
work-in (*noun*)
work·ing
work·load
work·man (*plural* ·men)
work·man·like
work·man·ly

work·man·ship
work-out (*noun*)
work·people
work·piece
work·room
works
work·shop
work·shy
Work·sop English town
work·table
work-to-rule (*noun*)
world
world-beater
world-beating
world·li·ness
world·ling
world·ly (·li·er, ·li·est)
worldly-wise
world-shaking
world-weariness
world-weary
world-wide
worm
worm·cast
worm-eaten
worm·er
worm·hole
worm·like (*or* ·ish)
worm·seed
worm·wood
wormy (wormi·er,
  wormi·est)
worn
worn-out
wor·ri·er
wor·ri·ment
wor·ri·some
wor·rit *Dialect* tease
wor·ry (*verb* ·ries, ·ry·ing,
  ·ried; *noun, plural*
  ·ries)
wor·ry·wart worrier
worse
wors·en
wor·ship (·ship·ping,
  ·shipped; *US* ·ship·ing,
  ·shiped)
wor·ship·able
wor·ship·ful
wor·ship·ful·ly
wor·ship·ful·ness
wor·ship·per
wor·ship·ping·ly
worst
wor·sted fabric

worst·ed defeated
wort soaked malt
worth
wor·thi·ly
wor·thi·ness
Wor·thing
worth·less
worth·less·ly
worth·less·ness
worth·while
worth·while·ness
wor·thy (*adj* ·thi·er,
  ·thi·est; *noun, plural*
  ·thies)
Wotan Germanic god
would
would-be
wouldn't
wouldst
wound
wound·able
wound·ed
wound·er
wound·ing·ly
wound·wort
wove
wo·ven
wow
wow·ser *Austral* puritanical
  person
wrack seaweed; *variant*
  spelling of **rack**
wraith
wraith-like
wran·gle
wran·gler
wrap (wrap·ping,
  wrapped)
wrap·over (*or* ·around,
  ·round)
wrap·per
wrap·ping
wrasse fish; *compare* **rasse**
wrath anger; *compare* **wroth**
wrath·ful
wrath·ful·ly
wrath·ful·ness
wreak
wreak·er
wreath (*noun, plural*
  wreaths)
wreathe (*verb*)
wreck
wreck·age
wreck·er

wreck·fish (*plural* ·**fish** *or* ·**fishes**)
Wre·kin English hill
Wren member of WRNS
wren bird
wrench
wrest
wrest·er
wres·tle
wres·tler
wres·tling
wretch miserable person; *compare* **retch**
wretch·ed
wretch·ed·ness
Wrex·ham
wried contorted
wri·er *variant spelling of* **wryer**
wri·est *variant spelling of* **wryest**
wrig·gle
wrig·gler
wrig·gling·ly
wrig·gly (·**gli·er**, ·**gli·est**)
wright maker or repairer
wring (**wring·ing**, **wrung**)
wring·er
wrin·kle
wrin·kly
wrist
wrist·band
wrist·let bracelet
wrist·lock
wrist·watch
writ
writ·able

write (**writ·ing**, **wrote**, **writ·ten**)
write-off (*noun*)
writ·er
writhe
with·er
writh·ing·ly
writ·ing
writ·ten
Wro·cław Polish city
wrong
wrong·doer
wrong·doing
wrong·er
wrong-foot (*verb*)
wrong·ful
wrong·ful·ly
wrong·ful·ness
wrong-headed
wrong-headed·ness
wrong·ly
wrong·ness
wrote
wroth *Archaic* angry; *compare* **wrath**
wrought
wrought-up
wrung
wry (*adj* **wry·er**, **wry·est** *or* **wri·er**, **wri·est**; *verb* **wries**, **wry·ing**, **wried**)
wry·bill bird
wry·ing
wry·ly
wry·neck
wry·ness

Wu Chinese dialect
Wu·han Chinese city
Wu-hsi *variant spelling of* **Wusih**
Wuhu Chinese port
wul·fen·ite mineral
Wu-lu-mu-ch'i *variant of* **Urumchi**
wun·der·kind (*plural* ·**kinds** *or* ·**kind·er**) child prodigy
Wup·per·tal West German city
wurley (*or* **wurlie**) Aboriginal hut
wurst German sausage
Würt·tem·berg former German state
Würz·burg West German city
wus Welsh term of address
Wu·sih (*or* **Wu-hsi**) Chinese city
Wy·an·dotte domestic fowl
wych elm (*or* **witch elm**)
wych hazel *variant spelling of* **witch hazel**
Wyc·lif·fite (*or* **Wyc·lif·ite**)
Wye British river
Wyke·ham·ist member of Winchester College
wynd *Scot* lane
Wyo·ming
wy·vern (*or* **wi·**) heraldic beast

X

xan·thate chemical compound
xan·tha·tion
xan·the·in plant pigment
xan·thene chemical compound
xan·thic chemistry or botany term
xan·thin plant pigment
xan·thine chemical compound
xan·thoch·ro·ism animal skin condition

xan·tho·ma (*plural* ·**mas** *or* ·**ma·ta**) skin nodule
xan·tho·phyll plant pigment
xan·tho·phyll·ous
xan·thous having yellowish hair
Xan·thus ancient Asian city
x-axis
X-chromosome
xe·bec (*or* **ze·bec**, **ze·beck**) ship
xe·nia botany term

xe·nial
xeno·cryst
xe·noga·mous
xe·noga·my cross-fertilization
xeno·gen·esis botany term
xeno·genet·ic (*or* ·**gen·ic**)
xeno·glos·sia language ability
xeno·lith geology term
xeno·lith·ic
xeno·mor·phic geology term

xeno·mor·phi·cal·ly
xen·on chemical element
xeno·phile
xeno·phobe
xeno·pho·bia
xeno·pho·bic
xer·arch ecology term
xe·ric of dry conditions
xe·ri·cal·ly
xe·ro·der·ma (*or* ·mia) dry skin
xe·ro·der·mat·ic (*or* ·ma·tous)
xe·rog·ra·pher
xe·ro·graph·ic
xe·ro·graphi·cal·ly
xe·rog·ra·phy photocopying
xe·ro·mor·phic botany term
xe·ro·phile
xe·rophi·lous living in dry conditions
xe·rophi·ly
xe·roph·thal·mia (*or* xe·ro·ma) eye disease

xe·roph·thal·mic
xe·ro·phyte
xe·ro·phyt·ic
xe·ro·phyti·cal·ly
xe·ro·phyt·ism
xe·ro·sere ecology term
xe·ro·sis dryness of tissues
xe·rot·ic
Xer·ox (*Trademark*)
Xho·sa (*plural* ·sa *or* ·sas) African people
Xho·san
xi (*plural* xis) Greek letter
xiphi·ster·num (*plural* ·na) part of breastbone
xiph·oid anatomy or biology term
xipho·su·ran zoology term
Xmas
X-radiation
X-ray (*or* x-ray)
xy·lan biochemistry term
xy·lem plant tissue
xy·lene chemical compound

xy·li·dine chemical compound
xy·lo·carp botany term
xy·lo·car·pous
xy·lo·graph wood engraving
xy·log·ra·pher
xy·lo·graph·ic (*or* ·graphi·cal)
xy·log·ra·phy
xy·loid woody
xy·lol chemical compound
xy·lopha·gous wood-eating
xy·lo·phone
xy·lo·phon·ic
xy·lopho·nist
xy·lose sugar
xy·loto·mist
xy·loto·mous wood-boring
xy·loto·my preparing wood for microscopy
xy·lyl chemistry term
xyst (*or* xys·tus, xys·tos) portico
xys·ter surgical file

Y

yacht
yacht·ing
yachts·man (*plural* ·men)
yachts·man·ship (*or* yacht·)
yachts·woman (*plural* ·women)
ya·hoo (*plural* ·hoos) coarse person
ya·hoo·ism
yak (yak·king, yakked)
Ya·kut (*plural* ·kuts *or* ·kut) Soviet people
Ya·kutsk Soviet port
Yale US university; (*Trademark*) lock
Yal·ta Soviet port
yam
yam·mer
yam·mer·er
yang Chinese masculine principle; *compare* yin
Yang·tze
yank tug

Yank (*or* Yan·kee) *Slang* American
Yan·kee·ism
Ya·oun·dé (*or* Ya·un·de) Cameroon capital
yap (yap·ping, yapped)
ya·pok animal
ya·pon *variant spelling of* yaupon
yapped
yap·per
yap·ping
yap·py
yar·bor·ough bridge or whist term
yard·age
yard·arm
yard·stick
Yar·mouth
yar·mul·ke skullcap
yarn
yarn-dyed
Ya·ro·slavl Soviet city
yar·row
yash·mak (*or* ·mac)

yata·ghan sword
Ya·un·de *variant spelling of* Yaoundé
yau·pon (*or* ya·pon) shrub
yau·tia plant
yaw
yawl
yawn
yawn·er
yawn·ing·ly
yaws disease
y-axis
Y-chromosome
ye
yea
yean·ling goat's or sheep's young
year
year·book
year·ling
year·long
year·ly (*plural* ·lies)
yearn
yearn·er
yearn·ing

yeast

yeasti·ly

yeasti·ness

yeasty (yeasti·er, yeasti·est)

yell

yell·er

yel·low

yellow·bark

yellow-belly (plural -bellies)

yellow·bird

yellow·hammer

yel·low·ish

yellow·legs bird

yel·lows disease

Yellow·stone

yellow·tail (plural ·tails or ·tail) fish

yellow·weed

yellow·wood

yel·lowy

yelp

yelp·er

Yem·en

Yem·eni

yen (yen·ning, yenned)

yen (plural yen) Japanese currency

Ye·ni·sei Soviet river

Yen·tai (or Yen-t'ai) Chinese port

yeo·man (plural ·men)

yeo·man·ry (plural ·ries)

Yeo·vil

yer·ba beverage

Ye·re·van Armenian capital

yes

yes-man (plural -men)

yes·ter·day

yes·ter·year

yeti

yew

Ygg·dra·sil mythological tree

Yid·dish

yield

yield·able

yield·er

yield·ing·ly

yield·ing·ness

yin Chinese feminine principle; compare yang

Ying·kow (or Ying-k'ou) Chinese port

yip·pee

ylang-ylang (or ilang-ilang) tree

ylem original matter of universe

yob (or yob·bo; plural yobs or yob·bos)

yo·del (·del·ling, ·delled; US ·del·ing, ·deled)

yo·del·ler (US ·del·er)

yoga

yo·ghurt (or ·gurt)

yogi (plural yo·gis or yo·gin) yoga master

yo·gic

yo·gism

yo·gurt variant spelling of yoghurt

yo·him·bine medicinal substance

yoicks huntsman's exclamation

yoke frame; burden; link; part of garment; compare yolk

yo·kel

yo·kel·ish

Yo·ko·ha·ma Japanese city

Yok·ya·kar·ta (or Jog·ja·) Indonesian city

yolk part of egg; compare yoke

yolky

Yom Kip·pur

yon (or yond)

yon·der

yoni female genitalia

Yon·kers US city

Yonne French department and river

yon·nie Austral stone

yoo-hoo

yore

York

york·er cricket term

York·ist

York·shire

Yorkshire·man (plural ·men)

Yo·ru·ba (plural ·bas or ·ba) African people

Yo·ru·ban

Yo·semi·te US national park

Yoshkar-Ola Soviet city

you

you'd you would; you had

you'll you will; you shall

young

young·berry (plural ·berries)

young·ish

young·ster

Youngs·town US city

your of you

you're you are

yours

your·self (plural ·selves)

youth

youth·ful

youth·ful·ly

youth·ful·ness

you've you have

yowl

yowl·er

yo-yo (plural -yos)

Ypres

Yquem French vineyard

yt·ter·bia chemical compound

yt·ter·bite mineral

yt·ter·bium chemical element

yt·tria chemical compound

yt·tric

yt·trif·er·ous

yt·trium chemical element

yuan (plural yuan) Chinese currency

Yu·ca·tán Mexican state

yuc·ca

Yuga Hindu age

Yu·go·slav (or Ju·)

Yu·go·sla·via (or Ju·)

Yu·go·sla·vian (or Ju·)

yuk

yuk·ky

Yu·kon

Yu·kon·er

yu·lan tree

yule

yule·tide

Yu·man language group

yum·my (·mi·er, ·mi·est)

Yün·nan Chinese province

yup Slang yes

yup·pie

Yve·lines French department

Z

za·ba·glio·ne
Za·brze Polish city
Za·ca·te·cas Mexican state
zaf·fer (or zaf·fre) pigment
Zaga·zig (or Zaqa·ziq)
   Egyptian city
Za·greb
zai·bat·su Japanese wealthy
   families
Za·ïre African republic
za·ïre (plural ·ïre) African
   currency
Za·ïr·ese
Za·ïr·ian
Zama ancient African city
Zam·be·zi (or ·se)
Zam·be·zian
Zam·bia
Zam·bian
Zam·bo·an·ga Philippine
   port
za·mia plant
za·min·dar (or ze·) Indian
   landowner
za·min·dari (or ze·; plural
   ·daris) estate
za·ni·ly
za·ni·ness
Zan·te Greek island
zan·thoxy·lum tree
zany (adj zani·er,
   zani·est; noun, plural
   zanies)
Zan·zi·bar
Zan·zi·ba·ri
zap (zap·ping, zapped)
za·pa·dea·do (plural ·dos)
   dance
Za·po·rozh·ye Soviet city
Za·po·tec (plural ·tecs or
   ·tec) American Indian
Zapo·tec·an
Zaqa·ziq variant of Zagazig
Za·ra·go·za Spanish city
zara·tite mineral
za·reba (or ·ree·ba)
   African enclosure
zarf coffee-cup holder
Zar·ga (or Sar·ka)
   Jordanian town

Za·ria Nigerian city
zar·zue·la Spanish opera
z-axis
zeal
Zea·land Danish island;
   compare Zeeland
zeal·ot
zeal·ot·ry
zeal·ous
zeal·ous·ness
ze·bec (or ·beck) variant
   spellings of xebec
Zebedee biblical character
zeb·ra (plural ·ras or ·ra)
zebra-like (or ze·bra·ic)
zebra·wood
ze·brine (or ·broid)
zebu ox
zec·chi·no (plural ·ni) coin
zed
zedo·ary condiment
zee US zed
Zee·brug·ge
Zee·land Dutch province;
   compare Zealand
Zee·land·er
zein protein
Zeist Dutch city
Zeit·geist German outlook
ze·min·dar variant spelling
   of zamindar
ze·min·dari variant spelling
   of zamindari
Zen
ze·na·na women's part of
   house
Zen·ic
Zen·ist
zen·ith
zen·ith·al
zeo·lite mineral
zeo·lit·ic
zeph·yr breeze; fabric
Zephyrus Greek god
zep·pe·lin
zero (noun, plural zeros
   or zeroes; verb zeroes,
   ze·ro·ing, ze·roed)
zero-rated
zeroth

zest
zest·ful
zest·ful·ly
zest·ful·ness
zesty
zeta Greek letter
zeug·ma figure of speech
zeug·mat·ic
zeug·mati·cal·ly
Zeus
Zhda·nov Soviet port
Zhi·to·mir Soviet city
zho variant spelling of zo
zib·el·ine fur
zib·et animal
ziff Austral beard
zig·gu·rat (or zik·ku·rat,
   ziku·rat) temple tower
zig·zag (·zag·ging,
   ·zagged)
zig·zag·ged·ness
zig·zag·ger
zila (or zil·la, zil·lah)
   Indian administrative
   district
zilch
zil·lion (plural ·lions or
   ·lion)
Zim·ba·bwe
Zim·ba·bwe·an
zinc
zin·cate
zinc·ic (or ·ous, ·oid)
zinc·if·er·ous
zinc·ite mineral
zinck·en·ite variant spelling
   of zinkenite
zincky (or zincy, zinky)
zin·co (plural ·cos) short
   for zincograph
zin·co·graph zinc printing-
   plate
zin·cog·ra·pher
zin·co·graph·ic (or
   ·graphi·cal)
zin·cog·ra·phy
zincy variant spelling of
   zincky
Zin·fan·del wine grape
zing

zin·ga·ro (*fem* ·ra; *plural* ·ri *or* ·re) gipsy

zin·gi·bera·ceous botany term

zingy

zin·jan·thro·pus fossil hominid

zin·ken·ite (*or* zinck·en·ite) mineral

zinky *variant spelling of* zincky

zin·nia plant

Zion (*or* Sion)

Zi·on·ism

Zi·on·ist

Zi·on·is·tic

zip (zip·ping, zipped)

zip·per

zip·py (·pi·er, ·pi·est)

zirc·al·loy

zir·con

zir·co·nia chemical compound

zir·con·ic

zir·co·nium chemical element

zith·er

zith·er·ist

Zla·to·ust Soviet town

zlo·ty (*plural* ·tys *or* ·ty) Polish currency

zo (*or* zho, dzo; *plural* zos, zhos, dzos *or* zo, zho, dzo) cattle

zo·di·ac

zo·dia·cal

Zo·har Jewish text

zois·ite mineral

Zom·ba Malawian city

zom·bie (*or* ·bi; *plural* ·bies *or* ·bis)

zom·bi·ism

zon·al (*or* zona·ry)

zon·ate (*or* zo·nat·ed)

zo·na·tion

Zond Soviet spacecraft

zone

zone·time

zonu·lar

zon·ule

zoo (*plural* zoos)

zoo·chemi·cal

zoo·chem·is·try

zoo·chore botany term

zoo·geog·ra·pher

zoo·geo·graph·ic (*or* ·graphi·cal)

zoo·geo·graphi·cal·ly

zoo·geog·ra·phy

zoo·gloea (*US* ·glea; *plural* ·gloeas *or* ·gloeae, *US* ·gleas *or* ·gleae) bacterial mass

zoo·gloeal (*US* ·gleal)

zo·og·ra·pher

zoo·graph·ic (*or* ·graphi·cal)

zo·og·ra·phy

zo·oid

zo·ol·at·er

zo·ola·trous

zo·ola·try worship of animals

zoo·logi·cal

zo·olo·gist

zo·ol·ogy (*plural* ·ogies)

zoom

zoo·met·ric (*or* ·ri·cal)

zo·om·etry

zoo·mor·phic

zoo·mor·phism

zo·ono·sis (*plural* ·ses) pathology term

zo·opha·gous feeding on animals

zoo·phile

zoo·philia fondness for animals

zoo·phil·ic

zo·ophi·lism sexual attraction to animals

zo·ophi·lous pollinated by animals

zoo·pho·bia

zo·opho·bous

zoo·phyte

zoo·phyt·ic (*or* ·phyti·cal)

zoo·plank·ton

zoo·plas·tic

zoo·plas·ty surgical transplantation

zoo·sperm

zoo·sper·mat·ic

zoo·spo·ran·gial

zoo·spo·ran·gium (*plural* ·gia)

zoo·spore

zoo·spor·ic (*or* zo·os·por·ous)

zo·os·ter·ol biochemical compound

zoo·tech·nics

zoo·tom·ic (*or* ·tomi·cal)

zoo·tomi·cal·ly

zo·oto·mist

zo·oto·my animal dissection

zoo·tox·ic

zoo·tox·in

zo·ril·la (*or* zo·rille) animal

Zo·ro·as·trian

Zo·ro·as·tri·an·ism

zos·ter shingles

Zou·ave French infantryman

zounds archaic exclamation

zoy·sia grass

zuc·chet·to (*plural* ·tos) skullcap

zuc·chi·ni (*plural* ·ni *or* ·nis)

zug·zwang chess position

Zui·der Zee (*or* Zuy·)

Zulu (*plural* Zulus *or* Zulu)

Zu·lu·land

Zü·rich

Zwickau East German city

zwie·back toasted rusk

Zwing·lian denoting religious movement

zwit·teri·on

zwit·teri·on·ic

zyg·apo·phys·eal (*or* ·ial)

zyga·pophy·sis (*plural* ·ses) part of vertebra

zy·go·dac·tyl ornithology term

zy·go·dac·tyl·ism

zy·go·dac·ty·lous

zy·go·ma (*plural* ·ma·ta) bone

zy·go·mat·ic

zy·go·mor·phic (*or* ·phous) botany term

zy·go·mor·phy (*or* ·phism)

zy·go·phyl·la·ceous botany term

zy·go·phyte

zy·gose

zy·go·sis (*plural* ·ses) biology term

zy·go·spore

zy·go·spor·ic

zy·gote fertilized egg cell

zy·go·tene stage of cell
  division
zy·got·ic
zy·goti·cal·ly
zy·mase enzyme
zy·mo·gen enzyme
  precursor
zy·mo·gen·esis

zy·mo·gen·ic
zy·mo·log·ic (*or* **·logi·cal**)
zy·molo·gist
zy·mol·ogy
zy·moly·sis fermentation
zy·mo·lyt·ic
zy·mom·eter

zy·mo·sis (*plural* **·ses**)
  disease
zy·mot·ic
zy·moti·cal·ly
zy·mur·gy branch of
  chemistry
Zyr·ian language

First Names

Aaron
Abbey (or Abbie, Abby)
Abe
Abel
Abigail
Abner
Abraham
Abram
Absalom
Ada
Adah
Adair
Adam
Adamina
Adamnan
Addie (or Addy)
Adela
Adelaide
Adele
Adelheid
Adelina
Adeline
Adlai
Adolf (or Adolph, Adolphe)
Adolphus
Adrian
Adriana
Adrianne (or Adrienne)
Aeneas
Afra
Agacia
Agatha
Aggie
Agnes
Agneta
Aidan
Aileen
Ailie
Ailis
Ailith
Ailsa
Aimee
Aine
Ainslie (or Ainsley)
Aisling
Aislinn
Aithne
Al
Alain

Alan (or Allan, Allen, Alun)
Alana (or Alanna)
Alaric
Alasdair (or Alastair) variant
    spellings of Alistair
Alban
Albany
Alberic
Albert
Alberta
Albertina
Albertine
Albin
Albina
Albinia
Albreda
Alda
Alden
Aldhelm
Aldis
Aldith
Aldo
Aldous (or Aldus)
Aldred
Aldreda
Aldwyn (or Aldwin)
Alec
Aled
Aledwen
Alethea
Alex
Alexa
Alexander
Alexandra
Alexandria
Alexandrina
Alexia
Alexis
Alf
Alfie
Alfonso variant spelling of
    Alphonso
Alfred
Alfreda
Algar
Alger
Algernon
Algie (or Algy)
Alice (or Alys)

Alicia
Alick
Alina
Aline
Alison (or Allison)
Alistair (or Alasdair,
    Alastair)
Alix
Allan variant spelling of Alan
Allegra
Allen variant spelling of Alan
Ally (or Allie)
Alma
Alonso (or Alonzo)
Aloysia (or Aloisia)
Aloysius
Alphonse
Alphonsine
Alphonso (or Alfonso)
Alphonsus
Althea
Alun variant spelling of Alan
Alured
Alva (or Alvah)
Alvar
Alvie
Alvin
Alvina
Alvis
Alwyn
Alys variant spelling of Alice
Amabel
Amalia
Amalie
Amanda
Amaryllis
Amata
Amber
Ambrose
Ambrosina
Ambrosine
Ambrosius
Amelia
Amias variant spelling of
    Amyas
Amice
Amicia
Aminta
Amos

Amy
Amyas (*or* Amias)
Anastasia
Ancel
André
Andrea
Andreas
Andrée
Andrew
Andy
Aneira
Aneurin (*or* Aneirin)
Angel
Angela
Angelica
Angelina
Angeline
Angelique
Angelo
Angharad
Angie
Angus
Anis (*or* Annis, Annice)
Anita
Ann *variant spelling of* Anne
Anna
Annabel (*or* Annabelle)
Annabella
Annalisa
Annaple
Anne (*or* Ann)
Anneliese
Annette
Annice *variant spelling of* Anis
Annie
Annika
Annis
Annora
Anona
Anouska
Ansel (*or* Ansell)
Anselm
Anselma
Anstey
Anstice
Anthea
Anthony (*or* Antony)
Antoine
Antoinette
Anton
Antonia
Antonina
Antonio

Antony *variant spelling of* Anthony
Anwen
Anya
Aphra
Apollonia
Appolina
Appoline
April
Aquila
Arabella
Araminta
Archelaus
Archer
Archibald
Archie (*or* Archy)
Ariadne
Ariane
Arianna
Arlene (*or* Arleen) *variant* spellings of Arline
Arletta
Arlette
Arline (*or* Arlene, Arleen)
Armand
Armin
Armina
Armine
Arnaud
Arnold
Art
Artemas (*or* Artemus)
Artemisia
Arthur
Arthuretta
Arthurina
Arthurine
Artie (*or* Arty)
Asa
Asher
Ashley
Aspasia
Astra
Astrid
Athelstan
Athene
Athol
Auberon
Aubert
Aubrey
Aud
Audra
Audrey
August
Augusta

Augustina
Augustine (*or* Augustin)
Augustus
Aulay
Aurea
Aurelia
Aurelian
Aureola
Aureole
Auriel
Auriol
Aurora
Aurore
Austen
Austin
Ava
Aveline
Averil
Avery
Avis (*or* Avice)
Avril
Axel
Aylmer
Aylwin
Azariah
Bab
Babette
Babs
Baldie
Baldwin
Balthasar (*or* Balthazar)
Barbara (*or* Barbra)
Barbary
Barbie
Barclay *variant spelling of* Berkeley
Bardolph
Barnabas
Barnaby
Barnard
Barnet
Barney
Baron (*or* Barron)
Barrett
Barrington
Barry (*or* Barrie)
Bart
Bartholomew
Bartle
Bartlett (*or* Bartlet)
Basie
Basil
Basilia
Basilie
Basilla

Bastian
Bathsheba
Baubie
Bea (*or* Bee)
Beata
Beatrice
Beatrix
Beattie (*or* Beatty)
Beau
Becky
Bedelia
Bedford
Bee *variant spelling of* Bea
Belinda
Bella
Belle (*or* Bell, Bel)
Ben
Benedict (*or* Benedick)
Benedicta
Benet *variant spelling of*
Bennet
Benita
Benito
Benjamin
Benjy
Bennet (*or* Bennett, Benet)
Benny
Bentley
Berengaria
Berenger
Berenice
Berkeley (*or* Barclay)
Bernadette
Bernadina
Bernadine
Bernard
Bernardina
Bernardine
Bernhard
Bernice
Bernie (*or* Berny)
Berry
Bert
Berta
Bertha
Berthold
Bertie
Bertram
Bertrand
Beryl
Bess
Bessie (*or* Bessy)
Beta
Beth
Bethan

Bethany
Bethel (*or* Bethell)
Bethia
Betsy
Bette
Bettina
Bettrys
Betty
Beulah
Beverley (*or* Beverly)
Bevis
Bianca
Biddy
Bill
Billy (*or* Billie)
Bina
Bing
Birdie
Birgit
Birgitta
Bjorn
Blaine (*or* Blane)
Blair
Blaise (*or* Blase)
Blake
Blanche (*or* Blanch)
Blane *variant spelling of*
Blaine
Blodwen
Blodyn
Blossom
Blythe
Boaz
Bob
Bobby (*or* Bobbie)
Bonamy
Bonar
Boniface
Bonita
Bonnie (*or* Bonny)
Boris
Botolph (*or* Botolf, Botulf)
Boyce
Boyd
Brad
Bradley
Bram
Brandon (*or* Brandan)
Branwen
Brenda
Brendan
Brent
Brett (*or* Bret)
Brian (*or* Bryan)

Brice *variant spelling of*
Bryce
Bride
Bridget (*or* Brigit, Brigitte)
Bridie
Brighid (*or* Brigid)
Brigitta
Briony *variant spelling of*
Bryony
Brita
Britannia
Britt
Brock
Broderick
Bronwen (*or* Bronwyn)
Bruce
Brunetta
Bruno
Bryan *variant spelling of*
Brian
Bryce (*or* Brice)
Bryn
Bryony (*or* Briony)
Bud
Burt
Buster
Byron
Cadel (*or* Cadell)
Caesar
Cai
Caitlin
Caius
Caleb
Calum (*or* Callum)
Calvin
Cameron
Camilla
Camille
Camillus
Campbell
Candace
Candice
Candida
Candy
Canice
Cara (*or* Kara)
Caradoc (*or* Caradog)
Carey *variant spelling of*
Cary
Carina (*or* Karina)
Carita
Carl (*or* Karl)
Carla
Carleen (*or* Carlene)
Carlo

Carlos
Carlotta
Carlton (or Carleton)
Carly
Carmel
Carmela
Carmelita
Carmen
Carol (or Carole)
Carola
Carolina
Caroline
Carolus
Carolyn
Carrie
Carter
Carthach
Carthage
Cary (or Carey)
Caryl
Carys
Casey
Casimir
Caspar
Cass
Cassandra
Cassie
Cath (or Kath)
Catherine (or Katherine, Katharine, Catharine)
Cathleen variant spelling of Kathleen
Cathy (or Kathy)
Catrin
Catriona
Cecil
Cecile
Cecilia
Cecily (or Cecilie)
Cedric (or Cedrych)
Ceinwen
Celeste
Celestina
Celestine
Celia
Celina variant spelling of Selina
Celine
Cerdic
Ceri
Ceridwen
Cerys
Chad
Charis
Charissa

Charity
Charlene
Charles
Charlie (or Charley)
Charlotte
Charlton
Charmaine
Charmian
Chas
Chattie
Chauncey (or Chauncy)
Chay
Cherie (or Sherry, Sherri)
Cherry
Cheryl
Chester
Chloe
Chris
Chrissie (or Chrissy)
Christabel
Christian
Christiana
Christiania
Christie (or Christy)
Christina (or Kristina)
Christine (or Kristine)
Christmas
Christopher
Christy variant spelling of Christie
Chrystal variant spelling of Crystal
Chuck
Cicely
Cilla
Cinderella
Cindy
Cis (or Ciss)
Cissy (or Cissie, Sissy, Sissie)
Claire (or Clare)
Clara
Clarence
Claribel
Clarice
Clarinda
Clarissa
Clark
Clarrie
Claud (or Claude)
Claudette
Claudia
Claudine
Claudius
Clayton

Cledwyn
Clem
Clemence
Clemency
Clement
Clementia
Clementina
Clementine
Cleo
Cleopatra
Cliff
Clifford
Clifton
Clint
Clinton
Clive
Clodagh
Clotilda
Clyde
Colette
Colin
Colina
Colleen
Colley
Colm
Colum
Columba
Columbina
Columbine
Conan
Concepta
Concetta
Conn
Connie
Connor (or Conor)
Conrad
Constance
Constancy
Constant
Constantia
Constantine
Cora
Coral
Coralie
Cordelia
Corinna
Corinne
Cormac
Cornelia
Cornelius
Corney
Cosimo
Cosmo
Courtney (or Courtenay)
Craig

Cressida
Crispian
Crispin
Crystal (or Chrystal)
Cuddy (or Cuddie)
Curt variant spelling of Kurt
Curtis
Cuthbert
Cy
Cynthia
Cyprian
Cyril
Cyrus
Cytherea
Daff variant spelling of Daph
Dafydd
Dagmar
Dai
Daisy
Dale
Damaris
Damian (or Damien)
Damon
Dan
Dana
Dane
Danette
Daniel
Daniella
Danielle
Danita
Danny
Dante
Danuta
Daph (or Daff)
Daphne
Darby (or Derby)
Darcy (or D'Arcy)
Darlene
Darren
Darryl (or Darrell, Daryl, Darrel)
Dave
David
Davida
Davina
Davinia
Davy
Dawn
Dean
Deanna
Deanne
Deb
Debbie
Deborah

Debra
Decima
Decimus
Declan
Dee
Deirdre
Del
Delia
Delilah
Della
Delphine
Delwyn (or Delwen)
Delyth
Demelza
Denholm
Denise
Dennie (or Denny)
Dennis (or Denis, Denys)
Denzil
Derby variant spelling of Darby
Derek (or Derrick, Deryck, Deryk)
Dermot
Derry
Deryn
Des
Desdemona
Desiree
Desmond
Dewi
Dexter
Diamond
Diana
Diane (or Dianne)
Diarmuid (or Diarmait)
Dick
Dickie (or Dicky)
Dickon
Digby
Diggory
Dillon
Dilys
Dinah
Dion
Dione (or Dionne)
Dionysia
Dionysius
Dirk
Dodie
Doll
Dolly
Dolores
Dominic (or Dominick)
Dominica

Dominique
Don
Donal
Donald
Donalda
Donaldina
Donna
Donny
Donovan
Dora
Doran
Dorcas
Doreen
Dorette
Doria
Dorian
Dorinda
Doris (or Dorice)
Dorita
Dorothea
Dorothy
Dorrie
Dot
Dottie
Doug
Dougal
Dougie (or Duggie)
Douglas
Dowsabel
Dreda
Drew
Drogo
Drusilla
Duane (or Dwayne)
Dudley
Dugald
Duggie variant spelling of Dougie
Duke
Dulce
Dulcibella
Dulcie
Duncan
Dunstan
Durand
Dustin
Dwayne variant spelling of Duane
Dwight
Dylan
Dymphna
Dympna
Eamon (or Eamonn)
Earl (or Erle)

Earnest variant spelling of
  Ernest
Eartha
Easter
Eben
Ebenezer
Ed
Eda
Eddie (or **Eddy**)
Eden
Edgar
Edie
Edith
Edmund (or **Edmond**)
Edna
Edom
Edward
Edwin (or **Edwyn**)
Edwina
Effie
Egbert
Egidia
Egidius
Eileen
Eiluned variant spelling of
  Eluned
Eilwen
Eily
Eira
Eirian
Eithne
Elain
Elaine
Eldon
Eldred
Eldreda
Eleanor (or **Elinor**)
Eleanora
Eleazar
Elena
Eleonora
Elfreda (or **Elfrida**)
Eli
Elias
Elihu
Elijah
Elined variant spelling of
  Eluned
Elinor variant spelling of
  Eleanor
Eliot variant spelling of
  Elliott
Elisabeth variant spelling of
  Elizabeth
Elise

Elisha
Elissa
Eliza
Elizabeth (or **Elisabeth**)
Elkanah
Ella
Ellen
Ellery
Ellie
Elliott (or **Elliot, Eliot**)
Ellis
Elma
Elmer
Eloisa
Eloise
Elroy
Elsa
Elsie
Elspeth
Elspie
Elton
Eluned (or **Elined, Eiluned**)
Elvie
Elvin
Elvina
Elvira
Elvis
Elwyn
Emanuel (or **Emmanuel**)
Emanuela (or **Emmanuela**)
Emblem
Emblyn
Emeline variant spelling of
  Emmeline
Emelyn
Emerald
Emery
Emil (or **Emile**)
Emilia
Emily
Emlyn
Emma
Emmanuel variant spelling
  of Emanuel
Emmanuela variant spelling
  of Emanuela
Emmeline (or **Emeline**)
Emmie
Emrys
Ena
Enid
Enoch
Enos
Eoghan
Ephraim

Eppie
Erasmus
Eric (or **Erik**)
Erica (or **Erika**)
Erin
Erle variant spelling of **Earl**
Ermintrude (or
  Ermyntrude)
Ernest (or **Earnest**)
Ernestine
Ernie
Errol
Erwin variant spelling of
  Irwin
Esau
Esme (or **Esmee**)
Esmeralda
Esmond
Essie
Estella
Estelle
Esther
Ethan
Ethel
Ethelbert
Etheldreda
Ethelinda
Ethelred
Ethne
Etta
Ettie (or **Etty**)
Eugene
Eugenia
Eugenie
Eulalia
Eulalie
Eunice
Euphemia
Eustace
Eustacia
Eva
Evadne
Evan
Evangelina
Evangeline
Eve
Eveleen
Evelina
Eveline
Evelyn
Everard
Everild
Evie
Evita

Evonne *variant spelling of* Yvonne

Ewan (*or* Ewen)

Ezekiel

Ezra

Fabian

Fabiana

Faith

Fanny

Farquhar

Farran (*or* Farren, Faron)

Faustina

Fay (*or* Faye)

Feargus *variant spelling of* Fergus

Fedora

Felice

Felicia

Felicity

Felix

Fenella

Feodora

Ferdinand

Fergie

Fergus (*or* Feargus)

Fern

Fernando

Fidel

Fidelia

Fifi

Finlay

Finola

Fiona

Fionnuala (*or* Fionnghuala)

Fitzroy

Flavia

Fletcher

Fleur

Flora

Florence

Floretta

Florette

Florian

Florinda

Florrie

Floss

Flossie

Flower

Floy

Floyd

Fluellen

Flurry

Fortunatus

Fortune

Foster

Franca

Frances (*fem*)

Francesca

Francesco

Francie

Francine

Francis (*masc*)

Francisca

Francisco

Franco

Frank

Frankie

Franklin

Frannie (*or* Franny)

Fraser (*or* Frazer)

Fred

Freda

Freddie (*or* Freddy)

Frederica (*or* Frederika, Fredrica, Fredrika)

Frederick (*or* Frederic, Fredrick, Fredric)

Freya

Frieda

Fulbert

Gabby (*or* Gabbie, Gabi, Gaby)

Gabriel

Gabriella

Gabrielle

Gaenor *variant spelling of* Gaynor

Gail (*or* Gayle, Gale)

Gaius

Gamaliel

Gareth

Garfield

Garnet

Garret (*or* Garrett)

Garrick

Garth

Gary (*or* Garry)

Gaspar

Gavin

Gawain

Gay (*or* Gaye)

Gayle *variant spelling of* Gail

Gaylord

Gaynor (*or* Gaenor)

Gemma (*or* Jemma)

Gene

Genevieve

Genevra *variant spelling of* Ginevra

Geoff (*or* Jeff)

Geoffrey (*or* Jeffrey, Jeffery)

Geordie

George

Georgette

Georgia

Georgiana

Georgie

Georgina

Geraint

Gerald

Geraldine

Gerard (*or* Gerrard)

Gerda

Germaine (*or* Germain)

Gerontius

Gerry (*or* Jerry)

Gershom

Gert

Gertie

Gertrude

Gervase (*or* Gervais)

Gerwyn

Gethin

Ghislaine

Gideon

Gil

Gilbert

Gilberta

Gilbertine

Gilda

Giles (*or* Gyles)

Gill (*or* Jill)

Gillian (*or* Jillian, Gillean)

Gilroy

Gina

Ginette

Ginevra (*or* Genevra)

Ginger

Ginny

Gisela

Giselle

Glad

Gladys

Glen (*or* Glenn)

Glenda

Glenna

Glenys (*or* Glenis)

Gloria

Glyn

Glynis (*or* Glinys)

Godfrey

Godwin

Goldie

Goldwin (*or* Goldwyn)

Gordon
Grace
Gracie
Graham (or Graeme, Grahame)
Grainne
Grania
Grant
Granville
Greg (or Gregg)
Gregor
Gregory
Grenville
Greta
Gretchen
Gretel
Griffith
Griselda
Grizel (or Grizzel)
Grover
Guendolen variant spelling of Gwendoline
Guido
Guinevere
Gulielma
Gunter (or Gunther)
Gus
Gussie
Gusta
Gustave (or Gustav, Gustaf)
Gustavus
Guy
Gwen
Gwenda
Gwendoline (or Gwendolyn, Gwendolen, Guendolen)
Gwenllian
Gwilym (or Gwylim)
Gwladys
Gwyn
Gwyneth (or Gwynneth, Gwynedd)
Gwynfor
Gyles variant spelling of Giles
Hadassah
Hadrian
Hagar
Haidee
Hal
Halcyon
Ham
Hamilton
Hamish
Hamlet

Hamlyn
Hammond
Hamnet
Hamo
Hamon
Hank
Hannah
Hannibal
Hans
Hardy
Harley
Harold
Harriet (or Harriette)
Harriot
Harrison
Harry
Hartley
Harvey
Hattie (or Hatty)
Haydn (or Haydon, Hayden)
Hayley
Hazel
Heath
Heather
Hebe
Heber
Hector
Hedda
Hedley
Hedwig
Hedy
Heidi
Helen
Helena
Helene
Helewise
Helga
Héloïse
Hennie (or Henny)
Henri
Henrietta
Henriette
Henry
Hephzibah
Hepsie (or Hepsey, Hepsy)
Hepzibah
Herb
Herbert
Herbie
Hereward
Herman (or Hermann)
Hermia
Hermione
Hervé
Hervey

Hester
Hetty
Heulwen
Hew variant spelling of Hugh
Hezekiah
Hieronymus
Hilary (or Hillary)
Hilda (or Hylda)
Hildebrand
Hildegard (or Hildegarde)
Hillary variant spelling of Hilary
Hippolyta
Hippolytus
Hiram
Hob
Hobart
Holden
Holly
Homer
Honor (or Honour)
Honora
Honoria
Hope
Horace
Horatia
Horatio
Horry
Hortense
Hortensia
Howard
Howell (or Howel) variant spellings of Hywel
Hubert
Hugh (or Huw, Hew)
Hughie (or Huey)
Hugo
Huldah, Hulda
Humbert
Humph
Humphrey
Huw variant spelling of Hugh
Hyacinth
Hyacintha
Hylda variant spelling of Hilda
Hyman
Hymie
Hypatia
Hywel (or Howell, Howel)
Iago
Ian (or Iain)
Ianthe
Ibbie (or Ibby)
Ichabod

Ida
Idonea
Idris
Ifor
Ignatius
Igor
Ike
Ilma
Ilona
Ilse
Immy
Imogen
Ina
Inez
Inga
Inge
Ingeborg
Ingram
Ingrid
Ingvar
Inigo
Iola
Iolanthe
Iolo
Iona
Iorwerth
Ira
Irene
Iris
Irma
Irvin (or Irvine)
Irving
Irwin (or Erwin)
Isa
Isaac (or Izaak)
Isabel (or Isabelle)
Isabella
Isadora
Isaiah
Iseult
Ishbel
Isidora
Isidore
Isla
Ismay
Isobel
Isolda
Isolde
Israel
Issy (or Izzy)
Ita
Ithel
Ivah
Ivan
Ives

Ivo
Ivor
Ivy
Izaak variant spelling of
    Isaac
Izzy variant spelling of Issy
Jabez
Jacinta
Jacinth
Jack
Jackie (or Jacky, Jacqui)
Jacob
Jacoba
Jacobina
Jacqueline (or Jacquelyn)
Jacques
Jacquetta
Jacqui variant spelling of
    Jackie
Jade
Jael
Jago
Jake
James
Jamesina
Jamie
Jan
Jane (or Jayne)
Janet
Janetta
Janette
Janice (or Janis)
Janie (or Janey)
Janine
Japheth
Jarrod (or Jarred, Jared)
Jarvis
Jasmine
Jason
Jasper
Jay
Jayne variant spelling of
    Jane
Jean
Jeanette (or Jeannette)
Jeanne
Jeannie (or Jeanie)
Jeannine
Jed
Jedidiah
Jeff variant spelling of Geoff
Jefferson
Jeffrey (or Jeffery) variant
    spellings of Geoffrey
Jehane

Jem
Jemima
Jemma variant spelling of
    Gemma
Jemmy
Jenna
Jennifer (or Jenifer)
Jenny (or Jennie)
Jephthah
Jeremiah
Jeremias
Jeremy
Jermaine
Jerome
Jerry variant spelling of
    Gerry
Jess
Jessamine (or Jessamyn)
Jesse
Jessica
Jessie
Jesus
Jethro
Jewel
Jill variant spelling of Gill
Jillian variant spelling of
    Gillian
Jim
Jimmy
Jinny
Jo
Joachim
Joan
Joanna
Joanne
Job
Jocasta
Jocelyn (or Joscelin)
Jock
Jodie (or Jodi, Jody)
Joe
Joel
Joey
Johanna
Johannes
John (or Jon)
Johnny (or Johnnie)
Jolene (or Joleen)
Jolyon
Jonah
Jonas
Jonathan
Jonquil
Jordan

Joscelin *variant spelling of*
  Jocelyn
José
Joseph
Josepha
Josephine
Josette
Josh
Joshua
Josiah
Josias
Josie
Joss
Jotham
Joy
Joyce
Juan
Juanita
Judah
Judas
Judd
Jude
Judith
Judoc
Judy (*or* Judi)
Jules
Julia
Julian
Juliana
Julianne
Julie
Julienne
Juliet (*or* Juliette)
Julitta
Julius
June
Junior
Juno
Justin
Justina
Justine
Kane
Kara *variant spelling of* **Cara**
Karel
Karen
Karin
Karina *variant spelling of*
  Carina
Karl *variant spelling of* **Carl**
Karol
Kate
Kath *variant spelling of* **Cath**
Katherine (*or* Katharine)
  variant spellings of
  Catherine

Kathleen (*or* Cathleen)
Kathryn
Kathy *variant spelling of*
  Cathy
Katie (*or* Katy)
Katrina
Katrine
Kay
Keeley
Keir
Keith
Kelda
Kelly (*or* Kellie)
Kelvin
Ken
Kendal (*or* Kendall)
Kendra
Kenelm
Kenneth
Kenny
Kenrick
Kent
Kentigern
Kenton
Keren
Kerenhappuch
Kerry (*or* Kerrie, Kerri,
  Keri)
Kester
Keturah
Kevin
Keziah (*or* Kezia)
Kieran
Kim
Kimball
Kimberly (*or* Kimberley)
Kinborough
King
Kingsley
Kirby
Kirk
Kirsten
Kirsty
Kit
Kitty
Kris
Kristen (*or* Kristin)
Kristina *variant spelling of*
  Christina
Kristine *variant spelling of*
  Christine
Kurt (*or* Curt)
Kyle
Kylie
Laban

Lachlan
Laetitia (*or* Letitia)
Lalage
Lambert
Lana
Lance
Lancelot
Lanty
Laraine (*or* Larraine)
Larissa
Larry
Lars
Launce
Launcelot
Laura (*or* Lora)
Lauraine
Laureen (*or* Loreen)
Laurel
Lauren
Laurence (*or* Lawrence)
Laurencia (*or* Laurentia)
Lauretta *variant spelling of*
  Loretta
Laurette (*or* Lorette)
Laurie (*or* Lauri, Lori)
Laurina
Laurinda *variant spelling of*
  Lorinda
Laverne
Lavina (*or* Lavena)
Lavinia
Lawrence *variant spelling of*
  Laurence
Lawrie
Layton *variant spelling of*
  Leighton
Lazarus
Leah
Leander
Leanne (*or* Lianne)
Lee (*or* Leigh)
Leighton (*or* Layton)
Leila (*or* Leilah, Lela)
Lelia
Lemmy
Lemuel
Lena
Lennox
Lenny (*or* Lennie)
Lenore
Leo
Leofric
Leoline
Leon
Leona

Leonard
Leonie
Leonora
Leopold
Leroy
Lesley (*fem*)
Leslie (*masc or fem*)
Lester
Leta
Letitia (*or* Laetitia)
Lettice
Letty (*or* Lettie)
Levi
Lew
Lewis
Liam
Liana
Lianne *variant spelling of* Leanne
Libby
Liddy
Liesl (*or* Liesel)
Lila
Lilac
Lili
Lilian (*or* Lillian)
Lilias (*or* Lillias)
Lilith
Lilla (*or* Lillah)
Lily (*or* Lillie)
Lina
Lincoln
Linda (*or* Lynda)
Lindsay (*masc or fem*)
Lindsey (*fem*)
Lindy
Linette *variant spelling of* Lynette
Linnet
Lionel
Lisa
Lisbeth *variant spelling of* Lizbeth
Lise
Lisette
Lita
Liz
Liza
Lizanne
Lizbeth (*or* Lisbeth)
Lizzie (*or* Lizzy)
Llewellyn (*or* Llewelyn)
Llinos
Lloyd
Lois

Lola
Lolita
Lolly
Lonnie
Lora *variant spelling of* Laura
Loraine *variant spelling of* Lorraine
Loreen *variant spelling of* Laureen
Loren (*or* Lorin)
Lorenzo
Loretta (*or* Lauretta)
Lorette *variant spelling of* Laurette
Lori *variant spelling of* Laurie
Lorin
Lorinda (*or* Laurinda)
Lorna
Lorne (*or* Lorn)
Lorraine (*or* Loraine)
Lottie (*or* Lotty)
Lou
Louella (*or* Luella)
Louie
Louis
Louisa
Louise
Loveday
Lovell
Lowell
Lucas
Lucasta
Luce
Lucetta
Lucette
Lucia
Lucian (*or* Lucien)
Luciana
Lucie
Lucienne
Lucilla
Lucille
Lucina
Lucinda
Lucius
Lucky
Lucrece
Lucretia
Lucrezia
Lucy
Ludo
Ludovic

Luella *variant spelling of* Louella
Luke
Lulu
Luther
Lydia
Lyle
Lyn *variant spelling of* Lynn
Lynda *variant spelling of* Linda
Lyndon
Lynette (*or* Lynnette, Linette)
Lynn (*or* Lynne, Lyn)
Lynsey
Lyra
Lyulf (*or* Lyulph)
Mabel (*or* Mable)
Mabella
Mabelle
Maddie (*or* Maddy)
Madeleine (*or* Madeline)
Madelina
Madge
Madoc
Mae
Maeve (*or* Meave)
Magda
Magdalena
Magdalene (*or* Magdalen)
Maggie
Magnolia
Magnus
Mahala (*or* Mahalah)
Mahalia
Maidie
Mair
Maire
Mairin
Maisie
Malachi (*or* Malachy)
Malcolm
Malise
Mallory (*or* Malory)
Malvin
Malvina
Mamie
Manasseh
Manasses
Mandy
Manfred
Manley
Manny
Mansel (*or* Mansell)
Manuel

Manuela
Manus
Mara (*or* Marah)
Marc
Marcel
Marcella
Marcelle
Marcellus
Marcia
Marcie (*or* Marcy)
Marco
Marcus
Margaret
Margareta (*or* Margaretta)
Margarita (*or* Marguerita)
Marge
Margery *variant spelling of*
  Marjorie
Margie
Margot (*or* Margo)
Marguerite
Maria
Mariabella
Mariam (*or* Mariamne)
Marian *variant spelling of*
  Marion
Marianne
Marie
Mariel
Marietta (*or* Mariette)
Marigold
Marilyn
Marina
Mario
Marion (*or* Marian)
Marisa (*or* Marissa)
Marita
Marius
Marjorie (*or* Margery)
Mark
Marla
Marlene
Marlin (*or* Marlyn)
Marmaduke
Marnie (*or* Marni)
Marsha
Marshall (*or* Marshal)
Marta
Martha
Marti (*or* Martie)
Martin (*or* Martyn)
Martina
Martine
Marty
Marvin (*or* Marvyn)

Mary
Matilda
Matt (*or* Mat)
Matthew
Matthias
Mattie (*or* Matty)
Maud (*or* Maude)
Maudie
Maura *variant spelling of*
  Moira
Maureen
Maurice (*or* Morris)
Mavis
Max
Maximilian
Maxine
Maxwell
May
Maynard
Meave *variant spelling of*
  Maeve
Meg
Megan (*or* Meghan)
Meggie (*or* Meggy)
Mehala (*or* Mehalah,
  Mehalia)
Mehetabel (*or* Mehitabel)
Meirion (*or* Merrion)
Mel
Melania
Melanie (*or* Melloney)
Melba
Melicent (*or* Melisent)
Melinda
Meliora
Mélisande
Melissa
Melody (*or* Melodie)
Melva
Melville
Melvin (*or* Melvyn)
Melvina
Mercedes
Mercia
Mercy
Meredith
Meriel
Merilyn (*or* Merrilyn)
Merle
Merlin
Merrion *variant spelling of*
  Meirion
Merry
Merton
Merv

Mervyn (*or* Mervin)
Meryl
Meta
Mia
Micah
Michael
Michaela
Michelle (*or* Michele)
Mick
Mickey (*or* Micky)
Mignon
Mike
Milborough
Milburn
Mildred
Miles (*or* Myles)
Millicent
Millie (*or* Milly)
Milo
Milton
Mima
Mimi
Mina
Minerva
Minna
Minnie
Minty
Mira *variant spelling of*
  Myra
Mirabel (*or* Mirabelle)
Mirabella
Miranda
Miriam
Mitch
Mitchell
Mitzi
Modesty
Moira (*or* Moyra, Maura)
Moll
Molly
Mona
Monica
Monique
Montague (*or* Montagu)
Montgomery
Monty (*or* Monte)
Morag
Moray
Mordecai
Morgan
Morna
Morris *variant spelling of*
  Maurice
Mort
Mortimer

Morty
Morwenna
Moses
Moshe
Moss
Moyna
Moyra *variant spelling of*
    Moira
Muir
Mungo
Murdoch
Muriel
Murray
Murtagh
Myfanwy
Myles *variant spelling of*
    Miles
Myra (*or* Mira)
Myrna
Myron
Myrtilla
Myrtle
Mysie
Nada
Nadia
Nadine
Nahum
Nan
Nance
Nancy
Nanette
Nanny
Naomi
Napoleon
Narcissus
Nat
Natalia
Natalie
Natasha
Nathan
Nathaniel (*or* Nathanael)
Neal *variant spelling of* Neil
Ned
Neddie (*or* Neddy)
Nehemiah
Neil (*or* Neill, Neal, Niall)
Nell
Nellie (*or* Nelly)
Nelson
Nerina
Nerissa
Nerys
Nessa
Nessie
Nest

Nesta
Netta
Nettie
Neva
Neville (*or* Nevil)
Newton
Niall *variant spelling of* Neil
Nichola *variant spelling of*
    Nicola
Nicholas (*or* Nicolas)
Nick
Nicky (*or* Nikki)
Nicodemus
Nicol
Nicola (*or* Nichola)
Nicolas *variant spelling of*
    Nicholas
Nicole
Nicolette
Nigel
Nikki *variant spelling of*
    Nicky
Nina
Ninette
Ninian
Nita
Noah
Noel (*or* Nowell)
Noeleen (*or* Noeline)
Noelle (*or* Noele)
Nola
Nolan
Nona
Nora (*or* Norah)
Norbert
Noreen
Norm
Norma
Norman
Norris
Norton
Nova
Nowell *variant spelling of*
    Noel
Nuala
Nye
Nyree
Obadiah
Oberon
Octavia
Octavian
Octavius
Odette
Odile
Odilia

Odo
Ogden
Olaf
Olave (*or* Olav)
Olga
Oliff
Oliva
Olive
Oliver
Olivet
Olivia
Olivier
Ollie
Olwen (*or* Olwyn)
Olympia
Omar
Ona
Onuphrius
Oonagh (*or* Oona)
Opal
Ophelia
Oriana
Oriel
Orlando
Orrell
Orson
Orval
Orville
Osbert
Osborn (*or* Osborne)
Oscar
Osmond (*or* Osmund)
Ossy (*or* Ossie)
Oswald
Oswin
Otho
Otis
Ottilia
Ottilie
Otto
Owen (*or* Owain)
Owena
Ozzy (*or* Ozzie)
Pablo
Paddy
Padraig
Palmer
Pam
Pamela
Pamelia
Pandora
Pansy
Paolo
Parker
Parnel (*or* Parnell)

Parry
Parthenia
Pascal
Pascale
Pascoe
Pat
Patience
Patricia
Patrick
Patsy
Patti (*or* Patty, Pattie)
Paul
Paula
Paulette
Pauline
Peace
Pearl
Pearlie
Pedro
Peg
Peggy
Pelham
Penelope
Penny
Pepin
Pepita
Perce
Percival (*or* Perceval)
Percy
Perdita
Peregrine
Peronel
Perpetua
Perry
Peta
Pete
Peter
Petra
Petrina
Petronella
Petronilla
Petula
Phebe *variant spelling of*
  Phoebe
Phemie
Phil
Philadelphia
Philemon
Philibert
Philip (*or* Phillip)
Philippa (*or* Phillipa,
  Phillippa)
Phillida *variant spelling of*
  Phyllida

Phillis *variant spelling of*
  Phyllis
Philomena
Phineas (*or* Phinehas)
Phoebe (*or* Phebe)
Phyllida (*or* Phillida)
Phyllis (*or* Phillis)
Pia
Pierre
Piers
Pip
Pippa
Piran
Pleasance
Poldie
Poll
Polly
Pollyanna
Poppy
Portia
Preston
Primrose
Prince
Prisca
Priscilla
Prissy
Pru (*or* Prue)
Prudence
Prunella
Queena
Queenie (*or* Queeny)
Quentin (*or* Quintin)
Quincy
Quinn
Quintin *variant spelling of*
  Quentin
Rab
Rabbie
Rachel (*or* Rachael)
Radcliff (*or* Radcliffe)
Rae
Raelene
Rafael *variant spelling of*
  Raphael
Rafaela *variant spelling of*
  Raphaela
Rafe
Raina
Raine
Rainer *variant spelling of*
  Rayner
Ralph
Ramon
Ramona
Ramsay (*or* Ramsey)

Ranald
Randall (*or* Randal)
Randolph
Randy
Raoul
Raphael (*or* Rafael)
Raphaela (*or* Rafaela)
Ray
Raymond (*or* Raymund)
Raymonde
Rayner (*or* Raynor, Rainer)
Rebecca (*or* Rebekah)
Redvers
Reg
Reggie
Regina
Reginald
Reine
Rena (*or* Rina)
Renata
René (*masc*)
Renée (*fem*)
Renie (*or* Rene)
Reuben
Rex
Reynard
Reynold
Rhea (*or* Ria)
Rhiannon
Rhoda
Rhona
Rhonda
Rhonwen
Rhys
Ria *variant spelling of* Rhea
Rica (*or* Rika)
Ricarda
Ricardo
Rich
Richard
Richenda
Richie
Richmal
Rick
Ricky (*or* Ricki, Rikki)
Rika *variant spelling of* Rica
Rina *variant spelling of* Rena
Rita
Roald
Rob
Robbie
Robert
Roberta
Robin
Robina

Robyn
Rochelle
Rod
Roddy
Roderick
Rodge
Rodger *variant spelling of*
    Roger
Rodney
Rodolph
Rodrigo
Roger (*or* Rodger)
Roisin
Roland (*or* Rowland)
Rolf (*or* Rolph)
Rollo
Rolly
Rolph *variant spelling of*
    Rolf
Roly
Roma
Romaine
Ron
Rona
Ronald
Ronalda
Ronna
Ronnette
Ronnie
Rory
Ros
Rosa
Rosabel (*or* Rosabelle)
Rosabella
Rosaleen
Rosalia
Rosalie
Rosalind
Rosalinda
Rosaline (*or* Rosalyn)
Rosamund (*or* Rosamond)
Rosanna (*or* Roseanna)
Rosanne (*or* Roseann,
    Roseanne)
Rose
Roseline (*or* Roselyn)
Rosemary (*or* Rosemarie)
Rosetta
Rosie
Rosina
Rosita
Roslyn (*or* Rosslyn)
Ross
Rowan
Rowena

Rowland *variant spelling of*
    Roland
Roxana
Roxane (*or* Roxanne)
Roxanna
Roxy
Roy
Royal
Royston
Rubina
Ruby
Rudolph (*or* Rudolf)
Rudy (*or* Rudi)
Rufus
Rupert
Ruperta
Russ
Russell (*or* Russel)
Ruth
Ruthie
Ryan
Sabina
Sabrina
Sacha
Sacheverell
Sadie
Saffron
Sal
Salamon
Salena (*or* Salina)
Sally
Salome
Salvador
Salvatore
Sam
Samantha
Sammy
Samson (*or* Sampson)
Samuel
Sanchia
Sandra
Sandy (*or* Sandie)
Sapphira
Sapphire
Sarah (*or* Sara, Sarra)
Sarai
Saranna
Sarina
Sarita
Sarra *variant spelling of*
    Sarah
Saul
Saxon
Scarlett (*or* Scarlet)
Scott

Seamus (*or* Shamus)
Sean (*or* Shaun, Shawn)
Seb
Sebastian
Sefton
Selby
Selina (*or* Selena, Celina)
Selma
Selwyn
Senga
Septima
Septimus
Seraphina
Serena
Serge
Sergei
Sergio
Sergius
Seth
Seumas
Seward
Sextus
Seymour
Shamus *variant spelling of*
    Seamus
Shane
Shani
Shannon
Shari
Sharon (*or* Sharron)
Shaun *variant spelling of*
    Sean
Shauna
Shaw
Shawn *variant spelling of*
    Sean
Sheba
Sheena (*or* Shena)
Sheila (*or* Shelagh,
    Sheelagh, Sheilah)
Sheldon
Shelley (*or* Shelly)
Shem
Shena *variant spelling of*
    Sheena
Sheridan
Sherry (*or* Sherri) *variant
    spellings of* Cherie
Sheryl
Shirl
Shirley
Sholto
Shona
Shushana (*or* Shushanna)
Sian

Sibbie (or Sibby)
Sibella
Sibilla
Sibyl
Sibylla
Sid (or Syd)
Sidney (or Sydney)
Sidonia
Sidony (or Sidonie)
Siegfried
Sigismund
Sigmund
Silas
Sile
Silvana
Silvanus (or Sylvanus)
Silvester
Silvia
Sim
Simeon
Simon
Simona
Simone
Sinclair
Sine
Sinead
Siobhan
Sisley
Sissy (or Sissie) variant
  spellings of Cissy
Solly
Solomon
Sonia (or Sonya, Sonja)
Sophia
Sophie (or Sophy)
Sophronia
Sorcha
Spencer
Stacey (or Stacy)
Stafford
Stan
Stanford
Stanislas (or Stanislaus)
Stanley
Steenie
Stella
Stephanie (or Stefanie)
Stephen (or Steven)
Steve
Stevie
Stewart variant spelling of
  Stuart
Stirling
St John
Stuart (or Stewart)

Sue
Sukey
Susan
Susannah (or Susanna,
  Suzanna)
Susie (or Suzy)
Suzanne (or Susanne)
Suzette
Suzy
Swithin
Sybella
Sybil (or Sibyl)
Sybilla
Syd variant spelling of Sid
Sydney variant spelling of
  Sidney
Sylvanus variant spelling of
  Silvanus
Sylvester (or Silvester)
Sylvia (or Silvia)
Sylvie
Tabitha
Tacey (or Tacy)
Taffy
Talbot
Taliesin
Talitha
Tallulah
Tam
Tamar
Tamara
Tamasine
Tammy
Tamsin
Tancred
Tania variant spelling of
  Tanya
Tanith
Tansy
Tanya (or Tania)
Tara
Tarquin
Tatiana
Taylor
Ted
Teddy (or Teddie)
Tegan
Tegwen
Temperance
Terence (or Terrence)
Teresa (or Theresa)
Terry (or Terri)
Tertius
Tess
Tessa

Tessie
Tetty
Tex
Thaddeus
Thea
Thekla (or Thecla)
Thelma
Theo
Theobald
Theodora
Theodore
Theodoric
Theodosia
Theophania
Theophila
Theophilus
Theresa variant spelling of
  Teresa
Thérèse
Theresia
Thirza (or Thirsa)
Thom
Thomas
Thomasin
Thomasina
Thomasine
Thora
Thorley
Thornton
Thurstan (or Thurston)
Thyra
Tibby
Tiffany
Tilda
Tilly
Tim
Timmy
Timothea
Timothy
Tina
Tirzah
Tisha
Titus
Tobias
Toby
Todd
Tolly
Tom
Tommy
Toni
Tonia (or Tonya)
Tony
Topsy
Torquil
Totty

Tracy (*or* Tracey)
Travers
Travis
Trevor (*or* Trefor)
Tricia (*or* Trisha)
Trina
Trissie
Tristan
Tristram
Trix
Trixie
Troy
Trudy (*or* Trudie, Trudi)
Tryphena
Tudor
Turlough
Tybalt
Tyra
Tyrone
Ulric
Ulrica
Ulysses
Una
Unity
Upton
Urban
Uriah
Ursula
Val
Valda
Valentina
Valentine
Valeria
Valerie
Vanda
Vanessa
Vashti
Vaughan (*or* Vaughn)
Velda
Velma
Venetia
Venus
Vera
Vere
Verena
Verity
Verna
Vernon
Verona
Veronica
Véronique
Vic (*or* Vick)
Vicky (*or* Vicki, Vickie, Vikki)
Victor

Victoria
Victorine
Vida
Vilma
Vin
Vina
Vince
Vincent
Vincentia
Vinnie (*or* Vinny)
Vinny
Viola
Violet
Violetta
Violette
Virgil
Virginia
Vita
Vitus
Viv
Viva
Vivia
Vivian (*or* Vivien, Vyvyan)
Viviana
Vivienne
Wade
Wal
Walburga
Waldo
Wallace (*or* Wallis)
Wally
Walt
Walter
Wanda
Ward
Warner
Warren
Warwick
Washington
Wat
Wayne
Wenda
Wendell
Wendy
Wesley
Wilbert
Wilbur
Wilf
Wilfred (*or* Wilfrid)
Wilfrida (*or* Wilfreda)
Wilhelmina
Will
Willa
Willard
William

Williamina
Willie (*or* Willy)
Willis
Willoughby
Wilma
Wilmer
Wilmot
Win
Windsor
Winfred (*or* Winfrid)
Winifred (*or* Winnifred, Winefred)
Winnie
Winston
Winthrop
Woodrow
Wyatt
Wybert
Wyndham
Wynford
Wynn (*or* Wynne)
Wystan
Xanthe
Xavier
Xenia
Yasmin
Yehudi
Yolanda
Yolande
Yves
Yvette
Yvonne (*or* Evonne)
Zacchaeus
Zachariah
Zacharias
Zachary
Zak (*or* Zack)
Zana
Zandra
Zane
Zara
Zechariah
Zedekiah
Zelda
Zelma
Zena
Zenobia
Zephaniah
Zillah
Zinnia
Zita
Zoë (*or* Zoe)
Zola
Zora (*or* Zorah)
Zuleika

Biographical Names

Aalto, Alvar
Aaltonen, Wäinö
Abbas
Abbas, Ferhat
Abd Allah (*known as* the Khalifa)
'Abd al-Malik ibn Marwan
'Abd ar-Rahman III an-Nasir
Abdelkader
Abdulhamid
Abdullah
Abdul Rahman, Tunku
Abel, Sir Frederick Augustus
Abel, Niels Henrik
Abelard, Peter
Abercrombie, Sir (Leslie) Patrick
Abercromby, Sir Ralph
Aberdeen, George Hamilton-Gordon, 4th Earl of
Absalom son of King David
Absalon 12th-century Danish statesman
Abu al-Wafa
Abu Bakar sultan of Johore
Abu Bakr first caliph
Abu Hanifah
Abu Nuwas
Accius, Lucius
Accoramboni, Vittoria
Achard, Franz Karl
Achebe, Chinua
Acheson, Dean (Gooderham)
Acton, John Emerich Edward Dalberg-Acton, 1st Baron
Adalbert
Adam, Adolphe-Charles
Adam, James
Adam, Robert
Adam, William
Adamnan, St
Adamov, Arthur
Adams, Charles Francis
Adams, Henry

Adams, John
Adams, John Couch
Adams, John Quincy
Adams, Richard
Adams, Samuel
Adamson, Robert
Addington, Henry, 1st Viscount Sidmouth
Addinsell, Richard
Addison, Joseph
Addison, Thomas
Adenauer, Konrad
Ader, Clément
Adler, Alfred
Adler, Felix
Adler, Larry
Adrian, Edgar Douglas, 1st Baron
Aelfric
Aeneas Silvius
Aeschines
Aeschylus
Aesop
Aetius, Flavius
Afghani, Jamal ad-Din al-
Aga Khan
Agassiz, Alexander
Agassiz, Jean Louis Rodolphe
Agathocles
Agee, James
Agesilaus
Agha Mohammad Khan
Agnesi, Maria Gaetana
Agnew, Spiro T(heodore)
Agnon, Shmuel Yosef
Agostini, Giacomo
Agricola, Georgius
Agricola, Gnaeus Julius
Agricola, Johann
Agrippa, Marcus Vipsanius
Agrippina
Ahad Ha'am
Ahmad Khan, Sir Sayyid
Ahmad Shah Durrani
Ahmed

Ahmose
Aiken, Howard Hathaway
Ailred of Rievaulx, St
Ainsworth, W(illiam) Harrison
Airy, Sir George Biddell
Aistulf
Akbar
Akhenaton (*or* Ikhnaton)
Akhmatova
Akiba ben Joseph
Alain-Fournier
Alanbrooke, Alan Francis Brooke, 1st Viscount
Alarcón, Pedro Antonio de
Alarcón y Mendoza, Juan Ruiz de
Alba, Fernando Alvarez de Toledo, Duke of
Albee, Edward
Albéniz, Isaac Manuel Francisco
Alberoni, Giulio
Albers, Josef
Alberti, Leon Battista
Alberti, Raphael
Albertus Magnus, St
Albinoni, Tomaso
Alboin
Albuquerque, Alfonso de
Alcaeus
Alcibiades
Alcmaeon
Alcock, Sir John (William)
Alcoforado, Marianna
Alcott, Louisa May
Alcuin
Aldanov, Mark
Aldhelm, St
Aldington, Richard
Aldiss, Brian W(ilson)
Aldrich, Thomas Bailey
Aldridge, Ira Frederick
Alegría, Ciro
Alekhine, Alexander
Alemán, Mateo

Alexander, Sir William,
  1st Earl of Stirling
Alexander of Tunis,
  Harold, 1st Earl
Alexius Comnenus
al-Farabi, Mohammed
  ibn Tarkhan
Alfieri, Vittorio, Count
Alfonso Spanish king
Alfvén, Hannes Olof
  Gösta
Algirdas
Algren, Nelson
Ali
Ali, Muhammad
Ali Pasa, Mehmed Emin
Alkan, Charles Henri
  Valentin
al-Khwarizmi,
  Muhammed ibn Musa
Al-Kindi, Abu Yusuf
  Ya'qub ibn Ishaq
Allbutt, Sir Thomas
  Clifford
Allegri, Gregorio
Allen, Ethan
Allen, William, Cardinal
Allen, Woody
Allenby, Edmund Henry
  Hynman, 1st Viscount
Allende (Gossens),
  Salvador
Alleyn, Edward
Allingham, Margery
Allston, Washington
Alma-Tadema, Sir
  Lawrence
Almeida, Francisco de
Alp Arslan
Alphege, St
Altdorfer, Albrecht
Althusius, Johannes
Altichiero
Alvarado, Pedro de
Alvarez, Luis Walter
Alvárez Quintero,
  Joaquin
Alvárez Quintero,
  Serafin
Alyattes
Alypius
Amadeus the Peaceful
Amalasuntha
Amalia, Anna
Amanollah Khan
Amati, Andrea

Amati, Antonio
Amati, Girolamo
Amati, Nicolò
Ambartsumian, Viktor
  A(mazaspovich)
Ambler, Eric
Amenemhet
Amenhotep
Amherst, Jeffrey, Baron
Amici, Giovanni Battista
Amiel, Henri Frédéric
Amin Dada, Idi
Amis, Kingsley
Amis, Martin
Ammanati, Bartolommeo
Ampère, André Marie
Amr ibn al-As
Amundsen, Roald
Amyot, Jacques
Anacreon
Ananda
Anastasius
Anaxagoras
Anaximander
Anaximenes
Anchieta, José de
Andersen, Hans
  Christian
Anderson, Carl David
Anderson, Elizabeth
  Garrett
Anderson, John, 1st
  Viscount Waverley
Anderson, Sherwood
Andrássy, Gyula, Count
André, John
Andrea del Sarto
Andrewes, Lancelot
Andrić, Ivo
Andropov, Yuri
  Vladimirovich
Aneirin
Angelico, Fra
Angell, Sir Norman
Anglesey, Henry William
  Paget, 1st Marquess
  of
Angoulême, Charles de
  Valois, Duc d'
Angoulême, Margaret of
Ångström, Anders Jonas
Ankhesenamen
An Lu Shan
Annigoni, Pietro
Anouilh, Jean

Ansbach, Caroline of
Anselm of Canterbury,
  St
Ansermet, Ernest
Ansgar, St
Anson, George Anson,
  Baron
Antelami, Benedetto
Antenor
Antheil, George
Antigonus
Antiochus
Antipas, Herod
Antipater
Antiphon
Antisthenes
Antonello da Messina
Antonescu, Ion
Antoninus Pius
Antonioni, Michelangelo
Anville, Jean-Baptiste
  Bourguignon d'
Anzengruber, Ludwig
Apelles
Aphraates
Apollinaire, Guillaume
Apollonius
Appert, Nicolas
Apuleius, Lucius
Aquaviva, Claudio
Aquinas, St Thomas
Arafat, Yassir
Arago, (Dominique)
  François (Jean)
Aragon, Louis
Arakcheev, Aleksei
  Andreevich, Count
Aram, Eugene
Arany, János
Arbuthnot, John
Arc, St Joan of
Archer, Frederick Scott
Archer, Thomas
Archer, William
Archilochus
Archimedes
Archipenko, Alexander
Archytas
Arcimboldo, Giuseppe
Ardashir
Arduin
Aretino, Pietro
Argyll, Archibald
  Campbell, 1st
  Marquess of

Baez, Joan
Baffin, William
Bagehot, Walter
Baily, Francis
Bain, Alexander
Baird, John Logie
Bairnsfather, (Charles)
  Bruce
Baker, Sir Benjamin
Baker, Dame Janet
  (Abbott)
Baker, Sir Samuel White
Bakewell, Robert
Bakst, Léon
Bakunin, Mikhail
  Aleksandrovich
Balakirev, Mili
  Alekseevich
Balanchine, George
Balboa, Vasco Núñez de
Balchin, Nigel
Balcon, Sir Michael
Baldwin, James Arthur
Baldwin of Bewdley,
  Stanley, 1st Earl
Balenciaga, Cristóbal
Balfour, Arthur James,
  1st Earl of
Ball, John
Balla, Giacomo
Balliol, Edward de
Balliol, John de
Balzac, Honoré de
Bana
Banda, Hastings Kamuzu
Bandaranaike, Sirimavo
  Ratwatte Dias
Bandaranaike,
  S(olomon) W(est)
  R(idgeway) D(ias)
Bandeira, Manuel
  Carneiró de Sousa
Bankhead, Tallulah
Banks, Sir Joseph
Bannister, Sir Roger
  (Gilbert)
Banting, Sir Frederick
  Grant
Banville, Théodore
  Faullain de
Barbarossa
Barber, Samuel
Barbirolli, Sir John
Barbour, John
Barbusse, Henri

Barclay de Tolly,
  Mikhail Bogdanovich,
  Prince
Bardeen, John
Bardot, Brigitte
Barents, Willem
Barère, Bertrand
Barham, Richard Harris
Bar Hebraeus
Baring, Evelyn
Barker, George
Barker, Harley Granville
Barkhausen, Heinrich
Bar Kokhba
Barlach, Ernst
Barnard, Christiaan
  Neethling
Barnard, Edward
  Emerson
Barnardo, Thomas John
Barnave, Antoine Pierre
Barnes, William
Barnum, Phineas Taylor
Baroja, Pío
Barras, Paul François
  Jean Nicolas, Vicomte
  de
Barrault, Jean-Louis
Barrès, Maurice
Barrie, Sir James
  (Matthew)
Barry, Sir Charles
Barrymore, Ethel
Barrymore, John
Barrymore, Lionel
Bart, Jean
Bart, Lionel
Barth, Heinrich
Barth, John
Barth, Karl
Bartholdi, Frédéric
  August
Bartók, Béla
Bartolommeo, Fra
Barton, Clara
Barton, Sir Edmund
Barton, Elizabeth
Baruch, Bernard
Basie, Count
Baskerville, John
Bassano, Jacopo
Bates, H(erbert)
  E(rnest)
Bates, Henry Walter
Bateson, William

Báthory, Stephen
Batista y Zaldívar,
  Fulgencio
Battani, al-
Batten, Jean
Battenberg, Prince Louis
  of
Baudelaire, Charles
Baudouin
Baum, L(yman) Frank
Baumgarten, Alexander
  Gottlieb
Baur, Ferdinand
  Christian
Bax, Sir Arnold Edward
  Trevor
Baxter, Richard
Bayar, Mahmud Celal
Bayard, Pierre Terrail,
  Seigneur de
Baybars
Bayezid
Bayle, Pierre
Baylis, Lilian
Bayliss, Sir William
  Maddock
Bazaine, Achille
  François
Beadle, George Wells
Beale, Dorothea
Beardsley, Aubrey
  Vincent
Beaton, Sir Cecil
  (Walter Hardy)
Beaton, David
Beatty, David, 1st Earl
Beaufort, Henry
Beaufort, Margaret
Beauharnais, Alexandre,
  Vicomte de
Beauharnais, Eugène de
Beauharnais, Hortense
  de
Beaumarchais, Pierre-
  Augustin Caron de
Beaumont, Francis
Beaumont, William
Beauvais, Vincent of
Beauvoir, Simone de
Beaverbrook, Max(well)
  Aitken, 1st Baron
Bebel, August
Beccaria, Cesare
  Bonesana, Marchese
  de
Bechet, Sidney

Becket, St Thomas
Beckett, Samuel
Beckford, William
Beckmann, Max
Bequerel, Antoine César
Becquerel, (Antoine)
  Henri
Beddoes, Thomas Lovell
Bede, St
Bedford, John, Duke of
Beebe, Charles William
Beecham, Sir Thomas
Beecher, Henry Ward
Beerbohm, Sir Max
Beethoven, Ludwig van
Beeton, Isabella Mary
Begin, Menachem
Behan, Brendan
Behn, Aphra
Behrens, Peter
Behring, Emil Adolf von
Behzad
Beiderbecke, Bix
Béjart, Maurice
Belinsky, Vissarion
Belisarius
Bell, Alexander Graham
Bell, Gertrude
Bellay, Joachim de
Bellingshausen, Fabian
  Gottlieb, Baron von
Bellini, Gentile
Bellini, Giovanni
Bellini, Jacopo
Bellini, Vincenzo
Bello, Andrés
Belloc, (Joseph-Pierre)
  Hilaire
Bellow, Saul
Belmonte y García, Juan
Belyi, Andrei
Bembo, Pietro
Ben Bella, Ahmed
Benbow, John
Benchley, Robert
  Charles
Benda, Julien
Beneš, Edvard
Benét, Stephen Vincent
Ben-Gurion, David
Benn, Anthony (Neil)
  Wedgwood
Benn, Gottfried
Bennett, (Enoch) Arnold
Bennett, James Gordon

Bennett, Richard
  Bedford, Viscount
Bennett, Richard Rodney
Bennett, Sir William
  Sterndale
Benoit de Sainte-Maure
Benson, Sir Frank
Bentham, Jeremy
Bentinck, Lord William
  (Henry Cavendish)
Bentley, Edmund
  Clerihew
Bentley, Richard
Benton, Thomas Hart
Benz, Karl (Friedrich)
Ben-Zvi, Itzhak
Bérain the Elder, Jean
Beranger, Pierre Jean de
Berdyaev, Nikolai
Berenson, Bernard
Berg, Alban
Bergius, Friedrich
Bergman, Hjalmar
  (Fredrik Elgérus)
Bergman, Ingmar
Bergman, Ingrid
Bergson, Henri
Beria, Lavrenti Pavlovich
Bering, Vitus Jonassen
Berio, Luciano
Beriosova, Svetlana
Berkeley, Busby
Berkeley, George
Berkeley, Sir Lennox
  Randal Francis
Berkeley, Sir William
Berlichingen, Götz von
Berlin, Irving
Berlin, Sir Isaiah
Berlinguer, Enrico
Berlioz, (Louis) Hector
Bernadotte, Folke,
  Count
Bernadotte, Jean
  Baptiste Jules
Bernanos, Georges
Bernard, Claude
Bernardin de Saint-
  Pierre, Jacques Henri
Bernhard of Saxe-
  Weimar, Duke
Bernhardt, Sarah
Bernini, Gian Lorenzo
Bernoulli, Daniel
Bernoulli, Jaques

Bernoulli, Jean
Bernoulli, Nicolas
Bernstein, Eduard
Bernstein, Leonard
Berruguete, Alonso
Berruguete, Pedro
Berry, Chuck
Berry, Jean de France,
  Duc de
Berry, Marie-Caroline
  de Bourbon-Sicile,
  Duchesse de
Berthelot, (Pierre
  Eugène) Marcelin
Berthollet, Claude Louis,
  Comte
Bertillon, Alphonse
Bertillon, Jacques
Bertolucci, Bernardo
Bertrand, Henri Gratien,
  Comte
Bertran de Born
Berwick, James
  Fitzjames, Duke of
Berzelius, Jöns Jakob,
  Baron
Besant, Annie
Besant, Sir Walter
Bessarion, John
Bessemer, Sir Henry
Best, Charles Herbert
Bestuzhev-Riumin,
  Aleksei Petrovich,
  Count
Bethe, Hans Albrecht
Bethlen, Gábor
Bethmann-Hollweg,
  Theobald von
Betjeman, Sir John
Betterton, Thomas
Betti, Ugo
Beust, Friedrich
  Ferdinand, Count von
Bevan, Aneurin
Beveridge, William
  Henry Beveridge, 1st
  Baron
Bevin, Ernest
Bewick, Thomas
Beza, Theodore
Bhoskhara
Bhutto, Benazir
Bhutto, Zulfikar Ali
Bialik, Chaim Nachman
Bidault, Georges
Biddle, John

Bierce, Ambrose
Gwinnett
Bilderdijk, Willem
Billroth, Christian Albert
Theodor
Binet, Alfred
Bing, Sir Rudolf
Binyon, Laurence
Birendra Bir Bikram
Shah Dev
Birkbeck, George
Birkenhead, F(rederick)
E(dwin) Smith, 1st
Earl of
Birkhoff, George David
Biró, Laszlo
Birtwistle, Harrison
Bishop, Sir Henry
Rowley
Bismarck, Otto Eduard
Leopold, Prince von
Bizet, Georges
Bjerknes, Jakob
Bjerknes, Vilhelm
Friman Koren
Bjørnson, Bjørnstjerne
(Martinius)
Black, Joseph
Blackett, Patrick
Maynard Stuart,
Baron
Blackmore, R(ichard)
D(oddridge)
Blackstone, Sir William
Blackwood, Algernon
Henry
Blake, Peter
Blake, Robert
Blake, William
Blanc, Louis
Blanchard, Jean Pierre
François
Blanqui, Louis Auguste
Blasco Ibáñez, Vicente
Blasis, Carlo
Blavatsky, Helen
Petrovna
Blenkinsop, John
Blériot, Louis
Blessington, Marguerite,
Countess of
Bligh, William
Bliss, Sir Arthur Edward
Drummond

Blixen, Karen, Baroness
Blixen-Finecke (pen
name Isak Dinesen)
Bloch, Ernest
Bloch, Felix
Blok, Aleksandr
Aleksandrovich
Blondel, Maurice
Blondin, Charles
Blood, Colonel Thomas
Bloomfield, Leonard
Blow, John
Blücher, Gebhard
Leberecht von, Prince
of Wahlstatt
Blum, Léon
Blunden, Edmund
Charles
Blunt, Anthony
Blyton, Enid
Boadicea (or Boudicca)
Boas, Franz
Boccaccio, Giovanni
Boccherini, Luigi
Boccioni, Umberto
Bodawpaya
Bodhidharma
Bodin, Jean
Bodoni, Giambattista
Boehm, Theobald
Boehme, Jakob variant
spelling of Böhme, Jakob
Boethius, Anicius
Manlius Severinus
Bogarde, Dirk
Bogart, Humphrey
Bohemond
Böhm, Karl
Böhme (or Boehme), Jakob
Bohr, Aage
Bohr, Niels Henrik
David
Boiardo, Matteo Maria,
Conte di Scandiano
Boileau(-Despréaux),
Nicolas
Boito, Arrigo
Bokassa
Bolden, Buddy
Bolesław
Boleyn, Anne
Bolingbroke, Henry St
John, 1st Viscount
Bolívar, Simón
Böll, Heinrich

Bologna, Giovanni da
Bolt, Robert Oxton
Boltzmann, Ludwig
Eduard
Bolyai, János
Bonaparte, Carlo
Bonaparte, Jérôme
Bonaparte, Joseph
Bonaparte, Louis
Bonaparte, Lucien
Bonaparte, Napoleon
Bonaventure, St
Bond, Edward
Bondi, Sir Hermann
Bonham-Carter, Lady
Violet, Baroness
Asquith
Bonhoeffer, Dietrich
Boniface, St
Bonington, Chris
Bonington, Richard
Parkes
Bonnard, Pierre
Bonnet, Charles
Boole, George
Boone, Daniel
Booth, Charles
Booth, Edwin
Booth, Evangeline
Booth, John Wilkes
Booth, William
Booth, William Bramwell
Borden, Sir Robert Laird
Bordet, Jules Jean
Baptiste Vincent
Borelli, Giovanni
Alfonso
Borg, Bjorn
Borges, Jorge Luis
Borgia, Cesare
Borgia, Lucrezia
Borglum, Gutzon
Borlaug, Norman
Bormann, Martin
Born, Max
Borodin, Aleksandr
Porfirevich
Borromeo, St Charles
Borromini, Francesco
Borrow, George Henry
Boru, Brian
Bosanquet, Bernard
Bosch, Carl
Bosch, Hieronymus

Bose, Sir Jagadis
  Chandra
Bose, Subhas Chandra
Bossuet, Jacques
  Bénigne
Boswell, James
Botha, Louis
Botha, Pieter Willem
Bothe, Walther Wilhelm
  Georg Franz
Bothwell, James
  Hepburn, 4th Earl of
Botticelli, Sandro
Botvinnik, Mikhail
  Moiseivich
Boucher, François
Boucher de Perthes,
  Jacques
Boudicca *variant spelling of*
  Boadicea
Boudin, Eugène
Bougainville, Louis
  Antoine de
Bouillon, Godfrey of
Boulanger, Nadia
  (Juliette)
Boulez, Pierre
Boulle, André Charles
Boult, Sir Adrian
  (Cedric)
Boulter, Hugh
Boulton, Matthew
Boumédienne, Houari
Bourbaki, Nicolas
Bourdelle, Émile
Bourgeois, Léon
Bourmont, Louis
  Auguste Victor de
  Ghaisnes, Comte de
Bouts, Dierick
Boveri, Theodor
  Heinrich
Bovet, Daniel
Bow, Clara
Bowdler, Thomas
Bowen, Elizabeth
Bowen, Norman Levi
Bower, Frederick Orpen
Bowie, David
Boyce, William
Boycott, Charles
  Cunningham
Boyd-Orr of Brechin
  Mearns, John, 1st
  Baron
Boyer, Charles

Boyle, Robert
Bo Zhu Yi (*or* Po Chü-i)
Brabham, Jack
Bracegirdle, Anne
Bracton, Henry de
Bradbury, Ray
Bradford, William
Bradlaugh, Charles
Bradley, Andrew Cecil
Bradley, Francis Herbert
Bradley, Omar Nelson
Bradman, Sir Donald
  George
Braganza, Catherine of
Bragg, Sir (William)
  Lawrence
Bragg, Sir William
  Henry
Brahe, Tycho
Brahms, Johannes
Braille, Louis
Bramah, Joseph
Bramante, Donato
Brancusi, Constantin
Brandes, Georg Morris
  Cohen
Brando, Marlon
Brandt, Bill British photog-
  rapher
Brandt, Willy German
  statesman
Brant, Joseph
Brant, Sebastian
Branting, Karl Hjalmar
Brantôme, Pierre, Abbé
  and Seigneur de
  Bourdeille
Braque, Georges
Bratby, John
Brattain, Walter Houser
Brauchitsch, Walther
  von
Braun, Eva
Brazza, Pierre Paul
  François Camille
  Savorgnan de
Bream, Julian Alexander
Brébeuf, St Jean de
Brecht, Bertolt
Brendel, Alfred
Brentano, Clemens
Brentano, Franz
Bresson, Robert
Breton, André
Breuer, Josef

Breuer, Marcel Lajos
Breuil, Henri
Brewster, Sir David
Brezhnev, Leonid Ilich
Brian, Havergal
Briand, Aristide
Bridge, Frank
Bridges, Robert
  Seymour
Bridgman, Percy
  Williams
Bridie, James
Briggs, Henry
Bright, John
Bright, Richard
Brillat-Savarin,
  Anthelme
Brindley, James
Brissot, Jacques-Pierre
Britten, (Edward)
  Benjamin, Baron
Broadwood, John
Broch, Hermann
Broglie, Louis Victor,
  7th Duc de
Bronowski, Jacob
Brontë, Anne
Brontë, Charlotte
Brontë, Emily
Brontë, Patrick Branwell
Bronzino
Brook, Peter
Brooke, Sir James
Brooke, Rupert
  (Chawner)
Brookeborough, Basil
  Stanlake Brooke, 1st
  Viscount
Broome, David
Brough, Louise
Brouwer, Adriaen
Brouwer, L(uitzen)
  E(gbertus) J(an)
Brown, Sir Arthur
Brown, Capability
Brown, Ford Madox
Brown, George (Alfred),
  Baron George-Brown
Brown, John
Brown, Robert botanist
Browne, Hablot Knight
  (*known as* Phiz)
Browne, Robert Puritan
Browne, Sir Thomas

Browning, Elizabeth
Barrett
Browning, Robert
Brubeck, Dave
Bruce, James
Bruce, Robert the
Bruce of Melbourne,
Stanley Melbourne,
1st Viscount
Bruch, Max
Bruckner, Anton
Brueghel, Jan
Brueghel, Pieter
Brummel, George Bryan
Brunel, Isambard
Kingdom
Brunel, Sir Marc
Isambard
Brunelleschi, Filippo
Brüning, Heinrich
Brunner, Emil
Bruno, Giordano
Brunswick, Caroline of
Brutus, Marcus Junius
Bryant, William Cullen
Bryce, James, 1st
Viscount
Buber, Martin
Bucer, Martin
Buchan, John, 1st Baron
Tweedsmuir
Buchanan, George
Buchanan, James
Büchner, Georg
Buck, Pearl
S(ydenstricker)
Buckingham, George
Villiers, Duke of
Buddha
Buddhaghosa
Budé, Guillaume
Budge, (James) Don(ald)
Bueno, Maria (Esther)
Buffalo Bill see Cody,
William F(rederick)
Buffet, Bernard
Buffon, Georges Louis
Leclerc, Comte de
Bugatti, Ettore (Arco
Isidoro)
Bukhari, al-
Bukharin, Nikolai
Ivanovich
Bulganin, Nikolai
Aleksandrovich
Bull, John

Bülow, Bernhard
Heinrich, Fürst von
Bülow, Hans Guido,
Freiherr von
Bultmann, Rudolf (Karl)
Bulwer-Lytton, Edward
George Earle, 1st
Baron Lytton
Bunche, Ralph
Bunin, Ivan Alekseevich
Bunsen, Robert Wilhelm
Buñuel, Luis
Bunyan, John
Burbage, Richard
Burbank, Luther
Burckhardt, Jacob
Christoph
Bürge, Joost
Bürger, Gottfried
Burgess, Anthony
Burgess, Guy
Burgh, Hubert de
Burghley, Robert Cecil,
1st Earl of Salisbury
Burghley, William Cecil,
Lord
Burgoyne, John
Buridan, Jean
Burke, Edmund
Burke, Robert O'Hara
Burke, William
Burlington, Richard
Boyle, 3rd Earl of
Burne-Jones, Sir Edward
Coley
Burnet, Sir Frank
Macfarlane
Burnet, Gilbert
Burnett, Frances Eliza
Hodgson
Burney, Charles
Burney, Fanny
Burns, John Elliot
Burns, Robert
Burr, Aaron
Burra, Edward
Burroughs, Edgar Rice
Burroughs, William
Burton, Sir Richard
Burton, Richard
Burton, Robert
Busby, Matt
Bush, Alan Dudley
Bushnell, David
Busoni, Ferruccio

Buss, Frances Mary
Bustamante y Sirvén,
Antonio Sánchez de
Bute, John Stuart, 3rd
Earl of
Butler, Benjamin
Franklin
Butler, Joseph
Butler, R(ichard)
A(usten), Baron
Butler, Reg(inald)
Cotterell
Butler, Samuel
Butler, Samuel
Butor, Michel
Butt, Dame Clara
Butterfield, William
Buxtehude, Dietrich
Bylot, Robert
Byng, George, Viscount
Torrington
Byng, John
Byng of Vimy, Julian,
1st Viscount
Byrd, Richard E(velyn)
Byrd, William
Byron, George Gordon,
—Lord
Caballé, Montserrat
Cabot, John
Cabot, Sebastian
Cabral, Pedro Álvares
Cabrini, St Frances
Xavier
Caccini, Giulio
Cadbury, George
Cadbury, Richard
Cade, Jack
Cadwallader (or Cadwaladr)
Caedmon
Caesar, (Gaius) Julius
Cage, John
Cagliostro, Alessandro,
Conte di
Cagney, James
Caillaux, Joseph
Cain
Calas, Jean
Calder, Alexander
Calderón de la Barca,
Pedro
Calhoun, John
C(aldwell)
Caligula
Callaghan, (Leonard)
James, Baron

Callas, Maria
Calles, Plutarco Elías
Callias
Callicrates
Callimachus
Callot, Jacques
Calmette, Albert Léon
  Charles
Calvin, John
Calvin, Melvin
Cambacérès, Jean
  Jacques Régis, Duc de
Cambyses II
Camden, William
Cameron, Julia
  Margaret
Camões, Luís de
Campanella, Tommaso
Campbell, Colin, Baron
  Clyde
Campbell, Donald
  Malcolm
Campbell, Gina
Campbell, Sir Malcolm
Campbell, Mrs Patrick
Campbell, Roy
  (Dunnachie)
Campbell, Thomas
Campbell-Bannerman,
  Sir Henry
Campi, Antonio
Campi, Giulio
Campi, Vincenzo
Campion, Edmund
Campion, Thomas
Camus, Albert
Canaletto
Candela, Felix
Canning, Charles John,
  Earl
Canning, George
Cannizzaro, Stanislao
Cannon, Walter
  Bradford
Cano, Juan Sebastián
  del
Canova, Antonio
Cánovas del Castillo,
  Antonio
Cantor, Georg
Canute
Cao Chan (or Ts'ao Chan,
  Zao Zhan)
Capablanca y Graupera,
  José Raúl
Capone, Al

Capote, Truman
Capp, Al
Capra, Frank
Caracalla
Caratacus (or Caractacus)
Caravaggio
Cardano, Girolamo
Cárdenas, Lázaro
Cardigan, James Thomas
  Brudenell, 7th Earl of
Cardin, Pierre
Carducci, Giosuè
Cardwell, Edward,
  Viscount
Carew, Thomas
Carey, William
Carl Gustaf Swedish king
Carlos, Don
Carlyle, Thomas
Carnap, Rudolf
Carné, Marcel
Carnegie, Andrew
Carnera, Primo
Carnot, Lazare Nicolas
  Marguerite
Carnot, (Nicolas
  Léonard) Sadi
Caro, Joseph
Carossa, Hans
Carpaccio, Vittore
Carpentier, Georges
Carpini, Giovanni da
  Pian del
Carr, Robert
Carracci, Agostino
Carracci, Annibale
Carracci, Ludovico
Carranza, Venustiano
Carrel, Alexis
Carrington, Peter
  Alexander Rupert
  Carrington, 6th Baron
Carroll, Lewis pen name of
  Charles Lutwidge
  Dodgson
Carson, Edward Henry,
  Baron
Carson, Kit
Carson, Rachel Louise
Carte, Richard D'Oyly
Carter, Elliott (Cook)
Carter, Howard
Carter, Jimmy
Cartier, Jacques
Cartier-Bresson, Henri

Cartwright, Edmund
Caruso, Enrico
Carver, George
  Washington
Cary, (Arthur) Joyce
  (Lunel)
Casals, Pablo
Casanova, Giovanni
  Giacomo, Chevalier de
  Seingalt
Casement, Sir Roger
  (David)
Cassander
Cassatt, Mary
Cassiodorus, Flavius
  Magnus Aurelius
Cassirer, Ernst
Cassius Longinus, Gaius
Cassivelaunus
Casson, Sir Hugh
  (Maxwell)
Casson, Sir Lewis
Castagno, Andrea del
Castelo Branco, Camilo
Castiglione, Baldassare
Castilho, Antonio
  Feliciano de
Castlereagh, Robert
  Stewart, Viscount
Castro (Ruz), Fidel
Catesby, Robert
Catiline
Catlin, George
Cato
Catullus, Valerius
Cauchy, Augustin Louis,
  Baron
Cavafy, Constantine
Cavalcanti, Guido
Cavalli, Francesco
Cavallini, Pietro
Cavell, Edith
Cavendish, Henry
Cavour, Camillo Benso
  di, Count
Cawley, Evonne (maiden
  name Goolagong)
Caxton, William
Cayley, Arthur
Cayley, Sir George
Ceauşescu, Nicolae
Cecil, Lord David
Cecil, Robert Gascoyne-
  Cecil, 1st Viscount
Céline, Louis Ferdinand
Cellini, Benvenuto

Celsus, Aulus Cornelius

Cennini, Cennino (di Drea)

Cervantes, Miguel de

Cetshwayo

Cézanne, Paul

Chabrier, Emmanuel

Chabrol, Claude

Chadwick, Sir Edwin

Chadwick, Sir James

Chadwick, Lynn

Chagall, Marc

Chain, Sir Ernst Boris

Chaliapin, Feodor Ivanovich

Challoner, Richard

Chalmers, Thomas

Chamberlain, Sir (Joseph) Austen

Chamberlain, Joseph

Chamberlain, (Arthur) Neville

Chamberlain, Owen

Chambers, Sir William

Champaigne, Philippe de

Champlain, Samuel de

Champollion, Jean-François

Chandler, Raymond

Chandra Gupta

Chandragupta Maurya

Chandrasekhar, Subrahmanyan

Chanel, Coco

Chaplin, Charlie

Chapman, George

Charcot, Jean-Martin

Chardin, Jean-Baptiste-Siméon

Charlemagne

Charles, Ray

Charlton, Bobby

Charlton, Jackie

Charpentier, Gustave

Charron, Pierre

Charteris, Leslie

Chartier, Alain

Chateaubriand, Vicomte de

Chatham, William Pitt, 1st Earl of

Chatterjee, Bankim Chandra

Chatterton, Thomas

Chaucer, Geoffrey

Chausson, Ernest

Chebishev, Pafnuti Lvovich

Chekhov, Anton Pavlovich

Cheng Ch'eng-kung *variant spelling of* Zheng Cheng Gong

Cheng Ho *variant spelling of* Zheng He

Chénier, André de

Cheops *Greek name of* Khufu

Chephren *Greek name of* Khafre

Cherenkov, Pavel Alekseievich

Cherubini, Maria Luigi

Cheshire, (Geoffrey) Leonard

Chesterfield, Philip Dormer Stanhope, 4th Earl of

Chesterton, G(ilbert) K(eith)

Chevalier, Maurice

Chiang Ch'ing *variant spelling of* Jiang Qing

Chiang Ching-kuo *variant spelling of* Jiang Jing Guo

Chiang Kai-shek (*or* Jiang Jie Shi)

Chicherin, Georgi Vasilievich

Chichester, Sir Francis (Charles)

Ch'ien-lung *variant spelling of* Qian Long

Chifley, Joseph Benedict

Chikamatsu Monzaemon

Childers, Erskine

Childers, Robert Erskine

Chippendale, Thomas

Chirac, Jacques

Chirico, Giorgio de

Chodowiecki, Daniel Nikolaus

Choiseul, Étienne François, Duc de

Chomsky, Noam

Chopin, Frédéric (François)

Chou En-lai (*or* Zhou En Lai)

Chrétien de Troyes

Christie, Dame Agatha

Christoff, Boris

Christophe, Henri

Chrysoloras, Manuel

Chrysostom, St John

Chuang-tzu *variant spelling of* Zhuangzi

Ch'ü Ch'iu-pai *variant spelling of* Qu Qiu Bai

Chulalongkorn

Churchill, Charles

Churchill, Lord Randolph Henry Spencer

Churchill, Sir Winston (Leonard Spencer)

Churriguera

Chu Teh *variant spelling of* Zhu De

Chu Xi (*or* Chu Hsi)

Chu Yuan

Ciano, Galeazzo

Cibber, Colley

Cicero, Marcus Tullius

Cimabue, Giovanni

Cimarosa, Domenico

Cimon

Cincinnatus, Lucius Quinctius

Cinna, Lucius Cornelius

Clair, René

Clare, John

Clarendon, Edward Hyde, 1st Earl of

Clare of Assisi, St

Clark, Jim

Clark, (Charles) Joseph

Clark, Kenneth (Mackenzie), Baron

Clarke, Jeremiah

Clarke, Marcus (Andrew Hislop)

Clarkson, Thomas

Claudel, Paul

Claude Lorraine

Claudian *Roman poet*

Claudius *Roman emperor*

Clausewitz, Karl von

Clausius, Rudolf Julius Emanuel

Clay, Cassius *original name of* Muhammad Ali

Clay, Henry

Cleanthes

Cleisthenes

Cleland, John
Clemenceau, Georges
Clementi, Muzio
Cleon
Cleopatra
Cleveland, Stephen
  Grover
Cleves, Anne of
Clinton, De Witt
Clive of Plassey, Robert,
  Baron
Clodion
Clouet, François
Clouet, Jean
Clovis
Coates, Joseph Gordon
Cobbett, William
Cobden, Richard
Cochise
Cochrane, Thomas, 10th
  Earl of Dundonald
Cockcroft, Sir John
  Douglas
Cockerell, Charles
  Robert
Cocteau, Jean
Cody, William
  F(rederick) (known as
  Buffalo Bill)
Coen, Jan Pieterszoon
Coeur, Jacques
Cohn, Ferdinand Julius
Coke, Sir Edward
Coke, Thomas William,
  Earl of Leicester of
  Holkham
Colbert, Claudette
Colbert, Jean-Baptiste
Coleridge, Samuel
  Taylor
Coleridge-Taylor,
  Samuel
Colet, John
Colette, Sidonie
  Gabrielle Claudine
Coligny, Gaspard de,
  Seigneur de Châtillon
Collier, Jeremy
Collingwood, Cuthbert,
  1st Baron
Collingwood, Robin
  George
Collins, Michael
Collins, William
Collins, William Wilkie
Colman, George

Colman, Ronald
Colombo, Matteo Realdo
Colum, Padraic
Columba, St founder of Io-
  nian monastery
Columban, St founder of
  monasteries in Gaul and It-
  aly
Columbus, Christopher
Comaneci, Nadia
Comenius, John Amos
Commodus, Lucius
  Aelius Aurelius
Commynes, Philippe de
Comnena, Anna
Compton, Arthur Holly
Compton, Denis
  (Charles Scott)
Compton-Burnett, Dame
  Ivy
Comte, Auguste
Condillac, Étienne
  Bonnot de
Condorcet, Marie Jean
  Antoine de Caritat,
  Marquis de
Confucius
Congreve, William
Connors, Jimmy
Conrad, Joseph
Conscience, Hendrik
Constable, John
Constant, Benjamin
Constantine, Learie
  Nicholas, Baron
Cook, Captain James
Cook, Sir Joseph
Cook, Thomas
Coolidge, John Calvin
Cooper, Gary
Cooper, James Fenimore
Cooper, Samuel
Copernicus, Nicolaus
Copland, Aaron
Coralli, Jean
Corbusier, Le
Corday, Charlotte
Corelli, Arcangelo
Corelli, Marie
Corneille, Pierre
Cornelius, Peter von
Cornforth, Sir John
  Warcup
Cornwallis, Charles, 1st
  Marquess

Corot, Jean Baptiste
  Camille
Correggio
Correns, Carl Erich
Cort, Henry
Cortés, Hernán
Cortot, Alfred
Corvo, Baron pseudonym of
  Frederick William Rolfe
Cosgrave, Liam
Cosgrave, William
  Thomas
Cosmas, St
Cosway, Richard
Cotman, John Sell
Coulomb, Charles
  Augustin de
Couperin, François
Courbet, Gustave
Courrèges, André
Court, Margaret
Cousin, Jean
Cousin, Victor
Cousteau, Jacques Yves
Coverdale, Miles
Covilhã, Pêro da
Coward, Sir Noel
Cowdrey, (Michael)
  Colin
Cowell, Henry
Cowley, Abraham
Cowper, William
Crabbe, George
Craig, Edward Henry
  Gordon
Craik, Dinah Maria
  Mulock
Cram, Steve
Cranach the Elder,
  Lucas
Crane, Hart
Crane, Stephen
Crane, Walter
Cranko, John
Cranmer, Thomas
Crashaw, Richard
Crassus, Marcus Licinius
Crawford, Joan
Creed, Frederick
Creeley, Robert
Cressent, Charles
Crèvecoeur, Michel-
  Guillaume-Jean de
Crichton, James

Crick, Francis Harry
Compton
Crippen, Hawley Harvey
Cripps, Sir (Richard)
Stafford
Cristofori, Bartolommeo
Crivelli, Carlo
Croce, Benedetto
Crockett, Davy
Crockford, William
Croesus
Crome, John
Crome, John Bernay
Cromer, Evelyn Baring,
1st Earl of
Crompton, Richmal
Crompton, Samuel
Cromwell, Oliver
Cromwell, Richard
Cromwell, Thomas, Earl
of Essex
Cronin, A(rchibald)
J(oseph)
Cronje, Piet Arnoldus
Crookes, Sir William
Crosby, Bing
Crossman, Richard
(Howard Stafford)
Cruden, Alexander
Cruft, Charles
Cruikshank, George
Cruyff, Johann
Cruz, Sor Juana Inéz de
la
Csokonai Vitéz, Mihaly
Cudworth, Ralph
Culbertson, Ely
Culpeper, Nicholas
Cumberland, Richard
Cumberland, William
Augustus, Duke of
cummings, e(dward)
e(stlin)
Cunningham, Merce
Cunobelinus
Curie, Marie
Curie, Pierre
Curry, John (Anthony)
Curtin, John Joseph
Curtiss, Glenn
(Hammond)
Curwen, John
Curzon, Sir Clifford

Curzon, George
Nathaniel, 1st
Marquess
Cusa, Nicholas of
Cushing, Harvey
Williams
Custer, George
A(rmstrong)
Cuvier, Georges, Baron
Cuyp, Aelbert Jacobsz
Cuyp, Jacob Gerritsz
Cymbeline
Cynewulf
Cyrano de Bergerac,
Savinien
Czerny, Karl
Dadd, Richard
Dafydd ap Gwilym
Dagly, Gerhard
Daguerre, Louis-
Jacques-Mandé
Dahl, Roald
Daigo
Daimler, Gottlieb
(Wilhelm)
Daladier, Édouard
Dale, Sir Henry Hallett
d'Alembert, Jean le
Rond
Dalhousie, James
Ramsay, 1st Marquess
of
Dali, Salvador
Dallapiccola, Luigi
Dalton, John
Dam, Carl Peter Henrik
Damian, St 4th-century
martyr
Damien, Father 19th-cen-
tury missionary
Dampier, William
Danby, Francis
Danby, Thomas
Osborne, 1st Earl of
Dance, George
Dandolo, Enrico
Dangerfield, Thomas
Daniel, Samuel
Daniell, John Frederic
D'Annunzio, Gabriele
Dante Alighieri
Danton, Georges
Jacques
Da Ponte, Lorenzo
Darío, Rubén
Darius

Darlan, Jean (Louis
Xavier) François
Darling, Grace
Darnley, Henry Stuart,
Lord
Darrow, Clarence
Darwin, Charles Robert
Darwin, Erasmus
Datini, Francesco
Daubenton, Louis Jean
Marie
Daubigny, Charles-
François
Daudet, Alphonse
Daudet, Léon
Daumier, Honoré
Davenant, Sir William
Davenport, Charles
Benedict
David, Gerard
David, Jacques Louis
David ap Gruffudd
Davies, Sir Peter
Maxwell
Davies, W(illiam)
H(enry)
da Vinci, Leonardo
Davis, Bette
Davis, Sir Colin
Davis, Jefferson
Davis, John
Davis, Miles
Davitt, Michael
Davy, Sir Humphry
Dawes, Charles G(ates)
Dayan, Moshe
Day Lewis, C(ecil)
Dazai Osamu
Deák, Ferenc
Deakin, Alfred
Dean, James
Deane, Silas
de Bary, Heinrich Anton
Debray, (Jules) Régis
Debré, Michel
Debrett, John
de Broglie, Louis Victor,
7th Duc
Debs, Eugene V(ictor)
Deburau, Jean-Gaspard
Debussy, Claude
(Achille)
Debye, Peter Joseph
Wilhelm
Decatur, Stephen

Decius, Gaius Messius
  Quintus Trajanus
Dedekind, (Julius
  Wilhelm) Richard
de Duve, Christian
Dee, John
Defoe, Daniel
De Forest, Lee
Degas, (Hilaire
  Germain) Edgar
De Gasperi, Alcide
de Gaulle, Charles André
  Joseph Marie
De Havilland, Sir
  Geoffrey
Dekker, Thomas
de Kooning, Willem
Delacroix, Eugène
De la Mare, Walter
De la Roche, Mazo
Delaroche, (Hippolyte)
  Paul
De La Rue, Warren
Delaunay, Robert
Delcassé, Théophile
Deledda, Grazia
Delescluze, Louis
  Charles
Delibes, Leo
Delius, Frederick
della Robbia, Andrea
della Robbia, Giovanni
della Robbia, Girolamo
della Robbia, Luca
Delorme, Philibert
Delvaux, Paul
de Mille, Agnes
de Mille, Cecil B(lount)
Democritus
De Morgan, Augustus
Demosthenes
Dempsey, Jack
Deng Xiao Ping *variant
  spelling of* Teng Hsiao-
  p'ing
Denham, Sir John
Denikin, Anton
  Ivanovich
Denis, Maurice
Denis, St
Denning, Alfred
  Thompson, Baron
d'Éon, Charles de
  Beaumont, Chevalier
Depretis, Agostino

De Quincey, Thomas
Derain, André
Derby, Edward (George
  Geoffrey Smith)
  Stanley, 4th Earl of
Desai, (Shri) Morarji
  (Ranchhodji)
Descartes, René
De Sica, Vittorio
Desiderio da Settignano
Desmond, Gerald
  Fitzgerald, 15th Earl
  of
Desmoulins, Camille
des Prez, Josquin
Dessalines, Jean Jacques
Destutt, Antoine Louis
  Claude, Comte de
  Tracy
Deus, João de
De Valera, Eamon
de Valois, Dame Ninette
Devine, George
Devonshire, Spencer
  Compton Cavendish,
  8th Duke of
de Vries, Hugo Marie
de Wet, Christian Rudolf
Dewey, George
Dewey, John
De Wint, Peter
Diaghilev, Sergei
  (Pavlovich)
Dias, Bartolomeu
Díaz, Porfirio
Dibdin, Charles
Dickens, Charles
Dickinson, Emily
Diderot, Denis
Diefenbaker, John
  G(eorge)
Diels, Otto Paul
  Hermann
Dieman, Anthony van
Dietrich, Marlene
Digby, Sir Kenelm
Dilthey, Wilhelm
Dimitrii Donskoi
Dimitrov, Georgi
D'Indy, Vincent
Dinesen, Isak *pen name of*
  Karen Blixen
D'Inzeo, Piero
D'Inzeo, Raimondo
Dio Cassius
Dio Chrysostom

Diocletian(us), Gaius
  Aurelius Valerius
Diodorus Siculus
Diogenes
Dionysius
Diophantus
Dior, Christian
Dioscorides Pedanius
Dirac, Paul Adrien
  Maurice
Disney, Walt
Disraeli, Benjamin, 1st
  Earl of Beaconsfield
Djilas, Milovan
Djoser (*or* Zoser)
Dobzhansky, Theodosius
Dodgson, Charles
  Lutwidge (*pen name*
  Lewis Carroll)
Dodsley, Robert
Dogen
Dohnányi, Ernö
Dolci, Danilo
D'Oliviera, Basil Lewis
Dollfuss, Engelbert
Dolmetsch, Arnold
Dolmetsch, Carl
Domagk, Gerhard
Domenichino
Domenico Veneziano
Domingo, Placido
Domino, Fats
Domitian(us), Titus
  Flavius
Donatello
Donatus, Aelius
Dönitz, Karl
Donizetti, Gaetano
Donleavy, J(ames)
  P(atrick)
Donne, John
Doolittle, Hilda
Doppler, Christian
  Johann
Doré, (Paul) Gustave
  (Louis Christophe)
Dorgon
Dornier, Claudius
Dos Passos, John
Dostoievski, Fedor
  Mikhailovich
Dou, Gerrit
Doughty, Charles
  Montagu
Douglas, Gavin

Douglas, (George)
Norman

Douglas-Home, Alec,
Baron Home of the
Hirsel

Dowding, Hugh Caswall
Tremenheere, 1st
Baron

Dowland, John

Dowson, Ernest
(Christopher)

Doyle, Sir Arthur Conan

D'Oyly Carte, Richard

Drabble, Margaret

Draco

Drake, Sir Francis

Drayton, Michael

Dreiser, Theodore

Dreyer, Carl Theodor

Dreyer, Johan Ludvig
Emil

Dreyfus, Alfred

Driesch, Hans Adolf
Eduard

Drinkwater, John

Droste-Hülshoff,
Annette von

Drummond of
Hawthornden, William

Dryden, John

Drysdale, Sir (George)
Russell

Du Barry, Marie Jeanne
Bécu, Comtesse

Dubček, Alexander

Dubuffet, Jean (Phillipe
Arthur)

Du Cange, Charles du
Fresne, Sieur

Duccio di Buoninsegna

Duchamp, Marcel

Dufay, Guillaume

Du Fu (or Tu Fu)

Dufy, Raoul

Duhamel, Georges

Dukas, Paul

Duke, Geoffrey E.

Dulles, John Foster

Dumas, Alexandre

Du Maurier, Dame
Daphne

Du Maurier, George
(Louis Palmella
Busson)

Du Mont, Allen Balcom

Dumont d'Urville, Jules
Sébastien César

Dumouriez, Charles
François du Périer

Dunant, (Jean-)Henri

Dunbar, William

Duncan, Isadora

Dundee, John Graham
of Claverhouse, 1st
Viscount

Dunlop, John Boyd

Dunois, Jean d'Orléans,
Comte de

Dunsany, Edward John
Moreton Drax
Plunkett, 18th Baron

Duns Scotus, John

Dunstable, John

Duparc, Henri

du Pré, Jacqueline

Dupré, Marcel

Duras, Marguerite

Dürer, Albrecht

Durham, John George
Lambton, 1st Earl of

Durkheim, Emile

Durrell, Gerald Malcolm

Durrell, Lawrence
George

Dürrenmatt, Friedrich

Duse, Eleonora

Duval, Claude

Duvalier, François

Duvalier, Jean-Claude

Dvořák, Antonín

Dylan, Bob

Eadred

Eads, John Buchanan

Eadwig (or Edwy)

Eakins, Thomas

Eanes, António dos
Santos Ramalho

Earhart, Amelia

Eastman, George

Ebert, Friedrich

Eccles, Sir John Carew

Ecevit, Bülent

Echegaray y Eizaguirre,
José

Eck, Johann Maier von

Eckermann, Johann
Peter

Eckert, John Presper

Eckhart, Meister

Eddington, Sir Arthur
Stanley

Eddy, Mary Baker

Eden, (Robert) Anthony,
1st Earl of Avon

Edgar the Aetheling

Edgeworth, Maria

Edison, Thomas Alva

Edwards, Jonathan

Edwy variant of Eadwig

Egmont, Lamoraal,
Graaf van

Ehrenberg, Iliya
Grigorievich

Ehrlich, Paul

Eichendorff, Josef,
Freiherr von

Eichler, August Wilhelm

Eichmann, Adolf

Eijkman, Christiaan

Einhard

Einstein, Albert

Einthoven, Willem

Eisenhower, Dwight
D(avid)

Eisenstein, Sergei

El Cid (or Rodrigo Diáz de
Vivar)

Elgar, Sir Edward

El Greco

Eliot, George

Eliot, Sir John

Eliot, T(homas)
S(tearns)

Ellenborough, Edward
Law, Earl of

Ellington, Duke

Ellis, (Henry) Havelock

Elton, Charles

Éluard, Paul

Elyot, Sir Thomas

Emerson, Ralph Waldo

Emin Paşa, Mehmed

Emmet, Robert

Empedocles

Empson, Sir William

Enders, John Franklin

Endlicher, Stephan
Ladislaus

Enesco, Georges

Engels, Friedrich

Engler, Gustav Heinrich
Adolf

Ennius, Quintus

Ensor, James Sydney,
Baron

Enver Pasha

Epaminondas
Epictetus
Epicurus
Epstein, Sir Jacob
Erasistratus of Ceos
Erasmus, Desiderius
Eratosthenes of Cyrene
Erceldoune, Thomas of
Ercilla, Alonso de
Erhard, Ludwig
Ericsson, John
Erigena, John Scotus
Erik Swedish king
Erlanger, Joseph
Ernst, Max
Erskine, Thomas
   Erskine, 1st Baron
Erté
Esarhaddon
Eschenbach, Wolfram
   von
Escoffier, Auguste
Essex, Robert Devereux,
   Earl of
Estienne, Henri
Estienne, Robert
Ethelwulf
Etherege, Sir George
Etty, William
Eucken, Rudolf
   Christoph
Euclid
Eudoxus of Cnidus
Eugène of Savoy, Prince
Eugénie empress of France
Euler, Leonhard
Euphronios
Eupolis
Euripides
Eusebius of Caesarea
Eustachio, Bartolommeo
Evans, Sir Arthur John
Evans, Dame Edith
Evans, Sir Geraint
Evans, Oliver
Evelyn, John
Evert, Chris(tine)
Ewald, Johannes
Exekias
Eyre, Edward John
Eysenck, Hans Jürgen
Fabergé, Peter Carl
Fabius Maximus,
   Quintus
Fabre, Jean Henri

Fabricius ab
   Aquapendente,
   Hieronymus
Fabritius, Carel
Fabry, Charles
Fadden, Sir Arthur
   William
Fa-hsien *variant spelling of*
   Fa Xian
Faidherbe, Louis (Léon
   César)
Fairbanks, Douglas
Fairfax, Thomas, 3rd
   Baron
Faisal
Faisal Ibn Abdul Aziz
Fakhr ad-Din II
Falla, Manuel de
Fallopius, Gabriel
Fangio, Juan Manuel
Fa Ngum
Fantin-Latour, (Ignace)
   Henri (Joseph
   Théodore)
Faraday, Michael
Farel, Guillaume
Fargo, William
Farnaby, Giles
Farnese, Alessandro,
   Duke of Parma
Farouk
Farquhar, George
Fassbinder, Rainer
   Werner
Fateh Singh, Sant
Fatimah
Faulkner, William
Fauré, Gabriel (Urbain)
Fawcett, Henry
Fawcett, Dame Millicent
   Garrett
Fawkes, Guy
Fa Xian (*or* Fa-hsien)
Fechner, Gustav
   Theodor
Feininger, Lyonel
   (Charles Adrian)
Fellini, Federico
Fénelon, François de
   Salignac de la Mothe
Ferlinghetti, Lawrence
Fermat, Pierre de
Fermi, Enrico
Fernandel
Ferrar, Nicholas
Ferrier, Kathleen

Ferrier, Susan
   Edmonstone
Feuchtwanger, Lion
Feuerbach, Ludwig
   Andreas
Feuillère, Edwige
Feydeau, Georges
Feynman, Richard
   Phillips
Fibonacci, Leonardo
Fichte, Johann Gottlieb
Ficino, Marsilio
Field, Cyrus West
Field, John
Fielding, Henry
Fields, Gracie
Fields, W. C.
Fife, Duncan *variant spell-*
   ing of Phyfe, Duncan
Filarete
Fillmore, Millard
Finlay, Carlos Juan
Finney, Albert
Finsen, Niels Ryberg
Firbank, (Arthur
   Annesley) Ronald
Firdausi
Firth, J(ohn) R(upert)
Fischer, Bobby
Fischer, Emil Hermann
Fischer-Dieskau,
   Dietrich
Fischer von Erlach,
   Johann Bernhard
Fisher, Andrew
Fisher, John Arbuthnot,
   1st Baron
Fisher, St John
Fitzgerald, Edward
Fitzgerald, Ella
Fitzgerald, F(rancis)
   Scott (Key)
Fitzgerald, George
   Francis
Fitzsimmons, Bob
Flagstad, Kirsten Malfrid
Flaherty, Robert
   (Joseph)
Flamininus, Titus
   Quinctius
Flaminius, Gaius
Flamsteed, John
Flaubert, Gustave
Flaxman, John Henry
Flecker, (Herman)
   James Elroy

Flémalle, Master of
Fleming, Sir Alexander
Fleming, Ian (Lancaster)
Fleming, Sir John
  Ambrose
Fleming, Paul
Fletcher, John
Fleury, André Hercule
  de, Cardinal
Flinders, Matthew
Flood, Henry
Florey, Howard Walter,
  Baron
Florio, John
Floris, Cornelis
Floris, Frans
Flotow, Friedrich von
Fludd, Robert
Flynn, Errol
Foch, Ferdinand
Fokine, Michel
Fokker, Anthony
  Hermann Gerard
Foley, John Henry
Fonda, Henry
Fonda, Jane
Fonda, Peter
Fontana, Domenico
Fontane, Theodor
Fontanne, Lyn
Fontenelle, Bernard le
  Bovier de
Fonteyn, Dame Margot
Foot, Michael
  (Mackintosh)
Forbes, George William
Ford, Ford Madox
Ford, Gerald R(udolph)
Ford, Henry
Ford, John
Forester, C(ecil) S(cott)
Forman, Miloš
Forster, E(dward)
  M(organ)
Fortescue, Sir John
Foscolo, Ugo
Foster, Stephen Collins
Fothergill, John
Foucault, Jean Bernard
  Léon
Fouché, Joseph, Duc
  d'Otrante
Fouqué, Friedrich
  Heinrich Karl, Baron
  de la Motte

Fouquet, Jean
Fouquet, Nicolas
Fourier, (François
  Marie) Charles
Fourier, Jean Baptiste
  Joseph, Baron
Fourneyron, Benoît
Fowler, Francis
Fowler, H(enry)
  W(atson)
Fowles, John
Fox, Charles James
Fox, George
Foxe, John
Fragonard, Jean Honoré
Frampton, Sir George
  James
France, Anatole
Francis, Sir Philip
Franck, César Auguste
Franck, James
Franco, Francisco
Frank, Anne
Frankfurter, Felix
Franklin, Benjamin
Franklin, Sir John
Fraser, (John) Malcolm
Fraser, Peter
Fraunhofer, Joseph von
Frazer, Sir James
  George
Frazier, Joe
Frederick Barbarossa
Frege, Gottlob
Frei (Montalva),
  Eduardo
Frémont, John C(harles)
French, John, Earl of
  Ypres
Freneau, Philip
Fresnel, Augustin Jean
Freud, Anna
Freud, Clement
Freud, Lucian
Freud, Sigmund
Friedman, Milton
Friedman, Rose
Friedrich, Caspar David
Friml, Rudolph
Frisch, Karl von
Frisch, Max
Frisch, Otto Robert
Frisch, Ragnar
Frobisher, Sir Martin
Fröding, Gustaf

Froebel, Friedrich
  Wilhelm August
Froissart, Jean
Fromm, Erich
Frontenac, Louis de
  Buade, Comte de
  Palluau et de
Frost, Robert Lee
Froude, James Anthony
Fry, Christopher
Fry, Elizabeth
Fry, Roger (Eliot)
Fu'ad
Fuchs, (Emil Julius)
  Klaus
Fuchs, Sir Vivian
  (Ernest)
Fugard, Athol
Fuller, J(ohn)
  F(rederick) C(harles)
Fuller, Richard
  Buckminster
Fuller, Roy (Broadbent)
Fuller, Thomas
Fulton, Robert
Furtwängler, Wilhelm
Fuseli, Henry
Fust, Johann
Gabin, Jean
Gable, Clark
Gabo, Naum
Gabor, Dennis
Gabrieli, Andrea
Gabrieli, Giovanni
Gaddafi, Moammar al-
Gaddi, Agnolo
Gaddi, Taddeo
Gagarin, Yuri
  Alekseevich
Gage, Thomas
Gainsborough, Thomas
Gaitskell, Hugh (Todd
  Naylor)
Galbraith, John Kenneth
Galen
Galerius
Galileo Galilei
Gall, Franz Joseph
Galle, Johann Gottfried
Galli-Curci, Amelita
Gallup, George Horace
Galois, Évariste
Galsworthy, John
Galt, John
Galton, Sir Francis

Galuppi, Baldassare
Galvani, Luigi
Galway, James
Gama, Vasco da
Gambetta, Léon
Gamliel
Gandhi, Indira
Gandhi, Mohandas
　Karamchand
Gandhi, Rajiv
Gandhi, Sanjay
Garbo, Greta
García Lorca, Federico
Gardiner, Stephen
Garibaldi, Giuseppe
Garland, Judy
Garrick, David
Gaskell, Elizabeth
　Cleghorn
Gassendi, Pierre
Gasser, Herbert Spencer
Gates, Horatio
Gaudier-Brzeska, Henri
Gaudí y Cornet, Antonio
Gauguin, Paul
Gaunt, John of, Duke of
　Lancaster
Gauss, Karl Friedrich
Gautama Siddhartha *original name of* Buddha
Gautier, Théophile
Gay, John
Gay-Lussac, Joseph
　Louis
Geber
Gediminas
Geiger, Hans
Gell-Mann, Murray
Genet, Jean
Genghis Khan
Genseric
Gentile, Giovanni
Gentile da Fabriano
Geoffroy Saint-Hilaire,
　Étienne
George, Stefan
Gérard, François (Pascal
　Simon), Baron
Géricault, (Jean Louis
　André) Théodore
Germanicus Julius
　Caesar
Geronimo
Gershwin, George
Gershwin, Ira

Gerson, Jean de
Gesner, Conrad
Gesualdo, Carlo, Prince
　of Venosa
Getty, J(ean) Paul
Geulincx, Arnold
Ghazna, Mahmud of
Ghiberti, Lorenzo
Ghirlandaio, Domenico
Giacometti, Alberto
Giambologna
Gibbon, Edward
Gibbons, Grinling
Gibbons, Orlando
Gibbs, James
Gibbs, Josiah Willard
Gibran, Khalil
Gide, André
Gielgud, Sir (Arthur)
　John
Gierek, Edward
Gigli, Beniamino
Gilbert, Sir Humphrey
Gilbert, William
Gilbert, Sir William
　Schwenk
Giles, Carl Ronald
Gill, (Arthur) Eric
　(Rowton)
Gillespie, Dizzy
Gillray, James
Ginkel, Godert de, 1st
　Earl of Athlone
Ginsberg, Allen
Giordano, Luca
Giorgione
Giotto
Giraldus Cambrensis
Giraudoux, Jean
Girtin, Thomas
Giscard d'Estaing,
　Valéry
Gish, Dorothy
Gish, Lillian
Gislebertus
Gissing, George Robert
Giulini, Carlo Maria
Giulio Romano
Gladstone, W(illiam)
　E(wart)
Glanville, Ranulf de
Glaser, Donald Arthur
Glazunov, Aleksandr
　Konstantinovich
Glendower, Owen

Glinka, Mikhail
　Ivanovich
Gluck, Christoph
　Willibald
Gneisenau, August
　(Wilhelm Anton), Graf
　Neithardt von
Gobbi, Tito
Gobind Singh (*or* Govind
　Singh)
Gobineau, Joseph
　Arthur, Comte de
Godard, Jean-Luc
Goddard, Robert
　Hutchings
Gödel, Kurt
Goderich, George
　Frederick Samuel
　Robinson, Viscount
Godiva, Lady
Godolphin, Sidney, Earl
　of
Godoy, Manuel de
Godunov, Boris
　(Fedorovich)
Godwin, William
Goebbels, (Paul) Joseph
Goes, Hugo van der
Goethe, Johann
　Wolfgang von
Gogol, Nikolai
　Vasilievich
Gold, Thomas
Golding, William
Goldoni, Carlo
Goldschmidt, Richard
　Benedict
Goldsmith, Oliver
Goldwyn, Samuel
Golgi, Camillo
Gollancz, Victor
Golovkin, Gavril
　Ivanovich, Count
Gómez, Juan Vicente
Gomułka, Władysław
Goncharov, Ivan
　Aleksandrovich
Goncourt, Edmond de
Goncourt, Jules de
Gondomar, Diego
　Sarmiento de Acuña,
　Conde de
Góngora y Argote, Luis
　de
González de Mendoza,
　Pedro

Goodman, Benny
Goodyear, Charles
Goolagong, Evonne *maiden name of* Evonne Cawley
Goossens, Sir Eugene
Goossens, Leon
Gordon, Charles George
Göring, Hermann Wilhelm
Gorki, Maksim
Gorky, Arshile
Gorton, John Grey
Gossaert, Jan (*known as* Mabuse)
Gosse, Sir Edmund
Gottfried von Strassburg
Gottsched, Johann Christoph
Goujon, Jean
Gounod, Charles François
Govind Singh *variant spelling of* Gobind Singh
Gower, John
Gowon, Yakubu
Goya (y Lucientes), Francesco (Jose) de
Goyen, Jan Josephszoon van
Gozzi, Carlo
Gozzoli, Benozzo
Gracchus, Gaius Sempronius
Gracchus, Tiberius Sempronius
Grace, W(illiam) G(ilbert)
Graham, Billy
Graham, Martha
Graham, Thomas
Grahame, Kenneth
Grainger, Percy Aldridge
Gramsci, Antonio
Granados, Enrique
Granby, John Manners, Marquess of
Grant, Cary
Grant, Duncan James Corrowr
Grant, Ulysses S(impson)
Granville, Granville George Leveson-Gower, 2nd Earl

Granville, John Carteret, 1st Earl
Granville-Barker, Harley
Grappelli, Stephane
Grass, Günter
Gratian(us), Flavius
Grattan, Henry
Graves, Robert (Ranke)
Gray, Asa
Gray, Thomas
Greeley, Horace
Green, Henry
Greenaway, Kate
Greene, (Henry) Graham
Greene, Nathaneal
Greene, Robert
Greenough, Horatio
Greenwood, Walter
Gregory, Lady Augusta
Gregory, James
Greig, Tony
Grenville, George
Grenville, Sir Richard
Grenville, William (Wyndham), Baron
Gresham, Sir Thomas
Grétry, André Ernest Modeste
Greuze, Jean-Baptiste
Greville, Fulke, 1st Baron Brooke
Grey, Charles, 2nd Earl
Grey, Sir George
Grey, Henry George, 3rd Earl Grey
Grey, Lady Jane
Grey of Fallodon, Edward, 1st Viscount
Grieg, Edvard Hagerup
Grierson, John
Griffith, Arthur
Griffith, D(avid) W(ark)
Grillparzer, Franz
Grimaldi, Joseph
Grimm, Jakob
Grimm, Wilhelm
Grimmelshausen, Hans Jacob Christoph von
Grimond, Jo(seph), Baron
Gris, Juan
Grivas, Georgios
Gromyko, Andrei
Gropius, Walter

Gros, Antoine Jean, Baron
Grosseteste, Robert
Grossmith, George
Grossmith, Weedon
Grosz, George
Grotefend, Georg Friedrich
Grotius, Hugo
Grove, Sir George
Groves, Sir Charles
Grünewald, Matthias
Guang Xu (*or* Kuang-hsü)
Guardi, Francesco
Guardi, Giovanni Antonio
Guarini, Giovanni Battista
Guarini, Guarino Italian architect
Guarneri, Andrea Italian violin maker
Guarneri, Giuseppe
Guercino
Guericke, Otto von
Guesclin, Bertrand du
Guevara, Che
Guicciardini, Francesco
Guido d'Arezzo
Guillaume de Lorris
Guinness, Sir Alec
Guiscard, Robert
Guitry, Sacha
Guizot, François (Pierre Guillaume)
Gunn, Thom(son William)
Gurdjieff, George Ivanovitch
Gustavus II Adolphus
Gustavus I Vasa
Gutenberg, Johann
Guthrie, Arlo
Guthrie, (William) Tyrone
Guthrie, Woody
Guzmán Blanco, Antonio
Gwyn, Nell
Haakon
Haber, Fritz
Hadrian
Haeckel, Ernst Heinrich
Hafiz, Shams al-Din Muhammad
Hagen, Walter Charles

Haggard, Sir H(enry)
Rider
Hahn, Kurt
Hahn, Otto
Hahnemann, Samuel
Christian Friedrich
Haig, Douglas, 1st Earl
Haile Selassie
Hailsham, Douglas
McGarel Hogg, 1st
Viscount
Hailsham of St
Marylebone, Quintin
McGarel Hogg, Baron
Hailwood, Mike
Haitink, Bernard
Hakluyt, Richard
Haldane, John Burdon
Sanderson
Haldane, John Scott
Haldane, Richard
Burdon, 1st Viscount
Hale, Sir Matthew
Halévy, Jacques
François
Halifax, Charles
Montagu, 1st Earl of
Halifax, Edward
Frederick Lindley
Wood, 1st Earl of
Halifax, George Savile,
1st Marquess of
Hall, Sir Peter
Halle, Adam de la
Hallé, Sir Charles
Haller, Albrecht von
Halley, Edmund
Hals, Frans
Halsey, William
F(rederick)
Hamilcar Barca
Hamilton, Alexander
Hamilton, Emma, Lady
Hamilton, James, 1st
Duke of
Hamilton, Sir William
Rowan
Hammarskjöld, Dag
(Hjalmar Agne Carl)
Hammerstein, Oscar
Hammett, Dashiell
Hammond, Dame Joan
Hammond, Wally
Hammurabi
Hampden, John
Hampton, Lionel

Hamsun, Knut
Hancock, Tony
Handel, George
Frederick
Handley Page, Sir
Frederick
Handy, William
Christopher
Han fei zi
Hardecanute (or
Harthacnute)
Hardenberg, Karl
(August), Fürst von
Hardie, J(ames) Keir
Hardinge of Lahore,
Henry, 1st Viscount
Hardinge of Penshurst,
Charles, 1st Baron
Hardouin-Mansart, Jules
Hardy, G(odfrey)
H(arold)
Hardy, Oliver
Hardy, Thomas
Hare, William
Hargreaves, James
Harishchandra
Harlan, John Marshall
Harley, Robert, 1st Earl
of Oxford
Harlow, Jean
Harmsworth, Alfred, 1st
Viscount Northcliffe
Harmsworth, Harold, 1st
Viscount Rothermere
Harnack, Adolf von
Harriman, W(illiam)
Averell
Harrington, James
Harris, Joel Chandler
Harris, Roy
Harrison, Benjamin
Harrison, George
Harrison, William Henry
Harsa (or Harsha)
Hart, Moss
Harte, (Francis) Bret(t)
Hartley, L(esley) P(oles)
Hartmann, (Karl Robert)
Eduard von
Hartmann, Nicolai
Hartnell, Sir Norman
Harun ar-Rashid
Harvey, William
Hasan al-Basri, al-
Hasdrubal (Barca)
Hašek, Jaroslav

Haselrig, Sir Arthur vari-
ant spelling of Hesilrig,
Sir Arthur
Hassall, John
Hassan
Hastings, Francis
Rawdon-Hastings, 1st
Marquess of
Hastings, Warren
Hathaway, Anne
Hatshepsut
Hauptmann, Gerhart
Haussmann, Georges-
Eugène, Baron
Haw-Haw, Lord see Joyce,
William
Hawke, Edward, 1st
Baron
Hawkins, Sir John
Hawkins, Sir Richard
Hawks, Howard
Hawksmoor, Nicholas
Haworth, Sir Walter
Norman
Hawthorn, Mike
Hawthorne, Nathaniel
Hay, Will
Haya de la Torre, Victor
Raúl
Haydn, Franz Joseph
Hayes, Rutherford
B(irchard)
Hazlitt, William
Healey, Denis (Winston)
Hearst, William
Randolph
Heath, Edward (Richard
George)
Heaviside, Oliver
Hebbel, (Christian)
Friedrich
Hébert, Jacques-René
Heenan, John Carmel,
Cardinal
Hegel, Georg Wilhelm
Friedrich
Heidegger, Martin
Heifetz, Jascha
Heine, Heinrich
Heisenberg, Werner
Karl
Heller, Joseph
Hellman, Lillian
Helmholtz, Hermann
Ludwig Ferdinand von

Helmont, Jan Baptist
van
Helpmann, Sir Robert
Helvétius, Claude Adrien
Hemingway, Ernest
Henderson, Arthur
Hendrix, Jimi
Henry, Joseph
Henry, O.
Henry, Patrick
Henryson, Robert
Henze, Hans Werner
Hepburn, Katharine
Hepplewhite, George
Hepworth, Dame
Barbara
Heraclitus Greek philoso-
pher
Heraclius Byzantine emper-
or
Herbart, Johann
Friedrich
Herbert, George
Herder, Johann
Gottfried
Hereward the Wake
Hermann von Reichenau
Hermite, Charles
Herod
Herodotus
Hero of Alexandria
Herophilus
Herrera, Francisco de
Herrera, Juan de
Herrick, Robert
Herriot, Édouard
Herschel, Caroline
Herschel, Sir John
Herschel, Sir William
Hertz, Heinrich Rudolf
Hertzog, James Barry
Munnik
Herzen, Aleksandr
(Ivanovich)
Herzl, Theodor
Herzog, Werner
Hesilrige (or Haselrig), Sir
Arthur
Hesiod
Hess, Dame Myra
Hess, Rudolf
Hess, Victor Francis
Hesse, Hermann
Hevesy, George Charles
von

Heyerdahl, Thor
Heywood, Thomas
Hezekiah
Hickok, James Butler
Hideyoshi
Highsmith, Patricia
Hilbert, David
Hill, Archibald Vivian
Hill, David Octavius
Hill, Graham
Hill, Octavia
Hill, Sir Rowland
Hillary, Sir Edmund
(Percival)
Hillel
Hillery, Patrick (John)
Hilliard, Nicholas
Hilton, James
Himmler, Heinrich
Hincmar of Reims
Hindemith, Paul
Hindenburg, Paul von
Beneckendorff und
von
Hines, Earl (Fatha)
Hinkler, Herbert John
Lewis
Hinshelwood, Sir Cyril
Norman
Hipparchus
Hippocrates
Hirohito
Hiroshige
Hitchcock, Sir Alfred
Hitler, Adolf
Hoad, Lew(is Alan)
Hobbema, Meindert
Hobbes, Thomas
Hobbs, Jack
Hochhuth, Rolf
Ho Chi Minh
Hockney, David
Hoddinott, Alun
Hodgkin, Alan Lloyd
Hodgkin, Dorothy Mary
Crowfoot
Hodgkin, Thomas
Hoffman, Dustin
Hofmann, Joseph
Casimir
Hofmannsthal, Hugo von
Hofmeister, Wilhelm
Friedrich Benedict
Hogan, Ben
Hogarth, William

Hogg, James
Hohenlohe-
Schillingsfürst,
Chlodwig Karl Viktor,
Fürst zu
Hokusai
Holbein, Hans
Holberg, Ludvig, Baron
Hölderlin, (Johann
Christian) Friedrich
Holiday, Billie
Holinshed, Raphael
Holland, Henry
Holland, Sir Sidney
(George)
Hollar, Wenceslaus
Holles, Denzil, Baron
Holliger, Heinz
Holmes, Oliver Wendell
Holst, Gustav
(Theodore)
Holt, Harold (Edward)
Holyoake, Sir Keith
Jacka
Home, Daniel Douglas
Home of the Hirsel, Alec
Douglas-Home, Baron
Homer
Homer, Winslow
Honecker, Erich
Honegger, Arthur
Hong-wu (or Hung-wu)
Hong Xiu Quan (or Hung
Hsiu-ch'uan)
Honorius
Honthorst, Gerrit von
Hooch, Pieter de
Hood, Samuel, 1st
Viscount
Hood, Thomas
Hooft, Pieter
Corneliszoon
Hooke, Robert
Hooker, Sir Joseph
Dalton
Hooker, Richard
Hooker, Sir William
Jackson
Hoover, Herbert (Clark)
Hoover, J(ohn) Edgar
Hope, Anthony
Hope, Bob
Hopkins, Sir Frederick
Gowland
Hopkins, Gerard Manley
Hopkins, Harry (Lloyd)

Hopkinson, John
Hoppner, John
Hore-Belisha, (Isaac)
  Leslie, 1st Baron
Horn, Filips van
  Montmorency, Graaf
  van
Horowitz, Vladimir
Horta, Victor
Horthy de Nagybánya,
  Miklós
Hotspur see Percy, Sir
  Henry
Hotter, Hans
Houdini, Harry
Houdon, Jean Antoine
Houphouët-Boigny,
  Félix
Housman, A(lfred)
  E(dward)
Hovell, William Hilton
Howard, Catherine
Howard, Sir Ebenezer
Howard, Henry, Earl of
  Surrey
Howard, John
Howard, Leslie
Howard, Trevor
Howard of Effingham,
  Charles, 2nd Baron
Howe, Elias
Howe, Sir (Richard
  Edward) Geoffrey
Howe, Richard, Earl
Howe, William, 5th
  Viscount
Hoxha, Enver
Hoyle, Edmond
Hoyle, Sir Fred
Hsia Kuei variant spelling
  of Xia Gui
Hsuan-tsang variant spell-
  ing of Xuan Cang
Hua Guo Feng (or Hua
  Kuo-feng)
Huascar
Hubble, Edwin Powell
Huddleston, Trevor
Hudson, Henry
Hudson, W(illiam)
  H(enry)
Huggins, Sir William
Hughes, Howard
  (Robard)
Hughes, Richard
Hughes, Ted

Hughes, Thomas
Hughes, William
  M(orris)
Hugo, Victor (Marie)
Huizinga, Johan
Hull, Cordell
Humbolt, (Friedrich
  Wilhelm Karl
  Heinrich) Alexander
  von
Humboldt, (Karl)
  Wilhelm von
Hume, Basil George,
  Cardinal
Hume, David
Hume, Hamilton
Hume, Joseph
Hummel, Johann
  Nepomuk
Humperdinck, Engelbert
Humphrey, Hubert
  Horatio
Hung Hsiu-ch'uan variant
  spelling of Hong Xiu
  Quan
Hung-wu variant spelling of
  Hong-wu
Hunt, Henry
Hunt, James
Hunt, (Henry Cecil)
  John, Baron
Hunt, (James Henry)
  Leigh
Hunt, William Holman
Hunter, John
Hunter, William
Huntingdon, Selina
  Hastings, Countess of
Hunyadi, János
Hus, Jan
Husák, Gustáv
Hussein (ibn Talal)
Husserl, Edmund
Huston, John
Hutcheson, Francis
Hutten, Ulrich von
Hutton, James
Hutton, Len
Huxley, Aldous
Huxley, Sir Andrew
  Fielding
Huxley, Sir Julian
Huxley, Thomas Henry
Huygens, Christiaan
Huysmans, Joris Karl
Hyde, Douglas

Hyder Ali
Ibarruri, Dolores (known
  as La Pasionaria)
Ibert, Jacques
Iberville, Pierre le
  Moyne, Sieur d'
Ibn al-'Arabi, Muhyi-l-
  din
Ibn Battutah
Ibn Ezra, Abraham Ben
  Meir
Ibn Gabirol, Solomon
Ibn Khaldun
Ibn Saud
Ibrahim Pasha
Ibsen, Henrik
Ictinus
Ignatiev, Nikolai
  Pavlovich, Count
Ignatius Loyola, St
Ikhnaton variant spelling of
  Akhenaton
Illich, Ivan
Ilyushin, Sergei
  Vladimirovich
Imhotep
Ine
Inge, William Ralph
Ingenhousz, Jan
Ingres, Jean-Auguste-
  Dominique
Innocent pope
Inönü, Ismet
Ionesco, Eugène
Ipatieff, Vladimir
  Nikolaievich
Iqbal, Mohammed
Ireland, John Nicholson
Ireton, Henry
Ironside, William
  Edmund, 1st Baron
Irving, Sir Henry
Irving, Washington
Isaacs, Jorge
Isabey, Eugène
Isabey, Jean Baptiste
Isherwood, Christopher
Isma'il Pasha
Isocrates
Ito Hirobumi
Itúrbide, Agustín
Ivanovna, Anna
Ives, Charles (Edward)
Jabir ibn Hayyan
Jackson, Andrew

Jackson, Glenda
Jackson, Stonewall
Jacobsen, Arne
Jacopo della Quercia
Jacopone da Todi
Jacquard, Joseph-Marie
Jagan, Cheddi Berrat
Jagan, Janet
Jagger, Mick
Jahangir
James, Henry
James, William
Jameson, Sir Leander
   Starr
Janáček, Leoš
Jansen, Cornelius Otto
Jansky, Karl Guthe
Januarius, St
Jaques-Dalcroze, Émile
Jarry, Alfred
Jaspers, Karl (Theodor)
Jaurès, Jean
Jawara, Sir Dawda
Jawlensky, Alexey von
Jay, John
Jayawardene, J(unius)
   R(ichard)
Jean de Meun
Jeans, Sir James
   Hopwood
Jeeps, Dickie
Jefferies, Richard
Jeffers, Robinson
Jefferson, Thomas
Jeffrey, Francis, Lord
Jeffreys of Wem,
   George, 1st Baron
Jeffries, John
Jellicoe, John
   Rushworth, 1st Earl
Jenkins, Roy (Harris)
Jenner, Edward
Jensen, Johannes
   (Vilhelm)
Jenson, Nicolas
Jespersen, Otto
Jevons, William Stanley
Jewel, John
Jiang Jing Guo (or Chiang
   Ching-kuo)
Jiang Qing (or Chiang
   Ch'ing)
Jiménez, Juan Ramón
Jimmu
Jinnah, Mohammed Ali

Joachim, Joseph
Jochho
Jochum, Eugen
Jodl, Alfred
Joffre, Joseph Jacques
   Césaire
Johannsen, Wilhelm
   Ludvig
John, Augustus (Edwin)
John, Barry
John, Elton
John, Gwen
Johns, Jasper
Johnson, Amy
Johnson, Andrew
Johnson, Cornelius
Johnson, Lyndon Baines
Johnson, Samuel
Johnson, Virginia
   Eshelman
Joinville, Jean de
Joliot, Frédéric
Joliot-Curie, Irène
Jolliet, Louis
Jolson, Al
Jones, (Alfred) Ernest
Jones, Bobby
Jones, Daniel
Jones, David
Jones, Inigo
Jones, Jack
Jones, John Paul
Jones, LeRoi
Jones, Sir William
Jongkind, Johan
   Barthold
Jonson, Ben
Joplin, Scott
Jordaens, Jakob
Jordan, Dorothy
Joselito
Joseph, Sir Keith
   (Sinjohn)
Josephson, Brian David
Josephus, Flavius
Josquin des Prez
Joubert, Piet
Joule, James Prescott
Jouvet, Louis
Jovian, Flavius
Jowett, Benjamin
Joyce, James
Joyce, William (known as
   Lord Haw-Haw)
Juantorena, Alberto

Juárez, Benito (Pablo)
Judah ha-Levi
Jugurtha
Jung, Carl Gustav
Jussieu, Antoine de
Jussieu, Antoine-Laurent
   de
Jussieu, Bernard de
Jussieu, Joseph de
Justinian
Juvenal
Kádár, János
Kafka, Franz
Kahn, Louis I(sadore)
Kaiser, Georg
Kakinomoto Hitomaro
Kalidasa
Kalinin, Mikhail
   Ivanovich
Kamehameha
Kamenev, Lev
   Borisovich
Kandinsky, Wassily
Kang Xi (or K'ang-hsi)
Kang You Wei
Kant, Immanuel
Kapitza, Peter
   Leonidovich
Karageorge
Karajan, Herbert von
Karamanlis, Constantine
Karloff, Boris
Károlyi, Mihály, Count
Karpov, Anatoly
Kasavubu, Joseph
Kassem, Abdul Karim
Kästner, Erich
Katsura Taro
Kauffmann, Angelica
Kaufman, George
   S(imon)
Kaunda, Kenneth
   (David)
Kaunitz, Wenzel Anton,
   Count von
Kawabata Yasunari
Kay, John
Kazan, Elia
Kazantzakis, Nikos
Kean, Edmund
Keaton, Buster
Keats, John
Keble, John
Keegan, Kevin
Keene, Charles Samuel

Keitel, Wilhelm
Kekulé von Stradonitz,
  (Friedrich) August
Keller, Gottfried
Keller, Helen Adams
Kelly, Grace
Kelly, Ned
Kelvin, William
  Thomson, 1st Baron
Kemal, (Mehmed)
  Namik
Kemble, Charles
Kemble, Frances Ann
Kemble, John Philip
Kemble, Roger
Kempe, Margery
Kempe, Rudolf
Kempis, Thomas à
Kendall, Edward Calvin
Kendall, Henry
Kendrew, Sir John
  Cowdery
Kennedy, Edward Moore
Kennedy, John
  Fitzgerald
Kennedy, Joseph Patrick
Kennedy, Robert Francis
Kennelly, Arthur Edwin
Kent, William
Kenyatta, Jomo
Kenyon, Dame Kathleen
Kepler, Johannes
Kerenski, Aleksandr
  Feodorovich
Kern, Jerome (David)
Kerouac, Jack
Kertanagara
Kesey, Ken
Kesselring, Albert
Ketch, Jack
Kettering, Charles
  Franklin
Keynes, John Maynard,
  1st Baron
Khachaturian, Aram Ilich
Khafre
Khalid Ibn Abdul Aziz
Khalifa see Abd Allah
Khama, Sir Seretse
Khlebnikov, Velimir
Khomeini, Ayatollah
  Ruholla
Khorana, Har Gobind
Khosrow

Khrushchev, Nikita
  S(ergeevich)
Khufu
Kidd, William
Kidinnu
Kierkegaard, Søren
Kilvert, Francis
Kim Il Sung
King, Billie Jean
King, Martin Luther
King, William Lyon
  Mackenzie
Kingsley, Charles
Kingsley, Mary
  Henriette
Kinsey, Alfred
Kipling, (Joseph)
  Rudyard
Kirchhoff, Gustav Robert
Kirchner, Ernst Ludwig
Kirk, Norman (Eric)
Kirov, Sergei
  Mironovich
Kissinger, Henry
  (Alfred)
Kitagawa Utamaro
Kitasato, Shibasaburo
Kitchener of Khartoum,
  Horatio Herbert, 1st
  Earl
Kivi, Alexis
Klaproth, Martin
  Heinrich
Kléber, Jean Baptiste
Klebs, Edwin
Klee, Paul
Klein, Melanie
Kleist, Heinrich von
Klemperer, Otto
Klimt, Gustav
Klinger, Friedrich
  Maximilian von
Klint, Kaare
Klopstock, Friedrich
  Gottlieb
Kneller, Sir Godfrey
Knight, Harold
Knight, Dame Laura
Knox, John
Knox, Ronald
  (Arbuthnott)
Kobayashi Masaki
Koch, Robert
Köchel, Ludwig von
Kodály, Zoltan

Koestler, Arthur
Koffka, Kurt
Köhler, Wolfgang
Kokoschka, Oskar
Kolbe, (Adolf Wilhelm)
  Hermann
Kolchak, Alexander
  Vasilievich
Koldewey, Robert
Kolmogorov, Andrei
  Nikolaevich
Koniecpolski, Stanisław
Koniev, Ivan
  Stepanovich
Konoe Fumimaro, Prince
Korchnoi, Victor
Korda, Sir Alexander
Kornberg, Arthur
Kornilov, Lavrentia
  Georgievich
Koroliov, Sergei
  Pavlovich
Kosciuszko, Tadeusz
  Andrezei Bonawentura
Kossuth, Lajos
Kosygin, Aleksei
  Nikolaevich
Kotzebue, August von
Koussevitsky, Sergei
Koxinga see Zheng Cheng
  Gong
Kozirev, Nikolai
  Aleksandrovich
Krafft-Ebing, Richard
  von
Krebs, Sir Hans Adolf
Kreisky, Bruno
Kreisler, Fritz
Křenek, Ernst
Kreutzer, Rodolphe
Krishna Menon
Krochmal, Nachman
Kropotkin, Peter, Prince
Kruger, (Stephanus
  Johannes) Paul(us)
Krum
Krupp, Alfred
Krupp, Alfried
Krupp, Arndt
Krupp, Bertha
Krupp, Friedrich
Krupp, Gustav von
  Bohlen und Halbach
Kuang-hsü variant spelling
  of Guang Xu
Kubelik, Jan

Kubelik, Rafael
Kublai Khan
Kubrick, Stanley
Kukai
Kun, Béla
Kuo Mo-jo
Kurchatov, Igor
  Vasilievich
Kurosawa, Akira
Kusunoki Masashige
Kutuzov, Mikhail
  Ilarionovich, Prince of
  Smolensk
Kuznets, Simon
Kyd, Thomas
Kyprianou, Spyros
Labiche, Eugène
La Bruyère, Jean de
Laclos, Pierre Choderlos
  de
La Condamine, Charles
  Marie de
Laënnec, René
  Théophile Hyacinth
Lafayette, Marie Joseph
  Gilbert Motier,
  Marquis de
La Fayette, Mme de
Lafontaine, Henri-Marie
La Fontaine, Jean de
Laforgue, Jules
Lagerkvist, Pär (Fabian)
Lagerlöf, Selma
  Ottiliana Lovisa
Lagrange, Joseph Louis,
  Comte de
La Guardia, Fiorello
  Henry
Laing, R(onald) D(avid)
Laird, Macgregor
Lalande, Joseph-Jérôme
  Le Français de
Lalique, René
Lally, Thomas, Comte de
Lalo, (Victor Antoine)
  Édouard
Lalor, Peter
Lamarck, Jean-Baptiste
  de Monet, Chevalier
  de
Lamartine, Alphonse de
Lamb, Lady Caroline
Lamb, Charles
Lamb, Henry
Lamb, Sir Horace
Lambert, Constant

Lambert, Johann
  Heinrich
Lambert, John
Lamerie, Paul de
Lampedusa, Giuseppe
  Tomasi di
Lancaster, Sir Osbert
Lanchester, Frederick
  William
Land, Edwin Herbert
Landau, Lev Davidovich
Landor, Walter Savage
Landowska, Wanda
Landseer, Sir Edwin
  Henry
Landsteiner, Karl
Lane, Sir Allen
Lanfranc
Lang, Andrew
Lang, Fritz
Langland, William
Langley, Samuel
  Pierpont
Langmuir, Irving
Langton, Stephen
Langtry, Lillie
Lanier, Sidney
Lankester, Sir Edwin
  Ray
Lansbury, George
Lansdowne, Henry
  Charles Keith Petty-
  Fitzmaurice, 5th
  Marquess of
Lao Zi (*or* Lao Tzu)
Laplace, Pierre Simon,
  Marquis de
Lardner, Ring
Larkin, Philip
La Rochefoucauld,
  François, Duc de
Larousse, Pierre
Lars Porsena
Lartet, Édouard Armand
  Isidore Hippolyte
La Salle, Robert
  Cavelier, Sieur de
Lascaris, Theodore
Las Casas, Bartolomé de
Las Cases, Emmanuel,
  Comte de
Lasdun, Sir Denys
Lasker, Emanuel
Laski, Harold Joseph
Laski, Marghanita
Lassalle, Ferdinand

Lassus, Roland de
László
Latimer, Hugh
Latini, Brunetto
La Tour, Georges de
La Tour, Maurice-
  Quentin de
Laud, William
Lauda, Niki
Lauder, Sir Harry
Lauderdale, John
  Maitland, Duke of
Laue, Max Theodor
  Felix von
Laughton, Charles
Laurel, Stan
Laurier, Sir Wilfrid
Lautréamont, Comte de
Laval, Pierre
La Vallière, Louise de
  Françoise de la Baume
  le Blanc, Duchesse de
Laver, Rod(ney George)
Laveran, Charles Louis
  Alphonse
Lavoisier, Antoine
  Laurent
Law, (Andrew) Bonar
Law, William
Lawes, Sir John Bennet
Lawler, Ray
Lawrence, St
Lawrence, D(avid)
  H(erbert)
Lawrence, Ernest
  Orlando
Lawrence, Gertrude
Lawrence, John Laird
  Mair, 1st Baron
Lawrence, T(homas)
  E(dward)
Lawrence, Sir Thomas
Laxness, Halldór
  (Kiljan)
Layamon
Layard, Sir Austen
  Henry
Leach, Bernard (Howell)
Leacock, Stephen
  (Butler)
Leadbelly
Leakey, Louis Seymour
  Bazett
Leakey, Mary
Leakey, Richard
Lean, Sir David

Lear, Edward
Leavis, F(rank) R(aymond)
Le Brun, Charles
Le Carré, John
Le Châtelier, Henri-Louis
Leconte de Lisle, Charles Marie René
Lecoq de Boisbaudran, Paul-Émile
Le Corbusier
Lederberg, Joshua
Le Duc Tho
Lee, Bruce
Lee, Gypsy Rose
Lee, Jenny, Baroness
Lee, Robert E(dward)
Lee, Tsung-Dao
Leech, John
Lee Kuan Yew
Leeuwenhoek, Antonie van
Le Fanu, (Joseph) Sheridan
Legendre, Adrien Marie
Léger, Fernand
Lehár, Franz
Lehmann, Lilli
Lehmann, Lotte
Leibniz, Gottfried Wilhelm
Leicester, Robert Dudley, Earl of
Leichardt, (Friedrich Wilhelm) Ludwig
Leif Eriksson
Leigh, Vivien
Leighton of Stretton, Frederic, Baron
Leland, John
Lely, Sir Peter
Lemaître, Georges Édouard, Abbé
Le Nain, Antoine
Le Nain, Louis
Le Nain, Mathieu
Lenclos, Ninon de
L'Enfant, Pierre-Charles
Lenglen, Suzanne
Lenin, Vladimir Ilich
Lennon, John
Le Nôtre, André
Lenya, Lotte
Leonardo da Vinci

Leoncavallo, Ruggiero
Leonidas
Leonov, Leonid
Leopardi, Giacomo
Leopold
Lepidus, Marcus Aemilius
Lermontov, Mikhail
Lerner, Alan Jay
Lesage, Alain-René
Leschetizky, Theodor
Lescot, Pierre
Lesseps, Ferdinand de
Lessing, Doris
Lessing, Gotthold Ephraim
Leszczyński, Stanisław
Le Tellier, Michel
Leucippus
Leuckart, Karl Georg Friedrich Rudolph
Le Vau, Louis
Leven, Alexander Leslie, 1st Earl of
Leverhulme, William Hesketh Lever, 1st Viscount
Leverrier, Urbain Jean Joseph
Lévesque, René
Lévi-Strauss, Claude
Lewes, George Henry
Lewis, C. Day
Lewis, C(live) S(taples)
Lewis, Matthew Gregory
Lewis, (Harry) Sinclair
Lewis, (Percy) Wyndham
Libby, Willard Frank
Lichtenstein, Roy
Liddell Hart, Sir Basil Henry
Lie, Trygve (Halvdan)
Liebig, Justus, Baron von
Liebknecht, Karl
Liebknecht, Wilhelm
Lifar, Serge
Ligeti, György
Li Hong Zhang (or Li Hung-chang)
Lilburne, John
Lilienthal, Otto
Liliuokalani
Lillie, Beatrice

Limburg, de
Limosin, Léonard
Linacre, Thomas
Lin Biao (or Lin Piao)
Lincoln, Abraham
Lind, Jenny
Lindbergh, Charles A(ugustus)
Lindsay, (Nicholas) Vachel
Lindwall, Raymond Russell
Linklater, Eric
Linnaeus, Carolus
Lin Ze Xu (or Lin Tse-hsü)
Liouville, Joseph
Lipchitz, Jacques
Li Bo (or Li Po)
Lippershey, Hans
Lippi, Filippino
Lippi, Fra Filippo
Lipscomb, William Nunn
Lissitzky, El
List, Friedrich
Lister, Joseph, 1st Baron
Liszt, Franz
Littlewood, Joan
Litvinov, Maksim Maksimovich
Liu Shao Qi (or Liu Shao-sh'i)
Liverpool, Robert Banks Jenkinson, 2nd Earl of
Livia Drusilla
Livingstone, David
Livy
Llewellyn, Harry
Llewellyn, Richard
Lloyd, Harold
Lloyd, Marie
Lloyd George, David, 1st Earl
Lloyd George, Dame Margaret
Lloyd Webber, Andrew
Lloyd Webber, Julian
Llywelyn ap Gruffudd
Llywelyn ap Iorwerth
Lobachevski, Nikolai Ivanovich
Lobengula
Lochner, Stefan
Locke, John
Locke, Matthew

Lockhart, Sir (Robert
Hamilton) Bruce
Lockhart, John Gibson
Lockyer, Sir Joseph
Norman
Lodge, Henry Cabot
Lodge, Sir Oliver Joseph
Lodge, Thomas
Loeb, Jacques
Loeffler, Friedrich
August Johannes
Loewe, Frederick
Loewi, Otto
Lomax, Alan
Lomax, John Avery
Lombard, Peter
Lombardo, Antonio
Lombardo, Pietro
Lombardo, Tullio
Lombroso, Cesare
Lomonosov, Mikhail
Vasilievich
London, Jack
Longfellow, Henry
Wadsworth
Longhi, Alessandro
Longhi, Pietro
Longinus
Lonsdale, Gordon
Arnold
Lonsdale, Dame
Kathleen
Loos, Adolph
Lope de Vega
López, Carlos Antonio
López, Francisco Solano
López de Ayala, Pero
Lorca, Federico Garcia
Loren, Sophia
Lorentz, Hendrick
Antoon
Lorenz, Konrad
Lorenzetti, Ambrogio
Lorenzetti, Pietro
Lorenzo Monaco
Lorrain, Claude
Lorraine, Charles,
Cardinal de
Los Angeles, Victoria de
Losey, Joseph
Lothair
Loti, Pierre
Lotto, Lorenzo
Louis, Joe
Louis Philippe

Louvois, Michel Le
Tellier, Marquis de
Lovecraft, H(oward)
P(hilips)
Lovelace, Richard
Lovell, Sir Bernard
Lovett, William
Low, Sir David
(Alexander Cecil)
Lowell, Amy
Lowell, James Russell
Lowell, Percival
Lowell, Robert
Lowry, L(awrence)
S(tephen)
Lowry, (Clarence)
Malcolm
Lubitsch, Ernst
Lucan
Lucas van Leyden
Luce, Clare Booth
Luce, Henry R(obinson)
Lucretius
Lucullus, Lucius Licinius
Ludendorff, Erich
Lugard, Frederick
Dealtry, 1st Baron
Lu Hsün
Lukacs, Giorgi
Lull, Ramón
Lully, Jean Baptiste
Lumière, Auguste
Lumière, Louis
Lumumba, Patrice
(Hemery)
Lunt, Alfred
Lynne Fontanne
Lurçat, Jean
Luria, Isaac
Luther, Martin
Lutoslawski, Witold
Lutuli, Albert (John
Mvumbi)
Lutyens, Sir Edwin
Landseer
Lutyens, Elisabeth
Luxemburg, Rosa
Lvov, Georgi
Yevgenievich, Prince
Lyautey, Louis Hubert
Gonzalve
Lydgate, John
Lyell, Sir Charles
Lyly, John
Lynch, Jack

Lynd, Helen
Lynd, Robert Staughton
Lyons, Joseph Aloysius
Lysander
Lysenko, Trofim
Denisovich
Lysias
Lysippus
Lyttelton, Humphrey
Lytton, Edward George
Earle Bulwer-Lytton,
1st Baron
Maazel, Lorin
Mabuse see Gossaert, Jan
McAdam, John Loudon
MacAlpine, Kenneth
MacArthur, Douglas
Macarthur, John
Macaulay, Dame Rose
Macaulay, Thomas
Babington, 1st Baron
Macbeth
MacBride, Seán
McBride, Willie John
McCarthy, Joseph
R(aymond)
McCarthy, Mary
McCartney, Linda
McCartney, Paul
McClellan, George
B(rinton)
McClure, Sir Robert
John Le Mesurier
McCullers, Carson
MacDiarmid, Hugh
MacDonald, Flora
Macdonald, Sir John
(Alexander)
MacDonald, (James)
Ramsay
McEnroe, John (Patrick)
McGonagall, William
Mach, Ernst
Machaut, Guillaume de
Machel, Samora Moïses
Machen, Arthur
(Llewellyn)
Machiavelli, Niccolò
McIndoe, Sir Archibald
Hector
Macintosh, Charles
Macke, August
McKenna, Siobhán
Mackenzie, Sir (Edward
Montague) Compton

Mackerras, Sir Charles
Mackinder, Sir Halford
  John
McKinley, William
Mackintosh, Charles
  Rennie
Maclean, Donald
Macleish, Archibald
Macleod, Iain (Norman)
Macleod, John James
  Rickard
Mac Liammóir, Micheál
Maclise, Daniel
McLuhan, (Herbert)
  Marshall
MacMahon, Marie
  Edme Patrice
  Maurice, Comte de
McMahon, William
Macmillan, Alexander
Macmillan, Daniel
McMillan, Edwin
  Mattison
Macmillan, (Maurice)
  Harold, 1st Earl of
  Stockton
MacMillan, Sir
  Kenneth
Macmillan, Kirkpatrick
MacMurrough, Dermot
MacNeice, Louis
Maconchy, Elizabeth
Macquarie, Lachlan
McQueen, Steve
Macready, William
  Charles
Madariaga y Rojo,
  Salvador de
Maderna, Carlo
Madison, James
Maecenas, Gaius
Maes, Nicolas
Maeterlinck, Maurice
Magellan, Ferdinand
Magendie, François
Magnani, Anna
Magritte, René
Mahavira *title of*
  Vardhamana
Mahdi, al-
Mahler, Gustav
Mahmud
Mailer, Norman
Maillol, Aristide
Maimonides, Moses

Maintenon, Mme de
Maistre, Joseph de
Makarios
Malachy, St
Malamud, Bernard
Malan, Daniel F(rançois)
Malaparte, Curzio
Malcolm, George (John)
Malebranche, Nicolas
Malenkov, Georgi
  Maksimilianovich
Malesherbes, Chrétien
  Guillaume de
  Lamoignon de
Malevich, Kazimir
Malherbe, François de
Malik-Shah
Malinowski, Bronisław
Malipiero, Gian
  Francesco
Mallarmé, Stéphane
Malmesbury, William of
Malory, Sir Thomas
Malpighi, Marcello
Malraux, André
Malthus, Thomas Robert
Ma'mun, al-
Manasseh ben Israel
Mandela, Nelson
  (Rolihlahla)
Mandela, Winnie
Mandelstam, Osip
Mandeville, Sir John
Manet, Edouard
Manin, Daniele
Manley, Michael
Mann, Heinrich
Mann, Thomas
Mannerheim, Carl
  Gustaf Emil, Baron
  von
Manning, Henry
  Edward, Cardinal
Mansart, François
Mansfield, Katherine
Mansfield, William
  Murray, 1st Earl of
Mansholt, Sicco
Mansholt Plan
Mansur, Abu Ja'far al-
Mantegna, Andrea
Manutius, Aldus
Manutius, Paulus
Manzoni, Alessandro

Mao Tse-tung (*or* Mao Ze
  Dong)
Marat, Jean Paul
Marc, Franz
Marceau, Marcel
Marcellus, Marcus
  Claudius
Marchand, Jean Baptiste
Marconi, Guglielmo
Marcos, Ferdinand
  E(dralin)
Marcus Aurelius
Marcuse, Herbert
Marenzio, Luca
Margrethe Danish queen
Mariette, Auguste
  Ferdinand François
Marinetti, Filippo
  Tommaso
Marini, Marino
Maritain, Jacques
Marius, Gaius
Marivaux, Pierre Carlet
  de Chamblain de
Mark Antony
Markiewicz, Constance,
  Countess of
Markov, Andrei
  Andreevich
Markova, Dame Alicia
Marks, Michael
Marks, Simon, 1st
  Baron
Marlborough, John
  Churchill, 1st Duke of
Marlborough, Sarah
  Churchill, Duchess of
Marlowe, Christopher
Marot, Clément
Marquand, J(ohn)
  P(hillips)
Marquette, Jacques
Marryat, Captain
  Frederick
Marsh, Dame Ngaio
Marshall, George
  C(atlett)
Marshall, John
Marsilius of Padua
Marston, John
Martel, Charles
Martel, Geoffrey
Martí, José Julián
Martial
Martin, Archer John
  Porter

Martin, John
Martin, Pierre-Émile
Martin, Richard
Martin du Gard, Roger
Martineau, Harriet
Martini, Simone
Martinu, Bohuslav
Marvell, Andrew
Marx, Chico
Marx, Groucho
Marx, Gummo
Marx, Harpo
Marx, Karl (Heinrich)
Marx, Zeppo
Masaccio
Masaryk, Jan (Garrigue)
Masaryk, Tomáš
  (Garrigue)
Mascagni, Pietro
Masefield, John
Masinissa
Masolino
Mason, A(lfred)
  E(dward) W(oodley)
Masséna, André
Massenet, Jules
Massey, Anna
Massey, Daniel
Massey, Raymond
Massey, William
  Ferguson
Massine, Léonide
Massinger, Philip
Massys, Quentin
Masters, Edgar Lee
Masters, William Howell
Mastroianni, Marcello
Mata Hari
Matisse, Henri
Matsuo Basho
Matteotti, Giacomo
Matthews, Sir Stanley
Mauchly, John W.
Maudslay, Henry
Maugham, Robin
Maugham, W(illiam)
  Somerset
Maupassant, Guy de
Maupertuis, Pierre Louis
  Moreau de
Mauriac, François
Maurois, André
Maurras, Charles
Maxim, Sir Hiram
  Stevens

Maxwell, James Clerk
Mayakovskii, Vladimir
Mayer, Julius Robert
  von
Mayer, Louis B.
Mayer, Sir Robert
Mayhew, Henry
Mayo, Charles Horace
Mayo, Charles William
Mayo, William James
Mayo, William Worrall
Mazarin, Jules, Cardinal
Mazzini, Giuseppe
Mboya, Tom
Mead, Margaret
Meade, Richard
Meads, Colin Earl
Mechnikov, Ilya *variant*
  spelling of Metchnikov,
  Ilya
Medawar, Sir Peter
  Brian
Medici, Catherine de'
Medici, Cosimo de'
Medici, Lorenzo de'
Medici, Piero de'
Médicis, Marie de
Meegeren, Hans van
Mehemet Ali
Meiji *title of* Mutsuhito
Meir, Golda
Meissonier, Jean-Louis-
  Ernest
Meitner, Lise
Melanchthon, Philip
Melba, Dame Nellie
Melbourne, William
  Lamb, 2nd Viscount
Melchett, Alfred Mond,
  1st Baron
Melchior, Lauritz
Mellon, Andrew William
Melville, Herman
Memling, Hans
Menander
Mencius
Mencken, H(enry)
  L(ouis)
Mendel, Gregor Johann
Mendeleyev, Dimitrii
  Ivanovich
Mendelssohn, Felix
Mendelssohn, Moses
Menderes, Adnan
Mendès-France, Pierre

Mendoza, Antonio de
Menelik
Menes
Mengelberg, William
Mengs, Anton Raphael
Menno Simons
Menon, Krishna
Menotti, Gian Carlo
Menuhin, Hephzibah
Menuhin, Jeremy
Menuhin, Yaltah
Menuhin, Sir Yehudi
Menzies, Sir Robert
  Gordon
Mercator, Gerardus
Mercer, David
Mercouri, Melina
Meredith, George
Meredith, Owen *pen name*
  of Robert Bulmer-Lytton,
  1st Earl of Lytton
Mérimée, Prosper
Merleau-Ponty, Maurice
Merneptah
Mesmer, Franz Anton
Messager, André
  (Charles Prosper)
Messalina, Valeria
Messerschmitt, Willy
Messiaen, Olivier
Messier, Charles
Meštrović, Ivan
Metastasio, Pietro
Metaxas, Ioannis
Metchnikov (*or*
  Mechnikov), **Ilya Ilich**
Methodius, St
Metsu, Gabriel
Metternich, Klemens
  Wenzel Nepomuk
  Lothar, Fürst von
Meyerbeer, Giacomo
Meyerhof, Otto Fritz
Meyerhold, Vsevolod
  Emilievich
Michelangelo Buonarroti
Michelet, Jules
Michelin, André
Michelin, Édouard
Michelozzo di
  Bartolommeo
Michelson, Albert
  Abraham
Mickiewicz, Adam
Middleton, Thomas

Mies van der Rohe,
  Ludwig
Mihajlović, Draža
Miles, Bernard, Baron
Milhaud, Darius
Mill, James
Mill, John Stuart
Millais, Sir John Everett
Millay, Edna St Vincent
Miller, Arthur
Miller, Glenn
Miller, Henry
Millet, Jean François
Millikan, Robert
  Andrews
Mills, Hayley
Mills, Sir John
Mills, Juliet
Milne, A(lan)
  A(lexander)
Milner, Alfred, Viscount
Miloš
Milstein, Nathan
Miltiades
Milton, John
Minamoto Yoritomo
Minamoto Yoshitsune
Mindszenty, József,
  Cardinal
Mingus, Charlie
Minnelli, Liza
Mintoff, Dom(inic)
Mirabeau, Honoré
  Gabriel Riquetti,
  Comte de
Miró, Joan
Mishima, Yukio
Mistinguett
Mistral, Frédéric
Mistral, Gabriela
Mitchell, Margaret
Mitchell, R(eginald)
  J(oseph)
Mithridates
Mitterrand, François
  (Maurice)
Mizoguchi Kenji
Mobutu, Sese Seko
Mocenigo, Andrea
Mocenigo, Giovanni
Mocenigo, Pietro
Mocenigo, Tommaso
Modigliani, Amedeo
Mohammed (or
  Muhammad)

Mohammed Askia
Moholy-Nagy, László
Molière
Molina, Luis de
Molinos, Miguel de
Molnár, Ferenc
Molotov, Vyacheslav
  Mikhailovich
Moltke, Helmuth, Graf
  von
Moltke, Helmuth
  Johannes Ludwig von
Mommsen, Theodor
Mond, Alfred, 1st Baron
  Melchett
Mond, Ludwig
Mondrian, Piet
Monet, Claude
Monge, Gaspard
Moniz, Antonio Egas
Monk, Thelonius
  (Sphere)
Monmouth, James Scott,
  Duke of
Monnet, Jean
Monod, Jacques-Lucien
Monroe, James
Monroe, Marilyn
Monsarrat, Nicholas
Montagu, Lady Mary
  Wortley
Montaigne, Michel de
Montale, Eugenio
Montcalm, Louis Joseph
  de Montcalm-Grozon,
  Marquis de
Montefeltro, Federigo,
  Duke of Urbino
Montefiore, Sir Moses
Montespan, Françoise
  Athénaïs de
  Rochechouart,
  Marquise de
Montesquieu, Charles
  Louis de Secondat,
  Baron de
Monteux, Pierre
Monteverdi, Claudio
Montez, Lola
Montezuma
Montfort, Simon de,
  Earl of Leicester
Montgolfier, Jacques-
  Étienne
Montgolfier, Joseph-
  Michel

Montgomery of Alamein,
  Bernard Law, 1st
  Viscount
Montherlant, Henry de
Montrose, James
  Graham, 1st Marquess
  of
Moody, Dwight Lyman
Moore, Bobby
Moore, G(eorge)
  E(dward)
Moore, Gerald
Moore, Henry
Moore, Sir John
Moore, Marianne
Moore, Thomas
Morandi, Giorgio
Moravia, Alberto
Moray, James Stuart,
  Earl of
More, Henry
More, Sir Thomas
Moreau, Gustave
Moreau, Jean Victor
Morgagni, Giovanni
  Battista
Morgan, Charles
Morgan, Sir Henry
Morgan, John Pierpont
Morgan, Thomas Hunt
Mörike, Eduard
  Friedrich
Morison, Stanley
Morisot, Berthe
Morland, George
Morley, Edward
  Williams
Morley, Robert
Morley, Thomas
Mornay, Philippe de,
  Seigneur du Plessis-
  Marly
Moro, Aldo
Moroni, Giovanni
  Battista
Morphy, Paul Charles
Morris, Desmond John
Morris, William
Morrison, Herbert
  Stanley, Baron
Morse, Samuel Finley
  Breese
Mortier, Édouard
  Adolphe Casimir
  Joseph, Duc de
  Trévise

Mortimer, Roger de, 1st
Earl of March
Morton, James Douglas,
4th Earl of
Morton, Jelly Roll
Morton, John
Moseley, Henry Gwyn
Jeffries
Mosley, Sir Oswald
Ernald
Moss, Stirling
Motherwell, Robert
Mo-tzu *variant spelling of*
Mo-Zi
Mountbatten of Burma,
Louis, 1st Earl
Mozart, Wolfgang
Amadeus
Mo-Zi (*or* Mo-tzu)
Mu'awiyah
Mugabe, Robert
(Gabriel)
Muhammad *variant spell-
ing of* Mohammed
Muhammad Ahmad *origi-
nal name of* al-Mahdi
Muir, Edwin
Mujibur Rahman, Sheik
Muller, Hermann Joseph
Müller, Paul Hermann
Mulliken, Robert
Sanderson
Mulready, William
Mumford, Lewis
Munch, Charles
Munch, Edvard
Münchhausen, Karl
Friedrich, Freiherr von
Munnings, Sir Alfred
Munro, H(ector) H(ugh)
(*pen name* Saki)
Munthe, Axel
Müntzer, Thomas
Murasaki Shikibu
Murat, Joachim
Murdoch, Dame Iris
Murdock, William
Murillo, Bartolomé
Esteban
Murray, Gilbert
Murray, Sir James
(Augustus Henry)
Murray, Len
Murrow, Edward
R(oscoe)
Murry, John Middleton

Musgrave, Thea
Musil, Robert
Musset, Alfred de
Mussolini, Benito
(Amilcare Andrea)
Mussorgski, Modest
Petrovich
Mutanabbi, Abu At-
Tayyib Ahmad Ibn
Husayn al-
Mutesa
Mutsuhito
Muybridge, Eadweard
Muzorewa, Bishop Abel
(Tendekayi)
Myers, F(rederic)
W(illiam) H(enry)
Myrdal, Alva
Myrdal, Gunnar
Mzilikazi
Nabokov, Vladimir
Nadar
Nader, Ralph
Nader Shah
Naevius, Gnaeus
Nagarjuna
Nagy, Imre
Naipaul, V(idiadhur)
S(urajprasad)
Namier, Sir Lewis
Bernstein
Nanak
Nana Sahib
Nansen, Fridtjof
Napier, Sir Charles
James
Napier, John
Napier of Magdala,
Robert Cornelis, 1st
Baron
Narses
Nash, John
Nash, Ogden
Nash, Paul
Nash, Richard
Nash, Sir Walter
Nashe, Thomas
Nasser, Gamal Abdel
Nazianus, St Gregory of
Nebuchadnezzar
Necker, Jacques
Neer, Aert van der
Nefertiti
Negrín, Juan
Nehru, Jawaharlal

Neill, A(lexander)
S(utherland)
Nekrasov, Nikolai
Alekseevich
Nelson, Horatio,
Viscount
Nemery, Jaafar
Mohammed al
Nennius
Neri, St Philip
Nernst, Walther
Hermann
Nero (Claudius Caesar)
Neruda, Pablo
Nerva, Marcus Cocceius
Nerval, Gérard de
Nervi, Pier Luigi
Nesbit, Edith
Nesselrode, Karl Robert,
Count
Neto, Agostinho
Neumann, (Johann)
Balthasar
Neumann, John von
Nevsky, Alexander
Newcastle, Thomas
Pelham-Holles, 1st
Duke of
Newcastle, William
Cavendish, Duke of
Newcombe, John
Newcomen, Thomas
Ne Win
Newman, John Henry,
Cardinal
Newman, Paul
Newton, Sir Isaac
Nexø, Martin Andersen
Ney, Michel, Prince of
Moscow
Ngo Dinh Diem
Niarchos, Stavros
Spyros
Nicholson, Ben
Nicholson, Jack
Nicholson, William
Nicias
Nicklaus, Jack William
Nicolai, Otto Ehrenfried
Nicolson, Sir Harold
(George)
Niebuhr, Barthold Georg
Nielsen, Carl (August)
Niemeyer, Oscar
Niemöller, Martin
Nietzsche, Friedrich

Nightingale, Florence
Nijinsky, Vaslav
Nikisch, Arthur
Nilsson, Birgit Marta
Nimitz, Chester
  W(illiam)
Nirenberg, Marshall
  Warren
Nithsdale, William
  Maxwell, 5th Earl of
Niven, David
Nixon, Richard Milhous
Nizam al-Mulk
Nkomo, Joshua
Nkrumah, Kwame
Nobel, Alfred Bernhard
Nobile, Umberto
Noble, Sir Andrew
Nobunaga Oda
Noel-Baker, Philip John
Noguchi, Hideyo
Nolan, Sir Sidney
Nolde, Emil
Nollekens, Joseph
Nono, Luigi
Nordenskjöld, Nils Adolf
  Erik, Baron
Norfolk, Thomas
  Howard, Duke of
North, Frederick, Lord
North, Sir Thomas
Northcliffe, Alfred
  Charles William
  Harmsworth, 1st
  Viscount
Northrop, John Howard
Northumberland, John
  Dudley, Duke of
Nostradamus
Novalis
Novello, Ivor
Novotný, Antonín
Noyes, Alfred
Nu, U
Nuffield, William
  Richard Morris, 1st
  Viscount
Nureyev, Rudolf
Nurhachi
Nurmi, Paavo Johannes
Nyerere, Julius
  (Kambarage)
Nyssa, St Gregory of
Oakley, Annie
Oastler, Richard

Oates, Lawrence Edward
  Grace
Oates, Titus
Obote, (Apollo) Milton
O'Brien, Conor Cruise
O'Brien, Flann
O'Brien, William
O'Brien, William Smith
O'Casey, Sean
Ockham, William of
O'Connell, Daniel
O'Connor, Feargus
O'Connor, Frank
Oda Nobunaga
Odets, Clifford
Odoacer
Oehlenschläger, Adam
  (Gottlob)
Oersted, Hans Christian
Offa
Offenbach, Jacques
O'Flaherty, Liam
Ogden, C(harles) K(ay)
Ogdon, John
Oglethorpe, James
  Edward
O'Hara, John (Henry)
O'Higgins, Bernardo
Ohm, Georg Simon
Oistrakh, David
Oistrakh, Igor
O'Keeffe, Georgia
Okeghem, Jean d'
Olbers, Heinrich
  Wilhelm Matthäus
Oldcastle, Sir John
Oldenbarneveldt, Johan
  van
Oldenburg, Claes
  (Thure)
Oliphant, Sir Mark
  Laurence Elwin
Olivares, Gaspar de
  Guzmán, Conde-
  Duque de
Oliver, Isaac
Olivier, Laurence (Kerr),
  Baron
Omar Khayyam
Onassis, Aristotle
  Socrates
Oñate, Juan de
O'Neill, Eugene
O'Neill, Terence, Baron
Onsager, Lars

Ophüls, Max
Opie, John
Opitz (von Boberfeld),
  Martin
Oppenheimer, J. Robert
Orcagna, Andrea
Orczy, Baroness
  Emmusca
Oresme, Nicole d'
Orff, Carl
Origen
Orlando, Vittorio
  Emanuele
Orléans, Charles, Duc d'
Orléans, Louis Philippe
  Joseph, Duc d'
Orlov, Aleksei
  Grigorievich
Orlov, Grigori
  Grigorievich, Count
Ormandy, Eugene
Ormonde, James Butler,
  1st Duke of
Orozco, José
Ortega y Gasset, José
Ortelius, Abraham
Ortoli, François Xavier
Orwell, George
Osborne, Dorothy
Osborne, John
O'Shea, Katherine Page
Osler, Sir William
Osman
Ossian
Ossietsky, Carl von
Ostade, Adrian van
Ostrovskii, Aleksandr
  Nikolaevich
Ostwald, (Friedrich)
  Wilhelm
Oswald, Lee Harvey
Oswiu
Otis, Elisha Graves
Otto, Nikolaus August
Otway, Thomas
Oudry, Jean-Baptiste
Ouida
Ouspensky, Peter
Outram, Sir James
Ovid
Owen, Alun Davies
Owen, Dr David
  (Anthony Llewellyn)
Owen, Robert
Owen, Wilfred

Owens, Jesse
Oxenstierna, Axel,
   Count
Pabst, G(eorge)
   W(ilhelm)
Pachomius, St
Pachymeres, Georgius
Paderewski, Ignacy (Jan)
Páez, José Antonio
Paganini, Niccolò
Page, Sir Earle
   (Christmas Grafton)
Page, Sir Frederick
   Handley
Pahlavi, Mohammed
   Reza
Pahlavi, Reza Shah
Paine, Thomas
Paisley, Ian
Palaeologus, Michael
Palestrina, Giovanni
   Pierluigi da
Paley, William
Palgrave, Francis Turner
Palissy, Bernard
Palladio, Andrea
Palma Vecchio, Jacopo
Palmer, Arnold
Palmer, Samuel
Palmerston, Henry John
   Temple, 3rd Viscount
Pandit, Vijaya Lakshmi
Pan Gu (or P'an Ku)
Panini
Pankhurst, Dame
   Christabel
Pankhurst, Emmeline
Pankhurst, Sylvia
Papadopoulos, George
Papen, Franz von
Pappus of Alexandria
Paracelsus
Paré, Ambroise
Pareto, Vilfredo
Paris, Matthew
Park, Mungo
Park Chung Hee
Parker, Charlie
   (Christopher)
Parker, Dorothy
   Rothschild
Parker, Matthew
Parkes, Sir Henry
Parkinson, (Cyril)
   Northcote

Parkman, Francis
Parmenides
Parmigianino
Parnell, Charles Stewart
Parr, Catherine
Parry, Sir Hubert
Parry, Sir William
   Edward
Parsons, Sir Charles
   Algernon
Partridge, Eric
   Honeywood
Pascal, Blaise
Pasić, Nicola
Pasionaria, La see Ibarruri,
   Dolores
Pasmore, Victor
Pasolini, Pier Paolo
Passy, Frédéric
Pasternak, Boris
Pasteur, Louis
Pater, Walter (Horatio)
Paterson, William
Patinir, Joachim
Patmore, Coventry
Paton, Alan
Patti, Adelina
Patton, George S(mith)
Pauli, Wolfgang
Pauling, Linus Carl
Paulinus of Nola, St
Paulus, Friedrich
Pausanias
Pavarotti, Luciano
Pavese, Cesare
Pavlov, Ivan Petrovich
Pavlova, Anna
Paxinou, Katina
Paxton, Sir Joseph
Paz, Octavio
Peacock, Thomas Love
Peake, Mervyn
Pears, Sir Peter
Pearse, Patrick Henry
Pearson, Lester B(owles)
Peary, Robert Edwin
Peckinpah, Sam
Peel, Sir Robert
Peele, George
Péguy, Charles
Peirce, Charles Sanders
Pelagius
Pelé
Pelham, Henry
Pelletier, Pierre Joseph

Penda
Penderecki, Krzysztof
Pendlebury, John Devitt
   Stringfellow
Penn, William
Penney, William George,
   Baron
Pepys, Samuel
Perceval, Spencer
Percy, Sir Henry (known
   as Harry Hotspur)
Percy, Bishop Thomas
Perelman, S(idney)
   J(oseph)
Pérez Galdós, Benito
Pergolesi, Giovanni
   (Battista)
Pericles
Perkin, Sir William
   Henry
Perón, Evita
Perón, Isabel
Perón, Juan (Domingo)
Pérotin
Perrault, Charles
Perrin, Jean-Baptiste
Perry, Fred(erick John)
Perry, Matthew
   C(albraith)
Perse, Saint-John
Pershing, John J(oseph)
Perugino
Perutz, Max Ferdinand
Pestalozzi, Johann
   Heinrich
Pétain, (Henri) Philippe
Peterson, Oscar
   Emmanuel
Petipa, Marius
Petit, Roland
Petöfi, Sándor
Petrarch
Petrie, Sir (William
   Matthew) Flinders
Petronius Arbiter
Petrosian, Tigran
   Vartanovich
Pevsner, Antoine
Pevsner, Sir Nikolaus
   (Bernhard Leon)
Phaedrus
Phalaris
Phidias
Phidippides
Philadelphus, Ptolomy

Philby, Harold Adrian
  Russell
Philby, H(arry) St John
  (Bridge)
Philemon
Philidor, André Danican
Philidor, François André
  Danican
Phillip, Arthur
Philo Judaeus
Phiz *see* Browne, Hablot
  Knight
Phryne
Phyfe (*or* Fife), Duncan
Piaf, Edith
Piaget, Jean
Picabia, Francis
Picasso, Pablo
Piccard, Auguste
Piccard, Jacques
Piccard, Jean-Félix
Pickford, Mary
Pico della Mirandola,
  Giovanni, Conte
Pieck, Wilhelm
Piero della Francesca
Piero di Cosimo
Piggott, Lester Keith
Pilate, Pontius
Piłsudski, Józef Klemens
Pinckney, Charles
Pinckney, Charles
  Cotesworth
Pinckney, Thomas
Pindar
Pinero, Sir Arthur Wing
Pinkerton, Allan
Pinochet, Augusto
Pinter, Harold
Pinturicchio
Piozzi, Hester Lynch
  (*married name* Thrale)
Piper, John
Pirandello, Luigi
Piranesi, Giambattista
Pisanello
Pisano, Andrea
Pisano, Giovanni
Pisano, Nicola
Pisistratus
Pissarro, Camille
Pissarro, Lucien
Pitman, Sir Isaac
Pitt, William

Pitt-Rivers, Augustus
  Henry Lane Fox
Pius pope
Pizarro, Francisco
Place, Francis
Planck, Erwin
Planck, Max Karl Ernst
  Ludwig
Plantagenet surname of
  English kings 1154–1485
Plath, Sylvia
Plato
Plautus, Titus Maccius
Pleasence, Donald
Plekhanov, Georgi
  Valentinovich
Pliny
Plomer, William
Plotinus
Plowright, Joan
Plunket, St Oliver
Plutarch
Pocahontas
Po Chü-i *variant spelling of*
  Bo Zhu Yi
Podgorny, N(ikolai)
  V(iktorovich)
Poe, Edgar Allan
Poggio Bracciolini,
  Giovanni Francesco
Poincaré, Jules Henri
Poincaré, Raymond
Poisson, Siméon Dénis
Poitiers, Diane de,
  Duchesse de
  Valentinois
Polanski, Roman
Pole, Reginald, Cardinal
Polignac, Auguste Jules
  Armand Marie, Prince
  de
Poliziano
Polk, James K(nox)
Pollaiuolo, Antonio
Pollaiuolo, Piero
Pollock, Jackson
Polo, Marco
Polybius
Polycarp, St
Polyclitus
Polycrates
Pombal, Sebastião José
  de Carvalho e Mello,
  Marquês de
Pompadour, Mme de
Pompey

Pompidou, Georges
  (Jean Raymond)
Ponce de Leon, Juan
Poniatowski, Józef
Poniatowski, Stanisław
Pontiac
Pontormo, Jacopo da
Pope, Alexander
Popov, Aleksandr
  Stepanovich
Popov, Oleg
  Konstantinovich
Popper, Sir Karl
  Raimund
Porphyriogenitus,
  Constantine
Porphyry
Porter, Cole (Albert)
Porter, Katherine Anne
Porter, Peter
Portland, William Henry
  Cavendish Bentinck,
  3rd Duke of
Potemkin, Grigori
  Aleksandrovich
Potter, Beatrix
Potter, Paul
Potter, Stephen
Poulenc, Francis
Pound, Ezra
Poussin, Nicolas
Powell, Anthony
Powell, Cecil Frank
Powell, (John) Enoch
Powys, John Cowper
Powys, Theodore
  Francis
Praetorius, Michael
Prandtl, Ludwig
Prasad, Rajendra
Praxiteles
Preminger, Otto
  (Ludwig)
Prescott, William
  Hickling
Presley, Elvis (Aaron)
Prester John
Pretorius, Andries
  (Wilhelmus Jacobus)
Pretorius, Marthinus
  Wessel
Prévert, Jacques
Previn, André
Prévost d'Exiles,
  Antoine François,
  Abbé

Pride, Thomas
Priestley, J(ohn) B(oynton)
Priestley, Joseph
Primo de Rivera, José Antonio
Primo de Rivera, Miguel
Prior, Matthew
Priscian
Pritchett, V(ictor) S(awden)
Proclus
Procopius
Prokofiev, Sergei
Prokop
Propertius, Sextus
Protagoras
Proudhon, Pierre Joseph
Proust, Joseph-Louis
Proust, Marcel
Prout, William
Prud'hon, Pierre Paul
Prynne, William
Psamtik
Pseudo-Dionysius the Areopagite
Ptolemy
Puccini, Giacomo
Pucelle, Jean
Pudovkin, Vsevolod
Pufendorf, Samuel von
Pugachov, Yemelyan Ivanovich
Pugin, Augustus Welby Northmore
Pulci, Luigi
Pullman, George Mortimer
Purcell, Edward Mills
Purcell, Henry
Purchas, Samuel
Pusey, Edward Bouverie
Pushkin, Aleksandr
Puvis de Chavannes, Pierre (Cécile)
Pu Yi, Henry
Pym, John
Pynchon, Thomas
Pyrrhon
Pyrrhus
Pythagoras
Pytheas
Qaboos ibn Sa'id
Qaddafi, Moammar al-
Qian Long (or Ch'ien-lung)

Quant, Mary
Quasimodo, Salvatore
Queneau, Raymond
Quercia, Jacopo della
Quesnay, François
Quesnel, Pasquier
Quiller-Couch, Sir Arthur Thomas
Quine, Willard van Orman
Quintilian
Quisling, Vidkun (Abraham Lauritz Jonsson)
Qu Qiu Bai (or Ch'ü Ch'iu-pai)
Rabelais, François
Rabi, Isidor Isaac
Rachmaninov, Sergei
Racine, Jean
Rackham, Arthur
Radcliffe, Ann (Ward)
Radcliffe-Brown, Alfred Reginald
Radek, Karl
Radić, Stjepan
Radiguet, Raymond
Raeburn, Sir Henry
Raeder, Erich
Raffles, Sir Thomas Stamford
Raglan, FitzRoy James Henry Somerset, 1st Baron
Raikes, Robert
Raine, Kathleen
Rainier, Prince
Rais, Gilles de
Rákóczy, Ferenc
Raleigh, Sir Walter
Ramakrishna
Raman, Sir Chandrasekhara Venkata
Ramanuja
Rambert, Dame Marie
Rameau, Jean Philippe
Ramón y Cajal, Santiago
Ramsay, Allan
Ramsay, Sir William
Ramses
Ramsey, Alf
Ram Singh
Ramus, Petrus
Ranjit Singh, Maharaja

Ranjitsinhji Vibhaji, Kumar Shri, Maharajah Jam Sahib of Nawanagar
Rank, J(oseph) Arthur, 1st Baron
Rank, Otto
Ranke, Leopold von
Ransom, John Crowe
Ransome, Arthur Mitchell
Raphael
Rashi
Rasmussen, Knud Johan Victor
Rasputin, Grigori Yefimovich
Rathenau, Walther
Rattigan, Sir Terence
Rauschenberg, Robert
Ravel, Maurice
Rawlinson, Sir Henry Creswicke
Rawsthorne, Alan
Ray, John
Ray, Man
Ray, Satyajit
Rayleigh, John William Strutt, 3rd Baron
Rayleigh, Robert John Strutt, 4th Baron
Razi, ar-
Razin, Stenka
Read, Sir Herbert
Reade, Charles
Reading, Rufus Daniel Isaacs, 1st Marquess of
Réaumur, René-Antoine Ferchault de
Reber, Grote
Recamier, Jeanne Françoise Julie Adelaide
Redford, Robert
Redgrave, Corin
Redgrave, Lynn
Redgrave, Sir Michael
Redgrave, Vanessa
Redmond, John Edward
Redon, Odilon
Redouté, Pierre Joseph
Reed, Sir Carol
Reed, John
Reed, Walter
Reeves, William Pember

Reger, Max
Regiomontanus
Regnier, Henri François
 Joseph de
Regulus, Marcus Attilus
Rehoboam
Reich, Wilhelm
Reid, Sir George
 Houston
Reid, Thomas
Reinhardt, Django
Reinhardt, Max
Reith, John Charles
 Walsham, 1st Baron
Remarque, Erich Maria
Rembrandt
 (Harmenszoon) van
 Rijn
Remington, Eliphalet
Renan, (Joseph) Ernest
Reni, Guido
Rennie, John
Renoir, Jean
Renoir, Pierre Auguste
Resnais, Alain
Respighi, Ottorino
Retz, Jean François Paul
 de Gondi, Cardinal de
Reuter, Paul Julius,
 Baron von
Revere, Paul
Reynaud, Paul
Reynolds, Sir Joshua
Rhee, Syngman
Rheticus
Rhine, Joseph Banks
Rhodes, Cecil (John)
Rhodes, Wilfred
Rhys, Jean
Ribbentrop, Joachim von
Ribera, José de
Ricardo, David
Ricci, Marco
Ricci, Matteo
Ricci, Sebastiano
Riccio, David
Rich, Richard, 1st Baron
Richards, Frank
Richards, Sir Gordon
Richards, I(vor)
 A(rmstrong)
Richardson, Henry
 Handel
Richardson, Henry
 Hobson

Richardson, Sir Ralph
Richardson, Samuel
Richelieu, Armand Jean
 du Plessis, Cardinal de
Richler, Mordecai
Richter, Hans
Richter, Johann Paul
 Friedrich.
Richter, Sviatoslav
 (Teofilovitch)
Richthofen, Manfred,
 Freiherr von
Ridley, Nicholas
Ridolfi, Roberto
Riebeeck, Jan van
Riefensthal, Leni
Riel, Louis
Riemann, Georg
 Friedrich Bernhard
Rienzo, Cola di
Riesman, David
Riley, Bridget Louise
Rilke, Rainer Maria
Rimbaud, Arthur
Rimsky-Korsakov,
 Nikolai
Rivera, Diego
Rizzio, David
Roach, Hal
Robbe-Grillet, Alain
Robbins, Frederick
 Chapman
Robbins, Jerome
Roberts, Frederick
 Sleigh, 1st Earl
Roberts, Tom
Robeson, Paul
Robespierre, Maximilien
 François Marie
 Isidore de
Robey, Sir George
Robinson, Edward G.
Robinson, Edwin
 Arlington
Robinson, John (Arthur
 Thomas)
Robinson, Sir Robert
Robinson, Sugar Ray
Robinson, William
 Heath
Robson, Dame Flora
Rochester, John Wilmot,
 2nd Earl of
Rockefeller, John
 D(avison)

Rockefeller, Nelson
 A(ldrich)
Rockingham, Charles
 Watson-Wentworth,
 2nd Marquess of
Roderic Irish king
Rodgers, Richard
 Charles
Rodin, Auguste
Rodney, George
 Brydges, 1st Baron
Rodrigo, Joaquín
Roebling, John Augustus
Roebling, Washington
 Augustus
Roentgen, Wilhelm
 Konrad
Rogers, Ginger
Rogers, John
Roget, Peter Mark
Röhm, Ernst
Rokitansky, Karl,
 Freiherr von
Rolfe, Frederick William
Rolland, Romain
Rolls, Charles Stewart
Romains, Jules
Rommel, Erwin
Romney, George
Romulus Augustulus
Ronsard, Pierre de
Roon, Albrecht, Graf von
Roosevelt, Eleanor
Roosevelt, Franklin
 D(elano)
Roosevelt, Theodore
Root, Elihu
Rory O'Connor
Rosa, Salvator
Roscelin
Roscius, Quintus
Rosebery, Archibald
 Philip Primrose, 5th
 Earl of
Rosenberg, Ethel
Rosenberg, Julius
Rosewall, Ken(neth
 Ronald)
Ross, Sir James Clark
Ross, Sir Ronald
Rosse, William Parsons,
 3rd Earl of
Rossellini, Roberto
Rossetti, Christina
 Georgina
Rossetti, Dante Gabriel

Rossini, Gioacchino
  Antonio
Rostand, Edmond
Rostropovich, Mstislav
Roth, Philip
Rothermere, Harold
  Sydney Harmsworth,
  1st Viscount
Rothko, Mark
Rothschild, James
Rothschild, Karl Mayer
Rothschild, Lionel
  Nathan
Rothschild, Mayer
  Amschel
Rothschild, Nathan
  Mayer
Rothschild, Nathaniel
  Mayer Victor, 3rd
  Baron
Rothschild, Salomon
  Mayer
Rouault, Georges
  (Henri)
Roubillac, Louis
  François
Rouget de l'Isle, Claude
  Joseph
Rousseau, Henri
Rousseau, Jean Jacques
Rousseau, (Pierre
  Étienne) Théodore
Roussel, Albert
Roussel, Raymond
Roux, Pierre Paul Emile
Rowe, Nicholas
Rowlandson, Thomas
Rowley, Thomas
Rowse, A(lfred) L(eslie)
Royce, Sir (Frederick)
  Henry
Royce, Josiah
Rubbra, Edmund
Rubens, Peter Paul
Rubinstein, Anton
Rubinstein, Artur
Rublyov, Andrey
Ruggles, Carl
Ruisdael, Jacob van
Ruysdael, Salomon van
Ruiz, Juan
Rumford, Benjamin
  Thompson, Count
Rundstedt, (Karl Rudolf)
  Gerd von
Runeberg, Johan Ludvig

Runyon, Damon
Rurik
Rushdie, Salman
Rusk, (David) Dean
Ruskin, John
Russell, Bertrand Arthur
  William, 3rd Earl
Russell, John, 1st Earl
Russell, Ken
Russell, Lord William
Russell, Sir William
  Howard
Rutherford, Ernest, 1st
  Baron
Rutherford, Dame
  Margaret
Rutherford, Mark
Ruyter, Michiel
  Adriaanszoon de
Ryder, Sue, Baroness
Rykov, Aleksei Ivanovich
Ryle, Gilbert
Ryle, Sir Martin
Saarinen, Eero
Sabatier, Paul
Sachs, Hans
Sachs, Nelly (Leonie)
Sackville, Thomas, 1st
  Earl of Dorset
Sadat, Anwar
Sade, Donatien
  Alphonse François,
  Marquis de
Sa'di
Sagan, Françoise
Saigo Takamori
Sainte-Beuve, Charles-
  Augustin
Saint-Exupéry, Antoine
  de
Saint-Just, Louis
  (Antoine Léon) de
Saint-Laurent, Yves
Saint-Saëns, Camille
Saint-Simon, Claude
  Henri de Rouvroy,
  Comte de
Saint-Simon, Louis de
  Rouvroy, Duc de
Sakharov, Andrei
  Dimitrievich
Saki pen name of H(ector)
  H(ugh) Munro
Saladin
Salam, Abdus

Salazar, António de
  Oliveira
Sales, St Francis of
Salieri, Antonio
Salinger, J(erome)
  D(avid)
Salisbury, Robert Arthur
  Talbot Gascoyne-
  Cecil, 3rd Marquess of
Salisbury, Robert Cecil,
  1st Earl of
Sallust
Samudra Gupta
Samuel, Herbert Louis,
  1st Viscount
Sand, George
Sandage, Allan Rex
Sandburg, Carl
Sandwich, John
  Montagu, 4th Earl of
Sanger, Frederick
Sankara
San Martin, José de
Santa Anna, Antonio
  López de
Santayana, George
Sapir, Edward
Sapper pen name of
  H(erman) C(yril)
  McNeile
Sappho
Sardou, Victorien
Sargent, John Singer
Sargent, Sir Malcolm
Sargon
Saroyan, William
Sarraute, Nathalie
Sarto, Andrea del
Sartre, Jean-Paul
Sassetta
Sassoon, Siegfried
Satie, Erik
Sato Eisaku
Saud
Saussure, Ferdinand de
Savage, Michael Joseph
Savage, Richard
Savery, Thomas
Savonarola, Girolamo
Saxe, Maurice, Comte
  de
Saxe-Weimar, Duke
  Bernhard of
Saxo Grammaticus
Sayers, Dorothy L(eigh)

Scaliger, Joseph Justus
Scaliger, Julius Caesar
Scarfe, Gerald
Scarlatti, Alessandro
Scarlatti, Domenico
Scarron, Paul
Schacht, Hjalmar
Scheel, Walter
Scheele, Carl Wilhelm
Schelling, Friedrich
Schiaparelli, Elsa
Schiele, Egon
Schiller, (Johann Christoph) Friedrich (von)
Schlegel, August Wilhelm von
Schegel, (Carl Wilhelm) Friedrich von
Schleiden, Matthias Jakob
Schlesinger, John
Schlick, Moritz
Schlieffen, Alfred, Graf von
Schliemann, Heinrich
Schmeling, Max
Schmidt, Helmut
Schnabel, Artur
Schnitzler, Arthur
Schoenberg, Arnold
Schopenhauer, Arthur
Schreiner, Olive
Schrödinger, Erwin
Schubert, Franz (Peter)
Schuman, Robert French statesman; *compare* Schumann, Robert
Schuman, William (Howard)
Schumann, Clara
Schumann, Elisabeth
Schumann, Robert (Alexander) German composer; *compare* Schuman, Robert
Schuschnigg, Kurt von
Schütz, Heinrich
Schwann, Theodor
Schwarzenberg, Felix, Fürst zu
Schwarzkopf, Elisabeth
Schweitzer, Albert
Schwitters, Kurt

Scipio Aemilianus Africanus grandson of Scipio Africanus
Scipio Africanus
Scofield, (David) Paul
Scott, Sir George Gilbert
Scott, Sir Giles Gilbert
Scott, Sir Peter Markham
Scott, Robert Falcon
Scott, Ronnie
Scott, Sir Walter
Scriabin, Alexander
Scullin, James Henry
Seaborg, Glenn Theodore
Searle, Ronald William Fordham
Seddon, Richard John
Seeger, Pete
Seferis, George
Seghers, Hercules Pieterzoon
Segovia, Andrés
Segrè, Emilio
Selden, John
Seleucus I Nicator
Selkirk, Alexander
Sellers, Peter
Selwyn Lloyd, John, Baron
Selznick, David O(liver)
Semiramis
Sempringham, St Gilbert of
Senanayake, D(on) S(tephen)
Senanayake, Dudley
Seneca
Senefelder, Aloys
Senghor, Léopold Sédar
Sennacherib
Sennett, Mack
Sergius of Radonezh, St
Servetus, Michael
Sesostris
Sesshu
Sessions, Roger
Seton, Ernest Thompson
Seurat, Georges
Severini, Gino
Severus, Lucius Septimius
Severus Alexander

Sévigné, Marie de Rabutin-Chantal, Marquise de
Seymour, Jane
Shackleton, Sir Ernest Henry
Shadwell, Thomas
Shaffer, Anthony
Shaffer, Peter
Shaftesbury, Anthony Ashley Cooper, Earl of
Shah Jahan
Shahn, Ben
Shaka
Shakespeare, William
Shankar, Ravi
Shapur
Sharp, Cecil (James)
Shastri, Shri Lal Bahadur
Shaw, Artie
Shaw, George Bernard
Shaw, (Richard) Norman
Sheene, Barry
Shelburne, William Petty Fitzmaurice, 2nd Earl of
Shelley, Mary Wollstonecraft
Shelley, Percy Bysshe
Shenstone, William
Shepard, Ernest Howard
Shepard, Allan Bartlett
Sheppard, Jack
Sheraton, Thomas
Sheridan, Philip H(enry)
Sheridan, Richard Brinsley
Sherman, John
Sherman, William Tecumseh
Sherrington, Sir Charles Scott
Shockley, William Bradfield
Sholes, Christopher Latham
Sholokhov, Mikhail
Shostakovich, Dmitri
Shostakovich, Maxim
Shovell, Sir Cloudesley
Shrapnel, Henry
Shute, Nevil
Sibelius, Jean
Sica, Vittoria De
Sickert, Walter Richard

Siddons, Sarah
Sidgwick, Henry
Sidmouth, Henry
  Addington, 1st
  Viscount
Sidney, Algernon
Sidney, Sir Philip
Siemens, Ernst Werner
  von
Siemens, Friedrich
Siemens, Karl
Siemens, Sir William
Sienkiewicz, Henryk
Sieyès, Emmanuel
  Joseph
Siger of Brabant
Signac, Paul
Signorelli, Luca
Sigurdsson *variant spelling*
  of Sverrir
Sihanouk, Norodim,
  Prince
Sikorski, Władysław Po-
  lish statesman
Sikorsky, Igor Ivan US en-
  gineer
Sillitoe, Alan
Silone, Ignazio
Si-ma Qian (*or* Ssu-ma
  Ch'ien)
Simenon, Georges
Simeon Stylites, St
Simms, William Gilmore
Simnel, Lambert
Simon, John Allsebrook,
  1st Viscount
Simonov, Konstantin
Simpson, George
  Gaylord
Simpson, N(orman)
  F(rederick)
Sinatra, Frank
Sinclair, Upton
Singer, Isaac Bashevis
Singer, Isaac Merrit
Siqueiros, David Alfaro
Sisley, Alfred
Sitwell, Edith
Sitwell, Sir Osbert
Sitwell, Sacheverell
Sivaji
Sixtus *pope*
Skalkottas, Nikos
Skanderbeg
Skelton, John

Skinner, Burrhus
  Frederic
Slade, Felix
Slánský, Rudolf
Slim, William Joseph,
  1st Viscount
Sloane, Sir Hans
Sluter, Claus
Smart, Christopher
Smetana, Bedřich
Smiles, Samuel
Smith, Adam
Smith, Bessie
Smith, Harvey
Smith, Ian (Douglas)
Smith, John
Smith, Joseph
Smith, Sir Keith
  Macpherson
Smith, Maggie
Smith, Sir Ross
  Macpherson
Smith, Stevie
Smithson, Alison
Smithson, Peter
Smollett, Tobias
  (George)
Smuts, Jan (Christiaan)
Smythe, Pat
Snefru
Snow, C(harles) P(ercy),
  Baron
Snowdon, Antony
  Armstrong-Jones, Earl
  of
Snyders, Frans
Soames, (Arthur)
  Christopher (John),
  Baron
Soane, Sir John
Soares, Mario
Sobers, Gary
Sobieski, John
Socinus, Faustus
Socinus, Laelius
Socrates
Soddy, Frederick
Söderblom, Nathan
Solon
Soloviov, Vladimir
  Sergevich
Solti, Sir Georg
Solzhenitsyn, Aleksandr
Somers, John, Baron

Somerset, Edward
  Seymour, 1st Duke of
Somerset, Robert Carr,
  Earl of
Sommerfeld, Arnold
  Johannes Wilhelm
Sondheim, Stephen
  (Joshua)
Song (*or* Sung), T. V.
Song Qing-ling (*or* Sung
  Ch'ing-ling)
Song Mei-ling (*or* Sung
  Mei-ling)
Sophocles
Sopwith, Sir Thomas
  Octave Murdoch
Soranus of Ephesus
Sorel, Georges
Sosigenes of Alexandria
Soter, Ptolomy
Soto, Hernando de
Soufflot, Jacques
  Germain
Soult, Nicolas Jean de
  Dieu, Duc de
  Dalmatie
Souphanouvong, Prince
Sousa, John Philip
Soustelle, Jacques
  (Émile)
Southampton, Henry
  Wriothesley, 3rd Earl
  of
Southcott, Joanna
Southey, Robert
Soutine, Chaim
Soyinka, Wole
Spaak, Paul Henri
Spallanzani, Lazzaro
Spark, Muriel
Spartacus
Spassky, Boris
Spearman, Charles
  Edward
Speke, John Hanning
Spence, Sir Basil
Spencer, Herbert
Spencer, Sir Stanley
Spencer, Thomas
Spender, Stephen
Spengler, Oswald
Spenser, Edmund
Speranski, Mikhail
  Mikhailovich
Spillane, Mickey
Spinoza, Benedict

Spitz, Mark (Andrew)
Spock, Benjamin
  McLane
Spohr, Louis
Spooner, William
  Archibald
Ssu-ma Ch'ien *variant*
  spelling of Si-ma Qian
Staël, Anne Louise
  Germaine Necker,
  Madame de
Stahl, Georg Ernst
Stainer, Sir John
Stalin, Joseph
Stamitz, Johann
Standish, Myles
Stanford, Sir Charles
  (Villiers)
Stanhope, Charles, 3rd
  Earl
Stanhope, James, 1st
  Earl
Stanislavsky, Konstantin
Stanisław, St
Stanley, Sir Henry
  Morton
Stark, Dame Freya
  (Madeline)
Starr, Ringo
Staudinger, Hermann
Stauffenberg, Claus,
  Graf von
Steel, David (Martin
  Scott)
Steele, Sir Richard
Steen, Jan
Stefan Dušan
Stein, Sir (Marc) Aurel
Stein, Gertrude
Stein, Karl, Freiherr vom
Steinbeck, John
Steiner, Rudolf
Steinmetz, Charles
  Proteus
Steinway, Henry
  (Engelhard)
Stendhal
Steno, Nicolaus
Stephen, Sir Leslie
Stephenson, George
Stephenson, Robert Brit-
  ish civil engineer; *compare*
  Stevenson, Robert Louis
Stern, Isaac
Sternberg, Josef von
Sterne, Laurence

Stevens, Wallace
Stevenson, Adlai E(wing)
Stevenson, Frances
Stevenson, Robert Louis
  Scottish novelist; *com-*
  pare Stephenson, Robert
Stewart, Jackie
Stewart, James
  (Maitland)
Stewart, Rod
Stieglitz, Alfred
Stiernhielm, Georg
  Olofson
Stilicho, Flavius
Stilwell, Joseph
  W(arren)
Stirling, James
Stockhausen, Karlheinz
Stoker, Bram
Stokes, Sir George
  Gabriel
Stokowski, Leopold
Stolypin, Petr
  Arkadievich
Stopes, Marie Charlotte
  Carmichael
Stoppard, Miriam
Stoppard, Tom
Storey, David
Storm, (Hans) Theodor
  Woldsen
Stoss, Veit
Stowe, Harriet Beecher
Strabo
Strachey, (Giles) Lytton
Stradivari, Antonio
Strafford, Thomas
  Wentworth, 1st Earl of
Stratton, Charles (*known*
  as Tom Thumb)
Strauss, Johann
Strauss, Richard
Stravinsky, Igor
Strawson, Peter
  Frederick
Streicher, Julius
Streisand, Barbra
Stresemann, Gustav
Strindberg, August
Stroheim, Erich von
Strong, Sir Roy (Colin)
Struve, Otto
Stuart surname of Scottish
  and English monarchs
Stuart, John McDouall
Stubbs, George

Stubbs, William
Sturluson, Snorri
Sturt, Charles
Stuyvesant, Peter
Suárez (Gonzalez),
  Adolfo, Duke of
Suarez, Francisco de
Suckling, Sir John
Sucre, Antonio José de
Su Dong Po (*or* Su Tung-
  p'o)
Sue, Eugène
Suetonius
Suger of Saint-Denis
Suharto
Sukarno
Suleiman
Sulla, Lucius Cornelius
Sullivan, Sir Arthur
Sullivan, John Lawrence
Sullivan, Louis Henry
Sully, Maximilien de
  Béthune, Duc de
Sully-Prudhomme, René
  François Armand
Sunderland, Robert
  Spencer, 2nd Earl of
Sun Yat-sen (*or* Sun Zhong
  Shan)
Suppiluliumas
Surrey, Henry Howard,
  Earl of
Surtees, John
Surtees, Robert Smith
Suslov, Mikhail
Sutcliffe, Herbert
Sutherland, Graham
  Vivian
Sutherland, Dame Joan
Sutton, Walter
  Stanborough
Suvorov, Aleksandr
  Vasilievich, Count
Sverrir (*or* Sigurdsson)
Svevo, Italo
Swammerdam, Jan
Swan, Sir Joseph Wilson
Swedenborg, Emanuel
Sweyn Forkbeard
Swift, Jonathan
Swinburne, Algernon
  Charles
Swithin, St
Symonds, John
  Addington

Symons, Arthur (William)

Synge, John Millington

Szell, George

Szent-Györgyi, Albert (von Nagyrapolt)

Szewinska, Irena

Szilard, Leo

Szymanowski, Karol

Tabari, Muhammad ibn Jarir al-

Tacitus, Cornelius

Taft, Robert Alphonso

Taft, William Howard

Tagore, Debendranath

Tagore, Rabindranath

Taine, Hippolyte Adolphe

Talbot, William Henry Fox

Taliesin

Talleyrand

Tallien, Jean Lambert

Tallis, Thomas

Tamerlane variant of Timur

Tancred

Tange Kenzo

Tanguy, Yves

Tanizaki Jun-ichiro

Tannhäuser

Tasman, Abel Janszoon

Tasso, Torquato

Tate, Allen

Tate, Harry

Tate, Nahum

Tati, Jacques

Tattersall, Richard

Tatum, Art(hur)

Tatum, Edward Lawrie

Tavener, John 20th-century British composer

Taverner, John 16th-century English composer

Tawney, R(ichard) H(enry)

Taylor, A(lan) J(ohn) P(ercivale)

Taylor, Brook

Taylor, Elizabeth

Taylor, Frederick Winslow

Taylor, Jeremy

Taylor, Zachary

Tchaikovsky, Peter Ilich

Teach, Edward

Teck, Mary of Tecumseh

Tedder, Arthur William, 1st Baron

Teilhard de Chardin, Pierre

Te Kanawa, Dame Kiri

Telemann, Georg Philipp

Telesio, Bernardino

Telford, Thomas

Teller, Edward

Temple, Frederick

Temple, Shirley

Temple, William

Teng Hsiao-p'ing variant spelling of Deng Xiao Ping

Teniers, David

Tenniel, Sir John

Tennyson, Alfred, Lord

Tenzing Norgay

Terborch, Gerard

Terbrugghen, Hendrik

Terman, Lewis Madison

Terry, Dame Ellen (Alice)

Tertullian(us), Quintus Septimius Florens

Tesla, Nikola

Tetrazzini, Luisa

Tetzel, Johann

Teyte, Dame Maggie

Thackeray, William Makepeace

Thais

Thales

Thatcher, Margaret (Hilda)

Themistocles

Thenard, Louis-Jacques

Theocritus

Theodorakis, Mikis

Theodoric

Theodosius

Theophrastus

Thespis

Thibaud, Jacques

Thiers, Louis Adolphe

Thistlewood, Arthur

Thomas, Dylan

Thomas, Edward

Thompson, Francis

Thomson, Sir George Paget

Thomson, James

Thomson, Sir Joseph John

Thomson, Kenneth Roy, 2nd Baron

Thomson, Virgil

Thomson, William, 1st Baron Kelvin

Thomson of Fleet, Roy Herbert, 1st Baron

Thoreau, Henry David

Thorndike, Dame Sybil

Thornhill, Sir James

Thorpe, (John) Jeremy

Thorvaldsen, Bertel

Thrale, Hester Lynch (maiden name Piozzi)

Throckmorton, Francis

Throckmorton, Sir Nicholas

Thucydides

Thurber, James

Thutmose

Tibaldi, Pellegrino

Tiberius

Tibullus, Albius

Tieck, (Johann) Ludwig

Tiepolo, Giovanni Battista

Tiepolo, Giovanni Domenico

Tiglath-pileser

Tilak, Bal Gangadhar

Tillett, Benjamin

Tilley, Vesta

Tillich, Paul (Johannes)

Tilly, Johan Tserclaes, Graf von

Timoshenko, Semyon Konstantinovich

Timur (or Tamerlane)

Tinbergen, Jan

Tinbergen, Niko(laas)

Tintoretto

Tippett, Sir Michael

Tipu Sahib

Tirpitz, Alfred von

Tirso de Molina

Tissot, James Joseph Jacques

Titian

Tito

Titus (Flavius Vespasianus)

Tobey, Mark

Tocqueville, Alexis de

Todd, Alexander
  Robertus, Baron
Toghril Beg
Togliatti, Palmiro
Togo Heihachiro
Tojo Hideki
Tokugawa Ieyasu
Tolkien, J(ohn) R(onald)
  R(euel)
Toller, Ernst
Tolstoy, Leo
  (Nikolaevich), Count
Tom Thumb see Stratton,
  Charles
Tone, (Theobald) Wolfe
Tong Zhi (or T'ung-chih)
Tooke, John Horne
Torquemada, Tomás de
Torricelli, Evangelista
Tortelier, Paul
Toscanini, Arturo
Tostig
Totila
Toulouse-Lautrec, Henri
  (Marie Raymond) de
Touré, (Ahmed) Sékou
Tournefort, Joseph
  Pitton de
Tourneur, Cyril
Tours, St Gregory of
Toussaint-L'Ouverture,
  François Dominique
Townes, Charles Hard
Townshend, Charles, 2nd
  Viscount
Townshend, Pete
Toynbee, Arnold
  (Joseph)
Toynbee, (Theodore)
  Philip
Tracy, Spencer
Traherne, Thomas
Trajan(us), Marcus
  Ulpius
Traven, B(en) US novelist
Travers, Ben(jamin) Brit-
  ish dramatist
Tree, Sir Herbert
  (Draper) Beerbohm
Trenchard, Hugh
  Montague, 1st
  Viscount
Trevelyan, George
  Macaulay
Trevelyan, Sir George
  Otto

Trevino, Lee
Trevithick, Richard
Trevor-Roper, Hugh
  Redwald, Baron Dacre
Trilling, Lionel
Trollope, Anthony
Tromp, Cornelis
  (Martenszoon)
Tromp, Maarten
  (Harpertszoon)
Trotsky, Leon
Trudeau, Pierre Elliott
Trueman, Freddy
Truffaut, François
Trujillo (Molina), Rafael
  (Leónidas)
Truman, Harry S.
Tryggvason, Olaf
Ts'ao Chan variant spelling
  of Cao Chan
Tshombe, Moise
  (Kapenda)
Tsiolkovski, Konstantin
  Eduardovich
Tsvetaeva, Marina
Tubman, William
  V(acanarat)
  S(hadrach)
Tu Fu variant spelling of Du
  Fu
Tull, Jethro
Tulsidas
T'ung-chih variant spelling
  of Tong Zhi
Tunney, Gene
Tupac Amarú
Tupolev, Andrei
  Niklaievich
Turenne, Henri de la
  Tour d'Auvergne,
  Vicomte de
Turgenev, Ivan
Turgot, Anne Robert
  Jacques, Baron de
  l'Aulne
Turishcheva, Ludmilla
Turner, Joseph Mallord
  William
Turner, Nat
Turpin, Dick
Tussaud, Marie
Tutankhamen
Tutuola, Amos
Twain, Mark
Tyler, John
Tyler, Wat

Tylor, Sir Edward
  Burnett
Tyndale, William
Tyndall, John
Tzimisces, John
Tz'u-hsi variant spelling of
  Zi Xi
Uccello, Paolo
Udall, Nicholas
Uhland, (Johann)
  Ludwig
Ulanova, Galina
Ulbricht, Walter
Umberto
Unamuno y Jugo,
  Miguel de
Undset, Sigrid
Ungaretti, Giuseppe
Updike, John (Hoyer)
Urban pope
Urey, Harold Clayton
Urfé, Honoré d'
Ussher, James
Ustinov, Peter
  (Alexander)
Utagawa Kuniyoshi
Utamaro, Kitagawa
Utrillo, Maurice
Valdemar (or Waldemar)
Valens
Valentinian
Valentino, Rudolf
Valera, Eamon De
Valéry, Paul
Valla, Lorenzo
Valois, Dame Ninette de
Valois, Margaret of
Van Allen, James Alfred
Vanbrugh, Sir John
Van Buren, Martin
Vance, Cyrus
Vancouver, George
Vanderbilt, Cornelius
Van der Post, Sir
  Laurens
Van der Waals,
  Johannes Diderik
van de Velde, Adriaen
van de Velde, Esaias
van de Velde, Henry
van de Velde, Willem
van Dieman, Anthony
Van Dyck, Sir Anthony
Vane, Sir Henry
van Eyck, Hubert

van Eyck, Jan
Van Gogh, Vincent
Vansittart, Robert
  Gilbert, 1st Baron
Van't Hoff, Jacobus
  Henricus
Vardhamana *see* Mahavira
Varèse, Edgard
Vargas, Getúlio
Varro, Marcus Terentius
Vasarely, Victor
Vasari, Giorgio
Vauban, Sébastian Le
  Prestre de
Vaughan, Henry
Vaughan Williams,
  Ralph
Vavilov, Nikolai
  Ivanovich
Vega (Carpio), Lope
  Félix de
Velázquez, Diego
  Rodriguez de Silva
Vendôme, Louis Joseph,
  Duc de
Venizélos, Eleuthérios
Ventris, Michael
Vercingetorix
Verdi, Giuseppe
Verhaeren, Émile
Verlaine, Paul
Vermeer, Jan
Verne, Jules
Vernon, Edward
Veronese, Paolo
Verrocchio, Andrea del
Verwoerd, Hendrik
  Frensch
Vesalius, Andreas
Vespasian
Vespucci, Amerigo
Vicente, Gil
Vicky *pen name of* Victor
  Weisz
Vico, Giambattista
Victor Emmanuel Italian
  king
Victoria, Tomás Luis de
Vidal, Gore
Vidal de la Blache, Paul
Vignola, Giacomo da
Vigny, Alfred de
Villa, Pancho
Villa-Lobos, Heitor

Villars, Claude Louis
  Hector, Duc de
Villehardouin, Geoffroi
  de
Villeneuve, Pierre
Villiers de l'Isle-Adam,
  Philippe Auguste,
  Comte de
Villon, François
Vincent de Paul, St
Viollet-le-Duc, Eugène
  Emmanuel
Virchow, Rudolf
Viren, Lasse Artturi
Visconti, Luchino
Vitruvius
Vittorini, Elio
Vittorino da Feltre
Vivaldi, Antonio
Vivekananda, Swami
Vivés, Juan Luis
Vladimir, St
Vlaminck, Maurice de
Volta, Alessandro
  Giuseppe Antonio
  Anastasio, Count
Voltaire
Vondel, Joost van den
Vonnegut, Kurt
Voroshilov, Kliment
  Yefremovich
Vorster, Balthazar
  Johannes
Voysey, Charles Francis
  Annesley
Voznesenskii, Andrei
Vuillard, (Jean) Édouard
Vyshinskii, Andrei
  Yanuareevich
Wace
Wade, Virginia
Wagner, (Wilhelm)
  Richard
Wagner, Siegfried
Wagner, Wieland
Wagner von Jauregg,
  Julius
Wain, John British novelist;
  compare Wayne, John
Wajda, Andrzej
Wakefield, Edward
  Gibbon
Waksman, Selman
  Abraham
Walafrid Strabo
Walburga, St

Waldemar *variant spelling*
  of Valdemar
Waldheim, Kurt
Waley, Arthur
Wallace, Alfred Russel
Wallace, Edgar
Wallace, Lew(is)
Wallace, Sir William
Wallenstein, Albrecht
  Wenzel von
Waller, Edmund
Waller, (Thomas) Fats
Wallis, Sir Barnes
  (Neville)
Walpole, Horace 4th
  Earl of Orford
Walpole, Sir Hugh
  (Seymour)
Walpole, Sir Robert, 1st
  Earl of Orford
Walsingham, Sir Francis
Walter, Bruno
Walter, Hubert
Walter, John
Walther von der
  Vogelweide
Walton, Ernest Thomas
  Sinton
Walton, Izaak
Walton, Sir William
  (Turner)
Wang An Shi (*or* Wang
  An-shih)
Wang Jing Wei (*or* Wang
  Ching-wei)
Warbeck, Perkin
Ward, Artemus
Ward, Barbara, Baroness
  Jackson
Ward, Mrs Humphry
Ward, Sir Joseph
  George
Ward, Sir Leslie
Warhol, Andy
Warlock, Peter
Warren, Earl
Warton, Joseph
Warton, Thomas
Warwick, Richard
  Neville, Earl of
Washington, Booker
  T(aliaferro)
Washington, George
Wasserman, August von
Waterhouse, Alfred
Watson, James Dewey

Watson, John Broadus
Watson, John Christian
Watson-Watt, Sir
  Robert Alexander
Watt, James
Watteau, (Jean) Antoine
Watts, George Frederick
Waugh, Alec (Raban)
Waugh, Auberon
Waugh, Evelyn (Arthur
  St John)
Wavell, Archibald
  Percival, 1st Earl
Wayne, John US actor;
  compare Wain, John
Webb, Beatrice (Potter)
Webb, Mary
Webb, Sidney (James),
  Baron Passfield
Weber, Carl Maria von
Weber, Ernst Heinrich
Weber, Max
Weber, Wilhelm Eduard
Webern, Anton von
Webster, John
Webster, Noah
Wedekind, Frank
Wedgwood, Dame Cicely
  Veronica
Wedgwood, Josiah
Weelkes, Thomas
Wegener, Alfred Lothar
Weil, Simone
Weill, Kurt
Weismann, August
  Friedrich Leopold
Weiss, Peter
Weissmuller, Johnny
Weisz, Victor (pen name
  Vicky)
Weizmann, Chaim
  (Azriel)
Welensky, Sir Roy
Welles, (George) Orson
Wellesley, Richard
  Colley, Marquess
Wellesz, Egon
Wellington, Arthur
  Wellesley, 1st Duke of
Wells, Henry
Wells, H(erbert)
  G(eorge)
Wenceslas
Wentworth, Thomas, 1st
  Earl of Strafford

Wentworth, William
  Charles
Werfel, Franz
Wergeland, Henrik
  Arnold
Wesker, Arnold
Wesley, Charles
Wesley, John
Wesley, Samuel
Wesley, Samuel
  Sebastian
West, Benjamin
West, Mae
West, Nathanael
West, Dame Rebecca
Weyden, Rogier van der
Wharton, Edith
  (Newbold)
Wheatstone, Sir Charles
Wheeler, Sir (Robert
  Eric) Mortimer
Whistler, James
  (Abbott) McNeill
Whistler, Laurence
Whistler, Rex
White, Gilbert
White, Patrick
White, T(erence)
  H(anbury)
Whitefield, George
Whitehead, A(lfred)
  N(orth)
Whitelaw, William
  (Stephen Ian), 1st
  Viscount
Whitgift, John
Whitlam, (Edward)
  Gough
Whitman, Walt
Whitney, Eli
Whittier, John Greenleaf
Whittington, Dick
Whittle, Sir Frank
Whorf, Benjamin Lee
Whymper, Edward
Widor, Charles Marie
Wieland, Christoph
  Martin
Wiener, Norbert
Wigner, Eugene Paul
Wilberforce, William
Wilde, Oscar
Wilder, Billy
Wilder, Thornton
Wilkes, John

Wilkie, Sir David
Wilkins, Sir George
  Hubert
Wilkins, Maurice Hugh
  Frederick
Williams, John
Williams, J(ohn) P(eter)
  R(hys)
Williams, Roger
Williams, Shirley (Vivien
  Teresa Brittain)
Williams, Tennessee
Williams, William Carlos
Williams-Ellis, Sir
  Clough
Williamson, Henry
Williamson, Malcolm
Willis, Ted
Wills (Moody), Helen
Wilson, Sir Angus
Wilson, Charles
  Thomson Rees
Wilson, Colin
Wilson, Edmund
Wilson, Edmund
  Beecher
Wilson, (James) Harold,
  Baron
Wilson, Sir Henry
  Hughes
Wilson, Henry Maitland,
  1st Baron
Wilson, Richard
Wilson, (Thomas)
  Woodrow
Winckelmann, Johann
  Joachim
Wingate, Orde Charles
Winkler, Hans Günter
Winstanley, Gerrard
Winterhalter, Franz
  Xavier
Winthrop, John
Wise, Thomas James
Wiseman, Nicholas
  Patrick Stephen
Wishart, George
Wissler, Clark
Witt, Johan de
Witte, Sergei Yulievich
Wittgenstein, Ludwig
Wodehouse, Sir
  P(elham) G(renville)
Woffington, Peg
Wöhler, Friedrich
Wolf, Hugo

Wolfe, Charles
Wolfe, James
Wolfe, Thomas
Wolfenden, John
   Frederick, Baron
Wolf-Ferrari, Ermanno
Wölfflin, Heinrich
Wolfit, Sir Donald
Wolfram von
   Eschenbach
Wolfson, Sir Isaac
Wollstonecraft, Mary
Wolseley, Garnet
   Joseph, 1st Viscount
Wolsey, Thomas,
   Cardinal
Wood, Aaron
Wood, Enoch
Wood, Sir Henry
   (Joseph)
Wood, John
Wood, Ralph
Woodville, Elizabeth
Woodward, Robert
   Burns
Woolf, Leonard (Sidney)
Woolf, (Adeline)
   Virginia
Woollett, William
Woolley, Sir Leonard
Woolworth, F(rank)
   W(infield)
Wootton, Barbara,
   Baroness
Wordsworth, William
Wotton, Sir Henry
Wouwerman, Jan
Wouwerman, Philips
Wouwerman, Pieter
Wrangel, Ferdinand
   Petrovich, Baron von
Wrangel, Peter
   Nikolaievich, Baron
Wren, Sir Christopher
Wren, P(ercival)
   C(hristopher)
Wright, Frank Lloyd
Wright, Judith
Wright, Orville
Wright, Richard
Wright, Wilbur

Wu Hou
Wundt, Wilhelm
Wyatt, James
Wyatt, Sir Thomas
Wycherley, William
Wycliffe, John
Wykeham, William of
Wyss, Johann Rudolph
Wyszyński, Stefan,
   Cardinal
Xanthippe
Xenakis, Yannis
Xenophanes
Xenophon
Xerxes
Xia Gui (*or* Hsia Kuei)
Xuan Cang (*or* Hsuan-
   tsang)
Yamagata Aritomo
Yang, Chen Ning
Yeats, Jack Butler
Yeats, William Butler
Yesenin, Sergei
   Aleksandrovich
Yevtushenko, Yevgenii
Yoko Ono
Yonge, Charlotte
Yong Le (*or* Yung-lo)
Young, Andrew
Young, Arthur
Young, Brigham
Young, Thomas
Younghusband, Sir
   Francis Edward
Yuan Shi Kai (*or* Yüan
   Shih-k'ai)
Yukawa, Hideki
Zabaleta, Nicanor
Zadkine, Ossip
Zaghlul, Saad
Zaharoff, Sir Basil
Zamyatin, Yevgenii
   Ivanovich
Zao Zhan *variant spelling of*
   Cao Chan
Zapata, Emiliano
Zarathustra *variant spelling*
   of Zoroaster
Zátopek, Emil
Zeami Motokiyo

Zedekiah
Zeeman, Pieter
Zeffirelli, G. Franco
Zeiss, Carl
Zenobia
Zeno of Citium
Zeno of Elea
Zernicke, Frits
Zetkin, Clara
Zeuxis
Zheng Cheng Gong (*or*
   Cheng Ch'eng-kung;
   known as Koxinga)
Zheng He (*or* Cheng Ho)
Zhivkov, Todor
Zhuangzi (*or* Chuang-tzu)
Zhu De (*or* Chu Teh)
Zhukov, Georgi
   Konstantinovich
Zia ul-Haq, Gen
   Mohammad
Ziaur Rahman
Ziegfeld, Florenz
Ziegler, Karl
Zinoviev, Grigori
   Yevseevich
Zinzendorf, Nikolaus
   Ludwig, Graf von
Zi Xi (*or* Tz'u-hsi)
Žižka, Jan, Count
Zoffany, Johann
Zog
Zola, Émile
Zorn, Anders (Leonard)
Zoroaster (*or* Zarathustra)
Zorrilla y Moral, José
Zoser *variant spelling of*
   Djoser
Zsigmondy, Richard
   Adolph
Zuccarelli, Francesco
Zuccari, Federico
Zuccari, Taddeo
Zuckerman, Solly, Baron
Zurbarán, Francisco de
Zweig, Arnold
Zweig, Stefan
Zwingli, Ulrich
Zworykin, Vladimir
   Kosma

FOR THE BEST IN PAPERBACKS, LOOK FOR THE 🐧

In every corner of the world, on every subject under the sun, Penguin represents quality and variety – the very best in publishing today.

For complete information about books available from Penguin – including Pelicans, Puffins, Peregrines and Penguin Classics – and how to order them, write to us at the appropriate address below. Please note that for copyright reasons the selection of books varies from country to country.

In the United Kingdom: Please write to *Dept E.P., Penguin Books Ltd, Harmondsworth, Middlesex, UB7 0DA*

If you have any difficulty in obtaining a title, please send your order with the correct money, plus ten per cent for postage and packaging, to *PO Box No 11, West Drayton, Middlesex*

In the United States: Please write to *Dept BA, Penguin, 299 Murray Hill Parkway, East Rutherford, New Jersey 07073*

In Canada: Please write to *Penguin Books Canada Ltd, 2801 John Street, Markham, Ontario L3R 1B4*

In Australia: Please write to the *Marketing Department, Penguin Books Australia Ltd, P.O. Box 257, Ringwood, Victoria 3134*

In New Zealand: Please write to the *Marketing Department, Penguin Books (NZ) Ltd, Private Bag, Takapuna, Auckland 9*

In India: Please write to *Penguin Overseas Ltd, 706 Eros Apartments, 56 Nehru Place, New Delhi, 110019*

In Holland: Please write to *Penguin Books Nederland B.V., Postbus 195, NL–1380AD Weesp, Netherlands*

In Germany: Please write to *Penguin Books Ltd, Friedrichstrasse 10–12, D–6000 Frankfurt Main 1, Federal Republic of Germany*

In Spain: Please write to *Longman Penguin España, Calle San Nicolas 15, E–28013 Madrid, Spain*

In France: Please write to *Penguin Books Ltd, 39 Rue de Montmorency, F–75003, Paris, France*

In Japan: Please write to *Longman Penguin Japan Co Ltd, Yamaguchi Building, 2–12–9 Kanda Jimbocho, Chiyoda-Ku, Tokyo 101, Japan*

FOR THE BEST IN PAPERBACKS, LOOK FOR THE 🐧

PENGUIN SELF-STARTERS

Self-Starters is a new series designed to help you develop skills and proficiency in the subject of your choice. Each book has been written by an expert and is suitable for school-leavers, students, those considering changing their career in mid-stream and all those who study at home.

Titles published or in preparation:

Accounting	Noel Trimming
Advertising	Michael Pollard
Basic Statistics	Peter Gwilliam
A Career in Banking	Sheila Black, John Brennan
Clear English	Vivian Summers
French	Anne Stevens
German	Anna Nyburg
Good Business Communication	Doris Wheatley
Marketing	Marsaili Cameron, Angela Rushton, David Carson
Nursing	David White
Personnel Management	J. D. Preston
Public Relations	Sheila Black, John Brennan
Public Speaking	Vivian Summers
Retailing	David Couch
Secretarial Skills	Gale Cornish, Charlotte Coudrille, Joan Lipkin-Edwardes
Starting a Business on a Shoestring	Michel Syrett, Chris Dunn
Understanding Data	Peter Sprent

A CHOICE OF PENGUINS

Adieux: A Farewell to Sartre Simone de Beauvoir

A devastatingly frank account of the last years of Sartre's life, and his death, by the woman who for more than half a century shared that life. 'A true labour of love, there is about it a touching sadness, a mingling of the personal with the impersonal and timeless which Sartre himself would surely have liked and understood' – *Listener*

Business Wargames James Barrie

How did BMW overtake Mercedes? Why did Laker crash? How did MacDonalds grab the hamburger market? Drawing on the tragic mistakes and brilliant victories of military history, this remarkable book draws countless fascinating parallels with case histories from industry worldwide.

Metamagical Themas Douglas R. Hofstadter

This astonishing sequel to the bestselling, Pulitzer Prize-winning *Gödel, Escher, Bach* swarms with 'extraordinary ideas, brilliant fables, deep philosophical questions and Carrollian word play' – Martin Gardner

Into the Heart of Borneo Redmond O'Hanlon

'Perceptive, hilarious and at the same time a serious natural-history journey into one of the last remaining unspoilt paradises' – *New Statesman* 'Consistently exciting, often funny and erudite without ever being overwhelming' – *Punch*

The Assassination of Federico García Lorca Ian Gibson

Lorca's 'crime' was his antipathy to pomposity, conformity and intolerance. His punishment was murder. Ian Gibson reveals the truth about Lorca's death and the atmosphere in Spain that allowed it to happen.

The Secrets of a Woman's Heart Hilary Spurling

The later life of Ivy Compton-Burnett 1920–69. 'A biographical triumph . . . elegant, stylish, witty tender, immensely acute – dazzles and exhilarates . . . a great achievement' – Kay Dick in the *Literary Review*. 'One of the most important literary biographies of the century' – *New Statesman*

The Diary of Virginia Woolf
Five volumes edited by Quentin Bell and Anne Olivier Bell

'As an account of intellectual and cultural life of our century, Virginia Woolf's diaries are invaluable; as the record of one bruised and unquiet mind, they are unique' – Peter Ackroyd in the *Sunday Times*

Voices of the Old Sea   Norman Lewis

'I will wager that *Voices of the Old Sea* will be a classic in the literature about Spain' – *Mail on Sunday* 'Limpidly and lovingly Norman Lewis has caught the helpless, unwitting, often foolish, but always hopeful village in its dying summers, and saved the tragedy with sublime comedy' – *Observer*

The First World War   A J P Taylor

In this superb illustrated history, A J P Taylor 'manages to say almost everything that is important for an understanding and, indeed, intellectual digestion of that vast event . . . A special text . . . a remarkable collection of photographs' – *Observer*

Ninety-Two Days   Evelyn Waugh

With characteristic honesty Evelyn Waugh here debunks the romantic notions attached to rough travelling; his journey in Guiana and Brazil is difficult, dangerous and extremely uncomfortable, and his account of it is witty and unquestionably compelling.

When the Mind Hears   Harlan Lane
A History of the Deaf

'Reads like a suspense novel . . . what emerges is evidence of a great wrong done to a minority group, the deaf' – *The New York Times Book Review* 'Impassioned, polemical, at times even virulent . . . (he shows) immense scholarship, powers of historical reconstruction, and deep empathy for the world of the deaf' – Oliver Sacks in *The New York Review of Books*

BIOGRAPHY AND AUTOBIOGRAPHY IN PENGUIN

Jackdaw Cake   Norman Lewis

From Carmarthen to Cuba, from Enfield to Algeria, Norman Lewis brilliantly recounts his transformation from stammering schoolboy to the man Auberon Waugh called 'the greatest travel writer alive, if not the greatest since Marco Polo'.

Catherine   Maureen Dunbar

Catherine is the tragic story of a young woman who died of anorexia nervosa. Told by her mother, it includes extracts from Catherine's diary and conveys both the physical and psychological traumas suffered by anorexics.

Isak Dinesen, the Life of Karen Blixen   Judith Thurman

Myth-spinner and storyteller famous far beyond her native Denmark, Karen Blixen lived much of the Gothic strangeness of her tales. This remarkable biography paints Karen Blixen in all her sybiline beauty and magnetism, conveying the delight and terror she inspired, and the pain she suffered.

The Silent Twins   Marjorie Wallace

June and Jennifer Gibbons are twenty-three year old identical twins, who from childhood have been locked together in a strange secret bondage which made them reject the outside world. *The Silent Twins* is a real-life psychological thriller about the most fundamental question – what makes a separate, individual human being?

Backcloth   Dirk Bogarde

The final volume of Dirk Bogarde's autobiography is not about his acting years but about Dirk Bogarde the man and the people and events that have shaped his life and character. All are remembered with affection, nostalgia and characteristic perception and eloquence.

QUIZZES, GAMES AND PUZZLES

The Book Quiz Book   Joseph Connolly

Who was literature's performing flea . . .? Who wrote 'Live Now, Pay Later . . .'? Keats and Cartland, Balzac and Braine, Coleridge conundrums, Eliot enigmas, Tolstoy teasers . . . all in this brilliant quiz book.

The Ultimate Trivia Game Book   Maureen and Alan Hiron

If you are immersed in trivia, addicted to quiz games, endlessly nosey, then this is the book for you: over 10,000 pieces of utterly dispensable information!

The Penguin Book of Acrostic Puzzles   Albie Fiore

A book of crosswords and a book of quotations in one! Solve the clues provided, fit the letters into the grid provided and make a quotation. It's the most fun you can have with a pen and paper.

Plus five trivia quiz books:
The Royalty Game
The TV Game
The Travel Game
The Pop Game
The Business Game

Crossword Books to baffle and bewilder

Eleven Penguin Books of the *Sun* Crosswords
Eight Penguin books of the *Sunday Times* Crosswords
Seven Penguin Books of *The Times* Crosswords
and Four Jumbo Books of the *Sun* Crosswords
The First Penguin Book of *Daily Express* Crosswords
The Second Penguin Book of *Daily Express* Crosswords

Penguin Crossword Books – something for everyone, however much or little time you have on your hands.

FOR THE BEST IN PAPERBACKS, LOOK FOR THE 🐧

PENGUIN DICTIONARIES

Archaeology
Architecture
Art and Artists
Biology
Botany
Building
Business
Commerce
Computers
Curious and Interesting
  Words
Curious and Interesting
  Numbers
Decorative Arts
Design and Designers
Economics
English and European
  History
English Idioms
Fairies
French
Geography

Geology
Historical Slang
Italian
Literary Terms
Microprocessors
Modern History 1789–1945
Modern Quotations
Physical Geography
Physics
Political Quotations
Proverbs
Psychology
Quotations
Religions
Rhyming Dictionary
Saints
Sociology
Telecommunications
The Theatre
Troublesome Words
Twentieth Century History

FOR THE BEST IN PAPERBACKS, LOOK FOR THE 🐧

PENGUIN REFERENCE BOOKS

The Penguin Guide to the Law

This acclaimed reference book is designed for everyday use and forms the most comprehensive handbook ever published on the law as it affects the individual.

The Penguin Medical Encyclopedia

Covers the body and mind in sickness and in health, including drugs, surgery, history, institutions, medical vocabulary and many other aspects. 'Highly commendable' – *Journal of the Institute of Health Education*

The Penguin French Dictionary

This invaluable French–English, English–French dictionary includes both the literary and dated vocabulary needed by students, and the up-to-date slang and specialized vocabulary (scientific, legal, sporting, etc) needed in everyday life. As a passport to the French language it is second to none.

A Dictionary of Literary Terms

Defines over 2,000 literary terms (including lesser known, foreign language and technical terms) explained with illustrations from literature past and present.

The Penguin Dictionary of Troublesome Words

A witty, straightforward guide to the pitfalls and hotly disputed issues in standard written English, illustrated with examples and including a glossary of grammatical terms and an appendix on punctuation.

The Concise Cambridge Italian Dictionary

Compiled by Barbara Reynolds, this work is notable for the range of examples provided to illustrate the exact meaning of Italian words and phrases. It also contains a pronunciation guide and a reference grammar.